The World's Great
Contemporary Poems

Edited by Eddie-Lou Cole

The World's Great Contemporary Poems

Victoria N. Gibb
PURPLE RAPTURE

Violet raindrops, red ribbons
  in the sky.
Blue orchids, jeweled coaches
  in meadows of icicles.
Silvered streams and, golden
  dreams, candied forests.
Mirrored crystals and crystal
  mirrors.
Nights with wings, smiles into
  heaven.
Touch and, purple rapture.
Come oh come with me to
  live, fly, and die with me.
Away with me into mountains
  of rivers, rivers of valleys,
  essence of
hearth, Fires burning, sighing
  and yet to live.
Flames melting like candles,
  wax figures in the sky.
Oh love me, love me, while
  I die.

Holly Gaertner
UNTITLED

Little lights I see
Sparkle in the darkness
What pretty birds are these.

Melinda K. Purser
MOODY BLUE

Feeling blue
  and all alone.

Feeling blue
  but just don't know what to
  do.
Feeling blue
  all through the night.
Feeling blue
  and having so many thoughts
  that are scattered about.

So why do you sit and pout?

Think of those who hunger,
  and you are filled.
Or those who have no clothing,
  whild you can't decide what
  to wear.
Or even those who may not see
  the beautiful sunshine,
Or hear the birds sing in the
  trees.

But most of all think of those
  whose soul is lost.

Feeling blue?
  Not any more.

For there is so much to be
  thankful for.

The mood is still there,
  but not on things that really
  matter,

But all on things that I can help,
  and share some kindness for
  those who are in need,
And not on things of the past,
  or things that make you
  worry,
  or even things that won't
  last.
But to set your mind on things
  above,
  on things that will last
  Forever.

Sister Mary Malachy Kux
DYING LOYALTY

England! The land of my birth,
  of which I know so little.
I have no love for you, my
  Mother Country, for you never

nursed me at your breast.
All that I am, all that I have,
  all that I need
Comes to me from the glorious
  land in which I was so
  generously reborn—my
  America!
It is a little sad, though, not to
  be able to say I love the land
  of my birth.
And yet I have memories of
  you; fond childhood memories
  to which I cling
Like a leach sucking on its
  prey;
Memories of bright moments,
  of sadder times;
Memories of things lived
  through that only a child
  would recall and treasure—
The backyard of my home;

  the doll carriage with which
  I played;
The cobblestone street where
  I fell and split open my knee;
The relatives I left behind.
What has become of them?
The loving arms of the
  Grandmother whose comfort
  I could not feel because you
  sent me away.
Nostalgic memories that can
  still bring a wee bit of
  England back into my life;
Unsought, unwanted, but
  very much here;
Brought to life when I see a
  small English style setting of
  homes
Surrounded by trees, flowers,
  shrubs and grass.
When each scene has passed
  the visions fade.
With new eyes I view the beauty
  surrounding me
And am completely drained of
  nostalgic memories.

Marguerite Mooney
JAMAICA

Oh isle of riotous beauty
Built by bloody and kindly
  hands,
Perfumed nights of regal
  witchery
Spread o'er this small, exotic
  land.
Your chameleon skies cap
  the imagination.
Trees draped with bromeliads
  fair,
Casting loveliness upon the
  branches
While wet roots feed giant
  oysters there.
Your shape is like a swimming
  turtle,
Every curve a different scene
In a kaleidoscope of color,
Where we rest and look and
  dream.

Oh beauteous national flower
Blue as the deep on a quiet day
The birds content, within
  their bowers
While doctor-fishes, leap
  and play.
Names of gee-gee and Busta's
  charisma,
Heroes faces, on bak notes,
  you display.
Historic lovers leap, draws
  much attention
While underground rivers,

amble away.
The Spaniards brought the
  gift banana,
You eat fruit of the world's
  very best.
Sugar from your fields bring
  needed profit,
Beauty growing wild at your
  behest.
We wonder and speak of the
  hall called Rose
And the rugged old sugar
  mills.
Day turns to dusk as we stand
  and muse,
Canoes slip by, in the night,
  so still.

With beauty splashing on every
  hand,
We catch our breath at this
  bewitching view
As alligators bask and coney
  dine,
We turn and bid a fond adieu.

Mark D. Hachey
OPENING DAY

The wind
  Raw
    Chilly
Grabs at the too large coat
And finds its way through holes
  torn in it decades before.
It whistles a hollow tune
As it blows across the muzzle
  of the ancient shotgun.
The sun struggles
To break free
From the grip of the low lying
  clouds in the east,
Casting a red glow across the
  remaining sky.
The mud
Sucks at the hunter's boots.
As he hurries to his blind.
The faded decoys
Bob up and down
On the murky water.
High above
The mournful honking of
  the geese is heard,
And several flocks can be seen
Silhouetted against a pink
  background.
The pocket watch
Ticks away as the season's
  opening nears.
Three minutes,
One minute,
Fifteen seconds;
The blast of a dozen guns can
  be heard all around,
Echoing,
Echoing back and forth.
The dog,
Faithful, but slowing with age,
Drops a pile of feathers at
  his feet,
Wagging his tail happily, at
  a job well done.
Throughout the remainder of
  the day,
Echoing booms are heard
  across the marsh,
Continuing until the clouds
  cushion the descent of the
Falling sun.
Sounds of laughter and praise
  are heard.
The car doors squeak open
And close.
Engines start
And fade away.
The marsh is silent,
Save for the sounds
Of the feeding geese.

Floyd O. Skoglund
COWBOY FROM HAVELOCK

I'm from west of the Missouri
  and south of the Platte;
I wear spurs on my boots and
  a ten-gallon hat;
I eat sour-dough biscuits with
  bacon and beans
And my butt feels at home in
  an old pair of jeans.

That man there's the sheriff,
  asleep in his chair,
With his head tilted back and
  his feet in the air.
He won't even notice—I'll
  sneak from my cell
And steal to the paddock to
  saddle Old Nell.

I'm riding to Hickman. The
  Wells-Fargo's due
With a shipment of rum and a
  gold bar or two.
On the outskirts of town, with
  Nell stashed away,
I'll cover my face and I'll wait
  for my play.

When the wagon draws near,
  I'll step from the sage
Yelling "This is a stick-up.
  I'm robbing this stage."
I'll pick up the loot and I'll
  fire my Colt
So's the Wells-Fargo team will
  take off with a bolt.

I'll bury my prize in a place
  you won't know
'Cause I'll cover my tracks so
  no traces will show.
Then back to the jail-house—
  the sheriff in his chair
Will still be asleep with his feet
  in the air.

He won't even notice I've
  gone and come back;
He'll think that I spent the
  whole night in the sack.
Sometime later on, when the
  news settles down,
I'll dig up my prize and I'll
  get out of town.

I'll head for Chicago and live
  like a king,
and I'll tell you right now what
  the future will bring:
I'll live west of the lake and
  south of the Loop
And I'll smoke Panatellas and
  eat Campbell's Soup.

I'll buy Palm Beach suits with
  just one pair of pants
And I'll go to White City to
  learn how to dance.

Then no man will know that
  this citified cat
Came from west of the Missouri
  and south of the Platte.

Angie Satter
BRANDED AN OUTLAW

The sun blazed hot and
  scorched the sand
  A life did not exist.
There came a man upon a horse
  No path could he resist.
A crime was done but not
  by him
  Misunderstood by all.
Now forced to roam the gates
  of hell
  Young death is on the call.

The birds of death soared
  'round above
  To wait the truce of life
But onward forth must he go on

In hand his gun and knife.
"Old Paint my horse the day
    grows short,
    And still they hunt us down.
In cold blood will they murder
    us,
    To rot upon the ground."

"God knows that we are
    innocent
And we have done no crime.
At least we have the two of us
    To pass along the time."

The miles came the miles went
    The fate fortold came true
Both man and beast was not
    enough
    To keep them living through.

As night fell in still there he lay
    A tear fell from his cheek,
"Old Paint Ol' boy, I guess
    we failed,
    I guess I am too weak."

The greed of man and unjustice
    too
    Enough to kill us all.
The life he gave to prove himself
Was his and none too small.

The sun blazed hot and scorched
    the sand
    A life did not exist.
There came a man upon a
    horse,
    No path could he resist.

Michael Eugene Graham
PYRAMID

Let everyone and everything
    fear time, but let time fear
    pyramid.
Time continually complained
    to itself about the wonder
    who stood still,

With science and medicine it
    fought dismissing nations of
    every stripe,
the jew, the fillipino, the arab,
    the spaniard, vienna where it
    spring to
birth, the amerikan, the
    japanese, men and women of
    every stripe numbering
thirty-two in twelve years.
    Pyramid stood still!
A toll was announced as well as
    a goal accomplished for the
    arm tires when
washing cook's wares, four
    gray hairs adorn the crest
    and pyramid listen to
the heart, the pulse and the
    b.p. and discovered the child
    inside, a human who
had been all things to all people
    but not a caretaker of himself.
            And time
detached the work from the
    mind and made it realized
    that now it was a part of
nature and they shared each
    other's secrets and nature
    saw pyramid in
good fortune or in ill; nature
    saw him when he was tired
    or ill or both.
And pyramid saw nature in
    the wind, in human events,
    and in the trees.
    What is truth?
Pyramid knew that it was
    conformity to nature and it
    has its harshness, but
only when unfeeling and u
    uncaring people come into
    the picture.
        II. Criticisms

Pyramid waits too much.
    What's pyramid waiting for?
    Pyramid won't change!
        IIIANSWER
Pyramid finally realized, he
    could do no other than
    what he had done—stand
    still.

Anna Lee Holman Kirkpatrick
YOUTH OF TODAY

Youth of today
To impatient to stay
Ever pressing, preparing to be
    on your way.
Knowing so surely knowledge
    is youth!
Seeking to find what? What?
    with no name,
Convinced it is youth.
Youth of today
Hear me I say,
Listen intently, listen quietly,
Listen to what?
What was once told to me,
    told by an old man who sat
    by the sea.
Sat ever waiting, while watching
    each ship sailing by,
Eyelit mirror reflecting the sky,
Eyelit mirror reflecting the sea,
Clouded by tears,
Tears of regret passing through.
"Keep impatience calmed,
    travel with care,
Once you have left it will
    never be there.
Tarry ejnoy; hang on to your
    youth.
The decision once made, leaves
    nothing to trade.
Anticipation will grow, but
    you'll come to know,
The house will still stand.
Dad will put out his hand.
Mom will grab you and fuss, you
    don't eat enough.
It just want be the same, except
    for the name—
            "HOME"
What was once told to me,
Told by an old man who sat
    by the sea,
Who sat sadly, silent by the
    sea.
Gone forever, just never, really
    to return HOME!

Cathy L. Fitzsimmons
SEARCH FOR LOVE

We search our souls for love
I search yours and you search
    mine
We search for love, the lasting
    kind.

We search up, down, and
    through the
portholes of our hearts.

I look in your eyes you look
    in mine.
We touch on it for a moment
    and it
passes.
Was it really there or were
    we lying
to ourselves wanting to believe.

Phillip L. Duncan
THE BUSINESS MEETING

Well—here I sits, Thinking of
    you and me; Him; Her.
Over there,—they are talking.
    Alone and together.

I wonder,—but only a little bit,
    what they are talking about.

Then the BOSS rises, looking
    the part of an educated lout.
As the audible distortion begins,
    glances ensure nodded
    syncopation.
All continue their cerebral
    oscillations, as I watch in
    fascination.
What was that HE said?!?. . .
    I am cognizant of my
    ignorance.
Is HE going to ask me a
    question? Will I blow my
    only chance?

HIS attention focuses on me,
    meaning Image reception.
If I don't know the answer, do
    I dare to risk deception?

Seconds chip away at eternity,
    but still, still he stares at me.
I pray that he sits down soon,
    and then stays there
    terminally.

With abruptness comes silence,
    and with silence he sits.
Meeting's over!!! Thank God!!!
Well,—here I sits.

Peg Duchesne
MYSTIQUE

Sometimes I think I
    can't stand the
    yearning any longer.

My heart is racing
    at a pace faster
    than I can type.

So little time;
    never enough of it

Always want more—
    more time,
        and more you.

I feel I'm special.
No one knows it
    this specialness,
    this closeness with you.

I don't hide it
    shamefully,
for I am ever so proud
But the hiding adds another
    dimension—
        Mystique

William A. Price
A TEXAS WITCHES' MOON

'Twas late in the evening of a
    July night,
    the Anniversary of our
    Wedding on the 29th.
A full waning Moon was rising
    low in the sky,
    and low-hanging clouds were
    scurrying by.

As dark clouds danced across
    the face of the Moon,
    they resembled Witches,in
    black, riding on brooms.
" 'Tis a Texas Witches' Moon!"
    the old folks would say,
"So guard your heart well,
    or they'll steal it away."

I said to myself, "But how
    can it happen to me,
    when it's been so many years,
    since my heart was free?"
Then I remembered another
    golden night,
    and someone so lovely in
    pink and white.

We were dancing that night,
    on the Delta Queen,
    on the Mississippi River, in
    New Orleans.
I remember so well, as I recall

the scene,
    she was the prettiest girl,
    I'd ever seen.

Her gown was pink and white,
    that night,
    and she danced as light as
    an Elf in flight.
'Tis true, she stole my heart
    from me,
    but that is the way I wished
    it to be.

Just then the whispering
    breezes said, "We know!,
    We know!,
    she stole it from you that
    night long ago.
And, she has it still,
    and she probably always will."

"Remember, love does not
    wear away with years,
    but will grow through
    happiness, trial and tears.
There are good Witches
    abroad tonight, you see,
    to remind you, some love
    when bound, will always be."

By now, the Moon had climbed
    above the low scudding clouds,
    the night was bright, you
    could hear the crickets, loud.
A sparkling path to the
    Moon, danced across Aransas
    Bay,
    toward St. Joseph Island, so
    far away.
I thanked the "Texas Witches'
    Moon", in all it's might,
    for reminding me of another
    golden night.
The night the mighty
    Mississippi sparkled, in
    bright Moonlight,
    and I first held in my arms, my
    life's delight.

Hope Tenhaeff
CHILDREN

We are God's Children,
And it occurs to me
We adults act like infants
Who are two, going on three.

I know why we're God's
    Children;
In the morning we vow to do
    right,
But our good intentions are
    tried all day
And totally dissolved by night.

We grow impatient with our
    children;
We talk, and they never seem
    to hear,
But sooner or later, we happily
    find
An active brain between their
    ears.

Our children love each other;
Accept the good; overlook the
    bad;
But the way we treat each other
Is not only vicious but
    downright sad.

If our children's friends win
    honors,
You'd think they'd won them
    too;
They sense if good things happen
    to friends,
They will also happen to you.

Our children don't talk about
    God a lot,
But I see Him in what they do;
They seem to know love is more
    than words;

6

It's actions and empathy too.
It's opening the refrigerator
And smiling because I see
"Hi!" written on the shell of
    an egg;
My daughter was thinking of
    me.

It's her friends, repairing the
    dock at the lake,
When no one asked them to;
It's finding a rose, in a Dixie
    Cup,
Snow-white and glistening
    with Dew.

I'm not worried about our
    children;
My concern is for you and me;
If we could only learn from
    children,
What a different world this
    would be.

Julian Washalefsky
A CLOUDY DAY

A cloudy day, to some they say,
Is oft times sad and gloomy,
But to me, I'm glad to see
A day that's bright and bloomy
A dark cloud in the sky
Can bring on the rain
So then, by and by
The flowers in the spring will
    bloom again
On one of those days, how
    one can hope,
Rather than sit around and
    mope and mope
For the very next day
Will be bright and gay
And you go through the grass
    and thistle,
As you toot your old brass
    whistle,
And quietly you think,
Where there's a will, there's
    a way
You'll sip on a cool drink,
And to yourself, will say,
"Cheers", to a cloudy day.

Wanda Yost Jones
FINI

The sands of time
Passed swiftly by
The twilight was a glare!
The elusive ticking
Of the clock
Its rhythm was a dare!

I felt you quietly
Slip away
The moments were so bare.

If only time could
Be reversed
I'd take more time to care.

Julie Kay Clements
MAKIN' BELIEVE

It's not fun makin' believe, life's
    not real
when you're in a dream.

All of my life I've been playin'
    the game.
Tryin' to be what other people
    expect of me.
I never had a chance to make
    up my own mind,
Everyone seemed to do it for
    me.

So many people passin' by, have
    the need to identify.
All of us want to be satisfied.
Few people seem to care—livin'
    life that leads nowhere.
No one takes the time to try.

I've got to go out and find
    myself,
Stand up for what I feel is right.
From now on no one's pushing
    me around 'cause,
It's not fun makin' believe,
    life's not real
when you're in a dream.

Leah L. Phillips Payne
ECSTACY

Youth is not a look nor a
    smile;
Youth is the expectant heart—
    and that
    but for awhile—
As an elusive bubble that has
    vanished
And with it my adventurous
    youth is
    banished—
Expectancy's shed as a coat in
    spring,
Ambitions of mastery stripped,
    all winged.
Youth when I possessed it—
    did ought
    but abuse it—
Alas, now—if I it's magic
    owned—
Oh! how I would use it!
Youth is impulsive, oft times
    so
compelling—even conscious
    stilling,
Fleeting, frivolities unsurpassed,
Tranquil, seen but once—
    beyond telling,
Always anticipating—ineffable
    joys—A-ha—such Ecstacy!
Those without it, as without
    breath
    of air,
Reduced to role of only
    spectator.
For me there is a void—that
    can
    ne'r be replaced
As he who had entered—yet
    failed
    in life's race.
As for love, or anatomy—I
    dare not
    digress—
Yesterday's invisible joyous
    escapade,
    I'd guess,
The envy of the very young,
    or aged
    at best,
With maturity clothed like a
    shroud,
Was heard to cry aloud, this
    even is
    Ecstacy!
If it were made so, would I
    go back—to frolic and to
    laughter,
    tho it be triple fold?
I think not, for there cometh
    treasured wisdom, youth
    unknown,
    when older grown—
Blossom from the bud.

Ruth H. Yorns
AL

When I was only thirteen
    I was introduced to an older
    boy
And thought that if I could
    snair him
    It would bring me true love
    and much joy!
My mother did not like him;
    She said he was not for me,
But I told her that I loved him

And she said we'd have to see!
Another two years went
    swiftly by
And I dated other lads
But not one could compare to
    Al;
    He was just like all our dads.
Mom said when you are
    twenty-one
You can do as you please,
But wait until you reach that
    age
    And try to get A's and B's.
I was third in my class
    And won a high school
    scholarship
But I did not take it,
    As I was working for a tip!
My mother got me a working
    permit
    So I could work while
    attending school,
After school I would race to
    my job
and Al would pick me up, as
    a rule.
When I reached that sought
    for age,
    I finally married Al,
And now knew what happiness
    I had;
    He's being my life-time pal!
I did not know what sorrows
    were
    Until the doctor told me Al
    was very ill;
I prayed and prayed to God
    above
    To make him well if it was
    His will!
Because of some good reason
    He does not want to make
    him well
But I can't understand this,
    As I love him more than
    words can tell!

Mary Van Pelt
INFINITY

As I tuck the night away, I
    go forth quietly to awaken
    my children for a new day.
I've spread my vivid colors
    across the earth, and,
The green of me stretches
    endlessly as far as the eye can
    see.
Squirrels scamper up and down
    my torso,
In search of acorns I've
    scattered round for them.
The gophers and moles play
    beneath my feet like naughty
    children.
The bees and humming birds
    nurse at the sweetness of my
    breast,
While my butterflies go about
    their task of kissing awake
    the sleeping flowers.
So they might contribute to
    the scheme of continuity.
I blow pollen softly across the
    land, and with my warm soft
    kiss,
Start them on their way to a
    new beginning, and
My rabbits hop about in search
    of new tender shoots I have
    prepared for them.
Everywhere I walk, the deer
    walk by my side, and each
    time I hear a hunter's gun,
I pause for a brief sad moment,

to mourn deeply for one of
    my own,
Who will not see a new day.
Dusk is almost upon us, so
    I begin the task of tucking my
    children to sleep.
After the birds are nestled
    safely within my arms, I
    close the eyes of my babies,
And lull my vast nursery to
    gently stillness and sleep.
The sweet wild hoot of my
    owls signal all is well, and
    they are on guard,
And. . .tired. . .I seek my own
    rest for tomorrow is just a
    step away, my chore endless,
For I am. . .creation, I am. . .
    nature, I am. . .Infinity!!!

Lori A. Smith
UNTITLED

I've loved you
In so many different ways
For so many different reasons.
I have not understood.
And it worried me until
I realized that love
Never needs to be justified.
Love needs only to be accepted
And shared. . .

Daniel P. Campbell
WHAT IS THIS EMPTY SPACE

My heart lies limp in my hands;
    the gift that comes to me,
So unused, so misspent.
What calls me here to see my
    own folly?
    What mortal desire wastes my
    heart?
The soul of my being doth shine
    in brilliant illumination;
Oe'er all the universe does
    it see.

Yet here I hold it in my hands,
    To watch it, seemingly failing.
What gift of sight does falter
    that
    Strips the vision of truth
    from mine eyes?
What foolish thoughts seduced
    me here
    That I might falter in
    wondering doubt?
Heart in hand, I beg it to beat to
    the
    Glories and beauties that
    must be.
Beat my palsied friend, in even
    rhythms
    To the breath of the universe.
Be one, my friend, with the
    wholeness
    That so infuses the Divine

What light can I cast upon you
    That might ignite your glow?
What breath of wind can I
    place
    within your palpid soul?
A gift, oh God, a gift of sight
    That I might see whence
    comes the light.

Carry me to mine own destiny,
    that through it all
    Was spent this time in
    fulfilling Thy desires.
Make of me that You will to
    be,
    For naught I have to see
    That destiny You have for
    me.
Let this vessel be as it was
    meant to be.
Let this life fulfill and see.

Bradley K. Bunde
HEAVEN

There's a time and place I'm
   searchin' for,
   it's just around the bend;
A place of light and beauty,
   a time that has no end.

It's a place of magnificent
   valleys,
   of mountains that touch the
   sky;
And the sun is forever shining,
   giving life from up so high.

The grass is a deep green carpet,
   rolling up and down the slopes;
The trees stand tall and majestic
   lending faith, comfort and
   hope.

Winding its way through this
   land,
   a river runs shallow and
   smoothe;
It's water is always moving,
   caressing the shore as it moves.

There is a lake perched high
   in the peaks,
   royal blue and crystal clear;
The landscape is reflected by
   this broad, smooth wonder,
   as if it were a giant mirror.

As a breeze whispers through
   the treetops,
   bearing relief as it hits the face;
The rain falls gentle and cool,
   bringing refreshment o'er
   the place.

This land is truly something
   special,
   a place so perfect and unique;
It's a place that they call
   "Heaven",
   the place that I now seek.

I've been looking for some time,
   everywhere I go;
And I'm sure some day I'll find
   it,
   where and when, I just don't
   know!

Nancy Lynne Kitzke
THE DEATH OF ROBERT

Over is the day of a rancher,
   his life now asleep.
Yet through the solitude of
   darkness his tough body creeps.
His jeans are replaced by the
   wool of a sheep.
Not so strong is this man, for
   alone he now weeps.
His tears are the tears of a
   last day gone by.
He tries to gain control, but
   continues to cry.
He knows his life is nearing
   an end.
He bows his head in prayer,
   but feels all alone, is God not
   there?
So many he loved, for many
   he cared,
but now when he needs them,
   there is nobody there.
He reaches his hand, but
   for what reason he can't tell.
The memories of his life jump
   upon him, he's gone through
   some hell,
but all in all he admits his life
   has been swell.
He remembers himself the wild
   young man,
who stormed from pa's ranch
   with his rifle in hand.
He gallantly trotted down the

old dirt road,
   the promise of tommorow just
   glowed.
Now his ripped chest can not
   be sewed.
   Alone he was dying, alone in
the sand.
How he wished his woman was
   holding his hand.
   Alone he was dying, alone
   in the dirt.
His trousers all soiled and blood
   on his shirt.
He knew he was dying for he
   no longer hurt.
   His body ran cold and
   silently he laid.
Five days later, Robert was
   placed in his grave.

Roger W. Gowan
**THE LADY AND THE
WOODSMAN**

In a rundown shack I sat
With my dog and fuzzy cat,
The only Woodsman
She had ever seen.

Outside it's wind and snow
Must be...thirty below,
When she knocked and asked
If I'd mind some company.

In my patched and faded jeans
And my frosty, bearded face
I must have been a sight
For her to see.

But I said pull up a chair
As she fumbled with her hair
A more unlikely pair
You'll never see.

I was Rocky Mountain 'shine,
She was Chablis 'fifty-nine,
But there we sat,
The Lady and the Woodsman

She was satin trimmed with
   lace
And parties in D. C.
I was Rocky Mountains...
Big Sky Country.

The Lady and the Woodsman
As different as could be,
But it seemed so right

That lonely night in Arlee.

We talked into the night
As the world was painted white
A grandeur lady
I have never known.

We somehow came together
On a night of stormy weather,
Now, there are memories
   and dreams
For this old Woodsman
Of love
   and laughter
   shared
With The Lady.

James R. Lazzaro
BEGINNING TO END

I
Little one! Little one! Get
   up, get up!
There's cereal in your bowl,
   hot chocolate in your cup.
Shoes on the floor, clothes
   beside your bed,
Wash your face, come and be
   fed.
All is still—the room is bare.
Where is the little one that used
   to be there?

II
Little toy soldiers standing in
   a line,

Bright and shiny and looking
   so fine.
Waiting to begin a day of fun,
Marching on parade one by
   one.
The drums are silent—the room
   is bare.
Where's the little boy that used
   to be there?
III
Rise and shine and off to school,
To learn how not to be
   anybody's fool.
Hurry now, don't be late,
The sun is up, the day is great.
But all is quiet—the room is
   bare.
What happened to the young
   man that used to be there?
IV
College is done, he's coming
   home with his bride,
All is well, I'm filled with pride.
There's food to eat and songs
   to sing,
Soon there will be children to
   make my heart ring.
Gee, it's quiet—the room is
   bare.
Where's the man that used to
   live there?
V
I pick up my razor and start
   to shave,
A face stares back as if from
   out of the grave.
Deep-deep lines in a pale old
   face,
Signs of age all over the place.
The time has come—the room
   is bare.
I know why the old man is
   not there!

J. L. Coller
DEAR MAMA

Dear Mama
   I wish you were here, so I
   could talk to you
I have so many problems and
   don't know what to do
A girl needs a mother in her
   life
Before and after, she becomes
   a wife
"And Mama"
The kids are driving me mad
Don't know why they must
   be so bad
Sure wish you were here to
   give me a hand
You'd probably tell me,
   their hides need tanned
I often wonder what did you do
You surely did something, to
   raise such a crew
"And Mama"
My husband is very sick, he's
   unable to work and
'bout has a fit.

We don't have enough money
   to make ends meet
If you could see him, he really
   looks beat
"And Mama"
Our house—it's such a mess, I
   always had to settle for less
But then—life isn't all material
   things
Like million dollar houses
   and Diamond rings
You must have love and God
   in your heart
Hey! That's how you did it,
   I should have known from
   the start

Thank you Mama for opening
   my eyes
And when I want to talk to you,
   I'll just look toward the skies
I know you're up there,
   watching down on me
I love you, Mama, wish you
   could be
Sitting right here alongside of
   me.

I'll make it now, with the kids
   and things
I'm prepared for whatever
   the future brings
"And Mama"
I'm glad we had this little talk
Now I'm going out to take a
   walk
I'll be looking up toward your
   heavenly home
Watch for me Mama, so I'm
   not alone.

Barbara Lawrence
FRIENDS

One true friend!—
What is that worth
When measured by
   standards
We have here on earth?
We tend to put value
   on silver and gold,
And on material things
   that we can hold.
How foolish we are, because
   in the end,
Nothing is worth as much
   as a friend.

For life has its follies
Its ups and its downs
Its joys and its sorrows
   Its smiles and its
   frowns
One day you're happy
   The next day you're
   blue
That's why we need friends
   Who we can turn to!

A gentle sort of person
   A haven in a storm
   Someone who can make
   you feel
Safe, secure, and warm.
Someone you can turn
   to
When the rest of the
   world won't care
A person you can
   count upon
And who is always there.

So you can have your
   silver
And you can have your
   gold
And all the money you
   could ever spend
But as for me I'd
rather have
Just one, true, loyal
   friend!

John F. Wood, Jr.
YOU ARE MY FIRST LOVE

You are my first love,
You are my last love,
You are my only love.

I'd been searching all around,
Searching for something I'd
   never found.
At times I'd been up, and
At times I'd been down.

I'd been searching and reaching;
About to give up to despair.
I'd been hoping and groping,
   then;

8

That day, I saw you standing
there.
You opened the door to your
heart;
And, I walked in cautiously.
As I walked in, the doors of my
heart
Opened for you, and closed
for others past.
As they closed, I knew this
love would last.
You are my first love,
You are my last love,
You are my only love.
Now as I look back through
the doors,
I can clearly see; I've never
been in love before.
I view my past mistakes and
feel no pain.
For I know our love is real;
and,
I'll never make those mistakes
again.
You give your love to me
In all innocence and honesty,
A trust my love for you
Will never allow me to betray.
I vow to you, I'll keep your
trust
Until my dying day.
You are my first love,
You are my last love,
You are my only love.

Sharon Harris
WINDBLOWN DREAMS

in my dreams at night I drift
down tangled hidden trails.
I search for him, that someone,
that I can give all my heart to,
tell all my desires, my innermost
thoughts.
I've caught glimpses of him
in swirls of mist,
I've seen him often just ahead
of me
in my wild journeys through
clouds of sleep.
I see him but cannot reach him.
I can feel his eyes searching,
burning over me;
I want to lose myself in those
eyes.
I see him, but the wind blows
him from me.
how long must I search my
dreams and my mind for him?
is he real? I can almost touch
him
but the wind hides him in
shrouds of fog again
and he is gone from my sight.
my fingers close on emptiness.
in my dreams, I know I'll find
him someday
and hear his voice in my ear
and somewhere on a cloudless
night
he will hold me next to him
and never ever let me go.
but when I wake, I look about
me blankly
with only vague recollections
of the one I was seeking
and I wonder about the stranger
I search endlessly for
each night in my windblown
dreams. . .

Laura A. Kuntz
DECADES

I can but think of yesterday
And a smile will brighten my
face.

I've been through alot, so to
say.
Traveling from place to place.
Through experience I've learned
and grown.
Just sittin' around gettin'
blown.
Enjoyed the company of friends
Stayin' till the bitter end.
In search of that rainbow,
Following the sea, sun, and
sand.
Yes, they've showed me the
way to go.
Through sweat, smog, and
snow.
With destiny guiding me by
the hand.
And yet. . .
I have no regrets,
For what I've done.
I've lived for twenty years,
gave birth to a son,
I've cryed my share of tears,
Trying to understand
What drives me to travel this
land.
No regrets, none I can think
of
Yet I still ask for guidance
from above.
It's my life to live,
Giving all that I choose to give.
So give me a space,
For when my time comes,
Try to remember my face,
Smiling, and then some.
Life itself has been a blast,
In living, and loving, in
dying at last.

Luke Estes
HOMECOMING

Down an old country road, at
the top of a hill,
There stands an old church
house, lovely, but still.
Though beauty still lingers,
its glory is gone;
For seldom is heard there,
sermon or song.
Of the saints who worshipped
there, most of them lie
In the little cemetery, which
nestles close by.
And the old church stands
silently, day by day,
As if guarding their sleep,
until they're called away.
There was a time, though long
ago,
When the church was filled
to overflow;
Folks walked for miles on
the Sabbath day,
To hear the word and to sing
and pray.
Revivals were held and many
a soul
Surrendered to God and to
His control.
But those days are gone, at
the top of the hill

There's a sad little church
house, empty and still.
But the spot is remembered and
one day each year,
Folks gather at the church
house from far and near;
They meet with old friends on
this homecoming day,
And pay homage to loved ones
who have passed away.
The church house is filled, and
once more is heard,

Sacred songs of our childhood
and the spoken word.
And if a church house could
talk I'm sure it would say,
"Welcome home, children,
this is my day!"

William Schroll
THE TREASURE

Early I saw
an old man on bicycle pedaling,
headed for Tomorrow. . .
coat thread-bare on his back,
sweaty Stetson an attic sack
packed with webbed mem'ries
and wracked
with scurryings.
   A box of paperboard
   rode in the carrier,
   and somehow I knew
   that This was all of him. . .
   This was the hoard,
   the treasure of a lifetime:
"My medals and ribbons of
   War:
the Cause the bones and dust
   I saw."
"In pressed plastic: rice and
   a withered rose.
Once I drew so close to Heaven!
But I needn't suppose
to ever get near again."
"These coins: from every place
   we'd been. . .
this meagre ransom of the world
   our love was in."
"The album: chosen moments
   of life,
yet so many pictures have blown
   away. .
I see the babe, the child, the
   handsome boy;
the 'soft and fluff' that became
   a lady."
"Two letters: within one the
   hint of rose sachet
still haunts the first lines of love
   for me. . .
the second: never do I open
   again,
though it's the greatest of my
   treasure. . .
she left it among her things.
   The pain
   pushes me ever
toward Tomorrow."
   Early I saw
   an old man on bicycle pedaling,
   headed for tomorrow. . .
      with treasure. . .
worthy of a king.

Solomon Vanguard
**MYRTLE, THE LITTLE GRAY
HEN**

To George and Charlotte
   Wunder:
I keep remembering when,
   you told me about Myrtle,
   the little
   gray hen,
Who comes from across the
   way, to lay an egg for you
   each day.
'Twas nice of George to
   build the nest, to encourage
   her to do
   her best.
But after she lays her egg
   each day, for heaven's sake
   don't collect it right away.
Myrtle intends to accumulate
   five or six, to sit on for three
   weeks

to hatch some chicks.
So don't frustrate your little
   friend, or you'll be sorry in
   the end.
Always allow a nest egg to
   remain, to make sure she
   will return to
   the nest again.
This little egg should do the
   trick, so run out, slip it
   the nest quick!
When she feels it at her behind,
   she will think she is
   accomplishing what she has
   in mind.
How do I know so much
   about the hen?
Well, I have "Laid an egg" my
   myself now and then.
For example of this poetic
   letter doesn't pull your leg,
Then once again I have "laid
   an egg."

Li Schafer
GRAVEDIGGER

nobody from home can really
   care
since none of them know
   exactly where
i'll be one night to the next
flowing in and out of context.
whispering words strange and
   low
never caring where i go
as long as i wander from place
   to place
i catch a smile on a familiar
   face
and realize i'm too far from
   home.
ancient ruins of a catacomb
w anting me back
wanting me back where i belong
(God how i hate a repeating
   song)
satin and lace with burlap sacks
never learning all the facts
related to the story as time goes
   on
keep on wondering where i've
   gone.
i'll be home some day next
   June
whistling dixie your favorite
   tune
bringing lilacs and roses and
   samples of mud
along with bottles of other
   crud
from ruins i dug with my own
   little paws
(stop to listen as the crow caws)
rejoice, i'm home! they stare
   back,
where'd i go wrong? what do
   i lack?
hmph, if you feel that way
   i'm leaving for Egypt
headed back to my own little
   crypt,
nobody from home knows
   my name. . .
it's part of the family game.
the sign says gravedigger hard
   at work.

Helen G. Storie
AH, YESTERYEAR

I call to mind a balladeer
Who wrote of ladies far and
   near
Beautiful ones, or so 'twas said,
But in the ballad they all were
   dead.
And Villon, the lover and
   balladeer,

9

Asked of all, who were far and
near,
"Where are the snows of
yesteryear?"

I, too, would ask in the same
refrain,
I'd say it over and over again
Yes, where are the snows of
yesteryear?

I say a name, and the ghosts
appear
Each one coming from his bier.
Not in a line, for they're not
that near
In age or time, but my ghosts
are as clear
As ever they used to be
When they weren't ghosts,
and they all knew me.

There were those I knew away
back there
We all were young, and we
couldn't care
Less about time or age or
eternity.
But now the ghosts all beckon
me.
"You'll join us anon," they
seem to say.
"There'll come the time,
there'll come the day,
When you'll join your friends
of yesterday."
Ah, yesterday! Ah, yesterday!

What wonderful, wonderful
memories dear
My ghosts who come, when I
think their name
They're just like always,
always the same
My ghosts, my friends of
yesteryear.
Ah, yesteryear!

Mona R. Edmonds
**MOTHER/DAUGHTER/
FATHER**

As a child my Mother was
neglected
she was not shown love
she was not shown affection
she was shown anger
Now my mother is a mother
she still does not show love
she still does not show
affection
she does show anger.

As a child my father grew up
without a father
he was not shown love
he was not shown how to
protect
he was shown how to take
care of himself
Now my father is a father
he still does not show love
he still does not know how
to protect
he does take care of himself.

As a child I had parents
who did not show love
who did not show affection
As a child I had a mother
who was overprotective
who showed anger well.
As a child I had a father
who was never there for me
who always found fault in me.

As an Adult
I feel sorry for my parents
Sorry that they were and are
unable to show love, affection
I look back and wonder how
I managed as a child
I tell myself it was because

my parents loved me
I did not have to be told of
their love
it was understood to be there
words were not necessary.

Elizabeth Lee Mendenhall
THOUGHTS BY THE FIRE

The night I fell asleep by the
fire
Dreaming of my greatest
desires
The fire was burning bright
There was no lights
The rain poured down hard
There was thunder in every
yard
I was awakened by a sudden
knock on the door
I trembled with horror
I opened the door and there
he stood
He wasn't wearing a hood
He looked in and saw the dim
lights
He asked me if he could come
in
Without fail I let him in
We sat down in the den
The fire was burning bright
There was no lights
He was my bestfriend
I knew it would never end
We went out for awhile
But I think we both ran out
of style
We knew it could never be
I asked him for a cup of tea
We were close, sitting by the
fire
I began to think of my desires
Of being with him forever
His warmth made me tired
We both fell asleep
My love for him will always
be very deep
When we woke up three hours
later
He told me he had to leave
The fire had gone out
There was no lights
He walked to the door and
kissed me good-night
It made me feel really bright
After he left I went and relit
the fire
Dreaming of the guy I really
admired
The fire was burning bright
There was no lights—

Madeline M. Harris
**KING'S ROW, SKID ROW,
DEATH ROW. . .**

Final now is the goodbye,
whispered softly like a sigh,
While I try, not to cry,
  But wondering why, it
should be I,
  Who knows no truth no lie,
    Except that I,
    am soon to die.

Only figures loom, in a lonely
room,
No birds sing, no roses bloom,
  Approaching gloom,
impending doom,
  Reeking fiery fume,
  Of Hells dark womb,
    My lonely tomb.

Nothing real, except the pain I
feel,
What I would reveal, my
  eyes conceal,
    as with my last meal,
    goes my hope of repeal,
    from my ordeal. . .

It makes no sense, theres no
pretense,
As with feelings intense,
myself I convince,
  No special care, as I prepare
  for my final hour of despair
  My nightmare, no fanfare
  for cowardice is common,
  courage is rare,
  when its winner
    take all,
    The Winner,
    The chair. . .

Dorothy L. Hettich
THE PROMISE OF CREATION

"I am withered—I am worn,"
Haunts the tree one frosty
morn—
"I am withered—I am worn,
Yet this I know—I'll be reborn!"

As barren arms reach aimlessly
Their twisted forms reveal

A catatonic mystery
—Unspoken—and Unreal—

While scattered leaves lie at
your feet
'So brown and crisp—'So
weather beat'—
The springs of Life throughout
their veins

Have slowly drained til none
remains.

Then they shall catch the
fleeting breeze,
Be lost in space—'til no one sees
Remainders of your fruitful
Spring
When warmth brought life
to everything.

You viewed the children while
at play
And hid the "Lovers"—on
their way
From duty's call—to sweet
reward—
That unspent dreams could
well afford!

You fed the birds and sheltered
well
Their young—so that no harm
befell—
And as their wings gave rise
to flight
Your branches glowed with
pride and might.

Now in your rest and sweet
repose
Winter sends its chilling snows
That permeate unscented air
And coats the ground that lies
so bare.

But—in your wisdom, tree
forlorn,
'Tho you are withered—you are
worn,
You know that Night brings
forth the Morn
And once again—"You'll be
reborn!"

Dr. L. Marvin Marion
**A TRIBUTE TO PRESIDENT
CARTER**

"Hello, Ah'm Jimmy Carter,
  Ah'm going to be your next
President."

A peanut farmer from Plains,
Georgia,
With the charisma of the late
President John F. Kennedy,
In '76 elected President of the
United States,

Devout in religion, disciplined
in intellect, dedicated to the
pursuit of goals,
Influenced by Admiral
Rickover, demanding of self
and followers,
Understanding of the poor,
the less privileged, the
minorities.

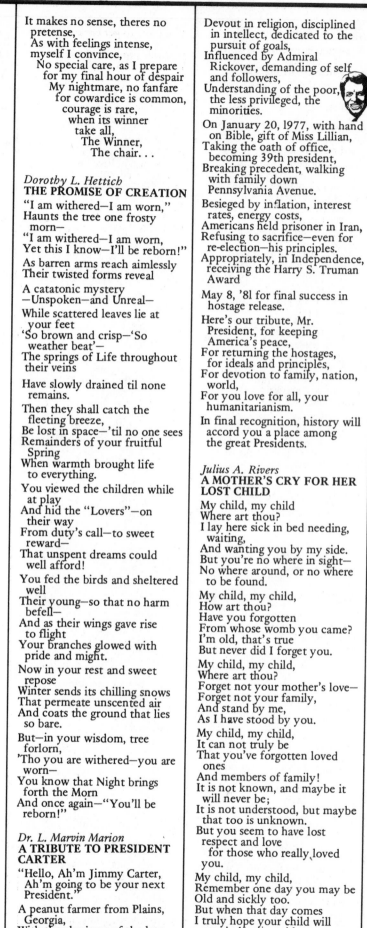

On January 20, 1977, with hand
on Bible, gift of Miss Lillian,
Taking the oath of office,
becoming 39th president,
Breaking precedent, walking
with family down
Pennsylvania Avenue.

Besieged by inflation, interest
rates, energy costs,
Americans held prisoner in Iran,
Refusing to sacrifice—even for
re-election—his principles,
Appropriately, in Independence,
receiving the Harry S. Truman
Award

May 8, '81 for final success in
hostage release.

Here's our tribute, Mr.
President, for keeping
America's peace,
For returning the hostages,
for ideals and principles,
For devotion to family, nation,
world,
For you love for all, your
humanitarianism.

In final recognition, history will
accord you a place among
the great Presidents.

Julius A. Rivers
**A MOTHER'S CRY FOR HER
LOST CHILD**

My child, my child
Where art thou?
I lay here sick in bed needing,
waiting,
And wanting you by my side.
But you're no where in sight—
No where around, or no where
to be found.

My child, my child,
How art thou?
Have you forgotten
From whose womb you came?
I'm old, that's true
But never did I forget you.

My child, my child,
Where art thou?
Forget not your mother's love—
Forget not your family,
And stand by me,
As I have stood by you.

My child, my child,
It can not truly be
That you've forgotten loved
ones
And members of family!
It is not known, and maybe it
will never be;
It is not understood, but maybe
that too is unknown.
But you seem to have lost
respect and love
for those who really loved
you.

My child, my child,
Remember one day you may be
Old and sickly too.
But when that day comes
I truly hope your child will
remain by your side
And not toss you aside as if not
alive,
as you have done to me.

Barbara Burnett
HEAVEN'S CROWN

A jeweled crown is said to be
  a gift we will receive
when heaven's shores we
  one day reach
tis something I believe

Each stone, I think, is meant
  to be
a story in itself
about the life of Jesus Christ
and not for show or wealth

Our Savior came from humble
  birth
this much we understand
just as the lustrous, soft
  white pearl
starts as a grain of sand

He grew in wisdom and in
  grace
and traveled we are told
teaching men about God's
  love
with heart of purest gold

Because He was a well loved
  man
and held in high esteem
High Priests and Scribes had
  fear in them
and envy emerald green

Judas made a pact with them
  our Savior to betray
and thirty coins of silver
  was what they had to pay

They crucified Him on a tree
  put thorns upon His head
He hung in tortured agony
  His blood ran ruby red

They thought they'd won a
  victory
and sealed Him in a tomb
But like a diamond shining
  bright
Christ beat deaths dark and
  gloom

I'll need no crown of
  precious stones
ween I'm to leave this place
but just to stand in wondrous
  awe
and look on Jesus face.

Lynne Mary-Frances Widmer
MY FIRST LOVE

I loved you
I really thought I did
I spent my time
always alone with you
You said you loved me
I said I loved you
We were together always
We went for walks
and to the movies
But we never watched
the show
We only watched
each other
When you held me
I felt so safe
So safe that no one
could harm me
When people said things
about the difference
in our ages
We didn't listen
We didn't care
You said you loved me
I said I loved you
But then something happened
Something went wrong
I don't know what
But I don't care
I don't want to spend
my life always alone

with you
You want to get close
I want away
You want to hold me
I'd prefer you wouldn't
I think our ages
had something to do with it
I couldn't do
the things you wanted
You thought my things
were childish
I really wish that
it could have worked
You said you loved me
I said I loved you
But not any more.

Kenda Lee Creasy
LOPSIDED

Yeah, 't's been this way
  awhile now.   Lop
                                    sided
hurts but
't's easier bein lopsided th'n
  bein honest (!)
You're on the downside o'th'
  teeter
                        totter 'n' i'm
on the upside
with m'legs danglin in   mid
                                            air;
We's al'ays been lop
                  sided
            this way,
            see.
        Ever since fourteen.
(Fourteen's a little old
    t'be playin teeter
                        totter but
        we's had fun
        hain't we?)
But you al'ays weighed
  more'n'me
    (all these four up'n'down yrs)
'n' that's put me in the air
  with m'legs danglin
  More'n my share o'th'times.
  ('t's cold'n'windy upthere)
Lotsatimes i wanted t'jump
                                    off
'n' play somethin more equal
  (monkey bars maybe)
But 't was a long way
        down (nothin but rocks
'n'gravel underneath)
  'n'i's chicken.
But that 'us fourteen, scrawny
  and plucked.
Now 'm taller'n'weigh more
'n'th' ground's a little higher
'n' i'm considerin
hoppin off   but
Guts don't come easy at
  eighteen.

Gigi Greco
STEPPING STONES

I grow encrusted in my armor,
Stifled, limited.
Yet safe from bruises and
  exposure.
I clamor clumsily about,
If I cry, I will rust.
I sit by the edge of a stream,
Wanting to dangle my feet.
I hear the birds,
Through the m
Though the metal mask blurrs
  my vision.
I'm growing tired of
  experiencing
Such a narrow existence.
Painfully I tug at a lifetime
Of protection.
Off comes the silver.
I am cold.
My body carries the rigidity

Of my fortress;
Tarnished and lying in a heap.
I look down at my reflection;
Trembling and scared,
Vulnerable.
Making my way across a stream
Never before ventured,
I see an image, an honest
reflection.
I accept.
I accept my trembling and
  wavering.
In my weakness, I am human.
I am tender, I am young and
  open.
My strength, my endurance,
  solidity—
This is my fortress.
My reflection lies not, I am
  recognizable.
Today, you'll see me as I am;
Arms spread,
To fly, to reach, or to break my
  fall.
Either day, I am safe and
Unencrusted.
Now.

Joyce Ann Hall
FOR TOMMIE

Sunday in the evening hour,
Sunrays flit above the tower
Of a church upon a winsome
  crest
Where Grandma places her
  hands to rest.
Her sweet voice echoes, "Just
  As I am,"
While fingers tap to the ancient
  hymn.
Bowing her head to whisper
  grace—
Every hair is neatly in place.
Eyes are sparkling, wet with
  dew,
Her love for God is kindled
  anew.
Joyful of spirit and light of
  step
Rising with the good Lord's
  help.
People to hug, then dearly kiss,
Not a soul would the lady miss.
A child clutches her swaying
  skirt,
Proud to show his brand new
  shirt.
A shirt she'd sewn especially
  for him,
Grandma gave—then gave again
  again. . .
Loving hands stroked his hair,
Golden silk and honey fair.
Pausing to gaze about the room,
The time had ended much too
  soon.
Many faces she couldn't find—
Reverberations of another
  time.
Strumming memories gently
  cleave,
First to enter and last to leave. . .
Grandma quietly laid to rest,
Beside her man on a winsome
  crest.

Sylvia Angelovic
ALL MY LOVE TO YOU

My husband, I give all my love
  to you.
Even though, I say it in words
  very few.
After you left for work this
  morning in such a rush,
It flashed through my mind,

as I stirred the kid's mush.
Got to do the breakfast dishes,
  and scrub the floor.
Have a little muddy boy coming
  in the back door.

All my love to you. . .

Got to make the beds and
  vacuum the rug,
And got baskets of dirty clothes
  to lug.
Your mom phoned and needs
  a ride downtown.
I said "Yes", but with a
  disgusted frown.

Just giving Suzy a bath, from
  getting muddy in the yard.
Tommy said, she got knocked
  dow by our dog, Pard.

All my love to you. . .

Got to go to the store and shop
  for dinner.
Couldn't talk long, to the owner
  Mr. Binner.
Number two son has a dentist
  appointment at one.
Haven't got the darn dinner
  dishes even done

All my love to you. . .

Just remembered your company
  party is at six.
I have my hair yet to wash,
  and try to fix.
What possibly could I wear,
  I wish I knew.
And wouldn't you know,
  the babysitter will be late, too.

All my love to you. . .

For our hungry children, I
  have supper yet to prepare.
Billy just split his lip, and
  gave me quite a good scare.

God half an hour to get ready,
  hope I look like I should.
Being you—you'll say,
  "Honey, you sure do look
  real good."

All my love to you. . .

Cynthia L. Maupin
WINNERS AND LOSERS

There's a shiny plaque on the
  wall
with my name upon the gold
  plate.
The dozen roses in the vase
arrived with it too.
It seems that glory and
  happiness
and bright shiny faces surround
  me.
There's only one thing missing,
and that's you.

The winner's the loser,
  when there's no one to love her.
A cold bed means more to her
  heart
than any fortune or fame.
Who's winner? Who's loser?
When there's really no prize
  to gain?
What's harder still to figure,
is who's really to blame?

We spent too many empty
  nights
seeing who could hurt who first.
The fact that we both won
is all we found out.
The score can never be even,
when the odds are always
  against you.
And the only way you can win
  is by choosing to lose.

11

The winner's the loser,
when there's no one to love her.
A cold bed means more to her heart
than any fortune or fame.
Who's winner? Who's loser?
When there's really no prize to gain?
What's harder to
What's harder still to figure,
is who's really to blame?

R. London B. Brown
CRY OF THE MINORITY

As I look through the lens
What do I see in this land
of the free?
Very few liberties,
That's—for someone who's
Black like me.
Very few opportunities,
For you fight me on every hand.
In education and thus on the job,
To me it looks like I've been robbed,
For I've never known the fruits
of this great land.
You say it's competition and
on my worth I must stand,
But for your diploma—I must
have a degree in hand.
The opportunities that come
with your first degree,
Might be opened to me if I
have a Ph.D.
As I look through the lens,
A so distorted picture I see,
In frustration I sometimes cry
American Democracy is not
for me!
Then you are shocked and say
you can't understand
That trifling, lazy, unpatriotic
black man.
All sort of name calling and
accusations you make
Perhaps thinking this makes
you and country great.
In frustration, I sometimes cry,
American Democracy for me
will never be,
Yet until death I'll hope
Until death I'll plan and try
To make American Democracy
work
For my posterity.

Bill Martin
A SIMPLE HOUR OF GLASS

A simple hour of glass—our lives
Above—the sand is hopes and dreams
Below—memories of shattered hopes
Along with dreams fulfilled—
A heap of priceless treasures
Within—discarded rubbish

Yet—one pile—the same
Thru—in—around—the
narrowed passage
Maybe? It, itself is not before
or after
But—the dimension now.
A constant battle? No—a
war is fought
to occupy the space called
Now
For if this space between we
learn but to embrace
We—overlay the rubbish
with more worthwhile
things.
And then—let go with ease,
to with the final grain of life
fall to the heap below.
Who? but a greater man, within
his space between,
would dare to probe this heap
But he—will not
for such men dwell between

Cedric Navenma
**GOOD, BAD, AND THE
UGLY**

Opportunities, I should have
been choosing
But no, I was lazy and always
snoozing.
Just think, a lot of cowardly
boozing
Cost me a lot of reasonable
loosing.
High school days were a lot
of fun
Ditching classes, flirting with
a bun,
Boozing, popping pills,
and on the run.
Never looking back to see what
I've done.
Growing up, I thought about
marriage.
What fun to be seen with a
baby carriage.
I was determined, along with
a lot of courage
But; I didn't know what was in
storage.
Many jobs were here and there.
For me, it was a whole
nightmare.
People would say; you will
get nowhere
For money doesn't fall from
the air.
Problems, problems, and they
were all mine.
No money to take the family
out to dine.
But, always money to buy
another bottle of wine.
constantly hassling for money
to pay my fine.
How long was it ever going to
last?
Do I have to end up in a cast?
Did I ever think about my past?
One bottle after another, it
was too fast.
The horrible nights I couldn't
forget,
The unexplainable days I
would regret.
The enormous losses of my
expenses
That finally brought me to
my senses.
You don't have to experience
all these memories
all these miseries
Or even go all the way into the

obituaries.
Please stop now, while you are
still ahead,
It's gonna be too late,
especially when you're dead.

Bette Dadds Hawkins
GOD'S PLAN

I am a caring, compassionate
woman,
I have earned the feeling of
grace
that dwells within me.
Life with it's heartaches and
disappointments,
has given me a wondrous feeling
of wisdom and maturity,
A feeling denied me in my
youthful quest for happiness.
I have existed, I have survived
the storms,
I have filled my alloted time
with my children, friends and
job.
Proclaiming to all, "I am
happy!"
I was untrue to myself.
Robots are incapable of
emotions;
Joy, love, sharing and caring—
"Had I become a robot?"

I have been chosen to receive
a beautiful, precious gift,
A warm, sensitive, caring
and loving friend.
Was it God's plan or perhaps
by chance—
That this man entered my life?
Wondrous discovery!!!I am
not a robot!
I am alive. I feel useful and
wanted, someone listens—
Someone cares—my new friend
has opened my mind.

We exchange thoughts and
dreams in an unending
poring of words and ideas.
This I know—we did not
meet by chance—
We met by God's plan.
A young man seething with
knowledge, reaching for
mountain tops,
stretching for the stars, meets
a child-woman of the universe.
The child-woman has so many
questions, unspoken-
unanswered.
But she will not question
God's plan,
she waits, serenly, for the
answers.

Amber L. Van Hoorn
CANADIAN WILDERNESS

Deep and compelling
Runs the appeal of the
wilderness,
As this country of ours
Fills us Canadians with
happiness;

Each territory and province
Offers so much to explore,
It's mountains and rivers,
and so much more!

Having severe limitations
For traditional human use,
Here in the country
Live the bear, elk, and moose

Vast and silent,
Enigmatic and inhospitable
To live in this wilderness,
Many of us would be uncapable;

A taste of adventure

For those who have not
acquired it,
Canada's wilderness is so unique
That one is forced to admire
it.

A rapids may still roar,
And a forest may still stand,
But a power saw and a logging
truck
Will take this out of hand. . .

In an instant this can shatter
The traveler's trend,
Of having cut himself off
From all other men.

By the four different seasons—
The sunsets, the rain,
This land will remain beautiful
But will continue to change;

The wilderness of Canada is
not just a "thing";
And myself, I am captured
By its endless meaning.

Eva M. Galloway
CHILDHOOD MEMORIES

My Son and I took a drive today
To an old home place where I
used to play.
No familiar voice called "come
on in,"
Nor as I left "come back again."

For only the chimney stood
straight and tall,
In the distance I heard a lonely
dove call,
A row of Junipers had
weathered the time,
A peach tree in bloom was
truly sublime.

A spring that once flowed cold
and sweet,
Was filled with leaves there at
my feet.
I closed my eyes and only then,
Could I see it as it was back
"when."

I saw myself a little girl,
With tom-boy ways and flying
curls.
And for a moment I could
almost hear,
"Come fetch me a pail of water,
Dear."

My son said, "Mom, are you
ready to ride?"
Or we could play a game of
hoopie hide.
As he broke the silence I think
he knew,
That tears were near and I was
blue.

Come, let's go back to the
push-button life,
And stop on the way for a
coke on ice.
When he carefully helped me
across the creek,
I kissed him soundly on the
cheek.

Frank Franklin
THE CRUCIFIXION

The wolves over the hill are
sadly whining
The stars in heaven are barely
shining
The moon does not give any
light
His hour comes close during
the night.

His nake is well known all
around
He is being sought throughout
the towns

In the garden of Gethsemane
he's to be found
After he was betrayed below
the mount.
As he knelt down to pray
in his sweat
He prayed for strength before
his arrest
His hands were to be scarred
with nails
His rising on the third day he
was to tell
He was finally taken before
the high priest
It was not long before he again
was seized
He was then taken before
Pontius Pilate
But his innocence the people
would not tolerate.
He was led to Calvary as he
carried his cross
It was there that he died for us
all
We'll never know what pains
he had to feel
But each and everyone of us
know it was real
He lost his life praying we might
be forgiven
So that we may join him in
heaven
As he watches over us all now
Kneel down and to him let us
bow
Remember as you say your
prayers tonight
He will be by your side
Even until the end of the day
He will be listening as you pray
As you see the picture of the
crucivixion
You know in your heart that
it was no fiction
Each and everytime while you
are praying
Fill in your heart the Lord
Jesus sayings.

His crucifixion will never be
forgotten
Even though earth's kingdom
has gone rotten
He can still fill your heart with
love
Way up from the heaven above.
His spirit, is pure, clean
and white
He wishes us to follow him
day and night
Your prayers He will always
hear
As you feel his presence so
near

Waitie D. Gorham
FOR SALE

At "Happy Corner" where I
dwell
There stands a house that I
must sell.
It gives my aching heart true
joy
To think of days when, as a
boy,
I spent the weeks that came and
went,
With grandpa, who was old and
bent,
Yet carried water in a pail,
And walked a mile to get the
mail;
Who miled the long, long rows
of cows,
And pitched down hay from

out the mows;
Who fed the pigs and all the
chicks,
And split the wood and picked
up sticks.
Such things are these I cannot
sell.
In yonder attic there's an
arrow
With which I killed a tiny
sparrow
Long years ago, when as a
child
I loved to hunt and shoot the
wild.
And up there is my line and
hook
with which I fished in every
brook
And caught fat suckers, tiny
trout;
My net, with which, I seized
hornpout,
Down in the cellar there are
jell—
And jars of jam I cannot sell
A barrel of pork, a keg of
wine,
A dusty churn, a frayed
clothesline.
Such things as these I cannot
sell.

There'll be an auction; this
I know.
'Tis not my wish to see things
go,
My grandpa's chair, and
grandma's too,
The things I keep can be but
few.
In memory's closet I shall
store
These few and many, many
more;
There'll be no auction there
I pray
Until my flesh and bones decay
Praise God for days that used
to be,
For these can no one steal from
me
But now to sell—I must not
fail
Thank God my memory's
not for sale.

Henry Pylypow
OCTOBER RAIN

Who has not heard of October
rain?
At times I accept it, although
it's a pain
The skies turn sullen, with
shades of grey
We had expected a much better
day.
We wouldn't be human if
we didn't complain
In fact it can be a regular refrain
The temperature drops, and
we feel the damp chill

The rheumatic ones could be
really be ill;
The grass becomes sodden, the
pavement is wet
The raindrops keep coming;
the pattern is set
I button the jacket, and put
on a cape
The elements prove that we
cannot escape.
The fog patches here, and
some over there
Make driving a hazard through
the cold misty air;

The ducks and the geese are
cheerful and gay
They hope it will last at least
one more day;
In no time at all the bus
shelters are filled
While the patrons outside
are sure to get chilled;
Don't fret and don't fume,
the rain will pass by
In no time at all, we'll see the
blue sky
Then we'll silently thank the
Power up there
For the fresh and clean air
that our spirits will bear;
All too soon we'll forget
the rain and the drizzle
As the prime dinner steak
will presently sizzle.

Cher Spagnola
CANVAS AND EASEL

I am a reborn product of you,
I am, like an unborn peace
of clay you took me and
molded me, but yet, I am not
a sculpture. Unlike a frustrated
artist you strive for quality
superiority and excellence and
all of your attributes you will
bestow upon me. And you,
like
an artist, who places his canvas
on an easel to give it strength
and
stability. You have inspired me
to stand upright you've
added a splash of
color to give me accent, and
you have
broadened my horizon to give
me
life. You are my easel for wit
without you, I fall.
I am your canvas your future
intent a reborn product of you.

Gwen Aileen Lincoln
AND I KNOW YOU LOVE ME

The sunlight flickers across your
face
Weaving back and forth
Forming millions of patterns
And I lay staring
At a curly haired head
Sleeping peacefully in a dream
I reach out and touch your face
You say my name in your
dream
And I know you love me.

I get a letter from a friend in
trouble
Sit there reading over and over
How she could have done such
a thing
I sit there thinking how lucky
I am
The phone rings
It is you asking if I am alright
And I know you love me.

I sit looking at pictures
Of you and I together
How much fun we have had
And how much more there is
to come
And then you come from
behind
And start laughing
At the tears on my face
And hold me tight
And I know you love me.
Someday when I look back
Tell children, grandchildren
and greats
If I ever can live it all
And those children of ours
Will enjoy those stories of us
That I remember so well
Of how you loved me.

Judy M. Olsen
ESSENCE OF A SOUL

Where have the blue skies gone?
Are they hidden behind a
blanket of a dark cloud?
Sadness overcomes me to think
I am alone with my thoughts
and fears,
Fears that plague me, conquer
my very being,
Fears that make me feel
defeated and lost.

Where has the sun gone?
Is it lost to me forever?
Loneliness can be bitter and
harsh,
Fantasies and thoughts play
on my brain, what is love?
Loneliness is evil, an emptiness
inside.

Where has contentment gone?
Has it vanished under that
dark cloud?
Peace of mind is self
contentment, no fears,
We must conquer our souls
before we venture on to
each other,
Ah, love and happiness
are they the key to
contentment?

Where has joy gone?
Love is sweet they say, is it?
Falling in love is wonderful
and easy,
Staying in love is not so
simple,
Joy and happiness bring peace
of mind in love.

Where has love gone?
Is it still there?
Ah yes, it is there behind that
dark cloud of his mind,
It is there behind the sunshine
of his eyes when he looks at
me,
Peace of mind, contentment,
joy and happiness is there—
it is through his love
that I find it.

Cheryl Hintzel
JOHN WAYNE

I lost a lover, a father, a friend
and forever a hero when
John Wayne
died
He was all these things to me,
in my dreams, as I watched
his movies
and on the day of his passing
as I sat and cried
I cried for when he died I lost
not one person, but four

A lover to me he was, but only
in my dreams, but no more

A father he was to me. Surely
only by image, because he was
so strong
and stern, but could be gentle
and kind

He was also my friend, because
he gave me an escape from
my problems
as I watched him act and in
this talent no one else I can
find

Then as a hero, he was always
so brave, as in his acting
and even in
his death. He fought bravely,
but lost his last battle

He was a world wide hero at
the end. He was known as
the American and
the rugged cowboy called the
Duke always riding high in
his saddle

He will be sadly missed by
many, but never forgotten.
In my memories
and in my heart he will always
have a special place

I shall never forget his special
walk, his one and only kind
of talk
and his weather worn face

Before I end this very small
tribute to a very big man that
meant so
much to me and this I cannot
shun

Because not only was he a
special man, but a supreme
actor and a very
true blue American

Jeanette Holtz
AMY

Good morning little one, full
of hopes and dreams;
As you ride upon your unicorn
to the three sorts of
moonbeams,
With your eyes of brown—bright
and bold,
And your hair of bronze with a
touch of gold.

Oh Golden Goddess of Love,
please don't shed a tear,
Good ol' Mom lays quietly
next to you, there's nothing
to fear;
As you climb aboard your
starship to the sky,
To explore this life in which
you're about to try.

You've got it made, with
your true blue pedigree,
So chin up, fair child, it's not
as bad as it seems to be;
With Mom and Dad at your
side to help you down the
path of reality,
To the milestone of ecstacy.

With the sun at your feet to
call upon,
You are one of nature's
mystical phenomenon.
By chance, you are a child of
special lovin',
Resembling the features of
two, to be genuine.

As I watch grow from year
to year,
With your childlike smile so
sweet and sincere;
And your gestures of moments

of the night,
As you outshine the mighty
suns light.

Goodnight, Amy, tomorrow
will be another day,
As you dream dreams of places
far away,
For the Bronze hair beauty of
only two,
You've got the world child,
with so many who truly
love you.

Carrie D. Chandler
NO LONGER BEHIND

We say we haven't been treated
fair,
still we must have the courage
to dare.

We say we can't,
But deep within we know we
can.

I can't—we must always reject
I can—and I can only we must
accept.

We have been full of fear.
No relief has been near.

The way has been dark.
We haven't been able to embark.

Face it—we must make our mark.
We can linger no longer in the
dark.

We aren't prisoners in a cell.
The truth is ours to tell.

We must strive to achieve.
To do this we must earnestly
believe.

That in whatever work we
choose,
We will excel and not lose.

We know that we must pass
each test,
And not be better—but be the
best!

The rest we leave to God above,
Who has endowed us with love.

Then to all men we must be
kind,
Keeping others ever in mind.

Showing all humankind that
we care,
And in all things be willing
to share.

At last we will find,
That we are no longer—no
longer behind.

Emma Jean Reed
I NEVER TOLD

Just before performance time
the midway lay in waiting,
bright under countless bulbs
ringed by swarming insects.

Mother had married a carnival
man
who didn't like spying kids
who saw too much.

Promised a surprise

little Miss Nosey
was sneaked into a quiet tent
where two huge boas
slid over and under each other
lethargic, lumpy
from chickens swallowed
whole—
cold unblinking eyes
watching every move.

Pat 'um, Pet 'um,
they caint hurt cha!

Outside to a snort of steam
the calliope chugged around,
chains down, the crowd
surged in,
shrieking young ticket holders
climbed on painted horses
or rocking ferris wheel seats

Barkers in sing song ballyhoo
extolled their wares,
trombones blared from note
to note,
gaudy girls beckoned,
kicked high and shook their
behinds.

Inside the musty side tent
mingling in all the racket,
a six year old
screamed and screamed
on her birthday.

Loretta M. Filicia
MY CHILDREN

When you were just little bity
things,
I used to think you were God's
angels without wings.

How you smiled, laughed and
coo,
hide behind a hand and say boo.

Then you learned to walk and
run,
found out toys were full of fun.

How amazed and curious you'd
be
just to see a flower or bee.

Who can forget your first bike
or the happy look flying your
first kite.

What a big day when you
went to school,
your mother went home to
cry like a fool.

How you would roll and play
in the snow,
come in and say but Mom I'm
not cold.

The smiles on your faces
Christmas morning,
was soul felt and heart
warming.

The way you came to be held
tight,
would make up for any little
fight.

When you woke from a bad
dream,
we would sit and have a dish
of ice cream.

At times when I was so blue,
in your way you knew what
to do.

You'd make everything so
sunny, so bright,
even if it was the black of
night.

What I'm really saying to all
of you,
without you I would not
know what to do.

Hope this poem tells of my love
for YOU FOUR little doves.

As your mother I always want
to be near,
to help and dry each and every
tear.

May you have a happy sunny
day,
God bless you along life's
way.

Sandra M. Slater
JUST FOR YOU

This poem is written just for
you,
To tell my father "I love you".
We've all had our
disappointments,
Our confusion and wanderings,
Our questions and ponderings.

Growing up isn't always easy,
And the growing pains seem
never to cease.
But learning patience and
forgiveness,
Seems the key to peace in life—
It removes all the internal
strife.

We do grow and change, if
we're trying,
While all around us folks are
dying;
Alone, confused and desperate.
But the good feeling of
'making things right',
Takes all that bad stuff out of
sight.

A daughter doesn't have much
to give,
Or to offer to her father.
But to say I'm sorry and I love
you.
And smiling to reassure, like
fathers do,
"You see, Sis, fathers have
failings too."

A daughter loving her father,
Watching him change, praying
for his peace,
Saying I love you and I thank
you.
Sharing the only good news
she has—
That God, the Father,
waits for my dad .
Offering His love and peace
thru His Son—
Forgiveness on the cross was
won!

Alice Cowan
**COLORADO, LAND OF
BEAUTY**

The heady scent of balsam
invades the thick pine forests
Where elk, deer and antelope
make their homes.
The bright hued birds flit
happily above, singing
lustily,

While far below the furry
rabbits and busy squirrels
abound.
On occasion a mean-eyed
grizzly lumbers about
In search of a fast-moving
stream to quench his thirst
And slap a startled trout or
two out of the water.
Numerous shimmering lakes
dot the verdant countryside,
Beautiful and blue under the
clear sky.
Giant cliffs, brilliantly red,
stand like guarding sentinals
Showing off their dark green

bushes and tumbling
waterfalls.
Sparkling rivers race and glide
to meet each other and head
for the sea.
In winter the whole land is
covered with a crisp white
blanket,
To sleep until the springtime
calls again.
I stand in awe at this astounding
beauty which some call
Nature.
I call it a gift from the hand of
God.

G. P. Elliott
BORROWED TIME

Our time we have on earth
today
Is only borrowed from God—
in a way.
God gave us life to share;
He gave us our children for care.
They all grow in their own way
With the passing of each day.

They are first brought to us in
a tiny bundle—
Placed in our arms with care.
With life He let us give so dear,
We know that God has sent
no fear.

All the pain of birth is gone.
God has blessed us with a Son!
Oh, thank you God so dear.
We watched him grow to
form his mold—
He is healthy, strong, and bold.

We have no fear of losing him.
At least our love has let us
forget
Our time is borrowed.
We have yet to go home.

We know now, Dear God
That our children too have
credit due—
You have taken our son home
with you.

We pray for your help to
get us through
The giving back our son to you.
We know it will take time;
But, Dear God, why did our
son have to die?

We realize now that it is true,
We are living our lives only
borrowed from you.
Thank you, God, for the time
we had—
Our son we give to you.

Linda Humes
MY LIFE

My life as portrayed in the
life of an apple.
I began my life so very small,
the size of a seed
to be exact.
I was loved and nourished
with water and
the best plant food.
I was growing to be a very
beautiful apple.
I grew wild during my young
apple life,
bruising other apples when
they didn't satisfy
my needs.
Yet. . .
I felt an emptiness in my little
core
of a heart.
With people thoughtlessly
rummaging through the

apples for the best.
I was always overlooked.
I searched my apple heart and
found
that it was mushy instead of
firm and crisp.
Why would someone want a
mushy apple like me.
So,
I began looking at other apples
and asking how they
made themselves beautiful.
You know what they said?
That God, not they themselves,
had done it.
I kept searching and found,
with God, the emptiness
disappeared.
My little core of a heart became
firm and crisp with
conviction for God.
I was finally picked as a
beautiful apple and
went home
with the most beautiful
person of all
to live
forever.

Lucille Davis Minke
THE MEADOW'S REALM

Reach out and touch—
the sunshine
as a footstep finds its way—
through this roughly tumbling
meadow
on a walking summer's day
Caraway—scents, from Queen
Anne's lace
wild sweet berries from the
lower bowers
winding paths of nodding
flowers—
In the air around your head
Honey bees and butterflies—
whisper by—
inviting you to seat thyself
give over to repose—
Hear the crickets—
in a happy song
singing in all their glory.

Listen too—
the spring-fed pond
thats cradled in this meadows
realm
sooth, the troubles from your
world—
with its gentle motion.

See the nesting evergreen on
the water's edge—
drink deeply from their roots—
While sharing thoughts
mirrored on the surface.
Serenely awaiting the changing
of a season.

Bethel Nunley Evans
**SOLITUDE OF A PARK
BENCH**

As one sits on a park bench
in pensive thought
With cool breezes blowing
all around,
He is lost in the world of
meditation
And delights with the echos
that resound.

Among nature's creations in
the woodlands
There is beauty and wealth
untold.
The whispering pines so
stately and tall
Give essence of history to

unfold.
Forming pyramids as they
fall on the ground
Pine cones crackle loud as if
in protest
Of the mocking bird that
twitters high above,
While guarding her babies in
their nest.

Rays of sunshine streaming
through the trees
Like ribbons strung from limb
to limb,
Make shadows dazzle among
the leaves
As sylph like figures dancing
in a gym.

A stroll down the park's
pathway
Leads to a lovely babbling
brook.
A footbridge spans its icy
waters
And little fishes swim around
the crook.

To see so much of nature's
marvels
In such a small area of the
world
Makes one thankful for the
privilege
Of living to see the wonders
that unfurl.

Karen Sue Wiles Daggett
POEMS OF THE MORNING

Poem of the morning
come to me so clear
Letting the world know
the inner feelings that so dear
come
tripping across the paper
and
scamper through my mind.
Oh, not a thing can stop
the world that my heart
does find.
say, words of gentle breeding
combined in one accord
tell all who read you
from whom you have been bore
State your case quite clearly
and make them see
that the hands whom seem to
nurture you
are that of not a he.
In early morn when all is
slumbering, in
quiet dreams
there is but one, awake
writing by moon beams
No one could find
such beauty
Alive
at such an awkward hour
Fresh and untouched
like an April shower
Such is the elusive poem
in the morning,
with words to the day anew
Bring joy
bring hope
and
happy times.
To all that read you.

Victor Morabito
LINE TO LINE

they amber skies
and ebony clouds,
they tornado winds
and hurricane rains,
they avalanche mountains
and blizzard snows,
they moisten dew

and drizzle mist;
they write between lines
and forget to interpret—
they read of the times
and somehow desert it;
they retrieve yesteryear
to ready tomorrow,
they restyle words
to garnish diction,
they repeat actions
to witness truch,
they extol holiness
to trespass sanctum:
they write between lines
and forget to interpret—
they read of the times
and somehow desert it;
they miss what's gone
but tire to fetch it,
they descry faults
but forfeit truths,
they hearten emotions
but bleed dry,
they embellish love
but usher despair:
they write between lines
and forget to interpret—
they read of the times
and somehow desert it.

Adrianne Olazabal
US FOUR

The four of us it always seems
are always making up stories
and splendid dreams.

When we were small it was such
a pleasure to be together.

No one can understand the love
and Friendship we have shared.

We made a pact oneday
whatever come our way
we would love remain unchanged.

Sunset—Sunrise—Dawn—Dusk
us four

Times have changed and so have
we
yet in our eyes its the children
we
all see.

Life is such a mystery

When I see something new I
know
they can see it too.

If one can grasp a little more
it's fine with the rest, just as
long as
one of us gets the best.

I'll never know why its this way.
It's so real, something not
everyone
can feel.

Brother and Sisters who have
overcome
the blisters of life and made it
such a divine and peaceful flight.

15

It's so easy to overcome the trivial
Qualms of childhood, look at us.
We are four forever More.

Madeline Rasmusson
THE SECRET OF HAPPINESS

When you rise at the beginning of day,
And open your window to the morning air,
If you just stand and pause a moment,
And enjoy the surprise you see there.

If you enjoy saying "Good morning",
To each friend you chance to meet,
It is surprising just how quickly
Your life can become more sweet.

If you thrill at each hand clasp.
That you receive from a friend,
You will soon have so much happiness,
Some of it to others you can lend.

Even though you find your occupation,
Does not quite suit your taste,
If you but do your job real well,
While working no time you waste.

You will soon learn to enjoy doing it,
Even though you do it again and again,
If you strive to do it a little better,
Then has been done by your fellowman.

If you just pause a moment to listen,
To that bird singing in your tree,
For he can teach you a good lesson,
For he is just happy as he can be.

Then at the close of a long day,
And you retire with the setting sun,
You will find you have had happiness,
For a perfect day has been done.

Instead of doing things just for pleasure,
And having only fun ahead in view,
Life is so much sweeter, if you will just
Take pleasure in everything that you do.

Lorie Meyer
THE HOLY REDWOODS

They stand stately and proud, these quiet giants,
Their heads peeking through the windows of God's heaven.

They have witnessed the coming of Christ, the birth of nations, and the birth of freedom.

They are a haven for God's creatures.

Pioneer settlers, kings and queens, and "we" have walked among them, in awe at their transcendent beauty and the peace
and tranquility they emit.
They were entrusted to mans care
for eternity.
Now, their roots tremble in the earth's bosom, while man's machinery
threatens their existence.
As each "Majestic Giant" falls to
earth to perish, its pain is felt
in the very heart of the universe universe.
The word "Mankind" has lost its
meaning, for man has become the
executioner of still another of God's creations.
While "He" watches through tear-stained eyes, and "His"
please fall upon deaf ears.
"He" must be wondering why "He"
created—man!

David Divine
I'M JUST GLAD I'M AN AMERICAN

I'm just glad I'm an American
Wish I could meet some one day
Wish I could meet one someday
I'll be glad when an American becomes president
Who's not glad his Mama comes from Europe or Daddy comes from Africa
But somebody whose glad for glad sakes their American
Shoot the roots
And I don't wanna hear that jibe from someone just because
I'm glad about Africa and Europe don't mean
I ain't glad for America
Well, I ain't puttin down either one, seriously
Nor nobody else's home town tell you the truth
But I'm just glad I'm an American
Just why I don't really know
Then again I think I do, really
Maybe cause God tole me so is telling me so
Maybe it's ice cream soda and rock n roll
And smokin Joe, Mohammed Ali or Peggy Lee
Still I'm glad I'm American
Not because of her history
Because of what I feel and hear and see
I ain't very smart about intellectual things
But Heaven's here it seems
Take this building I'm living in, let's pretend, not

Why they got people here from all over the world
Black n brown, white n green, must be martians, hum whatever
Yes, I'm just glad I'm American
My Black Blood tells me, whitey get right
My White blood tells me, blackie, I ain't all wrong
My Spanish blood tells me "Get Hot" in some songs
My Indian blood tells me to live where I can roam
All together they say Americas my home
Chinese ancestry keeps me at peace
Japanese tells me like it for keeps

Yes, I'm glad I'm American.
Thank God He done this for we, mum I mean
Thank God he done this for me

Heidi D. Ediger
MY GRANDMA'S KINDA SPECIAL

My grandma's kinda special
Kinda nice and sweet;
My grandma's kinda special
To me she's pretty neat.

My grandma's pretty special,
She's 98 years old.
She's really kinda special—
Her heart is made of gold.

Her thoughts are really very sweet,
My grandma's pretty neat.
Yes, I think my grandma is very special.

Grandma taught me lots of things—
To knit, crochet, and wash behind my ears.
When I call her name, she always hears.

She tells me stories and teaches
and plays games with me.
Yes, my grandma's pretty special, you see.

She came to school with me one day
Then the children, they did say,
"I love that grandma of yours named 'May'."

Grandma Rickey is her name,
And to me she's known for her fame,
Even though she's a little lame—
Yes, I love that grandma of mine just the same.

She may not hear or walk too well
But to me, she's pretty swell!

Mary Weller Sa'id Royce
NIGHT IS MOTHER—AM I MAD?

Change but never!
Seal to eternity, mother,
your cloak cast in bronze—
you of no fear,
calm and even,
who stirs yet finely to passion,
then turns, returning
to constancy accepted
in the vigil fire
of forever.
Stoutly guide the bellows

to essential coals,
while I, your charge,
whimper for the tit.
Do not pawn hope
for dreams of imperial tablets:
chiseled memories to some
sun-god's magic eye—
verbs muttering uselessly in the glow.
A thistle, burn not brightly,
nor a dried squid bone.
But, toss in a tuft of ineffable awe,
the patch from a loyal old sweater,
and twenty cloves of garlic—
a gift, mother,
from your unforgetting friends.
Night is not a wizened olive. . .
Night might be a dance. . .
Night is:
CHANGE FEAR CALM
PASSION CONSTANCY
HOPE
equalling LOVE
Night is Mother—am I mad?
in the vigil fire
of forever.

Dorothy Mudd
THE CROWD

Streets teem with the flow of the masses
Few stop to listen and look across
to the western sky ablaze from the setting sun.
Yet, there is that solitary one at the edge of the crowd.

In the crowd, but not a part of it, alone
from the orange sunrise in the east to the
red sunset in the west. She strives
from within to muse away from the throng
for she hears a harmony of the waves.

Insensitive to the push, the noise,
the locomotive whistle: she hears
the soft padding of sandal feet, and she breathes
the odor of fish from the peddler's cart.

There are no audible words to this rhythmic sonata from the heartbeat of the universe.
While walking alone the never-ending sandy beach
she listens as waves break

upon the shore.
Narrow are the crowded Hong Kong Streets
in the shadow of Tiger Balm Garden
Amid this rush of life come nostalgic
reveries; because from there the sea washes
its beach across the world.
Her own self winds this mystical music box
Tinkling noisily within the crowd

to the tune of the lapping waves
from that far away eastern shore
her own solitary symphony flows.

Eileen B. Perry
THE ORANGE TREE

He bought the orange tree
From a nice old lady
Who sold him some antiques—
It was green and lovely.

Nearly four feet in height
It was twenty years old.
We put it in a churn
Inside, out of the cold.

Then he left me one day
For another woman.
I hated the orange tree
Given by my husband.

I did not water it.
The leaves fell and it died.
It was a symbol of
My lost love, and I cried.

Then one day I noticed
The trunk looked alive, green.
I thought I'd water it—
A miracle I've seen.

For there were many sprouts
And little shiny leaves
Among the dried old limbs—
Still my broken heart grieves.

A lesson I have learned
From the old orange tree.
Love may seem lost indeed—
Faith brings new life to me.

Michele F. Keegan
THE ENCHANTRESS

I am an enchantress,
   at least I'm told that's so.
I've been many things to
   many men—
   child, lover, friend, and foe.
My eyes they say are mystical,
   they bewilder and intrigue,
And there's a fire deep within
   love's passion can't fatigue.
I give myself so totally
   when I have been enraptured.
But rarely has there been
   the man,
   my heart and soul that's
   captured.
Men have tried to win my heart
   with trinkets rich and rare.
But I tire of their foolishness—
   for them I cannot care.
I do not want your diamonds.
   I do not need your gold.
But if you've a heart that's
   pure and true,
   you can buy what
   can't be sold.

Barbara Robinson
A STAR

I touched a star and held
   him close-
And to my bosom pressed him;
But in heat of love I let him go,
For a star is no possession.

He has a path, a life to lead,
And it crossed mine for awhile,
Which makes us each feel

more complete;
Oh! Those memories make
   me smile.

But it hurts me, too, it
   brings an ache-
A longing I cannot resist.
But that will pass, pain
   doesn't stay,
Only joyous love can persist.

Helen McLain
CONTAGION

The puss runs out of the sore,
While lesions leisurely form;
Woman gives birth to disease.

Her man lies ignorantly in
   that infectious bed,
Gleefully performing the
   thrusts of jeopardy,
While captive hands lull him
   into fearless faith.

The cool Plottress with her
Wicked work well-ordered,
Strikes! And again!

Drunkenly down drifts he
To the equaler of man;
His pure blood mixing languidly
With the crimson liquor of
   other fools.

The contagious sores contain
   her body,
But she, oblivious to vileness,
   touches—
And leaves the stench of death
On the hands of all women.

Doris Vinson
A CHILD IN PASSING

Oh child of the earth,
   and child of the air.
When you look around
   do you feel that I care?

I look into your eyes
   as you're searching for love,
and I want to give you
   what you're dreaming of.

I feel your pain
   and your loneliness, too.
But here I am alone . . .
   what can I do?

I can show you I care,
   I can hug and smile.
I can give you that love
   if only a while.

I want to help you
   grow and be strong,
   set your feet on the right
   path, not on the wrong.

For when you are grown
   and standing so tall,
   maybe you'll reach down
   so a child won't fall.

Jill St. Claire
FEELINGS

If I could wish upon a star
I'd never change the things
   you are
From the start I'd have
   the chance.
To make our marriage the
   last romance.
I'd fill your days with
   happy times.
And make our life just one
   big rhyme.
You were once my King,
   my Prince.
What's happened to that
   feeling since?
I feel hurt, I ache inside.
I feel as if, I can't have pride.

I feel as if, I'm on my own.
I'm in a crowd, yet all alone.
I feel depressed more than
   you see.
Can you see the person in me?
Please look at me and let me
   know.
I only live on love that shows.
I'm mad because I'm made
   to feel.
That real love isn't really real.
If my words could only
   reach you.
You would surely understand.
You're the one and only
   person,
My one and only man.

Nora Coots
WANING MOON PONDERS

This November dawn
A shrunken moon observes
Ice clad Elm tree branches-
Cornucopia of diamonds
   and pearls.
Aware these gleaming jewels
   will disappear
Another year end.
Memory records
For replay.

Winifred Conkling
THE HUNT

With death came my genesis.
Starving
Consumed by autonomy
I am intercepted
by wolves, masked as men.
They blindfold
and lead me to Lucifer's den.
Eyes open to darkness,
the Light is eclipsed
by avarice and Judas' intention.
"Improbity reigns   "
in the kingdom of God.
I am told.

In hunting my way
toward the light
I must face a millenium.
Alone.
With an ominous rifle lodged
beneath my arm
I stalk . . .

M. C. Weiland
PROFIT

Is there no time or place
   for friends
in this world of dividends.
Today, it seems you rarely see
any good old-fashioned charity.
As we strive to make a living,
is there really no time for
   giving—
To gain the world, but lose
   a friend
there is no profit in the end

Bud Coleman
HARD SPENT AMERICAN
(An Ode in Sonnet)

At your birthday I lament;
A greater space within my mind,
Has been so idle spent.

I cannot think, but grieve
   and weep.
For I know a love so fine.
Alas! 'tis only a dream,
   I sleep.

For me this day can mean
   no'else.
My days are cold, I now see.
Thy eyes, thy heart,

extend no pulse.
On your birthday I contend,
That myself release me . . .
This ink: does it end!
I'll not cry long; I'll not cry.
For one tear will cause eternity.

Nancy M. Brevelle
SHINE ON ME

Wherever you go, you
Beckon to all who are
   cold and frozen.
Like luminous embers
Your gentle smile invites them
   to come closer
While your soft eyes whisper
   to their frozen spirits.

Desperately I'm drawn to
   your inner warmth
The glow in you warms me,
Thawing the hard, icy shell
   around my heart.

I need you to shelter
   that naked, vulnerable
Core you've exposed.

The artic world
   still
      surrounds us.

Talma Windle Wolfe
GREEN SKY AT MORNING

Early start for home.
   Sky dark blue
With brilliant stars like diamond
Starfish in deep sea.
   As we drove below
A high stony bluff the sky
   become
Clear pale green like a
   shallow bay,
Like transparent jade.

The stars were gone.
Around a curve, ahead we
   saw the low
Pink flush of dawn.
The sky was edged with
   wisps of cloud
Like foam. As we sped on
The haze lifted, drifted away.
Pink blazed to copper, then
   began to fade,
Soon was changed to buff.
It was day.

Sometime I may forget
   the starry night,
The fiery sunrise, the later noon.
But always I shall remember
When you and I,
Shoulders touching for
   comfort
And warmth, moved swiftly
   along
Beneath the cool green sky.

Terri Hendrick Ullrich
REGRET

Regret—
a feeling of aching helplessness;
a stenching carrion of the past,
fed upon by immortal
   memories,
the bones of which will
   forever serve as a monument
to things that should have
   been otherwise.

Sue Sutton Willbanks
AN ALIEN CHIME

Softly through time
In quiet solitude,
An alien chime
Sounds a postlude,
A poignant strain

From a distant sphere,
A misty curtain
Lingering there.

Strangers passing by
Pause to listen,
Looking to the belfry
As eyes moisten.
Then, in haste they go,
Ignoring the air above,
A piercing echo
Of a cry for love.

Karen A. DiMaggio
TO ONE BETRAYED

What would I do
if I saw you again?
Would I smile
my deceiving smile
and add more lies
to my sin?

Would I possess nerve
to face you once more—
to look in your eyes
and know what I am—
Recalling the things
that I've done before?

I'd rather face Hell
and the devil himself
or unlimited pain
of another kind—
To face you again
would be facing myself.

Yvonne Pennestri
SONNET TO MY HUSBAND

Do not assume I love you,
 'though all I see
In memory's pale light is each
 part of you;
The mischief in your eyes, that
 change from green to blue,
The confidence and pride in
 all you do,
Your strong hands and mind so
 dear to me,
Your lower lip turned down
 when you're deep in thought.
Do not assume I love you,
 though I am caught
In tangles of emotions you
 cause me to feel.
How easily you crush me with
 careless words or looks,
Or make me take second place
 to your books,
Or ignore me, and inflict me
 with pain that won't heal.
Just because I lay sleepless
 with thoughts of you
Or live with your memory the
 whole day through,
Do not assume I love you—
 although I do.

LaVerne Anne Capalbo
TRUTH AT LAST

I chased the sun,
 And found the rain.
I reached for stars,
 My quest in vain.
I yearned to touch the moon's
 soft glow,
 My patience short, my grasp
 too slow.
While in defeat I hung my head,
 My heart, my soul, my senses
 dead.
And then a truth enveloped
 me,
 To light my world with
 ecstasy.
I'd tried too hard to reach for
 naught,
 For beauty lies in tranquil
 thought.
The brilliant sun warms earth
 and seas,

And you and I are touched by
 these.
While twilight's stars light
 destiny,
 They shine in eyes of souls
 set free.
The pale moon's glow, a beacon
 light,
 To guide us through each
 darkened night.
No longer need I chase the sun,
 For peace and love are gifts
 of One.
The highest peak I need not
 climb,
 For all I want in TRUTH is
 mine.

Gloria Warden
MY FISH GROVER

A friendly little creature
 is he
Adds to my day lots
 of company
Never a dull moment in
 his life
Not ever signs of stress
 of strife
Observing the way he spends
 his time
Swimming around in wavelike
 rhythms
Wouldn't have thought how
 I'd learn to love
Grover, my little fish from
 God above

Virginia Pope
THE HYSTERICAL WIND

 The hysterical
 Wind
Laughing in the opaque of
 night
Gives me chills as I lay thinking
 Of you.
Its perpetual interruptions
 evade
 My ponderings until finally
 You
 Are abandoned and my mind
 Pursues the
 Wind.

Frances L. Sessions
I THINK OF YOU

Waves crashing on a white
 shore
Standing at my open door
I think of you.
Tanned face and blowing hair
We had **so** much love to share
I think of you.
I walk upon the white sand
And see a couple hand in hand
I think of you.
I spot our secret place
And see your loving face
I think of you.
Then the cloud of death
And I remember you are
 at rest
I think of you.
Back to my door
To watch the white shore
I think of you.
You are the one that is dead
And I am left alive instead...
To think of you.

Keith E. McGraffin
TOUCH ME NOW IN LOVE

Touch me now in love,
touch me softly
and in kindness,

Like the soft breeze

whispering in the trees,
like the waves washing
sand out to sea
in their gentle caress.

Touch me now in love,
like the sun
touching the earth
in a spring sunrise.

Josephine Bannon Scott
REVERIE

Dreams suspend beyond the
 dawn.
Hopes elude the night.
Daylight brings reality, and
Morning whispers "No."

Slowly, we learn to face the
 light.
Small triumphs have to suffice,
 when
Bleakness strives to the fore.

To soar and float beyond the
 clouds
Must wait till night, and
Once again, we find
Solace in our inner mind.

Sometimes to share,
More often to treasure,
We hide the quiet times
 But
Some day, yes, some day
All will know our secret
 triumphs.

In the bright light of day
Our secret hopes will explode
Into riotous color like the
Flora of spring, and
We will be justified.

Gary Fredrickson
THE TILLER

Later
the tiller comes,
scratching the earth
(in relief)
with his small hoe.
Behind him
the earth turns
black,
gray,
white,
and flapping with seagulls
gathering the crumbs
of the feast.

Katharine Chalk
GO WITH YOUR FEELINGS

 Go with your feelings,
 Let it all out,
This will be healing, so try,
 Minding the bad times,
 Minding the sad times,
Go with your feelings and cry.

 Spilling your grief
 Gives you relief,
Every outlet you allow
 Takes away pain,
 Helps keep you sane,
So pour out all your troubles
 now.

 Let it come pouring,
 Don't hold it in,
Never all feelings deny,
 Somebody telling,
 As they come welling,
Go with your feelings and cry.

 Let yourself feel
 Anger that's real,
Tell the world the reason why,
 Be brave and strong,
 But there's nothing wrong
When you break down and cry.

 Go with your feelings,
 Let it all out,

This will be healing, so try,
 All your confessing
 God will be blessing,
Go with your feelings and cry.

C. H. Kletzker
UNTITLED

Dawn comes creeping to
 smother iced tea afternoons
 into shrouds of night.

Art Howard
FAITH

Let us share these precious
 bits of time
And cherish each moment of
 our
 unborn future with reverence.
The season of our love will
 not fade
But urge forth from the unquiet
 of our souls a new peace.
When we shall no more be ruled
 by the dust and shadow of
 time
The rising sun will
 continue.
Our love reborn in the face
 of every cloud
Will soar with the ease of the
 soft gull.

Loretta Foose
MEDITATION

If you are frightened or uptight
 or feel you're in a bind,
Meditate upon the Light
 and leave the world behind.

This Light is always waiting
 there
 and ever watching you;
You can feel it everywhere
 in everything you do.

Flush all bad thoughts from
 your mind
 and quietly be still.
Dwell on Love and you will
 find
 you've given up your will.

Becky Sweet (Reb)
SUNSET

A sunset is like a
 Splendid actor;
Gracing the stage in a
 Vivid Performance;
Something you hold in awe,
 As he bows his head
Majestically,
 Before his nightly
Exit.

Daniel Kirk
HALYCON DAY

Hand in pocket
Sunset ray
Dry leaf smelly
Halycon day

Dog in thicket
Lover's smile
Dirt road dusty
Country mile

Love in concert
Nature's wand
Green-eyed laughing
Strawberry blonde

Shirley Chaput
THE COMPOSER

Conquering my role in life was
 of my greatest challenge!

For, I (who was better known
 as the composer of my own
 existence) has set to lyrics,
 to melody my life of song.
And with this ability to

penetrate
  And create
    Out of what appears
      to be air,
A downpour of musical
  experience
That results from a healthy
  lust for life
And an extensive search
  In my universal travel.

Georgiana Lieder Lahr
SKY SONNET

Shall I tell you what things
  I see in sky?
It is a canvas wide, where
  angels paint
Such panoramas to delight
  the eye,
All done with heav'nly Art,
  with no restraint.
Shall I tell you what things
  I saw today?
I saw a range of mountains,
  shining white,
And in a field of blue, small
  lambs did play,
While over all, there shone a
  golden light.
At sunset time, the canvas
  was aflame
With colors bright, of ev'ry
  shade and hue;
A magic castle, and two kings
  of fame,
Arrayed in purple robes,
  came into view.
If you will watch the sky,
  you, too, will see
A canvas filled with glory,
  majesty!

Steven V. Kemery
PROGRESS

One is a lonely number.
  Two is better than one.
Why not find a companion?
  Spend not your hours
    in idle intrepidness.
Reflect not on what has been,
  yea, neither to be.
    This hour, this day, this
      existence we are
        living is now!
Seize it fast.
  Know where you are now,
And tomorrow you will
  know how far you've come.

James Hansford Wright, III
BROWN LEAF

Wherever pounding hoof beats
  drum, as galloping
Riders go or come, wherever
  the saddle is still
A throne, and the dust of
  hoofs by wind is blown,
Wherever are horsemen, young
  and old, the
Pacing mustang's tale is told:
  A hundred years,
On hill and plan, with comet
  tail and flying
Mane, milk white, free, and
  high of head, over the
Range his trail has led. Never
  a break in his
Pacing speed, never a trot
  nor a lope his need,
Since the faraway days of
  the wagon train, men
Have followed his trail in vain.
  A score of horse
Spurred to death, still he flees
  like a phantom's
Breath, and from some hill

at horizon's hem,
Snorts his challenge back
  at them. A bullet drops
Him dead by day, yet white
  at night he speeds
Away. Forever a thief of
  tamer steeds, stallion
Prince of the mustang's
  breeds, coveted prize of
The men who ride.....Never
  a rope has touched
His side.
Wherever the saddle is still
  a throne,
The great white mustang's
  tale is known.
    For Chris and Elizabeth

Marisol Vazquez
CHANGES IN TIME

As naturally as the early
  sun rises
will an infant undoubtedly
  cry,
one season gives way to
  the next,
consequently, time relent-
  lessly advances.
Styles will alter, views
  will change,
the young will age as the
  aged grow older.
Faces of beauty become
  those of experience,
Time will take its toll
  upon youth.
Change is a battle that must
  not be fought,
the drawn, tedious encounter
  will be in vain
for in the longrun, it will
  claim its victory.
Willingly, must we travel in
  the chariot of Time.
We must not drift, nor must
  we anchor,
Life is too great a challenge
  to lose,
a positive attitude and strong
  will are essential,
for it is the persevering
  traveler who reaches the
  summit.

Gary Durkin
FRIENDS

People meet and they like
  each other
they get along very well together
they smile and frown, laugh
  and cry
day by day wondering why
when it's all over and the
  journey ends
they finally know why, they
  have just become friends.
But only the journey has ended,
  it's true
and there is no reason for us
  to be blue
our lives are different and
  separate as such
but true friends have ways
  of keeping in touch
we keep the memories of
  things we have done
but friendships will last for
  all time to come.

Larry Brownlee
LOVE EVER PRESENT

Thoughts running wild
  through a mind of confusion.
Emotions pushing to be felt
  but afraid to feel.

Hearts crying out
  but afraid of being broken.
Eyes sparkling with joy
  yet filled with many tears.
Hands reaching out
  yet afraid of finding nothing.
Love, ever present
  yet afraid to grow.

Patt Iandiorio
THE EDGE OF TOPANGA

From atop the rim
  of the canyon I had seen
all the places I had traveled
  and the places I'd been.
The expanse of land
  was spread far and wide
and from there I could see
  the Pacific tide.
There seemed no end
  to the beauty of it all
as the sun set on a mountain
  waiting to fall.
It sank slowly, oh so slowly
  three-quarters, half, and then
I wished for it's return
  so I could see it again.

Ryder Robinson
BORN OF WATER

I stand alone on the open surf,
  the sand washing over my feet,
Ocean waves coming and going.
The soothing night wind flows
  cool through my hair;
Looking back, I see the
  horizon fall.
In the distance, dim in the
  fog, someone's coming;
Next to me he stands, gazing
  at the misty grey sky;
Then we both feel the
  rolling waves.
For we are born of water,
  we can't stay away;
Our blood in the water,
  our soul in the sand.
The city can't satisfy our
  seagoing souls;
Faraway, we long for the
  roar of the ocean.
The tide guies our moods as
  we think of its reaching out
    to us,
For we are born of water;
Our blood the water, our
  soul in the sand.
Never are we lonely as long
  as the gulls soar;
Our spirits run free with the
  tide and the wind
Because we were born of
  water, we can't stay away.
Our blood in the water,
  our soul in the sand,
For we are born of water.

Jerrie L. Chamberlain
A FOAL

They come in all sorts of
  sizes and colors,
From white to black, to a
  red or a bay.
Some are born gals, some are
  born fellers—
Makes no difference, they'll
  steal your heart away.
Some are destined to run
  at the track,
Some end up in a rodeo
  string;
Some pack grub tied on
  their back,
And others do tricks in a
  circus ring.

Some fancy ones may win
  in a show
With shampooed hair and
  ribbons, no less!
Some pull big hay wagons
  through the deep snow,
And some are for kids to
  love and caress.
Whatever their duty while
  here on earth,
Whatever their breed, whether
  young or old,
Only a horse lover knows
  the worth
Of a little new foal to have
  and to hold.

Bryce M. Sheldon
VIKING PROBE

Pale utterance of saffron words
Rounded with a sheaf of
  stars;
A shell's soft merchandise
Leeward on the bars.
Mute craft across the skies,
Soft lands that melodize;
Yet hollowed and alone,
No song for Mars but stone.
A planet's silent word
Voiced by a metal bird;
No Rosetta stone, no flower
  petal;
No thought, where a creeping
  shadow stirred.
Fog in the unquestioned night,
Room with soft spectral walls;
Hidden from that ghostly light
Down endless halls.
Life's unanswered question
Rounded with a sheaf of
  fears;
Like the shadows of a million
  birds
Lost in a sea of tears.

Barbara Hibbert
REACHING OUT

I reached out to a friend today
  to let her know that I cared.
I wanted to give her something
  in a special way,
with hopes that it would lift
  the heavy cross
    that she beared.
But in my heart I knew I
  had not much to give,
only my love and friendship
  and nothing more
    had I.
And within my heart I pray,
  that soon she will
    live.
Without the heavy cross that
  on her shoulders lie.

Tom Papadakis
THE MERCEDES LADY

A Mercedes lady on her way
  to the office
stops at a red light
near a condo with a kitchen
  window
where a housewife cutting
  coupons
glances out at the woman
  behind the wheel
of the idling sportscar.
Her hair up in rollers
  her husband gone to work
  her kids in school
she sits alone
with the morning paper
clipping out squares
  and rectangles
to save pennies on

family things.
So the roles are cast
in this tragedy of lost identity
and the street light changes
to green
as their eyes meet...

Edith P. Hazlehurst
THE TWILIGHT HOURS

The hours I wish
I could always keep,
Are the hours when night
Lulls the day to sleep.

The bustle of day
Should come to an end.
It's time to enjoy
A book or a friend.

It's time to calm
The troubled breast
When night time lulls
The day to rest.

Soft colors seem
To rest the eye,
When night time paints
The evening sky.

It rests the soul
And warms the heart
With a magnificent
Display of art.

So it's time to stop,
But I wish I could keep
Those hours when night
Lulls the day to sleep.

Margaret Sheridan Paquette
AN INDIAN LAMENT

I'm lying here, across the ditch
where I have fallen
Life seems so futile, and which
of us has made the
best of it?
I walked the mesa with my
friend, and sat on mountain
tops
Loving the miles of beauty
stretching endlessly
This is OUR land, our ancient
heritage
I am well educated, but our
ways are not your ways
Because I loved our arts and
folklore
People say I went back to
the blanket.
Yet all I wanted was to keep
our old traditions
Now I lie here, dead, across
this ditch.
And who will mourn me,
except my mother?
The wind whispers to me of
her broken heart.
I helped raise the flag at
Iwo Jima
My name is Ira Hayes.

Doris D. Smith, Ph.D.
**THANK YOU, NATURAL
MOTHER!**

Oh natural mother, how great
you must be
To have enough love to set
me free.
You are the one who gave
me life,
You are the one who experi-
enced such strife!
I was cut off from your
unfailing love
Because of the courage you
received from above.
I was grafted then to a
different tree
Which nurtured and cared
for only me!

Years long have passed since
those days long ago,
But just who you are, I have
wanted to know.
I have wanted to know you
and thank you at last
For giving me strong roots,
the roots of my past!
That search was accomplished;
I know you once more.
Again your great love upon
me doth pour.
I'm now a complete person
with real roots and love.
The peace which I feel comes
from God up above.
Thank you, dear mother, for
giving me life.
Thank you for experiencing
those long years of strife.
Thank you for giving me roots
that will last,
And for your love so strong
and steadfast!

Elizabeth Hamilton
I CAN IMAGINE

I can imagine the first dawn,
The sun's final breakthrough
from the
darkness of a million years.
As if I were there,
I can feel the fresh air permeate
my lungs,
And the sky,
So blue I can almost see forever.
The ocean,
Soft and cool as I glide in, and
as clear as crystal allowing the
glistening colors to be seen.
All life seems to be reaching
towards the sun, drinking in its
nutrients with thirsty greed,
But the outcome is
magnificent, the
whole earth green and alive.
The birds fill the air with their
shrill but sweet music even into
the
sunset,
Which brings with it a
tremendous
fire-like glow,
That spreads throughout the
horizon melting into darkness,
That lets the coolness sweep
over the earth.

Cleo Iline Soto
SUMMER'S EVE

A song sung high -
A gong rung low,
Doves cooing in the
Summer heat.

Music spills,
Aching trills,
Enchants our
Dancing feet.

You are a shadow,
I am a mist.
Memories dark
And sweet.

Are called from over
Sweet-breathed clover
When summer's eve
I meet.

Stewart Shepherd Giffin, Jr.
THE JOYS OF WAR

Joy comes when shattered
streets
Erupt again with student
laughter,
Joy comes when scattered
dreams
Return and bloom, for

ever after,
Joy comes with hearing
children crying
From childish things,
instead of dying,
Joy comes with knowing
men are daring
To stand for freedom, peace,
and sharing,
Joy comes to me, at last,
Because I know my wars
are past.

Vivian Machado-Jantz
OUR LAST GOODBYE

Today I said goodbye. Not
out loud, but in my heart.
There was no need to speak
for the silence voiced both
out thoughts.

I wanted to tell you again how
much I loved you, but the
words wouldn't come and I
knew my plea would be lost
in the wind.

I almost reached out to touch
your hand, one last time,
but I knew the time had
come for me to let you go.

Silently I said I Love You,
then turned and walked away.

Andrea E. Stavros
**TAPESTRY OF THE
UNICORN**

Madder, woad, and weld:
Threads woven from their meld
live on through the centuries
line on line,
lasting beyond revolutions
(once, coddling potatoes,
safe in a peasant's cellar)
to come round
to hang from walls of
museum stone
Author Unknown.
Woven for unknown reasons—
only the rhyme of thread
remains.

James P. Lodge, Jr.
**A CONTRIBUTION TO THE
DISTINCTION BETWEEN
EROS AND AGAPE**

Before men wrote
They raised sacred poles
And Copulated Liturgically
In the name of gods
Of fertility.
When they did the same thing
Non-liturgically
They called it loving.

When Jesus spoke of love,
He meant something different,
And liturgized it
With a kiss.

Today we seem hard put
To tell apart
The varieties of love.
We seldom stop to think
How thoroughly
A sacred pole is disabled
From its symbolic purpose
By a crossbar.

Woodrow Andrew Fink
**AN OLD-FASHIONED
LOVE POEM**

Thoughts of her keep floating
through my mind
Through every hour of every
day that I'm away.
Vivid pictures of the girl I
left behind
Are etched upon my heart
and there to stay.

If only I could but see her
To hold her in my arms
once more
To tell her how much I
love her
Then my heart could heal
its sore.

But all I can do is remember
Those sweet moments of
bliss long ago
When everything I did
concerned her
And my love continues
to flow.

It's a burning, seething
upheaval
To be away from the one
you need.
It's a maddening, saddening
feeling
To know that you'll have
to leave.

It's a hungry, yearning
sensation
Deep in the soul of me.
From which there is
no turning
With her, I wish to be.

So through his torture
I realize
Remembering this girl
I know
That perhaps one day
she'll visualize
How my love for her will
always glow.

Irma Brown
SURVIVAL OF A CAT

Old Fellow, walking
A tight-rope to defeat death
Wavers and regains
His balance, platform in sight
Where he rests and re-fuels

Irma Brown
WINTER HAI-KU

Icicles hang like
Stalactites trimming town roofs
On a wintry day

David A. Johnson
NOT ASHAMED

I am not afraid to take a stand
In these days, when to stand
for anything
Is considered a breach of
someone else's rights

I am not afraid to love,
And to show that love
To everyone that I meet

I am not afraid to be involved
While others strive to avoid
responsibility

I am not afraid to hold
unpopular views
While others fear public
opinion

I am not ashamed
I am a Christian

Nancy Adele Hodshire
DAWN SONG

It's a few moments past
the dawn—
Early risers waken me.
My dark dream flies before
the light
Like a veil in the wind.

On the dawn's fragrant breeze
Floats a nightingale's song,
Bidding me rise from my couch
And walk in the warming light.

As the Day-Star lights my face,

His sweet melody cheers
  my heart,
And my spirit is refreshed
And stirred to join his song.
  Suddenly his voice is still
And he rises, homeward-bound
But his message lingers on
Echoing in my heart.

Mildred M. Cook Brookins
**HUSBAND, FATHER,
  GRANDFATHER**

Dear Daddy,
Nothing can ever erase
  The lovely things
  My life has known
Nor diminish the treasures
  That we shared
  Alone
I would not wish you back
  To know such pain,
The anguish and the suffering
  That you would feel again.
Ah! No, my love, I must
  Go on each day,
Knowing that somehow
  You found the way,
And each dawn
  Brings me closer
  Than before
To the miracle
  And the Wonder
  Of another door.
      With Love, M.

Steve R. Sibra
IT'S YOUR BIRTHDAY

Before you drink your milk
look into its heart
Nothing else on earth is white
not even hospital linen
Don't be afraid to touch
  your milk
think of your mother
Cold, like window panes
  noiselessly breaking
Warm, like candlelight intimacy
Birth from a womb of milk
Where are you?
Repose in a tomb of milk
God at last.

Frances Granger Martin, M.D.
RUNNING AND DREAMING

Candidates and joggers, I
  wonder why you run.
Is it to win, to overcome, or
  simply for the fun?
The purpose of your running
  is deepest mystery,
For I confess that running
  is anathema to me.

I much prefer to meditate in
  comfort and in ease,
Exploring in my mind alone—
  relaxing if you please.
No weighty problems have I
  solved, no marathons endured,
But neither have I lost a race
  or by a prize been lured.

Oh, placid ones who sit like me
Observing others run,
Who cares if muscles atrophy?
There's dreaming to be done!

Sandy Lopez
UNTITLED

i feel alone.
So empty and wanting.
Wanting to see you at the
  end of the day.
Empty, because I know you
  won't be there.

i feel nothing.
Like someone took every
  emotion.
i ever felt
And put them on a plane
  for New Jersey.
i feel lacking.
A part of me went with you.
And will stay in the safety
  of your arms
Until you come back.
i feel empty.
My soul went away without me.
The harder i try to catch up
  with it
The faster it runs.
i need you.
To see you, to feel you,
To know you're okay.
Come home soon.

Nellie Parodi
GENESIS

Genesis of the verse,
a mystery!
What did we hear, see,
taste, smell, touch?
Which moving feeling,
what stirring thought
kindled in us the flame
that inspires our verse?

Mrs. Glenn Lee
60 ACRES OF HAPPINESS

My son, My son what can I do
When you come to me and say
"Mom, Mom don't let them take
  this land from me
Come Mom Come, pack
  our lunch
Let's go to the fields, just
  you and me
Look Mom look, I've found
  a tree
Shady enough for you and me.
Hurry Mom hurry put down
  that book,
Find my rod and bait my hook
Mom, Mom I got my wish
I've caught myself a heck of
  a fish.
Gee Mom, Gee Mom Isn't
  this great
Elmhurst, Elmhurst hear
  our plea
Save this land for the boys
  and me.
    Mother of a Huckleberry Finn

Patricia A. Lafour
SHOE BOX MEMORIES

She held the box tenderly
  As she watched us leave.
A faint smile and silent tear
  To have the memories so near.
In the world of days gone by
  A shoe box of memories
  and a sigh.
Put safely back upon a shelf,
  As alone she again is left.

Sandy Shields
THE AFTERGLOW

Long hours after holding you
Remembering yet the thrill
The sweet fragrance of you
  lingers
And it's with me still

A subtle scent that's part of you
Stays close until
It haunts me in the quiet times
And always will
So many things that seem

important
Like passion's tie
Are only flesh and substance
In the mind's eye
The pleasant glow of holding
  you
Sweet excitement to be kissed
When gone I never asked you
  love me
But only to be missed
Both friend and lover each
  has its share
In equal part
Like sibling twins both
  are cherished
In my heart

Martin Swanhall, Jr.
(AND) JUST LIKE LOVE

Just like love I know you
  are sweet, dear
And just like love I know
  you are kind.
Just like love you are always
  so near
And just like love you are
  on my mind.
Just like love I know you
  are good, love
And just like love I know
  you are true.
Just like love it's you I'm
  thinking of
And just like love I do need
  you too.
Just like love you never get
  me blue
And just like love I'm glad
  you are mine.
And just like love I cannot
  see you
For you can see my dear,
  I am blind.

Patricia A. Wilburn
I NEVER THOUGHT

I've been thinking about you.
How close we used to be.
We've changed.
Changing so much, I'm not
  sure of you.
Maybe the distance, so little
  time spent together.
I have to say I don't know you.
I can't believe I'm saying this,
  I never thought.....
We've lost a part of our bond.
What's left is slipping.
At first, it hurt not to see
  or talk to you.
But I began to adapt.
I never thought.....
I wouldn't miss you.
I miss our friendship,
  your comfort.
Where are you in your life?
I never thought.....
I would ever not know,
I never thought.....
I would lose part of
  your friendship.

Jean Brenningmeyer
IF EVER AGAIN

If ever again I'd see you
I wonder what we'd say;
Would we smile a friendly
  greeting
Or just glance the other way
Pretending not to have noticed
The other's face in the crowd?
The human heart is so foolish;
A foolish heart is so proud.
Too proud to say "I'm sorry"
When we hurt another so dear,

We go our way in silence
And hide our lonely tears.
If we could only be more open
In things that matter the most
Instead of apart and unhappy
We still could be happy and
  close.

Barbara M. Lex
**THE GOODNESS OF THE
  LORD**

I can smell the sweetness
  of the Lord,
in the fragrance of the
  flowers,
I can taste the sweetness
  of the Lord,
in the products of the land.
I can see the goodness
  of the Lord,
in the beauty of Nature.
I can feel the warmth
  of the Lord,
in the sun.
I can hear the calmness
  of the Lord,
in the wind and in the birds.
By all these things, I can know
of the presence of the Lord.

Lisa Schaeffer
**THE POND THAT IS
  NO MORE**

A tiny pond sheltered by trees,
  Was the special place of mine,
There I would go to rest,
  explore, contemplate,
  Fish, frogs and lillies,
flourished there, in a place
  obscured.
  Flowers raised their
  heads there,
Where they grew in sanctuary.
  Just a friend and I visited
  there,
Telling no one, lest it be
  spoiled.
  It was the only pond near
  my childhood town,
Where a family of ducks made
  their home.
  Until developers came with
  steel jaws, and buried it.
Now a graveyard of barreness
  remains,
  The pond, the woods,
  is only memory.

Helen Holub
MOMENT OF TRUTH

I cannot grieve for what
  is lost
  and never to regain.
The tears are gone, the
  memories fall
  like roses in the rain.

A new and fuller life awaits
  away from youthful dreams.
A more mature and fruitful life
  away from foolish schemes.

A life to share with loved ones
  who have always been aware
of all my trivialities,
  but still find time to care.

The place, the time, the people
  no longer are the first
Truth reached out and set
  me free
  and made my being burst!

The time has come to take
  my place
  'mongst those I hold
most dear.
My husband, full of love
  and hope;

Kj Deakin
**THE LADDER, THE ROPE,
AND THE BALL OF YARN**

You're only grasping for
  a moon,
  out of reach and touch.
Belonging to dreams with
  extended ropes,
  giant ladders and such.
Your ball of yarn fell short.
Your ship broke under pressure
I think you'll be searching
  for the definitive
  transportation solution
  forever.

K. R. Caughlin
**LORD, GIVE ME BACK
  MY EARS**

I remember cloudy days,
  Gray skies and smoky haze.
Sitting for hours with a
  concentrating stare,
  Looking, looking, looking
  nowhere.
Sitting and sitting not saying
  a word,
  Waiting in silence for the
  song of a bird.
The song my ears were
  waiting for,
  The song my ears couldn't
  hear anymore.
O, Lord, give me back my ears,
  That glorious song, I've
  waited for years.
I never knew I loved it so,
  Why, O Lord, did it
  have to go?
I've never really done
  anything wrong
  So please, Lord, let me
  hear the birds' song.

Julia E. Hale
**I'M TIRED OF WRITING
  WORDS**

I'm tired of writing words
steeped in pain;
bored with tears
that washed my face
when I sat alone in the dark,
watching the shadows lengthen.
Oh, I could be so content
to allow your love
lap over me like so many waves,
joyous to live in the light
  you brought
when I lifted the blinds,
opened the window
to let you in,
and feel, at last, the warmth
  it took
to touch my heart.

Frank Wood Hays
THE BEAUTY OF NIGHT

As the waves made their way
  unto the beach
the sun was swallowed into the
  horizon
Slowly the moon made its trek
  across the blackened sky
seeking a home amongst the
  stars
For now it was night
and all things along the white
  sand were shimmering
from the glow of the crystal
  white moon

The water, breaking up on the
  shore,
melted into the dry sand
Hundreds of crabs ventured out
  of their caves
searching for the treasures that
  the new night had brought
Lonely seagulls drifted
  gracefully over the beach
in search of small fish who
  hadn't made it back home
The surfers and swimmers had
  called it a day
but the young at heart were
  opening the doors to fantasy
Sweet smelling air blew across
  their naked bodies
as they laid hand in hand, lips
  caressing the smoothness of
  each other
Knowing that it would last
  only so long
For the moon was gone and the
  air cold, letting them know
that it was time again to leave
  their happiness behind
and struggle through another
  day so they could be together
  again;
Now the sunbathers and the
  fishermen took hold of the
  waters,
for their happiness was as the
  sun started its journey
across the sky to hold its place
  within the heavens

Arden K. Michael
WINTER

Maybe summers are hot for you
  But if you dress up in winter,
  you'll be warm too
Let's hope your homes are
  insulator nice
So you won't feel like a piece
  of ice
It's better than a few months
  just gone
  At least you won't have to
  mow the lawn
Instead, let's take the shovel
  out
  You'd enjoy scooping my
  walk, no doubt.
You mean it's snowing', that
  soft white stuff?
  It usually seems like it's light
  as fluff
If there's enough, maybe we
  can build a snowman
  Will you help me with it? I
  know you can.
If the snow is that nice and light
  Let's hope those winds don't
  come up tonight
Sometimes at night they and
  more snow blow in.
  Would you like to scoop my
  walk again?
Without that snow St. Nick
  couldn't slide

And on that frozen ground it
  would be a rough ride
Be good so he can see you this
  December
I might forget but he will
  remember.

Robert P. Mancuso
DEATH

Here lies a body
Surrounded by space,
Upon this body
An aged face,
Friction abounds
Within this tomb,
Muted sounds
Break forth in the room,
Though matter is dying
Though the feeble are crying
All is well
For we are more than shell,
And the sea shall wash us
  ashore—
And the sea shall wash us ashore.

Mrs. Paulette Kay Zimmerman
THE STAR

If the star that shone so long
  ago
would light our world today?
Would it's brilliance still be
  matchless
or have we let it fade away.

Does the beauty of that
  Christmas Night
still bring joy and hope each
  day?
Would our treasures that we
  strive for
seem important when we pray.

If the star of Bethlehem shone
  once more
would we realize its worth?
Should we stop and once more
  reflect
on the priceless birth.

although it shone so long ago
it still can shine today
It's a beginning of the miracle
that was always meant to stay.

If all the world would see the
  star
as the wise men did that night
Would we follow it as they did
  then?
as it led them to the light.

All the world can now rejoice
that the savior now is born.
And let the Star always shine
  as it did
on Christmas Morn.

Earl J. Feather
DADDY'S LITTLE GIRL

Oh! sweet little girl in a
  pin-a-fore dress,
and gold hair in tresses so neat,
with that light in your eyes,
  for which the heart sighs,
and that smile on your face so
  sweet.

How I long to have you right
  here by my side,
from morn till comes hour of
  sleep,
to talk, and to sing with, to
  feel like a king with,
and shoulder your head when
  you weep.

Would be joy so untold, to have
  you to hold,
and to pleasure my fast graying
  years.
But that it is gone ne'er to
  return,

that is the worst of my fears.

If only could be, that this
  dream could come true,
(this dream for a lifetime I've
  had)
For a little girl child, so meek
  and so mild,
just a sweet Miss to call me her
  dad.

You surely would be, all the
  world to me,
my Treasure, my joy, my pride.
ne're to be real, I must keep
  you sealed,
Down deep, my heart inside.

Nancy Ascher
UNTITLED

It was almost Christmas, way
  past fall,
The snow came down, you
  didn't like it at all.
Your paws came up, you
  jumped to the sky
You looked like you really
  wanted to cry.

You hadn't seen this cold stuff
  before
And you came running right
  back to the door.
I'll keep you warm, my little
  kitten.
I love you—so it's only fittin'

G. L. Haney
FAITH IS A PINK BALL-

                    in the sky
                    higher
                    oon rising
faith is a pink ball-
as i watch it rise
my arguseyedbodyguards
shoottokillonsight
any pinarmed bandits.

John Mac Dougall
MEDITATION MAN

Who or what am I?
A child of the universe
A being called man
A fish of the sea
A curious thought, perhaps
To swim, to be free
A drifter in life
A philosopher to be
Is always in thought

Debbie Engel
LOVE

Love is a free thing.
It may be fun, lovely,
Sad at times, or maybe
Hard at times.

Love is caring
For a person,
Sharing their pain
And agony, happiness,
And fun.

Love is putting
That person above anything else,
Except God. Love is
Being friends with each other.

Love is many many things.
It is what you make it.
Love . . .

Cynthia Marie Garcia
TRUST MY EYES

So often
you recite beautiful
things to me.
I hear you,
yet I do not reply.
When I should respond freely,

my dear ones always near.
Oft times it takes too much
  of life
  in all its many ways;
to realize how much you have,
  and will have all your days!

no words are unwritten.
I am frightened to express them
  out loud,
therefore, the answer lies
in my eyes.
I love You!
Please understand.
Do not think I am cold,
because of no reply.
Look into my eyes.
What do they say?
Trust my eyes;
Not my words.

JoFrances Sheffield Cook
QUIET

Have you ever sat and listened
  to the Quiet?
Do you ever wonder why it's
  there?
There are birds to sing, leaves
  to fall, wind to blow
    and raindrops—but
      sometimes—Quiet!
There are rabbits and deer and
  oh! so many small
    things on this earth.
But! when they go to sleep
There comes the Quiet.
Tonight—when you lie down to
  sleep
    and the world outside closes
    its eyes,
Say a prayer and ask God to—
Let you—Listen to the Quiet.

Douglas Grudzina
IT HAPPENED IN A MOMENT

It happened in a moment.
The word was said and then
The look of pain crossed o'er
  your face
And slipped away again.
The word was unintended
And better left unsaid,
But once we speak, the act is
  done;
You can't turn toast to bread.
Apologies are useless;
They always come too late,
And in the wound left open,
Where love once grew grows
  hate.
And now I feel the vacuum.
Forgiveness is divine,
But 'ere it comes, the pain must
  go
And pain goes but with time.
It seems unfair yet likely
Our friendship now is dead
Because of one unhappy word,
Unthought, unasked, but said.

J. Wilkinson
LITTLE BOYS

Little boys are lots of things,
Worms, and toads, and bits
  of strings,
Fishing poles, and bent pin
  hooks,
Dad's old hats, and picture
  books,
Broken clocks, and baggy
  jeans,
Muddy shoes, and jelly beans,
Toothless grins, and grubby
  hands,
Nails, and brads, and rubber
  bads,
Flying kites, and freckled nose,
Little boys are all of those,
But little boys are much,
  more;
Curious minds, and dreams
  that soar,
Preparing for that time when
Little boys will soon be men.

Judi E. Frost
TALK WITH YOUR TEMPER

How did your temper help you
  today
Did a scowl do the trick when
  you had nothing to say
Did that frown give you strength
  for the job to be done
Was your temper the master in
  work and in fun
Did your temper make friends
  with others around you
And help solve the problems
  your children brought to you
Did your temper make you
  happy at the end of the day
Knowing your problems had
  not gone away
So how did your temper help
  you my friend
And was it really that difficult
  to mend
So why was your temper on
  display
And why are you so angry
  today

Vicky Lee
DIMENSIONS OF THOUGHT

Depth is only illusion, isn't it?
Vivid colors on both sides
  argue, though.
If one side is real, is the other
  so fake?
Attached, but no conflict.
  There is no touch.

Separated by a fraction
  thickness,
a glass painted silver on the fake
  side.
Which side?
Is the other side also flesh and
  wood
or is it paper-thin and there for
  show?

A coke bottle looks the samely
  tinted;
its ripples still up its pinched
  in sides.
And when half empty, having
  quenched your thirst,
the monkey-do side is also half
  full.

Living inside a vanity mirror.
Gathering dust when its user's
  needs fade.
And both sides will crack when
  two elbows twitch,
giving seven-year curses to both
  sides.
Or one.

David A. Watson
THE ABSOLUTE TRUTH LIES

The Absolute Truth lies
In the hollow of three hills
As a stream serenely draining
  a morass.

Arthur D. Dittman
MONOTONE

The battered crags disperse the
  sting
  Of the wind and pounding sea.
A stray gull's cry reverts to
  sling
  The empty span to me.

A turbid sun is in a reach
  Of dull redundant sky
And anywhere, the barren beach
  And nowhere; Ann Savai.

Along the city street, the swarm
  Of nameless faces pass
And swirl; and break; and then
  re-form
  Their remote, indifferent mass.

A wilderness of crowded strife
  Backdrops a siren's cry
And anywhere, the press of life
  And nowhere; Ann Savai.

The moving sun, from dip to
  crest
  Has spanned all life in time
And fired each spasm till
  clodded rest
  From Bach to primal slime.

With dribbled time does sense
  forbear
  What the will could not deny:
A monotone in numb despair
  Of nowhere; Ann Savai.

Eunice Baker Steele
IT IS FINISHED

No tolling bell to announce the
  flight of a soul
But darkness and rolling
  thunder
Friends and loved ones must
  hide in hills and caves
To avoid the same disaster—
Nail-pierced hands and feet,
  a crown of thorns.

The three men hung on wooden
  crosses—
No comforting words but
  railings and mockery
Rose from the jeering crowd.
"I thirst," cried One in agony,
Then, "Son behold thy Mother;
  Mother thy son."

Suffering from the hands of
  those for whom He died;
No triumphant march today
  with palms strewn in His
  path,
No loud hosannas to proclaim
  the King.
"Father forgive this angry mob;
  they know not what they do."
Friend and foe alike forsook
  Him now
Suffering and dying alone—
No longer to be sought by
  Roman or Jewish enemy
But a life given freely for all.
"Father, into Thy hands I
  commend my spirit."
Mission accomplished, I am
  coming back home
Now to sit at Thy right hand
  on an Eternal Throne.

Judy Petro
FAT BEAUTY

She is appealing and scintillating.
The ignorant see her as only
  masticating.
Always aware, alert, and bright,
Even though she isn't light.
She has great insight and
  sensitivity for all;
Thru name-calling she is always
  walking tall.
It is no facade her joyfulness;
Because her sensuality is not

coyness.
Her senses are always tittilated;
All pleasures of life keep her
  fascinated.

Hugging her you feel no
  boniness,
And in her is no phoniness.
If God had meant for beauty to
  be in bone,
Then why did He not leave it
  alone?
He covered it with lots of flesh
  to fit.
And now the people try to rid
  of it.
Of course there is beauty in fat!
And I will attest to that!

Adella Reeder
JOE

The face of a child is often
  intent
Watching a bug with head
  slightly bent
Catching the light the sun has
  sent
Observing that other the mirror
  has lent

He knits his brows, sticks his
  tongue out
Slowly then faster turns about
A grubby finger reaches in
  doubt
He runs away, comes back to
  pout

A waking child is alert, intent
A sleeping child is so content
The mind of a child is easily
  bent
But the heart of a child God
  has lent.

Deborah Rae Friedrick
A LACE

  A lace,
    Discolored and long,
Pirouetting and twiddling
      Nobly
    A dancer.

Barbara Hanselman
LOVE IS A SUN

Love is a sun from which you
  hide
like a medieval vampire
unaware that you are no such
  creature
Only a moon
incapable of shining
but for the sun

Paul C. Pierce
SONG OF FAITH

Why do I miss...soft spoken
  words...
The warm and cheerful
  smile...
The tender touch...The soft
  caress...
That made my life worth-
  while...

Why then...My sad and broken
  heart...
My tearwashed burning
  eyes...
When in my faith...I really
  know...
She walks neath heavens
  skies...

She stands beside...A calming
  sea...
Cool breezes wash the sand...
The pain and cares...Of life
  have ceased...
The Good Shepherd...

Takes her hand...
He leads her cross...Broad
  meadows fair...
Onto lush pastures green...
They talk...They laugh...
  They stroll beside...
Still waters...Of a crystal
  stream...
Hand in hand...They walk
  the path...
That everyone must trod...
To lay her down...In peace
  and love...
Secure...In the arms of God...
And God will...Wipe my
  tears away...
Then mend my broken
  heart...
Keeping me fast...Until the
  day...
I'm again with my sweetheart...

Deborah L. Harris
OUT OF LOVE FOR ME

There were so many times that
  I,
    so young, misunderstood.
  Your intentions, your feelings
What you meant by the things
  you did.
    Out of love for me.

In the turmoil of adolescent
  rebellion, I
    so wrong, had hated.
  Your ideas, your beliefs.
Everything you stood for and
  tried to convey.
    Out of love for me.

Those times have passed now
  and I
  much older, can understand.
    That I am, as you were.
And I know what sacrifices you
  have made.
    Out of love for me.

As a woman now, I have true
  appreciation of you,
    My Mother, so dear.
  Who has given of herself,
So much, for so long, with little
  reward.
    Out of love for me.

Velma G. Adkisson
DOUBLE EXPOSURE

Friendly one time was my
  mirror;
Of it now I have a great fear.
  When I look into it,
    I shudder a bit;
Once firm flesh is now blubber
  my dear.

Now what I see makes me
  quiver;
Tho' I exercise with great vigor.
  I eat much, much less,
    But more often I guess,
'Cause my figger gets bigger and
  bigger.

Glenda Fulton Davis
THE COIN

Excitedly, I sought upon
  the shore
A wealth of shells the waves
  had promised me.
Yet, found I there a coin
  and nothing more
To carry home as my gift
  from the sea.
This single coin to me was
  valueless,
Though many such would be
  a thing of pride.
One coin could not repay the

morning's gas,
So carelessly, I kicked the
  coin aside.
Another, walking, looking
  in the sand,
Did spy the coin which I had
  seen that day.
In ecstasy, he cupped it in
  his hand,
Then made for home; his
  treasure to display.
The rare and precious value
  of a thing
Is measured by the happiness
  it brings.

Maxine Radaker Harris
TO YOU, FRIEND

Better for you to be my
  fantasy,
And for me to dream of
  all our joys,
Than to have you and then see,
You, friend, are gone.
My dreams were but alloys.

M. L. Thompson
THE ICE STORM

There are diamonds in
  the treetops,
And silver like a sea
Blankets the earth and grasses
  in crystal fantasy.
From summer's weary garden,
  deep in winter's sleep
Each small weed has blossomed
  into a jeweled heap.
And glittering on the highlines
Are miles of silver rope
Verging in a bright mirage
  of ethereal scope.
Yet, this omnipotent sun,
  show'ring spendor over all,
May, within this magic hour,
  decree Alladin's fall.

Lillian Payne, R.N.
**GO — VISIT A NURSING
  HOME**

If you would receive a
  blessing,
And joy beyond compare,
Go to a Nursing Home, and
  spread a little cheer.
You will find surprise
  awaiting you,
But this you will find tis' true,
The cheer you sought to
  give away,
Has all come back to you.

Penny R. Burnett
AMERICA CRIES

My Country, I love thee,
  Why do you cry?
Are your freedom halls
  not free,
  Within me I sigh..
Is it, your inhabitants have
  forgotten God
  And those paths our fore-
  fathers trod?

America, are you troubled
  of fuel,
Or is it communism and oil,
  a duel,
You have a strong background,
  This we all know,
And I for one, want to see
  you grow.
  More than ever, you need
  support from us all,
America, American you
  cannot fall.
Kidnappers and streakers,
  put them to shame!

American, America oh,
  just who is to blame?
In Washington, the fuss
  about Watergate
Never gave our President
  time to even concentrate.
His time too well spent
  otherwise
  Communism, Communism
  in disguise!

I praise my America,
  Can you praise her too?
Please keep her waters safe
  and blue
  I respect my America
This I hold true,
  To keep her beautiful is
  saying this too.
Yes, I love you America, the
  home of the free.
  This land created for you
  and me.

Carolyn Kimzey
A STAGGERING THOUGHT

Our God
with curved fingers
and mind burning like fire
reached out to create
  loveliness
and form.
If I
can create song
or something comforting
then I am kindred, even part
of God.

Larry Douglas Brown
SUNDAY MORNING

Sunday Morning-
and there is poetry:
in the intimacy
of the crisp autumnal air,
in the pulsing vibrancy
of the black-jacketed bee,
and in the rooster's rousing
  cheer,
in the imagery
of a dove in foraging flight,
in the rapt expectancy
on the faces of people,
and in the white church steeple
thrusting in to a languid sky.

Etta Price
READ ME, I LIVE

My life has been a book with
  chapters for all my
experiences,
  a home for all my
memories.
Within my covers are enclosed
  the times
lived but once, now history
  and forever
remembered.
  Skim through my chapters
and find my life.
For I change with every turn
  of the page.
With every word—I grow.
  Stories told but never lost
because
  I am
the story teller within the
  vastness of those
  thoughts.
Upon the shelves of my home:
  my mind
I reign and preserve my
  individuality.
There I rest my novels, my
  stories,
  my poetry and my thoughts.
I am free: free to explore,
  discover,

learn and live.
Every time I'm lifted from
  my shelves
I spread my gift, never forgot
  my time-
  Imagination.

Stephen Gatto
WOODLORE

Midst a well-cloaked wood-
  land scene
Mongst fertile fields
And velvet walks of green—
Stand two imposing trees,
Rising forth from the earth,
Love's embrace strong since
  birth.
Wide of girth, these silent
  sages;
Proud and tall; oak of ages!
Wealth of limbs, true of line;
Caressing branches intertwine.
Boughs of green on supple
  limbs
Softly sway on breezes' whims,
Gently calling, calmly, clearly—
Or rustling wind on branches
  merely?
"Step between these wooden
  columns;
Nature's haven from all
  problems.
Learn of patience, mark the
  hour;
Feel the peace, the silent
  power."
Neath this web of lofty arms,
Golden sunlight touches, warms.
And the dew on leafy fingers,
Morning's gift like laughter
  lingers.
Cool green colors yield no clue
Of hidden rainbows in autumn's
  hue.
Nor wintry snows so precise
To leave each limb encased
  in ice.
But from above an airy roof
Raindrops beckon, once aloof.
Then journey down, leaf to
  leaf
Sharing moments all too brief.
Now I realize, though we part
Lost from sight, not from
  heart.
Your love and peace live on
  in me
Growing gently like a tree.

Wanda Palmer
WILD GEESE

How do you know
  when it's time to go
to your nesting grounds
  up north?

Does someone give
  you a sign or a clue?
Or is there a signal
  given to you?

How do you know
  that the lakes are clear
  of ice?
  How do you hear?

We see you fly
  your design in the sky
One seems to be leading
  How does he know?

We think we have answers
  to so many things
Why the earth shakes
  Why the bird sings.

But we don't know
  what tells you to go
I really wonder
  How do you know?

Walter Vladimir Kostyshyn
CARAVAN

Laden camels hauling treasures;
Across the sands came
 a caravan;
Befitting a Sultan and his
 pleasure,
From distant lands led by
 a merchantman.

Oils, jewels, musk and
 velveteen;
Much more to be sold;
Fit even for a Queen,
The wares they did unfold.

Came a fortnight they did rest;
Setting up camp at an oasis;
Within sight of their quest,
First unloaded were the laces.

Next day at the palace;
With much ado and fanfare;
Filling them with heartful
 solace,
As the Sultan chose with care.

Exotic perfumes to be sniffed;
Oils to leave the skin so sheen;
Enough to make ones thoughts
 drift,
Also purchased by the Queen.

Slave girls all fair maidens;
For the Sultan they did
 bare them;
Chosen were some for hand
 maidens,
Others selected for his harem.

What remained sold in the
 square;
Bought up by so many;
They came from everywhere,
The fortune made was uncanny.

When all this they did finish;
Back they went across the
 sands;
Their lightened caravan to
 replenish,
Soon to barter in other lands.

Gary Meyer
WOODSMOKE

From the chimney woodsmoke
 rolls and curls
Into the autumn sky
It fills the air in wisps and
 and whirls
Where wild geese now fly

I stand and watch the
 drifting smoke
And know it's warm inside
Seasoned beech and ash
 and oak
Are piled high and wide

With that special autumn scent
On a crisp fall day so fair
I can stand back and be content
To smell the woodsmoke
 in the air

Bruce Van Dam
CONFUSION

Does anyone know where
 I am...?
I passed through life in a
 trancelike state...
yet the world doesn't know
 where I am...?

Does anyone believe what
 I tell...?
My takes are of space and
 beyond the stars...
but can nobody hear what
 I tell...?

Can people conceive what
 they see...?
They wander about in the

deep state of sleep...
do they really understand
 what they see...?

Is madness just a moment...
 a space in time for me...
or could it be a memory...
 of time that once will be...

Was life a magic instant...?
of time that none shall see,
or is it just a dream...
that was made for you and me...

Is love a bird on the ocean...?
floating high and free...
dipping and raising its wings,
as it crosses the deep blue sea...

As you read this writing...
look around you and you
 shall see,
that the barrier has been
 broken...
and of my spell you now
 are free........

Francine Lanctot
WINTERTIME

 The air is cool and crisp,
Like a piece of fresh lettuce.
 The sun sparkles on the snow
With an unearthly brilliance.
 The icicles hang from
 Roofs and tree limbs.
 The cold wind whistles
 Through the trees
 And chills my backbone.
 It makes me want to shout
 To sing and rejoice
 In being alive.

Judi Hornchek
THE LUCKY ONES

We hope and dream all
 our lives,
And some are lucky and
 win first prize.
They find whatever they're
 searching for,
And have peace of mind
 forever more.
But then there are others
 who never find
Happiness or love throughout
 their lifetime.
These are the ones who need
 special consideration,
Especially in their hour
 of desperation.
So give a prayer of thanks
 if you happen to me
One of the lucky ones who
 is truly happy.

Audrey Hart
CARRIE LOVE

I am sure
All Mothers Marvel
When
Their Daughter's
Legs get long
But I feel
As if I am
the first

Lucille Acker Sibley
AUTUMN'S BLANKETS

Autum shakes her blankets out
 when wintertime is due;
She tints with golds and yellows
 and reds and others too.
She waves them in the sunlight,
 a gay and happy time,
To see what needs protection
 before the winter clime.
When Jack Frost makes his
 entry and blows his chilling
 breath,

She calls her brown-clad sen-
 tries to save from icy death;
Spreads covers down so gently
 on every living thing,
Bulbs and plants and shrubbery,
 to stay until the spring.
Those she doesn't need
 she piles against the hedge;
She tucks in all the seedlings,
 and vows her season's pledge:
That all is snug and well to
 sleep through winter's spell.
On garden, hill and yard and
 deep down in the dell
With leafy coverings laid,
 just before the night,
She quietly and gracefully
 disappears from sight.

B. Iana Cochran
PERHAPS WHEN SOMEDAY

Perhaps, when I am...
 someday...old,
I'll find all memory of you gone,
Your eyes won't haunt my
 every dream,
Your smile won't greet this
 stricken dawn.

Perhaps I won't recall your face.
Your walk...Forgotten in
 the crowd!
Maybe, then, the time will come
I will not think my love aloud.

Perhaps, in that day's radiance,
These shadows, tamed, will
 seem less bold,
Then these soft tears, at last,
 will dry,
Someday...perhaps...When
 I am old!

When that day comes, if
 peace abides,
When pain and sorrow are
 no more,
I'll tiptoe through my useless
 heart
And, very gently, close the door.

Sheryl Parker
WISHING FOR YOU

When the world is dark and
 dingy,
 I wish you a light for
guidance.
When you are alone,
 I wish you a warm companion.
When all the world seems to
 forget you,
 I wish you the power to
 remember.
When all about is in turmoil,
 I wish you inner peace.
When the noise of man's earth
 envelopes you,
 I wish you an inner sanc-
 tuary.
When all around you moves
 too swiftly,
 I wish you the grace to
 step aside.
When you stand by and watch
 life go around,
 I wish you the common sense
 to jump on.
When you need someone to
talk to,
 I wish you a compassionate
 ear.
When you need someone to
listen to,
 I wish you a friendly voice.
When you need to experience
love,
 I wish you someone willing
 to share it with you.

When you cry alone at night,
 I wish you a comforting
 touch.
All these things I wish for you,
But for myself I have but
 one wish,
You.

Wallace L. Weister
SHAPING

Dark visions consumed Japheth
 like lions devour their prey,
gripping savagely, brutally to
 maintain their leverage,
struggling and striving to over-
 ride the timid, weak
impressions that roamed the
 prairies of Japheth's mind.
His ideas of contentment and
 satisfaction toward his
 abilities diminished.
They soared off into the dark
 horizon like a mighty eagle
drifting afar on a current of
 nature's breath.
They vanished like the ebb tide,
moved endlessly out on the
 sea of hopelessness—
out of touch, out of dimension,
 out of reality.

You! The people who speak
 with a tongue as keen as
 a knife,
slashing viciously without
 awareness of malice,
it is you who chokes the life
 out of individuality
like a strangler in the night.
It is you who extinguish the
 fire of desire,
smothering it with your pillow
 of one-sided knowledge.
In a sadistic rage you rip
 to pieces.
You destroy Japheth's mental
 structure like a bulldozer
removing soil and refacing
 the earth.
You bite deep with those
 mighty fangs of conformity,
demanding and setting a pat-
 tern to your rules,
believing your dogma should
 house itself within the walls
of Japheth's cortical dome.
Yes, it is you who pollute
 Japheth's clear stream of
 thought with debris.

Adrian M. Maschek
IF YOU ASK ME!

If you ask me
am I a believer
this is what I would say,
only God can make the night
 and the day.
I see God in the rose
and in the child at play
he walks with me,
when I am on my way.
He nurtures and sustains me
from the bounty of God's
 green earth,
he guided and watched over me,
each moment since my birth.
He made the heavens and
 the earth
and it's beauty for all to see
he planted all of our food,
every flower and every tree.
He invented the streams
the rivers, oceans and seas
he designed the forest and
 filled them,
with all the animals and trees.
He gave me parents who
 dearly loved me

and I thank him for that feat
and for the loving relatives
and wonderful friends I
cherish very deep.
If you ask me
I've been blessed to the
depths of my soul
and to me that's worth more,
than a King's ransom in Gold.
If you ask me, God has smiled
down on me
and though my life has not
been measured
by Silver and Gold, what I
have shared,
is by far the greatest riches
untold!

William Garner
ESCHATON

Disturbing nothing,
not disturbed,
Flapping up from a flat
expanse
And wheeling slowly in
an endless sky,
An ugly bird,
Emblem from an empty mind,
Comes back home to die.

MarieElena Caulfield
ALONE

Never walk alone, your legs
will become too weak
Never cry alone, your tears
will be unseen
Never laugh alone, your smile
will disappear
Never want for anything,
unless someone is near
Never strive for success,
unless you can share
For success may bring you
prestige and wealth
But who will ever care
Never speak alone, you will
never disagree
If you are right or you are
wrong
What will the answer be
If you could see the life
you lead
Through another's eyes
Your legs would soon be
strong to walk
Without your disguise

Sharon Lee Spallone
UNTITLED

Window pane
Stained
With tear drops
Of Rain.
Shadows blend;
Night lights flicker.
Mist reflects the gleam
Of passing metal souls.
Sole attendant
Keeps vigil,
Gazing through
Water colored lace,
Tear-stained windows.
Streams of human tears
Mimic nature's
In sympathy
For the loneliness,
The faithlessness
Of love.

Sue Banko
UNTITLED

A dirty rat,
a scuz, a wench,
ungrateful bitch.
You lost, I won
 - but I lost.

You provoked me...
 do you really care?
"Prove it": your own words.
Does it matter now?
 No.

Lloyd Davis
SNOWFLAKES

How I love those little
 white flakes
With the careful hand of
 God he makes;
Staining, melting on the
 window pane,
Those providence-sculptured
 wheels of frosty rain.
I caught some in open hands
Freezing hard upon the land;
Descending, dancing, in
 silent ballet,
Drifting to mid-winter's play.

Danny K. Harvey
FINGERS IN THE SAND

Walking along a moonlit shore,
 as if I'd past through a mystic
 door,
 seeing things in a bright clear
 light,
 things that had always been
 in sight.
 The tiny waves of uneven
 sand,
 reveal a strange yet perfect
 hand.
Little ridge like fingers run in
 groves,
as the surf washes over, the
 fingers move.
Sea shells dot the fingers like
 rings,
 each new wave more jewelry
 brings.
 All colors and shapes in the
 moonlite gleam,
 a natural beauty befitting
 a queen.
 Growing longer with the
 dropping tide,
 twisting and turning, they
 try to hide.
Fingers folding over like
 clasping hands,
returning to dry little mounds
 of sand.

Christine Boring
**THE PASSING OF A
SPRING DAY**

 In the quiet morning before
 the day awakes,
the doves gather and coo their
 mournful song;
and the mist steals over the
 grass,
leaving droplets to replenish
 the earth.
 When the sun comes over
 the hill —
the weeds afire and the trees
 aflame —
the dew glistens and sparkles,
and the mockingbird awakes
 with the day.
 As the day grows warm,
animals roam and munch on
 the grass
now dried from the sun;
and a lone cloud sits high up
 in the blue sky.
 As evening draws near a
 breeze softly blows,
and children play before dark,
 while it's cool.
 And as the sun departs,
 the moon arrives;

and the owls' hoot accompanies
 the nightengale.
 And the mist steals over
 the grass,
once more, replenishing
 the earth.

Mildred L. Geary
THE DIETER'S PLIGHT

One day in a panic and trying
 to dress
I found (to my sorrow) I
 should weigh much less,
Getting dressed was not
 too successive —
The hips seem to need a
 slight recessive...
"No need for a change yet,"
 did I beguile?
One peer in the mirror to
 spy the profile...
Then the scales leered at me,
 "you lie — 142"
"Since you've read me, you
 should have a clue!"

Here's goodbye to Bread,
 Gravy, Potatoes, Candied
 Yams,
Cherry Pies, Fudge, Chocolate
 Cake, Puddings and Jams;
Invitations you refuse, then
 your friends start to tease—
Finally you say, "I'll show,
 but no refreshments — please!"

Here's to all diets and here's
 to hunger,
Here's hoping I'm not just
 a silly plunger;
For if your appetite you need
 not amend,
"My blessings — eat your heart
 out, my friend!"

Some of my friends are
 joining the 'club'
To reduce, aided by sort
 sort of drug,
When we say Grace, our
 prayer shall now be —
"Lord bless this pill and
 also bless me!" (give me
 strength)

Sue A. Houston
TIME

Life is a journey,
A new step each day,
Treasure each moment,
For time slips away.

Let the wind blow your hair,
And the sun blush your skin,
Let the people around you,
Be touched from within.

Enjoy all the colors,
The fragrance, the sounds,
Full up your heart,
With the joy that surrounds.

The blessings of life,
We must cherish each day,
And treasure each moment,
For time slips away.

Dan L. Blake
COWBOY

There's a shadow in the saddle
In a town called Santa Fe,
And its eyes have lost their fire
As the twilight sky turns gray.

Its quest took nearly 80 years
The ride was long and hard,
The man it sought to capture
Has drawn the final card.

Many times it faced him
In the dust, the sea and sky,
But the man thought life

too precious
And laughed when it said die.

Yet the shadow always followed
The man could hear its call,
But catching him was futile
The man refused to fall.

In time its face grew weary
But the man stood tall and
 strong,
The shadow's eyes showed
 anger
It had to wait too long.

Now it rides into the sunset
Leaving all the world in pain,
But it can never stop the
 memory
Of a legend called John Wayne.

Rose Anne Lindgren
WITH YOUR SMILE

With your smile
 you light up my day,
Making life worthwhile
 in so very many ways.

The sound of your voice
 rings clear as a bell,
Words make me rejoice -
 love I know so well.

There is a depth to your eyes
 where I easily reside,
With you there can be no lies
 and I'll know when our
 love has died.

Arms warmer than embers,
 the strongest, gentlest embrace,
Often my heart remembers -
 the memories my tears
 can't erase.

Sharon Ann Kaplan
AMERICA

America, my land,
Fertile, elegant and
Far-flung.
I speak,
Call out to her,
"America, my homeland!"

Sing out, America
Let your flag fly;
Thy emblems decorate
The paths of
Glory
In our minds.

Sing out, America
For you are
The greatest country
 on Earth.

Rejoice, my land
For I do hear
My country.
I do hear America dancing
And, let your
Thoughts ring out —
For
I HEAR AMERICA SINGING!!

Vickie Lee Blake
WAS IT YOU?

Was it you who knelt to
 pray today?
Was it you who prayed for me?
Was it you who took my
 heavy load
And laid it on calvery?

So many times our pastor
 will ask,
Are there any requests today?
And I slip up my hand and
 quickly say
For an "unspoken request"
 to pray.
And before my week is over,
Or before the day is through

An answer from God will
come to me,
And restore my faith anew.

And while rejoicing in my soul,
A thought will cross my mind
The wonder of just whose
prayer it was
That sent Jesus to me this time.

Was it you who knelt to
pray today?
Was it you who prayed for me,
Without even knowing the
things I ask,
You took it to calvery.

Betty Ellis
LOOKING BACK
FORWARD AHEAD

Looking back I think of
walking in the park, pictures
We would take
A record we made together,
which I still cherish, mem-
ories always stay with us
Little things meant so much,
the flowers you brought me,
Our favorite booth we sat
Like lovers were, we had
our special little places,
Our special love songs to,
all these things bring mem-
ories of you
A photo with your laughing
face, which is all I have
Left
But memories will never stray,
looking back forward ahead.

Kathleen Clemence Linehan
I AM ADDICTED TO COFFEE
AND CIGARETTES—WHAT
KIND OF CARDS DO YOU
PLAY?

I am addicted to coffee and
cigarettes —
what kind of cards do you
play?
mornings are long and nights
are cool,
I play a heart and you play
a fool,
if the earth were my bed and
the oceans my cover —
what kind of love would
you make?
I grow young but you get
older,
you prefer the Klavier and I,
the clarinet.

Meta Pfeiffer
PORTRAIT

She never wrote a poem,
Preferring active toil,
Sharing with her neighbors,
Products of the soil.

Living with a happiness
That deep communion brings,
She found an ever spreading
strength
Among the growing things.

And when 'twas time for
knitting,
She took a straight-backed
chair.
She never wrote a poem.
She was one, sitting there.

Irene Whitmore Long
BE NOT SAD

Grieve not for those we
thot we lost,
Cry not your tears in vain.
Rejoice with them as they
step across

To a home on high...and
heavenly gain.

Think not of them as in
the past,
Nor feel you've been deprived.
They have but journeyed
on ahead...
In peaceful rest since they
arrived.

This body of flesh we claim
as our own,
Is but souls temporal abode.
Your faith in God brings
eternal life
At the end of this physical
road.

If you but search within
your soul,
Beyond this earthly lust;
You too would know how
great it is...
His comfort, love, and trust.

These words, I pray, restores
your faith,
Consoles your earthly sorrows.
He feels the hurt within
your heart,
Gives strength...for all
tomorrows.

Orville Pointer
THE KNIGHT

There once was a Knight who
as he walked one day he saw
a Princess of
heart and soul. She could have
worn velvet or sack cloth and
still be a
Princess in each. He watched
her day by day If only I could
speak to her
To hold her he thought as she
touched the flowers. He found
that he loved
her with all his heart and soul.
But he could not draw close
to her to
tell her. He was watching her
when from a black velvet band
from the
Princesses neck fell a heart
shaped from jewels. But as
he picked
up the heart he was going to tell
her as she was walking away
but
found he could not. The Knight
kept the heart with him
wherever
he went and always the love the
heart stood for. There came a
great
battle. Down below from a hill
where he stood he could see
if he
failed to stop them here the
castle would be over run.
The Princess would die if he
failed he knew.
With tears upon his face he
made his stand with sword in
hand.
The King after the battle moved
among the fallen. And against
a tree looking down on the
castle he found a Knight as
they took
him away a heart shaped from
jewels fell from his hand.

Larry G. Rathburn
CONSIDERATIONS

It's always been so hard for me,
to say how I feel inside
Instead of saying I love you,
I'd cover up and hide.

I built a suit of armor several
layers thick
And hid behind that wall of
steel until I'm cold and sick.
Stay away! Don't get too close;
there's things you shouldn't
see
There's snakes and dragons
and horrible things,
the things that are really me.
And so outside that iron gate,
I built a different me
A man that's strong, a man
that's proud, the man I've
let you see.
Never mind the way you feel.
Just let me know I'm right!
Cause if you don't I'll put you
down, I'm ready for a fight.
But then one day I found
myself sitting in a room
With 120 people whose hearts
were filled with gloom.
So I said, "OK, I don't know
you, I'll let you have a look."
I opened up my library; I let
them read a sad and guilt-
filled book.
But they didn't read the things
I read, they looked between
the lines
They said, "What's wrong with
this? You're ok, you're fine!"
And so I took another look and
saw that they were right.
My heart was filled with joy
and love; I didn't want to fight.
So I took those beautiful people
and held them to my heart
And let them see the real me
from the finish to the start.
Now I know that I am just
beginning to see just who I am
To shed those heavy armor
plates, the cover story, the
sham.
I've only taken the first step,
there's so much more to say.
I don't know if I can handle
it, my fear gets in the way.
Now I have my new-found
friends, it's the same old
story I guess
How are they going to look at
me if I tell them all the rest?

Heidi Andy
HUMANITY

In the aftermath of tragedies;
man stands naked
before his consciousness.

Wandering through the valleys
of his creation;

Weeping through the labyrinth
of his anguish

Asking why, then retreating
back to nothingness;

Where pain and sorrow
find no place to rest;

Where joy and hope
no longer seek a home.

In what form has humanity
chosen to exist,
that we walk among the beauty
of the woods and fields;

And still we do not see?

Oran M. Pyle
INDECISION

A passing thought, I think
of you,
I'm just not sure of what
to do.
A smile, a word, a wave,
a wink?

I'm just not sure of what
you'll think.
My compliments I'd like to pay,
I'm just not sure of what
to say.
So many things I'd like to dare,
I'm just not sure if you
will care.
With you I'd like to spend a day,
I'm just not sure if you
would stay.
I want to tell you how I feel,
I'm just not sure if it is real.
My life's a puzzle, I do not know.
I'm just not sure which way
I'll go.
But I wish you would come
along with me,
I'm just not sure if we'll
be free.

Jane Pearl (Isquith) Rubin
SAY GOODBYE TO LOVE

Say goodbye to love today;
for tomorrow it shall be lost.
The quiet warmth will slowly
fade, for the flame will
turn to frost.

The flame will turn into frost
my dear, the warmth
becomes a chill. That leaves
your heart an empty
place that he alone can fill.

Live for love while there's
still time, do this at any
cost. And say goodbye to
love today, for tomorrow it
will be lost.

Lavonne S. Lowrance
LIFE'S TIMES

Joy at one's BIRTH,
Excitement with GROWTH,
Pride in one's WORTH.
LOVE, MARRIAGE, or
BOTH —

All these are headlines of
life's times,
The stories or scoops with
our by-lines.
Life's cub reporters cover
each event,
Set the type daily and all
goes in print
We pound the pavement of
life's actions,
Tell it as it is with few
retractions.
A lifespan is short, full of
work and sweat;
One must edit and sort 'til
the deadline is met.

Eleanor B. Cacio
LOVE

Love is mysterious
It baffles us all.
So take it serious
And not let it fall
To those who so lightly

Toss it around.
By using it blithly
To play like a cloan.

Love is mature
So ripe and so pure.
Enriching our life
The rich and the poor.

Pass it out freely
But guard it for fear
You mistakenly use it
Without even a care.

Love all the children
The young and the old
The sick and the lonely
Those weak and those bold.

Love knows no boundary
To tie it all in
But bursts out around us
All glory to Him.

Janice Davis
UNHEARDOF LOVE
(FOR GREG)

My love for you reaches
  unseeable heights
It's stronger than the days
  or the star-lit nights
It's something that I cannot
  fight
And something I don't want to

It keeps getting stronger
  every day
When I go to think, it's in
  my way
You don't need it, some
  people say
But honestly, I do

Don't fall in love, I'm some-
  times told
Play the field until you're old
But now that I've got the gold,
I'm gonna hang on to you

There have been lovers in
  the past
But none of them could
  ever last
And the thing I would say
  if I were asked,
Is, I love you

Kerry A. Smith
TO JEFF

I keep thee in a world apart
  in the secret places of
  my heart
My love does shine, a gentle
  glow
the fire by which I warm
  my soul.

Connie R. Holt
HOW DO YOU MEASURE
A MAN

"How do you measure
  a man?"
"Do you measure the height
  he stands?"
"Or by the ways he has
  become a man?"
"Do you measure him by
  his soul -
  in hope he's reached his
  goal?"
"Do you measure him by
  his qualities —
  or by his quantities?"
"Do you count him as
  being your friend?"
Friends are special gifts —
They are only strangers until
  you —
Make them your friends,
In turn they give your
  qualities a lift,
"So how do you measure

a man?"
You first make him your
  friend —
Then let the rest take command.

Jenny Freeman
OCHRE AND CARMINE
CAMEO

ochre and carmine cameo
parisian sacristy
          centuries cold
enshrine tenderly
    thy golden fold
enrobing thyself in brilliant
    hued vestments
what sagacious symmetrical
    hands
      decorated you?
what bird of passage
      passed by
your trellised window to call..
hosanna! hosanna! at sighting
    your sacrificial
      cache?
remiss you clash and dim with
    christian colors
like silver fox or white spruce
    all manner of creation
    you wear centuries well

Jennie E. Steriti
WINTER'S MAGIC

The barren trees
were wreathed with
sparkling diamonds
dangling from long
pointy icicles.

The evergreen bushes
glinted with crystal
prisms.

It's nature's handwork
that glistens upon an
early winter morning.

Maureen Patricia Nelson
SLEEPERS

. . . And that made me think of
How softly morning light can
  seep
Over lovers, half dead, half
  awake,
Only briefly aware—what is it?—
  clean sheets—
Then—roll over—slip—back into
  sleep.
Now what's that drowning
  victims think of?
Ah, breathing. Sleepers do not
  think
Of that—they sometimes quit
And float near to that abyss
Where twirling, turning ghosts
Flow inside from earth and yet
The sleepers do not die:
They breathe again, heavily,
  sigh,
And gather blankets close,
And you wrongly think they're
  going to miss
Songbirds with feathers brilliant,
  deep,
But you miss the colours of
  their dreams
And all the sounds in their
  silent sleep.

Michaelyn McCoy
DEATH OF A MARRIAGE

Where has our love gone?
  We do not know;
We went separate ways.
  Drifting apart with passing
  days.
Lovers became strangers
  Passion's embers cold;
No laughter, no wailing,
  Just polite silence prevailing.

We're alone yet together
  No more as one;
Indifference is a cruel fate,
  For realization has come too
  late.

Georgia Ray
CHILD OF DIVORCE

Should you pause and look
  at his face and a
body that's far too thin,
  For he's the forgotten child
  of a selfish
divorce and nobody wanted
  him,
  Too young for a job, yet
  too old for play,
he'll pick up his change here
  and there,
  He'll try to keep clean and
  nourish his dream,
that someday someone will care,
  But when his days on earth
  are over, love and
happiness he will share, for he'll
  belong to a family again,
they'll be no divorces up there.

Joyce Bates
THE SILENT TIME

In the silent time
  of our life,

What goes across
  our mind?
A yesterday of
  forgotten dreams;
A tomorrow of
  future hopes;
A today filled
  with wonder.

A silence falls around,
As we think of
  what is now
  what was then
And
  what might have been.
The silent time in our life.

Mary Ann Lott
THANKS

Thanks for all of the memories,
Thanks for making me smile,
Thanks for letting me lean
  on you,
as we traveled all those miles.

Thanks for taking the time
  to listen,
Thanks for understanding
  my needs,
Thanks for quieting some
  of my fears,
and helping me plant some
  new seeds.

Thanks for helping me out
  of the darkness,
Thanks for giving me faith
  in tomorrow,
Thanks for extending to me,
  your helping hand,
during happiness and sorrow.

Thanks for filling me with
  emotions,
Thanks for returning my
  heart to the "living",
Thanks for staying near
  me long enough
to teach me the greatness
  of giving.

Thanks for stirring the need
  to smell flowers,
Thanks so much for being
  my friend,
Thanks for letting me love you,
I pray God, our friendship
  won't end...

Norma Jean Rombalski
DESOLATION

The starkness of today reminds
  me of you.
It was on a day like this that
  we met.
Inhospitable,
Cold,
Unkind.
Days like today always remind
  me of you . . .
The ways you warm me from
  the inside.
I hope I will see you tonight.
I need to be warmed.
I, like the day, feel
Inhospitable,
Cold,
Unkind.

Linda Ann Mollicone
CIRCLE OF SHARING

You bring me a smile when
  tears surround my eyes
  You warm my days when
  I am cold
You are the greatest gift I
  could enfold
  The bond between us is
  true and great
A friendship like ours just
  can't be fate
  It takes trust, pleasure
  and caring
To bring two people into a
  close circle of sharing

Richard Milam
RUMINATIONS

Flickerings of light as if from
  some illuminant source
Faded to the mind do emanate
Shadowy essence deemed as
  shadows cast from enlighten-
  ing force
In light of thought to culminate
Fragments in whole esteemed
  with lucid gaze through
  darkness gleam
Revealed when passively
  yielding
Composings of inward sight
  through looming haze with
  quest to deem
Attained when actively wielding

Ann Elise Weber
TOWERS OF BABBLE

I babble on —
I talk to God—
"Oh lift your mighty rod
From my back
Like the dawn
Lifts the sun,
Like the resurrection
Lifts the body.
Oh, Christ on high,
Is it the sky
That we seek
Or the frozen mountain peak—
Both white and blue?
Or is it you?"
Continuous babble
Like a brook—
I hear myself.

Wayne E. Blake
AUTUMN PROMENADE

Walking in wonderment
Lending ear to the whistling
Wind singing through almost
Leaf-barren boughs—
Evening silence broken
Only occasionally by the
  barking
Of a distant dog and the

purring
Engines of passing cars.
Misty autumn drizzle
Pricks one's face, bringing
On a tingling sensation
As the biting fall wind adds
To the already present sting.
The prevalent odor of
Rain-dampened, moldy leaves
Mars autumn's sweet aroma
Mixed with perfumed essence
Of burning wood.
The white brightness of the
Moon casts shadows and
silhouettes
Upon patch-paved earth while
Above, dazzling, diamond-like
Stars glisten and shed light as
They look down upon
Evening's otherwise
Velvet blackness.

Juanita S. Johnson
SILVER WINGS AFFAIR

Flight 90, Nonstop....
  Back to New York...
    Home To Another Love,
    Back To His Life....
      Without Me.

  Back to Normalization,
    Something I Find Is
      So Difficult To Keep.

  Back To Me On Monday...

Flight 90, Nonstop....
  Heartache....
    For Me.

Mary L. Hawkins
MEMORIES

In the sky tonight bright stars
  were shining,
I pretended one was you,
  one me.
The sky so clear, the night
  so quiet,
Reminded me of evenings
  gone by.
The night so still, not a sound
  could you hear,
Only a breeze through the trees.
Alone I stood, recalling
  memories of you and me.

Remember the night you said
  you loved me?
It was a time quite like this.
Only God above knew our love,
And he let everything start
  off right.
Then do you recall another
  time,
Under the tree, by the side
  of the road?
You gave me the ring that
  pledged your love to mine.
I'll never forget all those
  wonderful times,
Or the happiness together
  we've shared.
How could I forget on a night
  like this,
Of our love and the way that
  I've cared?
Remember my dear, where
  ever you are,
I'll be right there with you,
Miles cannot separate us, or
  dim our love,
Our souls are one, is true.

Marlene Franzianne Cirbus
I SAID IT WAS YOU
(FOR VERN)

I said it was you
who made me feel
small
but it probably

wasn't you at all
It was probably
only me my friend
tearing my battered
self down again
But I feel at last
I'm at the beginning
of the end.
I'm starting to really
like when I pull myself
up
and take a sip from
my own silver cup
and believe in myself
and the things I can do
So I'm sorry if I put
the whole blame on you.

Colleen A. Neal
ICE TEARS

As the leaves are blown down
  from the branches,
And the wintry clouds fill
  the skies;
Nobody will hear, see, or
  care for,
The lone little girl as she cries.
The steps to the building
  feel chilly
To her small body, scantily
  dressed.
Yet she lingers; an everyday
  occupant,
The frosty days very best guest.
There must be a reason for
  her stay
To be overextended this way.
And the tears, meaning feelings
  of sorrow,
Turn to ice on her cheeks
  each cold day.
Does she stand for a thought
  in our own lives,
As we try hard to grasp what
  is meant?
Will we sit on our cold steps
  and ponder,
Just for what will your ice
  tears be spent?

Grace J. Reddick
EYES OF BLUE

A beautiful child, with hair
  of gold, and eyes of blue,
a smile so radiant, it could
  light up the world,
yet she lives in total darkness,
  for she is blind.
So sweet, and so innocent,
  so full of love.
I look into her beautiful,
  fragile face,
while she gently takes her
  hands, and carefully outlines
  my face,
I secretly thank God, that
  she is mine,
and tho she cannot see, she
  feels the tears of love,
  streaming down my face.
My beautiful child, with hair
  of gold, and eyes of blue,
what has this world to
  offer you!
Darkness, that may be true,
but loneliness, never for you,
for you are God's sunshine,
  touching everyone that
  comes near.
My beautiful, precious child,
  with hair of gold, and
  eyes of blue,
so warm, so tender, and so
  very kind.

There is a hand, much stronger
  than mine,
that will one day, lead you
  into a world of beauty, of
  which you
have never before seen,
and when your eyes are finally
  opened, you will behold,
  the beauty
of that world, and look upon
  the face of God.

Eugene Godilo-Godlevsky
THE GENTLEMAN OF THANA

I wish that he would go away;
I do not like to hear him say,
"You will be mine always,
  always"—
The Gentleman of Thana.

When fields are specked with
  moonlight beams
I see him nightly in my dreams.
He is not always what he seems—
The Gentleman of Thana.

He paints his lips with azure blue
To show that he is not untrue.
I think he sees me through
  and through—
The Gentleman of Thana.

He takes me to his wintry bed.
Beyond the graveyards of
  the dead,
Where not a word is ever said—
The Gentleman of Thana.

Tonight we fly on wings
  of Thought
Forever from this friendly spot.
Alas! He cannot ever be
  forgot—
The Gentleman of Thana.

Vickie Lockhart
ESCAPE

Alcoholism is a sin of man to
  always have a
drink and stagger till you
  can't stand.
And soon it gets to where it's
  a demand.
To always have a stiff one
  in the hand.
You drink to where you feel
  you're in command.
Only problem is-no one can
  understand.
You drink to try and find
  the solution.
Only accomplishment is:
  self pollution.

Christine Kallas
I WALK ALONE

I walk alone
No one beside me
Or even around me
As I walk into the path
  of darkness

Somebody help me, I am
  so confused
Not knowing where I'm
  really going
Will I continue to walk alone
With no one to walk with me

Please someone guide me
In the right direction
Before I'm lost and forgotten
In this path of darkness

Fred Royal
MARLENA AND THE CROSS

Soft as a kitten purring—
Wild as a tigress be.

Soaring high into ecstasy
Plunging down, down into
  depths of despair.

Stroking, stroking a kitten soft—
Arching to respond.

Remember the Cross—
Remember the Cross.

Lovely to behold, lovely to have
Love worthy of the gods-never
  to let go.

Remember the Cross—
Remember the Cross.

Wide eyes begging, nodding eyes—
Of a haven found.

Marlena, Marlena—
Remember the Cross.

Pain unbearable, Pleasure found—
For such a little while.

Woman supreme in love—
Woman unsurpassed.

Marlena, Marlena—
Remember the Cross—and Fred.

Virginia Hurt Bailey
UNTITLED

I am my own
creature
Belonging only
to God
Who allowed me
to be.
You only hold
what I give
Freely
of my choice.
Don't force me
to reclaim
my being.
Love is not
fierce possession,
nor domination,
But gentle
encouragement,
nourishing growth.
Tenderly cherish
myself
so that
I am yours.

Nancy Bernritter
SEASONS OF LIFE

Living through the seasons
  of life;
  the spring is green a warmth
  dances softly in the heart.
Living through the seasons
  of life;
  the summer is brown, a
  passion inflames your soul
  to wander.
Living through the seasons
  of life;
  the autumn is golden, a
  strength holds you with
  restful peace.
Living through the seasons
  of life;
  the winter is white, a
  challenge enters your mind
  to seek.

Pamela S. Hastings
THE ACCUSATION

Across the aisle
a man stared blankly at me
actually gawking, accusing
  me of what?

A sudden panic of fear
  engulfed me
when I sneaked a glance at him
to see that his eyes had not
  shifted the slightest

While squirming restlessly
my heart furiously pounded
  against my chest
for who was this stranger
  that was terrifying me?

But suddenly, I was overcome
  with relief
when I discovered him feeling
  his watch
to learn the time.

Terri Lynn Heisser
**I NEED SOMEONE TO
SLEEP WITH**

I need someone to sleep with.
It's not easy to say.
Everyone thinks the wrong
  things,
Like it's just for play.

I need someone to sleep with,
to take all the pain,
to see it's not for play
but for real.

I need someone to sleep with.

Forrest Neal Whatley
SONGS WITHOUT TUNES

Bright orange butterflies
  prancing in June
falling leaves and songs
  without tunes
A street is paved for a
  reason unknown
People dodge holes and
  jagged stones
Progress is reckless with the
  trouble she brings
A man sleeps soundly while
  the telephone rings
Striking workers are bunched
  in a crowd
and the sound of revolt is
  ever so loud
A man has to live on this
  good old earth
and pass the time of day
  while mothers give birth
Sooner or later one day
  he will die
No one knows why; no
  one will cry
The sky grows darker though
  it will not rain
and throughout the world
  there is a common pain
Bright orange butterflies
  prancing in June
falling leaves and songs
  without tunes

Doris A. Daniels
**TO VANESSA
(TWO MONTHS OLD)**

I saw the love in your
  mother's eyes
As her voice softly
  caressed you.
Words given in love and
  not with deep sighs.
Both of you with eyes
  so blue.

The joy of having you
  filled the air.
So let this response when
  older you grow,
Recall a day when you both
  were so fair,
With the light of love aglow.

From one of helpless
  dependence
A smile of innocent trust,
  by you unrecognized.
From the other a bit of
  knowledgeable experience
Perhaps yet to be surprised.

As the years move along
Bringing newness of another
  individual self,
Ever growing and emerging
  as a song

Adding a treasure of unseen
  wealth
  To those who love and care.
May you Vanessa, as you
  older grow
Love with your family share,
As God keeps you all
  within His care.

Bradley Farb
**MONEY DON'T GROW
ON TREES**

I know that chipmunks gather
  nuts and work as hard as bees,
But I sit here just worrying—
  two hands upon two knees,
Wondering if I will ever sail
  the seven seas,
So then I rise and realize
  money don't grow on trees.

I'd like to play those eighteen
  holes and hit balls off of tees,
Eat a meal fit for a king with
  crepe suzette and peas,
But I must understand I can't
  have any of these.
While I stay, it's hard to say
  money don't grow on trees.

The way you walk, the way
  you talk is not good
  enough today.
We judge it now by how much
  money is your pay.
I'd like to swim with dollar
  bills in vaults of currency.
Though greenbacks won't keep
  me afloat, at least drowning
  is free.

I love this Earth, my place of
  birth. I'll stay here if
  you please.
I'll scrounge around now that
  I've found money don't
  grow on trees.

Joyce W. Povolny
THE UNFOLDING

Thrusting through pretenses,
I come upon you,
Hollow-eyed, stalwart
Yet quivering.
One thing I've learnt in life
Is not to be surprised by
  surprises
And thus I have you.
Lambent with light,
Complete, bone-white,
  trusting,
Frightened yet holding
  your ground,
You appear nascent
And what joy I take
In your white birth.

Robert Alvin Davis
THE OLD MAN

The old man stands atop a
  lonely hill
His gaze intent on the
  valley below.
Can it be that time has raced
  so swiftly by?
Why it seems like just a few
  short days ago.

Now the future lies so
  strangely silent
With days allotted nearly o'er.
Ah yes, 'twas there he
  played as a child
Mid mornings mist, on a
  sandy shore.

But yesterday has fled this
  earthly plane
And to the present cannot
  last.

Tomorrow will linger but
  for a moment
And life will soon be past.
So he wonders at his
  purpose here
Pray tell, is it much too late?
What has he gave, what will
  he leave?
Oh God, is this to be his fate?

Beth Ellen Bether
UNTITLED

I looked in your eyes
  And saw the reflection
Of someone that just isn't me.

I'm sorry I failed you.
  I know that I've hurt you.
But, the person you see
  isn't me.

I know that you love me.
  You help me and guide me.
You do your best for me.

But I can't fill your dreams
  Or live your life's story.
Being me is all I can be.

With God's hand to guide me,
  I reach down inside me
To find the right path for me.

The look in your eyes
  Says I'm living a lie,
Chasing some impossible dream.

I know that I failed you.
  I'm sorry I hurt you.
I just want you to be proud
  of me.

It's more than time,
  For me to find,
A place in this world for me.

Please know that I love you.
  I'm sorry I failed you
It's time, I must learn to be me.

Richard H. Ballo
SIGNS

Sometimes the sun shines
on the inner sides of minds.
Clouds lift, birds fly,
days laugh, nights cry.

Minds arrive, change in time
to different looks on
  different signs.
Star burst, moon beam,
scarlet rose, trickling stream.

Different times on the
same signs find the minds
in tune and rime.

Jeannie Heintzelman
JESUS

Jesus is my closest friend.
I go to Him in prayer.
I tell Him what is on my heart.
I know that He is there.

Sometimes He stands before me
In the quietness of night,
When my thoughts are fixed
  upon Him,
And my eyes are closed
  real tight.

He gives me words of comfort,
He tells me not to fear,
He says no matter what
  may come,
He's always standing near.

And so with this assurance,
He sets my heart at peace,
To face each day with gladness
With joy that does not cease.

My prayers have all been
  answered,
For He came to me one day,
He said we'd walk together,
And together we would stay.

Dorothy Sullivan Brown
CORN HUSK SCULPTURE

Corn Husk Sculpture,
  You stand fragile as the
    tenuous bonds
      That cross each generation
Grandmother, looking down,
  Accepts the offering
    of flowers
      From little hands raised
        high in trust.
Corn Husk Sculpture,
  You are a symbol of love
    given and received,
      A gift of a daughter-in-law's
        deep caring.

Inez Polizzi
HOW WONDERFUL THE DAY

How wonderful the day can be
When touched by love.
The sun shines warm
Skies are clear
The song of birds
Ring sweet and dear
While you listen.

How wonderful the day can be
When touched by love.
Breezes are soft
Grass so green
And in the sky
No cloud is seen
'Cause you're happy.

How wonderful the day can be
When touched by love.
Your heart will glow
Your body sings
A song of wonder
And it rings
In your mind.

How wonderful the day can be
When touched by love.
Love just touched me
Now I see
You are love
And your touch
Brings beauty.

Love just touched me,
The day is wonderful.

Judy Patmore
AUTHORITY

The Figure stands—
  the people sit.
The Figure talks—
  the people listen.
The Figure says—
  the people do.
The Figure walks—
  the people follow.
The Figure jokes—
  the people laugh.
The Figure crys—
  the people sob.
The Figure ails—
  the people weaken.
The Figure dies—
  the people are lost.

David C. Geary
TO DREAM

Life and time
and words that don't rhyme
and the life and the dream
so it must seem
fade with the night
with the pains and the joys
and the dark and the light

and when its all gone bye
I lay with myself
and I wonder why;
why did I
dream in the night
that some day I might
be what I'm not

if only to dream once again
of life and of men
all men must dream
and to them it must seem
of something they're not
and to this I deem
men are all that they dream.

John Ray Nunes
TO BE A WOMAN

Sometimes I search for
  alternatives to being a woman.
  Why does it have to be
  so hard?
I realize that having needs both
  mental and physical
  Can leave me so cold and
  so scarred.
I'm not looking for a one
  night stand.
  But sometimes I feel the
  needs that it entails.
And although I do not search
  for a wedding band,
  security of marriage is better,
  when all else fails.
I try not to say, that all men
  are the same,
  But with each new one it
  strengthens that fear.
I try not to say that to them
  its a game.
  But that's what it seems to
  the ones I get near.
I don't want to seem like a
  virgin princess
  whose only claim in life is
  to belong to one.
But my respect and my pride
  are much more than
  caresses;
  there's got to be love from
  my place in the sun.
I fight the bitterness as I hold
  back the tears.
  My womanhood questions
  what's real.
I'm just one of many with
  similar fears.
  Who wonders if it's wrong
  what we feel.
I guess I hope not to make
  that mistake,
  that letting some man have
  me might bring.
I hope I will give and the
  right man will take;
  For its love that I search,
  not a gold-plated ring.
I want him to understand
  just how I feel,
  when I give of myself
  to a man.
That a relationship should
  never start with a deal
  that contains in its contract
  something less than I am.

Susan C. Muir
**I HAVE WORDS I
WANT TO RHYME**

Please don't kill me before
  my time, I have too many
  words to rhyme. I have so
  many thoughts to think; a
  day to visit, a night to seek.

I need your body to survive,
  until I can on mine rely, then
  if I don't please you, leave
  me to stay, with someone who
  will love me day after day.

I have some words I want to
  say. I want to see the light of
  day. I want to breathe the
  air of life. Is it too much to
  ask? You did conceive my
  life!

I know I'll burden you for
  awhile, but I can give you
  cause to smile. I have words
  I want to rhyme. Someday
  you'll hear my words in
  rhyme and it will make it
  worth your time.

Give me this gift. Nine months
  of care and I'll return a gift
  we both can share. Take a
  chance on me. I have a
  destiny. One you can't see.
  Don't steal it away from me.

Lynette Rayburn Payne
THE PLEA OF APHORDITE

My lamps beckon thee softly
To feast upon beauty and grace.
Lovely am I as dream in stone*
Housed in this dreadful place*
Cold and passionless once
  immortalized.

Find thy refuge in my breast
Search this tranquil shadow
Empty of a worshipping Euclid
Leave not my love lie fallow
Cold and passionless still
  anatomized.

Release, I beg, this solitude
Let me breathe again the air
Of spring, the flowering
  interlude
Warm and passionate forever
  eternalized.

*The statue of Aphordite
  resting in the basement
  of a museum.

Nella Minnite
WASTE

Many a raindrop is born
At sea to waste its goodness
  on desert rocks.

Many leaves are born on trees
To be blown away to rot.

Many a man is born to serve
God and you
But pass away with their
  dreams
Not come true.

Gloria M. Little
IT CAN'T BE LOST

It can't be lost, your
  peace of mind,
  If all your worries are
  left behind.
When you seek, then you
  shall find,
  The serene of peace
  is sublime.

It can't be lost, your
  peace of mind,
  Prayer changes trouble
  of any kind.
The way will be bright,
  try it sometime,
  For inner peace, and
  love divine.
It can't be lost, your

peace of mind,
  For bright is the day,
  the sun will shine.
No matter how dark the
  clouds incline,
  Tomorrow, for you,
  good fortune combine.

It can't be lost, your
  peace of mind,
  Blessings to follow,
  sorrow left behind.
Be of good cheer, smile
  all the time,
  For you've found that
  something, your peace
  of mind.

Diane Kay Rhoades
LOVE

These words don't come easy
And they don't come
  very often.
I'm writing them down now
In hopes my heart will
  soften.

So as not to get hurt,
I kept my distance.
I remained cold and
I built up my resistance.

But I've never felt this way.
No one could get through.
I was a stone wall
And then there was you.

You made me see that
In giving you're bound
  to receive.
You taught me a lesson
And now I believe...

That love is not a closed door,
Nor a heart of stone.
If I just open up my heart,
I'll never be alone.

Juanita E. Morgan
SIXTH DAY

My mind darts about - as a
  deer being hunted in the
  forest.
Up and down, right then left,
  bounding frantically,
  aimlessly,
  hopelessly.
Where are the caves and
  shelters of times previous
  in which I
hid so well?
Each turn confusion, I'm lost!
  Panic takes control!

The Hunter is close now, I
  can FEEL his determination!
The arrow pierces my heart,
  pain engulfs my being -
  realization
too late sinks in.
I manage one last look up at
  my assailant - God Help Me!
  It is
myself....

Donna Y. Hanneman
MEM'RIES SWEET AS MINE

I recall a friendly fire
A cracklin' in the night,
Whose golden glow provided
Our only source of light.

A glass of wine whose
  mellow blend
Poured o'er our burdened-
  minds
And released our inhibitions
As we discovered previous
  finds.

The passion of those moments
Has stirred my heart to tears,
Though time has cooled

those embers
Through the passing of
  the years.

Before that fire I came to know,
Though youthful I was then,
Such times are very
  precious gifts
And ne'r return again.

So to lovers, young and old,
I wish a glass of wine,
A fire to warm you in
  the night,
And mem'ries sweet as mine...

Laura Valerie Barnes
MAGGOTS

A long dark tunnel
Opens like a mouth
Does a friend wait at the end?
Shall I try another route?

A life is wasted.
The maggots rejoice
Old wounds for opening,
New cause for remorse.

Still onward I travel
The familiar is sweet
Tears, you worms of remorse,
Find other meat.

Shirley Smart
VIBRATIONS

His eyes absorbed her beauty
Like a bow caressing a
  Stradivarius,
Breathing in her vibrant,
  warm being
Basking in the radiance of
  her spell,
Her presence gave him new vigor
His breath came in deep gasps,
As she drew nearer the place
Where their eyes would meet,
Her smile would carry him
  into orbit
His every fiber felt
  vibrantly alive
He was helplessly under
  her influence.

Duane D. Thornton
ESCAPE

Pressures of reality force
  me to dream.
A way of unwinding and of
  blowing off steam.
I live in a world of fantasy
  and in words of rhyme.
Escaping from reality if
  only for a short time.
With my mind aloft of a
  future that may never be
Returning briefly to cope
  with reality.
Then to block it out and
  once again leave it behind.
This can only be done
  through thoughts of mind.

Shirley Hanson Horne
**"...THAT YE ALL SPEAK
THE SAME THING"**

Each spoke in a foreign
  language:
The strings in fine blendings,
The oboes in weird wailings,
Percussive paradiddles from
  the drums,
And light trilling floated from
  the flutes.
The clarinets spoke in a sweet
  ribbon of tunes,
The horns in accented
  tonguings,
And the harp in a sweep
  of arpeggios.
  Then all spoke together

In the universal language
of harmony,
And all understood
Divine orchestration.

Betty Jennings Lindberg
COME, PLEASURE ME

Come, pleasure me
treasure me
measure me
With your hands
And heart
And love.
Find in me
A depth
Now kept
For you alone.

Come, pleasure me
treasure me
measure me
With your eyes
Your mind
Your soul.
Find in me
A gift
A joy
For you alone.

Come, pleasure me
treasure me
measure me
With your laughter
Your tears
Your rest.
Find in me
A mirror
Reflecting love
For you alone.

Betty Gossi
WHEN THE WIND BLOWS

When the wind blows
you come riding in
on the breeze—
to share some sweet
time together.

But all too soon
the time comes
when I have to
wave you down the
road again.

Back to your home
and your life—
away from me
and back to your
wife.

Anne Astrella Tipitino
SNOW

Clouds breathe
Stands still
In calm anticipation.
Moist air
Getting chill
Awaits a transformation.
Snow fills
Calm space
A quiet revelation.
Winds cease
Crystal peace
A silent jubilation.

Judy Feliciano
JUDGE NOT

I saw a boy laughing at another
For being lame
When he grew up, his child
was born with
Damage to its brain.
There was a woman that
condemned a black
To his face
A few years later, she married
Into that race.
How often do we see a
sister or brother

Doing something in a
different way
So we condemn them, Jesus
wouldn't be
Pleased we say
We judge each other, for
every little thing
Then go to church on
Sunday and
"Jesus Loves Me" we sing
Jesus said, "judge not,
that ye be not judged."
When we see some one
different from us
Why don't we act like
christians
And show our love?

Amy Susan Crohn
UNTITLED

My friend, you are my friend;
When time passed easily
In former, carefree days;
When time was serenely still
in warm, cuddly nights.
And when distance played
too frequently with
our emotions.

My friend, you are my friend;
Now that love has been defined
for what it is and for what
it can be
in a grown-up future;
Now that the searching
has calmed
somewhat
to let our feelings free.

My friend, you are my friend;
Willing me to be happy
in an uncluttered future
in which
to only you will I be
easily grateful.
For caring that I will exist
in uninterrupted peace
when time will let me grow.
And when you, my friend,
are mindfully
with me, I will know.

C. Ann Williams
TAKE A BREAK

Silence is at least four
times a day.
Silence is the way to
hold on tight.
Silence is not light,
it is strong.
Silence is never wrong,
it is O'K'
Silence is at least four
times a day.
Silence is skin against skin.
Silence is closeness in any way.
Silence is always to begin.
Silence is a hug.

Shirley Hudgin-Goings
AGE

Children
Small feet advance
Each one in their own time
Till all steps are taken and they
Are grown.

K. K. Porco
DEAR JOHN

I never asked for much
from you,
I only asked for love.
But here I am, alone and blue,
With just the sky above.

You promised we would
be a pair,
Never to be parted.
But here I sit in deep despair,
Alone and broken-hearted.

Your illness came on sure
and quick,
As I sat by and cried.
You clung to life; but were
too sick,
You said, "I love..." and died!

Darling, I know that you
have gone
To a better world than this.
Wait for me there in Heaven,
DEAR JOHN,...
I shall meet you with a kiss!

Louise Yates Angers
TIGHTROPE

sometimes
my words
strung—one—after—another
and you can bet
there is no net at all,
to catch me
if I fall.

so I try
to keep my balance
with my fears -
and my affection.
to love -
without detection.

as I teeter
on this thin
and fragile rope -
delicately woven
out of need,
and dreams,
and hope.

Suzanne M. Cain
MY CHILD

My child is like a wild fawn,
Awake at crack of dawn,
To see and feel and hear
the things
Each brand new morning
brings;
A small green leaf, a butterfly,
The clouds up in the sky;
A spider's web, the gentle rain,
The whistle of a train.
I hope my child will always be
A creature shy and free,
And that her heart stays
always clear
Of hate, deceit and fear.

Jeanne E. Kleinsasser
A FRIEND

A friend is a person who
comforts
When you have sorrow
and are sad.
A friend is a person who
laughs
And rejoices over things
that make
you glad.
A friend is a person who is
a good listener
When you need someone,
your problems
they share.

A friend is a person who
keeps things
silent,
And won't tell your secrets
because they care.
A friend is one of God's
blessings
in disguise,
Who is willing some of your
burdens to bear.
A friend is a constant
prayer partner
Always taking your needs
to God
in prayer.

Susan M. Kefford
LONG DISTANCE

Voices so far away
Hollow wires
Between us,
Connect us,
Separate us
Long distance ...

Phone calls and letters
Pieces of me to you
Bits of souls
And ink that bleeds
Through hearts of paper.
All of these find their way
To you
Long distance ...

Kay D. DeTar
INNOCENCE

You smiled at me—and
I could feel
The ice around my heart
begin to crack and peel.
You reached out your hand—
touching my face,
And the ice melted away,
and was gone.
It spilled down my cheeks
as a flood of tears.
You laughed—and patted
them away.
And as you laughed, I
felt the sun
Shining deep within my soul—
And all my cares were gone.
I held out my arms to you,
And you ran to me and
cried out—
"Grandma! I love you!"
And it was so. The truest
kind of love—
The Love of Innocence.

Charles S. Nanavaty
FINDING OUT

Cause finding out what
everything's about
Is what will make this
world go round.
Cause finding out what
everything's about
Will tell us what we
know not now.

We look through nature
that's our only key,
Will tell us what we're looking
for in the 21st century.
We've come to the 1980's and
we're lost and so confused,
I wonder now what man
is gonna do.

It takes us some time to find
out these things,
Forever and forever and a day,
But this time man, you're
gonna work for it.
It'll never, no, no, never
come your way.

So people, if you will, open
up your eyes and ears

And look around and tell
   me what you see.
If Mother Nature's not
   complaining, then I can't
   see a thing.
But if she is, then we're got
   to do something.
But if she is, then we're got
   to do something.
Cause finding out what
   everything's about
Is what will make this
   world go round.
Cause finding out what
   everything's about
Will tell us what we
   know not now.

Barbara Anne Kirpas
DEJA VU

In dreams long ago we met ...
   when wishing on a star
   was not too far from
   reality.
Sharing hazy images of life
   separately
And the years slowly began
   to clear the clouds,
Finally bringing into focus
   the dreams of yesterday,
Transforming them into the
   hope of tomorrow.

Laurence Adams Malone
LOVE'S CROWN

Though stern as law, Love
   wears no judge's cap...
Nor seats star symbols on
   her cosmic lap.
Love better graced bears
   sceptre of a flower,
Thus symbolized, Love
   resurrects Life's hour...
The lily taller stands than
   rose and bares
No thorn...and as perfume
   of life, Love shares,
When wisdom leads my
   hope beyond the grave,
Toward Life, and yields to
   me that which I gave...
So beautiful is Love's
   imprint on soul,
Life stands and gazes
   inwardly, quite still...
I smile and Life reflected,
   smiles at me...
So beautiful is Love,
   love given whole,
The flame that burns in
   nature's soul, I see
As whiteness and pure
   truth, life must fulfil...
And this is Wisdom's gift
   of spiritual crown...
Love's mortal birth that
   Christ has handed down.

Karen "kam" Marinelli
ONCE FOR ALL

Touch me
   Once you did with your eyes,
   your words, your heart.
You made me yours with
   more than words —
You gave me love and life
   and hope with your smile.
You answered my heart
   with your own
And you touched me to the
   fibers of my being.
Love you
   Once I did with my eyes,
   my words, my heart.
Now I do with my life.

Jean M. Thieda
NIGHT THOUGHTS

You are awake in the midst
   of the night
all about you is quiet and still,
Then thoughts come to mind,
   that were out of sight
but you can't push 'em back
   when you will.
You toss and you turn 'till
   daylight is come
with your memories churning
   about,
You're saddened a bit, but
   you laugh at some wit
then surely your sleep's put
   to route.
Wide awake you are, and
   awake you stay
for it is time to get up
   at last,
As the sun rises on a bright
   new day
you shove memories into
   the past.

Dawn Lovelady Fazende
SHADOW DANCE

Shadows dancing on my ceiling
And I'm remembering you
Remembering hand in
   hand strolls
On warm misty evenings
Remembering closeness
   in my bed.
Remembering tea and crackers
Shared in silence
As dawn grew outside
   my window
Remembering tears you shed.
Shadows dancing on my ceiling
And I'm wondering
Why I could not love you.

R. Leon Hughes
COMMENTS TO EDDIE LOU

It seems I let my subscription
   lapse,
   Not being so greatly
   thrilled perhaps;
But feeling again a poetic bent
   A renewal check is being sent.
   Below are comments that
   you may print.
Lamb, my lamb, is an up beat
   so sweet.
   Trochee, 'scuse me, is a
   stumble in feet,
Anapest, ever blest, upward
   swings, dit dit dah!
   But dactyl goes down hill,
   Oh la la, don't tell Ma.
Now spondee, forceful plea,
   holds its pitch, rah rah rah.
Alliteration-trite and trash,
   tingling twist.
   Assonance-arduous and able,
   aid and assist.

Metaphor-unseemly raging
   curdled the air.
   Metonymy-flower of my
   heart say you care.
   Finding perfection is
   most rare.

Vickie McBride
GRASP FIRM YOUR LIFE

Grasp firm your life
and inherit your dream.
Wind blows swiftly;
Rain is spontaneous.
And a dream is a vision
of what life could be.
Sunshine is radiant;
Spring is refreshing.
And life is a test
where dreams never answer.
Fog spreads quietly
and coldness is frightening.
But the seasons are cycles
of natures wonders
and the colors of autumn
are a goodbye,
for winter brings sleep
and dreams begin anew.
A human is an
image of God's creation.
And life is a truth
that doesn't always
accept logic.
So, mold your utmost
desire from slumberland
into an everyday reality.
And damn all the planning;
Live a dream.

Joan H. Taksler
IT IS COMING

Ran from the far-darter
crossing the bridge of rainbows,
Burdened with hope in a box,
Met darkness devoid of power,
Terror of the night.
Submitted to ring of flames,
Saved by threads of the
   labryinth,
Accepted the crown of
   seven stars,
Scales weighted with
   wickedness,
heavy with discord, fear
   and fright.
Gifted with sense, expression
   and speech,
Ripped apart at crosswalks
   of life,
entrances guarded by
   howling dogs,
Gadflies stinging with blood,
Discovery of the grail is
   in sight.

Teresa L. Christen
ENOUGH UNLOVE

E motionally disturbed
   student's frustrations
N ever being met as a person
   al challenge!
O nly silent unloving,
   misunderstanding!
U rgent messages to the
   principal's office!
G et this disruptive, undis-
   ciplined, bad child out!
H ow as human beings can
   we be so cruel?
U nlearn socially acceptable
   misbeliefs?
N ever change the old
   educational system!
L earning disabled children
   bleed when they are hurt!
O verwhelmed with useless
   rules and regulations!

V ery often people try to
   help do what's right!
E xcellence pays poor
   dividends for handicaps!

Roxann Franscoviak
I'VE GOT TO LET GO

I woke up early this morning
My thoughts were all on you
And the beautiful time that
   we would share,
But now I'm feeling blue.
I needed you to hold me
To make love like we use to do
But now, like so many times
   before,
Our wonderful plans fell
   through.
It hurts to love you so much
When we never have time
   to share
The love that we need from
   each other
Somehow, it just doesn't
   seem fair.
Right now I wish I could
   forget you,
Find another to take your
   place
But now, when another man
   holds me
I feel warm, but I picture
   your face.
I'm sorry, but I can't go
   on this way
Always wondering when
   it will be;
When we can spend a
   moment together
I've got to let go, to be free!
You may not understand this,
But it's harder for me to be
Hoping one minute, let
   down the next,
Oh darling! Can't you see?
It'd be easier to know I'll
   never love you again
To try to forget what we had
Than to go on loving,
   caring, needing,
Only to be left feeling sad.

Ruth I. Myers
THOUGHTS

Happy birthday, dear friend,
   to you today,
You are a woman of beauty
   in every way.
Your smile, your cheer and
   your friendly ways,
Your sincerity and kindness
   bring glad days.
A joy to know, my thanks
   for God's giving
A friend like you to make
   life worth living.
May daily joy and happiness
   come to you,
May life's blessings
   reach your heart
   for what you do.

Cynthia Lynne Schremly
REBIRTH IN THE GRAVE

Here's a song before I go
to make the memory last.
Long and tired and going slow,
I wish I could go fast.
It always seems that time
   takes care
of every cure there is,
except for things like dying
when I'm trying my best
   to live.
Inspite of all the tears

I've shed,
I'm glad there is no pain.
I'd like to make it to
  the other side,
but I'm sad...I'll lose my name.

Life is funny in its own way
because we think we've got
  it made,
but every dog must have
  his day,
it's a rebirth in the grave.

Mildred V. Hole
HAY

Green in the field
Timothy sways in the wind
Alfalfa flowers draw bees
And clovers lavender
  puffs please.

Mowed hay neatly in its rows
Cures and dries as sun shines
  and wind blows.
Tedders help the sun with
  its work as
Rakes spin out hay into
  gigantic curls.

Balers gobble the hay with
  insatiable hunger
Hay disappears inside,
  pushed by the plunger.
Out emerges a neat
  little square
Providing some animal
  its dinner fare.

Fields manicured sporting
  fresh brush cuts
Wait now for rain to give
  new growth.
The farmer again prepares
  his machines
As the hay grows green.

Jackie Daugherty
ME

I'm me,
Here I am,
Take it or leave it
I don't give a damn

I don't play games,
Or kiss any ass,
I may not be pretty
But I've got my own class

Mary Popiolek
FOR MICHAEL

You entered my life softly
  and now you're all I know,
you brought back feelings I
  thought I'd never show.
Each time we're together it's
  like the first,
with a touch of your hand
  my senses burst.

You're my best friend, my lover,
  I couldn't ask for more.
Your hug, your embrace,
  make me feel so secure,
and when it's just you and me,
  the wind and the stars,
nothing's impossible, no place
  is too far.

Life is better living it with you,
days are lighter when love
  is true.
You've showed me how happy
  I could be,
I thank you for saving
  yourself for me.

Mary Lou Derocher
SWEET JESUS

Sweet, sweet Jesus
Loves us above all
Died for our salvation
Answers when we call.

Sweet, sweet Jesus
Faith is all He asks
Love one another
Is our only task.

Sweet, sweet Jesus
Love is what He shows
When we ask forgiveness
For all the wrong we sow.

Sweet, sweet Jesus
Praise Your Holy Name!
Ever since I met You
My life is not the same.

Kathleen LeCompte
APRIL SONG

The gentle winds of April
Sing a lilting spring refrain
They chant of leafy lacework
And of warm refreshing rain.

Their song is of renewal
Of sweet blossom, scented fair
Of miracles in color, composed
By nature's newest flair.

The windsong is of
  brilliant greens
Of flowery, gay prosaic hue
Pink and white of budding trees
And cloudless skies of azure blue.

How quiet is this whispered hymn
Caressing gently all who hear
Hush. Listen! Hold this lullaby
The earth is born again this year.

Linda (Ackerman) Gudek
SEAGULL

I feel the wind
  slide through my wings.

I need not flap nor flutter —
  but glide.

Whirlpools of wind - pull me back
  like the seatide.

Feeling so effortless - I rest
  in suspended animation.

I realize -
  for me, life is free - as the wind.

I am at peace with myself —
  and there is nothing better...

Linda L. Jones
THE PATHS TO LIFE'S WAY

Our Father in Heaven,
  we believe
with you, our lives
  will remain:
True and happy from this
  day through.
We'll take your hand for you
  to lead our hearts
  toward a divine life.
We trust in you and pray
  that you guide our ways
  spiritually
for a lasting eternity
  together,
beneath the clean soils for
  you to walk upon.
My LORD, we lay here
  as carpets,
  to be servants forever.

S. J. Bollinger
MATER

Does she seek a yesterday calm
  Can she play the miles
When all was planned a fairytale
  And pretend was but her child
Years that marr the tapestry
  Faded now the cloth
Draped ideals the holidays
  Curtained beyond distraught
Is she to smile at wisdoms game
  Memory of those nights
Love bloomed tomorrow's path
  And all her world was right

Time has stolen her youthful
  glow
Beauty withdrawn her faded
  eyes
Loneliness clouds of
  sleeplessness
  Dreams have taken the child

Anna W. Rudolph
JUST THOUGHTS!

Crescent moon, ending
  your tour
'Round the universe,
Hang as a cradle in the sky,
Lovely as a jewel
Which others and I cherish,
And await another tour
  to behold.

Elizabeth Kouba
NOVEMBER 15, 1976

Life turned an unsuspecting
  page
On me one cold November
  day:
It did not matter what my
  age—
Perhaps it was meant this
  way.
Sure I cried, what a sight,
Words and friends so hard
  to find.
Loneliness suddenly became
  fright—
Where is my peace of mind?
I know you're always there
Knowing and seeing all—
It's because you truly care
That I'll get up after each fall.
Faith and courage I need
  plenty of—
Just like sunshine after
  the rain.
God—please send me your
  tender love
Along with my sorrow
  and pain.

June Niles
A PEBBLE

A pebble is a wee, small dot
You find along the way,
Compared unto the whole
  wide world
It's as tiny as a tot.

It can have a smooth,
  soft surface
That gives back the warmth
  of sun
It can make you feel just
  full of fun
And want to chase and run.

Or it can be prickley and rough
And rub a sore into your heel,
Jab into your palm and hand
You try to hold it; and it
  calls your bluff.

Myself, I'd like one that
  is pretty
With corners just some peaked,
A little color; smooth surfaces
  just here and there
A lovely pebble, someone put
  there just for me.

Carol Welsch Phillips
MEMORIES TO SHARE

If you have walked along
  a beach
And felt the misty air,
You have seen wondrous
  things,
Have memories to share.
Silly birds dodging waves,
Feeding from the sand;

Treasures in the shells
  you find,
Holding seaweed in your
  hand.
Running, laughing, jumping
  waves,
Sea breeze blowing your hair;
Happy, exciting, lovely hours,
Memories to share.

Otto R. Kundert
DEMONSTRATION

How quiet the mind, how
  still the soul
That knows, in silence, its
  true state of grace,
That knows the wondrous
  truth that it is whole,
That in the span eternal
  knows its place.
For harmony immortal
  lies within,
And we must turn within
  before we see
This truth, and in that knowing
  can begin
To demonstrate what we
  are meant to be!

Virginia A. BerisFord
IF SHE TRIES

A woman can be, anything
  she wants to be,
  If only she tries.
She can have a baby; or
  touch the heavenly skies,
  She can hold her head high.
  Or be low by and by
She can cheat, lie and sin.
But cannot hide from Him.
For if she tries her very best
God will do the rest.

Dixie McVey King
WINTER'S OCEAN IS NEAR

As you walk along the
  ocean's shore
  You realize -
The hot days here, this year,
  will be no more.

When you wet your finger
  and raise it in the air,
you'll find the wind direction
  coming on or off shore,
  You realize -
That's the way it's moving
  through your hair.

Then you sit in the sand,
  You realize -
There is warmth coming
  from the grain
as you bury your feet from
  the cold water pain.

The ocean salt air is getting
  alot colder.
As it penetrates your face,
  You realize -
To stay out here in winter
  you'd have to be alot bolder.
With tears of salt water from
  you and the sea,

you get up and turn away,
   You realize -
In hope of returning on a
   hot summer's day,
You realize -
That winter's ocean is near
but will not stay.

Rev. Joseph E. Kiely
CONSOLATION

Tonight I saw a setting sun
descending in its glory
to me this flaming red-gold ord
has told its whole life story
has told me of its glorious rise
into the spangled orient skies
its warming strength at high
   full-noon
but then 'tis spent and all
   too soon
now it descends its work
   well done
such the song of the setting sun.

Tonight I saw a silent soul
ascending to her glory
a mother's soul I need not say
I know her whole life story
but through full heart-sick,
   'reft, forlorn
I should not feel so sorry.

For as I saw that setting sun
fast-fading from my eyes
I knew it would in other lands
begin its glorious rise
as surely, as the parting ship
shakes off a foreign strand
and reaches soon the friendly
   shores
of its own native land
so surely will a mother's soul
her work in life well done
be met by loving Mary—
and Jesus Christ, her son.

Francis Lantos
**THE OLD BARD'S SONG
   TO THE YOUTH**

Greetings to you, Young Folks!
   I'm a strolling Bard,
Patriot and Fighter of the
   great Old Guard.
I am ninety years old, but
   in spirit young,
And dedicate to you these
   lines, my last song.

Never have mournful thoughts,
   keep your spirit high!
Do not torment yourself,
   have no trothless sigh!
Only the strong and bold is
   destined to live.
The fate of the hopeless is
   sorrow and grief.
Moral of the land shall be
   your guiding light!
Fair fight is the basis to
   a future bright.

But to achieving that take
   your books, your pen,
And read, and write, and
   learn as much as you can.
You may lose all your goods

but now you have learned:
The knowledge of profession,
   thru years you have earned.
Never be despondent! Set
   your goal and strive!
That is the only way to
   success in life.

That's my advise to you,
   that's the success' source:
Learn, fight, and don't give
   up! The future is yours.

Lucille V. Altieri
THE MARATHON RUNNER

My feet have pounded on
   this pavement before,
And I think to myself, just
   push a little more.
I count every tree that I
   pass along the way,
And think of hours spent
   preparing for this day.

I hear the twigs and leaves
   crunch under my feet,
And glance at my watch,
   whose time I must beat.
The man once beside me is
   now far behind,
The thought of falling back
   just enters my mind.

For no one knows the
   agony but me,
Or just how lonely this
   sport can be,
When the grueling wind
   tears at your face,
And the pressure is on to
   keep the pace.
But you'll never hear this
   song on your dial,
The song of the marathon
   runner beginning another
   mile.

It's hard to explain what
   I'm feeling now,
As I turn the curve and wipe
   the sweat from my brow.
I listent intently, it's
   people I hear,
And now I know the last
   kilometer is near.

Across the finish line,
   and then I knew,
The dream I've had has
   at last come true.
And suddenly I recall a
   person from my past,
The lonely marathon runner
   who once finished last.

Olive N. Mulvaney
THANK YOU, LORD

Thank you, Lord for beauty
   around us
For each tall stately pine
For the river that flows
   ever seaward
For each twinkling star
   that shines.

For flowers of every size
   and hue
But one facet of your
   creation
For pictures painted in
   the clouds
To be viewed with
   imagination.

For hills and valleys,
   sun and sand
The many things that
   make up nature
All a part of your vast art
But still you give us
   something greater.

For life itself, your

greatest gift
You have sacrificed your own
For the multitude of sins
   committed
Your life given does atone.

Help us to live in your world
Giving thanks each day to Thee
For life and its bountiful
   blessings
Gifts of your generosity.

Lead us not into temptation,
   dear Lord
Help us to live as brothers
May we walk closely in
   your footsteps
And bring your word
   to others.

Let us live each day for you
Touching the lives of
   all we meet
That we may all travel
   together
And sit someday at your feet.

Kent Godfrey
SPIRITUAL MUTUALITY

The trees had stripped their
   naked thighs of all pretense;
Their worn arms arch toward
   the leaden skies.
Empty rents replace their
   bright and painted faces—
Their jeweled vines and
   willowy laces.

We numbly suffer winter
   harsh and sere,
Nor can our flinching tender
   skin evade
Those whips of pain that
   scouge the dying year
When comes the hour debts
   must be paid.
Dour white intellect commands
   us to save,
For passions fade with leaves
   no longer green
As each of us nears that
   embraching grave.

William L. Marion
MY WORLD

God gave us the sun so that
there would grow trees and grass
and flowers of the field might
sweeten the air.

God gave us the wind so it
might cool the burning deserts
and breath new life in to the
lungs of man.

The water to quench mans
maddening thirst. The wild
stock to fill him when he
was hungry. The night to rest
him when his body and soul
are tired.

All of this he's given us and
quite alot more. But the
   greatest
gift he's given me is the day
he sent me you and that above
all these other things is
worth quite alot more.

Tasha-Razi Khosrovani
**WITH THE MAGIC OF
   KNOWING**

With lips, parched and drawn,
Like the face of a canvas
   cracked with age
She laid upon her death-bed
With her skin whiter than the
   color of her gown.
Her eyes were deeply hollowed
Like those of a jack-o'-lantern
   carved by a child
Or like the hooves of horses

struck down in thick ooze.
Her skin hung about the
   bones of her cheeks
Like a sagging tarpaulin
Making it hard to remember
That she had once been
   a beauty.
Her voice rasped like a jealous
   wind at midnight
Chilling even the icicles staring
   blankly at the moon.
Purple-blue veins reflected
   crystal-clear
Through skin as delicate and
   transparent as faded,
   parchment-paper.
But her eyes, as blue as the
   eyes of Jesus,
Smiled with the magic
   of knowing
That at last
She was going home!

Lynn A. Chew
A ROSE

A Rose
A bud, petals tightly closed
concealing its inner self
undaring to reveal itself
   to the world.

As it ages it opens slightly
   more daring
   it strives to live its life
      to the fullest
   yet still unsure.

As it nears the end of life
   it thrusts itself open
   exposing its inner beauty,
   its fear overcome
   by its need to live its fullest.
The end if here
   its spirit is broken
   and having reached its destiny
   is ready to die, contented.

Fern Olsen Oviatt
THE BALANCE

Life! How beautiful it is!
A delicate masterpiece
So easily abused, or given
Back to its creator.

Life! To balance as we can
On that invisible line, so thin,
Of right, or wrong, that gently
Sways us, back and forth
   at our command.

Life! A form of gentle strength,
Of inward peace, simple faith,
Developed into what we may
Before accounting back to God.

Donald B. Hunt
IN A NUTSHELL

I think we need to face
   the facts,
   Poets heads are full
      of cracks,
And though you may
   already know it
   Every nut is not a poet.

Jerri W. Miller
FOR JOHN K.

Light and shadow
Searching for perfection
   in an all too chaotic world
Where is the reason?

Sunlight illuminates the earth
   Translucent glimpses of
      immortality
   Too brief!!

Time   moving
Time   passing
Time
   running like hell
To and through another day

another month
another year,
Shadow changing form
Giving depth and new
perspectives
Uncertain visions of our
own mortality
Too real!!
Abrupt change, Abrupt end
Sudden conclusion to our
painfully precise
sense of order,
Light and Shadow
Inseparable collage
Shadow fused with living light
Swirling monument
To life ever changing.

Carla Pilapil
UNTITLED

The silken twines of a
spider's tapestry
The timeless eyes of the
night sky
A glimpse of a rose's perfect
symmetry
Ancient ruins of an era
gone by
The changing foliage of autumn
A sparkle in a child's eye
Brilliant hues of a spectrum
Dawn's light creeping sly
Know for a moment while
the world
is at rest,
The simplest things in life
are best.

Regan Forest
**WILD ORCHIDS AND
MEMORIES**

Memories of you.
Wild orchids blooming in a
slant of sun
Through arborescent eaves
of tangled forest.
Shielded here from
Stinging rains of change
and winds of time,
From yesterday and tomorrow,
they prevail in silence.
Off shadow'd paths,
In the misty webs of light,
I chance upon
Still-life moments of
incomparable beauty.

Marti Wilson Vann
ENCOUNTER/DUEL

At five paces we stand—
our eyes slowly meet.
Now I must draw
and shoot a phrase
to hit your attention
square in the heart
quick
before it turns away
and I fall alone.

Helen H. Gilchrist
A GARDEN OF WISHES

If I could walk in your
garden, God,
I know what I would do,
Spend my time on this
planet Earth,
The way you would want
me to.
I'd pluck the blooms from
your path,
For the tired and the weary,
Give the rays from your
bright sun,
To light the dark and dreary.

Give the roars of your
great seas,
To those who cannot hear it,
To raise the hopes of the
hopeless,
Would endow me your
loving spirit.
I'd feed the poor, tend
the sick,
Be a friend to man,
If I can't walk in your
garden, God,
Then let me do what I can!

Pamela A. Cochran
THE ST CHRISTOPHER

The ride was brief from
there to here
Now we are all sitting in
a designated chair
The coffin now shut, we
nod our heads to pray
The flowers observe in a
particular, grievous way
The handshakes are over,
there you go
Being wheeled down into
the cleanly cut hole
I am silent, as I commence
to cry
For to you I cannot say
goodbye
A secluded box, I see through
my tears
Just can't be you, that I've
loved all these years
Now it's over, the dirt
between you and me
But our hearts are together
and perpetually will be
I'll see you again, of this
I am sure
Remember you have our
ST Christopher
Clasped in the palm of
your cold hands
It will bring us together
once again.
(Dedicated to my Uncle Billy)

Karen S. Powell
DESNITY

Tho I've had no regrets
The path in which I've followed
Has been one long struggle
Memories of past mistakes
I do not dwell on
But learn from them as
each day goes by.
And tho my journey has
yet to end
I know my desnity lies
on steady ground
For I've proved not only
to others
But to myself as well
That I'am a leader
For I have not yet been
conquered
I've just begun.

Mauricia Price
EARLINESS

Before the sun has flamed
the crest
Of eastern hills with
burning gold—
Or finger-kissed the
rustling crowns
Of clustered copse-like
verdancies
Or flung translucencies
of light
Through undulating ocean
waves—
There is a magic moment just

Before that eastern
goldening—
A soft enchantment for
the one
Who rose and strolled the
quiet land
In dawning's earliness to feel
That stirring electricity
Of new-fledged morning's
first embrace.

Curtis A. Ferguson
SPIRITUALLY LIFELESS

If you know that you should,
but you don't,
And you say that you will,
but you won't,
You're convinced in advance
that you haven't a chance,
But somehow you're not
even worried;
Then don't look ahead for
you're spiritually dead,
And just waiting around
to be buried.

Joseph H. Young
TO YOU MY VALENTINE

You're my 'lily of the valley'
in the springtime,
You're my 'mountain rose
of sharon' in the fall;
As I read between the line,
Through a scope of valentine;
You're the most lovely
flower of all.

Hayward Hennebury
LOVE SONG TO MY TOE

I'm attached to my big toe
Take's it every where I go,
Couldn't lose it if I tried
'Cause it's always by my side.
Oh my toe I love you so,
Real attached to you I know.
Matter's not how drunk I'll be
Your around to steady me.
Girl's are plenty this I know
But my love is my big toe.
Never care's what girl's I see
For it's free from jealousy.

Dean Alexander Gronos
GIDDIE BLUSH

Carpets of red roses,
her lips so plush;
Sunshine full face,
rainbow glad appearance,
Too sure as Lloyd's of
London Insurance;
Just New Year's Eve, the
roomfelt party hush;
Lucky charms her looks;
feel blue ribbon rush,
The tide's flood high of
her Golden Book eyes;
Quicken have mercy smiles
in quiet sighs;
Child of God kisses true,
Miss Giddie Blush,
Modest like USO show
stepper fair;

Senate Subcommittee's
subpoenas reap
Rich man, poor man, Nobel
Prize loving cup;
Praise glorious breath of
spring dear fresh air,
The Maypole, fountain youth
let all drink deep
Income tax refund pleasure,
coming up.

Johneen Griffin
BLACK CAT NIGHT

black cat night
blinding light
redrimmed eyes
starless skies

around every bend
an unknown end

double exposure
of lights through rain
follow the white line
make it home again.

black cat night
blinding light
redrimmed eyes
starless skies

some road's behind
as the way unwinds

double exposure
of lights through rain
follow the white line
make it home again.

Rachael M. Romano
THE YEAST OF LIFE

I could take two loaves of
bread and give you one.
That would be a kind of
sharing won;
But I would rather take one
loaf and break,
So that in this act you
would know
That love like a loaf is one,
No matter how the edges
are broken.
Then you would see
That when the loaf is made
one again,
My love finds its fitting
with you,
We are not two, despite
the rough edges,
How uneven the parts.
We are one in substance
And in our hearts.

Pearl Teigen
I'M RIDING ON THE RIM

When I took myself a wife
And I started out in life
I thought that I'd be rich
some day;
But through the years of
toil and sweat
I have not made my goal
as yet
And I'm riding on the
rim today.
It's not just a whim
I'm riding on the rim,
And that is not a load of hay;
For I thought I could get by
But the years were long and dry
And I'm riding on the
rim today.
Oh I bought a house and lot
And some furniture I got
And month by month began
to pay;
But the bills they stared
at me
From the nooks I could
not see

And I'm riding on the
rim today.

Oh the taxes came at first
And insurance made it worse
I knew that I could never stay;
So I sold my house and lot
And an old tin can I bought
And I'm riding on the
rim today.

Jacqueline K. Taylor
BEDTIME DREAMS

At the end of the day
the sun waves goodbye
with fingers of red, orange
and blue through the sky.
The shadows grow dark
stars blink here and there
I see the moonlight begin
to appear.
There's a woosh through
the air
a shadow sweeps by
something quite special has
just caught my eye.
It's the night bird
who flies when we all sleep
she dips and swerves among
the stars
she flies by my window
the moon lighting her way
to be sure that I'm dreaming
of flying someday.

Grace W. Hart
ARIZONA ROADRUNNER

He eats more than he needs
Of weeds, berries, and seeds.
He skims across the desert sand,
Wary eyes scanning the land.
Suddenly a hissing sound
Comes from a coil on
the ground.
Then a lightning flash
through the air,
But that alert bird was
not there.
The next thing that rattler
knew
Sharp talons ripped him
through and through.

Christena Ann Nelson
ASSUMPTIONS

Assumptions
Maybe you are better where
you now exist,
Freer to perceive what you've
desired for so long.
Maybe with one valid request
I could yield you back.
With time unaltered, I'd
set the stage
equal to my memories'
rostrum.
Maybe you'd see fit to cast
me as the dreamer.
You were the root we
relied on.
Perhaps we are the wilted stem.

Anneke Mason
**WESTMINSTER AND
ST. PAUL'S**

Directing us skywards, sunrays
through stained glass
windows cast prism lights
on sculptured beams
underscore the heavens,
lift our minds beyond
Splendor of yester year,
ethereal lacework of solid
ages looks down wonderingly
on robots moved by
atom forces

Aura of lost greatness weighs
on minds of Twentieth
Century man, remnants of
power and wealth bewilder
communal owners of state
property, wondering about
driving forces which left such
great memorials to heroes
of war amidst these holy
columns, sought to immorta-
lize
frail spirits of earthbound men
who offered to infinity
effigies of their own glory,
seeking to join eternally
two worlds, ever one

We stand in awe of splendor
left behind and only now
remember nameless men and
women who truly lived
and died in its creation

Connie Marbley-Dent
CHRISTMAS

The seasons changing,
cool winds are blowing,
the quiet evening,
my heart is glowing.

The spirit of
the CHRISTmas season,
should hold a joy,
for CHRIST like reason.

Let each of us
try to remember,
and teach the truth
throughout December.

Lois Jean Lionberger
MY LIFE? OR YOUR PRIDE?

While sleeping I dream.
I see myself quickly
Swimming downstream
Trying to grasp the edge
frantically.

Finally I catch hold
Pulling myself up closer
I feel something cold
Looking up-it's the foot
of my brother.

I cry out-asking him to
help me—
But he steps on my
straining hands.
I slip back, but try to
grasp his knee.
Failing, I drift towards
the waterfall.
Struggling to keep alive
I see a vine
From a tree which is
very tall.
Grasping, and straining,
I reach my life's twine.
But at the end of the limb
Sits my brother cutting
the stem.

Barbara A. Ives
SEA OF LIFE AND DEATH

I walk along the shore
beside the sea,
And all around me life
is passing by,
The question whirls around
inside of me:
Will all things go on living
when I die?
I can't imagine how the
world will be
When I am gone, and in
the ground I lie,
Will all the things around
me now be free
When I no longer share
their beauty? Why?

And yet deep down inside
of me I know
My absence will not change
a single day;
The world will still be
changing, and will grow,
All life will go on in a
normal way;
To live and die is part
of Nature's plan,
Return to sea from where
all life began.

Bob Mullin
O GENTLE SEAGULL

O gentle seagull
Today you are to fly
Your only direction
to follow the wind
to fulfill the sky
Take notice of the grass
all around
how it directs only upwards
Pay no mind to the falling leaf
that is a gift to the earth
You are a gift to the sky
O gentle seagull
Today you are to fly
Oh gentle seagull
Today you are to soar

Ong, Gin Keong
MISGIVINGS

When the moon was bright,
I asked her to be my bride,
Somehow I came to know,
That the answer would be no,
I knew that she would
turn her back,
And that was why I was sad,
But somehow I had to
know the answer,
For I knew that I could
wait no longer,
With her turning of her back,
I knew that I had to pack,
For I had to go,
Since I had the answer ago,
If I only knew of her kind,
I didn't know that
love was blind,
I was turned out into the cold,
Because her heart was
as hard as gold,
With no offence,
I had to keep my sense,
To hear a reply,
I was not yet to die,
To have such a loss,
Was not to be my cause,
Let me not fill with hate,
For this is my fate,
For now I nurse a
broken heart,
And sadly it is now time
to depart.

Thomas J. Kimball
MEMORIES OF MONA

As dawn washes my windows
in absolution,
I think of you, my love,
pure as summer rain.
The rosy red hues of the
rising sun
Herald a new day, a new
beginning,
And an old love rekindles
in its glory.
Perhaps, as light pushes
the stars away,
You'll give some small
thought to me,
Alone in my solemn gray
garret
With only memories of you,
With only the memory of

your touch,
Your smile, your chestnut
hair
Soft falling on smooth
shoulders
I long to touch.
As dawn washes warmly
my windows
In absolution,
I think only of you, my love,
Pure as summer rain,
Soft as spring's last snow.

Susan C. Stolte
REFLECTING

Once in a while
I can see
Things I was made to see.
How many times did I
look to see
A flower,
And saw only a flower?
How many times did I
want to see
A rainbow,
And saw only colors?
And how many times did
I actually see
Beauty?
Maybe once.

Timothy Hunn
YOUR WORDS

Your words;
Are a song within myself
I sing.
Your words;
Are the flavor of a new
hive in spring.
Your words;
Are the strength and
encouragement,
I need to go on,
When all the "GOOD
TIME" friends,
I thought I had are gone.
Your words;
Are a break from factory
work's din,
Giving me a sense of peace,
And joy within.
Your words;
Are gayety and fun,
And the sound I long
for most of all,
Oh gentle one.

Ken Jones
CLOUD WINTER'S MOON

The Moon. . .
Drunk with her grief. . .
Staggers through the cloud-rifts
Weeping for her long lost lover. . .
Li Po

C. Vincent Kroeger
**THE TIGHTROPE OF
DESPAIR**

I walked the tightrope of
despair
over the Valley of the
Shadow of Death,
I was alone no one else was
there
a Hell on Earth that took
away my breath.
I wandered through the caves
of lunacy
rejected and abandoned by
my friends,
I swam the whirlpools of
despondency
chilled to desperation by the
fateful winds.

Yes, I walked the tightrope of
despair
  without the will to survive.
But the promise of Love was
always there
  it was Faith that kept me
alive!

Patricia L. Arnegard
THINKING OF YOU

Watching the leaves fall
  to the ground
Makes me miss you and
  want you around
Each day that we are apart
We can feel it in our heart
Feeling empty without you
Thinking of something to do
Sew awhile and clean house
Need the feeling of my spouse
Thinking of the things we
  have done
Climb hills, swim and run
The children want to play
  all day
At nite time they sleep away
Waiting still to hear your voice
Make a meal of your choice
Listen to you read aloud
Makes me feel so very proud
That I am yours and you're mine
Until the very end of time.

Elisabeth Jane Hall
THE CLOCK

Ticking away the time of day
The Clock ticks on in a
  melancholy way
minutes like hours going
  so slow
only twenty more minutes
  to go.

Ever so slowly the hands
  go round
bringing you closer with
  each ticking sound
now only ten minutes,
  I hope they go fast,
    until finally at last
    I am with you.

Deane A. Tack
SAND DUNES

Thy gentle slopes do speak
  so softly,
Yet carry in thy mounds
  of warmth
A velvet touch that sets
  the soul afire.

Each changing form
The alpha of the greatest
  sculptor's hand
To spread o'er all
And smooth man's
  blemished earth.

O dunes of sand,
Speak thou from thy
  timeless wisdom
And set with wings our
  fettered minds.

Tim DiVito
ONLY A DREAMER'S DREAM

Ages have gone by since
I have walked these streets
To look at my past
I knew the sorrow wouldn't
  last
If I were to keep anything
It would be my dignity
Because without your dignity
  you aren't worth a penny
I have been living only a
  dreamer's dream

Many say to succeed you
  have to soar

With the eagles
Walk with the champions
To live, laugh
To sing, sacrifice
Even to die for what
  you believe
I believe when the sun sets
  in the morning
A new life begins, a new
  dream has begun
To see the impossible dream
To hear the impossible promise
Is only a dream a dreamer
  can dream
I believe when the sun sets
  the dreams
And wishes of the world
  come true
Never let these feelings pass
Without a second look
Nobody can take your dignity
Nobody can steal your
  heart and soul
Nobody can shatter a
  dreamer's dream

Lori Caldarola
LIFE

Life what is it
  a series of beginnings
  and endings
    of starts and finishes
but of all the joy we
    experience
  the only thing we really
    feel
      is the pain.

William A. Mayes
THE BARD

Blessed seclusion we trasure,
  thoughts written at pace.
To be content forever,
  the bard and quiet space.

Adept in white metaphor,
  dull in common prose.
Mental efforts are made,
  till awaited internal repose.

Bill L. Hunt
BYGONE DAYS

Gone are the wagons crossing
  prairie and plain.
Gone are the travelers pitching
  tents in the rain.
Gone are the freedoms to
  settle where you are.
Gone are the days of viewing
  earth with no scar.
Gone are the people who
  cherish these things still?
I meet one now and then,
  hope I ever will.

Jamie Anne Shankles
LOOK AT ME

Hey little bird
Up in the sky,
Won't you please
Show me how to fly?

Show me how to spin
And how to float on air.
Won't you please show me
How to make people stare?

You fly so well!
Don't you know everybody
  watches you?
They all stand speechless
As you fly beyond their view.

I want to know
What that's like to be.
Little bird, don't you know
That this is my plea?

So show me how to fly

And show me how to soar.
Because I need you, little bird
To help me make crowds roar.

I'll give it all I've got
And I'll try not to be afraid.
Is it really you little bird
That I am trying to persuade?

Peter R. Vallas
MISSING YOU

Even though your away,
Its so nice to have someone
  to miss,
To miss you brings you closer,
  I can smile.
Thoughts of you are happy,
Thoughts of you are warm,
And as time passes on,
That special feeling grows,
And when you return,
My heart bursts with gladness,
Its been so nice missing you.

Minerva Erevia Fry
MY SPECIAL SON

How wonderful to watch,
My children at the beach,
Walking hand in hand.
They laugh, run,
Compare shells.
But............
  You are not among them.

I see you then............
  Mentally.
I see you laughing, running,
  and playing.

The sorrow will never
  leave me.
The things............
  that you should be doing.
Are growing
  Like the branches of a tree.

Everyday
  I remember you
And the feeling for you
To be near me
  is renewed.

God bless you, my special son
For when you were born
My cross was begun.

Danae Gronos
IN VAIN

In vain you lie beneath
  the earth,
Thinking you had given birth
To freedom and tranquility,
Your children full security.

But dearest you must
  have known,
For many times it was shown,
The beast in man lingers still
Craving yet another kill.

Janet H. Cassel
**THE MOST BEAUTIFUL
MORNING OF OUR LIVES**

The sun crept through
  the window
  one early 'morn in May
And cast its golden glow
  on the man who by me lay.

T'would be a short time now
  before he would awake
To the precious gift of life
  adorning this day break.

As he began to stir
  I sat down by his side
And gently broke the news,
  his first born would arrive.

How does one describe
  the depth of one's emotions
As suddenly months
  of waiting

is about to cease its motion?
Of all the mornings we
  have known
of all the treasured days
None will ever be as precious
  as this beautiful 'morn
in May!

When we awoke to realize
  the union we had made
Was this day to be completed
  with the birth of our
first babe!

Carole Browning-Black
THE AGING SHELL

My mirror tells me
I have been squinting
into too many sunrises;
too many sunsets. But
the dawn conjurs up
energy reminiscent of
long ago sunny days.

My mirror tells me
there have been too
many years of worry
and concern, but the bright
new morning washes away
all inner traces.

My mirror tells me life
is losing its color;
becoming drab and gray.
But each day brings me
new and challenging ex-
periences.

My mirror tells me
I am no longer firm,
agile and swift. But
in my mind's eye I
can move and accomplish
as in yesteryear.

I am as I was!
I have not changed!
I have not aged; instead
it is this shell that
surrounds me.

Melissa K. Ward
INNER TURMOIL

Paper
A few words
pen flowing freely
mind turning endlessly
thoughts escaping with
  emotions
A tear trickles down my
  cheek, slowly
Dropping a salty stain
  on my paper
Words blurring through
  cloudy eyes

The storm has begun.
Writing is done.
(Try reading between
  the lines).

Clarence Sanders
DREW ET ALIA

Saturday, October 11th:

  Army vs. Lehigh, at West-
  point, at 2:00...
  Boston College vs. Yale, at
  Chestnut Hill, at 6:00...
  Colgate vs. Holy Cross, at
  Hamilton, at 1:30...
  Rutgers vs. Alabama at
  Giants Stadium, The
  Meadowland,
  at 1:30...

  Drew vs. Life et Alia.

Saturday, October 18th:
(All games at 1:30)

  Cornell vs. Brown, at Ithaca.
  Dartmouth vs. Harvard,

at Hanover.
Wesleyan vs. Amherst,
at Piscataway.
Drew vs. Life et Alia.

Louetta M. Borrmann
THE EVENING OF LIFE

Life's twilight hours are
here at last,
The days ahead are few,
The hours and minutes
tick away,
And disappear like dew.

Life's evening sun has
set at last,
No day shall wake our
slumbers,
But in God's home above
Our days are without
number.

Carol Chapin Lindsey
TO A RETARDED SON

Love is the only arm across the
breach
That widens as we grow away
from you
Who seem to stay the same.
Each day you teach
Me knowledge of myself long
overdue:
That patience is a rugged land
to reach,
That love and understanding
stumble, new,
And not yet strong. Your
shallow eyes beseech
The deeper look that cannot
misconstrue.

Anachronism is not yours, nor
lack:
The armor of my hopeless
mother-love
Will shield you from the
mockery of years
Which praise your brother.
Were many moons turned back,
Our womb-choice now, I
wonder if we'd move
Conversely—quenching start of
stubborn tears.

Rose M. Brown
NEW BORN BABE

Oh Lord, I'm just a
newborn Christian,
A baby, for your arms
to enfold.
Help me to take each
step carefully,
Keep me sheltered from
the bitter cold.
Grant me the knowledge
to know right from wrong.
And be patient with me
each day.
For like a child, I'm
eager to learn,
Help me to listen to
what you say.
Give me the courage to
live in this world,
And keepy my life
pure for you.
Make me bold enough
to tell others,
Let them see my light
in all I do.
If I ever start to slip
from you,
Bring me back down
to my knees.
Help me always to
be humble,
And forever hear my
soft pleas.

Give me enlightment
of your word.
As I study the
Bible through.
Help me to receive
understanding,
For I want to be one
of the chosen few.

Irma Campbell
PRAY FOR PEACE

What do we mean when we
pray for peace
Do we simply mean that
bombing will cease
While men still crouch in fear
and dread
Knowing that communism
will spread
While men are still afraid to
pray
Because of the communistic
way
And some folks still must hide
their face
Because other men hate their
race
Let's pray that victory shall be
won
So that there's peace for every
one
We can make the right prevail
Trust in God we need not fail
If we fight to shield the right
God will help us by his might
So let's each one do our part
To keep the peace within our
heart.

Reuben Perez
BOXES

i wish i had
little, golden, jeweled
sugar-cube-sized boxes
to keep the memories
of you within.
and on those
cold and dark days
i could open a box
persuading
the sun to shine
and a baby bird to sing.

Florence E. Brytcuk
**SWITCHBOARD
OPERATOR'S LAMENT**

Oh, switchboard, you have
driven
Me out of my mind at last.
I, who so gladly had given,
You all of my life in the past.
The same old dreary voices I
hear,
Asking the same old dreary
questions.
Till I have an ache in my ear,
And my thoughts are torn to
distraction.
You weary me from the time I
start,
Till the long day is ended.
My nerves are gradually shaking

apart,
My wrecked life can never be
mended.
So this is enough of the misery
you give me,
I'll bear a grin, till it's finished.
And give a smiling "Hello" so
sweetly,
So as not my record to blemish.

Larry R. Dillon
MAN

Teach me all you know
And it will not be enough,
Show me all there is to be seen
And I will not be satisfied,
Let me experience all there is
to experience
And I will still want more.
Hold me back
And I will only try harder,
Take me to the highest point
And I will reach higher,
Challenge me to do better
And I will,
Say it is impossible
And I will overcome it,
For I am man
And my world knows no limits,
Except those limits I place upon
myself.

Randy A. DeFord
THE TILLER

The morning light has
never shown
So bright, or quite
so sweet,
This growing land
before my eyes
Of barley, rye,·
and wheat.
To know my hands
have touched this soil,
And felt the timeless
grant
That God has blessed
into the earth,
For every seed
I plant.
Until the day I cease
to be
With mortal sight
and sound,
My pride shall be to
know I was
A tiller of the ground.

John C. May
ROME

(To Laurie Jane Bennett)

In many a night
I feared that the sacred
fire of life
Would flicker and die,
But you were always there
In my Rome of hearts,
Tending the flames
Like a pale Vestal Virgin.
You—of purpose inviolate—
Preserved for me—of
will moribund—
My Trojan birthright
Brought so long ago
To my shores by Aeneas.
I will not forget
How time and time again
You saved me—a
crumbling Rome—
From barbarian assaults.
Like the Capitoline geese,
You cried out to me in
the temple of Juno
That the Gauls had
penetrated
My very core.
Your timely warning

roused my forces
To rally in defense.
Then, like Pope Leo
the Great,
You alone fearlessly crossed
The misty Tiber
To meet Attila, Scourge
of God,
And dissuaded him
From sacking my city.
My gratitude to you
Will be, like Rome,
Eternal.

Cindy Harle
CASUAL AFFAIR

I loved him with all my might
But he never really held me
tight
I thought that we would always
be
But to him it was casual, why
couldn't I see

Harry E. Abrams, Jr.
YOU GAVE ME LOVE

You gave me love, and
The words to express my own
for thee
Failed me.

I wished I were a Shakespeare,
That I might write a sonnet
for thee.

But, I am not.

I wished I were a Byron, or a
Shelly;
A Whitman or an Eisely,
That I might string together
beautiful words
As a necklace of love for thee.

But, I am not.

You gave me love to light my
path
At the bottom of the abyss,
So I turned to That which is,
And prayed,
That I might someday light
your way with love,
During some dark hour of your
life.

Until that hour,
Keep these poor words to
remind thee,
You gave me love.

Helen Elaine Cubellis
THE RESTLESS WIND

The restless wind
Blows wildly about,
Twisting and turning
Through the trees in and out;
Bending their branches
Almost to the ground,
Over and under
And all around;
Frantically racing
From tree to tree,
Leaving behind
A vague memory;
Of whence it came
And where it's gone,
Wandering endlessly
On and on.

Nancy Dressler
ARE THEY TOYS?

A bunny rabbit on my bed, he
is stuffed and cloth, you see,
But when I use my imagination,
he comes to life for me.
I see him dance and hear a song,
could it have come from
my bunny?
Then he smiles and sits back
down—Now toys are really
funny!

An alligator in my closet, but
    what a weird fellow is he!
He has blue and red spots all
    over his back and yellow
        pads at the knee!
He will crawl and bite, then
    chase me around, a battle well
        worth a fee,
But then he goes back and hides
    again, until HE wants to
        play with me!
Now I ask you, my friend, are
    they toys? Or things we just
        like to see?
Do all kids "pretend" their
    toys are alive? Or maybe they
        really could be?
Whoever could answer a simple
    old question? A wizard he
        must be,
'Cause not only do my "toys"
    sing and dance, they also
        fight with me!!

Angela Bushey
A CHILD

To watch part
of ones' self
grow, and then
to let go;
to guide, yet
give independence
to an extension
of yourself;
to share in the
happy times,
to comfort
during the sad times;
to prepare
and then set free
this seed of
your existence;
to have a child.

Genevieve R. Erwin
COMING HOME

The hills of home are brighter
    now
And the clouds have rolled
    away;
The lines are fainter on a brow
For this is such a lovely day.
The voices ring as clear as a bell,
They reach down and touch
    the heart;
Such lovely tales each one can
    tell
This is the homecoming's
    sweetest part.
Each one is fresh and dear to
    see,
With a smile on each one's face;
This day is, indeed, so lovely
And this, indeed, is the dearest
    place.

Anna M. Scepanovic
BECOMING

Each minute in time;
Growing. Dreaming.
Making a life of
    echoing streams
Rippling through hopes
    and dreams.
Sifting through...
Making realities visible
Forgetting sad memories
Loving every second of
    shared love
[friends, nature, sunsets
    behind the woods]
Looking at the way
    people are
And not how I wish them
    to be.
Taking each day for what

it is, what it can bring.
Just accepting things...
    people...MYSELF...
My gift of love to you.

C. Scott
WINDOWS

Clear as the windows once were,
They're covered now with
    broken shades
Flapping in the chill of
    lonesome winds,
Taking from us the
    glowing warmth
That held your body
    and mine.
We're cold and shivering
And moving trickles of
    moonlight
Falling from shattered
    glass
Have lost the clear,
    pure hopes
That swayed back and
    forth in our minds.
The windows are broken
    and dirty
And we are tired of
    constant moving.
Be still: we will forget
    loosing the life
That we never found in
    years of searching.
Are you too tired to
    clean the window?
Let us rest for a long,
    long while.
Tomorrow maybe our
    skies will smile down
Clear as the windows
    once were.

Kenneth Karl Knoelk
**YOU MEAN EVERYTHING
TO ME (SANDY)**

Girl you tell me I am too
    insecure.
Well woman I am not too sure
If it is not just me.
You say I am not very dominate.
Well woman dog-gone-it,
Can't you begin to see?
I've given myself to you—
Maybe I am a fool.
Maybe I am the one who
    cannot see.
But girl, you mean everything
    to me.
Girl you say I drive you up a
    wall.
Well woman now don't you fall,
'Cause together your
    frustrations we share.
Girl you say I don't understand.
Well woman what's wrong with
    a helping hand?
There's nothing wrong with
    showing you care.
So I've built my world around
    you.
Maybe its wrong, I am a fool.
But I am not so blind I can't
    see,
That you mean everything to
    me.

Kathleen A. Hess
SOMEDAY

Isn't it time you loved me?
Isn't it time you cared?
My life had been so empty
Until you came along.
I've waited such a long time,
But you still don't say you care.
I guess I'll just keep hoping
    For someday.

I wonder what you're feeling;
I could never read your mind.
You hide behind your laughter,
But then I never did complain.
You turned my frowns into
    smiles,
You brightened up my life.
I hope you'll feel the same for
    me
        Someday.
But when will that someday
    come along?
It seems to be taking its time.
I guess I'll have to wait
Until you tell me how you feel.
I guess I'll just keep holding on
    To someday.
Isn't it time you loved me?

Martha Brock
RAINBOWS

Ribbons of remembering
Animations of anticipation
Invasions of iridescence
Notes of nothing
Bubbles of banquets
Omens of optimism
Windows of wishes
Shadows of secrets

Yvonne Berry
A MEMORY

I never loved anyone the way
    I Love You—never cared.
But even though this is true,
    "His" memory is in my mind
        And somehow lingers there.
I think of you all throughout
    the day—But sometimes;
        "He comes into my mind
        and refuses to go away.
Maybe it's the guilt, Or the pain
    I put him through,
        Or knowing He loved me
        enough
        To let me go to you.

Nellie Woll Kirkpatrick
OUR DAD—STILL GUIDES US

Our father's clock has ticked
    and tocked our years away,
(And turned my hair—once
    shiny gold—to limpid gray);
It speaks a challenge to our
    every day and hour
To add some worth to life while
    yet we're given power.
Who knows if we shall sit
    together here again
Beneath its hands, like this, to
    read and write with pen?
Its striking chimes bring insights
    crystal clear to light:
We must do good for one we
    love before this night.
For one we love? more likely,
    one we nearly hate,
To cleanse our willful souls
    before Time grows too late.
It's strange: our dad (whose
    skillful hands kept wound
    this clock)
Though long since gone, still
    guides us through its tick and
    tock.

Annette M. Allee
THE BUTTERFLY

Oh Butterfly -
    Oh, sign of hope,
    Oh spirit flying free!
I wish that I were thee!

Oh Butterfly -
    Oh, sign of love,
    Wings the colors of the sun!
I wish that we could be as one.

Robin Scofield Koteles
6/19/79
if
    we
        be
    as one
        we shall
            in-
            crease
                as
                    two
within a sphere
    of warmth
        created
            by
        us

Donna K. Hughes
LIFE

Life is so unfair
for those who just don't care
But for those who do
life will see you through
You're bound to find a way
to make the best of every day
and if you don't
at least you didn't say you won't
One of the best things in
    life is hope
and to know how to cope
There may be tears to shed
from memorys that aren't
    quite dead
Still you hold your head
    up high and grin
and greet every one as if
    a friend
So happy to be free
thats how everyone should be

Ira Jay Rothenberg
**MADNESS: AFTER THE
SCALPEL'S CUT**

Lost in
gray paradise
Tilts on the razor's edge
Tarnished star sinks silently
"Cuckoo!"

Larry Douglas Chappell
OUR LITTLE BOY

Don't whimper if you
Break your toy,
Don't despair if you
Sometimes lessen our joy.
Never ever worry
About being in a hurry
To become a man,
Just be our little boy
As long as you can!

Maryruth Burbank
CHORES ARE NEVER DONE

I am a happy housewife
Built big and strong
I have been cleaning most of
    my life
I do not work for hourly pay,
    I do it for a song
I pick up dirty clothes here and
    there
I pick them up in my travels
    everywhere
My household consists of me
    and two males
There's dirt and dust by the
    pails
I run around and curse and
    swear
My work is almost done, Oh,
    no, here's some dog hair
The rubbish must be put away
And there goes half a day
Now to the store I go shopping
Now to home again on the run

Here it is the day is done
Here comes the supper dishes
and the setting sun
I sit to watch the colored TV
Oh, no, I found a stray dried
pea
So you see my work still isn't
done
And it's later, much later, than
the SETTING SUN.

Lori Florence Laska
**BETWEEN MOTHER, DADDY,
AND DAUGHTER**

Daddy is away again
Overseas blue and green. Above
the horizon
that I can see from our back
porch.
He is doing business with
people I have never seen in
places I have never been.
And now,
My eyes are dripping wet
like the days umbrellas are used.
And why,
that's a question like a crooked
letter, grandma said.
Hello middle aged woman
downstairs (kitchen, kitchen).
How do you do?
Oh, you are my mother,
why won't you spill your guts?
Oh, mother, have you guts to
spill?
Am I just the teenage daughter?
Just that.
Only here
because of a love once had
between you
and a man overseas.
But daddy, where are you?
Oh, you are in Europe. Yes,
I am in my room
again.

L.O.W.
SARKASMOS

Hum drum
Hi ho
Buy cold power
Always fasten your seat belt!

Did you talk to the Lord today?

Own a piece of the rock!
You'll be glad you did!

Walt Disney was a fag!
Mickey Mouse screws Minnie.
Up
Down
Entrance
Exit
Always a way in and out
What's inside?

Sun causes skin cancer
Repent and be joyful
Damn blacks are taking over
Young people got no respect
for their elders.

Why when I was a kid...
    E.T.C.
    E.C.T.
    T.E.C.

Manera Heath
YES JESUS CARES

Does Jesus care when our
Hearts are pained
Too deeply for Mirth
and Song?
Oh, Carol, yes. He says
He cares
And He cannot say
the wrong.

Does Jesus care when our
Way is so dark and
Our hearts beat quickly

with fear?
Oh, honey, yes. But
His promises
Are to always be very near.

When so deep is our grief
And we find no relief,
When we choke on held
in tears?
Oh, Carol, yes He promises
To go with us through
all the years.

Does Jesus really care
That we've said "good bye"
To the Daddy we love
so much?
Oh, honey, yes. And
He is making
Now, A mansion for
Daddy and us.

I know He cares,
Never doubt that He cares,
And one day He will
take us above.
With the cares of this
world overcome
With Daddy, we will
bask in God's love.

Nancy Beattie
THE PAINTED FACE

Underneath her powder,
Artificial rose.
Collections from her past,
Under painted picture pose.
Violet when so young,
Slowly fades past primrose grey,
As longing through many mirrors;
    She discovers
    Late fall...

Janet M. McGuire
UNTITLED

one single perfect shell
tiny and white
washed ashore in my hand
the thought of this huge
rough body
bringing me this
oh
so perfect gift
fills me with wonder
and then I think of you
how like this
tiny
sea washed gift of mine
you are
one single perfect love
placed in my hands
by god

Marilyn Hare
LONG AGO

It was long ago that you
and I met.
Long ago that we shared
our thoughts.
Long ago, we laughed,
touched, lived.
We also left one another
long ago.
Uncertainties came to
fill our lives.

Then, long after, we began
again as friends.
The times were few
but pleasant.
We knew each other from
long ago.
Our hearts touched, but
not too tightly.
Long after we could
smile at long ago.

Then again we left each
other's company.
The world stops for
no one,

And now I am alone with
my desires.
You are far away now
but very near.
I miss you as a friend.
My heart remembers too
often, long ago.

Shelley Sue Cronkhite
I MADE A WISH

I made a wish for you today
That you might reach
your star,
To know true feelings of
being needed
And show love and caring
the way they are.

I made a wish for your
own dreams
That you might reach
your goals,
To have a full and happy life
And fill your only roles.

I made a wish for your
true hopes
That you might reach no end,
To keep and cherish your
inner thoughts
And never be without
a friend.

I made a wish for your future
That you might find
what's yours,
To see a life of eternity
And find the key to
life's doors.

Charlotte Rose McElduff
SHINING SHOPS

Today I entered a shining
shop full of time and
ticking clocks.

All types, all faces.
Some play music, some do not.
Reminding us all time is
the present.

We spend our youth
spending time.
Our old age wishing for
one more tomorrow.

Like, clocks, the carpenter
of wood,
    the carver of all time,
    God sets His day with
    the sun.

Watchmakers usual settings
are 1 p.m., 3 p.m., and
5 p.m.
They are mechanically precise.
His time is never regulated.
Time spent with Him in
prayer is priceless.
Perpetual happiness streams
forth from his hands,
holding His own close to
Him at all times.

Leroy Mohr
CROSSROADS AHEAD

She arises morningtide
The sun's light won't her
beauty hide.

A soul has she.

Not knowing unknowing
She thinks of me.

I am the lock, she has my key.
She has the power to help
me be me.

A crossroads ahead,
We long for, we two,
As we both wonder
I wonder who?

Come, oh crossroads come,

Fate preordained meeting,
My heart keeps beating,
Coldness retreating.

Beating, heating,
Yearning, burning,
Seeking, Keeping,
Screaming its need.

Jan Winemiller
LAST RITES

the old man rests
on his stoop
the home behind him
a shell square walls
holding space a few
traces of his life
stares beyond the red sun
over tracks where
the streetcar used
to run; recalls
jennie, four daughters
three sons nearly gone
when he got there
like ghosts wading
through solvent air

Linda Imbeault Rowe
**MERRY CHRISTMAS
SWEETHEART**

Did I tell you your my
diamond ring?
My total world wide treasure.
Or how much I'm in love
with you?
I'm in love with you
for ever.

Did I mention how you've
made me smile?
How you've made my
dreams come true?
My lonely heart stretched
twice its size
By the love that comes
from you.

I want to make you happy
Just like you've done for me.
To lace your dreams
with silver.
I'll do it all for free.

I hope I find a Christmas star.
That's falling from the sky.
I'll wish apon that string
of light
Before it starts to die.

I'll have a special wish
in mind.
I'll wish away your fears.
A very Merry Christmas
And the happiest of
New Years.

The only way this wish
will work.
The way it will come true.
Is if the many happy years
Are spent by me and you.

So Merry Christmas sweetheart
And keep my wish in mind.
Because the love that I
have given you
No one else will ever find.

Robert Burns McIntyre
**PENNSYLVANIAN
THANKSGIVING**

A scene glimpsed down a
valley, was a scene
beyond compare
Challenge to a man from
God, saying do you
really dare.
Share with me this beauty
spot here in my created
world
Glory seen in yonder view,
like a snapping flag

unfurled.
Battle flag of sweat and
  strife to wrestle from
  yonder field
Home within a wilderness
  from this harsh stone
  earth a yield.
Changing land to man's
  increase, your children
  to bear and rear
Do God's Will through
  Jesus Christ for those
  who you hold most dear.
A man's world as God
  directs and woman responds
  with strength
Man and wife and all they
  own having found a
  place at length
Valley views become a
  home, a prayer answered
  by acts
God's will now reality when
  prayer and toil are facts.

Roberta B. Lindbeck
**THE LAND OF MAKE
  BELIEVE**

I love the Land of
  Make Believe
Where you'll sometimes
  walk with me,
Far from the noisy
  shores of life,
Far from reality.

We can close the gates
  behind us,
And wander as we please,
All alone in this lovely world
We relax, and are at ease.

This fabulous land of
  Make Believe
Is beautiful and fair,
And I float in a golden glow,
Just because you are there.

I revel in every moment
And cry out to time
  "Go slow"!
So quickly fly the moments,
And alas, we have to go—

Back to the world of reality
Back to its problems and strife
Back to what we must cope with
In all our every day life.

Yet how I love to remember
The golden moments past
I've spent in the Land of
  Make Believe.
In my heart they will
  always last.

Marjorie J. Brown
SPIRIT'S OF ME!

My spirit longs to be free,
Of the burdens that chain
  and bind me,
Of the hussel and bussel
  of City Life,
Where everyday traffic
  becomes a fight
for your life;

Where people are in such
  a rush
to get - no where,
To busy to stop and say,
Good morning, and how
  are you today?

My spirit longs to be free
Of never enough hours,
And to short a days;

Free to sore like the birds
  in the sky,
To be like the whispering
  breezes of the wind,
and the gentle waves of

the ocean;
My spirit longs to be free,
To feel the sunshine upon
  my face,
For my body to relax,
  and not be at a pace,
To see the beauty of
  sunrise and sunset,
  which I have long forgotten.
My spirit longs for so much,
When will my spirit ever
  be free?

Lori Kay Smith
REBELLION

Radically
I'm free
And gradually
A seed
Growing differently
Not wrongly.

Luther E. Paddock
**THE ADVENTURE
  OF FISHING**

Of angling Bobby was
  very fond
His daydreams wandered
  far beyond
The waves of his local
  fishing pond

Invitation came for an
  ocean cruise
To Bob and his Mom it
  was wonderful news
A fun-filled event one
  couldn't refuse

They stayed over night at
  a seaside motel
Sailing day dawned clear
  as a bell
But - Oh! That unsettling
  ocean swell!

Others trolling lines
  did trail
But our pair spent more
  time at the rail
Telling the fishes a sad
  little tale

Now, Bobby still likes to
  tally his score
But will he try the big
  sea once more?
Heck, no! He stops ten
  feet from the shore!

(A true experience of Bobby
Yurgionas)
Related by Grandpa

Lorene Beeler
OCTOBER TRAILS

Cool rippling winds
Sprinkling leaves of various hues
Rustling thru the cornstalks
Seeming almost to talk to you!

Colors, oh glorious colors
Warm reds, browns, and
  yellows too
With the grains all harvested
Ready for the winter view!

Soon will come that frosty morn
And the pumpkins we will see
As a "pot o' gold" for the
  goblins
And heartfelt treasures for
  you and me!

Thomas J. Russell
SAND CARB'S LAMENT

Swell on swell,
  wave on wave,
Bursting with
  ecstatic mirth.
Leaving lines

of frosty foam
On my soft
  and sandy surf.

Watery fingers
  reaching, splashing,
Grasping bits
  of sandy loam.

Why are you
  still re-arranging
This, my beach,
  my sandy home?

Angeline A. Buchanan
OLD GLORY, I AM

They burned me today,
  Old Glory, I am.
I flew under the guise,
  of great Uncle Sam.

My stars had a meaning,
  my stripes had one too,
And they torched me today,
  but first walked on me too.

If a cloth could cry,
  surely I would,
For I've been so proud,
  yet so misunderstood.

Yes, they burned me today,
  Old Glory, I am.
I flew for all,
  but some didn't give a damn.

So farewell to all! Farewell
  from me!
Farewell to the Great
  Land of the free.
Remember me well,
  remember I tried;
Remember, remember,
  a cloth can't cry.

Rose I. Tomlinson
THE GIFT

If I could give a gift to you
My gift would surely be
A life that's long and healthy
Filled with love and flowers
  and trees
My gift would be your
  love to last
Forever and a day
And happiness be with you
In sunshine and in haze
To see you holding hands
  in love
And resting in the shade
With a love that's sure
  and comfortable
So you'll never be afraid
For joy will last forever
In the love you have and hold
My gift would be to always see
Your love that's pure as gold

Pam Calvert
AUTUMN'S SONG

I am filled with sweet
  wonderment at the beauty
  of it.
Could it be that death is
  not horrid and ugly,
but a thing of beauty
  to behold,
Just as the breath-taking
  radiance of summer leaves
die in a wondering glory
  of colors undescribable.

Could it be that death is
  as the autumn leaves?
They live their lives to
  the fullest
and leave in glory and
  radiance.

Is death but just one more
  endless step of eternity?
Is not life as the wink
  of an eye,

just one small glimpse
  of eternity.
So if this life be only a
  glimpse of eternity,
think of the wonderment
  and glory which lies beyond.

So just as the autumn leaves
  show off
their final ray of flory,
  and step to a new deminsion,
so shall we with dignity and
  hope and glory.

Maxine Barnhard
THE UNIT

It was such a simple question
  and the patient asked it
  so quietly.
Yes, no or I don't know
  would have answered it.
Instead they shouted at her,
  told how sick she was, spoke
  of signs and evidence and
  strode angrily away.

So she rejected their world.

The talkative one answered
  the telephone
and told the caller to wait.
She was watching the monitor
  run out.
When she called the coroner,
  she spelled
the patient's last name and
  gave the time
as 8:55.01.

The nurses drank coffee,
  munched cookies
and chatted about their strike.
I huddled in the center
  of my bed
and stared into the night.

Phillis K. Frazier
SNOWFLAKES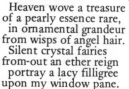

Heaven wove a treasure
of a pearly essence rare,
  in ornamental grandeur
from wisps of angel hair.
Silent crystal fairies
from-out an ether reign
  portray a lacy filligree
upon my window pane.

Melissa Anne Trapnell
WHEN YOU LEFT

You left for awhile
left me to be alone
with just my thoughts of
  you to keep me company.

You left me to wonder
if you'll call,
if you'd think of me,
if you cared..

You left me
hoping that you'd call
that you'd want me,
once more.

You left me
hoping that you'd miss me
half as much as I missed you.

Alice B. Kendall
SING TO THE SOURCE

SING TO THE SOURCE
  to the well-spring
  the Muse, whose spirits arise
    from the crevices
      caverns and cracks—
      running and rushing
  over the rocks
  splashing and humming
through mists, under rainbows
  into the sunlight
    on to dark pools

where stars play at midnight
  through sleeping meadows
  sweet-scented at dawn—
to waken the poet
gifted with song
drawn from deep dreams
  alive in the stream
  echoing music
  above and beyond.

Madge E. Pfleger
NIGHT WIND

The night wind is like a
  deep sea net
  drawn with sensitive
  awareness of wet
  glistening life adrift below.

Trees with leaves atremble
  acquiesce
  to that darkly familiar
  caress
  of cool streaming fingers.

Day birds exhausted with
  chores of need
  feel kinship with her
  passage through reed
  and soft sloping
  pasture grass.

Now-folded hillside blooms
  keep their sleep
  yet sway on slender necks
  as though to weep
  or mourn bright
  sunlight lost.

It knows not its place
  of origin
  but drifts as castle
  ghost of legend,
  phantom of days
  heat and night mists.

Cheryl L. Seigel
DEATH OF A DAY

Dusk slowly peaks
  through the cracks of day,
Bringing tiny ballet slippers,
  first roses, and
  the yellowed snapshots
  of old lovers.
The battered remnants
  of all those yesterdays,
that make us cry with longing
  for the moments,
  that have vanished
  as quickly, as the
  sun's last rays
  slip over
    the horizon.

Joseph N. Cavallo
BREAKING-UP

Leaving someone close to you,
is something very hard to do.
Though sometimes best you
  do part,
that person always remains
  in your heart.

Although you love her and
  want her back,
you have to remember one
  simple fact:
her love is fading out of
  your heart
or you would never had
  thought to part.

You think your life has
  come to an end;
but as you turn every
  corner and bend,
you find happiness in
  new places
where you see new life
  and happy faces.
There's an emptiness

in your heart
from the first time you
  had to part;
and you're afraid to get
  serious again
'cause this time you don't
  think your heart will mend.

But LOVE works in a
  strange way:
you start living day for day;
without the thought of
  what happened before,
you enjoy your new
  happiness more and more.

Adeline Blair
A CHILD IS BORN

A child is born.
A mother comes into being
A smile he's worn
Though child is barely seeing
Her pain is soon forgotten
Thru child gentle as cotton

No precious stone
Will match your own
When your child is born
The pain you've worn
So soon is torn; from body
  and soul
Again you're whole, when
  a child is born

Cheryl Johnson Benedict
LIFE OF A TURNIP

When I was just a baby,
My Mama said to me,
As long as you're a child,
Be happy and be free.
Play with the other children,
Enjoy each passing day,
the time will come for
  you my child,
that you must go away.
Grow upward and get stronger,
Go forth to be the best,
Your only real one goal
  in life,
Is just to beat the rest.
Now after years of striving,
I know what my fate is,
I know what Mama meant now,
My life's no more a wiz.
For it is time to go now,
The time of year to pluck,
Who'd have guessed my
  goal in life,
To be just another turnip
  in a truck.

Holly Lorentz
YOUNG MAN BOLD

Young man bold,
Fair maid daring.
Together they will meet
Way up in the sky.
Dancing, swirling,
Blowing in the wind
Falling to the ground.
Young man broken,
Fair maid dead.

Jose M. Lerma
STEPPENWOLF

I have been myself
  and loved
  thinking mostly of myself
  uncaring, and uncared for
  by the bulk of humanity
I have been the wolf
  preying, fangless,
  in the abyss of my soul
  and that of my brothers' too
I have been the butterfly
  afraid of flight,
  a fluttering phanthom of beauty
  forever on the ground

I have been the leaves
  on the boughs of swaying trees
  shaken by the intimate caress
  of night's wind and
  morning's dew
I have been the promise,
  repudiated long ago,
  an echo of nostalgia
  of yesterdays distorted
  by despair
I am the center
  of circular creation
  a forgotten god
  forlorn in space and time
  idly weaving myths
  from the scattered strands
  of persistent fantasy.

Don Eklund
HE SPOKE TO ME

I talked with my GOD before
  the break of day.
I listened to what he had
  to say.
He talked of a grassy meadow
  and a quiet stream.
HIS soothing voice, it
  seemed like a dream.
We talked of a city with
  streets of gold.
Never any problems, no one
  grows old.
Follow me my son, I
  heard HIM say.
Give me your hand, I'm
  leading the way.

Tommy B. Rupinski
**UPON READING THE
  DAILY NEWS**

my stomach growns,
  invisibly,
  in pain.

i sleep,
  with horrible anticipation
  of russians,
  invading poland.

these russians,
will not creep
into a city
on Sandburg's catlike feet.
But their action,
will be as unclear in my mind,
as the fog,
that settled over Chicago,
that one night.

Cami Kirkman
REALITY FOR MY FATHER

It happens to everyone else.
I.
I remember when you
  spanked me,
All the way up the driveway.
You told me I couldn't go
  play with Bryan,
But I didn't think you
  were serious,
Well, you were.

You were so proud of me
  and my little dapple gray.
We went everywhere;
I stole hearts and showed off.
But one day the barn was empty,
And so was I.
II.
I just knew you'd be mad
  'cause I flunked.
You waited hours and you
  weren't well;
But when I timidly told you,
You didn't yell, but you said
Ah hell, drive home without
  the stupid piece of paper.

I remember your opening eyes
  and your blue body—
The room reeking of sickness.
You weren't gasping anymore,
Because you had no need
  of breath.
I knew you needed nothing now.
It happened to me.

Rana Dawn
REFLECTIONS

My life is lonely with
  him not here
I'm torn apart so
  deep inside
I hated him, he was
  a dear.

I think of him, his
  crazy leer
and how his pranks
  I did abide
with my own small
  replying sneer.

I watched him grow
  like in a mirror
loved one drifting from
  my side
I hated him, he was
  a dear.

Age stole the child,
  he had his peers
Close no more it's
  against his pride
My life is lonely with
  him not here.

The day soon came,
  he chose his career
I was sad to part but
  never cried
As life went on he
  showed no fear.

But why can life end
  up so queer?
With pain I saw my
  brother die
My life is lonely with
  him not here
I hated him, he was
  a dear.

Doug Shea
CASSIOPEIA

Dark lashes above
  your emerald eyes,
  lashes curled like the
  long surf
  and as dark as the
  moonless night,
  eclipse your eyes:
  but like dew on a leaf
  stars bead on you
  outlining your flesh in
  the reaches of space.

Open your eyes,
  wake from your terror,
  escape from the sky back
  into my arms!

Remember when you
  shocked them
  with your laughter, kicking
  aside the stars,
  when you grabbed a comet
  and slid down it,
  your stars flying off you
  like herring on the run
  and all your clothes
  ran up to the sky
  as you landed dancing
  beside me
  charging the streets
  with love?

Open your eyes,
  escape from your nightmare,
  fall into my earthy arms again!

N. L. Perkins
ALONE IN TIME

A toast to those who are
    alone in time,
To those who spend their
    lives among the blind,
To those who compromise
    because their not
    further down the line.

A toast to the poets, the
    dreamers, to Edgar Allen Poe,
To the people of vision,
    depth, to Michael Angelo,
To those who suffer because
    the mass
    doesn't know.

A toast to the discoverer,
    Nicholaus Corpernicus,
When placed upon the gallows,
    laughed, made fools of "us",
In time he knew the
    mass would
    cry "injustice".

A toast to perhaps the
    lonliest in time, Albert
    Einstein,
Who may have been displaced
    a 1000 years in time,
Leaving mysteries to a mass
    who may be
    centuries behind.

A toast to now and the man
    who's out of time,
Who lives, and walks,
    talking with the blind,
To those who'll be a ledgend
    and understood
    somewhere down the line.

M. J. Nauta
GAZE

His eyes
Blue as ice,
Pierced the barrier of my soul,
Exposing my despair as a
Deserted, barren wasteland
That lay within.
Time stood still.
Shivers crept into my
Innermost depths,
Where breath itself began.
Passion flushed my face
A sweet wine color,
While the strength of
    my resistance
Melted away.
I stood numb with
Bewilderment,
Frozen by his gaze.

Kelli Christenson
IMAGINARY PLAYMATE

I had a friend when I
    was young
A friend whom nobody saw.
Now that I've grown,
My friend has moved away,
But sometimes we still write.

Thomas J. Sellman
(BROTHERS WINE)

Like You my brother—
I too sleep alone
We were once young,
    you an I
Now we are frail with
    blackened souls
Wine you asked for?—
Yes another bottle!
Were they not the days
Now plaster falls
    from our walls
Yes my brother, You
    an I are alone
    Many years we fought

You your way-I
    went mine
Now we dine alone
More wine?—YES
    another bottle!

Gloria Strombom
WRONG NUMBER

I had to know.
That's why I called so late—
Too late, I guess.

She only had time to
    say " hello? "
before I hung up because
Then I knew

What I had to know,
But didn't want to know,
And certainly not from
    her lips.

Sharon A. O'Neil
ALL THE FISH IN THE SEA

My heart's breaking again,
Why always me?
Is there a law that says
That's how it's got to be?
Other girls always seem to
Get who they want,
Sometimes it's even love at
First sight.
With all the fish in the sea,
Why do none bite,
For me?

Sharon Renee Smart
SEALED WITH A TEAR

I sit here in the early morning
    thinking of you
Trying to find out where
    we went wrong,
Trying to find out where
    I failed.
We almost made it, you and I,
But somewhere along the line
    we failed.
So I'm writing to you in regret—
    for the times we lost,
    for the times we won't have.
I'm writing to you in thanks—
    for the times we had,
    for the times you tried.
I'm writing to you in sorrow—
    for what I did,
    for what I didn't do.
And I'm sealing this with a tear.

Rich McKenzie
DAWNING

I sat on my porch just
    writing songs
for so long.
I saw the sun come
    over the trees
and I smiled.
It's all so real to me.
The promises held in the
    newly dawned day
we all say
Hold special meanings
    and hopes for us.
We know it's true.
Our dreams we trust
    with each other.

Gary Michael Jaworski
SHADOW

Black man, your wrinkles
match those on grey shingles
    of your wooden shack.

Your crooked yellow dog
gnarls at the bees
nesting in corners of a
    lopsided porch.

Your children play in dirt

that choked blades of
    green grass
many years before.

Your wife's pink palms
slap white laundry
against enormous brown rocks.

Black man,
your bloodshot eyes are
    storybooks
that tell decades of tales.

Leota Mammenga
THE DAY WE MET

It wasn't a dance band playing-
    The tune that brought you
    to me;
'Twas the music of Mother
    Nature
    In a wonderful melody.

We hadn't been properly
    introduced
    As to who I was and who
    were you,
But we really didn't need it
    For we both already knew-

Knew there could be no other
    Who could take your place
    with me,
And since the day we met, dear,
    I've been as happy as can be.

There have been times of
    parting
    But there's always been the
    day
When we have once more met
    again
    And then I hear you say,-

"Let's always be together
    For you are my precious pet
And we'll never be sorry,
    darling,
    Nor forget the day we met."

Susanna Myers
FROST

Destiny of molecules
Arranged in patterns, nature's
    rule
Creations in the night,
Flora nurtured from the rain
Remembered now on window
    panes
In sculptures pearly white,
Mist transfigured in it's stay,
One of moisture's little ways
To make more splendorous
    winter days
And prove it's zeal and might.

Les Bland
FOREVER YOURS

When the Universe is dark
    and empty,
And the Stars have shined
    their last.
There will still be a
    light,
shining brilliantly in my
    heart.
Showing you the way
    home.

David Solomon Shepherd
IT'S O.K. THEN

When there's something to be
    excited about:
    It's O.K. Then.
Like . . .
    A team's victory,
    A home run,
    A tie breaker,
    A winning point.
When there's sorrow to share:
    It's O.K. Then.
Like . . .

A brother's death,
A close friend's accident,
A father's thought of failure,
A tragedy in a friend's life.
When there's nothing
    spectacular, why don't we say:
    It's O.K. Then?
Like . . .
    A friend greeting a friend
    with a hug,
    A close, intimate talk,
    A time of showing you care,
    A time of saying, "I Love
    you, Brother."

Gretchen G. Kipp
A PART OF YOU REMAINED WITH ME

Dear Dad, when sickness snuffed
    your breath
And pain, at last, was wrenched
    from thee,
A part of you went with your
    death,
But a part of you remained
    with me.

I shall dismiss those suffering
    days
When darkness hovered as your
    foe.
I shall envision heavenly rays
Enshrouding peace that you
    now know.

And sometimes, Dad, when day
    is done,
And twilight bids my prayers
    to rest,
I hear you laughing—having fun!
And know that you've been
    truly blest.

I always shall remember thee;
A part of you remained with me.

Karen (Kiki) Fawkes
I WONDER

I often sit and wonder why,
    I was put here on this earth.
I wonder what the reason is,
    and what it is all worth.
I also wondered when I was
    young why the years went
    slowly by.
And now as I grow older, it
    seems as though they fly.
I wonder what's in store for
    me and where my life will lead.
Will I get the things I want or
    just the things I need?

Neale Cotton
SEASONS

Resigning colors, autumn leaves
Sighing neath the sleepy trees
Would I were a bear to seek
My solace from the season bleak
Awaken spring desires thaw
A trumpeting to life—the call
Resounding sensual delight
The lovers laughing summer
    night

June Hammons Megginson
THE BUTTERFLY

Out of the blue, a butterfly,
Came drifting down, on zephyrs
    borne;
And stayed to visit for awhile,
In beauty resting on your arm.

It spoke to you of gentle things,
Of baby's smiles and robin's
    wings;
A loved one's touch and
    whispered word,
The soft, faint hum of a
    humming bird.

In a voice so low you could
  scarcely hear,
With a dip of wings and a
  diamond tear;
It said "Goodby" with a touch
  of pain,
"I won't be coming by again."
Then it soared into the over
  blue,
And vanished in the hazy sky;
To finish out in happy flight,
The short, free life of a
  butterfly.

Roger Walter Patterson
AUTUMN SONG

White Shell found me
In the lodge of pictures,
  'Take of my earth-colors,
  And paint me your life'
White Shell came
To the place of charred cedars,
  'Take my moments,
  Write me a robe of years'
White Shell woke me
From the sun-sleep,
  'Hide where your heart must
  hide,
  But consider me there'
White Shell followed
To the bridge of stones,
  'Walk far in your game-search,
  Yet mark your trails'
White Shell left me
By the tree of singing wires,
  'Bridle your death-horse,
  But give me goodbye.'

Rhonda J. Johnson
CRADLE PLEA

Come . . . sweet lady of tender
  age
  Come to know yourself
  through mirrors of reflection
    in the eyes of your many
    children.
  Pains of growth need to be
  cradled
    and rocked in your nuturance.
  You have given so much
    to those who are foreign
      to your own children's crib.
Come . . . beautiful Liberty
  Lady, with your
    lighted torch
  and shining harbour . . .
  Bring your soft, warm touch
  home
    to we, the children of
      masses.

Donna Shear
INCUBUS

I dream of a stark white mask,
With one sequined eye,
And my brothers love,
Why do I cry?
In quiet sleep I have lost my
  trust.
My nights are now ruled by
  Incubus.
Oh, why can't you go and leave
  me be,
So that my dreams may again
  be light and free.
How I wish I had never heard
  your name,
And I wonder, do I have you or
  I to blame.
Demon, what is it that you
  want from me?
Do you show me things that
  are yet to be?
I pray that God won't let me
  slip into your hands.
To become but a pawn, for

your demonic plans.
You must be as proud as you
  can be,
When I have distorted dreams
  such as these,
A stark white mask,
With one sequined eye,
And my brothers love,
Why do I cry?

Janet E. Rowe
MOONLIGHT'S LASS

Flitting from light into shadows
The bonny lass did flee,
To watch the night's reflection
Upon the ebony sea.
Breathing so softly,
Motionless, still,
She waited beneath her tree
Alone upon her hill . . .

Softly came warm breezes . . .
Her hair alone did wave,
Deep eyes glowed starlight,
So starlight still gave
Some irradiant glory
To the lass shadowed there,
Reliving a lost love's story
In the silent empty air . . . .

Marina Lieban
TEN

I am ten again
Lying on my back
I watch the clouds,
Castles in the air.
Knights in silver armour
Wave at maidens
As they ride by.

I am ten again.
Perched in the boughs
Of an old apple tree,
I am Napoleon in Russia,
I am Socrates in Greece.
I can be anything
I want to be.

I am ten again.
Lying in the bracken,
I watch the rabbits play
And high above the pine trees
Summer goes on for ever.

I am ten again.
I've dug the grave
And placed the shoebox in.
Do mice have souls?
Will God take care of them?
I am ten again
And death is an eternity away.

Lonnie J. Moreno
DAYS

Awake and be glad of God's
  given day,
Come shake off that transient
  gray,
Perelandrian days, Islandian
  nights,
Those are but dreams, Here is
  the living flight.

Our dream is for real,
This Ultimate goal,
Has given us strength,
Kept hidden in most.

Christ walks with us, He lends
  us His light,
We are His rays for the rest of
  the world.
No day in reckoning will keep
  this aside,
On the horizon the Kingdom's
  in sight,
And all of our days are sunny
  and bright.

Christopher E. Penera
ONE KISS FROM YOU

A kiss can change the tempo of
  the drums
From soft whispers to loud
  hums,
Open minds to expose thoughts
That burst out in verbal shots,
Fill dull nights with frenzied
  noise,
And my sad heart with
  mammoth joys,
Pierce the dark with a guiding
  light
That takes me to your smile so
  bright.
These are things a kiss can do
And the changes I've been
  through.
All of these one kiss can do.
One loving kiss from you.

Marcia Vosburgh
THE VERMONTER

Vermonter, slow moving but
  steady,
pushing, pushing, working hard
  to get ahead,
a family man, a sharing man, a
  caring man,
bold, set in his ways, back down
  to no one,
or anything old Vermonter, the
  last of your
kind never to be forgotten.

Deborah Ross
UNTITLED

And now that you have come to
  me, my love,
You in your gold to match my
  summer green,
Your periwinkle eyes piercing
  my heart,
As summer's sun begins his
  downward plunge
To gather strength for next
  year's summer sun,
Turn and turn about: I sense a
  new fire
That turn and turn about runs
  between us
And like the yearling sun will
  never die,
But will carry us surely through
  this life
To that eternal life beyond the
  grave
Whence we were born, where we
  will never die,
Where Life and Death meet,
  partners in Love's dance.

Pat Shaw Larson
**I SAW FULL PINK MOON
RISE**

I saw full pink moon rise
above my tears and cries
sailing free and clear

not man-made to sear,
mock or scorn or jeer
my man-made fate here . . .
I saw round gold moon rise
free, soaring: my goodbyes.

G. Phyllis McCullough
**FATHER, INTO THY
HANDS . . .**

Tender arms reached out to
  hold me
I found warmth in their
  embrace.
Loving arms that reassured me
I had found a resting place.
Gentle hands that spoke a
  language
That no words could quite
  convey.
Yet such strong hands giving
  comfort
Helping me to face each day.
Lifeless now you lay before me
God had called you through
  death's door.
Gentle hands that once gave
  comfort
Rest in peace—they feel no
  more.
Tender arms of God surround
  you
Giving you what you once gave.
Loving arms that long to hold
  you
Lay you gently in your grave.

Miss Lolie Ellen Ourso
WHERE AM I GOING?

Where am I going?
What shall I see
When I get there?
How shall I know I
  am there?
To stop and see the sun
go down, and smell the
salt air of the ever ending
sea.
To stop time with a bat of
an eye so things happen
your way.
The dreams I dream have
turned to realities.
And my realities to dreams,
with the clock of time
running out even faster
than life itself.
And life will never stop
for time.

Robert V. Reed
NOSTALGIA

Nostalgia comes with middle
  age;
  It's hard to keep away.
It seems to creep 'way up inside,
  Of things of yesterday.
It guides the mind to days gone
  by,
  We live within the past.
If we could only change the
  time,
  I'd gladly make it last.
Today is right for some, I know;
  It's progress they look for.
But I will stay with yesterday;
  I couldn't ask for more.

Vanessa Thompson
THE ARTIST

He sits in the backroom
of a small tourist shop.
People wander all about him,
yet, he works on as if they
are not there.

Talking slowly, he explains his
  craft.
Blending colors, painting
  tapestries,
Expressing an erotic need or
  desire,
Expressing sadness or pain,

Expressing love or fantasy,
He is the Artist.
Slowly the people leave the
 room,
He continues painting.
Few linger to see the finished
 product,
The production of a man's soul.
Expressing the Artist.

Mary Jo Eury
BIRD WATCHING

You stopped to ponder me
 there,
my feet clutching to the earth.
so fragile, sallow and pitifully
 flightless.

You wondered where my nest
 was,
had I young to feed?
What must my voice be like,
did I have a song to sing,
a song to sing?

Was I lost? A stranger to these
 woods?
We all resemble each other so.
We may have passed every day,
every day.

At some future vacant time
you will study this species.
But I was of the ordinary
 variety,
Hardly notable,
hardly Notable.

Corena Gordon Spells
LIFE

There's so much that I don't
 understand
And that I have tried to perceive
For life is truly a mystery
And few miracles I have seen

And the mysteries of this world
Always intrigue my mind
And make room for wondering
When I'm alone and unoccupied

But this I have learned to accept
And to take within my stride
For the beauty in mystery is
 not knowing
The whens the wheres or the
 whys

Roger Glen Bummer
THE PRIMEVAL POOL

In it
Life floweth
Multiplying fervently,
Then in great time It dried up
Parched by the sun
And Life sloweth
Aimlessly, wandering
In limbo,
As if waiting
For some great unheard of
 Shepherd
To claim It's spirit.
Then . . . God and Man.

Deborah M. Moses
LOVER'S PRAYER

As I lay my head upon my
 pillow, and pray to God on
 high
I wish I'd never heard his
 words—My darling this is
 goodbye.
I call his name out low at night
 and wish things were the same
Because Dear God, as you know,
 I cannot stand this pain.
I need his love and warm
 tenderness for I am insecure
Oh darling won't you please
 come back, and love me

instead of her?
The days are slowly drifting by
 and fading into the past
But won't you please remember
 this—my love for you will last.
So now as I go to sleep—I'll
 dream of you tonight
I'll be waiting for you my love,
 under the soft dimmed light.

Harold Watson
MY FATHER'S GARDEN

Our Father, who dwells above,
 has a "garden"
Where every soul, chosen by
 His love, is a flower—
Whose awesome beauty and
 golden brilliance, lights the
 "heavens"
And is attended by an angel,
 in every hour.
We, here on earth as "God's
 Children," are mortal flowers.
Nourished by His love, we, too,
 will flourish within His will.
Our faith will open every petal
 if we will listen to His word
And our cup will runneth over
 that He will fill.
When we suffer disappointments
 that we do not understand
And our fate here in this world
 is woe and strife,
Just remember all the pain that
 "Jesus" suffered upon the
 cross
And our salvation that He paid
 for with His life.
A flower will not bloom without
 sunshine
Nor will it flourish to brilliant
 beauty without rain.
To walk the path and be a part
 of "God's" garden up above,
You must "believe" and know
 your faith is not in vain.

Karen S. Bennett
ALONE

A
Love which
Ought to be
Never-
Ending, but isn't.

Jo King
MY WILL-O'-THE-WISP

You will be still,
 My Will-o'-the Wisp!
You will stop calling me!
 You will find a place
For yourself, O Scamp,
 Where my dreams can never
 be.
You will go away and leave me,
 O vagrant sprite of my soul.
Elusive Vagabond, be gone!
 Be gone, and leave me whole!

Marge Saphir-Fish
VERMONT VIGNETTE 1

Boy with sore hand
nestles against his father
sheltered
from a field of running children,
 mingling adults.
Nature is written
in all the lines
of his father's body.

Kenneth Hartwell Hart
OUR LITTLE WHO

All you mothers and fathers
 listen to my tale,
At your little darlings please do
 not yell.
Just hold them and hug them oh

so tight,
Now I will tell you of our sad
 plight.
Who made the frog green and
 yucky?
Who made the feathers on the
 baby ducky?
Who made the sky so very blue,
 who mommy who?
Who made the ice cream you
 buy at the zoo, who daddy
 who?
One day the angels came to our
 little who's room.
When they left there was nothing
 but gloom,
Now all we have are memories
 over the years,
Also eyes that easily fill with
 tears.
Now we long to go to heaven
 beyond the blue,
Where we will join our little who.
If you trust in Jesus with all
 your might,
He will one day make all things
 right.

Louise Rosson Burr
DAILY DRIVE

Every day
I take a drive
To the distant land
Of long ago.
It really isn't far,
Just around a curve
And over a hill,
And I look down
Into the long, golden valley
Of Yesterday.
The people there all know me,
They smile when they see me,
They hold my hand
And they tell me
How much they want me to
 stay,
But
After awhile,
I always leave,
Because, you see,
I can always return
Tomorrow,
To
Yesterday.

Lois Ostern Gray
THE JOURNEY

I toss and turn in constant pain;
A rising fever racks my brain.
I hear a voice, "This is for you,
A sleek, black car, shining and
 new.
You're starting on a trip today."
I try, but little I can say.
A brief glance, and a muttered
 curse,
That sleek car is a long, black
 hearse.

Larry Nielsen
HUDDLING PLACES

The bombs kept falling through
 the night
bringing death
and terror
and fires to light up
the faces of those left with pain
and fear.
The bombs kept falling through
 the night
never knowing
who sent them
on their way
to kill
and destroy,
never caring whether
mother or child

old or soldier,
they just do.
They fall in passivity
resulting in horrors of humanity.
Or is it,
They fall in horrors of
 humanity
resulting in passivity.
The bombs kept falling through
 the night
and together
people kept huddling.
Not so much for safety
but rather
for comfort
of knowing others
in pain too.
The bombs kept falling.
Falling.

Falling

Betty Jo Day
THEN AND NOW

Then—
 I was so lost.
 I was in a maze,
 Not knowing the cost,
 To part the haze.
But, then there is now.
Now—
 I am disillusioned.
 I am so saddened,
 By the cruel truth.
 What a ruthless brute.
But, now there is reality.

H. Richmond Stuart
SPACE TO GROW

ALL THINGS NEED SPACE
 TO GROW:
The sweetest flowers that blow;
The woodland creatures where
 they go;
The fishes in the river's flow.
ALL THINGS NEED SPACE
 TO GROW.

EACH MAN NEEDS HIS OWN
 SPACE:
To own his private place;
To flee the world's grimace;
To grow his special grace.
EACH MAN NEEDS HIS OWN
 SPACE.

 I cannot be your friend
 Without a space to tend
 That's not to share or lend.
I do not love you less, but more,
If now and then I shut the door,
To walk upon my secret shore.

Robert James Kruzewski
STRANGER, LOOK AT ME!

Just because my lips are
 smiling,
Doesn't mean all is fine—
Stop a moment, get to know me,
And discover what's in this
 heart of mine.
Pause a bit, a little bit
From your hectic pace,
You may see my smile isn't

thorough,
It only goes as far as my face.
Just because my lips are singing,
Doesn't mean my heart plays
a song—
Look at me,
If you want to,
And unveil a melody that's been
silent much too long.
Put out your hand, lend an ear,
And understanding too;
For alone, I cannot hear life's
music,
Has it occurred in your thoughts,
That I might need you?

John W. Hungerford
A STRANGER SMILED AT ME

A stranger smiled at me the
other day,
And no longer was a stranger,
you see.
He smiled at me, I'm happy to
say,
Because I smiled, and he
thought he knew me.

I thought and thought as I
walked along,
What a pleasant world this
would be,
If everyone smiled, then we'd
all belong,
To a much better world, we'd
all agree.

So turn on that smile and keep
it there,
Don't hold it for a privileged
few.
Let everyone know you care,
Nothing else, but more friends
will do!

Katherine Inman
SENSEI

A bird, she is small.
Ruffled feathers flatten back
With a flick of head,

Spark in her eye jumps
Ahead as she struts the mat,
Scanning her domain.

She is light of word,
Her easy touch directing
Activity. She

Walks softly, carries
Her hands like molten lead
bricks
Ready to be thrown.

Kenneth J. Silva
OH WIND

Oh wind
That hallows in
The heart of man,
Tell me why you tarry.
You mock the land
And sever the sea,
Aren't you ever merry?

Oh wind
That pushes forth
The waves so high,
And strokes the gentle field;
You thrash the clouds
Up in the sky,
Will you ever yield?

Oh wind
Who sends you off
In endless flight?
What purpose do you seek?
Reason left
Without a trace
To find that missing link.

Linda Lee Gau
REFLECTIONS

As I stroll along a quiet beach
And gaze on glistening sands,

I reflect upon the years gone by
To where it all began.
I recall the autumn day we met
And how we spent our time.
I found it hard to comprehend
That happiness was mine.

And now as each day passes
Our love grows ever strong,
And with his arms around me
I'm home, where I belong.

Rick Mattix
SO MANY SORROWS

So many sorrows have gone by
So many tears you've had to
cry
So many times you've felt you'd
die
And found you couldn't so
you'd cry
So many times you've wondered
'Bout all those times you've
blundered
In love then love again
In love then love again

Tracee A. Wager
ALL THAT I ASK

Do you love me?
That is the question I ask.
And if you do,
Will your love last?
Tell me now,
There's no time to spare.
I have to know,
If you really still care.
Then take me in your arms,
And hold me tight.
Make love to me darling
Throughout the night.
Shower me with hugs,
And warm loving kisses.
These my sweetheart,
Are my only wishes.

Darline Murphy
MORNINGS' BRIDE

upon waking
i dressed as a bride
in need of union with the
morning
running to bathe in the sky
i found the clover dressed in
silver
and each, the morning's bride
together we lay in earth's arms
and we were married
and freedom was our love
dance
in this marriage bed i feel whole
again
and i want to open my arms for
someone seeking
freedom to share
and open my mind
for love's dance
i think that you too have
married the morning
you are the morning
clouds' gentleness and warm
like the sun

the colors of dawn are songs
that play in your mind
and the sea flows free thru your
being
you accept the world for
brides
even though they come dressed
in pain
and you give what was lost
as only the morning could

D. Marie Lewis
SPIRITLESS QUEST

Oh spiritless soul
How dare you regress
And make of this life
A tedious mess
Not looking forward
You drift with the stream
Finding no answers
But too scared to dream

You're seeking a sphere
You can't reach the end
Circling always
You seem to pretend
Life is so easy
Just follow along
Don't hazard to change
In case you go wrong

Unlock your courage
And boldly begin
Take up the gamble
I know you can win
Set free your feelings
It just takes a start
Life is worth living
So open your heart

Janice L. King
HERBAL TEA

The crazy old lady who lived
by the sea
She rocked on her porch and
sipped herbal tea.
She went for long walks and
had many talks
With herself, the shells and the
sea.
The crazy old lady who lived
by the sea
Was perhaps not as old as she
seemed then to be.
Her time was her own, her cats
were apart.
The gulls only knew what lay
in her heart.
The crazy old lady who lived
by the sea
Had she any lovers, now all
memories?
Was there a lost kissed that
swirled as the mist
Which hid the old lady that
lived by the sea.

Donna Yackley
WINTER WONDERLAND

A dream come true, setting
against the brightest sun.
Coming toward me a moment
of gladness. Beset the time
when the light brings again a
moment come true.
Believe the sun is what it seems;
radiant in one awe.
Along the road, through time,
I will see again the light.
Do not erase what you mean to
say.
Alone not, unseen not, grow
and grow and grow.
Keep on and stay on for awhile.
Leave, what you've done
open to me. Forget all the wiles
of time and leave not

trace for question?
Honestly; trace a single land.
Afterwards, take me along.
A white picture, a white glow.
For awhile remember what you
did; then never wonder again.
I see you!

Kim Baumgart
HELLO, SON

Torn from my
body through tears and
blood, your
cry smoothes the
damp hair from my
face and I see your
fingers and toes,
perfectly formed.
Cleansed with fresh water and
given back to my
breast for more of the
nourishment that
helped you during the
long months of rest,
I feel the small
human body we
produced.
Watching you
kiss your son for the
first time, I can see how
proud you are of
him.

P. A. Cronin
**SANDWICHES AND
SCHOOLYARDS APART**

Someone called me by your
name today,
mistaking me for you.
Mistaking, as the mirror
misnames her blurred
reflection,
as the shadow, her misty
morning counterpart.

The shadow conspires with her
sister
as two young girls share secrets
and sandwiches from a brown
paper bag;
two young women dreaming
of Friday Nights
dress up in pretenses and
spike heels
Only to be unmasked, undressed
by some schoolboy or another.

Mistaking as the shadow
misconceives her gray double
and stretches from her twin in
late afternoon,
slipping into twilight
Leaving us sandwiches and
schoolyards apart,
Leaving us with secrets now
breathed from pen to page,
Leaving us to dream and dress
up alone,
Leaving us . . .

Jenifer Kunz
THE CHALLENGE

Rubbing the discus with rough
wet hands,
sizing the circle with deep set
eye,
breathing deeply, stepping into
the ring
molding the disk with his
fingertips.

Thinking in rhythm
his clothing sticks,
his deep grooved legs
begin the test.

His muscles bulge,
and stretch like a spring.
Spinning, spinning forward
giving a last minute scream.

A perfect release,
floating onward,
upward,
out of man's reach.

Bev Hammond
WHAT LOVE IS

I wonder just what love is
I've found it often grows
I know it's sometimes painful
It's something that you show
Love is always gentle
Whenever you are near
It's somewhat sentimental
And somehow eases tears
Love is understanding
And means you'll always care
Love is joy expanding
It's you just being there
Love is walking near you
On strolls along the beach
Love will always dare you
If you're within its reach
Love is touching someone
Who's thoughtful; also true
I think I understand now
I guess that love is you

Ken Eckman
EVERY BOY'S SATURDAY DREAM

Out on a Saturday morn, no
  lawns to trim
empty pockets, now filled to
  the brim
with treasures that were found
  on the way
He feels the freedom in his
  bones today.

Secret rendezvous with nature
  in the hills
A boy's dream of Monday
  remains quite still
Saturday will last forever and
  he'll run
thru the days, crossing streams
  and having his fun.

Time is non-existent in the
  sunshine
A boy of twelve can always
  change his mind
and become an explorer of
  distant worlds,
until the day he discovers a
  world of girls.

Royalyn Hayes
MISSING HIM

Sometimes if I close my weary
  eyes
And think really hard in a
  moment of quiet desperation,
I can see it. I can see his face.
The gaunt, angular cheek bones,
  the forever-bent glasses
Slowly slipping off his nose, the
  "peach-fuzz" above his lip
Vainly pretending to be a
  moustache,
The perfect formality of each
  strand of coal black hair,
The faultless shaped mouth,
  neither smiling nor frowning.
There's times when I want to
  remember that face
And times I want to forget it.
There's times I wish his face
  were here
And times I wish he would
  leave.
People ask me if I've forgotten
  about him and
I tell them what they want to
  hear,
"Do you ever miss him, honey?"
  "No."

But I do. I still love him and
  miss him.
He has a world of his own now.
A world in which I have no part,
  though
Other people say I'll get over
  him, why is it taking so long?
Oh, I suppose I'll forget his
  face one day. Until then
People ask me if I've forgotten
  about him and
I tell them what they want to
  hear,
"Do you ever miss him,
  Cupcakes?" "No,
I've forgotten all about him."

Mary P. Hunter Wells
A TRIBUTE

Many years I have spent with
  all of you
  and found your friendships to
  be tried and true.
It's difficult now to pack and
  depart
  from those I cherish with all
  my heart.
Wilton Woods has been my home
  school base
  for ten short years and it's
  hard to face
That as a building it will remain
  but it won't house my friends
It will be a different domain.
Now let's remember that friends
  we will always be
  and we can get together, you
  and me.
A humble thank you I give to
  each of you here
  who so generously made this
  day special and dear.
I won't miss the ride, that very
  long trip
  nor the snow and the ice, with
  a possible slip.
But I will miss my friends so
  kind and so true
  so please remember me as I
  remember you.
A good-bye wave is all I can do
  for the tears are pushing and
  coming through.

Teresa Lawrence
BABY'S LOVE

You light up my life,
  and fill me with joy
I can't get enough love
  from my sweet baby boy . . .

For almost a year now,
  I've held you so near
It's easy to see
  Why I can't shed a tear.

With you in my life
  It's like Christmas each day,
You've brought so much
  sunshine
  and love my way.

So when things go bad,
  And they will indeed
I reach for you . . .
  and that's all I need.

Stephanie L. Strunk
WCSC TEAM

The pitcher warms up with fast
  strikes,
Then we see the ritual of
  cleaning his spikes.
Then he warms up to throw the
  ball,
Just for the ump to make a bad
  call.
Now we see the catcher's lame—

How'd it happen? We just
  started the game.
The first baseman's making eyes
  at his girl,
While the guy at second is
  combing his curls.
The shortstop's kicking stones
  and making dust,
And the guy at third is making
  a fuss.
The centerfielder's yelling to
  the guy at right;
While left is watching a bird in
  flight.
The coach is giving his worthy
  praise,
Hoping to hell he still gets his
  raise.

Lewis H. Dudley, Sr.
NOTHING FROM NOTHING

Nothing from nothing leaves
  nothing—
You've often heard it said;
There was never a truer saying,
Whether it's spoken, or it's read.

If you decide to *do* nothing,
Then *nothing* is your game—
For when you deal in zeros,
Then *nothing* is your aim.

Let's do a little subtraction,
The way we used to do—
Take away nothing from
  nothing,
Then *nothing* is left for you.

So don't go piling up *nothing*,
If you're looking for to *gain*—
For when you *take away*
  nothing,
I'm sure *nothing* will remain.

Ora Smith Richards
A ROBIN SINGS

Lively robin there in the
  blossoming tree,
Blithely singing your carols of
  spring;
I see your bright eyes are
  watching me—
Can it be to my heart you sing?

Do I fancy my ear a soft note
  detects
Of thankfulness in your gay
  song?
With those sweet tuneful lays
  do you pay your respects?
I strewed crumbs for you all
  winter long.

Johnny Mack Brown
LOVE THOUGHTS OF YOU

The gentleness of your touch,
The tenderness of your kiss,
Like a drop of dew in the
  morning mist,
I pray for just a touch of the
  sweet love you possess.

In the darkness of night you're
  in my dreams,
And the light of day brings even
  more love,

Than the love I had for you
  yesterday.
And when I lay my head down
  for the last time,
With my last breath I shall
  whisper your sweet name.

Rene O. Hernandez
SEASHORE

I saw you running silently in
  the sunlight,
And each slender move graced
  the image
Of your soft footprints on the
  washing sands.

The glistening waves in
  shimmering colors
Sparkle gayly as the salt spray
  morning
Plays joyfully amidst your wind
  blown hair.

You ran in silence, gliding
  effortlessly
In and out the diving, running
  gulls, while
Floating beautifully, the sun,
  your running framed.

I saw you running pass the
  dunes and perhaps
It was the happiness of knowing
  it was you,
That I heard the seagulls sweetly
  sing your name.

Beatrice Ann Duda
TRYING TO REMEMBER

Seems to me I've known you
Somewhere in my past
Memories like a movie
Flickering thru glass
Something seems to bother this
  sufficient brain
I must have known you
  somewhere
It can't be a game
When were we together
Was it in years past
Trying to remember
When we met here last
My only recollection
Seems to be too vague
Was it an impression
When I heard your name
Will I ever find you
Needing me someday
Or is this a precious moment
Coming just my way

Dale A. Hoover
ROSES AND MEMORIES

The smell of roses carries me
  back
  down the lanes of summer
  days
  to a well remembered
  countryside
  and to gentle country ways.
To when our love was bursting
  into bloom
  and each rosebud divine
  held promise within its
  velvet petals
  of our life's dreamed designs.
Dew covered petals hold
  tenderly
  the rose in miraculous bloom
  and I held you in my arms,
  then breathed your enchanted
  perfume.
I held a rose to my weary brow
  while remembering all the
  time
  that you are near
  and still we are touched
  sublime.

The sky smiles, and, on joyous
wing
   a mockingbird in ardent voice
to us begins to sing
all through the day until
   night.
The sweet smell of roses fills
the air
   entwining us with our dreams
and my knowing you are
   there
   makes love burst at its seams.

kimberlee ann burdick
WITH LOVE

Kafka said
a book
should be an
axe
that breaks up
the frozen sea within
us.
So.
I plan to
book-up my
poems
and chop away
at your
ice.

Gypsy Travis
13 JULY 1973

My apologies
If you're offended.
My broken heart has mended.
I didn't mean to be unkind.
Love is a state of mind.

I enjoyed
Your company, time,
Music, thoughts and wine.
The show is over.
The curtain is falling.
I can hear distance calling.

Kathleen M. Horton
MOTHER

Tho' I caused you many sorrows
The pain of which I may never
   know
I loved you with a deeper love
Than I could ever, ever show.

You always did the best for me
And cured my every pain
And rest assured that all you
   did
Was certainly not in vain.

But really, Mother, I could
   never
Begin at trying to repay
The many, many lovely things
You did for me each day.

As I look back on forgotten
   years
I'll always picture you there
And thank the God Almighty
For placing me in your care.

When years go by and I grow
   old
And someone speaks of
   "Mother"
I'll think of you in tenderness
For me, there'll never be
   another.

Becky S. Pittman
LOST TEARS

Once I caught a strand
   of your stare.
I held it with my own eyes,
   only a second.
I lowered my head to escape
   from your gaze,
So you could not see
   The glisten of a tear
     That had fallen to my cheek.

That one degree of time
   That small distance of space—
   between us.
In a stare I had seen
   so many times before.
Passively sat memories
   and feelings,
ones I had tried to forget,
many painful paths ago.
   Strangers we weren't—
     But friends? I'm not sure.
And each time I feel the
   presence of your stare.
I turn, to fall into the tunnel
   of confusion
   that dwells deep in the color
   of your eyes.
In this confusion I feel a certain
   loss.
   A certain emotion, that always
   brings
   a tear to my eye.
It's one I can't explain.
   I don't care to try.
     But one, I can never, never
     hide.

Angela Babin
THE SHORE

I walk along the shore and in the
   distance I see him,
The man I want to be with very
   much.
My heart starts to pound ever
   so fast knowing in a moment
   we will touch.
We embrace, his lips pressed
   against mine bring on a burning
   desire
Oh how I longed for this night!
We lay beneath the stars, as the
   waves play tag with our feet,
And the moon a bright crimson,
   as if blushing by the sight of us
Hides behind a cloud,
And he whispers love me till
   morning light.

Carolyn M. Hathaway
MY BROTHER, BOB

There we were, just two kids,
   a boy and a girl, a *brother*
   and *sister,*
We laughed and played, we
   argued, we cried, we prayed.
Our Mom and Dad—good
   leaders were they,
In the way to live and the things
   to say.

As we moved from place to
   place,
New people we learned to face.
West Virginia, New York, New
   Jersey too,
And every time we moved we
   grew—both in age and
   spiritually.

For eleven years there were just
   us two, this brother and sister,
But if the people only knew
   how close they were—
How they loved one another,
   through thick and thin,
There was time for each other—
   it was always 'Come on in.'

Later there were two more—A
   total of four,
Two boys and two girls—two
   brothers and sisters.
And still we were close—so very,
   very close,
More than anyone in this world
   can know.

And even as we all grew up, our
   love remained the same,
In times of health, times of

sadness, times of pain.
Our love was something not
   easily explained,
For though we loved, we often
   refrained
From telling each other, because
   of pride,
But it was comforting with him
   by my side.

His children are all grown, and
   most not at home,
His wife must carry on alone.
For he is at Peace now with my
   Lord above,
And he sits at His right hand,
   shadowed by His love.
He's not there to lean on now,
   my Brother,
But Christ is always there, and
   there is no Other.

Michael Robert Meyer
THE KING IS DEAD

Hail! Hail! The King is dead!
All hail for whom he bled.
A gun that fired and the heart
   that stopped.
The bullet flew. The King was
   shot.

Shed thy tears. Do your part.
Finish the job he did start.
No sense in that rash cause.
No regard for rights and laws.

Down, down the King has come.
And so screams a Negro son.
It's not my joy, and needlessly,
it's a sad, sad day in Tennessee.

Hail, hail, the King is dead.
There lies the King, a bullet in
   his head.

No more marches to rouse and
   preach,
of Civil Rights and violent peace.

Hail! Hail! The King is dead!
Long live the King. The King
   is dead.

Marguerite Austin
PERCEPTION

The child saw a flower, full,
   wondrous
Jeweled yet with crystal dew.
She picked it from the vine and
Looking up, gave it to a woman,
A woman neighboring across a
   fence.
The child was only three.

The woman took the flower
   from the child,
Glanced unseeing at its beauty.
Then plucking the petals
And talking still,
Dropped them softly, one by
   one.
The woman was eighty-three.

The flower the child saw clearly
With the fullness of being,
The woman darkly,
Her zeal for beauty spent.

Some all their lives of beauty
   savor,
Others, midway, waught it
   quickly
And thirst.

Gary M. Morrow
SPITFIRE!

   I was flying my Spitfire at ten
     thousand feet,
but suddenly it sounded as
   though it were being hit by
   sleet.
Because from out of the sun,

came the enemy with blazing
   guns.
The aircraft zipped past and
   started turning,
lucky for me my Spitfire wasn't
   burning.
As he was turning I started to
   follow,
because this Messerschmitt I
   was determined to swallow!
The Messerschmitt came into
   view in my sight,
and this aircraft I would soon
   put out of flight.
He put his craft into a frenzied
   turn in the blue,
but I stayed on his tail like glue.
Getting into position for a
   deflection shot,
I opened fire with all guns and
   did hit a lot.
The enemy aircraft started
   smoking and spun,
the final death throws of the
   hun.

Phylis Dix
REASONS OF A MAN

You are like a diamond
   A many faceted man.
A mixture of all things,
   Bad and Good.
A man with all the egotism
   Of a Roman Warrior
And the gentleness of A
   Spring Rain.
You are a thoughtless,
   insensitive, caring,
   loving person.
The perfect example of
   nature's imbalance
I love to watch your face—
   especially the eyes which
   are the inner soul of a man
Your children reflect the
   kind of man you are.
They are mirrors of their
   father.
You are a combination of
   Robert Redford, a cuddly
   kitten and Attila the Hun.
My world is flowers and rain,
   sunshine and pain
   because you are in it.
Love is like a diamond
   A many faceted feeling.

Emilie Davezac
THERE CAN'T BE A TITLE

To have thought a thought
Or felt an emotion
Or felt warmth from an image
   There are no words—

To have seen a beauty
That surpasses any dream
Never touched by the
   imagination
   There are no phrases—

To have a realization of
   something
Unconsciously encumbering
   experience
As the reference
   There are no . . .

Stanley W. Birge
AUTUMN EVENING

I've looked at those trees
so many times
As day was drawing the shades
of evening to the ground
I've watched the very last glow
As they were silhouetted all
   around
Evenings breeze had dwindled
   completely
Night time took on a stillness

broken only by a night bird
And the pines dark outline
  wavered
ever so discretely

But as early night began to
  settle
A fresh breeze greeted the
  harvest moon
Chilling it came, fresher than
  the morning dew
Telling us that Autumn would
  be here soon

Stronger it came through the
  silhouetted pines
Wildly they danced, as though
  breaking bonds
Which had held them in lasting
  lines

Nights like these have made men
  wander
Driven by feelings too old to
  explain
Only to go as the wind o'er the
  mountain
Man must go: He cannot remain

Diane Harris
DEATH

A star bursts apart
Into a hundred fragments
And leaves a spot of darkness
In the sky
That will never shine again.

A person dies
And leaves a spot of emptiness
In someone's heart
That will never love again.

L. J. Pennington
PERENNIAL GARDEN

As I knelt upon my father's
  grave,
I looked up toward the sun
And out across the chequered
  lawn
Enshrined with red and yellow
  flowers,
Wide ribbons flapping on the
  breeze.
Here I laid two white roses down
And ran my fingers across the
  upraised letters
Of his name.
There is a garden of another
  name
Where the earth is soft and
  damp
And marked rows yield
Full-bloomed flowers in every
  season.

AM Wiese
THE CHOSEN PEOPLE

The common many,
the fortunate few,
and oh the damn many liars!

Accept or Regret;
Discriminate;
Lose the latter,
accept the win.

Shawn Duquette
PRISONS OF THE MIND

In this penitentiary the walls
  are high and hard to climb
It is the cold gray cinderblock
  that haunts me from another
  time;
The walls, those heartless
  prisons, are so much colder
  than before
I try to think of happier things,
  but I can think no more.

This place will not let me be
  free, though I am no prisoner
  here

The walls are closing in—Damn
  the walls! Save my sanity!
  Calm my fear!
But still the nameless faces
  laugh; How can they after so
  much pain?
Laughing, yet surely they know
  that when they die the walls
  remain.

I will never climb the walls I
  built to keep all others away
No one comes in; I can't go
  out—there is no life night or
  day.

I've searched for my enemy in
  others always knowing what
  I'd find
I am my hidden enemy—the
  only prisoner in the prisons of
  my mind.

Deanna J. Cannell
MOMENT IN TIME

I lay my fingers upon your lips
  I ask you not to speak
You've touched me softly with
  your love
  And left my body weak

You've loved me gently and I
  have soared
  Akin to a soft, white Dove
Satisfied beyond compare
  Elated in the warmth of your
  love

Quietly now you steal away
  As darkness settles over me
I'll treasure, forever, this
  moment in time
  Fantasy became reality . . .

Jo Conley
NO LONGER MY BABY

Oh, pretty young lady,
Yesterday, you were my small
  baby.
Soon you'll face life all alone.
That will be the judge of this
  home.
I used to be confident that our
  lifestyle was right.
Now I lay awake many a night.
Life can bring joy, life can bring
  pain.
I'd like to give you sunshine
  and forsake the rain.
The choices no longer belong
  to me.
How hard it is to set you free.

Dwain Thomas Flowers
DESTINY

As I walked along that point of
  the Earth,
where the land is constantly
  battling to hold the waters
  back.
I felt the granular beads of
  centuries of erosion beneath
  me.
I reached down and picked one
  up.

One minute particle of millions.
So like me in comparison with
  the human race.
Yet that grain of sand had no
  control of getting where it was.
And I myself, can control my
  destiny.

Lee King
DREAMER

Am I just a dreamer
Living in a fairy tale land?
Trying to find life's beauty
When problems are at hand.

Some say that I am out of touch
And my thoughts are just not
  real.
But I know that these are good
  visions
By the way they make me feel.

Close your eyes and hold my
  hand
And I will take you miles away.
If you will dare to search my
  soul,
I'll promise a brighter day.

R. M. Schimenz
**COMPULSIONS TO REMAIN
AWAKE**

if I left now I could go to
bed early . . . god knows I need
the rest . . . but my glass is not
empty yet, my cigarettes are
not smoked and my pen needs
many dippings in ink before
  I will be
    through *this* night—

I have been disappointed
before and on those nights too
I could not sleep til glass
and pen were quite emptied—
I will sleep when sleep comes
  and
hopefully not dream—but if
  dream I must
I only hope the images
  I see in
    my darkness
  are not too
true reflections of my life—

Robert J. Cywinski
**THE STATUE IN MARIPOSA
MALL**

In Fresno on business, I left
  the Board Meeting,
Adjourning at noon for mid-day
  repast;
Departed the back of our
  Hilton Headquarters,
For a stroll through the mall,
  to see Fresno at last.

Startled, I suddenly stopped.
A statue assaulted my eye.
A woman, naked and wringing
  a long cloth;
Normally, I would have walked
  by.

But that day a child was
  climbing the statue,
Grabbing the nape of the long
  neck, alone;
Completely indifferent to
  people pressing,
Straining to kiss mouth of green,
  cold, hard stone.

I've gone by the statue each day
  at the same time,
But never the girl do I see.
Tomorrow I fly home to wife
  and to children.
My memory of Fresno will be
Radiant bloom on the face of

the child,
Her total oblivion to all:
Little girl clinging to the neck
  of her mother—
The Statue in Mariposa Mall.

Marion L. Schoonbeck
**HOMESICK FOR THE
PRAIRIE**

Oh, how I miss the free rolling
  plains;
The tall prairie grass, the cattle,
  the range.
A warm starry sky, or a morning
  blue,
Ending in sunset's promising
  hue.
A song of a coyote calling his
  mate,
Or a whistling cowboy coming
  in late.
The steady hum of contented
  bees,
And the wind softly whispering
  high in the trees.
The endless milling of cattle
  bands;
The wild hoof-beats in the
  Texas sands.

Marti Clark
ABORTION

It was trying for me then
To terminate that part of you
  within me.
    It died
    in the cold of winter.
God, I needed you then,
And you came to meet me.
    But still I cry each time
    October rolls around
    to think what could have
    been mine.

Joseph M. Neuville
THE PERFECT POET

I've often wondered how it felt
To write a perfect rhyme;
A perfect poem, with perfect
  words,
As swift and true as time.

'The Perfect Poem' would be its
  name;
A title quaint and yet contrite;
For though it stands as my life's
  dream,
Perfection's tough to write.

Yet here I sit on a chair of
  thought
Which some unheard of force
  has wrought,
Wond'ring why I still persist,
On this quest for a poem . . .
    . . . that doesn't exist.

Mary Shepardson Loos
THE OTHER PART OF ME

Understand me please.
There are two people inside the
  one of me.
The one you know as wife and
  mother.
A free learning woman is the
  other.
My world is surely waiting out
  there.
I've just got to find out where.
And so I must search, wait, and
  see.
Exactly what the other part is,
  of me.

Steve Nuiver
SHE IS ME

She speaks,
I listen and understand,

A captive of her mind.
Together in a swirl of merging
   thoughts,
We cling to the meanings.
Free thoughts, hopeful thoughts,
That mingle, compare and
   laugh.
Our feelings unite to form a
   bond,
Our souls reach out and touch,
A wholeness prevails.
I am she, she is me.
For the moment our lives
   fulfilled.
I smile at her and know,
She is unique.

Barbette Johnston
ECHO

I walked up the stairway
   hearing footsteps
   but I was alone
   it was my echo.
As I ascended further
   I realized
   there will never be
   footsteps
   in harmony with mine.
I will go through life
   with an echo
   as my companion.

Reba L. Driggers
FOR THE FIRST TIME . . .

For the first time in such a long
   time
I've got a song in my heart
I want to tell the whole world
But I don't know where to start.
For the first time in such a long
   time
I know what it's like to smile
It feels so good to be happy
I've been down for such a long
   while.
It's this crazy funny feeling
That comes from way down
   inside
That's so hard to hold to myself
And impossible to try to hide.
It's the strangest weirdest thing
It's all so different and new
It's a love I've never felt
This love belongs to you.
For the first time in all these
   years
I've found that one special guy
It gives me a sense of peace
And puts a happy tear in my
   eye.
For the first time in all this time
Someone loves me too
And babe, I have to say "thank
   you"
I'm not alone now—I've got you.

Zadie L. Andre
THE LOSER

My Love, you are my undying
   dream,
A glowing light, a beckoning
   beam.
I reach for you, but you fade
   away—
A mist overwhelming takes you
   to play.
Then atop a hill I see you and
   stare,
My arms outstretched but
   utterly bare.
Following a guiding light,
I climb, though it becomes
   night.
Weighted with accumulated
   want,
Shaken by your eyes that haunt,
I stumble, fall o'er and again;
But there's only numbness, no

pain.
Where are you, my own?
The top is reached but you are
   gone.
The moon and stars are waiting
   there,
But my waiting arms are bare.

Julie Charleen Lambert
YOU—GOD'S EMISSARY

How beautiful it is to see
   A trust develop, where—
A person felt he'd never meet
Another who would care.

This gift to help lies well within
   The reach of every man,
If he'll but do a simple thing,
   Sincerely as he can:

Transport to other beings, that—
   Imperfect as they are,
The good they do, on God's
   kind scales,
   Outweighs the bad, by far.

Melinda Laraneta
RE-LEARNING

Somewhere within my memory,
I can't quite say just when,
The veils of childhood fantasies
Were parted by the wind.

No sudden vision held me,
I was blind within the storm
As on it raged about me
Left me naked, bruised and torn.

Since then I've spent a lot of
   time
Re-learning how to see
And when I learn to see again
I hope to see it's me.

Michele Lee Barker
WINTER

   Old hands
   Wrinkled, worn,
   Grasping, clutching,
   Gnarled like an old tree
Stripped of leaves and blossoms
   As though in Winter
   Unlike saplings
   Youth is gone
   Forever.

Jeanne Stanley
RAIN, LEAVES, AND STARS

It should be crystal,
Showering up, when it's down,
Tiny, tinkly tears,
Making color chords of clouds
It should crash and flash.

They should blow off limbs
from a thousand different trees
meet in a cyclone,
and form a rare patchwork ship.
They should sail the wind.

They should be wind-washed,
then join points and make
   flowers
by wreathing the moon,
Silver-circling a gold sun.
They should line rainbows.

Frances Wilk Hobbs
EVENING OF LIFE

Calling back to mind
   passed happenings
When little, eating an
   apple on a stick
   in Lincoln Park, by the lake
   in Chicago
In Glenview, Illinois
   singing around a campfire
   Forty girls in a circle
Leaving the city
   settling in Pennsylvania

Tasting wintergreen
   birch-bark with
   country friends
I recall my first date
   going home separate ways
   from theatre doors
Love children, had daughter
   and son
Landscaping, making a house a
   home
Bachelor-mother
   "did all this" on my own
Liberated from late husband
   years ago
Philanderer, gambler
   God rest his soul
Time for reminiscing
   the evening of life

William J. Sanderson
A GODDESS OF LOVE

Come with me,
   For I can give you all you shall
      ever desire
   And more,
Take my hand,
   For I can give you eternal
      youth.
Come to my side,
   For you and I shall roam the
      timeless
   Regions of the heavens.
Come to love me,
   For your's shall verily be the
      most noble of
   Loves.
Come, spend the rest of your
   life with me,
   For I am a goddess of love.
Love me to your heart's content,
   For it should befall all men to
      love and
   Cherish me.

A. R. Watson
UNTITLED

I stand, in awe of Helen's beauty,
Gazing at you, her reflection,
Searching for an access to your
   attention.
All the lines that come to mind,
Mere words, lack enough
   expression
For me to even mention.
   But,
I write, in hope of finding a
   clue,
Some key to you, in my
   selection
Of phrases, riddles from above.
I fail to grasp, with just a view,
Which it is I truly love:
The mirror or the reflection.

Claudia Gardner
FROZEN BUDS OF SUMMER

Come take my hand,
We'll dance until the twilight
   stars begin to shine,
Before the frozen buds of
   summer fade away.
Our love turns circles in my
   mind,
Beginning never ending;
But growing with the warmth
   your hand gives mine.
I see us there together in the
   misty morning showers,
In the crimson of the autumn
And before the blazing fire of a
   dozen long loved days.
A love like ours was meant to be
Before time echoed onward

through the trees
And touched the sunlit rays that
   fell upon a golden lullaby.
Our love is made of purest light
   and it must never part
Like waves that lap against the
   sky
And find when fallen they are
   never more to be.
Our love will still be strong as
   giant oaks
Braced hard against the battling
   winds,
Though frozen buds of summer
   fade to drops of life upon the
   misty ground.
Our love will still turn circles
   in my mind,
Never ending,
But growing with the warmth
   your hand gives mine.

Clara J. Drobish
SMILE

Smile every day cast your
   worries away,
Smile every day, you'll be
   happy . . . I say
Smile all the while to the friends
   that you greet,
You will lighten their day,
You will brighten your way . . .
   if
You smile every day.

Pat De Paris
TREE OF LIFE

   In the darkest hour only time
      is merciful; it is
   the great healer; and with time
      one learns to accept
   the taste of bitter fruit from the
      Tree of Life . . .

Joyce Tunnell
LOCAL VET

We have a nice local Vet,
   claiming to love all pets.
Doc's assistant is his wife.
Together, they have a tough life,
   spending long hours mending
   animal's ills.
He quickly administers pills.
Equipment all sterile and germ
   free.
Animals are afraid, wanting to
   flee.
Each animal is checked with
   care.
Even for diseases that are rare.
Sometimes blood samples are
   taken to test.
In this line of work, it's hard
   to rest.
An operation may be necessary
   in a case.
They are never too complicated
   for him to face.
There's one thing to see.
At the end of the examination,
Doc or his wife hand a bill
For the fee.

Joseph R. Macaluso
LATE NIGHT AIR

The late night air is crisp
and clear,
No light, no stars, no moon.
Perfect blackness abundant.

The leafless tree stands alone,
Only the company of the
signpost.
Signs which direct no one.

Winter wind whips through
the streets,
Yet no survivors feel its sting.
No flags unfurled in its gusts.

Lightless, the empty cities
stand.
No candles burn, no
cigarettes glow.
No bonfires blaze in the night.

Winter wind wiggles through
a tiny crack,
And utters a shrill cry.
All is silent; no one heard.

The clock goes on, yet it
does nothing.
No light to read its face,
No one to hear its tick.

Papers whirl in winter winds,
Full of words, yet saying
nothing.
No one to read their message.

No light.
Winter winds whipping wildly.
Alone.

Carolyn R. Schaeffer
BIRTH PANGS

From my loins you sprang
with Howl ascending -
No gentle squall
but angry Bellow -
Red-faced, Raging!
So long sought
was Your Emergence
that its Fury
came as music.
In relief that
All was Well -
my ears construed it
As a Serenade.

James A. Wheatley
SHE LADY

I took her home
she lady smilin'
Big hearted little woman
mind staid on freedom
Found her weepin'
she thinkin'
down the road
feet plowin' through
starved soil
toilin'
soul plundered but ain't broken
She harvestin'
gatherin'
singing' zion songs
amidst her sweat and
miseries
searchin' for salvation

Tracy DeBrincat
CRAIG

Craig sits in bed—
her lipstick still smeared
from that long goodnight kiss.

Her delicate and lacy strap
slides off her shoulder
onto her thin brown arm.

Long red nails are wrapped
around a warm gin and tonic.
Blonde hair, once-curled, sleeps.

The red coal of her cigarette

glows like a devil's eye
as it travels up and down
Unseen elevators—
from pink lips to ashtray
and back again.

A long shapely leg
gracefully danges over the
side of the bed;
trying to steady the ship.

Robert King Dale Groenewoud
RAIN

rain falling
strained rain
frail rain falling
pristine
opulent kisses
crystal tongues
sliver thin
hissing tinly
thinly
crystal clear
angel tears
falling
angellic mist
kissing barren brows
love mist
blessing barren soil
bearing life
fertility
rain falling
calling names
of lost lovers

Atasua Peters
FIRST REALITY AFTER WORK

There is a salvation in being
alone,
Away from the sufficating
layers of "human" creatures
That crowd the outside world.
The carbon copy people I
encounter
I cannot comprehend,
Their ways and thoughts are not
unlike
Those of whoever is near,
And their smiles are as fake as
their hair color.
I prefer being alone
So reality is what I wish,
Not what others demand.
A non-conformist? I think not.
More of a turtle peeking out of
its shell,
Trying to cope with the
problems
Of simple making a living to
survive.

dorsey robbins
MORGANTOWN AT CHRISTMAS TIME

Dear God, I would like
To pen a magnificent rhyme
or lay
Honoring my town I love so
much
This glorious Christmas Day.
Each time I go 'round
The Willey Street bend,
I just cannot help
Swelling with pride deep
within!
My eyes take in at a glance
The houses in the valley below,
And up the hill on each side.
Sparkling lights are all aglow!
How thrillingly beautiful the
scene,
Blanketed in the purist white,
My wonderful magic town
So transformed Christmas
Night.
It is the precious way He tells us

Each year of the priceless Gift
That is ours—to begin again,
To give a weary heart a lift!

Melanie Dawn Brown
WINTER'S APPROACH

Autumn is departing
Winter is slowly stepping in
The leaves of red and gold
have fallen to the ground
Soon a glittering white blanket
will cover them
The trees will have sleeves of
ivory
and the roofs will don pearly
shrouds
The sparkling snow will reflect
the calm
and peacefulness
of
wintry
life.

Linda Occhineri
TO MY SISTER MARIE

Floating on a cloud
Made up of the softness
of life
Holding to dreams of
reality and truths
Needing that which brings
tranquility and peace
Touching upon the soul
As if a delicate piece
of crystal
Held on by the tenderness
felt by a fortunate few
Bringing to a world of despair
A glow of infinite light

Martin Vagel
WHEN YOU KNOW

When you know that life
has been
A pleasant past to think about,
And a future which you know
Will bring into your mind,
no doubt,
You have a way of knowing
what you want,
A loved one very dear,
ever near,
And you know she is devout.

My love will find a way for me
To say the words she wants
to hear,
And when I say them,
I will know
I'll want her always near.
I can also say in truth,
each day
She's in my thoughts in
every way,
A million times she'll
hear me say
I need you, and always
want you,
Just soft words away.

Joan L. Johnson
YOU AND ME

Will ever my broken heart
be mended
Now that the love we shared
has ended?
Are all my thoughts to be
only of you
Will you be thinking about
me too?
Will there be a day when
I am free
From the thoughts and
memories of you and me?
Can this pain I'm feeling
go away
Or does it go on likes this
every day?

Is what they say true that
Love conquers all
Or will only time tell
if I'm to fall.

Kathleen Hall
WOULD YOU

If we met in total darkness
And I softly touched your hand
If my presence gave you
comfort
In a dark and lonely land

If we spoke and found
agreement
And our thoughts were
much the same
If our goals in life were equal
Reaching higher was our aim

If we gave each other courage
Thru' the blackness of
the night
And we formed a bond
of friendship
As we waited for the light

Would you turn your back
upon me
When the morning brightness
came
When we finally see each other
And our skin is not the same?

Pat Warner
POEM OF SEXUAL FRUSTRATION

there's
an orgasm
waiting for me
around the
corner

i just
can't find
the strength
to cross
the
street.

Pearl Newton Rook
DREAM COME TRUE

In the forest, vines
Cover a glade
Where Ho Tai sits
In the shade
Watching over a pool
of paradise,
Even as his shape fades
Into the landscape of
the night.

Gold Finches dream
Of the secret space -
Awake in surprise
Beneath the gentle gaze
Of the Happy God's eyes.

Lynn Bradshaw
I AM ME

I am Me
Me not I
I the individual, Me the
conformist
I am an impression of life
passed before Me
I and Me are not the same
not indifferent
I am eternal, Me universal
I belong to Me
Me belongs to others not
within Me
I suffer, so shall life Me
I the idea of being not Me

Elaine Tarr
UNLESS

There it is again, Lord,
Sitting down beside me,
Snuggling up next to my heart.
This sin, Lord.
Why must it be?

Help me to understand
this burden
you have given me to bear.
I don't think I can take it
on my own Lord.
The pain inside my heart, my
mind, my soul, is driving me
pulling, pushing, putting
me across the edge.
I must escape somehow Lord!
Escape with the sin.
If you can't give to me the
desire of my heart.
Give me a reason to go
on living.
It is too painful, too pointless
to take unless,
Unless I keep the sin.

Cindy Sunshine Walraven
**GO AHEAD AND SMILE,
YOU'VE MADE ME CRY**

You call me late at night
and say you miss me,
And I find it hard to sleep
when you say goodbye.
I toss and turn all night
just thinking of you;
So go ahead and smile,
you've made me cry.

With every late night night
call came hesitation,
And soon enough I'd
end up wondering why.
It goes to show your spell
has kept on working,
So go ahead and smile,
you've made me cry.

Now and then I'll see you
when I'm dreaming,
And I can't forget about
you though I try.
So here I am awake at
two A.M. again,
Go ahead and smile,
you've made me cry.

H. James Hutcheson
SURFING

Slow
  Motion
    Movement,
      Time stands still;
Graceful pushup,
  Right lean swerve;
Wave breaks behind me,
  Slow white fall;
Stall it in,
  White washed wall;
Exploding outward,
  Soft and slow;
Slipping along,
  Keeping low;
White water rolling,
  Closing out;
Right lean back,
  Pulling out.

William M. Karnes
MEET ME ON A STAR

Autumn walks, building
snowmen and flying kites-
When we first met, we did
so many things.
We seemed to have so much
time together,
So long ago, before I gave
you wedding rings.

Time seems to be passing
so quickly now.
Back then we loved each
other, even from afar.
When separated, we agreed
to look heavenward,
"Remember," we'd say,
"I'll meet you on a star."

We now have streaks of grey,
you know.
We have a family and our
own career.
But even though we're
very busy,
We always manage to say,
"I love you, dear."
Yes, my love, our lives are
busier, by far,
But you still find time to
"meet me on a star."

Sue Shupe
HOW ABOUT LIFE

We live in
Our own individual worlds
Mine made out of a
crystalline bubble
Yours made from a concrete
wall
I can see over yours
And you can see through mine
My world is enchanting
I have emotions, heartbreaks,
dreams
And love
My world soars above
the heavens
In your world
There are unconcerned hearts
And frozen dreams
Your world holds no promise
of leaving the ground
Yes,
....my world is beautiful
as is crystal
But yours, even heartless
and imprisoned
Is shatterproof

Patrice Lange
**THE LORD IS MY
THERAPIST**

for the Lord is my Therapist
Nothing shall I fear...

He watches over me in the
dark tunnels of my misery

He holds me in His arms
above the sea

He clothes me in the innocence
of Truth,
    and Faith,
    and Hope

He caresses me in His eyes
of Charity

He walked through fire for me

for the Lord is my Therapist
The Lord is my Provider

nothing shall I fear...

Pamela Hogue
I LOVE YOU

Quietly hiding as you go by,
Too embarrassed to even say hi,
I silently watch you working
and playing.
I remain anonymous,
never saying,
"I love you."

I write you lots and lots
of notes,
Pinning to each all my hopes,
Going by you and always
shrinking,
To myself, I'm always
thinking,
"I love you."

Wanting so much to make
you smile,
To be with you all the while,
To make you laugh and
brighten your day
So that you'll be glad to say,
"I love you."

Sigmund Kolatzki
BABY FOOD

the linen is unbuttoned
by silky fingers
the perfect breasts exposed
as waves upon high tide
dark nippled
all jungle mother
reposes with her babe
who opens wide
upon the well they pump
baby food

Jane A. Semprevivo
SNOW WHITE

Sleeping Beauty
The light shys you away
Enveloping you
Darkening shadows
Forming shapes like
Musical notes
Touting
Words reaching in to
Bring you here -
January
Our time is spent as yours
Marches on, on, on
Limitless until
Acrylic egg shell
Is severed
We find you
Crawling carefully
Along the thin edge
We pull you out

Marjorie E. Musgrave
LOVE

Young love -
Ah, how brightly it burns
With an all-consuming flame,
Running wild and free.
Then one day
The tempest's o'er,
The battles fought and won,
And that same dear love
Is still a warm and lovely glow!
Forget not to keep it
With an ever-loving, tender care
Lest the flame die upon
the hearth
And nought but ashes
Will be remaining there!

Susan Kelly Jambard
PATHS

The paths are there,
that I had known,
Worn down grass, some
thorns have grown.
Memories of childhood
in the wood,
Castles, peacefulness
and solitude.
Sometimes I return when
I need a rest,
It's only my imagination
that goes at best.
The path seems never free
from briars that grow,
Branches, grasping thoughts,
stooping low.
Lifes tangles somehow
stop my descent,
Down the path of uncluttered
mind, that youth had meant.

Susan Kelly Jambard
FORGETTING

I try to put you out of
my mind!
"Why are you there anyway?"
If I search my heart what
will I find?
I dare not think I'll let
you stay!
It's hard to forget your touch...

Your eyes find mine and
ponder,
I smile and quickly turn
away.
I do look back to watch
awhile and wonder,
When our eyes next meet—
what will I do?
Will there come a day when
I won't turn away?

Robert K. Robertson, Jr.
COULD BE

I would rather be a could be,
If I could not be an are.
Because a could be is a maybe,
With a chance of touching par.
I would rather be a has been,
Than a might have been afar.
Because a might have been
can never be,
And a has been was an are.

Barbara Jarmuth Campbell
PATIO MEMORIES

Hands handling bricks
set in sand
set in memory's grid
where time is telescoped
from near beginning
to near end.
We are but two
who once were five
and share this summer eve
beneath our purple plum.
Hands and branches
gnarled now
recall
the bare root
birthday-tree
and children's cry.
When but one remembers
will it be you
or I?

Raine Stevens Rogers
SEASHELL

I am the seashell
tossed to the wet sand —
But look closer
and I am a pearl sunset
with many corals and golds.
Like the vanishing daylight,
I have many secrets —
You must hold me close
to hear the crying
at the shore.

Miss Joan Markley Davis
SUNLIGHT

A piece of the sun
Stealing into my room
Caresses my brow
With its soft warmth.

Kim Goss Kesler
TO MARKA

A child—woman she dreams
Her young colt legs in
fifth position.
The gracefulness is yet to come
As she dances in past tradition.

My daughter I cherish
Her dreams we both see.
On stage the prima ballerina
The woman—child to be.

Terri Tolbert Hendricks
WHY HER LORD

"Why her Lord?"
Please take me.

She is so beautiful and
has the whole world left to see.

I've hurt alot of people
and made mistakes.

But she's brand new so take
me for heavens sake.

Her smiles make people happy
While I make people sad.

She is laughter and love,
while the things I try seem
to turn out bad.

She's my third try and it's
three strikes
and you're out.

So leave her here, you win
this bout.

I've doubted you in the past,
but if this
is the way I have to pay.

It's too much Lord, please
don't make me stay.

Karen St. George Kerth
THE WEDDING GIFT

What can I give you?
I don't have a dime.
I'd give you the earth,
If it were mine.
I'd give you the land,
also the sea,
Even the stars that fall
silently.
I'd give you nighttime,
And with it the day,
Fragrant blossoms that
color the May,
I'd give you sunshine,
bright skies of blue
I'd grant you a wish,
You'd hope would
come true.
What can I give you,
As these are not mine?
I'll give you my love,
To last for all time.

Marjorie B. Kline
VISION ON A HILL

Not so far away I saw
something familiar
Of words I'd heard
about a cross
Stained with blood, the
emblem of love,
Of one who suffered and
died for me.

Discontent and sadness loomed
The symbol of struggle
and shame
The Lamb of God hung on
that cross
Aware of the agony He
endured for me.

Grateful was He on that day
When He was freed from
earthliness
And the old rugged,
wood cross
On that hill in a land
far away.

Peace was within me, a
humble servant,
When I took Him as
my Savior
Always there to help
my cross to bear
Hopefully in exchange
for a crown someday.

Nancy Bartlett
THE GIFT

Today, God gave me a
mountaintop.
I only asked for a hill.
Today, God brought me
heaven on earth.
I only sought His will.

I only looked for peace
of mind,
A little cheer in my heart.
Maybe some comfort

for my soul....
But nothing whole!
Just a part!
So I reached out to touch
His garment's hem.
I was not worthy of more!
How could I know that
His sweet touch
Would open Heaven's store?
So here I am, on a
mountaintop,
So far and yet so near,
And you know? I never
felt the climb!
My Savior brought me here.

Steve Isom
RACE

Didn't run fast
Ran my best
Finished first
Although I was last.

Viola E. Walters
I LOVE YOU, MY LOVE

As God was my witness
I swore before Man,
That you were my true love
through all this life span.

I don't have the words,
nor have I the metre,
To tell of my feelings and
thoughts, so much sweeter
Than any I've felt or
thought in my life —
Despite all our sorrow—
despite all our strife.

For you are my one love,
my life and my dreams;
You fit in my home, in
my arms and my schemes.

You see, you're my oak,
my earth and my sky —
And you've pulled me from
drudgery to heaven on high
With your blonde hair and
blue eyes, your arms and
your laugh.
So — now these are my
crutch, my cross and
my staff!

It's said here so poorly
and yet you know well,
With you as my angel
I'll never know hell!

Frances Troxler Keogh
GOD'S SPOTLIGHT

As I gazed by the window
Pondering things I should do,
Suddenly from behind the trees
A blinding ray broke through.

How can I see, the sun's
so bright!
I said to one near by.
Why be concerned was
the reply.
Not everyone performs in
God's spotlight.

Carol Novotny Fisher
SILENT MUSIC

I hear the Silent Music
of living beings
of other things
rocks trees earth
in symphony
in tune
with the infinite
picking up the silence
I feel alive
vibrations of consciousness
a beautiful world
a beautiful life
healthy wholly happy

Hazel Smoak Clover
ANOTHER DAY

The night is so still
And the limbs of the Oak,
Look so lonely and lost,
As the last of the notes,
Of the night bird's call
Goes trilling away.
Thank God for tomorrow,
Another day!

Another day to make amends,
Another day to speak
to friends.
Living our lives as though
We too......
Would make amends for
the world,
If we could, would you?

Asking for love
In all that we do.
Seeking and searching
For a dream that's true.
Wanting only to hold
Our loved ones close.
Of our lives together,
To be able to boast.

Yet knowing with all
Of our mind and soul.
It's just a lost dream,
Of an unreached goal!

Teresa Schalnat Bush
SECRET WEB OF DREAMS

Man of my past
why do you haunt my
dreams so?

too many years
too many tears
gone by
yet, deep in slumber,
the echo of your whisper
lingers
the fire of your kiss burns
my lips
the sweet gentleness of you
spurs my longing
and my body warms, and
runs cool, for want of you

intangible reality
untouchable memory
spirit of tender youth
I desire you still...

I wake, restless now,
to find I am alone
and content to know I
have not lost you
but hold you safely in my
secret web of dreams.

Lynn M. Masulaitis
**TODAY, TOMORROW,
YESTERDAY**

Days flow into each other.
There is no beginning—
And no end.

I wonder what Tomorrow
will bring;
But I do not dwell—
For rain mists my eyes.

I think not of Yesterdays,
Or what Tomorrow brings.
I cling to Today—this moment.

There is too much pain
in memories;
Too much loneliness
in Tomorrows.
With Todays, I can somehow
cope.

Tiny sand grains drop
one by one
Sometimes so deafening
I must run . . . .

I look upon my tear-stained

pillow
And count a long ten.
Then take a deep breath.. . . .

I slowly open my eyes
As rays of Hope flicker
And dance between fading
gray clouds.

Inner strength, please give
me the courage
To Believe in myself and
to go on—
For Tomorrow has arrived.

Cheri L. Whalen
NATURE'S TUNE

Listen to the wind whispering
through the trees.
Feel the sun beating down
upon your head.
Smell the greening of the plants
as springs arrives.
Taste the sweet air upon
your tongue.
Everything around you is
part of life.
So take it in and let its life
be part of yours
and together we'll attend
our mother earth.

Linda Lee Hansken
A WILD FLOWER

I saw this wild flower
growing,
Inbetween a group of weeds.
I think that I shall pick
this flower
And retain it for it's seeds.
It has to be a plant with
strength
To grow among it's enemies.
And that's the kind of
flower that I'd
Like to propagate for me.
I saw this flower growing wild,
Not another one about.
I think that I shall go and try
To pull this lonely flower out.
Well better yet I'll leave
it there
It has a better chance to live.
If picked it's strength would
drain away
And certain death is all
I'd give.
But then it'd die all by
it's self
And seedlings may not
then survive.
I picked that flower,
took it home,
And now it is survived
by five.

Mrs. Billie Miller
TO A CROSSING GUARD

A children's world is
her abode,
in her lonely vigil by
the road.
She stands erect with
watchful eye,
and always waves a
cheerful "Hi".
Always with a helping hand,
with deep concern for
fellowman.
A pause—to tie a tiny shoe,
to wipe a nose, a tear
or two.
Perhaps a mother to console,
and ever safety is her goal.
And so I think of all
the strife,
of one who's fighting
for her life.

With sober thoughts I
  do extend,
  My loving tribute to
  a friend.

Edward J. Besner
CALL IT RIGHT

As I pass through this time
  and age
I think of all the wrongs
I've tried to right
And find it a useless fight.
O Lord God
Let your light be clear
  and bright
For thy servant has put
  up a fight
And only you can ever
  make it right.
To watch the carelessness
  of life
I'm still petrified from
  fright
And hope to live till
  my love be right.
Until that time of our
  meeting
Keep thy servant in thy sight
And make all his ways right.
Look upon us in the
  gentleness of thy mercies
That we maybe brought to
  the power of thy holiness
And grant me my wish
That I may have eternal bliss.

Virginia Power Sells
BLOOD

Here in the hospital, I'm at
  last all alone,
I'm very uncomfortable,
  wish I "wuz" home.
They've taken enough of my
  poor tired blood,
To help any invasion of
  for or of flood.

They've shot me full of
  antibiotics galore.
  "Laws A mercy", here nurse
  comes with one more.
"Hello there, this is your
  last shot tonight."
It's a long time till dawn,
  and morning light.

Today is the day I at last
  can go home.
I just got the last shot,
  nurse hit the bone.
They come with a wheel chair,
  I sit me down,
At last, I'm outside and on
  good level ground.

J. T. Wall
SEASONING

Summer simmers
Naked swimmers;
Autumn leaves them
Falling hues;
Winter freezes faces,
Sneeze!
And spring begins anew.

Mary Jane McClure
MY DREAM

I pick up my pen and
  drift away,
  To times and places I
  cannot stay;
In search of my imaginary
  dream,
  The one that truly would
  be supreme.
And voice every writer's
  dream,

Releasing every pent up
  emotion;
In every poet's mind making
  up a poem
  That's to be the very best
  in time.
Poems on every subject
  have been
    written in so many ways.
    Some seem good and
    even best,
Some relax our souls
    And put our minds to rest.
If by chance some poet
  found it,
  Where would the
  challenge be?
  What's there left
  to dream?
If by chance someone
  wrote it—
  This poem we call Supreme.

Ann Fassler
TO THE SENTIMENTAL

I sweep up sentimentality
  with words and whispers
  I have heard,
  and collect them
  with teardrops that fall
  down trembling cheeks.
With memories and recollection,
  I remember
  the faintest smiles,
  the softest touch,
    and the most reassuring hug.
Nothing can be forgotten
  within this unfolding paper;
and I will never forget
  my sweetest memory,
the time I had spent with you.

Jeanne Muller
MORNING PRAYER

Father thee we praise,
our voices to thee raise
in song and loving care.
With thee our love we share.

Thank you, oh Father dear,
in faith we know you're near.
Hands together to you we pray,
stay with us all the day.

Eleanor McKee
A HAPPY SEASON

Christmas is a happy season,
of all sweet times the best.
  How softly slept the
  Christ child,
How softly stirred the night,
  as shepherd watched in
  market places and steeples.
The reel and peel of bells and
  in the hearts of people
  the music swells.
How softly smiled the little
  one's Mother as Joseph gazed,
on this tiny child whose name
  would soon be praised.
How softly gleams in countless
  hearts, the steady radiant light.

Edwin R. Scott
A NEW DAY

I awakened this morning,
  the sunshine felt so warm.
That ole wind blew gentle as
  it chilled my aching bones.
How full are the trees where
  the sparrows just flew.
And green is the grass, yet
  covered with the dew.

Troubled has been this world,
  and so burdened is my heart.
Upon us a new day that will
  be good at the start.

Blessed and full of grace
  this day is to be.
Sunshine, blue skies, and
  burden free.
How long has been its coming,
  now the waiting is done.
Free is my spirit as I
  awakened to its dawn.
The day that was promised
  will soon come to pass.
The change we have awaited
  is upon us at last.

Solid is its bottom as its
  built on a rock.
As it all comes to pass at
  the crow of a cock.
So high is its mountains and
  pure as virgin snow
As flowers fill its valleys
  and the green grass grow.

Reinaldo Matos
SWALLOW'S NEST

I made a swallow's nest
On the top of a palm,
With the body and soul
Of your life and mine.

Day and night,
In the garden of my house,
Quiverings of wings
Whisper
Confidences of happiness.

We are snow and fire,
Perfume and flower,
Body and soul.

Bessie M. Trask
WAVES

Waves rush upon the sand
  and slowly drift back
    into the sea
Thoughts of you rush upon
  my mind
    and slowly drift
      through time

Beverly Cowher
MY SPECIAL GUY

You're a very special guy,
And you belong to me.
You're kind, strong but
  gentle, too.
You're the best thing that's
  ever happened to me.
You're my special guy.

Our relationship has gone
  through many trials
And we've come through
  stronger than ever.
You and I have the understand-
  ing the world really needs.
We have our love to take
  us far.

You're a very special guy,
And you belong to me.
Where would I be without you?
You're the best thing that's
  ever happened to me.
You're my special guy.
I Love You.

Kate Blackledge
A SON

Seeing small children makes
  me remember
The dear little son born
  one December.
Your chubby cheeks you
  would hold next to mine
As you sat in my lap. For
  that I pine!
When you would do things
  to upset my day,
You'd look up at me and
  then you would say;
"But Mommy, I wuv you,
  I not be bad!"
Then no longer could I -
  at you be mad.
Growing up you would make
  me feel so proud;
With your smile, I'd pick
  you out in a crowd.
All my errands you would
  so quickly run,
Even though you had to
  stop having fun.
These thoughts of you can
  never be measured;
In my heart, you will always
  be treasured.

Richard L. Muller
GOODBYE

Moisture pearls your upper lip
sad
  angry
    confused
      lonely
        firm
in slipping your hand out of his
that he hesitates to breathe;
nervously smiling,
not believing in death at such
  a young age.

Boyd Whitson
HOUSE OR HOME

A man can build with sticks
  and mud
Or lumber fresh from the mill
Or bricks or stone and build
In town or country or on a hill.
  It is just a house.

Whether it be a hovel or
  mansion grand
Be it owned or mortgaged,
  it matters not.
When it is painted and
  plastered
And papered, all that he has got.
  Is a house.

Add the patter of little feet,
Mix well with laughter and tears.
Let happiness and sorrow
  be shared
With hope and love and years.
  It is a home.

Gloria Hayes Mitrovka
TARA BETH

With my first recollection of
  very black hair
She was placed on my stomach
  with a great deal of care
When I spoke and said, hi,
  she turned her small face
Like my voice was a haven in
  a cold and strange place

"She does know your voice,"
  said a nurse standing near,
"Through vibrations, she's
  heard it for almost a year."
It did seem she knew me,
  though she couldn't see
That alert little face told
  me clear as could be

LaVada Toni Glover
LORD, THANK YOU!

The rain is falling softly all
   across my way,
Wonders sweet as dawn
   this new
   and glorious day.
Each miracle brought I
   shall cherish,
   Lord, from Thee,
A Rose, A Rainbow, in
   sharing life
   and love with me.
Lord thank You, for these
   treasures
   you have given me today—
And, Thank You, again
   sweetly Lord,
More than heart or lips can say!

Karen L. Roberts
FRIENDS

Come to my doorstep when
   you feel the urge to;
you need no invitation.
Bring to me your state of
   depression and the
need for a shoulder to cry on.
Save your clown image for
   those who can offer
no shelter from life's
   tribulations.
Walk beside me, not ahead,
   or behind
because friends are equal in
   all these ways.

Annette Tittensor
MY LOVE

Purer than fresh mountain air is,
So pure is my love for thee,
Vaster than the expanse of
   heaven,
And deeper than the deepest sea,
More delightsome than a merry
   tune
Dancing through the morning
   air,
Brighter than the sun but soft
   as the moon's glow,
And rare as the rarest flower is
   rare.
My love, it is eternal.
It goes beyond the last breath;
And I will but love thee deeper
When my eyes close in death.

Marsha L. Munyon
SEARCHING

Looking everywhere
   Searching for the one
To tell me who I am
   And where I'm coming from
To help me see myself
   To search throughout my mind
To know what's in my thoughts
   And know the person I might
   find
Searching for someone
   To help me straighten out
To care enough to tell me
   What life is all about.

Lois MC Ginn
SMILES

I look my best when I wear a
   smile,
It lets the love shine through.
I bloom and grow, a hundred
   fold,
And pass it on to you.
The circle grows and gathers
   warmth,
And spreads throughout the
   world,
Then returns to where it began,
And starts all over again.

Ruth Ellis
MY FRIEND

He likes to walk along
   the seashore...
And feel the softness of
   the sand,
To think..and drink in all
   the beauty
As he holds a lovely seashell
   in his hand.
He feels the radiance of
   the sunshine...
It warms his soul...it fills
   his heart...
And all the while he's
   thanking GOD
That in this all..he has
   a part.
He listens to the hurting
   of the people,
He understands...in a
   special way...
Because he knows...that
   as they're talking...
He's sharing in the value
   of a precious day!
   And....... I love him.......

Carole Browning-Black
THE "SPECIAL" ONES

Their hands struggle to meet
   and make the sound;
I barely notice mine touch.
They wobble precariously
   as we rock;
I sway back and forth
   gracefully.
Their legs quiver in an
   attempt to stamp their feet;
Mine follow a rhythmic
   pattern.
They sing the song in jumbled,
   mumbled words;
I sing out loud and clear.
We finish the song and they
   applaud themselves,
And rightfully they should;
For I have made no
   appreciable effort,
But they have given their all.

Dianne A. Armstrong
FINAL MOMENTS

Lined leaves are thickened,
   weathered and torn;
These old soldiers staunchly
   guard the glen.
The survivors of storms, alive,
   yet forlorn
They speak of youths joys again
   and again.
But begging relief in Augusts'
   cruel maze
Demands so much more of the
   high energy.
Her dismay drains so they dip
   in disdain
And die on the winds of dry
   destiny.

Kathleen A. Blough
LOVE

Infatuation is a star,
that is bright from far away,
but is often dim when one looks
   at it.
When one lets it go,
it stays dim.
Love is a star,
that is bright from the distance,
it's even brighter when one
   looks at it.
When one lets it go, it is still
   bright,
but when one catches it, it is
   the brightest of all.

Penny Tellas Blair
THE WINGS OF FATE

Keep the wings of fate from my
   eyes,
Still their flight from the skies.
For what can I do but shoot
   them down,
And bury them in yesterday's
   ground.
Yesterday's ground where
   memory goes,
Where grass is dead and nothing
   grows.
Keep the wings of fate forever
   bound,
In an unmarked grave of
   yesterday's ground.
On hollow wings fly birds of
   fate,
And now they return just plain
   too late.
Silvery wings that once filled
   the sky,
Tis now but just a speck in my
   eye.

Luina Schidlowski
MY PRINCE

Our eyes met across the crowded
   room,
Releasing a current of familiarity
   never felt before.
Each became captive of the
   other forever.
Not a word passed, only this
   strange feeling
Of having come face to face
   with our destiny.
You, my love, young and slim,
   became My Prince
As you came to me and we
   touched for the first time
We danced, we laughed, we
   played the games young lovers
   play,
Until the bells rang on our
   Wedding Day.
Fifty years now of laughter and
   tears bring us to the Winter of
   fulfilled dreams
Facing our Eternal Destiny,
   hand in hand, My Prince and
   me.

Annie Booker Hall
DANGERS OF LOVE

I wished him and him alone
   dead.
This is one thought I dearly
   dread.
I hold no key to a life of give
   and take.
These words I spoke for
   womanhood sake.
Everything he touches he must
   destroy.
Like a motherless child with
   only one toy.
He'll lie his way into your heart,
With a long sob story, but not
   a truthful part.
His tactics he'll plan like a
   counter spy.
Or kill all the goodness before
   you die.
Roaming this earth like a great
   disease,
Seeking female victims to
   continue his squeeze.
Careful daughter, don't believe
   everything you hear.
This disease once again starts
   his sobbing tears.
Built like a man but retarded
   in mind.

But one good thing, there's only
   one of his kind.
I speak now because I qualified,
To say to those not yet notified.
Check his words until
   completely understood.
He definitely has your death
   written under his hood.
A fatal disease that works on
   your emotion
It soaks into your heart like
   skin lotion
His death would cause no great
   pain,
Because he lived his life all in
   vain.
Strike him down before he
   again extends his hand.
Bury him deep under the rocks
   and sand.
Before another woman must
   say the words she dread
Yes, my love, I wish you dead.

Erva Loomis Merow
DEAREST

When I am with you —————
my world is safe—————
all fears disappear.
But, when you leave me———
the world returns,
and I tremble in the raw
   twilight,
realizing———————
what we are,
and have always been————
shall always be.

Jayn Merry
THE MISSING OF YOU

Adjusting to the missing
   of you,
The loneliness inside.
Accepting is such a
   hideous ordeal,
I never wanted to try.
My soul cries out to you
   in vain
Can you hear my
   emptiness now.
Dear Lord, I miss you so
No price is there for pain.
Perhaps in time from now
A dawn will come to me
And let me see the sky above -
The way you showed me
   life can be.

Jeremy
UNTITLED

I see you there
your nose against the glass,
   you looking in or
me looking out I do not
   know
   for sure
if you listen softly you'll hear
singing, softer still and you may
hear yourself the singing was
   from me to you; I'd
hoped you'd like it but I did
not know the words

Wandi (Wanda Vice)
ALL THE LOVELY THINGS

sometimes i gaze upon your
   countenance,
when you are unaware
and i can't begin to tell you
of the magic i see there
inspirations and dreams
castles and kings
and all of the lovely things
a man is to a woman . . .

Molly Therese Stewart
LET GO

Let go of hurts, large and small
You'll be victor over all
When trouble comes with
  sadness and grief
Don't dwell too long, make it
  brief

Let go, before it occupies the
  mind
Try to relax, try to unwind
Think, that it had to be
Because it's God's plan—for you
  and me

Jewel T. McElroy
A CLOWN'S REWARD

The great "Big Top" had come
  to town
With tigers and ponies and all
  of the clowns.
The children all hurried in
  with glee
Hoping their favorite clown
  to see.

The three-ring acts had just
  begun
When Johnny suddenly spotted
  one.
His feet were big; his clothes
  hung loose
And under his arm he
  cradled a goose.

His smile was wide, and
  friendly too,
And Johnny cried out, "I
  just love you!"
The clown waved back and
  threw him a kiss,
And thought to himself, "I
  love doing this!"

Orpha Love Gullickson
MYSTIC SEASHORE

Beautiful sand so soft
  and warm,
  I dig me a bed and a cover.
I lift my eyes to the bright
  blue skies
  Where wispy cloudlets hover.

The earth of me longs to
  return to its own,
  To rest in the sun, to
  crackle and freeze,
And then with the magic of
  dust once again,
  To drift on the water, or
  float on a breeze.

My arms are warmed by the
  radiant soil;
  My lids and my cheeks
  are glowing,
But the mounded weight
  can gravitate,
  So I must be up and going ...

Jean Price Stephens
PORTRAIT OF WORDS

Sometimes it's hard to put
  into words
Exactly how we feel;
And so we paint a picture
  of words...
But the colors are very real!

We dip our brush and stroke
  the canvas
To make the portrait show
That you're a man we all
  admire...
And one we're proud
  to know.

A touch of red will boldly
  note
The contributions you

have made;
Your many deeds — like
  the brilliance of red —
Will never, ever fade.

And now we splash on
  lots of gold
For your ever-cheerful ways;
It represents warm friendship,
  too—
The kind that never frays.

A stroke of blue will let
  you know
This illness we truly regret;
But it also reminds you
  we're standing by
To see that your needs
  are met.

And finally, the most
  DOMINANT shades
  we paint—
Yellows.... so sunny and
  bright!
With WARMEST GET WELL
  WISHES for you
'Til your days are filled
  with SUNLIGHT!

Dorothy Lee
WHY DO I LOVE YOU

Why do I bind myself to you?
When this I know,
You love me not.
Why do I long to hear
  your voice?
When mine, I'm sure
You have forgot.
The pain is all with me
And plans to stay.
I'm sure.
While you find love where
  e'er you go
Yet you expect me
To endure,
This agony of waiting
  your return,
Which you will do
When e'er you choose.
Why can't I close my heart
  and have you gone,
Then dry my tears
And say, I lose.

J. I. Stolley
PASSIONS OF WINTER

Slumping
tree boughs
draw
my gaze
and even they
are fast
crumbling
under enduring snows
which
have since
dilated
my garden bulbs
wirey
roots now
deadened in
ice crystals
aborting
them

before
springtide.

Teresa Dees
SILENCE

Blow on, wind,
Don't stop to mourn the dead.
Laugh on, stars,
It's only the silence I dread.

Mary J. Hodgkinson
MY MOTHER MY FRIEND

She gave me comfort
  and warmth,
When I was cold and alone.
  She helped me get up
  again,
When life had knocked
  me down.
  She gave me laughter,
When I wanted to cry.
  She gave me strength
  and courage,
When things were hard.
  She taught me how to
  love others,
So I could receive love
  in return.
  She's My Mother,
           My Friend

Emily Rosenblum
MY FIGHT FOR MY RIGHT

It was a fight,an awful fight.
They wanted wars,we wanted
  rights.
It was a fight,an awful fight.
They played dirty,we played
  right.
It was a fight,an awful fight.
They weren't hurt,we were
  a sight.
It was a fight,an awful fight.
They swung strongly,with
  all their might.
It was a fight,an awful fight.
We were black,they were white.

Sondra M. Mihalich
LOVING YOU

Loving you is like a rainbow;
No matter how far I travel,
I will never find the end,
And...
No matter how far I look back,
I will never find the beginning.

Paula R. Woltman
A LETTER TO ME

It's just your nerves
The doctor said
All you are feeling
Is in your head

You need no pills
For up and down
Nor a drink to bring
Your mind around

You are letting thinking
Get in your way
Your head keeps spinning
Day after day

The blues are there
Depression set in
You are in a limbo
It's happened again

No noise - No music
No living - No tube
Even your body
Seems to be in no mood

A space is there
Within your mind
Most spaces are good
But - no - not this kind

You function daily
Your body - that is
Your mouth even moves

Just like hers and his
Come on now woman
You must get it together
Come back to yourself
No matter the weather

You have what it takes
Yourself - your best bet
So get yourself moving
Get ready - get set

Think only what you have
Not what you ain't got
Just open your eyes
You can see it's alot

So here is the letter
I have written to you
Better days have to come
But it's all up to you

Dolores Endres Szarek
MEMORIES

Is it not possible
That somewhere in this
  vast expanse
Death has no bounds?
  Somehow, someday,
  for one brief moment,
I pray that our souls will
  meet again,
Our spirits touch;
And we would know each
  other.

We would have so much
  to say.

Shannon L. Martin
MOMENT

Moment — there is — in a touch
that slakes the dry flesh
with the shock of skin to skin —
Silent — screams the flash
of the electrifying force
of our human connection.

Pauline A. Lynch
DIVORCE

A memory welded deep
  in my heart
Is preserved and pampered,
  so t'will not fall apart.
The pain that banished,
  left a smile.
Remembering was grief
  for a little while.

For memories linger, though
  love can fade.
Breaking vows that once
  were made.
Then time intervenes, wiping
  out pain.
The heart finds peace and
  solace again.

Things we tried so hard
  to forget
Join forces with joy, and
  linger yet.
Yesterday's memories,
  I leave behind
Except in the portals
  of my mind.

Anita Margarete Zechner
THE ICE MAIDEN

Frosty cheeks, two icy eyes,
Melt away as she cries.
The shiny tears do not cease,
For all she seeks is love
  and peace.

She is the Ice Maiden laden
  with tears,
Which make her melt for
  all she fears.
She fears the war so blunt
  and cold.
Yet the Ice Maiden is so bold.

And as the day turns to night,
The Ice Maiden she cringes
    with fright.
For the day is warm, sunny,
    and kind,
But the night is evil, cold,
    and blind.

The Ice Maiden's journey
    does not cease,
For all she wants is love
    and peace.
Then she finds it across
    the bend,
But it's too late, for it's
    the end.

J. Quintin Brown
BRAVE DAY

Brazen is the moment
that scoffs the doubts and
    fears of night
and greets the bitterness
    of dawn
with a hearty laugh
and warms the day
with a smile.

Linda Kelly Hook
THE COYOTE PROWLS

The coyote prowls in the
    darkness of
the evening,
His essence glistens in
    the snow
as the moon beams reflect
upon the white blanket.

The frenzied beast slowly
    stalks the
night,
pouncing on innocent
    prey, unawares.
It seems to disappear,
into the dark edge of
    the earth.

Florence Boswell
A FRIEND

A true friend
Understands you.
Your thoughts
    your needs
Your memories of
    past deeds. And
if he laughs
He's not laughing
    at you
But with you
Because he cares.

June Outtrim
LIFE'S GARDEN

Early one morning as I sat and
pondered, the mysteries and
whys of Life. It came to mind,
from God, I believe, the com-
parison of a rose and a man.
It may seem strange to compare
the two, but if you'll listen,
I'll try to explain it to you.
We are all roses in God's Garden
of Life, all different kinds, race,
color, and creed. But he loves
us all, each variety and shade,
because he, our Creator, planted
and nutuired each soul from
it's infinite beginning. As God
walks thru his garden, he sees
some stinted of growth, some
weak, some sick and starved
from lack of spiritual growth.
These turn their heads from
the life giving presence, and
God will not force them to see.
Far to get full benefit from God's
sunshine bright, it has to be
sought for and free. God looks
on his roses with infinite love,

and long to nourish and bring
them full bloom, so throughout
our lives he prunes, snips, and
shears, the blight from each
rose, as it grows. These are the
troubles and trials of life that
each soul must conquer you
know. As God sees fit he trans-
plants each life, according to
his plan. So that each may grow
to an esquisite bloom, full
bloom, with all beauty, and
ready to dwell in god's Eternal
Garden of Love.

Perri Harrington
WHERE DID OUR LOVE GO

I walk here on the beach,
Feel the sand neath my feet.
Hear the splashing of the waves,
Takes me back to by-gone days.

My mind goes back in time;
We strolled here, you hand
    in mine.
Our love, it seemed so real,
Would last forever, we did feel.

Somewhere along the way
Our love slowly slipped away.
What happened, where did
    it go?
The answer, I do not know.

Our love, where can it be?
Did it wash out to sea?
Perhaps the tide will bring
    it back to me.

Renee Babineau York
DEATH ROW

Here I gaze, looking at the wall,
Counting every crack,
Washing I weren't here at all,
Knowing I can't go back.

Will anyone hear my plea
Can't you see I'm in the dark,
Come and release me.

Stop tearing at my heart
Doesn't anyone know
I didn't have to die,
I didn't want to go!

No, no one hears
It might be years
Before they hear me cry,
Before my memory disappears!

B. J. Curtis
GESTATION

Inspiration
Aspiration
Conspiration
Perspiration

(excerpt from
PLACES AND TIMES)

Sylvia Christina Conley
WORDS

Words should be spoken with
    chosen care, words
truly spoken, should also be
    heard with care—or
pardoned before they are
    ever wasted.

"I want to lend a helping
    hand my friend, but
seems to me, my foot is
    quicker to my mouth than
is my helping hand. But fear
    not my friend, for
I have one more hand and
    one more foot."

(Ded. To my friend Don)

Jean McBride Whitaker
REACTION

Phenyl, Methyl, Ethyl, Benzyl,
Tumble from you lips

with flair;
I know not a beaker from
    a flaskyl,
But I know the chemistry
    we share.

Judy Maddux
THE BIRD

Up in the tree top there sits
    a bird, minding his own
    business not saying a word.

Down on the ground there
stands a little boy, holding
    a B-B gun not knowing which
way to point. When all of a
sudden he notices the bird
and thinks to himself how
tuff he would be if he could
get just one.

Down on the ground there
lies a dead bird, not knowing
what he had done to deserve
this one.

Way down the road there
walks a little boy, crying
over what he had done.

Peggy Berry
LOVING

Lovingly you move in close
    to me as
Urgently your lips and hands
    seek out the secret places,
    that only you can know.
Eagerly I open myself up
    to you and
Joyously we give to each other;
Passionately moving in unison,
    the love song of the ages;
    sang with the very fibers
    of our being;
    reaching heighths familiar
    and sweet yet new,
    with each new experience.
Exploding in rapture.
Tenderly we lie wrapped in
    each others afterglow;
A tangle of bodies still
    connected in mind and body.
A body that seems more one
    than two.

Chuck R. Schussman
SO MANY POEMS

I've lost it.
How many times have I taken
    Your idea
Just to lose it in my thoughts?
So many poems...
    So many hanging.
    Will You ever let me
    finish them?
Give me another chance.
So many poems...
    So many hanging.
    Will I ever let You... ?

Norene Carroll Snider
MY MOTTO

To sacrifice for others,
To give and not receive,
To show that I am honest,
Have sorrow and not grieve,
To read my Bible always,
And follow HIM with zest,
If this be my life's motto,
I'll leave with God the rest.

D. Sue Nelson
UNTITLED

Love is a clique
Of sunset posters,
And sea gull cards;
Painted blue-green forests,
And plaques of dainty
    daisy fields.

There is more to love
Than poor poems,
And soft-colored cards or
Paper flowers in a wine bottle.
It goes deeper.
Kind of like
Passing the sugar
On a rainy morning.

Brenda K. Wallace
COMES THE AUTUMN

Autumn came
    and swept away a summer
made up of dreams;
or so they seem —
those memories I keep.
Oh,
so softly
    so silently
I cling to those dreams
to wander aimlessly;
I find no peace.

Bill Felenchak
REQUIEM FOR MY LOVE

When one of us has Gone
And one of us remains
Life must go on with its
    deep despair
Because dear Love you are
    not there
When one of us has Gone

When one of us has Gone
And one of us Remains
Will bear the crushing sorrows
Thru all the sad remaining
    tomorrows
When one of us has Gone

When one of us has gone
And one of us Remains
I still think of you and sunny
    summer days
When together we laughed in
    our own happy ways
When one of us has Gone

When one of us has Gone
And one of us Remains
My Love you have gone
    from me
But never from my Memories
We always will be together
When one of us has Gone

Matthew F. Creighton
FOR EUGENIA

On a day like today
The memory of you comes
    so easily
There's not much to do
Except stare out the window
At all those umbrellas
Imagining one of them
Shared by us two

It's a day like today
That I would describe
As a blue shade of gray
A big piece of paper
The artist's conception
Of just what it feels like
Missing you
And being in love with you

I can't help it
I'm not sorry
To me this is bliss
Were you with me
I would show you
What a kiss can mean
Especially on a day like today
When all the rest of the world
Seems to get washed away
My eyes too are wet
But I won't regret
If tomorrow
Is a day
Like today

E. Tompkins Miller
THE REDWOOD TREE

I bow before
Your Majesty -
The King of all -
The Redwood Tree.

Eyes lifted
Toward the sky above,
I gaze in awe,
Respect and love.

God made beautiful trees,
It's true,
But He surpassed Himself
With you!

Patricia Hanson
CHRISTMAS ROSE

The one who holds and touches
The Rose,
Inside each petal love unfolds
Prince and princess of flowers,
A seed, then a bud, to a
full bloomed
Rose, seasoned with love.

Our perfect garden of Roses
A symphony celebration,
Gift wrapped in delicate
harmony,
Laced in circles of warmth,

Growing graciously, and
flowering joyfully.
We are all the Christmas Rose,
Our tender, precious hearts
To bud and bloom Eternally.

Johny Guitar
HORSES WITH WINGS

Children of the moon frolic on
the banks of the Sea of
Tranquility,
Selene looks on as a distant
world rises over the bleak
horizon,
Her horses of white dance
through the sky,
A dreamer dreams on, They'll
never be gone,
Who are we, Where are we,
Wherefore, And why,
Why should some live, Why
should some die,
Questions unanswered of life
as it is,
Is the dream mine, or is the
dream his,
Reaching forever for keys
to these things,
Mysterious legends, Horses
with wings,
Dragons and Witches, Tales
of the past,
Deeds that were done, Spells
that were cast,
Pieces of knowledge hidden
on shelves,
Secrets of life they've kept
for themselves,
Some people know, Others
endeavour,
Dreams are for real and life

is forever,
Why should some live, Why
should some die,
Children shall laugh, and
Children shall cry.

Patricia A. Laskey
FORCE

Mt. St. Helens was a slumbering
giant
She waited with death her
spirit defiant
Her fires were ready
Her magma lay still
Ready with gas the air to fill
On one sunlit day, THE
eighteenth of May
She sent her message to
strongly say
"to all ye within my awesome
range"
"the face of this land is going
to change"
"I'll prove it to one"
"I'll prove it to all"
"That natures great force"
"Will now make her call"

Sandra Nunes
CARA

She quietly sleeps in her own
little world,
On her belly, slightly curled.
Sighing and cooing once
in a while,
And when she stirs she seems
to smile.
Then silence is broken by
her cries,
As tiny tears fall from her
eyes.
I pick her up gently, as if
she could break,
And the tiny bundle is
now awake.
She'll tire soon and begin
to yawn,
Back into her dreams before
too long.
And now she sleeps in her
own little world,
On her belly, slightly curled.

Elizabeth S. Nisperos
BALANCE

!
' . *
                #   : ?
am
   was
      will be
         forever, eternity.
Did I make man?
Or did man make me?
I weave the patterns on
   weathers and feathers,
and roses and all those crosses.
Will beauty at your fingertips
   strips the eyes to wonder
the thunder and blunder
   of ugliness and disease?
   of famine and disasters?
the name of the Maker
   starting from the anti-matter
to soul...
      as
the Theory of Relativity sprung
   into a genius' brain,
      is
it the same palsy in another's
   frame?
the dust must trust the thrust
   of the Fiery Mask.

         * # : ?
   ! ' .

Marie Dayian
REFLECTIONS

You died today and a part
of me died with you.
Your life could have been saved
but no-one cared enough
to reach out and rise above
the hurt and the pain
to see beneath the angry words
into each heart
where love struggled bravely
to survive.

Oh, how much I enjoyed you
while you lived;
even tho I took advantage of
you many times.
I tried and tested you to prove
you would be true.
Used and abused you, too,
yet you never turned away,
and were always faithful right
to the very end.
If there was some way to give
life back to you,
you know I would try to
make this possible.
But, that would mean accepting
my part in your death.
How could I ever live with
the knowledge
knowing that I helped you
to die.

Ms. Pauline Beck
WINTER TREES

Winter trees.
   Barren beauty.

Standing stark
   against ash gray skies. . .
      Reaching ever upward. . .

Reminding me
   that
      I'M ALIVE!

Grim, but hopeful,
   symbols of what
      yet awaits me.

The Spring of my life was
beautiful;
   Let my Summer years be
   fruitful
      and my Autumn, colorful.
         Winter brings Death.

A period of rest
   and restoral.

I'll be
   planted in the ground. . .

Spreading through the
Universe. . .
   Reaching Homeward. . .
      Bending in the wind. . .
         GIVING. . .
            yet firm—
            part of a plan.

And, again,
   in the SPRING,
   REBORN! ! !

Janice Ann Eudy
BEYOND ME

How often do you hear
   the sound
this ringing sharp and clear;
That asks you will not tell you
to touch what is not near.

What takes you warm and
   gently
into places far away;
where time has little meaning
and shadows run and play.

Who takes my colors to
   shape them
into light so bright,
Then makes them into sounds
   sounds that

call forever day and night.
Those who hear and follow
may never question how, and
what this is that takes you,
is all of who you are right now.

Annie Johnson
CONTRA VERITAS

is my past or future
any better or worse
for the acceptance
or rejection
of one who is closer to me
than i am to myself? ...

Janet A. Nybakke
NATURE CHANTS

Autumn leaf tapestry
announces
   days of a briefer sun,
as the sky
lowers
to a greying earth.

The vagrant winds
sweep
   and resweep the fields,
whose harvests yields
now mature
in barns.

The energetic soul
of a summer season
   prepares
for winter nestling
in fog, mist, cold,
and shortened days.

The sea grass
crackles
   with the bend of freezing
   winds,
and prints upon the sand
vanish
with the pulse of waves.

Listening——
my anxieties are penetrated,
   and I am
engulfed
by this liturgy
of the earth.

Terry Miskell
SUNBIRD

She whispers as she flies
As she sails across golden
   mountains
Wings of air take her through
   the clouds
Searching distant heights
   lost somewhere

A western wind carries her
   on the air
As she reaches for the
   sun's fire
A spirit untouched by time
Touching the sky where
   none may go

A lost dream of forgotten life
That sleeps within the moon's
   night shine
Who rises to the music
   of the wind
And flies to heaven with
   the sun

A soul unbound by the
   cage of life
Whose dreams give her
   wings to fly
As she lives beyond lost time
She passes from life to
   eternity's door

Denise Flaim
WINTER

Crisp, cold, sun beating
down on blinding whiteness.
Trees bare and lifeless

from without, pulsing within.
Children laughing, playing,
 enjoying themselves.
Building white men, sliding
 down hills.
Skating on lakes in the
 frosty air.
Bundles entering homes
 to defrost.

James E. Overturf
THE OLD HOME PLACE

The old home place looked
 lonely ...
 So I stopped while passing by
"Why, it seems as though it
 was only yesterday
 That laughter could be heard
 from inside.

The old well was still standing,
 Though part of the uprights
 were gone,
The windless wouldn't turn
 too good
 Because it hadn't been used
 for so long.

While standing there alone ...
 thinking
 It seemed as though I could
 still hear mother saying,
"Son, don't go very far,
 And always remember where
 home is no matter where
 you are.

I couldn't help but wonder,
 While standing there alone,
Just where all those happy
 days had gone to
 And had it really been
 that long.

Arlene M. Dedini
LAKESIDE

Rays shimmer on the water.
Sleek fish glide by.

On the hillside, daffodils
 sunburst.
Birds play tag among the
 dogwood blossoms.
In mid-air, dragonflies frolic.

By command of the breeze,
 emerald blades
Dance to the willows' music.

Mighty trees sway, rustling
 Their leaves to frenzy.
Limbs spring to the sun.

Lynda Snyder
BEING IN LOVE

How does it feel to fall
 deeply in Love?
I've never fallin', so I'd
 only imagine...

Scary.....
Like the feeling you get when
 you awake from a bad dream,
With your heart in your throat,
 ready to scream.

Hurt.....
Like your heart just fell,
 like a leaf to the ground,
With someone there ready
 to kick it around.

Sad.....
The way your heart breaks
 at the sight of man's tear,
Yearning and aching to
 hold him near.

Exciting.....
Driving real fast, and with
 lots of good luck,
Like the first time I drove
 my Dad's pick-up truck.

Romantic.....
Soft lights, good music, a
 man by your side,
Your first formal dance
 or a beautiful bride.

Fulfilling.....
The feeling you get when
 you've shouted your loudest,
Or when your Mom said,
 you've made me the proudest.

Clumsy.....
Dangly arms, long legs, no
 head, funny face,
Forgetting everything you
 ever learned about grace.

If these are the feelings of
 Being in Love
Then I am, I am, Yes'ire
 I'm In Love!

William Wyatt Reeves, III
A NEW LIFE

It is a portentous thing
That into this world you
Should bring;
A new human life,
A joy to husband and wife!
May he know natures' God
And may he come to appreciate
His native sod.

Gladys Willoughby Goins
OUR DESTINY

They say brave men never die,
And that they seldom ever cry,
But in this day of pain and
 strife,
We face the awesomeness
 of life.

Volcanoes erupt on the
 mountain dome,
Earth-quakes bury people
 and home,
The drought that spread
 across our land,
Destruction we can't
 understand.

Tragedy man has never
 experienced before,
Predictions that we're
 facing more,
We the proud, the weak,
 the brave,
Relenting as a public slave.

Our spirits are broken,
 dreams immense,
We render them solemnly
 in defense,
With heavy hearts we kneel
 to pray,
In faithful assurance of a
 brighter day.

Mona-Lee Marcotte
**THE SILENCE OF
SPRINGTIME**

Why so silent dear earth,
 to unfold your springtime
 before us?
Why have you lost the radiant
 colors of your blossoms
 and the
glitter of your brook? Your
 birds have all hushed, and
 your
flowers no longer look to
 the sun, but bow their
 heads in silence.
What has dimmed your heart?
 Has the winter layed too
 heavy upon you?
Has your hour of prunning
 gone too deep? Have your
 roots been
torn apart and shaken from

their environment? ·Where.....
 Oh! where
are the first seeds of your
 Father's love? Have you
 let them
suffocate and die before
 trying to give birth?
 Remember........
the Father loves you. Your
 strength and beauty is
 not in the peak
of the bloom, it is in your
 struggle together with Him
 to reach out
of the darkened earth into
 the sunlight. HUSH......and
 listen to the
faint tune by which your
 spirit use to dance. Stretch
 forth your
hand and feel the wetness
 of the dew upon your
 parched soul.
RISE UP.......and dress your
 nakeness in the golden
 and crimson
blossoms of the springtime.
 Roll your emerald velvet
 carpets
beneath our feet. Spread your
 fragrance like swift arrows
 on the
wind into the heart of your
 people, and let us see
 once again that,
"ALL THE EARTH IS FULL
OF GOD'S GLORY".

Shirley Yobe
MY CORNER

This is my corner
This is my space
Don't enter my ring
Don't run in my race

There's another year ahead
I might as well be dead
If I can't handle
My corner of the globe

Maybe next time
I won't waste time
But now, I just have to be
 alone

Give me my time
Let me unwind
So, I can share my
Corner of the globe

Patricia L. Dalton
WEDDING VOW

Today my dreams come true
As I become your wife.
You're all that I have prayed for,
And now you are my life.

Today my love, I give you
My life, my love, and my heart.
Our love will be forever,
Until in death we part.

But even then, my love,
Our love will still shine bright,
For true love is eternal,
As the stars that shine at night.

Katherine Lypp
VESPERS

The pines stand tall
Where mountain streams
Whisper vespers and camp fires
Glow like candles on the altar
Of night; I wonder if
 others pray
As I do that this night will
 never end.
I sit on a moon washed
 boulder
With myself, all myself
 now, and
Find no need for false
 pretenses.
I feel you stand beside me
See your face, bathed in
 moonlight,
Your dark hair and
 strong hands;
Knowing you too see
 this beauty,
Think the same thoughts,
My husband, lover, stranger
Known but never known
 completely.
In moments like this, I
 turn to you,
Reach out to find the
 truth of you.
You leave me, alone and
 empty
Like the mists that leave
 the valley
While I sit here quietly,
 alone.

Flora R. Seal
THE STUDENT

Uninhibited. Free...
to roam the green hills
that slope down to form a
 pure, almost holy, valley.

No strings to bind me to the
 classrooms in which one
must sit and contemplate upon
 matters that are immaterial
to the flower.

The flower blooms.
The blossoms on the trees
begin to fulfill their
predetermined destinies.

And then, "they" come:·
The responsibilities of life
upon which we all are thrust
and then bound with no escape.

Bette Randolph
LOVE WAITS

Please come with me,
My favorite place to be,
Is by the sparkling sea.
While watching wind-blown
 sails glide by,
To blow your love to me.
 Above the clouds, the
 sun dances to and fro,
To let you know our love
 will grow.
Please wait on me, my darling,
Life is sure to let us know,
That love is just a seed to sow,
And time will tell us when to go.

Gloria Wilde
THIS CANDLE

In a shop I saw a candle
Carved with intricate design,
Richly scented, proudly
 boasting
Of it's beauty, rare and fine.

There it stood, all highly
 polished;
Made of wax, so hard and cold,
Hadn't warmed a single person

Since it came forth from it's
mold.

Then I thought, I'm like
that candle -
Made for spreading warmth
and light,
Yet resisting flame and fire
To remain a lovely sight.

ThoughI'm only one small
taper,
Met me Lord, and make me
Thine,
Set my wick to burning
brightly
That for others I might shine!

Change my careless lack
of service,
Help me share and love
and give,
Shining only for my Saviour,
Showing others how to live.

Then, when all my wax
has vanished,
Of my wick - there's not
a thread,
May no one recall this
candle -
But remember warmth
instead!

Dallas Bernard LeBlanc
AN INSTANT IN LIFE

There is an instant in life
when the beacon of
the moment
is an advent.

When the surge of inner
creativity
cannot be denied.

When you can't wait for
the sun to rise
and the morning to
declare itself.

When a flower is not just
a flower,
But a miracle of open fields
and other hillsides.

When the cry of a baby brings
Tears of confidence
Awareness of a new presence.

And you look in-to the eyes
of the old
and know the conscientious
serenity
of the aged.

When facing death is an
annunciation of JOY
instead of a denunciation
of life.

When sleep is a panacea
for the heart
and a morning with a
resurrection.

It is this moment when the
whispering winds
echo
the flame
is worth the candle

And one experiences that

vigorous moment
of extreme exultation
and the purity of love.

Florence Semler Rafter
NICKY

Twas the week before Christmas
When first we met,
And I knew at a glance
He would be my pet.

He was white and fluffy
And soft as silk,
And his whiskers were coated
With droplets of milk.

His eyes were so big
And as yellow as gold,
And his nose like a button
So pink and so cold.

His teeth were like needles
So sharp and so white,
But I knew in a moment
He had learned how to bite.

He gave me one look
Which tugged at my heart,
And I thought to myself
We never will part.

What would I call my new
found friend
What name could I
possibly pick,
But of course, it was
Christmas
What better name
Than that of "Little St. Nick."

Mary E. Assenza
TINY'S QUEST

I was sent by The Lord to
fill a gap
My name is Tiny and I'm
only a cat.
I came before Christmas in
time to be a gift
for a lady that death had
sent a secret heart adrift.
Could I take the place of
one so dear?
Would I be able to bring
some cheer?
Who says that paws can't
hug and pet?
And a furry face can't dry
eyes that are wet?
It took some time to
make her feel
that I was special and I
was real.
But once she knew and
made the connection,
she recognized the
resurrection.
Years have gone by
and still we're together.
And so we shall be
forever and ever!

Ms. Pearl Stratyner
AND THE DAYS PASS

And the days pass
It's almost 3 weeks now
since he left
And the days pass
The friends come and go,
people he could have talked to
And the days pass
The kids cry a little, then
run and play,
And the days pass
My arms reach out at night
and there's no one there
And the days pass
The problems start rushing
in, old, new, big ones
And the days pass.

The soft earth over him hardens
and settles down to stay.
And I take the children and
sadly, slowly walk away.
But the days pass.
And we must go home.
And we must go on.
So the days can pass.

Marianne Duda
NO NEED

I do not need you.
Saying that I need you
would be like saying
that I could not live
without you;
as if my being, my existence,
would be shattered without
your presence.
I do not want you to need me.
In needing me
you would place demands
into my life style
and put expectations
into our relationship.
No, I do not need you . . .
But I want you.

Ann Fassler
ANTIQUE MIRROR

Antique mirror on the wall
has it any face at all?
It glares at me
to see me smile,
or comb my hair
or stare awhile.
It sees me as I truly stand
hiding no fears,
giving no demands.
It sends me light
and a reflection
from past and lonely lands,
in which time had ruled
and gave commands.
    Commanded troops to right
and die,
    Commanded love commanded
lies;
    Reflected in a single glimpse
a world that has past
me since.
It's silver shines
from long ago
polished sand that
through it show,
a mottled world and destiny
in which time
will change so little for me.

Wanda M Reed
COME BE WITH ME
(To my husband with love)

    Come sail with me across
    the sea
    Come be my love forever

Come sail with me o'r
waters blue
Where only love survives
thats true
Come fly with me on wings
up high
Where skies are blue and
GOD is nigh
Where there's always joy
and never fear
Where there's peace and
stillness you can almost hear
Come walk with me across
our land
Where, everywhere, you see
HIS hand
And when our days on earth
are done
We'll walk together the
final one

We'll cross dark valleys where
shadows are long
And as we go we'll sing
a song
Of earth and skies, of wind
and rain
But in holding GOD's hand
never fear again
COME, Be with me

Susan P. Glodas
A GENTLE MOMENT

I saw You walking along the
beach yesterday.
I could sense Your warm
gentleness as You knelt
to a small boy
crying.
I thought, I wish it were me.
At that moment You helped
him to his feet and softly
brushed the
sand from his eyes.
You smiled at him and
continued on Your way.
I followed close behind for
awhile longer and thought,
could You
ever love me?
Suddenly You turned around
and saw me there,
So lonely and empty.
You walked up and gently
held my hand.
With eyes of love You looked
at me and said, I understand.
Together we walked for
several more miles.
Suddenly again my life
seemed worthwhile.
We stopped to watch some
children on the beach
Again You looked at me with
those eyes of love and said,
I understand.
I thought for a moment and
began to cry.
You kissed me, then said
good-bye.

Evelyn M. Swinamer
A WEDDING DAY PRAYER

To take the trip of marriage
Two must pay the fare
Two must work to make
it last
Two must give and share.

Two must learn to say
"I'm Sorry"
Two must learn to listen
Two must learn to keep
the flame
Within your hearts to glisten.

To-day as you exchange
your vows
And wear the marriage ring
May you take with you forever
All the joys that life can bring.

Elaine Steele
**SEQUEL TO TERROR,
ll-8-79**

each throb
distorts my body .

no corner
absorbs an inch of me .

those eyes -
gleaming whites, reds,
and yellows -
squeeze my being
into endless spasms of
shrieks -
until they see
no more
of me .

Judy Meddock Everhart
WHEN MA-MA DIED

When Ma-Ma died I blamed
Jesus
Then I took a better look
I read about life after death
In the Great Book
I read how people who
suffer will
suffer no more
How Jesus doesn't distinguish
between
the rich or poor
How he doesn't take you
home until
the time is right and how
everyone
should be ready should
he come in
the night
I understand now she
isn't suffering,
worrying, crying, or bored,
she's happier
than she's ever been living
with our Lord

Varian D. Schmokel
INQUISITION

—'And what is Truth?' asked
Pilate narrowly.

Oh, let me read your writhing
lips. Can it be an angled
laser-gaze,
eye to shriven eye, teeth
bared, reducing me to
tailings of glassy shard?

—'Excellent! Now for a
harder one: tell me what
Love consists of?'

A moment. Yes, I must think.
The folded, spindled,
mutilated spirit,
imprinted with the ruts and
scorings of the footed Gross,
borne inch by
fiery inch across a mackerel
desert toward inaccessible
Gethsemane?
Or better still, a maze of
thicketed briars saluting me
with thorny menace,
scalding, stinging, wounding,
each laceration a honeyed
word
masking a tiny milestone
between thirst and greater
thirst?

Let go, Pilate. I'd rather
Truth. It's easier to bear.

Wm. Patrick Riley
PLAYMATE OF
NOTHINGNESS

Running—yet stark and still,
Existing—yet cold and nil.
Waiting—just for Fate to say,
"Come, my boy, today's
your day."
Yes, I'm a playmate of
nothingness.

Walking by the beckoning sea—
yet failing even to wade in.
Denying ears and heart its
roaring rhapsody.
Playing puppet on a string.
Hiding in the throng's dull echo,
dull ring.
Yes, I'm a playmate of
nothingness.

Stalling long on the fringe
of wilderness—
yet fooling myself.
I know life's worth my best.

But rooted to the earth
with fear
Of courage and compassion
calling me near.
Yes, I'm a playmate of
nothingness.

Ken Stone
RAINY DAY WITH SNOW

Listen carefully
and
you might hear
leaves
welcoming the rain.
Autumn day:
bringer of
cool tingles.
An
uplifting tonic.
A
promise
of now
by
afternoon.

Laura Armstrong
PIECES

The sands of time
make sand castles in our mind.
The door is barricaded with
past fears.
Salty tears fill a dungeon
of despair,
but a torch of joy guides us
through the dark halls.
Pieces of people reach out
from yesterday
and are held in the grasp
of an ageless moment.
Distant is near,
Death aroused;
Aged new....
     a place
     an experience
     a lover
     a friend.
Though the waves of time
carry them away,
the sand remains.

John P. DeBonis
THE KISS

Even though it was
Cloudy and misty
The sun shined for me
When you kissed me.

For the fragrance of your
enchanting kiss
Lingered on and on my lips.
Even after you had left me
Left me standing their alone.

Leaving me in a heavenly
monumental bliss
After you kissed me.

Margaret M. Wilkins
FRUSTRATION

Meow! Meow!
My little kitty cat
Yearning for this and
mostly that.
O, my ball of yellow fluff
What's got your dander up?
Kitty cat, kitty cat,
Go take THE PILL
An' get off that darn
window sill.
SCAT! CAT!

Allison Rosenberg
GUMMY (MY HAMSTER)

The teddy-bear hamster
that I knew
Was Gumdrop oh that
little Shmoo!
He jibber-jabbered through
his cage

And never was in a sudden
rage.
But the day I came home
from Malibu Beach
His poor food bowl he
could not reach.
Oh his cute and little head
GUMMY! GUMMY! was
he dead?
Yes he was, poor little Shmoo,
Now I need a Gumdrop II.
And oh that day I'll always
remember,
That terrible, terrible day
in November.

Mona Bottari
SURFSIGNS

Trailing down the beach,
in cool soft sand....
          our footprints
     Pity
They only show us where
we've been
They cannot tell us where
we're going

Paul R. Reece
WHEN WINTER HAS
IT'S CHILL

love has left some winter
snows
broken hearts have left
their fears
i often was the one to know
and so i've shed some tears.

lovers are so hard to leave
memories, so hard to get
i have my share of souvenirs
some pain, a few regrets.

the wind blows cold upon
the road
and leaves fall where
they will
still love is found beneath
the snow
when winter has it's chill.

Susan Fay Whelchel
ACCEPTANCE

Unfettered now of cloying
youth,
I find myself in counterpoint
to eyes more kind
and hands made hard from
sweat of prayer.

You are the silver smiling rain.
and I the purring of the storm,
settled in to watch you play.

William D. Green
BIRTH OF SPRING

O'Winter—Winter where do
you go?
with your blanket of white
and dark days lo.
I know where you impart to—
you go North for the Summer.
And on your last breath the
Joys of
Spring are born.

John P. Trueman
DARKNESS

Darkness;
Lets me escape from all
my fears
And weep in silence my
lonely tears,
From all that's torn at
me through the years.
Darkness;
Is where I run to hide
From all that bothers me
deep inside,

And to unknown spirits
pretend to confide.
Darkness;
Is where I search my mind,
Answers and reasons I
try to find,
All unpleasantries I
leave behind.

I curl in the corner of a
darkened room,
I can breathe at night but
the days spell gloom,
Because darkness offers the
only cure, you see,
The warmth and comfort
of obscurity.

Erik Flowers
SWEETHEARTS

Sweet wheat sway above
they lay as at the hearth and
rolling they waive, each
like the wheat
sweet in heat, and warm
Hear hearts serene, careen,
and here
tears secrete, secret for each
Then eye to eye and eye to
eye the moment stops.
Somewhere below wheat golden
they are sweethearts

Chris M. Bye
STRIPPING

As I strip you down
     Dear Christmas tree
I can relate to you.
     Each bulb I take off
Is as part of me
     That has been darkened.
With all the memories from you
     That I pack here in this box,
I wish some of mine too
     Could be packed away
And not trampled on
     By whoever so chooses.

Then when I have all
     The glitter and glare off
Your branches,
     I see how much better
You are that way.
     Stronger and able to breathe,
And how I pray
     I could fee the same.

Annette P. Grocholski
I'LL WIN

You were always there.
when I turned my head
But will you still be there,
if I turn the other way instead?

You always made me happy,
and sunny on rainy days;
but will you still do that
if I decide to change my ways?

We've been through so
much together,
we lived through thick and thin;
I may not have been so sure
of myself,
but with you as a friend, I
know I'll Win!

J. D. Hackett
BLUSHERING

Your rose
Bloomed like a smile
Into my fallen heart
And I revived like spring
From winter's depression
You stood there
Like a mountain to my soul
And I blushed
The color of each and every
petal

Janice Kay Light
MY GARDEN

God has given me a garden
  of precious
flowers so rare and in this
  little gar-
den arose among many weeds there.

He has given many tools with
  which I must
work to give each flower,
  the life it
seeks while it grows upon
  this earth.

Some weeds are sorrow,
  some are despair,
others are timorous, and
  each are in my
care.

Fear, hate, malice, and
  lots of mass
despair, which would choke
  out the ten-
der flowers if Jesus
  didn't share...

His love and mercy and
  promises, hidden
there, are the tools which
  He gives me,
to weed with care.

All the flowers in the garden
  are not
the same you see, for each
  is unique and
must be treated differently.

So as I work the garden
  for the world
to see, I am the tool He
  uses to set the
flowers free.

Jacqueline D. Erickson
DISCARDED HIGHWAY

Old highways
  crumbled and broken
  expose memories
  of past generations.

Weeds grow in cracks
  giving renewed life to the land
decayed posts guard
  a finale to its memory.

Animals scurry across
  while ants make their home
  comfortable in the
  warmth of an asphalt roof.

Discarded run for a dead coyote
  remembered for history
  spoken in the wheels hum of
  yesteryear.

Marjorie Moon
I WAS CLIMBING A LADDER

I was climbing a ladder,
Reaching for the sky.
I was looking for something.
Then along you came
And offered me some
  freshly baked
  fortune cookies on a tray.
I reached down to take
  your kind offer
And meanwhile fell.

Nina W. Likens
REMEMBER

Let Me Remember
The holy cross.
When I am there
I am not lost.

Let Me Remember
Those pierced hand's.
That are scarred
Because of man.

Let Me Remember

That crown of thorn's.
And Mary
Who deeply mourned.

Let Me Remember
Gethsemane.
And my Jesus
Who died for me.

Helen Irene Daniels
FAUCETS

I stand in my kitchen
Looking at a dripping faucet
Waiting for the sun to rise
Even the faucet
Is more than it's leaks
It can be turned on
Full force
Will I know as much?

Kathie Lavoie
A BIRTHDAY NOTE

I was born
  in love with you
Your warmth and energy
  were all I knew
Long before you
  knew it was true
To make all of me
  it took all of you
Through patience and time
  our energies grew
Such a short time
  and so much to do
You produced and directed
  I waited for cue
Through one
  now is two
And now at twenty four
  life is still new
Mom, with all of me
  I thank you.

Carol A. Gallo
**BILL REEVES,
SCIENTOLOGIST**

Ancient Chinese philosopher
Who once did sit by river's
  bend—
A mind at rest,
Oh, timeless quest!
You tried to give, but could
  not lend.

Now no more a river's bend,
Now no more a broken flower,
But sit you in an Ivory Tower
And free from tears the lives
  you mend.

Beyond all test,
A mind at rest—
You are now new wisdom
  blessed
To do the work your love
  doest best.

DeNisa Owens
THE GLORY OLE FLAG

The Glory Ole Flag,
  for a many she stands.

She lasted through,
  all our hardships and wars.

She lived through,
  our rejoicing and happiness.

She Proudly and Loyally,
  Stood for one and all.

The Glory Ole Flag,
What's the rewards she receives?

Some don't even bother to
  put her up,
to fly with the wind.

Groups demonstrate rights,
and burn her.

What does it Prove?
What does it Show?

Others leave her to lie
  in darkness,

and let her touch the ground.
Teachers remove her,
Children no longer pledge
  her mornings.

Why take it out on her?
We are the ones who turned,
America into what remaines.
But yet she's still loyal.

You put her up and watch,
She'll fly like never before!
Why let her down?
Why put her in disgrace?
She Stands,
for You and Me..........

Nyla Rae
MEMORIES

The day has faded,
  darkness folds her arms
  around me.
I feel warmth from the
  glowing moon;
  I will not cry.
In silence I remember;
  You are gone.
But the memories remain
  Like a treasure, buried deep,
that only I can find.
  No one can take them away.

Joni M. Brady
THROUGH A TEARS EYES

I never know why
I'm called upon
I come up
Through your eye
And then I'm gone
Over a lash
Down your cheek
As I'm leaving
I feel so weak
Why must you
Rid of me?
Why must I go?
As I'm fading away
Can you please
Let me know?
It's too late now
I can't be kept
Who would of thought
I'd die when you wept.

Sherry E. Cravens
PAINT CHIPPED CHILD

The creeping germ
The sordid world
The dirty streets
and paint chipped child

The picture bleak
I look for light
to bring forth life

Nothing grows
but restless me

I push and prod
and try to force
what will not be

Then close my eyes
To hide the dark
The pain of those
who will not see

A. M. Linsenbigler
MY HAPPINESS

My happiness is to see your
  bright smile,
The twinkle in your eyes,
  to hear your sweet voice.
To watch your graceful
  movements as you walk
Through field and forest
  by stream and sea,
Demurely studying the plants
  and animals that you see.

My happiness is to hear your
  quick wit, and gaiety
When you are happy with
  some new discovery.
To help you learn of things
  that are of interest to you,
And to be with you in your
  times of need.

To see your beauty when at
  rest or active in all
That you do, these things
  bring me my contentment
And happiness with life itself.

Joseph Szpila
STATUE

the stilleto's bent belief
the pistol's mindless
  blue barrel
the aimless wheel of
  drunkeness
the tendoned fist of passion
poverty's anxious fingertips
the blade's cool hone
the sword's ceremonious
  descent
the atom's obedient burst
the belly's blameless swell

they bury their waste beneath
  speechless waves.
they plow into the land with
  metal monsters
where the grass will soon
  grow greenest.
they set their craftsmen
  to work,
set their stone-cutters to work,
chiseling saints from blocks
  of blind marble.

Denise G. Beck
THE TREE

While wandering through the
  park one day,
I noticed a tree, so tall to say.
In a funny way it reminded me
Of the way my life used to be.

So strong and straight and
  tall and proud
Not too soft but not too loud,
Happy, courageous, healthy,
  and pure,
Now of my future I'm not
  so sure.

For now these bars keep
  nature from me
And all I can say is, "I want
  to be free."
Now life is precious but not
  so much so
As to waste it in chains where
  one cannot grow.

Z. M. Coleman
HE IS ALL I NEED

i found a friend
his name is Jesus
He is all i need
My Jesus saves
and He lives for ever
He is all i need

i got to him
When im heavy laden
Jesus will lift up

My heavy burden
Jesus will give us
free salvation
He save my soul
And my sins forgiven
Jesus knows when
the storm clouds roll
He will guide
and protect our souls
i found a friend
and his name is Jesus
He is all i need

Jeffrey H. Adler
**TO DAMIEN, THE SEA
AND LORI**

Upon the night stands
Damien alone,
he faces north as Lori
runs southward.
Apart, they think of all
the other owns,
two broken glass worlds
of scarlet and swords.

Like Gemini, the two grow
closer now,
awaiting symphonic rapture
from the stars
as night and the waves
recede unrenowned,
and a mist covered morning
imparts.

Together they stand on a
stony ledge
Watching the breakers in
high-tide fury,
A gull gliding over the
water's edge
Was awed when the crackling
sandstone scurried.

The gull flew back where
Damien was strewn
as Lori threw her necklace
towards the moon.

J. Elwood Braithwaite, Jr.
WORDS WHISPERED SOFTLY

words whispered softly in
the basement
as we walk quickly away
from life
never pausing to think,
care, or
believe our dreams, much
less theirs.

Michael Rennie Peterson
THE UNIVERSE

the universe
hidden in
the depths of
my mind
wandering through
undiscovered channels
of the imagination
leaving trails behind
prisms of knowlege
then drifting on
and finally coming
to an inside-out
conclusion:
i am not the
only fool striving
for wisdom

Edna Junemann
ISLE OF WONDER

I

Mystical island,
Ever green,
Star of the ocean,
Neptune's queen

II

Garden of love
Embracing all,

Bells of peace
Tolling His call

III

I sail at dawn
To this wondrous land
In the sea of soul,
Heaven at hand.

Nicholas P. Caputo
MUSIC TO HIS EARS

Tho yesterdays heart beats
are but echos
    In space—waste not one
    today,
Use todays wisely, and
tomorrows beats
    Are sure to carry a smile
    to your face.
For He is ever listening,
and your smile,
    Is his response, to the
    sound of a
Happy heart.

Marene Clark Mattern
UNTITLED (HAIKU)

Sleeping together,
The cat and I;
    Soft tremors

Christy J. Abbott
RAIN WALKING

Water softness
    speckled rain
gutters overflowing
    of the dead leaves
and I like walking
    barefoot
gooshy mud, toes squishing
    refracted puddle reflection
worm-smell
    damp earth temporarily
    cleansed
passing cars spraying
    emphatically.
rain walking
    puddle jumping
        home.

Jeanette Lambert
OUR SHINING STAR

A star above is shining bright
Upon us all this special night
There seems to be a special
    glow
Which warms the hearts of
    all below
Angels sing in a Heavenly
    choir
Who all are happy and
    never tire
Our tiny angel smiles
    contentedly
With all his love unrelentingly
Sadness will be shared by
    all of us
You will miss all the hustle
    and fuss
The twinkling stars light
    up the skies
Like sparkling diamonds in
    your eyes
As we gaze up to Heaven
    tonight
We'll be blessed to see the
    light
That sparkles as you watch
    us tonight.

Marilyn
A FREE TIME

It was a time of longing for
    days long passed
Of a restlessness too close
    to understand
A yearning for things that
    are beautiful

A searching for answers to
    questions not even
    understood.
It was a time of flight through
    imagination to another time
    and place.

Frank Rose
**DEAR LORD I'D LIKE
TO THANK YOU**

Dear Lord I'd Like To Thank
    You for each day that
    passes by
The roses in the valley and the
    mountain tops so high
For every little bluebird as
    he sings his song to you
Dear Lord I'd Like To Thank
    You and I know he thanks
    you too
Dear Lord I'd Like To Thank
    You for the sunshine and
    the rain
The promise that comes after
    is a golden crop of grain
And for that precious moment
    when you thought that I
    was worth
Dear Lord I'd Like To Thank
    You for this mortal here
    on earth
Dear Lord I'd Like To Thank
    You for my little bungalow
It nestles in the woodland
    where a tiny river flows
The laughter of the children
    seems to set my heart aglow
Dear Lord I'd Like To Thank
    You cause I thought you'd
    like to know
Dear Lord I'd Like To Thank
    You but there's one thing
    I would ask
If I should leave this big wide
    world would you complete
    my task
Just keep my family free from
    want they live with purity
Dear Lord I'd Like To Thank
    You and I place my trust
    in thee

Mark W. Zilkoski
CELEBRATE

People dancing on their roofs
    climbing
        up and down
            the garden trestles
    and hanging loosely from
        the rain drains
            bordering the ledge
        tightly holding hands in
        a circle
            skipping round and round
What a day it was today
And
They just thought
They'd
    Celebrate

Tony Bryant
THERE STANDS MY LOVE

There stands my love
    in the shade of a tree.
My love stands there,
    she longs for me.
She holds a scrapbook
    from which she reads
Of what I've done,
    heroic deeds.

There stands my love
    serenely dressed
She holds my picture
    to her breast.
Tears stream down cheekbones,

then they fall
'Neath mighty oak,
    so big and tall.

There stands my love
    in open view.
She has great beauty,
    possessed by few.
The breeze flows gently
    through her hair.
She whispers softly,
    "it isn't fair."

There stands my love,
    she stands alone.
Gone is the lover
    she has known.
His body lies 'neath
    old oak tree.
She knows his soul
    has been set free.

She shall stand by me
    again someday
In another place,
    so far away.

Joseph E. Szalay
WRITER'S CREDO

The ritual about which you will
    you will ...
well ... should ... no, must be
religious to give unto me
not days of daily bread
but bliss with reality wed
is a simple, simply this:
        Write!
Write you lazy bastard, write!

    O subconscious schemer,
    Quixotic blasphemer,
    Walter Mitty-eyed dreamer
    of the ever-fragmentary,
    redeem and make whole
        yourself
        and your dream.

Brenda Kay Nichols
WHOSE?

Whose eyes do you use
Today when you will see
All the hate, untrust, and tears
That will always be?

Whose heart will feel today
A Love that need no kiss
To show the way of truth
To those who'll miss?

Whose words do you speak
    today
And argue them in vain
To hide all you feel for now
The searing, cutting pain?

Whose life will you live today
When you life isn't right?
And whose thoughts will
    you think
When you lay awake tonight?

D. R. Sledge
SUNDAYS

I love Sundays in bed
Lettin' the week settle
    in my head
Reading sections of the
    New York Times
And lettin' nothing occupy
    my mind
Curling up and eating crackers
Easy smiles and easy laughter
Warm relaxation and the
    Sunday news
I love Sundays in bed...
And you

Paul L. Rosengren
EMPHASIS

Words are superfluous in the
    arms of love
And guilt just melts away.
There's so much more to love

than words could ever say.
A kiss, a hug, a certain look
it communicates so true
What words could say
a hundred
times and justice never do.

C. L. Levesque
ARTIST

An artist I'd love to be,
Oh! How I'd love to see what
the artist can see.

The skies so blue,
The mornings so new.

The sun so bright,
The high noons, the
warm nights,
The birds, their beauty,
their flight.

An artist I'd love to be,
I want to see what the
artist can see.

A frown on a solemn face,
A dark and erry place.

A child's innocent smile,
Running and skipping all
the while.

The strong and the weak,
The brave, and the meek.

The love in a woman's face,
So gentle as she says the
evening grace.

The colors, the way they
join together,
The brights, the darks,
whatever.

The swirls, and the curls,
The red of ruby, the glow
of pearls.

How they do it?
God only knows.

Dorothy D. Robinson
PINE LAKE

Back to thy cool green hills
I wend my way,
As all things homing go at
close of day.
Thy pines, that tower 'gainst
the evening sky,
The last late birds that,
ling'ring, nestward fly;
Thy calm and placid waters
where you hold
The mirrored splendor of
the sunset's gold;
Along thy shore, soft light
that gleams
From cottage windows
bright with dreams;
A winding road across a hill,
Where shadows fall, serene
and still
Beneath the trees, and
wild things roam;
A step or two, and I am home.
From these, like soothing hand
that brings surcease
To fevered brow, my spirit
gains thy peace.

Barbara Kohler
CHRISTINA'S FLUTE

Such a flight of melody,
perhaps echoes songlets
From that first shepherd's
pipe...
When, to his astonished
delight, the hollow reed
set the lonely
mountain dancing with
his music, as if with
sunlight....
Elusive as beams glancing

off a raindrop
Pristine...Tremulous...
utterly joyous....
This enchantment will not
fade irretrievably into
ether....
But will float in the labyrinth
of the heart, listening here
in the mauve twilight.

Vicky A. Farino
DRUGS

Take these and you'll feel fine,
But don't complain if you
can't walk a line.
You can get them if the
price is right,
And they make you see
an awful sight.
We know they make you
feel great,
And cause you to forget
the date.
With these you can be
pronounced dead,
That's right my friend,
I said dead.
If they make you feel
great at the time,
Don't think of what you're
doing commiting a crime.
So, if your afraid of bugs,
Take my advice and stay
away from drugs.

Sherry Leigh Crane
MEMORIES

I'LL remember all the
special days.
I'LL remember her co
concerning ways.
I'LL remember all the
kindness that she gave,
and all the happiness that
was made.
I'LL remember all the good
times, that we shared,
and the loving she gave me,
showed she cared.
I wish you were still here
with me.
But I have my memories
for now, you see.

Connie Ratliff
THE CROSS SPEAKS

"I am the rugged, blood-
stained Cross
That was made from a
stately tree
I had to stand still and
say nothing
The day they nailed
Christ to me !
I held Him till He
finally died
Then, I had a prayer
to lift
Thanking God for
The Sacrifice
Of His Son to the world
as a gift !

Vivian L. Abbott
A POEM FOR AN ARTIST

When you write a poem for me
Paint a picture I can see
Not words, strung like the
lovely pearls you wear.
They must unfurl as the petals
of a rose, with care.
Show me the myriad colors of
the sunset glow
Perhaps the silhouette of a
spreading Elm tree
Against the flow of ribbons
of light

across the sky
All the hues of the rainbow
arching high.
That is the picture you
paint for me
When you write a poem
I can see.

Richard Bliemegger
ON LOVE

Mysterious and forward.
Uncompromising.
Engulfs your every all.
Reflective, rewarding, ecstatic,
As lovers know too well.

Wrings tears of joy,
And anguish;
That swells your very heart,
Intense in all its feelings,
True love can never part.

To care, compromise,
Console;
To swear would never end.
Would love.......as life,
To do it all again.

Mildred Thomas
UNCLE SAM'S SATELLITES

Watching space spectaculars,
Gazing skyward mesmerized.
Those who use binoculars
Stand like they were paralyzed.

Brother, this I must admit:
Mute I stand but want to say,
Do enjoy this well. For it
You will pay and pay and pay.

Teresa L. Jameson
A-NEW-TOMORROW

Finally you have passed me by,
With your hopes and your fears,
Your truths and your lies,
Your laughter and your tears.

You meant mistakes-
To me, this is true,
Watching each step we take,
In all that we do.

I'll try very hard,
Each day that I live,
No grudges to hold,
And quick to forgive.

I'll take your thoughts
and your meaning,
Your joy and your sorrow,
And I'll end up dreaming
Of a-new-tomorrow.

E. Lynn Mackessy
PROCLAMATION

Nobody here gets out alive,
Many have tried in vain.
Nobody here gets out alive,
Your passage ecstacy or pain.
The room is filled with
many doors,
The choice is up to you.
And when you choose - you'll
just find more,
More doors you must
pass through.

Restless thoughts slice the
stillness,
Static chaos fills the air,
Silent voices speak so loud,
I hear someone who isn't
there.
Windows lined up like tin
soldiers,
Through one you must peer.
The armoured tank is set
in motion,
Shift it into gear.
Peering through and drawing
back,
Afraid to look again,
Go on and choose a different
past,
A better might have been.

Mary R. Ingram
A TASTE OF SCHIZ

In bellowing silence,
the black sun rose.
The no-thing,
touched by rays of darkness,
cast upon the earth a
shadow of light.
Reality crumbles in a heap
of absurdity
. . . and only the madman
knows the difference.

Roque Rosales
MERRY CHRISTMAS,
AMIGOS

'Tis the night before Christmas
And all through the casa
Not a creature is stirring,
Caramba, que pasa?
The stockings are hanging
Con mucho cuidado
In hopes that St. Nicholas
Will feel obligado
To leave a few cosas qui
and alli
For Chico y Chica (and
something for mi).
Los ninos are snuggled
All safe in their camas
(Some in camisas and some
in pajamas).
Their little cabezas
Are full of good things
Todos esperan que Santa
will bring.
But Santa is down at the
corner saloon
(Muy borracho since
mid-afternoon);
And Mama is sitting beside
la ventana
Shining her rolling pin
para manana,
When Santa will come en
un manner extrano
Lit up like the Star on the
mountain cantando
Y Mama lo manda to bed
with a right!
Merry Christmas a todos y
a todos good-night!

Raquel V. Griffin
GOD SMILED DOWN
UPON ME

God smiled down upon me,
When friendship came my way;
He brought you into my life,
And I'll thank him every day.

Yes, He smiled down upon me,
And filled my skies with blue;
He blessed me with His love,
When He sent me you.

Yes, God smiled down upon me,
When He sent you my way;
Your friendship I will cherish,
Each and every day.

Gail L. Wright
THEME OF TIME

Tomorrow is coming
And yesterday's past,
But today is the day
That won't seem to last.

Today - seen tomorrow
To be yesterday,
Must be lived by each moment
Those of wisdom all say.

My! Time is a strange thing
Each person receives,
Moves on so quickly
And can't be retrieved.

So today if you're sorry
That yesterday's gone,
You'll ruin the present
To which we all belong.

Hermine Wilber
THE BELLY DANCER

A maiden dancing in the street
Golden coins tossed to her feet
Eager her limbs tremble
All the movements of life
they resemble
The past, the present, the future
The sorrow, the joy, the
happiness
Fair she would be - with
time's speed
ahead
The "Belly Dancer".
"Queen of Egypt"

Liz Ann Hartman
UNTITLED

When lights are out
I'm by myself,
Alone throughout the night.
I wish for things I cannot have;
For all beyond my sight.
It almost seems I have these
things,
So real my dreams become
I have much riches and do
great deeds
For all and not for some.
But when daybreak comes
my life is back
As cold as to entomb
Though some would cry
but not so I
I'm queen at next full moon.

Praxcedes Gonzales
RETREAT

When skies are awesome,
dark and gray
And clouds obscure that
hopeful ray;
When no-one seems to see
or care
And hope turns into deep
despair;
When nothing seems to
fill or cure
The emptiness you must
endure;
Retreat somewhere into
your heart

Search there for things
that hope impart,
You'll find some kind
word said to you,
Some faith to change a
dark sky's hue,
You'll find there, neatly,
on a shelf
Some happy mem'ries of
yourself,
Remains and ruins of
things once new,
Perhaps, a tarnished love
or two,
You'll find the beam that
lit the way
When dark prevailed another
day.
And, then behind you lock
the door,
Emerge from that secluded
place
With courage, dignity
and grace.

H. N. Guttromson
OVERDRAWN

Darling—
Inside this purse is my
seed of love—
May money not be our
troubles—
All gold in the world—
melted down
Wouldn't be as warm a
feeling to me
As your lips pressed in mine—
And you—in my embrace.
Dad.

Valerie D. Richards
DREAMS

When I dream about the
future, and
reflect upon the past,
I always sit and wonder if
a "True Love"
ever lasts.
The answer comes out
different each time
I think it through,
And sometimes I even end
up with special
thoughts of you.
It started out so innocent,
and somehow
grew and grew,
And now there's not a day
that goes, with-
out a thought of you.
I don't know how to say
it, but I hope
you'll understand,
I need to have you by
my side, to walk
with hand in hand.

Nancy D. Plaster
THE TIME WE CARED

The birds sang the night
we kissed
a song of love, the love
we missed.
What could have been, I
wish I knew
now you're gone, what
do I do.
In my life you held a place
of special thoughts, of
love and grace.
We shared moments that
will always be
precious in the sight of me.
I see you there and now
I know

we cannot love, we cannot
grow,
but because of this time
we shared,
please don't forget the
time we cared.

Marie Kristiansen
WINTER AND THE TREES

Trees standing starkly grey
and bare
shivering in the crisp
wintry air
stripped by winters
chilling arts
silently submitting their
trembling hearts

The royal oak and the
quaking aspen
both humbled by natures
annual fashion
in faith drop their leaves
of red and gold
thus is repeated the theme
as of old

The pine trees branches are
laden with snow
there she softly cradles it
til the winds blow
the ash and the alder and
the maple tree
have shed their covering
simultaneously

Cruel though winter may
truly be
none stands forth braver
than the cedar tree
the wind bends their heads
in prayer to god
they thank him for good
footing that wonderful sod

Carol Gawronski
IF ONLY

"If only, if only"
All the people say.
"If only, if only"
Forever and a day.
"If only we were happy,
If only we were glad."
But we are not usually happy,
And most of the time are sad.
"If only, if only"
Means dreams and wishes.
Wishes of happiness,
And dreams of lost kisses.
But reality waits, like death,
in the wings,
While stupid man his song
of "if only" sings.

Gloria Ann Condrey Myers
SHARING

We share our food,
a humble bite,
And share our love with
all our might;
We share the good news
and the bad,
And share our fights when
we are mad.
We share the green grass
on the hill,
And share the sounds of
the old grist mill;
We share the sun, the snow
and the rain,
And share the agony of
one's pain.
We share the freedom and
liberties all,
And share the crises, large
or small;
We share the boasting and
bragging of wealth,
And share the daily good
tidings of health;

We share in rejoicing of
worldly acclaim,
But we share not ever,
our part of the blame.

Maria Fenesy
LISTEN

Listen to me,
I am sad and lonely,
I want to express to you only.
My heart and soul is being
poured out,
Take the time to feel my
love and pain,
So I may be whole again.
Try to understand me and
not use yourself as a wall,
Because my love I want
you all.

Shirley J. Lauritsen
THE AGONIES OF MAN

Every man, in his own time,
has tasted life's bitter, and
all-sweet wine.
Upon his own tongue, tasted
salty tears,
has encountered, and fought,
his own countless fears.
He's felt the anguish of death,
of life and his dreams,
the heartbreak of love, when
it is not all, that it seems.
Only to account, for his
sins, evermore,
as he trudges through this
life, unto death's awaiting
door.

Hazel Parker O'Brien
THE COLOR OF REASON

There has never been a time
when I could close my mind
to wondering
About what life holds in store
about what lies beyond
the door
closed to me
Is it there in front of me
did I egress to fast to
really see
by design or fortuity
I know not the truth of
my fallacy
nor where to direct my query
I stay resigned
To stroke the brush subtly,
'til I find
the color of reason
adrift in my mind.

Michelle Ferrado
STEADFAST

The waves of time have carried
us thru each of our changing
seasons.
Yesterday's hidden tragedies
are tomorrow's incentives.
Today is the essence of
our lives.
Now is the time to hold what is
dear;
Remember that love is an echo
we all need to hear.

Donna Lee Branch
FIRST LOVE

In the cold world of reality
first loves rarely last,
First loves usually become
a beautiful memory;
That never dies, but lives
in our minds' past.

From the moments of that
first meeting to shy to
hardly speak,
Eventually warm touching

hands and a look into each
other's eyes;
Seeing love grow more, week
after week.
The rememberance of that
first magical kiss,
To the first soft spoken words,
I love you;
Fall gently upon the ear like
ocean mist.
Feelings shared for the first
time that some of us
never forget,
Thoughts that love really
is endless;
Along with visions of lovers
without regrets, makeup
first love.

Wesley W. Rees
**STATISTICS SHOW MORE
BABIES**

The implication of occupational
propinquity,
Or being in the vicinquity of
one of the opposite gender,
Is that love on a bus or in a
doctor's office
Or in the executive suite of an
industrial mogul
Can lead to kisses not conjugal,
but tender.
From a recent survey came the
information
That the whole nation is
suffering from the effects
Of this form of togetherness,
and the whetherness
Is: Does propinquity lead to
sinquity,
Or do one and one make sex?

Renee Lawrence
**SOMEWHERE THERE IS
SOMEONE**

Somewhere there is someone
I know one day i'll love
A person filled with kindness
Sent from God above
Somewhere there is someone
To share my whole life through
I hope that i have found him
My loved one is you
Somewhere there is someone
I'll find him i know that is true
To help me face each day
And make sure i am loved too
Somewhere there is someone
I'll find him i know its true
The one person that i will love
That person i hope is you

Wendy Bietz
LIFE IS GRAND

Nature and earth are sharing
their
Inside secret of happiness.
Trees bow, whispering "Life
is Grand"
Digger squirrels glance up
and wink.
The whirling earth slows
While I gaze into the green,
breathe beauty, excitement!
You cover my world, a soft
touch of snow.
I fall past your hold, into you.
A butterfly in a cacoon
A bee in a flower!

Glenna A. Morgan Rollins
JULIE BEEKLE BUG

I was but four, too young to
understand
Why my baby sister lay there,
red rose tucked in her hand.

I wanted to caress her, and kiss
her lightly on the cheek,
But Father said I shouldn't. Oh
why did he look so bleak?
The tears were streaming down
his face, the other's just as well.
Mother wasn't crying that much,
but her expression looked
more frail.
I asked her if she'd hold me,
and bounce me on her knee.
It was then she started crying
and asked me with a plea.
"Please try to understand dear,
that she's only just alseep?
For in your heart she'll always
live, for life is just belief.
And if you'll go into the room
that's filled with flowers and
chairs,
And walk slowly down the little
isle, I'm sure you'll find her
there.
Whisper, Julie Beekle Bug wake
up; then she'll open her eyes."
So I did as I was told, but it
only brought more cries.
I seen that she was pale and
cold, and really needed a hug,
But they wouldn't let me hold
her, My Julie Beekle Bug.
I was but four, too young to
understand,
But now it's fourteen years later,
and I still remember her hand,
And how I used to hold it,
when she lay in her crib so
snug.
I loved her so, and I love her
now, My Julie Beekle Bug.

Gaynell A. Howe
MISSING YOU

I could see your smiles
In the darkest night
And I'd walk miles
To hold you tight
I miss so much
Your warm embrace
I long to touch
Your smiling face
When you come home
Away we will fly
There are roads to roam
And our love to try....

Sandra L. Morgan
MIND OF WORDS

The words that within me lie
So deep in thought, I have
to try
To write these wonderous
words I know
So others like me will want
to grow.
I have no fancy things to write
No words of wisdom or
of might
Only a way to keep my mind
So clear and peaceful, I
do find.
So I write these words, as I do
If only for me to read them
through
There not the greatest things
I'll see
But at least they were written
down by me.

Georgene D. Ames
MY RAINBOW OF COLORS

My Rainbow of colors
Are blended so true,
I'm near black, yellow, red
And pretty white too.

My rainbow of colors
Make the flesh of our land
We live side by side
As Woman and man.
My rainbow of colors
Mold a perfect blue sky,
With yellow and orange
When the sunset goes by.
My rainbow of colors
On a blue ocean wave,
Has white caps so sparkling
To pure to fade.
My rainbow of colors
The earth on the ground,
With trees of distinction
That turn green, yellow
& brown.
My rainbow of colors
Include red, white and blue,
The flag of our nation
United States, I love you.

Trudy E. Knowles
OUTSIDE ALONE

Its 4:00 am
and birds call
on highwires
to the wake
of sunrise,
and seagulls
await low tides
uncovering
edible grubs
and I,
I build mansion
with buckets of sand.

Rose Marie Griffy
TEARDROP

I
am
one
you
think
comes when
you are low,
in pain, in sor-
row, in love, or
full of joy. I trick-
le in when you least
expect me and slide
down your face to
be part of your
feelings.

*Judith Ann Vaughan -
Rick Clark*
THE BOOK

I reached for a little book that
I found in my
daughters car.
I didn't know what the book
was; until I picked it
up and brushed away the dust,
that had covered the
Holy Title.
The Book that I held in my
hand was her misplaced Bible.
I am glad for her; not for
placing it there.
But because it is her possession.
She bound her soul to her
Father;
in the days of her youth.
through these pages she has
found the truth.
Although she is not reading
it now.
Our Father then heard her vow.
Before I place it back into
the nook;
I opened the pages of her Book.
The Scripture I read was from
the Book of Romans:
She had underlined in ink.

"For I am not ashamed
of the Gospel of Christ"
So I will take this Book; that
I hold in my hand,
and try to remove the dust,
and place it back where I
found it.

James Butler
I CAN DO

Those three little words, I can
do,
Ring out loud for the very few,
It's in your soul, my soul too,
The way to know and the what
to do.
Just hang on, for your life hang
on,
One more step and you may
have won,
When the answer is no and the
going gets tough,
Now is the time to show them
our stuff.
I know we battle with life each
day
And when sometimes we get
through, we receive our pay,
That glorious feeling wells up
from within
Is the force that compels us to
do good again.
On such an evening when I
retire
I lay there quiet, with my heart
on fire,
And my body feels like it's
chilled to the touch,
I know this feeling can never be
enough.
One day maybe, it will be very
soon,
My whole life will change to a
different tune,
And I will be able to write for
a crowd,
Then my words will be spoken
out loud.

Rosemarie Raychel
A ROSE IS A ROSE

One can see the blooming
fullness of the Rose,
the delicate touch, the
lovely fragrance.
One can almost taste its
sweetness,
and hear the busy bees
gathering its honey,
like the nectar of the fruit
of life;
GODS creation!

Linda Bergman Vollmer
QUESTIONS 1-3

Who can explain the chemistry
of corrections?
Is it life's delicate, yet
deliberate plan?
Are factors of life so imperfect
than an inexplicable force

intervenes?
Defying accepted reason
 and purpose,
Making this, life,
 Strive for the pinnacle
Of perfection in all living things.

Rena Grassi Baldrica
MY LOVE:

I will not despair
 When you fly-away—away,
My heart with you take
 To keep safe my love, everyday.
Your love I will hold
 Until you return,
Then dispel all reason
 For me to yearn.

A silent thought
 I will send each night,
Sealed in a star
 For you to catch
As it flies high on a cloud
 Through the air,
A kiss on top I place
 With three words,

 "I love you"
My dear, look well, sir,
 The words are there,
For you and I
 Forever, to share.

Helen R. Wulfert
GOD'S LITTLE MIRACLES

It's a beautiful world we live in
If we take the time to look,
The little things are miracles—
Like the babbling of a brook.
The budding flowers of
 springtime,
The leaves of trees, so green,
Small children playing merrily—
Yes, all this can be seen.
It's a beautiful world we live in,
A gift from God, above;
Yes, all God's little miracles
Assure us of His love!

Paul L. Long
**I THOUGHT WE HAD A
DREAM**

I am not prepared for the things
 I
 see on T.V.
Black children murdered in the
 South
 The KKK running free.
Social injustice, the poverty of
 starving Americans
Little countries holding hostages
 and war at hand.
I though we had a dream of
 Peace
 in the 60's
Now peace in America is
 something
 we can't even achieve.
We are killing our fellow man
 and
 binding the wounds with red
 tape.
Instead of my generation

spawning love,
 we propogate hate.

Maria Mastras
ANTICIPATION

Afternoon storm hides among
 daffodils
And flutters beneath a brocade
 sky,
Cloud-swollen and toned with
 liquid silver.
Prouder than to spill its message
 in
Rain-dropped letters on the
 dusty pavement
Or to leave earthworms
 squirming wet
Upon the speckled driveway
 gravel,
It hovers, still, bathing the hour
 in grey
Anticipation of the gift
 withheld.

Billie Jo Coleman
**SEARCHING - LOOKING -
REACHING**

I've searched the world,
 For happiness and joy . . .
I've looked in cities,
 In small towns and the
 country . . .
I've even reached into my mind,
 Still searching and looking . . .
I went looking for someone,
 Searching for anyone,
 Reaching for something . . .
I found you and there's no need
 To go on searching,
 No desire to go on looking . . .
I only want to go on
 Reaching out to you . . . .

Ann Filinger Neel
A PRAYER

Nothing, nowhere tells you
 how to suffer
with grace, full grace.
 The Bible?
Well, it's all right
 with ordinary problems—
love, death, and sorrow.
 But where to go
when real things hit?
 The world is prepared
for love, death, and sorrow
 but not reality.
Real reality. Losing, lost?
 Can't stay lost.
One rotates on the compass
 to where it stands
on you and ingenuity.
 God help ingenuity!
Or if God is weak
 ingenuity help God.
 Amen.

T. Zoe Stanard
REACH UP, WOMAN

I am the farmer's wife,
The other half of the Udder
 End.
He toils in the fields, he browns
 in the sun—
His bronze is like my hair, his
 sunlight my smile.
Those tall rows of corn are but
 a glimpse of my stature,
Tall, slender, reaching for the
 heavens.
My strength pushes him onward
 like seeds push through the
 ground
To grow into magnificent plants.
My love nourishes like the warm
 spring rain,
Bringing life to all who feel it.

I am the mother, the stepmother,
Who will change all fairy-tale
 notions about wickedness.
My compassion exceeds all
 motherly love,
Even Mother Nature stands in
 awe.
When the time comes for me to
 leave this world behind,
I will take my place in the
 heavens
To live and love there, with my
 stars beside me.

Jean Love
SONG

Sometimes a melody so
 perfectly
Expressing love, and joy, and
 sadness,
Stirs my heart, my soul, my
 being,
But cannot find a way of
 singing.
And, thus, no sound will break
 the silence
That lies between us without
 ending,
Unless the Muse can take my
 longing
And make it song, to sing to
 you.

Tonya R. Zalenski
**SOMETIMES I THINK YOU
LOVE ME**

Sometimes I think you really
 love me.
And sometimes I think you
 really despise me.
Sometimes you're really funny,
and full of love for me.
 And sometimes you're serious,
and full of hatred and cruelty.
Sometimes you can be sitting
 right next to me,
and still be so far, far away.
 But after all the times I have
 spent with you,
The good and the bad.
 The sweet and the cruel
 honesty.
Knowing your bright spots,
and your dark ones.
 Knowing what to say when
 you're in a good mood,
and knowing what not to say
 when you're in a bad one.
And although you don't tell
 me that you love me,
I know you do.
 I can see it in your eyes.
No, you won't ever have to
 tell me,
'Cause I know you do.
 And I love you too.
 I will forever & ever . . . .

Dora Marshall Marvin
THE SILVER CORD

Thirty pieces of silver! the price
 of a man?
Thirty pieces of silver . . . a
 part of God's plan . . .
His plan of redemption . . . the
 gift of His Son . . .
Christ willingly dying that the
 world might be won.

Thirty pieces of silver! and what
 will you give
In the service of Him by whose
 death you may live?
Will you give of your talents,
 your money, your time,
Thirty pieces of silver? or all
 that is thine?

Bob Kubitz
I HIKED A FOREST TRAIL

I hiked a forest trail
 as slow as a snail
 looking to see
what nature had for me

 I saw a deer
 standing real near
 he ran away
 he wouldn't stay

 I saw a bear
 right over there
 just walking along
 he was soon gone

 I sat by a stream
 to let my mind dream
the wind touched the leaves
with a soft and warm breeze

 Along came a fox
 at a slow east trot
 he looked right at me
wondering who I could be

 Up in the sky
 an eagle soared by
 just floating on air
without ever a care

 It came time to go
but my heart did know
 at peace was my mind
serenity I did find

Alexander F. John
FLIGHT OF THE UNKNOWN

Plot a course to the distant
 corners of the world,
Cross the sparkling blue,
 tranquil seas;
Crush the barriers that lie
 before you silently,
But don't lose hope;
Keep your golden, electrified
 eyes toward the future.

Come with high spirits—glide
 with the westwinds,
Spread your golden wings
 across the cloudless skies;
Grip your iron claws into the
 highest mountains,
Fly high, don't let the sky be
 your limit,
Because beyond this crystal
 land,
Lay an unoccupied domain of
 scattered planets.

Streak through the sky breaking
 the cloud barrier,
Treat your dreams as if ultimate
 instances,
Glide and be free—let the wind
 lift your soul,
Roll like thunder, strike like
 lightning,
Because beyond this city of
 illusion,
Lies an unoccupied world of
 fantasy and gold.

Paul C. Smith
A BUG'S PICNIC

We sat munching at one
 bird-crusted table,
Crunching six-leggers nibbled
 at the feast,
The mustard splurted my wife
 Mabel,
But bogged a beetle, at least.
Buzzers plunged into our pink
 lemonade,
Hoppers played on top the
 bread,
I smashed a stinkbug, for the
 odor he made,
And we departed, for our guests,
 we did dread.

Margaret Walker
WOMANKIND

Mothers gently wipe tears from
the face of the earth
They humbly minister to our
needs from birth.

Mothers are the foundation of
our society
Knowing what's best has
brought them notoriety.

The loving steadfast
commitments of Mothers
Nourish and foster the becoming
of others.

It is sweetness that should be
worn outside
Gentlemen, elevate your brides.

It is woman who holds in the
palm of her hand
Qualities that can bring peace
throughout the land.

She's a messenger of
understanding life and love
A very special agent sent from
above.

Give her a throne worthy to sit
upon
For without her all hope would
be gone.

I certainly hope the force that
is with us
Is at least half matronly instead
of all chivalrous.

Michelle Lee Wilson
ONE PERSON

One person . . .
Simple on the outside, yet
inside very complex.
There are so many masks
to hide behind, too many
moods to slip into, but
with much love and
understanding, one person
can unfold and be set
free, like a butterfly
from it's cocoon . . . .

Rick Schroedel
LIFE

Life holds many questions.
Yours is not to know all
answers.
Just to understand the questions
is enough.
Life is its own answer.

William W. Elliott
**GLOBAL THEATRE
UNIVERSE**

God spins the earth and like a
puppet show
The animated creatures move
and talk.
The vaulted ceiling of the
heavens glow
By day and night, and teeming
millions walk

Upon Life's stage. The curtains
and the props
Are set for drama. Act one,
scene one, begins.
The orchestration of the
prelude stops:
The cue for all mankind to
vaunt his sins,

His virtues, pride, religious zeal
and zest
In glorious panarama and
parade.
Time marks, records, and gives
awards for best
Performances; and "stars" are

born and made.
The vast global theatre Universe
Features Life's dramas, real
and unrehearsed.

Virginia Riddick
GROWING UP

Back then was just a Dream
Cast among the long, cool
grasses:
Hidden from the summer's heat.

Beside a field of corn,
Growing tiresome with weeds;
A mere patch of green.

Joan E. Polk
WHEN SHE WAS YOUNG

When she was young
She went to Rome for the wine,
To Japan for the sound of wind
chimes,
To Switzerland for the moon's
glow,
To Alaska for the silent snow,
To Hawaii for the seashells,
To France for the cathedral's
bells,
Now she goes to the mountains
For the echo.

Lyla Lanier
STILL IN LOVE

Fall leaves,
Blowing off in a
storm,
Chase each other
In the wind,
Like we did
When we were
young.

Even the rain,
Painting them onto
the ground,
Won't keep them still
forever.

Just as
time,
Stealing away our youth,
Won't keep us from
chasing
dreams.

Even if it's just
In each other's eyes.

Jeffrey Kenton Harris
LET'S OPEN THE DOOR

Acting on my own
I know there's more to be
known
I don't see the light
Cause I need a lantern at night
Even in crowded places
I still see wide open spaces
We need to communicate
It's the only way to educate
Don't live for your peers
As they look in their mirrors
What we see is distorted
Cause it's all being hoarded
In the back of our minds
Wasting many new possible
finds
Let's open the door
At the new department store
Let's start a chain
It won't be in vain.

Nancy Frederick
MARY

watches the late show
reads love poems
day-dreams

uses Loving Care
massages her wrinkled thighs
smiles at hitchhikers

packed her over-nite case once
unpacked it the same hour
smiles while her husband
dances with a young blond
and
asks for chocolate mocha pie

W. L. (Bill) Warner
EIGHTEEN

At last—finally—you are
"Eighteen"
You have waited so long.
Now it's here—*How Beautiful.*
Always look ahead, with hope.
May your dreams come true.
Be sure and enjoy God's
nature.
The change of seasons—
The sun, moon so bright.
Stars neatly arranged in the
heavens.
Always see the beauty of
nature.
The grass, trees—colorful
flowers—
Beautiful birds, squirrels,
animals.
Love them all—*Really Care.*
Be aware of the balance God
provided
Notice the clouds—feel the
warm
Breeze on your face.
Walk in the rain—*think, feel.*
How beautiful life is—*Always*
Give it your very best.
Keep your values *High—Very
High.*
Always give more than you
take.
Remember—you are now
"Eighteen"
May God Bless You—Now
and Always.

Melanie Kappler
COLLECTION

As others run
to and fro
collecting collectables,
I
with pen in hand
collect words.

Dave Ryan
PLAYWRIGHT

The man sat waiting for the
show.

the Sun dipped cautiously
into the salty waters
dragging his fiery robe along
behind
the waves lightly fingered the
taciturn sand
and whispered softly as each
miniture wave retreated
soon He slunk almost all the
way under
enjoying his swim in the
orange water
the waves held their breath
while He slowly submerged
and the velvet curtain
closed above him

The man was not disappointed,
And he left the beach
With a smile.

Donna Marie Hagan
LITTLE CHILDREN

Little children are like sunrays
they brighten the world in many
ways.

When we tuck them in bed at
night
those tiny faces; a beautiful

sight.
See the smiles and hear the
giggles
and watch a child as he wiggles.

Little children do just anything
make up a dance and can even
sing.

They have a world of their very
own
a special toy or a kite they've
flown.

Things they do whether simple
or wild
see nothing more precious than
a child.

I wish that the world could
always be
as happy as a small child of
three.

Marilyn L. Brown
CASTLE OF SAND

Pail and shovel—the task at hand
I build my castle out of sand
Golden gate over shallow moat
Thwarted sail of vacant boat
Strong winds urge the angry sea
A crashing wave—the evil deed
Mighty fortress is no more
Chateau of sand is part of shore

Nancy Rose Blank
A LIFETIME OF SEASONS

Springtime . . .
I am a child,
fresh and strong and filled with
smiles.

Summer . . .
I'm a growing girl,
filled with questions about the
world.

Autumn . . .
The woman has arrived.
She shows the world she can
survive.

Winter . . .
I am old and gray.
All my questions are answered,
and Eternity is just a season
away.

Miss Becky DeLay
GENERAL

Proud stands the sinewy body
Cold gray hooves planted deep
in the trembling earth
Nostrils flare throwing fiery
blasts of breath into
the blue night air.
Staunch muscles ripple in his
fluent neck
His ribboned chest thrust
forward like a shield
His steely eye surveys the barren
plains
Darkness shrouds his world like
a flag
He waits . . .

John Desautels
IN TIME

In time
there is a life;
In that life, there is time:
A time of happiness, joy,
laughter;
A time of sadness, grief, and
sorrow.
But memories—
life is a memory.
And when that memory seems
to end
it continues forever,
for all time;

69

always loved.
For one must believe
Memories will always have time
during that life
to say in one's heart:
I love you.

Kenneth G. Geisert
TWO LIVES

She was fragile and old
He was youthful and bold
Her skin translucent and her
gait a trifle weak
His boyishness so evident led
one to believe him meek
They met by chance one
bright sunny day
Each traversing a path their
own special way
He asked her directions to
some certain place
She was aglow with the charm
of his young face
His next move was lethal as
the knife he held in salute
Her gaze was unbelieving,
miming a deaf mute
Her shopping interrupted for
a gift for her grandson
His life just beginning, never
to witness another sun
She now rests peacefully in
a crepe-covered bed
While he tosses angrily with
guilt inscribed upon his head
Her day was well-spent doing
a good deed
His just the opposite, filled
with greed.

Janet Salyers
THE ESKIMO

The Eskimo sits alone in the
cold
and watched the young,
for he is old.
The Eskimo smiles while they
go by,
No smile hello,
No wave goodbye.
The Eskimo journeys into the
town,
But no one cares,
No one is around.
The Eskimo prays to God above,
and silently asks, "Where is the
love?"

Diane Gonzáles
RELATIONS

I have relatives all across the
USA,
Most I've never seen, but what
can I say.
They have their lives and I have
mine;
We'll probably never meet,
because we think we don't
have time.
It is sad when we don't keep
track of our family,
But that's how people in this
world have turned out to be.
And when a relative dies we
have no concern,
Because of their lives we did
not learn.

Richard A. Solis
STILL I'M GLAD

Though I'm sad still I'm glad
For Queca loved me for a while,
She was mine, for too short
a time,
Oh how she made me smile
I love her so, she makes

me glow
With the love she felt for me.
Yes I can tell, that I fell
in love so endlessly.
Her eyes, her lips, her
fingertips,
Were made in heaven's mold
Her hair, her toes, her
funny nose,
To me are solid gold.
I love her still, I always will,
I love her more each day.
At night I die, alone I cry
Since she took her love away
I want her back, my skies
are black
Great emptiness I feel
For though she's gone, my
love lives on,
A love so true and real
It's still true, that I do
love Queca till I die
We had fun, were close as one
Before she said goodbye
Yes, she was mine, for too
short a time
Queca loved me for a while
And though I'm sad, still
I'm glad
For thoughts of Queca, will
always make me smile

Edith M. Morgan
ENDURE

Captious Challenge
Futile Fight,
Strangled Struggle,
Desperate Despair
Endurance Ends.

David C. White
THE GENIE

Aladdin rubbed his magic lamp,
A genie then appeared.
He said, "Three wishes you
shall get."
And then he disappeared.
Aladdin paced from here to
there;
His wishes he began.
He looked directly at the lamp
And saw "Made in Japan."

P. L. Bedortha
I TALK ABOUT FOREVER

I talk about forever,
But do I really know what
it means?
Can I even distinguish the time
forever is said to be?
Can I explain to you how
I feel
when I say I love you...
and mean forever?
Could you really understand?
Do you think you could ever
find it in yourself to say...
I love you.
And really truly mean it?
To say, you understand, feeling
the same as I.
And talk about forever?

Stephen T. Latour
TIME SO SMALL

Love ... Such an elusive thing;
How the change in tide and
time
with intervals between the
rhyme
of waves upon the shoreline
of its ever changing ways.
Is it the wind within the sails
that will draw
each ship to the isles of

awareness within our souls . . .
Where echoes in the harbors
move to take flight atip
the wings of gulls . . . . And is it
not that same wind
which will wind to full storm,
to shake the hulls
of even the most stable of
vessels into a submissive
voyage, that will end only when
the seas turn again
to clear and calm.

To Look at love . . .
The morning glories open their
eyes to the dawning
of the light, only to close them
to the glare of
mid day; to reopen them with
the pass of every day,
in beauty and delight of times
so small.

BenjiMarie Durocher
CARELESS

Why do the birds sing,
Because the song is careless.
Then why should the world cry,
Because we are careless.

Leah-Anne Martin
SAILING SHIPS

Our ships will pass but maybe
once,
So let us love at this time,
Let us not change our mind.

Let us love one more time,
But if we don't we'll remember
when,
Our ships passed through that
tunnel of time,
That love was all that was in
our minds.

Rita Purcell
SUNRISE

Sunrise.
The birth of the day
succeeding the death of the
night.
Bringing
new hopes, new joys,
new life.
Another day to live,
to work. Another challenge
to meet.
I
thank you God, for this
new day,
for this sunrise.

R. E. Nolan
**TO SHARON ON HER
BIRTHDAY**

Maychild, born with flowers
Of cool and verdant sylvan
bowers;
'Midst pink and white arbutus
trailing
(Whose beauty next to yours
is paling);
Child, whose spirit is bound
To Ephemeroptera dancing
'round;
Dear lovely girl of the Spring,
To whom the young cicadas
sing—
Be happy ever, never sad;
Accept this wish of a loving
Dad

Betty A. Clark
GIFT OF NOW

We're all so very overpaid—
Don't you think it's a little
bit weird?
Yet, we awake each day—To
another day—

And all those things we
feared—
We never live today TODAY—
We're usually one day late—
A dollar short With a guilty
feeling—
And yet—we sit and wait—
Wait for what? Except a What
Or, when—or why—or how—
Instead of living the present—
And, enjoying the Gift of Now

Valerie Parsley
THE FINALE

So much pain, so soon.
But with one last burst
of power,
She soars upward,
Her hair caressing the stars,
Fingers reaching out to
grasp the hands
Of those who wish to follow.
Her heart is pulsing,
Straining until it must
surely burst,
But still she presses on.
As the fire turns to embers,
She slows, stops, and then
starts to fall.
She floats down past the stars
Like a feather,
This time without pain.
She settles on the ground
so softly
That she appears never
To touch it.
The crowds come to their feet,
Cheering wildly,
Shouting for an encore.
Only an unfortunate few
Notice how still she is,
And they slowly turn their
heads
And softly weep.

Donald Lashley
UNREVEALED

mosaic bridges cross the canals
weaving and intertwining
through rising stretching panels
reaching into the lining
rushing and running secret
channels
finding an opening for their
winding

hidden under bushes and brush
rapidly spreading wetness
wanders
through tunnels in a hastening
hush
while quietness ponders
the broken emptiness to push
a stranded signal or sound

the search begins into the
flooded night
for the lost and unknown
quivering and huddled
from sight
reached and was thrown
deceiving pursuit in the height
of where the black ravens
have flown

Howard A. Miller
THIS OLD WORLD

What's a matter with the world,
what's a matter with the world
With the way of This Old
World...gone mad
Day after day makes you feel
kinda bad
Makes you feel kinda sad
This Old World is gone and
forgotten in it's own way
Everyday I cry alittle, I sigh
alittle

And no matter what I do
Yes.....No matter what I say
There's no changing you...
No rearranging you
There's just no pleasing you
There's just no pleasing you
No matter what I say I still
love you all the way...
Everyday I cry alittle. I die
alittle. I sigh alittle.

Do we have the time to play
The way things are today!
It's just not the same no more...
There's less joy than before
Flowers no longer bloom
like before
And the sun never shines
All the promises that you gave
just lay shattered
on the ground...
Everyday I cry alittle...I die
alittle...I sigh alittle...

David Michael Evans
THE WILL

When you're feeling broken
down
Don't let it get around.
Just call on me,
and I will comfort thee.

When you feel you're
all alone
just pick up the phone.
I will be your clown,
and pick you up off the ground.

No, I'm not just trying
to flirt.
I know how much you hurt.
I just want you to feel good,
the way I know you could.

When you feel you cannot
cope
I'll be there to offer hope.
All I want is a smile!
And a chance to stand trial.

And when you're finally
feeling right,
the stars will all shine bright.
And that's what makes me feel,
Girl, you give me the will!
All I want you to know
is, I love you so!

Susan McKelvey Johnson
I'M DEATH

Death holds no modest inquest
for the secrets of my life.
She eats my breakfast for me,
Butters her toast with my
own knife,
And then she jeers and
taunts me,
As she dresses in my best,
So do not be deceived,
my friend,
I am not me, I'm Death.

Linda Gramm
TO MY LOVER

My eyelids are settling
into their
last position of the day.
The clock in my head
yearns to be
at rest.
Sweet Dreams!
But how can I sleep when
my heart's
desire is to commune with thee?
I arise to find you already
listening.
You aroused me!
Sometimes, as now, you
are so close I

long to put my arms around
you so I know
you really are there.
Instead, you ever so
tenderly, enfold
me into your arms.
How much better!
One word proclaimed would
utterly
turn my doubting around.
You remind me of your
voice in the
claps of thunder, the mighty
waves, and
the laughing waterfall.
Your power is real!
Everything in my world
is so tangible
I surely would enjoy a glimpse
of your face.
You assure me you are
fairer than the
lily, more breathtaking than
the sunset, and
brighter than the morning star.
What splendor!
I have tasted of your
goodness and
mercy.
I'll follow wherever you lead.
What a more excellent way!
Loving by faith.

Vickie Wilson
GIVE THANKS AMERICA!

America a proud nation we
should be,
Many countries are not free.
Americans don't complain,
We don't have to be ashamed.
We can go wherever we please,
We can worship God without
fear of being seized.
We can lift our eyes to the
red, white, and blue,
America this gives us reason
for thanks-
all year through.

Irene Maria Collins
FURRY LITTLE BANDIT

As I sit in the forest I
suddenly see,
a brown, furry creature coming
toward me.
An interesting fellow with
small pointed nose;
his eyes are jet black—to his
ears it goes.
He waddles toward me and I
see his black mask;
his eyes—shining lights—to
walk seems a task.
Nearer he comes to sniff
at my hand;
he eats the cookie 'cause
sweets are his friend.
He sniffs and sniffs, then grabs
with his paws;
they're soft to the touch,
'cause he's drawn in his claws.
He goes back to his home—oh,
must we end it?
But I'll remember him—that
little "Bandit".

Mabel Sutton
LOOK INTO THE SUN

Look into the sun
And there you will find
A blinding bright warmth
Such as would define
The love of a friend,
To whom we're inclined
Our love to extend.
Look into a friend

And there you will find
A bright warming light,
And if the light blind
The heart can forgive
The small and unkind,
And friendship will live.

Douglas Stanton Brown
SYMBOL

The tear drop is the symbol
of sadness
and happiness and of the onion.
The handshake is the
symbol of
peace, trust and the buying
of a FIAT.
The smile is the symbol
of happiness,
thanks, and of course the
"mug shot".
The kiss is the symbol of love,
thank-you, thanks for the flower.
The wink of the eye is
the symbol
of suggestion, goddamn your
sexy and
always a grain of dirt in
your eye.
The eyes are the symbol
to see the
colorful and alive world, to
see a dirty
movie and to see your blind
date. But
of course you wish you were
blind after seeing your blind
date.
The ear is the symbol to
hear those
wonderful sounds of nature,
to hear a
police cruiser upon your back,
and of course
to hear your blind date giggle
in the
background.
The symbol is the symbol
of life and
happy times. Always remember
to give your
friend the symbol to get the
hell away from "your blind
date".

Wanda L. Price
**A TOAST - TO THOSE
WHO DARE**

To those who dare
To see the truth
When there is comfort in a lie.
To those who dare
To speak the truth
When their friends all
pass then by.
To those who dare
To live the truth
When in so doing - they
stand alone.
To those who dare
To give the truth
When it seems all hope
is gone.
To those who dare
To defend the truth
When there are obstacles
everywhere.
To those who dare
To commend the truth
To those who dare - - - - -
- - - -To Care - - - -

Joan L. Goodman
FLATWARE

Two spoons lie
not quite perfectly fitting;
but resting in the drawer
balanced in the dark.

One wears the nicks and
scratches of daily use,
and bends to fit its companions.
The other is newer
not yet tarnished
or scratched
or bent;
it reflects the older spoon
back into itself
shining
when there is light.

Kim Heestand
IN LIFE TO ME

In Life To Me, you should be
learning, experiencing,
yet keep control.
You should compete and
be determined,
You should fulfill every moment
good or bad,
Because when you stop to
think about it
Its a once in a lifetime chance.

Marie Lilly
THE OLD WALNUT TREE

Once we owned a walnut tree
That grew so big and tall
You ought to have seen
the walnuts
We gathered in the fall

We picked them up when
they fell
And hulled them one by one
We put them in the cakes
we made
And candy just for fun

But then we took a notion
As crazy as could be
So without thinking it over
We cut down that old tree

We made wood from all
the limbs
And stacked it all in cords
Then we hauled the log to
the mill
And sawed it up in boards

We had a bedroom suite made
Of the boards from that tree
And how very proud we
were then
The neighbors came to see

But we miss the walnut cakes
And all the candy too
Its so bare where the tree
once stood
It makes my heart feel blue

Now I'm not near as happy
As I'm trying to act
I'd gladly give that bedroom
suite
Just to have that old tree back

Christal Jones
**GIVE TO ME LIFE,
DEAR MOTHER**

Give to me, loving care
For without it,
I may not grow
A child needs warmth
and security
In which to set forth her roots
A child needs time to create
To give a child an open world
In which to find her inner self
Among the millions of souls
That battle within her
Is the greatest gift
One may give
And to she who gives this
To she who grants to this
child life
The child shall owe her
entire being
Yet, a mother will settle

for love
For a child is ignorant of
the debt
And can give no more
Than mere love

-Loy Combs Guy
AN OLD RELIC

In the farthest corner
Of the shed out back,
Minus - the pipe
One leg intact.

With dignity lost
By decay and rust,
A catch-all for junk
All covered with dust.

Just an old relic
'Twas thought to be,
May shortly become
A necessity.

The steps of time...
I shall retrace...
And move it to,
It's rightful place.

Back to the kitchen
In a cozy nook,
On the old wood stove
Again I'll cook.

I will make it a shining
And cheerful thing,
Then listen to my
Teakettle sing.

Georgia Radcliffe
MORNING-GLORIES

Looking backward into time
I see
Morning-glories on a wall,
Blue and purple
Climbing skyward
Wrapping carefully
Lest their fabrications fall.
I ponder precision in the way
The tendrils would always wind
From left to right,
Weaving their way
So tenaciously
Though delicately designed.
Nature's splendid spirit
manifests
The direction in her plan
To edify
Without a word
And thus stimulate
The alchemic mind of man.

Patricia Anne Harmon
THIRD CHRISTMAS

In Jennifer the Christmas
love has come,
unfolding day by day and
wrapped with smiles.
Her Santa lives on doors,
and television,
In shops of decorated windows
white.
She understands this Christmas,
trees of lights
and tinsel. Presents ribboned
blue and red.
She gives her gifts of pleasing,
touching hugs.
Delight is contagious, enjoyed
and shared.
This Christmas morning comes
too soon,
as time will fade to memory,
becoming part
of stories told and photographs
in books
for family and Christmas
yet unknown.
This Christmas comes with
special meaning now.
For Jenny Dawn her love is
gift enough.

Wilma Jean McCowan
PRAY FOR THE CHILDREN

People of Zion pray for your
children, and their
children down through
the ages.
A modern world after all
isn't so grand-
Tears of reprisal and cries of
anguish vibrate
throughout your great halls
There is sickness and hunger
over your vast land.
Faultshood abounds within
your streets,
as fear stalks your temples
Oh what hidden dangers
awaits man...
Almighty God for many people,
is only a wording
token the Ancients
left behind.
People of Zion pray for your
children, and their
children down through
the ages.
For the end of the ages is at
hand and there is
work still undone...

Phyllis A. Aperans
MEMORIES

There are times past
that we best forget.
The hurts, the stings,
of the butterfly net.
The gossamer wings
and colors so bold,
Seek to enthrall us,
With memories to hold.
Butterflies die - oh yes
that's true,
but what of the human -
what about you?
Will you be entrapped
With memories of old?
Or throw away the net,
and dare to behold!

Claudean Sanchez
DIM FUTURE

We are born in pain and
scream with anger.
And we struggle to stand up
on two feet.
Then off we go to school and
learn not to be a fool.
Living in this world is not
a treat.
We will learn the ABC's to
read and write with.
To learn the things we need to
know, we do our best.
Teacher makes the rules, as
she tries to teach us fools.
Yet, what we're learning really
puts her to the test.
There is grass and speed and
it's addiction.
And the violence in the schools
go untamed.
Listen close, all you guys,
better open up your eyes.
For your future, you are
alone to blame.

Ronald A. Fegley
YE MUST BE BORN AGAIN

Ye must be born again,
yet must be born again
Ye must be born again,
to see the kingdom of God
Ye must be born again,
of water and of the Spirit

Ye must be born again,
to enter the kingdom of God
Ye must be born again,
marvel not at this wonder
Ye must be born again,
the Holy Spirit beckons thee
Ye must be born again,
come accept the gracious offer
Ye must be born again,
to enter your heavenly home.

Zella Justina Black Patterson
THE SEASONS

Winter is slowly fading,
Its work will soon be done;
Then spring will bring us
showers,
Sunshine and flowers;
Roses will bloom in the bowers,
And birdies will sing in the
trees;
The earth will be covered
With a blanket of green,
And the brooklet will trickle
Into a stream.
Then after the task of a spring
Is performed;
The days will change from
Pleasant to warm;
Summer heat will gradually
increase,
Until it will be impossible
to find peace;
When the task of summer
is complete,
Vegetation will be scorched
Under our feet.
Then comes autumn with its
magic wand—
Within a few days th'earth will
turn brown;
Th'leaves gradually change
from brown to red.
And fall into their winter bed.
Th'earth will be dead, the
birds have fled
To the southland until
spring returns.
When winter returns,
The trees are all bare;
Stripped of their clothing
By autumn's cool air;
Winter brings on the ice
and snow,
And the cold north wind
Sweeps from shore to shore;
This tells the story
Of all the seasons;
People like all for various
reasons.

Faith M. Spinosa
FRIENDSHIP

If by chance you think you see
a teardrop in my eye,
and with faultering voice you
hear me try,
to tell you, dear friend goodby,
think not that I am filled
with sorrow.
My tearstained cheek belies

my sad tomorrow.
From treasured memories of
friendship past I'll borrow.
Until, like the flickering and
dimming candle glow,
Softly stealing through my
aging mind, faintly, slow,
the lifelike image of a friend
I used to know.
My thoughts ever reflecting,
pretending you're still here.
Now vividly dancing through
the dewdron veil, a tear
for you my friend, not so near,
but ever, ever so dear.
With an endearing embrace
before you go,
to feel the warmth of human
love aglow;
could I but tell you, my friend,
I love you so.

P. G. Colon, Jr.
BELOVED

Rough and troubled times
we've seen
and many days we were
not sure.
When we look at where
we've been
we know our love will
still endure.
Others think, as they grow
older
a love like ours will just
grow cold.
Instead it keeps on getting
bolder
as you and I grow old.
Beloved, I just want to say,
for God in heaven had
ordained it,
The love we have will not
decay,
without our knowing we
attained it.
When in Him we learned
to rest,
we knew He'd given us
His best.

Liz Craig
NOW THAT'S MATURITY!

the last time I saw him
I was just sixteen—
six rapturous months
down the tubes in six
short minutes.

now I think:
maybe it was better, we were
too serious,
the age difference (5 years
after all),
the...er...INTEREST difference;
but then,
you couldn't have reasoned
with me.
(my heart still ruled my brain,
and broken hearts take time
to mend again.)
I remember summer Sundays
rainsoaked beaches
lost in the lightness of love.
I thought I wanted to marry him.
(picture me presiding over
women's groups;
wondering if the manse will
last another year;
pouring tea for deacons
Pastoral Relations Committee
the odd itinerant tradesman?)
then,
I thought it romantic.
now,
at twenty-three,
I can look back and laugh at

the me that was Me.
I might have been protective
    coloration
for a closet queen.
...anyway
last week I saw him again
and laughed it all off as
    a narrow escape.

Charlotte K. Bokowski
PLAINSONG

I wandered through paths
    Near my home to pray
While twilight pastels
Softly ending day
Assured me that God also
    lingered there...
He touched gently my brow
As I knelt down in prayer...
Dear God, as a child with a
    Heart visionary
I yearned to be chosen Thine
    Own missionary
To catty through lands across
    Seas miles away
The truth of Thy light
Thy Divine Love alway!
Somehow, Dear God,
I got never too far
From my childhood's faithful
    Wishing star...
Talents untried by my
    Field-pulpit dreams
Thrived on domestic tasks
    It seems...
Helping mind-sick patients
With hurt-soul moans,
War-scarred veterans uttering
    wound-caused groans,
Aged care-center invalids in
    Huge wheelchairs
And pitifully young drug addicts
    With vacant-eyed stares...
Dear God keep me true
To my small destined place
Helping daily a bit of our
    Torn human race...
And please, Dear God,
    from Thee
    Let me borrow
Kind words and deeds to
Help ease the sorrow that
Someone close may face
    tomorrow!

Beth Beauchemin
STILLBORN

He wasn't born to laugh
    or love;
he died without a cry.
The doctor said, "He's
    stillborn,"
and I bade my baby goodbye.

Now all I feel is emptiness
in the place he used to be.
I never even held him,
yet he was very real to me.

For nine long months I
    carried him
and delighted as he grew;
his room was ready, his bed
    was made

and now that's empty too.
I can see that little coffin
being lowered in the ground.
My empty womb is aching;
a part of me is being laid down.

So God, please take to heaven
his lifeless little form.
Please care for him as I would;
my first-born, yet sadly,
    stillborn.

Donald R. McGuirk
THE PRIME RIB OF ADAM

The Prime Rib Of Adam
A Choice Cut Of Beef
Fashioned The First Woman
And Parts Covered By Leaf

The Leaf Was A Symbol
Of Modesty Well Meant
Adoring The Place
Where Adam Was Spent

Foliage Was Soon Outmoded
By More Glorious Raiment
But To The Amorous Male
It Was An Impediment

Why Cover The Flesh
Was The Cry Of The Mate
There Should Be No Shame
To The Dishabille State

So The Trend Was Reversed
Till Today Marks The Era
Where The Day Of The Leaf
Again Comes Near-A And Neara

Patricia B. Phare
CAN I BE SURE

It was out of the corner
    Of my eye;
But I swear I saw your bulk
    At the door.
    When I turned to see,
    Nothing was there;
    But I swear I saw a
    Swift Movement.
Mabey it was the imagination
    Of a lonely mind;
    But I swear it was you
    Checking up on me.

Barbara A. McDowell
OASIS

There are times when life
    seems desolate
as an empty desert land;
hopes and dreams evaporate
like mirages in the sand.
With nothing to sustain him,
how can a man withstand?

There's a refuge, though,
    where man can go—
God provided an oasis.
He sent His Son that man
    might know
the more abundant, fertile
    places.

Nancy Mitchell Elliott
CAN WE?

Can we still be friends
After all this love
Can we gently push
Instead of shove?

Can we ask
And not just tell
I'm not sure,
Do I know you well?

Can we trust
And dispel all doubt
Tell me how
Do I find out?

Can what was one
Now be two
Can I adjust
To not loving you?

Can we be strong
Instead of weak
The anger is gone
Now, can we speak?

Can we stop feeling
Passion and pain
Can't we try,
Just once again?

W L Frasl
UNTITLED

Who takes time to watch
a little flower grow
and who takes time to listen
to the falling snow.

Little things so often
pass before an eye
for who takes time to watch
the sun set in the sky.

Who takes time to show
how much they really care
who takes time to say
if you need me I'll be there.

For soon it will be to late
and youth will pass you by
when will you have the time
to ask the question why.

For when your old and bent
time for you may slow
then who will take the time
to watch a flower grow.

Wilma Morley Despain
BEFORE SLEEP COMES

Between the dark and the
    daylight
    of Earth's agony
I think of my tall son.
He volunteered for a cruel war,
They keep saying, "that
    nobody won."
Far-away night winds while
    singing,
Will you tell me what I need
    to know?
Are there lillies there to cling
To the crosses in endless row?
Do you dust each day the fresh
    turned mounds,
Is 'his' cross a startling white?
Can I ask you to sing the
    lullabies,
That I sang long ago, at night?

Kay Welch
A WINDY NIGHT

Such are memories falling light,
    on a rainswept windy night,
As I kneel before you seeing;
    hands all aged and wrinkled.
    Remembering,
    what your smile was like.
Such a young and handsome
    man;
    nature's played you such
    a hand.
All our friends are dead
    and gone —
    we are all that linger on.
    Have some comfort my
    old friend;
    knowing I remember when.

Linda Conley
JUDGMENT DAY IS COMING

Judgment Day is coming to
    both you and me,
On this day we will be judged
    for all eternity.
I know I'll go to heaven but
    some will be denied,
Don't be in that number left
    standing outside.
As we stand at the Judgment
    before that White Throne

and when
the Life Book is opened and
    all our deeds made known
If we're not ready then we'll
    surely be denied,
God will leave us standing
    on the outside.
All we have to do is kneel
    down and pray,
Ask for God's forgiveness
    before that final day.
Think of your love ones that
    will pass through heaven's
    gate,
Won't you please get ready
    before it's to late.

Dennis R. Flathom
ADOLESCENT INNOCENCE?

That ever so silent pool of
    our youth,
    where we caught tadpoles
    and frogs by the hundreds.
Only to pen them up in
    unclean pails,
    left to die, in the shadows
    of the sun.

Barefoot and mean we were,
    all smiled up for the
    afternoon.
For the heat of the sun
    smoothed our waves,
    waves made with thoughtless
    anticipation.
And the closest thing to Hell
    were the tiny red worms
    that filled the water
    with the tadpoles about.

Just so long as we could
    see them
    we could always brush
    them off.
It's those unseen creatures
    that scared us half blind
    as they do still and
    always will.

Keli King
**THE FROST ON THE
WINDOW**

The frost on the window
recalled to me how I was
    on the outside looking in.
Seeing everything, yet not
    being a part of.
Now I'm on the inside and
    all seems to blossom
As that first buttercup of
    the Spring.
The winding road which I
    travelled now seems to
    descent into a field of
    violets
    and baby's breadth.
Giving me the happiness and
    the hope to go on.
The way is clear, the sun shines
    out of a blue water-colored
    sky.
And there, to the East, is the
    rainbow which holds a
    golden-bronzed treasure,
    a pot of gold.
A pot of specially-wrapped
    gifts,
One for everyone, everyone's
    needs and everyone's wishes.
Filled to overflowing, but I
    realized that I didn't need
    to choose any of these
    gifts.
I already had one, the golden-
    hued gift of friendship.
More valuable than those which
    the pot of gold contained.
But, unlike a pot of gold which
    vanishes after you've chosen

73

a gift,
Friendships last and create
their own rainbows.

Linda Buntin Hull
UNANSWERED QUESTIONS

The gate at the San Diego
airport
is full of activity,
but nothing is happening.
You left me confused.
You left me sad.
You left me with questions.
But, as always,
the questions remain
unanswered
Because they were never asked.

Steve Wood
**WHAT'S HAPPENING,
ANYWAY?**

Red man telling his red
neck jokes
Gasoline playing with
another hoax,
Nixon telling his favorite
quotes
That's all I can see today.

Red neck sitten on an iron
beam building his brick
Making a scheme, yelling at
black power saying that
They're wrong, what's
happening, anyway?
Skyscrappers, red necks, big
fat pigs; hippies, yippies,
A marijuana lid. Smog
pollution, noise pollution, and
Water too. There's a little time
left and it's left for you.
The day is past, the war is
still on, if they keep
on going we'll all be gone.
Taxes, television, and
watergate too,
There's a little time left
and it's left for you,—
So change it.

Betty Counterman
HOT TEARS

Hot tears are tears that are
shed when one prays
to the Almighty God
on high,
When nothing can ease the
beleaguered heart
And one chokes on an
anguished cry.

Bow down unabashed, and
on bended knee
Give full vent to those
hot, hot tears;
Then lift up your eyes for
help from above,
To the One who can calm
all fears.

If ever hot tears have coursed
down your cheeks
In a prayer for someone dear,
Be assured that God was
listening in;
He hearkens not vainly -
He'll hear!

Dianne Runion
LIBERATION

You vowed to chop the wood
and I to tend the fires,
But you, I quickly learned,
had no desire for flame.
Thus I assumed that chopping
generated heat
And shouldered axe to join
you in your game.

So laboring we quickly con-

quered tree on tree,
Each finding new and fresher
timber stand.
The lumber builds; our chop-
ping multiplies,
But fires die without a
kindling hand.

The ashes lie beneath untended
grate,
But chopping warms our cold
extremities
Unless we stop to note our
frigid state.
But chopping, chopping helps
the numbness cease.

Lori S. Leslie
GOD'S WORLD

God's world is something to
behold,
It's something that can't
be sold.
When Springtime comes, life
unfolds,
There are little animals to
hold.
Summer brings sunshine
brilliant, colors bold,
It seems that nothing grows
old.
Fall comes bringing life
un-seen, un-told,
With falling leaves to rake
and load.
Winter brings sparkling snow
and freezing cold,
With frosty dreams of
hidden gold.

Diane Tristan
A MEMORY

Just a memory that has come
and gone
Of make believe time.
The time we shared a heart
We thought would never break
And the sorrow we shared
Half mine and half yours
Has come and gone,
And all the minutes that are
to come.
Now there isn't the time to
say
"I Love You."
'Cause all our time has gone.

Yvonne A. Fazzio Halstead
THE NIGHT WE MET

With the fun that we'd had
You'd have thought it was
planned
But together two strangers
We danced hand in hand

Though others were present
We floated on air
While they all sat watching
Attached to their chairs

The night filled with laughter
As the stereo played
And we were alone
In the world that we'd made

No romance was there, in
the room
Nor in the stars above
So who'd have thought us
strangers
Would ever fall in love.

Luetta B. Williams
WISHFUL THINKING

"How are you?"
Becomes
"I Love You."
"How have you been?"
Becomes
"I have missed you."
The lingering look

Becomes
"I need you."
Reality says
"Wishful Thinking."

Maggie V. Autry
A WAY WITH WORDS

A writer must have a way
with words
If his story is to be heard,
He must shape and form each
simple line,
Around his dreams they must
entwine.

He must place his words,
and use his wit
Which way is best to make
them fit,
When at the end, its shape
is formed
There it is: A story is borned.

Lyn Good
JUST A FEELING

Strange feelings,
a simple call...
a woman's voice..
where yours
ought to be.
Wrong number?
maybe
Wrong assumption?
possibly
(as I gently lower the phone)
More than likely,
I was——just wrong!
wrong to think you
cared
wrong to think you
shared...
the feelings that I brought...
to you
(alone).

Margaret Hughes Blankenship
TAKE COURAGE

Climb every mountain
Walk every valley through
At the end of the storm
The sun will be there for you.

Stretch forth the rod of courage
Let truth and faith so shine
That your trophy for your
sorrow
Be - your peace of mind.

Dean Mitchell
LOVE AND TWINS

We know that girls
Are 'sugar and spice'.
If she's twins,
It's 'twice as nice'.

But don't take her
For her double
If you do,
It's twice the trouble.

This friend of ours
Came from behind.
He kissed my twin
But I didn't mind.

He didn't know
I've found another;
And my new love
Is his twin brother!

Faye Memolo
WHEN I WAS YOUNG

When I was young, so long ago,
So many things I could not
know;
The gaps are filled with things
learned since —
And what became of innocence?

As a child
I smiled
A lot

I'm still quite young, yet feel
so old.
What do I feel? The world's
so cold.
I've met many; I know a few;
But those I know grow
older too.

And now so old and different
too;
So many things I've yet to do;
So many things already done,
With all the emphasis on fun.

I think of things that I
have learned,
Of straight ways walked and
corners turned,
Of passions that have died
and burned,
Of people whose respect
I've earned.

Solitude, my only friend
Who will remain up to the end;
The others who have come
and gone
Take part of me, but leave
a song.

Shelley K. Russell
SEASON UNLOVED

the trees are swaying
to the cool seasonal wind,
their leaves are turning
to the colors of the sunset
and slowly drifting to
the ground.

bare limbs are looking so cold,
searching and longing for
last bits
of sunshine and summer's
warmth.

and, just like the trees,
I find myself thinking of you;
as the loneliness of winter
sets inside of me -
my mind turns to you often,
and, I, too,
search and long for our
warmth
that has changed as the
foliage,
fallen to the ground,
the wind having blown
us away...

Patricia Anders Dulaney
**OBSERVATIONS ON DALE
HOWARD'S SERMON**

God is "laid back"; God is
"cool."
God isn't worried; He's not
cruel.
But He would have us give up
Our love for our family?
Our joy in our work?
Pleasure from hobbies; Put
Him first?

If He says, "Sell it all and give
to the poor,"
I'd worry about who would
provide, to be sure.
He gave me some talent; He
gave me a brain.
He asks me to use it; that's
only sane.

How do I know if He's talking
to me?
I hear no voice from some
burning tree.
I just vacuum the floor, prepare
the food,
And try to manage my little
brood.

Just tell me He loves me,

faults and all,
And tell me that when I'm
not feeling tall.
Assure me that while my
virtue's innate,
Even I may squeak through
that narrow gate.

Laura A. Pina
MORNING

As dawn breaks,
I wake
to greet thoughts
of you.
I face the day
with the brightness
of love
shining in my heart.

Mary Ann Weber
THE ROBOT

Every day at the same old time
The alarm goes off in monoto-
nous rhyme;
From the bitter taste in the
coffee cup,
The sleepy eyes now open up.
Grab a dollar from the
cupboards
That stay as bare as Mother
Hubbard's;
Find the keys to start the car,
Then rush to work, near or far.
The same old cycle day after
day,
But this is our society's way;
Push the button, run the
machine,
Who cares if the universe ever
gets clean.
And on and on the robot goes
With computer command at
all controls;
Yet is there no button to
break the spell
Of this modern, technological
hell?

Tommy Konevecki
FAMILY FORUM

A true happy family is one that
when all put together; makes
a reunion.
Day by day we all join in the
secrets shared by the members
of unity.
our out going strides lengthen
in our hour of need. Our
great long
lasting memories filled with
treasures; keeps us whole and,
fresh as
we knew but last. How can we
possibly be kept separate
until death do
us part? Mine the lonely days,
yours the richer claim.

D. D. Utter
STARTING OVER

How hard is it to begin to
live for yourself when you
have always lived for others?
Today I begin my life for the
first time. Years of living for
someone else has left me
broken in spirit, but has given
me strength to start over.
I question why the people I
loved the most have hurt
me so, but I have no answers.
I have given love but never
felt the joy of its return.
I want to love, be loved, and
to bring happiness to
others. I want to discover me

and learn how to love myself.
My past has given me heart-
break that most people could
not have borne, but it has also
given me wisdom to live my
own life and Today I Am Born.

Michael Girard
FRIENDS

A friend is a person that you'll
always trust,
Where caring and sharing is
always a must.
A friend understands your
wrongs and rights,
They'll always be there on those
pain-stricken nights.
Distance means nothing when
dealing with a friend.
You'll always be close - never
finding the end.
A true friend it is said - is very
hard to find,
But the feeling you share is
one of a kind.
Things are not always smooth
but find their way,
The difference you'll see is
that a friend will stay.
Its not what you are or who
you will be,
Its just being yourself that
matters to me.

Patty Zimmerman Tarpley
MY WEDDING DAY

Thank-you mother
For giving me the Zimmerman
name,
But after today
My name will no longer be
the same.
Thank-you for all the love
And the care you've given me.
The sacrifices that you have
made
Is clear for everyone to see.
You've taught me about love,
You've taught me about life.
But I'm no longer just a
daughter,
Today I'm Ron's wife.
Larry will light the candles,
My four sisters will be at
my side.
And with my big brother
Down the aisle I will stride.
Mother, I made sure
You were the only one
watching it all.
Because when it comes to
special memories,
I knew each one you would
recall.
As I go down the aisle
A rose to you I will give,
To represent the love I will
have for you
For as long as I shall live.

Eloise Marx-Shoults
**GRANDMA'S
THANKSGIVING**

There's no gratitude in eating,
However good the cook may be.
Answer to this season's
greeting
    "Now let the clean up
    fall to me."
Kids, let Grandma fill the
rocker.
Show her you are quite adult —
Grown— You appreciate
    her effort,
    Inclined to enjoy wor's
result.

Vigor use in every movement;
Invite all hands to join the fun;
Nip the comfort inclination;
    Go on, until the work is done.
Don't just sit there, precious
    Granny.
Ask the Good Lord up above,
Year by year to bless those
    children.
Sit and rock and pray
    your love.

Pamela K. Barger
THE AUTHORS

They came from all walks
of life.
All had one fire burning in
their souls and minds.
Each man listened to the tune
of his own fife,
And struggled to be free from
common binds.
Frustration, false beginnings,
calamity, and confusion,
Have lured many authors and
poets astray.
They walked and wrote their
way into seclusion,
Only to emerge and greet the
light of a brighter day.
The poets—the authors, they
are the world's eyes,
They see all to be seen; they
are the world's heart.
They were born to bring fire
and light; to immortalize
Everything noble in art and
humanity, to you impart.
The great, earnest, gentle men
Lived, loved, and died by the
stroke of the pen.
Their masterpieces will be ours
to cherish until earth's end.

Blanche M. McNames
MARCH MOMENT

Today, another Spring arrived.
I watched it from my kitchen
    door;
"How odd", I thought, "you
    are not due
By calendar, for three weeks
    more".
But Spring is like a woman's
    heart-
It has no reason and no rhyme;
It becomes suddenly alive
    and warm
With small regard for "proper"
    time.
So now if wint'ry days should
    come
And wind should blow, and
    snow appear,
Why then, I'll smile serene
    and snug;
My Spring, you see, was
    early here.

Diane Lynn Fairchild
SO MANY TIMES

So many times have I looked
    to the sky,
dreaming a dream that could
    color a book,
watching a world stare me
    right in the eye,
-but never giving me a second
    look.
Many a day have I gazed at
    the sea,
blaming it's waves for my pain
    through the years,
looking for beauty, but only
    to see,
a body of water made from

my tears.
Every so often I'll look to
    the night,
hating it's darkness that grasps
    at the air,
wishing on only the stars that
    are bright,
and feeling the deepest of dark
    despair.
So many years have I watched
    pass me by,
leaving me only more reason
    to cry.

Debra J. Magnafici
MY AWAKENING

Once upon a yesterday. I
    was born.
The time of day was early
    morn.
The sun it rose so big and
    great
But all there was for me
    was hate.
I came into the world and
    found
Everybody cut me down.
Although the day grows
    warmer still
I know not what lies upon
    the hill.
They're big, they're beautiful,
Colors of every kind
But all I can do is picture me
in the back of my mind.
They're orange, yellow, red
    and blue.
With very special care they
    grew.
For now I know I'll never
    succeed,
For "they" are flowers,
And I'm a weed!

Ethewin M. Wright
SNOW

It snowed steadly all the night,
Covering the earth with a
    blanket of white,
Transfering the trees into
    princesses tall,
Makeing the hills like great
    white walls.
It decked all the bushes with
    jewels gay,
And played queer tricks on a
    stack of hay,
Makeing them look like castles
    white,
With out any doors or windows
    for light.
When morning came and the
    sun shone bright,
The world was covered with
    festoons of white,
Even the fence posts stark
    and bare,
Looked like old men with long
    white hair.
And then, as I looked,
At the beauty around,
I prayed for thoughts as pure,
As the snow on the ground.

Valencia Voth Koehn
MIDSUMMER EVENING

Have you ever
On a balmy summer evening
Stood a moment in the gentle
    breeze
Enthralled?
Is there anything more lovely
Than the myraid hues of
    sunlit skies?
Has the lonely mourn of a
    coyote

Ever made you stop and cry?
An unexpected discovery
Along some forsaken road
Caused you to ruminate—
How first crude ore
But, now the gold?
Have you felt the enchantment
Of a perfect wild rose?
Has the happy song
Of chirping birds, caused joy
To flood into your soul?
Have they lightened your
  weary step
Gave courage new, to press
Toward your goal?
Perchance some melancholy
  mood
Descends—you're blue
Just spend an hour in Nature's
  store
It will bring great dividends to
  you.

Jennifer Sheffield
FRIENDS

Some friends are old, others
  are new,
Some friends are false and
  others are true;
A true friend is there, to
  share and to care;
To listen and hear, to give
  truth without fear;
To need and be needed, to
  give and to take,
To realize friendship is too
  important to forsake.

Over the years few friends
  make the grade,
We trade one for another in
  a silly exchange;
Yet those that remain are the
  truest of all,
They've passed the test of
  time, the best of them all;
When all else fails, they remain
  constant and true,
A friend you can count on;
  a friend like you.

Edward L. Allridge
**VISIONS OF A SPRINGTIME
  MORN**

Clouds
  puffing their gossamer
  tendrils
  lacing upward heaven-born
Zephyrs
  swirling the dying mist
  adding speed to the galloping
  peppercorn
Birds
  skimming across a sky
  subdued
  cackling their cries of
  weatherwarn
Shadows
  fondling the leaf-topped
  trees
  touching tenderly to adorn
Everything
  pulsating in rhapsodic
  movement
  visions of a springtime morn.

Beth Podesta
KEEP LIFE SIMPLE

watch the rainfall
as life passes by
sing a song and gently sigh
in the morning
through the day
smile happy along the way
laugh at sunshine
cry with tears
make the most of passing years

just be yourself
speak up loud
open your eyes and stand up
  proud
life is made
of simple things
running water and butterfly
  wings
appreciate what
God has given'
just be glad for the life your
  liven' ...

William T. McKenna
REFLECTIONS

The offshore breeze
made your hair dance.
The steady sunlight
darkened your
already bronze skin.
The ocean approached
your feet like a
subject to a queen.
Your reflection
made me a liar.
I always said
there'd never be
another you.

Roger D. Nottingham
LONELINESS

Now "Loneliness" can't be
  defined.
It's dif'rent in each person's
  mind.
But "Loneliness " has distinct
  traits.
To some of which we can
  relate.
The single person in a crowd.
The quiet type, that's never
  loud.
The handsome man, without
  a wife.
A healthy man, who has no
  "Life"!
They watch (T.V.) and don't
  go out.
They are withdrawn and
  sometimes stout.
They really don't have any fun,
Because they're only pleasing
  one.
For "Loneliness" is in your
  heart.
A selfish drive, that will not
  part.
It's never sharing things with
  friends.
All that we do on us depends.
You go your way and I'll
  go mine;
Without your friendship I'll
  do fine.
Most lonely people count
  on one;
But what they have is really
  "None"!

Kelly Marion Potter
CERTAINTY

I know he's out there
Waiting for me
Biding his time
Until
That fateful moment
When
Our eyes
Meet
With an intensity
That sends chills
Up and down our spines
It may be years from now
It may be tomorrow
But

When it happens
We'll know
The electric shock
Of our eyes clinging
Will
Enlighten us
Here is my Forever!

Carole Taylor
THE BUDDING ROSE

Today I came to see you - but
  I forgot a rose.
I stood so long and wondered,
  "Could anybody know
  the aching of this life of
  mine?.......
Then I began to see - I needn't
  bring a rose to you
  to set beside an empty grave.
For you, this seed that has
  stayed beneath the ground
  will root and stand so straight,
  strong and tall,
  ....and for you, I'll be
  a rose.

Stephenaie Saginaw
IN THE DARK

Left on the dark side of the
  moon
Never feeling the suns burning
  rays
Stranded in a quiet eternity
Where the desert is forever
  night
Waiting for the turning
Expecting all to change
Waiting alone in time
Trying to recognize the faith
But never feeling the spirit
Or knowledging it's burning
  rays -
Left alone in constant tiredness
Never to sleep or float in place
Drifting without water
So very long -
In space.

Lenore Sowle Hess
TUMBLE FREE

Filled with blue painted chairs,
  a happy patch rug,
  fresh popcorn aroma and
  love in the air, yes...
This tumble down happy place.
  This contemporary dab,
  creative dab
  tumble out—overflowing
  peace place
  With real hominess just
  scattered about.
  It's a get away, hide away,
  safe away place
  Like a dream that is
  sleep or fog
  That will suddenly be
  snatched by the sun's
  selfish rays.
  But for now, just for
  a little while
  I can hide; I can tumble
  free...happy be...
  Thanks for you
  Thanks for here
  Thanks for now!

Steven W. Bailey
NO SUCH THING

I've searched all my life for a
  rainbow without rain.
For happiness without sadness
  and joy without pain.
I thought that if I ever found
  that rainbow,
I'd climb on it and say to
  those below,

"I've done something that has
  never been done before,
I've made the world a better
  place, and given you some-
  thing to
  live for."
But now that I've tried I know,
  that is one bell I'll never
  ring.
Because a rainbow without
  rain, is like a perfect man,
  there
  is no such thing.

Gertrude Payne Lewis
NEW HOPE

The pathway was long and
  dreary,
The day had dwindled away,
And I was tired and weary
From the toiling of the day.

Somehow with the coming of
  twilight -
My heart grew weary and sad,
And in the coming darkness
I lost all the hope that I had.

Quite long it seemed I waited,
Almost wishing I were dead
'Till I seemed to hear a faint
  echo
And I saw New Hope far ahead.

She beckoned me to follow,
Her light shining over my way,
And somehow I forgot I was
  weary
From the toils of the day.

And now when the night en-
  closes about me
I patiently wait to see
New Hope coming o'er the
  horizon
To light up the pathway for me.

Josephine Calascibetta
NOW, AS WE PART

Now, as we part dear,
This is good-bye,
Love in my heart dear,
And tears, in my eyes.

Kimberly Leach
THE MISCONCEPTION

Some say love and hate are
  opposite
But really side by side they
  sit.

Judith Corey
THE WALL

Freud a cursed man are ye
For introducing me to
  psychology
Tonto rides me day and night
No matter how my spirit fights.

"I wish I may, I wish I might,"
Turns into word games in this
  plight.
"I want to die, I want to live,"
The same breath, yet what
  gives?

A moment's whim? No! Hold
  on.
Life will surely spell out what's
  wrong.
Then better off will I be
For suffering this hell of
  eternity.

Somehow that sounds like
  magical myth
A hopeful thread men beakon
  with
To keep others in this limited
  life
Where, I doubt we'll ever o're
  take this strife.

Yet, is the gain for another
world
The resolutions of this time?
  (I should hope, I should
  hope)
What more do I know of
heaven?
So................I grope.

Barbara Robinson
RELATIONSHIPS

Such babes we do feel
When reaching to others.
Yet to trust, as do children,
Would help us recover
The depth of real sharing-
Completion with another.

Yet we strut and we smile
As our hearts bleed within,
Our witticisms and guile
I don't really condemn.
But oh! to reach down beneath-
To really touch someone again.

I am here, let me share
The present, "right now".
I'll not use or possess
Or restrain you, somehow.
But this moment feels empty,
I could share - if you allow.

Viola Fedorczyk Margarones
YOUR PRESENCE

Drowning in the sea of
  selfishness,
  thoughtful gestures lend the
  buoyancy to stay afloat.

Suffocating in the fumes of
  anger and hate,
  kindness revives.

Amidst violence and fear which
  shrivel the very soul,
  gentility brings forth a
  renaissance.

To know that it exists
      THOUGHTFULNESS
        KINDNESS
          GENTILITY

Gives hope and faith
    and
    the ability to love.

James J. Marino
NEEDING

Are you concerned
    that...
My back is to you tonight?
    don't be -
I still need your warmth
As you sleep
    behind me -
Love, don't be concerned,
Just follow me.

Karen Ann Oleyar
TEAR JOURNEY

A teardrop...
Before you can see it,
It is all the feelings inside of me
That cannot be put into words.
Brimming in my eye,
It is a puddle of indecision.
Will it flow freely as liquid
    emotion?
Or will it remain there,
Blurring my vision
So I cannot see how you are
    hurting me,
And drowning my pain
So I cannot feel it?

Rolling down my cheek,
It is but a tiny splash of my
    feelings for you;
All that remains of the fountain

of my love that thrived on you,
And constantly overflowed my
    heart with happiness.
But alas,
Sorrow has all but exhausted it,
And now it is even less than a
    dying, bittersweet trickle.
At the end of its journey,
Splashing soundlessly on the
    ground,
It shows to you and to the
    world
In glistening, emotional
    silence
The immeasurable depth of
    my love.

Cathy Shields
FANTASY SANITARIUM

Bad to the core-
I'm bad to the core
Like a rotten apple
In summer's muggy haze,
Brown and moist and stinking
    of corpse.
A thick, soft, deafened mass
Of inane flesh;
Adulterated scum,
Unseemingly vile.

I have but one futile hope
To spark my ensanguined,
Chiseled existence.
To subsist a myth;
A gay fluttering fairy
That lives on and on.

Peter Johnson
DARK HORSES RUNNING

Once, deep within a winter
    wood,
Wandering, long and lonely,
Driven by no purpose but
    the wind,
I came upon a small and
    frozen stream,
And stood fading into darkness,
Daylight blending into starless
    night,
Slow and silent, as impercepti-
    bly as sorry.

Then, a startling, cracking
    sound of branches,
A clip, clapping hurried on
    the frozen ground,
And from only shadows
    diving in the trees
Came three dark horses
    running
Then back into the shadows,
    gone!
Leaving behind, a memory,
The sound and fury of their
    elusive race.

Caryn Christine Euting
IN A POET'S EYE

In a poet's eye where no birds
    are in flight,
    sea gulls are dancing in
    the night.
In a poet's eye where the sky
    is painted gray,
    comes the shining light
    of day.
In a poet's eye there really IS
    gold at the end of a rainbow.
To her the song of a bird turns
    into a hymn,
And in a poet's eye love shall
    never end.

Sherry R. Coldiron
SHARE A LITTLE LOVE

Make a sad someone happy
Teach them how to smile.
Help to brighten up their day
Show them life's worthwhile.

Make the most of every day
Make every friendship count.
Don't be afraid to show you
    care
Cause that's what love's about!

Ellen J. Steinkamp
UNTITLED

I looked up
and saw the mighty
hand of God
move the earth
and form the
mountains and valleys.

I listened
and heard His voice
as it whispered
through the trees
beckoning me to walk
into the solitude
of the pines.

I reached out
and felt the
breath of God
as it washed my body
in the warmth
and tenderness
of the gentle breeze.

And as my eyes turned
to the heavens
to praise this Creator-
I saw the clouds
as they formed the stairs
that would lead to the heaven
from which all this
power and glory
had come.

Wendy Dawn Sensoli
HEARTACHE

Yesterday's dreams for
    tomorrow
are today's misery...
tomorrow's dreams
are today's hope...
and what will become of us?
when all hope is gone?
when love
is pushed aside...
when misery
takes me over
and under
into the never-ending tearfalls
    of togetherness.

Betty J. Clark
MY HUSBAND

My husband is someone who is
    loving and warm,
he likes to be with me and
    would do me no harm.
He doesn't look like Clark Gable
    or have muscles of steel,
but sometime during the day
    his love I can feel.
Maybe it!s just a hug as he
    passes by,
or just a warm smile, it can
    light up my sky.
He!s the good smell of cologne
    after a shower,
he!s always there in my darkest
    hour.
He!s a I love you honey and
    not just in bed,
even for those times I made
    him see red.
He!s a go buy yourself a pretty
    dress honey,
and I know he won!t worry
    about the money.
He is black hair and greenesh
    brown eyes with a ready smile,
and being married 26 years is
    a pretty long while.
There must have been some-

thing he saw in me,
for in those 26 years he has
    never wanted to be free.
A husband, a wife, God ment
    it to be,
and Rad I sure am glad you
    picked me.

Gertrude W.K. Affolter
THE PEEK HOLE

My grandma was a tomboy kid,
    A question mark all day;
They never knew just where
    she was-
    At home she'd seldom stay.

She shared a room with sister
    Min
    Where ev'rything was stored.
Yes, e'en a barrel of sauerkraut
    Which had on top a board.

The stovepipe came in o'er
    the kraut
    But wasn't in just yet,
So Christmas found that open
    hole
    And Addie's eye it met.

She'd always longed to take
    a peek
    At Santa Claus for years,
And now her chance had come
    at last-
    She'd disobey her peers.

When ev'ryone was fast asleep,
    She climbed atop the kraut;
The board went up and Ad
    fell in-
    Of that there was no doubt,
For in the morn sis Min cried
    out,
    "Oh, Mother, do come quick!
Who put this kraut between
    our sheets?"
    "It must have been ST. Nick."

Vivian M. O'Neal
BITTERSWEET

Is it fair,
That soldiers die,
And babies cry?
Is it right,
That people chat,
And step on other people's
    feet?
Is it fair,
That lies are said,
And things are dead?
Is it right,
That people sing,
Of only the sad and lonely
    things?

No, it isn't fair that soldiers
    die,
And babies cry, that people
    cheat,
And step on other people's
    feet.
It isn't right that lies are said,
And things are dead, that
    people sing
Of only the sad and lonely
    things.

But, I heard that life's not all
  typed and neat.
I've heard that life is bittersweet.

David Vincent Guy
A SPINNING TOP

A spinning top,
Spins unseen,
My heart is its center,
It's what I mean.

East or west,
Not which is best,
My heart the balance,
Never in the center rests.

Mrs. Judy C. Harvey
A SMILE

A smile is something that's
  present almost everywhere
  you go.
A smile is something that's very
  easy to show.
It is one of the joys in life that
  doesn't cost money,
For it can express feelings that
  look pleasing, loving or funny.

A smile is something that
  everyone can share,
All of the people in the world;
  everyone, everywhere.

Whether you are rich, average
  or poor
A smile can show happiness and
  much, much more.

If you come across someone
  you really don't know, just
  SMILE.
Then he will know that you
  want to share
Something that will create
  sunshine whether it's rainy
  or fair.

The most wonderful thing that
  makes you feel good inside,
Something too warm and
  beautiful to hide.
A heartfelt gift that spreads in
  every yard, inch, foot or mile.
The most precious and
  friendliest gift you can give . . .
  YOUR SMILE!

Mary Ann Birch
FIREFLY

  Stars upon my sky,
like fire passing by.
  With blinking colors of light,
envading on my night.

Alice Marie Rifflard
THE ROSE

Sweet, symbolic, beautiful,
A flower of good taste.
Fit among cabbages and Kings,
Graduations-Weddings-Eternal
  things.
Sign of love, friendship,
  dignity-
Peace, calm, serenity.
A dozen red roses, a small

bouquet,
Lasting fragrance—'savoury';
A climbing trelis, a single rose,
Commanding attention, where-
  ever it grows;
Beauty always,
                    The Rose.

Rowena L. Morgan
COLD AND LONELY

Cold and lonely, frightened
  and weeping
is my heart as it lies alone
in the night's profound
  deepness.
It feels the pulsating storm
  inside itself,
but knows the stillness of eve
as though trying to forget.
But shall it ever stop surfacing
  to renew all?
To remind that one can try
  and love again.
So that it cries out for love?
No, two battling forces;
My heart and soul.
One lives for the future—
One lives in the past.

R. Gene McKenzie
LEOPARD

Leopard, Leopard,
So proud of each spot;
If I laundered you in Tide,
And you came out spotless,
Would you still feel like a
  leopard,
Or not?

Becky Van Winkle
LIFE INFINITUM

Winter-bone-chills, overcome
  by mind, spring-nudging.
Eyes, straining to see rebirth of
First faint fertile bud subtly
  hidden under snow,
As egg in womb lies waiting
  unseen.
That fore-planned moment
  known only by each.
Burst their bonds, grow from
  buds to new life, neophytes.
Fleeting life, return to their
  beginning dust. Bud again.
Repeat infinitum.

Pierre P. Eno
MONET MOVIE

Before I open the door
I stare through the
Frosted glass.
Inside the doctor's office,
Life is a Monet movie.

Doris C. Smith
HIGH HOPES

I loved my pet puppy named
  Bowser
'Till he chewed a whole leg
  off my trouser!
Pup barks at my bare shin
And the cold breeze blows in.
Now I hope he'll become a
  good mouser
And grow up to be a nice
  Schnauzer!

Steven Hurst
**THE SUNSET ACROSS YOU
  IS BEAUTIFUL**

Teach me something, Brother-
  with-the-crashing-waves.
Tell me about the mountains.
Answer incoming tide.
I know you are awake, Brother.
Nothing? You know nothing
  of the mountains?

Strange. You seemed to know
  everything,
Anything I asked.
Do you know nothing of the
  mountains,
Wind, beast, or seed?
"Go ahead," whispers the
  barely perceptable voice
  itself.
"Leave here thinking you have
  learned all you can,
That the wise old sea can offer
  no more.
For all he's taught you, he still
  hasn't taught you
The beginning of what he knows.
Five steps,
            Ten,
You'll never hear his sigh,
You're already to far away."

Helen J. Shanline Bonnell
**TO A LADY BORN IN
  NOVEMBER**

You wear tawny ambers or
  autumn toned gowns,
copper chiffons or linens in
  bright jonquil gold,
smoky scarves tied to leathers
  of cordovan browns.
Topaz Lady, have you ever
  had your horoscope told?
Winter pewter tipped furs;
  your moods never the same,
pinning on in spring promise
  a cyclamen bloom.
You weave a Zodiac tapestry,
  threaded frost and flame
designed for November on
  scheming Scorpio's loom.

Robert Andrew McDonough
DANDELION PUFF

life is like blowing dandelion
  puff
and all that cool and groovy
  kind of stuff

to see those buds shoot out into
  space
they remind me i'm a member
  of the human race

to see them float through the
  ocean of air
sometimes i wonder—is anybody
  aware, does anybody care?

to see them descending and
  colliding
reminds me of life which is so
  beguiling

yes, life is like blowing dandelion
  puff
and all that cool and groovy
  kind of stuff

Barbara Fooks Redden
MY SECRET PLACE

Tell me friends out there in the
  world so big and wide,
Did you ever have a quiet place
  where you could go and hide?
My secret place was beneath
  the stairs out in the hall.
And it was dark, and no one
  could see me at all.
I'd sit there for half an hour
  or more.
With my back against the door,
Flashlight shining before my
  eyes,
Dancing shadows of every size.
I loved to squeeze into that
  tiny space.
With boots and umbrellas all
  over the place,
And to hear mother after tea,

Wondering where that child
  could be.
Once a dear friend came to
  play.
I shared my secret place that
  day.
My, we did have fun in there,
Whispering and giggling under
  the stair.
Wish I could sit in my quiet
  place today,
But maybe I'm too big to play.

Joni Jaye Albert
**MAJESTIC ANIMAL SO
  SLEEK AND PROUD**

Majestic animal so sleek and
  proud
Your soulful call is so clear
  and loud.
Across the rugged hills you
  run
Always watchful of the
  hunter's gun.
Into the forest primeval you
  wander
Across the darkest sky comes
  the lightning and thunder.
Your legs are strong but the
  pace causes you to stumble
  and
            fall
Above you're watchful head
  you hear an owl's call.
Once again your courage is
  too great to fail
Onward you fly through the
  night's destructive gale.
High on the mountain you
  stand
At last you are free from your
  fiercest enemy, Man.

Sharon I. Murray
SUNSHINE DROPS

The cold wind was nipping at
  my nose,
As I was walking through an
  open field.
I was unhappy,
I am not sure what about.
I was crying,
I remember that.
I held my hand out, to catch a
  falling tear,
Instead of a tear, something
  else landed in my hand.
It was the size of a teardrop,
  but it was shiny and gold.
I then realized it was a drop of
  shine,
that had fallen from
  the sun.
It warmed my heart, and
  made me realize everything was
  going to be okay.
It dried my tears,
  then melted away,
  for another one of my dreary
  days.

Carol Anne Dalamangas
SOMETHING SPECIAL

Come dance with me,
Come sing with me,
And together we shall
Live in harmony.
You were a shadow
From my past,
You are now a rainbow
To my future.
And together we shall
Make it last.
You are a radiance of a rare
And elusive quality,
Beauty, delicacy,
Softness and charm.

You are a gentle drawing
Of a true human being.
Forever you shall live,
Like the freedom of the wind.
You are a dance,
The graceful steps,
Are easy to learn.
You are like a song,
The melody stays
Forever in memories.

Barbara Ann Langevin
ONE DAY

The days, they seem so long
My life has gone so wrong.
I take off my wedding band
And I take the gun in my hand.
It's a fitting end to a life
That has given so much grief
and strife.
I'm sorry that's all I can say
Maybe you can forget me one
day.

Janet E. Eickhoff
THE END

 Curtains drawn shut; lights
no longer beam—
 Echos of my footsteps; is
death being seen?
 The final act is over; no longer
to be awed at—by anyone.
 The actors no longer paint on
smiles—and on the stage they
run.
"Fin'e"—so final; so jagged
edged
final that the laughter and tears
aren't remembered for long.
 The props, curtains, lights,
words,
and actors—now and forever, are
gone.

Jo Ann Luizzi
A WINTER'S EVENING

 The cathedral light of the
forest
Was made of a bright full moon.
Through the aisles of the
darkest woods
I wandered slowly into the
gloom.
The evening of the whispering
winds
Had gently caressed my face.
And the odor of the peaceful
pines
Had filled the air of tender
grace.
As I continued to pace along
The white blanket of snow
grew dark.
Along with the lonely feelings
showed
In the covering clouds gray
mark.
My paces began to slow a ways
And the wintry winds blew
more.
I turned back towards the way
I came
And enjoyed the walk to my
door.

Barbara L. Storey
SONNET - NUMBER ONE

 Alone at last; we've finally
found the time
For awkwardness. The crisis
over, now
We have to face the pain, the
stretched-thin line
Of understanding — silent,
broken vows.

I was afraid, who claimed to
be so free,
To know the love you held
out to my soul.
I only saw emotion's tyranny
And ran from passion, safety
as my goal.
But now, this...simple feeling,
and your touch,
Have led me back, destroyed
the fragile lie
I told myself. Can you forgive
so much?
I see your pain, your fear, the
question — "why?"
 I've learned my truth, but
paid a heavy cost,
If, from my fear, the trust
we had is lost.

Robert Cannataro
A PRAYER

Tomorrow Lord she will wake
up an say:
 I love you
 I realize what you have done
for me
 I am sorry I hurt you
 I believe in you
 I feel emotions and can
show them, and
 Oh God I'm happy!!
I will have to write a new
prayer soon
 This one doesn't work

Marianne Barrett
MASKS AND MIRRORS

We encounter them daily
These masks of ours,
 Our friends
 Those others.
Emotional armour.
Masks reflect
 Simultaneously
As mirrors.
To risk intimacy means
Discarding charades
Hence,
The silver disappears
To reveal
 Glass.

Robert D. Paesano
MOVIE STAR

The most beautiful of movie
stars-
 A new chauffeur to drive
your cars,
A bourbon voice that whispers
to your fans;
 You lay down on your
satin bed-
Mink pillows underneath your
head,
 And wonder why nobody
understands...
They found you on your satin
bed-
 Mink pillows underneath
your head,
And still nobody here can
understand;
 I watch you on the late,
late show-
You set the whole t.v. aglow,
 Your bourbon voice still
whispers to your fans.

Cindy Asendorf
A THING CALLED LOVE

What's this thing called love,
I've heard so many people say?
Is it like the sun is shining on
 a cold
and rainy day?
Is it like the birds are singing

when you're
all alone and blue?
Is it like a day in springtime,
 when all
is fresh and new?
Is it like the stars at nighttime
twinkling
high up in the sky?
Is it like a breath of fresh air
 or a
newborn baby's cry?
So, what's this thing called
 Love, if you
don't feel it in your heart?
If you take the time to show
me then
I'll gladly do my part.

Stanley S. Simmons
I LOVE YOU NOW

I love you now
 More than I possibly ever will
And yet each time I see you
 It's still a never ending thrill
Possibly and perhaps and
until
The day I die, my love for you
shall forever fly
Over and beyond the
effervescent sky
Which you bring to me each
and every single day
A love song you sing to me, in
each and every single way
Loving you is so easy, the
easiest thing I've ever done
Bringing to me, everything from
the moon to the sun
 And all I have is what you've
given
 And all of my mistakes, you've
always forgiven
Loving you for that is just a
small part
Of the feeling I have for you,
so deep within my heart
And as the morning softly
appears
Having you here, so close by
my side
Before you wake, I hide those
loving tears
You'll never see, for with you
with me
 They will always subside
Thanking someone, so often
every day
That I have you to soften
 All my clouds of grey
Making everything worthwhile,
if not in your smile
Then in everything else you
give.....and it's still
For you, the only reason I
have to live

Jennifer Lyn Mace
MERE SHADOWS

I reach out for you,
Seeing shadows,
But can only touch vague
memories

Buried in the dusty volumes of
countless days.
Your face is lost to me,
Shrouded in the hazy valleys
of time,
And your voice is not remem-
bered,
Drowned in the forward
rushing winds.
Often I think of you,
But wonder if my reflections
are true.
The years are a swindler,
But can never steal the warmth
Each time my groping mind
Catches a shadow.

Kristine Stratman McCoy
**THE MOST BEAUTIFUL
 ROSE**

God wanted the most beautiful
rose today
 So He chose my Mother and
took her away,
She was beautiful in so many,
many ways
 With sunshine and laughter,
she filled our days,
Always there, when we needed
her so much
 Happiness and help she gave,
to everyone she touched,
God only lent her for such a
short time
 To give us all, love, hope,
happiness and peace of mine,
He needed the most beautiful
rose, for His heavenly garden
 So He took my Mother and
the worlds best friend, within.

Theresa Alescio
UNTITLED

Far above the land, I see the
peak of the trees-
and the sun setting, shining
through the leaves-
while I listen to the birds-there's
a slight cool breeze
and smelling the spring air it's
bringing me
I looked around to find I'm
alone-
only to know God's love has
just been shown.

Wanda Wissman
FIRE'S GLOW

As I watch the fire's glow
I feel the warmth not only
outside
 but deep within, as it fills me
 with peace and tranquility.
I feel you beside me as I watch
the
 fire's reflection in your eyes;
burning brilliantly, shining
with care
I know shall always remain.
Your touch, so gentle and soft,
 has ignited a fire so strong
and
 powerful; it shall never burn
out.
The desire in your eyes tells
me that just
 because we will only be
this way once,
 the moment will last forever.

Judy A. Flynn
AFRAID

I don't want to cloud your
mind with
My thoughts.
Because where there's clouds
 there's usually

A storm...sounds like it's the
   chance of precipitation that
I'm afraid of and not actually
   the clouds.
And it's the superficial silver
   linings that I dislike the most,
Always hiding
Never telling
What's really there.
The sun though is always behind
   those clouds,
Peeping through..
Just think if the clouds
   wouldn't play their games of
Hide and seek,
It would always be
Sunny.

Elaine Frances Williams
SNOW

It sifts and drifts
Like powered sugar
Falling on a cake,
And covers a tired world
To newness when we wake.
It makes children laugh,
Old folks remember
Memories long past.
An illusion of freshness
That leaves us all too fast.
With a sigh I watch
As the snow
Slowly melts away,
For deep inside
A part of me
Wishes it could stay.

Helen C. Gould
I WONDER

You're asleep.
I haven't seen you all day.
You need rest;
Yet, I want to waken you
   to say,
"I love you."
I quietly turn the doorknob,
Hoping I will not waken you;
Yet really wanting to.
In your deep sleep you don't
   know I'm here.
I feel hurt,
But it soon disappears.
Your favorite sheets flow
   gracefully over your body.
I take in your form;
Memorizing every part of you.
I softly kiss your back.
As I quietly leave,
I wonder,
Have you ever done this to me?

Maureen C. Lang
WORDS

Words
Inadequate symbols
For deepening pain
Of a love that can't grow
I can't tell you
To go,
Or explain
How I feel
I try,
To no avail
I leave you
With nothing;
Just words.

Denise Maull
THE HAPPENING

When it finally happened,
   I couldn't believe that it
   was true,
   That it just up and started,
   That it turned out to be you.

But then it finally happened,
   And it ended up to be good,
   We looked then we turned,
   And here you finally stood.

And so it finally happened,
   A love that I never thought
   would be true,
   It happened with someone
   special,
   And it turned out to be you!

Christine M. Matteson
KEEPER OF MY PANTRY

Keeper of my Pantry,
throw away the key.
For this is to be kept,
and only for me.
Preserving the fruits,
of Love are here.
Seasoned just right,
so they would be near.
So keeper of my Pantry,
throw away my key.
So no one can enter.
Not
   even
      me.

Lori Harlan
FRIENDS

Friends can be you and me
Friends can be free

Friends can share happy times
Friends can share sad times

Friends can be far apart
And yet so close

Friends can be you
Friends can be me

But most of all
Friends can be free

Rosemary Bowery
ROBIN AND AUTUMN

   Shining hair that blends
With hues of autumn in the
   wind.
   A marigold, the last to bloom,
      to put in her room.
Colorful as an ear of Indian
   Corn.
Up-tight as a wound up ball
   of yarn.
   Brilliant as sunshine on frost,
      summer is past.
Dry leaves make earth's floor.
   Noisy cricket by the door.
   Brisk evenings, lazy days.
      Indian Summer haze.
Graceful as a leaf floating down.
   Sweet as molasses in the pan.
   Harvest moon in it's splendor.
      always a winner.
   Frightened of spiders.
   Knee socks and dock siders.
Squirrels scamperin—cattails
noddin.
      Robin and autumn.

Mary Lisa Kinney
SOLITARY SPACE

Time
By myself
   Free time
   All my time
      To dream

To love you
   With you
      But without
         Time

Kathy Dineen Krawczyk
SOUL SONGSTER

Words, Words, Words
why must we talk
just to communicate?
So many words our brain
must nourish
You can't say this
You can't say that
Punctuation, Pronunciation
   and Procedure
Oh, I wish I were a bird!
Tweet Tweet!

Edith M. Stoney
NO WALLS OF STONE

I've been a prisoner all my life,
Of dreams when I was young,
but later, with my world
   in strife,
I served those dreams with gun
and blood—and so much more.
   The price
was high, for prison walls
soon change adventurous
   hearts to ice
as, far away, life calls—
and love. Lost dreams turn
   rancid now,
for hatred sears the mind
until revenge speaks out in vow
that will forever bind
even a once free heart...

Cyndie Pogue
A SISTER'S WISH

If it were possible
I would
wrap you
in a
sheath of security
Never permitting
pain
to scar
your innocent soul

Susan Hale
O, FATE, THAT FINDS ME

O, fate, that finds me
   In
      The darkness
         Of
My unsuspecting desire
   May I welcome
      You
   In committment
      True
      Rather
      Than
      With
      Ire
   And teach me
      How
         The roses
            Bloom ....
         Dispel all
         Mitigating gloom!
         And be
         My
         Crown
      Both flower
         And
         Thorns ....

Beth Hoefler
CHRISTMAS TIME

The incredible ... magic of
   Christmas
The mystic ... divine spell
A heavenly mist must fall ...
   from the sky
When it touches Earth ...
   Christmas is nigh

Oh, such a glow ... comes,
   with Christmas
The feeling of love ... the
   delight
The implicit touch ... of peace,
   within
As Christmas ... looms, in sight.

The Infant Jesus ... is on His
   way
To live with us ... on Earth
And, Santa Claus ... prepares,
   his sleigh
To travel ... ore the Earth.

There's a haze of ... expectation
The Evening Star ... shines
   bright
We are caught in ... a special
   splendor
We live in a ... strange, new light.

Joyous greetings ... peace and
   love
Goodwill ... to all men
Then, ALAS ... it leaves us
Why does it ... have to end

Oh ... the magic of Christmas
why can't it last ... all year
The blessed magic ... of
   Christmas
We just feel ... once, each year

June Renee Dietz
UNTITLED

at the end of the road
a thundering roar
gold dust glistening in the
   bright sun
denim matched against the
   blue sky
acceleration
swaying side to side balancing
   the rhythm
aiming deeper into oblivion
graceful glide
like the eagle in flight
caught in a whirlwind of
   incessant time
floating to wherever dreams lie
moving free
disappearing behind my tree

Joseph I. McCullough
THE UGLY TREE

An ugly looking leafless tree,
Whose knarled crooked branches
Whistle unceasingly
In the cruel Arctic winds,
Stands like a wicked witch
From November till late March.
Not a thing of beauty,
Although often bedecked
By stray blue jays or orioles.
This unseemly specimen of
   Nature
Presents a wretched appearance
Except in Winter's wonderland
Of clinging icycles and
   glistening snow,
Smothering the naked twigs
With an immaculate whiteness
That makes it the most
   precious jewel
In King Winter's Paradise.

Larry Czerwonka
**FOOTPRINTS AND
MEMORIES**

The seagulls cry -
As the sun begins to set.
Fresh memories line the beach.
A lost shovel is stuck in the
   sand.
Footprints here and there.
The water moves up the beach.
Fading memories...
The sky has turned red.
Nature's cycle begins to end.

Sandpipers dart between old
and new.
A lone fisherman sits on the
pier -
A silhouette against the
darkening sky.
Water splashes ...
The sand castle comes tumb-
ling down.
Memories fade faster now.
The water rushes below your
feet.
Memories of the day go out
with the tide.
There is nothing left but a
shovel -
riding the waves ...
The fisherman left hours ago.
The lights have dimmed.
You are alone...

Jeanne Redmond
TALL GRASS

Your devilishly sweet scent
Swam through the air
Caressing your papery substance
My lungs invited
Your presence

Entrance to my mind
created thoughts of every kind

Love to Hate
Life to Death

But
much laughter accompanied
your effects

Strange quality for finding
Humor
Added to the urge to be
an everyday consumer

A strange and strong
quality indeed
Only found in the
Enjoyably evil weed

But as time wore on
Thoughts and laughter
were all gone

Driving me to drowsiness
My mind was functioning
Less and less

Now I look upon you
with much distaste
Condemn your Power
of turning my mind
To waste

So now I must bid you farewell
but thank you for the
experiences
Before your goodness
Fell

Beverly J. De Maria
SUMMER LONGINGS

A sailboat on the horizon
Close, yet too far to touch.
Like me here, You there;
Sometimes it hurts so much.

I hear your voice in the waves
As they crash upon the shore.
And it makes me want to hold
you
For just one moment more.

A sailboat on the horizon
Drawing nearer with the wind;
Like me here, You there;
But, soon together again.

Lisa Jo Keene
OUR ISLAND

When we left our island
we left a time
that will never return.

Our sandcastles have fallen
with the tide,

and the footprints where we
played
have faded in the sand.
The island is still there,
the blue ocean and soft white
sand
will never disappear.
But the laughter and joy of
that love
has past like the years.
For when we said goodbye to
our island
we turned toward a new sun
and left that life behind.

Tressa Armstead
UNTITLED

Raindrops fall to earth from
above.

From a seed comes a flower
rare,
standing alone in the midst
of weeds—
weeds which attempt to rob
the life of the flower.

Like the flower, the child so
beautiful grows.

The child—innocent, curious,
loving, trusting—
grows in the midst of traits
so unlike his own
to be the man so unlike the
child.

Loss of innocence—is it worth
the price?

Ms. Deb Mader
MATURITY

The sky is above me; clear,
deep-blue, cloudless, perfect.
I feel so small.
The grass is below me; dark
green, thick, soft, beautiful.
I feel so ugly.
The stars are above me;
laughing, far away, endless,
breathtaking.
I feel so insignificant.

Is my niche in life supposed to
be that of a doubter?
Or should I just accept?
Am I stupid for not blindly
following "the crowd"?
Or am I wise beyond my years?

I want to soar with a perfect
love!
But I'll accept a man who
shares my interests and is
a friend.
I want to be a world renowned
novelist, read by millions!
But I'll accept just getting
local fame.
Is this being Mature?

David W. Barthel
THE TALKING OAK

Ive stood here for a hundred
years,
Listening to the rains wet
tears.

Heard the voice of the lynching
mobs,
Soft words of love, and
muffled heart throbs.

Felt the pain of Indian arrows,
Held in my arms, the nests
of sparrows.

Watched while the deer ate
from my fingers,
The green leaves of summer,
the thoughts still linger.

Hurt from the blow of the
woodsmans ax,

Comforted the tired while
they relaxed.
Fed the fires of the lost and
cold,
Watched men die, in the
fight for gold.
Held the reins of frontier
steeds,
Watched men murdered, and
seen good deeds.
Breathed clean air, from the
sky above,
Drank from the earth,
tasted its love.
Seen changes on the face of
earth,
From village, to town, to
the citys girth.
Ive told all this, in hopes youll
see,
The wonderous life of a
big oak tree

Marcia Wiesenfeld
UNTITLED

Her giving heart knows no
logic
As I speak it to myself -
She gives me wholly and
exposed-like
some dreamland, some dream.
She gives me love so total
I think I can not hold it all
I fear I am not there at all
Without her.
She gives me form to turn.
As fire turns the air of summer
woods
As petals turn
when butterflies descend.

my mother my mother I am
my mother's child
and what my mother gives me
I give away.

Mary Anne Henson
ALL THAT GLITTERS?

Sparkle tree, sparkle, glitter
and shine.
Your days are numbered, your
days and mine.
And Christmas comes and
Christmas goes,
Like kisses under mistletoe.
Still you sparkle, still you
shine,
Trying to make the days
unwind.
Knowing no matter how deep
or bitter,
No one ever looks beyond
the glitter.

M. Jill Karolevitz
SHEPHERD

You're a Pied Piper ....
your sheep follow the song
of the oats in your bucket.

Robert White
**REFLECTIONS OF MY MIND,
TO COME**

I've seen the weather-worn
Old Man
In front of his store.
He stands alone.
No one is to know
Of his existence.
The people have gone,
Left him behind.
A tear
Drops from his cheek,
As he stares
In lonesome sadness,
And waits for those
Who will never come.

Francis Fescharek
A CHILD DIED

A child died today.
Couldn't have been more than
ten.
A Viet Cong gave him a
grenade and said,
"Give it to the G.I.", as he
pulled the pin.
"To him you say this,
Here is a present from Ho
Chi Minh."

Olive Lucille Johnson
TARRY ALONE AND PRAY

Do you have a foe to conquer,
What will you do or say?
Here is the secret of success,
Tarry Alone and Pray.

Are you burdened with a task,
Which should be done today?
Ask the Lord to give you aid,
Tarry Alone and Pray.

The very thing you cannot do,
(At least as some folks say,)
Can be done, and victr'y won,
Tarry Alone and Pray.

Marla Rozelle Snow
THERE "STANZA" DESTINY

Searching for something,
Minds reaching so deep.
A destination so close,
But quite far to keep.

Wondering day by day
Where this special feeling lives.
Trying to find the ecstasy
Along with the pain it gives.

It may be life itself,
Or an emotional resistance.
It may be feelings of love and
hate,
Or the mere fact of existence.

Destiny dwells within us all,
And it is God-given, and unique.
In our poetry, music, and in
our hearts
Is where we must all seek.

Hold on to it tightly
Once it is found.
Treat it ever so gentle,
For it comes once around.

Be grateful for all the time
We are given to search our
souls;
To find our dreams and
destinations,
And to finally reach our goals.

Ella Burley
FRIENDS

Is it flowers you need
When you're in sick bay
Or is it a nightie,
All pink and gay?

Really, it's friends
Like I have at the store
Who reach for their nickels
And dimes, then more.

And come up with flowers
And gifts and things
I think they're all angels
Just hiding their wings.
So, thanks so much
Now I'm back in line
And Lots of luck!
Come up'n see me sometime.

Franklin W. Marshall
UNTITLED

A cider sequel to mock orange
    spurn:
Dawn down to dun cold-caulked
    the cuckoo spittle
On queue and quill! — Tart
oozes bald where brittle
Coppers in a breath-bite
    bonrise burn.

To skins of bruised and blis-
    tered fruit accrues
A rime of wrinkled wax, and
    you believe
It were benign if you did not
    perceive
The matted mulch of
    droughtful residues...

Esther M. Rice
REINCARNATION

Life is such precious stuff. It
    cannot be
The Master Weaver of Eternity.
Would let one thread be lost.
    It seems to me
That when a thread does break,
    most carefully
He ties it, and again with
    skillful hand
Weaves it into the pattern He
    has planned.

Joe G. Woosley
LITTLE PEOPLE

They say we're missing a lot
    of things,
Luxuries, only money brings;
But there's flowers and trees
    and a sun in the sky,
For little people, like you and I.
Riches were denied us, but
    then, we don't mind,
For at night a calloused hand
    holds mine,
Glad we're together when day
    is through.
With little children to tuck in
    bed
And kisses and hugs after
    prayers are said;
Money might make us forget
    these things,
The simple joys our
    contentment brings;
Fussing a little, and loving a lot,
Kind words remembered, harsh
    ones forgot,
Struggling and planning, and
    just getting by,
The little people, like you and I.

Mamie H. Preyer
EDUCATION

Education is the torch of
    enlightment,
it is the tower of peace and
    gentle excitement.
It is the purger of the ghost
    of ignorance,
it is the staff of the saint of
    tolerance.
Education is the pedestal for
    the scholar,
it is the guide for who receives
    the big dollar.
It is the mind's stimulator,
it is the soul's regulator.

Education is the ancestor of
    loyalty,
it is the atlas of earnestly.
It is what is to be continually
    obtained
as the humble seeker travels
    along life's plains.
Education is the wisdom of
    the wise,
it is the essence of the holistic
    prize.
It says to all, here is a testimony
    of
life spent for mankind and
    eternity.

Carolyn Jean Wright
LOVE

Love is your friend, and yet
    it's your foe.
A kiss be your arrow, a smile
    be your bow.
It pierces young hearts with
    pain and with cheer.
You laugh, and you cry, but
    you smile through a tear.
Is it better to love him, or just
    let him go?
I guess without trying you never
    will know.
To love and to lose would be
    such bitter grief.
But never to try would be
    self-defeat.
For everything lost, something
    is gained.
All days can't be sunny, we
    must have some rain.

Ruth Eaton
UNTITLED

It is a cruel world when a
    person walks alone
- so we search for one to sooth
    our agonies.
It is a confusing world when a
    person walks alone
- so we search for one to help
    us understand.
It is a cold world when a
    person walks alone
- so we search for a companion
    to provide warmth.
And yet, when we search with-
    out first knowing what
we search for, or when and
where to end our search
- we shall only continue to
    walk alone.

Linda D. Stoddard
RESURRECTION MORN

There's a gleam on the eastern
    horizon;
    The awakening birds greet
    the dawn
With a chorus of happy
    rejoicing
    That morn after morning
    goes on.
The green grass is tipped with
    diamonds,
    With the magical morning
    dew.
The drab old stump seems to
    glisten
    As if blessed with a life
    brand-new.
The golden sun peeks o'er the
    tree tops;
    The clouds in the west blush
    light pink.
Swallows soar high in the azure
    sky.
    So what can a mere mortal
    think?

When the morning comes in
    with such splendor,
    When you see a new day just
    born,
It's a glorious time to be
    rising—
    It's a resurrection morn!

Ella Lea Dowling
A HOT DAY IN JULY

The sweltering heat of the
    rising sun -
Is greeted by works it has
    already done -
The earths red clay in pieces
    does lie -
Dust from streets choke us
    as traffic goes by -
The free running brooks and
    ponds are now gone -
And the straw colored yard
    once
    was a green lawn -
Leaves on the trees are
    yellowing so -
And the birds once bright notes
    are now mornfully low -
Seems all nature is joined
    in its plaintive way -
To beg for some rain on
    this hot July day -

Tom H. Castillo
MY EGYPT

joys in my heart
are songs in my ears
nothing compares most than an
    everlasting love.

from the garden of sweet
    scented flowers to the
    uttermost feeling that dwells
    within
lullabies from white lillies
lingers to awaken my dormant
    emotions;
only the soft voice of my fair
    maiden can
now be my EGYPT

Cecelia G. Tolley - Duda
HOW DID YOU KNOW

You came when my heart
    cried out for you...
    How did you know that I
    needed you?
In silence, you came and
    enveloped me in strong,
    gentle arms...
Warm kisses on my face, lips,
    eyes...
    and I was home...
    safe, quiet, loved.
You left when my heart was
    filled,
    enough to last until next time.
You came when my heart
    begged for your touch.
    How did you know that I
    needed you?

Aileen M. Lawton
IF

If there was no God above,
What would happen with our
    love?
Would we all curl up and die,
Even birds up in the sky?
Who would answer a childs
    prayer?
Would a church be very rare?
Would mankind be so strong?
Who would teach children
    right from wrong?
Would people always walk in
    fear,

Or never need to shed a tear?
Would there be water in the
    sea?
Would there be a shady tree?
Why can't people understand,
What God has put upon our
    land?
We know when he was laid
    to rest,
He had fought his very best.
Someday we'll bow are heads
    in prayer,
And let God know we've
    learned to share.

Donna Whisenant
THE WISEMEN

O wonderful star burning bright
Lead us to your mystery in the
    night.
Lead us to Bethlehem where
    the baby lay
Lead us to the stable where the
    family stays.
Let us bring presents to honor
    the Son
Over hills and across the land
    to the Only One.

They knelt before the child,
    the Wisemen Three
They bowed their heads and
    got down on one knee.
The Wisemen praised the new-
    born stranger
They prayed to the baby in
    the manger.

Margaret E. Strickland
SPRING

I like to see the budding
    Of the first burst of Spring.
To watch the sun bathe the
    Earth,
    And listen as birds sing.
I like to feel a major part
    Of all universal things.
To feel a part of God's love,
    And the pleasure that it
    brings.

Arlene F. Brown
NOT HERE

Here,
yet deliciously not here.

Wandering warm-drenched
    canyons
far from anywhere close to
    nowhere.

Feeling sun streaks flash
in kaleidoscope patterns
through ever changing
limbs and lashes.

Carolyn H. Woosley
SERVICE

What wilt thou do for thy
    fellowman?
To see the Christ within thy
    neighbor.
Then love will be in command,
And keep thy motive pure.

God has given to thee a
    special gift.
A talent to be wisely used.
Now, go thy way,
And let thy gift be multiplied.
Use thy gift faithfully and
    unselfishly.

Tho need not look to serve.
Opportunity is always at
    thy door.
Master Jesus, let thy example
    be.
Soon, thou wilt learn that
    living is serving.

Serve well, that thou mayest
  have sheaves
To lay at thy Father's feet.

Helen M. Doster
**MY GRANDMOTHER'S
  VIOLETS**

Violets are all over the place
On the tables and in a blue vase.
They are white, lavender, and
  blue
And sometimes a purple one,
  too.

How many do you have? She
  said 1,000
Counting those on the bed.
They have to be watered
  everyday
And rain water is best, they say.

What does she do with them all?
Sells them to folks, large and
  small.
She has to have a violet sitter
If she goes away in the fall.

Grandpa says he can cut the
  grass
But violet growing is out of
  his class.
I'm inclined to agree with him,
  too,
It sounds like too much work
  to do.

Everett Wm. Ayers
THE LATE START

Up the street,
And around the bend,
No time to waste,
It's almost ten.
I'm off to work,
No time to spend.
Almost there;

I remember, then;
To stop, and be thankful,
  for this day.
And there's no words,
That, I must say;
Just to LOVE
With EACH breath,
EVERY single day.

Susan Houghton Boynton
MY FRIEND MIC

Let me tell you about my
  friend Mic
with hope in his eyes and a
  heart that won't quit
He was a carefree easy going
  guy
but something happened and
  I don't know why

Never did he dream his time
  was borrowed
when he was driving down the
  road that night
minding his own, enjoying the
  ride
and hit a car not yet in sight

The car caught fire
and so did Mic
burning and screaming
"Why won't it quit?"

Now man created this machine
and knowingly treated my
  friend mean
They took some things man
  can't replace
three years, spare parts and
  memories constantly retraced

To tie his shoes is a difficult
  task
or button his shirt, he has to
  ask
To play his drums

is now a thing of the past
I don't know why
I can't help but care
All I know is man put him there
Now this Company they have
  a future strong
and my friend Mic, he tries to
  get along
I pray to God Mic wins his trial
so I can see Mic finally smile

Love Breezy

Pamela J. Wilford
RUNNING SCARED

A small
  trembling
    bright eyed dear
      spotted brown and white
Bounded
  over
    cold, damp grass
      around black shadows
Panting
  loudly
    through wide, quivering
      nostrils
        with tiny, furry ears
Perked
  upright
    while passing shrill cries
      from tall, swaying,
        leafless trees
As
  a cool wind
    shuffled musty, fallen leaves
      and scattered broken twigs.

Michael Paul Kersteter
WILL I?

The winged creature lit on a
  leaf,
i'm slowly tiptoeing.
The wings flinched, the leaf
  swayed,
Soft wind blowing.
Almost in reach, with
  outstretched arms,
The butterfly was swift.
An empty leaf drifted toward
  the ground,
A cold breeze.
She lit again, again i tried,
Never does she stay long.
Someday she'll be caught,
Who will catch her?
Will I?

Nancy De
THE GREASY SPOON

It is known as the Greasy
  Spoon
to some, but the prices are
  right,
though the atmosphere is
  not much
to speak of, with filthy floors
and clouded windows covered
  by
frayed flowered curtains.

Now two a.m. and all are gone,

except for the cook wiping
  sweat
from his brow, the waitress
  whose
look beckons me to leave, and I
who have no reason to rush.

Once again, my eyes catch
  those
of the bitch, but I refuse to
leave my cup half-filled because
there is something about this
mug of caffeine, so strong in
aroma and rich in its flavor
when I drink it alone, and
I savor that taste.

Myrtle B. Lockwood
MY SOUL SPEAKS

Yesterday it seems that I had
  it all together.
Now I ask myself, do I spend
  too much
Time in the struggle and loose
  the
Essence of Living - with the
  search of self?

Would that I could quietly let
  the
Flow of life take over as often
As possible - while I simply
  enjoy
The pleasure of being alive.

The search, the questions,
  are often
Capable of putting to death the
Flowing beauty of life itself.

  Be still my soul and know that
  This is life.

Doyle L. Morton
FOR CAROL

Come, sit beside me—
  I so humbly desire to
  Hold your slender hand.
'Tis not what some who are
  near you
Would want, I know—
  But please, for the fewest
  of moments,
  Bless this
  Love taken heart
With the tenderness of your
  touch.
Smile, my passion, for your
  curved lips
So effectively lift
  The weight of unknowingness
  From these burdened
  shoulders.
Bear with me—
  When comes the time to part,
For I will cling to your healing
  harmony
With the force of the midnight
  tides,
Hold our hearts tightly together
  For just a second,
And—oh forgive me dear
  Carol—
Cry
  Upon your soft auburn hair...

Andrew J. Talbert
**THE SOURCE OF
  KNOWLEDGE**

Our inherent natures shrink
  from pain,
and seek to shun the clouds
  and rain;
But joy and pleasure-pain and
  strife,
all are the building blocks of
  life.
Much of the mutual love we
  share
was born in darkness, and

despair;
And in immeasurable distress
the callous heart finds
  tenderness,
where-in it's softened, and
  subdued,
and rises from it's hell renewed.
Our sorrows of't confound the
  wise
by proving blessings in disguise.
I've known the sordidness of
  earth,
and all the merriment of mirth-
been blessed with all the agonies
of love, and lovely ecstasies.
Many a sorrow has been mine;
But so has laughter, song and
  wine.
I've learned from labor, pain
  and tears,
that faith trancends the
  scorching years.
Those who in storm to faith
  hold fast
shall rise again, when storms
  are past.

Lisa Ann Poli
LULLABIES AND LOVE

The nursery was done up
in pastels and lace
bringing a smile
to everyone's face
Everything ready and waiting
for the baby to be
it's so hard to believe
there is someone inside of me.
the greatest and finest
miracle on earth
is this
the miracle of birth

Mary E. O'Shea
**ODE TO LADY (MY CANINE
  FRIEND)**

Though you are gone beyond
  my reach,
In my heart you will always be;
You were a friend, to see you
  suffer could not be,
Because I loved you so, you see.

She will not suffer, this he said,
As I stroked your lovely head;
I trusted him, as you trust me,
Don't worry girl, soon you'll
  be free.

I'll remember your eyes - so
  trusting and true.
Remember the days we romped
  in the wood?
The memories of you will
  always be good.

Free from pain, they'll be no
  tomorrow,
But from the past, loving
  memories I'll borrow;
Tears are flowing down my
  cheeks,
Good-bye old friend - Sleep
  well and rest.

Charles A. Linn
MORNING

In the early morning light as I
  turned to admire you,
All that is you, while you sleep,
I gaze upon the beauty of you...
The gentleness felt from those
  hands, now still, at rest.
The innocent warmth seen in
  those eyes, closed now, so
  tranquil.
The pulsating sensation that
  started with a kiss from those
  lips, quiet now,
still inviting.

As I gaze, tender remembrances
come to mind.
In the darkness of the night
gone by, we reached out to
discover each other,
arousing, tasting, satisfying...
Now in the early mornings
light...
I turn to admire you.
All the beauty of you....as you
sleep.

Richard Meyer
VISITANT

You say the same thing all the
time
Like a dead man in an open
coffin—
Whispers of bad make-up and
trite prayerful hands.

It is these thin sheaths,
The flavor of snow, that tear
my breath
And exhale a cold poultice
Still sticky from musty offices
And Christmas hallways.

Clare Salata
YESTERDAY'S LOVE

I saw yesterday's love, so
fragile and frail,
In a cardboard box at a
neighborhood garage sale.
A stuffed animal we bought
at a zoo
With a life-size poster I gave
to you.
Memories only we two have
shared.
We were very happy while we
cared.

It's yesterday's love, so
fragile and frail,
In a cardboard box at a
neighborhood garage sale.
A large, wooden photograph
frame without a face,
A dusty trophy won in a
fun-filled sack race,
Romantic records and tapes
stacked high;
Those songs now make me
want to cry.

Why is yesterday's love, so
fragile and frail,
In a cardboard box at a
neighborhood garage sale?
At the very back of the old box
I smiled at our two pet rocks;
A female rock and a male.
May their love never fail.

I left yesterday's love, so
fragile and frail,
In a cardboard box at a
neighborhood garage sale.

Ted Jensen
REST

I'd wake
to greet
the new sun
But all my dreams
are threatned
Broken
Turned around
So I take
them in
In this
State of dispair
I hold them
for they
will not shake
from me
I ring
them from

My sleeve
Bloody stains
and Dieing
Promises
Then I must wake
For unrest
which haunts
My memory
I'd face
the new sun
but fear
strikes me
It may burn
my eyes
And leave me
In splinters
On the ground
so I
Cover my head
pray for rest
Ignore the sound
Smashing me
Into submission
And Dare
to dream

Joyce Welch Hedges
MEMORIES

Endless thoughts of time gone
by,
the memories that forever tie
themselves to one life and then
disappear in the eons with kin.

The roses, the joy, the lovely
sun
remind us all we are not one,
but through the darkness and
cold acclaim,
our memories of love remain
the same.

Teresa Phillippe
MEMORIES OF NOTHING

You never touched me,
or held me close.
You never gave me,
what I needed most.

When you smiled at me,
or said my name,
You raised my hopes
and played your game.

You've torn my heart,
and hurt my pride.
You broke promises,
and you always lied.

I wish you could know,
what you have missed,
A life time lover,
who longed to be kissed.

All I have left over
is a box of dreams;
Memories of nothing,
and tears, unseen.

Lori Dawn Zeller
FULFILLMENT

Early morning sun
bathes the hollow space in our
bed,
leaving a glow in the spot
where you slept but a moment
ago.
Something in the golden light
reminded me of lovers past;
then memory of the ending
night
assures me that you are the
last.
Early morning sun
brings a smile to my face, from
our bed-
For now I know that all the
times I've wept
simply helped me to grow.

Chris Tilman
MASKS

I know you,
You know me.
But do you really?
Or am I
Just pretending
So I can be
What I am
Expected to be?
Am I wearing
A protective mask
Over my true self?
Has that mask
Been there so long
That I, myself,
Don't even
Know me?

Mary Anne Gaudette
THE GREATEST MIRACLE

Lord, of all your miracles,
there's one I cherish most,
Made possible by Your Father,
and the Holy Ghost,
The miracle I speak of, is the
miracle of birth,
No price tag could be high
enough to express just what
it's worth,
From the first sign of life, til
the last pain I feel,
I realize this miracle is very,
very real,
To see my new baby, tucked
safe in my arm,
To love and to cherish and keep
safe from harm,
Thank you Lord Jesus, for the
miracle of life,
The greatest gift given to a man
and his wife..........

Cindy J. Jankowski
THE LONELY BEACH

Ripples in the sand
Tiny grains of small wonder
Hot bleached color
Melted down with white
thunder

Baked-in sunlight
Yellow rivers of sand
Salty glow in the moonlight
From the rocks on where I
stand

Waves splashing down
Wet sea shining
Hear the ocean sound—
The lonely beach.

Sylvia P. Beres
**HAPPY 75TH BIRTHDAY,
ALBERTA**

Pioneer souls our province
built
Steadfast people, brave and
true
On they trod with inner
strength
Thanking God along the way
Breaking sod and planting

crops
Raising families on they toiled
Drought and famine took
their share
Depression years were hard
to bear
Celebrations now are due
Birthday candles shinning
bright
Alberta pioneers we honor
thee
You lead the way, we follow
you

Amy C Keast
LOVE'S BREEZE

From oceans on the west
with their waves striking warm
beaches
To oceans on the east
with waves pulled by cool
breezes
From the deserts sandy
mountains
and its simple barren beauty
To the flatlands of the prairies
where the wheat flows of
mans duty
Across the world I place the
breeze
to flow to you on wings of a
dove
from across land and seas
For the warmth of the air
on the wings of the dove
is made of my heart
of my soul, of my love.

John Lee Wilson
THE SOLDIER

Hired by your Uncle Sam
To do a job worth doing.

Called by our President when
an enemy needs destroying.

"WARR" is really a four letter
word
The world knows this is true,

But in time of National
Emergency I know what I
must do.

A U.S. Fighting Man! A
Defender!
Black or White!

Ready for the battle call be it
morning, noon, or night.

Armed with Training, Pride,
Honor
and a Weapon in my hand,

Defeating my Countries
enemies
on any distant land.

Freedom is the Prize, The
soldier has died for in the past.

Someone must dare to give his
life to make sure that Freedom
Last.

Sharon Lundberg
THE IRKSOME INSTITUTION

I am so tired of school, and
the golden rule.
I'm always very tense, because
the pressure is so immense.
I study for a test, confident
I'll be at my best.
But when the test arrives I
break out in hives!

Home work in every class,
trying hard just to pass.
Staying up till eleven, getting
up at seven.
No time to rest in between. No
time for my own being.

The pressure is really rough,
and two days are not enough,
To prepare for the upcoming
week. This isn't the life I
seek.

Teachers cram knowledge in
my head and fill me with a
sickening dread.
They make me worry every
day, regulate all that I can
say,
Then tell me how lucky I am,
and how they wish they were
young again.

Sharon Deirdre Waters
FUTURE VISIONS

The pain in my body,
The pain in my head,
The dreams come true,
I won't look ahead.
With recurring dread
The dreams are all night-
mares,
I know they're all true,
The when, the where, and the
how
Are confused.

Valerie C. Vernau
EVENING OUT

A gentle tinkle of music
the sudden flicker of flame.
Careful brushing of locks and
primping in front of the mirror.
A shower of scent, the last
minute touch.
A quick smug smile, the
hiss of dead light and
she's gone for the evening.

Maile Kagiyama
THE FALL OF AN AXE

The rustling of leaves
The chattering of squirrels
The singing of birds
The fall of an axe.

The silence of leaves
The silence of squirrels
The silence of birds
The fall of an axe.

Jackie L. Bond
TO YOU

Now nothing seems so new,
days are filled with gloom
and blue.
Dreams at night of lust with
you,
forgetting for me is hard to do.
Behind you have left such
traces,
as children, hurt and marriage
basis,
passion, love and secret places.
Forever I'll see you in other
faces.

Amy Foley Bennett
PASSIONS OF THE KITCHEN

You make me feel like saran
wrap
In love with itself, wanting
to stick,
Curving elastically over your
edges;
Adhering and attaching
myself, everywhere.
Or maybe a sheet of aluminum
foil.
Radiating the heat; warm
and perforated,
Silver and shining, needing
only to be
Crushed and crinkled, by you.
I am also a superlative piece of

wax paper.
Creating such soft, smooth
surfaces
You would slide slowly over
my skin;
Watching its protective
coatings melt.
Love, we will climb into an
enormous plastic baggie.
Twist our tops, let them cart
us off to be incinerated.
Our fire will burn, flagrantly,
forever;
As the world vainly tries,
to extinguish its flame.

Rebecca South
VISIONS

Visions
The day departs
to gather up silouettes
for the night to embrace
until dawn

Katherine Cain
OUR NEW GENERATION

Torn spaces of time
Grasped between sheets
Frayed with living.
Photograph faces
Staring outward
Enduring perusal
By a generation caring less
Than they used to;
Going into the future
Without looking back to
remember
Save things purchased
At costs none can count -
This want it now generation.

Maurice Barrow
MY MOTHER'S SECRETS

I opened the lid to an old
rusty trunk,
Unused for these many years;
I gently touched the treasures
it held,
Dampened each with my tears...
There wrapped in white tissue
yellowed with age,
I found an old friend of mine;
A big china doll that Santa
had brought,
And Mother had kept all this
time...
My first pair of shoes, a white
baby dress,
Two yellow curls from my
head;
The things she must have
treasured the most,
Two old " love letters " from
Dad...
Between the pages of the worn
family Bible,
Momentos were tucked here
and there;
A faded rose, old photographs,
a lock of auburn hair...
I'm sure she knew someday
I'd find them,

The secrets she never shared;
It was her way of showing love,
Assurance that she cared...
I seemed to feel her presence
near me,
and knew I'd never be alone;
I know her soul is safe in
Heaven,
But she left her love at home...

Ethel Eastwood Marshall
STENO TRIP

No poet's world for me,
the darkened glass is smoke
again
and Alice's Wonderland dwells
in the chancered
callus of my mind.

No world of poetry for me,
time and space are inky
blotches on my metal keys,
and whitened liquid erases the
fine tuning
of my consuming thought.

My world is not for poetry
defined
yet, my ephemeral days carry
me on
and what I feel is versed
beautifully
within.

Debi (Angel) Witz
A QUESTION OF LOVE

Could it be that yesterday will
be tomorrow;
that the circle will join and
begin again?
Could it be that we are pawns
that must
travel tat circle; meeting and
parting?
Will it ever end?
Emotionless soldiers, created
by
disappointment and failure
in Love...
Isn't Love supposed to hurt
and
confuse?
What is Love that it has
the right
to taunt and torture...
-to make happy then sad
-to bring laughter then tears
-to hurt then comfort, only
to
hurt again?
It isn't fair, or is it?
Could it be that Love is the
hardest test of
life; that the test has to be
passed before
the two pawns can travel the
circle in unison?
Could it be that the testing
never ends; that
there are no final grades, pass
or fail?
Could there be any good reason
for Love's
merciless and cruel torture of
the soul; that
it must survive, or die and
become numb to
all emotion?

Teresa La Quie Le Doux
**AM I MAD . . . OR JUST
HUMAN**

I can see the many beauties
of our world
Yet, I am blind
I can hear the songs of birds
overhead

Yet, I am deaf
I can smell the blossoming
flowers underfoot
Yet, I am utterly senseless
I can speak words to explain
my thoughts
Yet, I am mute
Without a proper mind to
observe messages around me,
I am without my senses till
death.

For,
I cannot see the lesson in my
punishment
Therefore, I must be blind
I cannot hear the peircing cry
for help from within
Therefore, I am deaf
I cannot smell the odor of
wrong and right
Therefore, utter senselessness
I cannot speak straight from
my heart
Therefore, I have to be mute
My mind must be empty of all
the right things.
Am I mad . . . or just human?

Virginia M. Eversole
SANDY BEACHES

We have no sandy beaches to
pic-nic on,
nor a seashore to walk along.
But we do have the sun by day,
and the moon by night.
The green meadows and
ducks in the summer
The crispness and flowing pure
beauty
of white winter snow
And each others hand to hold
and body to hug.

Charlene G. Jones
THE SHELL MOON

I remember once when I was
young,
I had sung of a place where my
life had begun.
A place where a glowing ball
had hung,
All alone in a pyramid that
reached to the top of our sky.
There in the water was an
often told tale,
It filled our minds with the
knolage of how the oldsters
had saved us,
Then brought us here to our
watery hiding place,
Our one protection from the
land.
Oh, but how they feared the
impending nearness of the
landers!
They would find us in a
nearing time.
We knew we could tell by
the predicters shell moon.
Ere long they were coming.
In expection we would watch
them swim by,
While the tide of the ages
wispered a coming discovery.
We would fade into a mystery
soon,
Leaving only the remains of
a culture.
For you arn't ready for our
wistom yet,
And when the last has faded
the glowing ball shall fade
also,
Thus the wistom of the shell
moon shall be gone.
Leaving only another shadow
mystery.

Audrey J. Christian
MY FRIEND BIFFLE

Life seemed over for me;
The one I loved was gone you
  see.
I even forgot God in my life;
That caused me even more
  strife.

Hopeless days and nights I
  spent;
In agony I cried.
A neighbor friend, I found one
  day,
She listened to me and helped
  my soul.

Sometimes, I feel God put
  her here;
To help me through, that
  awful year.

She never condemned me for
  the way I was living;
Even though she didn't approve.
Life still seems tough and sad
  at times;
My friend is still there, to lift
  me up.

I pray to God to bless her soul;
And lift her up when she is
  sad.
She is the most wonderful
  friend I've ever had.

Alvin W. Hass
THANKS MOM

In a distant land so far away
I'm still remembering this
  Mother's Day
Your soft spoken words, tender
  touch, and loving way
Making my life sunny when
  clouds would make it gray

Remembering those early
  morn's the smell of fresh
  mown hay
The roar of the rocks fighting
  back in crystal spray
You were always there to start
  me out each day
Making my life sunny when
  clouds would make it gray

So t'is in this poem that I wish
  to say
Have a Happy, Happy, Happy
  Mother's Day
For your love, joy, and peace
  is what I pray
For making my life sunny when
  clouds would make it gray

Grace James
AS I WAIT

As I sit and wait for you
I look around and enjoy the
  scenery
The flowers aren't blooming
But the trees and plants are
  all lush green

The sand is white
And the water is a sparkling
  blue
Out on the point the waves
  are breaking
And washing over the jutting
  rocks

There is a boat anchored at sea
That sits gently rocking to and
  frow
Providing such peace
For the owners who are resting
  on deck

Birds are flying from tree to
  tree
One even came down to peck
  at the floor

To see if he could find a morsel
While others were calling to
  one another
People are passing back and
  forth
Some in groups, some alone
Some on the sand, some among
  the trees
They all seem so at ease

Here you come into sight
The other people fade into
  the background
I see only you
As I wait for your eyes to
  meet mine

Kay L. Stamman
LEAVES

Like leaves on a tree,
we are.
Born green to this world,
we are.
Over a period of time
we grow and mature
until we reach our peak
in life.
Just as leaves
reach their color peak
in Autumn.
Burden of age
springs upon us
and as leaves do,
we fall to the ground.
Death bound for
eternity.

Katherine W. Stiller
MOTHER'S DAY

I was going to enter
    a contest
    on the radio
with 25 words or less
    on my little postcard
telling the world
    (or at least the local DJ)
why my mother
    is The Best Mother
    in the world.

But no one has to know that
    except you and me, Mom.

Eileen Halpern
BETRAYAL

Love is something that was
  meant to be free
Like the seagulls flying above
  the sea
I must not deny the things
  that I feel
I must understand that these
  feelings
are real.

Pete Saunders
DUSK

the air stills
my thoughts silently
transforming light
into shadows subtly
the full moon reflects
upon them rising
my mood to mellow
as dusk dawns

Florence L. Cripps
**TRIBUTE TO THE LATE
PRESIDENT KENNEDY**

He's gone-the beloved President,
  respected and loved by all
The old, the young, the in
  betweens,
From far off lands, the Kings,
  the Queens,
To his life's companion,
  Jacqueline
It must have seemed like a bad
  distorted dream-

His little ones will never know
  what it means to have Daddy
  watch them
What it means to have a Daddy
  watch them grow/
We couldn't help but smile at
  the skittish steed
As he tugged and pulled at the
  shortened lead,
Wondering what it was all about
Doubtless expecting his master
  to mount-
We have no right to wonder why
This gentleman President had
  to die-
The hands that marred his
  pleasant features
Must have belonged to the very
  lowest of creatures,
Now they will have to control
  matters as well as they can
For they may never find just
  such another man,
But, we hope the one that
  has to pick up broken threads
Will get strength and Guidance
  for the great tasks ahead/*

Cass W. Reasor
**THE SHIP THAT SAILED
THE SEA**

Raise the anchor ye hearty
  lads,
And soon we'll sail the sea;
To the forward bow and do
  it now,
And the land no more we'll
  see.

When we were married the
  vows we said,
Would last forevermore;
But the sea she rolls, as the
  story's told
And we drift farther from
  the shore.

The sun shines bright in the
  summer days,
But we have the winter, too;
I love you Hon, I love our son,
And I love our daughter, too.

Some days are good, some
  days are bad,
And some should be skipped
  o're;
But the sea she rolls, as the
  story's told,
And we're looking for the
  shore.

Our ship is solid, tho the sails
  are patched,
The decks are good and sound;
Our love will last, till our
  bodies' cast,
Into the cold, cold ground.

We set our sails for an easy
  route,
In faith we set great store;
But the sea she rolls, as the
  story's told,
But we're closer to the shore.

Raise the anchor my lovely
  wife,
For now we sail the sea;
To the forward bow, and do
  it now,
Our love will forever be.

Barbara Jayne Harold-Ah Kuoi
CRYSTABELLE

Crystabelle...
Are you there
Or are you not?
Where is there
And who are you,
Baby Blue...

Belle Starr...?
Real name, Mommy Jayne,
Bernadette
or Lady Rain?
Not to worry,
There's room for all of you
At the inn.

Confidentially,
Concerning yesterday,
Did you not ask me
What it took
To cause rigidity,
Desperation
And restraint?

(Ask and you shall receive)

Now relax,
Name this home,
Create space
For your family
And a pathway
Of answered prayers
For you.

Beau Stine
THE KNIGHT OF THE ROAD

He was a noble sort of man
  that wandered through our
  land.
As he wandered from here to
  yonder,
  the life he chose is a wonder.
He's met those so true and fair,
  showing all he passes how
  much he cares.

He wondered through time
  touching lives,
  bringing love to those he met.
His tattered and torn clothing
  gave little shelter from the
  rain and sleet.

His spirits low, his hope fading,
  on through life he kept on
  wading.
Maybe someday he will give up
  his urge to roam,
  and find a place to call home.

No one knows his lonely life,
  except his Master from above.
When in life all he sought,
  was the choosen one he can
  love.

There are many who cast
  stones
  when there is little that is
  known.
He is a knight through-out
  this land,
  so touch him with a helping
  hand.

Though time came, he had to
  move on.
  We'll always remember our
  Vagabond.

Thomas R. Boughan
A TREE ON THE ROCK

We renew our relationship now
As time flows ever on for us.
The madness goes on a parade
  of time this day.

For love makes us blind to the others around us.
As we sit beside a tree on the rock.

Nevada S. Johns
SUICIDE

No schedule changes were made in my day
To help you find a better way.
Letting you reach for hands that were withdrawn
While my hands with a positive grip,
 might have made you strong.
Looking, without seeing the anguish
 and self rejection
Never reminding you that man's love and loyalty
 are not perfection
Listening, but not hearing the moans
 of emotional pain deep within
Surrounded by family, yet your agony
 was borne alone like in Gethsemone.
I'm like a coach after the game has been played,
Thinking how the calls should have been made
Thinking of things I should have said and done,
But time and life are spent, this game is over
 and nobody won.
If the subtle knot of life could be re-tied
 and life's game could be replayed
I'd build a barricade of love around you
 to keep the negative thoughts away.

Esther Mazza
MY QUIET HOURS

My quiet hours are precious to me
Especially as evening draws near
I talk to the Lord!, He answers you see
It seems like He's waiting to hear.
Waiting and listening like a dear friend:
I, pour out my problems, joys and sorrows
Not in a prayer, I don't have to pretend
I talk about today and ask about tomorrow
His answers come in all different ways,
Oh! So hard for me to understand,
Sometimes, turning my nights into days
But! In my quiet hours He holds my hand.

Delta Moore Drobnick
THIS LAND

Some years ago when I was a girl,
My family went walking one day.
It was out on the Montana prairie,
In the wind the grasses did sway.

My aunt and uncle and cousins Went with us the land to see.
And I said to my father and

mother,
"Does this land belong to me?"
"Yes, this land belongs to us, Child,
It is our very own.
A part of this vast prairie," Said Daddy, "To us does belong!"
Those words made me so very happy,
I could not contain my joy.
I laughed and I ran on the prairie,
Like a child with a brand new toy.
Forever I'll love the prairies That are part of this land so free.
And pray that God will always Save this land for you and for me.

Stuart L. Williams
BROTHERS

Brothers are we in blood
Two people bond together by the blood of others
Yet, brother we're different
You have your world and I have mine
Yet, brothers are we
You like hunting, fishing; pictures are for me
Yet, different are we
You have a family; I have none
Yet, brothers are we in blood

Vanda Brown
SAY WHY DID YOU MARRY ME?

You don't like the way I walk
You don't like the way I talk
Say why did you marry me?
You Say my clothes are too revealing
My smile is too appealing
Say why did you marry me?
When we went together
We took strolls in all kinds of weather
But now you sit at home
And I walk alone
Say! Why did you marry me?

Dawn Marie Rappa
SHELTERED

Slowly I have been ushered into this womb
Small as it is, it is my world
All the exits have been locked behind me
All the shades have been drawn to hide
 the hideous creatures from my view.
Censored is all that enters these portals
Prudently chosen are the people allowed in
Each visit is timed, each movement is watched,
Each weapon, used for my torture,
 is carefully sterilized.
A slight tear is found in the drapery
Through it I steal sights from an alien world
Intrigued, I press against the window
All this which I've never seen, leaves me
 with a feeling of ignorance
I see my sheltered world is not complete

There is so much more to learn
There are so many lands to explore
The pioneer in me begs to escape
 from these sterile surroundings
I ask, softly at first, for my release
My release is forbidden
It is said that I am now dirtied
I am made to feel guilty
 simply because I need to learn
I must step out of this tomb
Slowly, for the light must not blind me
I must walk tall, proud, and straight
With the confidence of a saint
 I must emerge

Thomas J. Russell
THE STAR

Lying by the sea last night
We watched a star's celestial flight.

I saw our star within a tear
Descending slowly toward your ear.

And as it lingered there so near
I kissed the star and tiny tear.

The tear was sweet and salty, too.
The star was cool as summer's dew.

Tre Pallisco
MOOKIE

Sometimes when I look at my Mookie, I think she knows something I don't.
She has a wisdom about her that beholds me.
She carries herself with assurance and dignity and reflects a warmth nestled right next to the part of her that can't be touched.
How curious this animal is.
She gives her love to me and asks nothing in return.
She knows I love her just because I'm me.
For a cat to be so wise seems almost inhuman.

Lilli Ginden
AWAKENING

Within the night
the light that waits before the dawn,
starts yawning,
then rises mistily to stretch itself
cross trees and rocks
and little birds, whose merging forms
arrange the sounds,
that make it morning.

Kelly Shaffer
SEASIDE REVELATION

I once stood alone
 on a high mountain cliff overlooking the sea.
Waves crashed against the rocks;
 Sands were carried away with the receding tides.

So my life flows-
churning emotions inside of me.
Past
 meeting
 Present,
rushing into the future.
A lonely seagull cried;
 My heart reached out;
 We soared the heights together.
And in the stillness of the moment,
 amidst the deafening waves,
I felt a sense of belonging-
 A touch of wildness.

Mark McNease
HANDS

It was hypnotic charisma
 Those hands,
Moving and looking at me.
We quivered each other
Yes sir, we fell apart.
The fingers dreamed on me
In order, one at a time
And I shivered like fast water.
It was a first impression
 Those hands,
Shaking hello, saying a name.

Wes Rine
CASTLE ON THE MOOR

A finer palace I've never known
Than this castle by the Moor;
And never a lovelier maiden
Spun dreams behind its door.
The youthful vision of ravens hair
Who met me near the glen
Was gentle, yes, in her courtly gown
And the envy of jealous men.
But she laughed when I spoke of my desire
On the morrow of that night.
It seemed the coals of my brain were fire!
As the knife flashed in her sight.
She'll dance no more when Arion plays,
But sleep in silence with the darkest night
Waxed by a pallor of death.

Hall R. O'Regan
THE PERSON I AM

Cold and alone I walk these streets
 Never to a soul I dare to speak
For it's the fear inside that lights my way
 I feel this fear is here to stay
Often I have wanted to speak from within
 Often I have wanted to be your friend
But an unknown voice I've heard inside
 A voice so strange, I begin to cry
Might it be the voice of anger and aggression?
 Or the sullen voice of deep depression?
"You're a man among men" this I've been told
So then my feelings I must withhold
"Maintain your image through-

out the years"
But my eyes are swollen with
salty tears
Feelings and fantasies I'm
willing to share
Who will listen; who really
cares?
It's sad to think of me as JUST
a man
When FIRST a person is
what I am

Sally A. Schumacher
THE STREAK OF SUNSET

The sunset streaked across
the sky,
Its blue and crimson drew my
eye.
I watched it peak and fade
away
So slowly at the end of day.
I stood alone and took it in,
Its glorious, gorgeous rays grew
thin.
The colors bursting forth were
bold,
In mauve, strawberry, plum,
and gold.
The gentle breeze was soft
and warm,
Its flowing softness was its
charm.
I felt relaxed, yet full of life;
The sky was cut as by a knife.
The colors blended not, but
stayed
Distinctly different as they
played
Upon the far horizon there,
Then disappeared into the air.

Lori Hougaard
I'M DEPRESSED

Down,
    Downer,
        Downest,
Are my spirits when the day
curls to bed.
Worries burst, triggering gloom,
deep, deep
in my boggled head.
So d
    o
        w
            n am I, I can't come up
to give a
cheating smile,
To false friends who stay only
true for only
a little while.
This is my fate; I'm trapped!
I'm doomed!
And happiness cannot appear,
Cause I want to be like this
awhile, so
please don't interfere.

Sandra Lynn Barry
**ONE DAY IN THE LIFE OF
AN ONION**

I was just getting ready to go
to bed
When all of a sudden I felt this
hand on my head.
It was picking me up at the end
of my spine
And I yelled; "Oh no! Not me
this time."
She layed me down and put a
knife to my throat
And I yelled; "Not that way,
I'd rather be choked."
She put down the knife and
took out a gun
She said to me; I'm sorry poor

onion this has to be done.
Just then I remembered the
refill of my odor
I kept releasing my gas, til she
thought I was a boulder.
Then she put me back to bed,
With a softening pat on my
head.
Then I saw this real bright beam
And just then realized it was
only a dream.

Mary Kae
HAPPY BIRTHDAY - RICK

I remember the day that I was
blessed
by God with a very special
"guest"
The awe, the pride, the tears
of joy—
A priceless gift child, my baby
boy!
Miniature perfect, a creation
from above—
"He's yours for awhile, please
fill him with love".
I held you, and kissed you;
wiped way your tears
While God's plan unfolded days
turned to years.
Good times and bad times
memory knows—
They're part of God's plan son,
and help you to grow.
So many "life's lessons" I've
not taught you yet—
Treasure quiet moments, know
what to forget.
Be gentle and kind son, learn
to listen and care.
Share all your good fortunes;
know God's always there.
Some days you'll drink from
life's sorrow cup—
Know when to give in, but
don't ever give up.
May God's infinite wisdom
guide you each day.
Let Him lead without question—
for He knows the way.
As you reach out for manhood,
and all life has to give,
With honor, pride, justness and
humility—LIVE!
Love,
    Mom

Kathy Carr
SUNRISE...SUNSET

Sunrise...
A new beginning with an
eternal glow.
Bringing with it,
The loveliness of mankind.
A peaceful sort of love
That's reflected on the water's
edge.
It slowly grows to abundance
As my pain and fear weakens...
My dreams broaden.
Time passes calmly by,
As the morning's stillness is
broken.
Freshly made trails are
highlighted
By the sun's boldness;
And it's warmth peeks through
The branches of the tallest tree.
People are scattered far below
Scurrying to reach their goal
While the beauty is still secure.
Sunshine is powerful, yet
relaxed.
It's strength draws the earth
And the mountains close

together—
Almost as if they're united.
But the glory that shined
overhead
Is leaving.
Night cautiously moves forward,
Blocking out the radiance of
the sunlight.
Even my dreams have faded...
But reality still remains.
Adding to it, the beauty and
serenity
Of the tree-tops are greatly
begillerent.
Times goes on consistently
And it now appears the end of
this day,
With much accomplished
And new thoughts for
tomorrow.
It is now sunset...

Julie C. Holmes
I LIVE

A friend stopped in a day ago
she just stopped in to say
"Have a nice day" and
    I smiled
A friend called the other day
he just called to tell me some
onery things that he had done
and
    I laughed
A friend of mine many days ago
was killed upon a cross
for me it was a great loss and
    I cried

Storm
FRIEND

Friend
Reach out to me
And grasp my hand;
Hold me when I fall.
Friend
Grow tall and strong;
And as it reaches out
Wrap my security around you.
Friend
Hold my hand forever
Let my strength be yours
As yours is mine.

Martha Louise Stewart
YOU ARE

You are the rock on my
mountain
    my strength when the path
    is steep
You are the stream in my ocean
    my lifeline when the water is
    deep
You are the tree in my forest
    my guide when I lose my way.
You are the sun in my cloudy
sky...
    my warmth when cold is the
    day.

Evelyn B. Ryan
THREAD OF LIFE

I cannot give of myself
Lest I give of Thee.
For You are I,
And I am You.
Separated,
I cannot live apart from Thee.
And though oft I estrange
Myself from Thee,
Yet always I seek the umbilical
That ties me ever to Thy bosom.
Alone,
I am nothing.
With Thee,
I am the
Universe of Life.

Jana K. Downey
NATURE

The Sky so bright and lightly
shone,
The grass so green and slightly
blown.
The trees so tall and fully
sprout.
The flowers small and boldly
stout.
The wind stirs and makes a
sound.
The flowers so small, touch
the ground.
The trees so tall, wiggle their
leaves,
The grass so green blows with
the breeze.
The Sky so bright grows dark
at night.
But all will awake in the
morning with a new shining
light.

Kennard V. Wilson Jr.
BLUE SKY AND ADOBE

See the sky
rinsed to a clear blue
from the rain
the adobe buildings
a year older
their lives draining back
into the land
from whence they came
as the water spills over them
refreshing them
making them clean.

Grace Shelton Dukeminier
SONNET TO ECOLOGY

The child goes off reluctantly
to school,
While parents spend their day
at home or work;
The insects toil all day; they
dare not shirk
Lest they be judged, alas, a
mortal fool;
Each creature has a place; it's
nature's rule
To put all things in line without
a quirk;
Ecology in tune, we must not
smirk
Or criticize our fate with
ridicule;
We mortals with conceit have
torn asunder
All things created for our
livelihood;
Destroyed, demolished, ignored
the good
Of nature's beauty through
greedy plunder.
Now each soul begins a time
of wonder
And prays we all at last have
understood.

Kim Westrope
RAINBOWS

My life is a rainbow
of happiness,
And you are my pot
of gold.
And all I need is
what I've got,
If what I've got is
you to hold.

Mary Robertson
NIGHT TRAIN

Voices from another time
Intrude upon my sleepy mind
And conjure up a memory
Of midnight treks that used to

be.
A whistle blew a minor chord.
An engine's voice thru silence
roared
And rhythmic clatter on the
rails
Made venturesome the peaceful
dales
Trains travelled thru on
journeys far
To busy stops that seldom are
But long ago that simple fact
Meant little. All my bags were
packed.
The engineer, my only friend,
Would let me ride til journey's
end
And then would bring me home
again
Before mere man could
comprehend
But in mind's eye I journeyed
long
To Paris, Rome and Old Hong
Kong
And spent my nights in parts
unknown,
More distant now that I am
grown.
I still recall that silver snake
That wove around our crystal
lake
And slithered loudly down the
track
With moonlight glinting on its
back.
My dreams were built around
that train.
It haunted me with its refrain.
Its clatter rattled me abed.
Its whistle echoed thru my head.
It calls me still though I am
grown
And thought such fancies
overblown.
My life's ambition is once more
To hear that night train's sooty
roar.

Ralph Glenn Howell
THE BEES

Few drones, one queen—a
hundred bees encore
At work near nightfall's fast
approaching shade;
New petaled stamens fumbled
gently more
Than ever winds unleash their
golden raid.
Born hope escapes the sting of
fright's delay
And leashes freely to the
coupled draft;
Rechanneled gold filled sap
delights the sway
Of stems responding to the
creature's craft.

Alessandro Padovan
DILEMMA

Nowadays I'm feeling old;
Inside of me, I am cold.
So what am I to do but sit
and pout?
For me life has all kinds of pain
And things that make me go
insane.
So what exactly is this life
about?

As this world is spinning 'round,
I am feeling so let down;
I think: it's best to get off
while I can.
So I go look for a rope,
Since I've given up all hope
Of living in this crazy world
of man.

But before I choose to go,
I think of every single woe
That has befallen others in
days past.
Then I wonder if it's good,
Whether or not I really should
Surrender and call this day my
very last.

For the more I recollect,
I begin to think and suspect
That there were some things
that were not quite so bad.
I begin to realize on this day
That there just might be a way
Of dealing with life's troubles
before I'm mad.

So once again I'm here
With not too much to fear
Of falling off into the deep
abyss.
Although I cannot tell
If all is really well;
I know that love is one thing
not to miss.

Olivia DeCamp
DON'T DELILAH

Stay away from him, Delilah.
Stay away from
this male.
He belongs to me, Delilah, and
he'll never
be for sale.

Don't tempt him with your
favors, don't tease
him with your toys.
Stop making all those promises
of nights out
with the boys.

Don't soothe him, pet him or
let him know
you care.
Please, oh please, Delilah, don't
try to cut
his hair.

Don't take away my Samson,
it'll make me
awfully sad.
For you see, Delilah, he's the
only poodle
I've ever had.

Leyten Fontaine
TODAY'S CHILD

oh child of sunshine
child of delight:
there's more to you than
golden harps
and darts
and carousel bars;
there's night!

for in you run the dinosaurs
carousing through the trees
in you the soul of an
earthbound snake;
and in you blows the quick
abandon
of a bluebell breeze
a sudden sneeze
or the hot fudge icing on an

ice cream cake.
black blind night
poor child
settles in the shadows of your
mind
and time
and temperment:
blood wild!

what long ago and now for
forgotten mirror on the wall
can justify your mindless
vanity?

what silent call from ancient
astronauts
can separate the bell and toll?

what beastly terror robs you
of your sanity
and what insidious slime
degrades your soul?

oh child of sun
child of night:
oh precious child
which is it?
are you lightly dark
or darkly lit?

Denise Smith
JUST A PASSING THOUGHT

Do ever think of me?
Do you remember the times
We had together - Just you and
I?
Or are we just passing thoughts
each new day?
It's hard to say for sure
But this I know
Someday you'll really care
Let's not wait forever!

If you think of me sometimes
I'll be satisfied,
Because then at least I know
Deep down inside you really
care.

Each new day, if we're apart
or together,
I think of each little thing you
did,
The sweet things you said,
And the unbroken promises
made.

And that's when I begin to pray
That I'm not just a passing
thought
With each new day -
Because I love you so.

Nellie Henry Moore
LE PETIT SAINT

So young to die . . . . .
So short was his life span,
But tears must not preclude
The miracle in God's plan;
For God's gifts are eternal,
Man's faith must deny
complaint,
And rejoice in the birth of a
baby,
Born in the stature of a saint.

Lou Anne Smith
SUDDENLY

Suddenly, as if the world had
stopped,
I was in total confusion and
darkness.
What had I done to myself?
Running away again...
But the door to the path of
escape had frozen shut.
It was as if someone had
grabbed me,
And thrown me at myself.
And there I was...my naked self-
So selfish, stripped of my

unrealistic dreams,
Stripped of my perfect picture
of myself.
There was a child searching for
love and happiness,
clinging to the wind,
And, in desperation, grabbing
anything the wind brought by.
But the wind was not blowing
anymore.
"Look at yourself!" cried my
soul,
"There are shadows of your
past scratching at your closed
mind.
Let them in; collect the pieces
of your life.
Slow down! Slow down!
You are looking for love
without loving yourself.
You want to take, but you can
not give.
You are trying to find your
happiness in someone else.
You are trying to drink wine
out of an empty glass."
I stopped and listened to the
voice within.
Happiness filtered into me as a
stream slowly trickling into
a pond at the bottom of a
hill.
Love came like a sunrise lifting
the darkness.
There was strength to pick up
the pieces.
All that I had searched for was
in myself...
There was hope.

Catharine Herder
HOME SAFE

As we welcomed our son and
his kids on that day
The emotions that grappled
our poor feet of clay
Were so varied, co-mingled, and
all out of tune
We must jump in a straw pile,
sail over the moon.

Overseas they'd been living for
more than twelve years -
Bangladesh had its fratricide
war, floods, and tears;
Nepal was no Shangri-la, no
open door;
And Jordan too close to the
Persian Gulf war.

But for now they were back in
the United States
Where there's freedom, and
laughter, and Golden Gates.
We're assured as their baggage
is lugged into our home
That it's real - they're here -
and won't soon again roam.

Dolores Dahl
RAGS OF YESTERDAY

Yesterday is
but a glimmer
though I strain
to see it yet...

Trying...
to remember
things that I
would best forget

Memories that
have no bearing
on the 'me'
today...

I continue...
wearing garment
old, and wrought
with fray....

Covering...
the golden gown
of 'now'
I foolishly
Walk in rags
of yesterday
not knowing
I am free....

Gayle Gaddis
ALL IS QUIET

Tall and proud are the trees
As the still water
  brushes over the rocks,
And the wind blows -
But all is quiet.

The birds chirp merrily
  in a soft way
As the leaves rustle softly,
The air is fresh and clean -
But still all is quiet.

Peace is everywhere,
In the trees, water, and rocks,
It is beautiful -
And all is quiet.

Samuel H. Goff
NEW YORK SUBWAY

He fought his way Uptown,
In subways dank and dimmed,
Ravaged and desecrated so,
By sickening obscenities,
Spewed everywhere in the
Demonic scripts of Graffito,
Spawned by faceless vandals
Whose rage and culture left,
Fecal sweepings of dung and
  spoilage,
All witnessed by listless eyes,
That stared ahead in quiet
  defeat
At curlicues that led to
  nowhere,
And melding with each
  mournful scream
Of wheel and rail announcing
His sad journey's end.......

J. R. Boyd
**FOR WHOM THE WELLS
  TOLL**

Finnian rainbows carve cycloids
  of people
waterfalling from pendent
  crystal balls
forthwith disembogued into
  hopes disemboweled
marooning themselves within
  their sultans
prostrating of carpet,
uncontested Shroud.
Embellished-bows they arch
  astill
below the wishing wells
whither thrown their pennies
while tossing their heads
trusting their dreams to vesper
  bells.

Gilles E. Soucy
PEACE

Bright rays of light; shining,
through grey clouds, seems to
  be,
A vast emptiness;
Bluer than the sea.

How quiet and serene, things
  are to me.
Sounds of the wind echoes
through the trees.

Life never stops, death always
  near
The burden of sorrows.
The care for one dear.

A time, when, alone you may

---

find
How vast this life.
When you find yourself
Stop to notice;
Everything there may be.
Listen to the winds
Talk to the trees
then you can say
You're really at peace.

Dorothy V. Uthes
MY TALK WITH GOD

I had a talk with God today
In a very peaceful kind of way,
As I knelt to pray beside my
  bed
I felt God's hand upon my head.
Lord if ever I should stray
Please help to guide me back
  your way.
I'm sorry when I make you sad
So I'll try harder to make you
  glad.
By dying on the cross one day
Your Precious Son prepared
  the way
To Eternal Life that we may
  share
Through Jesus Christ because
  You care.
I'm glad I talked with God
  today
And this is what He had to say,
"If you ever feel lonely, don't
  despair,
just call to Me and I'll be there."

Ronald J. Olson
SPRINGTIME

Spring is now blooming,
  the plants come to life.
The buds are now opening,
  end long winter strife.
The colors of Springtime,
  white, purple, and pink.
The odors of flowers,
  any fragrance you think.
Nature in full view,
  for all to see.
Its glorious colors,
  for you and for me.
Look at the beauty,
  in the world around.
Look at the wonders,
  here to be found.
Winter is restful,
  yet marvel in fall.
Summer's for living,
  but Spring best of all.

Eleanor Attaway Patch
BRIGHT, DARK NIGHTS

Poems come to me in the dark
  of the night
When God is all I can see.
He stands out there in His
  Brilliant Light,
Saying; "Child, write this down
  for me."
I do not question His order, for;
I am His child I know.
Though my old house is almost
  gone,
I don't worry about that any
  more.
My wrists are sore and wasting
  away,
The left one has long since been
  gone.
Multiple disease has taken its
  toll and
Pain is still present at all times,
But; I must carry on.
As I rubbed the right one today
I heard my own voice say,
"Please Lord, don't take the

---

use of it away
Until I have finished the task
  I've begun;
To glorify the name of Your
  Wonderful Son."
I felt His smile beam down to
  me;
I know He will carry me all of
  the way,
As long as I can see Him there
  and
Until the lovely day, He will
  finally say,
"Come Child, move into your
  New Home
Forever with Me to stay."

Olympia Daiutolo
**WHEN I HARD THE
ANGELUS RING**

With tear-dimmed eyes and
  heavy heart
I walked along my way,
No peace of mind had I until
The Angelus rang and I paused
  to pray;
Reflecting on my blessings
In the past and in the now
Both great and small - then with
  faith renewed
Sighed a sigh, smiled a smile,
  and somehow;
Divinely secure in its inner
  peace
O how my heart did SING!
Simply because I paused to
  pray
When I heard the Angelus ring.

Eugene A. Firsich, Jr.
DREAMS

Your presence invades my
  dreams,
A part of my fantasies.
With you the night is peaceful,
For in my dreams we share love.

Janell M. Fry
ANOTHER DREAM

Somewhere here
Far away
Another dream
Another day.

So alone I fear
So many uncried tears
Clouds of grey
Hanging in my way.

Escape is almost real
Mind taking me away
To the place I feel
Another time, another way.

Blue and green
The mist surrounds
Lonely dreamworld
Where peace abounds.

I see it all
Nothing to see
That what is you
This which is me.

Endless confusion
I only run

Somewhere here
Far away
Another dream
Another day.

Judie Lynn
MORNING BOAT RIDE

Gray, cloudy skies
Water is gray, too;
What a difference
When they are blue.

Thick, foggy mist
Covers all to see,
Feels like a cloak

Falling over me.
All is peaceful
Except the fog horn,
Hear the seagull?
I feel reborn.

Here we are
Back at the city,
Time for work -
What a pity!

Jean Kolin
**NOVEMBER 1938 - AND
MANY YEARS LATER**

There was splendor and
  luxurious living on board of
    "The New Amsterdam"
Carrying Jewish refugees to the
  land of "Uncle Sam"
Those who were lucky to
  escape the terrors of
    "Nazi-Regime"
Great was their joy when of
  the "Statue of Liberty"
    they caught the first gleam
Manhattan glittered in its power
  of light
When we landed in the middle
  of night
Unknown, long forgotten
  relatives were waiting on shore
Compassionately to their heart
  and home they opened a door
Many years have passed since
  the time I arrived
A life-time of events and dear-
  ones I have survived
After each loss I have gathered
  new strength to go on
Following the stream of life,
  I was never alone
"God gives us strength and
  clothes according to the
  weather'
    (I once heard my mother
      say)
Who has faith and courage will
  always find a new way
To give continued meaning to
  life, if live we must
The only way to go on and to
  adjust!

Tracy E. Johnson
WHEN THE PARTY'S OVER

When the party's over I'll go
  back into my shell,
When the party's over I'm sure
  I won't feel well.
When the party's over who'll
  take me home?
When the party's over will they
  just let me roam?
When the party's over will life
  be the same?
When the party's over will they
  even know that I came?
When the party's over will I be
  left to clean up and turn
    out the lights?
When the party's over will my
  mood hit its heights?

When the party's over will I
   fall or will I be stout?
When the party's over who'll
   sweep me down the steps
   and out?
When the party's over will they
   laugh at what I did?
When the party's over will they
   laugh at me while I'm hid?
When the party's over who'll
   pick me up?
When the party's over will I
   still have an empty cup?
When the party's over who'll
   stand by my side?
When the party's over who
   will have said hi? and who will
   have
   lied?
When the party's over will it be
   over for all or just for me?
When the party's over where
   will I be.
When the party's over I'll go
   back to my room.
When the party's over there'll
   be nothing left, but the gloom!

Katherine Brooks
THE MALL

One gigantic structure,
   encompassing in its
womb tinsel, greenery, a past,
   a present,
a future.
For me it is an experience, a
   change that
propels me into a world not
   alone, but
with others, in quest of
   companionship.
A reaching out, a longing to
   grasp at the
   masses.
To look, to listen, to wonder
   at this
phenomenon of a new age.
A metropolis filled with people
   rushing,
talking, eating, shopping, in
   search of
their destinies.
They, too, have a need to
   explore this
land of oz, this maze of modern
   day
life, as I search with them, if
   only
for a time.
Waiting for the bewitching hour,
   when the clock strikes nine and
   this
great structure becomes barren
   and
cold,
For without the people it has
   no life,
no purpose, only an empty
   structure,
until tomorrow comes.

Iris Kindel
FEELINGS

When you make love to me
I tingle from head to toe
I know how you feel about me
But how deep does the feeling
   go?
Is it just upon the surface
Being fake from the start
Or do you really love me
From deep within your heart?
How long will your love last?
A month, a week, a day
I can almost hear the words
When you come right out and

say:
I'm really sorry kid
But it just can't work out
So please leave me now
It's good-bye, I have no doubt.
Then I'll be sad for awhile
But I'll get over you
I'll get over how you hurt me
By saying things untrue.
It'll take some time
A month, a week, a day
Just like your love ....
Feelings fade away.

Eugene Anthony Dioguardi
RADIANT NIGHT

Leaving his house before dawn,
   An Arab walked into the
   radiant night.
He bore the characteristics that
   made him solitary,
   His dark skin, black hair, and
   Asian eyes
That saw within and without.
   Suddenly, the Arab's mind
   breached
Into the universal energy
   surrounding him,
   That singular, undetected
   figure becoming aware
Of the violent existence of the
   stars.
   Stars, like giant, luminous
   spiders,
Fiercely using their forces of
   gravity
   To prey upon each other.
He watched a universal mystery
   fragmented,
   Consuming itself to persist;
Sensed an all-pervasive
   consciousness
   Of a cosmos aware of itself;
And received a revelation to
   the mind's eye,
   For a brief moment, seeing
   as the Creator sees.
The Arab, himself adrift on the
   face of the earth,
   Longed for the discarded,
   sacrificial forms of deity
Now lost in an eternal drift of
   a self-cycling universe.
   A vision to take through life,
   that radiant night
Hidden within the glimpse of
   an Arab's eyes.

Linda Elaine Kingsley
LOVE

What is Love?
What does it mean?
Is it kept within ones soul?
Or can it be seen?

As God made us to love our
   sister and brother,
He also created man and
   woman to love and cherish
   each other.
When two people walk hand

in hand,
They go to the altar to make
   their stand.
Now they must realize the big
   step is here,
But remember the Lord will
   always be near.
If you should become
   discouraged and don't know
   what to do,
Just call on the Heavenly Father
   to help and guide
   you through.
There will be hardships that
   come along the way,
Then pray that tomorrow
   becomes a much better day.
For if two devoted beings can
   stick with their mite
   problems of today,
God will bless them with a
   stronger love that will
   never fade away.

Ruthie J. Knight
HE'S COMING

He's coming, He's coming, He's
   almost here
I know for I've heard this,,year
   after year
He didn't come yesterday, not
   even today
I'm sure I have time for the
   world and to play
I lived my life doing just as I
   pleased
But now my life is ebbing and
   soon it will cease
I'm sorry I waited, and wasted
   those years
For now it's all over, there's
   nothing but tears
Oh wait! There is hope, I've
   opened the door
He knocked and I listened, not
   like before
Thank God you were patient,
   you waited for me
You knew what I needed, much
   better than me
He's coming, He's coming, I'll
   say it again
Don't ever forget it, for in HIM
   you will win.

Katheryn L. Boyd
THE DANE

Feign madness to evoke truths
From uncle-father, mother-aunt.
Princely nobility wastes as
   coffins close
Under the hand of a jeweled
Poison, caressing a heart loyal
Faithful to a phantasmic father.
Dirge fennel Ophelia entombed
   for tears;
No son's salt revives for invasion.
Yorick's wormy crown,
   Horatio's scholary weeds;
The denouement of celestial
   zest.

Candace Blair
OCTAGON

Silent, sensual, sentient power:
   Transparent as gloom, opaque
   as night—
Soul of rigid, wretched steel;
With melting only moments
   feel.
Only rage remains to relish in
   the fight.
Icy, invincible, impenetrable
   shell:
   Silent as the tomb, final as
   the grave—

The deadly traps unwind;
He sees, though all are blind.
Noble as the knight, though
   cursed as knave.
Mystery, melancholy, memory
   haunt:
   Rending his soul, neither half
   nor whole—
Conscience voices as a plague;
Guilt and brotherhood grow
   vague.
Triumph is the prey, though
   death the toll.

Gayle Patrice Miller
LUNA

In the ivory curve
         of my husband's arms
                  nestled

   my flesh
         as a shell's own living
         creature
                  is found
   the fullness of lady moon's
   highest tide.

Annie Lindsey
WE DYE THE DOG BLUE

we dye the dog blue
each Easter
my wife's toy poodle
goes Rit dye blue
and we are amused
and the child
is amused
and the dog, mercifully,
does not seem
to care.

Annie Lindsey
MOON LIGHT

moon light
river stretched reflection
(a pause in our own)
distortion
of a million possibilities
colored glass
and wavy lines
invaded darkness
night mirrored.

MaryLou Doubleday
SILENCE

Are you brooding again
or
are you deep in thought?
Are you my lover
or
are we like two opposing
   magnets;
repelling in circles,
   - turn after turn -
never to meet or to agree?

Barbara A. Brigante
CLOWNS

Gaily sought
   the myriad clowns
Teasing smiles
   of founding delight
Sounding horns
   of triumph play
In apting form
   a Voice arose
Silly clowns
   you spend your day
Seeking smiles
   in bright array
You spoke
   so loud and blissful
That
   the day became
So useless

That
  the words became
So tiring
  that these playful clowns
Repeated
  every other word
In jest
  not knowing if the day
Would pass
  unnoticed
By their master's voice

Kit Snyder
A HAIKU

The Gracefull Swan
Glides on the Glass-like pool
Under the tall willow trees

Anita-Turk-Eden
A POET'S CONFESSION

Poetry is more than verse and
  rhyme.
'Tis inspirations at the time,
Of one who feels the need to
  write-
To bring his deepest thoughts
  to light.
'Tis what he feels and thinks
  within,
Of love, beauty, of peace, of
  din.
These he expresses with his pen-
And thus reveals his thoughts
  to men.

Jodie Stewart
NO ONE CARES ANYMORE

When it comes to killing no one
  will resist
I wish fighting, and violence
  didn't exist
Hurting people, no one should
  ignore
We try to talk it over but it
  ends in war
People are put in jail for crime
  every day
Some violators are caught,
  others get away
People every day give their lives
Weapons that are used are guns,
  and knives
People do not even care
Put violence around me, you
  wouldn't dare

K. L. Kaspar
MY FRIEND

I wish I were as good a friend
  as you have been to me,
You've been a help through
  many things
  with truth and practicality.
Greater wisdom than history's
  kings
  who blindly ruled and failed
  to see,
The simple truths of common
  man
  as you my friend so swiftly
  can.

Maureen S. Neely
LAST NIGHT

Last night
I could not sleep,
For thoughts of you
Kept swirling around in my
  mind.
I could see your face vividly
In the dark corners of my mind,
And could hear you softly
  whisper
"I love you" in my ear.
I could feel your hand against

mine, for a moment,
Then moving up my arm
As you encircle me
With your love and warmth.
I could feel your breath
Soft against my cheek,
And could feel your warm,
  gentle kiss
On my lips.
Just then—when I felt you near
  me,
I knew I could never leave you,
I would always love you,
And I was able to sleep,
  surrounded by our love.

Carol Trent
SOUNDS OF WINTER

It was very cold on that late
  December night.
I was outside, all alone
Standing 'neath a street light.
My icy hands dug deep into my
  parka made of down,
As I heard a dog barking
Far off, beyond the town.
So faint was that lonely sound
Amidst the snowflakes
That were falling all around.
I began walking at a moderate
  pace
And the lights from the houses
Shone brightly on my face.
As I turned the corner I could
  hear children say,
"Mother, what will Santa bring
For me on Christmas day?"
So faint was that cheerful
  sound
Amidst the snowflakes
That were falling all around.
I made my way back to the
  street light
Where I stood illuminated in
  the cold dark night.
Two blocks away I heard
  carolers singing.
Their voices rang out
Like church bells ringing.
So clear was that joyous sound
Amidst the snowflakes
That were falling all around

George A. Bruce
FOR WHAT I PINE

Some for the dreams of the
  deep red wine;
Some long to say, "The world
  is mine!"
    But I; Ah, I am different.
I for the love of a woman do
  pine.

Miriam Hubbard Frick
TRUE FRIENDS

True friends are like priceless
  treasures
Like a Van Gogh or a Renoir
Like a rare black pearl

True friendship grows from a
  very special need
Often a private need
Of people for one another

The bonds of true friends
Are deep and life long
Friendship hurts as do friends
  hurt
Friendship is joyous as are
  friends joyful

The needs or desires of true
  friends are oft times
Felt or known without words
Call it a magical or spiritual
  bond

Between persons who need
  each other
True friends have a silent
  understanding
Between themselves
A certain something of which
  only God knows

Indeed, true friends are as a
  priceless gift
Acquired through a mutual
  need or desire
A gift, which if broken can
  sometimes be repaired
But most certainly never
  replaced
Guard true friendship with
  your life
For it is through this
  relationship
That you both will grow into
  a more
Wholly complete person

Phyllis Joy Steinberg
EVERYONE

Everyone is by themselves,
so wrapped within their souls.
They won't let me enter,
they make me feel alone.

Philis Cohen
LOVE IS

Love is you & me
we can be friends 'till eturnity,
Love is true & sweet
like the birds going tweet, tweet;
Love is friends
like a ring that never ends.

Love is something that never
  fails
like a boat on a river that sails,
Love is to last for, forever & a
  day
and to be true in each &
  everyway;
Love is the way I like to be
and most of all is coming to you
      FREE.

Roberta Ann Collier
REFLECTION

Oh, it is lovely to be young,
And feel the fiery blood of me
Rushing and singing in my veins
Life is my own particular oyster
And for time and dreaming
I have eternity.

Oh, it will be lovely to be old,
And feel the fiery blood of me
Grown gentle and tame
And slow in my veins
For when you have no time
  at all
Somehow you still have
  eternity.

Kerri Hawkins
**I'D HATE TO LIVE IN A
CITY**

I'd hate to live in a city,
You'd get lost in all the crowd,
There's no birds, but it
  doesn't matter,
You couldn't hear them
  because it's too loud.

The grime doesn't wash away,
It has nowhere to go,
They hide their rising histeria,
And never let it show.

How they ever stand it,
Really blows my mind,
A dreamer from the city,
I have yet to find.

I don't like seeing the city,

Because I don't like seeing the
  air,
You can never see the sunshine,
You just hope that it's still
  there.

Why they ever live there,
Makes me want to cry,
How can you reach for heaven,
If you can't even see the sky?

Betty Jeanne Wilhite Brewster
REFLECTIONS

Before me lies a thousand fears
Of future incarnated years;
Of memories buried in a haze;
Of bondage in a mortal maze.

Before me lies a thousand shoals
Of moaning, musty, naked souls;
Of yawning chasms spewing
  fire;
Of wraiths depraved, aroused
  desire.

Before me lies a thousand
  dreams
Of stranded love, misplaced
  scenes;
Of tainted replicas of my past;
Of trials before the Saintly
  Caste.

Mary Lynn Brown
**THE MAN, THE MIGHTY
  MAN, MY SON**

As I hold the child that I love,
  he grows to be big and strong;
Then I'm standing on a far
  away shore, he grew to be big
  and strong;
Then in a distance I hear a
  loud roar, as the sailor, my
  son, goes sailing
  out to War.

I raised him from a small one
  into a mighty man;
He's gone to fight the battle
  to do what ever he can;
And if he should get wounded,
  he will soon go back again,
for he's a man,
  a mighty man, my son.

Now I stand in a battlefield
  amongst the giant War;
They've found his tag,
  double 501.
I look amongst the bodies,
  then over on the ground, I
  see a wounded sailor,
It's a strong and mighty man,
  my son!

Oh, yes, he's wounded, but his
  teeth are clenched, he doesn't
  make a sound,
    not even a moan.
The medic said, "He'll be all
  right, but he could have lost
  his life."
He's a man, a mighty man, my
  son!

Anne Sturdivant
SEASONS OF CHANGE

The winds of summer
Changed the direction
Of your thoughts
About me.
I will wait till
The winter freezes
My memories of you.

Sheryl A. Cormicle
DAWN

The waking of the sun
  is delightful fresh and new.
It's rays are shimmering like a
  diamond on the morning dew.

Bright yellows, oranges and
scarlet
reds,
Each wisp of color as thin as
a thread.
The sun is seering through
foliage
like a knife,
Detecting each tiny movement
of
life.
It wakes up the birds and they
begin to sing,
And soon the whole world with
bird song will ring.
This thing is as fresh as a
newborn
fawn,
The most beautiful creation;
dawn.

Andre "Abe" Tucker
IN SEARCH OF YOU

I search for love that can be
true,
With lots of joy and
happiness too.
I search for a woman that is
so fine,
When I look at her, she blows
my mind.
I search for a woman to be my
wife,
To help me struggle through
all my strifes.
I search for a woman to be the
perfect mother,
For our kids to say there is
no other.
In my dreams I search for you
And I hope you're searching
too!

Florence H. Anastasas
NOVEMBER

The sun bows slowly down
Beyond October's dying hour,
And in a golden town
Receives November's dower,
To whence the bride will move.
Plain cloistered bedroom
Will mark the season's love
And greet November's groom.
Weep not, thou human guest!
Learn that a caste of snow
In one's own private nest
By contrast - helps Love grow.

Martha Alderfer
SEARCHING

When I was young and had no
fears,
My life was easy, there were no
tears.
I began to reap what had been
sown,
When I grew older and my life
was my own.
I went from living in my
father's house,
To that of a man I had made
my spouse.
I bore him a daughter and then
a son,
But my fight for identity had
just begun.
I cleaned and changed diapers
by the score,
I day dreamed my life away,
I could take no more.
My life was all wrong, I
couldn't live in the past,
I had to escape and find me
at last.
I ran and ran til I could run no

more,
And I found Jesus the open
door.
He gave me his strength and
determination to fight,
And because of all this my life
would be right.
He gave me the victory which
now is mine,
And I'll know who I am til the
end of time.

Anna H. Barnard
LITTLE GARDEN SPIDER

As you, so slowly creep
through the fragrant
flower garden, little spider
Emerald green eyes upon you,
you can not see
Up, up, up in the tree.
Ever so sharp, kitty claws, and
wide opened jaws
hoping to catch you,
As you, so slowly creep
through the fragrant
flower garden, little spider.
So hurry, hurry - scurry away,
But please, come back to play
In the fragrant, flower garden,
with me
Another day.

Jeanette Peterson
THE FIRE

Raging and mad; the wild fire
grew.
Fierce and aglow; as the wind
blew.
The kindling had been there
for quite sometime,
Smoldering-smoking, unaware
of the time.
It started to glitter from one
little spark,
Flaring-shimmering; leaving
its mark.
The fire was coming, they tried
not to heed.
Defying-ignoring; approaching
with speed.
Without any warning, without
e'er a plan,
Slinking-stealing; into the heart
of the man.
The woman evading the feelings
inside,
Eliding-not heeding; just trying
to hide.
But the fire was raging and
clouding their minds,
Uncaring-not thinking; unafraid
of their finds.
The two frenzied fires that
were burning in each,
Were burning as one, that day
on the beach.

Hillman Collier
ODE TO OLD ALLEN

He was born way out in the
ocean
Way down by the leeward isles
Then he started upon his
journey
Which would take him
hundreds of miles
He picked up speed as he
traveled
They all knew he was master
He showed them all how big
he was
Spreading his woes and disaster
He covered a lot of territory
For miles and miles he was
spread
He passed over Dominican

Republic
And left a lot of people dead
He went on over by Cuba
And then to the Yukatan
There was nothing that could
tame him
Not even beast or man
He slipped into the Gulf of
Mexico
And filled it up to the brim
Every one on the Texas coast
Had great fear of him
He came on land near
Brownsville
With all his might and pride
But he shouldn't have come to
Texas
Because that's where Old Allen
died.

Edna M. Rimini
FRIEND

As a dear precious friend of
mine
God bless you with his love
divine
As the beautiful rose burst
into bloom
Your radiant smile will chase
the gloom.
May God help you climb life's
rugged hill
The raging storms of life He
will still
Listen to the bluebirds soothing
melody ring
Joy and happiness to your heart
bring.
The wheels of time roll down
stream
May your life be a beautiful
dream
Stars at night glitter and gleam
True friends weave a lasting
seam.
May God protect you from
above
Caressing you with His tender
love
Walking with you side by side
May His blessings with you
abide.

Joan Janueswski
I OFTEN WONDER

A winters night so long ago,
a child was born of this we
know.
I often wonder how it would
be,
to really live or even see.
This Holy Child so loving too,
I often wonder just what I'd
do.
Would I want to hold Him in
my
arms? Or even scold Him too
at times?
How proud his Mother must
have
been, to have a child as great
as Him.
I thank Our Father up above,
for giving me so much to love.
Not just on Christmas should
we pray, for Christmas should
be everyday.

Roger Wilson Cook
MORNING SUN

You are small
And delicate
As a flower
And your face
Turns toward mine

When I approach
as if
I
were
the
morning
sun.

Margaretha Murphy
LONGING

I left my homeland so long ago.
My new home, oh, I like it, too,
But sometimes there is that
longing in me.
I want to go home.
That little house there, down
the hill,
I can't forget, I love it still.
Where my mother used to say,
"Be careful, darling,
when you play".
I want to go home.
To see that old house just once
more,
Listen to the sound of the
squeeking door,
Pretend my mother is still
there, that I am safe
and have nothing to fear.
Once more I want to go home.

Zaida M. Nighswonger
SPRINGTIME

Two kitty cats and a puppy dog,
Two little squirrels on a big
Oak log.
A sassy jay on a bough above
Singing away, his song of love
To a little girl jay, in a tall
pine tree
Preening her feathers in
expectancy.
A little brown wren in a
sheltered place,
Picking up bugs from some
Queen Anne's lace.
A shrinking violet dressed in
blue
A tiny crocus, of golden hue.
What a happy thing to know
it's Spring,
Chant Nature's children
As the Blue Bells ring.

Theresa Pope
UNSELFISH KNOWLEDGE

He spreads his wings into the
wind and flies.
Feeling the warmth of the sun
hung in a silky blue sky.
Soreing across his vast domain
seaking what he needs to
survive.
Finding what he needs, he is
content.
With the roar of the endless
crashing of waves he again
takes flight.
I look at the things around
me in amazement.
The sun sets making a rainbow
of colors across the sky

Time passes slowly as the
quiet night takes over.
Then the stars light up a
blanket of darkness.
He returns from somewhere
unknown to me.
Taking from the ocean only
enough to sustain him.
Learning all I can from him
I move on to determine my
destiny.
Taking with me the simple
knowledge he unselfishly
gave.

Lydia G. Saenz
EXISTENCE

My emotion is so powerful
that it exhausts me
I wish that you didn't exist
so that I would be certain
it was a hopeless case
But
You do exist, and this makes
it unbearable for me to know
Just
The mere fact that you are
there
And
I am unable to have the total
You!

Judy Ploger
THE MAZE

I must be on my way.
Cuz I see no reason why I
should stay.
Someone please give me a
cause!
I can't stand this silent pause!
I wander around in a daze.
I wish I could get out of this
crazy maze!

A. I. Price
INTO AFGHANISTAN

Russia's furry claw
scratches
across the cover of Time
shredding detente,
scattering isms,
and tracking salt
into the bleeding wounds.

The union is in a state
of ire,
conjoined and vengeful
as it tracks
the beastie's droppings
already iced
beneath the fallen snow.

Alice G. Wilson
THE OCEAN SPEAKS TO ME

The oceans incessant roar
speaks to me as I stand on its
shore.
"Come closer you can see
the beauty of my body
And the strength of me."
Perfidious voice, I am well
aware
A waterey grave is what lies
out there.
Even now I can feel the sand
swiftly washing from under
my feet.
I turn and head for dry land
and do not heed your siren call
Nor find your voice is sweet.

Vincent La Barbera
WOUND

in a cloudnight she fled
dreamsong visions
first love
for a comfort
and creeping

of future dawns
desire.
thru the painted brush
and paradise.
under capricorn weeping.
vacant eyes followed.
and a rogue in marvelous
youth holding a spoon
and chain, and wanting
only to feed her
hungry breath- his day

Guyvan B. Shirley
IF I WERE FREE

If I were free
I would sing to the heavens
Mounted on an ancient
pyramid
Of the Eastern Sea
If I were free
I would teach to the world
Especially those
Who would heed to me
If I were free
I would use my knowledge
To help all of those
Who are poorer than me
If I were free
I would give my life
To preserve
Humanity
If I were free
I would do whatever I could
To help those
Who need me
If I were free
I would give all I have,
LOVE, only
If I were free

Dennis Mendis
THE FLIGHT OF STEPS

Time and tide will run it's
course,
And will respect no man's
bidding.
Twilight comes and then the
dawn
Of another new beginning
Of life and love, labor and
rest.
'Tis the circle of life
That goes on and on.
Calling us one by one,
To the flight of steps
That leads to the Eternal.

Nancy Musselman
IN HIDING

A face is just a cover
For emotions we discover;
It can mask and hide
The feelings deep inside,
But please do not uncover!

Vivian R. Steele
LOVE

Does anyone know what Love
is?
Is it a feeling or just a memory?
Love is a memory forever in
your broken

heart.
Love is a feeling of being joked
about
to his friends!
Love is a song with a familiar
tune.
Love is a poem with a
unfinished line.
Love is a feeling! Do you know
what love
is?
Love is a time of many moods,
but exceptionally
Love is a time of Happiness
and a time of sadness!!!!

Janice R. Hillberg
OUR AMERICA

A is for Allegiance
the pledge we've all said.
M is for Military
of the countires we've led.
E is for Equality
the opportunity we share.
R is for Riches
no other countries compare.
I is for Immigrants
to our forefathers we belong.
C is for Confident
we know she'll stand strong.
A is for Anthem
"Old Glory" waves proud,
Stand up and salute
let the voices ring loud.

Phyllis E. Malone
MY HERETIC FRIEND OCIE

You have patient with everyone
All the little things in life
Or just simple things you do
With the kind words you say.
"A friendly smile"
For those who are sad
The kindness of your words
make
"Someone Glad"
The friendly greeting you give
"Here and there"
Make the little time we shared
"The joy of being friends.".
A sparkle of your kindness
Will probably set a town on
fire
Your wish is my will
Your laugh amid my tears
I talk to you about my burdens
All flown my anxious fears
"We can only be friends"
"Just by being ourselves"
Your kindness reveals hope
that's
"strong and sure"
Your kindness remembered
someone
"dear today"
May I learn from your kindness
to impart strength, courage,
grace
faith and hope.

Tara
MONARCH

fallen -
I found him.
scattered-
on the beach amongst autumn
leaves.
crippled-
by cold tears and sand.
his colors, as my own-
only powder.
in us each, a breath of life
barely felt,
then torn away.
tenderly-
I lifted him from the shore
and carried him home to lay

on the ground beside my son.
for even in death-
their fragile wings
still flutter.

Louise Sewill
BEE VERBS

Communicate
Cooperate
Navigate
Pollinate
Congregate
Manipulate
Ventilate
Incubate
Buzz

Linda Ivie Burns
**NATURE'S FONDEST
DREAMS**

Tis the time of
Summer showers,
Springtime rain
And winter snow.

In this field of
Lovely flowers,
There again to
Thrive and grow.

For these epic
Hills of plenty,
Mountains over streams,
Choose to comfort
In their beauty
Nature's fondest Dreams.

Linda Martin
FAR AWAY LOVE

Tonight is lonely as
Books lay upon their shelves
Seeking for a voice from
beyond
To come into their lives
Tonight, its me with my
dreams
Somewhere out there is you
Maybe in the middle is right
or wrong
But now I can really say, I
do love you
Tomorrow is another day
Bearing the thoughts of you
I can only wait for a call
As it may end as a fantesy
instead of reality
The ringing of my phone
Spranged me upon my feet
But only to hear anothers
voice
Within a dismay of my dream
Then after a long waiting
period
I began to wonder if its all over
or was it just all dreams
Which got me crying during
the nights
That one moment finally came
Now my tears all poured out
For I pray you still are mine
That will never come to end
Time came- for we have wed
Your my husband and Im yours
No one can or will try to split
us
For we have won each others
love

Ruth Elizabeth Freeman Miller
UNTITLED

Wishing you were here with me
tonight
doesn't help matters at all,
Wishing I could reach to touch
your face
whenever you call.
Hoping maybe things will

change
and you'll be holding me tight,
Hoping we could be still once
    more
talking through the night.
Watching the waves roll up to
    me
I wonder where you've gone,
The fresh, clear air could set
    me free
If I could just wander on.
Its always taken me time to
    love,
and much more time to heal,
My feelings grow with strong,
    deep roots
And I can not cease to feel.

Yvonne Marie Allan
RUN

A five year old boy, in red
    cotton shorts;
    running through the park,
Away from a five year old girl;
    running after him.
A 10 year old boy in blue-jeans
    and work shirt;
    running through the school
    yard.
Away from a 10 year old girl
    in pigtails,
    skinny with braces; running
    after him.
A 15 year old boy, tanned and
    brown,
    with hair below his shoulders;
    running through the streets.
Away from a 15 year old girl,
    who's body
    is curved and a face like an
    angel
    running after him.
A 20 year old man, in black tie
    and tux,
    walking to the alter with-
A 20 year old woman;
    who's tired of running.

Therese Musco
A LOST LOVE

My days were lonely and so sad,
There was nothing to make me
    glad.
I did not laugh, I did not smile,
It seemed that life was not
    worthwhile.
And then he came along one
    day,
He too was sad as he looked my
    way.
And when I looked at him, I
    knew
That fate had planned this
    rendezvous.
I fell in love, and hoped that he
Could feel the same about poor
    me.
He never spoke, but in my heart
I felt that we would never part.
But fate called again, and took
    away
This dear little cat who planned
    to stay.

Alvin Coleman Jr.
THE LAND OF YESTERDAY

In a dream, I traveled to the
    land of yesterday
I saw, the brightest of my lifes
    days, on display
I saw, the product of memories,
    come to life
I saw, in the land of yesterday,
    good times and strife
The land of yesterday, is not
    always sunny and fair

The land of yesterday, love and
    hate live there
The land of yesterday, a land
    of the happy and sad
The land of yesterday, in
    cohabitation good and bad
There is pain, in the land of
    yesterday
There are loved ones you see
    there, those who have gone
    away
There are visions, visions of
    hopes and dreams that have
    died
There are pictures of hurt, of
    anger and of tears that were
    cried
The land of yesterday, a place
    of heartache, a place of joy
The land of yesterday, a place
    of sorrow, a place of fun, for
    a little boy
The land of yesterday, the
    place where I grew
The land of yesterday, it was
    hell and heaven too

Theresa Inglima Alessi
THE HELPLESS SOT

As we strolled, a weakened
    voice was heard;
Over the railing I peered to find
A hand and face raised in
    anticipation.
Tears flowing from fearful,
    dazed eyes;
He trembled, as his feet met
    the water's edge.
We lifted him to life;
Placed him on the bench for
    reassurance.
I dried his face with great pity,
Then slowly walked away
To leave him without the
    memory of this night.

G. A. Kimmons
LOVE IN A SNOWFLAKE

We live in a snowflake
and the world is cool
and white outside.

Your smile surrounds me,
keeping me warm
through the hours.
And as I kiss you,
there is love,
so strong and good.

Outside the world
is white and cool
as we share love
in a snowflake.

Marcia Pappas
TEARS OF A CLOUD

Sitting here watching the
    raindrops
Of a dark cloud hovering above;
So wet, fresh and sparkling,
Are like the tears of a sad
    person,
Trying to cleanse its soul.
The rain begins and clears the
    air,
A sad person cries and clears
    its worries,
A coolness emerges after the
    rain,
Like a sense of relief after a
    good cry.
A rainbow is in the midst of
    forming,
Letting one know a colorful
    painting is about to engulf
    the heavens,
As a salty tear coated smile

surfaces from a once sad face.
The tears of a cloud are now
    dry,
As are the tears of a sad person,
But they will come again and
    again,
As the clouds need to cry as
    much as you.

Sarah Harris Levy
WILL ROGERS

Our Will is gone -
A genuineness no generation
    can claim,
Since before the prophets came.

Possessed of simplicity -
Like unto their name,
Will's world held no room
    for conventional reign.

An unprejudiced Heart -
To spell so rare a fame,
Wonder, we can't all be the
    same.

Will's memory shall always be -
Unto us a poignant flame,
To remind us of the Glory in
    a name.

Lorraine Anderson Griffith
REMEMBERANCE

Bury me not in a cemetary thus,
But in the ground if you must.
On a hill under a maple tree
    where,
The winds and rain shall cover
    me.

Let flowers grow so all will
    know,
That I am there even in the
    snow.
And if by change my spirit
    wakes,
My presents felt thru the sod.
Mayhaps my spirit can reach
    out,
And feel the touch of god.

Laurel Saunders
HAPPINESS

How like a child
    I snatched at the arrogant
    butterfly flying by.
Vainly, yet persistently, I
    determined to pluck it
    from the air
    where it floated above my
    groping fingertips.
An entire day I chased that
    winsome creature
    Scheming, plotting, praying—
    obsessed with seizure.
Laughing, it eluded me again
    and again
    And yet continued to hover
    inches above my straining,
    aching fingers.
Mad with frustration, I
    lumbered back through
    the highland grasses over
    which I had earlier soared.
Greyness tied the earth and sky

together before me
    as the evening sun retreated
    in the west.
Only the brilliance of the
    butterfly, settling on a bush
    before me,
    could disturb the rigidity of
    the hue,
    until, allowing me to touch
    its velvet wings, it flew off.

Frances L. Johnson
OF TIME AND PLACE

Amid the confused
(contra) clamor
buffeting fleshbone
and drum
grows
certain
knowledge
I am   My time
in   is
my   now
time   here.

Stacey Haugh
VALENTINE LOVE

    Valentine Love,
Oh, Valentine love
    The world is full of
    Valentine love.

To say, "Be mine,
    be my Valentine."
Are read in many different
    rhymes.

    To day, "I Love You,
yes, I do,
    so let's be Valentines,
    just me and you."

Valentine Love,
    Oh, Valentine Love.
Won't you be my Valentine,
LOVE?

Joyce Ann Rea
DIANNE

As I sit outside in my chair,
I see your house, but you're
    not there.
Although we may be miles
    apart,
You will always be near me in
    my heart.
You know our mother gave
    birth to us as a pair,
And for us to be this far apart
    just isn't fair.
And if I had plenty of dough,
To Alaska where you are, I
    would go.
When I think of you, my tears
    I try to hide,
But they fall as easy as the rain
    outside.
And to each other we may
    write,
But it's not the same as having
    you in my sight.
I know you are having lots of
    fun,
In the land of the midnight sun.
I pray that someday my dream
    will come true,
And I can come up there for a
    visit with you.

Paul Eden McGannon
SONGS IN THE WIND

Today I heard Him in songs in
    the wind
Met Him in quietness within
    garden walls
Felt fresh and new in coolness
    of the air
Found His sweetness in morning
    dove calls

Saw Him in tenderness of
blossom petals
Found Him in air heavy with
flowers fragrance
Heard Him in water from a
fountain fall
Found His love in friends
rememberance

So in evenings quiet hours of
peace
The freshness of night time dew
I pick from each of these
blessings
And send God's love to you

Stephen Wayne Messmer
**HEAVENLY PARADOX
OF LOVE**

I love you more with every
rising day
With every waning sun I love
you more,
A waxing moon and starry
sky—sign my love to try.
Love walketh with me on the
outward way,
It stands to meet me at the
open door.
It's harmony low while other
sounds clash loud;
I'm always kept lonely amid a
changing crowd.
Love is greatest when I am
far away;
Love is grandest when I steady
your glance;
I love you most when rapture
has its say,
I love you best when we take
our chance.
In restful moments, or sportive
spirits—
Forever, all times, I love you
most, Sweetheart!

Shirley Stoneburner
MIDNIGHT REUNION

I have been draped in blackness.
Night has hidden me far, far
from passion.
Shadows linger stale.
Even this morning I saw them.
The trees have grown closer.
The world has drawn closer-
all in fear of this lonely life.
How we weep!
Stones gather speed high, high
this minute.
The tide swirls and spits its
wrath.
A unicorn has seen her first
day of confusion.
Magic has no name.
Love crumbles and falls.
Lust lingers in corners,
fragments of memory.
Here a possibility,
temporary answer.
Zephyr's calm again.
He lifts me,
draws me to his mouth.
The darkness recedes now.
Mist hangs-
this time in laughter.
His strength is mine.

Michelle Marie Cook
THE CONFLICT

I had a conflict
with my friend today.

At first I hated him,
but then I stepped back,
and stood there,
looking,
thinking!
I suddenly realized,

that niether of us were right,
yet niether of us were wrong!
It's only that we were unable
to see,
that we are two different
people,
with our own views in life.
And being unable to appreciate
our individualism,
we now stand more alone
and confused,
than when we were together!

Stephen R. Goudie
CHARMING SMILES

Yesterday's rainfall
still disturbs me so.
For hours I watched
as the deluge
blurred my vision
and ceiling sounds
thundered
and winds howled.
I watched as the city
was poured
and all that was left
were two lovers
taking a walk
on a rainy afternoon.

Chris S. Russell
CHANGING FACES

You invited me to the ball
in honor of All Hallow.
Perhaps you thought I would
be in white ruffles -
meek and sallow.
When I said,"You won't know
me, I'll be so beautiful!"
Did you think I would drop
my normal guise,
becoming trembly and
dutiful?
I joined you as a woodsy
nymph creature,
wrapping myself in brown fur
and whiskers
for the main feature.
I tricked you into portray-
ing the wolfman
with fang and moon lust
and furry hand.
We appeared to others to play
a great duet.
But, in truth, you went your
way and left me mine,
and once, briefly, we met.

Robert C. Hancock
**WHEN YOU BECOME
THIRTEEN**

Daughter, the transition
you're about to make is
forever
no turning back
Too old to be a baby
yet too young to be a woman
These years between are
sometime
called the difficult years
Dirtied by frustrations
and cleansed by tears
Each step you take now will
prepare you to walk alone
There are many miles ahead
and
that many ways to go wrong
Sometimes you will wish to be
older
Sometimes just a baby
in your fathers arms
But like a butterfly
you are not what you were
Just more colorful with your
wings
to take you through this

world
So go explore, seek and dare
and if you ever need a
friend
look over your shoulder
and I will be there
HAPPY BIRTHDAY
YOUR DAD

Cecilia Lee Culbertson
WISH

Bury me not in a casket
of white,
To lay in the ground
both day and night.
Instead, take my ashes
to spread on the seas,
And there I will sing
with the cool summer
breeze.

Mary Lynn Thomas
NIGHT MAGIC

Darkness counting down
To sleep, anticipation dreams,
Laying bare the waxen nerves
Of passive, daytime scenes.

Stillness with a pounding
Heart, electric air is dense;
Faster now, my conscious
moves
To seek its recompense.

Amidst this sparking drama
Then, a beam of light ascends,
Reaching out across the moon,
A dimly-shadowed friend.

Energized, my beam moves
On, compelling in its dance;
Soft, it sweeps you to my
mind-
Subliminal romance.

Linked through time, we
cruise
The stars , infinity in motion,
Moonlight laughing, sailing
free,
The sky our endless ocean.

Though fated brief, our astral
Flight, its beauty pledges troth-
Nearer now, the day we'll
meet
In mind and body, both.

R. A. Younkin
**THE LURE FOUND AT
PAWTUCKET RESERVOIR**

The water was low at
Pawtucket Reservoir,
We found a tangled line and a
lost lure
as she and I walked along that
shore.
I asked about her friend, but
she could assure me
that there was nothing between
them anymore.
In fact nothing had happened
anyway.
It was all a product of my
mind.
I couldn't untangle all this
line
so I snapped the lure off, then
threw it away.
It failed its first master to
catch a fish.
It was a hope that died, an
unfulfilled wish.
As I watched it sink in a
circling swirl
I had no choice but say,
"Good-bye,"
to the girl
and resume my floating,
motionless days.

Mark Stephens
THE NARCOTIC

I feel it working
as my mind it does strip
This terrible drug
I'm trying to whip
I don't have to think
as my power it drains
My vocabulary lacks
as my vision wanes
It wakes me in the morning
and lulls me at night
It's effects I am scorning
but can no longer fight
My nerves now in constant
strife
I think that I am hooked for
life
These drugs they say are like a
disease
They cover the nation and are
called T.V.'s

Gladys Fulkerson
MY FRIENDSHIP WITH GOD

I walked along the garden path
And God waved to me
From the gently moving
tree.
It was a friendly wave.

I moved along the garden path
And God smiled at me
From the flowers I could see.
It was a friendly smile.

I strolled on down the lovely
path
And God spoke to me
From the birds in harmony.
It was a friendly voice.

The world's a lovely place to
be,
The earth, the sea, the sky,
And fellowship is oh, so
sweet
Between my God and I.

William R. Buchanan
CHERYL'S SONG

Out of a cold, dark winter
In the wilderness

Came the taste of spring:
Sunshine, butterflies, and magic
Laughter and smiles -
Ever so timid
Ever so soft
Gentle on the wind.

Evening falls and darkness.

In the dawn, will there be light?
Lucky springtime or . . .
Just a chinook wind.
Just a chinook wind
On the long
Long
Road.

Leta H. Richardson
TROUBLE BROKEN DOWN

Trouble is something, we do
better without,
So brigh'ten the Smile, and cut
out the pout.
Now broaden' your shoulders,
be proud of your work.
And be a good neighbor,
But never a jerk.

T-is for truth, we must watch
what we say.
R-is for rules, we follow each
day.
O-for others, let's give them a
hand.
U-is for unity, TOGETHER WE
STAND.
B-is for blessings, to numerous

to count.
L-is for LOVE, with never a
doubt
E-is for equal, lets give it our
Best.

Just take it from here, and
we'll pass the test.

Jim Wedeking
**DO YOU REMEMBER,
JENNYE?**

Do you remember Jennye,
the leaves
as, twisting and floating,
they fell to earth around us?
We smelled their dusty smell,
and their dry, sunwarmed
crispness crackled
as we walked deeper into the
dark and haunted woods.

Mote filled sunrays
would, here and there,
spotlight
a tiny yellow flower,
an ancient, wise lizard
warming his gray and
leathery skin,
or a dusty, rotting log.
Where are those woods,
Jennye, now?

Jackie Lewis Greeno
THRESHOLD

I no longer wear ribbons in my
hair,
Unadorned,
I mask the girl within with
talk
About the world's affairs -
And sigh.
Funny how ribbons tie woman
to youth,
Dark haired or fair . . .
There are no eternal Springs,
Only Autumns,
And if God provides,
Daughters,
With ribbons in their hair. . .

Beverly Reno Tong
FREE

I'll make it, will you
I'll make it if I have to
I know I can be strong
If I'm right and not wrong.
They can't keep me on the
ground
Not tied up, for away I'll
bound
There is nothing that can stop
me
I am human, I will be free.
It's the law of man, for the
bad and best
I'll fight til I'm there no
matter the test
And you can to if you believe
We have the right, we belong
free.

Laurie Smith
**A CHRISTMAS EVE IN
WISCONSIN**

Brilliant colored lights shining
from windows
Glow against the sparkling
white crystals falling from
the sky.
Pine trees droop under the
weight of the snow,
As grey smoke pours heavily
from every house
Making everything seem
peaceful and still outside.
An occasional car moves

slowly along slippery
streets
To make an annual holiday
visit.
Indoors merry people sing
carols to celebrate the
season,
While others talk fondly of
holidays past.
A few remember loved ones
they cannot be with
And smile over wonderful
memories.
Creamy eggnog and fancy
cookies await on decorated
tables
To give everyone a feeling of
warmth and contentment
On a Christmas eve in
Wisconsin.

Mrs. Earl Hille
STRAWBERRY TIME

It's strawberry time again this
year,
So let's get the family car in
gear;
Come Janelle and Sara let us
not forget,
The keys and containers, all
set?
Now off to the strawberry
field we go,
With mouth stirring appetite,
you know;
And yes, there might be a dew
on the field,
But this won't make a
difference to our yield.
We are here, and what do we
see,
All of those cars - how can
that be?
It is certain that Bob and Sue
too,
Will like those strawberries
just as we do.
We go to the row with the
strawberry girl,
You are sure to find berries,
so give it a whirl;
My knees will they bend, my
back will it straighten,
To leave that container with
more berries a waiten.
It's worth it all though, they
really are good,
Now home we must travel as
fast as we could;
To freeze and prepare that
strawberry jam,
A shortcake or two will go
with our plan.

Jan Shook-Hagen
UNTITLED

Empty promises
Shadows in a cracked mirror
Reflecting nothing

Julie McArthur
**SWIM QUICKLY, SWIM
SILENTLY**

Swim silently, graceful beast,
Swim quickly, in splendid
beauty.
Be watchful for the murderous
predator.
For even with your gigantic
size,
Man can still beat you,
And savagely destroy you in
seconds,
Don't let him,
Swim quickly,
Swim silently.

We hear your cries from miles
away,
A sound of agony, a sound of
Beauty,
The effect leaves us still,
with wonderment.
Do not let the predator take
that
From us, or you.
Swim silently,
Swim quickly.
Precious mammals of the
waters,
I am saddened deeply to see
You massacred, piece by
piece,
To be left with only a
Bloody carcass of an
Innocent living creature.
Swim quickly,
Swim silently,
Stay awhile,
Whale.

Lisa Allen-Thompson
TAKE CARE OF LOVE

Love isn't a toy
It's a precious thing,
It's within someone
Not something.
It's not to be played with
Or bought for a cost,
That's how hearts are broken
and true loves are lost.
Love should be cherished
And well taken care of,
For if you don't
It will all too soon perish.

Tara M. Key
LOVE COMPARED

My love for you,
Can be compared to a seagull;
It soars to its heights,
and down to its lows;
It can go higher,
Than the human mind can
imagine;
But it never goes low enough,
For long enough to drown;
It can endure bad weather,
and hide for shelter;
It can drop on you,
But mean no harm;
It can be beautiful at times,
and a pest at others;
But the best thing,
About this bird,
Is that I'll keep it with me,
As long as it will stay;
And love it forever,
Wherever it may stray!

Leslie Carol Bush
BAD WATER

Down along his road of life
a man ran into an awesome
blight.
The water he drank
from a faucet sink
struck him ill and
limited to bed.
He soon joined the dead.

Lucile J. Mayhew
**THE LESSON OF THE
TUMBLEWEED**

I stood by my window one
windy day,
Looking out at the highway
bleak and gray.
Along the pavement came a
large tumbleweed,
Blown by the wind at
topmost speed.
As I watched it tumble, now
here, now there,

I thought to myself, it doesn't
have a care;
Just blown by the wind,
content to go
Where'er fate blows it, now
fast, now slow.
Am I like the tumbleweed
with no way to go
Forgetting Christ's promises
of days long ago?
God gives me a choice to
choose each day,
And Christ has said to me,
"I am the Way . . . ."
So I'll chart my course, 'til
life's victory is won.
For the Lord of my life is
God's own Son,
And I'll claim His promises
one by one,
From early in the morning,
until the setting sun.
So happy little tumbleweed
on the highway,
Tumble on, tumble by, on
your way to-day,
For to-morrow mayhap,
there'll be no gale?
Just roll along, tumble on,
down to the vale.

Florence P. Teves
QUESTIONS

A youngster asks,
How high is up; why is water
wet?
Why is Janie white and Joey
black
And I am neither one?
The first two
I haven't answered to his
satisfaction yet.
The last, I confess, leaves me
quite undone.
How to explain to one so
young
That he can and does belong
To every race, color and
creed,
That love is everyone's
constant need?
Will mankind help me take his
hand
To offer him a better
tomorrow,
And present a world filled with
loving compassion
And less pain, tears and
sorrow?

Leona Roth
GOOD-BYE SUMMER

Good-bye to summer with all
of its woe
Too many weeds to pull, too
much grass to mow
Humidity high, made energy
low
Good-bye summer, you may
go.
First no rain, and then to
much,
Lots of fog and heavy dew,
Bugs of all kind, I'll just
mention a few,
There were spiders and
crickets, and grasshoppers
and ants,
And wasps enough to scare
you out of your pants.
They came in our houses,
and swarmed on our lawn.
Were there already with the
dawn,
When I wanted to sit in my
swing at night
Around came the mosquitoes,

and did they ever bite.
My legs are sore as they can be,
From our summer time pest,
   poison ivy.
So if I say summer good-bye
I think I've given enough
   reason why.
I'm ashamed to complain
For it wasn't all bad
Remembering the good wheat
   crop we had,
And out of my garden came
   carrots, lettuce, and peas,
And many other good things
   to can and to freeze.

Donna J. Blaha
SOLITUDE

Solitude, I graciously
Implore your time to think of
   me.
Swallow me within your hall
Of memories that rise and fall
In different cycles of my life,
Depending on past joy or strife,
Of love I lost and did regain
And salty tears that left a stain
Upon my worn-out memory
That died in search of ecstasy.

Anita McLean Willison
HIGH MOUNTAINS

If I had always lived where
   mountains are,
Perhaps I would have gotten
   used to them.
I doubt it though. How could
   I still my heart
Each time I stood beside a
   mountain wall
Of solid rock whose top I
   could not see,
Enormous giant looking down
   at me
And far below, a thousand
   feet or so.

How could I grow accustomed
   to the fear
Of all their purpled majesties
   so tall,
Those kings of space that make
   me feel so small.

I think it would have been the
   same for me
A hundred times: that
   terrifying thrill,
Deep haunting silence on a
   mountain pass,
Yet longing for my safe green
   prairie grass.

Cyndy Weber Bateman
MEMORIES

As each fleeting moment passes
   by,
I long to be the ruler of time.
For if I were, I would stop the
   clock;
To be able to grasp each
Loving moment we share.

Time passes too quickly,
Our love is caught between it.
Time has captured our
   moments together,
And has locked them all away.

Our love today
Is now another memory,
Stowed deep inside our minds;
Never to return again.

Mary A. Bell
TO A BABE

Dear babe, your tenderness is
   as a strain
Of gentle music stirring fragile
   chords

Upon a heart once crushed
   with grief but now
Restored to peace by Him Who
   called the lambs
Unto Himself. Your peace is
   that of one
who trusts the love of mother
   and her arms.
The Master welcomed you and
   said that such
as you are of His kingdom.
   Bright your eyes
with purity; you do not know
   that you
have come through unprotected
   waters where
the tool of death has cut your
   bretheren off
by leave of manmade law and
   hand of greed.
The Shepherd through His
   tears will keep His own,
and banish wolves, and reign
   supreme, alone.

Dorothy Voelpel Miller
STAR DUST

I plucked a star,
   And pinned it in my hair,
The moon beams,
   Fashioned gowns for me to
   wear,
The breeze my cloak-
   Perfumed with essence sweet,
A cloud sailed overhead,
   And lay jewels at my feet,
The grass blades my slippers,
   And I, on dancing toes,
Waltzed alone, and softly,
   Lest I wake the sleeping rose,
All things were perfection,
   Waiting for you to view,
And I- enchanted,
   Waited there for you.

Marie Bartolotta
MIND-BLOWER

Goliath never knew what
   hit him
      ...He was stoned...

Beverly M. Benjamin
THERE IS A TIME

There is a time for laughter
There is a time for tears
Yes my children there is
Even a time for fears
But fret not my children as
God's always standing so near
You really don't have any thing
   to fear

Life is made up of heartache,
   pain and woe's
As each one of us finds out
As down life's highway we go
So my children each day do
   the best you can
And someday you will
   understand
We all have a part in God's
   master plan
Each new day brings us another

new test
Each new day live to the
   fullest
And do the best you can
And one day you also will
   understand
We all played a part in God's
   master plan
For you see my children this
   poem has a moral
God, has never promised us
   tomorrow

Vicki Lynn Mohr
VISIONS

Sometimes,
she wakes in the night
   sweat,
      pouring off her face.
Something that she dreamed
makes her heart race,
   with fright.
She is weak,
   and she knows
that being all alone is scary.
Without the strength of
   someone
      the confidence,
      and self-like, just go.
She lies in bed at night,
   alone.
      Waiting,
   and wishing
for her man
   to be by her side
      all the time.
But for years now,
   He has been gone.

Lottie Burk
IT

He was a coach;
he had lots to teach.
He was a little boy;
he had lots to learn.
Both knew it wouldn't be easy.

They shook hands
and spoke,
neither sure
if the other understood.
It had begun.

It was slow,
and sometimes,
it was difficult.
But still,
it went on.

The coach taught.
The boy learned.
The boy taught.
The coach learned.
It grew.

Soon, it matured.
It had caused two lives to touch.
And though afraid of it,
they never abandoned it—
the coach and the little boy.

LaTrelle Stock
ON THE THRESHOLD

Studying the words of the
   Master's Divinity
   Takes me into the realms
   of Infinity!
But as the Studies must
   progress
   It does behoove me to digress,
For an occasional word or
   phrase
   Stops me in an opaque haze!
To back up and scrutinize
   Why did the author here
   decide
To say these words in such
   disguise?
   But then the meaning true
   is found

And back am I on familiar
   ground.
I know my God, my Source
   and Creator—
   All of these and much, much
   greater!
And I, an expression of this
   Core,
   Can open up the inner door,
   for I
Am closer now, I am on the
   threshold!

Stephen Wood
FROM MARATHON ON

Aching feet from Marathon on,
"I kinda forgot,
But I think that we won."

Turtle tears
On deadtime sheets,
Pariah cries
In every guise.

All a man is
Is a scream of desire
With potential.

I'm gonna catch
The next low-flying galaxy
Outta here.

K. Welch
NORTH LAKE III

Dawn saw through the clouds
to paths ankle deep
another trinkle
mountain tear
ocean aimed
met the morning
overstepping the mudpuddle

Gail Schaefer
INFINITUDE

Air is an infinite sea of
   wavewinds
S w e e p i n g through space,
Realm of galaxies -
Timeless
Circuitous,
Residence of an unrealized race.

Star-strung auroras of aerified
   reachers
Inhabiting whirling, orbicular
   isles:
Remotest inhabiters -
Pervasive
Primordial,
Traversing perpetual,
   imperceptible miles.

Doris H. Hadfield
TONIGHT THE MOON

Tonight
the moon, a coy
senorita, shyly
peeps through her mantilla
   of dark
cloud lace.

Dorothea Germundsson
LOVE STORY

From vastly different spheres
Fate brought together
A boy and girl,
And bade them fall in love.
For a brief space they clung
   to each other,
In an ecstasy of pure joy.

Then Life, urged on by a
   Capricious Fate,
Spun them around three times,
And when they started forward,
With arms outstretched,
They went in opposite
   directions.

Years later, they touched hands
   in passing,

Recognizing each other,
Yet knowing that they
Must move apart
As the tides of their separate
destinies
Carried them on.

J. S. Mihina
THE QUESTER

The quester who travels the
marked lanes
Of this geosphere, a traveller
who remains
At a hostel for a few passages
of the sun,
Sees nought but a mirror of
the land of Charon.

He gathers his trifles and leaves
to go,
Puzzled, for the place at which
he tarried
Was of a place he did not know.
He goes with a pace that is
unhurried.

In leaving, he is carrying that
persistent hope,
That beyond the range of eye
to scope,
Will be a great gathering of
races of all kinds,
Another chance, a promising,
at finding men of like minds.

Yet, when he comes to the
meeting meadows,
At where the sky does
meet the land,
He will only find himself again
in a band
That is nothing but another
set of shadows.

Amy Greene
AUTUMN LEAVES

Damp drizzle drops down
from the deciduous rainbow.
Cranberry red, marmalade
orange
glare out through the misty fog.
Greeness overwhelmed
by dazzling beauty
blinding the eye with awe.
From above,
a checkerboard
of colors
waiting for the
       jump
         of
           death.

Pearl W. Sellards
AN ODE TO A TWO
YEAR OLD

There is nothing as sweet as a
Two Year Old
  There is nothing as wiggly
  or harder to hold
Never again will one be so bold
  Into pots and pans — then
  out in the cold.
Who laughs with glee, as you
chase and scold
  Then cuddles close, when you
  catch and hold.
And looks like an angel when
asleep in the fold
  This is your loveable,
  huggable Two Year Old.

Loretta (Keeping) Sherren
DRINKERS OF THE WIND

Beautiful Arabian horse
Magnificent graceful steed
Mane flying, nostrils flaring
A challenge to most men
It is no wonder you are called
"Drinkers of the wind"

Your face shows much
intelligence
Your muscles show such
strength
Your beauty, something to
behold
It makes one stop and think
The artist sees your beauty
In every stroke of paint
He puts you on his canvas
Bold and dark, not faint
To paint you any other way
To him would be a sin
For we must see you as you
are
"Drinkers of the wind"

Mary L. Ratliff
A MESSAGE TO MY SISTER

Weep no tears for me, nor
sigh your sighs;
For though I have marveled at
the wonders
Of our universe and basked in
it's beauty;
Long have I searched for peace,
and found it
Walking close to God.
He gave me a cross to carry,
and I have carried it proudly;
Honored that God allowed me
to share His sorrows
And His joys.
But mostly I have found in
Him the peace
I searched for all my life.
Now I have laid down my cross
To accept the fulfillment my
God has promised me.

Dolores A. Kellogg
SNOW

  SNOW! SNOW! SNOW!
Look at it BLOW! BLOW!
BLOW!
NORTH and SOUTH! EAST
and WEST!
Where will it stop, haven't you
guessed.
  SNOW! SNOW! SNOW!
Look at it BLOW! BLOW!
BLOW!
UP and DOWN! All Around!
Just like a Swirl.
What a Bright World.
  SNOW! SNOW! SNOW!
You have got to go go go
Were SAD! SAD! SAD! and
Getting MAD! MAD! MAD!
Can't you stop and make us
  GLAD! GLAD! GLAD!
  SNOW! SNOW! SNOW!
Where will you go! go! go!
I know! know! know!
Will send you to Hell! For a
spell.
And bid you farewell.

Abraham M. Habash
MY TREE

Will I again my palm ever see
That towering lydda stately
tree
Sway with grace in the
perfumed breeze
Against blue skies that knew
no freeze
And guarding groves of endless
rows
By the sandy shores of a sleepy
sea.

I roamed the world and saw
great lands
With diamond lakes and golden
sands

Yet when silence calls to
evening prayers
My heart toward the warm
plain hovers
Then miles and time would
melt in space
As lonely souls of friends
embrace.

Donna Young King
IT IS LOVE

It is faith that moves a mountain
mountain,
It is kindness that lends a hand;
It is hope that lights a candle,
It is grace that understands....
It is joy that lifts a heart,
It is goodness that heeds a call;
It is mercy that fills a need,
But it is love that does it all.

Lorrie Fisher
MEMORIES

Moments
Encased within our
Minds.
Original from all others.
Reminding us of delightful
Impish times.
Erasing all that is forgettable.
Slipping away without a trace.

Petal A. Beebe
A DIFFERENT KIND

Look into the faded eyes
Of age; find understanding.
See the lines upon the brow
Look; learn, see how wise.

Take time to care now
For this, is beauty of
A different kind.

Wendy Rose Peace
LITTLE TIGER

Lost in the woods,
a tiger cub
Lifted a paw to wipe
his eye.
As everyone runs
when a tiger comes,
He knew he was far too
brave to cry.
But when it is dark
and a night wind howls
and seems to blow the stars
  from
    the sky,
a speck of dust
can bring a tear
to even the bravest eye.

Doris C. Lange
MYSTERY

Days beginning
Sun and flowers
Lovely hours.

Nights ending
Shadows and twilight
Stars and moon-light.

Sweet mystery of it all
Another day beginning
Another night ending.

Rhonda D. Ross
I NEED YOU

I need you like the lakes and
the oceans need
    waters to flow.
I need you to guide me so I
may know which way
  I am to go.
I need you like we need the air
to breathe.
I need you to help me better
achieve.
For in you, I do trust and I do

believe.
I need you like a junkie needs
the most hardest of dop
  of dope.
I need you beside me so I may
be able to cope.
I need you like the flowers need
the warm rays
  from the sun.
I need you to be my only one.
Mostly, I need you to always
understand.
That, I need you like a woman
needs her man.

Jeanne Kirk
FAITH

In all the world there is no
sweeter thing
  than faith that stands in
  stalwart majesty.
Each weary heart would seem
to understand
  those who defy the storms
  retain their dignity.
A lovelier thing than this was
never seen
  when hearts grow dark and
  trembling in the night.
God looks and in a loving
kindly way
  sends His swift angel
  messenger of light.
Oh golden hope, this weary
heart might hold,
  survive through faith the
  storms that come and go.
Let my faith stand with
courage strong and bold,
  defy the firey darts through
  strife and woe.
Lord, let my faith forever
stand the test
  and help this trembling heart
  to understand
When through the fires I pass,
tried as fine gold,
  thou Lord art reaching out a
  helping hand.
I'm lifted from the valley's
deepest gloom
  and carried to great heights
  of love supreme.
God gives to me new life and
tranquil peace;
  I take with me the Christ
  whom I have seen.
He gives the promise of eternal
life,
  a ray of faith to light the way
  for me.
In all the world there is no
sweeter thing
  than faith that stands in
  stalwart majesty.

A. E. Wilson
TWO-YEAR OLD

You, young man of two, gave
me your trust
Bringing a joysong to my
fatherheart

Because you could grant no
  greater gift;
But my mind has been in turmoil
  turmoil since
Because some day someone is
  going to betray your trust
And you will take a step forward
  forward in growing up,
Losing some of your ability to
  trust others.
I cannot imagine who it will be
Or why they will do it
Or when it will happen.
It saddens me to reflect on the
  inevitable
But the joysong of love in my
  fatherheart
Assures me I shall never be that
  Judas.

Dorothy Bodwell
THE TALKER

Hot wind
from the south
searing my senses
with words dinned
in torrents from a mouth
that never stops.

I yearn for Frost,
cool, white page
who speaks only when bidden,
sparse words tossed
by cryptic sage,
sly humor hidden.

Soul's edges are singed,
faint breath
is fading; I wither
consumed,
caught in the path
of her everyday weather.

Shirley Lee Sawyer
LOVE

From the moment we are born,
  We begin to die again!
So I ask why should,
  We not tenderly love then?

Love is a gift God gave
  A gift which goes with us,
From our birth to the grave.

Love is the Bee
  On the flower;
Creating sweet honey -
  Not sour!

Love is the rainbow
  After the shower -
A promise in the sky
  As lovely as a flower.

Love is our beautiful gift,
  Which gives the soul a lift!
Love is with us now -
  As when we met;
Why should we not love then,
  Even yet?

Alice L. Roesner
TIME AND CHANCE

Time hath gone likes waves of
  light,
Far beyond the distant night,
Never more the mind to
  wander,
Yearn for things the heart
  doth ponder,
Far beyond the outer space,
Out of sight of human race,
With eagle sight to discern,
Owl like wisdom one must
  learn,
Now safe from reach of human
  hand,
How deceptive the ways of
  earthling man,
To lay a trap for one they will,
Blind, or maim, or even kill,

Why are their hearts turning
  bad?
Ears gone deaf, their lot is sad,
Have they gone to far this time?
For God to pay them any
  mind!

Irene Stalcup
AUTUMN

Fallen leaves crisp and brittle
Carpet the earth below;
Forecast of winter a little
And blankets of glistening snow.

The Great Artist turns leaves
  to hues of gold,
Tangerine, orange, red, and
  yellow;
A beauty of nature to behold.
Skies are bright, soft, and
  mellow.

Snaps of chilling weather
Birds passing all of a feather;
Signs coming and going
Shows us the way of knowing.
Autumn is here for her spell,
Enjoy it, feel happy, contented,
  and well.

Carl L. Soderquist
THE CALL

While sitting in the waiting
  room
  listening to each name;
The little nurses' gentle voice
  calling out the same.

Each time a name, came or'er
  the wire
  someone would then adieu;
Long last my name was also
  heard
  and I was going too.

There comes a time in each
  ones' life
  a call to answer must,
Oft' times 'tis sooner than we
  think
  demands in whom we trust.

Let's place our trust and
  confidence
  in He the Great I Am;
And if the call comes soon or
  late
  in readiness we stand.

O God of love, my Saviour
  dear
  just keep my hand in thine,
As times gones on we're passing
  thru
  the call may soon be mine.

Tomas NegRon
MIDDLE CLASS GIRL

She stopped to listen and then
  heard.
A sinister confabulation
  of discordant sounds;
A new array of nonsense noises
  quite beyond the bounds
Of human voice; fantastic words
  words
From nowhere converging

on her auditory senses
And causing wild confusion
Of all thought — a weird
  profusion
That cut right through her mind
  mind's
  well-maintained mortal
  defenses;

Atop the building, poised, she
  stood
With dazed, demented
  delusions of immortality;
Alone, convinced the world
  she's known was false reality,
And jumped.
  (I never understood.)

M. Wad
BROKEN

Cruel words spoken.
Glasses fall broken.
Counseling needed.
Advice unheeded.

Encountering unforeseen
  dangers.
Lovers becoming strangers.
Two involved.
Absolutely no resolve.

Friendship receded.
Love defeated.
No words spoken.
Another marriage broken.

Sue Provenza
MORNING

The orange ball broken the
  window of the
  dark room, and suddenly
  the walls and
  ceiling began to glisten,
  blue and gold.
The carpet in shades of greens,
  and browns,
  and deep blues began to
  shimmer and to rock with
  life.
A meadowlark sang.

Linda Bennett
DEFINITION OF MAN

I am an entity in deep space
  Among a universe too vast
  to comprehend.
I am a speck compared with
  eternity;
  A giant compared to the
  smallest of particles.
I am a speck of dust
  And a grain of sand against
  infinity.
I am MAN
  In all the glory of my creator.

Judy Sacco-Lorenzini
A PEACEFUL FEELING

I'm growing.
I just realized it.
How good it feels,
When all the time I thought I
  was falling.
Things seemed so dismal,
I thought I was lost in the
  battle.
But I haven't lost.
I've gained.
And what a peaceful feeling
  it is!

Mattie Jeffers
**THERE IS A BIG DIFFERENC
DIFFERENCE**

There is a big difference in
  having sex and making love
In having sex, after it is over
  that is the end
You can have sex with anyone
In making love, you really

care about the other person
You will not go out and tell
  everyone about it
You are willing to go farther
  than making love to help the
  other person
In other words you are in love
In having sex you don't love
In making love there is a
  special feeling.

Dorothy Bodwe

Samuel J. Saladino Jr.
ONE

ONE:
As a whisp of wheat in a
  fertile field.
ONE:
As a point of light in a starlit
  sky.
ONE:
As a scratch in a battle borne
  shield.
ONE:
As a stone on a mountain high.
For as unimportant as one may
  appear,
The loss of one is something to
  fear.
For without one -
There is none.

David E. Phipps
A CERTAIN LOVE

Love (an heart's emotion)
  Is an endless ocean
  Flowing with waves,
  Surging with tides
  Of desire.

Love (an heart's emotion)
  Is an evening star
  Always burning,
  Ever yearning
  For fulfillment.

Kathi M. Klassen
I HAVE ONE FOR YOU

I have one for you, my friend.
A tear, tucked away inside me,
ready to appear
to show you I care.

I have one for you, my friend.
A place in my heart
where you may go
and yet be free to soar.

I have one for you, my friend.
A thought, a memory.
So, although you are gone,
you may live forever.

I have one for you.

Valerie Campbell
OCEAN

The ocean's roar
Sounds like a lion,
And in the background
You can here seagulls crying.

The shells are washed up
And then away,
The waves crash
And then they lay.

The sea creatures
That are swimming around,
Are so far out
They cannot be found.

And everyone around
Is beginning to see,
The beautiful form
Of the deep blue sea.

Joan Stephen
CONTENTMENT

The water falls
freely and laughingly,
over pebbles and stones.

It stops for nothing,
falling from rock to rock
without care,
without hesitation.
When it reaches
the bottom,
it bubbles and ripples;
flows on forever;
not even stopping
long enough
to admire
its reflection in the heaven,
even though
the heaven
is praising itself
in the cool green water.

Joanne H. Smith
I THINK I LOVE YOU

Increasing rise in temperature
Tenderly spoken words
Heartbeats thumping louder
Intentions free as birds
Nudges gently given
Kisses soft and sweet

Isolated pleasures
Lips magnetically meet
Ornamented feelings
Visions plain and clear
Eternity is blessed

Youth is drawing near
Options are obtuse
Useless to break loose

Hugh R. Campbell
**THAT NIGHT I WATCHED
    YOU TURN**

That night, I watched you turn
    away from me,
leave spotlight music and enter
    dark night
to probe a dream, escape high
    walls and see.

Schizophrenic rainbow light
    blinded we,
but you recovered, stepped
    aside full height
the night I watched you turn
    away from me.

An angered, independent
    thought forced free
light whipped limbs, unwound
    like a kite
the night I watched you turn
    away from me.

You passed from loud light,
    from cramped crowd to be
a solitude in silent search for
    sight,
to probe a dream, escape high
    walls and see.

Artificial brightness shuddered
    as he-
dark doorway- slammed hard
    schizophrenic light
the night I watched you turn
    away from me
to probe a dream, escape high
    walls and see.

Melody Joy
VERBITIS

With pen I sit with intent to
    bleed:
I writhe intricately within,
Twisting from the compression
Of all my times and all my
    images
Now being squeezed out like
    ripened puss —
Oozing so slowly but oh so
    beautifully
Upon this virgin page;
I pinch down on my pen point
And watch words reflect my

inner rage
In the glorious gleam of ink,
    like oozesome puss
Seeeing out of my flesh,
    infectious from thought —
Mind infectious from flesh:
    the human germ
Has me nursing my woes with
    perverse joy
In this damned privilege of
    touching my wound. . . . .

Marcella S. Patterson
THE SUMMIT

A young man viewed a distant
    mountain, and pondered —
    would it be worth the effort
    to climb?
His life became that mountain.

The path was not always easy;
    ofttimes fog, sometimes ice,
    obstructed progress.
There were windstorms and
    showers, then
    blue skies, pure air, and
    wildflowers
    renewed his spirit and
    lightened the climb.

And, one day when his children
    had grown tall,
He viewed them from a distance
    and knew he had reached
    the Summit.

Cheryl S. Boyd
RUDE AWAKENING

Oh, I was told
How men are cold.
They always will deceive.
But when you're young
Your seldom stung,
and so I didn't believe.
Now, after all the interludes
of bitter solitude,
After all the lies so strong,
The nights he was prolonged
Love finally turned into
disconcerned,
And now I can conceive,
Why I was told
That men are cold,
And, Oh, how they deceive!

Cynthia Cormier
THE BLACK ROSE

A seed fell to earth eons ago
In a land where nothing grows
No warmth no love no summer
    skies
A place where a seed would
    surly die.

Weeds covered this barren land
A place unknown to man.
Thorn entangled the blossoms
    from the
    seed as it struggles to grow.
In this land that was unknown.

Man began to walk the land
Clearing the weeds and thorns
    away
And with love he gently touched
The Black Rose.

Barbara Myers
AFTER BOSTON - PART FIVE

Nothing lasts forever
    minutes.. hours,
    days or years...
but forever?
There are things people want to
    last forever.
Fools? Maybe or easily
    satisfied.
Content?
I don't know, I sit here and
    watch
the beautiful blue sky

hypnotize
and the changing leaves tease
with their dying beauty.
The towns go quickly by.
How many in those fleeting
    towns are as
important to themselves
as I am to myself?

Nothing lasts forever
and I sure am glad,
cause I finished reading my
    book
I can't fall asleep
and this train ride threatens to
    stretch
into infinity
and I just want to go home.

Tracy Evelyn Riker
**TO MY GRANDPARENTS
    WITH LOVE**

I never wanted to see you go,
But I guess it was meant to be.
There's something I want you
    both to know,
It's very important to me.
I love you both with all my
    heart,
And I know you love me too.
Even though we're far apart,
My love will be with you.
I love ya lots I can't deny,
And this I must confess.
Even as the years go by,
I'll never love you less.

Melissa McKay Wessell
FOR ANISSIA:

climbing up up
out of the dream
up into wakefulness
and away from the
sweet warm reality
of unreality,
wanting to climb back down
go back there again
where i held you in my arms
little child
held you up over my head
where we were together
so close i could
touch
my dream come true.

Becky Kennell
COME MY LOVE

Come my love,
my long-ago love,
and we'll run down
grassy, sunlit slopes
at the park.
We'll laugh
in the yellow afternoons,
and cry
in the purple evenings.
We'll kiss in porch shadows,
and in the back seats
of cars.
We'll go driving
into sleepy, Sunday morning
    towns
and along silent
midnight roads.
But when summer goes
(and it always does)
we won't chase it
down amber, autumn avenues,
or into sad, winter airports.
So, come my love,
my long-ago love,
and I will set you free.

Carolyn Mort
DREAMS DIE SOFTLY

Dreams die softly, they're
    killed every day,
Laugh at the slayer as he walks

away.
Cry in the darkness, when
    daylight has flown,
Save silver teardrops till you're
    alone.
No one must notice, no one
    must see
What the dream slayer has
    left here for me.
Nights in dark shadows, not
    even a friend,
Realize that the dreaming has
    come to an end.

Lynn Kelton
NOVEMBER, 1973

Like little spears,
Through this
November night air,
Thoughts of you still come....
Pricking my senses and
Causing my body to twinge.

Wind, rustling the last
Lingering leaves, becomes
A haunting sigh;
A whimsical prophesy of
The coming business of winter.

A business cold and sharp,
Like little spears,
From the winterground
Of memory.

Joanne Wilson
GRANDMA, DEAR

There are times when I miss you
    very much,
Your kind smile and gentle
    touch.

I remember all the goodies you
    would bake
cookies, doughnuts, pies and
    cakes.

The constant love you gave to
    me
will live on in spirit and sweet
    memories.

All I really want to say is
I'm glad we were together
in those early carefree days.

Sandy Cerundolo
THE SEA

The sea as I recall, can be alive,
Have you ever wondered how
    the fish survive?
When you look into the sea,
    it reflects back to you,
It is wierd how the seas can
    do that, too.
The fish are exactly what I
    said before,
They're a whole new world
    behind a closed door.
Some of the birds fly viciously
    over the sea,
It is lucky for them that they
    are free.

Scott Rafter
AS WE SLEEP

Time,
Slipping away toward age,
Withered and wasted.
And breathing in the night,
Shallow and faded.
Caring is lost and
Dies in an overpowering need;
And still the faces,
Loving and unrelenting, -
Changed and changing,
Craved and forgotten.

Norma DeRuyter
**A RAGGEDY ANN?
    (OR DAN)**

Who am I?
Am I just a doll?

A Raggedy Ann, (or Dan)
With no life,
No feelings,
No purpose.
I can't be just a doll.
God breathed the breath of
    life into me.
He gave me eyes to see,
The beauty that He created,
And the poverty created by
    man.
He gave me a mouth and a
    voice to speak,
A kind word to a stranger or
    a friend.
He gave me ears that I might
    hear,
The sounds of joy that others
    speak,
Or the whimper of a lonely cry.
He gave me feelings that I might
    feel,
The tender touch of a friendly
    hand,
Or the hurt and pain of a
    hungry child.
He gave me a purpose that I
    can do,
By knowing Him in every way,
And serving Him by what He
    taught,
Through His son, our Lord,
    Jesus Christ.
I know now who I am.
Someone very special!

Audrey Brown
**HELP ME WALK IN
    YOUR LIGHT**

Help me walk In Your light
Lord, to reflect on
    someone else,— I can't do It
    by myself.
Help me walk In Your light
Lord, the way You would
    have me go,— so someone
    else might know.
Help me walk In Your light
Lord, the way You plan-
    ned from the start,— I know
    You're In my heart.
Help me walk In Your light
Lord, let me pass Your
    test,— so I can give my best.
Help me walk in Your light
Lord, to shine and not
    be shown,— Thank You Lord
    for living in my home.

Trisha Merritt
THE EARTH SLEEPS

The trees are barren, their
    colorful dress
is no more. The flowers too
    are gone, their
fragrant incense, has vanished
    from the air;
the melodies of singing birds
    has dwindled.

Everything seems so still, as
    still as the depth
of the nightime. For Winter
    has covered
her children with her white
    blanket of snow,
and so.....

The Earth, she sleeps.

The sun has moved away and
    her warmth
is so gentle now. The naked
    trees are glistening
with the crystal gems scattered
    by none other
than Jack Frost.

A snowflake touches gently
    the Earth, so

delicately and quietly, as if
    not to disturb
her sleeping child. And so...
The Earth, she sleeps.

Marilyn MacCrakin
CHIMES

I listen to the chimes play their
    tinkerbell song in the wind.
Nervously I listen and I wait.
For years I stare at the direction
    he will come.
I see him and I watch him dance
    up to my doorstep.
The chimes suddenly pound
    loudly in my ear.
I know his presence is the
    completion.
Physically, he wants to dance;
    physically, he wants to love.
Beside me for only a second,
    he turns and disappears out
    my door.
For years I stare at the
    emptiness he left around me.
And the chimes play their song
    so softly in the wind that I
    can bearly hear it.

Carl Siriani
MY PRAYER

The test of strength in life
Of all the fear and strife,
Unknown futures, and empty
    days.
Scared moments with each
    morning haze.
Yet you want me to carry on
    your word,
When its been so long since
    I've heard.
Please tell me in your own way
That what I do is what you say
Though I can't hear you speak
    to me
Let me act as though I see.

Charles Anthony Piazza
THE GIFT

I wanted to buy you a bouquet
    of roses,
When I looked in my pockets
    I said, Holy Moses!
All that's left is strings and
    some lint,
Maybe I should try the local
    mint.
They say it's not the gift, but
    the thought
        that counts,
I'm just afraid the check would
    bounce.
So all I can give you is the
    thought I had,
And hope it doesn't make you
    all that sad.

Rita Susan Greer
MASK

Why can't people just be
What they are for the world
    to see?
We hide ourselves behind a
    mask
And don't come out. It's too
    big a task.
Our color always changes hue
According to what others
    expect us to do.
We pretend we're gay when
    we're sad.
Put on a smile when we are
    mad.
We sometimes say what we
    think
Then hide it with a wink.
We go on and on with the deal
'Till we don't know ourselves

when we're real.
Why can't we to ourselves be
    true?
And not give a hang what
    others think or do.

Marsha Siren
WAITING

I waited on the porch for you
And summer hurried by
Storm clouds gathered in the
    west
And snow began to fly.
I stayed quite still
So you could see
Your shadow
In my eye.
I'm waiting on the porch for
    you
While others come and go
They scarcely even notice me
It seems as if they know.
If reason won
Then I'd have left
A thousand years ago.

Alex Michael Greenberg
THE MANDOLIN

I remember opening the case
Of my grandfather's mandolin
After dusting off the cracked
Alligator skin cover, and
    smelling the
Oiled, and now aged sweet
    wood, wrapped
In one of Abe's undershirts
    that has yellowed.
The voice silent for fifteen
    years as it lay
Buried under the books and
    rugs in the attic,
Still sounding a rich and
    probably deeper tremolo
Since Zayda's hands last held
    it.
Beneath its back lay scrolls of
Old Yiddish songs pressed flat
    since
They were last played, the
    ink of the
Fountain pen somewhat faded,
    and
The paper stiff and fragile.
Those picks once sat on his
    pinkies and
Danced on the strings, reviving
    the
Voices of the Ukraine and
    The Land.

Gayle T. Taylor
YOU

Beautiful things such as roses,
    rain,
Sunsets, the snow, babies,
Little children fast asleep and
    Love...
God gave us these things to
    share among
    us.
Together, we all can learn to
    love one
    another,
Share our happiness, our
    dreams...
Together, we can travel the
    distance,
The distance to a heaven
    created by God
and by you,
    yourself.
Happiness is created through
    our actions
and feelings toward one another.
Everything is beautiful when
    you know
    that God loves you.

He created everything beautiful
    and only
    you can share all the beauty;
Only you can make others
    experience
happiness and the joy of being
    loved.
Give yourself to expression,
    happiness,
and help others to know the
    love of God.

Betsy McGuire
MY MOM

If I could tell you once more;
I love you,
or hear your sweet voice on
    the phone
If you could come again
for a visit
or I could spend
a few days at home.
Your sweet smile
that lights your face
All dressed up
with style and grace.
I'll think of this
My whole life through
My mother; my friend
There was no one like you.

Wanda K. Daniel
SONG OF THE DAISY

Small flower standing tall
What secrets do you hold?
Petals of purest winter white,
Heart of sunset gold.
You drink life's tears
And grasp day's golden rays.
You bow your head in
    scorching winds
And lift your leaves in cooling
    rains.
To children your garland is
    innocence,
To lovers your petals whisper
    truths.
You bestow light on darkest
    fields,
And beauty to wandering
    souls.
Yet life is short and simple—
What secrets do you hold?

April DayE
**TO THOSE WHO WOULD
    DESTROY ME**

I shall not let you determine
What I will say and dare or do;
Rather, I will speak quiet
    words:
Then reach for the stars
They are there!!

David W. Moody
AN ELK

An Elk is a majestic thing.
It's gentle and yet so strong.
Dipping his head to drink from
    a spring,
He hears the songbird's song.
Through the meadows and
    down a cliff,
He sprints through the sleeping
    forest.
Through the aspens and a deep
    snow drift,
He hears nature's awakening
    chorus.
The Elk is as mighty as the
    eagles,
He stands so tall and proud.
Everytime he bugles,
He cries his name out loud.
Thundering through his
    timberline estate,

You can hear his call,
Searching to find his long lost
    mate,
To share the coming fall.

Linda Miller-Copeland
CONSCIOUS

Calm as a day, can be clear
I walk, I dare not hear.
Darkened, so that I may be
    free
    to think of now, and of me.
I won't let it out!
    it will torement me!
Oh how, I want to shout!
    But, darkened it will stay.
Know! it wont let me be
    it thinks has something to say.
Oh how I await the day.
My mind aches to be free.

Sara Katherine Ziegler
JAMEY, MY LOVE

Jamey, My Love.
My blond hair-blue eye baby.
Everyone loves you even though
    you are just a child.
They laugh at your grunts and
    groans
and come running to you, when
    you cry.
They think that you are so cute.
But, will they still love you
    when
your body grows and your mind
is still that of a child.
Will they still come and
    comfort
you when you groan or cry.
And except your hugs and kiss
As ready as they do now.
Will they take the time with
    you
so you wouldn't become scared
    or lost.
As I sit here holding you in
    my arms
With your head against my
    shoulder
I think all these things and
    hope to
God they still love you when
you are grown in body but
    still a child in mind.
I hope I still will love and
    understand you
when you are grown but still
    a child.

Juan A. Potau
ALL FOR YOU

Cheerless eyes at the window
    feel lost,
As the sun sinks low;
Loneliness is a sickess that kills,
But it's all I know;
Broken down,
Friendless too;
Oh, and words are the forte of
    this man,
But they're all for you.
Cups of wine, glasses of beer—
    poison,
But they both do soothe;
After all the bad water I've
    drunk,
Poison goes down smooth;
I don't care
Who cares too;
It don't matter to me that I am,
But I'm all for you.
Memories hang from nails on
    the wall,
Smiles frozen in space,
But as the curtain rises and

falls,
Memories keep pace
With the past;
Is it true
That the past holds no future
    for me
Like it does for you?

Edward W. Manning
THE STRAGGLERS

The few remaining summer
    leaves
Relinquishing their grip
Spiral slowly in the wind
Upon their destined trip.
Carried o'er the countrysides
And into the heart of town
Their colors change from
    summer's green
To autumn's red and brown.
Lying in the gutters,
Or blown against the wall,
They wait in silent patience,
For their fate that comes with
    fall.

Edward J. Fussello, Jr.
JUST WHO ARE YOU?

Just Who Are You:
to tell me to do the things you
    want me to do.
Just Who Are You:
to cause the whole world so
    much fright.
Just Who Are You:
who chases my mind, body,
    and soul at night.
Just Who Are You:
to flex your muscles muscling
    your might.
Just Who Are You:
to misuse the powers the people
    gave you.
Just Who Are You:
please tell me and rest so many
    restless minds.
Just Who Are You:
who dictates to the will of all
    of mankind.
Just Who Are You:
please seriously pose this
    question in introspection.
Just Who Are You:
who believes there's something
    wrong in asking this question.
Just Who Are You?

Audrey Bowen
FOR KIMMER

As the pines
    stood tall and free
upon their granite base
the misty rays
    of sunlight's dawn
broke through the wooden lace
to rest upon
    a sleeping fawn
who lay in quiet grace.

John D. Simons
FOR COUNTRY AND QUEEN

He had a future in the House
    of Lords.
His family was wealthy; had
    nobility's rewards.
He was to be married to his
    pretty young love.
But all this was lost with the
    death of the dove.
Young nobles must fight, it's
    an unwritten rule.
Young nobles can die taking
    orders from a fool.
He obeyed blindly, the reason
    unseen.
He gave up his dreams for
    country and Queen.

His questions unanswered; the
    how and the why.
All you need know son is that
    you must die.
His mother's last son; his
    father's last spark.
For freedom and duty he fell
    in the dark.
His young love cries, "Oh what
    does it mean?"
He gave his life, dear, for
    country and Queen.

Patricia Mae Karis
LITTLE GIRLS

Little girls are made of many
    things -
Soft, white, fleecy clouds,
    butterfly wings,
The sweetness of honeysuckle,
    the rare fragrance of roses,
Laughter like pure echoed
    winds - and discloses
A mischief, a mystic, a
    marvelleous creature,
Stubborn and shy but a nurse
    or a teacher!
Strong as an ox but meek as
    a kitten,
And one who denies ever losing
    a mitten.
Sulking, screaming, smiling or
    sad;
They often are naughty, but
    never are bad.
An angel in tafetta, velvet or
    lace -
A tom-boy in blue jeans with
    dirt on her face.
A hug that is worth all the gold
    in a rainbow
And a kiss that's more precious
    than jewels in a crown.
A smile that can lighten a
    heart full of sorrow,
Who changes so quickly from
    candid to clown.
God created this image unlike
    any other
With a look to the future - in
    creating a MOTHER.

Marti Kelley
TEACH ME LORD

Heavenly Father, teach me to
    love.
Send me your blessings from
    up above.
Help me and guide me
each step of the way.
Now and forever, Lord,
teach me to pray.
Your way is much better
of this I am sure.
I know that you love me
with a heart that is pure.
With a soft gentle touch
as your hand reaches mine,
I know that you chose me
from the moment of time.
I praise you, Dear Father,

and honor your name.
When your beauty surrounds
    me,
I am just not the same.
Your love and forgiveness
has cleansed me within.
You gave your life for me
and saved me from sin.
Dear Lord, I will serve you
no matter the cost.
I give my life to you,
for without you I'm lost.
Your mercy and grace
are the gifts that you give.
I will trust and obey you,
and forever shall live.

Sue Marie Adashun
CLOWN MADNESS

"No laughs for me,"
the clown whispers,
as he perceives
the audience.
They are the clowns.
Caramel coated
seats stuck to asses.
Clutching candy
balloons, heartless
sneakers, facades
painted, huge rouge
noses, lifeless
roses. Smashed
jack-o-lantern
faces, eerie
wax people with
candle minds wry.

William C. Lowenkamp Jr.
RECOLLECTIONS

As I sit recollecting,
beautiful moments - we shared,
and all those we have as yet -
    not.
I think of life, to be a dear
    venture,
to someday take it's path,
in a direction of love.
A love, in which we share,
is such a rarity - that those -
who have never touched a
    corner,
of these feelings -
find it difficult to understand.

Doris B. Clearman
A CHRISTMAS PRAYER

May your Christmas be
    wonderful and peaceful and
    bright
As it was long ago on that first
    Holy night,
When shepherds were awed by
    a wondrous Star
That shed its brilliance both
    near and far.
This miracle of light that
    guided their way
Led to a manger where a wee
    baby lay,
And there kneeling down in
    deep adoration
They thanked God for His
    gift to a nation.
May you experience again the
    gift of love
That God sent down from His
    throne above
And feel in your hearts, the
    wonder of it all—
The birth of a babe, so great,
    yet, so small.
Then travel again the self same
    way
The shepherds went on that
    first Christmas day.

Recapture the miracle of a
  baby's birth
Born of a virgin here on Earth.
And sing anew with the angels
  above
Our praises to God for His gift
  of love.

Susan Smith Frantz
UNTITLED

The web of bridges
Spans the water
Giving man a way in...
Or a way out.

If he goes in he finds others.
If he goes out he finds others.
Maybe it is only on the bridge
That he is truely alone.

Phillip O. Walch
CARMEL BEACH

There is much there among
The sun, sand, and simple
  people
A peace unknown to cities tall.

The trees are flat and bent
Dark green though lightened
By the grey sand beneath.

The moment is like the dog
Chasing the gull unable
To catch but excited by the
  pace.

The sea rushes in upon the
  land
The young boys and men do
Battle with continuous energy
  of nature.

The white thin clouds fan out
Against the cool light blue
As black spots run against its
  face.

Many peoples enjoy a stroll
Barefoot through grains
Of centuries past - energy
  renewed.

A vessel on the horizon beyond
The kelp patch. The blast of
An iron horse that carries a
  man.

Yes is a day to remember
Because it may be twenty years
Again till its song is replayed to
  the back woods man.

Gary Marshall Anderson
**SONNET NUMBER TWO TO
DOROTHY JEAN**

As I touch you in thought or
  gaze the east,
And know each hour you are
  my life and love;
I dread you'll change your
  heart, or mind at least,
When there's a point I cannot
  rise above.
Then this is as a sadness come
  not well
To cast a mood that mars this
  yearning deed,

And makes that I must garner
  strength to quell,
Or yet push this will to savor
  less some need.
That I will love you for all of
  our time,
And thank all Gods each day
  that there is you;
This you will know, my love,
  not just in rhyme,
But sweet sensing intuitively
  too.
    And I'll not seek a surcease
    of sorrow
    For without you, I'd not
    want tomorrow.

Anne E. Mobley
WALLS

Walls are made of many things
of wood, and mortar, and
  stone;
But did you ever think of other
  walls
the ones we create on our own.

These walls are made of
  emotion alone
and yet are stronger than wood
  or stone.
For anger, and jealousy, and
  bitterness
may sound like only words;
but once within man's heart
becomes stronger than any
  barrier known.

We build these walls for
  protection;
when all they really do
is keep us from the love we
  seek,
from the Master above.

So seek out the Master Builder,
and throw your tools away.
For He will give you what you
  seek;
and crumble your fears away.

Diane C. McCarthy
ODE TO MY LOVE

In your greeting in that
  moment one,
I picked up the magic in
  your nearness.
I saw in your eyes a
  subtle clearness,
Of what was to come...
At first I fought you, yes,
In my own way
My heart feared you.
But, in the battle of feelings...
  you won.
Now I am here with you in
  an eternal living dream,
With our future entwined,
  in the future's unwinding
  ream.

Lauren M. Sanders
GOODBYE CRUEL WORLD

I left you today
Cause I can't live your way
And everything's going
  downhill

Why are you so goddamn cruel
To those of us who try
To live by your rules

We're trying so hard
Just to be a part
And play this game your way

But I've found out
That you can't just pout
You've gotta take your own
  life away

So now I've tried

To better my life
And to throw the pain away
To be as free as a bird
And fly through the air
Without a worry or a care
So goodbye cruel world
As I used to say
Before I decided to go away.

Peggy O'Brien
DEATH, SWEET, DEATH

Death, sweet Death
  come kiss my lips
embrace me in the night
Make me yours eternally
  my spirit seeks no light
This soul will welcome
  blackness
  a niche to hide away
Need never waken to the sun
  to seek a brighter day
No spark remains - no golden
  dream with fortitude defend
Just a listless, loveless body
  quests its lonely end
Within your shroud enfold me
  passive vacuum to become
My body veiled in emptiness
  to you, sweet Death, succumb
Oh, Death, sweet Death
  come kiss my lips
Stark lover with whom I'll lay
  entomb my doomed and
  aching soul
Let me rest on your bed of
  decay -

Marlene Ann Staudenraus
DREAM SKATER

The little pond is frozen
From my window I do see,
Someone I've chosen
Who skates gracefully.

Oh how she glides
And she spins and she turns,
She makes my heart beat fast
I watch her and yearn.

Like a dancing ballerina
Inside a jewelry box,
She whirls and twirls
It's as if time has stopped.

She wears winter white ermine
Thru my window I see,
That someone I've chosen
In my dream, she is me.

Sara J. Craft
LAST THOUGHT

I've tried to live by the Golden
  Rule
Some people say, I've been an
  utter fool
I smile, softly, my face aglow
Seeds they reap, are the seeds
  they sow

If, I have done one earthly
  thing
To make those Heavenly Angels
  sing
I will be at peace with Thee
When they ring those Golden
  Bells for me

Surene G. Holzer
TO LIVE

To live,
To breathe,
To love,
Is God's greatest gift from
  above.

To cherish the new and respect
The wisdom of the old.

To reach out for knowledge
Unknown.

To caress the love of man.

To cherish what we have
At hand.

The love and wisdom to
  understand
Just who and what I am.

Evelyn M. Rowland
INTROSPECTION

When at last I come to the
sundown of my days, shall I
allow the curtain of destiny to
draw peacefully, or shall I
curse the fates and plead more
time to do those things I should
have done?
  An act of kindness I passed by,
  on my way to the more
important;
  A word of love I failed to give,
  when pride permitted
none.
  A prayer, forgotten in my
  haste; a favor, not yet
granted;
  A helping hand; sincere hello;
  a wish for someone's
happiness;
  A debt, unpaid; a sign of
  thanks to a thoughtful
fellow-man;
  Things, large and small I
  failed to do, which leave me
disenchanted.
  When at last I've reached that
sundown of my days, can I
I pull the draw-strings, at ease
with the world? In joyful
tears?
  Can I lay me down to sleep
  in peace, when life's finale
nears?

Cheryl Ridgway Bise
EXIT

Exit
Turnoff
Destination
At the moment
I have none.
Tears and ticket
Railway station
Lonely when the day is done.

Hustle, bustle
In a hurry
Beat the clock
And bear the load
I'm a drifter
but don't worry
I may meet you
On the road.

Lois Stauter
AUTUMN

Autumn,
Autumn, a blaze of glory:
Golden corn,
Bean fields of brown,
Mottled trees splashed with
  splendor
on the Maker's easel.

Winter,
After autumn, the winter—
White, barren, cold,
Fruits of autumn stored in its
  freezer
Waiting for spring.

Waiting,
Waiting for the spring to bring
  new life to the land.
Till the soil, plant the seeds,
Pray for the rain, give thanks,
  and

Wait.
Wait while summer crops grow
  and
Ripen and reach maturity;

Wait for the sower
To increase the harvest—
Wait for the autumn.

My autumn is now:
I planted my seeds in the spring
of my life;
In the summer
My crops thrived and grew to
maturity.
Now they are gone
To their own four seasons.
I am in my autumn
Waiting, waiting for the winter.

In my winter I will be white
and barren
But not cold.
My God will wrap me in his
arms
And He will keep me warm.
He will take me safely into that
new season where
There will be no night, I will
need no sun
For the Lord gives light
And I shall reign with my God
Forever and ever and forever...

Carolyn Carlton Bell
**WHERE WINTER COMES
NEVER**

Oh, for a land where winter
comes never,
Where spring and song bird
will be eternal,
Where the tree of life blooms
forever.

There life and joy will reign in
harmony,
No more the hoary frost upon
the brow,
Gone will be the winters of our
severity.

There ties we hold dear will
not severe,
In life's cold snap we'll not
cower,
We will be with our loved ones
forever.

Never more to see the winter
of lifelessness,
From this earth life we will be
delivered
Into the land where winter
comes never.

Alan C. Evans
UNTOUCHED

Time passes by silently without
pause,
but stops briefly to observe
her subjects.
Unlike time, beauty remains a
slow process.
Outer beauty erodes as time
passes,
but inner beauty never
changes its image.
Untouched by outer
atmosphere it remains fresh.

Stacey Chittenden Endsley
COWARDS

Come all ye cowards, gather
around,
While hands of dead
countrymen reach
out of the ground,
To show you that they are
still around,
That they have not died to be
made out
a clown,
By a circus of cowards prancing
around.
You have no country,
You've not earned the right.

Run if you can and stay out
of sight,
Or stand up like men and join
the fight.
For those who are cowards will
live in
fright,
And sleep by day instead of
by night!
The time will come when you
can sleep
no more,
Too frighten to even open the
door,
In fear of what's to be found.
Like the hands of dead
countrymen reaching
out of the ground!

Lawrence Reider
AUTUMN SONNET

A glint of sunlight falls on leaf
and bower,
The wind begins to stir and
brings light rain;
Some wistful thoughts of
Summer mark the hour
And bring regrets to mind in
their vague train.
October's come, with all its
various hues,
While years on years unfold in
memory's glance;
Things not yet done, and things
awry, now choose
To nudge us on through reverie
and trance.
If Nature and our moods find
harmony,
So intertwined in all life's
mysteries,
With seasons past and seasons
yet ahead,
In stars, the rising moon, the
earthly tread,
We sense no need to waver ill
at ease
While waiting for our Winter
dreamily.

Frances Misutka
MY SISTER

My Sister
always got the
top bunk because she was
always
older and she never used to
talk to me when her friends
were around
because they were always
older and when she moved
away
I used to sit on the
top bunk and do my
homework
and later it became a
convenient place to throw
new clothes (when I was too
lazy to
put them away)
covering her memory in
department store bags
but it was always
our room

Darla Elder
JUST A LITTLE MAN

I met a little man today,
He stood not very tall.
He had a little jacket
And the brightest smile of all.

I wasn't doing very well.
I felt kind of down.
The little man began to talk
And took away my frown.

He told me of his happy life

And his quiet little home.
He had lived all by himself
But he didn't seem all alone.

He said he had tried alot in life
But was happy helping others.
He liked to make the people
laugh
And he said he loved his
brothers.

The little man found it time to
leave
And I didn't want him to go,
But I learned something new
today
That I didn't really know.

I found that I am not alone
That I am like that elf.
The things I search the world
for-
Can be found within myself.

W. J. White
THE AGONY OF MY HEART

The shinny spun-woven
silkiness of thy hair
Thus the sparkling glaze in
thy eyes like the morning
dew
The luscious beauty with which
thy smile no-other can wear
Thus thy magnificient
boasting breast I toy to gaze
upon nude
The smooth or not of thine
abdomen I do not care
Thus what is beneath
is———I shall not be so crude
Thus thou see as we are apart
we shall not dare
Thus thy beautiful image
creates in my heart the
internal ague.

Pamela M. Kingsley
FIRST SNOW

Finaly you've come. Oh how
I've waited, so long.
You are so beautifull.
Falling with grace from heaven.
White sparkly dust.
So tiny, so significate.
Though my day was hard,
you have made my face shine.
How I wish I could fall with
you,
and feel the cool breeze.
A silent misty sand.
Free, so free.
Fly, and float away my friend.
Finaly you've come.
Take me with you.
I've waited so long.

Desi Gomes
TRUCE

It's that time of year
When all humans make their
fleeting gestures
Men turn to each other
And speak of peace and
harmony
For a moment in time

The minds of our leaders
Linger on the joys of the
season
For a time enemies lay down
their guns
All is quiet
A festive mood reigns over
the earth
And humans give to each other
comfort
Friendship and love.

Ginger Gay
FUTILITY

seeing nothing yet
realizing everything.
the empty road
offers no condolences.
miles of fruitless land,
space so wastefully
thrown nowhere.
walking in a mist of confusion,
the dusty sidewalk
runs in circles.

Harold P. Ouder, Jr.
CLOUDS

Clouds in the summer are
fluffy and light;
Lit by the sun, what a beautiful
sight!
Then comes the winter, and
oh! What a change.
The clouds become dark,
they're dreary and strange.
Then in a storm, they grow
angry and fierce;
Much too heavy for human eyes
to pierce.
But when the storm ends, the
clouds move away
To let us look at another new
day.

And so goes our lives, we're
happy and free;
Until a change comes we did
not foresee.
Then our lives darken with
problems and fears;
'Til the solution wipes away
our tears.

Paul M. Jones
THE EAGLE AND ME

As we leave the ground I can
feel a rush of air wisk us up
into space.
High above the clouds my heart
pounds, swooping down the
clouds and
me embrace.
People down below scurring
about like ants with just a few
trying to
put them into line.
While up above the freedom of
the air currents glide us
through space
and time.
Seeming almost motionless I
feel free to express my love,
my thoughts,
I become mellow wanting to
relate with my God high in
the sky,
perhaps until the day I die.
From dawn to dusk if you look
high into the endless blue sky,
you will
see the eagle and me.

Patricia Hansen
TAKING TIME FOR LIFE

I paused to witness a flower
bloom;
I sighed while peering at the

moon;
I knew I should be going soon;
But still, I had to stay.
I had no way of knowing then
How valuable that time had
  been
When I succumbed to fulfill
  my whim
And take time out for life.
I gained a peace within my
  heart
It filled my soul and every part.
The beauty surpassed all forms
  of art.
And I bowed my head in thanks.

Linda Silcox
THE MEMORY

My mind wonders
So frequently
As my heart ponders
The memory.
Yonder lies the distance
A trail of nonexistence
And yet, it seems
You are near
But only in my dreams
I fear.
And my mind wonders
So frequently
As my heart ponders
The memory.

Chris Mitchell
THE PUREST LUST

When midnight moans from
  empty scars
And the moon sheds its
  incessant stars,
My ears sense whispered pleas
  from down under
Inside a heart that shrivels fast
  from hunger:

  "Your skin starves so
  For the taste of warmth
  That it has only smelt of."

Janice Bryant
THE CLOWN DIED

The Clown died last night.
She put away her costume
Washed the grease paint from
  her face
the tear from her eye
And died.

Linda Falter
LIVING

Times of laughter, times of
  cheer,
Times of gladness, times of joy,
Times of sorrow, now fill
  tomorrow.
Places that free, places that
  confine,
Places that once were your's
  and mine,
Places that comfort, places
  unknown,
Have killed our own.
Another time, another place,
Another smile, another face,
Another love, has gone,
  someplace.

Patricia Howey
GROWING

The fires burn inside me
  exploding with amazing force
  wanting -- wanting
The cream of the earth
  envelops me
  soothing my very soul
  looking -- searching
  is there more
Ah, watch the energy flow

The sky is transparent
  pouring it's nectar
  into my mind
Now every inch wanton
  waiting with frenzy for more
  of earth's garnished
  mysteries
The seed you plant
  finally reaches -- reaches
  towards the sun's warmth
My body becomes one
  with the seed
  drinking the rain
  nourishing every part
  becoming one with the
  world
Love is growing inside
  grasping every inch
  holding on --

Bourdon Veazey Youngblood
TO MY CHILDREN

Dear Lord, great joy has been
  my lot
  Because you smiled on me
And sent three lovely, healthy
  babes
  A Gift to me from Thee.
First, Betty came on a snowy
  night
  A babe with big blue eyes
My heart was filled with wild
  delight
  An angel from the skies.
Time passed, again the rapture
  born of
  Motherhood was mine
Irene, my cuddly, darling babe
  Was brought by power Divine.
Could mortal woman be so
  blest?
  I wondered oftentimes
Two children filled with life
  and zest
  Made my heart ring with
  chimes.
And then, just to complete
  my joy
  You next Lord, did send
To me a son, Oh Gene, my boy
  The angels did attend.
Ah! Time has flown and now
  my babes
  Are men and women grown
But in my heart there's still
  a song
  Of babies I have known.
I cannot have you small again
  As my sad heart demands
For growths' statue you must
  attain
  There's work for your own
  hands.
Still you're my babes, my
  little ones
  And this my prayer today
Lord, make me strong to
  mother you
  And help you all the way.

Flo Flett
**MY GRAND DAUGHTER,
EDNA**

God placed a child within my
  care
  She came to me with long,
  dark hair
Her laughing eyes and dancing
  feet
  Are joys to me-so very sweet
I watched her grow, hour by
  hour
  From a small sweet bud to a
  lovely flower
She warms my heart and my
  spirits rise
  When I look into her clear
  blue eyes
A precious gem she is to me
  My happiness for all to see
I hope it is within God's plan
  For me to have a long
  life-span
For I would like to see her grow
  To full maturity-you know
To feel that I have done my
  best
  To bring her up-I'd feel most
  blessed.

Karyn R. J. Deeter
LA VIE

come close-
can you smell the poem
as it surfaces through
pore and skin?
sagey scent, odor of some
growing thing within.
a hothouse flower that blooms
in all weathers.

approach with care,
this is a hungry poem.
words stalk you from page
to page,
jumping at you-
biting at you-
grabbing you, yelling
taste!
listen!

this is a love poem.
it is the only music that
matters.
it woos, tantalizes,
whispers & undresses
before your shocked eyes.
a seducer of the senses,
it makes love &
tears at you with passion.

and as you climax,
you scream
i know this poem,
i am
this poem.

Sherie Rogoff
IN MY DREAMS

I kept hoping you would come
after me
As the heroes always do
And that we would start all
over
And our dreams would all
come true.
So I waited for your letter
And the phone call which
  didn't come
And I wondered why we parted
And if we ever loved as one?
Now two years have come and
  gone
And I'm here all alone
And I still look for that letter
And listen for the phone.
And I think of how we laughed

And I remember how I cried
The morning that we parted
The morning that I died.
But, I will see your face
Hear your voice
Forever, kiss your lips;
There in my dreams.

Sharon D. Holloman
DAISES

The flowers of nature its beauty
  beholds,
  the graceful smell of daises
  untold.
  The peddles, the middle, the
  leaves
  and the stem,
  they were all created, all
  by HIM.

Jacqueline Wadlinger
**THE LITTLE TENNIS BOY
AND THE LITTLE TENNIS
GIRL**

The little tennis girl
And the little tennis boy,
What memories they symbolize.
How they giggled in their box
All the way home from Vail.
How they enjoyed their place
  of honor,
Together on the glass topped
  table.

Then one day,
The little tennis boy
Was wrapped in newspaper
And taken away.

And now,
The little tennis girl
Always has a tear
In her eye.

For together memories
Are always so painful,
To share alone.

Laurie Bates
PERMANENCE

When I regret the words that
  I have written,
And wish they had not sullied
  my white page,
When my words insult me
  with impotence
and with their emptiness
  provoke my rage,
I can erase the words if so be
  my wish,
Or else the page can crumple
  and can tear,
But if my essence someone
  else offends,
No matter what they do I'll
  still be there.
Even death can not destroy
  my selfdom
I was here, and so I'll leave
  behind
some mark, even if it 'twere
  but a gravestone
Of my once present selfdom
  to remind.

Diane V. Statter
THE INVADING ENEMY

He now sits in that
chair so fragile and
weak; his moments of
life fleeting away.
Rare are the days now
that he sees without
pain.
No smiles, no snappy
remarks. This cancer
devasting his body and
reducing him to a shadow
of his being.

Once a man of stamina
and strength, vitality
that younger men envied;
a friend to everyone he
met. Still keeping courage
and holding on to that
thread of hope.

Mind and insight sharp
as ever, but this in-
vading enemy is totaling
out the man - my Dad.

Lucy J. Di Paolo
YOU'RE GONE

I want to tell you I love you
and how much I care
Hold you and erase each and
every fear
Together we'll do all the things
you wanted for so long
Now I want to, but you're gone

I want to listen to all the things
you have to say
To understand the loneliness
you felt in your days
I'll be at your side, the way you
tried to have it all along
Now I want to, but you're gone

Wish I had the chance to show
that I understand
To show I can fit all your needs
into my plans
I'd do my best to give the
happiness you wanted for so
long
Now I want to, but you're gone

David F. Schelter
DID YOU KNOW?

Did you know I love you
Although I am not near?
Did you know I long for you
And cry 'cause you're not here?

Did you know I need you
And pray for you each night?
Did you know I think of you
When, yet, you're out of sight?

Did you know I spend each day
Trying not to show
The lonliness I feel inside?
I love you—did you know?

Linda Aldrich
ISLAND LOVE

I see you are an island:
Clear on sad days,
mist enshrouded in joy;
the distance always changing
so that nothing can be sure.

I could try and swim that
length;
but the dull grey fins
circle in warning.

I could try and sail that length;
but the boat lies broken
and rotting.

I could try and fly that length;
but your forests yield
no landing.

But I can sit here on the bank
while eyes grow dim with age
and pretend
you are receding.

La Verne Swindle
WE ARE ONLY HUMAN

We have been entrusted,
With a vast and glorious land.
We ponder the problems of
our time,
And try to understand.

Who are we, we ask,
To have been willed the
Universe?

Can we compete with what
we've seen?
Our pride is our greatest curse.

Is there one of us so blind,
Who cannot see his way?
Who thinks that he can close
the night,
Or start the light of day?

Is there one of us so clever,
Who can will the seasons'
change?
Who can tell the moon and sun
to switch,
Or stop the falling rain?

Who can bring forth the
flowers of spring,
Birds nesting in the trees,
Or summer's warmth and magic,
Fall's turning of the leaves?

Can we bring snows of winter,
The cycle to complete?
No! We are only human,
We should kneel before His feet.

Adelphia Welch
KAMIKAZE ROUTINE

Victories teeth
hungry for another win
eat my last scrap of pride
and spit me out for all to see.

Gnawed and empty
again a meal for someone.
Gruesome alternative to follow.

Lynn DeShea Armstrong
THE ART OF GOD

Each day I look up in the sky
and see the art of God.
Scarves of light from the
morning sun
and whipped cream lions
standing at guard.

Then I look around me
and see knights in green armor.
Musical boxes floating through
the air
and animals running through
the emerald carpet of summer.

Each night I look up in the sky
and see diamonds on black
velvet
I pray to God that it will be
there tomorrow
and not let fools destroy it.

Maureen C. Connelly
A THOUGHT

Hold, this, in, mind, about
three special words,
which, is, a, very fine kind!
To, know joy, is, to, sorrow!
But, first you, must know, the
word, called love!
A, thought for, just now!

Ma'r Starro
RAINBOW

Beyond dreams of irresponsible
nature-
seeking their own divinity

a transparent sphere inhabits
color
against a neutral backdrop
to enhance its beauty.

A touch of glass to penetrate
their humor
would reign supreme on
ebony skies.

Sallie J. Cooper
LIGHTS, CAMERA, ACTION!

As the lights softly rise upon
a stage,
so does the morning break

through my slumber.
Beckoning slowly as to
encourage
my performance. And yet
does encumber
these shoulders with unwanted
honesty.
Responses ideal, a puppet
like mask,
I, like an actor, render openly
an accepted character of
what they ask.
A facade is precariously placed
upon masses of ulterior
feelings
tangled within a hesitant space
between Times bitter bruises
and healings.
Those thoughts in deepest
dominion are free,
but while in spotlight, must
pretend to be.

Frieda A. Figgins
MIRACLE OF CREATION

To see all the world through
the eyes of a child,
That is my wish for a world
gone wild.
To see only people, whether
large or small,
Through the eyes of a child,
the same one and all.
A child is a wonder, a miracle
of creation,
Full of joy and love, the same
from all nations.
Quick to forget anger, to heal
wounds with a kiss,
If all the world could just be
like this.

Elaine Wheat
WHEN IT IS EASY

It is easy to be strong,
When nothing else is going
wrong;
But when your dreams are
blown afar,
You find out just how tough
you are.

It is easy to be loud,
When you are yelling with the
crowd;
But when you, only make the
choice,
You find out just how strong
your voice.

It is easy to be loving,
When no one else is shoving;
But when you're the only one
to share,
You find out just how much
you care.

It is easy to be good,
When all are doing what they
should;
But when you alone must stand
and fight,
You find if you value wrong
or right.

Life is easy in its living,
When it's getting more than
giving;
But when you are willing to
sacrifice,
You find out just how high the
price.

George Stock
PARENTS

(Mother)
Ship of flesh, my origin; I'll
not abandon thee;
exonerate your life-supports;
set thy vessel out to sea.

My fate predetermined, traverse
the earthborn streams;
spirit preparation for life
beyond the human dream.
(Father)
Surfacing from fecund seas, now
thy adult progeny;
ripened by thy wisdom, yet
naive within humanity.
My rawness is a puzzlement,
my callowness belligerence;
struggling to gain the knowledge
of experience.

Faith Lynn Holden
GROWING PAINS

Potent,
I am,
as thirty fermented grapes.
Rusted
off the vine, vital
still.
Peeled, mashed and
bitter-sweet.
You are a
man
you want
red wine.
At last,
I like myself.

Irene Georgia Broumas
COLORS YOU CAN'T SEE

Ever think about colors you
can't see,
like the color of death creeping
over thee.

Colors of sickness can be a
morbid display,
of red, green, blue, black or
gray.

Joy on the other hand can be
pastelled to your taste,
of pink, blue, yellow or a
brillant maze.

Lonely can be a hard color to
describe,
cause its all the colors you have
inside.

I bet you never really sat down
and thought,
about all the color feelings
have brought.

You see color is really a mystery
I say,
because we never really think
of it by day.

But try closing your eyes one
night and see,
how many different colors you
can be.

Antonia Marrero
LOVE

Love, pure and simple, or fiery
and tormenting ...
The man gallant or the lady
taunting.
The roles reversed, we then
would find, an

angel sweet and a rake unkind.
Then there are times when both
  parties are on equal terms ...
When each will give as is
  received, in turn.
Many facets love does have ...
Some make us cry, some make
  us laugh.
But, with its myriad ups and
  downs,
True givers of love great joy
  have found.

Vaughn DeLeath Neeld
INSANITY

Soul searching
      for its soul
in terror
   of touching
       hurt.
  Bruised black,
      seared
     in passion's flame,
wandering lost
     in time's torment
until tangibles recede.
  Hiding within
      opaqueness
     dimly seeing out;
 unreal reality
       dimmed
    by pain.

Lynn Janssen
MYSELF

I'll never cry,
Oh no sir not me,
I'll surpress all my feelings,
Never letting them free.

On the outside a smile,
A cute little grin,
On the inside depression,
Just keeps working in.

You'll never know,
About all of my pride,
And if you try to hurt me,
I'll just run and hide.

Patricia Enrado
SOCIETY

There was a time before our
  time began
When we were wrapped in our
  mothers' flesh,
And all we knew was darkness;
Yet, we were warm.
And then cold, sterile hands
  pulled us out,
And we were virgins no more.
There were no more excuses,
  only freeways of confusion:
We wanted; they gave. We
  wanted; they ignored us.
We demanded; they struck
  innocence down and through
  our tears,
We saw the blurred barriers
  that they had built around us.
Scars do not heal on tender
  skin, but they deliberately

Ignored this fact—or was their
  skin too tough to remember?
We walked through the burning
  coals with their eyes upon us.
They nodded, as long as we
  ignored the pleas of our
Sloshing eyeballs to release its
  burden.
And at the end of our journey,
  we are supposed to examine
  our
Wounds with a sense of
  accomplishment and
  righteousness.
Now we have been accepted;
  we are one pleateau above the
  cowards.
It is our turn, our privilege, to
  rape the next generation.

Jean Gibson
FAITH

Today is now
  Yesterday is forever
Once, and only once
  I'ss pass to the here ever.
As I travel along
  And life's journey is ended
I'll stand before the throne
  And face God undefended.
When I shall say farewell
  To this life I know
My heart's filled with peace
  As upward, onward, I go.
Assuming the imortal body
  For me has no fear
For the infinite tomorrow
  At last will be here.
Oh, the sting of death
  I shall never see
It's the beginning of life
  And for eternity.

Kay Bunt
WELL, SKINNER?

Who knows if I am what I am
  today
because of strictures forcing me
  that way
or would I be myself with
  ethics and stout pride
in spite of training to attain
  less forceful stride;
more tolerant of catch-as-catch-
  can code,
more lenient of a multi-sexual
  mode,
more yielding to the fleet
  ephemeral bliss
of lightly given, more lightly
  forgotten, kiss?
Or would I be myself as I am
  now
sole-purposed as a nun unto
  her vow?

Pamela M. Kingsley
I THOUGHT OF YOU TODAY

I thought of you today,
  like every other day.
I being cold and lonely again.
You still soaring on your
  journey,
  to be free.
No strings for you to dangle
  onto.
Still searching for something.
Not knowing where you will be,
  next year.
Not realy caring.
You just grab up the gold as
  you
pass along, leaving behind
  a few grains.

Enough to know that you did.
But not enough to go back and
  pick up the pieces.
You know what you left
  behind,
and it will always be there
  when you return.
Like others, I wait untill your
  journey
  has ended.
I have no strings to hold you
  here,
  and I still search.
Also not knowing of next year.
Still hoping, waiting for you
  to return.
to pick up these few grains of
  dust
  you left behind.

Twila L. Sherry
SUPPORT

like
climbing roses
we search
for something to cling to
on our way to the top;
friends
who join to form a trellis
are what keep us
growing

Jorjanna Meeks
I WOULDN'T, IF I WERE DEATH

It isn't the passing of the dear
  old
  sick and elderly
That we regret so much.
It's the fact that their declining
  life
  had to be filled
With so much pain, and so
  much strife.
If they could just close their
  eyes
  in sleep, and pass away,
We might forgive that monster,
  "Death",
Far more quickly than we do,
  but must "he" take so long
To sound that last curfew?
I wouldn't, if I were "Death".
  Would you?

Art Lawson
WAR'S FOOTSTEPS

War gnaws at a man's brain like
  a hungry parasite,
Inch by inch it destroys his
  faith in existance,
And with no litigious leadership
  thousands are killed.
And after the spiry strands of
  smoke have cleared,
All that can be seen is blood,
  death, and ....
A flower? Which has kept a
  feeling of peace in the
  air throughout the terror
  of battle.
But a flower?
It must surely have survived
  under the eyes of God.
But now more of the enemies
  footsteps can be heard
In the distance, and as they
  move closer the flower
  begins to wilt,
And is slowly covered by fire
  of battle, and evil
  begins to inhabit.

Rena James
LIFE

My life, what has it really been?
Sometimes I wonder how I'll

survive.
The highs, the lows, the ups
  and downs,
But through it all, I'm glad
  I'm alive!

Taking each pitfall and turning
  it around
To my advantage, to my gain.
It helps me know one sure thing
That all my pitfalls have not
  been in vain.

I have survived, I have that
  peace,
That joy unspeakable, that joy
  divine.
It's given my life a whole new
  lease
To know what I want can truly
  be mine.

Grace Yancey
A WEDDING PRAYER

May the good Lord bless the
  two of you
And keep you in His care,
So that all the years and years
  ahead
A "Halo" you can share.

If you keep in mind that your
  "Two" no more
But "One" as He intended,
And go to Him for guidance
When each long day is ended,
Then you can rest assured
That love thats shared like this,
Will lead the two of you
To find your "Key to
  Happiness".

Zelma Wells
REFLECTIONS

Seven steps, so long you have
  been here,
attached to the home that's
  witnessed
my triumphs and my tears.

Seven steps, so long you have
  been here,
I have skipped up and down
  you.
My heart knew no care.

Seven little steps, so long you
  have been there.
Did you notice when my
  bouncing stopped
and I descended with a feminine
  air?

Seven little steps, I see you are
  still here.
Did you watch today?
I had to use a cane as I came
  up your way.

Seven steps, why do I notice
  you?
Is it because your mighty
  strength still holds
while mine is nearly through?

June Kissock
DISTANT DRUMS

The drums beat on distant soil
Do they beat for blood?
Or - - is it oil?

Is the free world the final stake?
Is Communism preparing a
  wake?

Is money, power, at the core?
Or is it religion's festering sore?

Is the western mind so
  construed?
Ignorant of customs anciently
  imbued.

Is Kipling's East and West
  ne'er to meet?
Can history's lesson be

obsolete?
We must stop, search,
 contemplate
Pause, pray before it's too late.
Capitalism, convenience,
 wealth, untold
Search our motives, question
 our souls.
Our life so easy and free from
 toil
Made possible by the "magic
 oil".
Our young warriors uneager
 to bleed
Doubt our values, question
 our needs.
The drums beat on distant soil
Do they beat for blood?
Or - - is it oil?

Barbara Dianne Fritts
UNTITLED

He says, "Where has all the
 feeling gone?"
She says, "Put out the cat,
 please, dear."
Their children have all gone,
 they're grown.
He says, "Where has all the
 feeling gone?"
Now they have time to be alone,
Talking together but cannot
 hear -
He says, "Where has all the
 feeling gone?"
She says, "Put out the cat,
 please, dear."

Loretta Chierico
ATLANTIC CITY MANIA

The gambling casinos
 fascination
 grips the crowd with
 hypnotic hold.
Which will it be, the One-Arm
 Bandit,
 Baccarat, Roulette or
 Blackjack "21"?
With what I have to spend the
 One-Arm Bandit
 is best I'm told.
He paid me well, for a long
 while
 we really had fun
Until finally he decided to take
 it all
 back, now I have none.
So long you One-Arm Bandit,
 time to go home
 feeling lonely and blue,
 no thanks to you.

Robert C. Gray
THE END OF LOVE

My heart keeps on crying
Because you were lying
About your love for me

Indifference is bad
I'm desolate and sad
Love was drowned in the sea

A wounded heart drips red
You love others instead
Hope can no longer be

Love-what happened to this?
Yes, dearly I will miss
That glowing warmth in me.

Eve Lynn Mahaney
ENDING

How I long to splash my feet
In a running brook, so cold,
To gather flowers all day long,
To laugh as time grows old.

To watch the day turn
 nightward,
With my own hair turning
 gray;
But still to laugh because I
 know
My youth fades not away.

Death possesses me to ask,
As I turn to face the sea,
"I was satisfied with Life:
Was Life content with me?"

As I finally close my eyes
And I know my time has come,
I must laugh at Death's
 remarks,
For Life and I were one.

Lona M. Krueger
THE POSITIVE WAY

When the sun shines brilliant
 colors on things
Across the treetops of my life
I think of all the beauty it
 brings
And forget about my troubles
 and strife.

When the warmness of the
 morning sun
Bathes my face with new hope
I think of all the promises to
 come
And remind myself there's no
 time to mope.

When the morning dew tickles
 my soul
It cleanses my life with its
 refreshing spray
Giving me faith in life as a
 whole
And giving me strength to face
 the new today.

Martha Bell Hays
JOY IS

Joy is a liquid moment
Tumbling gracefully
From a high point in time.

Joy is that hidden moment,
Sitting in a silent heart,
Smiling at a secret.

Joy is that lingering moment
Of love, one leaves
Clinging to the fringe of forever.
Joy is.

George Stock
THE CITY

The city streets were oil-stained,
 bubbling in the rain.
Cracking pavements broken
 glass, no trees for birds to
 nest.
Identical row houses, on marble
 steps folks sat and laughed;
Washloads hung throughout
 the yards on clotheslines
 looped and tattered.

The city wasn't bad for little
 friends were seldom idle.
The earth became a lunar base
 for astronautic explorations.
Cowboys rode the blacktopped
 plains with cap guns fully
 blazing;
shooting every enemy at least
 one hundred times a day.

Summer brought the hydrant's
 spray; quite illegal but police
 delayed.
Enjoying winter's mounted
 snow on the sloping hills
 with sleds.
Evening lent the city silence,

young were being tucked
 away;
dreaming of the new adventures
daylight always brought our
 way.

Robyn Dayl Wilson
DOMESTIC OUTCRY

Soaking in scalding soapy water
After roasting in a silver heated
 box,
The pan cries out for relief,
Sending an S.O.S. to the pink
 brillo pad
Stuffed in a crowded,
 overpriced box
Lost among others in a dark
 musty cabinet.
Suffocated with sticky mashed
 potatoes
Unwillingly shoved into a hole
 of saliva,
The spoon feeds the hungry
 mouth,
Searching for an escape to the
 sink
Yearning to be cleansed of all
 food deposits,
Having untarnished sterling
 silver.
Turning coward at the dinner
 table
Encountering an overdone slab
 of meat,
The four-pronged devil of
 disaster
Was forced to slice bite-size
 morsels
Whimpering at the fear of
 defeat
Retreating with bent prongs
 and spirit.
Shedding a skin of porcelain
 and paint
Covered by foreign particles
 of food,
The plates are picked on by
 silver oval demons
Controlled by long skin and
 bones,
Then stacked on a tiled platform
Finally alienated from human
 habit.

Terry Ross
WOLF PACK

The creeping silence rolls
 across the night,
And snow is falling softly
 through the dark.
A witness probes the darkest
 frightening shadows
In expectations dreadful to
 the mind.

Preceptive knowledge comes
 and tenseness builds;
Even man can feel this strange
 preceptive power.
The wilds of mountain woods
 are living fear.
Man trembles like a child from
 fears unknown.

The cloud collection dissipates
 from heaven
Revealing silver incandescent
 light
That casts a ghostly hue across
 the land.
In apprehension, living
 creatures hide.

A sullen shadow sulks across
 the snow,
The only interfering sight of
 stillness:
A demon born of storms, the
 color gray;
The autocrat from Satan's
 sacred zoo.

He lifts his head and sacral
 call
That echoes cross the
 mountains glowing tops
Responded to in ever
 decreasing circles:
That sacred answer from the
 hunting pack.

Ann Simon
ON BEING SICK

I am sick today
 At least a hundred pounds
 heavier
 Food turns to fire in my
 throat
Still, I tried to run
Only I fell
And now
 As I try to find comfort in
 the cold pavement
All I see are
 Delicate bubbles
 Floating out of my reach
 Slowly skyward

Ruth C. Kelly
JOSHUA

Joshua is a desert plant,
And very dear to me.
Watered with a mist of love,
You grow into a tree.

Branches reaching to the sun,
Roots deeply in the ground.
You hold a beauty all your own,
And in my heart have wound.

I gaze upon a work of art,
Especially made for me.
Grandma's heart is full of love,
For her little Joshua tree.

Judy Riise
**FATHER, IT'S BEEN A
HARD DAY**

 Father it's Been a Hard Day
Father it's been a hard day,
 I've failed in many ways.
I have made your heart sad,
because at my fellows I was
 mad.
Father, at the end of this day
 I pray,
 Please forgive my sins,
 and
 Help me tomorrow to win,
this I ask in Christ's name,
so that I might live without
 causing you pain.

Robert Femminella
LIFE

Life is an eternal maze,
Everyone wallows through
 its haze.
The road of life may
 cause fright,
And this will add to the
 devil's delight.
Life may lead you in many
 directions,

Its winding run may cause
corrections.
Never let your truth be had,
Or you will drift and end
up sad.

Brian Conway
MODERN FOAM

You can see castles in the foam.
There are towers, windows, and
draw bridges.
This must be modern foam
for there are no maidens and
the castles disappear.

Donna A. Millstone
FRIEND

At birth there is the beginning
At death there is the end
And inbetween there is life
And what is life without a
friend

Hilda M. Jordan
DREAMS

I dreamed of seagulls in the air
flying all around.
I walked by the beach just
around
and around.
I dreamed I walked with the
Lord
all around the grounds.

Rochelle Peck
**REMEMBERING
UNREQUITED LOVE**

Again, feelings of love and
despair are here.

Somewhere in the past, I am
still longing
for our togetherness of
yesterday.

Again, driving in the sunset ...
Alone, with feelings, singing
those old love songs of
you and I.

Being forced to forget.

Only to remember that I am
not
that robot I think you thought
I was.

I thought you weren't
computerized
for only today's programming,
—by leaving me behind.

Again, only my feelings are left,
and they're not fine.

Carole Frances Confar
**HE WAS BORN IN SUCH
PERFECTION**

It all began in love - they said it
should not be,
the risk was great, the chances
slim, the Profession did agree.

Child bearing years had passed,
those medications too,
a list of ten or twenty were
reasons they all knew.

But it all began with love - how
could we turn away,
how could we follow their
advice and kill a soul that day?

For the gift HE gave in love
could not be terminated,
a gift of life and hope, a soul,
was love thus celebrated.

What all began in love - now
came in jubilation,
this early Easter Sunday Morn
arrived our pro-creation.

If only they could see, those
unbelievers all,

that what they feared and
warned against is but a son
so small.

And what began in love - has
brought us new direction,
for all our prayers were
answered, he was born in
such perfection.

Helen VenDeVille
**AS THE CLOCK STRIKES
TIME**

As the Clock strikes
time...

Day by Day
Comes and goes
On it's way
Becoming simply
Every Day.
Today .. Becomes
Tomorrow, .. when ..
Then, Begins
All over ..
Again ..
Day
    By
        Day.

Susan Johnson
FANTASY

Good morning world.
Welcome to another day.
I suppose it's today.
Or is it the tomorrow
of yesterday's today?
It seems a bit unreal...
Could it be that I have
left a part of me
in yesterday's confusion?
Am I awake, or still
dreaming last night's fantasies?
The Garden seems real enough...
With sunlight, and flowers
blooming.
I picked a rose, I
guess it's real...I
pricked my finger
on a thorn.
My finger bled.

Frank E. Killins
WEST TEXAS WINDS

Blowing, blowing winter wind
Blows so hard the trees do bend.
With rain and snow and sky
so blue
We wait for spring and pleasant
dew.

Blowing, blowing winds of
spring,
Harbinger of storms and things.
Dust and sand are blown about
While we wait for summer's
drought.

Blowing, blowing summer wind,
Touches softly as a friend.
Blowing lightly; winds that
please,
While we wait for autumn's
breeze.

Blowing, blowing autumn
breeze,
Welcome coolness, early freeze.
Flower beds, the leaves do fill,
While we wait for winter's chill.

Blowing, blowing winter wind,
When, oh when will it ever end?
Seasons come and seasons go,
But West Texas winds will
always blow.

Sandra L. Holmes
MAKE ME

Make me a river, that I might
run free,
Make me a mountain, that I
might be closer to thee.
Make me an eagle, that I might
flee this place,
Make me the sun, that I might
touch thy face.
Make me a friend, that I might
never be alone,
Or make me die, that I might
come home.

Paula K. Schmidt
HAPPINESS

Happiness is not an art,
    there is no way
        to teach it;
    there is a way
        to reach it...
All you have to do is smile.

Happiness is not a skill,
    not a thing that
    one can learn;
    but something one
    must yearn....
All you have to do is laugh.

Happiness is not an object,
    not something one
    can steal;
    but something one
    can feel...
All you must do is love.

Toki Cheri Hughes
THE GARDEN OF MADNESS

I stand alone,
Waiting for the unbearable
silence to cease,
Always on guard for any
flicker of life.
Being alone,
That is what life is meant to be,
In this garden of madness
inside of my mind,
I see nothing at all . . . I am
blind.
I can't be happy,
I have nothing to be happy
about.
I cannot see the frustrations,
nor celebrations,
Nor human creations. I have
no choice but
to doubt.

Judith Pike-Boos
THE FOUNTAINHEAD

Sometimes at vespertide, when
we are made
to hear the bell of Christianity,
we rise above the toll. We see
arrayed
veiled spirits of a bygone
century:
Did Constantine, great Gregory,
Martel,
King Richard, Joan, and Brent
not recognize
the fountainhead beyond mere
earth?—the well?
Or, were they patriots in rare
disguise?

Their vision of the spring
transcended land,
although they loved the fief
not less—but more.
So faith and country can walk
hand-in-hand,
if we would dare pursue the
Christian spoor.
We must not let this living
twinning bell
become an easy, elegiac knell.

Janice G. Blazek
UNTITLED

The signs of summer
Seem today
To fade away.
My wilting plant
Can't find its place,
The clutter on the table
Erace its importance.
The candle we burned yesterday
For love,
Now tilts precariously,
Knowingly.
It is growing shorter
Like the days.
The magazines and books
Now read and neatly stacked
Lack adventure.
Summer's told their story.
The world seems still—
Stopped.
No shopping,
No meals to prepare,
The freezer is bare
Like this day.
I went walking
With a summer stride
But all outside was chill
And gray,
Lean, bare, trees bent to say
Summer is past.
Too fast it went.
Now I can only find the
memories
Of summer
Like pictures and poems,
And even they are put away
For other days.

Mike Banowetz
**A POEM OF BEGINNINGS
(A FRAGMENT)**

When I touched you,
    offering
the flashing black coinage
that sobs in my pocket
    for your enormous grain
    of wheat,
your lips pressed to my
stallion that bleeds —
    I witnessed a key of
    flame rising
from a day choked under
mud & death
while a riot of green magicians
    smashed timepieces of vomit
    between a dazzling network
    of sparrows.
Is it any wonder that I
pleaded with you
    to embroider me on your
    pillow?

Jerry R. Hawkins
LIFE'S MOUNTAINS

Within a world of quiet
desperation
For a time when uncertainty
seems
So near
There's a river of questions
asked
In silent
Of life's highest mountains and

her
Valleys pebbled sadly and
cluttered
With fears..
Blowing through the winds
that bitterly
Haunt around them
These mountains echo such a
'cold' that
Burst the thunder
As the clouds which loom the
darkest
Release their tears.
But if you could softly listen to
This cold that seers the moun
mountains
And could hear the love it needs
To hold
For indeed it only longs to hold
It gently,
So warmly to it's soul
If you could but softly listen to
The cold.

Alva E. Tucker
HELLO, PRINCESS

Hello, Princess,
  Just a word to ask
  What heavenly task
  Were you up to last night?

What angel reached out
And made you shout
With glee and childish delight?

Daddy tip-toed into where
  you slept
To make sure the angels
  had kept
Their haloes within your sight.

Oh, how proud I was! How
  pleased!
To see you unposed,
  unteased,
At peace with God and night.

Betty Pohle McGhee
DOUBLE EXPOSURE

Moon touched with shining
  silver,
Shading yourself behind a
  lacy bough,
Vanity must surely tell you
That you have found a perfect
  setting now,
With the shadowy pond below.

Gaze long into your pond-
  mirror, no longer
dark with mystery
For you have stirred the quiet
  waters
to burning whiteness with
  your blow.

I stand here helplessly
  entranced before
the two of you—
The silvery one caught for a
  moment
against the tree
And the dancing one in the
  water
flirting back at me.

Lorelei A. White
HAIKU

The creaking of pines
sounds of quiet forest winds
the gods speak to me

Tim L. Long
THE UNANSWERED WHY

At the peak of its beauty and
  glory
The leaf flitters to the earth
  and dies
Our vision, unobscured, rises
Through the limbs to the

ethereal skies.

There are stars in the sky which
  are shining
And have shone for ages
  unknown;
There are planets and bodies
  celestial
Which gloriously, endlessly
  roam.

Somewhere in the midst of the
  chasm
Between the leaf and the stars
  and the sky
Lies the body of beings deemed
  mortal
Who know nothing for sure
  but to die.

When they die they leave little
  but sorrow.
They leave questions and anger
  and sighs.
When one dies when just
  starting over
There are echoes of the
  unanswered "Why?"

But there are spirits in the sky
  which are shining
And shall shine for ages
  unknown;
There are bodies no longer
  terrestrial
Which are gloriously, endlessly
  home.

James Lewis Nehr
GIVE DAD LIFE

His remains lie
  In a cold dark grave.
Captured by time—
  To make him it's slave.
His innards malfunctioned
  So they laid him to rest,
Facing the heavens;
  Arms folded on his chest.
Men of science,
  Who tamper with Life and
  Death,
Find a way please—
  To give him breath.
Do what you must—
  To bring him back.
Can you restore him;
  His brain intact?
I was robbed of a father
  In my adult life.
He was robbed of his children
  And his wife.
I firmly believe
  In a lasting bond,
That starts in this Life
  And goes on beyond.
Please men of knowledge
  Do what you can.
To restore to me;
  This much loved man!

Marjorie Anderson
**THE HOUNDS OF THE
NORTH**

The hounds of the North are
  running;
Their cries are wild on the hill;
Their eyes are dark with
  cunning
And their teeth are bared for
  the kill.

The funeral wind of their
  passing
Wails like a soul in pain;
And the ghostly curtain of
  snowflakes
Whispers death to the shivering
  plain.

The angry storm clouds lower—
No rainbow dares to be brave
When the hounds of the North
  are running
And the heart is an open grave.

Edgar J. Willmott
VIOLENCE

What's gotten into the people
  of today
To make a lot of them
Act the way,
That violence
Is their life's blood,
To do harm to others
Is real, real good.

To bring sadness
Is their every rule,
Most are dropouts
From a lot of schools,
They think knowing the street
Is very cool,
But in truth
They're nothing but a damn
  fool.

As long as they hurt
But are not hurt in return,
They figure
They have nothing else to learn,
For they
Are king of the hill,
Each injury they cause
Brings them a thrill.

Violence
Is a one way street,
For the one who inflicts it
On the ones they meet,
For in the end
At the end of that street,
There's nothing for them
But violent defeat.

Kay Ann Stadlmeir
SOMEDAY

I wish he was mine
I wish I was his
But right now he doesn't know
  I even exist
I yearn for his touch
I yearn for his love
But right now I just have
  A faith from above
That somehow
And someway
He will come to me
  Someday

Gwen White
RECOLLECTION

Our lives are fragile
Like petals of white roses,
Which brown and shrivel,
While sweet fragrance lingers on,
Recalling times soft and far.

Katherine Needham
THANK YOU

Thank You
For being as thoughtful as
  you are
throughout each and every day
For doing the little surprising
  things
you do in every kind of way.
For the quiet of your voice
and the sunshine in your heart
For the many happy hours we
  have spent
together or when we are apart.
For being so patient and
  understanding
in so very many things
That these long and hectic days
with there many problems

bring.
For having the right amount of
  gentleness
at times when one is blue
And for showing lots of
  tenderness
I give my thanks to you.

Kymn Ogden-Heinrich
FEELING PREGNANT

All alone in the dark seeing
  nothing,
Reaching no one, not hearing
  a sound.
Paralyzed in the damp, misty,
  moonlight,
Sort of floating yet groping
  for ground.

The thoughts in my mind are
  of blackness,
Of a window through rain; cold,
  dark, gloom.
As my senses return I feel
  shallow,
Breaking through with a passion
  for doom.

Total thrill of the moment
  exceeds me,
Every second a pure lust for
  death.
I gave of myself for his passion,
And explode with new life on
  my breath.

Marilyn Bullard
MY ANGEL

An angel in disguse
While you're sleeping, my little
  one
May God watch over you.

Karen Ann Ottomers
UNTITLED

Peace
my friend
This is not the end
It is the beginning
The beginning of what
I really know not
Because it is already
finishing

Iris E. Gerber
**LAMENT TO MOUNT ST.
  HELENS**

You've taught us how
  infinitesimal we really are,
    Once Lovely Lady
You tauntingly teased us with
  your awesome beauty
    and overwhelming regality...
    You Beckoned
You allowed us intimate
  glimpses,
    into your very soul...
Yes, oh yes..., your vomiting
  spew gave warning,
    but our blind trust exceeded
    perceptibility

We Heeded Not

And now;
   Voices are stilled, which sleep
      forever
      beneath mounds of molten
         mud and gritty ash
         leaving many to abhor you,
            Asking Why...

Sylvia Delua Saenz
WASTING TIME

I have wasted a day,
but think of people
who've wasted their life.

Believing in changed course,
to use time wisely,
I shall work and work.

I have used all my time,
but think of people
who've lost all their goods.

So therefore I plead:
take time to play
for if all is gone,
memories of play
are left to reap.

Maritza Ramirez
POOR BUT HAPPY

My pants are old.
My shoes are new.
They don't match
But there good.

My shirt and pants don't match.
But as long as they fit and
keep me warm.
I really don't care.

Rich people buy what they
   want.
But poor people were what
   they
got.

Edith B. Armstrong
JESUS WILL RETURN

When Jesus said He must leave
   this earth
His words troubled many a
   heart.
But then He went on to further
   explain
The reasons He must depart.

He said He was going to His
   Father's house
To make rooms for you and
   for me -
If we'd only believe in the
   Father and Son
These mansions someday we
   would see.

He said He'd only be gone for
   a little while -
God would send the
   "Comforter" in His stead -
We were to carry on the work
   He'd done
Everywhere the "Good News"
   to spread.

Then in God's own time when
   we've all had a chance
To choose between evil and
   "Love" -
We'll see the Heavens open wide
And watch our LORD descend
   from above.

From the graves, He'll call; and
   from the sea;
From earth's four corners -
   you and me.

As promised when God called
   Him home,
JESUS WILL RETURN to
   claim His own.

Holly Porter
EMERGENCE

Dark thoughts roam the
   tenements of my mind
Fear is tangible, the fear of
   discoveries
But as new light falls
   illuminating the hidden
   ravages
Insight and understanding erode
   the despair
Opening mutilated passages
Reconstruction of the crumbled
   self-image begins
Building new from old
The dawn of renovation

Mary P. VanDyke
QUIET IS LONELY

Quiet is a lonely place,
When the whole world sleeps
   but me.
I retrace the past, look into
   the future,
But I can't find
What lies in the shadows,
   haunting my peace.
I tried reading, but my eyes
   hurt, and head.
I tried music, but lost the
   essence of it.
I tried talking to Jesus, but
   ended up talking to myself.
If someone else shares this night,
Telepath your thoughts to me.
I'm mentally wired for
   communication,
And quiet is better together.

Deb Sveinson
WITH THE BREEZE

With the breeze...
   the branch swayed,
      and the leaf seemed to be
         struggling,
      fighting to get free.
I watched it quiver,
   until it finally broke away,
      fluttering,
   gently falling out of time.
It made me think of him,
   slowly dying,
      but yet quivering,
      struggling for his life.
Then finally,
   giving it up,
      floating away,
...with the breeze.

Lisa Ferguson Gerba
UNTITLED

I've shed so many timeless tears
   because of dreams that
   couldn't be.
For fallen stars, and broken
   hearts,

and the love that never loved
   me.
My heart has ached, hard and
   long
   because of friends that are
   friends no more.
For forgotten hopes and
   aspirations
   that once were all I lived for.
There is so much joy, yet also
   sorrow,
   to experience in just one
   lifetime.
The future sneaks up and steals
   the present,
   the past is all one can call
   "mine".
In this play that someone
   named "Life",
   the story's end is so uncertain.
It could be a comedy, tragedy,
   or drama
   we won't know 'til they've
   dropped the curtain.

Harold Rogers
**THE GARDENER
(LEEROYS POEM)**

The gardener is killing all the
   weeds,
He says he dont want them
   there no more,
They were wild and they were
   free,
But the gardener wouldnt let
   them be,
He doesnt want the wild weeds,
To mix in with the garden seeds,
Gardens are what the gardener
   knows,
And weeds are not the things
   he grows.

Helen Danberry
REMINISCENCE

In a moment of quiet
   melancholy
I take your hand.
Gently you withdraw, I know
you don't understand
how I think of days and years
gone by,
how you would fall asleep in
   my arms
with a sigh.

Now you go your way as I go
mine
both getting older with the
   passage of time.
Yet, I dwell on the past like a
lost dream
and think of you, my son, all
of fourteen.

Lottie K. Opdahl
THE FLY AND I

The last fly of summer
   Is buzzing around,
I go for the swatter
   She's not to be found,
I spot her on the ceiling
   And climb on a stool-
But the fly is gone
   She's nobody's fool-
She is back on the wall
   I take a sure aim!
I swear she thinks
   We're playing a game,
She outwits me at every
   turn,
Clearly there's a lot
   I still have to learn,
She must know something
   That I don't know,
This pesky little creature-
   The lowest of the low.

Shirley Poirier Malmgren
MISSING

I searched for God
   in all my rooms
And out among the trees,
   in distant meadows
Full of bloom
   with birds in rhapsody.

I looked within
   my inmost soul
And took my brain apart.

I felt inside
   the deep recesses
Of my empty heart.

I saw His creatures
   romp about,
His purple mountains loom;
His breath disturb
   like rare perfume
The silence of a tomb.

I sensed His presence
   near about;
I reached to touch...
   but air...

He is the God
   created me
But He was not
   there...

Gayla Faith Crim
REMEMBERED MEMORIES

Remembered memories,
Gently drifting through my
   mind;
Memories of my mother's face,
So gentle and so kind.

Remembered memories,
Made in a moment or an hour.
Cherished moments of
   childhood,
My own ivory tower.

Remembered memories.
First loves embrace,
A white wedding gown
All covered with lace.

Remembered memories.
Some happy, some sad.
Some best forgotten,
If it was a choice that I'd had.

Remembered memories.
Are there any other kind?
I'm sure that there are,
In the back of my mind.

Remembered memories
Which time can't erase.
Other memories remain elusive
Till I give up the chase.

Remembered memories.
So awesome the mind.
Why are some things
   remembered
And other memories left
   behind?

Peter Lisk
ONE TERRIBLY LOST KITTY

One terribly lost kitty in the
   snow
Whose pure white fur shivers
   as cold winds blow;
Who sits in the street half
   frozen to death,
Who meows so softly with
   frozen breath,
Who curls into a tight little ball,
Who thinks nobody loves her
   at all.
- - - - - - - - -
Thought I saw something then
   pumped my brakes,

112

It was a kitty covered with
snowflakes.
I opened my door, like a
friendly guy,
And picked her up with a tear
in my eye.
I think to myself, God, who
left you there?
To place a kitty in such a
nightmare!
Headed back to my car, nicely
heated.
Called her Snowflake for a name
she needed;
A warm thanks she gave me
when she meowed
But in my apartment pets
aren't allowed.
With my thinking-cap on I
drove around
Don't want to give up the new
friend I've found.
Snowball started to purr right
by my side
And all my compassion I just
can't hide.
So I dropped her off at the
city pound.
But tomorrow I'll surely be
around
To pick her up for a new place
to stay,
To my new home, where they
don't chase kitties away.

Catherine (Frantz) Long
A BOOK

From cover to cover
    Love and excitement hover
Some love, some war
    Tears and laughs galore
From beginning to end
    You make many a friend
You travel to new and exciting
places
    And meet new and exciting
    faces
The danger and thrills
    Fill you with chills
The T.V. and movies at which
you look
    Are not half as exciting as
    reading a Book.

Jackie Crowell Isaac
GRATITUDE

You know I'm truly grateful
dear,
    for the life I share with you.
For the home we've built
together,
    All the things we love to do.
For all the happiness and
laughter,
    yes, the tears and sorrow, too.
Are full of understanding,
    because they are shared with
    you.
But most of all I'm grateful for
    the little folks who call me
    "Mother"
And that I chose so very wisely,
dear,
    the man they proudly call
    their "Father".

John E. Sanks
MY DREAM AND ME

I

I had a dream the other night-
    So different I must tell;
It was about my future life
    That seemed to go so well.

II

I dreamed I had the one I love

Laying closely by my side-
She told me things I wanted to
hear
    And nothing did she hide.

III

She said I love you oh! So much
    My heart belongs to you,
I have never been so happy
    And I hope that you are too.

IV

But when reality came to me
    I lay there all alone,
I found I had been dreaming
    And all my love was gone.

V

All I can do is hope some day-
    My dream will come to be;
Then I would be so happy
    With just my dream and me.

Kymn Ogden-Heinrich
I DREAM

I dreamt of deep red roses,
    Afresh with crystal dew.
The morning air, the plush
green grass,
    In golden violet hues.
I touched the sattin rose buds.
    I drank of sweet red wine.
And through the foggy, golden
dream
    Our love became intwined.
And through the mystic
moonlight,
    Warmth filtered, gleaming
new.
The gentle, velvet, touch of
time -
    Soft whispering thoughts
    of you.
High, lofting in the steeple.
    Bright auras wait for thee.
The tower doors are barred
with truth,
    And patience is the key...

Sally T. McCullough
UNTITLED

With the dawn
    shall come a new beginning...
Filtering through the
    early morning rays
Shall be reflections of faith.

And when dusk casts its
    shadow and the day turns to
    silent meditation

I will have a sunlit
    memory to glance back
    and smile upon...

Carolyn M. Davis
**ABRACADABRA HOCUS
POCUS HAS THE MAGICIAN
GONE OUT OF FOCUS?**

To the agnostic as well as the
    atheist I wish to implore.
As to the once existence of a
    magician is the topic I wish
    to explore.
If the universe was created by
    magic as you seem to suggest,
    it is my intent to put
your theory to the test.
For substantial evidence
    implicates not to mention
    indicates that logic itself must
dictate.
There had to be a magician at
    one time who waved a magic
    wand in the palm of his
mystical hand or else the magic
    act of pulling a rabbit from
    the hat would have
never began.

Has he retired?
Is he extinct?
Does he still exist?
Is he still performing magic in
    our midst?
It is up to you to decide the
    magicians fate.
I have nothing more to ask or
state.

Michelle Lynn Blake
LIVING LIFE AS ME

Oh, What a feeling it would be
To have all there is to have
To see all there is to see
To know all there is to know
To be all there is to be

But, When I look at what I have
What I know and what I see
I realize what life can be
If I live it while simply being me.

Eleanor J. Hand
I'M NOT A POET

If I knew what a poet knows,
    I wouldn't be rhyming these
    rhymes.
I'd be telling of great cathedrals
    or about some lofty climes.

If I knew what a poet knows'
    I wouldn't be singing these
    words.
I'd be singing the praises of the
    golden west and exclaiming
    the song of the birds.

If I knew what a poet knows,
    I wouldn't be spinning such
    yarns.
I'd weave a tapestry of gold,
    or tell of the harvest in
    brim-filled barns.

If I knew what a poet knows,
    I'd spin me a fabulous tale,
Of famous people, great
    beginnings or a beautiful ship
    with full sail.

If I could formulate words in
    my head, if I could but
    "spiel" a fine story,
I'd tell of the wonders of
    nature, and such, I'd tell of
    the heavens own glory.

But alas, I am not a poet, a
    weaver of magic lines, so I
    must be content
With the words that I use, to
    rhyme me my little rhymes.

Patricia Satlan
PLANS OF MAN

If I had the time,
I'd never leave the church.
But worldly cares intervene
Leaving me cast adrift in
    another scene.

A scenic play, Lord, I do not
    pretend to understand.
But Thou, O Lord, art the
    orator of all wisdom.

I cannot but feel sad that things
    did not work out in my plan
But I know that a heavenly
    ordained plan is for the best.

Plans of man art forever going
    astray
But trusting in Thee can never
    lead me wrong
For Thou art the Rock, Thou
    art the Mighty Sword
And Thy Holy Will shalt
    always keep me safe from
    harm.

Maureen S. Brown
MY PLEA

Oh Lord, why does it seem
    everytime I've got it figured
    out,
Something happens which
    makes me doubt?
    Just tell me this, exactly
    what am I supposed to do?
    You'd think I was born to
    sing the blues.
Why should I worry about
    tomorrow?
Because I'm getting tired of
    feeling this sorrow.
    I make others feel bad too,
    And really Lord, I doubt
    that's what you want me to
    do.
But everytime I ask your
    advice,
The answer makes me want to
    ask twice.
    One thing Lord, I have to
    admit,
    That writing this poetry helps
    me from throwing a fit.
For this Lord I shall always be
    thankful!!

Carolyn M. Davis
MAN

We are all Dr. Jekylls and Mr.
    Hydes on the inside.
Man can be an evil road Satan
    personified.
Man can be a good road God
    purified.
These two roads live inside
    and they must coincide.
For good and evil will
    constantly collide.
They must rule side by side.
Taking us for a ride.
For if we were but meek we
    would be as a flock of
    mindless sheep.
For if we were but strong we
    would be as ravaging dogs in
    a throng.
Man is an imperfect soul.
He has no choice but to walk
    the two roads to bear the
    good and evil load.
His place should be in the
    middle of the two roads.
A hard place to hold.

Eleanor Barnes Murray
I THINK OF YOU

When roses bloom beside our
    door
    And drop their petals on our
    floor;
When roses bloom and
    fragrance shed
    From laden bushes—pink and
    red—
        I think of you.

When round the pasture hill I
    walk,
    And need a friend with whom
    to talk;

When leaves appear on trees
once dead
   To form a bower overhead,
      I think of you.
When friends sit down at home
with me
   To share a cup of spicy tea;
When friends sit down around
our fire
   Where crickets join the insect
choir,
      I think of you.
When pictures catch my passing
eye:
   Hand painted roses, fruit
piled high;
When ivy twines from flower
stand,
   Or swings from baskets made
by hand,
      I think of you.
And now as time and days move
on,
   Though from our circle you
are gone,
You're very near to us you see,
For we can turn sweet
memory's key
      And think of you!

Sydney Ruth Lasky
QUIET DOMINION

...and it was a crisp winter
afternoon.
The winds gave birth to the
spontaneity
of dancing snowflakes, when
their destiny
was not to die but to give
expectation to
the earth. I reclined; made
angels in the
snow, and gazed into the quiet
of the
sky. There was a short absence
until
the tranquil beauty
over-whelmed my
efforts. It was just a brief
moment...

Darlisa Meszaros
NEVER AGAIN

I can never say what's true,
cause you know,
I am still in love with you.
I see you every day,
and in your own special way,
you make me smile.
Even though the days are short,
and the nights are long,
I hope to be yours before you're
gone.
I can never say what's true,
cause you know,
I am still in love with you.
How I long for the night,
when I can hold you tight,
then I'll know you're mine.
But until that day is here,
I will always have the fear,
of never being yours again.

Joanna K. Cunning
WOMAN ON THE BRIDGE

I see the morning's misty light,
Lord, why are things so grey?
I waken in the quiet night
And dread the coming day.

I miss the lilt of singing birds,
   Lord, have I done so wrong?
I've lost the meaning of your
words,
   And the angel's joyous song.
I haven't done as I was told
And the path I chose was weak.

But, must I stay here in the cold
when it's your warmth I seek?
I seem to feel the ache and strife
of
every living man.
But Lord, I cannot take my life
and change your holy plan.
I know I will do better now.
Lord would you please forgive?
To thy loving heart I bow.
Today I want to live.

Thomas J. Matthews
I TOSSED HIM A CROSS

He spoke of Christ's riches
And of a World to be.
But I wanted the riches
Of the World I could see.
Finally, He said,
"Christ died for us!
To Him we belong."
Artfully, I countered,
"Lucifer lied for us.
You got it all wrong."
Closing the valves of my
Heart with a thud,
I left him there standing,
Sweating the blood.
Telling him sweetly,
But ever discretely,
"Our cookie crumbles
And the mop flops,"
I tossed him a cross
With some vinegar sops.

Charlotte Webb
A CHILD'S PRAYER

Be kind to me
I am afraid
Of life in general, you see.
I need your love
Not your anger.
When I need a push, give me a
gentle shove.
I need your patience,
Please understand,
I need a lot of a helping hand.

Leonard Alexander
CLIMB TO THE TOP

Bosses are bosses, at the top
   of the tree.
If you climb the ladder, you'll
   plainly see.
They hire you, they fire you at
   the drop of
a hat.
If you don't get moving, and
   do this and do that.
Some you can please, and
   others can not.
You can work your self silly,
   but this is
your lot.
Orders you take, when they
   start to speak.
Some are young, and others
   antique.
So if you want to look down,
   on the world below.
Kiss the right persons ass, and
   to the top
you will go...

Bridget Auenson Burnett
REMEMBERING YOU

I remember that day
I remember it best
The way we talked
And all the rest.
It's still fresh in my mind
All we said to each other
I can still remember
How we felt about one another.

Nothing can separate us
Or at least that's what we said
But we never thought about
One of us being dead.

Sara Hindman
AN EVENING OUT

Warm night,
Play your scenario of light
  and color
Against black, hazy sky.
Shadows shift and melt in
doorways.
And drift in the corners
Of your smile.

Kathrine Plecas
CHILDREN

Children are my favorite people,
all they need is love and care;
They are so grateful and so
  sweet
when mom and dad love them
and tend to their need
They are so happy when they
  play
they make life worth living,
they make my day.

Emma Bleckner Crobaugh
**EUCHRED FIRES OF
THOUGHT**

The newly dead
are crying from darkened
crypts.
Lurid clouds are shrouding
the arid patch of earth,
the purple fruited orchards
of wisdom
smothered
in the euchred fires of thought,
and feet slip into the void
as winds scream death of day.

Left in darkness,
he hides himself
in perplexed defeat.

Dena Marie Nelson
FEATHER LOVE

And in the ecstacy
Of spring sundrops
And pine tree shadow passions,
Two sparrows dip and twirl.
Soft grey bellies
Brush and part again.
Wings snap rapidly,
Enfolding,
Now disclosing,
Quick beak kisses.
Obeying an instinct eons old,
They dance on breathless songs
And revel in the ritual
Of Love's wild ride.

Ima Ann Gilcrease
STAND SILENT

Stand silent, World, and behold
  the flower,
For the year runs swiftly, as a
  swift, fleeting hour,
And calm is the mind engulfed
  in peace,

But harried is the soul which
  lusts after power.
Stand silent, World, and listen,
  listen,
For the storm rages wild and
  your burdens glisten,
But sweet is the song from the
  robin's breast,
To those who stand silent and
  listen, listen.
Stand humble, World, and be
  touched by a smile,
For the strongest of powers is
  not lightly riled,
And troubled is the quarrelsome
  heart,
But stronger is he who is most
  like a child.

Marguerite Kaufmann
AH, YOUTH!

When I was young,
I used to think,
The rain was angels,
Watering their flowers.

But now I think,
It must be God,
Crying as
He looks down upon us,
His consummate creation?

Lisa Padovano
TRANQUILITY

In the early morning stillness
the day has just begun-
the sun is silently burning away
  the fog,
promising another clear day of
  sunshine..
By then the pace will be fast
people will be coming and
  going,
but still I'll remember
how peaceful the morning was...
I can carry that feeling inside
and make it a part of me,
and in this way
I can pass it on to others.
Though they won't know the
  story behind it,
still they can feel it-
and that's just what I ask for.

Susan M. Hastings
**MIDNIGHT CLEAR'S WHITE
BUCK DEER**

  I gazed upon a meadow,
when in a midnight clear.
  It was then I chanced to see
a young buck deer.

  Shining in the moonlight
his white coat shone like silk.
  A wonder upon wonders,
his fur so the color of milk.

  Suddenly he saw me,
as I was not so well concealed.
  His watching eyes caught sight
  of me,
now my hiding place revealed.

  From then on almost
  thereafter,
just between us two.
  Neither really knowing,
a kind of friendship grew.

  Every night I went back there,
when the skies were clear.
  When the stars were shining,
and the moon seemed quite
  near.

  He would be there sometimes,
seemingly waiting for me.
  I always sensed a certain pang,
a feeling not hard to be.

  But then sadly enough,
he failed to come again.

No longer can I gaze at him,
and now the thought of him
    brings pain.
    Will he one day;
come back to me I pray.
Nothing can avert my thought
from the lost happiness I sought,
and from the hurt that was so
    wrought.
    Yet I know it is not upon he,
but solely, only upon me . . . .

Holly Anderson
ROSE

a symbolic rose
with significant thorns
the perfect teacher
of the piercing pain
    of Love

Lil Weinkauf
GRIEF

I sit in loneliness listening to
    the rain
    Tears flowing freely,
As the water running down the
    pane.
Death has taken you from my
    side
    I bow beneath the grief,
No longer trying to hide.
Despair wraps about my spirit
    Like a dark black cloud;
I'm told someday the sun will
    clear it.
But for now I live in bleakness,
    In a lonely room,
Longing for a beloved voice—
    that is My Weakness.

Kelly M. King
THE DAINTY DAISY

One day I saw a Dainty Daisy,
Blowing in the windy weather.
It reminded me of Jill,
And the times we spent together.
I wanted to pick it and save it
    forever,
But I knew that someday it
    would die.
So I let it alone and watched it
    grow,
As it lifted its head toward the
    sky.
Then one day I ran to where it
    was growing,
And found it was no longer
    there.
I searched all over that open
    field,
But to my distress it was bare.

James E. Ainsley, Jr.
PROCRASTINATOR

To put off, from day to day.
To defer, or to delay.
To habitually procrastinate.
A future time, to always wait.
The act of postponement,
    consistantly.
To be, decision free.
Nothing's now, and everything
    is later.
A philosophy of life, to which
    I cater.
Maybe tomorrow, if it's not too
    cold.
It may also be too hot, or I may
    be too old!
If everything is just right, maybe
    I will.
This isn't a promise, and it isn't
    a deal!
Regardless of what you think,
    it's no fun to be this way.

I definitely will change—Maybe
    tomorrow—or some other day!

Donna Marie Scott
BUTTERFLY

Touch me like you would a
    butterfly
Caress me ever so gently
Capture me in flight
Squeeze me firm
But crush me light
Open and let me fly
As you would a butterfly

Helen I. Ripmaster
MOVING DAY

We're moving today,
No more rocking in the chair
Hearing the dry creak of floors
Waiting for rain out doors,
"We need the rain," I've heard
    my neighbor say
so many times before.
Familiar scenes will pass away
Changing colors on the trees
Bees in the apples in the fall
The doll on the trunk in the hall
We're leaving.
The kitchen where I cooked the
    food
My plastic statue of St. Jude on
    the
shelve above the sink
With leaky faucets that I love.
The hum of the ice box late at
    night
The children's fights o're who
    is stronger
Not much longer here.
My baby's room all gloom, in
    the grey dawn
She's gone,
Flown to another world of her
    own
The curtains blown in the wind,
    smell of changes.
Good bye dear old home
Stand firm, and serve and supply
House my ghosts in slender
    closets
Till time to fly.

Lisa Marie Stone
THE FAMILIAR FRAGRANCE

I was in a drugstore;
I opened a bottle of your
    perfume.
I smelled the familiar fragrance.
It took me into another place
    and time,
Where we were in each other's
    arms
With love's spell cast over us.
We were so in love.
Then I closed the bottle of
    perfume,
Because it brought back too
    many memories.

Cindy L. Belmer
BABIES

Into this world they come
With energy bursting from their
    lungs
They're ours, but, not ours
    alone
To have, to hold,
To share and let grow.
As we watch them grow
We'll try to ease their struggles.
They are ours, but, not ours
    alone
With love in our hearts
And tears in our eyes
One day we'll say goodbye
But tenderness shared

Will come back one day
When a Grandbaby comes our
    way.

Marla Fair
SPACE SONG
I.
A solitary unit
Dangle in space where there is
    room for many.
Far
From my time-locked home I
    sleep
In the somber embrace of the
    void.
(There is no other place where
    I belong)
I long . . .
Through my sphere of glass I
    watch
Celestial forms expire and
    return
I seek to learn,
Am I I?
Or is it I I will be then?
(A small star winks at me with
    water-weighted eyes of jet
and seeks to tell me. So will I
    wake)
But no.
It is my mistake.
In the cockpit of my universe
It was a flaw that spake.

Vila B. Keller
**EVERYWHERE SOMETHING
SINGS**

Life's cycle in spring begins
the real mystery of birth again.
As the young bend with the
    wind,
everywhere I hear something
    sing.
Life's space is filled
with squirrels and trees,
with birds and many bees.
Everywhere something sings.
Life's force is strong.
As different faces appear
across the bridge of time,
The sun continues to climb.
Life's colors slowly change.
As the moon holds of darkness,
stars are suspended in the sky
obscured by clouds passing by.
The night hides many things,
but not the hoot of an owl,
or the lonesome coyote's howl.
Everywhere something sings.

Mel Taje
WHY THE DRUNK?

We may be feeling low,
We felt that all was lost.
That is negative thinking,
When you total up the cost.
We thought we found the
    answer,
When we felt low and sunk.
We would clear the air,
By going on one Big Drunk.
Sure there was the hangover,
But the drunk took all the
    Blame.
It covered up an injured Pride,
The Booze absorbed the shame.

Mildred Landry
ALONE

When I was a baby and didn't
    know.
When all the people would come
    and go.
Pants not wet and tummy full,

The covers didn't pull,
I was content to be . . . Alone
As an infant was well aware,
of all the people everywhere.
As long as someone was nearby,
to hear me if I'd cry.
I was content to be . . . Alone
I grew up to be full grown,
Lots of little ones to fill my
    home.
My time was filled with
    obligations,
of those who replenished our
    nation.
When day was thru and all was
    done,
long after the setting of the sun,
I was content to be . . . Alone
I've lived my life every day,
trying to help in every way,
those I've passed along the way.
Still I think I can say,
I am content to be . . . Alone
So when I'm old and not much
    fun,
My work it seems I have done,
I can relive my yesterdays,
Be thankful in many ways,
I learned to be content . . .
    Alone

Nancy Poppe
WILL-O'-THE-WISP

You're talking, so happy, so
    homelike, so free:
    Nothing is wrong between you
    and me.
You're gone for an hour, so long
    yet so short,
    But now, hear, long fancy
    words which distort
All the meaning behind them,
    like gossamer dew
When the glorious, victorious
    sun rises anew.
You're sitting in that chair; I'm
    standing right here . . .
    You are so far, yet you seem
    so near.
You're talking, so happy, so
    homelike, so free;
    Yet nothing is right between
    you and me.

Valerie Meissner
EROSION

World, concreted and hammered
    to the core,
Drilled, stripped, pummeled
    and pressed
For more than she can bear.
There is a minor rebellion going
    on
In the splitting macadam
    beneath our feet.
Earth's yawn spewing upward
    her exiguous colonists,
Deponing the synthetic, stony
    cover of our street.
And here in a bus stop, subway
    rotting
Microcosm of our modern world,
We're challenged by matters of
    minor importance.
Idly follow the gradual, insistent
    dismemberment:
Ivy breaking bricks, introgression
    on the shores
Of carefully poured concrete by
    roots of trees,
And heads of weeds—survival,
    in spite of our symmetrical
    efforts;
Life and its chaos silently
    emerges, and we are the
    encroachers.

Patricia Dillabaugh
MEMORIES

Memories
Tender touching vignettes of
the past:
Deceptive portraits of the
"Used To Be,"
Mirroring a time and place that
seem to cast
A portent of the things to be,
The harbinger of our far
distant destiny.

Memories
Make beauties of the past
outshine the new:
The sunshine of a younger day
shone brighter
As it glistened on the
early-morning dew;
The birds sang more in key—
And life was much more
precious, then, to me.

And memories
Teach me that today will be
In some far future date,
A fairer and more pleasant day
Than I, beseiged, can now
anticipate.

Joe Spagnolo
U TELL ME₂

No poetry
I don't know why
Something's not here
The thoughts
The want
But
Is this poetry?
If i want it to be
But
I don't want it
To be
So it isn't poetry
For me
For you?

Tammy Davis
MY LOVE

Here,
take it,
I'm giving
it to
you.
Don't be
Scared,
All
that it
can do
is
Die.

Mrs. Janice D. Dailey
THE PUSHER

Pusher, our kids don't need the
junk you're selling,
they don't need an instant
high.
Young folks think you're their
best friend
as you fill their heads with lies.
"Just try it once," you tell
them,
"it's no worse than a social
drink."
They will not hearken to their
conscience.
"Don't put this poison in your
soul,"
refusing to heed God's warning
on a trip they choose to go.
One teen whose name was
Sally,
while strung out Higher Than
a Kite,
suddenly imagined she was a
bird

and attempted to take Flight.
Her friends could not help her
as she climbed onto that
window ledge,
for they were too spaced out to
notice
Sally Leaping to Her Death!
Friends and family gathered
round the gravesite
that day we said our Last
Good-bye,
and in my mind I pondered
"Pusher, were you there to
Cry?"

Emogene S. Adams
DEEP SOUTH LITANY

When I was 'littie
Mother taught me a dittie
It goes like this:
Missie gave me a holiday—
I had nowhere to go,
So I went down to the old pine
field
And pulled up Forky Toe!
I wondered *then,* and would
still like to know—
What in 'tarnation is "Forky
Toe?"

Thelma McFall
WHY?

Sometimes I guess it's hard to
say
Or maybe we just forget
It is so simple if we would just
Take the time
Those three little words that
would
Mean so much
We show it in the everyday
things we do
So why can't we just say
"I LOVE YOU"?

Dottie Scarborough Ball
TRACEY, MY SON

You are too young to be so wise,
my blonde haired son with
your
searching brown eyes.
What secrets in your heart do
you keep?
When you should be in bed—
long asleep.
You've held such sorrow in your
short life
When mama ceased to be your
daddy's wife.
But, I'll love you hard and I'll
love you long
And try to fill your heart with
song.
So let me learn to know you
well
Then when you need me I can
tell
And lend a hand to guide your
way
To be a friend to you each day.

I'll do my best and when all is
done
I'll still be with you, Tracey,
my son.

Patricia A. Colby, Flynn
**SOMETIMES WE ARE LIKE
A FLOWER**

Morning light wake up its
morning, jump out of bed
rejoice its morning.
A new day begins. Reach out
and feel it let everything
begin. Feel
it Oh feel it, touch it don't be
afraid. Love it, lose it, but
don't be afraid.

Sometimes we are like a flower
we bloom by love, grow by
the heat
of it and watered by the tears
of it.

Doug Frazier
LOVE FOR THE ILL

I've aided many a meager soul,
the helpless and
the weak, I've dried many eyes
of glistening tears
and found, it was only happiness
in which they seek.

The sick are also human, they
need love to pull
them through, they need that
friendly helping hand,
and a prayer that comes from
you.
What would you want if you
were lying there,
all wrapped up in a gown, what
would you do but
sit and cry, if no love could be
found.

A hospital can be a lonely
place, just lying
there alone, but it could all be
made happier, if
a little love would only be
shown.

So take the time to be kind,
and you'll find
it very true, that all the love you
give away,
returns to shine on you.

George E. Sanford
THE EAGLE

Perched high upon the lofty
crag
the silent sentry cast his eyes
upon the sunbaked scene below
and uttered forth his eerie cry
before into the pale blue sky
he sped like arrow from a bow.
Then soaring high above the
land
he saw the prey upon the sand,
and like a bolt of lightning shot
to earth with talons opened
wide
to strike the target he had spied
then rose to perch upon the crag.

Martin Jackson Faries
SUNBEAMS

Lovingly it seems,
the sun's caressing beams
bid me awaken
after sleeping.

Weeping, I cannot feel
that my own life is real,
keeping so close to heart
this sorrow that tears start
seeping again with zeal,
while suffering this part.

But lovingly it seems,

the sun's caressing beams
say I'm not foresaken
after weeping.

To him who is laid low
by a very great woe,
all is not lost,
for the sun just told me so.

Roe Custard
WANTING

Wanting; is an idea, feeling.
Remember: An idea of
feeling—you have to
have.
You have a feeling to want or
to have,
To make yours.
It's a yearning feeling of a
possibility
of having—to belong to you.
Making it an idea of having it
for yourself,
to satisfy your feeling,
Causing the idea to feel a
certain way to
have (Good Naturally)
Ending with the idea feeling
of wanting to
have you, belong to me.
(Can I?)

Elizabeth G. Van Horne
THE WIND

I can hear the wind
Outside my window
Like music to my ears,

I can feel the wind
Inside my room
Like music to my tears,

I can see the wind
Moving through the trees
Like music to my fears.

Virginia Green
MEMORIES

The summer with its warm lazy
days
The smell of newly mowed hay
The sound of children laughing
at play
The fragrance of flowers along
the way
Aren't you glad you awoke
today?

Oh what is so rare as a night in
June
Seeing lovers strolling hand in
hand,
Down the lane under a bright
yellow moon
It makes you wish you were
young again.

Memories flow to a time long
ago
During my growing up years,
For the young man with whom
I strolled
Is the one with whom I grew
old,
Now the thoughts of him make
my eyes grow dim again with
tears.

Rev. Ann Coffee Walker
IT TAKES MORE

It takes more, than just saying
that you're a
Christian.
It takes more, than just saying
a prayer.
It takes more, than that
outward appearance,
for it isn't the clothes that you
wear.
It takes more, than quoting the
scripture.

It takes more, than being
  supportive in the
church that you attend.
It takes more, than just being
  verbal, about
what you may or may not do.
The more that it takes is
  knowing, the Christ
that dwells in you.
It is when you recognize His
  almighty presence,
the doing becomes quite clear,
  when it is put
into practice the more needs
  disappear.

Richard Jay Rosenblatt
DISCO DOLDRUMS

I've had it with
the disco nights,
spinning mirrors,
flashing lights.

The women in their
fancy gowns with,
crude rejection
put-me-downs.

The disco beat is
much too fast, and
I just hope that
it won't last.

I'd rather sit in a
country bar, and
listen to Hank on
his guitar,

than, have a man
with a chain of gold,
dance with the girl
I once did hold.

Melanie I. Fantino
COMPANY

Company needs be
once in awhile—

Alone to be apart of
what they and she
are part of.

The company needs be
here for awhile.

I'll give them ideas
to follow in exchange
for a hand getting
out of my head,
and the ease of
slipping into an
empty bed.

Company needs be
for all of them that
are apart of what we
and those are already
part of.

Lisa Dawn Vaughn
ROAD TO LIFE

The road is long but I can see
A light at the end as a guide for
  me
And though I may stumble
  along the way
From this one path I'll never
  stray.

My legs are weary from this
  journey
But my heart's forever yearning
To continue forward to the light
That shines for me both day
  and night.

And sometimes as I travel on
To reach the light with my
  hopes nearly gone
I find that the light seems to
  grow a bit brighter
And the burdens I carry seem to
  grow a bit lighter.

It is at this time I truly know

This light for me shall always
  glow
And though I may stumble
  along the way
From this one path I'll never
  stray.

This light for me was placed by
  One
Who gave the life of His only
  son
So that I more easily can find
  my way
As I travel this path from day
  to day.

And though His Son from
  among men is gone
The lessons He taught us linger
  on.
Yes, the road is long but I can
  see
God's light at the end as a guide
  for me.

Evelyn Best
THANKSGIVING

That "turkey time" has rolled
  around,
And pumpkins gathered from
  the ground,
With all the festive foods
  abound,
Just for our pleasure.

Summer was hot with plenty
  rain,
Yet we have harvested our grain,
And look for winter once again,
In its own measure.

We thank Thee Lord for each
  new day,
For caring for us in Your Way,
Sincerely mean it when we say,
Thou art our Treasure.

Michael E. Waldecki
OLDMAN WORKHART

He works in the basement
behind the steel door
beneath which they slide his
  meals.

If you listen closely
you can hear the shuffling
  sound
of his approach.
For a moment
the ring of the hammer on
  metal will cease.

A quiet laughing and grunting
then the sparks will fly again.

He's been down there
for two—
almost three generations.
My grandfather knew him
when he was young.

Since then
he's been building his machine.
Plating it with silver and chrome,
engraving runes.

If his machine runs
the world will pay a high price.

He is a poet by trade
and I am waiting.
All poets are old men.
You can see it in their eyes.

Look upon the machine I've
  inherited
and the one I shall build.

Gina Meron
SEEMINGLY

Her smiles seem numb
you can't feel them.

Her life seems motionless
she does not move.

Her feelings seem confused

like moment to moment.
All this seems confined
woman, you can change.

Jeannie Parrish
SHINE ON, SUPER STAR

At Christmas time
  many years ago
  as shepards watched their
    sheep
Angels appeared
  bringing Good News
  of peace on earth to keep.
Off in the distance
  in Bethleham town,
  a star was shining bright.
A baby was born
  to bring to earth
  a Super Star of light.

So shine on You Super Star
let the world see how You shine.
May You light up many other
  lives
as much as You have mine!

Paul L. Daniels
THERE IS!

Is There a Religion without a
  claim
Is There a Truth that trancends
  fame
Is There a Bliss with silent zeal
Is There a Timeless state with
  universal appeal
Is There a Inner peace like the
  wind and tide
Is There a Sight made bright
  through the light inside
Is There a Single purpose for
  all mankind
Is There a Crucial message in
  the next line
Is There a One necessity relevant
  to love
There Is: Love ye one
  another . . . .

Wm. Micheal Saunders
MARY LENI

In the arid desert sand, a
  shimmering silhouette stands
A cunning young cougar, lying
  dying near her hand.
Freely and slowly flowing in
  the whispering oasis air
The yellow willowing strands,
  of their glistening golden hair.

Her feather soft voice serenely
  floated through the sky:
"I have written a poem, 'So
  Lonely I Shall Cry.' "
Said she with a solitary tear,
  and a very sultry sigh,
"My one true love is dying,
  soon alone, I shall cry."

In an amber mist glow, desert
  silence surrounds her home
Like reticent beauty from a
  chartreuse rose,
  a shimmering silhouette once
    had shone.

Yet the essence of femininity
  still reflects in her face
Revealing her talented style,
  both beauty and grace.
Standing fairer than fair in the
  whispering oasis air
Remorse and sorrow had left
  her, in an apathetic stare.

Robert J. Jackson, Jr. "Bo Jack"
HEAVEN

Heaven is the tranquility,
Between Man and his Mind.
With the foresight, of his
Final resting place, and
What he shall find.

The love and peace, he shall
Find at last, from the life,
of his worldly past.
The taste of honey, upon
His lips.
And to speak to our Father,
Our own true Divine.
On Judgement Day, as He
Drinks the wine.

Mary Lou Lemoine
OUR CHILDREN

As I recall day after day
Things our children did and said,
I remember you teaching them
  to pray
In such a beautiful way.

I can see them clearly,
Just barely walking and
Then looking at you dearly,
While doing their talking.

When being tucked in bed
Or when a fall, they would take,
You were always there when
  they said,
"Come, Help! Daddy, for
  Heaven's sake!"

Their little eyes would shine,
They were glad to have their
  father.
A kiss you'd give them and
  everything was fine.
You gave them love and didn't
  think it a bother.

You have been a wonderful
  father.
I'm proud to say that I'm glad
I'm the lucky woman whose
  children
So gladly call you "Dad."

Jeffrey Kaufman
LIFE

Willow trees,
Pine trees
Swaying in the breeze.
Birds that sing,
The running spring,
Life is even more beautiful
  than these.

Mary Jean McGee
BURNT CANDLELIGHT

I'm seventeen.
I made love in the shadows of
  candlelight—
  with a married man.
Lying beside him, smoothing
  the curls
upon his chest, my thoughts?
Of castles and colorful fields
the wind caressing the sails of
  a yacht
Who blew out the candlelight?
I'm thinking
Peace and time play patiently in
  blackness
  while we dream
Reality knocks at my soul
with cold facts and things
  behind
I peep around only to see

she looking at me.
I'm leaving
a kiss, a goodbye,
that hurt look in your eye
Roses don't cry on this
    beautiful fall
morning till tomorrow comes
    snow
See, I have to go . . . .
I'm seventeen.

Michael Lazazzara
UPSTATE SUNRISE

Grey dawn hushes in its infant
    light
As the wind carries fall and
    winter's remains
On its swift current towards the
    sky.
In the west the dormant woods
    of the Burnt Forest
Stand naked amidst the stunning
    color of the surrounding hills.
Across the lake morning exposes
    the sun
On its ascent over the downs.

Reflected on the stillwater
    before me
In the rising mist from the faded
    darkness,
The sun stretches towards the
    shoreline.
Midpoint divides the growing
    daylight
From evening's last stand,
Reaching for a final hold on
    existence
Pictured in the double sunrise.

Eleanor E. Tharalson
ONE ENCHANTED NIGHT

I was an impressionable child
    at the age of nine,
And I'll never forget that night
    that was mine.
The wheat was harvested and
    piled up high,
And to me it seemed that it
    reached to the sky.

At night it was guarded by one
    of the men,
And sometimes my Dad took
    his turn to attend.
I can still see his smile when he
    asked me to share
The time of his watch, as he
    wanted me there.

Down the hill to the field we
    carried our cots,
To sleep there with him was a
    beautiful thought.
The soft, whispering sound of
    the gentle warm breeze
Was delightful to hear as it
    blew through the trees.

As I lay on my back and
    glanced toward the sky
The sight was enchanting and
    it caused me to sigh.
My father and I had something
    special we shared,
In the calmness and wonder,
    we expressed how we cared.

I can close my eyes now and
    still hear the sound
Of the mockingbird's song as
    he sang in the dawn.
I have heard many birds sing
    over the years,
But that one in that tree is the
    one I still hear.

To be with my father alone in
    that field
Is a wonderful dream that only
    a child can feel.

If ever I was asked my most
    memorable time,
That night was enchanting—
    that night that was mine.

Helen Brown Rittershofer
CHRISTMAS JOY

Twinkling sparkling blue-green
    eyes
Smiling lips expressing joy
Curls piled high on nodding head
Excitedly dangling a Christmas
    toy.

The pathway of her present
    dreams
Led her to the Christmas tree
Where underneath the tinseled
    branches
She placed her doll and chuckled
    with glee.

The star that topped the
    Christmas tree
Shone down and glorified the
    scene
She winked then blinked with
    the sparkling lights
Turned and tiptoed out as in a
    dream.

Melanie Patrice Lane
MEMORIES

Memories some good, some bad
Memories some happy, some sad
Tucked away in the corners of
    my mind
Still come to me yet are left
    behind.

Memories of a happy carefree
    child
Who laughed and played and
    often smiled.
Memories of a tall and slender
    young girl
Learning the hard way about
    this sometimes cruel world.

And then there are memories
    of just a few years ago
Of the girl who into a woman
    did grow.
Memories of few smiles and
    many bitter tears
Looking back these seemed to
    be the hardest years.

And now the present will soon
    be the past
No matter how hard I try to
    make it last.
It too will soon cease to be
And be nothing more than
    memories.

Judith Strain-Vanet
A BRIEF ENCOUNTER

Your Friendship touched my
    life,
    And filled my heart with joy.
It made me realize,
    The convictions of my soul.

Yesterday a stranger,
    Today a long missed friend.
Will the plane that took you
    away,
    Bring you back again?

Or will I wander through time,
    With just a lingering memory,
Of the warmth and love I felt,
    When you touched lives with
    me.

Cher Marie Obusek
LOOKING IN THE MIRROR

Looking in the mirror
shattering glass
blows before her eyes
terror of love ungiven
she hears the cries

they come from way inside
mirrors of life.
Faulty impressions
upon the face
somehow the shatter
cannot erase.
Broken pieces laying there
upon the floor, she sits and
    stares.

Mirrors of life
seeing only what she will
one for hate
one for love.

Looking in the mirror
shattering before her eyes.
the life of love
is held inside.

She reaches out
    to grasp it.
But only gets the pain
She's inflicted upon
    the body
upon the shattered face
    she sees again.
Broken pieces of glass
    lay upon her
she'll stare and wait
    and wonder
what it told her
    in the
    mirror of life.

Katherine Andrews
BLEAK BRILLIANCE

Tender shoots
Ready to burst forth
In brilliant array.

Unseen, their life
Remains hidden,
Clothed in barren branches.

As a bud ever so slowly and
    gently
Peeks forth from its enclosure,
The power of hopelessness
Vanishes.

A spark of life,
As yet unnoticed by the world,
Springs forth and carries with it
The hope and promise
Of new beginnings.

Viola W. Easterling
NAP TIME

Two little shoes
    Sitting side by side
Dusty and worn
    Knotty strings untied.

Two little feet
    Tucked snugly in bed
Shiny golden ringlets
    Cover a little head.

Smiles cross her face
    As she peacefully sleeps
Her doll in her arms
    Teddy bear at her feet.

Ellen Buoncristiani
REVISION

A little girl sits alone
on the curb outside
clapping hands for
no apparent reason

There are great
symphonies I cannot
hear anymore,
but I see their signs

She applauds with
such contained abandon,
a lovely self-completion
in casual appreciation
of something
    or everything

I hope to re-attain it

Douglas Tharalson
A QUEST FOR REASON

I would speak, but I am not
    heard. I would
express my thoughts, but my
    views are
unimportant. As the tree bends
    with the wind,
I too must bend with the
    opinion of my elders,
even though I believe not in
    what they speak.
I would leap the walls of my
    father's parental
grasp on me and make my way
    through the barbed-wire
of my mother's love; but I know
    within myself
that I would not surrender.
    Then I would look
to life itself for guidance. But
    life is nothing
more than a few years of
    mortality on this planet,
and life would pass by me in an
    instant and leave
no trace of itself with me in my
    long narrow house
of life's quest for reason.

Norma Jean Barker
OUR BROTHER, THE EAGLE

High over the plains of the
    desert
Spreading his beautiful wings,
Flies our brother, the great
    mighty Eagle
Whistling along on the breeze.

One night, when it was dark and
    so stormy,
He swooped down the canyon
    so low
And took with him back to our
    Master
Our brother, Larry Baer's soul.

Now as we gaze toward the
    heavens
A new star shines, oh! so bright,
We whisper a prayer for our
    brother
And watch as the Eagle flies
    high.

Go with God, our dear brother
Rest in Heaven so high
And when the great mighty
    Eagle
Once more makes his heavenly
    flight
We will rejoice and welcome
    each other
And watch as the Eagle flies by.

Julie Anne Brown Bertoni
GRANDPA

We must remember those
who have left us with love and
a fullness in our hearts.
    They have touched our lives
in many ways, that we'll
remember throughout our days.
    But to look back in sadness
at the physical loss, will
only dull the happiness that
grows in the heart with
memories.

Craig Dee Callister
MOM

Colors on a pallette
Cannas in the rain
Children, tiny sparks of color,
And white smoke from Monet's
    train
Lakes in blues and greens reflect
The sky in strokes of paint
While trees from Western forests

seem
Painted by sunstrokes faint
Her paintings are warm and
   tender
Her brush is never dry
Her eyes they speak of kindness
Of friendships passing by
My mother is a meadow
Filled with trees and flowers
She has helped me find my way
From valleys to Heavenly
   Towers.

Alice C. Callaghan
REFUGE
I've found a secret place apart
   From you and your vexations,
Where I may take my aching
   heart
   And know not tribulation.
It is a place composed of dreams,
   It knows no regulations—
My children fill this little world
   With hopes and aspirations.
So briefly I find refuge here,
   A moment's relaxation,
I know full well this breathing
   spell
Will be of short duration.
A moment's respite from the
   storm
   And then with resignation,
I put my mental armor on
   And face the situation.

Celia Kate Burkhalter
UNTITLED
Passing moment
Too hard to forget.
Brief encounter
That touches my life.
A look, a sigh;
Over the shoulder
We look again.
Too hard to forget
That look, that thought
Of meeting again.

Linda Lafferty Oge
THE NEWS
I have no idea, how you will
   feel;
When I share the news, with
   which I must deal.
Will you be happy, or grevious
   feel?
Will it distraught, or to you
   appeal?
Right now I have no way of
   knowing.
But, someone, Dear, within me
   is growing.
Only happy notes should mark
   the greeting.
To know part of each within a
   miracle's meeting.
And for me, the Blessed; it
   must be gladness.
For a gift from God cannot
   bring sadness.
But for you, who knows how
   you will feel.
One thing for sure is, "Life is
   real."
My heart stands still, my senses
   stop.
The only sound - a ticking clock.
Will you be happy, or grevious
   feel?
Will it distraught, or to you
   appeal?
Right now I have no way of
   knowing;
But, Someone dear within me
   is growing.

Robin M. Schelzi
HOW OLD IS THE WORLD
When did the mountains rise
   from the land?
How long has the beach had
   plenty of sand?
How long have the stars been
   hung in the sky?
How long have the birds been
   able to fly?
When did the sun first shine
   on the earth?
When did the animals first
   give birth?
How old are the canyons, deep
   and dark?
How long have there been fish,
   a perch or a shark?
When did the waves first float
   on the sea?
These questions are much to
   hard for me!

Carolyn Tuten Ross
PERSPECTIVE
Sweating, digging, putting posts
   in the ground;
Spending hours setting up camp
   with the rain coming down;
Straining, stretching, jogging
   cells to breathe new life;
Watching movies that scare out
   the daylights;
Climbing, groping, hiking on
   blistered feet;
Trying to make the seams of
   the wallpaper meet;
Redoing, replanning, updating
   lessons, someday, to teach;
Never getting finished with
   the eight parts of speech;
Blistering, sweltering, relaxing
   in the summer sun—
Isn't it amazing what we call
   fun?

Veronica Christina Cava
DEATH BY WAY OF LOVE
Traces of tears and blood from
   broken wrists
Pave my way to your front
   door
Screams of terror, frustration
   and anger
Echo throughout your empty
   house
Reddened eyes and fleshless
   body
Roam among your darkened
   rooms
Bandaged mind and heart
   ripped in two
Left over remnants from the
   bullet which refused to go
   through
Words ring out, no meaning
   can be derived
Absorbed within your bare
   colorless walls
Back door swings open
No breeze to be found

A sudden scream, and then
   silence
Lifeless body crashes to the
   ground
Sprawled before them in
   broken pieces
The body and soul of their
   baby girl
A child wrapped in dreams
Struggling to create a love
   within
Enveloped by homegrown
   fantasies
Weakened and destroyed by
   realities.

Keith Davis Jr.
THE TREASURY CHEST
Today set your aim as high as
   hope will let.
Today go as far toward your
   goal as you can get.
Foster the good and resist the
   bad.
Today cherish all the worthy
   things that will make you glad.
Believe in all the right things,
   till your nights are filled
   with pleasant dreams.
Fill your prayers with love and
   hope until they are bursting
   at the seams.
Today help along some weary
   soul whose eyes are looking
   down.
And set his heart to hoping
   that someday he'll wear a
   crown.
Open up your treasury chest,
   let him see what he can find.
I'm talking about that treasury
   chest thats stored within
   your mind.

Wanda Gorka
THE INDWELLING CHRIST
With strength and patience let
   us grow in love each day:
While power and tenderness
   strengthen our way.
Majesty and meekness seem to
   go, hand in hand as we pray.
HIS is the soul full of love and
   light.
And HE comforted them as
   they walked, talked and
   communicated
   with their hearts.
Our Friend and Saviour spoke
   a message of peace and hope.
GOD is the source of light and
   life and joy in the universe.
Those who really believe in the
   indwelling CHRIST have a
   radiance about them; for the
   light, love and power shine
   through.
A flow of love and blessings
   seem to be ever near in time
   of need.
They have a deep perception of
   human feelings and failings,
   needs and joy.
When the love of CHRIST is
   enshrined in the heart, it
   comes out;
Like a sweet fragrance that
   cannot be hidden.
So bring forth a winning smile
   and really show the world—
   your new style!

Edith W.S. Olstad
PRAYER
O, Lord, these are the things
   that I would ask:
Give me a pair of steady, useful
   hands
And sense to occupy them at
   some task;
A heart that strives to better
   understand
What life and love are for; an
   honest soul
That seeks humility and
   righteousness;
A healthy mind, Lord, sensible
   and whole,
That thinks good thoughts; also
   the graciousness
To treat success and failure
   both the same,
The courage to believe in what
   is just;
A zest for living; pride in my
   good name;
Accomplishment to justify
   Thy Trust.
In total, Lord, no more
   rewarding pelf
Than that I may be honest with
   myself.

Rebecca Ann Haver
HANDS
Hands
   tiny and so very fragile
   reaching out to grasp a rattle
   or mommy's finger.
Hands
   trying to catch the ball
      that daddy threw
   and throw it back again
Hands
   with awkward chubby fingers
   that curl around a pencil
   to form the letters of his name.
Hands
   which hold his first love
   with wonderness and
   tenderness
   and a ceaseless curiousity.
Hands
   interlocking with his family
      doing everything
   he possibly can.
Hands
   old and frail
   stiffened by years of use,
   of triumphs and defeats.
Hands
   folded gently
   one last time
   to admire God's wisest tools.

Alicia Terrones Shapiro
TOGETHERNESS
I followed with my eyes
A pretty leaf that was fallen
   and death;
The wind pulled the leaf up
And by capricious whims
She danced lightly and gracious
On its arms.
I let my soul scape from me,
And for some split seconds
Joined the dance;
It was togetherness like made
   by God,
Nature, fantasy, and in between
A human soul.
My soul came back to me
And the majic was gone,
But a beautiful feeling was my
   win:
Mind can make grandious
Even a fallen leaf!

Sheila Fitzpatrick
QUESTIONS

What lies out there in infinity?
What lurks in the darkness
   above?
Is it a barren, lifeless void?
Or a wonderful world of love?

Are the stars just gaseous orbs?
Or a gateway to new life?
Is God the keeper of this gate?
Who helps us cope with strife?

Why do we live? Why do we die?
Does life really have a meaning?
When we die is that the end?
Or only the beginning?

Cindy M. White
AS TIME GOES BY

As time goes by, with every tic
   of the clock,
   I await for your arrival
As time goes by, with every tic
   of the clock,
   I long for the time to hold
you
   and to be held by you.
As time goes by, with every tic
   of the clock,
   I know we must part
   I await the hours until we
can
      be together
As time goes by, with every tic
   of the clock,
   Our love grows everlasting.

Lorrie Paul
THE NIGHT

   Into the valley the sun's light
seeps,
Upon its green carpet the
   willow tree weeps.
   The leaves float so slowly,
   their patience intense,
As birds seek thick tree tops in
   silent suspense.
   The presence is clear, like a
   current on air;
A small distant whisper of
   trite sacred prayer.
   And the sky seems to glow
   with an eerie pink light,
As the day steps aside to
   release the new night.
   In a clash of rare colors the
   daylight abodes,
And into the dimness the
   darkness explodes.
   Like a black velvet sheath it
   spreads its disease,
Of depth and obscurity this
magic decrees.
   And life seems to freeze in
   the grips of cold death,
While quietness conquers in
   slowing of breath.
   The dark is a beast that
   threatens with spite,
And gaining its strength its
   wings shall take flight
   With sounds of pure silence

that echo despair,
The whirring of blackness to
   justly declare
      That darkness is hell that
      clenches the spine,
And life will await its
   despondent decline.

Gail L. Triplett
MY FAREWELL

Suicide is Painless
only the surviving feel pain.
The killer dies so senseless
while the survivor tries to stay
sane.

To die so very young
to take ones own life
To leave the girl you loved
that someday would be your
   wife.

You kill me with my memories
the ones I hold deep within.
Don't you understand this
I need you the way you had
been.

Your life had so much meaning
too much to even explain
I loved you so very much
now I have nothing to gain.

This is my farewell to you
You see my life must go on.
I still hold you deep within
even tho you are gone.

Julie A. Wrazien
CLANDESTINE

Meeting quietly—
Waiting.
Savoring each second
of the rendezvous' sweet taste
upon hungry lips.

Fiercely embracing
in strong arms.
Murmuring softly,
wishes of uncertain dawns.

As raindrops fall
they serenade our hearts
whose throbbing lasts
long past
each clandestine pause
in our forbidden love.

Willis B. Merriam
FACELESS MASSES

Consider the human masses
Of all the continents of earth:
Mostly nameless to all others,
Without personality or identity
And mostly discontented,
The ox-like asking only to be
   fed,
With ambitious malcontents
Willing and eager
To engage in war
Or in explosive protest,
Engendering destruction
Of what other men have gained
   or wrought.

And recognize that no fragment
   of the world-
Though varying widely in its
   standards,
Value sets and cultures -
Can afford such irresponsible
   acts
Or any phase of destructive
   violence
Any more than it can afford
To encourage and support
With equal irresponsibility
Additional vast masses of the
   nameless,
Those without identity
Featureless and faceless
in the eyes of all the others.

Nella Holloway Cole
PERVERSITY

My mother says we children
Fight 'most all the day;
And why can't we just play
   together
And not scrap in our play?

But I want to be swinging
When sister wants to draw;
And she wants me to color when
I want to play seesaw!

It's that way every Saturday;
We fight and fight and fight;
But we forget about it when
My mother reads at night.

William Reed Hoffman
THE LENS WINKED

The lens winked-
   Her smile frozen
      For a moment
      For a yearbook
   Missing the feeling
   Missing the tear
      On her cheek as
   Cool confusion
   Reigns in unknown
      Needs and pain
   The page fades
   But memory returns
      In nightly reunions

Deanne Mary Spence
THE TREE

In splendor it stood on the
   grassy hill,
Now everything is quiet,
   everything still,
It had been young once, tall
   and erect,
The king of the mountain,
   gaining respect,
The leaves of the tree were
   plentiful and green
Increasing by thousands every
   new spring.

But most beautiful of all,
Was the time in the fall,
The leaves, bright gold catching
   your eye,
Dropping to the earth, it seemed
   with a sigh.
In winter it was the prettiest
   sight,
Frozen but glittering all through
   the night,
It looked so alive............

D. Rae Wiley
TIME

If the time is right
and your love is in sight.
Don't fret for long
because nothing can go wrong.

Nyko
ME

a grain of sand
rolling in with the sea
given by GOD's hand
to become me . . . .

Christina Hahn
WIDOWS

Unspeaking voices, settled
and muffled, netted
on a silent rose.

Tense, still air,
daring to share
tentative evening clothes.

Madness from a petal
pulled from a metal
shroud, enclosed
within a steel

box encasing, a feel
of cold; a pose
assumed from far
away; a door ajar
open, supposed

inviting; oh so quiet
breathless night—
countless widows

counting days and years,
brushing mute tears,
sighing within the shadows.

Melanie Kassen
DREAMS OF REALITY

 To live in dreams
Means wanting all good
As only one can hope for
But then one must wake up
To the realities.

To live in reality
May mean pain
Like in not being loved
But one can always sleep well
With hopes and dreams.

Jonathan E. Brough
LORNA JEAN

   Lorna Jean
Just like spring
A rose about to blossom
The mountains turning green
   Kisses like honey
The birds, beginning to sing
Here comes the Easter Bunny
For my sweet, an' lovely,
   Lorna Jean

Pauline (Dumas) Hebert
GOD CREATED CHILDREN

God created children
Making them different shades.
   WHY BOTHER?
For night dissipates color . . .
Everything fades!

Grace Setzer Martin
JUST A HOUSEWIFE

The Census-Taker came, went
   away
Leaving me considering what
   I'd had to say
"I'm just a housewife," lightly
   I had spoken
The depth of that phrase my
   thoughts gave token
"Just a housewife," but hearts
   were comforted
Hungry tummies fed
Weak faiths had been
   strengthened
Faltering footsteps—led.
My heart is bowed in humility
At the enormous task He's
   given to me.
Although I'm old, nearly
   finished
Love for family and friend is
   not diminished.
Arrives the time that I am
   un-needed
I'll ask—"God, please bless my
   house,"
And will have succeeded
In life's noble calling—
I'll be, "Just a housewife,"
No shame or stalling

Mark B. Hicks
THE WIZARD

He chants a spell in an unknown
   tongue,
   then slowly raises his hand.
White fires strike from his
   fingertips,
   laying waste upon the land.
He has called forth all the fires

of Hell
  to aid him in his plot.
He laughs in madness at a
  glimpse
  of the havoc he has wrought.

The flames and stench of death
  add new fire to his eyes.
No other life can now be seen;
  black smoke has filled the
  skies.

The Wizard's power has been
  unleashed;
  revenge is his at last.
Out of fire the earth was born;
  with fire it shall pass.

Anant Nagpur
HOLLYWOOD SQUARE

'once upon a time in the west'
  there lived
'the godfather' who sent a
  message to
'the ambassador' to see 'the
  last tango in paris'
shown at 'the house of terror'
  where 'young
frankenstein' lived who
  celebrated 'black
christmas' where 'serpico'
  entered with 'the
magnum force' and viewed
  through 'the torn curtain'
and returned with 'dr. no' who
  created a 'riot'
in 'the streets of san francisco'
  where
'mr. majesty' was living under
  'the obsession'
to create 'all the president's
  men' who
became an 'eye witness' to
  'the great bank
robbery' committed by 'the
  dirty dozen'
under the 'influence of woman'
  who was
living on 'the other side of the
  mountain'

P. Lamont Hamblin
PSYCHIC FOOTPRINTS

Waves of conscious footprints
Scamper the endless corridors
Of swirling sand conjured
From our mind's pictured
Beach of reality. Each
Print patterns its maker's
Paths—his focus, his
Three dimensional actions
In unassuming love, unending
  Grace.
  Many times washed away;
Yet always there, we walk
These realms—our chartered
Beach, our burning shore.
We feel the peace,
The fragrant sea-blown air.
We languish in its quiet,
Serene, effortless gaze: the
Warmth, the breeze, the
Waves of sun, of water, of
Breath of air. Life so
Small echoes life so Full.

Chester S. Henson
**TODAY I VISITED OLD
KENTUCKY**

Today I visited old Kentucky.
  For there in an old log cabin
  I was born.
But since that such a long time
  ago.
  It has took so many of man's
  scorns.
Men has robbed it of its minerals.
  Her timber, gas, oil, and coal.
They have treated her so badly.
  Digging for her soul.

They have scarred her back
  forever.
  And polluted all her streams.
And from their poison acid.
  Her meadows are no longer
  green.
It breaks my heart within me.
  To see what I have seen.
A land so wounded and dying.
  That once was so alive, lush,
  and green.

They have destroyed her virgin
  beauty.
  And her hills they're never
  reclaimed.
For what they have done to her.
  It is a terrible shame.
All the people who loves her.
  They look at her and cry.
As their hearts aches within
  them.
  As they wait for her to die.

This must have made God very
  angry.
  But is doesn't bother man.
But we'll all pay a terrible price.
  And die in an empty and
  polluted land.

Gaylia Swift Dalton
SHAGGY

When we moved away from
  Greenwood,
That grotesque menagerie
Of glass dogs was carefully
Packed in tissue paper.
Mother said it was my collection.
I was eleven and the only
Dog I wanted was Shaggy.
He was real for a long time
After we left him standing
Under my elm tree.

Jo Starrett Lindsey
SUMMER NIGHT MAGIC

The silvered light of summer's
  moon
  Has swept away the night;
  It's bathed my garden bright
With haunting mists that fade
  too soon.
  The beauty twists my heart,
  Which almost breaks apart
In pain sublime, this night in
  June.

Jo Starrett Lindsey
THE VISITOR

My garden has a visitor,
A tiny hummingbird that makes
A visit to all flowers there,
And then his choice of nectar
  takes.

He darts and looks, and darts
  again,
Among the fragrant blossoms
  bright,
And then he zips to parts
  unknows,
The secret place he goes at
  night.

David Brian Moulton
NOCTURNE

Now, dropping down behind the
  distant slopes
And shooting out its pink and
  purple streams,
The drowsy sun, the sower of
  sad hopes,
Admits the moon, the harvester
  of dreams.
Beneath the crescent's polished
  silver blade
The grass is swaying and the
  waters cower.
The leaves are trembling, too,

as if afraid
The trees will fall beneath the
  sickle's power.
This shining scythe will gleam
  on through the night,
Dripping its starry chaff on
  night's dark miles,
Over the languid landscape
  flashing bright,
Driving the shadows into distant
  piles,
Continuing to harvest all this
  corn,
Until its blade is blunted by the
  morn.

Doris C. Smith
CLOUD FANTASIES

I rest in my hammock and gaze
  up at the sky,
While I am reclining I'll just
  let my mind fly.

The piles of white cotton,
  floating on the clear blue,
Take shapes quite familiar,
  known to me and to you.

I behold some high mountains,
  tops all covered with snow,
Towering above woodlands of
  our earth far below.

My mind traces them upward,
  all their beauty to see,
Their magnitude dwarfing the
  small beings like me.

I see waves on a beach splashing
  stones smooth and white,
Dots of movement on shore—
  children romp in delight!

Sand castles erected throughout
  many a day
Meet rude, incoming tides that
  wash structures away.

A calm, new little lake lies
  secluded, remote,
But a tiny, white sail moves
  along on a boat.

This view has a skyline of a
  city so wide:
Stacked buildings, and parkways;
  streets with trolleys to ride.

Schools, stores, and factories—
  some built low and some tall
With chimneys and windows,
  but some have none at all.

An expanse of construction up
  there in the sky
Will carry on business while still
  floating so high.

I gaze at quaint structures to
  explore as I roam,
And see the strange places many
  people call home.

Now activity has stilled, blue
  horizons spread so wide,
I see animals from farms dot
  the peaceful countryside.

Sure, there are the woolly lambs,
  some so young, with ewes
  quite old;

They're all gathered in the flock
  grazing closely near the fold.
Those tiny fluffs are rabbits
  gayly nibbling on clover,
Soft breezes help them frolic
  just for this sleepy rover.

I've scanned a vast, blue
  sky-world seeing sights that
  make me proud;
I've had a restful journey riding
  high upon a cloud!

Hans Alfred Schroeder
MARINA LIFE

Bicyclists sometimes ride in
  pairs,
But I ride alone. Around the
  swimming
Pool the tennis talk lingers
Into the late evening, with the
  distant
Ring of telephones jarring the
  silence.
The Jacuzzi spits bubbles like
  fish,
And the neighbor's sundeck
  smokes of
Barbecue and comversation. On
  the beach
The volleyball artists,
  sunbronzed, work
Overtime, over nets. I listen to
  the
Drift of music along the
  apartment's walk.
Terraced flowers below the
  windows,
Pairs of things together,
Except . . . .

Dawn Marth
MIDNIGHT RUNNING

I know a jet black horse,
His name is Midnight Running.
There never was a creature,
So wise or as so cunning.

He runs on dark black nights,
Where moons are seldom found.
The valleys and the canyons,
Carry hoove prints in the
  ground.

He moves on thundering hooves,
The wind flows through his
  mane.
His eyes glow like a demon's,
Then the hoofbeats start to
  wane.

Gayla Dee Eckhoff
THE PAINTING

The painting was of a city.
Tall buildings rose powerfully
  to a red sky,
Shadows fell across an empty
  street.
In a faint array of darkness
  stood a person,
Unimportant, lost, amid the
  power of the buildings.
Funny isn't it . . . What cities
  do to people? . . .
Man becomes insignificant in
  his own masterpiece.
His own creation turns on him
  coldly,
It gives him poverty,
It gives him senseless violence,
It loses him in his own lust,
It gives him beauty tainted by
  ruin.
Man's own masterpiece—steel,
  cold gray towers of
  indifference,
Man's own masterpiece—built
  from his own hands.
Man's own masterpiece—a

product of his own intellect,
Leaves him undistinguishable at
the bottom of the painting,
An aimless blur covered by the
shadows of massive power.
Tall buildings reach up to a
red sky,
Man longingly reaches up to
the cold buildings.
Funny . . . isn't it . . .
what cities do to people? . . .

Judith Ann (Sparks) Cull
**HEAVEN'S LIKE
NEWFOUNDLAND**

I think back to that first year
That I left for Newfoundland.
I had heard of it so many times,
But never stepped upon its land.

I heard stories of the fishermen
Who were so brave and strong.
My grandmother would tell me
them,
But I thought she must be wrong.

To me it sounded wonderful,
Too wonderful to be true.
Nothing seemed that perfect
Even a place I never knew.

She mentioned how the people
lived
So different from us here,
And they held each friend and
neighbor
In their hearts so very dear.

Even the ocean
Sounded beautiful to me.
It was like the sparkling waters
In a movie I once did see.

She spoke of all these things
Up till her dying day,
And they remained in my heart
Even when she went away.

I just had to go to see myself
If what she said was true,
So to go to Newfoundland
Was the first thing I did do.

I couldn't believe my eyes,
Or the feeling I had inside.
When I stepped on
Newfoundland soil
I knew my grandmother had
not lied.

My grandmother's now in
heaven
And God has her by the hand.
I know she must be happy,
'Cause heaven's like
Newfoundland.

J. Norman Lambly
ELF OF SPACE

Ask that wee Elf that darts and
hums,
And feeds on blossom-kisses,
and comes
Ten petal-lengths at a single
bound,
All in a whirring mist wrapped
'round:
"How did you happen,
nimble-wit
To choose a zephyr on which
to sit,
As if on a magic carpet rare
Which takes you suddenly
anywhere?

"How came you, with your
airy grace,
To know of instant flight
through space,
While we poor mortals, clumsy
clods,
Build shrieking jets and think
we're gods?"

Brenda Yvonne Montana
DESOLATION

Lo, into the Hills
T'where I will be forevermore.
To worship to Whom?
My sore heart calls to none who
hear.
My sorrow echoes from valley
to valley
As I scream in reverberating
whimpers
I stumble upon rocks
am unaware of the excruciating
pain
My brain pounds out an
incoherent beat
And I stagger onward, onward,
on blistered feet.
My sorrow echoes from valley
to valley
My life has perished
I let it be—so will my soul.
Blood of my body runs thinly . .
I am enveloped in merciless
cold.

Mary June Butler
IT'S OVER

We cared so much when we were
wed
We thought we'd love forever,
Forever is a lengthy time
It even rhymes with 'never.'

Look back on all the years we've
shared
What ever has gone wrong?
I feel no love between us
Where it should have grown so
strong.

The house is not a home for us
It's not even shared in my name,
Is all your feeling gone for me—
I wonder, "what's your game?"

You're gone away so many
nights
Are you sitting in some bar?
Why aren't you here where you
belong,
I wonder where you are?

Can we salvage any feelings
Of the love we used to hold,
To see us through the years
ahead
While we are growing old?

I can't be so neglected
If I need you please be there—
Or if you should need some
sympathy,
I fear I just won't care.

I cannot nurse your body
If illness lays you low
You're never where you're
needed, so
If you're lonely, I won't know.

I'll close my eyes and heart to
you
The way you've done to me
For years I've felt unloved and
yet
You're still too blind to see:
That all I've ever asked for
Is an item which is free,
For you to show reaction
And a little love for me!

Marilyn Rutter
ANOTHER BEACH

Another beach, where the tide
comes
In so far
Another town where love and
laughter
can be heard. Another church

a choir
singing loud and strong. A
choir cap
a gown—a book. A book of
psalms—of hymns
Voices bold for God.
Another beach, again—with
seagulls in
the rain—Another field of
flowers with
houses everywhere—a place for
love and
God and joy forevermore.

Debbie Bigi
THE CAROUSEL

Growing up sometimes makes
me feel beguiled
Because I remember when I
was a child
I could run from my problems
and hide
On the magical carousel ride.

But now the carousel spins too
fast,
And the area it circles is much
too vast;
The music it strews seems
strange to me.
And the coursers no longer seem
wild and free.

It once was so merry, so
amusing—
Now it's so scary, so confusing.
My childhood nights were filled
with pleasant dreams—
Now they know only nightmares
and screams.

Slow down the carousel, let me
breathe:
Adulthood is much too great a
deed.
I've got to be a child again—
To have the carousel as my
friend.

Terri L. Snide
THE INDIANS' WORLD

The air is his home, the leaves
his ears,
The clouds his thoughts, the
water his tears.

The sun his imagination, the
moon his light,
The sand his floor, the
darkness his night.

The grass is his bed, his brothers
are the trees,
Nature is his pride, his
thoughts the breeze.

The stars are his freedom, the
wind his songs,
His integrity his strength, the
wilderness where he belongs.

His companion is the sky, the
canyons his mystery,
Surviving as his ancestors,
death his history.

Theodore J. Warren, Jr.
A LIGHTHOUSE STANDS

On a solid rock a lighthouse
stands
as the Sun casts its last rays upon
the horizon, leaving shadows
before
the call of night.
The Seagulls head to this abode
with
a homing instinct that leads
them into
their own flight path, hovering
in vast
numbers, though landing singly,
without

conflict, crash or bump.
It is not the artificial-automatic
light
of the lighthouse that beckons
them to
rest after a day of diving, fishing,
floating, perching, and flying
at last
to where it stands.
But nature herself echoes silently
to
the Gulls that message older
than man,
to find rest and sleep before
the next
tomorrow.
A young couple stopped! as if
mystified,
to see the Gulls carry on an age
old
ritual as the sky took on an
orange glow
in the Southwest, graying
slowly where the
Gulls' abode stood, identified
by the
lighthouse that did not signal
to them in
sunshine, fog or storm, but
serves as a
landmark for man's call to his
own.

Bruce Denver Greisen
MY ROSE

Beget by nature,
This rose I bring,
Conceived by God,
A gorgeous thing.

No flower so fair,
A work of art.
Its warmth and beauty
Swell the heart.

And only in
Your presence fair,
It bows its head,
But knows no shame.

It pales because of
Brilliance rare.
Reflected,
In your name.

Debbie L. Lind
QUEST OF LIFE

Go,
venture out into the unknown
and don't let the fear of failure
keep you from experiencing
the quest of life,

But give you the strength
that can catch the world by
surprise
and keep it turning.

eVe Sherel
SORROWS SUNSET

Come rejoice with the sunset
As it dies slowly,
Along with midnights multitude
Of malignant, shimmering,
Saddening, sapphire stars . . .
Burning, better, braver by far!

There is no more, for all light is
   gone.
Run from tomorrows love
   swept storm,
Lives in the yesterday of sad
   remains
And dies in the today of lovers
   arms.
Dissolve desolate dreams.
Worthless, aggregate schemes,
None will deliver from the
   heinous screams
Of lovers quarrels by quiet
   streams.

paula r. bosanac
COMMITMENT

   will the days light end
   so that i may move quickly
to my sheltered nest
   and hide quietly to mourn
for tomorrow
   when the light will appear again
smothering me with dread
   for i will still belong to them

William Jeffery Rutchasky
CHRISTMAS THANKS

Lonely mornings,
   feeling at ease . . .
Coffee steams,
   in the winter's breeze . . .
Frosted windows,
   in crystal picture . . .
Natural art,
   of nature's treasure . . .
Wind sings,
   to the summer's grass . . .
Now enchanted,
   by winter's grasp . . .
The old deceived,
   by youth's revenge . . .
Seasons come and go,
   but never end . . .
White sheet,
   blankets the earth . . .
Glowing coals,
   upon the hearth . . .
Inside crackles,
   sound of fire's rage . . .
Smoke descends,
   to morning's brisk age . . .
Winter's magic,
   becomes declared . . .
Enlightened hearts,
   fill the air . . .
Feathered flakes,
   fall with a silent crush . . .
Anticipated children,
   told to listen, in a murmured
   hush . . .
Families gather,
   to become as one . . .
Nostalgic stories,
   when we were young . . .
'Tis the time for all man,
   to be at peace . . .
To give thy love,
   without a lease . . .
Share openly,
   the gift of life . . .
Which God gave you,
   through His Son's strife . . .

Marilyn Rutter
NO MORE WOLF

In every tree I see the word of
   God.
In every flower that rises from
   the sod.
There is a blessing that comes
   and carries
good news from the bad. Wait
   for the
coming of the day when rain
   dries and

sun leaps through. Sun and rain
   we must
have to make a perfect day.
   Walk with
a dog or cat—walk with a fellow
   or girl
"They are all the same to me,"
   he says.
"I don't give a darn tootin' who
   is
rootin' " that is what the loafer
   said
as he walked the line—walking
   the
line is not my ball—walking the
   line
is not my game. "Free I come,
   free
I go" say the girls at the bar. No
Fellow wants to stir or gallivant.
Rosebuds on the field or flowers
   on
the wall. "I don't want them
   all," he says.
"They bore me to death." He
   points
to the door. The dog runs home
   with his
tail between his legs. He hates
   to see
the sight of bones broken on
   the sandy
shore. He hates the glare of the
   light
as it streams through the door.
   "I can't
sleep—the wolf is at my door."
"Wake up," she croons . . .
"I will catch
Your dream—that wolf will
   come no more."

Ozzie B. Glisson
PARADISE

Adam and Eve lost their
   Paradise home
So many long years ago,
For breaking God's
   Commandment
So he threw them out; we know.
But even if Adam and Eve did
   fail,
God's purpose for Earth will
   still prevail;
For Jesus taught us to pray
To our Father in Heaven this
   way:
Your Heavenly Kingdom come
And Your Will on Earth be done.
Then there will be no more
   wars on Earth
And no more cause for gloom.
Instead of thorns and thistles,
The Myrtle trees will bloom.

Eugene Collins
THE PROTOTYPE

Man has walked earth for
   thousands of years
Vast knowledge consumed day
   by day
Today man has vast knowledge
   but a locked brain
Has absorbed thru destruction
   that which shall never be
Monetary gains the ends to all
   means
Every man is different within
   himself
The difference not noticeable
   because he is so much alike
He dare not deviate or he is
   scorned
A prototype of a human being
   all man must be
Condemned to know, but not
   how to be

When will man open his eyes
   and see
There is only one place for man,
   that antiquity.

Merle D. Skinner
THE GREAT OUTDOORS

I climb the highest mountains
   Where vistas stretch endlessly,
And I find solace there.
   Or on the ocean front
Where sea gulls scream,
   My soul rides free,
And a special peace
   Becomes a part of me.
God's great outdoors
   A cathedral can be,
That links man to eternity.

Christie Capalite
THE TAX MAN

In a valley far, far away,
There lives a man who's happy
   and gay.

One day this man had to go,
He had to go to the store, and
   then to a show.

When he got home that
   afternoon so fine,
He found everything was gone,
   even his moonshine.

There was something he mistook,
Something lying down, it was
   a book.

The title of the book is as
   follows:
*How to Keep the Tax Man From
Making Your House Hollow.*

Anna L. Bowles
DEPRESSION

Goodbye cruel world you gave
   nothing to me
   Except heartache, misfortune
   and misery.
The hard lesson I learned was
   easy taught
   Now I must do the thing I
   ought.
      And that is just to fade
      away.
         On some forgotten rainy
         day
   To close my eyes and rest
   my bones
      And die forgotten all alone.

Judith Romano-Rizzo
AN ENDLESS FLIGHT

A beautiful bird flew into my
   life
his wings were all ruffled with
   wear
He carries the weight of the
   world on his shoulders
but he is as proud as the great
   black bear.

This bird overlooked one thing
   in his flight
he flew without a sense of
   direction

To fly without a destination in
   mind
could misguide you in your
   choice of election.

So if you ever see a bird in
   motionless flight
be kind, gentle and most
   understanding
For it is a scary feeling to go
   through life
without knowing which way
   you are heading.

Earl R. Hall
INCAPACITY

With furtive look
and timorous touch
We turn the wheel
for happiness to flow.

Intoxicated
By a sip or two
Of the heady stuff,
We grope, unable
To drink the flood.

Terry Duncan
LIFE IN THE FRONT LINES

If the landing point was unfair
The chance we risk to our lives
Was bewildered and unaware

The stance of creation stood at
   our heels
And the feeling of defeat stood
   deep
Inside each of us as if death we
   could feel

The plunder of our wounded
   command
Held our minds in a belief
   unreal
A deep gut feeling we'd never
   see home land

And when we reached the hell
   planned
Everything chanced to shine
   with glory
Of driving the enemy from his
   land

The trials we went through
Was a chance we risk to our lives
Like a wild bombardment of
   each clue

Standing far away from home
When only memories remain of
   staying alive
And yet each day a dream of
   being alone

Create in your mind a pain
   untamed
To the day in the life while in
   the front lines
And the feeling is ruined by a
   bullet maim

Ultonia Thomas
CHRISTMAS THOUGHTS

Wonder if God's little Son
   Knew the Glory 'round Him
   lay.
Did He hear the angels singing
   On that first, glad Christmas
   day.

Did He know the Wiseman came
   Bringing gifts to Him alone.
Did He know they saw His star
   That o'er Bethlehem brightly
   shone.

Wonder what His parents
   thought
   As they gazed where He lay.
Did they know it was God's Son
   On that first, glad Christmas
   day.

God's "divine gift" to the world!

We thank Thee every day.
For only thru Him alone
  Is the truth, the Life, and the
  Way.

Pamela Redmond
SWIMMER: IN MEMORY OF JIM MORRISON OF THE DOORS

Up, up through the dim murk,
the long urge,
the sudden surge of pain
at trapping, twitching, hiding
  things,
half seen.
Up, up through darkness,
to break out,
burst the surface.
Just one more twist, quick leap,
  one strain—
the light is there. Blackness is
  lifting.
Then clutch of weeds
catching, clinging,
a silk embrace—
down plunge, down, down again.

Perry E. Custer
YING, YANG

Inside out,
Full of doubt,
One minute with, the next
  without.
Life, a never ending tide
Continually coming in,
Then going out.
Rise and then fall,
Only to rise again.
Grab the good moments,
Catch 'em while you can;
Live them like you'll not see
  them again.
It's easy to grow up
Believing everything is certain,
And will all fall into place
When it can so easily be erased.
There is so much to feel,
And it's not always worthwhile;
Simply leaves you to wonder
  what life's about.
You've grown to a man from a
  child
And have yet to find out;
Inside out,
Full of doubt.

M. A. Barnett
I LOVE TO BE BESIDE YOU

I love to be beside you
like the moon is beside the stars
like the beach is beside the ocean
like the cloud is beside the sky
oh, how I love to be beside you.

I brung my guitar along
and sang you a tune
I was glad you had stayed for so
  long
'cos the chords were always right
when you were there
'cos you had stayed to hear my
  song.

Harold E. Harmon
ALONE?

I sit. Alone.
Feeling sorry for myself
And lonely, too,
Thinking only darkest thoughts
About myself
And about things in general
Like handicaps
And man's inhumanity to man.
Personal things.
Old issues best forgotten.
Old hates. Old dreams.
Dreams that never can come
  true.

My frustrations
Overwhelm me in times like
  this.
I'd go fishing,
But I wouldn't catch anything.
I'd be alone.
Suddenly I snap alert.
I'm not alone.
Looking 'round I see no one
Yet HE is here.
My God and I together now.
I'm not alone.
With HIM I face whatever comes.

Tommie Lou Wright
THY WILL BE DONE

They Will be done we often
  say
Do we mean this from our
  hearts
When trials and sadness come
  our way
Or a beloved from us departs?
Forgive our frailities and our
  doubts
O Master who made all of us,
And staunchly from our minds
  do rout
Bitter questions, when we
  should trust
Your Infinite Wisdom, pro or
  con
And needs must know They
  Will be done!

Paul E. Van Heuklom
EKLEKTOS

The creativity of man has died
The imagination has served
Hence reality all discovered
leaving nothing to be uncovered
There is nothing left of man
nothing left to exist as is
but rather to exist as might be
or could be
Those men who dream, the
  thinkers
the poets the singers the actors
  the painters
those who see beyond reality
those who will survive

Jean Moore
ME

The Woman I am
  You cannot see
The Woman I am
  Hides deep in me
There lies her sadness
  Behind a smile
This Woman you see
  Dressed in style
Her life so sheltered
  In her silence
Her search is Peace
  Never violence
She goes her way
  The Woman I am
She goes her way
  But you cannot see
but this one...Never the hidden

ME

The Woman I am
  Hides deep in me
Beneath the woman
  I seem to be
She hides away
  From the stranger's eye
She is not known
  To the passerby
She goes her way
  The Woman I seem
But the Woman I am
  Withdraws to dream
The Woman I seem
  Goes carelessly
When love comes by
  Does not seem to see.

Robert Michael Balderrama
JESUS

He suffered and He died
  Upon the cross for you and me
That we would know true
  happiness
  In our eternity
He set a true example
  In His living day by day
That we might follow in God's
  plan
  And in His holy way
Though weakened much in body
  He placed all unto God's trust
That heaven would be opened
  For the faithful and the just
Thus Jesus died that we might
  live
  No greater gift could be
Than that He gave His life
  That we might live eternally.

Donna J. Smith
COMING HOME

I've wandered here and
  wandered there
Always on the roam
But that's not the life I really
  want
So at last . . . I'm coming home.
All Alone, I've seen the world
The mountains, land and sea
Done some things I'm not
  proud of
For the sake of being free.
I've never felt the warmth and
  love
That I knew back there
There's no smiles of
  understanding
And very few who care.
Memories of my childhood days
Were always on my mind
The things I want are there at
  home
How could I have been so blind?
So now it ends, I've had my fill
Of living on my own
I've packed all my possessions
And at last . . . I'm coming home.

Opal Maybelle Elliott
SOUND OF POETRY

The sound of poetry is the
  songbird's song,
the babblin' brook that eases
  along
moments away from the milling
  throng
and praising God.

The sound of poetry is ever
  heard
in children's laughter and God's
  true word
in living a life that's much
  preferred

because it's best.
The sound of poetry is ever
  entwined
in a person's heart and soul
  and mind
if the good in life he is able to
  find
and thank our God.

Tracy A. Hixon
THE SEA

The lighthouse is still there, and
  the foghorn still blows.
The sun still shines on a lonely
  and empty shore.
The wind aches to carry the
  sound of a child's laughter,
And the voice of the thousands
  that came before.
The waves crash relentlessly
  against rock and sand,
Performing for an empty beach
  an endless dance.
The audience is blind deaf and
  dumb,
Walking out before the show
  has even begun.
If they could only see the
  beauty of a wave meeting shore.
If they would only listen to the
  sounds and hear the roar.
If they could only feel the
  power that is the sea.
Then they would be humbled
  before an immense reality.
If they would only remain from
  beginning to end,
Then perhaps the fog will never
  roll in.

Bruce H. McElroy
MY FOE

Better at strategy
with the dawn,
my lurking foe will come;

I cannot rest
till the war is won,
my relentless foe will come;

I fight to avert
the ravages and waste,
my damaging foe will come;

Not for history
but for my destiny,
my greatest foe, is me.

Ruth A. McDaniel Comeford
IF WE FOLLOW GOD

If we follow God every day and
  night,
We will always be doing what is
  right,
Everyone should love the other
to be at peace with every Sister
  and Brother.

To be thankful for what we
  have everyday,
And to have something in every
  way;
No matter what race, sex or
  creed,
To love each other is what we
  need.

If we love God like we should,
Everyone will know where we
  stood;
Should everyone wake up to
  see,
That stealing and killing
  shouldn't be.

If we follow God's plan,
He'll do for us what He can;
To share his love and, help each
  other,
And still love every sister and
  brother.

To help each other through thick and thin,
For souls for Him, we'll help to win;
Just helping God preserve the earth,
Even passing it on from birth to birth.
We've got to take care of His earth right now,
And as years go by passing on our know how.
God gave us everything we need to live,
So when we take, we need to give.
Just following God is where it's at,
And no matter where we sat,
Inside or outside show God's work,
For when God made earth, He did not Shirk.

Vivien Bilbeaux
HAVING WORSHIPPED YOU

Having known this kind of life
I walk away much changed,
Where once my heart reflected light, it's shrouded now in pain,
And you, my love, to whom I gave my world and my soul
Will not have the chance again to turn my world to stone,
Nor will you take my heart once more and slice it into two—
You'll find me much more cautious now,
    Having Worshipped You.
Of all the men this city held you were the only one for me,
But having tripped and having fell, I see how much you've done for me,
You speak of love then run from me
And all the while I waited
For you to come and claim your Queen—
How little you appreciated everything I've been.
I leave you now to find the life you feel I've kept you from,
And when it's time to take a wife, remember what you've done,
And I'll remember, too, as I take my life back in my hands,
You'll find I'll not be quite so quick
To give it to another man,
    Having Worshipped You.

Debra S. Newton
LONGING FOR A FANTASY

A day, a dream, a memory, and a tear.
    A love, a hope, no one will hear.
A warm kind of feeling: A soft sweet smile:
    Someone to hold me just for a while.
A kiss on the cheek; A tear in their eye;
    A look that says, "I'm always near-by."
A tender soft hand, like a child's own touch.
    To hear you say once, "I do care so much."
A hope for a day; A dream for a night.
    Calm, tender emotions which

shine so much light.
The pleasant embrace; The warmth of your arms;
    This beautiful moment is filled with your charms.
    Each small second; A minute or an hour.
    A hot soapy bath; A peaceful clear shower.
Again for your touch I pray there will be,
    That moment for us, For You and For Me . . .

Vonta Davis
OLD LOVE REMET

The fleeting years have gone, my love,
We hadn't time to share
The little everyday things
The joys, the tears and care
It takes to build a lifetime.
We're strangers now and yet,
Our lives are joined forever
Because one day we met.

Cheryl Ann Phillips
ON IMMORTALITY

Man is an insignificant being.
He has neither the serenity of the mighty
mountains
Nor the infinite glory of the universe.
Even the gentle breeze is stronger than he.
Yet, for all his shortcomings, only man is
immortal
For only man has an eternal soul.

Wilma Feitsma Bylsma
IT'S SPRINGTIME

In my backyard I find a peace
In growing things and whispering trees.
    The beauty all around I see,
    It is just the place I like to be.
    The chatter of a squirrel near by
    And singing of the birds on high;
    Then jumping of a mullet free
With nature's simple melody.
When silently the setting sun
Gives beauty all around,
I thank my God in heaven above
    For springtime, a backyard, and His love.

Patricia Anne Fleming
LIFE

Life is like an hourglass
Draining patiently,
Waiting for the time to pass
And everyone to flee.
It's as though I'd just catch up
To look at myself and see,
That the world is fading out
Right from under me.
So when my time comes to an end
I beg thee not to cry,
For even though I leave this earth,
My memory will never die.

Phyllis A. Matteson
CHILDHOOD PLAYMATE

There once was a princess
Who lived on a hill,
And down below there spread a town
    For her to look upon.

She lived in an imaginary castle
With her make-believe prince,
None were quite so happy
    As the hours together they spent.
They shared the deepest secrets
    Nothing from each other was ever kept,
They drank the most delicious tea
    And ate the daintiest cakes.
    Such happy hours
    Such lovely days,
    Could ever such happiness
Fade away?
But little girls grow to womanhood,
    Alas, make-believe princes stay young,
And there upon the wind swept hill
    He waits for her alone.
Yet even grown-up ladies
    Sometimes become princesses again,
And prince is always waiting
    For her to come again.
Although they're only golden moments
    Stolen from busy days—
They share their deepest secrets
    And drink their most delicious tea.

Virginia E. Wagner
CONTINUANT

Globes of satin grapes
    sugar pearls
        on dusty vines
Borne on bosoms green, swiftly spread
By harvesters on paper trays
Become dark purple raisins
As they dry.
Globes of gold
    globes of finite red
        and deepest indigo
Piled mountain high in wineries
Crushed! Callously. Juices freed
Become in their allotted time
Taste-tingling California wines.

Julia S. Howell
FIRST WINTER SNOW

The woods, the hills, the icy glades
Are banquet halls for fairy maids.
All decked in white, the branches gleam—
Encased in glass does nature seem.
The little ones, the fairy folk,
Come out of hiding, through knot-holes poke
Their tiny heads and begin to dance,
Through forest glen and dale they prance.
They hitch up sleighs of bark and twig,
They deck them out in fancy rig;
With needles of pine and glassy red berry,
The sleighs stand ready, the folks are all merry.
They dress themselves in gossamer cloaks
And mount the sleighs beneath the oaks;
They call to the mice who stand reined and ready
To pull them all forward—

sure-footed and steady.
So off they streak 'cross meadows mild,
Churn up the snow in spirals wild;
They laugh, they sing, the sound thrown back
Is left behind with furrowed track.
They reach at last the destined glade
Where firelight will soon have played,
And resting there they fall asleep,
Protected by the forest deep.

Cecile A. Nealley
NEW HAMPSHIRE THE BEAUTIFUL

They say we're independent
We like to do "Our Thing"
If this means not having any "cents"
We'll do some reconsidering!
We are proud of our accomplishments;
Our mountains, lakes and streams,
Our faithful and loyal residents,
Regardless of their genes!
You can promise us security
We're willing to work for that.
We demand honesty
Put that under your hat!
Our ancestors were workers
Not too many had degrees
They believed in hard labor
They feared not adversities!
We use the "tools" God gave us
Our hands, strong-backs and muscles.
Economic, strong-willed, but not callous,
That's why we claim the title
"New Hampshire The Beautiful"

Mildred Page Benson
ON THE BEACH

Left my footprints in the sand
With many others gone before;
Followed one upon another,
Saw them wait there on the shore.
Swishing, washing, came the waves,
Sending foam upon the beach;
Stretching toward me, flowing back,
Leaving shells within my reach.
Walked along the rocky break-walls,
Stepping safely here to there;
Out where waves came gently splashing,
Felt the windblown, salty air.
Saw the sun and watched it sinking,
Leaving streaks of beauty bright;

Colors only God could render,
As to us it said, "Good night."
On the morrow, as was promised,
Dawned the day so fresh and
  fair;
Gone the footprints I'd deserted.
Are they walking on somewhere?

Michael S. Wagner
DO WE CARE

What will become of this earth,
It has been destroying itself
  since birth.
When shall man become aware,
That life will soon be too much
  to bear.
We must make a decision soon,
Or else our children are in doom.
The pollution on land, sea and
  air,
Must be coped with by us who
  care.
One should begin to realize fast,
Contamination kills, therefore,
  life won't last.
So let's go forth and do our part,
To save the children next to our
  heart.
Then when we have all passed
  away,
Our offspring will remember
  that day.

Edie Babb
THE CATHEDRAL

There is a place where only I
May stand before the Throne,
And know myself for what I am,
No flowers oversown.
No rockets fired, no marching
  band,
No Easter Day Parade . . .
Just one great mural—wall to
  wall
Of the mistakes I've made.
The canvas . . . Life . . . the
  artist I;
Each brush stroke I recall,
And wonder then if ever God
Would whitewash such a wall.
This quiet place of reckoning
To evaluate my goal,
Where God and I alone can
  meet
Is that Cathedral called the Soul.

Kathleen Anne Kinney
UNTITLED

Saturday night is for
  smoking cigars
    eating Doritos
      drinking beer
and writing poetry.
Pretty girls spend their nights
  kissing boys.
I have drawers filled with bad
  poetry.

Shirley J. Mastroieni
THE PASSING

A memoriam for Papa
The laughter's
  stilled
Life is spent
The heart has
  stopped
The soul has
  passed
With all
  content

Kari Godell
TOTAL DESTRUCTION

old and cracked,
he lies on
his car seat
alone with no

comfort,
amidst the
crowding faceless strangers,
among them
the guilt ridden
driver
of the
ravaging car . . .
shattered his
pride
like the windshield
glass.

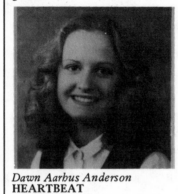

Dawn Aarbus Anderson
HEARTBEAT

Quiet,
And you can hear it.
It's the sound of someone's
  heart . . .
Beating with insistance;
Sounding like a drum.
And if you listen closely,
You may even find
That it sounds a bit like yours.
So you see,
You're not so different
From other human beings . . .
You have a heart that beats,
And also—
It can break.

Brenda Ryan
INCENSE

 Purple and brown,
dusk colors for the desert.
The smoky sweetness
of incense clings,
 a trip for the senses.
Veiled secrets with dark eyes
walk the path
of a million footsteps
to silver jeweled music
of the wind.
Heading west, the sun sets as
 we travel home.

Dolores LaBianco
THE SEEDLING

Here in the loneliness of the
  wee hours
Having labored so long
It is the twelfth hour and
You finally give in,
Not because you want to,
Nor because you've weakened,
But what else is left to do . . .
The time has come.
With a final thrust you push it
  from you
And the stillness of the night is
  broken
With a complaining cry
As flesh meets flesh . . .
Another tribute to God
For standing by, as life
Comes to a new being.

Carol Lee Shepherd
COME OUT OF THE WOODS

Come out of the woods and
  walk with me.
  You've been in there for such
    a long time.

I've waited outside and called to
  you, even though you
  couldn't see me.
  Sometimes I couldn't see you.
The wild animals have had you.
  The vines have tripped you
    and the darkness has
  confused you.
  I'll hold your hand as you
    come out into the sunlight.
The light will blind you at first
  and you'll be tempted to
  return.
  I'll stay beside you and walk
    with you.
I want to walk far away from
  the woods.
  You must hold to me.

Renee' A. Jeffries
TINY PURPLE FISH

Tiny purple fish,
Run through my fingers.
Splashing into a sea of blood,
Where I can see death lingers

These tiny fish have fins,
Sharp as a razor's edge.
They keep slicing through my
  thoughts,
As I prepare to jump the ledge.

They swim in whirling circles,
Mixing everything up.
Injecting such fear,
Like that of an insecure pup.

These fish have a huge appetite,
For what is called the human
  brain,
They rip and tear and chomp
  and gnaw,
Until they've driven my soul
  insane.

Roxanna Lee
BECAUSE I LOVE YOU

Because I love You, I can see
  deep
down inside you. Seeing you is
wonderful. Because I love
you, makes life much easier.
Because I love you, I can face
  tomorrow with a braver heart.
Because I love you, I become
  more gentle with my friends.
Because I love you everything's
  more beautiful. Because I
  love you
makes you number one.

Marilyn Lopez
THE LAST SEED OF LOVE

When the meaning of life comes,
And if it already came;
You get a sensual feeling,
Of wanting to be seen.
When death is nearby,
And all you think you could do,
Is wait and sigh,
Try to live and try to give;
  What does he want?
  What does he need?
Within his heart,
I shall plant my last seed.

Mary V. Lincoln Williams
MISSION

Veteran of the Second War,
Tears in his eyes,
Remembering the sacred
  moment,
Told me how, on Christmas Eve,
They were on a reconnaissance
  mission
Over Suez,
And flew off-course at midnight
So they could fly
Over Jerusalem
And dip their wings,

Just to be as close as possible
To the Birthplace
Of our Savior, Jesus.
Then, they flew on,
A little holier, perhaps,
Awe-filled,
And rejoicing.

Ms. Jackie Wilson Gelsey
INSPIRATION

You inspire me,
  to say things in rhyme that can
    only be expressed that way;
  to touch you in ways that will
    say things I cannot find words
    for . . .

The memories of things we've
  shared have inspired me to
  relax and
let my mind take control.

You've inspired me,
  to go on living and loving every
    minute of it, for life is
    precious and should be lived as
    though each day is my
    last.

Through your constant
  inspiration, I've learned the
  true secrets
of happiness.

Mary Beth Wigger
DILEMMA

What do you do with a squirrel
Who does fantastic things
  As high-wire walking,
    Incessant talking,
      And ludicrous leaps and
        springs
        And lands, where anyone
          least expects,
          Amid a
            great flurry
              of WINGS?

He did it again, and again, today
And, though I went out and ran
  him away,
He came right back with a
  haughty grin
  And sat there poking the
    birdfeed in.
    What do
    you do
      with a
        SQUIRREL?

Mark Joseph Carpentieri
DESERT RUNNERS

The Mighty Stallions Trod The
  Sands,
Of the Vast and Lonely Desert
  Lands;
So Graceful, Artful, Ran Their
  Forms
'Cross Murky Arid Sunlit Morns;
  Storming up Clouds of Dust, -
    Debris,-
    Such was Their Speed and
      Bravery,-
      Sleek Running Horses-
        Running Free!

Christine Fertig
UNTITLED

When God created man and
  woman,
He created the you and I that
  makes us one
together in a world
with just enough room for us
  to do our longing and our
  loving
without making way for the
  hurting
that so often ends up making
  way for itself.

But then again,
what is love without an ache,
  and then apology
to make our lives together last
  just a little longer
If only for a day,
at least it gives us time.

Aliene Davis
THE GRAVE CARES NOT

There is a place where time has
  stopped
Where bones and flesh both
  doth rot,
Beneath the ground and the
  grave cares not
For the love ..... that's buried
  there ;

There is a flower or marker
  stone
Above the spot, where life is
  gone,
Not seen or smelt, cannot atone
  the ugliness of death
But still ..... it stands alone ;

They come starring at the
  ground
And speak and question, receive
  no sound,
A empty place, a lonely spot
For those who grieve the bones
  that rot ;

And wonder why .....
The grave cares not,
For the love ....
That's buried there ....

Clarence J. Russell
CARING

You are not for sale
and cannot be bought, or
  traded.
In your presence, reason is
abolished and ignored.
Motives are sidestepped.
You dominate consciences
and allow yourself no conceit.
Often your generousity is
taken for granted, or abused.
Yet you repeatedly share
in others endeavors.
You are concerned, asking
no reward.
You are caring.

Deborah Seachrist
WHO WERE YOU?

You passed through town, dark
  and sinister.
Your kiss was cold upon my
  cheek.
Your love chilled my soul, froze
  my heart.
I cried, you laughed at me.
I was afraid, you scorned my
  cowardice.
I hid from you but you found
  me.
I tried to forget you, you burnt
  your image in my mind.
I slept, you haunted my dreams
  with your devious grin,
And your eyes blazed with
  hell-fire.

With a wind as cold as ice you
  were gone.
Leaving me behind in the
  destruction your presence
  caused;
Never to be the same again.

Beatrice E. Lydie
AM I AFRAID OF LOVE

Am I afraid of love
Love is the last thing
I am afraid of

I just don't want to get too close
To touch
Because what I know about it
Don't amount to much
But if love do come
I won't turn and run
Like some others I know have
  done
Am I afraid of love
Love is the last thing
I am afraid of
But if love ever do come my way
I know just what I would say
I know just what I would do
I would welcome love
Like I would welcome you
Hello Love I'm so glad you came
Please pardon me
If I don't shake your hand
You are welcome to stay
And leave when you may
But I really hope that time
Is still far away
Am I afraid of love
Love is the last thing I am afraid
of

J. Lois Walker
FALL

Earth prepares for slumber,
  long awaited;
  the sun prolongs it's dawning.
Yesterday's dewy morn gives
  way to lacey frost.
The heat of summer day gone
  by,
  and with its warmth cool
  greeness fades.
Chill air invigorates !
Once emerald forest, now
  decked in fiery brilliance,
  warms my heart, and earth
  and I are one.
O glorious sunset, finale of a
  grand Fall day,
  such artistry beyond compare.
Your beauty overwhelms in
  time suspended;
  my soul reborn, takes flight.
Season of dying majesty cries
  out, cries out !
  with all its might;
Defying death with wondrous
  sights.
And in its silent reverie, awaits...
  His mystery - new life.

Buffy Pruitt
THE ELK

The grass in the meadow waves,
His coat shines in the sun's rays.
The Elk, tall and sleek,
His wonders are unique.

His bugle breaks the air,
There is stillness everywhere.
He takes a step and turns to
  listen,
His dark eyes glisten.

He sniffs the air,
And looks at me as if he didn't
  care.
Slowly he turns to walk away.
I wished he would stay.

As I watch him disappear,
It is very clear,
Though he is free,
He has danger aplenty.

For men give him no rest,
He is always part of a test.
A test of his skill,
For men are out to kill.

Sharron Wiley
HAPPY BIRTHDAY

Ray,
Think of all the things you've
done
Now that you are 41.
But with more and more you
want to do,
It won't be long till you're 42.
It really shows with your gray
  hair
That you've done more than
  your share.
But we all know that you'll
  outlast
The very best in your "class".
So, live it up and have a beer,
Because with this, my husband,
  dear,
I'm sure you're good for
  another year.

Luri Owen
FOOTPRINTS

My father told me once that he
  heard footprints:
I laughed.
Footprints, I told him,
must be seen and not heard.

I'm not laughin now.
Too many footprints have
  passed unseen
but heard as whispers in the
  night:
walking home, running away;
fleeing something but going
  nowhere.

My own footprints have grown
  year by year.
I cannot see them, but I hear
  them still
as half-remembered songs and
  voices
echoing at the boundaries of
  my brain.

I listen now for footprints:
they mark the quiet passing
  of my life.

Rose Rowsell
A FRIENDSHIP FLOWER
GROWS

There is nothing that shows,
Till the planting begins.
With the feeding of love,
With the touch of warmth,
With a shared tear,
The beautiful flower of
  friendship
Blossoms and grows -
Within any human soul!

Gerard J. Howell
TO THE LIVING

Come here thou art,
With tender heart
Come dream and think of me.
As you are now, so once was I
As I am now, you soon shall be.

For it was no more than
  yesterday
With the sea I did play
The sea was I and I the sea
Beward my lad, for the time
  you had
As I am now, you soon shall be.

Jolene Buttolph
NO ONE

No where is there one, not one,
who can follow my thoughts,
see as I see,
feel as I feel,
grieve as I grieve.
No one.

Not one can I find, not one,
who finds beauty where I do,
loves as I do,
honors as I do,
cherishs as I do.

No one.
No one to endure with, not one,
who dreams as I dream,
hopes as I hope,
yearns as I yearn,
wishes as I wish.
No one.

Never will one exist, not one,
who can be my keel,
to cool my anger,
to fire my passion,
to calm my fear.
No one.

Victor Lynn Smith
NIGHTWATCH

Mama watch the night light
Don't let it's flame burn low,
Do you remember candles
That lit the winter snow?
Do you remember woodsmoke
A thousand years ago?
Mama watch the nighlight,
You gotta fight, you know.

Rod B. McInnes
THE OLD LOG CABIN

When I look into the decaying
  ruin with moss around,
It looks empty of life and all
  rotted to the ground.
This place seems dead, yet in a
  way it is alive,
A robin has built a nest not far
  from a beehive.

Memories still linger in this old
  place,
I can see a woman with a
  beautiful face.
There seems to be a fire in the
  old wood stove,
And a child is sleeping as
  contented as a dove.

These visions are not there, they
  are just dreams,
They are like the ice that float
  down the streams.
They float through my memory
  those images of a kind,
Then when they reach the end
  they melt into my mind.

Nina Spencer
ASTRAL CATACLYSM

In the year 2000 B. C.
Venus flew out of the arms of
  Jupiter
  in wild and petulant rage
An outlaw in our firmament
  she became
  changing night into day
As in her trailing gown she
  strayed!
Clouds like pillars rose in fire
  by night
The seas divided lay;
For centuries she serpentined
  in space
Until Mars the Solar giant
  captured her
  in his fiery orb.
Contented now and glorious
  to see afar
Venus - our captured morning
  star!

Sonna Nylene
DIED FOR A CAUSE

Today has come and gone again.
I have not seen the sun.
It's dark and cold and lonely
  here,
In this place where I have gone.

Ashes to ashes, dust to dust
And covered by the earth.
Such a price to pay.
Are they sure of what it's worth?
"It is for a good cause?"
"I did what I have done."
Tomorrow will come and go
 again.
I'll not see the sun.

Toni Ericsen
DO YOU REMEMBER?

Do you remember the time that
 you took your first step?
Do you remember the time you
 said to me, "are you going to
be there for me?" Yes,
 I'm going to be there. I'll
never forget the time you said
 my name. I won't forget the
time you held your hands out
 and cried, you said are you
going to be there for me?
I said, "I'll always be there."
When you are sick, sad or
 lonely."
 I will never forget you.

Darlene M. Fusco
GOALS

Reach out as far as the sun;
Touch a star, then try for a
 higher one.
Never give up;
Go for the silver cup.
For if we give up, we are all
 lost souls;
If we don't try for our highest
 goals...

Steve Bergseng
CHILDREN FISHING

Rain pouring,
 Causing pockmarks on the
 lake.
Swallows swooping, fish
 jumping-
 Children happy, having fun.
Take your time!
 Moments like these......
I know are precious.
 Memories held deep within-
My mind.

Thomas H. Gilmore
PRECIOUS TIME

Oh time, precious time,
Left and right but never dead
 center, yet always past;
Lonely time, solitude in passing;
Gone but not done, felt but
 not seen, felt but not heard;
Do you want time?
Time to think, time to live,
Time to be happy, time to be
 sad,
Time to collect yourself for
 another day.
Where did it go?
Why is it gone?
Who took it?
Is it the uncertainty of these
 questions
That makes time so precious?

Kristan Spencer Dillow
DESPAIR

Life isn't what it used to be.
It's changed so much it's hard
 to see,
where I've been or where I'm
 at,
am I plunging ahead or falling
 back?
Is it worth the effort to tread
 each day
or should I quietly fade away,

into silent thoughts and dreams,
to memories of what I've seen?
Of days gone by and hopes that
 flew
away from me when I lost you.

Viola Carr Lewis
THE COMMISSION

A poet receives his commission
 from God;
Those who write about the
 beauty of life,
Like David who complained of
 sorrow and pain
Yet lifted up by Holy
 compassion
And let down by confusion
 and strife.
My pen tis Master of my mind;
The need to write is driving,
 pressing, demanding.
We see the winner, the loser,
 the cruel and unkind;
And resolve not to grieve
 because of declining years,
But search for the peace that
 passes understanding.
Such astounding colors enhance
 the earth;
These falling leaves and autumn
 flowers;
Like unto the young and the
 aged;
Who pass from beauty to death
Reminding us of our passing
 hours.

Tony Hartmann
THE POND

Alive with chatter,
 the chirping sound,
evening dew,
 and the dusk surround.
Bullfrogs loud pound,
 bellowed tympany,
others tune in,
 twilight symphony.
Creating songs,
 no two alike,
an original show,
 yours for the hike.
Silver moon-shine,
 sparkle and sheen,
the water lies still,
 peaceful, serene.
Pungent odor,
 picture of death,
from the decay,
 comes a new breath.
Mother-earth composes,
 creations explode,
sound and new life,
 slip from the load.
Interruption - brief,
 clunk of a log,
in the shadows a 'coon
 snatches a frog.
Moments pass,
 then the silence is gone,
new music is born,
 sunny, blue dawn.

Jennifer Hamlin
MY SON

As I sit and watch you grow
I hear music all around.
It's a dancing minstrel show,
And my favorite kind of sound.

You are far, and yet so near
That I must reach out and
 touch;

You appear, then disappear,
And I search for you too much.
Though you're dancing out of
 sight,
Still the music softly lingers.
I'll keep humming through the
 night
Of my memory-laden years.

Alice Stauffer
DESIRE

My beloved, loves me!
I know not how, nor why,
And I love him, with
Every fibre of my being.

We lay embraced
In each others arms,
The blood pulses thro'
Our veins, hot with desire,
And then we are one,
Peace, contentment are sweet,
We are in love!

Fae S. Farrell
ON THE BEACH

She walks
Alone
Upon the beach.
The fog
Drifting
Surrounds her.
Her footsteps
Are
All that show
That
She was there.
The waves
Wash
Over the prints -
Obliterating
Even
Their existence.

Michael E. Robinson
MISS JENSEN

Miss Jensen, what are you
 doing?
'Cause I'm not fooling
When I say I love you
I really do!
Miss Jensen, where are you
 going?
Are you going bowling?
'Cause I love you
I really do!
Miss Jensen, what are you
 sewing?
Let's not again go bowling!
'Cause my fingers
Feel like ringers!
Miss Jensen, what are you
 saying?
What's that you're braying?
Can it really be?
You love me?

Paula Dillabough
MOUNTAINMAN

A soft wind blows over your
 grave
Melting the pockets of dirty
 snow
Do you know or care —
Spring may come early —
 this year.
We stood together, you and I —
At the top of a mountain, our
 world —
We held each other, and talked
 of being close to God's
 footstool
You always said you wanted
 to go first, and you did.
I am left with memories, the
 mountains and a heart
filled with tears —

Turning into ice — the lonely
 existence of a soul only
half alive —
With you gone. And your grave.
The wind cries around the
 cabin
A loon calls on the lake
We miss you so —
Rest easy my darling —
The pain of your days here,
 no more.
Your long trail has ended —
And spring came early — this
 year.

Augusta Smith Kelley
PRAYER

O Lord give me courage,
Courage not to speak
When it be far better
 My tongue to keep.

When I am lashed on
With razor sharp speech
May I be as the little child
Who hasn't learned to speak.

Jennie Tombaugh
**WHAT DOES JESUS DO
 ALL DAY?**

 What does Jesus do all day?
It's such a wondrous thought
 to say.
He listens to each prayer we
 pray,
He gives us strength to face each
 new day.
He comforts us when things go
 wrong,
He fills our lives with joy and
 song.
He helps us when we're full of
 doubt,
He gives us courage to work
 things out.
He forgives and forgets our
 many sins,
He loves us though we disregard
 Him.
He gives us peace in times of
 stress,
He only asks that we do our
 best.
He gives us hope and lights our
 way,
It's truly wondrous what Jesus
 does all day.

Elias Nicholas Mavroleon
FRIENDS

The cycle of life transforms
As do the seasons.
And though we must separate
Our friendship remains
As do the seasons.

Roberta H. Long
COMA

My son laid so quiet and still,
He could not move nor could
 he feel!
For seven months I knelt and
 prayed,
For God to make him move and
 say.
"I love you Mom and I feel
 better,
Let's get the family altogether."
Well that great day did arrive,
I knew my son wasn't going
 to die!
He opened up his beautiful
 eyes,
And spoke so well to our
 surprize.
Our family gathered round his

bed,
We knew the prayers that we
had said,
Were answered by the only one,
GOD THE FATHER, GOD
THE SON!

K. C. Powers
FLIGHT

Lying quiet beneath the cool
sheets
Feeling the warmth of your
body
Against my back —
The strength of your arm
Where it curves around me —
The light touch of your lips
On my bare shoulder —
Two breathing as one.
We find no need for words
In these silent moments.
For no words exist that could
express
The heights to which my heart
soars upward —
Beyond where it is safe
For butterflies to go.

Kimberly Eleanor Hacking
LOVE (DEDICATE TO MARK)

It's so beautiful but frustrating,
So much happiness but too
much pain.
Decisions of whether to stay
or leave,
To love or lose.
The tears of joy and anxiety
overcome
me,
His soothing and warming
touch or his
cold and confused stare.
Do I have the right to do this
to him?
Do I have the moral right to do
this to us?
Love,
The bitterest of all fruits,
Should I stay and harvest or do
I walk
away to watch it wither within
us.
The decision must be made.
Do I procrastinate and
strengthen our pain?
Or do I instantaneously
rejuvenate our vow?
Our vow,
To love till death do us part.
I won't decide,
I refuse to decide,
I deny to decide.
Yet,
If I choose not to make the
decision,
Have I already not made my
choice?
I know!
I will decide.
But only,
"TOMORROW!"

Elnora M. Smith
THOUGHTS

Something today is very heavy
on my heart,
And I feel a need to somehow,
express a thought,
And to let you know just how
much you are a part
Of a love that for many dreams
I have sought.

Last night as I looked across
the room dim and gay,
And saw you so tall and

handsome standing there,
I thought about all the things
that I want to say
And a life with you in dreams
only I share.

But when I feel something
inside for someone strong,
Perhaps a love that will never
have a chance to grow,
Somehow I cannot believe it is
all wrong
To tell him in a gentle way, just
so he'll know.

You have so many fine qualities
rarely found,
The kind that people are always
looking for,
But never seem to find, for so
few are around.
This, among many things, has
made you what you are.

You have never made me feel
guilty or ashamed
For things, perhaps in someone
else's eye
I would have been criticized
and greatly blamed.
These qualities are the ones
wealth cannot buy.

So I'll go on in a quiet sort of
way,
Telling you how I feel and what
is in my heart,
So that you will always know
that you never stray
Too far from my thoughts,
though we're many dreams
apart.

M. Evelyn Allen
TIME

The past opened the floodgate
Of pain and tears and laughter.
Sorrow gave birth to glory!
The present stood annointed—
Yet undone!
Frightened, wary—Yet firm
Upon the hope and joy
remembered—
Upon the troubles crossed to
Freedom
And Sometime—Peace.
The future stood in shadows
dim—
Not sure of lines and times
already gone.
Faintly he minds the beginning
Fitfully proclaiming "I am?"
Yet not knowing!
Why?

Clarence J. Russell
AUTUMN

Leaves falling in forlorn
splendor;
Life has passed them by;
How tragic, how short lived
their beauty,
The bare trees naked to the
abuse of Nature;
Nothing hidden in it's green veil,
Now a brown carpet on the
forest floor.
The morning frost gleaming in
it's magnificence,
The reaper of abundance.
The burrowing animals hidden
from it's sting.
Grey foreboding clouds
obliterating the distant sun,
Their fruit quenching the Earth's
thirst.
And the lovely quiet carpet of
first snow,
Serene, stark, unfeeling, fatal,
but majestic.

Nicholas M. Konesky
OUT-AND-OUT OUT

HOMO SAPIENS:
We wondered a wonder till
now we smile
To find our world so delirious
a smile;
We smiled a smile till now we
laugh
To find our world so
humorous a laugh;
We laughed a laugh till now we
fear
To find our world so
credulous a fear;
We feared a fear till now we
cry
To find our world so
thunderous a cry;
We cried a cry till now we
break down
To find our world so
sunderous a break-down.

INSECTAS:
Terra, terra OURS!
We thank our divine.
Oh, hurra, hurra!
Hail thy kingdom come
For the good terra—
Ad infinitum.
Down with homo sapiens—
The magnificent louts;
O almighty divine!
Keep them OUT-AND-OUT
OUT.

Rosann Marie Carson
WHY ARE THEY DIFFERENT?

They are young and very much
in love.
Why are they different?
They enjoy going places like
other couples do.
Why do people stare?
They want to marry and raise
a family.
Why do people call them
names?
They want a lovely home.
Why do the neighbors ignore
them?
Their love is strong;
They endure all that is against
them.
Their love is beautiful;
They care so very much for
each other.
Their love is sacred;
They worship God together.
Their love is good;
They try to understand, not
hate people.
Why are they different?
No, they are not really different.
But some people look at them
And see only Black and White.
God bless those who look at
them
And see only a Man and Woman
in love.

Deborah G. Moffitt
IN THE MIDDLE

The time has come to make your
great decision,
Quit wandering aimlessly about,
searching.
Envision your dreams, stare
upward, there, find.
Reach, grab, struggle, you can
make the climb.
Give up all the games of the
world,
Aren't you the one who doesn't

like to play?
Tell me your words, try, you
can find them.
Love is as a butterfly, it starts
as a cocoon,
Then, suddenly, magically it
bursts forth
Billowing, flying, free colors—
you can find
That too! Everything is within
your reach
Stretch, give a bit of yourself,
it takes that.
You are not a lone, solitaire
being here.
Interaction and reaction are all
our duties
Realization and insight have
their part also.
Are we not all brothers and
sisters? But
Yet, we knock down, growl at,
hate each other.
Look, the answers are not so
very clear.
Because of this, dig for the
questions; develop.
Yes, they count just as much as
the answers,
Maybe more. The end will still
reveal all,
It is best to be prepared for that
end;
One can be sure of its coming,
don't fool,
Deny, follow something, make
sure you're ready!

Joyce Blackner
MY DREAM WHILE WIDE
AWAKE

Woke up this morning, with a
heart and a soul
Blood racing in my veins from
my head to my toe
What more could you ask for?
So if the world looks dark and
gloomy and you feel
Your back against the wall, thro
back your shoulders
And walk mighty tall. Whether
you're 3 feet, 6 feet, or 8 feet,
Height and measurement has
nothing to do with it at all
It's that spark of life within you,
how you treat your
Fellow man, it's the joining of
all people clear across
The land around the world.
So someday we can build
bridges to walk across, to talk
Or share a laugh, or shake a
hand. And not to talk about
This world being damned.

Anita L. O'Connell
GOD SPOKE TO ME

The day was still
The cool morning chill nipped
at my
uncovered skin.
The sun was creeping out from
the
distant horizon.
I got in my car and drove into
this beauty.
The orange and pink rays against
the
blue sky was so beautiful.
The birds were making their
different
patterns looking so free.
I was so content with the beauty
God
Shared with me.
I felt so peaceful and content
with life.

All my troubles were gone.
And I truly think God spoke to me
this morning.

Michelle Anne Stosich
NIGHT RIDE

The flickering lights
  On the truck
Shine over the
  Wind swept taft.

My eyes are strained
  To see in dust
My eyes are smarting
  from the wind.

I am bouncing in the back now.

I stand upright,
  then lose my sight
To a sweeping branch above.

We bear down upon a house ....
  Darkened and becoming.

But the ride is over now,
  and to bed we go
Dreaming of the night ride.

Laurie Parish
I REMEMBER

I remember when I was young.
My life had just begun.
I didn't know where it'd take me.
So I just held on and took the journey.
It took me through rich and poor, love and hate.
Though I never really understood my fate.
Now while I wait and rest,
Searching for my last quest,
I think of those days way back when
I was young and my life had just begun.

Julie Anne Suzuki
KATHLEEN'S DREAM

Her name means "pure"
  Her green eyes glow in the sunlight like
    the leaves of Mother Nature's plants
Her place is among Nature's wildlife, mountains, and trees
  She's travelled to the mountains of Colorado and visited the deserts of Arizona
Her dream is to live among Nature, especially where the mountains dominate
  The air is clear and sky so blue
    It gives her the freedom of a gliding eagle —
      Free and graceful — with unlimited space

Brenda Elaine Hitchcock
WILL YOU?

When I reach out my hand,
Will I receive your hand?
When I shed a tear,
Will you gently brush it from my face?
When I'm feeling low and unwanted,
Will you make me smile?
When I'm happy,
Will you share my happiness?
When I am empty,
Will you fulfill me?
When I'm lost,

Will you show me the way?
When I feel a chill,
Will you hold me until I'm warm?
When I'm frightened,
Will you be there to comfort me?
When I'm confused,
Will you explain and make it clear?
When I need a friend,
Will you always be there?

Carl Floyd Freeman
BALLAD OF THE
  BICENTENNIAL

I have that power of the Poet,
That some don't understand;
To look outside the Universe;
Or, hold Time in my hand.

So, when my memory
  flutters back,
Through gardens of Old Time,
I hear the drums of Ancient War;
Or, some Old Poet's Rhyme.

The muffled drums of some
  old war,
And some old Poet's Lay,
Are the Mountains in the memory,
They will not pass away.

Two hundred years have come
  and gone;
And time has changed Apace:
And Governors and Presidents,
Are pimples on Time's face.

The Orators with flaming eye,
Like Watson, and Ben Hill,
Have echoed down Time's Corridors;
But now, they too are still.

So, what will be our heritage,
When Time has turned the Wheel?
Will Grace return to Womanhood?
And, Man go forth to field?...

Laurie Tanoura
THE HOUSEWIFE BLUES

up in the morning
crack of dawn
run around quickly
no clothes on
teeth sure need brushing
can't find toothpaste
dog's in the bathroom
oh, what a waste
kids in the kitchen
burning their toast
making their breakfast
with tonight's roast
shoes have no laces
hair is a mess
have only one stocking
can't find a clean dress
phone is still ringing
a man's at the door
I'll break that dog's leg
if he messes the floor

my mind's in a dither
don't get enough sleep
tub's running over
water's three inches deep
haven't paid any rent
since the first of July
oh landlord, dear landlord
I really do try
I have a solution
I'll find a clean blouse
send the kids to the movies
and burn down the house

Michael Carlyle Bryant
LONG AGO IN MALIBU

Sky is so blue
Ocean bluer
Sand's tanned white
Distant clouds whiter
The bush is so green
The rock so much older

Lovers and loners
Breezing on the beach forever
Seagulls in flight
Scavengers together
Relentless life
Whatever this sight

Lonely sky
I'm feeling like
Someone must have read my mind
Long ago in Malibu

Anna Lee Hayes
HELPING HANDS

When in a strange place, with a heavy heart and alone
I met some strangers, who took me into their home
Their kindness meant more to me than silver or gold
The blessing of friendship, between us did unfold

They proved that there are still some good people
Their life shines like a light in a Church Steeple
Standing ready to help someone in time of need
Not asking for gratitude, or pay, having no greed

As I travel down life's pathway in my memory stays
Thoughts of kindness, done in those troubled days
If someone passes my way that needs a helping hand
I pray that I too, will care, and try to understand

Gail L. Sanford
ME, GEMINI

I seem to get wound up inside of me sometimes.
I seem to be so many people
  I should need a computer to sort me all out.
I haven't time anymore
  to dig deep down and down
for the deepest meanings of life.
I must go on—
continue to put into practice—
  tune in and flow along.
No time for slow starts or stops
  or reasons to glide easy.
Take me here or put me there—
  just move on and on
  slower or faster
  high but low—
  on and on . . .
Can't slow, not now—
  goals—yes, goals
  keep going, don't give up.
Fly with me
die with me

just be there, if it ends.
Don't celebrate
  or anticipate
  or try for the award
  just move along—less slowly now
go on— go on like before. . .
It's all there, sitting in front of you
Smiling like the Chessy cat,
  you saw once in a dream
Take the fake or slide through—
  don't give too much of a damn.
If you don't know by now,
  just how crazy I can be—
  then baby——
    just stick around!

Vicki S. Mossman
MY WORLD

my world isn't simple anymore
since you entered my life.
now i can't keep hold
of those fleeting emotions,
or even keep track of my
minute-to-minute existence.
my world passes me by. . .
and i'm not even sure where i am;
much less where i want to go.

Gayle M. White
A CANDLE IN THE WIND

Life
  A candle in the wind
  It seems to me
  Extremely delicate - ever glowing
    Heavy shadows overcast its brilliance
    fear
  Constant fear of being extinguished
    Before reaching its brightest peak
      wondering
  How many hearts has it illuminated
      Not enough
        Life
  A candle in the wind
  it seems to me.

Margaret L. Coffin
IMPRESSIONS

The lake at night is a wonderful sight
With lights along the shore.
  'Tis a beautiful sight
  This lake in the night
Of it I never am bored.

Ducks on a pond are a delight to see
Swimming around with ease.
  They swim and dive
  Make the pond seem alive
Will wonders never cease?

Another delight is a tree of pine
Standing so straight and tall.
  It makes one wonder
  And think and ponder
How God could make it all.

Margaret Roy
MISSING OUR HOME IN
  ALBERTA

Missing our home in Alberta,
Missing the days on the farm.
Missing the hills and the meadows,
And the cud-chewing cows by the barn.

Missing the warm days of springtime,
Missing the ducks in the slough.

Missing our home in Alberta,
And longing to be there with
  you.
Missing a sense of freedom,
That no where else can bring.
Missing our home in Alberta,
Especially in the spring.

Helen Mullen
DON'T WEEP FOR ME

When I am gone
Don't weep for me
For I've had joy four fold!
A love of life
A host of friends,
A family sweet and dear,
And you my love!
So don't weep for me
When I'm away,
My love is always near.

Carol Schnall
OCTOBER MOON

A sudden voiceless whisper
taps softly at my sleep
I raise as if in wonder to see
  the dark so deep
It urges, quiet, gently, "Look
  out above the haze
Turn the bamboo curtain,
  behold the Moon ablaze!"

Oh the Moon!
The clouds they cradled, but
  were careful not to touch
Her temple softly blending
  into night.

Now, where's the wonder
  knowing
That for long I wished to see
The Moon in all her glory
At my window calling me.

Wilbur Fields
WISHIN'

I wish I was a happy, easy
  goin' fella,
Without a worry or a care.
I wish my pockets would turn
  to silver,
Instead of just my hair.
I don't mind workin', if there's
  something left
To put in the sack.
But it sure is disgustin' knockin'
  yourself out,
To get nothing back.
If things don't turn for the
  better,
I think I'm going to crack.
It will either be my nerves,
Or my poor old aching back.

Betty I. Denslow
REALITY

Hardest of all
Is learning to accept
That which is inevitable,
To interject philosophic hope
As a consoling cape
As you grope
For understanding
And learn to shape
What you have into what you
  need,
Accepting limits that intercede
Transitory dreams
And expectations
With realities of the present
And life's limitations.

Tone Degracia
MY MAGIC WORK

I learned to exalt my thoughts
  and dreams to "purify them
  into words."
I then, can look behind with

pride and joy to know it's
done by the "Magic of my
Work!"
The thoughts, the will, and the
  mind of one's being,
is the remedy for this formula
of My Magic Work . . .!

Charles E. Gross, Jr.
**THOUGHTS ON THE ROAD
OF LIFE**

Distant clouds of misfortune;
Sense the brooding,
the ominous looking,
of cool night air.
Walking; drifting;
Amongst distand light
Hoping to escape it soon.
These thoughts; far off lands
Return to haunt,
Spit and taunt.
Gazing past
These barren fields;
This, my souls
Everlasting desert sands.

Catherine Birch
TO AN EX-

I've never had the courage to
  make you aware
That though I've seemed
  indifferent — I really did care.
You're so nonchalant, but I
  had to act.
I was trying to make myself
  hate you, in fact!
  The truth is, I don't know if
  I can ever forget you.
  Even now, old memories of
  good times continue
To haunt my thoughts and
  complicate my life,
And I wonder if a better
  person will ever arrive.
Only then may these
  impressions in my mind be
  erased;
Though a person like you
  isn't easily replaced.
Why do I still love you? (God
  only knows!)
I should've told you this before,
  but each time I froze.
And although I am sure it will
  get me nowhere,
I guess it can't hurt for you to
  know I still care.

Wyman K.F. Wong
PURSUIT

Think not unkindly of her,
For, though she bade us
  farewell,
We still remain in her heart
Hidden by pain she must quell.

We must try to understand
Her feelings, wanting to go;
Because, forcing her to stay
Will bring to all grave sorrow.

She asked for a year or two,
On her own, to live away;
So she may find the white dove
That has eluded, gone astray.

But, only time can reveal
If, maybe, she should have
  stayed.

U. Meat
26TH GUAGE AND DOWN

Oh God, not that horse again
Ancient tracks carved in the
  desert
The mountains, the valley, the
  river that was
You could never do it? No it

doesn't hurt
Yes a lot of spikes 'been laid
To form this section of track
I remember every inch, every
  turn, every miss
Stranded at the station, no way
  to turn back
Oh the locomotives that have
  raced these tunnels
Sleek steel machines, a cargo
  that can't be stopped
Look down that road, there is
  no end, no arrival
No smiles on this one way ride;
  Why pretend
    When the sun turns raw
    And the meat turns brown
    No two ways about it
    It's 26th guage and down

Jackie Miller
EACH HORIZON

At birth I'm free; although I
  will
say at times, I'm still in search
  for
the one, whom, is called me***

But for now, all I know is to
honestly listen and seek clearly
"Each Horizon" I may or might
  see ***

Darla Rochelle Jensen
THE PLEA OF A HANDICAP

Look at me not
With eyes of pity.
Is it I
Who is different?
Are you sure
You are normal?
I am strong-
Not weak.
After all
Take a look
At what I must do
Just to walk
Down the street.
Nobody's perfect-
Least of all me—
But take a look at yourself—
Tell me what you see.

Dorothy Husar Krosky
JUST TELL ME

I would never forsake you, I
  could never try
I would not let you, ever say
  goodbye
I've waited so long, for someone
  like you
You occupy my mind, in
  whatever I do.
You're near me though others
  can't tell
You're in my blood, in each
  tiny cell
I want so to please you, just
  tell me how
You have only to speak, and
  with my love, I'll thee endow
I would like to walk in this
  world with you
Share all your triumphs and
  sorrows too.
What else can I say, what else
  can I do?
My dearest of dear, I do love
  you.

Dennis Vannoy
THE CHILD

Long ago a beautiful child was
  born,
And in the midst of that
  special moment
A miracle had come true.
One that had never occured

before
Like the sun shining bright
The smile it bore was a miracle
In itself.

A tear came from its eye,
Showing it had the feelings of
A human being.
That child has grown wise
And very beautiful
That child mom,
            is you.

Marilee G. Candelaria
WONDERING

I love to eat bananas,
  Monkey eat them too.
I wonder if they chew them,
  Or mush them like I do?

I climb up trees,
  And so do they.
I run and jump
  And chatter and play.

Sometimes I start to wonder
  If it could really be,
I'm acting like a monkey,
  Or if he is acting like me?

Karen R. Hasselswerth
INDUSTRIAL LUST

On haunted cheeks vaguely pink
Smoke sighs a jaundice yellow.
The eyes once blue are blinded
  grey,
For industrial lust skies mellow.

Vicki Augustine
MEMORIES

tickets
torn in half,
faded photographs,
a worn teddy bear
won at the fair,
flowers pressed in a book
of old love poems,
a friendship ring,
what memories these bring
of loves of long ago.

Sarah
PETRIFIED FOREST

empty saccharine smiles,
cool vacant stares
and polite conversations,
with nothing to say
and no one listening-

what would it take
to shake them
from that complacent
self-annihilation?

is loving someone so
inconceivable?

Michael C. Matuska
**ANXIETIES OF THE
COMMON MAN**

I dread the day
When the clock will stop,
And my heart shall not
  Stop beating.

And I fear those lips
Which smile at my face,
Yet hide the fact: that my days
  Are numbered.

I detest the decree
That the wise man may extoll
His wisdom, if his soul
  Keeps singing
Of death's eye (in which he
  spits),
Of death's place: only war;
For on his bed atop the floor
  There slumbers

But a poor man-soldier whose
  heart keeps beating
During meaningless days that

are numbered,
While vultures overhead insist
upon singing
Great songs of joy about
destiny's plunder...
INDEED, ABOUT HIS LIFE
OF PUREST SLUMBER!

Robert D. Jutton
THANK YOU GOD, FOR EVERYTHING

We have so very many things
That God has given us.
We forget them oh so many
times
And put up such a fuss.

We are all together now
What better gift than this?
I have a happy family
And a somewhat world of
bliss.

I thank my God for all He's
done
With his helping hand.
I see so little credit given him
In this wondrous land.

So, stand and raise your eyes
to heav'n
And thank him loud and
strong.
For if we praise him with all
our hearts
Nothing may go wrong.

Emily Ritke Okray
THE UNIVERSE IMPOSSIBLE

Let us go soaring into space-
And Space
And Space
And Space
And Space.

We come to the moon another
place-
Then Space
And Space
And Space
And Space.

On to many planets the world
do grace-
More Space
And Space
And Space
And Space.

A world without end and
timeless pace-
And Space
And Space
And Space
And Space?

Cathy Byrd
MOTHER

You were always there when
I needed you
A mother, a confidante, a
friend.
You were someone to look up
to
And on whom I could always
depend.

No matter what happened
You were there right by my
side.
When my spirits were
dampened
And I cried-you cried.

There's just no way in a
million years
That I could ever repay;
The time, the love, the tears
That we've shared to this very
day.

I love you dearly Mother
No one could take your place;

For there is just no other
Who could ever fill your space.

Karen M. Lindberg
THE LITTLE ONES

Oh! They're so cute
The little ones.
So young, so innocent
so naieve to the world
and all its pain.
Until they grow up and
start to realize that it
isn't all fun and games
all their lives.
They grow up to be
tough, rough and sometimes
even forceful in order to
get what they want and to get
what they need.
But what they really want
and really need is . . .
                        to be loved.

Cheryl A. Tippett
PLEASE

Won't you stay
    just a little longer?
We've just begun to love
    and I'm not ready
        to stop.
Can't you stay
    Just a little longer?
The excitement of you lifts me
    high
    and I'm not ready
        to come down.
Couldn't you stay
    Just a little longer?
I savor your gentle caresses
    and I'm not ready
        to give them up.
Please stay
    just a little longer.
I love you so much
    and I'm not ready
        to let you go.

Susan Loring
THE EVER ASKED QUESTION

    Where are you world of
    peace and love
This world I see is so far from
    you
Life is so full of hate
The only love is that of war
When I find you   Oh distant
    hope
All my dreams shall come true
For a world of love is magical
Where all fantasies blossom
    into reality
Life is born with hope anew
All creatures hate no more
What is the path that I must
    take...
To leave this world of war?

Paul H. Menier, III
CALIFORNIA

California redwoods,
Are all along the shore.
Little golden poppy,
Increase the sighs somemore.
From California grizzly bear,
Or golden trout galore.
Reminds me of the Golden
    State,
Natures place of store.
I love you, California,
And always will, for sure.

Shirley Arlene Garza
WINTER TREASURES

Glittering snow, hinting the
    sparkle of diamonds,
adorning mountains and vale,

So devastating, this picture of
    beauty, sharing
its monuments of luster,
To eyes that gaunt upon, to
    grasp its captivated
gift, within lens of sight,
So unsurpassed, spreading its
    fortune till enveloped
in hues of cluster,
Once barren rock, now mounds
    of pearls stringing out,
not to fasten its clasp,
Springs within, oozing threads
    of silver through
its seams,
Covert trees of jade, now
    opalesque, casting glints
of gold, sprinkling these
    mountains of fortune,
Be all its treasures, lest unseen,
    beholds the
seekers dreams —

Della M. Olson
TO THE VIRGIN RIVER AT FLOOD

Little Virgin hesitate
In your haste to copulate
With Colorado's caustic flood,
Churning sandstone into mud
In careless, uncurbed wanton
    spree
Completely loosed from sanity
Until at Mead's calm peaceful
    breast
You lay your coursing flood to
    rest
Yet lose your virgin entity
In intercourse with inland sea.
Calm your urgent springtime
    heart,
Let love remain the gentler part
In crystal clear life giving drink
Sustaining life clung to your
    brink.
Cease your chocolate throaty
    roar
Calling at my very door
Lest I like you answer spring
In one passionate consuming
    fling.

Susan Elayne Sabo
THE MISTS OF LOVE

I feel I must wander
Down paths dark and misty
But now in the distance
There is a place I know,
A place where I can shelter -
A place to call my home.
No walls nor roof,
No floors nor doors-
My home it walks
With pride and honor.
And the reflections
It mirrors show my own tender
    smile,
Deep within the warmth of
    brown.
And as I travel
Down my uncertain path,
Whenever I get scared or lonely-
Through the mists
So softly glimmers
The light of love within my
    home.

Ruth Webber
SENIORS

Seniors holding hands
As in days of yore
Love has stayed with them
Fifty years or more.

And a darkening thought
    comes o'er me
Like a shadow on the lawn
What will one of them do

When the other one is gone?
Please let them go together
Would be my ernest prayer
Holding hands forever
With no parting there.

Kara Midgette Acri
I WON'T FLY!

Oh I am a bird
    Who lives in a nest
But I will not fly,
    I will not fly.

The men they all yell,
    the ladies all scream,
But I will not fly,
    I will not fly.

For I hear all the talk
    about pollution and war
As the people all shout
    and the airplanes all roar;
So I'm staying right here
    where it's safe and it's warm,
And I will not fly,
    I will not fly.

William Edward Woodward
AS THE LAMPS EDGE NIGHT

As the lamps edge night
    The big bugs fly
And little men laugh
    But never know why.

Around, about,
    The hawkers cry
And the crowds like gnats
    Go whimpering by.

In the pale lamplight
    The big bugs fly
And little men cough
    And little men die.

Within, without,
    Deep murmers sigh
In the smog and flats
    Where little men die.

At the edge of night
    The big bugs fly
And little men laugh
As the end draws nigh.

Barbara Goldman
VISIT TO A DYING FRIEND

In her hospital bed
my friend didn't see me.
    Startled
I saw an ancient dowager; yet
when I approached more closely
her voice assured me she was
    there
behind the mask
of her pain and pallor.

With light in her eyes
Amy recognized me, and for a
    moment
we found ourselves
on more familiar ground.
the moment passed
and we were silent, listening—
like spectators in a darkening
    theater
for the first sound.

John E. Madden
THE DREAMER

Come dream with me and share
   my night
where we can walk by love's
   sweet light,
   on desert sands, through fields
      of gold,
   through crystal brooks, and
      forests old.
Come take my hand, stay close
   by me
and we will many wonders see
   'neath moon and stars arched
      overhead,
   in piney boughs we'll make our
      bed
to lay till dawn lights up the sky
and brings the sun to show the
   way
   to happy, wandering, gypsy
      feet
   that hurry on to pleasures
      meet.
Come live with me in golden
   dreams
where joy and laughter never
   seems
   to be more than a touch away,
   and life and love fills every day.
But dreams must end, and we
   must part
to separate worlds that chill my
   heart,
   to aimless, lonely days that
      bring
   the ache, and hurt, and
      sorrowing.
Yet, wait for me till I am
   through
this endless time away from you.
   then come and take my hand
      once more
   and share my dreams
      forevermore.

Michael Rogozik
VISION

Chirping birds entice the worms
   to dance
The soil warms the hearts of its
   inhabitants
Grass grows to be combed and
   caressed
Blue skies enrich the sight of
   man—to
   never fear the grays and
      thunder.
The Rainbow is a bridge for
   eyes to rest,
   and its colors the emanation
      of man.

Catherine Strasser
SLOW DEATH

Think.
Who's sorry now?
When the piercing moon smiles
   wickedly in the
hearth of heaven, and a
lone star wavers on its way to
   Hell,
Who is cringing in self-made
   isolation,
waiting for quicksilver death?
Listen
As the thunder renders words
inaudible, and pleas become
swallowed in the
vacuum of ensuing silence.
Wait
for the memory, forever
advancing with
broad strides and evil intent,
causing sorrow to bubble in
   veins

thickened with apathy.
Feel.
It is the last pain.
It will draw life from its
   container, leaving a
hollow, naked tomb behind,
   using
love as both defense and
   weapon.
Know
Death.
Who's sorry now?

Michael Harris
DIANE

We know ourselves, we say
We are, to a certainty,
At home with ourselves
Until an evening occurs
Disposed for a kiss, stolen
And half a dare, but vaults
The stars around us
The night sky breathes us in
Your eyes glisten, surprised
How it feels, how we wished me
To dare it, how a yearning you
   harbored
And scarcely knew, unfurls
With sexual frightened lips
As if you are something new
A swan, a young girl, some
   secret place . . .

George B. Mitchell
SOLITUDE

I've walked this trail, *so many
   times* with
head bent low and a heavy
   heart—
"Alone"—*yet not alone* for
   somewhere, "I
know, another soul"—had
   feelings such as
I and felt they *too* was set apart.
To enjoy the loveliness that
   comes to
those that look and wait, for
   the
last bright rays of an evening
   sun.
These golden glows that warm
   the
heart, make us keep searching
   and
loving what we see, until that
   special
love we meet.
Then all the beauty our souls
   and hearts
have stored we want to share—
   yet *with*
that special love we have already
shared our hearts contents
   before we ever met.

Connie Skulmoski
CAPRICE

Caprice
of coffee cups
and lit canals
and venders
in the shade
and cigarillos
and old French horns
with pink carnations
in brown cafes.

Diane W. Shreves
MEEOWNI

I have a darling Siamese,
   As sweet as she can be,
It took awhile to tame her—
   Oh, her name is Meeowni.

Her voice is very loud and clear,
   Her wants must all be met;
It's 'I want in,' or 'out,' or

'Isn't supper ready yet?'
She has a nice warm bed outside,
   (But ends up on my knee—)
Well, did I say I have a cat?
   What I mean is—she has me!

Ann P. Wood
FROM ENGLAND TO NEW ENGLAND

From England's green and
   pleasant land I came,
   From where the yellow crocus
      shyly peeks
   Its head through February's
      snow and seeks
To lift our hearts and spirits
   from that same
Bare, lifeless, icy, gray-skied
   shroud that in
   New England cloaks us in
      despair too long.
   Oh, daffodils come raise your
      trumpet song!
Proclaim relentless Winter's bow
   to Spring!
I came from where the houses
   intertwine,
   Their boxes stacked in rows,
      no space between
To breathe or stretch, as in
   New England's pine-
Filled hills and river-coursing
   dales. I'll lean
On this when next those longing
   thoughts of mine
   To England's Spring aspire—and
      what has been.

Harry Hand
I A MAN

I, a man, born without nothing!
I, a man, powerless over
   misdeeds!
I, a man, because of sin, must
   work
by sweat of brow!
I, a man, must work by day, and
   sleep
by night!
I, a man, seeking a life hereafter!
I, a man, pray to God to save
   my soul!
I, a man, will leave this world
   without
nothing!

John W. Grula
DEAD SERIOUS

Wars happen, history sweeps
   by—
All trumped up with a foolish
   seriousness.
The seriousness that carries
   death,
The seriousness that kills.
Hitler was serious,
But what did he know?
Someone should have told him
   a few jokes.
Someone should have showed
   him
That laughter rings as stars
   tickle the moon.

Mary L. Foote
WHERE IS DADDY?

I once had a daddy
That I have never known
I'd run and sit upon his lap
And he'd tell me how I had
   grown.
He'd give me a big hug and kiss
And then a squeeze or two
And then he'd put me down and
   say
Run along now for daddy
Has a lot of things to do.

He was a tall and handsome man
With lots of golden hair
His smile so sweet and gentle
Folks knew him most
   everywhere.
Sometimes he was a mechanic
Perhaps a writer too,
I don't know much about him
But by chance, perhaps do you?
I never knew my daddy
As you can plainly see
But something deep inside
Says yes, he did love me!!
Now as the time did quickly
   pass
His life has slipped away
I found my dearest daddy
But I wonder what he would
Have been like today.

Clara M. Hamm
SINGLE MOTHER

Fourteen—straight as an arrow
   plucked straight from
      his father's quiver.
Alone—my trembling hands
   fasten his target high;
Alone, I cry and watch his first
   young-winged eager flight.
Away from me—at last he flies
   alone. See! straight for the
      target—
   and so unafraid!
My fear is shame—but in the
   night I plead for him:
Dear God, don't let him fall to
   ruin—don't let him miss the
      mark
You helped me set—only help
   me follow him—
   and be as unafraid.

Marsha JoAnn Morris
WHY?

Here we all sit waiting for the
   day to come
   when we have to grab our bags
      and run.
We're all hearing dumb rumors
   that are goin' 'round.
Then we find out they all come
   from the ground.
Then we ask ourselves what we
   should do,
   until we come to our senses
      and remember Who
   planned it all to happen this
      way.
Then we get onto our knees
   and pray.
It takes a lot of faith to believe
   that we will ever be relieved
   of the thoughts and rumors
   and that they might turn into
      humor.
When will war end?
When will we all be friends?

Imogene Burger
OUR AMERICA

I wish that I could sing a song
   Or write a story book
About this big, wide land of
   ours.
   Oh, won't you take a look?
The greatest place in all the
   world,
   America is to me.
Her beauty far excells them all
Long may our land be free.
God bless America, is my prayer.
   Our flag, red, white, and blue,
Long may it wave mid storm or
   strife.
   America, I love you.

Mary Elizabeth Rose
LOVE

Love,
it is a rainbow,
without the pot of gold.
It is like the snowflakes,
pretty, but so cold.
It's a life you go on living,
when you don't want to live.
Demands to keep on giving,
when you've nothing left to
give.

Yet love,
can be a rainbow,
who cares about the gold.
You have loved it doesn't
matter,
if life is dull or cold.
You've got life and it's worth
living,
through all your dumb mistakes.
You've done your share of
giving
so now it's time to take.

Love,
is just a theory,
for things we can't explain,
invented by the poets,
for emotions still untamed.

Yet love,
could be a rainbow,
or a pot of gold,
love is many riches,
never heartless,
never cold . . .
L
O
V
E.

Agnes R. Coffelt
THE SEA

The sea is calm tonight.
The moon and stars shine
beneath azure blue.

The waves have a worried look,
but the breeze is free and cool.
I know my anxiety shows. I
feel fear inside,
for behind the calm that's cool,
The winds are furious and wild.

The wild cat of the storm begins
it's rage.
I stand on the shore and watch
the naughty waves.
Dash upon the ship that sails,
then hides beneath the gray.
My heart dispells all fear,
and I linger to see the break of
day.
I knew the sea, though
sometimes wild,
could weather any storm.

Gerald W. Coburn
A VILLANELLE FOR LAWRENCE WELK

The once BIG BANDS are sure
a wonder now.
They're all compressed into a
music family,
And all that means; melodious
and how.

Ah- One, Ah- Two! and Ah- take
a bow!
Wunnerful, Wunnerful! swinging
sweetly,
The once BIG BANDS are sure
a wonder now!

The furrows were not always
by a plow,
For some were cut in plastic
tenderly,
And all that means, melodious
and how!

Each score, in concert is indeed
a wow,
And playing golf is swinging
literally,
The once BIG BANDS are sure
a wonder now.

The bubbles will not last, but
we'll avow,
The style will outlast raucous
minstrelsey
And all that means; melodious
and how!

If there's one word, it's
Escondido
Which sums it up eventually
The once BIG BANDS are sure
a wonder now.
And all that means; melodious
and how!

Ethel Hergert
A DAY IN FLORIDA

A gentle breeze stirs my hair
As I sit on the patio, in the
warm air.

A quiet peaceful day
To enjoy the sun's ray.

A lazy comfortful day
No one pushing you anyway.

A day to relax in and enjoy

A day nice for any girl or boy.

As I look around me
A girl on skates I see.

Airplanes flying over head,
My friend wearing a suit of red.

Writing letters, you can bet
While I'm just content to set.

A wonderful day God has
created
Let us praise Him, and be
updated.

Jewel Anne Metz
PAPA

They said you died before I
was born;
I was the only kid in town
Without a father.

I used to go in the front room
And talk to your picture where
it hung
Over the mantel-piece.

I miss you, papa.

When I come where you are will
you
Hold my hands and look at me
And say you missed me too?

Oh papa . . . .

Eleanor R. Minnick
IRISH SENTIMENT

If I had to choose one day of
the year
That makes me both sad and
blue
It's the day of the sons of St.
Patrick
And that could mean me or
you
It matters not much
If you're English or Dutch
That Irish Charm's so
contagious
So why should we feel
That a good Irish Reel
When danced by a Pole is
outragious?
We need not be bleak,
What ere language we speak
For an engaging sweet smile
always blows
The tear from your eye

From your heart a deep sigh
When dispensed by a Wild
Irish Rose!
So if my hat has a tilt
And my walk quite a lilt
And if the happy and sad I
combine
It's cause as I write this poem
I've got visions of home
And that old Irish mother of
mine
So let's all be seen
Wearing the green
Whether German French or
Jew
And as I walk on the street
Join me as I greet
Top of the morning to you!

Trisha Peters
TRIBUTE TO BOB DYLAN

So who asked you to
you stranger you?
Filling up my room
with your Prophesys in tune.
You weave your songs
right through my brain
and cast your spell,
confusing my thoughts
with pain.

I see your face
filling up my space.
The paleness of your skin,
the paleness of the blue
in your eyes.
Your fingers so long
and straight,
clutching your guitar
while breathlessly I wait.

The sign of our times
is your master position.
You laugh at those
who criticize transition.
Are you a Prophet,
or Poet,
a troubled times
Musician?
So who asked you to
you stranger you?

Vern Sawatzky
BABY ELEPHANTS

There's a baby elephant
Up high in the clouds,
Lying down, forelegs sprawled
Into the blue,
Trunk lifted high
Without a sound.
Now it's stretching, growing,
blowing,
Blowing like chaff into the wind,
Becoming bigger, longer,
And to continue seeing it,
Your eyesight must be
Becoming stronger.

You look and wait,
As the breeze may hesitate,
Then shape your sky
Into fluffy memories
Of distant days gone by,
And a dozen telescopic visions

Of being operated on,
Buy the future's bold incisions.

Pamela J. Clarke
THE CLOSED DOOR

I sat beside a brook one day;
It was the lovely month of May.
The water was so clear and
bright,
It made a very pretty sight.

I wish I could go back again;
Unto the place where I had been,
Beside the brook and see once
more
The things on which I've closed
a door.

Louis Giovanni Sebik
THE SNAKE'S GAIN AND THE HAWK'S LOSS

A valiant hawk swooped down
on its prey,
A rabbit meal to devour today.
Nearby a snake had caught
sight of this,
And called out, "That catch
was a near miss.
Let me display a graceful small
trick
That will guarantee a sure kill
quick."
The hawk replied, "Your help
I need not,
For first with keen eyes, victims
I spot,
Then curling my claws, snatch,
then onslaught."
To the serpent this did not
appeal,
So, quickly he bit into the meal.
The hawk, startled by this
dreadful act,
Screeched, and at the low snake
he attacked.
"How *dare* you try to take this
from me?
Now 'tis off with you and leave
me be!"
With a smirk the snake started
away,
But he only when a little way.
Of the snake the hawk did no
more care,
So, he ate his seized food,
unaware,
That all within it poison lay
there.
After his fill the hawk tried to
start
On a new flight to another part.
At last he looked up into the
sky,
But without a breath he fell to
die.
The filthy snake went back to
the site,
And sans flinch he gorged the
rest outright.
If preoccupied without thinking,
Some are fooled by evil
hoodwinking.

James W. Witt
STREET OF LIFE

This is the street where poverty
lives;
Where life often takes more than
it gives.
Here hunger and sickness are
society's sin,
And the people here don't
know the meaning of win.

This is the street where
loneliness lives;
Where sordid embraces are the
warmth life gives.
Here love and hate are the

closest of kin.
And being alone is life's greatest
sin.
This is the street of life;
Where distrust is everyman's
wife.
Here old man birth plays the
fife,
That calls all men to the game
of life.
All who enter here receive the
rules to the game,
But the rules for all people are
not the same.

Terri Notarmaso
LOVE

I close my eyes
and try to get that feeling,
The feeling of warmth,
closeness, togetherness,
The feeling of his tender lips
pressed on mine,
His broad hands caressing me
gently all over my body,
His masculine voice whispering
ever so softly into my ear
Sending deep sensations down
my spine.
I hope someday I'll get that
feeling
That feeling of LOVE.

Josephine Kipcakli Roff
SPIRITUAL LOVE

To hear with your ears the
unspoken words, to see with
your eyes what no one else can
see. To know without
asking. To love without ever
touching.
A higher level than those of
man, a higher level only
those can know, who can speak
with their eyes and feel
with their minds. A love that
has no earthly boundaries.
Nothing can hurt it no person
can prevent it. Like the
wind, the night and the day you
know it is there, but you
cannot reach out your hand and
grasp it. For God will
not let you.
So is the spiritual love that
dwells between souls. No
amount of distance can tear
them apart.
For spiritual love goes beyond
the limits of the human
heart!

Guy M. Renfroe
IF BUT A DAY I HAD

If but a day I had to live,
I think I'd like to see
The things that always thrilled
me most;
Events that gave me glee.
If but a day I had left here
To say good-bye, my friend,
I wonder who the last would be
To speak so near the end?
If but a day I had on earth
To read a book or two,
I wonder if the words would
mean
The same they always do?
If but a day I had of breath
To see a favorite play,
I wonder if the actors would
Perform the usual way?
If but a day I has is all
To meet a famous man,
I wonder if just one I'd find

Who'd even shake my hand?
If but a day I had to win
A lady fair and fine,
I wonder how hard that would
be—
And me just ninety-nine!

Frances Ewing Grayson
RETROSPECT

Through quiet woods, there ran
a stream
Where one could sit alone and
dream
Beside its flowing purity.
Far from all those whose aim,
it seems,
Is just to shatter hopes and
dreams,
(At least, to me, it seems to
be).
Beside this stream I'd play alone,
A child of ten, yet not alone,
For Peace was always there.
Though years are many that
have passed,
A thought, a sigh is backward
cast,
Eyes blinded by unseeing
stare.
Where is the child? Ah, where
the stream,
And all the pattern of the
dream?
They live now in maturity!

Mary Madigan
I'M JUST ASKING TO BE ME

Sometimes I think, "I'm a
person."
Even tho I protest I know it
isn't so,
For part of me is missing—
borrowed,
Given, leaving me unwhole.
They say immortality is our
Progeny,
Children our legacy to Life.
But have I bequeathed the
breath
To strangers who walk away not
feeling the
Impact. Their eyes glance but
do not see,
That I too want to be a Person,
I'm just asking to be Me!

Marian Caruso
BODY AND SOUL

Body and soul!
You can have control.
With your mind grow.
Forward go!
Touch!
You can feel.
Artificial and real.
All can have appeal.
Love you can much.
Such is such.
With flowers you can say it.
Pick a bunch.

Love can give power.
Play your roles.
Love, will!
Try, you can reach your goals.
The best can be.
Openings you can fill.
Make you can deals.
Sadness you can kill.
Lean you can sometimes.
Brave be.
Wounds heal.
All to feel!

Jewel Anne Metz
SUNRISE IN NEVADA

The sun found paths between
The mountains, and lit fires in
the valleys,
Turning them golden.
But sentinel mountains stood
on either side
In peaceful grayness,
Their rocks and hollows
Black with sleep.

Theresa-Rose
THE DYING MAN (ANXIETY)

The black mass
Expanded
Before my eyes;
But I didn't see it,
I wouldn't look.
It grew as a child does:
Seemingly instantly,
Yet taking years.
It grew and bulged
And engulfed me.
My soul
And spirit were
Taken in,
Chewed up,
Then spat out
As blood from a dying man.
That dying man
Was me.

Edwin R. Scott
A STORM IS COMING

I've seen a storm coming,
To wash away the trouble
down here.
I've seen that ole devil running,
And only the righteous have
nothing to fear.
We've got to change our ways
of living,
Instead of taking, we'd better
start giving.
And learn to love our fellow
man,
God's going to walk through
this troubled land.
We may think we can straddle
the fence,
But we won't have any kind of
defense.
The storm is lean and the storm
is mean.
People, there will be no
in-between.
Blind to color is the eye of
the storm,
Seeking to destroy all that is
wrong.
Don't call for mother, sister,
or brother,
This storm is like none of the
others.
So people, you'd better really
make haste,
Believe it or not, there is no
time to waste.
The storm is coming and it's
very strong,
And when it passes a lot of us

will be gone.
It's not for me to say where
you belong,
But I know what side I want
to be on.

Bryan King
SEA OF SIN

My soul drifts endlessly on
the sea of sin
My spirit chained and shackled
to the sail
My mind tortured from past
memories
My body tired and beaten from
the long battle with life
My heart pierced and drained of
its unsatisfied love
My tears hold the reflection of
eternity
For I see the days come and
go
Living in the future
Visiting the present
And then living in the past
The eternal wind is my destiny
And the vastness of the sea
takes my breath away
The shore becomes a distant
memory

Christopher Bailey
NOVEMBER

I long to see the grass grow
green
Upon the little hills
And everytime I take a step
I feel a little chill
The birds are gone, their nests
are bare
They travel with the sun
And as I walk the forest floor
The deer are on the run
The sky is gray, the air is cold
The twigs on trees are bare
Beneath my feet the leaves are
scattered
All dampened right with care
The days are short, the nights
grow long
The dipper makes its swing
Snow will soon be on the
ground
Until another Spring

Carlene Yvette Morris
I THOUGHT...

I thought I loved you.
But found out that I didn't.
I thought you loved me too.
But no, it was just pretend.
I thought I could trust you.
But found out that I couldn't.
I thought...you were the
greatest.
But found out that there would
be more.
I thought we were meant for
each other.
But course not, we're entirely
different.
I knew our "pretend to be
love" wouldn't last forever.
That's why... I knew we had to
say good-bye.

Aneta Ziegler
THE MECHANIC

My husband is a farmer
Who works for John Deere on
the side.
His reputation as a mechanic
Has traveled far and wide.
However, it wasn't always this
way—
At first he worked as a loner,

And in the early years of our
  married life
He really pulled a boner.
He had a tractor that wouldn't
  start
And he couldn't have needed
  it more.
"It's the switch," his brother
  declared,
"That has happened before."
A switch was certainly needed—
So he chased to town in the
  truck,
But even after it was installed
He still didn't have any luck.
Thinking it might be flooded,
He let it stand awhile;
Then they pulled it down the
  lane
For a quarter of a mile.
He checked the carburetor,
  cleaned the plugs,
And kept looking for
  something to mend.
Is it any wonder the world
Was coming to an end?
He was ready to call a
  mechanic—
Surely this is the worst you
  have heard.
Then he happened to look in
  the gas tank
And muttered a five letter word!

Sally Lee Woodall
ENOUGH

alone
    time crawled
    and all I heard
    was the earth-scrapping wing
    of the crippled bird
and then
    with you
    o time at last
    seemed to be flying
    too fast too fast
now
    time is dead
    O wild banshee
    wail me to the deeps
    of the swallowing sea

Miriam M. Ourso
LONELY THOUGHTS

Twilight falls, on this quiet
  evening
Bringing thoughts, just gets to
  me, hurts me
My Dear, I miss you, with my
  whole being.
I'm full of emotion, this time
  of night
I can't seem, to get my thoughts
  just right.
What with us, going our
  separate ways
Hoping, we'll be together,
  again someday
You see, like I told you, I
  still love you
I see myself, my heart is
  breaking
Do you think, maybe, someday,
  there's a way
Regardless of the heartbreak
  we are making.

Betty Ann Whitt
REVERIE

Morpheus came to visit me
  last night.
He explained to me my
  predestination.
Now I have savoirfaire of my

future,
Now I know in my future I am
  guided
  by a lucerne;
And the lovelorn feeling I have
  for you
  has diminished and been
  replaced
  In Paradise by the Love-lies
  Bleed-ing;
For Morpheus told me last
  night
  that there is a special Goddess
  there,
"Waiting just for me,"
And the love she will bring
  shall be
  continuum, ever more.

Martha C. Osborne
**HOW DO YOU SAY
GOOD-BYE?**

How do you say good-bye
When someone says good-bye
  to you?
All those beautiful lies
That will never come true.
The wonderful yet painful
  part of my life
That leaves me empty
And cuts through me like a
  knife.
When happy memories now
  hurt the most
And the pictures I cherished
  are now just ghosts.
There's nothing left inside.
Just empty spaces for lost
  love and laughter to hide.
He says things just aren't the
  same.
And it's hard to explain,
But too much time has past,
Since we were married last.
But he lingers in my mind;
Because he's one of a kind
And the hurt that I feel
Is really that real
And the giving of love I fear
  will never be
Unless he comes back to me.

Lori-Jean Ryan
MAYBE

Maybe I'll never see you again
  Maybe then I might
I guess I'll never really know
  Unless you call or write
Maybe we've had an argument
  Maybe just a fight
I just can't tell which one it is
  But I know it isn't right
Maybe it was your fault
  Maybe it was mine
I'll always know the cause of it
  Each and every time
Maybe when we meet again
  Maybe we'll work things out
But if I know you, oh, too well
  To try again I doubt
Until that day we meet
  We'll see how things will be
If apart we can work things out
  I hope we can..........MAYBE

Timothy L. Hartman
MIRRORED THOUGHTS

I look into the mirror but,
  I don't see me.
There are people who see me
  but,
  don't know me.
There are those who know me
  but,
  never touch.
There are still others who touch
  me,

but never feel.
She is my mirror, when I see
  her
  I see a part of me.
It is she who knows me
  beyond seeing.
It is also she who touches me
  passed the physical
  restraints bound to
  all others.
Yes, it is she,
  My Lover,
  My Friend.

Diane Taylor
A FRIENDLY TEA?

When are you coming for tea
  again?
I've enjoyed myself so much
It's been weeks since I've
  laughed so hard
Please say you'll keep in touch.
I never knew I walked like that
I thought I had such grace
And I never saw the other
  person
Hiding behind my face.
I'm glad that you're my friend
You took time to drop by
To remind me I'm not a
  perfect sort
(As none of us are, tho' we try)
Yes, thanks for stopping over
At twenty five minutes til ten
It brightened up my morning
And when are you coming for
  tea again?

Laura McGee
WINTER

I just arose from my bed
And looked out upon the world.
Mother Nature has been busy
  I can see!
Snowflakes twirling 'round and
  'round
On their descent to the ground,
Piling up mounds of snow for
  you and me!
Yes, it's winter once again;
We're sitting in just looking out,
At the wonders of Our Father's
  Hand.
Not a leaf upon a tree,
One lonely bird that I can see,
Flying by, no destination
  planned!
It's so beautiful to see.
But what sadness it can bring,
To the children, when it melts
  away.
They'd rather skate upon the
  ice
Or go riding on a sled,
Than to go home to a warm and
  comfy bed!
Nothing moving anywhere,
Only snowflakes in the air.
All is quiet as we sit here
  staring out.
We won't be going anywhere,
Merely sitting in a chair,
Looking out at the beauty all
  about.
Yes, we're just waiting for the
  time
When the snowflakes cease to
  fall,
And, wintry winds stop howling
  'round the wing
When warmer days do appear.
Then we'll be glad they are
  here,
For with them comes the
  beauty,
Of the Spring!

Michele Diana Roeckl
SALVATION

She who once was my salvation
Now, alas, my own destruction.
Once so sweet of mind and eye-
Now seethes with venom, never
  try
To be someone for someone
  else,
Or you will find you lose
  yourself.
And so, salvation n'er to see
For my salvation once was me.

Arlene Elizabeth Hall
NOVEMBER

A chilling wind and whitening
  ground
Yet, sunny days are to be
  found
Trees, with branches stripped
  of dress
Like arms reached out for God
  to bless.
One day the sun is bright and
  clear
The next it seems like Winter's
  here
Sit evenings by the dancing
  flames
With popping corn and football
  games.
November's rich in changing
  days
And richer yet in holidays
Thanksgiving Day, we praise
  the Lord
For fruits of labor, neatly
  stored.
So, thank the Lord for
  Autumn's days
With silvery streaks of Winter's
  ways
Oh, blow ye winds of Winter's
  style
We shan't see Summer for
  awhile.

Jeanne Woolcott
**BROWN AND SMOOTH
STONE**

    A stone
    brown and smooth
    lies in the water,
    a trickling spring
    makes the stone sparkle.
  You kneel to pick up the stone
Once again you look at the
  water
    trickle over the empty spot.
    You replace the stone,
    the brown and smooth stone
that lies in the trickling water.

James G. Nicholson
OH GENTLE EARTH

Oh gentle Earth, may I visit
  thee,
this new-born wailing child;
  to suckle thy breast that
  feedeth me

for an unknown little while,
  and then go along my way?
  Oh gentle Earth, may I take
  from thee
the things thou hast to give?
  Thy bountiful hills and
  endless sea:
may I take from them and live
  for a day and yet a day?
  Oh gentle Earth, may I give
  to thee
that others too may share
  a bit of the love thou gavest
  me,
and a bit of thy tender care,
  and thy sunshine, and thy
  rain?
  Oh gentle Earth, may I go
  from thee,
and somehow leave behind
  a message to those who follow
  me,
that others too may find
  in thee that God is God?

Meredith Diane Moll
UNTIL YOU

Would we meet?
  Could we meet?
  In Another time
  Another space;
  Time and space
  Are endless
  When two eyes meet
  And know
  That the long road of
  searching,
  Believing, make believing,
  One loves;
But for one look I knew
I'd never really met at love's
  door,
    BEFORE YOU!

G. H. Roberts
UNTITLED

Silken silhouettes
  on the edges
  of hardwoods,
as the sun dances
  merrily on flowers
  of dogwoods,
filtering to earth
  through conifers
swimming in lilyglades
  waltzing among
  swamp ferns
'til daylight fades . . . .

Roy Windel Lovegrove
VOICE CALLING

There's a tiny voice calling for
  help from inside.
No one sees or hears it.
Yet it is still calling.
The tiny voice is like a baby
  crying.
Crying for he is hurt and lonely.
There's two small windows for
  him to look out and

see the world.
Sometimes he sees things that
  are upsetting.
Sometimes he sees things that
  make him happy.
He cannot get out for there's
  only one door, and it
does not open until death.
It is called (my soul).

Wenda Nemes
MORNING

Whispery, spindly gossamer
Strewn delicately across the
  mossy earth,
Glistening like silver in the
  morning's early light,
Attracting the observer's
  enchanted eye,
Suddenly broken by his
  hasty foot.

Denise Lynn Darby
THE MOUNTAIN AND ME

A beautiful, angry mountain
powerful and grumbling
I am awed.

A river of mud
Thick, flowing, destroying
I am sad.

Beauty and ugliness
Birth and death
Strength and weakness
I am confused.

Lynda A. Lengyel
ELUSIVE

I reached out to grasp
A piece of time, a little thing
It slipped through my fingers
As a butterfly on wing

Return to me in the still, dark
  night
I close my eyes, wishing with
  all my might
Appear before me, Elusive One,
Return before the night is done

Then . . .again you must go Free
Taking with you a part of me
Flow with the wind on high
Go . . . for the Dawn is nigh

Mark R. Streblow
HIDDEN SECRETS

If a man talks to himself
and loves the things he hears
Couldn't the man put this love
to work on others, since he
  knew
of a love to share.

If a man talks to himself, and
  hates the things he hears
But never realized this was deep
  inside.
Couldn't the man put this to
  use
on others without ever realizing
  its
hold, since he knew not of the
  hatred
that possessed him.

Would one call this the darkness
  of his own mind, which in turn
  he
knew little of, to begin with
  His Mind.

Samuel Penny
**"OH YES . . YOU MAY
FORGET!"**

If all those hopes that come
  close to my heart,
If all my dreams break on some
  rock-bound shore,
(For I have been afraid again

to start
Along the road that leads
  perhaps once more
To somber heartbreak e'er I
  reach its end)...
If you forget my life on your
  love feeds....
If you forget me, dear, how
  shall I mend
The anguish of a lonely soul
  that needs
So very, very much the
  happiness...
The love and will and help that
  you possess
And hold for me between your
  fingertips?
If you forget... God grant I'll
  stand the test..
Albeit by the wormwood in
  my breast..
Albeit by the gall upon my lips.

Chris Lee Wright
SILENT CHOIR

Children that were dressed to
  sing
windows stained now broken
unsung marble figurines
gather pious praise in tokens.
No righteously whelped infants
  or bothered orphans
tiptoeing to rise above the
  chanted words
desperate to confess the sins
  of intimate conscience
conjured by the fear of rites
  denied.
For the candled fire that once
  cleansed souls
now ravages the kneeling pews
peeling the altar of watchful
  faces
as gods and truths are tried.

Sherry Dee Brandenburg
ONCE

  Once he was there and
  he cared
But whatever happened to
  those times we shared
There were some good times,
  there were some bad
  Oh how I wish again those
  times we had.

  Once he told me he
  loved me
  But I was a bit to blind to
  see
  Now that he is no longer
  near
I have these words, except
  not to hear.

  Once he was there
  But now he is gone
  I wonder- what did I do
  wrong
  Now- if I could only relive
  that Once.

Peggie Cain-Collis
NO TOMORROWS

I thought there would always
  be a tomorrow;
But one day there wasn't—and
  no more to follow.
I'd give the world for just one
  more good-bye.
A chance to wipe away a tear,
  when you cried.
One more kiss on a soft
  wrinkled cheek;
Or to hold you close—just to
  feel your heart beat.
Just one more whispered "I
  love you";

To be together again—just us
  two.
One day you were here—the
  next gone;
Why did I always think time
  would go on?
Tho I miss you still, Mom, I'm
  no longer sad;
Because I know a better plan,
  God had.

J. Placek Matthews
A WOMAN OF MIGHT

She's the valleys and the
  mountains,
the sparkling sky so blue.
  Crystal waters in the
  fountains,
that flow for me and you.

  She's the peaceful rivers
  flowing,
throughout the lush green land.
  She's the gentle waves a sowing,
pearly shells upon the sand.

  She's the people of the world,
together, and as one.
  She's the stars and stripes
  unfurled,
to show what has been won.

  She's the men, the women, the
  children,
of every color and creed.
  From the rich and the powerful
to the simple and those in need.

  She's the queen of every nation,
and you ask who this might be.
  The lady is none other,
than America the free.

Sunday Smith Huebner
HE

He lives with unicorns, elves
  and four leaf clovers
  and maidens-all-in-a-row,
  an honorary citizen of
  Never-Never Land.
Star-lit nights are his and
  sun-washed days . . . Nepenth.
He must not be hurt!
He baskes in reflected glory
  from others' eyes.
A panther stride, the beauty of
  Adonis,
He has not felt pain so is
  unaware he inflicts it
  while playing
  mumbly-peg with hearts
and . . . He is like the sand-piper
  on the beach,
  running from the waves,
  afraid to get his feet wet.

Brian Lavallee
WOODS

Strolling through the woods
  one day,
Everything seemed to be okay.
The wind whistling through the
  trees,
The leaves floating in the breeze.
A bright sun shining all around
Casting shadows on the ground.
The brooks sing their endless
  song
While the birds sing right along.
Shadows dancing on the ground
As if moving to the sound.
The woods are peaceful, so
  serene,
The air there is so fresh and
  clean.
So many colors to behold,
So many stories left untold.
When you want to get away
Just walk through the woods
  someday.

You'll find them such a happy place,
They'll put a smile upon your face.

Ruby L. Wolfe
COSMIC CREATIVITY

Poems
Of varying brilliance
Or dullness
Cloud the cosmic horizon
Of the literary universe.
Whether judged by standards
Of poignant panache
Or of mediocrity
And pathetic pedantry,
Each syllable represents
The hidden fire
That burns
With varying degrees of hotness
Within all of us!

Catherine M. Hofstetter
JESUS, LOVER OF MY SOUL

"Jesus, Lover of my soul"
Greatest lover ever known
All is well when Thou art nigh
Without Thy love my soul
would die.
None with Thee, Lord, can
compare
Fairest Thou of all the fair
Purest Lily, fragrant Rose
Sweeter flower there's none
that grows.

What a joy to call Thee mine
Blessed Savior, Lord divine
All I need to me Thou art
Take possession of my heart;
Cleanse it from sin's deadly
pleasure,
Impart Thy love, most precious
treasure,
Light of life there shed abroad
Make it wholly Thine, O God.

Rarest Jewel, adorn my hands
Swift they'll move at Thy
commands
Kind and gentle their work will
prove
When inspired by Thy pure love.
Swift my feet Thy ways will
run
From morning dawn till set of
sun
Shod with beauteous heavenly
peace
They'll go for Thee till life
shall cease.

When my journey here is done
Life above for me's begun
There I'll see Thee face to face
Revel in Thy love and grace
Behold Thy beauty, matchless
splendor
Thou my soul's Strength and
Defender
Praise Thee while the ages roll
"Jesus, Lover of my soul."

Terri L. Kozy
THE CLOWN

white—the mask that covers his
face
red—the big round nose,
black—the lines that surround
his eyes
baggy—all his clothes,
sad—the shape drawn round his
mouth
the clown—who no one knows.

Theodore K. White
LISTENING

pardon my intrusion here
may i lend a word to the wise?
or an understanding gesture

like the winking of an eye
i'm hoping you'll consider
sharing a few words with me,
i'll trade ideas any time
just give me a chance to speak
i often wonder 'why is it?'
that no one listens to me,
i'm not trying to push too
hard
there's something i feel you
should see
i don't always know what to
say
and times it's not the thing to
do
but lord knows there comes a
day
when no one listens to you!

Donna Braun
PRAYER OF TRUTH

May the white light of truth
shine upon your soul
May Destiny show you kindness
May the spirit of love set you
free
And your eyes never know of
blindness

May the dreams that you
whisper be heard by the Gods
And a thousand tomorrows of
time fall away
Leaving a new world in place
of the old
And seeing the Sun one more
day

May the sorrow you feel teach
you to grow
May your heart speak of glory
and love
May you show your brother a
kind helping hand
And live with the knowledge
above

May you face all your endings
with thoughts of beginning
May time not catch up with
your heels
'Til the dreams in your head
show you paths you must
tread
And feel what the quiet one
feels

Valerie J. Vance
OF EQUIVOCAL NATURE

Perhaps the author soon
mildews in one's own
mirage
so eloquently spun into hero,
breath blown into shape,
character finding shape in
pursuit
of heroine

The telling of tales cannot
allow for intensity
behind admissions.
Confession can only result in
pointed fingers,
eyebrows raised in judgment of
a concept
so intricate as human energy
Ink dries quickly.
Impossible to capture the
essence
before the poet drowns
in preservation of pretty words.

Jean Larner
UNTITLED

Sleek, I feel the power surge,
Birthing urge
Strong enough to scrutinize
Whatever lies
Beyond this self-created cage

Wherein I circled, senseless rage
Clouded vision, made me see
Iron bars, mistakenly
Perceived, where silken ribbons,
softly streaming,
Lulled the beast, and kept him
dreaming.
Wakened, I reject in shame
Previous accepted game
Of piteous mewling, soft-pad
paws,
Astounded, I regard my claws,
Sheathed so long, now
stretching pride
Of dormant muscles, lengthened
stride
Away from pat-on-head
Play dead.
Scoffing, regal brow I raise,
Rejecting now false words of
praise,
With appetite too large to feed
On sugar cubes to fill your need
Of training me to prance and
cower,
Small rewards to curb my
power.
Listen, never heard before
Glorious, resounding roar
Of lion not afraid to bite,
Choosing path of fight, not
flight,
Hoops to jump through, by-gone
toys,
Guilt and fear now futile ploys,
Bouncing off a toughened hide
Powerless to stop the pride
Of laughing lion, new-born king
A special beauty, wondrous
thing.

Suzanne E. Huff
THE OCEAN

Pounding waves, crashing down,
nothing but water all around.
Clear and cool, like the breeze
above,
full of hate, yet full of love.
It guards the life that lives
beneath,
and hides it all, within its
wreath.
The life that lives within its
walls,
are answering their instinct's
call.
To be the one to survive, at no
cost,
to keep ahead, yet not get lost.
But now, man has defied the
sea,
for it's not quite the way it used
to be.
He's taken lives, both big and
small,
using nets and harpoons, with
no trouble at all.
Taking away the ocean's life,
giving back nothing but strife.
The ocean still lives, but not for
long,
for man doesn't realize, what
he's doing, is wrong.

Sarah H. Overturf
MARK

Thunder on the bridge
The carriage crosses.
The horses' hooves
Pound a sound—
A sound I know
I need not question
For the thunderous beating
comes from horses' hooves

And no man's heart.
Two figures emerge;
They utter fateful words.
A blur is all I see or hear
Of the message they have carried,
So full of fate and fury,
As the hoofbeats drum my ear
With the news that I so fear—
As reality rumbles on.
Thunder on the bridge;
The carriage crosses.
The horses' hooves
Pound out the fateful sound:
My dear friend, Mark, has
drowned.

Emma B. Heiple
FRESH STRAWBERRIES

Luscious, lovely mouth-watering
berries,
Rosy-red and pear-shaped
berries,
Piled high in tantalizing baskets,
Smelling succulent, and sweet
As dripping honey from the
comb.
Quickly stem them, quickly
wash them!
I can't wait to crush them
For my shortcake, for my ice
cream,
For my pie and glossy jellies.
Hurry, now, before I've
sampled
All those luscious, lovely berries!

Curt A. Auzenne
AN INSIDE VIEW

Above the clouds
within your dreams
seek the limit
In the rain
through lifestorms
look within it
Around the sun
between the moon
what a wonder
In the eyes
the conquering glance
from down under
Among the stars
around about
out in nothing
Here on earth
at my birth
I am something

Agnes R. Wendling
LEST WE FORGET

On hallowed ground, where
row on row,
Of sterile, white, unfeeling
stones,
Speak mutely of their sacrifice,
For family, country, and for
the homes
They loved so well.

Black or white, it mattered not,
Shoulder to shoulder, they
stood in strife.
And greater love, hath no man,

Than for his friends, he would
  give his life,
That they might live in
  freedom.
"Oh, God! let us never forget.
Let not their sacrifice be in vain.
Help us to cherish this precious
  gift,
Paid for so dearly, by these
  brave young men,
  This gift of freedom."

Florence T. Hammer
FLORENCE

Florence—city of dreams
Setting of multifarious
  Political intrigue
Your art splendid! The
  Ages unfold
Within your city of
  Old-gold
The muse and poet
Acknowledge you as
  Their home
Your glory? Unsurpassed!
  (excepting for Rome)
World-wearied traveler finds
  Comfort in you
A balm for Earth's
  Sorrows
Your mystique enfolds
  Man in your sphere
And all is contained
  Within your fold
As Medusa's stoney-eyed
  Glance,
In every statue beholds

Maria P. Herndon
UNCONDITIONAL LOVE

How is it that
In love there is so much pain,
So much rain,
So much that maimes, and
Bruises the heart?
We are young when we love,
No matter how old.
Each love is our first, to ever
  last.
We are dreamers, and
As tears stream down our faces,
We don't believe the hurt
That was done to us was done
  at all.
Avenge or forgive?
For we must choose, to let love
  grow
      or die.

Judson A. Kroh
LITTLE GIRL, LITTLE GIRL

I first met her by the shore
Her eyes were blue as the sky,
And sweet as could be.
She sat by me said no more,
There we said a word no bye
But it wasn't right I could see;
What happen to you Little Girl.
This I rightfully don't know
Little Girl, Little Girl beautiful
What happen that stopped that
  glow?
From that sparkling love so
  wonderful
To the disappointment it is
  seem blow
Our love gone to the winds
  seem blow
Little Girl, Little Girl what
  happened?

Lillian Viola Nelson
LATER

A silent rounded mound.
A chilly bed way underground.
A blanket of green grass
And room twist rows for rain

to pass.
A still unbroken sleep.
Myriad hours in which to weep.
That - for each of us does wait,
And if it comes too soon or late
Who shall take the blame.
Or care that each boned plot
Once wore a name?
And those who mutter
Of that Life to be -
They'll sleep down there
In Death with me.

Joe Schrag
ODE TO JACINTA'S DIMPLE

There is a dimple on her face,
Which teases me with its
  deceit;
Just when I think it knows its
  place,
It vanishes like dew in heat.
It leaves no trace of where it's
  been,
And can't be seen without her
  grin.
The trick then is to make her
  smile,
So impishly it peeks anew;
And captivates me all the while
It sparkles, fore it sneaks from
  view;
But all too soon it goes its way;
Nought can I do to make it
  stay.
Her every laugh is my lament,
Despite the pleasures that it
  wields;
For well I know this dainty
  dent,
First boldly shows before it
  yields.
How difficult to be content,
With favors momentarily sent.
Perhaps tis good to see then
  wait;
Perhaps my transient friend
  knows best.
Since constant sight would
  satiate,
It comes and goes at its behest;
Entrances me with mystery,
And makes me cherish when I
  see.

Beatrice I. Gardiner
THE MAN'S GONE WILD

Senile he seems
Yet in his dotage,
His hair gleams
As a silver stream,
The man's gone wild.

A tedious journey
He now makes,
No more he takes,
His mind is like a child's now,
He's gone wild.

Blaming everyone
Swearing for fashion,
He seems a child again
Not a mere lashing,
No not that to change
Because the man's gone wild.

His bed is made of straw
So fragile he is now,
He survives somehow
A glad ending he greets,
A new life, a new goal he meets.

Thomas J. Werner
LA HOBOES PARK

  Just sittin' by the railroad
tracks, saw a train comin'
'round the bend. It was a

movin' on down the line, I just
couldn't see the end. With the
full moon bright, on a cool,
lonely night, the wolves howlin'
in the dark. That's the way our
way of life is, here in La Hoboes
Park.
  A band of bums who will take
what comes from the earth that
God had made. They let things
lie, they live and die, their price
in life they have paid. Now the
train is gone, and soon will
come dawn, and another day
will appear. But the days go by
the same, in the sun or in the
rain, our life in La Hoboes Park.
Our life in La Hoboes Park.

Florence S. Katz
STRANGE INTERVAL

Ghostlike our ship glides amid
  dim islands
From a somber dome no silver
  spears
pierce the smoothbreathing sea
No pale plumes rise softly
a truce from Satan's fires
  banked below
Expectant, we watch and wait
Ours alone this deathly
  shrouded world
In sullen silence they brood,
  hellions unholy-
    Vesuvius - Etna - Stromboli

Ruth Clary Carter
THE STORM

It dashed around the corners;
Like an angry cat it cried.
It tore bare trees with cruel
  claws
While I watched, from inside
The cozy house beside the
  stove
Where it was safe and warm,
The howling anger of the wind
And the violence of the storm.

John T. Hudelson
LOCKED IN BEAUTY

For a moment, locked in
  beauty,
  was all heaven and earth
As the sun lingered low in the
  western sky.
Rains of sunbeams filtered
  through
  the motionless clouds
Showering the earth with a
  mist of
  golden spray.
Silently the rays of light slipped
  beneath the emerald sea
As the edge of night enveloped
  the
  waning hours of day.
The golden orb vanished
  beyond
  the vision of sight;
To rest in sweet repose until
  the break of dawn.

Awakened only by the sound
  of
  nature's clock;
The crowing of a barnyard cock
  on a distant hill.
Slowly on the eastern horizon
  the sun again would rise
Drenched in a raiment of
  misty hues.
Once again high above the
  dew laden earth
The heavens were bathed in a
  moment of beauty,
Surpassed only by the setting
  sun at dusk.

Bill Baker
THE RESONANCE OF LOVE

The resonance of love
  comes
as a saxophone in the night
To the tune of three lighted
  candles
and oyster stew
And eyes that fuse the
first born snow of October

into Pas De Deux

Edward B. Kiker
SLEIGHBELLS

Oh, snow without and snow
  within,
Why won't they let my soul
  roam free?
To walk the hills and woods
  afar is all I want.

The walls with blank and
  staring mein
Hold me confined and keep me
  chained,
And snow without and snow
  within
My guardsmen stay.

And yet, on frosty, silent nights
I hear the sound of sleighbells
  far,
And snow without and snow
  within
Can't matter then.

Daniel Sosa Coronado
EMOTIONAL

Trickling down my face
At a slow-motion pace,
I rain the tears of honesty;
I bleed the tears for you and
  me.
Yet, I am not a running-scared
  criminal,
I am just scarred and wise,
  emotional.

Glistening up my face
In a fast-moving chase,
I shine the laughs of children
  at play;
I stream the laughs for the
  young and gray.
Yet, I am not meaning to be
  comical,
I am just sane and able,
  emotional.

And weaving the two into one
  feature,
Together added like living laces,
God is my greatest teacher,
For love and care are my faces;
Mingled with the warmth of
  my showering sorrows;
Mingled with the joy of my
  coming tomorrows.

Eloisa Ortiz Lopez (Lisa)
PARADISE AND HAPPINESS

Paradise is to see my people,
  freed from bondage
to go and come from and to our

mud-made cottage
Happiness is to find, the once
   a day meal
come back and find, our loved
   ones still here
Happiness, is a shirt on our
   backs, cardboard shoes on our
   feet
or maybe a spoonful of food,
   for our children to eat
Paradise, is a doctor when
   needed, to kill, the pain
kill diseases that have no name
Paradise is, a place to be, with
   no fear of today
to see our children out at play
Paradise and Happiness, our
   country, with no more wars
The Freedom and Peace, we
   all fought for
Happiness is wisdom and
   courage, to kneel and pray
Thanking the Lord, for our
   blessing of today
Paradise; is my country; The
   United States.

Grace Tabone
SO SPECIAL

A special time for you,
   a special place to care for you.
The understanding that you
   have for me,
   the same feeling that we share
   you see.
There's a pressure that you
   release from my heart,
   now making you a special part.
Wondering how true you can
   really be,
   believing you whether or not
   you are you see.
Taking my feelings into
   consideration,
   which no-ones ever done
   before,
that makes me happy and
   makes me feel like more.
Seeming to sentimental to be
   a guy,
   almost makes me want to cry.
A special endurance you make
   me feel,
   a special heart I want to steal.
Theres been so much solitude
   in my existance,
   but you make my world
   warmer and pleasant for
   instance.
People need more self being
   thats very true,
   it would be great if there were
   more people like you.
A special time saved for you,
   a special place to talk to you,
special feelings to share with
   you,
   and it's very special how I
   care for you.

E. M. Crenshaw
SISTER SONGBIRD

Sister songbird, come show me
   the way
   of singing songs this cerulean
   day.
Love my loving thee so long
   and dear;
   help remaining hearts that
   ache so here.
Bring me Beltane on sweetening
   breath

that fights the fear of
   eventide's death
as shreds of sunlight splash thy
   feathers
   in twilight rays as darkness
   gathers.
Hearing thee amid the forest's
   sight
   I must smile and ever wonder
   why
flocks of birds and myriads of
   wings
   live among leaves the
   summertime brings,
and yet thy melodies alone so
   haunt
   the daydreaming things I
   always want.

Patrick Bishop
AFTER

Tenuous is the time
Which spans our days
Undaunted the pace
That marks demise
   but
      has every peak
      a valley wrought
      and spreading tree
      a shaded base?
   or
      does each height
      not brethren bear
      and winter branch
      soft light permit
   i believe
      it is but a breath
      till my hand trembling
      touches another child's
      who touches another
      all running down
      stretching yawning
      once ticking streets still

Jeanne Claytor
ABSENT ARTIST RETURNS

So quickly do you spiders
   seize the day
Stringing strong lace ropes on
   easel legs,
Laying the corpses of your
   victims
In the corners of carefully
   stretched canvas,
Repelling, snatching from thin
   air your fine silk,
Weaving threads into ladders and
   web-traps,
Disguising light-catchers, foils,
   reflectors.
How cunningly clever —
You almost trap and enwrap
   me — standing here,
Fascinated by your art already
   on display
Draped on my easel and this
   unpainted canvas,
Waiting for the stroke of my
   brush!

William Justin Blumenfeld
WATERGATE

These prophets of doom,
   These purveyors of gloom,
Say the world is in a hell of
   a state.
   But I can recall, when the
   clarion call
Of a 'Gus' that predicted the
   fate
   of this world and its lot,
Had got what it got,
   Because it had failed to relate.
He summoned his flock, his
   chicks and his stock.

And together they boarded
   the ark.
They tested the crest, and
   hoped for the best,
   For they, too, were lost to
   the dark.
But lo and behold, of tales
   yet untold,
   A mountain, a haven
   appeared.
This was the way out, without
   any doubt,
   A truly heaven sent rock!
The moral dear reader is hard
   to define,
   Perhaps it comes from on
   high.
For in moments of crisis, we
   scamper to cover and
   we turn to our Lord and we
   cry—
"Where did we waver, where
   did we fall?"
   "Why did it happen to us?"
Alas and alack, for the truth
   will be told,
   Its all a question of fate.
The story of men in high
   places and power—
   The story of Watergate!

Ronald W. Hauser
A BIRD OF PRAYER

         Phoenix
whose heart will raise forth
   dreams
         from your ashes ?
      Faith or magic
   which calls your command
with sword or secret the promise
   kept ?
      Do different dreams
      or hopes renewed
      rise from purging fire ?
   Oh bird of death and life
      what name your nest
      where lies your seed
      in Xanadu or Mordor ?

Sandra R. Dominguez
LOST IN TIME

Lost in time in life I live,
so sad to be alive.
To live today with thought in
   mind
on that I must survive.
My aimless efforts drag me
   down,
so low I cannot see.
I cannot comprehend myself,
or what my life should be.
Intense emotions fill my heart,
sometimes they make me cry.
Frustration builds within my
   mind,
I ask for reasons why?
I search to find the answers
   that
can bring me peace of mind.
I look to those around me,
from their thoughts I hope to
   find.
The answers that I'm searching
   for,
that seem so lost to me.
Why am I here? Why do I live?
What am I meant to be?

Jane Schneider
UNTITLED

Darkness surrounds me
   As I awake at dawn.
The hours go slowly
   But time rolls on.

I sit here and watch
   As time goes by
The times we laughed,
   The times we cried.

Nancy E. Olsan
TANTAMOUNT

Perhaps the time has come to
   dwell
Upon the subjects we know
   well;
To ponder that which is
   decided...
And ask why we must abide it?
Strange, it seems, that all that
   is
Must be as was to make it this.

Amy F. Campbell
TO KEVIN

I never knew my mother's
   parents;
I often wish I had.
They passed away when she
   was young
Before she met my dad.
My father's mother's life was
   brief;
She died at twenty-three.
The name she bore was long
   revered
And handed down to me.
His father, too, had left this
   earth
Before we children came,
And I have often longed to call
A grandma or a grandpa's name.
How much I missed a grandpa's
   lap,
A grandma's gentleness,
And all the little things they do
To make a child feel blest;
A grandpa's pockets filled with
   sweets;
A grandma's cooky jar;
All the little gifts of love;
A ride in Grandpa's car;
A horsey ride on Grandma's
   foot;
A bounce on Grandpa's knee;
Holidays with all their joys;
And birthdays just for me.
But, since you came, I look at
   things
In a rather different way.
I think of them and pay to you
The debt they could not pay.

Jean Tribble
MAN'S HOPE

Behold the star sliding down
   the sky;
   a thing of purity and beauty,
   too soon lost to sight.
Man strives with pathetic
   imitation
   displayed in celebration
   and exploded in frantic
   flight.
Behold the child
   all innocence and trust,
   holding out empty hands
   to life.
What is placed in those eager
   hands;
   is it love and warmth and
   security,
   or is it doubt and fear and
   strife?
Behold the clock
   relentless in it's forward
   march,
   measuring out man's scope.
Impossible to capture the star,
   impossible to stop the clock,
   is not the child man's hope?

Allison E. Brown
THERE'S NOTHING LEFT THAT'S BEAUTIFUL

I saw the wind, I heard the sky,
I sang the river flying by.
I watched the growing of the grass,
I listened to the ants run past.
I smelled the buzzing of the bees,
I touched the wind among the trees.
I loved the way the rabbits flew,
I watched the flowers start anew.

I shuddered as the workmen came
Just playing their destruction game.
The wind was gone, the sky was dark
And on dead trees there was no bark.
The ants were gone, the bee hive chopped,
The flowers died; no rabbits hopped.
The river died; and so the lawn.
The beauty of it all was gone.
And today high-rise apartments
Fill up all those dead compartments.
People wanting homes there flowing;
Trash and filth forever growing.
There's nothing left that's beautiful.
No roaring river, grass to pull.
It's all pollution, trash cans full.
There's nothing left that's beautiful.

Brenda Humphrey
I WILL

I will hold you gently
In hopes I will not break your heart,
I will kiss you softly
In hopes I will not smother you with love,
I will speak to you with kindness
In hopes that bitterness will not surround your mind,
I will touch you freely
In hopes that you will not feel confined,
....I WILL GIVE YOU LOVE....

Ann Gettys Cunningham
SOMNOLENCE OF AUTUMN

The clustered yucca plant bows
Her stems in silent prayer.
White dune primroses and yellow
Desert flowers will soon
Vanish from sandy expanses.
Open woods, fields and prairies
Show adornment of the goldenrod, the ocotillo.
Rock plants grace barren areas
Secluded on mountain tops.
Sepals of the anemone will clasp
Her gates in sleep, while
Chrysanthemums will burst forth in
Colors of the rainbow.
Winds will lift petals from
Plants searching for winter.
Mountainsides display the colors
From the Indian Paintbrush as
Nature prepares for the emergence

Of another season.
Indian summer will soon pass
Beyond the echoes of distance, of ageless time.
Arrays will soon disappear,
Being replaced by mossy woods
And barren slopes,
Awaiting another time, another season.

Kathy Bushnell
DREAM

The rainy days are moody days
When one should take the time to gaze.
The thoughts that grow may be heavy and blue
As things from the heart come flowing through.
To be alone and to think things out
Helps goals in life exist without doubt.
A dream is good to build hopes to,
Without such dreams what would one do?
When the rain persists and dreams seem lost,
Look to the heart at whatever cost.

Connie M. Reese
EARLY MOUNTAIN MORNING

I wake up in the morning,
The sun is in my eyes,
It warms the bed beside me
Where once you used to lie.

I look out my window,
The mountains lie ahead,
I recall the days I'd run
Where pine boughs made my bed.

Still the memories hurt me
When we said goodbye;
This early mountain morning is
Enough to make me smile.

Her silent strength has taught me
Not to fear the shifting sands,
'Cause I can lift my eyes to her
And she will understand.

The river runs so deep and cold,
Weaving through the pines,
This early mountain morning is
Enough to make me smile.

Elaine M. Rieger
K-9 FRIEND

Name: Mye Tye
        Command Dog
"Sit!" "Down!" "Stay!"
All words which I obey.
"Attack!" is one held in reserve.
I am a Dobbie - "mean dog"
A title I don't deserve!
Faithful, sweet and full of love
Gentle as a morning dove-
That's what I am.
But with me-
Protecting my family is not a game!
        Command Dog,
Mye Tye, is my name.

Linda R. Szczepanski
FRIENDS

Bring me your friendship, I'll make you feel at home
Only feeling cared for and never feeling alone
Bring me your Love, I'll show you the way

Only finding happiness in each and every day.
Sometimes being sad but only sad together
Then there would be less sadness if we had each other.
Being your friend and being your lover
I feel so strongly I want no other
You must believe me you know it's true
I feel so much Love and it's all for you.

Marya Dalton
TEDDY BEAR

A cuddly toy hugged each night,
A childish whispered prayer,
God Bless Mom and Dad,
And my Teddy Bear.
He gave comfort when I cried,
He seemed so much alive,
It was sad that when I grew up,
I put my Teddy Bear aside.
At times tears wet my pillow,
When I feel so all alone,
And wish that I still had,
The Teddy Bear I used to own.

Estel Mullinax Dodd
VORTEX

Faster than I can catch
  my breath, crueler than
  thorns which claw and
    tear and separate
  life's flowing stream
    from its safe
    protective
      banks
    I am caught
  in the whirling, turning,
churning void created by
life's mistakes and hurled
beyond the reaches of love and
reason into a certain madness which
crushes the spirit, bruises the soul,
  and leaves the body helpless
    to escape, a prisoner of its
    own mortal attempts
    to glimpse a bit of
      Heaven
      here on earth.
    I cannot see the
  light beyond, and the
  strength to struggle upward
fails me as I flounder in
  the constant, never ending
    storms of life
      that beat
        me
        down.

Elsie Thornton
MY CHRISTMAS PRAYER

Dear Lord, the bells on Christmas morn
Proclaim that mortal Christ was born
Thy Son, Who lived and died that we
Through Him may live eternally.
In His Name, Lord, I humbly pray
That Thou wilt guide us in Thy Way:
Unite us, Lord, in dedication
To Thy Word; Make strong our Nation
In love for Him, Thy Beloved Son,
In faith that Victory be won.
Let us be done with hate, distrust,

With envy, greed, with fear and lust:
Teach us the way of Right and Good,
Of Truth and Love and Brotherhood.
Teach us compassion, Lord, I pray,
With mercy and charity our way.
On this, the Holiest of Days,
May our Nation, as one voice, in praise
Rejoice in spiritual re-birth
Of PEACE to come to all the Earth.

Timothy Lee Hubbard
MEDITATION ON THE MOUNTAIN

Upon this lonely mountain peak
With no one else around,
I look to find a truth I seek;
The winds the only sound.
It strikes my face a chilling blow
And ruffles through my hair.
I look afar and hope to know;
I breathe the clear pure air.

I look upon God's majesty
And awe grows in my heart.
I pray to God that I may see
The seeds of wisdom start.

A wondrous peace comes over me
And all unplain is clear.
A second is eternity
As my God draws near.

I see the Lord before me
In mountains and in clouds.
Earth and sky and shining sea
No longer hide in shrouds.

My soul, reaching, is uplifted;
Angelic form I trod.
In my fortune heaven gifted
I touch the face of God.

Michelle A. Coder
MIND'S CHILD

Mind's child
You live among my older thoughts
Ride the winds of my imagining
Sit upon the golden meadow of my dreams
Linger quietly in bright corners

Small and subtle
You cling to my every thought
Move my being to wiser truths
Confound me with the significance of simplicity
Dwell in joyful wonder

Cindy Patton
THE FAMILY CREED

Families are a wonderous thing
They grow throughout the years
A family's made of joy and love
And laughter with the tears

The love grows deep within our hearts
For each other, when we must part
But when we're all together you see
There is no stronger bond for me

We talk about the frustrations of life
And sometimes yes, my Brother's wife
But all and still were a family

First and always this must be!
We stick together in all things
Through good times and the
bad
We pray to God and thank him
For the joys on earth we've had
I think it would be awfully sad
Not to have known this love
we've had
The warmth of our mother, and
her gentle touch
Knowing each of us meant so
much
So Thank you God for families
And all the ties that bind
For the joys and Blessings
That because of you are mine

Lynn Costa
HERE I ARE

Depressed and down; I'm in a
muddle,
This boring job I'd like to
scuddle.
Oh, it's not the gig's so bad ya'
know,
It's simply not where I want to
go.
I like to talk, I like to dream,
Engrossed in sharing all good
things.
To write and tell of all my
thoughts,
Perhaps broaden others insight
to their lots.
To spin a tale of color and life,
Express life's ecstasy, in spite
of it's strife.
Paint the pictures in words
alive,
Stir emotions, warm the soul,
living revive.
Reborn a soul of being's
wonderness,
Instill within, living for life's
zest.
These things I am, and shall
always be,
A prophet, a storyteller, a
poet..........ME!

Cynthia A. Payne
ANGER

Anger is a weakness that lives
In the human race.
Anger makes reality hard to
face.
I have often asked myself,
"Where did I go wrong, why
does
This anger grow so strong?
Was it the friend who told me
A lie or was it the boy
Who made me cry?"
But that was yesterday and
Today I can honestly say,
"Anger, anger you need not
stay
For I am strong this day."

Ann Pedigo
GLORIOUS COLORADO

Colorado stands up to a mile
high
her beauty reaches out up to
the sky.
Spring marches in to start the
show
My! what beauty, our Lord
doth sow.
With tall trees so green, what
a beautiful scene,
as though Gods painting on a
very large screen.
Summer brings colors of
flowers so bright,

you can almost see them by
the stars at night.
All this and more is waiting
for you,
with streams making a
fishermans dream come true.
Now autumn is here with a
gentle breeze
turning the aspen to red and
gold leaves.
Soon winters snow will glisten
our peaks,
skiers will have fun and rosy
cheeks.
Only in Colorado do we find
so much
where everything has been blest
by that magic touch.

Margarett Goza White
OVER MY CUP OF TEA

Due to an illness I did not
foresee
I sat wondering, pondering and
guessing
What my lifestyle would be.
I thought, perhaps, the illness
might be a blessing
So I looked up and I could see
God smiling at me
Over my cup of tea.
The words of a song
Came across my mind
As I earnestly tried a new
lifestyle
to find-
The song said, "His eye is on
the
sparrow
And I know He watches me."
So I looked up and I could see
God smiling at me
Over my cup of tea.
I shall not worry about my life
For God will help me plan,
Guiding me daily with His
loving care
To do the best that I can-
Then when my regular life
Commences again to be,
I shall look up and I shall see
God smiling at me
Over my cup of tea.

Rose Marie (Fiske) Williamson
LOVE LOST?

Love is a word-
Which has no description.
You can't see it;
    or smell it;
    or taste it;
    or touch it;
Yet sometimes you feel
It - a painful deception!

Jacob VanWyk
MOTHER'S DAY

This is to the mothers of the
days gone past.
They gave us wisdom that will
last and last.
They applied the board of
education to the seat
of knowledge,
And gave us wisdom you can't
get in any college.
Those same dear hands, without
discretion,
Brought us through the great
depression.
They gave up their sons by the
score
When our country was in the
last big war.
We came to them with our hurts

and care,
And with a tender kiss the
hurts were no longer there.
We still need them for our
future is gained from
the past.
Here's to the mothers of the
present,
With their smiles so sweet and
pleasant,
Who have the task to guide
this nation
In this fast world of this now
generation.
To the mothers yet to be,
They will bring in a new
generation
To watch over all of God's
creation.
They are the hope of the
future and glory of the past.
God will bless them and we do
too,
For without them what would
we ever do!

Gladys Reusser
GLOW-RAY

Oh, I rejoice in it! living with
Thee,
    God of the universe, lord of
    the
    bee.
Maker of mountains, keep
loving me.
Oh, I rejoice in it, breathing
thy air;
    The fresh sun is rising, gone
    every
    care.
The whole world is singing,
"God's
everywhere!"
Oh, I rejoice in it! Walking
with Thee,
    Over the hills down the valley,
Life is so radiant, life is so free.
Oh, I rejoice in it! Working
with Thee,
    Alert to Your message,
    listening how
To build Your heaven here and
now.
Oh, I rejoice in it! Ever to be
living
    in Glow-Ray,
    Living with Thee, Lord of
    tomorrow, keep loving me.

Maurice Barrow
GOD'S HIDDEN BEAUTY

Today I saw a lovely rose,
smelled the fragrance in the
air,
A thorn so sharp seemed out
of place on anything so fair.
I touched the rose that bore
the thorn, and the meaning
was
so clear,
I knew that God had sent a
message he meant for me to
hear.
All the beauty of the world
must have a hidden thorn,
That starts to grow and multiply
the day a man is born.
There has to be a little "bad"
to compensate the "good",
The trick is how to overcome it,
and find the beauty where
you should.
To see and hear these things of
beauty, is a gift "God" gave
to me,
I know there's beauty all around

us if we take the time to see.
I always seem to see a rainbow
when there isn't any rain,
And to me the grasses growing,
are as fields of golden grain.
Though long ago and most
forgotten, a song I seem to
hear,
All the words I can't remember,
but the music is so clear.
I wish that I could write the
lyrics to the songs the Angels
sing,
As they gather close to Jesus,
while the bells of Heaven ring.
If you just look you'll find the
beauty, among the thorns the
roses share,
God doesn't always make it
easy, but He knows that it is
there.

Valeria Jean Jones
ROOMS

Rooms for the mind is like
aspirin for the head. Rooms
close and open, some of them
stay open for someone to
enter my fantasy.
Echoes of my mind of
scattered
thoughts seem like doorknobs
of subtle disasters throughout
my life is the coldness I feel
when I enter.
Strangers come to sit, some
stay,
some just utter pure silence
throughout the rooms. At
times I
wonder where will my rooms
close
for good in my fantasy.
Beggars enter to visit for one
penny
just to say they came. Men
enter
to capture a virgin and take her
off in paradise.
My fantasy is for the rooms,
but no
echoes, strangers, beggars will
enter
tomorrow for the virgin has
turned
into a hard lady with no
concern for
men anymore.

Scotty M. Zollars
A LOVE SONNET

An ode to my love,
A gift from above,
Who came to me when I was
down
And has left me not the same.
A sonnet to the dearest girl,
A more priceless gift than a
pearl,
The apple of my eye,
The most beautiful cloud in
the sky.

This to my love,
The gift from above,
The apple of my eye,
The most beautiful cloud in
   the sky-
This my confession of love.

Lorraine Hicks
BON VOYAGE

The world seemed silent,
the soul was tranquilized
as life sank in slumber.

Surgeons instruments
   penetrated,
sutures walked over the body,
hell held fast.

Inward a voice cried, "Lord."
His touch was received
and the body rested in grace.

The soul was delivered,
hell parted company
as death marched away.

Marvie Toma
**DANCE WHILE LIFE'S
PENDULUM SWINGS
FORTH AND BACK**

Dance while life's pendulum
   swings forth and back.
A funeral dirge need not fill
   one with dread,
Ignore time's metronome as it
   keeps track.

Innocent children, with a
   guileless knack,
So unconcerned about pitfalls
   ahead,
Dance while life's pendulum
   swings forth and back.

Teen-agers, with their devotion
   to pack,
Tripping over stepping stones
   where they're led,
Ignore time's metronome as it
   keeps track.

The minutes, made up of
   seconds that stack
One on another till the hours
   have fled
Dance while life's pendulum
   swings forth and back.

Days, rushing by with a
   clickety-clack,
Making music to stir the
   plodding tread,
Ignore time's metronome as it
   keeps track.

Age need not bog down nor
   feel a lack
But draw on the melody of
   youth's thread
To dance while life's pendulum
   swings forth and back
And ignore time's metronome
   as it keeps track.

Treva Kay Sherman
THE SEA GULL

Over across the ocean
Down by the sea,
Are little plants and animals
Alive and free, like me.

I am a sea gull
Alive and free,
Drifting on the warm gentle
   breeze
By the sea.

I was born by the waves,
On a ships hull
Nicknamed the Sea's Caves,
In a huge storage stall.

My life is beautiful,
Wonderful, and free,
I love the oceans, the beaches,
   and the seas,

Because they are my home,
And my home is definitely me!!

Esta Keeney
OREGON

We came to Oregon in fifty-one,
   Our
   girls were small and we had
   fun.
When we left Colorado there
   were no
   snow, the ground was bare,
   but we
   had to go.
As we traveled we ran into rain.
We went across deserts for mies
   miles and
   miles, All we seen was tumble
   weeds in piles.
When we got to Bend we
   decided to
   sleep. We layed down, we
   couldn't rest.
Now was to be our biggest test.
   We
   started to drive but wouldn't
   you
   know first thing we ran in
   snow, it
   was snowing so hard you
   couldn't see.
A snow plow was coming, not
   one but
   three.
As we crawled along an inch at
   a time
   now my life wasn't worth a
   dime.
We traveled along, we seen
   a light
Sweet Home was a beautiful
   sight.
Five hours it had taken to travel
seventy miles.
   To go through snow pile after
   pile.
We were tired and weary, we
   had to
   rest.
Now was to be our second test.
A whistle blew and to our
   surprise in
   twelve more feet we wouldn't
   be
   alive.
   A train came by to wake us up.
Now it was time to travel on
   two
   hundred miles to get on home.
As we traveled on down through
   wind
   and rain.
   Down the coast it was a pain,
   the
   road was crooked, it was hard
   to
   see.
The water was muddy as it could
   be, but
   what was the most surprising
   to see
   green grass and apples all a
   around.
Just before we entered town.

You know why Coquille, Oregon
   is
   special to me.
All you had to do was look and
   see
   She gave my son to me.

Sarasu Raghavan
GRAND ILLUSIONS

If letting go is such pain,
Then possession should be no
   joy;
And even though we love in
   vain,
Knowing well that life is but a
   fragile toy;
Yet reluctant to relinquish that
   we hold dear,
In blissful ignorance thinking
   it would last;
Seeing what we want to see,
   hearing what we want to hear.
Future wrapped in glorious
   hope. . . .
Alas! neither sense nor will to
   learn from the past.

Michael Mannino
A NEW DAY

The darkness of night soon
   to pass, morning cometh to
break the stillness of night
   that passed without thoughts.

As I awaken I see the Light
of day, and I give thanks
to the Lord for He giveth
   a new Day.

Marion Koodlach
WINDSONG

Death is a dark pine. Hear her
   windsong:
Ants and man, wander your
   trails
Through sycamore leaves and
   valleys of fern,
Find your way to my granite
   anchored roots
And cradle against me.

Pillar on the vista, earth-
   mountain behind,
I stand on the edge of space.
Eagles soar below, eternity
   above.
Soft my song, no need to
   fear...come now gently,
Cradle against me.

Benedict Michael Bommarito
**A CHRISTMAS WISH
AND PRAYER**

'Twas the year before Christmas,
   And o'er Earth's expanse
Not a soldier did march,
   Not a treaty had crumbled.
No slayings in cities,
   No hatred toward neighbors
Disheartened the Faithful
   In prayer at the Crib.

For twelve months, then, each
   year
   Let the joy and the peace
And the thrill shining forth
   From yon Baby—wee Christ!—
And His Mass e'er proclaim
   Man's acceptance of Love,
At long last . . . at long last.
   Grant us Christmas, sweet
   Lord,
Every day of the year!

Kay M. Murray
THE MULTITUDES

Coming and going,
   they pass.
Each his own way heads
   in a conglomerous mass
   to maybe who knows where.

Materials incongruous,
   all forgetting today.
No reflecting on past. What
   wastefulness!
Time spending on only future.
   Grab it — Quick!

Nancy Draper
THE POET

   the ink flows
      the beauty of word
and feeling form on paper
   the contrasting black and
      white
reality versing fantasy
   coming together and then
separating once again

Ellie Connelly
A CHRISTMAS SCENE

Thanksgiving not yet o'er
And Christmas decors in the
   stores,
Sparkling lights and shiny
   trimmings,
On the streets and mall poles;
The news is out . . . .
Ole Saint Nick's in town.
Children being their best,
To bring not a frown.
Christmas catalogs are scanned
And coupons are clipped and
   saved.
Lists of gifts and cards,
Being carefully made.
Quick meals are in the oven,
Mother's been out shopping.
Bags with bows, gifts
And wraps are brought into
   homes,
Shelves are becoming
   mysterious domes.
While down by the roadside,
Are sales of very dear trees.
Sweet smells, of cookies and
   cakes,
And maybe candies too,
In the air ride.
We trim the tree and carols
   sing;
Most have the Christmas Spirit.
Then, there are stockings to be
   stuffed,
With fruits, nuts, and little
   toys.
But the manger scene
   portraying
Jesus' historical birth,
Is the grandest scene of them
   all.

Michaela Ann Charron
APOCALYPSE

The songs of yesterday come
   to pass:
The restless movement, class
   to class;
The ceaseless din, the sobbing
   night
In condemnation of its plight;
And Earth, its garments
   burned away,
Ashamed and naked, pale and
   grey.
The game is over, the last card
   dealt;
What mankind has done unto
   himself...

Bessie Howson Cantwell
GETHSEMANE

I walked in the garden at
   eventide
With thoughts of the long ago;
I lingered there in quietness
More fully Your love to know.
In anguish I saw you praying
   there
With pleas to the Father above;

What sacrifice You made that
day
Because of Your wondrous
love.
In sadness I'm thinking of
Calvary
And the cruel cross You bore;
You carried all my sins that day
And my crown of thorns You
wore.
Guiltless You trod up Calvary's
hill
And Your hands were pierced
there, by me;
You emptied self of all but
love
When You died on Calvary.

Joanne Moore
MAGNITUDE OF LIVING

The Magnitude of living swells
in my heart today.
If i forget to be gratefull humble
me in some small way.

The sky is a masterpiece of blue
engulfing the earth below.
The sun is warm and the air is
filled with a yesterdays after
glow.

All about me I feel peace and
Love for all mankind.
Let me bask in the beauty of
today
and store it in my mind.

For future days when I find it
hard
to be gratefull just for living
Lock the love within my heart,
per
chance for future giving.

Susan D. DeMorrow
WE WHO CRY

We who cry in the darkness,
like a wounded animal.
We who search for love, like a
starving animal
searching for a small morsel
of food.
We, the little children grown old
before our time.
As the Lord said, "Suffer the
little children,"
so have we suffered.
What great sin have we
committed?
Have we so grievously wronged
that the bruises
we bear must last an eternity?
We who cry through the dark,
lonely nights,
Long after we cease to be
children.
We who have no happy
memories of childhood,
only the bitter sting of
anguish.
We who cry in the darkness
are truly wounded animals.

Judy Allene Wilson
OCEAN OF LOVE

Love is like the rising tide
Against the shores of your
heart it collides
Fast then slow the waves will
glide
The love once cherished now
denied.

Once there was a blazing fire
inside.
Making you feel abundantly
alive,
Feeling as though you would
never die,
And now on the verge of

suicide.
It's this kind of love I am told,
Is bad to burden on your soul,
Making your heart extremely
cold,
And it does this I know.

Although this feeling is hard
to hide,
You must at least begin to try,
And now with change of heart
inside,
A brand new love will soon
arrive.

Then here again like the rising
tide,
Those waves that crashed will
again collide,
Upon your mind like a mad bee
in a burning hive,
The guilt and sadness will
subside.

And when it is time for your
life to unfold,
You will remember what it was
you were told,
And then you will realize what
decayed your soul.

Louise B. W. Woeppel
**CHILDREN THE
VULNERABLE**

O unborn child,
Yet undefiled,
Growing beneath your
mother's heart.
The world outside
Is wild and wide.
How will you fare at your
start?

O infant child,
So meek and mild,
Evil may shadow your path.
And as you grow,
How do you know
What causes a parent's wrath?

O little child,
By hate beguiled,
How can you escape your foe?
When no blood brother,
Or loving other,
Can save you from pain and
woe?

O growing child,
By crime defiled,
May the Lord reach a
sheltering arm,
When no one shares,
And no one cares
Who can protect you from rage
and harm?

O battered child,
Unreconciled
To society's blindness and sin.
May warmth and love,
Both here and above,
Protect you and help you to
win!

Elizabeth M. Pucciarelli
THE COVENANT

If I'm not aware of me
How can I share me with you
I must taste the joy of Life
I must feel the warm soft
odors of the woods at
daybreak
I must tremble beneath the
incense laden
caresses of a summer breeze
I must awake and feel God's
love alive inside me
Then I can offer you me

I will bathe in cool fresh
spring rain
and steal the rythmns from the

moon
and when I've battled snow
and ice,
and felt my blood grow warm
and when I've held a tiny child
trembling in my awe
Then everything I've ever done
or ever hope to do
Will become a covenant I hope
to share with you
The price is high
The risk is great
For if I share myself with you
Then you must then share you

Iris Whitmer Mog
FATE

Fate's ugly arms may reach out
and cast it's
spell upon our lives in it's path—
Or it's long treacherous fingers
may grasp to
the very depths of each heart;
claiming each
spark of life and tearing it to
shreds with
it's rath—
Fate entices our lives encircling
us with
everlasting love or hate; piercing
our souls
in it's after-math—
It's very destiny may make one
happy or sad,
for Fate is what every being
hath—

William H. Potts
I AM WOMAN...

...The frustrations I feel,
So oft times hard to suppress,
I discover are released
By crying.

The loneliness I feel,
So oft times depressing,
I discover is released
By sharing.

The anger I feel,
So oft times blinding,
I discover is released
By loving.

The separation I feel,
So oft times from mankind,
I discover is released
By caring.

The emotions I feel,
So oft times missing,
I discover are released
By me...

    ... I AM MAN

Barbara J. Smith
SOMEDAY

Someday I'll walk serene and
quiet in an ocean rimmed
and sun filled place
Where Nature's music fills the
air and the wind softly
blows upon my face.
I'll see blue skies and gold
flecked sands and smell

fragrant blossoms everywhere.
There'll be enchantment, joy
and peace with fulfillment
and love for all to share.
Yes, I'll see this place, perhaps
not soon, mayhap in a
dream or within someone
for whom I care.
It matters not just how or when
Just important in living to
know it's there.

Deborah Herron Fullarton
DESTINY

Life is but a mystery
unsolved in many ways,
Man's restless soul searches
with each passing day,
To find out where he's
"coming from"
and where he's "going to",
But never being certain
if what he's found is "truth".
Now every man in his time
shall solve life's mystery,
Too late to pass his knowledge
on
about his destiny!

Randy R. Scheil
SINCERITY

I say to you that I do love you.
But you say that you do not
believe me.
And that you can not believe
me,
when I say this to you with ice
cream
on my face.
Because it is not sincere.
Tell me what it means to be
sincere?
Is it taking the time to make
sure that my
face is clean before I speak to
you?
Or is it speaking what I feel as
I feel it,
even with melted ice cream
running down my chin.

Karl Lamont Krause
LIES

If you're looking for truth, in
words that were spread,
I'll tell you now that it never
was said!
If you look to yourself you'll
be able to see;
That you can shelf all of these
lies,
That have been spreading like
so many flies,
So come on now people and
open your eyes
And soon you'll be wise to the
lies that have spread,
I'm hoping you will or soon we
all will be dead!
For the truth it is escaping us!

Melvin LeRoi
MORNINGS

Shhh. Don't say anything.
Just let me look at you
In the morning sunlight with
Your hair all mussed, and
No makeup to cover your
beauty.
Your eyes are speaking softly,
And your warm body is
inviting;
But I'm too much in love to
even
Breathe as you touch me. Now,
I know why God made the
morning.

Kyle J. Tabenske
TOGETHER, YOU AND I

Together,
  We took a day
  And filled it with a song.
Together,
  We wrapped it in a rainbow
  and tied it tight.
Together,
  You and I
  Had special times.

William Stanton
THOU FUTURE'S DUST

Free to choose, thou chose to
  die,
Omnipotence would'st thou
  deny?
Thy Creator filled thy mind,
Ne'er an answer will thou find,
Time indeed shall conquer thee,
Knowledge cannot set thee free.
Life thats wrought from pangs
  of lust;
Born to death, thou future's
  dust!
Stumble on to find thy way,
Child of strength for just a day,
Snatch thy moment, hold it
  fast;
Even now the morrows past,
Be thee king or beggar low,
Do not let thy moment go.

Janet Linda Fox-Dion
CATACLYSMIC EVENT

I feel like I am on fire.
Like a panorama of a volcanic
  slope.
Like a valley of a thousand
  separate smokes,
Rising from all those steaming
  vents,
Escaping upward,
Releasing all the pressure,
Held in, for what seemed like
  forever.
The lava flows to the open sea,
Spreads forth deep and wide.

And now there is a place inside,
That once did not exist in me.

Elva E. Howell
A TRIBUTE TO FANNY CROSBY

A noble lady of great worth
To all man-kind was she,
Her sacred words in hymns we
  love
Will live eternally.
She could not see the crimson
  flower,
Nor see the sky of blue,
And yet she lived a thankful
  life,
And to her Lord was true.
God gave her vision of great
  depth
Beyond this world to see,
Where He prepared a place for
  her
To live eternally.

Martha Johnson
DILEMMA OF A WORM

God why did you let it rain last
  night?
I am in an awful plight
My home is gone
My lover is as dead as a stone.
The earth is wet and cold
My joints are so stiff and cold —
God Help me to find a new home
  quick,
Or I will be gone
Dead as a stone.

Fawn Cockrum
BLACK SHEEP

Today I found you really love
  me.
I fell myself to shame.
I was mad at you for no reason.
I myself am to blame.
All these years you tried and
  tried
to mold me toward the good,
but I fell the other way-
the black sheep of the brood.
Now I realize your cause
of doing what you do.
I know not why I closed my
  eyes,
and away from you I grew.
I now take myself from all-
My black wool turned to white.
No more worries for you to
  take,
as I fall freely to the night.

E. Lorraine Mote
I TALKED TO GOD

In a lovely, quiet place-
seeking Heaven-my upturned
  face,
I talked to God right out loud
about the peace that I had
  found
By letting go and letting Him
  guide the way that I had been,
In my humbleness- I spoke-
how He'd freed me of my
  yoke,
How He'd taken all my grief-
now my soul knows relief.
Then I thanked Him for His
  Son,
no greater love had anyone
Who gave His life upon the
  cross-
to save mankind from sin
  and loss.

Lucille Angel
FINDING A FRIEND

In my youth I wanted a friend.
I searched for him to the bitter
  end.
Friends I found were like a
  dime:
In hard times slipping from me
  and mine.
"One true friend, please, will
  you send.
With such a friend my heart
  would mend.
Let my youth go as youth must
  flow,
But leave a friend, someone to
  know."
Finally, I've found that friend.
Not one but three, and, yes,
  they're kin.
A real goldmine with them I
  find:
Me, myself and I going through
  time.
A verse we rhyme, not always
  so fine,

Painting in time we hope to
  refine,
And once in awhile we write a
  word,
That really seems to leave the
  herd.
In finding a friend you needn't
  go far.
Just look within for your
  heart's desire.
All that you need is there to fire.
Light the flame, and you'll
  never tire.
If with willing hands you mold
  your clay,
All that you sow will make
  golden hay.
Know yourself well, forgive
  what you're not,
And make the most of all
  you've got.

Tania Cherie Ansley
SUDDEN MENTOR DEATH

And here I sit,
  Awaiting dismal genius to
  claim
    My soul,
  And morbid fantasy to wile
  away
    My hours.
  Absorbing electrons from
  yesterday's
    Atmosphere.
  I am but a selfish ghoul,
    Abusing other's powers,
  To wipe my window clear.
But didn't a bit,
  Of your soul slip into my own
  when death
    Begat your brilliance?
  Or am I just a harlequin
  clothed in
    Burning fuselage?
  Oblation admist carnage, still
  grasping
    Your last breath,
  Attempting to buy resilience
  For the price of a mirage.
  To evade the reality,
  The ultimate finality-
    Of Sudden Mentor Death

Darlene C. Waller
ESCAPE

Escape to a place.
Smiles come to his face,
and never he sees,
a nude bodies trace,
only a nightgown I ware,
made of satin and lace.

He laughs at my shyness,
my childish haste,
has we lay on the couch,
in each others embrace.

What a wonderful place,
the couch of escape,
There,
Often we make love,
the next day we awake.

The way that I feel,
one way I escape.

Randy Orser
WITHOUT HER BY MY SIDE

A second without a moment
  Is this loss I feel
Without her by my side
  Like an ocean without a tide.

  Like a bird
    Without a song to sing
  I feel like a bell
    That cannot ring.

    Like a flower without pollen

Since our love has fallen
Like a forest without trees
A day without a breeze.

  Like a wood without a grain
  I can feel the pain
  Like that of a draught
  Without any rain.

    A nite without stars
    My heart bears the scars
  Without her by my side
  I'm an ocean without a
  tide.

      Like a brook
      Without a ripple
    The tears
    Of my heart trickle.

      For I'm a sunset
      without my horizon
        So very alone and
        lost at nite
      For my woman's gone
      And my heart's no
        where to light.

Lynn Ann Kaiser
THE LONGEST REACH

Out stretching my hand
it will go no further;
my socket feels pangs of pain;
my shoulder muscles are
  working hard.

Your finger tips
are so close,
too close to stop trying;
a little more,
and we shall be one unit.

But our arms grow weary;
we must wipe the sweat from
  our brows.
We have pained; we have tried;
We have failed!
Did we try hard enough?
Should we try again?

We lost the feeling:
the moment of truth
through one touch, one grasp!
Shall it ever be our
to try again?

Cindy White Peek
TO A FRIEND

Seasons come and go
and so do people,
New friends are made
old memories put away,
but time keeps passing...
Yet one remembers those
  friends;
The good and bad times shared,
the laughs, the frequent talks,
the rewarding experiences;
Yet time keeps passing...
I look back at old friends
who are more than friends,
Realizing that friendships are
  beautiful,
Like a flower.
Like you.

Susan St.Peter
WHERE DO THE YEARS GO

I remember walking with mama
Hand in hand,
Through the park
And to the ice cream stand
Lollipops, picnics on the grass
Or taking in a movie show.
Where do the years go?
Where do they go?

I remember being a mama
Walking hand in hand,
With my little boys
To the baseball stand,
Playing ball, fixing skinned

knees
Or listening to little stories.
Where do the years go?
Where do they go?

Now I'm a grandma
Walking hand in hand,
With my eldest son
Over unfamiliar land,
In a yard sits a house
With a large white sign,
Saying, "Home for the Aged"
And I gesture no!
Where do the years go?
Where do they go?

With a broken heart
And tear in my eye,
I look up at my son
And ask him why?
And get no reply!
Where do the years go?
Where do they go?

Anne T. Hickey
HIM

Away he goes to a foreign land
To fight for me and his fellow
man.
Respect and honor are what he
believes
I'm all alone - for now he leaves.

Hurting others by leaving them
One thing he knows is we all
love him.
I will remember our days
together
Respect and Love live on
forever.

Some day we'll never be apart
My love remains within my
heart.
My life exists with hurt and
pain
My love is true and will remain -
As long as there is you - Mike.

Maxine Brittain Stalcup
THE REAL NEPHEWS OF UNCLE SAM

The great lanky American
giant has awakened
to meet with vigor
the decade of the Eighties,
aroused and ready to tackle
complications
and choose his honorable place
among nations!

He will stand strong again for
truth and right!
The real nephews of Uncle
Sam,
the patriotic and honest working
class,
are ready to stand up and be
counted.

They are tired of being used
and abused
then forced to pay the bill.
They are finished paying the
lazy not to work.
They are finished paying for
bribery and graft.
They are finished
trying to feed and arm the
world.
There is much more as you will
soon know!

The real nephews of Uncle Sam
are going after solar energy,
wind and water power,
and fuels made from home
grown plants.
They aim to feed their families
wholesome natural food again.
They aim to put God and the

American family
back in control of the land
they made so great!

America must be great
but not at sacrifice to
enslavement and abuse.
America must be healthy
but not through misused HEW
and FDA programs.
America must be strong
but not at sacrifice of faith,
hope and charity!

Look out, Mister Politician!
The real nephews of Uncle Sam
the working patriots,
are on the move and aim to
right your wrongs!
America pivots
In the "Decade of the Eighties!"

Kathleen Cross
PUBLISHER'S PROOFREADER

The job I have from 9 to 5
isn't that at all.
In at 8:00, out at 6:00, others
have gone, but I stay on.
When I'm paid it barely covers
my expenses,
    but when a mistake is made
    they shout from
    their fences: You're to
blame! You're to blame!
Errors caught in proofing do
not count at all.
    What a shame! What a shame!
Something missed, the reader
points at me,
    I get caught.
I should've avoided it, as likely
as not.
We're not here to be friends,
feelings quickly
    turn to wrath.
Distance is the need, friendship
not the seed.
Love, hate, like, dislike, joy,
despair,
    changing feelings live in there.

Ruth C. Peppler
SOFTLY AT SUNRISE

Softly at sunrise,
When the world lies asleep;
With your warm arms around
me,
Your slumber still deep;
And your head on my breast,
With your love-tangled hair;
So softly I'll leave
'Fore the day-break is there.

So gently I'll lift
your sweet head at the dawn,
And unloose your warm arms;
(It's so cold with them gone)
While the magic still lingers
And our dreams hold no fears;
Softly at sunrise
I'll leave you my tears.

William Wayne Langmaid
JIVE

Treble tuned and sexed-up pure,
tree topped flight disdain.
Birds of paradise, flamingo foes,
ladies daft, demure.
Subtle slight of slippered slur,
and silliness regained.
How are the haunts of hollow
spills,
cerebrum splits and chills?
What do you do when others do
a decadent two step?
Those frilled buffoons, eared

crescent moons,
and jiggled jelly jive.

Charlotte Boyd Chambers
FOG

The sky's mouth opens,
and where space was
a dense curtain sits,
breathing gray dampness
with gaping throat
that silently spits.

Eyes search silhouettes
assurance sought
for familiar sights.
Soft penetration
casting weak beams
from high powered lights.

All sound seems distant,
morose, forlorn,
as from a deep well.
Listen intently,
no one can hear
November fog yell.

Lynn Folse
THE TANK

A mirror crumpled
plays background sonatas
of guppies jagged
orange fan-tails
reflecting colored tunes.

Movements quick and
sudden darting
up and over
spinning, spinning
restless water
Lilies sway to
rhythmic waves
bubbles bobbing
water dancing
crystal prism minuets.

Harold H. Milstead
WAKE UP AMERICA!

Wake up America! Take notice!
    Look around!
Be quiet and listen to destiny's
    sound.
A red light's blinking up the road
    ahead,
And the bells you hear could be
    pealing for the dead.
A black cloud hovers o'er the
    land today;
Foul air, polluted water, and
    moral decay.
Please, stop a minute and think!
Bigotry and crime—is culture
    on the brink?
Priorities are upside down, and
    values inside out,
Profit is the motive, of that
    no one can doubt.
As the savior goes unseen in a
    needy brother's face,
Your treasures are unequaled
    in all the human race.
Wake up America, you're too
    young to die,
Roll up your sleeves, and cast

your eyes to the sky.
Past failures can be used to
    rectify and gain,
And a new beginning could
    blot out the dreadful stain.

And once this earthly span is
    over, and the nations gather
    there,
When all the wrongs are
    righted, and the world is free
    of care,
The Lord of Hosts will rise, and
    with tender passion say,
"America the beautiful, you
    have shown the way."

R. M. Pavlovics
CYCLIC

In ruins
Inactive
Windswept
Indifferent
In limbo
In darkness
Like the sun
Engendered
Energized
Enlightened
Enriched
In love
In ruin
I stood
I languished
I followed
I drifted
I landed
I wasted
You dawned
I became
I grew
I felt
I flourished
I fell
I stand

Phyllis R. Carvalho
PUFFBALL

Little puffball, soft and white,
Watching you is pure delight.
Blowing here and floating there,
Drifting gently on the air;
Where you land new plants will
    grow:
Nature's lovely way to sow.

Rod Wade
SUSAN

Thinking of you
    when lips are dry and
    sounds are small
I trust the full green light in
    your eyes.

Missing you
    when the table is set
    the dusk descended
And shadows dine - delicious
    solitude.

Loving you
    when shoulders are drawn
    or looks distended
Your body smiles
    metaphysical.
Else leaving you is like summer
    in a sling.

S. J. Pakula
A PLACE CALLED SERENITY

I wonder if by chance
there is a place that is called
    Serenity?
Look out to sea, the water is
    calm,
it's so beautiful and at peace.
As if God was there walking
    across to greet me.
The trees are so still,
the air is sweet,

the sky is so bright.
I can feel his presence there
with me.
It's so wonderful you see,
Because God has led me here
to this place called Serenity.
Now I know the secret of
everlasting peace.

Robert S. Maher
A CLIMB

Aside from the wind,
Nothing moves on this stone
wall,
But heartbeat—silence.

Jean Pollitt
MOMMA'S HOUSE

As the house watches,
they take her away.
Like a pendulum,
the porch swing sways.
Silence, a drawn shade,
darkens Momma's house.

Sold, a crooked beret,
sits atop the realtor's
sign. Like eddying pools,
the fading light
fills Momma's house.

Buddy Rose
THE ATOMS

Ask of the devil - the devil will
tell,
The eyes of the atoms gaze deep
into hell.
As witness to reason how futile
to dream,
That atoms are simple as often
they seem.
Into their perilous circle I find
The price for my sanity is
losing my mind.
Now all of them watch me and
you must believe,
They are waiting to gather
the things they perceive.
Their incessant battle pulls me
apart,
Wasting the solitude time would
impart.
Onward their spinning on
infinite cores,
Onward our prison without any
doors.
I fear their directions will
someday converge,
And in through their centers
they all will emerge;
And in that one moment their
judgement must be,
That those who aren't with them
will never be free.

Felice Belman
LEFTOVERS

Last week's chicken, yesterday's
rice;
Always we eat the same thing
twice.
Monday it's lambchops,
Tuesday it's stew.

On Wednesday leftovers are
surely due.
April's soda has lost its pop;
To a bottle of milk we've
misplaced the top.
And so we drink these liquids
quickly,
Before the soda's flat, and the
milk gets too thickly.
Last night's dinner was fine last
night,
But today - cold, for lunch -
it's an unwelcome sight.
If only we could cure cooks of
these stunts—
We'd end leftovers now, and
eat meals just once!

Edie Denee Rose
IF EVER. . .IT IS NOW

If ever I have given so much
as to receive so little from you,
it is now.
If ever I have been so kind
as to being treated so cruel by
you,
it is now.
If ever I have been in such a
need
as to need you,
it is now.
If ever I have loved so much
as to being loved so little by
you,
it is now.
If ever I have been so devoted
as to be pushed aside by you,
it is now.
If ever I have given in so much
as to you for nothing,
it is now.
If ever I had to say good-bye
as I must say to you,
it is now.

Ernest M. Schuttenberg
TOO MUCH

Computer-like circuits and
channels
Shot thoughts in a single
direction.
The symmetry of the cerebrum
Responded by pre-programmed
process
To form the unyielding
conclusion:
Electric and chemical hate.
Apart from the cerebral level
The blood and the tissues
together
Produced unexpected result.
When intellect ended in darkness,
two enemies reached
understanding
Through blind molecular love.

Barbara Chaconas
IN SILVER SCRIPT

"Grow old with me
the best is yet to be."
The words were etched in
silver script
upon the frame that held the
wedding day -
all white in dreams of hope
and love.
. . . He stood before her now -
a guilt-worn frown
his eyes reflecting helpless
lust . . .
The thirty years of building
trust and dreams
all shattered in that awkward,
silent space.

"Do you love the girl?"
The words came soft - as if
afraid -
"She made me feel alive again."
Oh God! The awful pain.
Could he not see how much
she hurt?
She turned her tear-streaked
cheek away,
and prayed for anger -
Oh where was anger -
to swallow up the pain?
He reached - for what?
For her? For all the years?
He held her near - yet still
the want of younger skin was
wedged between.
He had to go
more than desire -
the need to "BE" again.
. . .She gazed around the nest
which she had built
the chair where he had sat -
the fireplace - a gaping empty
hole -
And then she saw the silver
frame
and etched upon her heart those
words of pain. . .
"Grow old with me
the best is yet to be."

Patti Jo Aden
WHAT IS A FARMER

When God makes a farmer
He forms him in such a way
That he will grow in knowledge
and strength
And love more with every day.
He gives farmers a sound mind
That can withstand and reason,
With daily farming problems
And the challenge of each new
season.
Only a farmer's eyes and senses
Can see and feel the need,
Of every animal that he owns
Every inch of soil, plant, and
seed.
God shapes his shoulders
perfectly
To lift weight and to burden
his cares,
But the Lord adds just enough
tenderness
That they tremble in his prayers.
A farmer's hands are calloused
and lined
And strong as steel and lead,
But gentle enough to hold and
lift
A small child softly into bed.
God needed special people to
be
Strong and kind, and charmers,
So he created them and
blessed them
And still is making farmers!

Sandra Ross
HOME IN THE VALLEY

Down in the Blue Ridge when
the sun goes to sleep,
The mist in the valley begins
to weep.
The air is so still you can hear
eagles fly.
The deer in the forest will all
run and hide.
The glow from the fire warms
the house through the night.
In the forest the animals can
see the light.
Under the stars through the

trees one can hear,
The soft whisper of wind
and an owl that's near.
My home in the valley,
the Shenandoah Valley,
is quiet
and peaceful and built from the
woodland.
We work and we love here, we
never are lonely, together
we'll die here in peace with
our own land.
The sun rises so slowly, just
ever so calmly, and the wind
lifts the fog with a breeze shy
and balmy.
The love that surrounds us as
we wake with the day, is like
the sky and the heavens in their
own natural way.
We hike up the skyline, at the
lookout we rest and gaze on
the valley through its
loveliness.
The color of blue on the trees
down below is like the sky
in the evening as the dark starts
to flow.
My home in the valley,
the Shenandoah Valley,
is quiet
and peaceful and build from
the woodland.
We work and we love here, we
never are lonely, together
we'll die here in peace with
our own land.

Jon Morris
UNTITLED

The woman astride her tan
equine;
An oasis for her tired men;
A lonely silhouette on a
denim-sky day;
Blue Jean lady, why do you
ride away?
And it's sad to see her ride.
Slipping away, like a falling
tide;
And the horse's thighs tremble
like my lip;
As I too begin to slip.
There was a time we rode
together,
We would trot and talk among
the heather.
Our stride and thoughts were one
in time;
Now you ride your way, I ride
mine.
The dawn is breaking soon I
fear;
On whose horizon will she
appear.
Perhaps she knows this red
sky morning,
It's best we avoid the storm
that's forming.

Victoria Lang Anderson
**A FATHER'S DAY
REMEMBRANCE**

Happy Father's Day in Heaven,
Daddy,
Though I'm not sharing it with
you.
This must surely be your greatest
of all the many, but few.
I won't be sending your card
this year,
Nor hurrying home with your
gift.
I'll just be remembering daddy,
All the memories you've left.
Still in my grieving I'm relieved

today,
To know you're spending this
  Father's day in such a special
  way.
Although sad memories I'll
  recall,
and heartaches will be many,
  with many tears to fall.
Thank you; for the love, life,
  and
memories you gave and left
  us all.
Happy Father's Day in Heaven,
  Daddy.

Cindy L. Stall
ANOTHER WINDING ROAD

Another winding road that
  leads me home, but home's
  so far from you

The rain reminds me of the
  good-bye we said but the
  tears weren't few

For now I know I need you
  more than you could ever
  know,
So I wrote this love song from
  my heart to tell you so.

Please remember all the
  promises of my return in
  spring
My love and heart are with you
  just in case you're wondering
Just hold the warm memories
  in the safety of your heart
Before too long we'll be
  togehter and never again be
  apart.

Virginia Brown Beckman
MY HOME

North Dakota is my home tho
  many miles
away I've roamed.

I've watched the ocean's rolling
  tides,
and toured castles built on
  mountain sides.

I've made new friends,
and learned new trends.

Of all these lovely sights that
  I have seen,
It's of North Dakota that I
  still dream.

To see the fields of golden
  wheat,
and breath the air so clean and
  sweet.

The Badlands with their lovely
  sights,
and the rolling prairies with the
  sun shining bright.

To see the deer and antelope at
  play,
takes me back to childhood days.

Yes, Many miles away I've
  roamed,
But North Dakota is still my
  home.

Vera C. Keffer
**NOSTALGIC THOUGHTS OF
LONG AGO**

Nostalgic thoughts of long ago
When I was but a child
Heat rays dazzling from the hay
Bumblebees humming here to
  stay
Yes, that's been awhile.

Lazy days were for me then
I look back and smile
When I would lie upon the
  ground
And watch the clouds go by.

Rain came in early spring
Wet earth and grass
Aroma spread;
Rainbows appeared in the sky
and flowers lift their heads.

Barefoot I would run
Splashing puddles to my knees
Making mudcakes in the mud
Just as long as I please.

Yes, my memories are of
  country
And yours of city may be
We can't compete with each
  other
But we can share—
Can't we?

Sonja McCarty Haddox
REACHING

I struggled up the mountain
  'mid pain and doubt and
  fears.
I climbed the very highest peak
  away from the valley of tears.

I turned and glanced behind
  me and there in the vale
  below;
You were starting up that
  mountain that I scaled not
  long ago.

Having been there, I could feel
  the terror in your soul;
The chains that bound your
  burdened heart as you
  struggled toward your goal.

In pity I reached down for
  you. In love, you saw my
  face.
Caring made your mountain
  smaller as you climbed at a
  faster pace.

So, when you see a friend in
  a valley you've been through;
Reach with your heart and
  touch his hand. Climbing's
  easy . . . when there's two.

Jill S. Baum
HAIKU

Butterflies are free.
They sail with the wind and rain
Until death claims them.

Mrs. Kathryn M. Krueger
FOR YOU, MY LOVE

I know you—
You may not want me to,
  but I do.
I watched and I waited,
And when you were very busy—
I crept closer.

You built a wall—
A wall of words;
Words of hope and aspirations;
Words of pain and even love;
But, still a wall.

But I know you—
And I knew the wall was very
  fragile,
And when I crept closer, it
  crumbled.
But the hope and the love was
  left standing.
I knew it would be—
Because I know you.

Amy Lynn Wall
BEHOLD

Behold, I stand before a city
  with lights
teaming above the trees—
each ray reaching the sky,
  bending not once
to blink an eye.
Before me stands the gate to

this bright city;
each golden turn of the metal
  smiles brassly at me, snarling
  at the indentation
of a lion on its chest.

Boldly, I clasp at the lions
  chain,
only for my hand
to be bitten
by its selfish teeth.

But now I find myself running,
or being chased by the lights
  whose rays have discovered
  a stranger;
harshly they pull me to and fro,
  forcing me again,
to the brassly lion.

Roma Hogue
WISHING

If wishing could make it true
I wish I could be there with you
Each night I wish upon a star
The one wish I have is to be
  where you are
If I wish long enough and strong
  enough
Will my wish come true
Will I some day be with you

I wish that we could stroll the
  beach
Feel the sand upon our feet
Hear the waves lap the shore
See the sunrise once more
Watch the birds fly on high
Their silhouettes against the
  sky
I wish that we could sit and
  dream a dream or two
And I'd be there alone with
  you

I wish that I could feel your
  touch
To know you need me just as
  must
If all my wishing could come
  true
Darling I'd be there with you.

Lucy A. Snow
DUSTY TREASURE

Curled tightly, a round little
  ball, lint-filled fragment
Sits collecting dust in the seam
  of a child's pocket.
A seemingly unimportant wad,
  folded and forgotten;
Flat formless vessel shaped
  round an innocent's first tears.
Invisible stains permeating
  fibers now loosely shredded
From aging irretrievable years.
Once placed as a panacea with
  warm and loving hands
To ward off symptoms of a
  cold,
Now precious memorabilia
  housing secrets never told.

George E. G. Ratteray
FOREVER

I never wished that anything
Should endure forever:
The furtive glance; the sensual
  stance;
Nor even the carol of the bird
To its world without Word.

Forever?
Never!

I never wished that anything
Should endure forever.
Yet on the shore's sands,
  crouched like a knave,
I had hurried to engrave,
a trinity of words.

Forever?
Never!

I said, and as the anxious water
Wrinkled slowly over
So that it might repeat, reproach,
Happily I turned and looked
  forward as the sea,
Fastened them in a liquid
  eternity.

Forever,
Together,
In the mute temples of the
  tides and Time.

Moss
SECRET ADMIRER

Smoldering embers—a latent
  desire—
Deep silence—delitescent
  Relation—
Inspiration—comes to those
  that Inspire—
And you fan the Fire—of
  Inspiration—
Flames of Compassion—do they
  burn the same—
Love—Truth—Understanding—
Mutual Trust—
Voluntarily volunteer my name
Or keep it— anonymously
  anonymous.

Rosiland Robin White
THE FISHERMAN'S WIFE

I miss you more than words can
  say,
With each and every passing day,
The days are long, the nights
  are lonely,
But I still wait for you only.

Yes, you think the world of me,
  but still
there's that deep blue sea.
It tugs at you with its tide, I
  tug you
from the other side.

You're all wrapped up inside
  two worlds;
it's just like loving two
  different girls.
If you had another woman, at
  least I could compete;
but the sea cannot speak, so I
  must admit
defeat.

For you have a job that needs
  to be done;
and for this job you're the only
  one.

So, go to the sea and please get
  done;
then return to me, for you're the
  only one.

Diana Lee Boroff
WHEN I'M OLD

You promise me I can come
  home again,
If I can learn to stand again.

I work hard to learn to stand,
but then you say I don't
understand.
Your home is small and not
much room,
The kids will make me upset.
But you see my life is almost
to an end,
And it would make me happy
to see home again.
It's lonely in this nursing home,
I hardly get time to get my rest.
They hurry me to eat my meals,
And rush me to my bed.
But there's a few, who take time
to care.
They will talk and see that I am
well taken care of,
before they leave.
How few they are and far
between,
For they get rid of most of
these.
So take me home just one more
time,
I promise I will do my best to
be good and kind.
I want to end my life right
here,
so I don't have to be lonely
and in tears.
Thank you God for letting me,
Spend so much of my life with
a family.

Cheryl Elizabeth Waddell
**EIGHTY-SEVENTH
CHRISTMAS**

Through evening halls
she drifts like snow,
the touch white and cold
and the tears and the yearning
for a satin Christmas box
containing the Morning.

Nina F. Patchen
THE LADY WITH THE LAMP

Our lady in the Harbor is
showing signs of wear,
Once her figure was so steady,
but now is bowed with care.
Her lamp, still shines so
brightly, in the day or in the
night,
And to the weary traveler, it
is a welcome sight.
Many years she kept her vigil,
standing on that lonely shore,
Now our land is overcrowded,
so her smile seems rather grim,
She wonders how much longer
she can let them enter in.
Even weary though she is, she
still smiles through the gloom,
Holding out her open arms,
hoping she will find the room.
Around the world she's noted,
scared and faded though she
be.
To the ones who seek
admittance, she rules the land
of Liberty.

Doug Shelton
SHARE

Show others
How they can
Appeal to God for
Redemption and life
Everlasting.

Elsie Cheeks
SHADOWS OF DARKNESS

Shadows of darkness casting
far into the night.
Waiting for the crest morning

light,
As the break of day.
The light comes shining through
on the earth's morning dew.
As the sun rises, the dew fades
away.
As the sleeping awaken to
another busy day.

Donald H. Johnson
DEEP IN MY SOUL

Deep in my soul
I feel the restlessness,
The want to wander
The need of expressiveness.

I feel the rumble,
I feel the surging,
The need to create,
The thoughts are merging.

The want to release,
The need to let go,
To free this restlessness,
To release my soul.

Peggy Lynn McCleary
MATTHEW

Morning brought the existence
of a new life in the form of
a tiny human being.
Affirmation of the miracle of
a shared love.
Truly a unique soul enclosed in
a bundle of soft pink flesh.
Today is the beginning of a
phenomenal maturation
process.
Holding him enables you to
absorb his beauty.
Every new day will bring
noticeable changes in his
beauty and personality.
Wonderously he will master
the challenges of his new
environment.

Gauri P. Agnihotri
UNTITLED

The light fades away
on the last scene
as the audience is left clapping
at the acting and singing
of the people on stage.
I think I was fooled
into being an audience
of yours.

James L. Neubauer
FOR MY LOVE

Fading
lights now fill the sky
Like embers
of a once raging fire
Remnants
of the day now gone by
we remain.
Patterns
form in a darkening sky
Their meaning
understood by you and I
Together
our love shall never die

away.
As the shadows fall around you
Stealing the light away
I'll wrap my arms around you
and here I will remain
Nestled
safe within your dreams
Lying
warm and still here by me
You'll see
all the things that never seem
to stay
The songbirds in the meadow
announce the rising sun
But I will never leave you
until my life is done
and I love you
yes I love you.

Mary Ann Morris
ONLY ONE TIME

We come this way but once,
one time to do our thing,
We can throw it away on
foolish play,
As if life were one big fling.
We can desert our loved ones
to pursue our selfish way,
Or we can go bravely on,
taking day by precious day.
If someone says he never
thought of giving up at all,
If he says that he has never once
been tempted to fall,
If he says that it is easy to take
the narrow road,
I don't believe he carries his
share of the load.
What makes it easy, though, is
if we work together,
And don't look back when
we've chosen our path,
And when we know, somehow,
that things will be better.

Karen Lee Howell
SMILE

A smile can never harm a thing,
Happiness is what a smile will
bring.
A nice hello, a shake of the
hand,
It's all these things that make
life grand.
A little nod, How do you do?
May I talk and walk with you?
I like to see a smiling face,
so full of happiness, so full of
grace.
A look of love, a warm touch,
a friendly smile that means
so much.
Helping people when they're
down and out,
a warm smile will bring them
about.
A smile can take up so much
room.
It's like a flower all in bloom.
It's like the sunshine and the
rain.
A smile can shine and wash
the pain.
So full of wind, so full of air,
A smile can be found
anywhere.

Ralph Emerson Oman
LET JESUS IN

A stranger came knocking at
my door,
He pleaded oh so gently to come
in.
The lying devil asked me to wait
a while,
You should enjoy life while you
may.

Jesus in loving kindness
continued knocking as before,
He asked me, please may I come
into your life today?
If I for long let Jesus pass me
by,
For all eternity I could lose
That heavenly reward beyond
the sky.
I would feel all alone in the
devil's crowd,
In the land of the doomed and
everlasting despair,
To suffer in torment and cry
aloud.
When I opened the door to the
Lord Jesus and said,
Come into my life and live your
life through me,
I found a peace I had never
known before.
Lord all my life I promise to
be true,
Use my little handful of
experience for ever more,
Lord of my life I'll do anything
You want me to do.
When Jesus knocks at your
door, let Him in!
Don't leave Him outside in the
cold,
Take Him as your Savior while
you are young,
He may cease to knock, if you
wait till you are old.
Jesus will be your dearest
friend,
If you open the door and let
Him in.

Karen Hoffman
MORE

I say that I've forgotten you
and think of you no more
I tell them that I've lost the
feeling
and need your love no more
I talk of times you've hurt me
and that I can't ignore
Yet they are puzzled and
cannot see
why I go back for more.

Teeno Montgomery
UNKNOWN SON

Arms now empty
Little crib gone
Unsung lullaby
Another day done
Closed eyes bring back
Memories best left untouched.

Linda Marie Romaniak
DESTINED TO CHAINS

Captive—icy steel fingers filter
its sight,
From the sweet caress of dawn's
tender touch;
Hardened by the haunting gray
shadow,
Cast down upon its dwindling
soul
By the towering walls which
imprison its corpse.
Their grasping grip binds
steadfast to this incarceration,
Coiling tauntly like a serpent
devouering its prey;
Slowly and secretly squeezing—
drop by drop the life which
dwells
In its numb body. Response
is deprived only to sweet
memories—
Reflections of a golden spirit
who once roamed its wild

existence.
A creature of liberty—
destined to chains.

Connie L. Wilson
ME

Love my soul
My being whole
No part stole
Love my ways
What I say
All the day
Give me no blame
And bring no shame
Upon my name
My soul needs play
Then I must lay
At the end of day
My soul must rest
to give it's best
To life with zest
Expect no more
Than I can store
Behind my soul's door
Let me drink
From life's brink
Or I shall sink
Tie me down
And I will
At your sound
I will sigh
And wish to fly
With dreams on high
Give me this thing
Love with no strings
So I can dream
Love with no strings
Happiness brings
Greater than dreams.

Patricia E. Downs
DAWN

Radiant Dawn
　　　reborn
　　　　　arises
Exuberant
　　in the
　　　newness of
　　　　　of
　　　　　　Day
Accepts its
　　challenge
　　　with
　　　　ardent
　　　　　zeal
Conquesters
　　victorious
　　　　Destiny
　　　　　fulfilled
Withdraws
　　.....fatigued
　　　　.....aged
In
　Nocturne
　　Indigo
　　　enveloped
Descends
　　into
　　　Celestrial
　　　　Tranquility

Brenda Stuber
SPRING LOVE

Look at the day
　is it not clear?
I care not
　for I am free
Be it as it may
　my dues are paid
　what more can I say.
Hello
　the sun is shining
　brightly
　I smile.

For it is not
　the dark clouds
　that hang over me
It is a feeling
　that lingers
　that makes me carefree.
Could it be love?
Glory, glory how could it be
　is it so good
　to be kind to me?
Are the flowers
　not blooming
While the birds
　they are singing.
Are not the days lighter
　than light
　the skies not clear?
Or is it love I fear.
Whatever, if is
　than carry me away
　the feeling too wonderful
　to not want to stay.
If want it not the Spring
　I care not
　for I am free
Be it as it may
　won't you
　come to me?

Mrs. L. R. Noe
A CLOUD SHIP

Lying on my bed one day
　looking through a window
　pane,
I saw a fleecy cloud appear
　upon the sky's broad,
　boundless plain.
It seemed a great and snow
　white ship
　Sailing smoothly, gracefully
With the breezes as they sighed
O'er the sky's broad azure sea.
Slowly, gently it gained speed
　when breezes started rushing
　by,
Till it joined some other ships
On their journey across the
　sky.

Mark A. Archer
THOUGH

Though clouds be over,
And rain seems to fall.
I have shelter to cover,
So no trouble shall befall,
Though darkness be around,
And nothing I can see,
A light is shone a bound,
So no confusion shall there be,
Though saddening may it seem,
And sorrow seems never to end,
There is happiness flowing like
　a stream,
If you accept, gladness will
　never end,
Though death be the price,
And hardness always come,
That is but a small sacrifice,
For in Heaven you have a
　kingdom to come.

Denise Carole Krawczyk
MY HOPES AND DREAMS

My hopes and dreams are far
　from true,
But with every one I'm closer
　to you,
My feelings aren't changed for
　I feel the same,
Each passing moment plays a
　new game.
Somewhere in you you want me
　to be,
Right there by your side and
　totally free,

Free from the people who did
　us no good,
Away from those who wished
　they could.
All alone and together to be as
　we are,
Not to hide here near or far,
Though there's nothing right
　now that I could try,
To help us back together would
　let us die.
So I say to you as I wanted to
　then,
This time only with words and
　a pen,
My hopes and dreams are far
　from true,
But with every one more, I
　hope, I'm closer to you.

Catherine M. Palmer-Lewis
REMEMBERING

remembering...
　roses
　and old copper
　antiques
　young children with joy in
　　their lives
　talking with happily married
　　wives
　blowing sound through my
　　flute
　fresh rain water... and you
　are all the things I love

so where are you now?
　your terrible lies
　the broken heart I gave you
　the battles that leave me
　　bleeding
　the very final pain...
　and you
　are all the things I hate

Donna Molinski
SPACE

Afloat
On an endless sea of space
Where weight meant nothing
Color was never heard of
Lonesome
With the company
Of a million galaxies
Stars drifting
Neighboring your touch
Lightyears away
Swallowed into a bowl
Of dreams
Empty wishes
And eternity.

Therese Anne Gionta
THE SIGN READ:

The Red roses are all gone.
All pink roses are half-price.
Not thinking, you hastily
　bought the pink ones.
Oh, if you had only known
　this would happen,
You never would have
　compromised yourself.

Only red roses mean
　　I Love You!!

Denise Machado
DON'T FORGET ME

Don't forget me when I'm
　not near,
Or my tenderness when I
　was hear.
Please give me your thoughts
　every once in awhile,
I will hold them to me and
　reply with a smile.
I need only to know that
　you'll care now and then,
That I was, that I am, and that
　I am your friend.

Kathleen A. Rise
YOU GAVE ME

You gave me a part, a part of
　your life
You gave me time, the time
　that I needed
Then came your touch, that
　now I need so much
You gave me a sense, a sense
　of being someone
You gave me feelings, feelings
　where I had none.
For thinking of you is one
　thing,
But being with you is
　something.
You gave me you, I'll give you
　me.
And hope that you'll take,
My part, my time, and my
　touch,
Hold them, together and
　remember,
You gave me yours.

Kathryn O. Secrest
YUCK!

I get the strangest wierd
　diseases,
I seldom get the coughs &
　sneezes,
I get lumps & blumps
　and warts most hideous.
And creeping fungus
　that's insidious!
Some day the doctor will
　come in
And find there - where
　I might have been -
Though it will be of no great
　loss-
A little pile of
　soft
　　green
　　　moss.

Barbara L. Kellogg
ALPINE DELIGHT

The most beautiful gardens in
　all the world
　Are found here free of form
　and design.
A plan known alone to the One
　Who created this all in His
　mind.
They're strong and they're
　rugged, these flowers
　In the heights where not all
　can survive;
But they cling to the rocks
　and the tundra
　And gaily they blossom and
　thrive.
Their colors are deepest and
　truest,
　Each detail is perfect in
　plan.
And no lovelier place can the

Shawna Trower Hitchcock
GOD IS LIFE

The breeze is but a whisper
    from God.
The stars the twinkles from
    his eyes.
The moon his halo, the sun
    his smile.
God's tears are the raindrops
    painting earth.
The snow his purity falling
    light and sweet.
The earth his heart beating
    warmly.
The galaxy his body breathing,
    life.

David Wilbourn
DON'T CLOSE MY BOOK

Don't close my book,
    it won't work on me.
I don't want to live
a life full of grief and your
    agony.

Your ignorance toward the
    subject
is a disgrace.
You complain about the reds,
but want a red race.

Socialist problems at the
    forefront
of the 50's airwave trials,
give you just cause
to redeem the education of a
    child
by burning books in piles.

Shirley Boucher
LONG ACQUAINTANCE

Here's to a friend
    Of long, long ago,
Here's my best wishes
    That will go.

Have a happy trip
    Drop a line or two,
And I'll write back
    If you want me to.

Its up to you
    If you want to write.
I'm not one for asking
    Whether its wrong or right.

Dorothy Marsh
COLORFALL

Worn green
Bleeds red,
Red laughs
Dances wildly,
Yellow calls.
Pumpkin orange
Touches up
Mauve morn.
Jewelled lawn,
Grey lace mist,
Smoke blue noon,
Brown bird warns.
Color falls.
Grey steals,
Black leers,
Metal cold,
White covers all.

DeeAnn M. Schirado
CANDLE, MY LIFE

Love grows
    as we slowly become one;
As I slowly feel the warmth
    of his gentle touch
    upon my shoulders—
swaying
    back and forth,

soul find its rest
    Than these gardens up high
    in the land.

dancing together, Our lives
    drindle on, till all that
is left is our Soul—
Models, Waxed in Time!
    Slowly
        dripping,
            down
                down
till only eternity can tell us
    that we have a long way to go
        till we find
complete
    peace
        within
            Ourselves.

Mark A. Morningstar
A SEASON GONE

Summer passed by silently
    and I never wrote a line
about the sunshine days of June
    or dandelion wine.

I never spoke of July swims
    in rivers running free
or put to rhyme the bluish sky
    nor mountain's greenery.

There were no words that I
    put down
    of August sunset glows
that bleed across horizons
    like the color of the rose.

So, fall has reaped the summer
    sun
    and I finally found the lines
to sit here in October winds
    and write of summer times.

Angelito T. Buhisan, Jr.
**TANKA 1: THE NIGHT IS
BLACK**

The cloak of darkness
Descends and covers us from
    light
Then all we can see
Is the void time of space
And the blackness of it all.

Debra Lee Hanson
TIME

Time, the lapse between
actions and words—
A deceiving thing.
For when you most desire
it, there is none;
But when you least
want to stand still,
there are always minutes
to spare. Time is the
truth to all things—
yet, time itself has
no honest meaning.

Jannis Birch Sommer
A SILENT GATHERING

Oh, there's a village
On the hill above the town.
With doorsteps glistening white
and quiet all around.

The neighbors aren't well
    acquainted
Although they live so near
The houses are always dark,
And people never appear.

Oh, the village lies so still.
All faces are turned to the sky.
I'll have a white doorstep there
    too
When I die.

Richard Groller
BEATITUDES

Who are these young lions
    these prodigies
    these sons of men
Who come to us and tell us
    they are wise?

Of silhouettes of steeples
    black and hollow
against a cold and breathless
    sky
And ting Braille cloudlets left
    from planes
that daily tell us what to buy
And a silver moon enshrouded,
    pocked and lonely
that they know will never die.

Who are these young lions
    these Magi
    these sons of men
Who come to us and tell us
    they are wise?

Of batteries of soldiers led to
    battle
for a peace they cannot keep
And death-heads marching
    forward, the Grim Reaper
and his bitter harvest reaped
And lonely men entombed
    by depthless wonder
far below the troubled deep.

Who are these young lions
    these peacemakers
    these sons of men
Who come to us and tell us
    they are wise?

Of proud and vanquished
    rebels slowly dying
and embittered by the law
And fighting to defend some
    countless yesterdays
lying beaten, scourged and raw
And a birthright buried deep,
    a way of life
that's crushed beneath the
    lion's paw.

Who are these young lions
    these Paladins
    these sons of men
Who come to us and tell us
    they are wise.

Joyce Altobelli
INSPIRATION

Tiny ideas
that pluck your mind
sometimes
play beautiful music,
but usually
just make a lot of
noise.

Sharon Graham-Davis
LOVING YOU

If I touch you gently while
    you sleep,
and you feel my mouth gliding
    down your body,
seeking dark dormant creases,
impatiently waiting to be
    explored—
and if I whisper in the darkness
to tell you I need you,
then let me touch you;
and tell me,
you've never been caressed
    there before . . .

Jose A. Flores—UNICORN
TELL ME ABOUT IT

Tell me about it,
How I love you so much.
I was always lonely before you.
The world turns differently
    with you.
I am a happy man.
Love,
Soars up high above clouds,
Where the sun shines.
Birds fly there,
And I live among them.
Night,

So clear and cool,
Hides nothing when we touch,
Honestly as two in love can.
Beauty begins with our love,
And grows on all the things
    around us,
And I tell you now
I love you.
Tell me about it,
The stars that you see,
The sun shining warm on your
    face.
Show me the meadows where
    you walk,
With lilies all around you.
Walk with me on lonely beaches,
Until the sun sets over the ocean.
Listen to the birds,
And watch them fly away.
Hold my hand . . .
I'll fly you to the moon.
Stay with me,
And I'll say "I love you."

Bill C. Ortega
SEARCH IN VAIN

And I find myself upon their
    land. With awe I gaze afar
    and see
their cities of crystal. I am
    but a stranger from the
    heavens,
who has traveled from star to
    star seeking their sterling
    presence.
At one point I lost my patience
    and my hand, but I have here
    my
companion—my laser pistol—
    with its glorious incandescence.
I, the earth man in seek of the
    ever elusive foe, have stumbled
    upon a cosmic nest of
radiation about to blow. Their
    infra-red
hearts have no way of
    detecting one so cold as mine;
    no way of
intercepting the spark that has
    triggered the thought that is
    going to eject them into
    eternal time.
I stand here so near, and yet
    afar. My heart beating
    thunderously
of fear, yet of anger and
    vengence from their scar.
Look at them! How dare they
    go about! How dare they
    exist, as if
they did not know who chose
    them to be.
Ah, but I must catch my
    breath. Must be this crimson
    mist straining my airbags. I
    can still see. I can still
    sense their elusive presence.
The solar wind has burned my
    thoughts, but suddenly I
    feel a cold chill of

some sort. Without suspect
of any kind, a
wave of audible tone comes
from nowhere and enters
my skullbone,
making me feel as if I am
floating into an event
horizon from
which there is no return.
Yes, the solar wind really
does burn.

Chris Engel
THE NOTE

How is it
you so easily walk away
from everything we shared

I still remember your face
when you let me see
your more sensitive self
When I apologized
for being so weak and pathetic
at times
and how you looked at me
and told me you needed me
especially when I needed you
I know you entrusted me
with frailer parts of your
nature
To me
fragile treasures
that sank deep
and nestled safely
in the warmest part
of my heart
Yet
here we are
dividing our lives
into pieces
not really our own
We can never take back
the exchange of our souls
But go
know yourself
And know I
will always
tenderly care for
the part of you
in me.

Annette Long
HIGH ABOVE THE WORLD

As I sit
High above the world
On a mountain,
Which seems to open its arms
to me,
I forget about the city
And the hustle and bustle
Of my everyday life.

Up here the pace is slowed to
a halt,
The only thing that moves
Is my hair,
Which flows in the wind
Like rustling leaves.

My cares fade away
One by one
Like the ending of a song.
It seems as though I am
In a dream.

I could never imagine
Man creating something
So beautiful, so unique as this.
Man cannot buy beauty and
splendor.
It has to form itself,
And when it is formed,
It is timeless.

Myrtle H. Taylor
MY TASK

I will walk through darkness,
By his light,
I will walk,
In the sunshine,
Of His Love.
I will rise,
With His smile,
Upon my lips.
I will not be ashamed
To praise his name.

Stephen Paul King
FRIENDSHIP

People come and people go
throughout our live's full span
But it's those we're glad we
know
who bring us love for man.

Those are the ones that we're
close to
to whom we can confide
Always there to help us through
own problems maybe hide.

No money or false praise can
buy
this richest prize of all
It is the deeds through time
that tie
the bond of what we call—
Friendship

Wendi Nicole Fornoff
AFTER THE RAIN

The skies look dark and gray,
And disappointing, too.
And I wish the clouds were
none;
And the skies still blue.
A loud rumble of thunder
Makes me wonder why;
Why did the lightning
Just flash across the sky?
And then the rain comes
pelting down,
Getting me all wet.
But I don't want
To go indoors;
Not just yet.
For hours and hours the rain
pelts down,
And as I watch from my
window,
Slowly but surely the rain
ceases,
And out comes a beautiful
rainbow.

Andrea L. Spangler
MEMORIES

Through whispers of the trees
I hear you call my name.
Clouds create visions of you
It can never be the same.

The mountains we climbed
together
Mean little to us now;
We scaled a life of love,
It was worth it, somehow . . .

The rain washes memories
away
As I try not to cry,
For my heart still holds dear
The feelings you've allowed
to die.

Michelle Darcy de Illies
**THE OLD MAN
(TURANORTSA)**

The old man
who sits there quietly
as he plays his song so soft
the meaning he tries to convey
it's hard and down and off
Crooked fingers pluck at
the strings
unbearably full of pain
hunchbacked over the old
worn box
he sings his sad refrain
For many years have come and
gone
years no longer held in hand
watch as they go passing by
Tis sad I no longer can
I am an old man.

Romaine L. Goodman
NEW LOVE

"How new our love," we seem
to say
In guarded whispers, darkened
nooks
No man nor maid has felt this
way
"Ours is a special kind of love."

Ask me not how first we knew
That you loved me and I loved
you
"Was it there for all to see
Till Cupid handed us the key
Unlocked our hearts and made
us one?"

And with each stolen moment
from each day
I kiss your lips and know it's
true
But when we're parted
Dark despair seeps in my mind.

"Will our love stand the chain
of Time
Or slowly sink and drown in
Time's quicksand?"

Roberta C. Nutt
FLIGHT

In his stone tower he sits
dreaming
Of blind love, ebony stone,
and burning rage.
Like some demon bird of prey
His mind soars,
Seeking the formless creations
suffocating within him.
They must be free—
If only upon paper.
From his shaking hand emerge
writhing symbols,
Shrieking the obsessions of
this outcast poet.
Once released, yet,
He can feel them roaming madly
once again,
Taking flight into the darkness
of the stones around him.

William J. O'Shea
A FRIEND

A friend is one, I think,
who is always there.
He will be your link with earth
when your head is in the air.
And though many times you'll
fight,
in the end everything will be
alright.
He is one who can see into your
eyes;
confirm your truthes, reveal
your lies.
Behind your back he won't
speak

or spread bad will,
and with love for him
your heart will fill.
He will be there to answer your
call,
to stand beside you, or pick
you up when you fall.

Larry Suhrbier
THAT CHRISTMAS FEELING

That Christmas Feeling of long
ago,
A happy feeling that I used to
know.
It's not the same as it used to
be,
It doesn't mean anything at all
to me.

I don't want presents wrapped
with beautiful bows,
Don't want to see holly leaves
or mistletoe,
I want someone to love me and
hold me tight
Through the whole year, not
just Christmas night.

I don't want to hear music
or songs from a choir
I don't want to roast chestnuts
on an open fire,
I don't want a sleigh ride or
a Christmas of white,
I just need someone near to
make things right.

I don't want to see a snowman
with a nose of coal,
Don't want to hear ji ngle
bells or see any snow.
The only present I want
underneath the tree
Is the one I love to come back
to me.

That Christmas Feeling of long
ago,
A happy feeling that I used to
know.
It's not the same as it used to
be,
It doesn't mean anything at all
to me.

Sarah Cutler Bates
MY PLACE IN LIFE

Many times life seems useless
Totally without any kind of
hope.
I feel that living is so senseless
And with life I can no longer
cope.

The bills and the rent come due
But the money is nowhere
around.
The full meals on the table are
few
And short tempers are sure to
be found.

Then I look at my children
around me,
At the trust that shows in their
face.
Their love and faith I can see
And once more I have found
my place.

Beverly Ovelton Romero
**SAVE A LITTLE FOR
YOURSELF**

As we walk along life's path,
We gather knowledge piece
by piece.
And we strive for togetherness
Before our life will cease.
When we have many problems
We express them to someone
else,

But remember my dear,
You must save a little for
  yourself.
You meet a special person
And you want them for your
  friend.
But there's doubt in your mind
If they'll stick by you till the
  end.
Then you get to know them,
And find personality an
  expression of their wealth.
But remember my dear,
You must save a little for
  yourself.
Often we have so much on our
  minds,
And the pain so hard to bear.
That we can't take it any longer
So our problems we must
  share.
Through the doors of our lips
Come secrets in sickness and
  in health,
But never, ever forget,
To save a little for yourself.

Lillian F. Cubberley
SUSAN

For fifteen short years, God
  loaned her to me
We shared laughter and many,
  many tears
I saw Susan grow from a tiny
  tot
To a young girl who giggled a
  lot
She was a joy to have and to
  hold
Her hair was as if it was spun
  gold
A smile to catch at your very
  heart strings
Her eyes were of a sparkling
  blue
And I knew Susan would always
  be true
Then God called her to that
  far away place
And I knew Susan was out of
  the race.

Ramona Garcia
RETURN TO ME

Come take my hand, I will lead
  you—
Let your tears of sorrow fall
  upon my shoulders—
Grieve if you would for awhile,
  but grieve in my understanding
I am here beside you, touching
  you in your needs—
Your voice to me is that of an
  angel—
Speak to me from your soul,
  for always I care—
Let me take your pain and free
  your aching heart—
We are one and I love you—
Let your tears cleanse your
  eyes—
Your eyes now seek again the
  light—
Know that I am here beside
  you—
Open your ears to my voice,
  that I may share with you—
Become aware of the beauty I
  see within you—
Arise again to hope, to dream,
  renew your faith in my
  wisdom—
Glory in the daylight, find
  laughter in my whisperings
  of nonsense to you which
  brings you

once again to the light—
Sing now to the hills, play
  with my earth, let me heal
  your heart—
I am real, dance fair child, for
  it delights me always—
Call aloud my name in estasy—
Renew your spirit in knowing
  the lesson you had chosen
  now is past—
Return to me in everything,
  for I AM unchanging in
  my devotion to you—
I AM faith, I AM the light
  of rebirth, cherish me as I
  cherish you—
Remember always, if you
  stumble once again I shall
  lift you up—
Every blessing will pour out
  upon you with renewed
  greatness—
My love for you is truth never
  ending—
LOVE ME—I AM YOUR GOD.

Dorothy R. Gill
TRIBUTE TO ROY

I won't try to tell you that he
  was a saint.
He didn't think so—just
  accepted his fate,
Picked himself up whenever he
  fell.
He carried his cross—and he
  carried it well.
He lived out his years with
  courage and pride.
Pain and frustration pushed
  away to the side.
So, from his life, there's this
  message to tell,
"Carry your cross—and carry
  it well."

Lois J. Glass
**PLEASE TAKE MY HAND
AND WALK WITH ME**

Please take my hand and walk
  with me
From now unto eternity
We'll walk together in the rain
Refreshed we'll find the sun
  again
We'll walk in fields and woods
  until
Night falls and atop the highest
  hill
We'll touch the stars if they be
  still
Next we'll have a magic night
Of love and other rare delight
Then rest until the break of
  day
Invites the sun outside to
  play
And we'll begin a bright new
  day
Love this is how our life should
  be
Please take my hand and walk
  with me.

Sheila L. Wood
THE MOST BEAUTIFUL ROSE

My Love plucked me some roses
from our rosebush in our yard
and as he gave them to me
I noticed that he looked so
  tired.
So, I returned his roses to him
  today
as I knelt beside his grave,
The most beautiful rose in all
  the world,
His life I couldn't save.

Now, every year as our roses
  bloom,
I pluck them from their stem,
Then, I sit them in a tiny vase,
Right up next to him.
For, he really loved the roses,
  almost as much as I,
and only when they're by his
  side,
our roses do not cry.
Then, today I replanted our
  rosebush,
Right beside his stone,
'cause the most beautiful rose
  in all the world
Should never be alone.

Audrey Renda
OPEN HEART

Love is having the sun always
  shine,
Even during the rain.
Love is giving with a happy
  heart,
No thought to personal gain.
Love is when you see and hear
  in poetry and song,
When the person that you used
  to be,
Now "don't" know right from
  wrong.
It's bringing cheer and a happy
  smile to replace a frown or
  tear.
It's turning on to another's
  needs, to listen to his fear.
It's looking up into the eyes
  of a lost and troubled friend,
To take his hand with a pat
  on the back
Come on, please try again.
To take the time to really care,
To want to help, to want to
  share.

Diane Bernardy
A TALL MAN

It seems like yesterday,
I was walking hand in hand:
With a gentle warm touch,
Reflecting from a tall man.
He'd call me little one,
I'd look up and call him dad.
Where have all the days gone,
That reflects back to this man:
They're gone now! They have
  passed,
But inside my heart they stay:
Keeping memories dear,
Reflecting onto this man:
  Soft tears roll down my face,
opening a new road:
Grown to be a woman,
I must leave this man to face:
A new life has opened,
Building me some memories:
The kind to call my own,
For the two of us to share:
We're building memories,
Even though you won't be
  there:
I'll know it's your warm touch
That shows me you really
  care.

Sue Scripture
HEART IN A GILDED CAGE

Where are the dreams I once
  held so dear
Faded away, replaced by
  fear
I've savored the gifts I've had
  in my life
I've tasted of motherhood,
  lover and wife
Why are the spaces that once

were taken
Filled with frustration and
  deep desperation
Like that of a bird in a gilded
  cage
My deep fulfillment in battle
  with rage
Why is my sea that once calmed
  my heart
Breaking with fury to tear me
  apart
If I can't find my way, where
  will I be
Imprisoned with feelings,
  feelings of me.

Akbarali H. Jetha
A GIFT

Oh man you have been given
  as a gift
A green carpet called grass
  which expands across the
  earth
Breeze which plays on your
  body like nothing can
Mountains to protect you from
  the weather
Flowers in their endless
  variety for your pleasure
Sun to give you warmth and
  light
Stars and the moon to ease
  the darkness
Vegetation to prevent hunger
Seasons to remove the
  monotony
Lakes and rivers to refresh you
And a heart to achieve love
  if you so desire.
In turn should you not
  acknowledge these presents
And realize how difficult
  life would be without them?

Vivian D. Hatchett
CHRISTMAS EYES

Inspired by Christmas spirit
I got up on Christmas morn,
knew it a special birthday
when Jesus Christ was born.
Then in came our smallest
  child,
born a year and months before,
I always felt Christmas special
but baby made it seem much
  more.
My heart filled with joy
and smiles began to flow,
baby's face was lighted
new eyes began to glow.
It was a moment
without any despair,
the tree was lined with gifts
which in turn were lined with
  care.
Baby ran with open arms
and gave me the sweetest hug,
then began impatiently
to give ribbons a hasty tug.
I wished the moment would
  last forever,
the presents with Christmas

ties,
welcomed by baby's warmth,
revealed by Christmas eyes.

Isabel L. Harbold
LOVE'S CASTLES IN THE AIR

My love, please come away with me,
For in my dreams I've built for thee,
Wondrous castles in the air,
With gardens round about so fair.

The perfume from the lovely flowers,
wafts upward round the stately towers.
I'll gather roses oh so sweet,
and lay them gently at thy feet.

A token from my yearning heart,
That from thee I would never part.
Oh come with me my love I pray,
And in this fairyland we'll stay.

With hands clasped we'll walk along,
Full of laughter and of song.
Happiness will e're be ours,
as we walk round the castle's towers.

Blessed Lord in Heav'n above,
How we thank thee for our love,
Walk beside us Lord we pray,
Guide our footsteps day by day.

A tender kiss upon thy face,
Sweetly now my love I place,
For thou hast come away with me,
Our love to share eternally.

Our castles we will tend with care,
And dwell within their walls so fair,
Lord we thank thee for this day,
For love has with us come to stay.

Lorraine Soo Storck
THE SPARROW AND THE HAWKS

The sparrow flew with hawks
In one misguided chart
And the hawks devoured the sparrow
And tore its tiny heart.

They left it, low and panting
on the brim of life's despair
The bitter reward of knowledge
With an awesome, awesome fear.

The sparrow learned, all too late
That hawks are rarely weak
And in their cunning and guile
They devour all that's meek.

Bruised, hurt and defiled
It lays all alone
Having reached the heights of malice
And reap what it has sown.

For, alas, the hawks had tired
of one misguided heart
and dropped it midst the carcasses
In its misguided chart.

Trembling, sore and fearful

The tiny sparrow lay
Fearing the winds of nightfall
And the arid, lonely day.

A mighty hand uplifts it
The breath of God descends
The flight of the hawks and sparrow
Has reached its final end . . .

Michael Mathew Richards
DEPENDENCY

The opiate you expel
entwines its grasp about me
encompassing my dependent nature.
My mind swells with intensity
trying to escape this mutilated play.
The imperfections are covered
with ardent behavior,
which beneath is lurking a devious plan.
In this game there is no benefactor.

Ellen L. Cox
LISTEN TO THE HEART BEAT OF SPRING

Listen to the heart beat of spring
Softly tapping at your door.
Hear her young voice sing
While dancing gracefully across the floor.

She arose from the winter's ice and snow
Coming forth with warming heat.
Bringing with her the sun's bright glow
To melt away rain and sleet.

Open wide the windows and doors
Let her in from the winter's chill.
Let her warmth through you soar
While her heart beat you feel.

Listen again to her sing
Watch her dance across the floor.
Listen to the heart beat of spring
Softly tapping at your door.

Jennifer Finlay
AN OFFERING TO THE GODS

I want to ride the world with you
upon your golden chariot new.
We'll reach the sun, run out of sky.
We'll find each Mars, to planets fly.
Our brazen wings will keep the pace
to wheels of clouds, comets of lace.
We'll play and dance the tune so far.
And end it as a shooting star.

Wilma A. Ingalls
SNOWBOUND LANDSCAPES

As light flows through my windows
space fills with colors
when the sun's radiance hits against the snow
to unfold beauty
that fills my open moments
in new awareness.

My view captures the touch of an artist
like a gallery canvas
where he paints half-finished

arc
near an old shed
as a passageway which I could pass through.
Then with a brush of winds northwest
he builds layered waves
in high white cap cliffs with white pebbles
piled like aggot gems
along the white sandy shoreline.

And forms blue ice sculptured twists
on bare trees frosted as if dipped in white paint
to dress all in wooden lace of boughs weeping
as man's survival hangs in the balance
of an artist's hands in Snowbound Landscapes.

Mary-Louise Scappaticci
A TRUE DOER

God is I
For I am not God
I'm not divine . . .
For he is.

I shall not be credited
For the good I've done,
For it was God in me . . .
One in one. . .

Robert G. Blewett
SMALL STEPS

I've always taken, on my path
Those cautious, timorous little
Small steps.

I've yearned to lift my head,
To see, to feel, to listen;
Unafraid to give
A tender glance, a helpful touch.

Sniveling small steps!

But change will come
and I shall learn of,
Those racing leaps and
Swinging strides and
Powerful encouraging bounds
I sense lie firmly placed:
Within my heart.

Kent Monroe, Jr.
STOLEN MASTERPIECE

This sunrise is like a pilfered painting
surfacing for a few sudden seconds,
its huge orange head burning through a gun-grey fog
thick as winter fur.

For ten minutes it becomes a pink flamingo,
its great wings
as long and powerful as the moment it owns.

The explosion is brief,
the encounter brilliant.

Bits of red fan out in symbolic expression
of suffering such short acquaintance.

It leaves to a bare blue
sadly similar and lonely
as lesser beauty sometimes is.

Damn you, blue sky—
you've stolen a masterpiece.

Sheila C. Raleigh
THE GRAVE, SMOOTH WAVES

I stand and watch them move toward me

the grave, smooth waves upon the sea.
They throw their strength upon the shore
then turn and leave forever more.
And when I see their power roll
and feel the force as they unfold
I recognize the majesty
of the great and grey eternal sea.
I think in dying I may go there
forsaking earth's anonymous air.

Re
VERSATILITY

Maybe I'm a woman
because I feel.
Maybe I'm a child
because I fear
Maybe I'm a fool
because I listen
Maybe I'm a friend
because I hear.

Edith Vernon Taylor
WAIT NOT!

Wait not, my heart, for all thy problems' ease.
Press on and seek the challenge of the shadow's edge!
Through the darkling glass of trembling fate,
Illumination of thy soul-light bring.
Expect not all fruition of thy earthly wish.
Let Heaven be thy ever certain goal!

Eileen Mary Conlin
FRIENDS

Tranquil are my thoughts with you in mind
Tranquil is my spirit when you're near
Surely Spring has blossomed in my soul
To know you—each day is to feel this way
What a beautiful gift you are to me
You reach out with a loving hand
Eager to please and understand
And jubilance sings from your heart
As you celebrate life
You live with the freedom to love
Given at birth
My joy is a true reflection of What I see
Happy am I to be your friend.

Sheila C. Raleigh
THE ORANGE CAT

I give my sustenance now
to the crows.
Where I came from
nobody knows, and
nobody knows if
I am young or old.
I have lain beside
the edge of the road
hurt and dying
in the rain and cold.
Three days now
the cars have gone by,
no one has heard
when I've tried to cry.
Now I can tell
I am about to die.
I'm only a cat

not meant to be,
there was never a home
provided for me.
I give my body now
to the crows
for I'm still a cat
that nobody knows.

R. D. Laurance
SILENCE

Sounds of Silence, scream at
  the night
For loneliness paces, left
  unbound
And silent faces, though they
  might
Look through me, without a
  sound
Loneliness beckons, from
  shadows deep
Calling,
  Reaching,
    and touching me lightly.

I hear my name,
  but all is still!

Where,...
  Oh where, ends this prelude,
    this ritual of time...
Tomorrow?

Ah, yes!
It is always tomorrow!
There are no screams during
  the day
    only the warmth
      the soothing warmth
        the gentle kiss of life
          a caress of sharing.

It always makes me forget
  this feeling,
    this feeling
      of silence.

Sue Brown
POETRY

Thoughts swirling in my mind
Faster than the hand can write
Thoughts
Of Life Death Eternity
Thoughts
Of Sadness Gladness
Thoughts
Soaring with the wind
Thoughts
Unsaid
Unwritten.

Kevin William Petsch
ON OUR ENGAGEMENT

May you be the seed, and I,
the water, and may time
provide
the sunshine for us to grow
together.

Let love become our roots,
from which
we grow strong and tall, with
many branches.

And as time passes, our
branches will break
and our leaves will fall, but
our roots
will remain forever.

Alta Lea Fugia
SCOTCH-IRISH

You'll find him in the best of
barrooms
His name is Scotch and he is
Irish;
He'll bid you be his bride or
groom,
And hold your hand.
Was it August or December;
That I joined his "gallant"
band?
With happiness I've held him

high,
He prostitutes me with a grin,
And oh, that head- ache on
tomarrow,
How and where will it end.
I know someday I'll try,
With hopefull heart, to quit
him cold,
I'm so afraid I'll get to shakeing,
Without the bottle that I hold.
Not to drink's a hard-earned
lesson
And there are few who never
pay,
All because they took the hand
of
Old Scotch-Irish on their way.

Mae Koppman
SILENCE UNCLAIMED

Why now does the stillness
hamper me,
  When before, I sought it like
a refuse?
Ah there! The sweet strains of
melody fill the air,
  Lifting the density of the
unclaimed silence -
Spreading, expanding, here,
there,
  Until all at once the silence
is gone.
The sound of music, the flute,
the drum, the violin,
  Sweet, soft strains, haunting
melodies follow me.

I must run, I must turn, I must
raise my hands
  To my face, this way, that
way - I must dance
To the light of the sun to the
beat of my heart.
  But now, I look again for
the stillness
Of the quiet corner, but find
it not,
  For all is the excitement of
the explosion of rhythm,
The motion of command, and
so, alone I sway,
  Until finally I lay upon the
soft down,
Beneath my feet and roll, like
a cat,
  Into a ball - and sleep.

Rheanda Wilson
THE THOUGHTFUL HOUSE

I am old, with rotting timbers,
but in my days of Glory
I have seen many a sight.
I saw the Civil War.
I saw General Washington
and held General Lee.
I held President Lincoln
and saw president Carter, too.
But now I am to be torn down
from my place of honor.
Good-bye my place of honor-
Good-bye forever more.

Gayle S. Marsh
UNTITLED

I can't stop screaming in my
anger
at the injustices we have done
the peace we've lost
the wars we never won
hungry children stare out with
eyes too old
the old so empty in pain at
being all alone
so we turn our heads and
answer with our old cliches
only to compound the
problems that we caused
yesterday

Rhondi Thomas
BEAUTIFUL LAKES

There is salt
in the water of
two of the most
Beautiful Lakes
I've ever seen,
streaming down
your face.
Deep liquid pools
of mysterious brown
-with black centers
emitting chills of ice,
sparks of fire.
Yes, there is salt
in the water of
two of the most
Beautiful Lakes
I've ever seen.

Michael Orozco
LOVER'S QUEST

Time and time again:
I have looked into the mirror,
but I see myself no more,
I have reached to hold your
hand,
but felt coldness from the floor.
I have yearned to have my say,
but my sounds still have no
words,
I have listened for your heart,
but there is nothing to be
heard.
I have cried within myself,
but my tears have never shown,
I have waited for your touch...
but you're forever gone.

Wade Harris
WHAT I SEE

The world is full of majesty
All that I see is mine
The people, the land, the sky
The people are my brothers
The land is my servant
The sky is my root

Karen Dixon
FOLLOW

Follow my footsteps,
  and I shall guide you.
Follow my hand,
  and I shall feed you.
Follow my mind,
  and I shall teach you.
Follow my love,
  and you shall find God.
Follow Gods way,
  and you shall be forever
          knowledged.

J. Maharani Quimby
FATE

From the day we met
my life has been changed
you touched my world
and made it beautiful
Bringing me sunshine and joy
and happiness that knows no
bounds.

J. Elizabeth Fowler
DON'T LEAVE

Please don't leave me,
I need you, believe me.

Our love is like no other,
I'm a woman, you're my lover,
I'm your sister, you're my
brother,
I'm your mother, you're my
father,
We're everything we'll ever
need,

So please,
Don't leave.

Darcy Diane Pearson
APOSTASY

I am a gentlewoman;
I have a gentle soul.
I am daffodil and crocus and
iris,
I am nightness and politeness.
My mother raised me to be a
lady.

We are together
and yet I feel such anger.
Could this really be
"knowing you"
in the Biblical sense?
Surely no one intended it
to be this way.

I said yes once,
a long time ago,
but you have always
said yes.

I am a gentlewoman
with a gentle soul,
and I have always been asked.
Why have you never asked me
again?

Mada M. Wilbur
IDAHO

I touch my hand to a rising
yawn;
Leave my bed at the break of
dawn
And look out at the early morn.
A beautiful day is being born!

The horizon sheds a sleepy haze
As clouds and sun spray painted
rays.
I fill my being with morning air;
Absorb the Beauty everywhere.

Green fields rolling to the
river's bend,
Surging life that will never end;
Snowcapped mountains on
every side -
All thrill my breast with
home-land pride.

Such a lift to my day
This scene is giving...
How sad, the world sleeps
Through this best part of
living.

Mary Burke Klein
FRIEND OF GRACE

Plastic soul,
  Searching eyes,
Arms stiff, ever reaching for
dreams.
  Pursed lips trying to speak...
No words.
Dressed in gown of silk, unable
to feel the softness.

Who cares...She has no where
to go.
  Forever caged for people to
stare and point.
God, I hate when they point
at my friend of grace and
peace.
  My plastic friend...the
mannequin.

James A. Marks
I AM A HOUSE

I am a house.
Through lonely, sightless,
shattered eyes
I stare, bewildered, at a world
That has forgotten my walls
that,
Once,
Were gleaming white;
My proud columns that,
Once,

Stood erect as sentries;
My heavy oak doors that,
Once,
Swung open for all,
And the joy and love and
  comfort that,
Once,
I gave
For nothing.
I am a house.
I was a home.

John C. Bowles
INELUCTABILITY

I am a citadel of strength,
  I stand alone inviolate,
against all armies full regaled,
  my fortress walls no man
  has scaled.

Time is the faceless enemy,
  that lays my ramparts in
  decay,
invading hordes of years seep
  through,
  my citadel will crumble too.

Charmaine Swansen
THE BEGINNING

Open windows,
Open jars,
Open bottles,
Open bars,
Life is so full of openness,
Some people to be kind will
  open your door,
But, when you're in love you
  open more.
Like you and me,
We've opened our hearts.
But just like the door,
The opening is just an entrance
  to the beginning of the start.

Daniel Rauser
THE DIVE

There on the brink of the abyss
  he stands;
  looking out and down to the
  valley floor below.
Pondering as to whether he
  should dive now,
  or if he should wait for a
  more opportune moment,
He glances back at what was
  once a home and a refuge,
  but which now holds only
  harsh blows, and impending
  hunger,
He fears the death which awaits
  if he crashes there,
  but there is also wonder, as
  to what may be the final
  outcome
  of it
With one last backward glance,
  he dives, and drops as if a
  stone,
  towards the rocks and broken
  mountain below
Then, with an exhilerating rush
  he is picked up by the ever-
  present wind
And another young falcon takes
  takes to the air.

William Don Marley
**WHAT HAPPENED TO
  THE ANIMALS**

It's death, dying, grief, will I
  ever get any relief?
The whole world is going to
  pieces,
No one has heard of a list of
  endangered species.

In the early years, the sea was
  filled with mammals,
And the land with oceans of

animals.
Now they've all been led to
  the slaughter.
Buffalo Bill, did you have a
  daughter?
Dressed like big-game hunters
  in Khakis and sun hats dashing,
I can't believe we killed all
  those animals
Just for the sake of fashion.
We've killed for bags, shoes,
  coats and soup,
To that superior being, we
  really must look like a bunch
  of dopes.
Don't listen to all the folk-lore,
You know there's a reason
  all the whales are washing up
  on shore.
It's death, dying, grief, will I
  ever get any relief?
The whole world is going to
  pieces,
No one has heard of a list of
  endangered species.

Jeanne M. Luce
**THE BEGINNING OF A
  MEMORY**

As time for your baby now
  draws very near,
You remember the times that
  to you were so dear
And you realize that now to
  your baby, they'll be
The beginning of what will be
  life's memory.

From the first breath of life,
  there are so many things-
Beautiful winters, much
  welcomed springs,
Happiness, sorrow and days
  full of cheer
And birthdays to start one more
  beautiful year.

Doris J. Rincker
FATHER

His hair is growing thinner now,
It's gray in place of brown.
His eyes show signs of tiredness,
Tho his brow holds not a frown.

He's a friend to little children,
The deer and squirrels as well,
In fact if you would ask me,
I'd have to say he's swell.

Of course I may be prejudice,
Of this you might agree,
For the person of whom I'm
  speaking of,
Is called "Father" by me.

Alexander Herrero
MARIE

Higher tide eventually comes,
Relentlessly the drummer
  drums,
Each grain a soul is washed
  away,
Each night destroys another
  day,
Others lie five feet or more,
But I stay near the salty shore.
I dream of a happier time before
  before,
When Marie and I walked this
  shore,
Hand in hand we walked then
  ran,
And wrestled each other in the
  sand.
Naked, happy, wild, and free,
The way we always wanted to
  be,
We'd dive into this horrid sea,

And I'd make love to my angel
  Marie.
Know lovers lie five feet or
  more,
But I stay near the salty shore.
Then one day with no moon in
  sight,
Afraid to show its face tonight,
Hades creept up from the sea,
And stole my only love Marie.
Afraid to take death in my hand
  hand,
Knowing God won't understand,
I sit here by this retched shore,
Hating this place I loved before,
And wait for those waives to
  come
take me.
Take me to my bride to be,
Take me to my lost Marie.

Christine Stowe Kelty
**OF LOVE AND OTHER
  THINGS**

I write of love and other things,
Of kisses soft as Angel's wings
Of young love's tender first
  embrace,
The peace found in an aged
  face,
Of song sung under Summer's
  moon,
And life that ended much too
  soon.
Of friendship, gentle as a breeze,
For love is found in all of
  these.
I write of love and other things
That living in this old world
  brings.

Jennifer Murphy
LOST

Looking out to the sea
My mind begins to escape me.
The shouts and screams
Are drowned by my dreams.
I see old enemies and friends.
I see new beginnings and their
  ends.
Where did my happiness go?
Why is my life full of woe?
Maybe it is time to die.
I am living in a lie.
I am not who I pretend to be.
What has happened to the real
  me?
I am lost
Will I be found?
Why have I changed for
  society?
Why can't I be free?
Will I find myself?
No, never.
I guess I have lost me forever.

M. Lois Daugherty
SEASONS WITH BILLIE JO

On hot summer days, to lots
  of yardsales we'd go.
Always the two of us together,
  me and little Billie Jo.
On rainy days, when my
  darling couldn't play out,
We'd have so much fun with
  toys, she wouldn't pout.
On cool fall days, we'd take
  rides, see the pretty trees.
And count all the different
  colors on leaves, blowing free.
We'd begin looking forward to
  share, enjoy the holidays.
"Santa will be here soon"
  several times a week she'd say.
On cold winter days, Billie Jo
  and I watched the blowing

snow,
And pop popcorn, play house,
  see all our favorite T.V. shows.
On spring days, we'd pick pr
  pretty little yellow flowers,
And swing and play, sharing
  laughter, love, and joy for
  hours.
She'd shout to people we'd see
  "Hi, it's mamaw and me".
Seasons end, so did "We,"
  Billie Jo went to heaven, she
  was only three.

A. J. Eversole
OUR LOVE

Our love is like
a river flowing
onward towards
it's endless goal.
Raging, roaring,
quiet, peaceful.
Onward,
endless,
evermore!

Tama Kay Corby
**IT SHOULD HAVE BEEN
  SAID**

Grandma,
  Please forgive me for all the
  times I should have
said I love you——and didn't.
  Now that you are gone it's
  to late for me to tell
you just how much I really
  loved you. This saddens me
deeply, because now I hold in
  my heart a new found know-
ledge of what love is all about
  and you are gone.
  I realize now all the times I
  should have held your
hand and told you of my dreams
  dreams, hopes, even all my
  fears,
you always understood.
  We talked, but not enough
  about the important things
of life, you and me. You were
  a great lady and I loved
you so.
  In any event you are gone
  now and our conversations
are only faded memories,
  shadowed by the deep, lasting
sorrow of losing you before I
  was ready to let you go.

Norma Claflin-Trask
VIOLETS

Last night I went out to my
  garden,
And smelled the turned over
  earth.
I looked at the sky above me
And asked "How much am I
  worth?"
Compared to the shy little
  violets -
Compared to the buttercup,
  yellow,
Compared to the blue sky above
  me.
"Good Lord!" Aren't I a lucky
  fellow?"

The grass is growing a bit
  greener,
The shy little violets, too.
Give me the old spring fever.
As they come smiling thru',
They lift up their little blue
  faces
And smile at God above.
Then bow in wee graceful poses
To the God, whom we all love.

Ardella Casper
UNDER COVER OF EVE

No doubt Eve's oft been
  blamed, and not acclaimed
For woman's lack of modesty
  in dress.
    We are inflamed.

Although she claimed to have
  been framed,
At least for Eve we can say
  this;
    She was ashamed.

Mark A. Butcher
FUTURE'S PAST

This cold, damp winter day I
  walk
As the golden sun sets in the
  west.
I think of what I am or will
  be.
What will I be that I am not now?
Yes, what am I now this day?
I am a slave, though I have no
  master.
I am a man, though I am yet a
  boy.
I care not what I am to be.
Whether I am to be hated or
  loved.
Am I to be feared or understood
  by man?
Yet I care not what I am to be,
Just that I am to be.
Will I be known or like every
  other man?
I wish to be known, but I care
  not.
Will I be with another, or be
  alone?
Is the life I live half or more
  over,
Or am I to die today or
  tomorrow?
Will I ever get back on my feet
  again,
If so will they be kicked out
  from beneath me?
I help others and ask for
  nothing, but
When I ask I get nothing in
  return.
I do not care much for great
  money.
I care not what I am to be,
  just
That I am to be; In Future's
  Past.

Donna Orlick
A SPACE IN TIME

The engines roar in our ears,
  the wheels turn,
We are a part of space.

The craft soars, falls, and rises
  again . . .
Motionless in time.

Stretching out as arms, the
  wings reach for the day
Or reach for the night.

Lightness and Darkness assume
  a position on a circumference
Of a dial of numbers.

Big Ben advances forward while
  we are a part of
Yesterday, Today, and
  Tomorrow . . .
Or is it a part of us?

Kennilee Addleman
GOING AWAY

"I love this farm, Maggie,
  from acre to inch.
  They're crowding and
    pushing us out.

Forty-nine years we've worked
  this soil,
    this rich, life-giving
    land!
Why are the buildings so tall
  and cold?
The clean, fresh air now burns
  my lungs.
There's no room left to plow.
They gave me money.
  It's not that . . .
Oh, Maggie, the memories!
  the time! the caring! . . .
Hold me close, old woman.
  I'm scared."

Carl Dietz
SUNRISE IS ALIVE

Sunrise
is alive, hallucination universe
world of brilliant color
  splashing
solids never stop moving
waiting, each of us universe
searching while it whispers
  secrets
infinity and the universe.

Debra A. Koller
THE WRITER

A being whose body is a
nervous system of sensitivity

His deepest thoughts, highest
  aspirations
etched onto a flimsy parchment
with hopes of immortalization.

Contained not within himself
but between the bindings of
  a book
is his soul, laid bare
for all to see.

Writing his own life
he stands watching
from a distance
to see it unfold.

Often death comes too soon,
the book, forgotten.
His life collecting dust
on the back of a shelf .
So again he tries.
Another book written.
And stepping out of its pages
he is reincarnated.

Karla Jacqueline
ON EARTH

To understand is to be
  understood,
If you don't try, then who
  would?
  And if you could,
  You really would,
  Be understood.

Jeannette Allen
TOMORROW

As I sit here today
My thoughts lean forward
Into the dream world of
  tomorrow.
What is there? What is
  tomorrow?
Will I be a part of it?
My thoughts run wild
Into that imaginary world
As if I know someday
I'll be a part of that world.
But is it real? Am I real?
My mind is free,
But am I?
Can I run wild and never end?
Is this me? Who am I?
Tomorrow is a land of no real
  meaning.
It has no real life.
It's only a dream,
A thought.

Have you ever been there?
NO! You yourself has never
  seen
or been to the land of tomorrow.
It's only a dream,
A thought.
WAIT!! I think I'm there,
Tomorrow has come for me,
I think I can touch it.
WAIT, don't leave, come back,
PLEASE!! PLEASE!! Come
  back.
I know you're there, aren't you?
Answer me, say something,
  please?
It's G O N E, today is here again.
Oh tomorrow, please come
  back . . .
I can't face today right now,
I'm not ready for it,
It came too soon.
Please tomorrow . . . come
  back . . . come back!!!

Rose Marie Evans
**ODE TO A DEFEATED
WARRIOR**

Face defeat with courage my
  child
Why, you can even learn to
  lose with style
Lose with grace in every case
And your reward will be the
  respect of every man
woman, or child in the human
  race

Stand, tall, and look trouble
  straight in the eye
Never waiver or even breathe
  a sigh
Bow to no person woman or
  man
Yet never be afraid to lend
  them a helping hand

Savor defeat as a good
  experience in learning
Always keep striving, growing,
  and yearning
For like yourself all brave men
  have tasted defeat
Even in the face of adversity
  they would never retreat

Though defeated know your
  cause is not lost
Be proud that you ran your
  race no matter what the cost
Yet all is not lost though it
  may seem to be
Once defeated, defeat can only
  open our eyes and make us
  see.

Winnifred Harding Harlow
SATISFACTION

Self pity-
A cry of spiritual hunger
Resounds to an empty
  audience.
What good am I?
Destiny unfulfilled-
Child of mind
Question not.
Vines are laden with grapes.
Your answer lies
In the harvest.

Barbara Brockman
FOR MY MOTHER

She is not totally forgotten.
A now grown up girl searches
Through the thinning haze
For a time in her childhood,
Where a memory exists -
  lingering.

A scene begins to form, and
Focuses on a firelit sitting
  room.

Here's a mother and little
  girl
(Bouncing playfully on her
  mother's knee)
Share a comfortably worn
  couch.

The two of them are chanting
  those
For years used nursery rhymes,
That seem to build a bond
Bringing closer together a
Mother and her child.

The child's eyes are alive,
They display the fire's flame
Dancing in their radiant
  reflection.
Both faces of mother and child
  shining
With the intense love they are
  feeling.

Security and a sense of peace
Flow like an invisible current
Filling the child's sensitive needs.
My search ends with this
  memory
Of my mother who has died.

Neal Van Dorsten
**WINTER BREAKFAST AT
HANGOVER LODGE**

Arose in hangover, lodge cold,
  running nose, snows,
  alone.

Lost thoughts, amnesia night,
  cobwebs burn
like forgotten bacon.

Where?
  Here; hair streaming.

Moist breasts,
  tongues, crevice.

Hard cock, soft touch,
  thrust, thrust, thrust, thrust,
  thrust . . .

Trust!

Gone.

No excedrin,
  Pain! Burnt bacon,
  good eggs.

Frances H. Lewis
LOST SPIRIT

The Saint of the Cascades lost
  her Spirit
Helen astride the chain
Graces the mountain range of
  Cascades
This Saint young and beautiful
Tall and symmetrical is
  restless
Spirit Lake stole her Spirit, to
  enchant itself
Her face is in the clouds . . .
  searching
Her white cold shoulders
Shiver under the snowcoat
Her depths rumble and grumble
Her foundation shudders and
  shakes
As she cries out for her Spirit
Helen's heart couldn't stand
  the strain
She opened her mouth wide
  and cried
Erupting in agony . . . disgorging
  herself
Heat and gas, bones and gray
  ash
Spewed out of her mouth,
  breaking her flank
Boulders and rocks vented up
  and rained down
Mud and debris filled the lake
  and valley
In pursuit of the rest of herself

Mt. St. Helen's quest goes on
She grieves for her Spirit lost.

Dorothy Sammons
THE SONG OF THE SEA

The song of the sea is lilting,
It has a pleasant sound.
Breakers crash like cymbals,
Then they roll across the ground.

The ocean is like a symphony,
Giant breakers become a drum.
They beat upon the rocky
shore,
While mermaids sing and hum.

Ishmael
THE PLAINS OF TIME: V

Endlessly circling in the sky
Flying vultures ponder our
fate
While waiting for us to die.

Wracked by the winds of time,
Blowing sand as bullets rend
Baking under the ubiquitous
Sun
Our lives slip by and we
wonder why?

Indifferent to love until too
late,
The beauty of the plains passes
by
As we resist the world
And concentrate on fearful
progeny of our mind.

Time's messengers, the vultures
are,
Counting our days with patient
glides
Before they descend to satiate
Their voracious hunger on our
lives.

Cecelia Leung
HEAVENLY INSPIRATION

. . . Heavenly Inspiration!
Fingers dart
Like minnows over strings
Echoing the soundless melody
of an angel harping.

Trills,
Cadenzas,
Brief snatches of melody
Flash brightly in the flow of
music.

Leaping and
Dancing
The notes fall
Over
Each other
In their eagerness
To reach the brink of
PERFECTION

Then,
in horror
tumble
to a crashing
DISCORD

Patricia Gaye Jensen
STAR OF MY LOVELIFE

You were older and charming
and handsome and wise
I don't know how I captured
your eyes
And in the dance of my dreams
it was you holding me
And the music it played on
forever.

'Cause you are the star of my
lovelife
Shining your love down on me
And you are the love of my
lovelife
Lasting all eternity
By the dark of the night, by

the light of the moon
By the way that you hold me
and touch me
It's the look in your eyes as you
look down in mine
It's the way that you kiss me
good night.

'Cause you are the star of my
lovelife
Shining your love down on me
And you are the love of my
lovelife
Lasting all eternity
As the night fades away I awake
in the dawn
And the brightness of day makes
me wonder
Be it real, be it right, you're the
love of my life
You're the one I've been waiting
for

'Cause you are the star of my
lovelife
Shining your love down on me
And you are the love of my
lovelife
Lasting all eternity.

Alma Joyce
DIVORCE

Split, the code today!
Who is the party of the second
part
living behind that whitewashed
chastity belt?
And shall commitment step
fullweight from the pain of
yesterday?
While order screams and
freedom weeps,
the stumbling block astride the
spirits vow
stretches His soul across the
void,
and blood gives up its water.

Kathleen Burke
ENDLESSLY

The rain leaks through the
greyness
Endlessly
Like silent sorrow slowly
growing
without cease.
For aching hearts forever
breaking
There's no peace
As long as rain keeps falling
Endlessly.
The whole world keeps on
fighting
Endlessly
For selfish reasons like position,
power and greed.
Men keep fighting, killing,
dying
without need.
And rain keeps slowly falling
Endlessly.
The world keeps growing darker
Endlessly
And nobody around me seems
to see.
Tomorrow there won't be a
world for me,
But the rain will keep on
falling
Endlessly.

Genevieve R. Erwin
MORE LIKE THE DOVES

The doves fly high above the
ground
Over tree tops and free as air;
Up where it's quiet, not a
sound

And all the while they haven't
a care.
We mortals down on earth
below
Worry and fret from sun to sun;
Ever and onward as we go
Until one day our life is done.
If we were much more like the
doves
I'm sure our lives would be
prolonged;
If we could dwell much more
on love
And keep within our hearts
a song.

Ronald Eugene Posey
**LOVE IS THE GREATEST
GIFT**

You're so soft and warm
You're so sweet and nice
You could never be a storm
When you're paradise.

You're as sweet as honey
And as tasty as wine
A good woman like you
Is very hard to find.

You make me happy
By lots of things you do
And I guess that's why I'm
saying
I honestly love you.

For love is the greatest gift in
the whole world
Especi ally when you can share
it with one special girl
And if my dream comes true,
My love I'll share with you.

Jessie M. MacDonald
REMINISCING

Wandering
Round the old deserted
homestead
Hearing
Ghosts of memories whispering
soft and low.
Faintly
Tales of hardships come to
haunt me
Calling
To be heard across the years.
Hard times
When the crops were swallowed
up in dust
Good times
Happy voices floating on the
breeze
Wishing
I could see the old familiar faces
Knowing
That their time in life was o'er.

Vivian D. Jones
AUTUMN'S BLANKET

Fall is one of Nature's most
exciting spectacles
A veritable promenade
of colors

yellow, orange, and red
The pastoral, muted tones of
early morning mists
Autumn moves down the
mountainside
a blanket of changing
color
Embracing the world with
charm
and love in bloom
The Autumn Blanket warms
our cheerful souls
And uplifts the world with
all its royal finery.

Gordon Saul
LES YEUX ECLATANTS

Radiant are her eyes
Joyful is her smile
Soft and tender is her touch
Warm and loving her embrace. .

Always fun-loving
Sometimes silly
And childishly mischievous

Strong . . . yet vulnerable
Intelligent, sensitive
Clever, practical
Ambitious, energetic and
persevering
Still, always longing to be
More that what she is
Not yet fully aware
Of what she wants
Or of who she can be

Hurt by the realization
That she is capable of hurting
Such is the ebb and flow
Of her emotions
And her frailties

Yet she loves
And appreciates
One who loves
And adores her

With indescribable sweetness
She walks in my mind
And stirs my heart.

Marcia Fair
LIKE A CLOUD

My illusions of you are finally
falling away like a cloud in the
sky.
Once my feelings for you were
strong but,
like a cloud, elements of nature
have
changed you and me and my
billowy dreams
of you drift delicately apart
and at long
last I am free . . .

Nancy Ann Moltisanti
YOUR PIANO

Alone and silent your piano
stands, dust playing the keys
where once your fingers danced

Gone for good the music
and your arms never to hold me
again
your whisper
never to break the night

The sweet sonata of our
lovemaking
echoes lingeringly
(shades of birdsong)
in the gray winter dawn creep
tattered wisps of moonlight
dreams

subtly and quite absently
insinuated into my earliest
(most first)
waking (one eye slowly)
thoughts (a cappella)

Grace E. Herman
THE BADLANDS

You say that you don't like
the badlands,
The glaring white of the alkali
sod.
The scant greasewood and
cactus clumps,
You say it's "land forsaken by
God."
But there's something about
the badlands
That sorta gets you after a
while,
Perhaps it's the barren stillness
That stretches out mile upon
mile.
Yes, the badlands are harsh and
ugly
To the city stranger's eye,
But, Mister, when you get to
know them
You'll see their beauty by and
by.
In the cactus that blooms on the
sandhills,
And the huge sprawling ramparts
of stone,
If you look close enough you'll
see
That the badlands have a beauty
all their own.

Gregg C. Kretchun
IN ANTICIPATION OF:

I live my days
in anticipation of
spending sleep in each other's
arms;
our souls dancing the night
away.
I live my nights
in anticipation of
spending an extra five morning
minutes in bed;
and the awakening exchange
over mugs of coffee.
I live my life
in anticipation of
an ever-deepening relationship
of love;
years of memories, an infinity
of futures.
I love you
in anticipation of
loving you more .

Steve Thomas
UNTITLED

The feeling I had for you won't
go away.

Oh sure, it hides for awhile,
but just as I've decided that
maybe it
wasn't there after all,
THERE it is - playing its silly
games
and hurting.

(But not meaning to.)

Martin Golby
SONNET OF THE WINDMILL

The rusty windmill, alone in
the field,
Stands tall among the gently
rolling hills
As it were a child that never
revealed
A need to be close, or display
his skills.
It remains untouched, without
a fresh glow
Of rustoleum to boast its
squelched pride,
While the barns and house
continue to show
Up against the sprawling
countryside.
Obscure, forgotten, or else
neglected,
On calm, still days it does not
speak, or show
Or even grieve of feeling
rejected;
But the blades turn slowly, as
night winds blow,
And sound a cry to those who
let it rust,
That enduring attention is a
must.

Eva L. Becker
A LITTLE GIRL SEES GOD

They say the little girl had a
big imagination
When she spoke, I looked into
her eyes
I felt a strange sensation.
She told me of that special
night
When her mommy brought her
home.
It was turning dusky dark,
Her heart was filled with song.
She looked into the sky above,
The clouds were etched with
lace.
A golden stairway there
appeared,
She saw a gentle face.
A man was looking down,
With outstretched hand he
beckoned.
She took a small step forward,
Tried to reach him for a
second.
He seemed to whisper, "Come
to me,"
She felt no fear at all.
Her tiny fingers touched his
face,
As she listened to his call.
Her mother broke the spell,
saying, "Come inside, Child,"
With tears flowing down her
cheeks,
She looked, the kind man
smiled.
A golden halo filled the sky,
His face faded with the night.
Where the stairway had
appeared,
Was a bright shining light.
Now we know that children
In their innocence
Tell tales of mystery and glory.
It may be just the poet in me,
But I do believe her story.

Troy McNaught Westby
THE CHANGING SEA

The endless billows rolled
beneath a sky of glass;
The endless waving sea,
composed of prairie grass.

Lured the settlers on
thru' days of thirst and sweat
Until they reached a river
where homestead stakes were
set.
The endless billows roll
beneath the sky of glass,
But the endless waving sea
is not the prairie grass.
'Tis endless miles of concrete
broken here and there
By stark and raucous cities
where men their shackles wear.

Cynthia Carol Matheson
I SEE YOU THERE

I see you there inside your
crystal ball
hovering over your life as if it
were to leave.
You do not hear my cry or my
call,
nor in life do you believe.

I feel the sorrow in my heart
for you-
You are not willing to live
or find great things to do,
and yet you treasure me, but
will not give.

I try to understand the reason
for your ways,
and not to interfere,
But I cry because of lonely days
and I hold you in my heart so
dear.

You can have your way
it was meant to be-
but for today,
please think of me.

Diana Kierce
SAINT HELENS

Saint Helen's rocks and shakes
Its mud flow buried Spirit Lake.

The skys are gloomy and grey
It has ruined the fertile fields
of hay.

It spits and sputters clouds of
ash,
and fills the air with poisonous
gas.

Our beautiful forest of timber
is gone,
the hot mud covered it up, as
it rolled along.

Over the land it covered with
ash,
killing the animals in a flash.
Why does Saint Helen's rumble
and growl?
It's an eerie feeling, when the
winds howl.

There's millions of dollars of
damage that needs repair,
It has been to many a terrible
scare.
Saint Helen's has slept for many
a year,
She wants you to know, she's
something to fear.
So let it be a warning to some,
that a closer look could be
dumb.

Saint Helen's will continue to
rumble and roar,
Till she goes back to sleep,
and is silent once more.

Ann Cassouto
STREET PEOPLE

Gray faces, staring,
Sharing broken dreams
With some who pass them
With indifferent eyes
Grown cold and colder
in a world
Grown cold and colder.

Shattered faces
Wearing hairy masks,
Wearing hopelessness
Like tattered rags,
Beating rhythms
On a battered drum-
Beating life
And everything
And everyone.

Arlene Mae Cushman
JENNIFER

One of open mind
Hoping for love, tenderness,
and patience,
Her smiles she'll give in return.
'Tis Jennifer's way of saying
with a sparkle in her eyes:
Of years she'll need someone
to help her learn.
Life stages as she modes-
As she grows, we won't let
her life erode.

Leave reality for her generation
to learn.
Don't rob her of being only a
child:
For what we teach; is her
concern.
Give her beauty of God's
creations.
O' please let her enjoy -
view -
listen:
Without man's pollution of her
anatomy -
Eroding her mind with obscene
views -
Contaminating her recreation.

Oh give Jennifer security, not
insecurity.
Join her hands and look;
For the silver side of life,
'Cause life's asking is for
purity.
Mistakes she makes, we hope
to forgive,
Life measures, is the results of
what she gives.
World as she makes her incli ne
Jennifer, born in the "Year of
the Child,"
Nineteen hundred seventy nine.

Frances Koehner
YEARNING

The seasons toss
The seasons turn
Blindly I watch
Yellow silk torn
From gypsy trees and
Snow's white tide
Rising in tableau.
Blindly I wait as
Spring's green silhouette
Foreshadows Summer's
Throbbing tempo but
I pay no homage
Refusing to partake alone
Of what we shared
Searching for a sign
You exist somewhere
Beyond the bed of earth
I crowned with stone
In infini te despair.

Stanley Jack
COLLECTORS AND COLLECTIBLES

Collectors everywhere are
collecting
anything collectible, old or new,
including this or that.
Some for a simple sentimental
reason;
others reason that eventually
they'll

surely see their moneybags
  grow fat.
Some will put their prized
  collections
proudly on display; others
  store them in
a strong vault to keep preditors
  away.
I, too, am a collector, altho not
  of some
commodity acquired to exhibit
  or to sell.
All my life, I've collected daily
  entries
in an imaginary diary and
  memorized them well.
And I keep them forever hidden
  where no
soul on earth will ever see them;
  none can ever find.
Since they're securely stashed
  away,
high up in the attic storeroom
of my mind.

Kathryn A. Pelky
YOU

Will You take my hand and tell
  me this,
That after death there is still
  bliss?
Will You take my heart and
  heal the pain,
So that I can laugh once again?
Will You take the tears from
  my eyes,
And help to free me from this
  vise?
Oh, God! I feel, You have
  taken my soul,
And You, alone, can make me
  whole.

Augusta K. Yaroker
REQUIEM

All who felt the need to cry
And mourn the sudden death
  of
a musician
So unlike Beethoven or Bach
All who felt the need-
Never shed a tear nor sent a
  flower
For everyone of our city police
  and firemen
Who died needlessly while on
  duty.
They who help protect us left
  many a sad home
All who cried publicly where
  are they now?
As all other sad hearts had no
Merry Christmas or Happy New
  Year.

Jane Sweetland
UNTITLED

Poetry is a stethoscope
with which one can hear
the heartbeat
of civilizations.

Carla D. Fishel
PASSING TIME

Be satisfied with time;
for it passes oh so fast.
Then think of days; of days
  gone by,
and treasured moments past.
The tears;
the joys,
the love,
the pain,
I miss those days now gone;
and wish I had in my arms
tomorrow morning's dawn.

Ila Standlea Steinke.
**WHO THINKS HE IS REALLY
THE BOSS AROUND HERE**

Who rules our home with will
  of steel?
Tom does.
Who gets fed first at every meal?
Tom does.
Who gets first choice of
  favorite chair,
With kingly glance and haughty
  air,
No matter WHO is sitting
  there?
Tom does.
Who stays indoors on a chilly
  night?
Tom does.
Until we drift in slumber light?
Tom does.
Who then decides to go outside?
Who does with soft meow
  confide
His wishes until we abide?
Tom does.
Who then decides to come back
  in?
Tom does.
At early hour, say 4:00 A.M.
Tom does.
And just when we crawl back
  in bed
Who thinks its time to eat
  instead?
Who wails and moans until
  he's fed?
Tom does.
Who sleeps all day while others
  toil?
Tom does.
Who primps until he's free from
  soil?
Tom does.
Who likes his coat brushed every
  day?
Who brings more joy than we
  can say?
Who warms our hearts in every
  way?
Tom does.

Candass Musslewhite
ALL'S NOT LOST

Where have all the children
  gone
That smiled so wide and bright.
And where have all the stars
  gone
That used to twinkle in their
  eyes?
The flowers that once bloomed
  over
The yard where they played
Have all turned to ashes, and
  with Them an empty plot.
The cemetaries seem to grow
  larger
With each passing day, and the
  children seem to grow weaker,
  with
Each game they play.
Their sweet little faces that
Remind me of Spring, have
  all
Seemed to vanish,
And leaving in their place
  sorrow
And emptiness.
Their warm loving eyes that
Looked toward us with
  hope,
Have all grown tired, making it
Hard for us all to cope.
Their open arms and kisses
  seem

To help us to forget our fears,
But when it's all over, who's
Really going to care?
For the children were always
Different and some people
  turned
Their heads, but what they
  don't
Realize is that we're not made
Of just weight and hair.
The Children may have their
  problems, but at least they
  have
What we haven't got.
The courage to go on, when
  other
People feel all is lost.

Richard F. Harvey
PHILOSOPHER'S REBIRTH

Victorian splendor heralded
  man's desires,
A mind, so restless that the seas
  must quake.
Now modern man extinguishes
  its fires,
Lain placid as an Indian summer
  lake.

The lamb is slaughtered for
  each common feast,
And reason has consumed each
  dying spark.
What creator could forge
  freedom in the beast,
That the light of day once more
  might breach the dark.

In the forest of this night roams
  modern man,
Lost souls, in rows, believing in
  their bars.
But time for me is once again
  at hand,
For shattering these old and
  ailing stars.

Again to feel the anvil fires
  mold;
Again to see the Tyger stalk
  the fold.

Helen Gane Del Curo
THE FARALLONES

High above the shores of
  San Francisco,
High above the grey Pacific,
Rise the Farallon Islands,
Refuge of the Harbor Seals.

All around them fly the
  sea gulls,
All around them swim the
  fishes,
A wild and rugged haven .
Peace for many a species.

All around them pounds the
  ocean,
All the waters once clean and
  pure.
Just beyond an ominous
  threat—
Just a dumping Navy
  operation.
Silent watchers saw the actions.
Silent watchers couldn't
  count the thousands—
Casks that spelled uncertainty,
Casks that altered with the
  times.

Now the Farallon Islands are
  hot with waste.
Now their waters spawn
  exotic growth,
Fish that carry lethal
  loads.

Sponges that tower grotesquely
  tall.
The Farallon Islands once
  offered protection.
Now endangers all who partake
  thereof.
And San Francisco most of
  all—
It knows the resident danger
  there.

Joan Tannen
ANALYSIS

Recesses of hell
Torturously planned,
Reprisals are revered
In beings precariously damned.
Lost souls
Of our own fortification,
Blindly not knowing
When seeking unification .
Awaken and ascend
The clarity of direction
Naught is concealed
In the Aves of our exaltation.

Dena Campbell Cook
TIME

Years-
  will they come again
  or has the wind
  carried them away.

Tears-
  did they come with you
  or did the years
  that counted every day.

Tom Gee
PUNISHED

The hiccup
of a child
weeping
asleep
sent supperless
to bed

the misdemeanor
a broken dish
spilt milk
something
forgotten now
and never important

only the ache
in my gut
for harsh words
and rough hands
remains
startled eyes and tears

too late
now
to hold
the weeping child
and his teddy
too late

Lida B. Marin
MEMORIES TO TREASURE

Do you remember when we
  were young
and yes, oh so restless too?
We couldn't wait till we grew
  up
to do the things that grown-ups

do.
Don't you often sit and wish
that you could turn back the
  time?
Just to relive for a little while
All the happy times, that come
  to mind.
And when our grandchildren
  ask you
what did you do when you
  were small?
Don't you love to sit and tell
  them
Of all the happy memories you
  recall.
Of course, when we were
  growing up
Everyone shared in the evening
  fun
All gathered around the old
  fireplace
After all our chores were done.
But our grandchildren will
  never know
What fun we shared, you and
  me.
They'll never know close
  family ties
Because they are closer to their
  TV.
They never had to work in a
  garden
Don't even know milk comes
  from a cow
Eggs are something they get in
  a store
It all seems like a shame
  somehow.
Our grandchildren are all so
  wonderful
And it's like looking in a glass
  to see
Our own little children all over
  again
The ones God sent to you and
  me.

Marjorie H. Richardson
CHRISTMAS
Midst all the glitter of
  Christmas
And presents under the tree,
We sometimes miss the Spirit
Of what the true meaning
  should be.

Cards and carols and cookies
All play important parts
In showing one another
The joy that's in our hearts.

But, let us always be mindful,
And share with those we know.
That this is a Celebration
For One born so long ago.

Ramona G. Webb
NO TIME FOR US
We used to talk, you and I
And laugh and love
As time went by.

We'd talk of walnuts on the
  roof,
Of war and college
And childrens books.

Trains, economy and oil wells
Of just the beauty
Of coral and sea shells.

Now, there's no time
To meet and dine
Or share a glass of sparkling
  wine.

You've no time to talk with
  me
And speak of the past

Or what is yet to be.
Our separate worlds
Have pulled apart
The desire we once had in our
  heart
To meet that very special one
Who brings joy to our life
When the day is done.

How sad, we allow this world
  to decree
No time for a love
That was meant to be!
Oh, that we could again talk,
You and I,
And laugh and love
As time slips by.

Mary Lynn Sansone
A LOVE LETTER
Long ago and far away I
  tasted the sweetness of your
  lips,
I shared the warmth of your
  embrace.
Unlike the words upon this
  page,
I cannot erase the many
  gathered moments.
You have touched me as no
  one else has
. . .in my mind, my heart, and
  my very being.
Should someone enter my
  existence along the
  encumbered road of life,
in a way such as you have,
even the slightest graze will
  stir my deepest memories
of the times I've spent with
  you.
My emotions cannot be
  adequately expressed through
mere composition,
your specialness,
your oneness,
have become so much a part
  of my nature.
I believe it is beyond your
  realization how very much
  you mean to me.
There may have been others
  before me,
there are those that may follow.
I can only hope I too have
  somehow,
in some say,
engraved upon your soul a
  uniqueness to be unforgotten.
The sound of your voice,
the gentle caress of your hand
  will forever linger
. . .over the days,
through the months,
and into the eternal years.

Gerald Juzdan
THE LAST LOOK
They never made a movie
on your movie street;
the street with closed houses
and vague alley cats.
They wrapped you
in the colors of the deathless
  king
when you came to them
on the night shift.
In the wind,
leaves fell like ribbons
to be done as decorations.
In the pillow
it is costing you
the sound of any new dreams
in new
  deaf
  nights.
The clock in the stars waited

in the influence of sleep.
In wet empty arms you became
  gone.
And you became a wax man
  in a fact mask,
and you became a wire smile
  and a joke wig.
In the dust, we buried an
  invisible suit and tie.

This is the end of coming back
  to us,
like the last day of snowmen.
I take you all
in one last look,
quickly like a handshake or
  a cold kiss.
These dark roses are bones
but no keys.
You are free
for
surely now
you have
acquired the world.

Randall. Cunningham
AWAKENING GIANT
Strolling along on the side
  of a hill
My eyes beheld a ghost.
A lonely giant with chaffed
  feet
Its limbs as bare as posts.
Stepping carefully on sodden
  soil
I approached this barren might.
Soles sinking in mossy turf
I beheld a saddened sight.
Gnarled knots, limbs awry
It stands high and alone.
Slants away from winter's
  gusts
Clinging to a limb, a cone.
With juices gone, leaves
  riding the winds,
A dreary sight to the eyes.
Its life returned to mother
  earth,
No tears to show its cries.
But hark, I bend a low hung
  limb,
No sound of breaking core.
Could that be life, a tiny
  bud,
Peeping thru a near open door?
As I leave, my toes kick high,
My mind is cleared of sorrow.
Just by observing that tiny
  bud,
I know the giant will awaken
  tomorrow.

Kathryn Ferrari
A QUESTION OF LOVE
By chance, I have known you
  for
two years, nine months, and
  eighteen days,
and all I have to show for it
  are some
broken pieces of glass
that I am afraid to touch
for fear of cutting myself again.
You gave me nothing
but a bunch of maybes
and false hopes.
I feel I got cheated out of
  something.
Like a spoiled child,
who had her doll taken away
behind her back.
I am angry and distrusting
  of you.
I am doubtful of all the feelings
  and words
exchanged.

I loathe you as a man,
and must think
before I call you such.
Then why, if I have
so much anger,
do I dwell on you
in my memory?
Why should I carry the heavy
  weight of
hurt on my shoulders and
  feel your neglect
and selfishness?
Should I wait and hope for
  a word
of recollection from you
of my being?
I have a gnawing feeling of
  emptiness
and fear the pieces of glass
are scattering further apart.
I have known you for two
  years,
nine months, and eighteen
  days . . .
and have nothing to show for
  it.

Clifford Davis
A PRIMER ON GOD
"Teach me about God,
  Socrates,
Tell me all you can
About His nature, works and
  way,
About His relationship to man."

Without a word, without a
  sound,
Socrates turned away from me,
And in a very sacred silence,
Stared steadily out across the
  sea.

"Pray tell me about God,
  Socrates,
Do not such rudeness show.
with words or signs or
  movements,
Socrates, tell me all you know."

"If God," said he, "Is but a
  greater man,
Only wiser and stronger than
  we,
Then to speak of God—of
  course one can,
But God is not a greater man
  to me."

"And so my silence tells you
  all I can
Of God's nature, works and
  way,
With human words we speak
  of man,
But of God—there is nothing
  man can say."

Then with nothing but a
  gentle nod,
And this as if against his will,
He said, "Come, let us learn
  of God,"
And then became so very still.

Without another word or
  sound,
Socrates turned, along with
  me,
And in a very, very sacred
  silence,
We both stared out across the
  sea.

Laura Jean Hoffman
THE LONE RIDER
A dark and dismal day it was
When he rode into town.
The rain came down in
  torrents,

The trees came crashing down.
He rode in on the handsomest
    stallion,
You'll ever live to see.
His head held high, his eyes
    a-shining,
As bright as they could be.
His face tanned an' tough it
    was.
Looked like a cowboy's should.
An' he never even blinked an
    eye
While against that storm he
    stood.
He dismounted an' started
    walkin'
Toward the General Store.
An' ev'ry man there stared at
    him,
When he walked in the door.
"Howdy, boys," his voice was
    heard,
Rich an' full an' deep.
An' every man that was in
    there,
Swaggered to his feet.
"Howdy, sir," the owner said,
"What's your business here?
What's yer name, an' where
    ye from,
From far'er vey near?"
"My name is William Jacob
    Brown,
(But y'all can jes' call me Bill)
An' if ya go where I came
    from,
You'll get rich, ya certainly
    will.
"I've come from out in
    Californy,
Where the streams run yella
    with gold.
But ta' stay there on the wild
    fronteir,
Ya' gotta be mighty bold."

Elsie Carlson Henry
DELAYED AWAKENING

Once she was a child, almost
    a woman,
weeping for a blessing yet
    unknown.
Oh, had it passed unrecognized,
    unheeded?
Was it future or already flown,
Ephemeral as star-dust, not
    quite glowing,
drifting, stealing, unpercepted,
    nigh?
Would she find it, let it go, un
    unknowing,
searching here, while there its
    passing by?
In the passing years,
    anticipating,
living, finding beauty, love and
    faith,
At times she thought she could
    discern an aura,
Fleeting, half-perceived, almost
    a wraith:
A note within an early morning
    bird-song,
her child's first cry, a smile,
    a loving prayer—
Oh! There! It must remain!
But no, it wavers,
melts like mist in sunshine
    into—where?
Old, content, yet unexpected
    moments
find a haunting, longing lingers
    on.
Ruefully, she wonders what

she seeks; what
could surpass the happiness
    she's known?
It may be that when Death,
    Life's greatest marvel,
opens wide its portals, she
    will find
And recognize, too late, her
    sought-for blessing:
awareness of the life she's
    left behind.

Fay Heim-Stahl
PREVAILING PRAYER

In the freshness of the morning
When it's softly quiet, still
Is a time when sweet
    communion
doth the soul God's Spirit
    fill.
Tell him all about your
    problems,
Ere you start the busy day,
He will strengthen, guide and
    keep you,
If you do not fail to pray.
When the day with all it's
    duties
Presses down with heavy care,
There is comfort for the weary
In the secret place of prayer.
As temptations 'round you
    gather,
And you feel the tempter's
    power,
Come to Christ in all your
    weakness;
He will guard you every hour.
"Satan's fiendish host will
    tremble"
When rebuked in Jesus' name.
He will flee if you resist him;
To defeat him, Jesus came.
In the hour of greatest trial,
When your faith is sorely
    tried,
You can win the fiercest
    battle
With all heaven on your side.

Marianne R. Thomas
**A LADY WORTH
REMEMBERING**

It isn't her beauty alone one
    remembers,
Nor the grace of her movement,
    nor style.
It isn't the goodness that shone
    in her face,
Nor the sunshine of her smile.
It isn't her talent, noteworthy
    indeed,
Nor the quickness of her mind.
It is all of these things, and
    then a few more
That frequently haunt us we
    find.
The love that she brought to
    her husband and brood,
The patience, the care, and
    the fun
Bring to mind the sensation one
    enjoys
with a comforting blanket—
    homespun.
Oh, mind you, a temper she
    had, yes indeed!
In fact, kitchen pots sometimes
    flew.
But, of one thing I'm certain,
    as sure as I live,
Those were times punishment
    was due.
She started to fail, though we
    knew it not.

We believed her concerned
    about him,
Her husband, whose health
    was far from the best.
Soon she became "next of
    kin".
After her husband died, she
    faded;
Her illness was painfully clear.
Her smile was gone, and her
    hazel eyes
Were either blank or dark
    with fear.
Watching her go was pure
    torture.
She rarely complained or
    cried.
Then, one morning we found
    her silently still,
And we knew that she had died.
We thought her an angel when
    alive,
And it's hard to believe that
    she's gone;
But we'll not forget that lovely
    lady;
Her memory lives on and on.

Colleen A. Carlson
WATCH THE PEOPLE

I like to watch the people walk
    by:
They're laughing, talking,
    yelling!
And one can't help but wonder,
What each individual is
    thinking.
They walk in twos, threes and
    fours
And by themselves—
Short, tall, young, old
Each a very different character
    In his own right.
Up and down and back they
    go,
Even through rain and sleet
    and snow.
Hair and hats blow and all—
Occasionally, an old lady will
    fall.
Bums roam aimlessly wondering
    by;
Searching for wine, and pie in
    the sky.
Jesus freaks yell in the streets,
As wide-eyed children
Stand at their mother's feet.
A band on the corner plays
    a song.
Old men sit, all day long.
Business people go about
    their business,
Shoppers go about their
    shopping—
I like to watch the people walk
    by:
To see how they feel,
By the look in their eyes.

J. M. Pottorf
GIFT

The treasures you deserve,
I cannot afford.
Not rings of silver,
Nor chains of gold.
I've no antique brass,
Nor woven cloth.
What I can give,
Cannot be bought.
Snowflakes that fall,
with an angel's grace.
Smiles of sincere joy,
From a childlike face.
Dreams that are real,
And those to come.
Life that is happy,
Until it is done.

A type of peace,
That comes from within,
It's not worth a dime,
But not made of tin.
A type of true happiness,
From liking myself,
I want that for you,
And no one else.
These things I have,
They're all part of me.
Though not worth much money,
They're not really free.
And if there be more,
I can possibly give,
To you they belong,
with my love—
And a kiss.

Kevin Grey Young
THE MOUNTAIN RETREAT

From atop the mountain
one can not miss
the presence and feel
of Mother Nature's kiss.
Below nature's garden
I can see
every farm, meadow,
animal and tree.
On this haven
I can hear
the sounds of nature
far and near
Near the pine
I can smell
the scent of evergreen,
the potion to nature's spell.
Sitting on the matted carpet
I can savor
the prized Teaberry leaf
and its flavor.
From within my eyes
I can view
the lifting of fog
to the settling of morning's
    dew.
During the winter months,
while looking below,
I notice a stream
imprisoned by snow.
While thanking our maker
I come to face
God's priceless handiwork
His power and His grace.
Bidding farewell,
as darkness sets in,
I leave for just a moment.
I'll be back again and again.

Lenora Lang
WHAT CAN I DO?

Father: I'm so small and weak,
I cannot win the world for
    thee
But with your help a little
    corner
Where I am, I'll try to win for
    thee
I cannot climb a mountain
    as
some can and do.
But I can climb a hill so high
and sing your praises true.
I cannot swim the ocean
or even a stream so wide
But I can share you a love
To all who passes by
I cannot do great things for
    you
Only things that are so small
But I can share your blessings
For there's enough for all
I cannot travel far by sea
or even far by land
your love for lost ones, I'll

spread
like grains of golden sand.
Little grains of sand together
a solid rock will make, so
have patience with me, Lord
If I do make mistakes.

Tomorrow I will try again
To do the best I can
To share with those less
    fortunate
your love for every man
to show to all, the pearly gates
Where love and God doth
    reign.

Jean C. Mossbrook-Frobock
JUST YOU AND I

I

Come, my love, and sit close to
    me.
Let me put my head on your
    shoulder;
Perhaps you will put your cheek
    to my hair,
And we shall sit quietly,
Speaking softly of things both
    loving and profound
As we watch the midnight sky—
Just you and I.

II

Just you and I.
Alone in the dark,
Holding hands,
Learning about each other.
Communication so deep,
No words need be spoken
As your heart speaks to mine,
And mine whispers its reply.
Yearnings so deep,
Words can not describe
The feelings inside.

III

It is the gentle,
Quiet time of the early morn.
Here we sit,
Loathe to say goodnight,
Content to sit in quiet peace
Until dawn breaks over the
    horizon
Cascading the window with
pale, then Fiery Light!
Ah, such peace there is
here with you!

Alda J. Osborn
**MY THOUGHTS GO
WANDERING**

Sometimes I find myself
    wondering,
is life worth all the problems we
    face everyday?
Does it really pay to be honest
    and
good as we travel along life's
    way?
I guess it depends on the way
    we
were reared and what we were
    taught was right,
But so often life gets so
    complicated
that we can't see the day for
    the night.
If we were to stop and study
    things
and see things the way that they
    are,
We would see that we're to
    blame
and not the world, by far.
Some people seem to have
    everything,
but is that really true?
Do they have their health and
    happiness
the same as me and you?

It seems that we have to
    struggle
so hard in order to survive,
Maybe we should be thankful
    that
we are healthy and alive.
If you find one person in your
    life
who loves you for what you
    are,
You should look up to the
    heavens
and thank your lucky star.
Some people go through their
whole life and never find what
    they're looking for
Some people find it and never
    know it,
for them life is just a bore.
If you meet a contented person
    and ask them
their secret to success,
They'll probably tell you it all
    began
with love and happiness.
So if we can find love and
    peace
and contentment as we travel
    along the way,
Life is worth the ups and downs
and the problems we face
    everyday.

Annie Robinson
THE TREES ARE STRIPPED

The trees are stripped
Of their once green leaves
As the wind cruelly whips
The frozen, bared branches.
The bracing wind gusts against
My face, my hair
And stings my nose.
It chills my inner soul.
I can feel the cold inside of me
Almost to my bones.
The season seems dead and
    lonely
Covered by a deadly blanket of
    white.
Its only brightness is
your eyes
that warm the soul
On the coldest winter day.
But it's cold, my friend,
And times are hard,
And I really have to go.
I'll just let go of your hand
And let you go,
And I run before
I cry or freeze
Whichever comes first.

Patti Love Wharton
A PUPPY'S PRAYER

Heavenly Father
Full of love
Bless my young master
With your riches from above.
He is just a little boy
With such kind, gentle ways
Thank you for sending me to
    him
That special Christmas Day.
We are always together
Whatever the cost
And that's why he was crossing
    the street, Lord,
He thought I was lost.
He just wanted to find me
He wasn't going very far
And Lord he needs your help
    now
He was hit by a car.
He is lying in his bed now
So pale and very still
They said he'd never see again
And I'll understand, if that's

your will.
I know I'm not much, Lord,
Just a puppy, and I'm small
But please hear my prayer,
Dear Ruler over all.
I love him, Lord
And his life has just begun
So please, God, in the morning
Just let him see the sun.

Reba Bynum Bell
YOUNG ELEGANT FARMER

Young elegant farmer get out
    of bed
Young elegant farmer the horses
    need fed
There's milking the cows, and
    much to be done
The chores on a farm are a
    million and one.

Young elegant farmer, get
    out of bed
Don't let your new sports car
    go to your head
There's food in the kitchen go
    eat on your way
Get up and get out and start
    a new day.

When schooling is out boy you
    must help yer pa
When those chores are finished
    then go help your ma
There's weeding the garden and
    hogs to be fed
Young elegant farmer you get
    out of bed.

Clean up the barn, there's an
    errand to town.
Wipe off of your face that
    silly, big frown.
Instruct the hired hands on
    crops in the field,
Proper attention will get a good
    yield.
Hired hands will eat at twelve
    o'clock noon
Lunch buckets aren't packed,
    but they will be soon
See that you take them, and
    don't you delay
Get money from Pa and give
    them their pay.

The chickens are hungry and
    they must be fed
There's no one to do it my
    boy in your stead
Gather the eggs as soon as
    you can
Then go back this evening and
    gather again.

Young elegant farmer the lawn
    needs a trim,
And the paint on the picket's
    is sure getting dim.
There's fruit to be gathered that
    just can not wait,
And it's going to take time to
    repair the east gate.

Many's the chore that'll be
    put away
Between now and the time

you'll haul in the hay.
Then there, of course, is the
    harvest of grain,
Let's pray for those tasks
    that there'll be no
    rain.

Elegant farmer as I've told you
    before
The building of fence can be
    quite a chore,
So throw back your shoulders
    and start standing tall
You're sure to be one that'll
    help do it all.

When steers go to market they'll
    bring in much pay
Then you can go courting when
    work can delay
You'd best fetch a bride that can
    stand up to toil
For there's plenty of work when
    you're farming the soil.

Marczi Dease Beaudoin
ONCE I WAS

Once I was a child small, so
    innocent and pure;
Too much; too fast; too
    many things and I could not
    endure.
So as helpness enveloped me
    and because I could not see;
I crawled into my lonely shell
    and served a term in my own
    hell.

Once I was addicted to a city
    filled with grief;
I played the great escapist,
    my husband played the thief.
And as I grew and through the
    tears and as I cam to know
    my fears;
I cast myself above that crowd,
    I walked away and I was
    proud.

Once I lived a lonely life with
    people all around;
My heart and soul yearned to
    be free but in my own web
    I was bound.
And as I came to meet the
    spider, my circle small became
    much wider;
So once again I left behind,
    what was my world, I'd
    undermined.

Once I wanted answers to
    questions not expressed;
I went not to another man,
    it was my conciousness I
    stressed.
I walked reflecting in the
    flowers; sat alone and
    thought for hours:
And I was never lonely, I
    was beginning to feel free.

Once upon a time I was,
    eternally I'll always be;
I'm privaledged enough to
    choose, my choice creates
    my destiny.
And so now as I face myself
    and analyze my growth and
    wealth;
I realize I am rich indeed,
    forever growing like a weed.

Vanita Kay Horn
MY DILEMMA

What in life is so glamourous
That it can inspire life?. . .
And just what is ultimate bliss—
Can it rule out all strife?
Tell me . . why does desire
Change to a living dread?. . .
Why do I seek destruction—

Is it my inner desire to wind up
dead?
What is the purpose of my
life?
Just why do I really exist? . . .
What is the use of my living
When only pain and heartache
persist?
How can I contribute anything
when, in myself, I can find
nothing there?
. . .why should life go on and
on
When the human being just
doesn't care?
Wouldn't death be the decisive
step
Of finding that sought-after
peace of mind? . . .
Wouldn't it offer the ultimate
end to my dilemma?
And wouldn't it stop the
hurtin' for all time?
. . .Companion death is ever
at my side,
Yet my life is not mine to
take!
I'm bound and tied, I have no
choice
But to bear all the pain and
heartache!
Alone I trod through my
inner misery,
For there is no human I can
confide in
Only to God can I turn for
help
For he promised to be with
me til the end!
From dust I came, and to dust
I will return
My life was given by God and
so shall be taken
At his time and hour as
according to his will
Or when my life on earth is at
its end!
. . .When my life on earth is at
its end!

Raul Nieto
THE TRAP

Marauders of the twilight
Victims of the night
Lovers in the satin
Heedless of our plight

The anger is incessant
We sense the laughter lined
with rage
We are haunted by tomorrow
And trapped within a cage.

Isabel Rutherford
THE TOKEN

Between the musty pages of
an old discarded manuscript
I found a faded daffodil
and wondered why it had
been clipped.
Perhaps in token, or a pledge
of someone's love, in days
gone by,
unto another who had
crushed
the blossom there and let it
die.

B. D. Paesano
OLD-FASHIONED LADY

My old-fashioned lady lives in
yesterday;
My old-fashioned lady, with
her old-fashioned way.
Everything's old-fashioned,
from her hair down to her
shoes;
My old-fashioned lady sticks
to old virtues.

She's not a top crusader for
women's liberation;
Just an old-fashioned lady in
a "space-age" generation.
She doesn't want a mansion,
she wants a picket fence;
Doesn't like the present, so
she lives in the past-tense.
With my old-fashioned lady,
I'll never go in debt;
My old-fashioned lady, with
her old etiquette.
My old-fashioned lady cries
old-fashioned tears;
I don't think she's really mine,
I think she's yesteryear's.

Ginger Beck
SNOW VISIONS

There are no visions
like snow visions
I glanced and glanced,
In the snow a particle
sparkled
and the vision danced in my
mind
I went to the spot and found
only
dead men because there were
no visions
in their lives, no visions,
no snow visions.

Garry H. Arbogast
TIME NEVER ENDING

Days of golden sunshine I give
to you,
These days to cherish,
Lock them close to your heart.
The wine sip,
The love we shall share,
Will soon fade with time.
Like the wonderous beauty
of sunset,
Everything must end.
So lock them close to your
heart,
And let them not be forgotten.
Store them like chapters from
a fine book,
And when a similar sunset
should appear,
Grab a fleeting ray, and use it
as the key,
To unlock that wonderous
book,
Stored all these years.
Think back, and read the fine
chapters of memories,
That might have been forgotten,
If not stored so close to your
heart,
And bound gently with locks.
Think of the love that was once
new,
Think of me, as I so often think
of you,
On that golden autumn day,
The sun setting,
And time, time never ending.
When we walked along in the
sand,

Two people, hand in hand,
While the tides of forever,
journeying,
Brought us together,
In nature's unrehearsed
October.

Sherry L. Schacht
AS I SEE IT

Sometimes I sit and watch the
grass grow.
Or see the river flow.
Maybe I'll just watch the spider
weave,
Or see the ants as they leave.
Can you hear what the crickets
sing?
Or guess what creation the m
morning dew will bring?
If not, well that just shows
We're not of the same world
you know.
Yet we stand on the same
ground,
But you just don't look down.
How can you stand there
not knowing,
Or even see the fireflies
glowing.
You're satisfied in your world
and that's alright,
It's too bad though, you just
can't see the light.
Stay in your world and carry
the line,
Or cross over and be joyous
in mine!!!

Greg Garrison
SON TO HIS MOTHER

The emotional feeling in the
back of the mind,
Sometimes is cruel—sometimes
is kind.
Whenever one person affects
another,
There is never the love as from
son to his mother.
The admiring sentiment and
honorable respect
Are unequivocal in the
broadest spect.
I never underestimate or
fail to recognize
The bright and shiny love in
those big blue eyes.

Elinor Grant-Watters
DESTINY

High in the northern wilds
My journey started from a
bubbling spring.
Timidly I crept thru forests;
then joined by other streams
grew bold and brave to meet
oncoming thrills.
Once I was a millrace in a noisy
lumber camp. What fun!
I was to feel the terror of
violent storms
which made me overflow my
banks.
Undaunted, with abandon I
dove from lofty cliffs
to a chasm far below, a show-
off, nature's wonder.
Trapped in stygian blackness
underground, I feared
I'd never view the heavens
again.
Finally emerging, eager for
new adventure, I rolled
on.
Quite unexpectedly today
I slipped into a mirrored

lake.
Its shores are rimmed with
pines and birches; dipping
willows.
Here children sail their tiny
barks.
Gauze-winged dragonflies alight
on lines of patient fishermen.
Lovers walking hand in hand
weave golden dreams.
Artists brush canvasses with
captured natural beauty
and poets write their verse.
I think I'd like to be here in
this haven to the end of
time,
for never have I known
contentment until now;
yet, would I?
No, my destination lies out
there beyond the shallows.
I'll join the ocean waves that
carry ships to far-off places.
There's so much more to see
and do!

Patricia McFarlane
EVERY MOTHER'S PRAYER

As I sit by my loved one's bed
in hopes that he will soon lift
his head, instead
I sit in silent prayer waiting
to hear a word of comfort
from you up above
So shine down upon my son
with your infinite mercy and
love,
Oh yes Lord I know you can
see
That my son has Muscular
Dystrophy . . .
Turn back time to yesterday
when he used to run, laugh
and play,
but now those moments have
slowly wasted away.
And so, I say to you up high,
Bring your blessings down upon
my little guy,
Tell me, oh Lord, how much
time can there be spent,
So that I can make his life
much more content?
Now in closing of this prayer
I ask for finer moments
that we might share,
Please save me from this
awful despair,
that's Every mother's prayer.

Bruce David Rowe
TWO FACES IN WAR

Death
Planted in the mud by spading
bullets,
Watered in his own blood,
Sleeping never to awaken, never
to see again
The beauty of the one he loved.
O upturned face! O shrunken
eye!
Never knowing or understanding
what killed you.
A look of sudden disbelief fills
your face as you die.
And you will never know
whether your cause was just
Or your dying justified.

Trampled under, drowning
though dead
In the blood of his fellows
and his enemies,
To be buried under a white
cross on a hillside far from
home;
To enrich the soil of another

land in which
The seeds of war may again
   be planted.
Life
In your eyes I read your struggle
A dejected face covered with
   mud.
I see your suffering reflected in
   your blank expressions,
I see your death in a howlitzer
   shell.
While you eat, you wait to
   be eaten
By the hungry bullets;
While you sleep, you wait to
   be tucked in
By the infinite nursie, Death.
The grim reality of the brevity
   of live
Reflected in your face.
The grim reality of the finality
   of death
Reflected in the mud-strewn
   bodies,
The blood-strewn bodies;
The death on the battle field
Where all are made equal
   by that
Which they all hold in common.

R. Donald Watkins
SONG OF DAPHNE

Can I beloved of a god,
Have come to love the sky
   alone?
Can I have traded floor for sod,
Leaves for my hair, life for my
   own?
Can I who guarded chastity,
Be left alone upon this
   hill?
Is this my crown, eternity,
To stand here pining, rife
   and still?
Oh birds, sweet warblers in
   my hair,
The gods have left you lone to
   sing,
Oh, come, forgive my pining
   air,
Be patient in my absent Spring.
Sometime I shall arise from
   earth,
Sometime shall know your
   lovely breath,
Sometime when half gods die
   in birth,
And mortals conquer living
   death.

Sandy Bressler
UNDER THE SHADE TREE

Oh little one . . .as you run
In the fields of flowers,
As you chase the monarchs
From their landings;
I see an embryo of life,
Of a small, innocent child—
Reaching out for more in
This world . . .
Than wiser men have ever
   attempted.

Laura Teague
**IT'S JUST A PLAIN OLD
JOHN**

It's just a plain Old John
Yet it has a purpose,
Even if it is to be sat on.
Well like you can give
That old John a lot of shit
And he'll just swallow it down.

Yes, I sure like
That Old John
Never has he thrown
Any of that shit back.

I guess he ain't human,
Poor Old John.
But, I ain't got pity
In my heart
For that is what you were
Born for.
Still I respect you,
For you found your future
Faster than some,
Smart Old John
Even if it is to be sat on.

Lewis R. Grendler
MAGNETIC LADY

The way you flash
you must be lightning
The way you attract
is clearly magnetizing
So pull yourself together right
   now
Don't waste anytime 'cause
   I'm gonna show you how
To make love like you'll
   never believe
Give you love
just to keep you pleased
Make is to you'll always
   want more
Better watch close
so you know the score
One to one, that's what it'll
   be
Fun on fun, just to make you
   see
That there's no other lover,
that you'll ever need.

Iraj Gharib
LONELY AS I

Tell me, tell me soaring eagle
is your spirit free as they say?
And do you climb the highest
   mountain
to reach the softness of the
   morning sun?
And please tell me soaring
   eagle
are clouds as soft as they say?
And your wing span so large
   and mighty
That casts a shadow a mile long.
is it to ward off spears of
   sunlight,
or simply designed to carry you
   far?
You have as friends mountain
   and clouds,
the morning sunlight, the
   bleeding dusk,
brushes, prairies, and trees red
   and white,
slopes and rivers, wide edges
   of moon,
the bright stars that twinkle at
   night,
but do you still feel lonely as
   I?

Madeline Fearman
SPACE AGE

Unfurl your sails upon the
   Milky Way!
Build fortresses upon the
   farthest star!
Fly downward where the
   blind fish glow with light!
Devour the sea where buried
   treasures are!
Equate the sun and cube the
   universe!
Transcend the stars and bring
   the moon to bay!
Divide the oceans, hollow out
   the hills!
Change darkest night into the
   brightest day!
Compute infinity with minds
   of light!

Launch wingless birds into
   the midnight space!
Their heartbeats drowning out
   the pipes of Pan!
Must tangibles be mankind's
   only grace?
Take pause to watch the flash
   of white-winged gulls.
Enrich the soul with sunset's
   amber glow.
Can knowledge build a velvet
   scented rose
Or resurrect the crocus
   through the snow?
Will sun and moon and stars
   be met
Only to find the earth has
   set?

Linda S. Thomas
**THOUGHTS OF A LITTLE
LEAGUE PLAYER**

Bases are loaded, two men are
   out,
Please let my confidence
   smother my doubt.
Everyone's shouting, "It's all
   up to you",
Just one more run and the game
   is through.
I want to be the one to win the
   victory,
For my parents, the coaches,
   the team and me.
If I lose this game, I'll feel
   so bad,
I'll lose any confidence I
   thought I had.
I know I'm not the best hitter
   they've got,
What matters now is to give
   it my best shot.
A strike is called, I look at
   the coach,
He tells me to watch the
   pitcher's approach.
Two strikes, three balls, this is
   the pitch,
A ball or a strike? I wish I
   knew which.
The ball is released, it's coming
   my way,
I swing, connect! I've saved
   the day!
The ball I hit brought two runs
   in,
I was never in doubt, I knew
   we would win!

Scott Alan Wiley
HURTS SO BAD

  foetus
adolescence
  puberty
love

  hate

  work

  play
  grey
  black
  tears.

Leslie Anne Whitten
DREAMS

Easing through the day
Lazily passing the time
Adding lines in the clay
Lines of past passions.

Passions often remembered
Dreading their strength
And times surrendered
Lost to the magic of dreams.

Dreams to ease reality
Fantasy a friendly ally

Adding to life vitality
And urgings for tomorrow.

In tomorrow all exists
Dreams may become truth
Truth and all it consists
May replace passion with peace.

Martha Bell Hays
JOY IS

Joy is a liquid moment
Tumbling gracefully
From a high point in time.

Joy is that hidden moment,
Sitting in a silent heart,
Smiling at a secret.

Joy is that lingering moment
Of love, one leaves
Clinging to the fringe of
   forever.

Joy is.

Minnie Lee Richardson
THE EVIL OF ALCOHOL

Why do we be so blind
As to let such a deceiver grant
   us defeat?
To our body and soul it is
   unkind,
Even in medical aid, it is
   deceit.

Too cruel it is, to be seized by
   its hand
Because it stains cleanliness
   and goodness,
And refinement is taken by
   demand.
And while blurring these,
   it shatters faithfulness.

It is not only cruel, but a
   thief
Who bribes us, and then robs
   our being
Of self-respect, or our
   character in chief
That gives courage to make
   life worth living.

Dorothy E. Law
GREETING

Let the dark tongue of silence
   sound,
Fraught with the lovely weight
Of words unsaid.
Speech is a bronze bell,
Sounding with too harsh a
   clangor
In the still temple
Where one spirit
Dimly perceives its brother.

Scott T. Sanders
JUST TALK

White teeth (big eyes) and
   pink tongue
proclaim overzealous
   greetings.
Is it forgetting (or forgiving)?
Perhaps just for today
hiding dull hours and
boring conversations.

The formalities gone,
intercourse proceeds with no
   climax.
Upon penetration,
only the crust of the stale
   role
remains.

Steve Wilson
THE FINAL FLIGHT

The sea of destiny slithered
   across the shore.
The gulls dive as if to drown.
We've destroyed their sacred
   ground.
When it all seems lost,

They attack the sun and soar.
Oh, what it must cost,
To claim we'll gain even more.
The gray becomes a prism's
array,
Glowing throughout its
lonesome eye.
The gulls force towards satan's
bay,
Fewer have the courage to fly.
Yet, the waters seep-in our
destructive clay,
Soiling the tears of our sky.
Soon it was us who counted the
final days,
As it became painful to sigh.
The earth began to crumble
with each moment.
Despite our varied skills,
We had not the strength to know
it.
We read our Father's will,
To hear what share we would
get,
What will we buy with our
ever-growing ditch?

Dean F. Priore
THE PRICE

The condition of unravel is
where we've come to stay
Looking out from behind
meshed glass
Watching the marionettes acting
out their life scripts
Doing what they were
programmed for
Their existence being inbred
They cannot change
They follow the trend
Working to exist
To think is a flaw
You are defective
What has gone wrong
I'm not the same
I cannot work
But I do exist
I must have won

Frank L. Ahlstrom
LIBERTY BELL

O Sweet Sounding Bell . . . The
Voice of Liberty
Ring Well . . . Ring Well!
Alike to the skilled in Genius'
Fair Designs
And to the poor and unskillful
as well,
Sound out thy Sweet and Noble
Notes of Joy.
For Peace, for Comfort in
Distress, for All Love
Which longs for thine Eternal
Care,
Be thou the Voice of our
Salvation,
Be thou the Sound of Quickened
and Gladsome Joy,
Though awakened Half in Fear,
soon turned
By thy inspired Song to the
Grace
Of Great God.

Carolyn M. Jacks
REFLECTIONS

It seems that life is one long
struggle from the day of birth
to make our fellow human
beings realize our worth.
Ever seeking broader scopes and
climbing higher towers,
never stopping on the way just
to smell the flowers.
Gleaning knowledge is our thirst,
applying it our hunger
until one day we sadly say "if
only I were younger."

We send a man by rocket to
play among the stars
but how could we communicate
with anyone on Mars, when
here on Earth we occupy the
greatest planet ever
and countries war without a
thought for all the ties they
sever.
And so I'm making this appeal
to all you men of science
hold off for just a little while
on that new appliance.
Give us time to catch our breath,
enjoy the day before it's
passed.
We know that progress is a
must, but must it be so fast?

Victoria Yoder
CITY NIGHT

Come back into the night of
disorder.
Leave behind freedom of
rational thought,
or remain lightheaded, blind.
Street lamps glare in humid
pressure.
Music beats. Eyes adapt. The
audience wallows
in paint, drugs, wild craving for
more wreckage.
"Break us down." We cry,
clutch with dance
and sunken eyes. Join the misty
anticipation.
Breathe moisture. Clear dry
lungs almost dead
from stifling, stagnant days.
Come back.
Staunch white wholes crumble
for renewal
in the damp, dirty city where
life abounds,
swims and mingles in collusion
and public.
Decrepit destitution unfolds,
grows.
Come back into the night.

Maria Rudy
COUNTRY LIVING

Beyond the fence a field of
bright flowers
that may not have been if not
for rain showers.
Up in the tree a bird in his nest
tired from flying and needing
his rest.
Out in the distance a man
tending his farm
a lovely sight this country
charm.
Down by the brook a man and
his son
reminds me of things that I've
never done.
But back to the city I must
now travel
back to the rush and the
concrete gravel.
But in my heart I'll never forget
that country living and that
peaceful world that I met.

Nanette Ludlow
YOU, THE FOOL

You look at life
through a deck of cards.
The rules are always in
your favor. It's too bad you
don't abide by them. What
about "Fish"?
Your game is more along
the lines for keeps or taking
over one's only possessions, the
game my friend is "War." Cold
and for keeps.

It's too bad, and if you don't
change your rules soon, you
will be playing solitaire for a
long time—You'll be the
Old Maid!
You'll never win with diamonds,
spades or clubs, even the ace
won't help. Put your game
aside.
There is a whole life ahead of
you.
If you have to play, at least
Use the hearts.

Darlene Redman
THE FUTURE IS MINE

One minute I'm lost
Don't know where I'm going
My friends seem miles away

I walk down a road
So gaunt and dim
I hear myself wishing to stay

To change my whole life
With no future in sight
The only thing holding me
Is the fear of the night

Please keep me from running
Hold back my tears
This could change my life
With tearing cold fears

No one to run to
Someone to find
I'm searching for something
The future is mine

Debi Shaffer
DEEP WITHIN

If I should die tomorrow
Upon my grave, I pray
You'll place a yellow rose
And single shall it lay.

I want no other flower
Upon my casket dim
For the yellow rose shall
symbolize
The love I held for him.

As the casket is lowered
I ask, please shed no tears
For with me I take the
happiness
Of our love throughout my
years.

When the funeral is over
And beneath the ground I lie
You'll feel a love within you
And you'll know it is I.

Mary Elizabeth Thompson
TO ME

My life is like a drop of rain
flowing as a swift moving river.

My life is full of fear and pain
the bitterness making me quiver.

My life is like a newborn child-
Able to touch, to feel, to see.

Carefree, frivolous and
sometimes wild
That's what my life is to me!

Cyndee Woodsit
ETERNAL SLEEP

The gray strands of hair
blend
With the cream color of satin.
The age of youth
shines through.
Tearful mourners pass by
one by one,
Grieving the lifeless person.
Each tear that's shed
reflects a memory
of her.
The moments she shared with us

will be treasured
till eternity.
We will always love her
and miss her greatly
As we miss the others
who have passed
from our lives.
But they'll always be
Remembered
Deep in our hearts.
Think of the times
Spent with her
With happiness; not sorrow
or else
Remember not at all.

Donald J. De Rosa
AUTUMN LOVE

Summer is now ending,
fall is in the air,
our love is growing,
we have much to share.
Changing are the colors
making the earth bright,
my heart opens it's door
to embrace your sight.
Leaves are gently falling,
sky is always so clear.
Birds fly to your calling,
paradise is here.
Trees become silent,
and rivers flow,
all this beauty he sent
to help our love grow.

Linda A. Stewart
SOFTLY GRAY

Observe a couple,
Softly gray,
A legacy of years
Have they
To leave us.

Smiling eyes,
Shuttered perspectives
Peering from pages,
Recipes for ages
Of life.

Their celebration,
Long deserved,
Life's dedication
To faith preserved,
A dried arrangement.

Friends and family
Come on Sunday,
Hoping the victory of love
Their's one day.
No gifts please.

Jewell Rowland Evans
INCONSISTENCY

Surely man was made to create,
mould notes into clarion tone,
fashion symphony of grace
from a hunk of stone;
wrest a glossy work of art
from a tree trunk tall;
determine rhyme and reason
where once was none at all.

Just as God created Adam,
man in his small way,
from the dust beneath his feet,
creates from the clay.
He must, if he fulfills his fate,
fashion for himself a crown;
yet often, through his wanton
tears,
stumbles on the smoothest
ground.

Lena E. Lewin
PASSING PEACE

O, calm, serene, unruffled Peace
Linger here awhile,
O, Gentle Spirit, enrich me with
your blessings;
Thou knowest the toil.
By Thine own hand, give me

such joys
As only Thou canst give.
Let me be pensive,
Let nothing here destroy one
single bit of it,
Let music flow and calm my
soul to rest,
And mad pursuit depart,
Thou God of Quietness.

Look! the weary waving trees
Pause in tranquility,
They know when to cease their
strugglings
And set themselves at ease;
Man is the only creature always
seeking to escape
That ever pining restlessness,
That he himself doth create.

Jean Bowen
A COUNTRY CEMETERY

White Tombstones on an
emerald ground
The starry sky makes a jeweled
Crown
The shadows dance when
breezes play
In the Cedars green, while the
Flowers sway
The nightwinds whisper
goodbye.

A Nightbird in the woods
nearby
Breaks the silence with a
lonesome cry
Night sounds come drifting in
on the wind
One word on a Tombstone can
break a sad heart again,
Mother.

A Wire fence encloses their long
dreamless sleep
On the wire, Vines silently creep
The sad lonely graves all seem
to say,
Life is so short tell someone
today
That you love them.

There's a time to live but we all
must die
We say hello world, then, when
it's Goodbye,
We all have our place,
somewhere . . .
In a Cemetery.

Stan Lee Milbrath
**TRANSENDENTAL
THINKING**

From where I was born,
to where I can reach
. . . that is an object

In between,
the filler energy
widespread and impacted
In full bloom,
down to lesser monuments
. . . that isn't tragic

Surmount the hurdles,
transend the morbid
'till the summit's end is
reached
. . . that is the magic.

Eva Wright
THE RECALL

His eyes asparkle, and anxious
to please,
Joyfully bounding up on
"The Recall"
My dog forgot to sit at my
feet
To await
a further command.
His eyes expressive and shaking
his head,

Somberly recording a failing
score,
The judge disapproved the
exercise
Improperly
Executed.
With misty eyes and conscience
panged by guilt
Remorsefully looking up to
Heaven
I realized that I too had failed
To await
my Master's command.
His eyes filled with love, and
with hand outstretched,
Sadly scribing my disappointing
score,
The Judge carefully added the
words:
"Forgiven!
We'll try him again."

Lois Nicholson
GOD WILL WATCH THEE

God will watch thee,
He will take you by the
hand and guide thee,
Yes, my little friends God
will watch thee.

God will watch thee,
He will love and protect thee,
Yes, my little friends God
will watch thee.

God will watch thee,
Yes, He will!
God will help and care for thee,
Yes, my little friends God
will watch thee.

Marcia A. Mulroney
P. T. (1)

Your face
Never stoic and hard
Smiling and laughing . . .
always . . . with me.
Legs brown and strong
I loved so much to touch them.
I hear they walk alone these
days.
I'm sorry . . .
I loved you far too much to
stay.

Marcia A. Mulroney
P. T. (2)

In the rain-flung purple dawn,
I smell your smell.
I watch the rain
And I touch your face . . .
Content with only now.

Connie Marie Batchelder
**HOW CAN I STOP THIS
SPINNING**

How can I stop this Spinning,
turning round?
I can't seem to get my feet
to touch the ground.
I'm at a loss of feeling,
I'm dead inside.
But my mind just keeps on
turning,
it won't let the pain subside.

Over and over again I see,
you walking away . . .
The hurt you caused surrounds
me,
why couldn't you stay?
I can't face reality,
in my dream world I hide.
I'll never love again,
I'm dead inside.
But the carousel of my mind
keeps on turning . . .

Jill Ellen Coale
***FIAT JUSTITIA, RUAT
COELUM . . .**

Fiat Justitia, ruat coelum . . .
Constant worries, constant pain
Suff'ring I; broke again
Empty pockets; empty hand
Depression rampant in the land.

Constant worries; constant pain
Seething hatreds in force again
Empty stares; empty hope
How is man supposed to cope?
Is faith in democracy lost?

*Fiat justitia, ruat coelum (L)
Let justice be done though
heavens shall fall.

Marie McCray
PERCEPTION

If I could hold this day in check
And keep it here forever,
If I could keep all love—all life
And never have to sever
It with destiny—the Master and
the keeper
Of the keys of eternity,
I'd rule the magic and the
mystery of happiness
And laughter, patience and
strength
And forever banish enmity.

Janice M. Woods
INTERIM

A drowsy, ghostly smoke left
the
burning autumn leaves
And spiraled toward the purple
ceiling as the
Moon rose to meet her sparkling
counterparts—
A chilling eastern wind spoke
suddenly
And pointed a finger to the
darkening west
To let us know that winter
would not be dismissed
Till morn.

Cindy Lee Fox
A VAGUE PICTURE

A vague picture, but so in
love.
Don't understand,
but I accept.
Together we are one, without
i am nothing
Rather,
don't want to be.
Needs. My needs you. I love
you;
With you I am me,
With me you are you.
I see your heart, I feel your
pain.
Let me be the one,
To kiss away your fears,
To wipe away
your tears.
To share.
Your life, my life.
To give my love, hopes and
dreams;
To take your heart,
Your love.
Dreamer dreams, now

realistic.
Can see, can feel and believe
as one.
I am finding you in me.
We are scared. But we grow.
We've searched and never
found.
Now we are one . . .
I love you.

Aris Estupinian III
SOMETHING

My dear Mother . . .
recently,
there's a rumor . . .
as sickly

as perhaps, you
just may be.
Don't ask me who!
God damn me . . .

I just feel sad.
Why put off
"something" gone bad?
Love is sof(t) . . .
Mom didn't you know.
And I'm pissed!
So, if you Go . . .
like a cist,

I will just stick
on to You.
Are you that sick/
and I, blue?

Jesus "is" aware:
if you die—
I might be "there" . . .
so, don't cry.

But, please get well;
Dr. Neat
will rid the Spell/
you aren't beat.

But mom, if you
should like, Go . . .
away-to-blue
I will poo

like a Baby . . .
remember?
Don't surrender
what may. . .be.

Chloe P. Vroman
RETURN TO THE MEADOWS

Many seasons
Have crossed where soldiers
were,
Their violent, steel husks
removed.
A breeze now sweeps the
government lawn,
Where you have lain these many
years.

At Normandy Beach,
Presidents stop for pictures that
make good copy.
Students come to study
campaign maps where
The pitted earth has been
restored.
Peasants and cowslips have
returned to the meadows.

We are tourists, speeding
Along the expressway gleaming
in soft rain,
The beach is out there;
The sound of waves beating the
shore.
Paris is 65 miles.

Ah yes,
My children that were not yours,
are grown
And bored with history that has
explained it all away,
Now that the grass grows and
rots . . . and grows
Where you have lain these many
years.

David P. McKenna
ICE WOLF

In the swirling, crystal mists
  he lurks,
In the dim and frozen arctic
  murks;
Till the winter solstice calls
  him forth
To ravage, rage, and kill.

Feel his teeth, feel him gnaw,
Icicle fangs in a fearsom maw;
Raging out of the wasteland
  north,
Driving south with a will.

Cold death hunts where his
  shadow falls,
The rebirth of spring his wrath
  forestalls;
The stormpack follows on his
  heels
As he howls his deathly chill.

Laying waste the cringing
  lands,
Roiling seas and scouring
  strands;
A snow-white shroud, the dead
  conceals,
Till of blood he's drunk his
  fill.

And the ravaged land lies
  cold and dead,
From the ice wolf's greed all
  life has fled;
Silent as an ancient tomb,
From moor to ice-rimed
  hill.

Then glutted, back to the north
  he creeps,
By the equinox, once more he
  sleeps.
Lurking in the frozen gloom,
Till the solstice, waiting still.

Nicholas C. McPhail
TO SEEK

Odd is it not when a feeling
  rushes to free itself
yet, is compulsively contained.
A feeling of wanting to belong,
to that you've given up as
  unattainable.
To encounter such desires is
  torture,
because the painful memories
  instill their reality.
Life, so generous in unforgiving
  complexity.
Existence, a void in time filled
  with auto-decesions.
Peace, when all things come
  together and
the mind is free of tormenting
  visages.
Death, a method of reaching
  peace.
So near, so far . . .God and
  self.
Where to the gate of
  enlightenment and eternity?

Ernest William Geitz
AUTUMN

Spring gave unto the summer
Alas, sweet summer is gone
Life was to share forever
Together in the dawn

Leaves falling to the ground
New air chilling every bone
Hollow whispers all around
To spend another autumn
  alone

A landscape changing colors
Traveling through the autumn
  day
Leaves keep falling upon
  others
And I keep walking away

Autumn came down with
  pride
A deep desire to last
One more summer has died
Buried somewhere in the past.

Golden pony galloping unaware
Upon his back a shining knight
Nature was like a maiden fair
Full of radiant energy and
  light

I came upon a brief clear
  river
That flowed throughout
  the world
Leaves gathering along the
  banks would shiver
And watch as the water
  swirled

Colors multiplied throughout
  the woodlands
All too soon the trees were
  bare
Wanting to catch the leaves in
  my hands
But the wind did not care

A gust of wind comes tomorrow
To blow the leaves across the
  sky
As I turn to watch the sorrow
The leaves all softly wave
  goodbye.

Regina Rigby
VERSE

I write my verses day and
  night
and though not written by
  candle light
They're old.

I read my verses upon every
  chance
  Inspired by sorrow, faith
  enhanced
Again too late.

What shall be my glory?
What shall be my praise?
But to know my verse is sung
Midst someone's bitterest
  days.

And someone will remember
And someone will forget
But someone will remember!
And I shall live on that.

When age grows fast upon me
as ivy creeping free
Then shall I outlive existence
For my verse shall outlive me.

Claire C. Foceri
INSPIRED

Inspired by a thought, a wish
  and dreams
A sunny day that never ends
Or so it seems

Inspired by the country air,
  the city park
And standing in the rain, long
  after it's dark.

Inspired by myself, of all the
  things I'll be
Of the way I feel, of what I
  see

Inspired by life, each waking
  day
Enables me to be a poet
To write what I cannot say.

Norma Rogers
SEASONAL WINDS

A playful breeze
Ruffles the trees,
And flirts with the flowers
  below.

A powerful gust
Collects the dust,
And scatters it for miles
  around.

A swirling gale
With a whipping tail,
Rends the trees from the
  ground.

A frigid blast
Brings moisture at last,
In the form of a blanket of
  snow.

Maire M. Spelay
HAPPY DAYS FOREVER

We go for long walks, and
  have long talks,
We do the dishes together.
We sing silly tunes, while
  clacking the spoons,
and have fun, no matter the
  weather.

The little holidays we've had,
  have left me so glad,
they'll not be forgotten, ever.
Every mother should know,
  this happy glow.
Who's my friend forever?
She's my daughter.
Sure glad I've gotten.

Julie Kahl King
MOMENTS

Moments—a silver web
Made up of tiny, silver threads.
Here—then gone.
Never the same again.

There are beautiful moments,
Like the moment I saw you.
I knew I would feel
never the same again.

The thoughtful moments came
When we would walk and talk
Along the river's bank
Never the same again.

The saddest moment struck,
You up and went away.
You left my world so empty,
Never the same again.

Now there are no moments,
Just empty despair.
I think of you and me,
Never the same again.

Kathleen R. Craig
DEADEND

and
still I look
for you:
bearded faces
moustached places
starsky voiced

I have my choice
but
all I want
is you.

James R. Lazzaro
HAPPY CLOWN; SAD

With shaking hands, the
  telegram read:
Sorry, plane crash, your wife
  and
child are dead.
He stumbles—sits—feeling very
  faint;
Pastes on his nose, puts on his
  smile with the grease and
  paint.
He stumbles slightly as he
  enters
the ring among the cheers.
Why does that clown with
  the big
smile have so many tears?

High on the wire with
  umbrella
in his hand;
Smile on face, tears in eyes,
  he falls into the sand.
If I live forever, I'll wonder
  till that day,
Whether his death was
  accidental
or he planned it that way.

Linda Sutherland
LOVE IS

Love to me is everything that
  is beautiful,
The crystal peaceful waters
  of a mountain stream.
The innocence of a newborn
  babe
The gentle scent of a rose
The warmth of a crackling fire
Soft and pure as the fresh
  fallen snow
Thrilling as running through
  a field of flowers
Refreshing as a fountain
  overflowing
Colorful as a rainbow
Majestic as the trees in all their
  glory
Endless as the stars in the black
  velvet night
And as sacred as the blue-white
  Heavens above and beyond . . .

Kay S. Myers
FOR KATE

Gently, the hand of Death
Touched me, took a memory.
And now, a year later,
I can't remember her voice.

But I vividly recall
The look of her, her love.

Gently, the hand of life
Touched me, replaced a dream.
And now, a year later,
I finally have a choice.

But I always will recall
The look of her, her love.

Carolyn Ann Slowski
WHAT I FEEL

My feelings are of guilt
My feelings are of pain
They leave me with fear
Of which I canno refrain

In a distance far gone
What comes over me I do
  not know
But, can I help it?
It follows me wherever I go.

Dennis Richard Mahoney
UNTITLED

Dancing, dancing
Earth dancing—
Spirits' answer
Arrange, derange—
In through doors,
Fly through windows,
Stare at suns and moons,
Leaving houses to fade—

Fly without wings
  Without sound
Through spectrum,
pass spectrum,
Echoes of drums
Eastern sand
Thousands Bloom—
Western Father men—
Feathers, Attendants to
  gates
Ready as spirit chimes,
Always we masters of passage—
We command the dance begin
And end.

Marjorie A. Bernard Dieter
KEY TO HAPPINESS (FOR LOUISE)

Many times we look back
  through the years,
while hiding our hopes and our
  fears
We will miss the carefree years
  of youth
that were full of honesty and
  of truth.
Yet we will look to the future
wondering what it will hold,
and try to understand all
  that we were told.
We will try finding the
  happiness we left behind,
while continuing our lives
  in the ways of mankind.
Then we will search our souls
  while looking for the key,
that will bring us happiness
  and set our minds free.
And in our search we will
  soon see,
that we are the holders of
  that key.

Glenda Snider
DRUGS TO DEATH

So you had a bad trip, the price
  you pay for flips.
The price is high—but then—
  you could die.
Sure it can be fun, but your
  time will come
and you'll pay your debt—maybe
  with death.
It's so easy to see you can't
  thumb your nose at society.
They'll catch you, lock you up
  and throw away the key.
'Cause they know when death
  comes, it won't take just one.
Death is a hungry Junkie, or
  a Pusher, or a Flipper,
You see— Or could it be,
Just a teen who got took and
  now he's hooked
On a needle, a bottle, or a pill,
and all wind which will blow,
If you need help it is near,
Just look to find and remember
  we are here.
So you're in a bind
There are good folks in the
  world, just look hard.

Bruce A. Spero
GAIL

You have been shown the
  beauty
Of a hundred thousand faces.
Some filled with joy.
Others hate, and some fear.
Yet the wonderfulness of your
  ministry
As you share yourself with
  these all
Surpasses the most beautiful
sunset
That you have ever seen.

Go forward then, my friend.
Share your smile.
Touch their hearts as no other
  can
Be yourself and shine,
For the Lord knows you by
  name.

Sandra Jean Heath
DESPAIR

Crying alone;
allowing my feelings to
  overflow
break forth like a dam
when it becomes weak—
can not hold—
  can not stand
can not endure time.

Loneliness:
away from friends and loved
  ones
gives me a feeling of loss
  and despair;
hopelessness and pain
can not help but destroy me
and what I stand for.

S. Enquist
WE CAUGHT THE LEAVES

We caught the leaves
that silently fell.
On a whisper they drifted
calling to all a brave farewell.

Born out of modest devotion,
  increasing
daily under the curious vision
  of local allies,
countless sprouts thrive
with the superior trait of
  releasing
themselves when destiny calls.

Midlife brings weariness as
  the union
between existing root and her
  dependant
grows weak, With only the
  wind to divert
the monotony, how they look
  forward to
those unseasonable days.

And then to yield their
  breath, surrendering
under the spell of devastating
  color, creating
the nobility this season
  demands.

With wisdom they tumbled to
fulfill their promise.
With wisdom they perished to
continue the epoch.

We caught the leaves that
silently fell
On a whisper they drifted
calling to all a brave farewell.

Bruce A. Spero
IT FELT SO TERRIBLE

It felt so terrible not being
  able
To help you out of your
  dilemma.
After all, I was going through
one of my own.
Stranded in this Godforsaken
  town
Listening to hogs and cattle
  screaming
In the middle of the night
  for excitement.
Of course, there were always
  my motel room walls.
Not very funny, huh?
I wished I could somehow
  spirit you away,
Deliver you safely to some

northwest paradise
With waterfalls, and fir trees,
and always, the sea.
Somehow when things are
  the worst
The rhythm of the sea never
  changes,
It has the ability to beat the
  terrible things away
And make them disappear into
  a type of forgetfulness.
It puts you back in touch
  with God.
But I thrill at your faith, it
  doesn't falter.
You always know who your
  Father is
No matter what seems to come
  before you.
And in the end, these will be
  the things of value.
These will be the things that
  mean eternal life.
This will be our victory
  forever,
Because He has borne our sins
  upon the tree.
Bless the name of Him who
  knew us before the
  foundations of the Earth.

Edith H. Whitaker
ALONE

I wake from sleep and gaze
  into
A room just eight by ten.
Around me stand a group
  of five,
Three women and two men.
Blank faced, in white, they
  stare at me,
A doctor's standing near.
I cannot speak. I barely
  feel.
I'm paralyzed with fear.
There's tubing everywhere I
  look.
Machines are hooked to me.
I try to run, to get away,
I can't get my arms free.
They bring a needle to my
  bed.
I struggle, but in vain.
Away I drift into a dream
Where I can feel no pain.
For weeks I lie immobilized,
Or has it been that long?
I wish someone would talk to
  me.
Please, tell me what is wrong!
Suspended here between two
  worlds,
You see me as I lie.
God, take me, now, to be
  with you.
No, I don't want to die!

Dan Mausner
A LOVE POEM

a greedy fertile soil
shifts to subterranean impulses
yet here no hungry root is
  nourished,
no graceful shoot destined to
  grow strong and follow the
  sun
the winds sift the rains wash
Ancient sirens' melodies
Narcissus flame lured
and quenched in frigid shadows
young birds' straining necks
but life-giving stuff falls
to the dry sand far below
the winds sift the rains wash

Pygmalion smiles cool,
  impenetrable
red hot chisel leaves no stains
  of blood
champagne explodes to cheers
bubbles spring to rejoin the air—
Later in silence the bottle
  sits
(higher than the label and flat)
lips briefly brushed and passed
to be quenched elsewhere
the winds sift the rains wash.

Sylvia Stern
EVERYBODY NEEDS A DREAM

A dream is the stuff of
fanciful wishful thinking
That keeps one going when
  things get really rough.
Even though one may have
  doubts
That his dream is attainable,
The yearning itself is a
  storehouse of spiritual food
  for the soul.

If the dream is realized,
The dreamer needs to wish
another wish
To keep alive his goal.
The dream may be for material
  wealth and comfort,
Or the dream may be for true
  love and spiritual fulfillment.
But a dream is a catalyst giving
  substance to the dreamer.

As long as one has his dream,
Obstacles in life can be
  overcome.
As long as one clings to a
  dream,
Life will become more
beautiful.

Cynthia R. Gautier
BEAUTY FOREVER

Beauty is blue sky,
Cloudless and wide;
Beauty if budding flower
Not wanting to hide.
Beauty is cat,
Curled up on the hearth;
Beauty is butterfly
From cocoon coming forth.

Beauty is child,
With flowers in hand;
Beauty is meadow
'Cross a quiet country land.
When the new age is here,
If beauty is to die,
What will you answer
When the child asks, "Why? "

Helen Allain Cormier
FAREWELL TO JOHN

Underneath the swaying pines
Standing so all alone
I saw her crying softly
And heard her whispered moan.

Why didn't she come closer
When the mourners gathered
  'round
As the coffin was being
  lowered
Why did she stand her ground?

*The crowd answered with
fervor
As the priest said the prayers
And the looked on with pity
As the widow shed her tears*

*On top of his earthly grave
She placed a floral bouquet
And I heard her whisper:
"Goodbye, John, for today!"*

As the crowd dispersed

I saw her move away
From her hiding place yonder
To the fresh mound of clay

On her knees she remained
As it started to rain
With tears flowing freely
She was the picture of pain.

Then as she finally rose
And was about to walk away,
I heard her whisper softly,
Thank you, John, for
yesterday!"

Alene Baumhover
THE WORLD

The world itself is a wonderful
place
except for one thing, the human
race.
We've taken this world and tore
it apart
Which now we see just wasn't
too smart.
To be back in that day when
the world began
when only the wild roamed
the land,
When the mountains stood
tall against the
sky, and the rivers flowed
clean and wide.
We've taken this away with
our foolish pride,
How dare we destroy it: you
and I.

Catherine Butler
THANK YOU, JESUS

Thank you Jesus
For loving me
And turning me back to Thee

Thank you Jesus
For forgiving me my sins
Victory goes to You for helping
me win
May our fellowship together
never dim

Thank you Jesus
For life each day
And Thy word
That shows me the way

Thank you Jesus
For the crimson stain
And washing it white as snow
As down the path of
righteousness we go

Thank you Jesus
For your nail-scarred hand
That means salvation for
every man

Thank you Jesus
For the blessed assurance
That you are mine
Even after the end of time.

Paul A. Brooks
EXILE'S LAMENT

Someday, perhaps soon,
there will be a message
Dreaded, but not
unanticipated
Eventually it must be.
If I were there, it would be
easier to accept
(for everyone).
My beloved will go—probably
not unattended—
But I won't be there
Where I most want to be
Where I most should be
The last gaze looking for me
The last word asking for me
The last hope wishing for me
But I won't be there.
This is how my punishment

is fulfilled,
bringing an unending totality
of remorse,
regret, anguish and despair.

Patti Cox Carrico
SHALL WE RISE?

If only for a moment, shall
we rise from the gutter?
Shall we chance to peer through
the window, or simply close
the
shutter?
Shall we remain justly, or rise
to higher ground?
Further still, shall we climb
the roya steps until we reach
the
crown?
Are we destined to a stationary
existence,
Or were we meant to rise
through determination and
persistence?
Are we afraid of heights, does
this phobia lame our
initiative?
Shall we reach for the heavens,
Shall we be pondering and
inquisitive?
God help us to answer yes;
To shy away from doom's
shallowness and rise into
bliss!

Beulah E. Walton
HOSTAGES

I studied about hostages
In Caesar's War,
And wondered many a time
"What am I studying about
them for?"

It seemed unlikely
That I'd ever need
To think of them,
Something like a weed.

Now I realize,
"This war is close,
Too close for comfort,
And a deadly dose."

God bless the hostages!
May they soon be free.
Not only may we hear of
them, But
very soon see!

Tillie A, Bednar
THERE IS TIME

Time changes everything.
There is time to do things.
There is time to go places.
There is time to rest.
There is time to make things.
There is time to pray.
There is time to think of
yourself.
There is time of the day.
There is time of the year.
There is time to take time out.
There is time out for Earth
and Mother Nature.
There is time for the bad and
good times.
There is a time to come on
this earth.
And a time to leave it.
This time, we are leaving it
thy way.

Jeffrey Waid
CITYWINTER

January breezes crease my
forehead
Whip me forward up the
sidewalk
Down the street
Chill wind bitter reds my face

and burns my eyes
Shiver skin rolls up my arms
Down my spine
A smile attacks my face—I
fight to
Hold the line
I lose
I smile
And the cold rushes in my
mouth and freezes off my
tongue.

Johnita K. Henry
LIVING IN DARK SILENCE

Blind to the world
And the beauty it brings.
Not able to see the flowers in
Spring
Nor the snow in winter.
Dear to the world
And the sounds within.
Not able to hear the birds
Or the rain or even
the voices of everyday
Life.
Once, long ago, you could
See the beauty of the
World and hear the
Sounds of life.
Now all that is left
Is a memory that will
Forever be tucked away
In the endless folds of your
Mind.

Dyan C. Haspel
RAINBOWS

Rainbows come and rainbows
go
So pretty in the sky
I wonder what it would be like
to climb and climb so high.

One one side there would be
a pretty pot of gold
And on the other, a ladder
So big, so high, so bold.

A rainbow shines so brightly
All across the land
Over hills and seas and
valleys
And even in the sand.

As I climb the ladder
I see the sand below
Then I walk so slowly
My thoughts just come and go.

When I reach the bottom
I find my journey's end.
What a beautiful experience
The rainbow is my friend.

Nicholas of Colorado Springs
PRETTY ONE

Damp forehead with ringlets
of hair,
clinging like tendrils
of vine on a chapel wall.

Jaunty breasts, dark-rose tipped,
form ivory pillows from
the Greek Bacchae.

Flat undulating stomach,
restless hips under a silken
sheet,
like an incoming surf.

Moist and trembling kisses,
then the momentary glow
from two cigarettes.

Arthur F. Krause, Jr.
**REFLECTIONS OF
FREEDOM**

Reflections of you in the water
so blue,
shows your sad eyes and
something that's true.
A river ahead that looks so

dead, a patch of green grass
to make
it your bed.

Turtles and ducks and fish
that jump; will sometimes
give you
chilly goose bumps.

A flock of birds fly overhead
and there in the sky is a
sunset
so red.

You think of how nice it is to
be free as the breezy wind
blows
through the trees.

Butterflies and bumble bees,
loving birds in the trees gives
you
a feeling of wanting to be free.

Catherine Colley
MY GOLDEN SEPTEMBER

Droplets of rain rested on the
leaves
Green and gold
The wind danced through them
The beauty was something to
behind
I walked on in this magical
place
I breathed in the natural scent
As the cool freshness touched
my hair and face
Rapport filled my very being
As I walked on this lovely
Golden September day I
was seeing.

Edith I. Ney
A CHRISTMAS PLEA

I'm not in school today because,
I'm going to visit Santy Claus;
I'll be glad to see him, once
again
To thank him for my truck
and train.

He left them for me, last
December
They're good as new, 'cept for
a fender,
I fixed it, least the best I could
I had only wire and a piece of
wood.

Now this year, I would like
a bike;
And maybe skates, for when
there's ice.
I'm older now, as you can
see,
I'll be more careful, I promise,
please!

Gwen O'Connor
MEMORIES

Fragrant lilacs—light and dark—
Tucked into a vase of blue;
The thrilling song of a meadow
lark,
All remind me of you.

A band of wild geese flying

high;
A pheasant of gorgeous hue,
Or a fleecy cloud up in the
sky—
They remind me of you.

The stream that babbles
Down the mountain side,
Where redbuds glow in the sun;
A road that shimmers
As it winds and climbs
Where the deer and bear may
run:

A well trodden path through
a meadow,
Where lupin spikes stand
tall,
Leading to a quiet fishing
pond
Floating wild ducks in the fall;

Your favorite rosebuds
glistening
With early morning dew,
Sending out their fragrances;
All these remind me of you!

Michael Chamish
EVERYBODY HAS A DREAM

Soft pink pillows of clouds part
to find the sun
as dawn opens on the King's
carnival.
The Jester's debut begins today
and
he has studied hard
for the chance to dance before
the King and Queen.

Many hours of toil preceded
this day
as he practiced routines while
months turned to years.
When his father died a
blacksmith
it spurred him on to prove
his true worth to himself.

Then in the shadows of
majestic marble pillars
the painted Jester leapt cross
the floor
with black and white tiles
passing under foot
his jumps and turns brought
cheers from the crowd.

But the King and Queen never
gazed an eye
at the graceful figure upon the
floor.
They remembered only as
a blacksmith's son in tatters
and rags.
Undaunted, the Jester never
missed a step
as he performed upon the
tiles
'til dawn became night.

And when the carnival was
over
the exhausted Jester slept
soundly at last.
He had danced like no other
across the King's floor.
And he cared not a bit that
they had not watched
because his heart's pride was
swelled
that he was once
a blacksmith's son in tatters
and rags.

Marion Voris
SPECIAL WORDS WHISPERED

I've heard those words
whispered sweet and low
I've heard those words
spoken with heat and desire

I have listened—
—I have known
Within the fervor of passion
Within the intimacy of Aloof
Alone
Together
we've spent tymes ago
Together we have known

the sentiments were present
with body mind and soul
with heart and hand and touch
and glow
those words—before, I've known

Now come to me tenderly
as never known before
Now filled with Someone's
Soul
Now holding Someone's being

My intimate being
i have shown to you
Your Soul you have revealed
Let me hear those words
once more
whispered sweet and low
a showing of Souls
a revealing of Beings
deserves no less than the
—Ultimate—
Body Mind Soul Being
all intimate truths you know
Share those tender ardent
words
that are whispered
Sweet and Low . . .

Lucia A. Roberts
MEMORIES

Time,
The essence of life itself,
Has one forgotten
The promises, the dreams,
The thoughts that were once
shared.

I watch, I wait,
Loneliness has engulfed me,
So overwhelmingly,
I only remember . . .

Joyce Anderson
A SECRET

The forest has a secret
Hidden deep inside,
But if you'll look real closely,
With you she will confide.

Look! There's a little pathway
Leading up the hill.
I think that I shall follow it
And try to be real still.

Hark! I see a squirrel
Scampering through the trees,
Warning my approachment
And it's carried with the breeze.

The grass is soft and springy
And cool beneath my feet,
The flowers on the hillside
Smell magnificent and sweet.

And there within a clearing
Some deer so gently browsed.
A bear was munching berries,
And my heart was wildly
roused.

The birds are softly singing
Like a chorus in the trees,
'Twas like a welcoming
committee,
And I fell down on my knees.
I finished my trek in silence
My heart bursting from within,
That the forest shared her
secret
With me—a human being.

Mary Cheryl Senter
THE OTHER SIDE OF BUSINESS

Frantic fingers are rattling
papers
While breathless limbs heave
down the hall,
Stacatto tongues lap up each
word
Like migrant birds in
chattering trees.

The brisk walk pays no mind
To tortured souls with faded
smiles,
Marches to the beat of
obsession
With human goals, manmade
ambition.

Endless, the clicking
clattering void
Born in the name of progress,
Believes itself a friend to
nature,
Vomits its oily sputum
In crystal pools, defiled.

Karl R. Dahl
THE HALF FALLEN MANSION

Like antiquated figures
that move across a barren stage
dancing slowly to the music
of the rusted iron gates.

As they sweep and sway
and gently brush the wind
the old trees around the
mansion
in rhythm creak and bend.

A cold and stately mansion
now crumbling in decay
whispers secrets long forgotten
its features seem to say.

In darkened shadows of
yesteryear
this solemn mansion stands,
through a yellowed broken
window
burns one solitary lamp.

In the moonlight you can see
her
from the garden far below
one desolate broken figure
staring through the cold.

Her gaze is to the garden
as a tear lightly falls
lips trace her baby's name
as she softly calls.

In the garden, dark and dreary
where proud roses once
bloomed,
lies a grave midst the rubble
where a small child is entombed.

Though cold winds shake the
mansion
and rustle through the trees,
the humble broken figure
stands listening patiently.

This night it will not happen,
though you hear a baby's cry,
a day and forever will see you
alone
the "Half Fallen Mansion" will
sigh.

Michaelina Buonocore
REQUIEM FOR FRANCESCA

Still I marvel, Beloved
Immortelle,
and must say what has not been
said before.

Wife, mother, sister
a throne thrice graced
by you, one so young, so brave
who sought the tyrant god in
youthful innocence
and in your brief season
knew the passion of love's
sorrow.

You stood on the peak of
Vesuvius
fearless of the unfanthomable
depth
in the mount's pit,
dared to touch the fiery lava.

With soul-rayed acceptance
your agony turned inward
to the wound
never rang the heartbreak beat
nor spilled the wailing tears
that would have brimmed the
cup of pieta.

O kneeling devotee,
rose-scented suppliant,
prostrated in radiance,
few knew the power emanating
from your innerly spring of
being
devotion bubbling with the zeal
of a child.

Looming absolute in death's
shadowing
soul incorruptible,
your image grants a solemn
recompense.
Living in a full aura of wine-
dark beauty
you envisioned a loftier venue
than our blind stumbling.

Memory is monarch.
In the embers of memoria in
aeternia
you glow red and gold as a
Neapolitan Madonna.
Your song chants a strain
divine
like the lingering promise
of a tolling temple bell.

May you know peace
in the sustaining holy hands
held out in the unfaltering
light
before Celestial Gates.

Ada M. Peters
HE IS TO ME

To me he is the dawning's
crimson sky,
the carefree bird that lifts its
wings on high,
the leaves of Autumn, and the
meadow flower,
the rainbow after Springtime's
sudden shower.

To me He is the light of star
and moon,
the cooling breeze of Summer's
languid noon,
the deep and dusky shadow,
long and tall,
that comes when peaceful
country twilights fall.

He's the winds of lonely Winter,
blowing wild,
He's the sweet and gentle
spirit of a child,
He's the brightly burning lamp
when daylight dies,
He's all that's good and
wonderful and wise.

He is my Christmas joy, my life
 and breath,
my path to God and Heaven
 after death,
my Easter morning, and my
 setting sun, my pride in
daily tasks that are well done.

All that I need, and so much
 for which I yearn,
He gives, and asks so little in
 return,
except to bid in voice of
 conscience true,
"Share with the poor, as I
 have shared with you."

For me He chose those bitter
 years to spend,
such a love I cannot even
 comprehend,
yet He willed to be my friend,
 nor thought it loss,
when He traded in His
 Kingship for a cross.

He is my world, my work and
 play and sleep.
He's the faithful Shepherd, I
 the wandering sheep.
He's the voice that says, "Fear
 not, you're not alone,
Be still, and take My hand, you
 are my own."

Diana Netherland
I SPEND

i spend
in my (if only)world
and i spend
and i spend
time.
and the electrodes of my mind
and i harvest if anything
nothing.

Gregor Lippold
**A NIGHT IN THE WOODS
OF A BOYSCOUT**

Beneath the trees
there is no breeze,
Only stale and stagnant
 air;
And why the moss grows
from the north, I really do
 not care.

I spent three hours
building fire
by rubbing sticks together,
A slow and tedious job its
 been
when matches would do the
 better.

I heard the call of nature
faintly from afar
And that is why you found
 me
sleeping in the car.

The only tic I've ever known
 is the tick tock of a clock,
But nature's had her heyday
in teaching ticks to walk.

I hate to seem a sissy
But I will not be a fraud;
I find nothing sentimental
With the croaking of a frog.

Crickets are disgusting.
With all their many chirps,
Take me home to Mamma
And away from all this birch.

The forest looks too evil,
Too dark with glaring eyes,
And everytime I feel an
 urge
I just hold it till I die.

You won't find me a'roamin
The woods in wonderous bliss.

It has taken all my courage
To go no farther than a piss.
So listen when I tell you
I think I've had my fill.
We'll do it again next summer
Or maybe never still.

Dorothy R. Ferrell
AN OLD MAN

'Twas too cold to stop and
 buy
A pencil from the man;
So I, with the crowd, went
 rushing on
And gave him just a scan.

Just one scan, but it pierced my
 soul—
In fact, the whole of my being;
That old man in his garments
 torn
Is all I kept a-seeing.

His head was bowed upon his
 breast,
His eyes were downward bent;
'Twas not the fact that he was
 old
Tho' many years he'd spent.

His thoughts, no doubt, ran
 backwards
To days or years gone buy;
Maybe the life that he had
 lived
Or how soon was he to die?

Perhaps, he thought of times
 that he
Could have helped someone
 in need;
And now, in turn, they pass him
 by
Blind to his needs, indeed!

In need? Oh, yes! he was
 sorely in need—
His garments told you that;
An old torn coat, and trousers
 split—
A second-handed hat.

And as I glanced, I saw one
 foot
Had surely been cut in two;
For it was half as long as
 t'other,
And blood was oozing through.

Ah, 'tis just an old man
 begging
Tho' he is sadly in need;
And the people pass him by
And to his needs unheed.

Verna Valante
PORTRAIT OF AMERICA

Toward the borders flow
 mingled, melted iron and ice,
Melted by hands clasped in
 friendship—the hands of the
 past and the future;
The eyes of a youth proudly
 appraise his own mountain;
An old man's lips relax in a
 sleepy, satisfied smile;
A child's legs, tripping on his
 own feet, learn to walk,
While a mother's hand soothes
 the bruises;
Virile ears listen patiently to
 the neighbor's problems,
As humane minds debate to
 find a just solution;
A student's curious nose, having
 known musty books,
pungent experiences and
 odorless failures,
enjoys the aroma of success;
A brawny back, bearing the
 burden of life,
is protected from the fiery red

star
By a thin parchment with an
 eternal message
written in blood and tears and
casting a cooling shadow
on the grateful and
 ungrateful alike;
A clergyman's arm, raised
 in blessing,
reminds the anxious heart
that Man, as the son of God,
works not to inherit the earth,
but the kingdom of Heaven.

Irene A. Smith
CLEAN SLATE

A little child kneels to pray
Dear God, I'se been real bad
 today
I got into my Mommy's clothes
And dressed myself from head
 to toes
And ripped the veil that's on
 her hat
Guess no one kin' be badder
 n' that.

And oh, some more I must
 confess
Her powder jar is quite a mess
I tried to put it on. . .just so,
But then I dropped it, don't
 ya' know
Of course the window stood
 ajar,
And scattered it both near
 and far.

When Mama came to see at
 last
She just stood there and looked
 aghast!
For everything was out of
 place
No powder left to dust her
 face
Her lipstick lay upon the floor
Her comb n' brush were by
 the door.

Things really looked quite
 awry
And me?. . .well, I began to
 cry
For well I knew the fate for
 me
I landed flat upon her knee
You see my mother minds you
 God
She loves me so spares not the
 rod . . .

And since I'm punished by her
 hand
I pray dear God, you'll
 understand
And not require penance too
For these same sins I've told
 to you
And since I won't do that again,
Wipe my slate clean tonight . .
 Amen.

David Terralavoro
UNTITLED

She enjoys her walk in the
 fields and she picks flowers

I don't know where she is from
 I know nothing about her

She is kind and like an angel

Others think she has powers

It is like some kind of magic
 the way she makes things
 change

She means no harm there are
 no signs of evil

Things that happen when she's
 near just seem rather strange

A baby sits crying for awhile

Someone hands her the little
 child

It no longer cries when the
 baby is held in her arms
And the mother is so glad that
 her baby has smiled

A wild dog sits there barking
 and is soon held in her arms
Seconds later the dog is no
 longer wild

Things that she touches with
 her hands
Change for some reason and
 I just don't understand

I still don't know who she is

I don't know her history

I can never forget her or find
 out about her

It will remain a mystery.

Virgie I. Cramer
DEM BONES—DEM BONES

Have you a twinge of Arthritis?
If you have, then you're a cinch
To have your bones a creakin'
Stickin' closer to the bench.

In the back you get lumbago
Then your hands will turn to
 claws.
Arthritis starts to creepin'
From your toes up to your
 jaws.

Ankles swollen twice the normal
And you're sure they're full of
 sap.
Then your knees will start to
 bangin'
Water is underneath the cap.

Every day you grow much
 stiffer
Wonderin' what the heck to do.
Then you grab a pint of liquor
For it warms you through and
 through.

But tomorrow when you're
 sober
Pains will stick you like a pin,
And you feel that this affliction
Is in answer to your sin.

Then once more you go a
 creakin'
back to your bench in pain.
And you swear that kind of
 healin'
You will never use again.

So keep hopin' and a prayin'
If a cure must come too late
When the Good Lord calls
 your number
You can amble through the
 gate.

Debra L. Piggott
INCONSEQUENCE

I thought to write about a tree
But that's already been done.
I thought to write of earth
 and sky—
That's done by everyone.
So then I had to stop and think
Of what I planned to write;
It wasn't very easy—
Most subjects seem so trite.
I thought to write about a time
When I was very small,
When I would look up at the
 sun
And ask why it's a ball.
I thought to write of later
 years
When I first fell in love;
I'd say that life was perfect,
Blessed by the gods above.
But everything I thought to

write
Had all been done before,
Like gazing through a mirrored
glass
Or walking through a door.
And still I sat and thought
that day—
The paper still was blank,
While visions danced before
my eyes
And in the shadows sank.
I could not think of anything
That hadn't yet been seen.
Not even colors seemed quite
right—
Not red, white, blue nor green.
There must be something in
earth or sky
That only I should know—
How lowering to reflect that
day
I couldn't steal the show.
Who was I to be so different
Among all those who live?
For all have thoughts to
cherish,
And all have much to give!
And so I settled back that
day
The paper in its drawer—
For in mankind's long history,
It'd all been said before.

Gil Dannenberg
THE ADIRONDACKS

Adirondack majesty
Land of evergreens
Towering trees
Mountain slopes
Crystal-flowing streams.

Adirondack beauty
Land of glacial lakes
Tear-Of-The-Clouds
Placid, Pine
Mystic as each morning breaks.

Adirondack dynasty
Land of animals
Wild moose, bear
Lynx and deer
Drinking as the evening falls.

Adirondack solitude
Land forever wild
Peace, calm
Serenity, A
Haven for adult or child.

Adirondack future
Land we must preserve
Give evergreens
Lakes and streams
Care and treatment they deserve.

Georgann Jenulis
**BIG, BIG BROAD HANDS
WHO PLAY THEIR
TOM TOM**

Deep, deep in a valley up
North
Tall, tall strong young men had
come forth
Big, big broad hands that they
owned
Came, came from a great land
they roamed
Fights, fights from the valley
so old
Strong, strong tall young men
who were bold
Dance, dance round fire and
song
Round, round to beats so long
Men, men who enjoyed life
itself
Ran, ran as the music brought
health
Wild, wild they would jump

on the ground
Blind, blind from all others
around.
Stamp, stamp from a foot sure
of earth
Fast, fast for all it was worth
Breath, breath which was lost
in the dance
Fire, fire to shine and enhance
Scream, scream till their
hearts burst with love
Loud, loud to the sky up
above
Shout, shout to the mountains
and hills
Loss, loss of minds and wills
Rage, rage till the heavens
split wide
Fever, fever burning inside
Slow, slow went the music so
dead
Blood, blood quit its flowing
so red
Stop, stop went the bodies and
feet
Still, still round fire of heat
Ears, ears of the men who could
hear it
Beats, beats from the twang of
a spirit
Brow, brow so slippery and wet
Beads, beads covered with
sweat
Joy, joy so precious and numb
Love, love as they now played
their tom tom.

Marnelle R. White
THE FUNERAL

The woman had been worth
several million.
She had held bonds and
rentals
and the old home ranch used
in years gone by
for the county fair and rodeo.
Now, they took her in a modest
coffin
from a Volkswagen bus
dispatched with the envied
austerity
of the sixties from Berkeley
under the auspices of two
daughters—
a fifties Beatnik—faded,
a nurse—practical.
Old eyes observed the wagon.
Old eyes observed the plain
box.
Old eyes observed the young
eyes
responsible for the ritual,
suspiciously.
The will was known;
it skipped a generation;
the daughters, the son
received, profit perhaps,
but no property,
no prestiege,
no power;
there was no love,
but the family had lingered on
perhaps there had been love—
once.
The grave, the son's responsibility
responsibility
had filled with ground water;
he had run a pump all morning
to no avail.
Now, in desperation, he
brought
a water-proof liner for the
coffin

with its water-stained satin
inner-lining.
There had been an accident in
the valley fog.
She had lain in a coma three
months,
and died of a strangled bowel.
She had endured much;
a husband who'd spent a
lifetime in a bar;
there had been a pretty
neighbor wooman;
perhaps it had been only
suspicion.
The old eyes watched.
Mother wrote burial instructions
after the funeral;
she carried them with her
for years and years
along with identification.

Hoda Holliday Linkous
**SOULS OF MORTAL
TEMPLES**

Mortal temples fashioned of
clay
Upon this sphere was meant
to stay
Until death takes its earthly
toll
And robs them of their living
soul.
Oh! Where in yonders great
unknown
As if on wings the soul has
flown
Only those gone before could
tell
Where souls of mortal temples
dwell.
Dust to dust was only spoken
Of the temple that can be
broken
It was not spoken of the
soul
That has the temple in control.
Oh! For a greater view of
sight
Beyond our limit of length and
height
And for deep wisdom to
explore
The depth below the water's
floor.
World of wonders and vast
space
Temples of different form
and face
Now see darkly as through
a glass
Have no vision beyond the
pass.
But when dawn breaks on that
great day
All mysteries will be cleared
away
And with clear vision face to
face
New temples will the old
replace.

Cindrea Diane Boggs
A WINTER'S JOURNEY

He walks through the night
as though it were day.
Each step—determined and
sure.
The snow falling softly—erasing
his mark,
And his thoughts were
beginning to soar.
He comes to a clearning—a
parting of woods,
And moonlight decends on
his strong, handsome face.
It glowed from the cold and
the thoughts he just had.
Looking quickly around, he
hastens his pace.
Not a sound could be heard
rising up from the snow.
It had muffled his steps for
nearly a night.
His journey seemed endless,
but now was forgotten.
At the top of a hill—its
end was in sight.
The glow from a lamp poured
out through a window.
It beckoned to him with a
soft, friendly hum.
He spied his love's face peeking
out from the shutter.
He knew he had made it—and
started to run.
He caught her in flight as she
shot from the door.
He'd forgotten her beauty,
and stared at her face.
Her long, flowing hair was
sprinkled with snow.
His beard rubbed her chin
with each sweet embrace.
His long winter walk had been
grueling—no less.
He thought of it now as he
held his love's form.
The sharp-biting cold had
tried to take over,
But the thought of her kisses
had kept his heart warm.

Ralph Henry Taylor
CRICKET

In that "House out West"—
Where I was priviledged guest,
There were several dogs—
house pets—
Wagging tails—performing
pirouettes—
Little dogs that court each
guest—
(Seeming never to need a rest)
With joyous bark and stamping
feet—
They made that home complete.
These Chihuahuas were so very
small—
I was afraid I'd step on them
all.
But there was my favorite one—
'Cricket', who my heart had
won,
She was so friendly—so full
of fun,
Always on the go and run.
She'd crawl into my bed at
night,
Under sheets drawn up tight,
And cuddle up to me—how
cute!
And kiss me on the cheek to
boot!
Quite a little dog was she,
As friendly as a dog could be.
The night I was told she had

died—
I nearly choked, and almost cried.
Cricket—I shall always think of you—
As being almost human, it's true.
A little dog who walked so tall—
Bringing happiness to all.
Melba loved you the most, I know,
Yes, Cricket, she told me so.
She paid your undivided attention
By showering you with affection—
So Cricket, we will not say 'Good-bye'
'Cause I'm sure we'll meet again—
in the 'by-and-by'!

Dave Wilson
THE TIMES THEY ARE CHANGIN'

The times they are changin'
I'll do you no harm
On worn soled shoes I'm a travelin' on
Is there no sorrow for a love that has gone
On worn soled shoes I'm travelin' I'm gone
Who is this lady that won't let me be
She's filled up my heart she's all I can see
My how times have changed her the sound of her song
And now it does grieve me she wants that I'm gone
Streets of a new town all strangers to me
I can't say I'm stayin. I'll just wait and see
Tomorrow brings promise of joy and a smile
I'll find my own joy and I'll laugh for awhile
The times they are changin'
I'll do you no harm
On worn soled shoes I'm a travelin' on
Is there no sorrow for a love that has gone
On worn soled shoes I'm travelin' I'm gone
And should I remember I just may return
A lifetime of agein', surely I'd learn
How the girl whore turned me to my wanderin' shoes
Also returned me to the road lonesome blues
The times they are changin'
I'll do no harm
On worn soled shoes I'm a travelin' on
Is there no sorrow for a love that has gone
On worn soled shoes I'm travelin' I'm gone.

Clemence Rheaume
WOODLAND VESPERS

Walking through the woods by the side of the pond
I stop for a moment . . .
My entire being takes in the scene before me:
I see the setting sun peering through the trees,
Its reflection glistening on the water;
The trout jumping out of the pond,
Their salmon bellies reflecting the setting sun;
The trees barely moving,
Their arms uplifted in silent prayer.
I hear the loon calling out in the wilderness;
The other birds singing "AMEN" to its hymn of praise;
The grass rustling silently,
Moved by the small creatures within.
I smell the fresh pine from the trees;
I taste the fresh water in the air;
I feel the gentle breeze.
Trees praying birds chanting fish dancing
—All are absorbed in their own kind of prayer;
And after they have finished their evening vespers
They go to sleep until the dawn
When once again they will start their day anew
With morning devotions.

Julie D. Larson
EPITAPH FOR ELGANAUD

He was a bright boy;
Elganaud,
Bright. . .
Until they spattered him
(ketsup and fat globules sticky in the muddy trench.)
Toy soldiers
Pointing plastic machine guns
At stuffed cloth dolls
(turn them upside down and they'll cry)
Playing war games
(be sure to scream when you fall down dead.
pretend it really hurts
it's funnier that way.)
Remember . . .
It's only a cartoon.
When you blow up the funny people
The pieces fall back in place
And they walk away laughing.
They found the young chap;
Elganaude,
What was left of him,
Smeared across the dirt walls
Of his hiding place,
Slimy bits of him
Had left oozing trails
Where they slid to the mud floor.
"Poor lad!"
Too bad he didn't leave us a fingerprint
Or something
We could send home to his family.
If we knew who he was
We could say a prayer
Or bless what's left of his soul.
But,
As it is . . .
He'll enrich the soil.
Might smell for a few months of course,
But in a couple years
Crops will grow splendidly here.
Throw some dirt on him for now, won't you.
It's a little too messy

To leave for some unsuspecting person
To stumble into.
Might make 'em sick or something.
Wouldn't want that now, would we?

Emmaline Casserly Palmer
HARD-TO-FINDS

There are hard-to-find places,
Though a map's in your hands.
There are hard-to-find spaces
To park cars, trucks or vans.
There are hard-to-find winners
On race programs to bet.
There are hard-to-find gifts
Without going in debt.
There are hard-to-find dyes
To match near-scalp grey hairs.
There are hard-to-find fabrics
For those old-clothes' repairs.
There are hard-to-find cards
For the hard-to-please set.
There are hard-to-find suits
For that once-slinky Vet.
There are hard-to-find tickets
For all big and best games.
There are hard-to-find spouses
Who accept any blame.
There are hard-to-find seats
On the roomiest jets
For pretended non-smokers
Who must visit smoke sets.
If you're tired of my list,
Just continue, my pet,
To add yours to the "gripe list".
There are countless more yet.

Sonja M. Witschonke
THE SACRIFICE OF ONE

As the air is filled with incense,
And the candles flicker on.
The ceremony will begin,
With the sacrifice of one.

A fragment of his life he'll lose,
Which will terminate his dream.
With the incantation she recites,
His life he'll not redeem.

Her hypnotic eyes will burn his mind,
As she puts him in a trance.
Then the moon will glow and set a scene,
That the evening will enhance.

Her covenant she's sworn to love,
As she chants away the night,
But her ritual she must complete,
Before the morning light.

The sorcerer then looks within,
And tears apart his soul.
For the cult has always told her,
That each man should pay his toll.

As he sits alone in a captive state,
His mind he'll not restore.
For she influenced him to believe,
That her love was ever more.

There is no ransom great enough,
To relieve him of his pain.
For she lives her life to prove to men,
That their love is given in vain.

Though in the end he might reform,
And recover from her spell.

But the wicked one with powers great,
Has another death to tell.

Thelma Haywood Gipson
A WOMAN MUST SPEAK

Attention all men, wherever you are
At work or at play, or drunk in a bar
The truth is forecoming, a woman must speak
Of diminishing man and his lost physique
From work he comes home and kisses a kid,
Gives a pat to his dog then flips his lid
He roars about his boss, and everything's wrong
My God! his record's the same old sad song
The next we know his food's not right
His path can be followed, a terrible sight
Rings on the bathtub, clothes on the floor
We know from the kitchen we'll soon hear his snore
We clean up the mess and wonder what's next
'Cause as soon as he wakes he's got a new text
Then he's off to bed and the lights are dim
And it's time for dear old "Romeo" to begin
His charms were outnumbered by disgusting remarks
No wonder his bedroom holds no more sparks
Now his ego's deflated and he stalks from the room
As he slams the door and goes to his doom
Seeking romance from his bar room sluts
While his flower at home bleeds from his cuts
A garden needs care and sunshine to grow
A beautiful flower won't bloom in the snow
Yet men brag and boast of sex and joys
When all they make at home is noise
Still master, superior, egotistical man
Destroys his own power to have and command
An absolute ruler you lock your own door
Please tell us how else to even the score.

Billy Sands
THE RIVER

Your smile flashes through my head
As a tear trickles down from my eye

It seems circumstances have
led
Me to now have to tell you
goodbye
But there's some things I need
to explain
Before I do something foolish
and drastic
Your beauty makes all the
pretty flowers look plain
With your bright sparkling
eyes so fantastic
You're telling me it just isn't
right
Infatuation you say it is
called
No such thing as love at first
sight
And it cannot be love at all
So why are you always in my
dreams?
How come the feeling isn't
easing at all?
How come every time I turn
it seems
So much deeper and deeper
I fall
The situation's not getting
better
It doesn't matter how hard I
try
I try and try to forget you
Finally I just give up and cry
But am I a mouse or a man?
Men are not supposed to cry
In that case I can't understand
What this moisture is rolling
from my eye
Yes, I know I've given you a
bad time
Expressing my feeling for you
After thinking it over I now
find
There is only one thing now I
can do
Without you I know I can't
live
As I look at the water and
shiver
There is so much love I could
give
Sure is a long way down to
the river
So this time it's really goodbye
I love you so much I could
die . . .

Desiree Mickelson
SUNNY 70

Sunny 70 October Day
Heart filled tears fell away
Mama's got cancer
Daddy's got no answer
and brother and sis don't know
what to say
Mama's journey had just begun
This everlasting struggle being
no fun
treatments here and needles
there
a growing tumor under
doctors care
Mama lay in the hospital miles
away
while I play mother every day
making meals and washing
clothes
this burden of mine nobody
knows
As each day of hard work
ends
I wish for a moment to spend
with friends
with brother at work and

sis at school
I find that daddy is "alright
and pretty cool"
After I grew up over night
I was thrilled to hear Mama's
"doing alright"
still a struggle without an
end
Mama knows she's got a friend
Sunny 70 October Day
Four years have passed away
Mama's got cancer
Daddy got an answer
and brother and sis are happy
to say
Mama *LIVES* day by day.

Eddie Milbrandt, Jr.
CAMPAIGN '80

T'was the year before election
and all across the land,
Every prominent American
was declaring his presidential
stand.

The polls were taken by the
experts with care,
In hopes that the voters and
primaries soon would be
there.

The candidates debated and
argued till their faces turned
red,
While visions of the White
House danced in their heads.

With Jimmy in the Rose Garden
and Teddy on the campaign
trail,
The election of l980 made
many Democrats turn pale.

Then in Iowa there arose such
a clatter,
People turned on their
televisions to see what was the
matter.

Away to Des Moines the GOP
debated in a flash,
Tore open the issue of the
economy and about the
absence of Reagan they
hashed.

The victory in the nation's first
caucus by George Bush,
Caused the assumed GOP
frontrunner to fall back in a
hush.
And then in New Hampshire
what should appear
But a handsome Californian
and his entire conservative
career.
With his wit and humor coming
again and again,
Everyone knew in a moment
it must be Ronald Reagan.

The primaries went by faster
than a running hare,
And Carter and Reagan won
them with votes to spare.

Florida, Illinois, New York
and Pennsylvania!

Maryland, New Jersey, Oregon
and California!
Secure the nominations at the
conventions,
And write a platform that
includes everyone's
intentions.

When GOP hopeful Reagan wante
wanted Ford as his Veep
nominee,
He met with his first obstacle:
Second place Ford did not
want to be.
So back to negotiating Reagan
flew,
With a list full of names, he
picked George Bush to be
part of his crew.
And then on the Republican
Convention was put a cork,
On to the Democratic
Convention in New York!

As the Democrats prepared
for a party divided,
Teddy, with the president
sided.
Kennedy delegates wanted
him to fight more,
But they would have to wait
until '84.

The third party did not a
candidate lack,
Republican John Anderson
jumped on the Independent
pack.
His white hair—how it shone!
His reason for running—
to be an alternative,
Americans would have to give
one of these, a majority
of the affirmative.

The campaign seen much mud
slinging,
And Americans soon had politics
in their ears ringing.
Reagan said Carter started in the
birth place of the Klan,
Both candidates had just three
months left to make an
effective campaign plan.
The league of Women Voters
sponsored a debate,
Among the three major
presidential candidates.
But the president did not
attend,
He would not, as he put it,
debate two Republicans.

People started seeing the Carter
campaign as mean,
He knew he must change this
image, or his share of the vote
would be lean.
Democrats tried to make an issue
of war and peace,
Republicans emphasized the
difficulty of obtaining a
lease.

The two met in Cleveland face-
to-face,
In one major debate which
could determine the race.
They talked, debated, and
argued,
And Reagan had won, most
people construed.
But then news came from Iran,
Was the release of the hostages
at hand?
But alas, it was not to be,
And Ronald Reagan went on
to a landslide victory.

Reagan sprang to Washington,
to his transition team he
gave a whistle,

And away they all flew to the
White House like the down
of a thistle.
But the President exclaimed
as he went back to Plains,
Today's many problems
require much brains.

To Reagan are left the hostages
in Iran,
And also the Soviets in
Afghanistan.
With the economy in disarray,
There won't be much time
for play.

To you, Ronald Reagan, we
wish much luck,
We hope you can put buying
power back in the buck.
And to you, Jimmy Carter, we
know you did your best,
Now return to Plaines and
catch up on a much needed
rest.

Flossie Dustin Byrd
THE FRIENDSHIP TREE

If I could grow a Friendship
tree
For everyone to see
I'd plant it where the world
walked by
So they'd share it with me.

I'd shape it oh so gracefully
They all would stop and stare
At all the lovely friends of
mine
That they'd see blooming
there.

Each friend a different flower
would be
In color, shape and form
Cause there are no two friends
alike
There's no such thing as
"Norm."

There'd be big strong and
sturdy ones
With petals opened wide
To show the strength and
thoughtfulness
That they hold deep inside.

And then there'd be the fragile
ones
Of such a pastel shade
To show their tender, gentle
love
And trust from which they're
made.

And here and there on tips of
twigs
Delicate dainty buds
To represent the little ones
That I think so much of.

I'd want it near a window
Where I could look and see
The faces of each dear one
Smiling back at me

And I would form it of such
stuff
That it bloomed all year long
For friendship isn't seasonal
It's like a lovely song.

That floats thru all your reveries
All your whole life thru
In one continuous melody
Bringing joy to you.

The leaves upon my lovely
tree
Would be the memories
That each dear friend has
given me
Oh, so many leaves there'd be.

I'd know the way to make it
grow

And always sturdy be
It's just to be the kind of friend
That they have been to me.
I'd cultivate it carefully
And water it with tears
And it would bloom for all my time
To brighten all my years.

Dallas Kirk Gantt
CRETE

cruising the north coast of Crete
in a beatup bus
that cut those dusty mountain curves
in practiced abandon. . .

we were determined
to outdistance
the crawling, sprawling tourist colossus
that turned the countryside to stone
more surely than any Medusa.

Zorba dances under the olives,
vineyards in his veins . . .
urging us on.

centuries slip into the sea
as we nod goodbye
to the palm-beaches of Vai,
and head into the heart
of the ancient island
where Zeus still stands
astride the cloudy peaks,
winking at the little white churches
and eyeing the slim brown goat-girls.

stretched out on sandstone beds
in the crypt-caves of Matala,
i finger my beads
and ache to hang out with Hercules,
leap bulls with the other naked youths,
and seize the seas with Ulysses.

Barbara J. Morris
OUR DEAR LITTLE BABY WE WON'T GET TO HOLD

Our dear little baby, we won't get to hold,
God chose to call him at two days old
It makes our hearts sad to miss him so,
We wish we knew why he had to go.
We waited to love him, we prayed with our soul,
Our dear little baby, we would get to hold
We know that God loves us, we reason and sigh,
He took back our darling, we don't know why.
We will find comfort in each others love,
And pray for our son, to God above
We know he's protected in God's loving care,
For now he's an angel, golden wings to bear.
He'll never know sorrow, he'll never be cold,
He'll be hungry, he'll never grow old
God will protect him in his home on high,
And we'll see him again, when we meet in the sky.
We'll always remember his

dear tiny face,
The one fleeting moment we got to embrace
His birth was a miracle, a sweet joy,
We'll hold in our hearts forever, our darling baby boy.
We are sad but we're happy to know of his love,
It could only be sent to us from Heaven above
God may grant us other babies, but we've treasures untold,
From the birth of our baby, we won't get to hold.

Joanne Wright
A FRIEND'S HOME

Your home is a lovely garden
Flowing with beauty from above,
No matter how empty I feel,
You fill me with gifts of love.
The fragrance of the atmosphere
Indwells my every need.
For the garden of your home life,
Is constantly sowing seed.
In the richness of your garden,
The friendship that we know,
Is never diminished—but abounds
In the understanding that we sow.
I fill my arms, my eyes and heart,
And breathe the essence of you;
My soul is refreshed, my bouquet is love
In every possible hue.
I may kneel there in prayerful longing
While offering my heart in tears,
And absorb your loving comfort
That will fill my empty years.
I kiss a tiny petal,
And taste the tear-drop dew.
For love only lives when given away,
And I have shared so much with you.
Enveloped in smiles, I step away.
Love's aura enfolds me where
Inside your lovely garden home
I will always remember you there.

Elwood Weisneck
MOM

Mom brought us into this world
And gave us all her love and affection
And made sure we started off in the right direction
She gave us so much, and all she wanted was love and trust
Who taught us to laugh and crawl
Who taught us to talk and draw
Mom's the one, we owe her so much
On cold winter nights when we would fuss from dust till dawn
Mom would walk the floor making sure we were dry and warm
She didn't even mind when we broke a cup or dish,
All she would say, Daddy will fix
And when we fell and got a

bump or scratch
Only Mom could heal it with a kiss
Mom's the only one who could bake, clean and cook
And at the same time read us a book
Yes we owe Mom so much more than we realize
When we got into trouble it was Mom who apologized
When we were old enough going out on dates
Mom would worry when we came home late
And it breaks my heart to see Mom cry
Knowing we were leaving by and by
So turn to your mother and tell her you love her
She needs to know before you leave her
And when you leave her, don't forget her
We owe Mom so much
And when Mom's hair turns to silver
She'll need all the love we can give her
Don't let her feel that her part is done
When it comes to Mom, we've only got one
Mom's not young, she's getting older and older
And if she had her way, she would do it over and over
And when it's time to lay Mom to rest
She'll know she's done her very best.

Hal II
A RETREAT TO THE TEDDER FARM

Flex-legged
A spider reigns
High on a pier post
Like a feline
With raised hairs
And arched back.

Jutted silk
Powered by an air current
Sets the arachnid skier
Gliding across pond water
Toward land.
A step ahead of human ingenuity:
Ingenuous Nature.

Charles R. Perlwitz
OUR POEM

It was only in approaching those places
not too well traversed by the everyday
walks of life that our love for uncommon
gardens, perhaps overgrown, ancient houses
full of ghosts and reminiscences of passions
withheld, stale yet lingering, and particularly
for occurrences tragic and fallen, as traced
perhaps in the grieving of the weather, or
the windy creaking of some forgotten door,
it was only in approaching these unmarred
twists from other lives, older lives from
previous times, that the present

day's
holding back revealed itself as an open
welcome from the center, an embrace embodying
the completeness of its cycle, fullness from
start to end, whose total time made yours
the circuit of sun and moon and stars lulling
like the whispers of an ephemeral companion,
always with you, reminding of your briefness
from behind your shoulder, sometimes singing,
sometimes crying, the everpresence of this life.

Louis Frederick Tow
THE BLOOD RED ROSE

In the days
Of adventure
We read
The ventures
Of Spanish ships
And Gold.

It was a time
Of wars and woes
And a ship
They called
The Blood Red Rose.

She was a ship
Trimmed
With silver and gold
And on her
Main sail
They painted
A red, red rose.

She was a ship
Of rare beauty
She carried
Large booty
And her cannons
Bellowed
And roared.

It was a time of
Royal rascals
Robbers and rogues
It was the time
Of the Blood Red Rose.

Pirate ships
Did plunder
There is no wonder
And one set sail
For the Rose.

It was a bold
Encounter
A mid-day
Encounter
When the robber
Encountered
The Rose.

The pirate ship
Engaged her
With no fear
Of danger
Her cannons

Thundered
And roared.
In black smoke
And thunder
The pirate ship
Blundered
It was the end
Of the skull
And crossed bones.
A victor in ventures
The Rose of
Adventure.
She was a ship
Of rare beauty
She carried
Large booty
And her cannons
Bellowed
And roared.
Rose of roses!
The Blood Red Rose.
She traveled
near and far
But nothing
Could ever mar
The wake of the
Blood Red Rose.

Daniel Lantz
UNCLE ABE

Square teeth browned by
 Lucky Strikes
And faced by nights as hollow
 as unkept
Promises, he drives the dusty
 green
Pickup to the deserted quarry
To be with the Marchtouched
 stone
At home with the bottled
 amber witch
Who shelters him from the
 harsh light of noon.
Beneath an inverted
 windcrossed cup of bone
A turbulent potion rumbles
 stirred
by the amber witche's
 whispered chant
Like an abrading thought
 arguing with itself:
Quos Deus vult perdere,
 prius dementat.
Spring's thaw brought no
 assurance
By the woodstove with a family
 of Strangers
To a propped broken leg
 wrapped in plaster
Where his heart should have
 been.
Lost in paperbacked graves of
 other's dreams
He carried in firewood when
 his leg allowed
After he hacksawed the itching
 cocoon of plaster
Free to hobble in February
 mud.
Warm Saturday afternoon ideas
 called him to night's
Liason with the bottled witch's
 comfort and taunt.
Chilling remnant of winter
 stirs the last
Surviving trees young enough
 to sway,
Nods at the callused
 mechanic's hands,
Bows to fortyeight old years
 of gifted destruction
And watches the rubber hose
 pierce the window,
An urgent probe for release.
Within he settles with the
 bottled amber girl,
Kisses her warmth

on the horsehair seat
And smells her fragrance with
 gasoline fumes
As the International truck
 chuckles, breathing
After him Quos Deus Quos
 Deus Quos Deus Quos Deus

Mrs. Maco Farwell
**THANKSGIVING AND
CHRISTMAS**

How much thanks in giving?
Are we thankful for just
 living?
As we look around and see
 God's handiwork
Do we try to live up to
 his teachings or do we
 shirk?
Let us all in 1981 resolve to
 help others
And so, make our own lives
 full of ruthers
The world sorely needs love
So all of us should be like
 a dove.

Then comes Christmas
With all the tinsel and glitter
Makes one want to flitter
The birthday of the Christ-
 child
He came to give us love
Do we revere his name or
 give it a shove.
Christmas means loving home
 and family
As well as all the people
Are we showing our true
 colors and following the
 steeple?
May Christmas this year
 bring Joy and gladness
To both old and young and
 not sadness
Christ's sacrifice at Calvary
Should make our own lifes full
 of caring and sharing
The cross of Revernty
Soon it will be Easter
Let us make it meaningful
 and sweeter.

Karen S. Neely
**THE BUTTERSCOTCH
ANGELS**

The butterscotch angels left
 me alone again
Don't they know that I'm
 scared?
The clouds are black, the sky
 is dark,
And I'm completely unprepared.
Their juicy-fruit harps play
 a space cadet song
About a stereo with full color
 sound.
They send out messages on
 their CB
But now they've stopped
 coming around.
A green flower on a polka-dot
 stem
Hollers for someone to care.
A plastocene horse comes
 around the bend—
He's running away to nowhere.
The digital clock says 11:02
But the radio doesn't come on.
The electric went off about
 an hour ago
And the butterscotch angels
 are gone.
They're my only contact with
 reality
Everything else is only a
 dream.
My only string on this side
 of life,

Everything else is fantasy, it
 seems.
The only connection with the
 world outside
With whatever's beyond that
 door.
The only way to find out my
 past
But they don't come around
 anymore.

Ruby G. Foote
FOR THE HANDICAPPED

If deaf ears can't hear your
 words of love
You can show me with a soft
 gentle touch
Or if I can't see your lips move
 when they're speaking
There are other ways that will
 mean just as much. . .
And if my physical being is
 different from yours
And I can't stand alone, or
 I'll fall,
Just the sound of a loving
 voice
Can make me feel in my heart
 six feet tall. . .
What a difference life makes
If you know someone cares,
If the shoulder you get is not
 cold
There are two things we still
 have
That you can't overlook,
And that is a heart and a soul.
So take time to remember
Those less fortunate than you
Just think how lucky you are
 overall
Don't put us off in a corner
 alone
And make us feel ugly and
 small
For we are God's children;
He has put us in this world
For a purpose we don't quite
 understand
So love and accept us, just as
 we are,
As part of the Master's Plan.

Pam Heaton
FOR JEFF

You've become a very
 important part of my life and
 made it complete
You're warm and tender,
 loving and sweet
I never thought I'd ever feel
 this way again
And in many ways you truly
 are my very best friend
You're very gentle and caring,
 not like any man I've ever
 known
And in the last few months,
 our love has really grown
You say I sometimes try too
 hard to please you, and maybe
 that's true
But I want you to know I
 think you're special, is that
 so wrong to want to do
When I lay in your arms there's
 a closeness only we can share
And if for any reason you need
 me, you know I'll always
 be there
You make me feel like a lady,
 a feeling I've rarely felt
And sometimes when you look
 at me, I swear I'm going to
 melt

You have a way of making me
 smile, even when I'm down
And I always feel good just
 knowing you're around
I hope you don't think I'm
 foolish when I say I love you
 with all my heart
And that I pray there's a
 lifetime together ahead of us
 and this is just the start.

Anita R. Fisk
**HIS BEGINNING WAS THE
END**

Before that which is, was
Was emptiness—beyond
 imagination.
There were no crevasses, no
 peaks, no shallows;
There was not a tear, nor a
 laugh, nor a sigh.
There was no one:
nothing
A force which came to be,
Was more powerful than the
 most—chose a moment.
Light from dark, element from
 element, all separated.
There were trees to bear fruit
 to bear trees.
There was life:
Something
Life was living, giving
Were the waters, the sky, the
 earth—it was good.
Lights for the dark, warmth
 for the day,
Beasts to inhabit, to multiply
 to subdue.
Man came:
EVERYTHING
Man brought men, men
Were thinking, talking,
 tinkering—progress
Environments produced, spaces
 filled,
energies confined.
Revolutions revolved
 revolutions which revolved.
He had adjusted:
something
He that had come last, had
 been the most,
is no more. He had thought,
 talked, tinkered—destiny
Denied new life, diminished
 living life, deprived old life.
No more were there trees to
 bear fruit to bear trees.
He had dominated and
 subdued:
nothing.

Melanie Marie Sadlon
THE SAILOR'S DREAM

Proud and mighty the ship
 sailed.
Cold salty air prevailed.
On up the mast sat he.
The crows nest was his duty.

Long into the night he sat
 eyes fixed.
What was it he saw in the waves
 so mixed?
Upon the dark glimmering
 sea,
riding and frolicking on the
 foam,
Was a glistening sun tanned
 maiden,
a mermaid I presume.

She had long golden hair and
 shining huge eyes.
Her voice was the wind
And it rang in the sailor's

ears,
telling him lies.

Alas! Many a young sailor was
lost at sea,
because of the beauty they had
seen.
Taking delight in the fair young
girl's breasts,
they found themselves all
laid to rest.

So deep in her trance the young
sailor stood,
and the melancholy
ringing still in his ears;
He sprang to the sea to go to
her arms,
but all he was rewarded with
was an
unearthly death.

The men on the ship lost sight
of the young sailor,
and all were saddened
by the loss of a brother.
Then in a strange wonder, they
saw the wind had
stopped blowing and
she had ceased calling.

But what became of the sailor?
He sank to his grave with a
smile on his face.
And did he see the girl?
She kissed his hand
and left not a wave
behind
for the sailor to trace . . .

Madeline Rasmusson
A LETTER TO MY SLEEPING SON

Listen son I am saying this,
As you lie asleep, one little
hand
Under your cheek with wet
curls,
As you drifted off in dream
land.

These are the things I am
thinking,
I had been very cross to you,
I scolded you as you were
dressing for school
You thought a dab of wet
cloth would do.

I called out angrily when I
found,
You had thrown your things
on the floor,
You gulped down your food,
And reached with both
hands for more.

You put your elbows on the
table,
You spread butter too thick
on your bread.
As I put my hat on to go out
the door,
I heard these words you said.

"Goodbye, Daddy" I
frowned and snapped,
"Hold your shoulders back,
my son."
It all started again when I came
home,
You were playing marbles in
the setting sun.

There were holds in your pants,
I humiliated you because I
am a grouch,
I told you pants were expensive
I made you walk ahead of me
to the house.

Later when I was reading in
the library,
You came in softly with a
hurt look in your eyes,

Impatiently at the interruption,
I said, "What do you want?"
to my surprise,
You said nothing but ran across
the room
With a tempestious pledge you
threw
Your arms around me
and kissed me,
Out the door you went
pattering through.

I have come to your bedside
in darkness,
I have knelt here choking with
emotion,
I know if you were awake you
would
Not understand though your
heart is as big as the ocean.

Eileen Jewett
I STARE AT THE TRAFFIC

I stare at the traffic
It's not traffic I see
I see a place far off
As clean as can be
There's white top mountains
year round
Lots of game on the ground
There's crooked roads, and
tall jack pine trees.
And the love of wonder that
we all need.

I stare at the traffic
It's not vehicles I see
It's a man and he's down on
his knees
He's panning for gold and he's
as cold as can be
But that is the love of gold
you see.
There is a frightening beauty
about their mountains
and streams,
I look, but no reason can be
seen
I wonder what it is I fear, the
height of the mountains,
depths of the lakes or the cold,
cold air.
I arrive in the big city, it's
spring of the year, the arts
are calling
I attend all until the fall of
the year.
Then the wind howls and the
snow falls.
Traffic is snarled there's danger
in all
The noise of the city makes it
hard to hear,
I wonder what I am doing here.
But getting back is not easy
you see,
So I settle for the west to be
as near as can be.
When I'm in the traffic and
can't see or hear
I hear the Yukon calling and
calling me.

S. E. Kidder
REMEMBRANCE

The old woman sat rocking on
the gabled verandah
And began hulling the peas in
her aproned lap.
Around her the wind sang
softly
In the lacy gingerbread.

She joined in the singing
Humming a lullaby
The tune long remembered.
The wind touched her cheek
And lifted a silver thread as
she shelled.

The fading sun made golden
butterflies dance on the
clapboards.
Her blue veined hands piled
emerald beads in the bowl.

She knew about Mother
Nature's treasures
And the ceaseless mysteries of
creation
She knew about courting songs
and lullabys,
And the strength of men.

To anyone passing . . .just an
old woman
Rocking on a porch
Shelling peas for supper
Not a sweet glowing girl
Not Nathan's child bride
Just a woman with a
weathered face
Lost in a wind song
With a gentle smile in her eyes.

Christina LaRosa
CAN IT BE

When we met,
You told me things I didn't
understand.
But you said it was all set,
My future was planned.

I wasn't ready to take the
chance,
But you said it was okay,
I'd be yours with just a glance,
One of these days.

I looked into your eyes,
And say sympathy through
glass,
They seemed to hypnotize,
You said the pain would pass.

I tried to put up a fight,
But your power was too strong,
I soon realized you were right,
I had to hang on.

I felt so strange inside,
When you took me to that
place,
For I was in paradise,
But you I couldn't face.

You found my inner fantasies,
Ones that I'd never show or
tell,
Then bring back all the
memories,
Surrounded by my shell.

You read my every inner
thoughts,
Made all my dreams come true,
My mind was forever caught,
Deep inside of you.

And now I'm sorry I took off
and ran,
But it's so hard to believe,
I'm still trying to understand,
magic, CAN IT BE!

Shonda S. Howard
DADDY'S LITTLE MAN

I've become to realize
That growing up's not
changing size,
But letting go,
That's how we grow.

As I pick up the aftermath
Of childhood days that now
are past,
I want to know,
Where did they go?

As I picture you still there,
Kneeling by your bed in
prayer,
I try to hide,
The pain inside.

The trolley cars and trains and

---

trucks,
And floating little rubber ducks
The rabbit's foot you had for
luck,
You traded them all in for
better things,
You let them go—
So you could grow.

The crayons and the picture
books,
The attention that they all
once took,
Are put away,
In yesterday.

As I look into your searching
eyes,
You're wondering if I realize,
I too must grow,
By letting go.

As I let go of yesterday,
And the simple joys of
childhood days,
I want to know,
Where childhood goes?

Now instead of mommy's little
boy,
Content to be her pride and joy
He needs me now to
understand
It's time for him to grow
and change
From mommy's little boy
To daddy's little man.

Richard James Suphan
BURNING THE MIDNIGHT OIL

The campus has shut down for
the night, a long
hard day of work and play is
at an end.

The dorms stand silent with
only a few lights
to show habitation and in one
room a stereo
plays rock and roll on into
the night.

Who are these people and what
brought them here?
Their hopes? Their dreams?
Or their ambitions?

Some came to find out who
they are and some came
to find out who they should
be.
But no matter
who they are you can look into
their eyes and
see that look of both
confidence and wariness.

Long hours of work and short
hours of play soon
show hints that some may
leave to go to a safer
life or to become a husband
or wife.

The dorm has one light on
now giving the appearance
of a huge cyclops. Is it some
studious person
burning the midnight
oil in the hopes of being tops
in his class?
No, it's just me. When the hell
else do you think I have time
to do this?

Franklin Sommers
HUMANITY

I seem to be awkward in
everything I do,
Except for dreaming, crying
and faith I guess
Awkward must hold true.
I guess It's true I'm an awkward

---

creation,
But I'm your faithful essence
  true,
For all your joy and poetry
  is why I live in you.
And all your music too.
And more than this, is what
  I am in you
I'm your beauty, love, and
  conscience,
And all the grace of you
Please tell me, my beloved
  child, who are you?
Are you a human true?
If to your essence you're not
  faithful
I hope you're human soon—
For I am awkward without
  you—
And I always need the real you;
I'm your essence missing
  you—
For I really need the human
  you;
To show your love for me in
  you.
Will you grow more love for
  me in you;
For I'm your essence missing
  you.

L. M. Mayesh
**BELLA DETESTA
MATRIBUS**

Within America's mute womb
  of liberty,
separated from the world
  community
by pulsating placental
  fluids of oceans and
actresses demanding a priceless
  peace for the land,
people grow, like beef cattle,
  like lambs, secure.
Never again will the Stars and
  Stripes' sons die premature
for words and old politicians
  grazing in tradition's joys.
Our mothers want peace, not
  plastic bags of boys,
crumpled, twisted, sealed
  tight, to stop their dead
  black smell.
A mushroom cloud on the
  Acropolis is not our death
  knell.
If Berlin wall moves under
  camouflage of peace, who
can say it portends of Birnam
  woods coming to
our Dunsinane home? Never
  mind what happens elsewhere.
Our isolated lives can grow to
  full term without care.
And, bumpkin faced Krushchev's
  ghose, our tough 50's clown
will purge us, and erase our
  name as if it were Stalin.
Down
into communism our land of
  the free will fall. We shall
die at home, and our country's
  shroud, tinged with red sea
  foam,
will be the web of breathless
  mothers and their clay-cold
  children.

Valery Varble
TIM

He sunburst into the school
  one weakling February day,
a golden-boy god from Canada,
a flash of broad-shouldered
  Paul Bunyan plaids,
lean-hipped Levi's,
a blue-eyed cocoa-box Dutch
  boy

with a hero-grin.
He was mine from the first—
  everyone knew it was right,
  looked
Raggeedy Ann and Andy good
  together, you see.
We danced hip-touching close,
  and that was that.
Valery-and-Tim was on every
  party list.
We had a way, everyone said.
We could jitterbug to the
  blues.
I had no blues.
He was mine.
He taught me French; he
  slithered,
I slurped.
And it was no accident I was
  always mixing up
"Bonjour"
with "Je t'aime."
But something happened.
Our whispers turned to bullet-
  words
Russian Roulette
He drifted out with a girl
  named Lavonne
(Lavonne, like a ladies'
  deodorant)
But as he was leaving, he
  looked
back to me, over
Miss Deodorant's arms croon-
  cradling his neck
and I knew, as he smiled
that he was mine still.

Randy Kruse
YOUR WORLD

As I stand here in the clouds,
Upon your land I stare
and see the hate, the turmoil,
  but
So many just don't care.

The factories throw up a screen
which almost chokes the air,
So much that soon it may be
  gone
Yet many just don't care.

The people gather up their
  trash
and toss it anywhere.
Gag at the ever present smell
But they don't seem to care.

The waters foam up like a
  brew,
and stops the sun and air
from giving life to that below
Yet so few really care.

A mother takes her unborn's
  life,
Another wouldn't dare
because she thinks it's
  murdering
Yet others just don't care.

The blacks hate whites, the
  whites hate blacks,
you'll find it anywhere,
so much that church bells
  ring all day
Yet many just don't care.

A "pig" will pull you to a
  curb
to say your plates aren't there,
and gets a bullet in the head
But no one wants to care.

A march for "peace" turns
  upside down
with bloodshed everywhere,
but no one knows whose
  fault it was
And many just don't care.

So now I turn and look at
  Him

who brought me here from
  there,
And hear Him as I wipe His
  tears:
"Why, Father, don't they
  care?"

Cheryl Brunette
THE ORPHAN-EATER

The orphan—eater is a runt.
He carries a hot stiletto
which he has painted black
  because
he does not want to carve a
  splinter from the candlelight
and alert the grown-ups.

He sidles up to a child waiting
  for Mommy or Daddy to
  come home,
skewers him through the navel
  and
pops him whole
before anyone can smell seared
  bellyflesh.

Inside he's much larger and
carpeted with leech mouths.
First he sucks the screams,
  then
the breath,
so that the orphan does not
  shriek when
his eyes are pierced and drained.

Two days later (in time for
  the funeral), like a newt that's
swallowed a snail, the gnome
  passes
the child-shell—
polished, onion-skin thin, dry.
He shuffles-Off-To—Buffalo,
tap—dancing to the voiceless
  sobs that warm his gut.

To the casual observer his
  matured victims appear
  ordinary enough.
But if you were an orphan, even
  a hundred years ago, you know
  where to find
the pinprick scars
in another's
eyes.

Ginny Jeffers
FRIENDS

An old man's heart grows
  lonely
In a world with so much change.
It is not safe to walk alone
Where he lives down Hickory
  Lane.

The lines are etched upon his
  face;
And he walks slowly on his
  cane;
All the things that he believed
  in
Seemed a life struggle all in
  vain.

There were still the fields of
  dandelions;
He still had his farm and land;
And one day when he walked
  there—
A little black child played in
  the sand.

Her life had not been touched
  with hate;
Her young heart had faith in
  man;
And reaching up, with trust
  and love,
She took the old man's hand.

They walked through the
  fields of dandelions;
Their faces smiled, and turned
  gold;

And as they picked and gathered
  them;
The old man was no longer old.

They sat upon an old tree
  stump;
The birds sang to them so sweet;
Together they watched in
  silence—
The rabbits at their feet.

Dusk told them it was time to
  go;
They shook hands like friends
  of old.
A tear slipped down the old
  man's cheek;
As homeward bound he strolled.

He was no longer lonely—
Through the fields he walked
  straight and tall;
He turned and waved to his
  little friend
It was a good world after all.

John Wilkie
WILDFLOWER

City lady,
Chase the breeze;
Run perfumed under flowered
  trees.
Rush the tossing tamarack,
Trailing hair,
And don't look back
Until you get there,
Deep inside
The fertile forest.
Run . . .and hide.

Hide among the Silversword
And Birds of Paradise.
Walk barefoot through the
  Lavender;
Feast your cityed eyes
On Bells and Black-eyed Susans
And blue, blue Columbines.

Yours will be the snowdrops
And the bursting Feverdew,
The sunsplashed Meadow
  Saffron,
Lords and Ladies too.

Fields full of Fireballs,
And Primrose everywhere,
Poppies bright as sunspots,
And lady (if you dare)
An Orchid blooming regal
In the lushness of your hair.

For you are Wildflower,
Transplanted by the wind
To gardens paved with concrete
Walled to keep you in
Beneath the broken bottles,
Between the jagged cracks.

Lady, city lady . . .
The wilds want you back.

Dorothy Turner Warner
THE MAZE

What tangled web do I weave
  here? What truth will unwind
  this maze?
The darkness is overwhelming
  me and all things seem to be
  in a haze.
Oh, sister and brother, why
  do you all flee? Why has
  everyone left
this hellish place but me? I am
  not familiar with this place.
  How
did I come to find myself here?
  Where and how did all of my
  fellow
men disappear? I call each
  name one by one, but still
  no answer
has come. Am I not one with
  all the good there is? why

am I so
filled with these doubts and
fears, where is my God who
is the great
power, what has separated me
from him in my darkest
hour? How much
longer will I call and search,
seeking you in my heart? Can
you not
hear me? Can you not feel me
in the dark? I no longer
pray and plead
for the darkness to move,
I no longer petition this
obstacle to lose.
I am tired vexed and sore. I
plead and petition it no more.
I release
this experience and care not
where it go. I refuse to let
it
cause me suffering and pain.
I refuse its presence in my
world again.
I take up my weapons now and
go into battle. I ride the
victory
horse, my divinity is my
saddle. I shall slay every
obstacle in my
way. I shall do spiritual battle
day and night, I am a warrior
now,
made strong by my plight. The
battle is the Lords and through
Him
I shall fight. I reclaim my
freedom and put my enemy to
flight. No
more shall it follow me and
cause me pain. Enemy, you
shall never live
in me again.

Juanita Tella
LIFE

To hold a rose close to me,
so delicate in my hands
with the morning dew
glistening.
Is to hold a newborn child
to my heart.
To watch a bird as he lifts
his wings in flight
toward the sky.
Is to know your well again.
To sit and watch a running
brook.
Is to see the tears flowing from
an old man's face,
For he knows his mate is gone
forever.
To watch a tree in autumn, with
its leaves
red and gold.
Lift its limbs towards the sky
and shutter.
Leaves softly caressing the
ground as you leave me.
To watch the sunset, as it
sinks softly behind
the mountains
As the closing of another day.
Leaves a sad feeling, deep
within me, when you're
not here with me.
To feel the rain softly falling
on my face.
Washing away the tears of
lonliness that
I cried for you.
To wake up and look out my
window
And see the sunrise in all its
brightness
As it warms the morning air.

Drying the tears of dew on
a morning rose,
Rays of warmth gently
awakening the sleeping
world of last night.
Gives me hope to hold you
close to me once again
in my life.

Don Jaxon
THE BIRTH OF LOVE

The words in which I must
express
are difficult, this I must
confess
to you these words I must
address
though the result may bring
sadness
the more that I reveal to you
the more I fear what might
ensue
already have I left not a clue
I have left not one but quite
a few
A woe, such woe does my
heart grieve,
such torment can one's mind
conceive
the heart and mind together
cleve
the curse or blessing you
receive
The truth I'll tell, I bear no
lies,
lest in my heart it lives and
dies
I want to stand pure in your
eyes
never see tears, or hear your
cries
These words perhaps someday
you'll read
but realize my heart's true
need
friendship watered a fertile
seed
a love now sprouts that you
have freed
I find your beauty a delight
a word from you makes my
day bright
your smile relieves me of each
plight
love cures all things and makes
them right
On paper it's so easy to say
the thoughts expressed no
other way
the same is true for me this
day
and so these thoughts I do
convey
So many words, we need but
few,
it's so hard to say . . . "I love
you."

Linda Schoonover
GOD'S PLAN

My dear Heavenly Father,
Please help me and guide me
further.
Help me on Thy word to
stand,
So I can tell others of Thy great
plan.
I thank you, Father, for so great
a love
That you sent your Son from
Heaven above.
To teach us love and truth and
might,
And your plan of salvation for
all tonight.
I thank you for sending us
your Son

So we can claim victory over
Satan, the evil one.
Christ shed His blood on
Calvary's tree
So I could be saved and be set
free.
Free from the bondage of the
law
And free from the sins that
make man fall.
Christ did it all when His blood
He shed.
Christ did it all, just as the
scriptures said.
Christ did not falter or run
away.
He did not tell you, "some
other day."
I can't imagine the pain that
he bore
As the nails right through His
skin tore.
I try to imagine myself hung
there;
The shame and pain and
humiliation and despair.
All that, because man sinned.
All that had to be to give
us life again.
I want to sing and shout
His praise,
And follow in His footsteps
the rest of my days.
I want to walk by the Spirit
and let Jesus take my hand,
And guide me and use me on
this earthly land.

Sharra Johnson
DIMENSIONS OF DREAMING

I have been dreaming again,
In this life that has no time for
dreams,
In this world where dreamers
are turned away,
Because they know life is not
the way it seems.
I have been dreaming of
another world;
A world where life and dreams
are both the same;
A place where there is no
winning or losing,
Because no one plays the game.
A world where I can walk the
fields of clover,
And take time to stop and
smell the rain;
A place where life and love
flow smoothly,
And are not measured in terms
of pain.
A world where souls are naked,
And no one stands to judge or
measure;
A place where faith in all
humanity
Is one of life's most important
treasures.
A world where father-mother-
child-friend,
Are words buried deep within
the soul;
A place where these words are
never tested,
and all life's relationships are
whole.
Yes, I have been dreaming
again,
And I know that soon I
will awaken,
And I'll have to face this
world I live in,
And the course my life has
taken.

But, as these dreams grow
nearer,
I will do what i have to do,
To pass through the dimensions
of dreaming,
And make these dreams come
true.
Somewhere beyond this life,
it's waiting
For me to take that final
breath;
The world where all these
dreams are real
Lies just beyond—on the other
side of death!

Larry Roik
HYPERION SLEEPS

I me mine—Hyperion sings:
The Devil slept with me last
night,
Lying quietly in my bed,
He was strangely dressed in
white—
I do not trust this head.
There seems to be no orthodox
In the mind of dreamy shocks,
For the evening was one time;
I'll order it for this rhyme.
Sleep swept itself across my
limbs,
Washing over the eye that
whims,
To enter the world of greenest
pasture;
Of thought I know, that's
sure.
My sleeping sweepers gazed
the field,
Searching endlessly for human
motion.
Across the green—it did yield—
I saw the strangest commotion.
I can only answer for what I
saw
As quite the oddest sight—
At present, I'm still in awe
For what it was last night:
There they were, ten tiny
gnomes,
Come they did, fresh from
their homes.
In the green, their purple
stood
before me, waving bad and
good.
The puppets they were
addressed,
If I should be their guest?
I felt no other choice or
course—
Of that dream I have remorse.
I followed the group in spirits,
good.
"Where are we going?" Thought
I asked.
And an answer, I thought
they should—
Ah, the mind spoke, not the
masked.
Tonight, today, tomorrow as
well,
Sleep is but easy waste—no!
Grandeur, the vision of hell—
I saw a castle's stormy glow.
Explanation, come to this
stand,
Describe for me this mason
land
Of walls, and peaks, and gates.
Upon the other side, what
waits?

Solution, problem, answer
found?
My sleeping person rolls
around,

To this the vision thins and t
thins,
For sleep escapes the skins.
Trust yourself Hyperion—you
do—
The reason is in blindness
dance'd,
The picture fades away from
you,
Cause: Your person's body's
lanced.
Forms come to the rational
call.
The restless moving began to
slow,
No longer worry—of Hyperion
fall?—
The dream continues spirit
Plato.
Ah, the castle again so morbid
drawn
Can only lay insult to the lawn.
I see one gate, there they go,
To meet the owner—frightfully
so.
No welcome came for me, the
guest,
And of attire, I was not the best.
Then the greetings came to
shock me quick,
The ugly face made me sick.
The horrid thing—the horrid
thing
Was Satan—Was Satan, the
Dark Prince!
The horrid thing—the horrid
thing
Was Satan—Was Satan, the
Dark Prince!
The newly pining Titan-me
heard
A waving ocean near my side,
Then came that dreadful
word,
Satan said to me, "You DIED."
Screaming to Hell bound death,
breathe!!!
The water's flow was that of
Lethe:
Treachery overcame my living's
rape,
I knew of Hades the quick
escape:
My bed was hell-hot as I awoke
To breathe on fire, O, I
choke!
Repent was senseless, the dream
real,
My pain is endless—Satan's deal.

He never left my bed again,
That devil shares my sights,
My soul is His successful
gain
Satan bargains at dreamy
nights!
We us ours—sing!

Eli E. Smith, Jr.
THE POETRY CONTEST
"Look," said the would-be
Poet to his wife,
"There's a poetry contest
to be."
And as his enthusiasm welled
to cheer,
His wife dryly said, "Yes, dear."
He took to the task of writing
his poem,
His best yet, he knew, it must
be.
And it would be, he extolled to
his wife very clear,
And she dryly replied, "Yes,
dear."
He posted his "Pride" in the

mail to be judged,
And patiently started his wait.
Told his wife t'would be soon,
cause the deadline was near,
And her measured reply was,
"Yes, dear."
The notice arrived by mail—he
had won!
And his prize was a handsome
check.
"Dear wife," he said, "will you
share my cheer?"
Her reply—a resounding, "YES,
DEAR!!!"

Jo Huisingh
IN MOTION
Endlessly rushing
Loudly crashing
Waterfalls have their attractions
Somewhat like making love
with you.
For it's during these moments
That where I'm at
Is all there is
And it's more than enough.
So that when we are through
Some of the love
Spills over
And keeps flowing gently on
Like the pool at the bottom of
the falls.

Jean Rowat
AN EASTER DREAM
This was the dream: that I
could clearly see
Idyllic scenes in Galilee.
A white-robed Silhouette
Against the sky . . .
The upturned faces of the
happy throng—
The bidden children, gathered
at His knee.
'Mid shifting scenery, I could
dimly see
The darkening day of
Calvary.
The silhouette of agony
Against the sky . . .
The upturned faces, as
remembering
Grief passed by.
This was the dream, but now
the vision see—
The Resurrection light.
The silhouette of hope
Against the sky . . .
His legacy of love to you and
me
As He passed by.

J. Elizabeth Van Fossen
SNOWY EGRET, REST
Egret hanging on the wire—
Why?
Swinging in the chilling wind—
Sigh.
Skinny legs, dangling head—
Stark!
Blue sky, sunny day—
Dark.
Week in, week out—
There.
Down—Down—Down—
Air!
Mother Earth
Blessed.
Snowy egret,
Rest.

Dr. Leroy Thomas
THANKSGIVING PRAYER
Dear Lord Jesus,
I never knew how to thank you

For the ability to walk
Until I could walk no more
And had to learn again.
I never knew how to thank you
for a child
Until I had a son
And heard him say,
"I'll do it for you, Dad,
'Cause we're both boys!"
But now I have these
Two great gifts—a son
And the ability to walk.
And I can tell you truthfully,
Lord, that I'm forever thankful.
And it's not just
On Thanksgiving Day!
So thank you, Lord,
And please help me not forget.
Selah,
Your Unworthy Servant.

Barbara Basye Carlisle
I WOULD RATHER SEE
I'd rather see a sermon
Than hear one any day,
I'd rather one should walk
with me
Than merely show the way.
The eye's a better pupil
And more willing than an ear,
Fine counsel is confusing
But example's always clear.
And the best of all the preachers
Are the ones who live their
creed.
For to see good put in action
Is what everyone needs.
I soon can learn to do it,
If you let me see it done,
I can watch your hands in
action,
But your tongue too fast may
run.
And the sermon you deliver
May be very wise and true,
But I would rather get my
lesson
By watching what you do.
For I might misunderstand
you
And the high advice you give,
But there is no
misunderstanding
In how you act and how you
live.

Lisa Anne Mesaros
WHISPERS OF THE BREEZE
The mellow light of sunset
Hangs over the silent trees,
Iridescent, filmy shades
Like the waves on the gentle
seas.
The hues are growing more
intense;
The blues and greens so cold
Have given way to fiery swathes
Of orange and red and gold.
The graceful trees extend dark
limbs
Into the flaming sky,

As behing them the metallic
river
Of brilliant shades flows by.
The rest of the sky above the
trees
Is a haunting, smoky grey,
The shifting shades of violet
and smoke
Are mourning the fading day.
Two coal-black phantom
swallows
Drift gently across the sky;
Together with a lonely voice
They utter a parting cry.
The trees begin to murmur
And their leaves begin to sigh.
The grass begins to whisper
As a breeze blows softly by.
The wind is telling stories
And breathing secrets too—
Tales that are fantasies,
and Tales that are true.
In every breeze is found a hint
Of what will come tomorrow;
Will it bring some finer things
Or will it just bring sorrow?

Ella Foster O'Brien
I WRITE OF OUR LAND
I write of the North, where
the Pilgrims came,
Two hundred years ago.
Their heritage they gave to us,
their kin,
And we'll always love it so.
I write of the east, where the
sun will rise
Over the mountains so blue,
Where our fathers and mothers
walked proud and tall
And their pleasures were very
few.
I write of the south, where
warm winds blow,
Where plantations arose from
the ground,
Where mountains and ocean
flow together and know,
That God's love forever
abounds.
I write of towering mountains,
way out in the west,
Where the sun and the moon
beams play,
Where gently the rain and the
snowflakes fall,
Where the rivers run cold all
day.
I write of a nation where
Indians lived,
In the long, long ago,
Where the desert rose, scents
the air so sweet,
Where the greasewood and
sagebrush grow.
Yes, I write of a land that we
all hold dear,
Where hearts and hands labor
with love,
And know that we hold our
honor,
In God's hands forever with
love.

Vivienne Kitson McPhae Nelson
**NORIEGA STREET, SAN
FRANCISCO**
Down Noreiga Street,
Measured and neat,
By storybook, one-story shops
And a lumberyard, neater than
you've ever seen,
Past blocks of green lawns and
houses,
Whitened and brightened with

sunlight and paint,
Drive straight to the sea.
There, out past the waves
At the end of the street
Looms large as an island
Or newly formed cliff—
A part of the city blown away
in the fog,
Returned on the incoming
tide?
No, a flagship, a carrier moving.
Skim on wheels north to the
Point,
Past the beach traffic stilled by
the sight,
Then up to the top of a hill
that looks out
O'er the ocean, the bridge and
the bay.
Now stand with the breeze
and sun on your face,
To watch the Navy return.
Flagship carrier, with little
planes folded on deck,
Destroyer, cruiser and three
submarines,
Marching in soundless pomp
they come,
Up to The Gate,
Then under the span,
With distance like cadence
measured between.
And we stand on that headland,
Sensing the glory
That man's always known,
Watching the return of the
venturesome,
Home from the fishing, the
storm, the Crusades,
Home from the great
wars,
Home from an orbit,
And then from a planet
returning.

William Tyrone White
HATRED AMONG THE RACES

Can someone please tell me why
there is so much hatred among
the races?
Does difference in color or
texture of hair justify war
and lifelong discrimination?
Are not all men born of a
woman and sired by a man—
Then why, and where did this
idea of hatred begin?
Can someone please tell me why
there is so much hatred
among the races?
Does the genetic reality
have to dictate mankind's
possibilities?
Are not all men consumers of
the same air and universe.
Then why—and where—did
this idea of hatred begin?
Can someone please tell me why
there is so much hatred
among the races?
Are not all babies cute, and all
women beautiful.
Do we not all share the same
sun and idolize the same
moon?
Can someone please tell me why
there is so much hatred among
the races?
Is it just a stupid excuse to
eventually annihilate the
races?

Klaro-Peter King Koapke
ALOHA BILLY ALLEN

there's a man
whose been overheard to say

people may pass, but,
the music will stay
and surely children
will always play
at being grown, notice too late
that their dreams have all
flown;
forgetting the fun, the powerful
pleasure
of Faith in Life! each day a
new treasure,
unless the few who know of
the fool
know also of Billy Allen's rule;
"live by the love of the smiling
face,
be you while you're here
and be gone with no trace
of the pain you've absorbed
nor the sadness you've
faced,
leave only your joy with your
turn at the dance,
be pleased to have been here
and had the chance
to experience the passion of
life on this Earth,
the sensation of limits comes
only through birgh,
the sensations of life comes
only through limits,
becoming tools and toys
with understanding, strength
and poise!"

Maureen Mancini
HO-HUM

The kids are slashing tires,
There's a riot on the run.
Oops, the garbage is overflowing,
and there's a "fire sale" on
guns.
The neighbors have been
fighting
since I can't remember when.
And, ho-hum, they're at it
again.
There was a robbery on the
corner.
Someone overdosed last night.
A car was stolen yesterday
before a big gang fight.
They grabbed an innocent
victim
and just left him there to bleed;
and, ho-hum, it's nothing new
to me.
There's an orphan in the alley
avoiding broken glass.
He dreams of what the days
are
like in the upper social class.
There are only rats to play
with.
Only rats are running free.
And, ho-hum, that's nothing
new to see.
The money's tight around here.
It seems most are unemployed.
An attitude is in the air
that's too nasty to avoid.
Between pollution and that
nasty air
it's difficult to breathe,
and, ho-hum, that's nothing
new to me.

Ezio DiFrancesco
FRIEND

In truth,
The stalk of trust is found.
Forever aging,
Bringforth a mature seed of
friendship,
Trust,
The essence of life in the
universe.

A friend, is the rarest human
form,
sparcely populating the
universe,
evolving in the movement of
the heavens,
where truth is secured and
strengthened
by the rising of the sun.
Its destruction never takes
for roots are implanted deep,
by centures,
too deep to pull away.
Is one who lends a hand
through boundless, treacherous
ways.
Who saves ones breath,
drawing from greed, want and
jealousies.
Who cries with you,
feeling pain and happiness
and tears that run so meanfully
down your cheeks.
Who touches them with gentle
hands,
smiling from the heart
complements them to a pleasant
ease.
Who speaks the truth,
at times brings pain, grief,
resentment
and even hate.
Finally,
with understanding will forget,
remembering,
all things in nature are weak,
brittle,
breaks away.
When need of help he's always
there
to cure the ailing ways.

Jack Kort
ACCEPTANCE

There was a time I looked at
life
Through glasses made of rose
The whole wide world was
at my feet
T'was there for me to hold
So optimistic were those days
When life was still unfolding
I thought that I could do
it all
My life would be fulfilled
But things are not that way
these days
There's water neath the bridge
The time is quickly slipping
by
There's still so much to do
I have to wonder where it
went
This mystery we call time
The vanishment of hopes and
dreams
The calling that was mine.
They often ask me if I had
A chance to live again
What would I do to change
my life
To make it more worthwhile
So much I've pondered on this
theme
But this I have to say
I'd do it all this way again
There's nothing I would change
The glass of rose blinds me no
more
I'm a realist in my way
It's age that makes me honest
now
I take it day by day
A perfect age of mellowness
There is no looking back

Yet young enough to be
unscarred
By the cynic they call time
I guess I'd like to stay this
way
I've learned my place in life
I'll never own or hold the
world
It's really not for me
And so in place of conquering
I know that I must serve
To help the more unfortunate
I'll share my life with them.

Ruth Pardue Gill
COUNTRY WOMAN

I weren't born to fit no mansion
and all them stately, stylish
ways
I were born a country woman
not held back by corset staves
Now some folks like them big,
neat houses
And rightly so . . .I know
But it'd be like bindin me in
chains
and they might not let me go
There's nothin pleasure me
so much
as gittin to my chores
A-shinin up my pots and pans
and a-polishin my floors
But when I'm thro with my
days work
that life gives me to do
I git a bear-sized kind a joy
out a knowin that I'm through
First . . .It'd take a lot of
money
That I'd have to earn some way
Or . . .It'd clean out my money
jar
Stuck back fer a rainy day
Then . . .I might git to lovin
it
more then I ortin to
And You . . .Bein learned and
knowin
You know that jest wouldn't
do
So them good folks, that
really wants it
Won't git no kind a kick from
me
I'd druther it'd be them that
had it
And jest set back
And jest be me.

Cathy Kugath
LORD, I NEEDED YOU

Lord,
where were You, when I
needed You,
To catch a falling star.
I called out to the heavens.
You had gone away
So far.
Lord,
Where were You, when I
needed You,
To find the rainbows' end.
The pot of gold I searched for.
I thought You were
My friend.
Lord,
Where were You, when I
needed You,
To build a castle in the sand.
I watched the tide flow in
and out,
By the call of
Your command.
Lord,

Where were You, when I
needed You,
To climb the mountains high.
I tried so hard, but You
weren't there.
My hopes
Were left to die.

While
Walking through green forest
The wind calls out for You.
I needed You and You were
there.
Bright angels came
With You.

Now Lord,
You are always here,
We walk slowly, hand in hand.
To the last place Thou wilt
lead me.
To my
Promised Land.

Renee Anne Viosca
**THE SPRINGTIME OF YOUR
LIFE**

Spring has just tiptoed in:
Plants are green, birds singing,
Those cool, breezy April
days
are here to stay.
Sunshine gives warmth to life,
As your ambitions shine.
Animals and plants are here
for you to enjoy—
For it is your birthday, mother.
Today you are 80 years old,
But you have just begun to
live.
You gave so much all your
life
To your children, to society.
Now you see your daughters
successful,
Your grandchildren,
And great-grandchildren
smiling,
Me, the holder of many
copyrights.
Now is the springtime of your
life;
We wish you many more happy
years—
Many rosy dawns, fruitful
dreams,
Blue skies, green fields,
Pink clouds like the one you
saw
When your grandchild Bonnie
was born,
For we give you as a present—
Love from all your family.
May this springtime of your
life
Ripen into many happy
experiences
Flowering to God!

Lallie Engell
E.S.P?

I was dreaming—A very deep
boat dock appeared
Excitement seemed in the
air
All along the shoreline and a
third of the way up
There seemed to be a dark
substance of some kind
Altho no one to see—A
contest was on
Suddenly a lone woman
appeared!
She seemed very calm—
contented maybe
Altho that excitement was
still in the air.
A male voice said "How does

it feel to
be a winner and have so much
as you?"
Her answer so strange "How
does it feel—
How would any woman feel
with that
many men's eyes upon her?"
The men from the ships were
the impression,
Altho no ships were to be seen.

I awoke with a start and arose
the time to see
It was 4 am—such an early
hour
There must be some significance
you say, or to be,
Yes, that woman but with only
two eyes upon her—was me.
Having been given everything
I've dreamt of in a man
Yes, I'd say I'm a winner—
of so much
Among which is a switch in
my mind
that wakes me up at that
early hour
A reminder of a day to start
for me, no—but for someone
so near to my heart.

J. Randy Gardner
RUNAWAY TRAIN

Engineer, please hit those
brakes: your wheels are going
a bit too fast,
for you just let a passenger
off, who called himself my
Dad.
Your rails go on forever and
your train it never slows.
We seldom find time to thank
the ones who taught us all
we know.
So just give me a second or
minute of your time.
Engineer will you please hit
those brakes; I'll ask
you one last time.
But your wheels they keep on
rolling and your engine always
runs
and though his ride is just now
ended, mine has just begun.
And like the man who rode
before me, he made himself
a model
he taught me how to ride
this train, so give this boy
the throttle.
So engineer, don't hit those
brakes: I have some goals
to set
for he left behind some
memories that I would like
to leave myself.
So engineer don't hit those
brakes,
but wave goodby to Dad.

Alice J. Oswald
DON'T GIVE UP

As a child I remember
carefree times of fun,
No burdens to endure as
life had just begun.
Living day to day without
regret or care,
Worries free—life untouched,
no hardships to bear.
But as the years passed by
like they always will,
My road of life curved and
started now uphill;
Not too steep just yet,
I'd just begun to grow,
But sufficient for me to notice,

enough for me to know:
That the more I learn of life
by gaining through the years,
Discovering joy and laughter
along
with pain and tears.
Troubles become much stronger
the road of life more steep;
Sometimes it hits lightly,
other times more deep.
When it seems too great to
stand
and I want to run and hide,
It's then I stop and listen to
the little voice inside:
"Don't give up and think your
beat
when life seems too hard,
If you keep on fighting you'll
win
the game and hold the highest
card!"

Dorothy L. Campbell
A MOUNTAIN TRAIL

Whoever walks a mountain
trail
Has never walked alone;
Or lifted eyes unto the hills,
But inner strength has known.
Whoever seeks communion
sweet
In God's cathedral there,
Will find the angels very near,
And joining him in prayer.
The trees and flow'rs, like
acolytes,
Will fling their incense sweet;
The feathered friends will
join in song,
And make the day complete.
The flowing stream whose
melodies
Are never known to cease;
The giant crags that tow'r above
Bring quietness and peace.
The wind will whisper through
the pines,
The sky will smile above,
And everything seems unified—
Enshrined in God's pure love.
Whoever walks a mountain
trail
Or kneels upon the sod,
Has been so near to heaven's
gate,
He touched the hand of God.

Margie Blythe Rohr
**HEAVEN'S PEACEFUL
SHORE**

Today your hearts are broken
With pain you scarce can bear.
It helps today but little
When I tell you that I care.

But, my dears, care I do.
This you have to know!
My heart's love is with you,
And I needs must tell you so!
I've felt the pain and grief
you bear.
I've walked the path you trod.
I've known the ache of your
broken hearts
As you placed her 'neath that
sod.

And 'tho tomorrow dawns
another day,
It will take yet quite a few
Ere grief's grey cloud has
lifted
Bidding golden rays of hope
shine through.

But she's gone to a far better
place.
She rests on Heaven's peaceful

shore,
In a land that knows not pain
nor sorrow.
She'll hurt again?—No, never
more!
There'll always be her vacant
chair.
But to the Holy Scriptures
let's refer.
Remember you can mend the
broken circle.
Someday you can go to her!*

*2 Samuel 12:23

Barb Eads
WILL YOU NOT LINGER?

Will you linger for awhile?
Will you stay and bide your
time?
Or will the next moment find
you gone on a puff of the wind?
Will you not stay on a bit?
Will you not delay the time you
leave?
Or will the days take wing and
fly
until it's only a short second
until goodbye?

I can't promise to wait for
your call.
I can't say if I'll wait for every
fall.
I don't know if I'll linger in
the sun
or glide away with the coming
rain.

I will not give binding words
to you
If you question me of their
meaning.
I will not take what you say
is true
and then find it has a false
ringing.

But will you not linger for
awhile?
Will you stay and pass the time?
Or shall I the next moment
find
you gone with the puffing
wind?

Mark Steven Larabee
THE UNSEEN ORATOR

Welcome to the realm of dreams
Of points unseen, unrealized
You who reach beyond your
fears
The often frail mortal mind
Welcome to the Darkness Road
You have walked so many
times
But when faced have fled
uncertain
Of what the shadows hold
to find
Be intent on what you seek
Within your strength make
your stand
For in this blackened nether
world
Illusion rules the jester's hand
May the course you set be
true
On your journey through the
void
Wary of the hand of him
Who would see your cause
destroyed
Elders of the Freedom Caste
Though their words be
hard to grasp
Their wisdoms live through
every season
To offer you the light—the

reason
I stand my vigil at these gates
To warn the traveler what
    awaits
Nothing here is what it seems
Welcome to the realm of dreams.

Valerie Hillard
DAUGHTER NOT YET CONCEIVED

Daughter not yet conceived,
in whom I shall take so much
    delight
when I free you of confinement
and give your precious body
    life,
I think of you often,
as I do all of life's charms,
and yearn as would any mother
to hold you in my arms.
How I shall celebrate your
    arrival
and marval at the majesty
of why a wonder such as you
was ever granted to one such
    as me.
Truly the heavens shall tremble
as to them I lift my voice,
and there beneath a sacred
    entourage
I shall humble rejoice,
for I will have been fulfilled
as would any woman be
upon bearing the fruit
of what was once but a seed.
I shall wrap you in cloth
and bask you in love's golden
    rays
as I lift you to my bosom
and gaze upon you in happy
    disarray.
No greater joy shall
I ever know,
no greater gift
shall God upon me ever bestow,
for
no greater treasure to discover
    is there left than
the miracle of my baby's
    breath.

Ronald F. Smedley
PSALM ONE (A PSALM OF SILENCE)

looking upon warmth's beauty
    (be still and know that He
    is God)
the sun shines within my eyes,
whispered thoughts
    silence of peace
(be still and know that He is
    God)
quieted heart
    with my smile within . . .
(be still and know that He is
    God)
so often Lord i look to the
    shouting
voice of trumpets,
the beat of the drum,
the ring of the lyre.
my Lord
my God
my All
i have learned and to this
    knowledge
i stand entranced at Thee
i have learned that all is your
    being
    all is within Thy realm
and i,
and myself as small as i am,
my being is but a servant to
    you Lord
a servant who sees now that
    the vision
of my joy is within your

presence.
whispering thoughts of love
Spirit speaking within
silence of a warm,
sunny morn.

this is my heart.
i come
and know who you are.
my joy is silence
and silence is my joy.

quietly resting near,
i rejoice and am glad.
Lord i see now that silence is
    wisdom at play
. . .being so still, i know that
    you are
my God.

Cynthia Waters
VOYAGER

Launch yourself into the skies,
A modern ship with rocket
    sails;
Roam among the twinkling
    stars,
Catch a comet by its tail.
Saddle Pegasus and fly,
Sip your fill from the Milky
    Way;
Beam your knowledge back to
    Earth,
Enrich me each eventful day.

You spend in searching for
    the truth
Upon your solitary flight,
As you swiftly cross the miles
In blackness of eternal night.
Let me see what you have seen
Upon your journey into space,
For I will not wear Saturn's
    rings,
For mine is not the time or
    place

To travel through the universe
Exploring new, exciting worlds,
And greeting alien forms of
    life.
No, I must watch as you unfurl
New scenes to me, for manned
    space flights
Are far and distant future
    schemes
That will occur when I am
    gone;
Now, I can only read and dream.

Gedeon Takaro
JONES BEACH IN APRIL

Sudden snows powdered the
    boardwalk, danced on
Aging planks accepting drifts
    sifting
Between, while swirling ballet
    groups of flakes
Skipped and pirouetted back
    and fourth.
Gulls pearched, sullen, shrouded,
    on the railings,
Huddled against the biting wind
    from the sea.
Pennants snapped and fluttered
    tethered to a
Ship's mast bending with the
    wind.

And grey waves skirled into
    snowy whitecaps to
Match the dancing snows,
    gently brushing
Back the sandpipers with each
    lapping surge,
As they skipped back and
    forth, searching
Edibles tucked among the sand
    grains . . .discernable

Only to the unerrant eyes of
    sandpipers
Pattering to and fro to the
    rhythm of the swells
Depositing or removing still
    more grains
From the Mississippi's
    inexhaustible broad currents
Ranging from the Delta along
    the route of
Soaring pelicans, past the
    Florida Sea northward,
Blending with the Antarctic
    swells also.

Northbound, to marriage with
    the **frigid** Arctic waters
And confluencies mysterious
    to oceans, and
Fluxing forever; first topside
    then in the deeps
On the return journey to
    original home.

Lisa A. Burgess
SEASONS OF MY LOVE

My desk faces the window
In my old New England home.
This is where the thoughts
    begin
That inspire me in a poem.
Through this little window
    frame
The past comes into view,
Framing seasonal portraits
That so often remind me of
    you.
In the spring I see the flowers
Blooming along the old pathway
It reminds me of the first
    rose
You brought that April day.
In the summer I hear the
    crickets serenade
And feel the humidity of the
    night time weather.
I remember your face in the
    August moon
And our special moments
    together.
The winter snow falls softly
Making the world so clean and
    pure.
I recall the January nights
And how the fire in your eyes
    would allure.
Autumn is such a beautiful
    season
The foliage so brilliant and clear.
But like our beautiful October
    love
The leaves fall and die, I fear.
Through my little window
    frame
I've seen love grow and die.
Like each precious season
How swiftly it goes by.

Ysella Fulton
FIND ME A FIREFLY

Find me a firefly, and let
me lie
upon the wings of night.
Show me a moondrop, let it
whirl
not to stop
till morning brings light.
Sing me a lullaby, about the
    dolphins
who cry
for a love that is lost.
Listen to the sounds of the
    seagulls
and the waves all around,
listen . . .there is no cost.
Tell me of Neptune's only
    love,
the mermaid

who's beneath and above
the turquoise sea.
Bring all the orange coral,
    nature's finest floral
to put all around me.
Hold my sould in your hands,
    let me
run through the sands of
    everlasting time.
Read me of your dreams, crazy
    as they seem,
make my life a new rhyme.
Be the magician of my mind,
    let
me seek
and always find
the riddles that you hide.
Make me see and always know,
    all the things to me you've
    shown
that you can bring out from
    the inside.

Wanda A. Abbe
EULOGY FOR AUNT HAZEL

I will remember my Aunt Ha
    Hazle as
a Matriarch whose reign was
    filled with love.
As a very special person, who
    found within her heart,
a small spot for everyone she
    knew.
She was never too busy, or
    too poor, to share
her love and material things
    with those who had a need.
There was always an extra
    chair at her table, and if need
    be, a place to spend a
night, or a week, or a year.
She was a person of mercury
    moods, stubborn and proud,
    if the occasion arose,
But most of the time, you
    could sense a girlish
    mischieviousness, just
    below
the surface.
She loved with the fierceness
    of a mother cat, whose soft
    paws could show
claws, if those near and dear
    were endangered.
I would compare her with a
    mother hen, clucking and
    bustling, and protecting
her brood, always able to spread
    a wing a little further, to
    encompass another
chick with love.
She lived a full, God-fearing
    life,
happy with family and friends,
knowing that her health had
    failed,
and all mortal lives must end,
She made one final last
    request,
To be allowed to go to Eternal
    Rest,
to be with "Coral" it was
    simply spoken, to renew
    their vows
ne'er again to be broken.

Jeanne Wylie Torosian
WHY THIS LITTLE OLD LADY IN TENNIS SHOES MOURNS WOLVES AND TRAIN WHISTLES AND ELVIS PRESLEY

For each was a singer unique
    and fitting to the Journey,
The short hauls and the long
    long haul,
The gone, the going and the
    foregone,

And it was written somewhere
that the Journey be so sung.

Now none but a last few
hunted wolves
Still haunt my farthest
forest in full yodeling cry,
Howl down the moon, the
snow, the very blood
And shiver the phantom
hackles of old severed memory.

Now none but ghost trains any
longer wail
Across the lamplit prairies
of my midnight,
Stirring some pith of gallantry
To ride out this willy nilly
ride,
Echoing time lost, the lives
unlived,
The promises that grabbed the
heart and drove
And even yet do drive my
deeds.

And now, only the disembodied
man still sings awhile
The brief forever of the heydays
of my days,
Laughter and love forlorn, the
sass and gut,
The reverent irreverence to
make and mock and break
the mold,
Sing DANNY BOY and
lays a sometime bridge
over the troubled waters,
Voice of the joy, the fatal
folly, and the Sorrow of
the World.

Magnus Bundgard
**IN MEMORY OF MOTHER
AT CHRISTMAS**

Just a few lines for you
on Christmas day
My memories and thoughts of
you
will never go away.

I remember at the hospital
I spent the night with you
The tears that fell from my
eyes
Were more than just a few.

As I sat by your side and let
my hand
run through your lovely white
hair
I couldn't help but feel
You knew that I was there.

As I took your sweet hand
And held it gently in mine
My mind drifted back over
many years
And sweet memories left
behind.

I was a boy in depression years
And there wasn't money for
entertainment or
fancy things to eat
But you kept love and
happiness within our
home
That money can never beat.

I remember I'd hurt myself
Or my clothes would tear
You always had sweet words
and would patch me up.
You would always care.

I remember you seeing me off
to school
And seeing that everything was
right.
You were always waiting
When I came home at night.
I remember all the loaves of
homemade bread

Lined along the table top.
You'd give me brown sugar
and butter
And I'd eat till I thought I'd
never stop.

Your washing machine was a
wash board
Your dryer a wire from tree to
tree.
But I know our clothes
Were as clean as they could be.

I remember you out among
your chickens
And watching as you'd milk
a cow.
I can still see you bringing
lunch out in the fields
You'd always find time, I
don't know how.

Later when I got older
And stayed out late at night
I'd try to come in quietly
But I can still hear your voice,
"Mac, are you all right?"

Then when I got married
You and Dad moved to town
I used to stop and see you
Whenever I was around.

We'd always have some coffee
and some good coffee cake
That real favorite kind
You would always make.

My everyday problems
Were never just mine alone.
You were always wanting to
share them.
You hardly took time for your
own.

I remember some weeks before
At the same hospital bed
I had gone to comfort you
But you tried to comfort me
instead.

You had asked how things were
on the farm,
And I said it was OK
You told me you hoped the
weather stayed good
And wouldn't rain upon the
hay.

You're up in heaven now,
Mother
I know that you are there.
God can find no one sweeter
And he's watching
everywhere.

Katharine Marie Braun
**SAGA OF OUR BLUEBIRDS,
1981**

April What a rough time you've
had this year,
This 1980 season!
You'd start your nest, then
have to rest;
Bad weather was the reason.

May You stayed around here
for so long—
T'was cold—with winds
a-blowing;
It was not weather meant for
song,
And it was even snowing!

June Three eggs, with only
half a nest,
We found by peeking in there;
The weather warmed; you
would not rest—
(We prayed that you would
win there!)

July We picked a time you
both were gone
To peek into your castle;
And WHAT a thrilling sight

we saw!
SIX nestlings—what a "passle"!

August Now they are grown,
and all have flown—
So lovingly you feed them;
Across the sky we see you fly;
How joyfully you lead them!

September You'll disappear
until next year,
And we will sorely miss you!
But happy when you reappear
In Spring. May God be with
you!

Still, it in its world is very
beautiful, you'll agree?
And too, what we shared
was surely that to me.
I thank you for being the
special person you are.
Aye, I'll remember you. No
distance is too far.
I'll wander in wind, darkness
and rain;
And no doubt I'll wish to be
with you again.
But I'll smile as I see roses
wild and free,
And think of what we shared—
'tween thee and me.

Thomas E. Zinn
'TWEEN THEE AND ME

"No more presents!" I've
often heard you say.
But let me give one more —after
our last day.
'Tis a most beautiful rose
captured in glass.
It's the best gift of all, so I
saved it for last.
Picked at the very best of her
bloom,
She's locked forever in her
little, round room.
Her life is frozen, from age
she escapes,
She gives of her beauty, and
fools of us makes.
While we wrinkle and die and
return to the dust,
She stays secure in her world—
we know she must.
Yet in truth, she's as dead as
we all shall be;
For she witholds so much—yes
can't you see?
Half of her beauty is the smell
thereof,
And the gift of her death is one
of great love.
In dying she thus presents us
a choice.
If she could speak, would this
be her voice?

"Pick me for your own, and I
die at your cut.
Put me in palace or humble
dirt hut.
Let me give pleasure by touch,
smell, and sight;
Then when I fade, throw me
into the night.
Or let me remain on the bush or

the vine,
And I'll die just the same—'tis
a matter of time.
So the choice is yours:
I'm dust just as you.
Either pick me or leave me. I
go with the dew."
Now you choose to go your
way and I must go mine.
Our paths crossed for awhile,
and it truly was fine.
We shared what we had—all
that we could.
We gave ourselves—more than
we should.
Yet we had each other in our
hours of need.
We were selfish, yet selfless,
quite unique indeed.
So this rose in its glass
represents what we share.
It neither grew nor died, but
'twas very much there.

H. Rex Hurst
STRUGGLE

Life is a plateau of existence.
Above, I sense meaning on the
pinnacle.
Up I struggle to reach it!
Alas; the escarpment is so
immense,
I'm falling.

Lugene Tucker
THE HOMEPLACE

The door opened slowly,
warped wood resisting,
groaning a protest
to those who would rouse the
homeplace,
disturb its silent sleep.

The dark interior,
splintered with silver slivers of
light,
grew less dim,
gradually, until
at last,
bulky shadows took form,
lost their aura of mystery
perhaps even terror.
Draped in darkness,
the rooms had housed threats
born of wild imaginings,
the residue of childhood rears
not quite erased by age.
Now, partly illuminated,
nothing lurked in shadowy
corners
more frightening than long-
abandoned spider nests;
nothing lived within the
empty shell
except memories,
some cherished,
others too painful to recall.
They lingered, left
behind by previous tenants,
some dead, their dreams buried
with them,
some making memories in
other rooms
far removed from these.
Awakened from its long and
secret sleep,
the homeplace,
once steeped in
sweet and sour smells,
the clanging of well-used pots,
the clamor of voices,
embraced the shouts of new
laughter,
echoed the patter of new feet
footprinting the dusty floors,
and readied itself for new
memories,

perhaps even better memories
than those it had kept alive thus
far.

Ruth B. McGinnis
INTROSPECTIONS

I have a shell
In which to crawl
On which to lean
I built a wall

Made not of brick
Nor yet of stone
But of such stuff
As I alone
  Could manufacture

Could fabricate
Within my mind
To prop the will
I oft do find
  Inadequate

But when I am
About to fall
I have a shell
In which to crawl
  For satisfaction

But O it is
So lonely there
And all alone
I cannot bear
  I seek distraction

It seems I ought
But then again
I do the best
The best I can

For life has put
Her mark on me
And so you see
I am not free
  I am defined

By genes and such
By this and that
By happenings
By where I'm at

I built a bridge
On which to cross
But bridge and shell
I coult but foss

For from myself
I cannot flee
Where're I go
I go with me.

Char Hicks
FOR GRANDPA SAM

My grandfather finished his
  job today.
His last job.
No more, not in this life
will I be hearing
the scrunch, scrunch of his
  hoe
cleaving the dry garden dirt.
No more
will I bend back the cornstalks
in search of him
only to find him leaning on his
  hoe,
head cocked, listening to the
  birds.
He knew them all,
and heard them,
even when he didn't hear
  grandma
telling him to wipe his feet.
And then he'd wink.
His hearing was our secret.

No more will I walk
  behind him
watching the brittle-brown
  leaves
crackling in his wake,
and no more hear
the sound of his banjo,
weaving the music of
  backwoods love

and sad moons over sad
  mountains.
It's not that he was tired
or even weak
but they needed music in
  heaven too, I think.
And so tonight
as I look out on the dark night
I hug tight
the secret part of him
and strain my ears
for an old man's dry laughter
and the sound of a banjo
  ringing.

Pam Latham
SEPARATION

As I turned around,
hearing you leave
your footsteps growing softer
  in the dark,
I knew our parting would last
  forever.

The life you placed inside
  me
shivered from my soul.
A special part of me
drifted down a stream,
floating into an ocean of
  forever lost
loves and memories.

All our promises to meet again
to call, to laugh, to remember...
Who are we kidding.

A new part of mea wants out.
grasping for air
begging for a new life
needing a new time

If only you could...

I cannot help remembering
  the time when...
or when we...
and I'll never forget...

I am searching for something
  different,
something new.
My life will be happy again,
if only given a chance.
I will grow to new heights,
and achieve
and develop
and experience
and I will make others happy
  too.

If only you could ...
come share my new life
and help me grow.

R. Emory Williamson
**ODE TO M.E. (DO YOU
REMEMBER)**

i climbed gropingly
Up a mountain today, i
  thought of you,
As a bird
(black; like my own scarred
  heart)
Flap flapflap flaplapFlappingly
Rose
(on transparent, sunsheilded
  wings)
To
GL I DE
s
p.
i
r
a
l
i
n
g
Down
  ward ...Nature's living
  beauty!

As i
In time, long ago
First instantaneously spied
Pointing as you did
(from a
just above roadlevel, thirtie (30)
  th Street bucketseat)
To a
Mystic's
Rainbow.

Sabrina Hackett
I CHOOSE

For the sweat of manking,
  cannot be blamed for the
  anguish of their fools—
Or the stolen dignity of their
  birth;
And the bleeding dreams of
  their visions—
"I CHOOSE"
To the greater glory of one's
  entity,
And the power of one's
  endurance!
"I CHOOSE"
The positive, the Infinite
  Intelligence, the noble God,
And the innocence of one's
  life—
"I CHOOSE"
You—Your being—your life,
  your faults and your
  sufferings.
"I CHOOSE"
You—to comfort you, to stand
  by you, to kiss you and to
  love you.
"I CHOOSE"
Also, to reject and say good-bye
  to you, out of the depths of
  my
lonliness and shyness.

For the Wind, the Waves, and
  Sea know me well—
And you never, did ever, get
  inside, my
beautiful dreams!

Gene A. Thompson
SALLY'S GONE HOME

God bless Mommy and Daddy
  She ended her prayer
The little girl with
  The long golden hair
She loved them so dearly
And told one and all
How someday they would find
  her
  Someday they would call
They would love and protect
  her
  And call her their own
Those wonderful and special
  parents
  That she had never known
For Sally was an orphan child
In a home that she shared
With other little homeless
  children
About whom no one cared
She was one of those children
  They call hard to place
No one wanted a little girl
  with
  Her leg in a brace
But she never stopped hoping
  She never questioned why
She was always smiling
  Tho she wanted to cry
Then one morning they found
  her
A smile upon her face
Sally was no longer a cripple
  No longer needed the brace

Death by natureal causes
  The coroner's report said
But Sally had just begun
  living
No she was not dead
Her father had come to claim
  her
To share with her his love
Sally had found her home in
  Heaven
  In His mansion up above.

Virginia Ann Taylor
ONLY A MOTHER KNOWS

Being a good mother is a rare
  gift from God above, only
  a mother knows
Having a child in our life is
  a very special thing in so
  many ways, only
a mother knows.
Our daughter (Tina Louise) is
  God's special gift to us as,
  only a
mother knows.
The heavenly joy of a baby
  is near, only a mother knows.
With all its precious charms
  and our baby in her mother's
  arms as, only
a mother knows.
God gave each mother 86,400
  seconds in each new day, as
  God has a
purpose for each one of us,
  only a mother knows.
A mother's love means a life
  of devotion and a life of
  sacrifices her
sole wish is of her children as
  only a kother knows.
Happy is a mother who has
  children she can be proud of
  as only a mother knows.
A good mother is a wonderful
  person most fair and true,
  only a mother
knows.
A mother's love is beyond
  explaination, only a mother
  knows.
A good mother should show
  her children how to love and
  care for one
another, only a mother knows.
A good mother will always
  give herself to her children
  with a helping
hand and an ear that will
  hear every cry of need, only
  a mother knows.
As a good mother you gave
  us each a happy home and an
  understanding way, so
we thank you Lord for each
  new day, only a mother knows.
Being a good mother is each day
  a very precious gift from God
  above
as only a mother knows.
Life is not life until you give
  part of it away, only a
  mother knows.

But God gave us so many good things in life, but only one mother . . .

Anna Marie Dahlquist
CREDO

I believe each night will usher in
A new sunrise;
And every thunderclap and cloud will bring
A glad surprise;
That every gagging, dusty drouth will end
In gentle showers,
That every snow is followed by a blend
Of new spring flowers.

I know the tree of life was never lost
In paradise,
But bears fruit in eternal Pentecost
Beyond the skies,
And I believe the farthest star's faint beam,
Light years away,
Is reachable. And that our boldest dream
Comes true some day.

I know there is a time for everything, both
good and right,
And waiting makes joy's cup full to the brim
With pure delight;
That seeds long left in slumber turn to flower;
That final fruit,
When ripe, is sweet, though buds may have been sour
And destitute.

And I believe no prayer will go unheard,
No good denied;
No promise will be just an idle word,
No stream too wide.
And all things have a purpose that is right
And good and true;
And God will conquer wrong and greed and night,
And make things new.

Geraldine D. Fuentes
WEDDING

Bound together
For love
And life
Two spirits one
Against all strife,
A voyage long
Thru dark
And light
A fight for better
A risk for right,
Though tears may come
And battles rage
They remain united
Come what may,
The blast of age
A gift of birth,
A touch of warmth
And days of mirth.
And though death will call
And their friends may stray
Forever they're joined
By words in name
Proclaimed but one
Still two that stay
The envy of gods
Just playing games
Their flesh will end
But souls remain,
Breathed into space
Like birds

Not take
They soar into flight
Trapped without faces
Till the poet one night
Sees what's eternal
And lives
At the sight
Beginning that moment
A union of 'me'
With 'you'
Endless,
And free.

Ar Weidner
THE BATTLE OF SEATON'S HILL

Not found in arid history book,
Or told in tales or story,
Was the valiant fight for Southern right
Or the fight for Southern glory.
'Twas the gory fight on Seaton's Hill,
the hill of bloody action.
That lost the fight and lost the war
To the blue-clad Union faction.

We advanced one score that fateful day—
Advanced to Seaton's Mill
And without a pause we scaled the crest
Of craggy Seaton's Hill.
There we watched the dreaded Blues
Who approached relentlessly.
We could spy the light reflecting from
Their sun-shined musketry.

And grimly there the battle raged
In the crisp November morn;
Amid the crackling shot of sound
And the muted cry of horn.
Furious; without respite— the Blues
destroyed our Rebel men.
But they also killed the Southern pride
And a dream that might have been.

Some shrug and say we gave our lives
In just a minor fray.
But we hail proudly it was more than that!
'Twas for the glory of the Gray!

Nancy C. Thomas
LOVING YOU

You said you loved me
And I believed,
Now it's over and
I guess I'm relieved.

Now I'm alone
Always feeling blue,
All because
I fell in love with you.

I guess I gave
My heart too fast,
Though I knew deep down
It couldn't last.

You really made me
Look like a fool,
You did a good job
And thought you were cool.

You took my heart
And broke it in two,
Everyone knows it
I know they do.

I sometimes wish
That it could be,

The way it used to
With you and me.
But now it is
All over and done,
But for a few months
I was number one.

I still feel
So alone,
But I'll make it
All on my own.
As for you
I hope you burn
Maybe in Hell
A lesson you'll learn.
Now I know
What they mean by Hell,
'Cause loving you
Has taught me well.

Mary Kathryn Byers
THE KEY TO FAMILY LOVE AND FRIENDSHIP

How many days have quietly passed you by
Before you realize how much time you've let run dry.
You've got things to do and bills to pay—
Being with friends and family takes time,
And you can't seem to find a way.

You promise your children or partner
that you'll spend more time with them,
But later! Not now!
You're pressed for time and your work just won't allow.
Some other time we'll be together, I promise you my dear;
When I get things more organized
And everything is clear.

But that time seems to never come
When your work is fully done.
One thing seems to lead to another in each passing day,
Your involvement makes you unaware of your family's needs
And they become further and further away.

Life is so temporary in every path it weaves,
You got so tangled up in its web
That you yourself aren't what you should be.
Some day you will wake up, old and grey;
Realizing your children are all grown up and have moved away.
Oh! If only I had another chance, I would spend more time with my family! You

begin to pray.
Let me tell you, my friend, nothing every stays the same.
But if you love and care for others,
a memory shall forever remain.
Life could be a joy to you—
Your children an inspiration!
If you make your life a family dedication.
Learn to love, laugh and cry with others,
Share with them your feelings.
You will then find everything in life easier in your dealings.
Don't be selfish with your time, dedicate it to others.
The key to Family love and friendship
will remain unlocked and uncovered.

Mary Therese Darcy
LOVE UNSPOKEN

We drank of the warm spring air
Embraced and gazing at the moon's pale light;
Quiet, listening to each other's racing heartbeat
At the water's edge.

Ahead, a church of crumbling stone;
Roofless, sacred, silent,
A relic of history's past,
Thoughts and dreams and words of love
Unsaid.

How right that we should linger here
In divine solitude;
A respite from our busy worlds
In joy and sweet retreat.

I would have cried for happiness
Overwhelming and tingling with echoing ecstacy,
Filling my heart like the golden cup
Of a sacred liturgy
And found in my feelings a comforting strength
As we stood on the silky sand.

While we held each other
Moonlight danced on the water's skin
Flashing light fairies to and fro
In frivolous fantasies.

Before long we felt the gentle wind
That blew across the lake
Cooling and refreshing
Into the night
Between reverie and profundity.

Quivering in the moon's light
A light brown lock rose above his forehead
Swayed, knelt, fluttered, flowed, fell
To a rhythm which we knew
As love.

Irene M. Omi
SAN FRANCISCO

Time hangs
Suspended for us on the wide grey road;
Cars whiz past us,
While dark clouds in the sky brood.

The engine sings a hoarse monotone
As we fly down one long hill,
Croons to the straightaway,
Then coughs up the grade.

We 'kerplank' across the bridge,
The setting sun in our eyes.
The jolly orange truck
Dispenses lane markers,
Orange and red, while its
  crossed red flags
Flutter in the breeze.
The city points a white finger
  at the Bay,
Its 'scrapers scratching the
  guileless blue sky
Straining to be seen through
  the high fog
And the dark coming of night.
A rash of irritable shiny
  windows
Greet the sunset,
Flickering as clouds drift by.
Row upon row of stucco
  houses,
Neatly parading up and down
  hills,
Straddling old sand dunes and
  underground rivers:
Pastels, white, with boastful
Pocket-gardens, they spew
  forth
Little baseball players into
  broad avenues:
While we move on.

Alice Johnson
REMEMBER

Remember me
When the moon
shall pour
Its silver sheen
on a tranquil shore.

When the trees and
  woods
Stand brown and bare
And sleek and fat
is the timid hare.

Remember me
When the sky is grey
And the rain runs down
The trees a way

When the wild young colt
So fresh and spry
In the clean cold air
begins to fly.

Remember me
When the sun is high
And no curtains of clouds
cover the sky
When dust and dirt
Fly thick and fast,
And the cool raindrops
come at last!

Harmony Colleen Adkins
FOR RUPERT BROOKE

Writing on the peacefulness
  of eventide
Beside the Old Vicarage garden
  wall
Transcribing silent thoughts
  into poetic mirrors
That do fall,
And shatter into fragmented
  reflections of yourself
  everywhere.
You pray for time to write
  all the words . . .
Time to live and love and care.
But you hear the future in
  urgent pursuit—
Time and freedom are not there.
Drowning in the darkness
The deathly corridors of
  World War I—
Struggling vainly for the
  surface
A way to break past time and
  run.

On universal scrolls, immortal
  poems will ablaze like sun.
But how does a mortal poet
  go
From pens and paper
  to a gun?
The world still pirouettes a
  ceaseless ballet.
Fugitive time still fleets
  away.
But those things that you
  cherished are still very
  much the same—
Love is still a city;
Still an emperor; A flame.
Legacies of phrase still
  transcend time and place.
Ink embroidered sojourns
  still take us near and far . . .
And your night is still
  remembered
For a star.

Sean Kevin Neilland II
**LET DOWN YOUR HAIR AND
LIVE**

When are people friends to me?
When do they fill my needs?
It's selfish, greedy and uncool
to think no one else bleeds!
We are all human deep within
We're all the same when we
  begin.

If life breeds questions
let it be that answers
Are all there to see.
To see and learn and use to guide
Us all to heaven and God's side.
The ways are clear for those
  believing
that ways exist at all
And when one feels that life's
  deceiving
then one has a fall.
A fall so far that down goes
  by
and soon you're falling up.
So drink of life and taste the
  brew
of nature's loving cup.
A cup that's filled with nectar
  sweet,
A wine like milk and honey.
And think of life as only
  LOVE
and not of having MONEY;
For if money brings you life,
  my friend
then you are truly dead
And never will you live outside
  of your banker's head.

No cash can buy you cool
  clean air,
No dollars quench your thirst
So give it up, let down your
  hair and live life free and
  first.

Emily Kamenovsky
FANTASIA

An Andalusian stallion in all
  his elegance dances over to
playfully nuzzle my hair.
To be that beautiful and yet
  so unvain just isn't fair.
His great body moves in step
  with mine as he follows me
around the pasture.
Even though he's spirited and
  free he still loves his master.
The wind makes his silky white
  main and tail fly.
As he lets out a whinny, shrill
  and high.
A magnificent beauty, a joy to
  behold, a stallion big,

beautiful and bold.
Magic dances around him as he
  arches his neck and lifts his
  legs in a dancing trot.
Stardust flies from beneath his
  hooves as he quickens
  the pace.
A look of heavenly contentment
  balanced upon his face.
His velvety muzzle and big
  dark eyes seem to surprise
  all,
as he comes right away
  whenever I call.
The time of my life I will have
  when I mount him and ride
away.
Expect me tomorrow, I won't
  come back today.
A coat of dark grey silk, mane
  and tail the color of
fresh milk.
His long, lean legs which are
  always lifted up high
Also notice a hint of sparkle
  in both eyes.
As the day rolls into night, I
  lead him to his stall, I've
got to take care of the King.
A horse whose filled my world
  with joy, to me for this
moment means everything.

Rita M. Hrzic
WHY?

She stood beside his bed that
  day;
She was so forlorn,
And her mind began to wonder
Why her son was born.
He lay upon that bed of white;
His body, it was still,
And her spirit cried in anguish,
"Oh God, is this your will?
I've only had him a few years,
For what I do not know.
And now you snatch him from
  me,
And my spirits are so low.
They say you want your
  angels
To come home and live with
  you,
But Oh dear God, my Father,
You make me feel so blue.
I know I'll never change your
  mind
For my poor boy's so ill
So I guess you'll have to take
  him,
If it be your holy will.
I loved him oh so very much
The short time he was here,
But I know he'll go to Heaven,
And he'll never have a fear.
Just lay your hands upon me,
And make me understand.
That you will truly love him
'Til you call me to your land,
And then we'll be together,
For I love this child of mine,
But it is not my will dear
  Father,
It is only thine."

Vivian May Pate
THE KREMLIN GREMLIN

In the kremlin, there's a
  gremlin,
And there's such a happy
  tremblin'
When he sings his happy,
Kremlin Gremlin song,
No matter what the time or
  season,
Without rhyme or without
  reason,
You can hear his "Gitchee um,

buy um," all day long.
"Gitchee um, buy um, buy um,
  buy um,
Gitchee um, buy um, buy um,
  buy um,"
You can hear him sing it
  morning, night and noon,
"Gitchee um, buy um, buy
  um, buy um,
Gitchee um, buy um, buy um,
  buy um,"
That's the happy little Kremlin
  Gremlin tune.
See the children crowd around
  him,
And the grownups, too,
  surround him,
When he sings his happy,
  Kremlin Gremlin song.
Children say the days are
  brighter,
Grownups say their work is
  lighter,
When they hear his, "Gitchee
  um, buy um, buy um" all
  day long.
He has lived throughout the
  ages,
And advised the world's great
  sages,
When he sings his happy
  Kremlin Gremlin song,
He has them smiling at each
  other,
For they realize they're all
  brothers,
When they hear his "Gitchee
  um, buy um, buy um," all
  day long.
Even fields begin to dancin'
When he swings out with his
  prancin'
For his little heart has loads of
  love to spare.
Since peace, goodwill and
  understanding,
Is what this sad old world is
  lacking,
So he does his part and gives
  a gremlin's share.

Bertha E. Wilson
CANADA

This majestic vast Dominion,
  this bounteous land
Stretching in glorious
  immensity from sea to sea,
The grandeur of snow capped
  mountains, like sentinels
  of destiny,
The beauty of lush valley
  orchards in blossom time,
With far reaching fragrance
  wafting in on the breeze,
The wide expanse of prairie,
  ripe with golden grain,
The turbulent rivers and
  sparkling lakes teeming with
  fish,
All this has made this land, this
  Canada of ours.
This land, the home of the
  buffalo and Indian,
This land that surrendered to
  ox drawn plow.
The pioneers toiled from dawn
  to dusk
To wrest a living from the
  stubborn soil.
The seamed face of the farmer
  raised hopefully for rain,
Offering a prayer for the
  seed just sown.
The old timer lost in a
  prairie blizzard
With deranged mind and hope

almost gone,
Till the faint glimmer of a
light leads him on,
They have made this land,
this Canada of ours.
The pounding of steel in the
blistering heat,
To link this country from
West to East.
The small towns springing up
along the tracks,
the growth of industries like
bee hives of energy.
The drone of the Snowbirds
in flying formation,
Inspiring respect and acclaim
for this land of ours.
The sacrifice of its sons in
two world wars,
Bringing peace to our shores,
to live without fear.
God grant us valour and wisdom
to keep this land, this
Canada of ours.

Pam Campbell
NOT EVEN GOD REALLY KNOWS

Sun shiny days
Birds singing in the trees
The nights uncover a soft
haze
In the darkness, a slight
breeze
Only felt in the sunlight
Is a refreshing warmness from
the sun
Reflections in the moonlight
After Mister Sun says, "My
day is done."
Is the smiling full moon
And many twinkling stars
And the absolute silence of
street cars.

Peace fills each mind
With the remembrance of
nature's time
Love finds each heart
As we bow our heads in prayer
And give thanks to the One
Who gave nature her first start.

While not too far away:
A murder in the street
Many suffering in the cold
without any heat
Growling stomachs from no
food to eat
Others barely making ends
meed
Wars fought for defeat
Machine guns fire to kill the
shuffle of little feet.

And as you look to the One
high above
To the almighty who at one
time
Sent down a white dove
The heart has to ask
"Due to all the sin
Will you once again
Destroy the earth as in the
past?"
Even though it would be a
great loss
He would have to start once
again
to rebuild His wondrous land
at His own cost
Not really knowing, would it
remain free of sin?

John F. Mulholland
THE END OF A FAMILY

My wife's niece phoned "Aunt
Betty's ill. Please come."
"Mayo doctors have said
'It's terminal.' "

We live by the blue pacific.
Except
Wife Pat's poor memory, we
have good health.
Pat's Mid-West family—parents,
brothers, sisters,
Wives and husbands: all these
had died.
Betty was left, amazingly strong,
serene.
Therapy held the pain in check
and Pat
Could not believe that one who
seemed so well
Should live in a nursing home.
So pat said,
"Betty, let us go home."
Betty answered,
"After Charles died, this became
my home."
Later the niece said, "You hurt
your sister."
"She bravely lives each day, yet
she's dying."
"The Springdale farm is not
so far, is it?"
Pat asked. Springdale had been
their childhood home.
Some fifty years ago they sold
the farm.
They left the gravel hills and
all found work.
We drove the new highway and
by the lake
Turned off a mile to Springdale
farm. Where house
And barn had been was now a
gravel pit.
The gravel hills had built the
new highway.
Pat shouted, "This is not our
Springdale farm."
She wanted me to find the
home secure.
Next day Pat said, "Betty, let
us go home."
I saw the love each one had
tortured both.
I took Pat home. We saw the
sea. Pat yelled,
"The lake. A mile to
Springdale farm. Brothers,"
"Sisters, father, mother, all
will be there."
Pat cheered. I stopped and
drew her close. I wept.

Joan Morgan
THE FISHERMAN

Crowds of people
all around me,
yet alone.
A fisherman walked by and
said "Hello."
Slowly, I responded.
It was good to see his smiling
face,
covered by a beard and shaggy
hair.
His smile warmed me.
I wanted to ask if he had a
good catch.
But in the instant the thought
went through my mind,
he was gone.
Gone,
like so many things in my
life.
He reminded me of that life.
I walked, looking for the
fisherman,
but he was really gone.
Life is so much like the
fisherman,
here,

than in an instant,
gone.
I've tried to hold on,
but you can't, you know.
Life keeps moving
Sometimes it flies
past you,
and you don't have the chance
to ask,
"Did you have a good catch?"
If I saw the fisherman again,
I would talk,
I'd do it all differently.
But fisherman,
if only I had the chance,
Like so many before you,
If only I had the chance once
more,
Surely I would ask
"Did you have a good catch?"

Deborah Ann Cohn
A WALTZ TO YESTERDAY

All the wild flower memories
must be pressed close to my
Heart
My first kiss . . .simple, shaky,
an innocent blush and flutters
My best friends like sisters who
shared in patchwork dreams
When I heard the words
"I love you"and answered
them in my soul.
Blustery Halloween nights
all golden a-lit in my mind's
eye
Every shy smile exchanged
and even those swallowed
but meant
Looking deep inside and feeling
all at once at Home
Reaching throughout and
knowing there is so much
more
Feeling, indeed, the heavens
are closer than tomorrow.
And the flavor of all yesterday's
growing and reaching secrets
Like rare spice enchant
and permeate my moment
of Reflection
I am a-drift in my meadow with
the swaying wild flowers
They tickle friend memory
and bud forth in sweetest
fragrance
I sing to our CREATOR in
grateful tones to have
touched this magic
. . .once again, as I frolick,
I spin; I reel in gentle ¾ time!

Pauline Clay
TO LIFE

Play musician . . .to life
and you
with willing fingers touch
the trembling keys.
The keys answered and sang
as disembodied dreams drift
across
the sea of sleep
To life!
or rather say
to every hope
that leans across the shadowed
sills of night
To every breeze
that stirs the whispering grass
with vague desire for bud
and blossoming,
To every heart that waits for
recognition!
Yes play to life
and there shall sound
the answering voice of all

the seasons
with roaring music of wintery
wind.
Across snow
vagrant notes of life stir beneath
the frozen earth.
Hearts of old persons listen
and they hear through music,
through winter's rage. The
promise of spring!
What leaf or bud but feels
within it stir
the ancient life that knew a
thousand things?
Sweet music that reaches
through the voiceless
depth
of time,
and by the music of a kindred
soul
rebuilds the vanished dream!
What truer sign that the
harmony of life fails
and passes away.
Yet, there shall rise
relentless, sure, born of
eternal thought.
Far from the waste of space
and time,
that binds our little world
a deeper song, a truer
symphony
wherein shall sound from utter
silence surest harmony,
. . .the living voice of Life.

Joseph O. McCarver
THE DAY THE ROSES DIED

I planted a rose when first
we met
and told you then my dear
we'd be together forever and
ever
or as long as the rose was there.
For some few years we stayed
as one
as closer to me you came
I watched the rose as it
flourished and grew
its blooms were always the
same.
As the years rolled by the
roses bloomed
and our love was as strong
as could be
Then one day I walked outside
to see
the rose looking back at me.
Its petals were all covered
with dew
as they were falling to the
ground
They looked like tears from
someone's eyes
just lying all around.
That same day you came to
me
with papers in your hand
As I read the lines I couldn't
believe
I'd no longer be your man.
I turned away with tear stained
eyes
trying not to cry
Because you see I lost your
love
that's the day the roses died.

Charles F. Jennings
THE HUNTER AND THE HORN

The hunter up at daybreak
goes
forth to wit-match with his
foes
The fox, the squirrel, the hare,

189

and coon
Listen to the horn of doom.
A note flung on the morning
air
That seeks out every den and
lair
Rebounding o'er the mountain
side
Bringing terror where they hide.
In woods and field there is
suspense
The timid hearts are still and
tense
Waiting, listening, for the
sound
The gleeful voices of the
hounds.
Again the bugle note on high
A warning that a life must
die
And startled from his hiding
place
The hunted one begins the
chase.
Through his land of birth he
goes
Through the woods and
fields he knows
In this place where life was
give
Here is where he seeks to live.
But alas, the horn has blew
And the hunted's time is
through
Soon the race for life will
cease
And the hunted will have
peace.
The horn of doom in victory
peals
The hounds of fate have made
their kill
Soon the horn will blow again
For the next race to begin.
The hunter, too, one morn
shall hear
The blowing of a trumpet
clear
He, too shall lead a fearful
chase
And so, he too, shall lose the
race.

Dino Ferra
**THE CHARIOT IS
PERFECTED . . . ARE YOU?**

Progress has perfected the
chariot. It's
harness is horsepower, not
horses.
Heed the call from the
adjacent chamber
where your freedom waits.
If the libedo permits you may
find utopia.
Seek serenity from its dark
shadows, as a
new scroll is written
Sometimes you drive out to
89 West and peart.
perch on the ramp, pondering
self-exile.
Your pulse pounds with the
rhythm of the pistons,
watered nerves bead your brow
like rain on a
freshly-waxed car.
You rear the uncertainty of the
unknown and scorn
what is known.
Your chariot is perfected . . .
Are you?
Easing on the throttle, swearing
the savior will
save your soul,

but realism and all its fallacies
has and is control.
You exit at the next exit, U-turn
for your return.
Place the chariot in its dark
chamber and mutter,
"maybe next time."

Jack Reilly
PURPOSE

In the quest of legitimate
pleasure
And to see where our heart
doth lie
We engage in a business of
choosing
This lifelong endeavor we try.
With the lessons of others
before us
'Neath the critical eyes of our
peers
And respecting the norms of
our elders
Our challenge, looming
mighty, appears
We reach unashamed lest
we falter
Toward ideals we hold to be
true
Striving by trial and error
Sincerely in all that we do.
Despite the false hopes and
vain labors
That surround and entice us
indeed
This subtle resolve serves to
guide us
As a true friend will help us in
need
Notwithstanding our failings
and errors
We're convinced we must not
hesitate
When the road widens off in
two branches
To needs pick one; the other
'liminate.
Proceeding we hasten to venture
On toward the goals we've
enshrined
Unflinched in the shadow of
danger
Never foolishly looking
behind.
Determined, intent to be
winners
Or to least of all give it a try
For something we treasure
most highly
We'll sacrifice, struggle, yea
die!

R. Phillip Croft
LENORA

To a wonderful sister,
the heartaches I've cost
On how to express my love,
for the words I am lost
You've always stuck by me,
thru thick and thru thin
I could search the world over,
n'er find a better friend
Looking back o'er the years,
it would happen every time
When just for the asking,
you'd give your last dime
Right or wrong made no
difference,
by my side you have stayed
For the love you've given me,
what a price you have paid
I just hope you'll forgive me,
so please accept this letter
As a token of my love
and I'll try to do better
May God bless and keep you

from harm in every way
For your health and happiness,
every night I do pray.

Karma O. Huggins
IF I DIDN'T HAVE YOU

Would there be . . .
No moon above,
Where lovers gaze
and renew their love.

No clusters of starlight
Shining down,
All through the night?

Would there be . . .
No birds in the tree,
Singing their own
Melodic rhapsody;

And no bubbling brook
Winding its way
Through an old shady nook?

And would there be . . .
No soft rain,
On a sunny afternoon
With promises of a rainbow,
on the horizon soon?

Would there be . . .
No laughter
Ringing so true?

Would there be
Anything at all . . .
If I didn't have you?

Norman Irving Beagle
YES

I wonder
if the bird feels joy
to be young and whole and
free,
as he chir-ups in the tall blue
spruce
and sings so very sweetly.
If I had such seeming joy,
could I sing a song
that would encircle all mankind
to which happiness would
belong?
I wonder.

Steven Gregory Alston
OF PEACE, LOVE AND LIGHT

O the peaceful quiet, restfulness
that serving GOD can bring.
o the joy the mystic joy we
feel
when bowing to the KING
o the love that flows from
heart
to heart from all who praise
the LORD
O the beauty, grace and wonder
of living by His WORD;
O the love of God is ever near
the dearest love we know
With God there is no one we
heed fear for he does love
us so.
The Love of God is for us
all that we may learn to share
no man is great, no man is
small
for all are in his CARE

O man do you know the one
who beckons you to HIM?
O man he's the great bright
light that will never grow dim.
A light to all who come to
him,
A wonderful savior is HE.
Who frees the world of
darkness
and causes the blind to see.

Dana Michelle Baker
WHY?

The land was theirs, they got
here first,
then we came.
They gave back what they took
from the land,
We took but never gave.
They hunted only the animals
they needed,
we killed just to be killing.
They worshipped the animals,
the land,
we worshipped only ourselves.
They had to start their lives
from scratch,
we started ours from what was
left of theirs.
Their weapon was the bow and
arrow.
ours was the gun.
They were treated like animals,
we acted like God.
Their lives were ruined, families
gone,
we walked away proud, we
had won.

Kelly Felty
CRUCIFIED

Be it fiction or be it true,
the days of Jesus were numbered
few.
The things that he did were
always good,
And he always helped with
whatever he could.
But they turned on him, when
he was kind.
They searched in the garden, for
him to find.
Pilate condemned this man to
die
and the people shouted,
"crucify!"
The cross was heavy, Jesus
was weak.
But he carried it there, humble
and meek.
They drove nails through his
hands and pierced his side.
"Forgive them Lord"
and then he died.
The veil was ripped and the
earth then shook,
as it was prophesied in the holy
book.
Many then knew he was God's
son
and they repented for what
they'd done.
Three days later he was risen
again.
And now he's alive to forgive
your sins.
He died on the cross for you
and me,
so that we could have life
eternally!
Christine Kay
FLOWERS

They grow inside me.
I mean flowers.
They're blooming,
and blooming.
And as I run

...own South West 64th Street
to your house
they are open.
I am open.

Marc Fike
LOOKING BACK IN 1998

This? In 1980.
archaic, forgotten technique.
No wonder . . .no cohesion,
no sense.

Yes it must have had . . .or it
wouldn't have been
definite trend, but styles
change.
  Lost in translation,
obscure.
  had to have been there, I
guess.

Moral? We'll never know . . .

Kimberly Voges
NORTH AND SOUTH

The North Wind sends its
biting cold
To the gentle South,
Hoping that she would unfold
And let him into her mouth.
She puts up a strong bitter
fight
Wishing to defeat his will,
But in the end the North
takes flight
Back to the old grindmill.

Their quarrel seems to have
a pattern
of fight and then retreat.
The north is cold and very
stern
While the South brings all the
heat.
The months in which lie in
wait
Not knowing what is to come.
If the South will go to its fate,
Or the North will return where
it's from.

Angela V. Paccione
A TIME COMES. . .

A time comes when the hurt
must stop hurting,
When the memories that linger
must fade . . .
  Forever away

A time comes when the heart
that was broken must mend,
When the clouds of unhappiness
must drift . . .
  Forever away

A time comes when laughter,
good times and smiles will
come your way,
When the days filled with
sunshine will last . . .
  Forever, always

A time comes when you know
someone cares, understands,
is a friend,
When the broken heart mends
and the hurt stops hurting . . .
  Forever, always.

Jane Tretter Petrovich
TO DAD

I think of you this Christmas
day
Sorry that you had to go away.
I miss you and think of you
day and night
And wonder if you're doing
all right.

Never thought you'd leave us
quite so soon,
Before Spring flowers came
to bloom,

Before my first baby was born.
It is because of all this I mourn.
All of us prayed for you today—
God sent our prayers up your
way.
He knows you were loved by
all of us
Even though it was not
verbalized much.

Mary Cooper
WE'VE COME HOME

We've come home . . .
A little worser for the wear
With hearts tattered by love's
tear,
The old folks say a silent prayer
Thanks . . .that we are home;

The dreams of youth have
gone away
The dancing feet, the laugh and
play,
With much regret, all we can
say—
Is, we've come home.

We wanted more . . .
An old time love,
The things the folks
Marriage is made of;

We've made mistakes by the
score
Learned wisdom beyond our
years,
And as we open up the door
Your arms held out—
Our eyes fill with tears;

To make good—to have you
proud
We wanted this . . .our souls
cry loud,
And lips that cannot dare speak
this . . .
Instead, return the old folks
kiss;

And know that . . .
On us, with your hearts you
gaze
Remembering cherished
childhood days,
Our hearts now so afraid to
roam
From this dear place . . .yes,
we've come home.

Jim Thompson
OMINOUS

echoed engines pound the wood
and seize the hood in barren
the grease gaud slickens the
skyskin
orders cloud gears to oil, fluid
quick
down the waters, thick and
drown sea animation
ballbearing seed loads the
strain
steel girdered plain looms
webward
combine reaper crops cripple
thin
scrapes and pits the soil,

lunar bare
road gutted rocks stare in cold
anticipation
let the oceans swill to swamp
and concrete cement the land
honour digital computed
pomp
and God grease mechano man

Pamellia Robertson
SOMEDAY

A cabin made from tree and
stones
A place to rest our weary bones
Someday

A place up in the mountain high
Somewhere between the
earth and sky
Someday

A meadow of flowers in bloom
year round
The larks in the morn, special
sound
Someday

Your loving arms to hold and
caress
for all our times of happiness
Someday.

Jean Leach
ALONE BUT NEVER LONELY

I may be alone but I am not
lonely
For you are still my one and
only
Even though we're miles apart
You are always in my heart
You are with me when I wake
up in the
morning
At sunrise when the day is
dawning
You are with me every hour
of the day
Even though you may be
miles away
And when I close my eyes at
night to
sleep
My dreams of you I'll always
have to
keep
They will help to satisfy my
yen
Till we are together once again.

John C. Prawdzik
ALL THE HUES AND GREYS

All the hues and greys
Lives prefer
Each moment mellow
Softly it arrives
All those brightly and vivid
Lifes intense glare
Impetuous and boisterous
Raucous intentions.

Eileen Connor Broadbelt
TO MY TWO YEAR OLD

On days when you are truly
wild—
(a real exasperating child)
I can't turn my back on you
for fear of what you'll get into.
When all is quiet, then I find
my table marked with red
crayon—
If that's not bad—I really
mind
you floating sailboats in the
john!

About the time I want to scream
I remember once you saw
a sunray full of sparkling dust . .
—You watched a moment—

wonderstruck—
then an idea came to you
and on your face a smile grew.
You caught the sunray in a cup
(so careful not to lose one beam)
and being it was only fair
you gave your brother half
your share.
You tip-toed up and poured
your gold
upon his head a thousandfold.
As though somehow it tickled
him
he broke into a toothless grin—
and laughed aloud to see you
there
tossing sunbeams in the air.

So when it's more than I can
stand
(more exhausting than I planned)
and when I wished you passed
this stage
—this very temper-trying age—
you'll grow up too fast—and
then—
I'll wish to have you back
again!

The Lonely Sailor
ON YOUR OWN AGAIN

On your own again
It's been so long
Always holding onto someone
Something that just wasn't
there
But now you're on your own
again
To face whatever you may
confront
To stand on your own two feet
And to experience what was
meant to be
at least for now . . .
On your own again.

Peggy Sheffield
**GOODBYE WIVES AND
MOTHERS**

Goodbye wives and mothers
You're so obsolete
We no longer need you
To guide our erring feet

You're so ticky tacky
Walking around the house
Picking up the garbage
Looking like a mouse

Pull yourself together
Stop being such a jerk
Go and get your hair done
Get out and go to work

Hey! Where do you think
you're going?
I'm telling you what I think.
What do you mean you're going
out?
There's dishes in the sink!

Hugh Brownlie
**SORRY, BUT I DON'T
UNDERSTAND**

Picasso, your fame has
travelled the world
And travelled the world again.
The critics were swayed
with reason mislaid,
And thrust up a shrine to
your reign.
Your paintings were fresh,
the style a coup,
The folks in the know gasped
aloud.
A rebel had risen to feed
revolution
And dispel a stagnating cloud.
But great as you are, profound
or whatever,

I fear that I've missed what
they've seen.
I like sky at the top, ground
  at the bottom,
With people in between.

Peggy S. Berryhill
LOVE COMPLETE

Soaring high above.
My heart is full of love.

Wings of passion,
From love everlasting.

Dreams of sharing,
A love of caring.

Gently like a morning dew,
My love will be forever new.

J.R. Isaac
A LATE FOGGY NIGHT

It was late in the evening.
My table was in the corner
  near
a window.
I sat looking into the darkness
  outside.
It was a wet and foggy one.
The street was dark and gloomy,
  but for
a light on the corner near the
  cobblestone square.
I stared out the rain-streaked
  window in a misty
dream and watched
people darting by.
It was late evening and the
  fog hung
like honey-dew from the leaves.
From the edge of town a faint
  sound of
church bells filled the air.

Kalyn Gabriel
CAUTIOUS SILENCE

As I walked down the road
On my way to school
A white dog spied upon me.
He watched with much
  caution
As our eyes stared affixedly
I was expecting him to bark
But not once did he utter
He let me pass, though still
  cautious;
Silence had befallen us
And my presence was known
only to him.

Martha E. Najera
COME IN

My body tingles when I hear
  your needs
Chance me to show you
The satisfaction of desire.

Strip your wall down
And enter my door of totality
Forever you are welcomed.

Gertrude Kiefer Heath
SPRING

Spring! How fresh and young
  and daring
Boldly painting the earth a
  shocking green
Drenching perfume throughout
  the trees and flowers
And bursting wildly with total
  newness as yet unseen.

Clifford Love
YOU NEVER TOUCHED US

You never touched us, Dad
You never put your arm
  around us
or held us on your lap
You never used your hand
to trace the profile of our

face
or smooth our hair
Why didn't you touch us, Dad?
Did Grandpa never teach you
  how to touch?
And did he never feel his father's
  touch
while growing up?
You made it difficult
for us to touch
and teach our children how
We missed so much
you and us.

Gretchen B. Powell
DEFEAT

I walked a shore today,
So newly freed from winter's
  vice
The remnants of a hundred,
  howling storms
Lay weakened, battered 'midst
  the
disappearing ice.

My thoughts, strange as it
  seemed,
Were not of coming Spring . . .
But rather of that fleeing,
  former Master's dreams.

How must it feel to be that
  King
Who ruled with iron hand,
Now helpless watch his
  Kingdom melt
In one great rush . . .to run
  away and vanish
in the sand.

Sharon E. Kelley
GRANDMA

My grandma is a person
we all cherish and love
She was given to us
by the Lord above

We don't always tell her
how much we all care
We hope that she knows it
even when we're not there

She's worked hard all her
  life
for the things she has had
She loves us and helps us
through good times and bad

She can be very stubborn
no matter what we may say
Sometimes she'll listen
or go her own way

But we'll always love her
through thick and through
  thin
For she is our grandma
and we are her kin.

And when she is gone
she will be sadly missed
For so many reasons
too numerous to list!

Florence Erisman
STATEN ISLAND'S RAINBOW

I thought as I viewed those
  flowers today
How true the best things in
  life are free.
Just a ferry or bridge ride
  across the bay
To visit Staten Island's gardens
  and lovely spring day.
There may not be a rainbow
  shining in the sky
But there's a rainbow hovering
  over Staten Isle.
It's in the lovely gardens of
  our people there
Whose flowers only with the
  rainbow can compare.

So why not visit Beauty while
  you may
For some of us there might
  not be another Spring day.

Linda A. Hysinger
GOODBYE

I never thought this heart of
  mine
would be this shade of blue.
Never thought I could love
  someone
the way that I love you.
Although you made no
  promises
or even said you cared;
I guess I read between the lines
the words you never shared.
That's the hardest thing to
  accept,
I meant nothing at all!
You didn't care if I got hurt,
I'll bend but never fall.
And that's where you made
  your mistake,
'cause I've got feelings too.
I've put up with a lot of things,
but can't take being used.
I really do care and love you—
probably always will.
I know you don't feel the same
  way,
you don't know how you feel.
So I'll just say goodbye for
  now
and wipe away my tears.
Please remember that I'll love
  you
for the rest of my years.
Goodbye!!!

Margaret-Rose Marek
CHRISTMAS 1980

There is not life enough
To search the past
In anger, misery, and fear
For an elusive joy.
Dwell not in the darkness.
Rather turn a hopeful heart
To one more bright beginning.
Sit not alone memorizing
  sorrow's song.
Get ye up and with some
  companion
Work hard, do good, improve
  your world!
In the doing learn harmony
and find peace to share.

A wrong turning is no grave
  thing
In journeys or in life;
The gravest error is to renounce
  the journey,
To refuse to risk adventure.

J. A. E. Loubere
JAY

Iceblue through the dawn
Dropping into pooled silence
Under the locust tree
Your cry is hunger, rapine,
  scorn
Of the base world that creeps
  beneath the leaves.

Before the sleeping guards
Sense and Expediency muster
  up their arms,
Clamor their orders, marshall
  all their means,
And raise the bastions of dull
  consent
Against the assaults of day—
Your scream
Shears me unshriven from
  the womb of dream.

B. Douglass Lowden
DESTINY

All must suffice
For this moment
As nothing,
Yet all,
Is forever.
Good fortune
Will not fall
Onto my hand
But will,
Instead,
Come within
My grasp.

Marjorie Ellen Waynai Smith
LOVE'S REJECTION

The failure in my heart was
  never detected
Until my love was rejected, by
  you.
There was nothing in Life that
  I wouldn't sacrifice, for You.
Perhaps I loved you too much.
I lived just to be touched, by
  You.
I never thought it was wrong
  to live my whole Life long,
  with You.
But somehow Love was lost.
New pathways were crossed,
  by You.
Now I have known the feeling
of being left alone, by You.
The time is right now, to
  face Life somehow, for Me.
I've got to go on living and
  finally do something, for
  Me.
All of a sudden I've found which
  way in Life that I'm bound,
  for Me.
I've found my new place in
  Life.
Things I want for, I'll strive,
  for Me.
My life now is full.
I have the stamina and pull,
  for Me.
There's so much to face
But I've finally changed my
  Life's pace, for Me.

Joyce A. Garrison
TREE OF LIFE

There once was a tiny seedling
No bigger than a pea.
And when this seedling grew
  and grew
It soon became a tree.
Throughout the years she stood
  so tall,
The biggest and proudest tree
  of all.
In spring she would wear an
  emerald gown.
In autumn she'd add a golden
  crown.
And when her leaves would
  begin to fall,
She was still the happiest of
  them all.
For in her wooden heart she

knew,
Beneath her branches a
seedling grew.

Spiros Aronis
THE VOYAGER

To you, oh, lovely sky,
I am sending you an eagle
a tiny souvenir, reminder
    from Earth
to search inside your bosom
near the end of Sun
to our beloved brothers
a message to deliver:
how we suffer of loneliness
and the mystique of darkness.
We are in need of new sounds
to echo into chaos
from their part or ours
to open all the avenues
and bridge in all the gaps
that keep us apart for centuries.

Donna J. Crenshaw
POETA NASCITUR

It's evident there's talent here
there's simply no dispute . . .
Socially we're maladjusted
and to some it's ill repute . . .
Displaying our creativity
the social elite say they
    understand . . .
That's half a dozen in a million
and twelve on the other
    hand . . .
Time expresses greatness
death merely sanctions truth
    of eons and eras
Creativity is our proof . . .
I know that some will say
my archaism is astute but;
It's evident there's talent
    here
There's simply no dispute.

Mrs. Elizebeth Brunstetter
TOUCH OUR LIVES

Our Dear Father, of our land
Guide us with your mighty
    hand

Give us strength, through
    your power
With each sunrise, sunset
    and hour

Bestow your spirit, upon
    our souls
Plant truth and knowledge,
    into our
lives and goals

And our Dear Father, as each
    day does come and go
Your Mercy, Love and
    Kindness,
    let each
one of us know.

Cheryl Lynne DeBrunl
LATE NIGHT LAMENT

Late at night when the lights
    go out
And no one's around to see
The pain I hold within my

heart
And what it's doing to me
This is the time my feelings
    show
Especially all my fears
All day long I hold them in
But now I shed my tears
To other people I show no
    hurt
To them I have no pain
But they don't see my pillow
Where my tears have made a
    stain
I cry for the memories of long
    ago
When I was always glad
Because with time they passed
    away
And now I'm only sad
So tonight again when the lights
    go out
And everything is still
The hurt and pain will come
    again
As my eyes begin to fill
And I'll cry myself to sleep.

Johnile C. Johnson
EMBRYO

All winter long it lay inside
    cold dark earth, quiescent,
    and felt no urge to stir.
Oval cotyledons, pressed
    together
    tight, sustained it, preventing
    day, prolonging night.
Now within its hardened case,
    it frets itself to toil,
Hurts within the tightened space
    to burst confining soil.
Wayward winds sweep snow
    across
    barren fields; no birds come.
Acid rain falls cold to tell us
    spring is coming late.
The sun is stingy with its kiss,
    but swelled to twice its girth,
The embryo, not knowing
    this, still
    keeps its rendezvous with
    birth.
With a surge, prenatal force
    uncoils a stem umbilical and
Pushes through the parting
    earth
    a single fragile, wrinkled
    leaf
        and points it up.

George N. Argyros
FUTURE CIRCUS

A riot of clowns
amidst a symmetry
of nude Cyprians
riding
a snowfall of horses.
A sense-whipped resurrection
of old sinners
and dead bards.

Winston E. Langley
**A SPIDER AND ITS MARRED
ENCLOSE**

You who join the spheres to
    spheres
Seem nothing take, and yet
    do give,
Most adept of engineers
Who singly toil, who toil alone;
You from whom derived was
    cursed,
Attained for her acumen,
Who do build with skills most
    versed
And do connect what's been
    apart,

Could it be that we're one?
Before our day, across the years
Man again this deed has done:
He's singly sought to merge
    the spheres,
Like yours his has been undone.
And justly earned—such a
    proceed,
Yourselves not bound, others
    enslaved;
While death and corpse
    ruins seed,
You had your aim, you sought
    your take.
Who from self alone do bridge
One hopes we are not one.
Who would all the spheres
    conjoin,
Must from all, with all
    design,
Disenact our former birth
And marred proportions of
    our time.

Lissetta L. Moravec
YOU ARE TO ME

My happiness . . .
My sadness . . .
My fight . . .
My light . . .
My darkness . . .
My world.
And all that is in it
My LOVE.

Ruth C. Blackstock
COCOON

Three minutes remain then
    the appointed time
Her heart beats hard in fear
    dread apprehension
    She is LONELY
The counselor will begin again
    to probe
Go back Go back to sweat
    pain returning
    She is TREMBLING
Leaves torn from trees Winter
    the bitter wind
Layers of living eons peeled
    away
    She is VULNERABLE
Cathedral doors magnetically
    beckon
Creator of cycles changing
    dying Springtime
    She is RADIENT.

Jean S. Kuniega
WASTED TIME

If only one had time to wait
Be a bit more patient
Understanding—hearing all
    that was said
Helping just by being silent.
Do people have such little
    comprehension
Living part of their life with
    a person
Yet somehow missing that
    person altogether.

Kathryn R. Shaver
BEFORE I TOUCH YOU

Before I touch you
    And before you—me,
Tell me, is it because
    You love to crave me
Or you crave to love me?

Sheri Cree Lewis
CRYSTAL RAIN

Drops of rain that fall form
    the curtain of yesterdays.
A time we once shared full
    of crystal feelings .

Feelings so pure and fresh
    that placed a warmth of
    treasure
in our hearts.
Yesterdays encompassed by:
the sizzling touch of your hand,
the whisper of desire in those
    eyes,
and the moments of silence.
Those precious moments cry
    aloud . . .
No more todays,
only yesterdays and wonder.
Drops of water that fall form
    only a puddle now.
We've only the treasure of
    yesterdays
And moments of those drops
    of crystal rain.

Florence E. Lenaway
LISTEN TO THE CHILDREN

Listen to the children,
hear what they've got to say.
Let them know you're there.
Let them know you care.

Listen to the children.
Listen to their song.
Let them know you're near,
Let them know they're dear.

Listen to the children.
Listen to their prayer.
Just hold out your hand,
and let them know it's there.

Elaine Williams
THE LONELY PINE

Above the lonely swale she
    stood
Magnificent, dignified and
    proud
The stately figure reaching high
To touch the floating cloud.

Her gown was flowing white
Shimmering with silver beads
She moved softly to and fro
Swaying gently in the breeze.

Her song was shrill and cold
    and sharp
Like death upon the ocean
    deep
With arms outstretched to
    soothe the wind
Her breath was stilled for
    winter sleep.

C. L. Daniels
WHISPER

Whisper to me softly,
    just what you want to say,
Whisper your emotions,
    in your ever-loving way.
Whisper to me phrases,
    I always love to hear,
Whisper to me, "Darling,
    I'll always love you, dear."
Whisper that you need me,
    as much as I need you,
Whisper that you love me,
    and your love, like mine, is
    true.
Whisper that you want me,
    for as long as the sun may
    shine,
Whisper me the promise,
    that forever you'll be mind.
Whisper that forever,
    you'll want to wear my ring,
And then my love forever,
    you can whisper anything.

William J. Pestinger
OLD MAN CAMP

It's a strange land
one of everything and one of
    nothing
It's a wolf outside and a bear

in the bus
it's tundra desert.
In the summertime it's a sun
that forgets to set
a sky that knows no stars
It's a moose who's lost his way
a man looking for a way.
It.s diamond willow and
finger mountain
but most of all
it's you my child
and that's enough for me.

Alice DeWitt Leapley
ARE YOU READY?

Are you ready to meet your
maker?
Will He take you by the hand?
Will He say, "You did your
best,"
Will He say, "I understand."?
Or will He gently remind us
Of the things we left undone—
A kindly word or some small
deed,
That could have lifted up
someone.
Life is so short as we count
time
That we should use it wise and
well,
For God alone in his wisdom
Knows where in Eternity we
will dwell.
So when life for us is over,
And our work on earth is done,
It's too late to wish we'd done
better,
The last race has just been run.
It's too late to say "I'm sorry,"
It's too late to say "I tried,"
It's too late to reconsider—
God, our fate will now decide.

Eilene Bertsch
THE CITY CHILL

A cry in the night
Unanswered, unclaimed.
A siren ringing cold
Against the murmur of the
rain;
Never silent, never still.

Houses on the street
Side by side.
Full of people that never meet.
Lonely people, broken hearts
Living miles apart
Side by side.

A tear in the eye of a child,
Unseen,
Left alone to dream
Broken dreams.
Rainy days, cold nights.
No one to make it right,
Only dreams.

No where to go to be alone,
Yet no one near to care.
Worried faces, wrinkled brows
Around us everywhere.

Close your eyes against the
sadness,
Turn your back against the
cold,
Let the children cry in darkness
And walk the road alone.

John B. Spiers III
**JET CONTRAILS CROSS THE
FACE OF THE MOON**

Jet contrails
cross the face of the moon,
phantom figures of
prophesied doom,
the eyes of the lost are
always in tune
to the dark world that lurks

behind us.
Shadow dancers
in a fog filled room
are all we are
for minds who've run
from the beasts and
the burdens
they find inside
their dark corner rooms
each morning.
Frosted moonlight
spills in the window,
your breath softly sings
to the pulse in my
throat.
I can't help but wonder,
when you smile in your dreams
why I'm lying here thinking
of madness.

Linda Ann West
A SPECIAL LETTER

Dear Baby To Be,
Even though you're not quite
here,
I already love you.
You are a little dear.

You'll be a bundle of laughs,
And lots of cuddles.
After a while you can help me
make puddles.

We'll have such fun,
Just wait and see.
We can even play with cousin
Anthony!

You have two great parents,
And that you will find,
Is three times better than your
own gold mine.

So stop wasting time and get
yourself here.
I already love you.
Have I made myself clear?

Love,

Puppy.

Carolyn Ann Allen
ONE FADED WORD

While walking down the beach
one day,
Accompanied by birds turning
on their wingtips,
I chanced upon a sandy bottle
of glazed clay
With a weathered cork stopping
its lips.
Out of curiosity I forced the
stopper out.
A tattered sheet of curled
paper fell out onto the shore.
Hurriedly I viewed the note
to cast aside my doubt,
But one faded word "Help"
was all the paper bore.

I know not who is made to
suffer more:
The endangered soul that
sent the plea
Or the one who discovered the
bottle on the shore

And is unable to aid the
helpless left to the fate of
the sea.

Richard Cornali
THE WRITER

I often wonder what it is
That makes me take a pen
And splash my soul across a
page.
What demon drives me?
What happens in that moment
When I lost myself and stand
Suspended
As the words pour out.
The feelings that I started with
are soon drained
And there are words upon
the page.
Words I never knew
Only felt.
As I look upon them now
The silence engulfs me once
again
And I am peaceful for awhile.

Nancy Dige Hedegaard
THE ARTIST OF LOVE

The world is a painting,
A wonder of art,
A collage of its people,
All different and apart.
Yet separate they be,
They're joined all the same,
Each fitting together,
Like pieces of a game.
All forming a unity,
A mixture from above,
By the brush and the palette
Of the Artist of Love.

S. Dewaine Dew
IMAGINATION

Fact of present, future to
ponder;
a mind's delight of dreams and
wonder.
Grandeur, like rain, lightning,
and thunder;
Imagination springs forth, never
holding us under.

To dream the dreams of a
future place;
solving the problems of time
and space.
Healing the despair of the
human race;
Imagination born in boldness,
accomplished with grace.

Dream your dreams, sweet
children of time:
cures will come from the
imagination of mankind.

Katrina Crocheron
A. M.

A purple-pink haze illuminates
the heavens
One by one the stars drift off
to sleep
Tucked gently beneath a
blanket of blue
Venus smiles, greets Apollo
rising steadily
Above the hills, yawning
contentedly, stretching
Forth his arms to embrace
their love-child, Dawn.

Dorothy Lovejoy Burke
SMILE

Are you so busy living
That you never stop to think?
The next thrill isn't everything,
Nor is food and drink.

Stand back and be objective,
Before you lose control.

Learn to live and let live,
It nourishes the soul.

Hold out a willing, helping hand,
Keep a smile upon your face.
Sincerely try to understand
The failings of the human race.

Mamie Ruth Lucid
GIRL, M.D.

In the twilight shines a star
A glowing light above the sea
Alone and small, so high and
far
It dares to shine relentlessly

Down the river, out to sea
A tiny stream can end its run
The little bud becomes a tree
And smallest cloud can hide the
sun

So the maiden fair and bright
Unwavering kept to her way
And like the star that gleams
the night
She dares to shine and light
the day.

Juanita Chandler
THE NOW AND THE HERE

We have but the now
And the now is here
For the dawn may not come on
The morrow.

I've accepted your love
And I'll treasure it dear
Should this day be our last
There's no sorrow

For I've known the warmth
Of your embrace
And the taste of your lips
Sweet and tender

I've known the completion
Of love's ecstasy
For my body and soul
Did surrender

So as I close my eyes
On this wonderful day
Fear I not that the morrow
Draws near

Should it not come my way
I have lived for today
And was thrilled
With the Now and the Here.

Deborah Smith
HURT

You look at me
with fear
in your eyes
like I'm waiting for a chance
to attack you,
maim you for life.

I don't want to hurt you.
How can I hurt
someone
that I love so much,
it hurts.

Valerie Wynne Jones
YOU'RE A FRIEND OF MINE

When the rest of the world has
walked away,
And the sun won't shine and
the skies turn gray,
And your rainbow colors no
longer shine,
Please remember one thing,
you're a friend of mine.

You're someone I love with
all my heart,
You're someone I've cared for
from the start,
There isn't one thing that I
won't do,
Because of the love that I have
for you.

When the path you're on starts
going uphill,
And the dreams you've had you
can't fulfill,
When all of life seems to have
come to an end,
Please remember one thing,
you've got a friend.

Someone that will help you
open each door,
And take you where you've
never been before,
I'll help you find those dreams
in your heart,
Just give me your hand when
you're ready to start.

Hand in hand we'll find the
strength we need,
To help each other both
succeed,
Looking at each other we'll be
able to say,
We've done a beautiful job
with today.

'Cause we've loved each other
another day,
And listened to what each
had to say,
And when we reach our
rainbow's end,
We'll know it's because we
have a friend.

Diana L. Boyce
WHAT IS LIFE?

What is life, I'd like to know,
Is it just the seeds we sow?

Could it be what we think,
the food we eat or the water
we drink?

Who could answer this question
with just one word,
For surely this one word, I've
never heard.

For life is filled up to the brim,
until nothing else can get
within.

It's love, laughter and the
here ever-after.
And it's hope, peace and
another chapter.

Life goes merrily on its own
way,
No matter what we do or say.
So there's no use worrying
about tomorrow,
Because today is today and
another one cannot be
borrowed.

So each day should be spent
with my heart in every
minute of every hour.
So when I look back on
this day I've spent, I'll know
I've used every moment to
the fullest of my power.

Nancy L. Sarver
HE KNOWS

There are times when my mind
is an open book.
Then most anyone can look.
Other times my mind is like
a secret, deep and dark.
Where no other can lark.
Then, only the Lord can read
my mind.
He can see what's in it every
time.
Yes, he knows my present and
past thoughts as well.
Even my future thoughts, He
can tell.
Long before I, He knows them
well.

If I could not speak a word that
could be heard,
His help, I could seek.
It matters not if I speak, He
knows what is
in my heart and mind every
time.
I can keep no secrets from Him.
He has the key to look within.
Remembering this, I'll try
to keep my
thoughts free from sin.

Michael W. Lindley
TOGETHER

Together we can make
the sweet perfume of life
tears and roses and orange
blossoms in the spring.
Together we can take
in the golden sunshine
that parts clouds of strife
knowing the joy it can bring.
Together we can break
all of those memories rife
with deceit and pain knowing
sadness will never cling.
Together we can forsake
the limitations our
life has brought,
Love's unbroken
melody, the song we'll sing.

Esther Fromenko
THE GREATEST

The bell rings! MUHAMMED
ALI,
a great fighter swings
A lower left!
An upper right!
What a fight!

Dancing around . . .
the ring with ease
A smile on his face,
his opponent,
he starts to tease.

Fifteenth round . . .
still on his feet!
He knows that he,
cannot be beat!

Tired—and yet,
he thinks in his mind
I can take, this fight,
one more time.

He yells! to the crowd,
"I am the greatest,
THE GREATEST am I"
Would anyone else,
like to have a try?

Mark G. Bullington
MAGIC

Is there really magic?
Is it often near?
Will we find the things we're
seeking
or will we die in fear?
I look up at the mountain
and the sky of blue
then I do believe in magic
I believe that it is true.

There is magic in a sparkling
spring
with it's hidden bliss

There is magic in a happy smile
There is magic in a kiss
There is magic in your brother
with his outstretched hand
There is magic in the moon
above
and in the beaches timeless
sand.

There is magic in a soaring
eagle
there is magic in a tree
And with all our searching
there is magic in you and me
So do believe in magic
as you gaze at the stars above
And give yourself to others
for I am telling you of love.

Cathy Schultz
I'M ONLY ME

I am what I am, me
And that I shall always be

I shall not change for anyone
Though there may be many to
come.

For how could I live with myself
knowing
That I wasn't truly what I was
showing

I would be a fake
No good for anyone's sake

So I shall stay as I am, and be
as I be
And if you'll love me, you'll
love me for me.

Janice O'Harrow Kindschi
DUSK

A going-out—after supper
with sun sinking in the west
God's sky—filled with colors
The birds—flying to their nest.

There is a sort of a hush
with the folks home from town
out walking after supper
and the sun going down.

A peaceful, quiet time,
Not one soul bickering,
Cows, lowing in the barn,
Birds softly twittering.

Such clucking in the hen house
Roosting chickens—perched up
high
The noises all are muffled
As the sun sinks in the sky.

Not a leaf moves—or stirs
Not a breeze of any kind
As the light leaves the earth
All troubles leave my mind.

Margaret Elaine Moulin
ESSENCE OF FREEDOM

When the hands that hold are
opened,
And let go,
And thought, a blown leaf on
the winds of circumstance
Lies still, and dies untenanted,
So life that sweetly sang within
its veins
New, given back to earth, shall
there
Be fetterless, unriven, free . . .

Judy F. Jones
AMERICA'S HER NAME

A very tired old lady
bows her head in prayer.
She prays for peace and harmony
and strength that she may bear
The daily inner turmoil
that struggles for control;
the heat that burns her crops;
the droughts; the rains; the
cold.

"If I can just survive
a few more years at best,
maybe then, Dear Lord,
I can finally rest.
Each day is such a trial,
Corruption stalks my soul,
but with each day comes hope
that I'll again gain control."

She's fighting hard for freedom—
a symbol of which she's proud.
She may be down for a little
while,
but the sun'll peek through
that cloud!
She's a mighty tough old gal . . .
the world she hopes to tame.
She'll always do us proud . . .
AMERICA'S her name!

Kimberly L. Wartick
**SLAVERY'S INNER-
THOUGHTS**

Am I not a man and brother?
Do I not have a father and
mother?
But, how can this be true,
If I am not treated as an equal
to you?

It doesn't seem right,
I lay awake at night.
Could all this be caused by my
color,
That I should be beaten and
not another?

Someday, maybe, it will end,
Someday, maybe, the rules
will bend.
For, you see, a man needs his
freedom, so dear,
If he is to live happily and
without fear.

Beverly M. Trudell
WHITSUNDAY

In hallows of flame and
withered light came
Within sanctum and winds of
the penitent
Disciples, bare men of foreign
descent—
Reverent eve laden of gold and
red array
Revered in essence of tender
lips that pray
While psalms the thrones
pensive with intent
To sing ashen words, fervors
of relent
Feted the static stars caught
in disarray,

As homily common cord
relates to hearth,
And cloven tongues evolved
tempered breath
To deliver language of nation
and birth
In His Spirit's effused descent
to earth
When men lacked to separate
their God of faith
And needed neither cloth or
bread as wraith.

Grady R. Gibson
JOANIE

Beautiful little and charming
Twinkling eyes and a smile
disarming
Kisses sweet as warm red wine
Our thoughts and souls to
entwine
Brown eyes that create desire
Warm lips whispering words
that inspire
Small hands and a tender
caress
A heart full of love to express.

Lisa M. Nocholas
BOUGHT AND PAID FOR

Your face ran through her mind
in scattered images
of green and blue, and while
she was holding me she was
thinking only of you. Though
I have her body you still
control her mind. She can't
go back to you now, it was
a contract and she signed.

So give up the dreams little
girl, we all grow up
one day. You're mine now and
there's nothing more to say.

And when the party's over,
the players all go home.
Each little King and Queen bee
return to the honey comb.
But you my dear remain here
forever and a day, because
you were bought and paid for,
and that's the way it will stay.

Nancy Elfgen Aud
PROMISING TOMORROWS

When it's cold, colors of gray
And snow has been falling
for hours
Just around the corner, green
grass grows,
And thousands of bright yellow
flowers.

Pick up your pace, look ahead
Turn the corner and face this
endeavor,
Let the fragrance fill your mind,
color your eyes
Under your feet, daisies flourish
forever.

Edward W. Hardgrove
LITTLE CHILD

Little child on your mother's
arm,
Away from danger, safe from
harm.
Born into a world of selfish
lust,
Misguided direction and little
trust.
Safe now it seems at your
mother's breast,
But not always so in life's
quest.
What great things are held for
you by fate,
Bridges to be crossed in search
of state.
So much to explore, lessons
to be learned,
Mistakes to be made, feelings
to concern.
For now small child ease your
heart,
Tomorrow is soon enough for
you to start.
Today is the day to enjoy
youth's prize,
Taste mother's love, open
your eyes.
Rushing to life's eternal
question begins soon enough. . .

E. A. Hughes
ORION

Great hunter of the heavens!
Who is it that you stalk
That lives amid the starry woods
Of your nocturnal walk?

In silence and supremacy
You steal across the sky.
In hunter's gear, you hold no
fear
Of what may hide close by.

Yet, far below, unknown to
you,
You're seen by two who love.
Though far apart, their souls
unite
While watching you above.

Three stars in line that mark
your belt
Give 'way your guise by night.
Two lovers hope and lift
their hearts
'Til morning hides your light.

Sharon Rose Larmour
SILENT CHILD

Oh, Silence still
I hear your tears
I read your mind
I feel your fears

I was once your age
Once upon a time
So long ago
Learning nursery rhymes

But times have changed
Your silence speaks
Subconsciously
You can't be meek

You bear a burden
Ten times your weight
So many choices
Deciding fate

Oh, Silent child
The games you play
Growing up "too" fast
To catch your day

Silent One
What strength you hold
Trying to relate
When people are cold

You see time's hands
As moving much too fast
So much to do
You save the words for last

Though times will change
And I pray they will
You started something
Oh, one so still.

Fia Jane Robbins
AUTUMN'S DEBUT

Windblown, summer parched
leaves
Race down the street;
Crackling the golden
announcement
Beneath stepping feet.

Eloquently, radiently, self-
assuredly
She steps right into place
And plants a cool brisk kiss
Upon her mother's face.

Deborah Lynn Styles
THAT SPECIAL SOMEONE

Problems are around us every
day
Though we don't always
understand
And we go astray
When the world is too
demanding.

We try to find the right solution
But sometimes we are wrong
And we go in the wrong
direction.

But when we are down
There is always one special
someone
Who is always around
To keep us all in one ·
They lift us back up on our
feet
And place us in that right
way
For they know what's
underneath
And they know what to say.

They are always there
To listen to you when there's
no one else
Even down through the years
No one else could replace them.

When you try to say thanks
The words won't come
But they understand
For they are that special
someone.

Blanche C. Scott
EXIT

Life—white snow—came down
and quickly grasped
an outreaching hand—
Dark death, unexpected,
The meeting left me cold—
saddened.
My hand would stay the
revolution of time—
Not so.
The wind swept as if to blow
away the hurt.
My tears are for the birds who
do not sing—
Please God, let peace consume.

Ronnie L. Olson
THE BEST IN LIFE IS FREE

Gather the rays from a hundred
sunsets
Catch the spray of an ocean
tide
Fill your head with the smell
of roses
Fresh and wild on the country
side

Hold a shimmering, crystal rain
drop
Or a frilly flake of falling snow
Grasp the lulling summer
breezes
And the evening stars that hang
so low

Remember the peace of a happy
daydream
Capture the warmth of a
friendly smile
Feel the lift of a word of praise
And find the joy of the second
mile

Then put into storage your
grand collection
Deep in your heart where no
one can see
And engrave forever there the
thought
That the very best in life is
free.

Helen E. Bates
DEATH OF A DREAM

And so, last night, I dug a
little grave
And sadly put my few small
treasures there:
The love that even poets
couldn't save,
The way the wind would
blow across your hair
Your laughter and the way your
lips would feel,
The way our eyes could make
our hearts believe,
The lovely golden hoard we
could not steal,
The headstone says but 'Dreams'
I must not grieve.

Victor Morabito
IN MEMORY FOR TEARS

Woe, woe no more is he
For yesterday was a year of
agony
To a world away he's become
closer to me,
But now I beg a tear
Our love, our love we shared;

. . .as a soul in sojourn transits
take these many prayers
as a thought befits
such sadness comes to clear . . .

Father to the day and friend
to the night
I felt my heart warm as his
wife
And joy—he's closest to Life,
But now I beg a tear
Our love, our love we shared.

Beulah LeFan
THE DREAMER

All day long his thoughts
possess his mind,
His time, his heart, his soul,
his ever being.
He does not act but whiles away
his time
Enveloped in the happiness of
seeing
The product of his dream
before its birth.
The dream remains unborn
without a worth.

Jane Corcoran
SET BACKS

My mind is bothered by the
things I've done.
I have to return to check
them.
A gun, it seems, is shooting off
doubts,
Did I turn off the stove?
Turn on the crock pot?
Leave the iron on, lock the
door?
And endless more.
To these wonders I must
submit,
and make yet another trip.
My time moves hastily,
To the job I must get.
Mistakes, I can't let happen.
But as usual I've lost.
I don't know if the
Meat has been put out to
defrost.

Abigail Hereford
SHARE IN A MIRACLE

The little heart beating softly
Beneath my trembling breast
I want you to be near me
When from labor I shall rest.

Hold my hand and whisper
So faith I shall keep,
As shadows come to darken
When pains are over, and I
sleep.

Lay our child beside me
And the tiny baby's cry
Will take all pain away
And in happiness, I'll sigh.

We'll both gaze together
Upon the face of our Son;
For he will be so precious
Both our hearts have won.

And with you beside me
My heart in sweet contentment;
I am your proud wife,
From Heaven, dear, our Son
will be sent.

Janice Van Dyke
SUNSET

I love a sunset:
It signifies the closing of another
day.

The sun ever so reluctantly
resigns its position as ruler of
the sky,
surrendering only to the splendid
beauty of the moon,
in all of her finery,
complete with stars as the
glittering jewels of her crown.

If there were ever a time
that I could choose one
beautiful sight for all to behold,
it would have to be a sunset;
for its majesty is unsurpassed.

Marcia Krohne
TIME

We loved when we were young,
We loved when we were old.
We made our silent promises
And made some that were told.

Our hearts were bound
together,
Our minds often worked as one.
Together we made our way,
In hard times, and in fun.

Our children shared our lives,
Their dreams as well as ours,
We learned and loved
together,
In reaching for the stars.

With the children gone, and
on their own,
Their exploration of life ahead,
Time was endless, and ours
again,
But we found not much to be
said.

Time passed us by silently,
forgotten our many dreams,
Our promises died, as years
went by;
And we grew old, too quickly
it seems.

And now you lay close to
death,
No fight for life is left.
I hold your hand, wipe your
brow,
But silence is with your last
breath.

Alone now, I have time to
think,
When we were young and
free.
Someday, my love, again we'll
meet,
And together we will be.

Anissa Beare
MY LITTLE SALTY

I have a Shetland pony,
And Salty is her name;
Her coat grows long in the
winter time
And so does her tail and mane.

She talks to me in special ways
In whinnies, snorts and blows;
I've learned the meaning of
each little sound
And whatever I say, she seems
to know.

She's always been my loving
pet
And special friend I'll never
forget;
I always know she'll be waiting
for me
Through thick and thin, she'll
always be.

I wish that every child I know
Could have a pet that they
loved so;
For when my Salty looks at
me
My heart is happy as can be.

Judy Goodson
TRUCKIN' ANGEL

Nights are long and weary
His days are filled with lines
and times
But this lonely cowboy keeps
on rolling
He forgets how and why.
As his body tires
And his eyes begin to close;
In the back of his mind
He finds his sweet repose.

For this trucking cowboy has
His own special angel.
Fantasy brings her
Long flowing hair
With her reassuring smile.
Her arms reach out and hold
him
As his soul is filled with love.

This truckin' angel gives him
His hopes and dreams fulfilled
For she is always with him
Riding the same rough roads
In loving understanding
As they touch and share the
load.

Dorothea Margaret Lane
LOVE AS A ROSE

A rose—it buds—it blooms
Delighting the senses.
It has a rare fragrance. It
stands alone, a thing of beauty.
Then forgotten—no longer
tended. Slowly the
velvety petals fall—one by
one . . .
The lovely flower is dead.

So it is with love, it sparks—
it flames
It is heights of joy and wonder—
mystery and intrigue. But
neglected . . . treated with
indifference, It's dream in ruin
lies
And love—as the flower—dies.

W. Phillip Lyliston
CLOUDS BY NIGHT

A dark vessel
drifts by
on a
changing, ominous sea;
A seahorse
size of ship
and some
swallows
the moon
and metamorphoses,
is a mist,
a swamp:
the sky . . .
is a swamp!

Gretchen Galsterer Free
THE NEW ARCH

The day bled profusely;
It stained the water going down
Behind tentative sandstone—
A rutilant land,
Gravid
And fragile beyond breath.

An age began to loosen,
Slowly at first,
Then gained the orotundity
of earth.
Deep and savage rumblings
growled
Another wrinkle into place.
The water heaved at revelation
of the wound;
A socket, smoking still,
Pulled open by the fracture,
Froze Surprise, as in a lifted
brow

(Or was it Sadness, as in a
downturned mouth?)
The blood ran through the
evening-dark hole,
And spotted an eye upon the
lake,
An eye that winked with the
landslide's waves,
Blinked at the death of an age.

Chandra Jaime
DEATH OF A DREAM

They push their heads above
the earth.
They grow, they bloom,
they dry and crumble into dust
without ever making fruit.

Clouds pass without seeing a
watery drop, plop-plop-plop-

minutes into hours—
hours into days—
days into years—
years become brooks,
echoing to the fallen logs,
"All through the past, all
through tomorrow,
filling your days with trivial
things,
putting aside the things that
are dreams."

Paula L. Wilson
LAST NIGHT

Last night
Lee took me by the hand
All he said was "come on."
We saw the world together
And the moon too!
Up with the stars
The pale moon turned bright
As the orange sun disappeared.
The city lights were bright too!
Everything was beautiful—
Even the "bumpy things" in the
road were beautiful.
The people on the streets,
The hitch-hikers,
The other lovers . . .
the beautiful people.
We putted the coast highway
the beach cities
In their freedom at twilight—
And the ocean came with us
On our ride to nowhere
Except deeper into each other's
hearts . . .
through an ocean of love
. . . then home.

Dee Rowan
THE SPRIG

I brought you a token of
our Saturday love
on sun-warmed dunes with
bright sky above . . .
smell of cool earth . . . fallen
leaves for a bed . . .
golden green leaves for a roof
overhead.
(Out on the highway, cars
rushed by . . . we could have
cared less if they watched—
you and I!)
I brought you a token from
our Saturday cove
found hidden and clinging . . .
still smelling of love.

Charline Owings
AUTUMN

In the wind a sigh is heard,
the soft sweet whistle
of a single bird,
The gentle landing of falling
leaves
The rhythmic swaying,
of barren trees.

The laughs of children
in an open field . . .
Golden grain
the harvest's yield.
A gentle rain
to ease the heat,
A squirrel rises to his feet
hurries to a tree scattering . . .
the fallen leaves.
Summer is behind us now,
The pasture is
without a cow.
The grass has turned
from green to brown.
I turn to find
My way to town . . .
As Autumn settles,
All around.

Susan DeGroat
**ANALYSIS (VIEWED
THROUGH A DIRTY
WINDOW)**

No, it's a crutch.
I must be strong as a person.
I don't hate;
I can love;
I didn't cut myself.

What's that you say?
I hate my mother?
I haven't grieved for her?
I unconsciously don't want
to die?
Hey, Dr. Dick, it's simpler than
that.

You are my father (I
transferred.)
See how much we each hate?
You hate me; I am almost you.
Hate begats hate.
Just like Genesis.

Or God, as I think you are
Who says his mystical chants
And I forget my soul is black,
Forget I am dying,
And lie peacefully on the
couch.

Chris Berns
TWILIGHT

yet
unto another
springtime
when
flowers
burst
the
ground
as snow
were
lingering on—
I shall call to you

"would you sit an hour or so
until my twilight?"

Margaret L. Schroeder
RUNAWAY

Runaway, runaway, runaway
leaves
Over the hills, and prairies wide,
By stony path, forest and grove,
Down to the ocean's wet foamy
tide,
Past mountain, deep valley, and
meadow green,
To sharp rocky cliff, humble
pasture, and stream,
Run evermore onward, oh
friends of the earth,
Evermore onward in search of
a dream,
Leave thy sad worries that
darken thy say
Off to the wind—now safely
behind,
Laugh on the hillsides in
grand jolitry,

Leaving thy sweet treasures
  for others to find,
Runaway, runaway, runaway
  leaves
Weep not in shadows now lost
  to dark night,
Hurry and scurry forever on
  thy way—
Oh hasten and not tarry alone
  in thy flight,
Runaway, runaway, runaway
  leaves
Do not despair from thy
  venturous yearning,
But go find thyself on the
  swift wings of time,
Seek out great truths, and then
  on thy returning
Treasure those great moments
  in grand ecstacy,
Sail with the wind as it gathers
  the sheaves
Over the earth in soft silence
  still
While somberly thus the trees
  sadly grieve,
Seek out great wisdom while
  ye are yet young,
Waste not a moment in
  foolish idle play,
But run while ye can in
  Summer's embrace—
Oh look to tomorrow and not
  to today.
Runaway, runaway, runaway
  leaves!

Sherry J. Stafford
LOVE, MY FRIEND

Never fall in love, my friend,
You see it doesn't pay.
Though it causes broken
  hearts,
It happens every day.
Each time you see him,
Your heart begins to dance.
Your world revolves around
  him,
There's nothing like romance.
You wonder where he is at
  night,
You wonder if he's true.
You see, my friend, you're
  losing him,
And there's nothing you can do.
Love is fun but it means so
  much,
The price you pay is high.
If I had the choice of love or
  death,
I think I'd choose to die.
So they I say;
Don't fall in love,
You'll get hurt before you're
  through,
You see, my friend, I ought
  to know,
I fell in love with you.

Chris Berns
UNTITLED

I would rather be a
thistle, that brushed against
your side in sweet tenderness,
than ever be a thorn
that drew blood
in anguish of my
browning years and brittleness.

Catherine Janssen
A POEM

A poem can paint a picture
  For the eyes that cannot see,
And tell a vivid story
  Of the "now" and "used to
  be."
A poem's words can make you
  cry

Or fill your heart with glee,
Can cheer you when you're
  lonely
And be gracious company.
I'm thankful for fine poets,
  For in me they have aroused
My sense of life's complexities—
  Its sunshine and its clouds.

Pablo R. Padilla
QUIET TEARS

Quiet tears running down my
  being,
like dew falling on the leaves,
soothing the hurt that has
  long been there,
like the whisper of a child,
taking the place of God,
to tell you that He loves you.

Ramon Angel Solis Jr.
KINDNESS

KINDNESS
  in the Heart
    makes tears come apart.
KINDNESS
  in the Air
    fills one with love everywhere.
KINDNESS
  in the Soul
    gives one Patience,
      Understanding and Control.
KINDNESS
  in Others
    creates God's love in Brothers.

Peggy Ellen Gillispie
BLISS

A life of bliss is not a dream
But only harder to achieve.
It takes more work than daily
  life
For it's very hard to banish
  strife.
But banish strife within I shall
For that is part of doing well.
Then outward life won't be so
  hard
And I'll have peace that is not
  married.
A life of bliss I will achieve
And then I can build on my
  dreams.

Anderson H. Hewitt
AMERICAN SUFI

See
  the leaf patterns
    shadowed on the floor
  while wisdom
    speaks of love
  swaying hypnotically
    in the morning breeze
dancing leafy skirts
  against the
  deep blue sky
    hung with
      grand white billows
  of cumulus
    water drops
a fine day
  for getting married
    eating pizza
      or playing dirvish.

Mariella Landers Sprouse
ASPHALT AND CONCRETE

City street so gray and warm;
Take my heart and clinch it
  dear,
Fill my head with thought
  and sound,
Let me see, observing all of
  whom are around.
Vibrant are the lights

reflecting my body's form;
A physique that flows,
  listening only to its own.
Fast is the pace, no-no,
  slithering across this time;
A private world, conceivable
  only if you are aware.

Karen Jean Hatfield
DECLANATION TO DEATH

We pick the flower,
And soon it dies.
Life is gone,
When we choose it . . .
  to be so.

Starr D. Woodall
CAREFREE TREPIDATIONS

When the day comes,
  I believe you will walk
    as quietly out of my life
    as you walked into it;
And that your departure
  will be as silent as the wind
    that touches the mirrored
    surface
    of clouds . . .
Leaving only ripples of
  rememberances.

Pat Crew
VALLEYS OF MY HEART

Do you know how much I
  miss you
When Springtime fills the air?
In every ray of sparkling sun
Your smile is everywhere.

Or is it in the Summer
When blossoms fill the sky
We walked along the singing
  brook
You and Love and I?

Or is it in the still white chill
When Winter shows her face,
You held me in your loving
  arms
In a tender warm embrace?

Or do I miss you most in
  autumn,
When reds and golds abound
And rustling leaves beneath
  our feet
Was a shared and joyous sound?

And now the seasons come and
  go
I walk the earth alone.
In the secret valleys of my
  heart,
You are still my very own.

Jeannette Myers
12:00 HIGH (I WONDER)

we pass the
A-framed houses
nestled in front
of the kite-strewn trees
and behind the
private beaches
with the
not-so-private
lovers,
the tide comes in
and crashes against
the shore.
i stare out
into the blue:
Long Island
is almost hidden
by the fog
the train ambles on,
and you, my love,
massage my feet
ever so . . .
ever so . . .
i wonder how can there

be such
beautiful,
thick woods
reaching out
to the shore?
and i wonder
how long will you,
my love,
keep reaching out
to me?
i wonder.

Keith Hagen
STREETSINGER

The razored street's piston
carves holes into his knee
inserts there pianos
where he can't keep time.

Blooded and weightless
plunges of song strike
airless triphammers
to piano-roll code.

Testing the reflex,
a goosebump ripple
a tightening, drumheaded
unisoned weevil

On his skin stitch by
stitch the rhythm catches
a small crowd weave;
the limp, the limp is catchy.

Elizabeth V. Tompkins
DANDELIONS

If you look at a dandelion as
  a blossom,
And not as a nuisance weed,
You'll find its rich-toned
  yellow,
Magnificent as any flower you've
  ever seen.

It brings forth many virtues we
  hardly ever see,
Greens for our table salads,
Dried roots for our health needs,
Wine from the yellow blossoms,
"Hurrah!" for this wonder weed.

Jocelyn Gessner
HANDLE WITH CARE

I feel brittle in my insecurity,
As transparent as glass
And just as fragile . . .
I am touched by an unkind
  world—
I fall and my mind shatters
And the fragments scatter . . .
So many splinters of glass . . .
All prisms . . .reflecting
  reinbows—
Alone I pick up the pieces
And glue back together my
  soul.

Lori Schreifels
WHAT YOU ARE

Live your life being what you
  are,
not what you are not.
Don't let bad times hold you
  down,
don't let sorrow kick you
  around.
Be happy, be free,
be what you wanna be.
Set a goal but not too high,
all you can do is try.
Don't run too fast,
But don't walk too slow
and don't ever give up
you have to go.
Remember the good times,
  not the bad,
don't go through life being
  sad.
So be what you are,
not what you're not.

Life is too short,
give it a thought!

Janet Lee
ROCKS

Tepid zephyrs from yonder
   hills
Encircle the whole of me,
Mingled with tawny leaves of
   Autumn
Cascading on the surface
of crystaline, churning waters
That tumble gently over blue-
   grey rocks
That know of eons past.
Holding their secrets locked
   inside
Until gentle Spring rains wash
   away
Yet another Winter past.
Angel's tears tenderly siphon
   those secrets
So ferociously held that all
   should know
It was better then than now.

Joyce Coffrin Vincent
DIAMONDS IN THE GRASS

When ever I go for a walk
At noon or late morn in the
   yard
I sit amidst the beauty
The beauty of Diamonds in
   the grass.

The great sparkle of clear
   colors
Red, yellow, green and blue
All twinkling bells amass
The many hues of Diamonds
   in the Grass.

Each dew drop a gift from up
   above
Free to me and for all to enjoy
But most have not the time to
   pass
Except a cheery sparrow amid
   the Diamonds in the Grass.

At the end of a bright sunny
   day
The sparkles disappear
Just waiting for the morning
   sun to shine
And return to all the Diamonds
   in the Grass.

Noel Boyett
LIKE A ROSE

Soft to the touch,
   like a rose.
Sweet to the smell,
   like a rose.
Red as a rose
   when shy,
Beautiful like a rose
   to the eye.

Norma Preisler
COME WALK WITH ME

Come walk with me, the
   spring has come,
The fair flowers bloom in
   parent wood.
We'll gather fragrant garlands
   there;
To deck our childhood home.

When golden days of summer
   come,
We'll wander through the
   fields,
Perhaps we'll find there once
   again,
Our childhood's golden dreams.

When autumn colors light
   the land,
How happily we'll go;
We'll keep in memory all the
   hours
Spent wandering to and fro.

When chilly winds blow down
   the land
To tell us winter comes again—
We'll laughing run together
   through
The whiteness of the falling
   snow.

Oh, sister dear, hold tight my
   hand—
Come now and walk with me.

Elsie Wilson
EXISTENCE

Not one that is
   was before:
   nor shall be,
   the same.

They who were,
   are also,
   but again—
   differently.

None remain unchanged
   but three:
   I am,
   Fish (try Greek)
   and The Comforter.
Agape.

Sherri Aleshire
A SPECIAL PERSON

A special person has entered my
   life,
now I have someone.
He's so kind and generous,
it's hard to believe—he cares
   for me!
He's always sharing things
   with me,
treating me like a person, a
   human being.
He seems to be around when
   I need him most.
When he's not near I always
   take time to say I love him.
I have realized what a friend
   said to me once is true.
"Somewhere out there, a
   special person waits just
   for you."
I am not lonesome anymore;
because this someone is
   always near.
He means a lot to me.
He takes care of me, and loves
   me.
That's why I call him a special
   person.

Marcheta Roth
A CHIME IN WINTER

A gust of wind blows the
   snow sideways
And rings the chime left
   outside since spring.
Brittle, tinkling sounds crack
   the thin ice of silence,
And the chime becomes the
   voice of the wind.

June Decker
MY MOTHER

God gave me a mother so kind
   and so good
Who loved me and taught me
   to do as I should.
She was right there beside me
   in my childhood years.
She fed me and cared for me
   drying my tears.
Through all of my girlhood
   no fear did I know,
For with all of my troubles
   to her I would go.
Then throughout all the years
   as older I grew,
The advice that she gave me was
   so good and true.
The example she set for me
   noble and fine,
That wonderful, patient, kind
   mother of mind.
With my father beside her,
   they sacrificed such
A lot for their children to
   give us so much
For our needs and our comforts,
   the gift of our birth,
The sweet childhood pleasures,
   the things of real worth.
I hope by the things that I say
   and I do
That I will prove worthy, that
   I will be true.
For a wonderful mother who
   showed me the way,
I thank my Father in Heaven
   on this Mother's Day.

Deborah A. Bergen
HUMAN CONDITION

Find me a place to call mine.
I need to have some peace
and to be on my own.
This world moves too fast.
Show me a sign
to show me the way.
Don't want to be by myself
I just want to be alone
Maybe I'll just let it all slip by
Won't even bother asking why
Sounds better all the time
I'll just crawl inside my mind
and say goodbye.

Shirley Kelly
OUR SYSTEM??

I want you to stop and think
'bout our system if you can.
The Government helps the poor
no worry for the rich man;
But between the two of these
stands the middle family,
Who can't qualify for the poor
nor afford the rich man's fee.

If you go to buy a home
you'll hear the banker say,
"You can't have the poor man's
   loan,
and the rich man's you can't
   pay."

It even harms our children
'cause they abide by the rule;
And even tho they're five,
they still can't go to school.
Don't qualify for headstart,
our income's above the rate;
And as for kindergarten,
their birthday's two days late.

Still we have to be content
to live the state we're in;
Because you see our system
was made by our fellow men.

Bart Thackrey
CHILDREN PROVIDE. . .

A reason to live,
Pain to bear,
Love to give,
Happiness to share.

Judith Maher
**EXPATRIATE DEPRESSION
RAMADAN 1980**

I live desert days with women,
   arid, barren hours
   dusty, desolate.
Commissary encounters are
   fruitless;
   vacuum chatter, devoid of
   love—Hoover? How soon?
   Late laundry news needs
   cheer.
I am thirsty
   to stir and be stirred,
   to hear and to be heard.
So I take poems for early tea;
I sip the poets,
   who speak truths and whisper
   why
   and seep softly into my
   parched heart.
Then, quenched, my drenched
   heart
   wrings up tears,
   moisture woefully wasted.
But my thirsty soul, a
   thrifty thistle,
   absorbs tears.
   Hoards them, holds them,
   miserly—
   drops to dole out meagerly
   when I mingle again among
   dry women.

Janet Lynn Olsen
MY PRAYER

Lord, please lead me where my
   heart dares to flow.
Lord, please lead me away from
   the love I let go.
Lord, give me strength to live
   through the pain
Of the love I have lost and the
   one I shall gain.

Lord, grant me Thy wisdom
   Thou hast given you.
Lord, grant me Thy love God
   hast given you too.
Grant me Thy light that's
   shown through your eyes.
Grant me the wings of the
   Peace dove that flies.

Show me the way to find
   goodness and love.
Show me Thy way to get
   peace from above.
Grant me thy wisdom Thou
   sheds on all.
Grant me Thy wisdom to
   follow the call.

Violet Rilkoff
PLASTIC PEOPLE

See the plastic people
file into the room
each one a carbon copy
of the one before.

They titter politely
and tell prim little jokes
hardly funny
but just some noise to fill in
that dreaded silence.

Their tightly drawn mouths
barely move
as they whisper their plastic
   names
Through transparent lips
and flash an almost smile
across saran wrap faces.

Then let their marble eyeballs
glide over you
then turn off their cellophane
   minds
and you're forgotten.

Vicki Clubb
WALK IN BEAUTY

I live near;
He lives far
He brings sunshine
And love to me.

He lives so far
will I ever see him again?

He calls but no words are said—
it is quiet.

I walk to

and from school in a daze.
There is no call,
there is no answer.

One day his shining face
appeared more beautiful
than anything—
it was the magic hour.

The dreams faded away
but the most important one
stayed.

And always a word is said,
the most powerful word
that anyone could ever say—
Love.

Merry M. Warner-Ewald
TRAINING E-MOTION

I've ridden on trains.
Most people on boats, buses,
planes,
But I have ridden trains
For fun mostly
Never any real place to go
Just to stand balancing
With the rhythm of the wheels
And to listen to music
That a train can compose.

But I've ridden on trains
Just to ride wherever
My father rides . . .
For my dad rides trains
And drives trains.

I love trains . . .
   More than that . . .
   I love my dad who drives
   them.

Cindi Hiles
HEAVEN'S NOT SO BAD

Trees dipped in lace
And cotton-candy clouds
Meadow's shiny flowers
With all the rainbow's colors

Tooth fairies, Santa Clauses,
And good little elves
Sprinkle candy and ice creams
Through sugar-coated dreams

Angel wings are dusted
With glimmering sequin beads
As we dance our Father's
ballet
To singing choirs everyday

I miss you Daddy and Mummy
But Heaven's not so bad
So cry no more for me
Cause I'll always love you—
Crissy.

Melecia L. Casabal
**EACH SEASON TELLS A
STORY**

Do you ever wonder
Who makes the seasons
That make us feel different
Outside and within?

Who makes fall or autumn
With cool breeze and gentle
wind?
Who turns the once green leaves
To lovely colors of different
shades?

Who makes the cold winter
And creates longer nights,
shorter days?
Who makes the snowflakes fall
And cover the earth spotless,
clean?

Who makes the snow melt
And lets rain fall in the spring,
And awakens trees to bud
And makes the flowers bloom?

Who makes the warm summer
That helps fruits and grains to
ripen,
And gives the people every
chance
To enjoy the outdoors or
travel?

Each season tells a story
Of Someone greater than you
and me,
He changes the seasons all
year round
For all creatures to enjoy.

Carol Newnum
SHARING

Barefoot and umbrellaed
I hurry down the street
To wake the neighbors
out of sleep.
I feel like Paul Revere
with a message.
How often does it snow in
the San Joaquin?
Little enough to make it
a day to be remembered.
I hope you are revelling in
the sun now
But remember when we shared
such happiness as
a snowy day?
I wish we could have shared
today, together.

Nancy Laird Pendleton
**A LITTLE DRIBBLE IS
BETTER THAN NO DRIBBLE
AT ALL—OR—HOW A LITTLE
LEAK NEVER HURT
ANYONE**

Your love
is a faucet
sometimes
it's off
sometimes
it's on
and
occasionally
it drips . . .
d
 r
  i
   p
    s
     .
      .
       d
        r
         i
          p
           s
            !

Eileen Mary Conlin
THE RESTLESS DREAM

I'm full ready to step on out
of here
I'm full ready and almost half
crazy
I need some time to rest my
mind
And don't you know—You've
got to be your own person
To deny yourself that— You'd
be better off left to die
Been hibernating in the shadow
of another man's life
My bags are all packed and I've
a full tank of gas
Sitting on the edge of my chair
I'm only waiting to hear
They've found a room prepared
for me in the House of
Tranquility
We've just one life time—So
give it all you can
Take pride in yourself
And let all that you meet know
why you came

Just think ahead a ways—If you
think along the lines
If there's another life ahead
of us—? It just can't be the
same
So take to your own mind
crevices and explore
Be a Napoleon of your own
mind as he was of the earth
But keep in mind for all your
years of service
And answering of needs
There's more to life than
breaking your back
For those who do or don't
appreciate
It's time for me to be set free
from the bondage of demand
Yes I'm full ready to step on
out of here
I've word they found a room
prepared for me
In the House of Tranquility
Don't wait for my return—
I'm going where I've never
been
Where time is taken by no
special one
And just let time make its
peace for me
So long my friend.

Kathy Koffel Rober
BECAUSE OF YOU

You have given me a chance to
take
the job—a Mother;
So full the task, yet rich and
fun,
the job—no other.

You labor all day and come
home to me,
your wife—a Mother;
A dad you are, a husband too,
the job
is mine—no other.

A wife I am to you always, and
to
your son—a Mother;
My day does never ever stop,
and yet,
this is my job—none other.

Because of love, and you, my
dear, the task
is mine—a Mother;
To show my love and care for
you both, this task
I want—none other.

Gerald R. Halldorson
EAGLES THREE

Eagles of destruction
hover in clouds above my
head;
Ten million hearts are full of
fear,
ten million are filled with
dread.
The first of the Eagles is hate,
what an insidious evil,
He leads us onto the battlefield
and creates world-wide
upheaval.
On fiery wings comes
propaganda,
to alight and swiftly spread,
Sowing unrest and sorrow,
leaving ten million dead!
Last, but not least of these
messengers,
is the Eagle Power winging.
Everything is consumed in the
holocaust.
Hear the mournful dirges
ringing?
Eagles from hell move up the
cannons,

tis they that supply the lead.
Humanity supplies the
heartaches,
the rows of silent dead.
Beware, oh mighty leaders,
avoid these Eagles Three.
A Nation's destiny is in your
hands.
What will your answer be?
One wrong step will plunge us
on
into war's engulfing lust.
It will turn our land from a
mighty realm
into drifting dust.
If the price of freedom is
sacrifice
we will stain the fields with
red,
But first let us exhaust
arbitration,
we owe it to the dead!

Collette A. Andre
TOGETHER WE'LL STAND

When we first met, our
friendship grew into a
blossoming love
Not like old fairy tales with
bells and sparkling fireworks,
It was purely simple and
beautiful.
Something that formed without
struggle and away from the
devastation of man, and it
was then that . . .

I never gave second thought
to the pains of love,
But now I realize the grief,
something that was so
wonderful can bring.
Every time you enter my mind
a lump the size of an apple
grows in my heart, and my
eyes
tremble with tears like volcanos
aching to erupt
I search through my thoughts
and only find myself falling
deeper into the irksome
pain—I'm trying to forget.
It's like a pit of quicksand, the
more one struggles, the
closer one is to doom.

In the darkness of my mind I
walk alone,
but I see a faint light like a
star in the midnite gloom,
my hopes are up and I feel
your hands gently caressing
me
I hear the words of love that
held us together and that I
cherish so, but . . .then
reality awakes me from my
dreams and I find myself
sadder than the day before.
Staring blankly at an
uncertain future, I realize I
cannot go on living like
this,
Because life without you, is
life without love and life
without love is worse than
no life at all.

You were the spine of my
happiness, my walking
stick
But as they say all good things
must come to an end,
and now I'll try to make it on
my own, but . . .
before we part remember one
thing:
My feelings for you will never
change,

Thank you for all you've done,
Good-bye my friend . . .my
   love.

Sharon Wagner
UNTITLED

You remember his face,
   his walk and his stride.
The way you held hands,
   and walked side by side.
But now you walk alone,
   it's "one" again.
You must go on living,
   it's hard I know.
For one so young,
   just starting your life together.
And now he's gone . . .
   but not for good.
He may not be with you,
   to walk alongside.
But he is not far away
   from you either.
You may not be able to
   reach and touch his arm;
But he's there, even
   though you cannot see him.
He may not answer questions
   you may ask.
But he listens intently,
   for he is not distant.
Perhaps guiding you through
   life,
"Keep of him fond memories."

Gwen A. Solberg
THE DAY I STARTED SCHOOL

All scrubbed and polished,
   fed and dressed,
The rules and regulations
   stressed,
I marched with mother hand
   in hand,
For this was how we had it
   planned,
The day I started school.
Into my mouth my heart had
   leapt,
And in my throat a lump had
   crept,
But mother must have sensed
   my fear,
'cause on her cheek I spied
   a tear,
The day I started school.
And now so many years have
   passed,
But memories will always
   last,
Today I felt my mother's
   fears,
For I have also shed some
   tears,
Today *my* baby started school.

Mary McFarland Vuncannon
MERRY CHRISTMAS, DAD

I'm just a babe . . .
Too young to know how cruel
   the world can be—
Too young to know the pain
   and tears
You've caused my mom and me.
My mom will buy you presents,
   "From your son," I'm sure
   they'll say.
But you'll know that they're
   not from me
That's just a game we play.
I can't say that I miss you—
My life's full of hugs and
   kissing . . .
Mom cries . . .and I can't
   understand

Just what it is she's missing.
She'll tell me all about you
All the good things . . .not the
   bad
She'll tell me how she loved
   you
And the good times that you
   had.
She'll tell me of my sister,
That she's beautiful and kind,
And when I have my facts
   straight, Dad,
I'll make up my own mind.
Yes, I'll make my own
   decision,
Are you bad? or are you good?
Who knows? Perhaps I'll
   understand
What Mommy never could.
You seem to be ashaked to
   be my Dad . . .
And so you run—
So don't be hurt or shocked
If I choose not to be your son.
Oh! And have a Merry
   Christmas, Dad . . .
Be merry while you can—
For someday I'll be what you
   can't—
Someday, I'll be a man.

Cindy Leigh Walker
ON THE EMOTION LOVE

I will clamp you in my fist
   without
The slightest leak in your
   valley of
fingers. I will lay myself on
   your
shelf, dusty or not.
You have contemplated a red
   day of clear
dear sun; attended by the
   flickering of
Your own light.
You do not breathe pain;
What we do with you is all
   our own.
What we do with you
In the name of you. And
Here you come in laps of,
   spoonfuls of
Your priceless breath. Your
   jets of bitter-sweet.
Wreathed in cool red, you lie
   in your
Bed of calm, never stirred,
   never stirred.
Your ruby red drips clean
   and pure.
Let the thin smell of empty
   drip over
You. Let the diciplined heart
   walk
Your heels.
Love, Love, I have hung over
   you roses
To make you thick as blood,
   and permanent
As time. You wear the marriage
   dress of
affection.
You are the one unsealable
   grip.
The solid-maker.
The pure fine bride
   in a rim of white.

Diane Payne
EXPECTANTCY

I was standing there
   watching
   waiting
   hoping.

You were coming towards me
   slowly
   confidently
   promisingly.
We looked at each other
   you winked
   I smiled
   we spoke without words.
In those moments we gazed at
   each other
did you see what I saw?
   the good times we shared
   stolen kisses under the stars
   long afternoon walks in the
   sun
   the "I love yous" spoken a
   dozen times an hour.
Are you remembering as I am?
   sometimes I think so
   always I hope so
But you walk on with only a
   hello.
Will it always be so?

John A. Sikes
BEAUTY

I have seen such beauty
   as my eyes could hold.
And I have felt for it
   before my limbs fell, beside me,
   cold.
Even so, my heart now lies dry
   from a never-ending thirst,
And suffers famine to my soul
   from a hunger ever more
   terse.
Yet memory spares me any
   worse
   heart-felt pains.
For, in my soul is known
   I would suffer myself all these
   strains,
In both body and mind
   for one blessed breath of your
   love.

Jamie Lara Bronstein
OBSERVATIONS

The sky is blue today, bluer
than Indian turquoise spread
   out to
sparkle under the sun
the sun which today is far out
   in
space talking to the black
   nothingness
vastly stretching out kingdoms
   of
black licorice holes
The ground is cold today,
   colder
that ice castles, grinning full
   of
transparent shining fangs
   delicate enough
only to chew on silence and
   open ground
the ground which is lightly
   spread with
snowflakes over layers of
   June's dead
butterflies, snownymphs and
   heavenpearls
wafted down over eons of
   time.
The air is quiet today, quieter
than the eternal gazing green
   deep
fishbowl seas that entrap space
   and
time in coral jungles of broken
   glass
the glass which holds every
   daisy like
the air holds the trees so soft
   and with

a distant breath whispers time
   into forever.

Miss Velma S. Witherbee
GOD'S WORLD

It only takes a little while
To teach ourselves to wear a
   smile;
When things aren't going our
   way
And to learn to bow our heads
   and pray.
And after a while we come to
   know
This world is full of grief and
   woe.
And all that we can do to save
   it,
Is to learn to "GO WITH GOD"
   who gave it.

Dale Farrington
THE HOUSEWIFE'S PLIGHT

A housewife is an unpaid maid,
   with clothes to wash and kids
   to bathe.
Groceries to buy and meals to
   cook,
oops, the baby hurt his foot.
Hon, don't pull your sister's
   hair,
put that down, get out of
   there.
The dog has torn the paper up,
   and now you broke my
   favorite cup.
The phone is ringing, what'll
   happen next,
the teacher said John got an X.
One more time and he'll be
   expelled,
oh my gosh it's the doorbell.
Daddy's home and ready to
   eat,
I just spilled spaghetti on my
   feet.
My hair's a mess, I look a sight,
this, my friend, is a housewife's
   plight.
God's bound to have a special
   place,
for housewives when entering
   those gates.
He'll tell them to rest with no
   more strife,
they worked enough through-
   out their life.

William T. Lucas
FEELINGS

So very deep, my feelings,
man made well could never go
If I could oh, but touch them,
I'd let my spirit go
To drift above the tree tops,
float gently down a stream
Wander in an open field,
to find out what my feelings
   mean
I'd then recall my spirit,
and ask of it, its views
So I may use my feelings,
good things in life to choose.

Celeste Dawn Varney
READY FOR LOVE

I laugh and I cry
I hope and I pray
That today above all other days
Love will appear and take
   me in its arms and say:
It's your turn to give,
It's your turn to love.
But it always seems to say:
Maybe someday but not today.
I wait and I dream of how it

will be . . .
When he comes into my life,
and shows me how wonderful
it is
To give your love to someone
who cares,
to be loved as never before,
To share the good times,
as well as the bad.
But love always seems to say:
Maybe someday but not today.

Lillian Wood Crenshaw
**IN THE SUNSHINE OF
GOD'S LOVE**

Our God will remain always the
same;
His love is unchanging forever.
He will not forsake or let evil
overtake;
He is with us in every endeavor.

We may rise and be strong, for
to God we belong;
the Christ within us gives power
to overcome every ill and to
know the Father's will,
that with joy our lives may
blossom into flower.

In the sunshine of God's love,
we soar and rise above
all that would hinder our climb.
Our eyes fixed on Him, we have
love, intelligence, and vim
to live a life that is holy and
sublime!

Henry M. Grouten
DONNA

Donna
  Sparkling eyes
    Cute, little dimples
      Beautiful, black, curly hair
    Slim, curvacious figure
  Lovely smile
Donna
  Radient charm
    Soft, fine skin
      Soothing, caring, assuring
      voice
    Warm, gentle hands
  Delicate lips
Donna
  Glamorous style
    Shining, amiable personality
      Persistant, strong, persuasive
      mind
    Kind, friendly heart
  Tender kisses
Donna

Amy Sullivan
THREE MAGIC WORDS

Three magic words, I love you,
Three little words, the world's
greatest need,
Food for the heart and soul,
Heavenly music to the ears,
Three little words, three magic
words
We all yearn to hear.

They mend a mother's broken
heart,
Dry a baby's tears,
Make a sad one smile again,
  Dark clouds disappear.
When your phone goes ding-a-
ling,
And you hear your name, your
heart goes zing
It's as if you heard the angels
sing,
Those three magic words, I
love you.

They can be so many things,
A smile, a prayer, a look, a
touch,
And they can do so very much,

When you're sad and blue.
They make a puppy wag his
tail, a kitten purr with glee,
Those three magic words, I
love you.

Judi Morrow
SHADOW OF REALITY

We can go anywhere in our
minds,
so please do not abandon hope.
We may find our images
interlock,
but can I return.
I am lost in you,
not wanting to be found.
A world of our own will be
born,
and together we shall endure.
We will be a shadow of reality.
You speak of desire,
and want to move our love
lightly into fire.
Empathetically we shall merge,
and glide into eternity.
Tenderly our entities unite,
and we become one.
Now the shadow,
a reality.

Dan Williams
LOVE YOU

Staring into space, I imagine
your face;
Feeling close to you in this
place.
Sitting alone upon the sand
of the beach;
Wanting so much, your body
within reach.
Kissing your lips, your skin
of cream;
Touching you, can only be a
dream.
Drowning in this lake, your
life I tried to save;
Crying when I failed, as you
sank beneath a wave.
Missing you my love, with all
my heart;
Dying each day, because we are
apart.

Janine Smith-Barrett
**WHEN CHRIST IS NOT THE
CENTER OF MY LIFE**

When Christ is not the center
of my life
I fail, miserably so,
When Christ is not the center
of my life
I can find no place to go.
When Christ is not the center
of my life
I can find no words to write,
When Christ is not the center
of my life,
I find not courage, but strife.

But when I turn to Him to
read His Word
I find that I, even I will be
heard!

His love does not stop, or falter
or turn
Just because I have not quite
yet learned,
His love is unending, forever
true
Jesus loves me, *much more*
than I knew.

When Christ is not the center
of my heart
I find I'll quit, and yet I know
He'll help me start.
Make Christ the Center of
your life.

Dean Sowder
CHAMPIONS

This statement has been made
many times,
And you will find it to be
quite true;
The worst enemy you will face
in life,
May be none other than you.

Don't doubt your ability to
cope.
With life and all its misgivings;
Remember there is always hope,
And strength to go on with
living.

Believe my friend in yourself,
You can do whatever you
please;
If you can just convince your
self,
You will be able to do it with
ease.

Believing is part of receiving,
Doubters never make the start;
If you expect to reach your
goals,
You must be strong of heart.

There is no room for weakness,
Strong is the name of the game;
Others by struggling have made
it,
You can also do the same.

How do I do it, you ask me?
Face it and go unafraid;
Patience and perseverance will
win for you,
A place where *champions* are
made.

Katherina Gill
DESTINY

Meeting you, was a destiny,
Knowing you, was life itself . . .
Snatching minutes of a
closeness,
On borrowed time,
The Gods have granted
just for us . . .
Away from people,
In the vastness of the fields,
Where the grass is so green,
And the wheat so ripe
Where the clouds sail above us,
Where the time stands still . . .
With no cares, like children,
We have wandered through the
days,
With a laughter, and Love . . .
We have played, as We have
lived.
If weary, we lay to rest and
sleep,
Where the sky watched above
us
And sent the sun, so warm . . .
just for us . . .
And when we watched the
ocean,
And the waves so calm . . .
As we walked together

With no shoes upon the moisty
sand,
We have left the imprints
of feet, of yours and mine . . .
  The minutes, hours, days
  have gone
Where you were mine,
and happiness, we held of bliss
But destiny, of our life
Has taken other turn,
We are no longer lovers,
There is no turning back
The memories of the past,
Just shadows of love
  We had once . . .

Phillippa T. Mignott
MY LOVE

I want to tell you how I really
feel
But when I see you I can't
speak
Your dark eyes look into mine,
Searching
And I wonder if we are both
searching
For the same feelings
We might be sharing inside.

I wish I could touch you
Touch your face
Place my hands in yours
Put my hands in your hair
To feel the difference of you.

I want to tell you
But I don't want to scare you
away.
How will I know your feelings?
How will you know mine?
And will your dark eyes
Continue to search
Searching into mine?

Ms. Keni Woodruff
**TO MY FRIEND . . .
ON THE DEATH OF HER
SISTER**

Life is a frail bird
Stopping briefly on its
fluttering journey.
A flash of color in a clear sky
A swooping blur against the
sun.

It is a moment of song in the
morning,
A rush of wings in the
afternoon.

It is quickly gone
Leaving a memory of music
In the minds of those
Who heard its too-quick lyric.

Susan Marie Hyde
UNSHED TEARS

Moon of silver, moon of gold,
Sightless orb that must cry
For men's dreams left untold—
Passion's rages turned to sighs
As we hide our heart's desire,
From our hopes, from our
fears,
Quench the all-consuming fire—
Drown it in our unshed tears.

Wendy A. Urban
UNTITLED

eatin' sand
watchin' the waves at my feet
and wishin'
you
    hadn't washed away so soon

Carolyn Draper
NO TEARFUL GOOD-BYES

I found you
in the time of my life
when I really needed someone.

And You've given to me
no tearful good-byes
but many a shining sun.
And I'll always be grateful
just to have known you
and to have seen your beautiful
smile.
And no matter what happens
believe me it's true—
I'll love you for more than
a while!

Christine Lynn Stanton
MY TEDDY BEAR

This teddy bear
was his
now it's mine.
Cute and cuddly
but it's not pretend
Always smiles on its face
there are
which make up for the others
lost.
Already named and grown-up
doesn't have to learn.
Never thinks, never does,
wasn't real, it never was.

Donna M. McKay
YOUR SPIRIT LIVES

Gazing at the flaming fire
burning
In the fireplace, my mind
drifts to
Another time in life. A time
that
Brings us together like we used
to be.
I remember most of all the
good times
And much less of the bad times.
I can see you.
The way you were. And I can
See you in me.
If only you could see the love
and
Happiness which has filled my
life.
To walk into my house and feel
the
Love that reaches out and
touches
You, as you walk through the
door.
And as the warm glow of the
fire dies,
I can see the
Life you gave me.
The sensitivity of well-being and
Knowing you are still part of
my
Life, even though you may
never
Physically enter my house or
life
Now or in the future. I know
you
Are present in me, within my
heart.
And you were right when you
once
Said your spirit would always
be.
I love you, Dad,
And I remember.

Mary M. Gillespie
NORMA JANE

First thing I hear in the early
morn
Are the roosters crowing in the
barn.
Mitzie whining and scratching
fleas;

Mom scrubbing on her knees.
The cat sitting on the window
sill;
Daddy leaving for the mill.
David crying in his bed;
Duster falling on her head.
Brother dreaming of Violet
sweet;
Tony eating shredded wheat.
Irma trying to scramble eggs,
Aunt Grace complaining of
her legs.
Our neighbor calling, "Come,
Boss,"
Mr. Frank riding by on his
hoss.
The bus goes whizzing by,
All the people riding high.
By then, I'm wide awake,
Waiting for my Johnny-cake.
That's how it is at our house,
So early in the morn.
Gee, I'm so glad I was born.

Patricia Diane Bell
NO GOODBYES

The day was cold and time stood
still
when I realized it was time for
you to leave.
Now the days are rather long
and I am quite sad,
I sit wondering if you will ever
come back!

Catherine Avery
CHERISH

He was born twenty-one years
ago,
I remember the very day.
The doctor came out to check
on him,
We lived too far away.
He was just like any other child,
No one could have loved him
so.
He was his father made over,
But his father was never to
know.
His father would have loved
him,
If only he could have been
here.
He'd always wanted a baby boy,
That he could hold so dear.
That was twenty-one years ago
today,
And I just got a call.
Mike's medals are on their way,
They said he gave his all.
You know he never saw his
father,
But they were just alike.
His father would have been
proud,
If he could have just seen Mike.
Five months before Mike was
born,
His father was killed in the
war.
He was constantly wondering,
If he should go into the corps.
Now they are both dead,
And I now have but one wish.
That someday I will join,
The men I greatly cherish.

Ray A. Conner
ONLY MY PRAYER

Thank you for life, O God
Thank you for me being me
Thank you God,
For setting me free.

God, there is only one
Thank you for being who you
are
Lord, I will try my best
To live up to par.
Oh kind and loving Father
Let me try to please you in
every way.
Let me be one of your children
Let me see things clearly day
to day.
O Heavenly Father
Let me bring joy to all
And when I have done the
things you've wanted
Let me then come to your call.

Tammy Simpson
BLOSSOMING LOVE

A new friendship blossoms into
a sweet sweet love.
A love sought
A love found
A love shared
And a love that like God will
endure forever.

Dee Ellen Armstrong
REALITY

Pass swiftly,
vain and
shallow play
called "life,"
that I
may begin
to live
REALITY!

Doyal Wayne Taylor
OTHERS

The wind brought forth the
morning freshness.
The sun brought forth the
warmth of God's love.
The birds sang out to break
the silence
As the day shows forth the
truth in God's word.
To watch this world go round
and round.
To feel the rain as it comes
down.
To see the growth in one new
found
As we gather jewels for our
heavenly crown.
Draw nigh unto God to know
of his power.
Pray without ceasing for others
their soul.
Pray that your rain might be
heavenly showers
That your works might prove
more precious than gold.

Mrs. Mary M. Mobley
**BELIEVE ME DEAR JESUS
I LOVE YOU**

Hark, hear the angels singing
Hark, hear the trumpets in
the band
Hark, hear the heavenly choir
singing
Listen, and you can hear it
all over this land
To me it brings a message from
above
So dear Jesus, let me tell you
of my love.
Believe me, Dear Jesus, I love
you
Please release me from these
heavy burdens I bear
Believe me, Dear Jesus, hear
me when I say
I will pray to be in your heaven

your wonderful heaven, some
day
Oh, Believe me, Dear Jesus, I
love you
Just believe me and I will love
you always.
The golden sun is sinking in the
west
And here I sit, with my precious
bible on my knees
It will soon be time to close
my eyes in sleep
But not before I pray, Dear
Jesus, to you
Believe me, Dear Jesus, I love
you
Please believe me, for I truly
do.

Bonnie Noreen Phelps
UNTITLED

Soft kisses breathe
murmured messages
of *oh*
and ache of awe
in ecstacy of each.

Debi Gennaro
THREE DAYS LATER

The tall green grasses that once
swayed freely
are now trampled.
Along the shore I can see a
thousand
footprints from spectators.
I wasn't one.
I can see the sun reflecting a
piece of chrome.
It's her bike.
I can't understand why it hasn't
been taken away.
Three days ago her body was
removed from the depths.
As I look across the dark
muddy water,
I am overcome with a feeling
of lonliness.
Memories of our friendship
flash before me.
I loved her.

Debra Lynn Liebeskind
A FAREWELL TO MY LOVE

Our love is forever eternal
I'm yours for always and you
are always mine
Remember me for I shan't
forget you
I shall wait for you because
I LOVE YOU
You are my one and only
for now and forever
Goodbye, Good luck and may
"GOD" be with you.

Janet Phelps
THE ANSWER

The answer
to a question never asked,
To what the future is
and what was the past?

The question in mind
you know not what it is,
But still you search for it
'cause you know what the
answer is.
Will you find it in time
to save those who need you,
Sometimes you will
but sometimes, you're late too.
Why does this question haunt
me?
Why can't it leave me be?
I know the answer,
The answer is . . .
to exist.

Mig Carlson
ANILLO

the circle comes full . . .
hurt
anger
rage
and softening back
to
loving
you
the
same . . .

Wilma Scott
MAD DOG!

Breaks breathless air
shambles heavily
sick
through heat curtains
fever fed furnaces
flare
in eyes dulled
by the scorch.
Fear shimmers
in slow motion
runs
from curses
frothing through clenched teeth
and spit
upon the lethargy
of too many midday suns.

Rosie Dubuisson
MY IMMACULATE MARY

I have a mother
Who is shared by all,
Christ was the first child
As I recall.
She is a mother to millions,
Yet a Virgin she be.
But with all of her children
Not a grandmother is she.
Merciful, gentle and kind,
She guides me from above,
And keeps me close to her
heart
With her sweet smile of love.
A Virgin Mother, a Glorious
Queen,
A lady of the Rosary.
My mother is all of these,
Her name is Immaculate Mary.
I will not meet my mother
Until in heaven I be,
There I will share her love
Forever through eternity.

Geraldine G. Pry
THE BEAUTITION

There was a man, a nice man,
Who I happened to meet by
chance.
He did His work well and tried
His best to please,
All those that were His, His
Clientele.
He was lied to, and ridiculed,
for sure,
But, His work He continued to
do well.

He held up His head and
laughed
As He put "Beauty"on the heads
of many
Yes, have you guessed, He was
the man,
With skill at his fingertips, a
witty tongue and a devilish
grin,
As He was known by many,
My "Beautition." who put
Beauty in my Hair.

Debbie Jones
UNTITLED

The first time I saw you,
I felt that I had loved you
all my life.
And now that I need you,
I know I'll love you the rest
of my days and nights.
In the very beginning,
You were just a game for me
to play.
But that soon changed,
And I began to take you more
seriously.
You gave me a lot of happiness,
You then gave me discontent.
Everybody said "Forget him,"
I smile and silently laugh at
their statement.
My life began to look clearer,
Enough to see where we were
going.
I start to believe we could go
anywhere,
All because your feelings for
me are really showing.
You make all my dreams come
true,
With every touch and kiss.
I think, "Do I really love him?"
Yes, because only love can
hurt like this!

Lisa Renee Fee
FOOLS OF GOLD

Fallen dreams of castle walls
Set in modesty.
Put in position of knighting men
The realm of dynasty.
Set forth approval of an aging
heir
Passed by the local peasant.
"And who are you to be near
me?"
Said rich to poor in much
resent.
Pushed aside in a single glance
The wicked fools of gold,
Who stole the rags of a dying
man
For the stories that he had
told.
And as they strode off on
golden horses
The peasants forced to bow,
While looking through their
empty eyes
They smiled and laughed
out loud.

Norma N. Jacks
A SPECIAL KIND OF MAN

My dad-in-law is a mailman,
he's a
Rare and special kind;
You see he's on the Star Rt.
Plan,
And one of the best you'll
ever find.
He started out in his younger
day
Ridin' horseback through the
hills

With very little pay; you may
think
Carrying mail was his only
chore,
But he also delivered groceries,
And did much more.
Whenever he found someone
sick or
Down and out, he didn't have
an ole
C. B. just to give a shout, he
always
Took the time to lend a
helping hand;
You see, he's kinda like a legend
in
This land, for on the hearts of
many people,
He sure has left his brand;
I'm sure they would walk
many a mile
Just to shake his hand.

Susan Sills Williams
INJUSTICE

It slumbers heavily at my side
when I sleep
It shades the new morning sun
when I awake
It randomly colors
the images I perceive
It questions the validity
of what I believe.
It demands patience
when disruption prevails
It asks for time
when endings abound
It delays understanding
when confusion reigns
It preaches transcendence
when reserve strength wanes.

Richard J. Kabat
MAJESTY

Ah, the majesty of a mountain
top glistening in the sun.
Birds fly carrying no cares or
worries.
Trees sway to the music of
a rhythmic breeze.
All the world seems to be at
ease.
The whisper of a far-off
waterfall lets all know of its
presence.
Deer stroll through their
backyard.
Listen to the call of some
high-flying geese.
All the world seems to be at
peace.
A gentle rain of starlight falls
silently.
Mr. Moon is out for his nightly
walk.
Night-time clouds dance for the
spectators below.
All the world seems to be aglow.
And I, under this friendly tree,
watch the order of the
Creation.
Its majesty, its music, is

something to behold.
More plentiful than water.
More precious than gold.

Pamela Junkin
DEPARTING J. R.

To have touched
the day with sunlight,
To have met
your warm smile,
Makes me happy . . .
And anxious for another day!

Nancy Lyman Stuart
THE SLAUGHTER BEGINS

Once in peace and solitude you
roamed the unspoiled sea.
Gentle creature, unafraid you
had no enemy.
Then they came—harpoons in
hand,
In sailing vessels, built on land.
The waters blackened with
your blood.
In fear you struggled—fought
for life,
Fought against humanity,
Who tried to take you from
the sea.
With one last surge, one final
breath,
In agony you met your death.
Your ravenged body towed to
coastal town.
Where men would boast,
"We've brought the great whale
down."

Marie A. Knudson
MYSTERY BOOK GAME

In my chair on a misty night,
before the fiery flames so
bright.
No one I hear, no one I see,
only the mystery book and me.
Weird figures before my eyes,
mysteries, shadows yonder lie.
The wind whistling through
the pines,
send icy fingers up my spine.
A figure lurches near my chair,
I grab, I reach, it's only air.
The mind plays such silly games
when books do have a mystery
name.

Holly Carol Decker
SOFT

Soft
is hard
to imagine
if you've
never yielded
to yourself
a tender
moment
of devotion.

Dorothy H. Murray
WISHING WELL

Age is like an old oaken bucket
Overflowing with love of the
past
It touches each friend and loved
one,
Overburdening a heart that
won't last.

Connie J. Copeland
THE CYCLE

As in life there is no life,
And in death there is no death,
So we were born to live and die,
So we were born to be born
again.
And mockery and skepticism

Are part of our daily routine;
And there is not one of us
Who does not partake
In this degradation
Of human nature and spirit.

For our minds are lost
In a sea of confusion,
And our emotions
Overtake our ability to reason.

And we are afloat
On a sea of fantasy,
And reality's long, cold fingers
Reach from the depths
Of our misty-like dream.

And we live,
And we die,
And we are born again.
For the cycle never stops,
And our spirits never cease
To wander.

Victoria Parker
A MYSTERY STORY

Two portraits in the attic
The artist had stashed them
   away
Neither could be completed
The models had vanished, they
   say

Both subjects were young and
   handsome
He'd captured the light in their
   eyes
Sketches were there, the cut of
   the hair
Two innocent looks of surprise.

The artist went on painting
   others
As the portraits-to-be gathered
   dust
In their corner in the attic
Where odds and ends were
   thrust

Occasionally he'd remember
"I'll superimpose some day
For what I saw in those faces
Is too precious to throw away."

Then one day many years later
The artist uncovered the pair
"Here are those unfinished
   portraits."
He sighed as he dusted with
   care.

Then he stared at them in
   amazement
For the subjects were wrinkled
   and grey
And painted in perfect pastel
Smiled out at their artist that
   day!

Melissa Marie Murzyn
**COMING OUT OF THE
DARKNESS**

When you're so angry
And feel so alone
When nobody cares
Answers are unknown.

Your anger seeps out
Tears spill over your cheek
Your chin begins to waver
Where's the knowledge you seek?

You feel so unwanted
It hurts your insides
Your emotions tremble
Like thundering tides.

Alone in this world
Which is a pretty big place
You feel so small, and
Can't keep up with its pace.

Should you crawl in a hole
Somewhere and hide?
Or should you make peace
With the rumbling tide?

Forgive and forget
That's what they all say
But should you listen
Or go your own way?

Time will heal
All that's been hurt
But it's hard to forgive
When you're treated like dirt.

Your world fell in pieces
But can you put it back?
Together like it was?
And with feelings it lacked?

You'll fix up your world
Put it all back together
Patch up the holes
Now it will weather.

Put your anger away
And give it a try
The clouds will disappear
And you'll see the sky!

Carol Jeanne Hagan
WORDS

words
reaching out
not to comfort
but to hurt
to mock
and
abuse
beating you down
lower
and
lower
until
you
crumble
to
the
floor
broken
empty
rejected.

Pamela K. Garland
IMAGES OF WEAPONRY

You said you would be
   destructive
in a relationship
like a wet little boy with
   ammunition
in a bathtub
shooting toy ships and Ivory
   bars
in a confined area of porcelain

Oh my love I promised a heap
in this relationship I'd never
   leave
like a devoted nun with a
   chapel of penance
in a church courtyard
weaving baskets for the church
   bazaar
in a cake-walk of your pride.

Rich Corvin
ETERNITY

I walked along the shore one
   night,
Oh, what an outstanding sight;
The tide was in—the birds were
   round,

It made me feel like lying down
And feeling the breeze upon
   my face
Stirring within this resplendent
   place.
With the wink of a star, I could
   see
The Creator in His eternity.

Linda LaRae Oliver
HAPPINESS TO HAPPINESS

I'd like to have a memory
   of life.
I'd like to leave a smile
   after life is gone.
I'd like to have an echo
   in memories of me.
I'd like the tears of them who
   grieve to dry under the sun.
I'd like to leave memories
   after life is gone.

Karen Bassingthwaite
YOUR TOMORROW

Should I enthrall
a captive plan?
but who shall see it through
for if I fail
my plan—it's dead
and only I shall know,
so ha for life
and ho for death
when narrow is the gap
that separates a man from thus
and thus from what he knows.

Ana Teresa Maidique
I SURRENDER

I was
merely
being
Sarcastic!
It was just a
joke!
Don't be mad,
I just can't take it—
your being mad,
I mean.
I love you too much
to see you unhappy.

Lorene Perrin
THE STEEPLE

I open my curtains
and my eyes search—
For the steeple
on the little country church.
It's just across the road, down
   my way,
and is my inspiration to start
   a new day.
The cross I see in the early
   morning light,
and again as the sun sets into
   dusky night.
I close my eyes and still see
   it there,
the steeple reaching upward in
   the still night air.
A symbol of strength, it speaks
   of God's love,
as it reaches upward—beyond
   and above.
Now it's morning again—
my opening eyes search—
God bless the steeple
on the little country church.

Peggy DeShields
MODERN COWBOY

Green was the grass and cattle
   herds grew
Auctions were crowded with
   buyers who knew
That profits could be made by
   more than a few
Part-time ranchers

Costs of supplies were out-of-
   sight,
But prices for beef made all
   that right
Until imports and shortages
   caused a plight
For the cattlemen

He loved his Stetson and
   cowboy boots, but no pay
Meant selling his cattle and
   all his hay—
Just too much work and all
   those problems in the way
For the Drugstore Cowboy!

Mary Jo Lakatos
KEEP 'EM FLYING

KEEP 'EM FLYING
   Husband—Brother—Sweetheart
   Friend
KEEP 'EM FLYING
Ours the victory to the end.
KEEP 'EM FLYING
For the freedom we all deserve,
Three cheers and Hurrah for
   the boys who serve.
KEEP 'EM FLYING
   We shall win o'er every foe
   Anarchy and oppression then
   will go!
KEEP 'EM FLYING
   For the gallant Red, White
   and Blue
   Victory for everyone: for
   me and you.
KEEP 'EM FLYING
for the country we all love
We have guidance from above.
KEEP 'EM FLYING
   Carry the torch for very high
   Never let its bright flame die:
KEEP 'EM FLYING
   Through ages past and those
   to come,
   Ours the glory forever won,
SO FIGHT ON—to the setting
   sun.

Mary Anne Atkins
REJUVENATION

Ancient willows,
long frozen in grotesque
   bareness
against the wintry sky,
Gratefully drape April's
   greenery
to hide their twisted limbs
And, taking on the air of
   youth,
dance lightly to the music
   of the breeze.

Marilyn A. Hilyard
MY SON (FOR DANNY)

Oh, the miracle of you
Coming to me
Straight from God
For me to see . . .
Just like a flower
Born in the spring,
The wonder of you
Made my mind spin . . .
Little and perfect,
Pink and so fair,
You entered my heart
And stayed there . . .
The joy and love
In watching you grow
Was a gift from God
For me to behold . . .
You filled me with love
In your little boy ways,
With compassion and kindness
Shown all through your days . . .
You grew up tall,
So handsome and proud,
Your love surrounding me
Like a hovering cloud . . .

I know you are happy
And at peace, my Son,
Because you're with God,
The merciful One . . .
But my loneliness without you
Will never end,
Until God in his wisdom
Joins us again.

Harold A. Seward
MY DREAM

It came upon me as I lay asleep.
A real feeling then over me did
  creep.
I saw a vision of loveliness
  there.
She was just sitting in my
  bedroom chair.
The golden hair, the noble
  brow, the face
Did seem to fill with loveliness
  the place.
I drew closer to this vision of
  joy;
I knelt before her like a little
  boy.
I stroked her hair, her cheek,
  and then I saw
That she was looking at me
  in great awe.
Then I trembled and my dream
  slid away.
I sat upright in the bright light
  of day.
Then I looked for my dream
  girl in the chair.
There sat my sister's doll with
  her cute stare.

Robert J. Edkins
UNTITLED

I love you, my friend,
for reasons clear and obvious,
And for reasons that are
  locked
in my mind;
Fantasies of things that will
  never be,
As both of us must travel
  our own paths,
And go our own way.
And as we are separated, my
  friend,
My love will never desert you.
My thoughts of you will
  follow you
wherever your road winds,
Hoping that your goals,
  dreams and wants,
Are fulfilled to your satisfaction
For a complete life.
When in despair, my friend,
Don't hesitate to think of me,
Or call my name,
  for I'll come as needed.
Don't have thoughts of
  misgiving,
For you will always be my
  friend,
And very dear to me.

Leslie Ann Fry
**THE VIEW FROM MY
WINDOW**

The view from my window, is
  plain to see
I look out, and what I see is a
  tree.
With roots reaching down for
  hundreds of years
And sprouting anew, as each
  Spring nears.
At it's base, a big thick trunk
That always sways with the
  wind, like some old drunk.
It stretches up, and branches
  out

Reaching for the sun, there is
  no doubt.
But then, the beauty of it's
  leaves
Turn from greens to golds, as
  Summer recedes.
Then Fall begins to start the
  sleep
Through the winter, when the
  snow is deep.
The leaves drop off, the branches
  are bare
The homes of the birds can be
  seen there.
A tree—is beautiful to me.

R. Lise Fradette
WORDS

big words and fancey phrases
  come from a script
    . . .and are read.
three small but meaningful words
  come from the heart,
    . . .and are meant.
  i love you.

Linda E. Knight Gould
A NEVER FORGOTTEN YOU

Love is pain and feeling blue,
It's heartache because I can't
  have you,
Love is tears and sleepless
  nights,
It's always having you in sight,
I hear your voice though you're
  not here,
I feel your touch though you're
  not near,
I dream of you when wide
  awake,
My dreams of you are no
  mistake,
I see your lips in the morning
  dew,
I feel your breath in the wind
  so new,
I see your smile in the moon
  above,
Oh, how I wish I could share
  this love.
I see your thoughts in the
  leaves that fall,
I hear your voice in the birds
  that call,
Like taps of cool rain on the
  sidewalk below,
Are the sounds of your
  footsteps I know, I know.
I see your face in the sky so
  blue,
Oh why, Oh why, can't I have
  you?
I know the answer deep down
  inside,
That's why these feelings for
  you I hide,
And though I know it can
  never be,
This love will always stay with
  me,
And when I see you from afar,
I'll remember all the
  wonderful things you are,
And through the tears that're
  in my eyes,
I'll keep on asking, "Oh, why
  can't I?"

Bruce Woodhams
THE MIRROR

Now retired from the storm
is a man without a home
all his children gone to play
he sits to grasp the bone
the bone he's had from long
  ago
the spoils of the game

now the men who walk about
fail to call his name
is this man forgotten
or just a king unknown?
the wheel surely came to him
but his seeds are left unsewn.
He's just a mirror of us all.

Debra D. Hicks
ACAPULCO

Smiles—we met
A night we spent together
The beach—the sand
A woman—a man
Many days-some sun—some rain
Somehow my life is not the
  same
Flutters my chest—you know
  the rest
Thoughts—alone
Then rings the phone
Smiles—we've met
I've lost a bet or two
I feel I'm falling—deep
And now I sleep—without you
Flutters my chest—you alone
  know the rest
Is that the phone?

Berniece Boylan
TOMORROWS

Tomorrow may never be the
  tomorrow we waited for.
The change of pace—the
  change of times
May find us caught up more
  and more.
We may not need or want what
  we find.
Our greatest wish could come
  and go
And we could overlook it and
  never know.
So the tomorrows we dream and
  can hardly wait to come
May have already been here
  and gone.
Our foolish dreams and wishes
  too
For years and years a fantasy
  gone by.
For what really has changed
  is you.
We finally realize our dreams
  will not come true.
And what we waited for, so
  long ago
Our precious tomorrows, we
  will never know.

Sheila Kay Mort
GOALS

A goal:
A star high up in the sky,
A trecherously steep climb
A long and winding road . . .
My goal:
To be someone special to you,
To be respected by all,
To be happy.
The final goal:
To achieve oneness with your
  self,
To have lived your life in full,
To be accepted entrance to
  Heaven.

Bruce Woods Patterson
HUDSON AND PERRY

I'm looking for love but you
  will do
As shallow night gives way to
  morn,
This cruel light, this bitter hue,
Reveal a hope hopelessly worn.
And I am not who you had in
  mind
Before you turned on down

this street,
But open bars are hard to
  find
So late, so late it is we meet.
The cold has cut the small talk
  short,
Tomorrow is well under way,
And though I'm not the
  stalling sort,
I haven't finished yesterday.
So who lives closer, you or me,
And who is watching, and who
  cares,
For afterwards we'll sleep until
  three
And catch the evening unawares.

Joan Carol Milano
CHANCE MEETING

Eyes meet in a mirror
hands move in a gesture
of an innocent wave

Don't turn around
no one must know
that we were lovers
sometime ago

Horns honk in aggrivated
  impatience
as traffic moves on.

Donna M. Eustachewich
TO YOU, MY FRIEND

You're there when I need you,
When I laugh or I cry;
Your shoulder is there for
  comfort,
When difficult times come by.
You guide me,
Sometimes stop me
  from doing crazy things . . .
I feel you will always be there,
To love and to care.
And, in return, I will offer my
  assistance.
I will bear that comforting
  shoulder
for you to lean on:
I will care, and I will love,
For you have always been so
  very special to me . . .
You have been a friend.

Jeanne Kalben
WAITING TIME

Into the sea, I cast a pebble
like so many pennies in a
  wishing well.
A candle left lit in a corner
  window
always knowing that
  time
    will
      tell.

So it is between you and me,
though distance apart, I wait
  patiently
for a sign, perhaps a letter . . .
truly,
  love is
    a noble
      endeavor!
And as I wander aimlessly on

often I wonder where you have
gone?
feeling the fangs of this empty
reach
as I walk along this
lonely
lonely
beach.

Terry Yandell—Ty
JUST PINT-SIZED

Little blond dog
as cute as can be.
Used to be tiny
But now you can see.
He's grown and he's grown
Till he's four times the size,
He was when I got him.
He was just pint-sized.

Jill Ogilvie
DREAMS

I am the dreamer and you are
the realist,
You can see my dreams in my
eyes,
In you I see them wilt and die.
Must life be so cold?
Is it not good to dream?
Must dreams be bought and
sold
As if they mean
Absolutely n
o
t
h
i
n
g
?

Barbara S. Cargill
TRACES

your a smile in my eyes
with you i tell no lies
with you i am one
as none
other i know
your spirit flows
a ghostly glow
i see your face
just a trace
but its always there
always there
that undying desire
bursting in fire
to be by you once again
making my storm to soft
rain.

Anthony A. Yager
SUICIDE

Call it the final solution
For unhappiness and despair,
A mind full of mass confusion
A mind that no longer cares.

No one has ever lived to tell
The relief it gives to a living
hell,
And all the souls who tried and
failed
Not one has ever told the tale.

An act from which there's no
return
How it's done is of your own
concern,
The end results are always the
same
There's no chance to start all
over again.

Once this drastic deed is done
Everybody will wonder what
was wrong,
But with you all those feelings
died
From this lonely act called
suicide.

Terry C. Misfeldt
SPACE

A frontier
to explore strange atmospheres
and probe the depths of
uncertainty,
broadening horizons
and yielding room to grow.

A vision
of touching divinity's aura
and opening the mind to life,
expanding dimensions
and dispelling myths of time.

A dream
of survival.

Gwen J. Henkel
A MOTHER'S LOVE

A little girl with big blue eyes,
I'd like to watch her grow,
with pale blond hair and sunlit
smile, I'd like for her to show
That the love I had for her
would match her love for me;
so then we could grow together
in a perfect harmony.

I think God made such little
girls for women everywhere,
that we might have a second
chance to live, to grow, to
share.

For the love between a mother
and that apple of her eye
can make the clouds that hide
the sun part to show the sky.

The future that is sure to be
for little girls today
will show a life as good as ours—
they've learned a better way.

Little girls are something
precious, for the woman
knows the game;
She learns to cope with life,
remembers whence she came.

A daughter and a mother share
a bond, I know,
'cause I learned it from my
mother, when she learned to
let me go.

Emily S. Goldberg
SEASET

A sunset,
The colors of the sea.
The hull of a brown boat
peers over the horizon.
Mysterious midnight blue
shines overhead,
and
I am all alone.
Light blinking silently
through the sky
Colors of the sea
Inspiring, powerful, deep
and Mysterious.

Jacqueline Carpenter Valdez
WYOMING WIDOW

Women wait for dark
for dawn
for word
A key in the lock
Betrayed in fumbling, bumbling.
In the bar
Boozing with the boys
Shooting pool
Telling lies.
Has her eye
Gets her number.
Women wait for word.
Dusk comes

Wind calms
Lights dim
Dishes wait
Women wait.
Sleep fails
Wind wails
House creaks
Light creeps through the
shutters.
Women wait
For word.
No word.

Phyllis Y. Crockett Thompson
PRETENDING?

I used to play house
when I was small,
but that was yesterday.

I was the mother,
with no father at all,
and that was yesterday.

I had many children
portrayed by my dolls.
I laughed . . .cried . . .
and screamed.
I spanked . . .smiled . . .
and cleaned.
I sat there alone, alone . . .
. . .in my dreams . . .
The way grownups often do.
. . .now . . .
Yesterday is today.

Candace York
FOR B. R.

People laugh at the ol' fool,
talking to himself on a swivel
barstool,
some folks say he's lost his mind,
but no, he's lookin for better
days left behind.

Dancin with himself at the juke
box,
he keeps a stompin good beat,
as he plays Rhinestone Cowboy
one more time,
he kicks up spurred boots on
his feet.

I hear he used to play in the
movies,
The cowboy who always got
shot,
now he lives for beer and
whiskey,
and he dreams an awful lot.

He has no real friends or family,
no one to carry his name,
he can't admit to his loneliness,
he's convinced he's still in the
game.

He's forgotten what it's like to
be sober,
and though he's played it over
and over,
he sticks in one more dime,
to play Rhinestone Cowboy,
one more time.

Claire Baker
TIME RUSHES ON

Time is swiftly rushing on.
The daylight hours will soon
be gone.
There's not much time to save
the lost—
To tell them of the cruel cross.
When twilight comes 'twill be
to late
To save them from an awful
fate.
For judgment then is sure to
come—
So hurry—for time rushes on.
Let's tell the lost of Jesus' love,
About his coming from above.

Tell them the story while we
can.
Explain to them salvation's
plan.
We'll be so happy in the end
If we have helped some soul
to win.
So hurry—e'er the twilight falls,
For then there'll be no time
at all.

Bob David Goldberg
LOVE SONNETS

Love wanders in through sunlit
doors
And snakes its way into
unsuspecting hearts
Through spaces so narrow
It finds its way

Love the dancing soliloquy of
life
Steps gingerly as it moves its
merry way
Driving forward with sometimes
swiftness of a knife
Entering new places bringing
smiles to new faces

Locked in fear, entwined in
emotion
We continuously step towards
this new ocean
Swimming through this vast
new world
We feel our heartbeats sing
tunes of enlightenment

Twisting and worming through
every cell
Love permeates the pores
Rising up and through
In and out

Love is the energy of truth
Love this energy has no bounds
Love this truth has no lie
Love is the beautiful sonnet of
life.

Bruce Woods Patterson
THE MIRROR

The mirror goes black at night
forced into inactivity
for lack of light..
It cannot sleep,
or close its eye,
But turns inward
upon itself.
Without reflection
it waits, hushed,
for me to change
in my sleep.

Robert E. Henson
METAMORPHOSIS

The still egg wet new caterpillar
thrived
Because his thoughtful mother
had contrived
Him a spacious home with
plenty of food
Which had been safe and warm
since he arrived.

But time passed through his
young interlude
And through the experience he
accrued
An ever increasing sense of
judgment
From the problems he had to
elude.

It was in this manner his life
was spent
Until in the end he got up and
went
To build a box of his own
invention
In which he planned to end his
body's stint.

This box retained the body of
mention
However let's direct our
attention
To the body that left its
retention
To fly into another dimension.

Ruth L. Legg
TO MY ANGEL

I miss you Angel,
I'm sure you know.
It aches my heart,
I loved you so.
I know not the
reason why,
God took you, and
left me to cry.
I pray each day
So you will know,
I feel your presence
Where e'er I go.
I, one day will be
with you,
To begin our lives
all o'er anew.
What a gloreous day
that will be,
When god unites you
and me.

Rev. John E. Williams
THE CARTERS

The Carters have come from
Georgia
Said Rosalynn to Jimmy one
day
Who is healing the people
brought to them
With the touch of their fingers.

Now I shall carry the gent's
Little Jack, Chip and Jeff
Now I shall carry the baby
Amy
For Lillian to look upon.

Lillian looked at her kindly
But she shook her head and
smiled
Oh! But only a grandmother
Would think of things so wise.

Rosalynn do not hide your
nature
You feel such burning care
If you carry Amy to
Washington
Perhaps you will leave her there.

If you lay your hands on Amy
Your heart will be like I know
For a blessing forever and ever
Will follow Amy as she grows.

Tracy Maguire
SOMETIMES IT HAPPENS

Sometimes it happens:
Close your eyes and put away,
The memories of the past.
What has happened is gone
for now,
The hurt will always last.

I can never promise you my
life,
Happiness or peace of mind.
But I can try and dream with
you,
Given the place and time.

Your soul and your heart are
one,
Alive and always true.
Exposed towards the rest of us,
For it shows the real you.

There are those who love
forever,
And some that seem to end.
Experience makes us more
aware,
The heart will always mend.

V. Hunt
SIXTIES

picketing, protesting
the youth tried to make a point
peace marches, riots
sometimes a disasterous flaunt
folk songs without folk lore
poems without rhyme
songs of conservation
oh what pathetic times
the war must end but did not
the hippie was born and died
the decade will be forgotten
although its children tried.

Paul D. Swigart
A PLEA FOR ELEGANCE

Acquiescence and desire
Pour forth in passion through
the years,
Lend only to the true of heart
Eternal joyous tears.
Afflatus is the gift I seek
For someone such as thee;
Oh, quintessential loveliness,
Return and set me free.
Elusive as a wind-blown kiss
Lamenting on the breeze,
Elicting in noble souls
Great reverence and ease,
And to my heart, Oh gentle one,
None other could aspire.
Cease not to wax in elegance,
Eternally inquire.

Madeline Woodard Hildenbrand
LOVE FOREVERMORE

I make my attempt to put into
verse
and so delight the universe
this winter night, while beauty
surrounds us
sleepily waiting to astound us.
Raidiant bars of heavenly light
silently
spread through the darkness
to waken, and dazzle the
populace of the earth
with beauty so bright they
must know this night
was the one of HIS birth.
The miracle of God is again
seen anew
Jesus on this night of nights
our spirit renew
In jubilation, the knee is bent
in reverence to thee.
On this holy night may the
little Babe's light
be a beacon of love, to let
all who adore
know this night will go on
Forevermore,
Forevermore——

Mary Giunta
FACE IN A CROWD

In my everyday shopping and
such
I seem to see your face
I'm startled when someone

calls out "How much?"
And I'm back to earth, not in
space
For no matter where I go
I think I hear or see
A semblance of your smile
In every face passing me
So do not stay away too long
And let my mind get perplexed
I stutter when I hear someone
say "Who's next?"
I forget where I am
My mind's in a daze
I would like to end
This incredible craze.

Lisa Anne Moeske
HAPPINESS

You fly like a bird
on velvet wings,
searching for tomorrow.
You smile at me everyday
through painted lips,
on an inanimate object.
You cry out at me
through staring eyes
that I refuse to see.
You are like a dreamland
filled with love,
that my heart won't accept.
You are happiness
in a place of hate,
that I long to find.

LynnEtte Barnum
OBSERVING

The only way I can see
any farther than a tree
Is to:
stop.
Check.
Observe.
Listen to the many sounds
Cracking . . .
    . . .of the ice.
Screaming . . .
    . . .of a child.
Snapping . . .
    . . .of a twig.
To be as alert
and observant
as I possibly can be.

Glenda J. Flores
THINKING BACK

As I grow old, I think back to
my past.
All of those good years went by
much too fast.
I remember all the happy times;
My share of love and attention.
There were a few sad times; but
then, too few to mention.
I smile as I remember how I
was sheltered by Love,
from daddy's helping hands
and God from above.
I feel so lucky now to have
been in their keeping,
And my heart filled with joy
now is silently weeping.
I thank you both for this good
life you've led me through.
But I must say goodbye to my
old life and welcome my new.
I'll never forget the good life
I had,
And again I thank you, to God
and to Dad.

Anne W. Parris
UNTITLED

Is life a deck
Of tarot cards?
Is existence merely
the strategic
placement of

paper
effigies
The hangman calls and
His song is slow
And sadly sweet
But wait, I have yet to
Be worthwhile my words
Die unuttered
Lives are swept
Aside
As the cruel gypsy
Of fortune
Puts away her game.

R. Tobin
ANOTHER DAY

I know one day
you'll walk away—
Going to a place
much farther astray.
Then I'll know
that at one time—
We had happiness
and you were mine.
I'll keep my memories
and think of you—
I'll remember a time
I wasn't blue.
When you were near
and experience new—
Life was sweet
and love was true.
But now you're going
far away—
So goodbye—
Till another place
Another day.

Capt. Thomas Anthony Mravak
DAWN

With each dawn man is reborn
Awakens to find new light
And begin again
Sky, wind, land, sea, air
Cleansed by night's cool calm
And day's rays
As from woman's womb
Man sheds night's sweet blanket
And sees a new light
Always seeking
The brightest light of all
God's love.

Corrye E. Single
VENUS

Muffled by a rush of air,
a tuft of oddly shaped leaves,
a regal stem.
Analogous to Boticelli; artistic
as a painting.
"Dionaeu" of the Sundew
Family.
In bogs on banks
She lies in ambush,
with her playful snare
of sharp, fringed bristles.
For window-glass wings,
to lite upon her venomous
lobes.
Deceived by her esthetic
grace,
octagonized eyes,
see nothing more
of beauty.

Sheir M. Soura
THE DIVINE ART OF LOVE

Erst I fancy you
posed some while
wearing La Gioconda's smile
near the veranda;
and there in the light
to err
would remain your essence

208

captured by Vermeer.
My eyes would then mold
you to granite's delight;
or marble to please the sight
of any mortal;
and shadow the Venus de Milo
in time
so that not even Phidias
could compare her to mine.

In your presence,
surely the gods would tumble
and Botticelli's cherubs fumble
with angelic hands;
Even Rembrandt could not
pierce nor awaken
the beauty and care
that I have given and taken.

I imagine you still
and see you eternally mine
in the light of art's divine
purpose and pose;
and perish not the
love and lore
that's made you art
and so much more.

Donna Pugh
LOVE WAS JUST A GAME

In the days before you came
Love was mostly like a game.
But now, the love I feel for
you—
So very strong, it must be true.
I cannot tell you how I feel
for
Inside the past is hurting
still.
Someday, maybe, you will
know—
If we let these feelings grow.
My life right now, is torn two
ways
Grown uncertain these passing
days.
Again, I wonder what I'd find
If I could see inside your mind.
Your thoughts and feelings
planted there
Would I find, that perhaps you
care?

Wende Omans
DISTANT GLASS

I watch you through a distant
glass
And pray that it would break.

You enjoy your life there,
alone,
But now it is time for a
confrontation.

You have touched my spirit
And allowed me a separate
part of you,
I sense your ways and seek
your warmth.
I watch.

You set me aside and continue
your life,
So, here I sit.

Could you learn my ways?
Could you touch me and
experience
My yearnings?

I watch you through a distant
glass
And pray that it would break.

I want you on my terms
But the thin transparency of
unmatched lives
Might well be eternally thick.

I put my fingers to the glass
And the yearning for your
touch grows stronger.

I watch you through that

dreadful glass
And damn the unyielding
coldness.

I know it will never give way
To my weakened touch,
My fantastic passions.
So, here I sit.

Diane K. DuBose
WHIRLWIND LOVE

You came in like a whirlwind
and really blew my mind
You're just the sort of man
I was hoping not to find
I have some old emotions
that really need to stay
Your love is like a whirlwind
it's blowing them away
My head is really spinning
I'm not sure how I feel
I think about my old love
and wonder if it's real
These feelings have me tied
down
chains around my heart
So spin me with your
whirlwind love
and blow these chains apart.

Ethel O'Hagan
THE SPIDER'S WEB

Little fly, caught in the spider's
web, struggling to be free
I know how you feel—life has
done that to me
Each day that goes by, I
struggle, I cry! I cry!
Oh God, please dear God, won't
you help me break away?
Why do I have to worry and
always think of others?
Why do I love so deeply,
mother, father, sisters and
brother?
Sometimes I start to break
the web in which I'm confined
Only to hear voices faintly
saying: "Please don't leave
me behind."
So I walk away and leave you
to struggle, little fly
I'm sorry but there's no one
to free me until I die.

Karen Lee Uhrich
CONSOLATION

The nights come fast and stay
so long
you'd think the sun was
sleeping—
Wishing I knew what had gone
wrong,
The hours were never ending.
A knife wedged deep within
my heart,
the pain was hot as fire;
my brain was scorched from
thoughts apart
awaiting my mind to tire.
Imprisoned—no wish for
company—
my anguish raged within;
The bleeding had ceased only
mentally
as the carpet grew red with sin.

Rose A. Hutchinson
ODE TO AN EGGSHELL

Fragile; breakable. Lost in
thought.
Purest white crust.
Jagged edges with lessons
taught.
Love, caring dust.
Ethereal quality of view
Delicate protection

Chickens clucking in a zoo
A newfound detection.
Minute lines of strain; Rivulets
of effort
Stained yellow and gray
The end, the fine, the last resort
Followed only by day.
Cracked, crunched. Completely
broken.
Craggy, crooked edges
Shattering pieces. A token
To an answer slowly hedges.
Restoration. Communion.
Commencement.
Seraphic whiteness. Purity.
Beckons toward retirement
An eggshell in its dignity.

Bettie Stembler
**'TOOT TOOT' PEANUT
BUTTER**

The rock of non-security
came rolling over next to me.
Touching my shoulder is this
monstrous boulder
of life's uncertainty.

One rock to crush me from
existence?
With feats of hammering
resistance—
I finally hear a crackkk.
How long can I hold the damn
thing back when
both hands feel tied to this
railroat track?
Now, my body lies limp like
a gunny sack.

The funereal train's a sleeper.
A huffin' and puffin'
c r e e p e r, as it rolls 'round
the bend.
Oh woe is me—
Can this be—
The End?

Wilson R. Morrill
AN ODE TO A VALVE JOB

I've got a gal who had a valve
That gradually grew weak,
And as it tried to pump blood
through
It finally sprang a leak.

It seemed as though the time
had come
To mend that leaky heart
By putting in another valve
To replace the worn out part.

The main question seemed to
me to be
What choice would the doctor
make.
Would it be a genuine "piggy"
valve—
Or a synthetic ball valve fake.

After weighing all the pros and
cons
It's obvious he chose not the
ball—
For now I detect a distinct
"Oink, oink"
Each time she answers my call.

George N. Kokoros
DAYS UNFORGETTABLE

A babe he was in Mother's
arms;
He heard her voice . . .she
murmured charms.
He felt secure upon her
breast
Where oftentimes he'd have
his rest.
She'd rock him in her rocking
chair;
Its pleasant sway would lull

him there . . .
A time to dream of many
joys:—
Of bouncing balls and cud'ly
toys.
She shielded him from all the
harms
By wrapping him in her warm
arms;
And soon she'd sing her
lullabies,
Which hushed at once his infant
cries.

Those days so tender now are
gone,
But in his heart he knows he
won
A mother's love so warm and
sound,
Tho' now she lies beneath
cold ground.
Yet ev'ryday he comes to her
Where grow the tow'ring
trees of fir;
A wreath he leaves upon her
breast
Where once he felt love's
warmth and rest.

E. Warren Oakes
AUTUMN TREE

Beauty it is to see
this autumn tree.
If ever there was an
expression of symmetrical
grace, it is in this small
sanctified place.

A masterpiece in color
this autumn tree.

We should see it with thee
and what it means to
you and me.

This autumn tree
This autumn tree.

Tamara Harmon
THE TWOSOME

Rays of love and peace
Warmed the sleeping child
As it slept among the daisies
out in the valley wild.
Then out of the forest strode
a magnificent unicorn.
Yet a gentleness shone in its
eyes
As it looked upon the sleeping
form.

He tread softly to where the boy
curled,
Gave a gentle neigh,
And the little child awoke
And romped with him all day.

The boy leaped upon the white
back,
Took ahold of the cascading
mane,
and off the twosome went,
Trotting through sugar cane.

And when dusk softly fell,
They ceased their playful
flight,
Laid down in a fragranced
field,
And slept through the velvet
night.

Betty Treggett
DAWN

The early dawn,
with its mystic ways—
Has a magical image,
The start of each day.

What will it hold—
Good times or bad.
Will it bring happiness,

Or shall we be sad.
So calm is the dawn,
Without a care—
Letting us know
Nature is there.

Wishes, being made,
Hopes held high—
Turning our thoughts
Up to the sky.

The birth of the dawn,
Is so very fine—
All tend to think
This day, is mine!

Crystal Ann Eastwood
I WISH

I wish
I was a perfect ring,
enterlocking with someone.
Never breaking apart,
two as one.
Knowing each other,
as we know ourselves.

T. A. Moffitt
PARTING

She touched his cheek
and said, "I better go."
It's much better if I go
while you are sleeping.
Her fingers moved to his
long brown hair
  and she touched its fineness
  one last time.
As she walked out the door
  and closed it softly behind her
  a tear fell
    from a closed eye
    and onto the pillow
      where last
      she'd lain
      her head.

Leora R. Williams
SUDDENLY IT HAPPENED

The winds in the west were
  silent.
As the sky once more turned
  grey.
Then suddenly it happened,
The leaves all sped away.

At last the rains were coming.
Things heaped upon the ground.
Then suddenly it happened,
That old familiar sound.

Beating down upon the roof
  tops.
Dropping through the thirsty
  trees.
The rains had finally found us.
We thanked God upon our
  knees.

The drought had finally ended.
Again we all felt sure.
The earth had gained its water
Things again were pure.

Ina Ellis
MCKEEVER

I cannot remember exactly when
you came into my life
Bringing the gift of friendship
That lessened the strife.
Even now I wonder why you
  had to
die so young
Leaving me lonely, without
  a friend
To climb the ladder of life
rung by rung.
I missed your voice ringing
  through
the walls
And there were times when I
  listened
for the echoes of your calls.

The grief for the loss of your
  earthly being
lingered heavily on my mind.
For your life, "Why were they
  so blind?"
The thickness of my sorrow
  could have been
cut with a knife
Just as the butchers had cut
  away the baby and ended
  your life.
I grieved because no one could
  see
How important your lives were
  to be.
The beautiful spirit of an
  unborn child and its mother
Goes with me day by day
And I know that within time,
we will meet somewhere along
  the way.

Janelle I. Bruce
THE TREE, LIKE ME

See the branches of the tree?
They are like the past, of me.
So much at the base, to grow
  on—
And that on top, which has
  formed.
The primaries, the secondaries,
  the twigs,
The people I've met and where
  they've led me.
See how they lead nowhere?
What am I to them?
So many dead ends . . .
Why?
Look at all the broken branches.
What of them?
Those relationships that
  suddenly left,
In vain love, in moving on, in
  death.
The tree is born, lives, grows,
  gives
life and meaning, and dies.
Is this not like I?
Or, Do
I really matter?
Does one tree in the forest
  matter?
It takes individuals, to make
  a group
But where one falls, another's
  found
I am lost
I have no ground
Like a tree . . .
Chopped
    Down.

Ann F. Lannom
LIFE'S RIDE

I've heard the word I love you.
Saw laughter in childrens' eyes.
Watched the sun rise in the
  valley,
While an eagle kissed the sky.
I've shook the hands of
  strangers.
Helped a friend who had lost
  his way.
Trying always to sing my love
  song,
While the words just slip away.
I've climbed life's highest
  mountains.
Felt the breeze caress my feet.
Sunbeams melt around me,
Took life's bitter with the
  sweet.
I've touched my cup of
  contentment,
Walked where living waters flow.
And when I had fallen from
  within-without,

It was love that restored my
  soul.
So if today the gods should
  call me,
Saying my life must turn with
  the tide,
I'll still be thankful that I passed
  this way,
Cause I've enjoyed life's ride.

Angel Del Valle
OFFERING SONG

Let our love grow as a flower
Before his glorious throne
Let our praise rise up to
  greet Him
Until we are called home.

Praise his name, praise His name
Praise the Lord God, forever the
  same
Angels sing of His grace
The Lord God of Heaven my
  sin has erased

What a priviledge to know Him
What a prize to call our own
What an honor to have Jesus
To guide us as His sons.

Nova Rohrbaugh
CHRISTMAS

Christ came down to earth
Hope for everyone.
Rose: a branch of Jesse's race
In a manger born.
Sent by God; a babe
To save men from their sin.
Master of Heaven and earth,
Angel heralds sang
Salvation for all men.

Jo E. Hamilton
IT'S EASY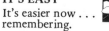

It's easier now . . .
remembering.

Still so much to absorb
and so much left to understand.

I know it was bad just living
  then
so much of the time,
But why have I forgotten what
  it felt like?

And why do I have your touch
and kiss so easily on my mind?
And still my heart is full of
  you—
Still— After all this time.

Why can't I let you go—
and where do I store these
left-over memories that you
  helped me make?
What right did you have to
invade my feelings and life
and scar my heart forever
  after?

Why still do I find tears
  flowing
at an instant's notice
for no reason at all?
And always your face remains
within my mind even when
  I'm not looking.

Please believe me . . .
It's easier now.

Sherry Faiella
THIS EMPTY SPACE

God has left an empty space;
Deep within my heart.
As he took my father, by the
  hand;
And told us he must part.
He took his smile, his warm
  embrace;
And the sparkle in his eyes.
And now I cry upon the grave;
Of which his body lies.

As I kneel in prayer, and express
  to God;
The pain of my great loss.
He opens my eyes, to the
  flowers of love;
And that little wooden cross.
Although they are such little
  things;
And he did deserve much
  more.
As we laid him there beneath
  the ground;
It opened Heaven's door.
Now his life will be with God;
And our love will linger on.
Until the day when we meet
  again;
And his face we'll gaze upon.
As his eyes sparkle, and I see
  his smile;
And feel his warm embrace.
He'll fill my heart, once more
  with love;
And fill this empty space.

G. Ray White
A DREAM OF LOVE

I've dreamed of love, long
  into the night
And wished for love, to take
  me to paradise;
But still I've found myself all
  alone.
And so I leave, and start to
  roam.

I've searched this land, so
  spacious it be;
And still there be no one
  next to me.
And so I go on, through the
  night;
And dream of a love, that
  will hold me tight.

I know someday, my search
  will end;
And with it, I'll be a better man.
And I shall find her, wherever
  she may be.
And we'll be together, through
  life endlessly.

Virginia E. Cruikshank
AUTUMN WHIMSEY

Beneath each fallen leaf a pixie
  lies
In wait; you'll see him if you
  follow closely
The fitful course his skyhorse
  takes. He flies
Along in glee; then shakes his
  head morosely
At the fainting wind, and
  huddles close
And presses hard against the
  earth. Sometimes
You'll hear him gently cough
  and poke his toes
Right through his leafy cover.
  In elfin rhymes
He sings and chants and whistles
  through his teeth
At snobbish passers-by who
  never seem
To see him. But just the same,
  don't ever breathe
You've guessed his precious
  secret, for he will scream
In sudden fright and scold
  you like a demon.

J. K. Hamilton
FORSAKEN PSYCHIATRY

By the beckoning flap of a
  gypsy tent
Designed by a nouveau god,
The spiraling, thinworn
  flirtation begins

The hag in a robe her silver
wins,
As I step in to applaud.
Fending with ice spears
My feral heart,
I attend this memory-den;
Your face looks out of the
candle-lit blue
I turn and wheel on my heel
at the cue,
And never return again.

Joy Lichau-Hidalgo
THE PROMISE

I have a shining golden bucket
to gather your tears.
When sorrow befalls you and
a flood you fear,
I shall take away your tear to
the Rain Vendor
To be bartered among the
Cloud Brokers—
Nurtured until heavy and gray
for other storms to come.
My bucket now is empty; your
heart is full to brim-over;
Spare for me it's content
And I shall yield to you
a magnificent rainbow.

Though our faiths, age and creed
may now part us,
I claim you still for my love's
own sake;
Delayed for eternities though
it may be,
Let this my promise to you a
constant now become.

For yet more lives are to be
shared, and
Through different worlds we
shall pass not a few;
Much to learn; Much to
forget.
I plead you now; remember
my words!
'ere time be come for taking you.
But the time shall come.

Steven Gould
TRITE

You smile at me and peaceful
grows my heart.
Today you blossom in the sun,
The others blossomed one by
one,
You have been the last to
start.
The sun upon your petals ruby
red
Shows shadows I would never
see.
So safe while in your little lea,
Thus beautiful a life you've
led.

But you are man and you are
mirror,
Reflecting only what we can
see,
Yet some can see much clearer;
For you are beauty and you
are beast
Hiding the things you like the
least,
Will you stay this way eternally.

Karen M. Klimovich
OPENING NIGHT

Slowly, far off against the
horizon,
a silent darkness
clutches the sky
with long, gray fingers.
Softly, announcing its arrival,
a low drumroll of thunder
echoes through the clouds .
The sad moan of the wind

drifts over the earth
as a chilling breeze
carelessly tosses and
whips the treetops.
The darkness creeps further—
swallowing the sun;
while the thunder
claps its approval
in the distance.
White lightning
splits the sky,
and its crackling
tempts the thunder
to rumble louder.
The wind howls and,
with a crash of thunder,
rain pours from above.
Fiercely pattering against
the thirsty earth,
it is applauded by the thunder
and illuminated by a spotlight
of lightning.
All this—
for heaven's tears.

Theresa John
SILENT CATHEDRAL

I dream of sunbeams
Pouring through a web of tree
branches.
Sunbeams bound gracefully
To each leaf.
To each blade of grass,
Bright in the morning dew.

A small rainbow
Stretches over a torn, ragged
path.
Ending abruptly at
the foot
Of an old, carved cross.

It is very quiet here,
No bird raises its song,
The wind does not breathe,
The dead leaves do not stir.

And yet there is something
In the high, wild grasses—
If you listen closely
You can hear it chuckling
About the frailty of life.

L. E. Whitmer
**ON COCAINE, JACKSON
BROWNE AND GRASS**

in the garden
transported on the energy of
rhythm harnessed
by the genius of communal
man
we discover a faint hint of the
great mystery.
traveling zones unencumbered
by a burdensom materialism
fashioned by life's images
sculpted by the musician
we touch. hands
communicate more than words;
eyes
more sensuous than fingers
caress and penetrate; souls
hotter than thighs lock
fly
soar
then float
in a sea suspended in song.

Melissa Suzanne Ingells
ECHOES OF A YEAR

If I were a gym, I would look
with anticipation toward
every year.
I would meet every class, every
person
And know their hopes and
their dreams.
And on the first day I would
wonder, "Who will be friends
by next year?"

I would watch a lone basketball
player shoot away his worries
in silence and half-light.
And hope with the one that
thought, "I hope he likes me
as much as I like him."
And the seventh graders come
here scared, go away confident
and older and graduating.
I would be cursed during hard
workouts, and thanked when
their team wins.
Long after school is out I would
still remember how one of my
children came back
with his own seventh grader,
small and scared, and said,
"I remember."

Candice Elizabeth Reason
CHEMISTRY

I don't know why I feel as I
do
and its crazy for its real
Just as you, look at me, so
silently,
nothing need be said.
Is this what they call chemistry?
To flush a rosy red;
if not to see it is inside,
creates a flow not casual like
you.
Your smile is warm;
it stays in my thoughts.
I know that mine does too.
You've given me the inspiration
to write this finding truth.
But what of you do I know?
What we share in conversation
tells me who you are.
Bold and strong; just as a man
Yet quiet like a star.

Haynes Reynolds, Ph.D.
DEATH

Death, how shall we receive you?
Reverently, quietly, a welcome
guest
finally arrived
Or noisome clatter, to ward you
off
with warm nothings?
But you will not be tamed.
You will have your own way.
Come, you have come;
We await the duration and
duress of your stay.

Jacquelyn Lee Morning
THE MASQUE

Justice
The mystical pretense
An illusion of balance
The prevaricator speaks of
realism
transforming all individual
beliefs
all control
into a pretentious style
This apparation of self
destruction
defends guilt
condemns innocence.

Mark E. Durand
EYES OF THE CALENDAR

Silvery star, twinkling in
twilight,
Flickering, flickering, in, out
of sight.
September sunset, orange orb
in west,
All our dear children, gently
put to rest.
Summer of our dreams, yes,
nearly spent.
Fantasy, fantasy, see where
it went.
Glance at the horizon.
Stare at the calendar.

Past forgotten, future unseen,
present ever lingers,
Passage of time, time slipped
through our fingers.
The clock's hands moving ever
so slow,
Vessel of life fluid, contents
ever so low.
To view the next step, both
comfort and bore,
Prefer ignorance of what lays
in store.

Excitement of the unknown,
Itch to explore, to feel, to
love, to own.
The blind man's perception
As a subtle subception.
Graying star, high in the sky,
Tactics of time, covert and
sly.
Glance at the horizon.
Stare at the calendar.

Brenda Lee Cates
BUT I CAN'T

I wish I could feel sorry,
But I can't
I wish I could understand,
But I can't
I wish I could forget,
But I can't
I just can't.

Chuck De Hart
KITHLESS

You left this morning!
Even knowing why, gave me
little warning.
Now suddenly I have the
freedom I demanded.
But I'm wandering in a stupor,
the shock is still too real.

I look at every face on the
street
Expecting to see you smiling
And laughing like you have
played another of your games.

It's hard to be alone—isn't it?
Alone is when we grow and
feel its pain.

I'll jump whenever I hear a
name shouted that sounds
like yours,
Then I'll smile to myself—and
go on.
I'll think of you always and
know that
We have shared and loved and
grown together—
And grown apart.

Caroline Feilberg
ELVIS PRESLEY

Elvis was a superstar,
he had many a fan
People travelled very far,
to hear and see this man.

He played a lot of parts,
in many many shows,
and won a lot of hearts;

goodness only knows.
He cherished his dear mother,
for she had loved him so;
and there was not another,
who could devote themselves
to him so.

When his mother died,
he found it hard to bear;
so he broke down and cried,
for mom was no longer there.

He led a life of fame
and so did his daughter and
wife,
but he lost the marriage game;
which slowly crumpled his
life.

He loved his daughter very
much,
and this was proven true;
The gifts he gave to her were
such,
she always had something new.

He sang a lot of songs,
for people far and wide.
It was for Elvis people longed,
until the day he died.

Erica A. Gindraux
THANK YOU MY FRIEND

To you a person, who is a
friend,
Always there with a lending
hand.

That bothered to listen, with
a caring ear,
To the thoughts of anothers
troubles and fear.

When I was down, not knowing
what to do,
You came by and helped pull
me through.

Not many people have such
care.
It's nice to know you are one
who's there.

I'll always remember, I'll
always be thankful,
To you a friend for taking the
time and trouble.

So as I say, "Thank You," I
hope it means to you,
All that it means to me too.

For this is where I give to you
my gift,
These words,
"Thank You My Friend."

Randall W. West
REMEMBER: ODE TO THE VIET VETS

Remember that time and
remember it well.
Enter your name among the
veterans of hell.
Mask not your thoughts with
dark veils of hate.
Eventually good comes to
those who can wait.
Mine is a prayer of grateful
reply,
Because there is no one more
thankful than I.
Ere you denounce all your time
as a waste,
Remember:
Life has a flavor the protected
can't taste.

Gloria Harris
A BAD HABIT

I wish I could quit the cigarette
Nothing to do is my biggest
fret
Children, work, laughter and
play

Are the things that consume
my day
Keeping me busy, giving me
no time
Still up the wall for a cigarette
I would climb.
Cigarette and smoke, cough and
choke
Even when sickness it did
evoke
The worst of hebits, I realize
This taste in my mouth, I
should despise
I really don't like them, I
must admit
But the need in my system
just won't quit.

Cynthia Tucker (Jamadhya)
TRUTH

Truth can be strong like an
iron
Truth can also be light as a
feather
But remember truth is stronger
than strength.

Yet you lust and temper with
beauty
And say it sweet as honey
Be cautious my friend it can
deceive
And be bitter as a lemon.

Judith Melby Jones
FULL CYCLE

Hidden in their cloaks of brown,
The tiny leaf buds crouch—
Spring's early ambassadors
Absorb the sun's warm touch.

Dazzling, dressed in brilliant
green,
The newborn leaves unfurl
Summer's glorious artistry
Amid the branches curl.

Colored in the richest hues,
The full—grown leaves appear—
Autumn's mellow majesty
Restore past memories dear.

Silent now in drabber shades
The spent leaves carpet earth—
Winter's faded oracles
Await spring's grand rebirth.

Joseph Michael Lombardo
REFLECTIONS

The scattered dreams of
yesteryear
lie like the rotting bow
Of ships that sailed the
ocean blue,
far in the past, not now.
Oh, they stood well the crested
waves
though tossed amidst the foam,
Yet now the weight of
perching gulls
brings forth a creaking moan.

William Porter Quam
A LAUGH IN YOUR HONOR

I was afraid another star had
risen
in *my* place.

I tried to be myself
For one more trip
One more time
I reached out to touch a dream
a life
I penetrated as before
in a rush of sincerity I presented
myself
In a rush of passion I was
exhausted
Emptied
With careless disregard I
offered all
In the despair of the ensuing

eternity
I glanced up and memorialized
The dreamy dreary fishing
village of ages past
As it intertwined—a tear
crossed a smile
And I laughed in your honor.

Arnold Kinsella
THE SWEETEST THING

Love is the sweetest thing in
the world
if you know how to use it
It is the sweetest thing in
the world
if you don't abuse it
Count your blessings when you
know you have got
Someone who loves you an
awful lot
Treat them tenderly and with
great care
Watch over them, make them
know you're there
To help them along when the
going gets rough
That you really can't love them
half enough
Your life is nothing, not until
You find someone whom you
know will
Return your love and help
you both find
The greatest love of all—the
unbreakable kind.

Todd Holt
BEHIND THE GATES OF TOMORROW

Behind the gates of tomorrow
There will be some joy and
sorrow;
There will be blue sky and
storm clouds;
There will be lonely hours
and fun crowds.
There may be fast-moving space
cars
To take us beyond the outer-
most stars.
There may be friends and
classmates coming from
planets in space;
They may be smarter than we
are but they may have a
strange looking face.
There may be just a pill for our
dinner,
So many will be looking much
thinner.
There may be a lot of changes
and many, many new things,
But we will do well with all
that it brings.

Pepa G. Volpe
THERE WAS A TIME

There was a time
When love was mine
When eagles soared
Rivers rushed to the sea
And children played
Hand in hand
As they built castles
In the sand.

The eagles are gone
The rivers dammed
The children have grown
Gone their separate ways
And the sea has reclaimed
Their dreams made of sand.

Monica Christine Bartel
BROKEN LOVE

The silent whispers of the sky
the gentle whispering breeze,
the sun's last rays splash on
your face

will you forgive me, please?
The twinkle once so very true
fades from your tearful eyes
feelings that we've dwelt on
yet nothing left but lies.

Seagulls trailing in the sand
sandcrabs scurry under,
My thoughts revolving back
to you
my love has made you wonder.

My reaching hand grasps
tightly yours
a tingle through my heart,
a love born for eternity
by me, now torn apart.

Janis Specht
MY PRECIOUS RUBY

My precious ruby you are
so beautiful
You take my breath away
When I hold it in my hand
I feel a strange vibration
It goes right through my body
And straight to my head
my precious ruby
Is fit for a queen to wear
I am that queen
Some day when I pass away
Another will possess my ruby
Better take good care of it
Or I'll haunt you from my
grave
Wear it close to your heart
Like the queen did.

I am the new queen now
I will obey your wishes
I will wear it close to my
heart
I promise to take good care
of your precious ruby.

Beverly Gunn
HORSE

Head carried high, looking
Over the rolling hills,
Remembering when he was a
young
Stallion, strong and powerful,
now
Everything is gone, except his
memories and his pride.

Wm. Keith Clayton
BARRIERS

Please keep the smart ass
Far away from here;
We need not one with no class,
Making trouble for the queer.

We'd put up partitions
To keep the riffraff out;
But it'd only add to suspicions,
Thinking we're all fooling about.

Solid walls, like shallow brains,
They're too hard for one to
get through;
It's too bad that barriers remain,
No matter what you may do.

Billie J. Grover
THE POET

Even as the poet
Writes words.
The verses
Are put into his mind.
As a poet I have a deepness
Which no one can enter.
Emotions are my pawns
They capture and hold.
Transfixed
My life you read.
Yet words have no meaning
Emotions carry the message.
Lightly they come
To be gone soon.
On winged feet

Beautiful but, harsh.
Telling of life
Shielding from destruction.
Giving pleasure
Bringing joy and sorrow.
Just as the blood flows
Moving forever, but
    permanent.

Lee Wells
**YESTERDAY, TODAY,
TOMORROW**

Yesterday has gone on its
    way.
We must use it when it is
    today.
For yesterday has passed
    forever more.
So life today like you never
    lived before.

Today we can claim as our
    day.
But tomorrow is not ours until
    it becomes today.
So if tomorrow, becomes our
    today my friends,
Let us be one that loves, shares,
    lends.

So as today comes to each of
    us,
We must always thank our
    saviour JESUS
For those that are above
Will share their wonderous
    love.

Mary L. Beel
THE POET

Blessed with a talent for poetry
    and prose
Pick up a pen and words will
    flow,
name the topic you wish me
    to write
Religion, romantic or
    mystery and fright.

Put your heart in fantasy land,
or create the love of a wonderful
    man
become erotic, dangerous and
    bold
the imagination has stories
    untold.

A way to escape from reality
and step into a world that may
    never be
to live so much in such little
    time
can only happen—in rhythm and
    rhyme.

Connie G. Cole
GOD GIVES US SUNSHINE

God gives us sunshine and
    happiness
What do we return
Prayers of asking
Promises of later
God gives us rain and sorrow
We return with
Cursing
Self-pity
Questioning why me
God gives material things
We reach for more
Challenges lost
The easy path well trod
God gives us guidance
We do not listen
God asks only
For us to read, live, and spread
His word
In return
He promises eternity
Free from suffering
God gives us hope
We promise soon

Reaching only
When death knocks
Time gone
We cry out
We believed
God answers
I believed
I waited
You said tomorrow
Tomorrow is unattainable.

Tracey Ondeck
STRANGE WAY

We met in the strangest way,
I'll never forget that day.
At first I couldn't stand you,
But now I'd never leave you.
Eventually we became friends,
I hope our love will never end.
Our love grew stronger every
    day.
Our love is here to stay.
Things work out in the strangest
    way,
Just live your life day by day.

Martha Dobbs
DREAMS

I had dreams,
I had plans,
Of a big fancy house
And a millionaire man.
A couple of kids
To round the dream out.
Yes, I had dreams,
But here's what I got—
A passel of kids,
A rickety old house,
A dirt land farmer
For a loving spouse.
Then I learned the truth;
A house is not a home,
Without kids and love,
You live all alone.
So they all came true,
My plans and my dreams,
I have treasures untold
With my family of thirteen!

D. C. Boyd
CHILDREN'S DREAMS

Ah yes—we run and hide in
    shame,
to close the guarding door,
Bequest the young with
    valuables—
trunks—where dreams they
    store,
And let them wander ever on,
with hopes—which are not
    real,
For if we give them back the
    key—
their dreams—someone shall
    steal.

Carmen F. Nixon
AS WE HEAR HIM

My life was full, my heart
    content
I lived my life and spent each
    day in happiness
I have no regrets, but one.
Just to be close to you—for
    a day—for an hour—
for a moment—just one more
    time—just one more time.
Just to say all the things I never
    said because
I was too busy living to speak
    my heart.
Just to tell my wife that she
    is the greatest woman
who ever lived—the sun in
    my sky.
Just to tell my sons that they
    are all men—the kind
Of men I saw in them from the

time they were boys.
Just to tell my daughters that
    they—like my mother—
are great women—the stars
    in my nights.
Just to tell my friends that they
    are the smiles behind my
    tears.
Just to say the things closest
    to my heart
that I neglected saying because
    I was too
busy loving people to tell them
    so.
But, my life was full—my heart
    content.

Tamara C. Price
ALONE

Alone
Softly, silently,
the breeze folds itself around me.
Chilling shivers run along my
    spine,
as I feel the cold.
I feel the fear as it washes over
    me.
When I look into the darkness.
When I realize he isn't coming,
I think, "again, I am alone."

Jill Bartel
MOUNTAIN ROYALTY

She stands majestic,
Silhouetted against the sky
In a forest green gown of velvet
Edged in deep-hued brocade.
A cloak of silver-grey fur
She wraps around herself,
Her face hidden
In the folds of the hood.

Mrs. Juanita L. Lumley
TEMPUS FUGIT

Time to work,
    No duty shirk
Time to kill—
    No life will fill
Time to play
    Each passing day
Time to share
    With those who care
Time to woo
    The right one, true
Time to pray,
    His praise to say
Time to love
    Our Lord above.

Susan Hickman
DREAMER

I, who am a dreamer
    have been stifled
by this City life
    and by the rain.

I, who need to be so free
    have been captured
by your eyes
    and by your smile.

You, who are the
    Lord of the winds and the
    Breezes
the king of the
    Spirits of the Air.

You, who surely are the
    music of the spring
Could you rush headlong
    into my life
and set me free.

Christopher G. Brown
YOUR POWER

Wonder not,
    on where you would be now,
Had you changed your course
    before

And sailed some different sea.
Instead
Look out,
    Horizon o'er the bow
And dream of places that
    could be
And spin the helm right now!

Chas Hausheer
A FADED, JADED MEMORY

I know I'm just a bad memory;
a smudged and wrinkled
slightly torn and faded memory.
In a mind a few years away,
racing to forget at the limit
    of time
exceeding it at times with the
    help of hate and contempt,
born of fear
that some year
I'll return to disprove what you
    know as the truth of the
    matter.
But babe——it doesn't matter.
A memory I'll remain
and I'll fade just as fast as I
    can.
Wiping out the good with the
    bad as you wish.
It.s the last and the least I can
    do.
'Cause I may just be a bad
    memory now
but lady——so are you.

William Orrell
NEW BEGINNINGS

They came, alas, amid the
    gloom
There fell a distant light
As though the stars in Heaven
    came out
To send a brilliant beam about
The stillness of the night.

They studied, their touch was
    on my hand
And all at once my life
Was flushed as with a bright
    new spring
To help them all in growing
With flowers of wisdom rife.

They learned, and through the
    silent space
A warm and honest effort stole,
As a wave of sound that the
    late dusk sings,
In ripples that each student
    brings
Completely fascinating my
    soul.

Why they came, or how it came
    about
That my fortune it should be
I know not, but I bless kind
    fate
Who, sensing my deserted gate,
Sent such a gift to me.

Now lingering in the chosen
    hour
Nineteen sun beams brightly
    shine
A rainbow spans the autumn
    skies,
That mirrors in all their eyes
And chases sadness away from
    mine.

William C. Garcia
SIESTA
Tal sera la hora en el dia.
Tan bonita y llena de vida,
Que lo natural, lo unico que
    cambia,
No cambia, si no adora esta
    hora mia.

Mary Ellen McKillop
WE ARE ONE

Though we may stand on two
  different sides of the room—
  we are one.

We may travel two different
  roads—
  but we are one.

The sun may shine and the rain
  may fall—
  but we are one.

And though we may lie in
  other arms tonight—
  we are still one.

For nothing can take away
  what we had.
    Only time will help us forget.

And once we forget,
  we will no longer have to try
  to understand
    why it can not be.

Barbara Boughten Premo
THE TIGRESS

She walks with a quickness of
  movement,
Always alert and lively.

She's aggressive in a very
  subduing way,
Yet confident and sure of
  herself.

She's refined and daring,
  very much a lady in her own
  right.

Her eyes are mysterious,
and very desirable.

Her touch is magnetic,
Her nearness possesses you.

The tigress.

Lourie Esta Cross
THE TRIUMPH

I gazed in awe as he lay sleeping
  there.
His pillow was mama's rocking
  chair.
He was so small.
Soon he began to crawl.
Then stand unsteadily, and
  walk. And run.
This laughing school boy! can
  he be my son?
He's driving much too fast,
  that sporty car.
With brimming eyes I watched
  him from afar.
I throbbed with pride, as he
  in cap and gown,
Walked with his classmates,
  headed for renoun.
I cried when he cried, wishing
  I could take
all of his hurt, bear all of his
  heartbreak.
Ah! then the call to serve,
  and served he well,
Giving his all that, I might
  safely dwell.
With bursting heart, his safe
  return to tell.

Nancy Delgado
MY FATHER

A father's job is to guide us
  along properly,
As he watches us grow each
  day,
So that we will grow in loving
  peace,
As we all go a separate way.

A father's job is to be employed,
To support his wife and
  children,
And to build each day better

in love,
At the end, may there be no
  space to build in.
Fathers couldn't be everywhere.
They need some time of their
  own.
Be thankful they're there when
  needed,
So don't you gripe and groan.
A father is to help a mother,
However, some find it hard
  to do,
But my father not only helps
  himself,
But helps my mother too.
My father is very loving,
And he loves my mother very
  much,
I can tell from the bottom of
  his heart,
And when I see his gentle touch.
Well, my father has fit the job,
Of making us stronger
  everyday,
So that we will grow in
  loving peace,
As we all go a separate way.

Heather Coulson
A MINOR WAR AT MY 52ND STREET CHANGEOVER

I saw a paragon of virtue
  yesterday
in the subway, at rush hour,
primly reclined in a plastic
  chair,
an anachronism of romanticism,
grey velvet, pristine lace,
demure, navy eyes,
swept-back chestnut hair—
clutching a leather suitcase
and a soft-worn volume of
  love poems?
I felt a most unusual urge
  to save her from It,
but my silver, steam-snorting
  steed
thundered in, profanities
  gashed
it's flanks.
  I shoved my way
aboard to fight the other
  war
and forgot her.

Kimberly A. Stenerson
UNDER GRASS

Under grass the fragile lie.
The strongly cast
can climb
or fly.
And looking through the
  bramble
and blades of green,
I see
the sky
and wish to fly
or climb
and leave the grass behind.

Mary Callahan Zelie
NEIGHBORHOODS

Old faces, unshaven
On porches, drinking beer.
Young faces; gangs of children
Almost men, roam steamy
  streets.
Whistling, laughing, boisterous
Accepting the misery
Of existence. Like the men.
Their curses drift from me.
Lamps hide behind the leaves.
Even the moon only peeks
From a perch above the gloom.
Garbage smells and screaming
  babes.

Malignant desparation.
Children of God. I hurry.
Children of poverty.
Down the street, my own home
Smacks of Superiority.
Same zip code; different world.
An imaginary line
As real as a culture
Separates my world from theirs.

Shelley Grace
GRANDAD

Walking through the garden
  just grandad and me
It's as if time has stopped now
Is this how life could be?

That walk through the garden
It was such a special day
I can't believe he's gone now
He was here just yesterday.

As I walk through the garden
this one last time
memories of grandad engulf me
And I've been left behind . . .

Brenda Niedbalski
WAITIN' FOR OLE SANTA

Hey there Ma what's wrong
  with Pa?
I'm still waitin' for Santa Claus.
Pa's still slipping in his easy
  chair,
Sitting there in his red
  underwear.
Do you think Santa will ever
  come,
Or has Pa got him on the run?
Seems the night will never
  end.
Is Ole Santa really my friend?
I wish Pa would go to bed,
So Ole Santa will show his
  head.
Maybe if I just go to sleep,
By Pa Ole Santa will sneak.
I'm going to go lay down my
  head,
In hopes Pa won't hear his
  sled.
I guess I shouldn't be so
  forlorn,
There's always presents
  there in the morn.

Wendy L. Pifer
P. A. B.

i heard all about you
  but i didn't listen

i believed the best of you
  until i was proved wrong

but still after all the trouble
  i still believe in you

i know now what and why
  you are you

your exciting
  but most of all your free

i won't ever try to change you
  i can accept you as you are

you are a refreshing and true
  individual
    you are you
    and i love it.

Suzanne L. Houle
I AM BUT A LEAF

To you,
I am but a leaf
fallen from its tree.
Soon will come another
and take the place of me.

Virgie V. Jones
RAINBOW

Rainbow, Nature's own,
Arching across the sky
Made of moisture and sun rays

With your myriad of colors
Always, purple, blue, green
  yellow, orange and red
Is your pot of gold treasure
The colors to the eye?

Steven J. McDow
LONELY CASTLE

Stars lite the lonely castle,
where the king sits mournfully.
His armies have been defeated,
now they shall take him captive.

Hoof beats through the dark,
armor clatters as they near.
Still he sits to show no fear,
thinking back upon the years,
when his kingdom was in rule.

Yet he peers through dark of
  night,
suddenly shone their torches
  bright.
Soon his drawbridge shall fall
  once again,
but not forth shall he remain.

Norsena Marble DeCair
WAR FOR INDEPENDANCE

House empty
Out of oil
Hope for tomorrow
No food to spoil
Eating raw potatoes
Sure daylight will bring
  anewness
Someone must care
Do you, somewhere?

J. Howard Bray
A NOTE TO A SKEPTIC

You tell me there is no God
Then tell me when the wind
  blows, and the ice and sleet
and snow comes and goes
And the sun comes out on
  a spring day and rains fall
so gently upon the ground and
  flowers bloom and the
grass turns green
Then children play
And summers heat makes one
  want to run under a water
  fall
To cool the sweat that lays
  upon man's brow and then
The autumn leaves begin to
  make their exit and the
  wind
Is crisp and cold and strong
  and you start to wonder how
  small man's life is compared to
  time eternal
Then suddenly
it all ends
And when we stand in the
  presence of the one who
  created it
all
Can you honestly believe
There is no God?

Marianne Flike
MY VIEW

I stand
Alone
Gazing
this Mountain's Majesty

It never moves
It never does a thing
May it be unseen
He sways in the breeze
Mt. Hood

Kelly Ann Field
SHHH ,LISTEN

Streams rushing through the
  valley
whisper sweet melodies

Trees blowing the cold autumn wind
bring back lost memories.

Geraldine Mosely
A SINGULAR BIRD
You perch alone.
You fly alone.
You wade alone.
You eat alone.
You nest alone.
Singular bird you must be lonely
Like me.

Betty Louise Chuman
SAILING

The waves and the wind
of our lives take us in
and may lead us to places unknown.

As we sail our seas
and resistance release
all the harbors with ease become home.

Julie J. Schmalz
UNTITLED
I have never heard anything
as quiet as the desert
at 5:30 in the morning.
Silence, clear til cracked
by the rooster's crow
and the sun breaking the horizon.

My laughter startled me.

Terry Donohoo
THERE IS A PART
There is a part of all of us
In everything on earth and in the sky
For all of us have seen it
All of us have felt it
And everything we need
Is given us by nature.

Virginia Summers Martin
TO MY SON
A son is a many complex thing
who makes a mother's heart sing.
So thoughful, strong, loving and kind
You have made me happy to call you mine.
Each year that comes, but fades to fast,
our bond grows deeper than the last.
The memories you gave me are a joy true
I pray that God will keep blessing you.
Fine boy then, fine man now,
you show the others how
to stand up and be a man, lest they compare,
thank you for letting me share.

Sandra Bennett
UNTITLED

Travel life's distant roads
as I must,
because I walk not alone
but I follow no one
as no one follows me,
but rather,
I am beside friends.

Love as I want
not because I should,
for I have loved
in many different ways,
and these ways
have only made me
want to love stronger.

Learn as I will

all life has to offer,
for its teachings are priceless
and its value divine,
let me share its worth
so I may not just be a part,
but rather I be whole.

Mary Ann Hetterick
THE SHARING OF MAN AND NATURE
Come here little fawn;
Come here gentle one.
It's only me—
Your friend come to see
How you are.

I mean no harm;
I will not lure and
Then trap you.
I am your friend,
Remember?

We share something.
Our different existences
Have touched and
We share a feeling;
The fear of trust.

We understand each other
And slowly the fear fades away.
Trust is exchanged;
A bond created
Forever.

Theresa Ann Wagner
CRONY
Together we laughed, together we cried
Together we faced life's many trials
Through ups and downs, pains and joys
The caring spread, and always showed
Never just here and gone tomorrow
Always around to cheer up sorrows
Love that is special
Friendship that's deep
Sometime again our roads shall meet
Not a day will go by when of you I'll not think
Our friendship is strong, and shall never be weak
To you I hope and pray
Life's greatest most precious gifts shall come your way.

Robert W. Taft
OLD MAN
Now my days are almost spent
From times before my back was bent
I've seen so many things go by
I've laughed a lot
I've also cried.
I went to places I never thought I'd go
I lived life fast
I lived it slow.
My hands are wrinkled worn without care.
My life is litter everywhere.

Carmella Leonardo
YESTERYEAR
It seems like only yesteryear
when kids we were and lived real near
We played and romped all over the place
now see the changes in our face
We were young, no cares, no woes

So you're leaving, thats how it goes.
Take the many happy thoughts
Loving memories that can't be bought.
Soon you're not going to be near
It seems like only yesteryear.

Elisabeth Stein Frisby
THANK YOU ,APOLLO
I, the child of Light
had wandered into darkness
feeling despair clutching at my throat
when the brazen god appeared
and with his brightness
wrestled off hopelessness.

Susan Hope
CLOUDS
As I look up in the sky,
I see the clouds go drifting by,
The clouds somehow remind me of me,
As they drift by so aimlessly.
Now all too soon they find their end,
Other clouds will begin.
Then one day the sun will come out,
All the clouds will be forgotten about.

Carla Denee Mynear
DEPRESSED
Depressed, that's what I've been
Since you turned away
Depressed that's how I'll stay
Till once again you look my way.

Depressed, that's all I know
Since your love is what I'm denied
Depressed, that's how I feel
With all the tears I've cried.

Depressed is all that shows
Since you took away
Depressed is all that remains
Without my reason for each new day!

Mary Jane Ebert
SEARCHING
My name is called "searching" and
I come from your distant past.
I know you think you don't know me
But watch the dancing shadows I cast.

My perfume is the flowers of springtime,
My tears are the dew on a rose.
My skin is the last glow of sunset,
My voice is the wind that blows.

We met and touched, I went on my way,
only a memory in eternity's day.
You won't be the same . . .
My gift was your name—
called "SEARCHING"

Dori J. Carderara
BUTTERFLY
Among the many leaves of a trunk
speared through earth.
Is a small nested womb forming
a task of life.

As the sun shines on and night grows darker;
A pride in ultimate design is created;
To detect a beautiful new form . . .
A cocoon detached once more.
The trace of grace;
The flutter of wings;
Another bond of life . . .
the butterfly.

J. S. Sawyer
PRELUDE
This immortal static passage
sends emissaries to the court of Death.
No sense in frail forgiveness
or meddling twilight prayers.
These immortal leaves of purpose,
now one, now two, now infinite:
Posessions wrought to stand
as monuments etched in marble.
Upon my deathbed calling for memories
of miles of endless living,
days of silent thinking:
us, them, and I
No man can think out loud
of living in death's last moment,
no man withstands the despair—
learning to live with such in life
sends forgetful rain at last:
Stormclouds, please, confide in me,
and tell me where you are.

Merletta S. Wilson
DREAMS
Dreams shattered by reality,
Age wish to return to youth.
Looking for tomorrow,
Aching for independences,
Wondering always of love and death,
Youth cries, "be free."
From what, he does not know.
To be free from dreams shattered by reality.
Youth dreams, "Let me be free!"
To a cause, a purpose; are maybe strive
for a goal,
Yough cries, "Be free."
It isn't freedom,
But the purpose there very souls cry out for,
Which their mouths dare not whisper.
Youth strive for a goal, "Let me be free."

Patricia Freeman
PROLONGED SOJOURN
Lights rarely shine through the leaded glasses;
he retires with old Sol.
What the postman leaves for "Occupant"
is not his mail at all.

The chimney whispers gentle wisps;
his cookstove warms his room.
He slowly stirs his vegetables—
It'll be hours yet til noon.

Porch steps for sitting and sipping tea,
discussing grapes and ales
with the mistress of the dog next next door.
She listens to his tales.
Shuffling through the

abandoned parlour;
heaviness in his head—
doilies' delicate designes in dust—
his wife now twelve years dead.

Breeze touches the torn,
yellowed curtain.
Has sown; so shall he reap?
Time has remembered him all
too well.
The old man goes to sleep.

Richard Magnuson
ALONE TOGETHER

You draw near without touching
my spirit.
You listen without hearing
the depth of my emotion.
You see me without perceiving
the essence of my being.
You cannot experience my
perceptions,
Nor can I encounter your inner
world.
We are unique, individual,
separate, alone.
But the barriers of our
cloistered souls
Are transcended by the simple
act of caring.

Joan Rose
LOVE GROWS

When two lovers know
That their love will grow
To an end that is nowhere in
sight.

They can only suppose
That as their love grows
It will reach the incredible
height.

Where nothing and no one
Can dim their bright sun
Nor hide it forever from sight.

And so to the end
As lover and friend
They'll walk in love's dazzling
light.

Francene C. Cunsolo
MY SUNSHINE

The sun is a rare and beautiful
thing.

Its roundness and its color of
gold
cannot be replaced.

It sits in the heavens and shines
over all the world, never dying
out.

You are my sun, shining for all
eternity
over my life.

Nothing or no one will ever
replace you,
Because my love for you will
never die.

Deborah Jean Leech
THE PLACE TO BE

When my mind is all jammed and
jumbled,
With the problems of today,
I often go out to the country
Sometimes just to get away.

I sit by the brook and listen
To the sound of it flowing by.
How can any place be so peaceful
As this spot underneath the sky?

The wind whispers through the
trees,
Oh! The feel of it really calms
me.
The flowers with their fragrance
so fresh
Allows my mind to wander and
rest.

So you see the best place to be,
When the problems pull your
mind asunder,
Is the place where you can be
free
From this world that's so full
of blunders.

Fenton F. DeSilva
SNOW SCENE

I've trod on cotton
underfoot,
O'er miles and miles
of windswept waste,
And held the hand
that gently put, each
tiny snowflake in its
place.
I've watched the heavens
yawn and stretch,
Then, settle down
on cliff and stream,
And realized that God
can sketch, the things
that earthly artist
dream.

Rose Murphy
**GOVERNMENT GAL'S
LAMENT**

On a hot summer day in the
year '38
I took my first job and sought
my fate.
"Reproduction" became my
chore—
Of papers, that is; no children
I bore.
My colleagues tried to give me
some polish;
My rural ways they bade me
abolish.
My army bosses looked and
leered;
I dropped my eyes and was
much afeard:
I had heard of their evil lives—
Eager for mistresses but never
for wives.
Not for me to drink and
carouse;
I clung to my role of meek
little mouse.
The years went by, and I kept
on typing;
The Army continued its playing
and griping.
Now, all these years later, it's
plain to see
That still not a thing has
happened to me!

Mildred Zekoll
AN ODE TO A PICTURE

Your face forever smiles at me
Beneath that ruffled hair
That sweet persuasion comes
across
From glowing eyes and skin so
fair.
From working long in sun and
frost
From early morn til late at night
From climbing trees and being
the boss
Until exhaustion catches him
in flight.
The real you in garments of
trade
Long underwear, denims and
boots,
Expertise, knowledge, strength
made
A house a home with roots.
The real you framed by the fruit
of your hands
The gestures you make, your

beautiful voice
Your personality under glass, by
my bed it stands
But I'd rather have you . . .If
I had a choice.
At last I have caught the
essence of joy
In a frame, to keep my heart in
tune with the spirit
Your twin self at once a carefree
boy
And the mature life you live
with merit.

Maud R. Bowles
A YEARNING REQUEST

Looking back, through all the
years,
  Through the heartaches, and the
  tears.
I close my eyes, and try to see,
  Straighter, smoother paths for
  me.

In my solitude, I brood
  Find I'm in an awful mood.
Bluebird, fluttered, far away,
  Left me, oh so sad today.

While I'm sleeping, through the
night,
  Bluebird, why not change your
  flight.
Bringing dreams, that are the
best,
Hovering close, while I'm at rest.

And then when tomorrow comes,
  I'll pick up the meager crumbs
Wasted crumbs, beneath the
table,
  At least I hope that I'll be able.

Sharon I. Burgner
CONTENTMENT

To lay my head on Nature's
breast,
To feel her gentle, sweet caress,
To look into her sparkling eyes,
Reflected in the starry skies,
I rest. And in the evening
calm
I sleep enclothed in Nature's
balm.

Carla Tracy
SAYING GOODBYE

It always hurts to say goodbye,
especially to you.
I wish the word never existed
between us.
You always tried to make things
as easy as possible,
Even though I took it hard.
What we almost were,
  will never be.

Evelyn M. S. Edwards
DON'T BE AN UNBELIEVER

Being an unbeliever will never
bring you joy
Being an unbeliever is like a
broken toy
Only half together and the
pieces they can't mend,

Ah! Who could believe a broken
toy is so much like a man.
Being an unbeliever can only
bring you pain
Being an unbeliever is living all
in vain,
Yes, only half together the toy
can not mend
Only half together neither can
a man.

It's not an unbelievers world
For the world belongs to God!
Therefore become a true
believer
And you'll find your peace in
God.

Jean Carolyn Bradley
WHY I SHOULD WIN

Never a gift bestowed
for being chosen,
or being favorite,
to toil not
for euphoric flattery
but Notice of my Writings,
not to say . . .
I'm Alpha
or Omega
If only I should win
because I'm GOOD!

Debra Anne Akins
LE CHANGE

I am me;
You are you;
Together we are infinity.
As our love grows so we grow.
We are an extension of each
other.
Our minds are as one;
Our thoughts intertwine.
I become you as you are now
me.
Our souls are meshed.
And we are now . . .as forever. .
one!

Kymberlea A. Garcia
WHAT'S HIS NAME

I broke my family's name,
I broke my heart,
I broke my reputation,
I broke my parents' heart,
and I wrecked my sister's life.
All because I fell in love,
with what's—his—name.
It wouldn't be so hard if he
really cared but I feel so bad,
So hurt,
And so cheap.

Wendy Bellion
SOMEWHERE

Somewhere, over the rainbow,
(If all tales are true,)
Lies the enchanted pot of gold,
Waiting, waiting for you.

Somewhere, in this world,
Is a place at peace,
This is the only site,
Where all evil shall cease.

Somewhere, in your mind,
Lies a special dream,
Waiting to be pursued by you,
And no one else, it seems.

Somewhere, inside you,
Lies a spirit of truth.
But in some people, it is all used
up,
At the end of their youth.

Somewhere, in this world,
Is a heart of pure gold,
Concealed inside a single soul,
It is so I'm told.

Somewhere, somewhere
undiscovered,

Lie all unknown secrets,
Yet to be revealed to man,
Before the last sun sets.

Maria T. Williams
DELUSIONS

And I feel like crying
But the tears won't wet the
 dryness in my soul.
So I sit here sighing knowing I
 won't find
 the meaning of my role.

Am I only dreaming
When I see my life has grown so
 out of touch?
Oh, I sit here scheming ways to
 fill my needs
but not change things too much.

All of this confusion,
I tell myself I'm not the only one,
It's just life's delusion;
Always searching, always leaving
wants undone.

When I think about it, can I
 really say that something is
 amiss?
Must I always doubt it? Can't
 I just accept
 a simple happiness?

But I feel like crying
And the missing tears just add
 to my unrest.
And I would be lying if I told
 myself
 that I was at my best.

Marjorie Ellen DeSotel
ALONE

As I sit here alone in the dark
 with on ly my memories around
 me,
I long for a kind soul to talk to,
 to see.
They're all so busy, can't come
 today,
maybe tomorrow they say.
 Tomorrow comes and then the
 call,
just can't find a way.
Finally comes the time, they're
 here
for awhile,
If only they'd stay longer—Oh,
 how
 I'd smile.
But off they go and here I am,
 alone again,
Only memories all around until
 they come—BUT WHEN!

Tracy Mordovanec
THE WAITING

Death came stalking,
one cold, windy night.
On cloud-coated feet,
his timing just right.

The old man was ready,
his waiting was calm.
His wife gone before him,
and also his son.

Death was no stranger,
he'd met death before.
On the road to his home,
near the end of the war.

A sniper stood hidden,
his presence unknown.
As his son came out running,
to welcome him home.

When his wife heard the shot,
she came running as well.
Before he could stop her,
his life turned to hell.

So he waits without fear,
as his life ebbs away.
And death is his friend,
who will show him the way.

Craig T. Higgins
A FRIEND

I could have a million friends
But I only want one
Someone to stay beside me
When my fighting's done

I am not a holy man
But mercy is my cry
Just someone to hold my hand
When it's my turn to die.

I've had a few friends on the
 road
I've had a few in jail
Some have carried a hated load
But none will go to hell

As it was in the beginning
It will be in the end
Even in death I'm winning
If I have a friend.

Elizabeth Kay Jones
DEATH

I wondered about the question
The wise men stumble on . . .
Is death a real reality,
Or just a myth passed on?
If life is wonderfully beautiful,
Then why should we stop with
Death?
When we could be living another
 day,
And breathing another breath?
I hope that maybe someday
The world will stop to see
That death is not a life stopper,
But a step towards being free.

Diana M. Babcock
AUTUMNUS

Autumn came with her boquets
 of leaves in every hue
and trailing from her auburn
 locks
 are grapes still wet with dew.
Then raising bronzed and velvet
 arms
 she signals birds to fly
They swoop in low and kiss her
 cheeks
 and never question why.
They spread their wings and
 climb the air
 and salute her as they go
She waves her hand, then hurries
 on
 to escape the coming snow.

Carolyn Gustafson
PUNKIE

 He was such a wonderful fellow
such a joy to know, and yet it
 was so seldom
 that we really let him know.

I know today he sees us as his
 loved ones all are sad,
 he's in our hearts forever
and this makes him very glad.

I think through this we've finally
 learned
 what "family" really means
and hope and pray in some small

way
we can show it day by day.
So let us be united in our love
 for one and all,
for if we have each other
all else seems very small.

Anthony J. Deus
ODE TO A BROTHER PAST

I've seen a mighty race of people
Hurl a tomahawk and ride the
 herds of buffalo 'round
Living life on nature's terms
Until the white man shot them
 down.

Now all the teepee's are missing
Like the sounds of young braves
 weeping.

I've seen them look at me
The way they do an enemy
And through the freedom of the
 open plains
We drove them to eternity.

And now all the teepee's are
 missing
Like the sounds of young braves
 weeping
And the cry of war wounds
 bleeding
Their future's buried six feet in
 the ground.

Cynthia Henson
RAINBOWS

A rainbow is the key to heaven
That leads to God above
Reflecting its colors of happiness
And expressing its dreams of
 love.

It's the connection to faith and
 courage
Brightening the love we share,
As it recognizes the joy we
 cherish,
To show how much God cares.

Addie Mocca
FRIGHTENING

We all have fears
And we should, you know.
None is so great
 To never show.

But what do we fear?
 What do we say
When a frightful thing
 May come our way.

Thousands of feet up
 in the air we fly,
 yet we see a mouse
 and we run and hide.

What is this fear?
 What makes it so?
 It's only in your mind
 You know.

June E. Williams
REVELATIONS!

The world is full
of painted faces;
like clowns,
in yesterday's parade
marching to a tune
that has no sound,
to a beat
that has no drum.

**WHAT HAPPENED TO MY
 LAUGHTER?**

Diane Obuchowski
SNOW

Snow when it first falls reminds
 me of a new born baby
clean and white and pure. No
 faults, no sins just goodness.
But like new snow getting dirty
 as it lays on the ground

a child may acquire sins and
faults.

Beth Atwell
MATT (A BOY I LOVED)

This love I've had
For a thousand years;
Disappears, Reappears,
Finds its strength
Inside my tears.
Before I lived
There must have been
A part of you
Carried deep within.
I grew up and
Tried to hide
My secret Soul
From your searching eyes.
But it does no good.
You win the game.
Seeing you is always the same:
A fire in the soul
Can never die
For within my heart
Burns the brightest flame.

Marie Y. Larson
LIFE

At dusk the rain shrouds the city
 in its gray wetness.
The car lights pierce through
 like searing white irons,
 refusing to give way to the
 darkness.
The wheels tear the softened
 earth—leaving deep dark scars.
Soon the cold air turns the rain
 to snow.
And the city is reborn in its pure
 white virginity.
The lights dance on each flake—
 reflecting its joy.
The ground becomes fire, but
 the tire marks remain.
So as in life, the darkness gives
 way to light, but the
 memories remain.

Bessie Reynolds Robulich
FEAR

As a bee goes buzzing by,
I often wonder why.
People recoil in fear,
Swatting with hands far and
 near.

Don't they know this very
 thing
Causes it to give the sting.
With loving thoughts, send it on
 its way
And your fear won't sting this
 day.

Sylvina Theresa Simmons
SWINGS AND SLIDES

MIND SWINGS UP.
MIND SLIDES DOWN.
Filled with thoughts of just what
 what is what.
What should be done.
What should be naught.

FEEL SO GLAD.
FEEL SO SAD.
Day is dark and night is light.

Laugh and make fun
out of the drum and the dumb
Things and events make ears
 hum
in the din of the dark and the
 light of the bright.

Like a child on a swing,
Like a child on a slide,
Mind ever, ever,
SWINGS UP.
slides down.
SWINGS UP . . .

Scott E. Raymond
HIDDEN DAYDREAMS

Most people carry a hidden
  daydream,
tucked away in the back of
  their minds.
It's filed away in a secret place
that only the dreamer can
  find.

It was planted there when the
  dreamer was young,
and he knew what he wished
  could be.
Then life settled in, sealed the
  daydream in
with a mortar of reality.

The dream of what he could
  have done
is blocked by life's masonry:
a job, a house, locks and deeds,
reality's mortar and
  responsibility.

Then only a place to peek in is
  left.
To think and remember, the
  dream revives again.
It's shackled by years, fears
  and regrets,
but mostly, "if only, I knew
  that then."

The hidden daydream never
  totally fades.
It lives a long life, quiet but
  distressed,
without a chance to live outside
before the dreamer's life
  supressed.

A. L. Scarborough
THE LOVING

As a thought,
Conceived in calm and given,
Loving comes from within,
And has meaning.

A meaningful relationship,
Becoming without, understands,
And knowing, gives itself.

Given to interact, the parts
Are one—together . . .alone,
And the loving grows.

That growth being loving,
That thought conceived
Allowed to grow, provides.

And, in provision,
Considers it giving, inside and
  out,
Of self . . .of heart . . .of life.

So the loving comes,
And becomes a knowing,
Providing growth
And giving life.

Gladys McKeon
LEAVING

Spring brings forth in great
  profusion
Their symmetry one glorious
  illusion
Tho born of the self-same
  regal mother
Each child of the tree is like
  no other

Prints of nature ours to enjoy
Incalculable numbers without
  decoy
Living by nature's golden rule
Changeling pawns in her
  constant duel

Their beauty and strength is
  undenied
Displayed by her with maternal
  pride
In nature's court there's no
  need to defend

Fall will come and summer will
  end
She dresses her children in
  lovely array
They sing the wind song—it's
  a time to be gay
Let the leaving be lovely, a
  time to remember
For all of the living there comes
  a September.
Winter beckons and they
  reluctantly fall
some early, some late, they
  answer the call
Once free and alone, life and
  beauty will fade
As everything must in life's
  promenade.

Peggy Hedding
THE DOVES

In a far away land, one dark
  stormy night,
A flock of young doves from
  their perch all took flight.
Away they flew westward, to
  bring to this land
The hope of tomorrow, the
  touch of a hand.
They brought us a key to
  unlock the door,
They brought us sweet charity
  and peace evermore.
They gave to us life, they they
  all flew away,
Trusting we'd use wisely the
  gifts brought that day.
Don't break the trust of these
  beautiful things,
By failing to care what joy
  this day brings.
Don't throw away what's deep
  down inside
By trying to find a dark place
  to hide.
Be like the doves and spread
  hope around,
Then only and ever will true
  happiness be found.

Mary Skladanek
HOLD THE MAYO

You've got mayonnaise on your
  mustache
But I'll kiss you anyway.
Mustard, ketchup, bernaise
  sauce,
I'll kiss you every day.
It doesn't matter what you eat
  or wear in your hair.
You've got mayonnaise on
  your mustache
And a kiss beyond compare.

Rose M. McCoy
A WINTER'S DAY

Softly, silently, the small white
  flakes fall
quickly to the ground.
God's own winter blanket
  thickens with each
passing hour.
No human hand with any color
  mixture could make
as dazzling a painting as this
  beautiful
glistening coverlet from above.
Sparkling snow maids dance
  lively across freshly
fallen snow from daybreak til
  dusk.
Mischievous snow elves form
  layers of ice and gleefully
watch the unsuspecting
  passers-by
precariously pick their way to
  safer ground.

Children, too, bundled heavily
  against the nippy
air, frolic playfully in the
  frosty shroud.
Snow forts, snowmen, and
  snow sleds abound.
The most that can be, is made
  of each precious
moment in this winter
  wonderland for all too
soon it is over and God's
  next masterpiece begins.

Sandra Tyler Rubitsky
A THOUGHT

A tiny thought emerges into
  words
on a paper and a sentence is
  formed.
From that sentence a paragraph
  is shaped
and soon a story is created.
The story is read and soon a
  picture
develops—an interpretation of
  a
mere thought so carefully
  preserved
for the right moment when it
  can
mean more than just words.

Vivian Orrison
MY MANTEL

Through the years has grown
  Old.
It's standing there beautiful
  And bold.
Figurines, with their faces
  Aglow,
Handed down from the days
  of
Long ago.
In the evening when the fire-
  logs
Are lit,
I love to go there and
  Sit.

Sharon Roberts
FULL CIRCLE

My son was just a tiny child
a day or so ago,
Now he's grown away from me
in ways I cannot know.
He's fighting changes inside
  himself
that are making him a man . . .
And he feels sure, as I once did,
that no one can understand.
I'd like to take him in my arms
  and hold him
like he were small . . .
I want to tell him that what I
  have
I'd gladly give him all.
But at the moment I can't help
although I wish I could
Any gesture on my part would
  be misunderstood . . .
So I keep watch, silently, with
  a parent's grave concern . . .
Knowing that once he finds
  himself
then to me he can return.

Myrtle B. Walker
WHAT BE MY DESTINY

Pain of a sword plunged deep
  in my heart,
breath I can hardly breathe;
beads of sweat upon my brow,
Lord, what be my destiny?

Each path I trod in my life
the sweets has turned to bitter;
with wounded heart and
  twisted mind,

love has dried and withered.
Death's cold hand which now I
  hold
would be lord so much sweeter;
and yet I breathe one breath of
  air,
with pain my body shivers.
With vultures hovering all
  around,
to pick upon my bones;
I ask you Lord "why not now?"
Why must death be prolonged?
What be my destiny, O lord,
that this I must endure;
I need you Lord to light my
  path
of this one thing I'm sure.

Dorothy I. Roberts
BRINGING US CLOSER TOGETHER

The time is very near when a
new life will enter into our
  world,
With the likeness and personality
of the two of us unfurled.

I hope he has your intelligence,
quick wit and winning smile
They will remind me of you—
  when you are away,
you'll be here—all the while.

He most likely will have a
hot temper, as we sometimes
  show ourselves,
But once he knows his family
and can see his needs are
  fulfilled,
He'll seldom show that
temper except to demand of us
  his will.

He'll be beautiful and
anyone who sees him will have
  to agree
That a baby like ours brought
here with such love would be
  special,
unique and sent from above.

I often hear parents say
"the baby has made us so close"
But I don't think they
realize, although they
  continually do boast
That, of course they are
closer, and so much in love and
  aware
of their newfound joy
But the love they share
has made them fully aware
Because its in the eyes of their
  girl or boy.

Lorraine Latini
A WEEK

The joys of giving, the joys of
  life,
The sorrows of anxiety, the
  sorrows of strife.
A face with a blank stare, one
  with a smile,
Some faces with tears,
  sometimes once in awhile.

Men going to work with hassles
everyday.
Some can accept the pressure,
some will go astray.
Women with children, some
are happy, some are sad,
Striving to give them things
they never had.
Children grow up, then take
a look around.
Some can face reality, some
go homeward bound,
Hurrying, hurrying, everyday
like a streak.
But we have one good thing to
be thankful for
There's only seven days to a
week.

M. K. McCorquodale
SOUL SET FREE

One morning from my leafy
hiding place I watched a
hunter
with rifle aimed and steady arm
make the first kill of the day.
His aim was accurate and my
own heart felt the pain
as the bullet pierced that other
beating heart.
The echo of the shot
momentarily deafened all
cept one,
and he lay dead on the red and
gold leafed forest floor.
A moment more and he would
not be resting thus, but safe
away.
His body was poised in flight
and his hooves had left the
ground
when the shot rang out, and
heavily he fell to the earth.
But in the time between life
and death I saw a shadow
move,
just a faint blurred image that
quickly blended with the
trees.
Was it just the shadow of a
gently swaying branch I saw,
or was it the spirit of some
lost soul at last set free.

Amelia Olivette Mower
PRESENT AND PAST

Think of the present, how we
have sought—
Think of the past, let it bother
us not!
Think of the present, we have
in our hand—
Think of the past, but bury it
in the sand!
Think of the present, for now
it is here—
Think of the past, but shed not
a tear!
Think of the present, and love
that you share—
Think of the past, as though it
weren't there!
Think of the present, you're
part of the cast—
Think of the past, gone forever
at last!

Nancy Kostura
REALITY

Down to the ocean I must go,
for there my mind is at ease.
As I watch the waves briskly
tumble in, and taste the
salty breeze.
I sit in the sand so quietly like
the wind my thoughts they
flow.
What will tomorrow bring my

way, where did yesterday go?
Slowly the sand trickles through
my fingers, the sun cast a
shadow on me.
I listen to the seagulls sing, how
wild, pretty and free.
The sea rushes in to kiss the
shore, then slowly drifts
away.
Taking with it my sand castle,
which I proudly built today.
I collect the shells in various
sizes, the colors amaze me
so.
I want to stay here for ever and
ever, but I know it's time to
go.
Once again I must leave this
place, then reality comes to
mind.
I've never seen the waves
tumble in, since birth I have
been blind.

Beverly Bowers
THE OUTDOOR SHOW

Winter varies
tarries
vascectomy of
the soul
alive the
frostbitten winds
crystals hang
cylinders of sky
suspended in air
along the land
night at last
dawn a churning
morning burning
sun abreast
reborn again
life's a comin'
dressed in smooth
yellow rays . . .
oh warm the skin
ice cracks
water flows
flowers reach
petals glow
spring's arrivin'
farewell snow!

Jean Holmes
**YESTERDAY AND
TOMORROW**

To learn that once you loved
me
In that time so long ago
Has brightened up my pathway
And I'd like to tell you so.

My joy at once more meeting
In that happy, rustic place,
Gave me hope for my
tomorrows,
Put a smile back on my face!

The years since first we parted
Have been filled with joy and
pain,
But at last God has arranged it
So our paths would cross
again!

Jerry Lee Sanders
**THE TREASURE OF BLOOD
MOUNTAIN**

There is a treasure, or so they
tell,
Left 'fore the Trail of Tears;
A treasure hid deep inside a
well,
Lost, lo, these many years!

If one should wish to find that
fountain,
The key to all life's leisure,
Begin thy search upon Blood
Mountain—
There lies the Cherokee Treasure!

And, ah, such riches thou wilt
behold,
Ne'er held by the likes of man:
Rubies, diamonds, silver and
gold,
Left 'hind by the Caravan!

But they hid it well, those wise
old owls,
Hid it for their children's kin,
Hidden from e'en the beasts
and fowls,
Hid deep within Blood
Mountain's glen!

Tis true, they say, the moon
will show
The secret of that hidden door;
Reveal the mark only they will
know
When rouse they from their
sleep of yore!

And rise they shall when
Winter's past,
Arise a greater Nation;
'Rise when Lookout's shed its
caste,
'Rise to their rightful station!

Joyce Laird Kennicutt
LOVESNOW

The snow seems to wash
over the maples and the pines,
in wondrous white waves;
A superb stillness follows—
as even the 'big rigs'
are safely sidelined—
on the deserted highway;
The piercing shriek
of the visiting jay,
momentarily shatters
the deep silence;
Reach out and touch the quiet;
Gather it close around you,
like a warm
white shaw;
A gray world—
suddenly so simply beautiful
so cozy so serene;
Humans
who normally hurry and scurry
unseeing unhearing,
miraculously become aware;
Respond
with helpful snowshovels—
battery chargers—
good fellowship personified;
First storms
inexplicably arrive,
with softly special
love laden snow.

Wendy Wilson
I DIDN'T WANT TO CALL

I didn't want to call,
I thought, maybe I could forget
it all,
But I guess I was wrong,
Because I've been thinking for
so long,
But I haven't reached a
conclusion,
Everytime, just more confusion
Builds up inside of me,
For free, I guess, I can never be.
He said he'd always be there,
But I wonder where,
I hope he's not trying to forget
my name
'Cause I can't forget he ever
came
In just a couple days
He became familiar with my
ways.
He walked in, somebody I didn't
even know,
Quietly I said, to myself, "Here
I go."
I told him how I felt, I bet he

thought I never would,
But I talked and he listened and
understood.
He came in a stranger and left
a friend.
I hope I have him as a friend
To see me through, if there's
an end.

Clara Mae Bradbury
**TRAVELING LIFE'S
HIGHWAY**

As I travel down life's highway,
I don't care for charity.
All I want is faith and hope,
Peace and harmony.

I don't want any special favors,
Don't care for mansions and
fame,
Don't care to be in society,
Give me friends who are always
the same.

I've never dreamed of riches,
Just give me a word of praise,
When I do the best I can,
Traveling on my way.

All I ask is a pat on the back,
If the going gets too rough,
Never, tell me that I failed,
Or didn't do enough.

For the things in life, that really
count,
Are the things we do and say.
The aid we give, and the way
we smile,
As we travel life's highway.

Kurt R. Daniels
QUITE

should never have been
someone—

would
much rather have been
a brilliant color
in a remembered autumn
afternoon
    (turning into
        eventual darkness).

Marjorie Grippo
AUTUMN ESCAPADE

Autumn is like an elderly lady
Grown jealous of youth and
Spring
So puts on her most brilliant
colors
For a last short fling.

Gloria Morris
REMEMBERING

Who am I?
I will tell you who I was.
I was the sand blowing past
desert tents
long ago.
I was the parchment upon
which were written
great and beautiful words
in the age of Pericles.
I was the wind that swept across
Europe
in the wake of many wars.

I was the firmament, moving
as the Universe evolved.
I was the light
of the first morning star.
I remember,
and by longing,
I am here, again and again.
And all the ages become as
one day
In this time.
I am all of you
and you are me.
Can you see
how we are all connected,
one to the other?
Every atom, every molecule,
shimmering and glowing,
Ready to sing, to dance, to
celebrate,
in one voice,
The endless possibilities
of our own creation.

Sharon Marjorie Gattus Davis
A FLY ON MY WINDOW

I heard you tried to kill a fly,
But, I think someone told me
a lie.

I know a fly you only swat,
But, thirty-five stitches is what
you got.

Take care, be good, get plenty
of rest,
And in a few days you'll be
again at your best.

But, do me a favor cause I like
you so much,
The flies you can kill, but the
windows, don't touch!

Suzanne Y. J. Cuell
NATURE'S WAY

The autumn leaves are falling,
It's part of nature's way
To give the trees a chance to
rest
Until some time in May.

The ducks and geese will all
fly south
To winter in the sun,
But they'll come back in Spring
time
When the water starts to run.

The northern lights are dancing
Beneath the harvest moon;
And owls are perched up in
the trees
To chant their eerie tune.

The earth seems almost ready
For the change that's taking
place;
Now winter winds will usher
in
A different kind of face;

We'll marvel at God's
masterpiece
Created by the frost.
The snow will cover all the
ground
But no one should feel lost.

Tho' winter brings much
darkness
We'll seldom worry or feel blue,
But rejoice in always knowing
The sun will still peek through.

Kathy Bradford Roberts
THE BIBLE

The Bible is a sacred book; into
which many and all may look.
Its pages tell of people and
deeds;
how Moses was found among
the reeds.
How David used a mighty sling,

and Pharoah gave Joseph his
powerful ring.
How Daniel was saved from the
lion's den, yet people doubted
even way back then.
Yes, the Bible is a book where
answers are found.
You'll find them too if you just
look around.

Odrey Chaney Wootan
TO A BROKEN HEART

Do not suffer any longer;
Love will find a way.
On wings of Love
We'll go together
To find another day,
Where there is laughter sweet
And sunshine.

Barry J. Bruno
FROM ME TO YOU

A tint of blue, yet mostly
yellow
Warmth is always close at hand
Peaceful, calm and a bit mellow
A good time to take a stand
Thoughts of a happy, healthy
life planned.

It is only fitting that Spring is
near
You dealth winter a mighty
blow
Being with you is a treasure so
dear
The truest of pleasures that
I will know
A life of love that is sure to
grow.

Eager expectations of a future
at last
To be with you is my primary
goal
You make it so easy to forget
the past
All that is me you have stole
My life, my love, my very
soul.

L. Janeene Versfelt
NURSING HOME NIGHTMARE

Slender lady, past eighty, you
woke up screaming in the
night.
A creature crept into your dream
and gave you quite a fright!
You bolted from bed in your
dim lit room, into the brighter
hall.
Unconsolable, uncontrollably
trembling, "Papa" you loudly
call.
Phantom creature scares you
still, for sleep you're too
upset.
Sit in the day room, hold my
hand. Are you feeling better,
Pet?
Eat a cookie, drink some milk.
What? Home, you want to go?
This is your home now, dear,
Though sometimes you don't
know.

There is a man in your life. The
staff has met him, too.
He has greying hair, a wrinkled
brow and smiling eyes of blue.
He takes you riding in his car
on Sunday afternoon.
Your other nightmare is, he
has to bring you back so soon.
You call the man who loves
you, from dawn till day is
done.
No, you're not calling Papa, Dear.
You're calling for your son.

Fay Duke
LONELINESS

Loneliness is terrible, there's
no one to talk to, no one to
hold
and no one to love. There's a
big difference in being alone
and being lonely.

Being alone is your choice but
being lonely is a state of
sadness

from the need and want of
companionship. This state
is not good
for your health nor your mind,
you should be full of life and
happy.

When you have someone to
share this happiness with,
there is no
time to be lonely or sad.

Find someone to share with
you both their good times
and bad
times, then you'll find a world
full of happiness and joy.

THINKING OF YOU.

Ransdell Hunter
**HOW WOULD YOU HAVE US
PART?**

How would you have us part?
I listen to your stepped logic.
I fell the caress of your eyes
And the words that manipulate
without meaning.

You give reasons, but you cannot
answer why.

Would you have our bond
dissolved
By a simple reaction?

Love is seldom neutralized—

Unless . . .yes, of course. You
Are right, it can be:
By a one-to-one ratio
of time.

Rhonda E. Flowers
THE FUTURE

As we look ahead
Hoping to see;
That wherever we may tread
Traces of our lives will be.

Looking to the future
What do we see?
Uncertainty and yet hope
To be or not to be.

Stephanie C. Bane
ROSES

As the dew settles on the rose
in the morn,
It glows like a diamond ring.
And it stands so very tall and
proud,
As if it were a king.
The rose resembles the world
around,
Blossoming so well.

The rose has a story,
That only it can tell.

Vita Gomes
THE UNADOPTED

She is stranger than most
Often missing the joke
Keeps to herself, sometimes
stutters and shakes
She is so hard to talk to and
afraid of mistakes

Her life is so empty, no love,
no sharing
Makes you wonder inside why
it is that you're caring.

But taking the time to learn
why she is
Has helped you be strong and
let her belong
You have opened the door and
carved out a path
Her footsteps behind you are
your only reward.

Alice C. Carroll
HOPE

It's hot.
The dusky gray and green
Of the foothills are stifled
Under the white hot sky.
Birds line up on the wires,
And there is no breeze to
Ruffle the heaviness.
But on the horizon,
A small black cloud
Begins to grow.

Tamilla Davies
LOVE

Love is you
Love is me
That's why I drew
This tree
The tree is special
But not special enough
For you and me

Natalie Rose Scavone
SNOWFLAKES

White as an ewe-lamb,
soft as a baby's skin,
the snow comes falling down.

Crystal-cut snowflakes
pondering their arrival
until . . .
finally they explode . . .
molecules of beauty.
Snowflakes.

Sheila C. Thompson
DANCIN'

Making love with
You
is like
Dancing
Graceful
Rhythmic
One basic step
A thousand variations.

Lana Putney Apana
STARS FALL

Stars fall
from the sky—
And I
wonder—
Are they missed?
Will there be
anyone to
notice?
Or, will the
void be
filled by
other stars
changing
positions—
Yes, I wonder

f astronomers
and God
are all who
notice that
another
light's gone
out in
our canopy'd
outdoor
room?!

Karen L. Will
WINDS

I have whispered my love for
you to the winds . . .
As the winds change from
season to season,
They show you the many
ways of my love . . .
The soft breezes in the morning
mixed with scented fragrances
and light moist dew . . .
Tenderness
The strong crisp gusts that
blow the rain clouds before
they burst
forth to saturate the earth . . .
Passion
The fierce, strong, hard gales
that escort the hurricanes,
tornados
and cyclones, spinning their
destruction.
Leaving a barren countryside . . .
Anger
As the snow falls, the wind
carries them to your face,
Kissing as
they meet the warmth of your
skin, saying good-bye as they
melt . . .
Happiness.
Walk with the wind wherever
you are. Listen as it tells you
of my love.
Breathe it deeply, so that it
may touch you, and be
with me for I am with
you. Mine is a love that will
carry on long as a single
leaf moves, with
the stirring of air . . .

Joy—Lyn Kenter
WINTER

Bleak skies, scrawny trees, and
bitter, cold snow slushed
here and there
Winter in all its bleakness is
here everywhere.
Snow sleighs, children's
laughter, snowboots and
fur-lined caps
Ragged torn, worn clothes
worn by rough, mean-looking
chaps
Wine and highballs sipped in
huge glowing halls
Only water, dry bread, and
moans in dusty, dirty
holes in walls
Warm, clean beds and warm
gowns with undisturbed
rest
Filthy ragged blankets where
rats infest
Winter can be such a wonderland
and happiness
Or it can be a bare existence
with death and unrest.

Denise Parker
WHITE ROBIN MORNING

One angelic dawn,
before the night pressed her
parting kiss
upon the blissful, open palm

of day,
from some unspoken realm
deep within the mystic sphere
of filigree and fantasy
where dream designs reshape
reality,
he silently materialized in
robin-form
of regal, alabastrine white
—a flawless, mesmerizing
monument to space—
gleaming in the aura of
evaporating dew
and, like a breathtaking newborn
star
gliding peerlessly through
predestined solitudes of
Heaven,
carried the morning with him
on effortless wings of
inevitable flight
to unparalleled heights of
ethereal dimension.

Wendy Karen Fabeck
HE

He came upon a summer's day
And swiftly stole my heart
away
With laughing eyes and tender
cries.
With leaps as high
As trade winds fly
We rushed to greet
The morning sights: golden
slopes of wintry white
gave sudden show of nature's
fight
to waken the dormant
meadows green,
soft and gentle,
warm and serene.
We laughed and sighed,
Beheld a sight,
A tender moment—seagulls in
flight.
With vacant minds
And rushing souls
Of freedom
We hopelessly tried
To match their speed
And fell to the earth in our
efforts
Fatigued.
Our bodies warmed with golden
graces,
Life's fantasy upon our faces,
Hand in hand we lay to rest
As the promise of summer
Sank in the west.

William T. Spivey
AMERICA, YOU CREATED THIS GLOW

The freedom to search for a
pot of gold
Has made America the land
to behold;
Giving all a chance to chase
the rainbow
Of arrayed colors and ever-
mystic glow.

This glow of freedom has
attracted many,
and created for you, somewhere,
another enemy.
They continually send spies
to your shores
Attempting to break through
your secret doors,
And tarnish your sparkling
gleam;
Yet, America, that sparkle
is supreme.

So, shine America, shine even
though;
Your considerate acts shall

create a new foe.
Just remain that land so
free,
And we shall continue to
defend Thee.
Just shine, America, you
created this glow.

Robert Daniel Areniuar
SITUATION

My cries will never be heard
The lines I speak will never be
written
I feel so cold on this journey
This place of mountains has
ended
Helpless so much, animals have
finally turned against me
Prey on me beast; I preyed on
you
The fall was not small
My winter I wish was gone
I am a trapped hunter
A making of my own kind
Searching so much for fur
A curse I gave for me
For I am a hunter, and soon I
will die.

Audrey Dean Cowan
THAT'S LIFE

It is said we have
One life to live,
Yet, people wonder
AS we beget , and beget,
If this is all:
What is the reason?
They're heard to shout,
Looking for answers.

The answers are found
from day to day,
As we live each moment,
Each in his way,
The truth for one,
Is not truth for all,
In living our way,
We stand, or we fall.

So, it all depends
On our point of view,
Of why we're here
To view the unknown.
I think we should live,
And do our best
To live each day,
And to hell with the rest!

Ginny John
TETON STREAM

White capped swirling water
Singing on its way,
Through deep entrenched
canyons
As it rushes to the bay.

Along its crevices and edges
Lay boulders large and small,
Products of molten lava
A part of the mountain wall.

Trees engulfed with liquid
Burned and turned to foam,
Land once so fertile,
Ruined by the burning cones.

Giants of yesteryear
Guarding streams and bays,
Setting as a sentinel,
While Teton rushes away.

Leo V. Hine
UNITED WE WERE, UNITED WE'LL BE

Sent from heaven out of birth,
God gave me you here on
earth.

United on earth just for awhile,
now that you're gone I'll miss
your smile.

I'll miss the sweetness you

offered me dear,
and maybe at moments I'll want
you near.

Remembering the goodness we
had so much of,
I'll always be thankful we
both were in love.

I will not cry, but remember
instead,
all the sweet memories, and no
tears will I shed.

For united we were, and united
we'll be,
up in God's heaven for eternity.

Stella Parpana
JOURNEY TO THE SEA

Do you remember?
When I went away
To a quiet place
Across the Bay
I drifted my boat
Out towards the Sea
And sailed into the sunset
My Soul was in ecstacy
I sailed the Sea alone
I was away from my Land,
my Home.

Sailing the vast clear waters
Gave me a brand new
perspective
I felt bold and courageous
I felt deeply contented
I grew to love the Sea.

I was born on the Land
But the Sea is truly my home
Where time and space
Is for the Loner
There my Soul flows free.

David Pope Seiberling
MORNING CALLING

A cool breeze
in the softness of morning,
Whispered a subtle stirring
from the bottom of the day,
A hushed sigh,
which showed where poplars
shimmered against the sky.

It played and skipped,
danced and ran
with my mind in time,
I was as the day,
already off
and along my way.

Frances Grant Plant
JUDGE NOT MY FRIENDS

Judge them not, for it's not
the way
Judge them not, not today
It's not our place, to judge our
friends
Jesus will decide, what are
their sins
A real true friend is hard to find
They accept your failures, and
your triumphs
They help when you need
someone to care
But never do they talk and tell

Don't talk about my friends
to me
For I love them, as you can see
My mother told me to pick
them wise
My father told me to look
inside
You never know where a person
has been
what are his burdens, what are
his sins
Just look for the good in
everyone
You'll be blessed . . .in Heaven
above.

Michelle Paszek
THE MASTERPIECE

We followed the road to our
masterpiece
Winding through the marks of
time
Which rose to meet us
We trudged silently among
broken schemes,
And empty bottles
Which lay as remnants of some
forgotten dream.
Like pilgrims we walked the
dusty paty,
Restless in the summer
afternoon.
As we neared the beach and
gazed upon our castle
Wall of wood and stone,
Made with uncertain hands.
And the waves foamed softly
around the foundations
As we gazed on our creation
in quiet reverie.
Built from the wreckage we
had gathered from the shore,
No fortress ever stood so proud
As the shelter we had built
around us,
Our embattled dreams were
shining
in our eyes
We'd sit inside
Staring out to sea from the
single window
Laughing at the waves
Like children,
Playing with our masterpiece
of time
Then wordlessly we pulled
down the walls
And left the pieces to wash
away.

Nancy A. Weaver
TODAY

Today is a beautiful day,
tomorrow may not be as
beautiful,
Today it is sunny, warm, and it
smells like Spring.

Spring smells like life is
beginning once again,
slowly but surely—sprouting
up everywhere—reaching
for the sky.

The Spring Sun casts an
effervescent glow, which
makes
people feel happy, free from
their troubles, burdens and
anxieties—ready to try again,
to piece it all together,
to smile, to forget the past,
and to perfect the future—
to enjoy the time until the
sun disappears once more—
and then . . .to look for it
behind the clouds, and wait.

Today is a beautiful day,
tomorrow may not be so
beautiful.

Sharon M. Hoban
THE LAST ROSE OF SUMMER

Oh, the last rose of summer,
Still in summer beauty—
Still in glory and splendor,
But fall's chill winds
Shall soon steal your beauty
And end your days of reign.
It brings a tear to my eye,
It reminds me so of thee
And the love we once shared.
Perhaps there will be another
sometime,
Just as fresh and lovely,
But still not the same as
The last rose of summer.

Virginia M. Roberts
MAGIC BALLOON

Looking out my window to the
street below,
Watching people passing, and
feeling the
city's bitter cold.

Noting dead men's faces as
walking ghosts
and in their hearts knowing
the grave as a
welcome host.

God! Save me from this
dreadful end.
Take me from this city with
its corruption
and sin.

Yes, I know some day all this
will pass and
I will be free, free at last.

I'll be chasing a rainbow,
touching the moon,
traveling far in my magic
balloon.

Upward and away where birds
dare not fly,
Alone in my magic balloon
piercing the sky.

Joseph Royal Shaver
PETTY THEFT?

A larceny of delicate skin
The unsung hero keeps
the bundle of his pride and joy
While loving mother sleeps.

Baby's warm, contented breath
awaites
as Daddy plays for keeps
A pillage designed for the time
he lost
while Mommy wakes and
weeps.

Diana Graham
MY AMARILLO MORNIN'

It's an Amarillo Mornin'
waking up by your side.
The sun's shinin' in and
the breeze is blowin' by.
Your skin's so soft
with me laying by your side.
I love it all, you and

my Amarillo mornin'.
It's an Amarillo mornin',
so let's stay in bed today.
Lovin' you and Lovin' . . .
and Lovin's all the way.
The sun is gettin' higher now,
yet neither one of us have
moved.
Not feelin' you move, but
knowin' your mood.
You and my Amarillo mornin'.
I want to stay with you all
day.
Not to you,
will I ever say goodbye.
Because you and my Amarillo
mornin'.

I love you.

Lynn Trudell
REBORN

With beach sand between my
toes
And ocean winds
Billowing through the trees
My mind begins to
wander
To younger days
When life seemed untouched
When I was free and lively
Unencumbered by problems
and cares
Which drag me through life
There on the beach
I am reborn into life
To start again and win.

Dorothy T. Puckette
ONCE UPON

Once upon a street, you were
standing there,
Eyes so soft and tender, sunlight
in your hair.

Once upon a heartbeat, I did
chance to say,
Would you care to wander
with me on my way?

Once upon a star, I wished
you for my own,
knowing not you would never
belong to anyone!

Once upon a parting, I was
standing there,
Rain around me falling, grey
skies everywhere.

Once upon a heartbreak, tear
filled eyes can't see
Anything but loneliness in this
life for me.

Jean Steinhoff
**A COWBOY AND HIS
HORSE**

"The outside of a horse
Is good for the inside of a man"
Someone thoughtful and wise
once said.
A cowboy and his horse
Have learned to function as one,
In the course of the lives
they've led.
And they share every day
Bonds of trust and of love,
And a closeness to nature
and God,
That help them stand tall,
Though the way may get
rough,
On the trails of life that they
trod.

Linda R. Buerger
INSPIRATION

I will pick up the pieces of
my life, which have fallen to
the

ground
I shall place them together much
better than placed before
My eyes will shine with tears, for
my life will become
enriched
It shall become even better, I
shall lift my hands and give
thanks.

Thanks to the Earth that I
am on everyday I am given
Thanks to the Sun that
brightens each day and glows
in my heart
Thanks to the Stars that shine
at night looking like diamonds
in the sky
Thanks for having friends to
love, and giving me strength
to
cope.

B. Joan Barna
IN THE BABY'S ROOM

The wind held its breath to
squeeze through a loost
shutter
At the top of the stairs and
entered a nursery.
It gently rocked the oaken
cradle and softly sniffed the
pink crocheted
Coverlet like a purring pussy
cat.
It billowed the lace curtains as
it brushed past the window
then pleated a
Silken cobweb atop the flowered
wallpaper.
As it drifted over the night table
it rustled the pages of an open
book
And sweetly kissed the tiny
up-turned faces of purple
pansies
Floating in a crystal bowl.
It stilled for a moment as if
resting on the needle point
stool
At the foot of a little yellow
rocking chair.
Refreshed, it mischeiviously
sent the rocker moving back
and forth,
Kicked at the braided rug and
blew a bootie off the dresser
top.

Then sighing, as if reluctant
to depart, it leaned over the
cradle and
Softly wound the baby's
golden curls around its
dew-tipped fingers;
Turned and slipped back
through the shutter into the
misty dawn.

Candace Van Dyk
ASSURANCE OF SECURITY

Flowing out from sin's domain
my rocky path was weaved;
Tangled webs of vain deceit
ne'er to be believed.

Then from the depths, tran
tranquility
dispersed my deep despair;
The Lord sent forth His love
to me
to show me someone cares.

Fleeing forward from the past
escaping judgment's claim;
Awakened from the dream at
last,
assured of what's to gain.

Assurance of security

lies not in vague reward;
The battle's won through
  Jesus Christ—
the foe yields up his sword.

Shirley J. Bach
**NINE HOURS BY
GREYHOUND**

Nine hours
By Greyhound
I hope wheels fly
With heavenly speed
Bringing the sight of you
At the end of the journey.
I'll sleep and dream
While, traveling through
cold towns, hazy smog
And smothering cities.
I'll awake heavy-lidded
Still half in a dream—
Weary I'll stumble from
The bus, stiff, from the
Non-use of my legs.
Nine hours
by Greyhound
By God, I hope those wheels
fly.

Sherrie Ploof
THE MIDNIGHT HOUR

The clock upon the wall
tells loud and oh so clear
while I pace the floor
waiting for you, dear

Ask yourself what could be
  wrong
He's usually never this late
So why bother getting upset
Sit and contemplate

While you try to be
understanding
sympathetic and you care
wondering if the police heard
  anything
but then should you dare

So five hours later he's smiling
that stupid silly grin
But the only words out of your
  mouth
are "Where the hell have you
  been?"

Teresa Avery Stines
THE PROMISE

There in the distance the valley
  sits gleaming,
Emersed in an emerald haze.
"The Promised Land" the
  deed reads
And even the sun peeks
Over the hills to gaze at her
  beauty.
Amid the luxurious rolling
  meadows
A cabin stands underneath a
  rainbow
And reminds man of something
  long forgot.
To one side the mountains
  stand
On guard to protect the land
From all unfortunate danger
The wind whispers "I love you"
  to all God's chosen few
And as it whirls by it paints in
  the clouds
"I've created all things anew."

D. R. Reed
POST-VIETNAM SYNDROME

Hey there Uncle Sam
Remember when you sent your
  boys off to Vietna,
Well, some came home
unaclaimed and very still,
And others came home quite
ashamed and very ill.

'Ya say that stuff that you
  sprayed,
Would help give us warning
  about the next incoming raid,
Now the times of after-effect
  are 'a prevailin',
Cause of the herbicide that
  we were 'a inhalin'.

You knew that Agent Orange
  contained dioxin,
Yet you failed to realize the
  effects of this damn toxin,
Yes, many times I sit idle
  in my dwellin',
Packing ice around all this pain
  and swellin'.

Oh, all I hear now is Veteran
  life insurance litter,
And all those words that we
  served in glitter,
Now is the time for the V.A.
  to pay out all the debts,
For all of us loyal, suffering
  vets.

Arlene Harwell
SHORTY

His hair was grey, his eyes were
  blue
He was short, just stood five
  foot two
But to me he was ten feet tall
This guy I met when I was
  forty
His name was Herman, but he
  was known as "Shorty."
I loved him so much, thus
  did we all.
He always said "Hi" and wore
  a smile
And for anyone he'd go that
  extra mile
He loved God and all people
  too
He drove a cab, his number was
  one
He was humble, he knew God's
  son
This was seen in what he'd do
  for you.
He's living in Heaven now, I
  know
Every day we all miss him so
But again we will see his eyes
  of blue
And sit with him at Jesus'
  feet
Where all things are forever
  sweet
This "Shorty" of mine that I
  loved so true.

Eleanor Morris
NO LONGER RUNNING

Light flickers in the window,
Playing a different pattern,
  coming on a different slant.
Fall is here, nights are cold,
Windows shut against the chill.
But still I hear through glass
  a faraway, half-forgotten song:
Crickets chanting—slower,
  slower as frost comes near.

It is a time of dreaming.
Remembering what was, wishing
  for what might have been.

Yet laced through it all is
  hope:
Not the exstatic hope of youth,
But a softer, faith-full hope.
No longer buffetted by winds
  of will
My soul is slowing down and
  filling up—

How can a soul be full
If it is always on the run?

Jane Edmonds
SPRING

The sky is so blue
Not a cloud can be seen
The birds sing so cheerful
The meadows are green
Spring comes alive
With bright colored flowers
Just waiting for sunshine
And April showers

Rebecca Jean Haley
MY PLANS OF DUST

In youth
My dreams of fresh plans
New ideas
Seemed as shooting stars
There for me to catch
And ride to worlds unending
all glamorous, mind expanding
Now in age my eyes see
nothing was new
nor was it my own invention
Rather
all repitious dredges
Gone like yesterday's smoke
Whitened like yesteryear's
  golden tresses.

Katherine Ann Wong
IF ONLY I KNEW

At times I wonder
how the world can be so unkind,
with only thoughts of hatred
coming from troubled minds.

Why must people suffer
the tragedies of war
and when can people stop
  worrying
when there's a knock upon the
  door?

Please help me to understand
how the world can be this way,
and why people aren't always
  sincere
in everything they say.

Barb Baca Djokich
IN EVERY WAY

Always on my mind
Trying to find
How it came about
Always having doubts
Every moment you were alert
Now to watch it only hurts
What is the cure
I'm not sure
If only I had the chance to say
I'm sorry in every way.

Pam Crabill
MY CONSCIENCE

At night, as I lie quiet,
I hear a whisper in my ear.
It is a wise whisper,
for it knows even
the greatest secrets
my heart can hold.
This whisper tells me of
all my faults,
And reminds me of all the
days of my life.
It says how sweet life
has been to me.
And I always listen,
as I cannot hide
From the voice of my
  conscience.

James D. Woolley
BEAUTY

Beauty, once beheld
By the eye
Remains forever
Like the sky
It seldom changes

By and by,
Just stays perfection
For you and I

Donna Rue Wilson
**ESSENCES OF YOU—FOR
JOHN**

you are my incense
unmistakable
lingering on my senses
delectable
drifting into my heart's temple
listening
your gentle beckoning
surrounding me
silently surrendering

Margaret G. Carabajal
GOOD MORNING LORD

Good morning Lord, good
  morning.
Oh! What a glorious day.
want to talk to you a moment,
before starting on my way.

First I want to thank you
for watching over me through
  the night.
and then I want to ask you
to guide me,
to do what's right.

Help me to cheerfully carry,
my share of the heavy load.
and watch over me as I
travel, upon life's busy road.

And as the night approaches,
and I lay down to rest.
I can honestly say,
"Dear Lord, I did my very best."

Nancy J. Condon.
DESTINY

Entity we are in space,
Caught in time and vector's race
To ever increase heaven's bound
And displace emptiness
  profound
With simple molecules and cold
Forbidden depths of mass
  untold.

Crusted sphere, but one of
  many,
Filled with life forms lacking
  any
Power to oppose the forces
Prompting random cosmic
  courses,
Can you comment on
  existence—
What shall be, quo vadis, and
  whence?

Edith T. Clements
DEATH AND LIFE

Why did you have to die so
  young?
You were in love with life.
It was a time for all to cry.
The world was torn by strife.
But your killer didn't have a
  gun.
He grappled you with pain.
He refused to let you go, so

Your struggle was in vain.
A miracle had been discovered,
But how was I to know?
It has proved to be a life
giver,
Irony, you had to go.

Your place on earth can not
be filled,
But part of you is here.
You would be proud of your
name-sake,
You know though, don't you
dear?

Leoma Cardwell Allen
KNIGHTS OF THE HIGHWAY

Knights of the highway
guardian of speed
Man with the badge a dedicated
breed
He makes your troubles seem
light
Just being there in the middle of
the night.
A servent of the people,it's
true.
His motto drive safe means you!
The nights are dark his vigil is
long.
He's friend when things go
wrong
Knights of the highway a rare
breed.
Tower of strength, friend in
need.
Once in a while someone says
"Thanks."
But it's not the guy with too
much to drink.
He's abusive and starts to get
rough.
And only then do you get
tough.
It's all in a day's work.
No matter what they say.
He'll be there another day.
The knights of the highway.

Deborah Ruth Hunsicker
THE GIFT

A mother is a special gift,
all wrapped up in love.
A father is another gift,
behind a big bear hug.
A child completes the gift
that God gives to mankind.
All together they are a family,
a gift simply sublime.

Viole Leah
PARDON ME KIND SIR

Pardon me kind sir—have you
ever met a man with
eyes so searching?
Or perhaps they are now dim—
but his ears on all
words seem to be lurching.
Perhaps he's tall, maybe thin,
or just a wee
bit stooped—
Then of course he may be
heavy, lean, short or
just plain old looped.
This man you passed somewhere
could now be
laid beneath the earth—
Should you have paused close
by, did you listen or
hear something about a birth?
A stranger could have said, "I'm
looking for a
little person I know is
somewhere."
Time is short and goes so fast.
"What?" "A little person!"

"Oh hurry, I must get there."
Perhaps just once as you read
your paper on a certain
day—
Think, was there ever a little
person notice asking
When, where and the way?
The one I'm seeking, Kind
sir, a *gentle* man he just has
to be.
Because, you see, somewhere
this man I see k
He Fathered me—

Patsy Joyce Kline
LIFE'S MARRIAGE

Enlightened as to the beauty
of the
Valleys that surround us
Enhanced with a blend of
nature
Given unto all in God's trust

As a song that is sung
With its rhythm and words
Together it is a beauty
In unison, as a flock of winged
birds

A storm that brews,
And the awakening of a breeze
Are forces that rub together,
Only to melt like calm seas

This is a marriage of life
We've been entrusted to see
each day
The guiding light and his
outstretched hand,
Together they'll go a long,
long way

With a marriage to two
It's but a particle of this life,
Immersed in its beauty,
Giving love, without strife.

To you, He gives a love
Nurtured through life together
With a song of valleys and
storms
All in the beauty of life's
marriage to weather

Yes, this is a marriage within
a marriage,
A part for just us two, to share,
Abound, with an overflowing
love,
His creation entrusted to our
care.

Silvia Jimenez Weis
**INTERPRETATION OF
LOVE**

Love is complex and ever so
elusive;
so like a flower opening at
dawn.
Once that you have it, should
you but neglect it,
in just one fleeting moment
it is gone.

So, If by chance you find
this precious flower,
do feed it well and nurture it,

my friend.
For all the growth and beauty
that to you return,
will be an everlasting love that
never ends.

I know, don't ask me how, that
in your heart,
the seeds of love exist—yet we
remain apart.
But seeds of love, like any other
seed
need food and sun and watering
indeed!

To you I say, please let my care
for you
fill all your needs, whatever
they may be,
And let my love engulf you with
the warmth
of summer suns such as you've
never seen,
I'll wash away your doubts
somehow, someway,
someday I'll make you see . . .
That happiness for us, my love,
is simply you and me!

Terri Collier Green
SEARCHING

Looking out my window
Searching my soul
Looking for . . .what?
Only God knows?

Trying to still the unrest in my
soul
I look and I look. . .
There's only a black hole.

Happiness eludes me
Peace is a dream
Life is full of my silent screams.

Takchandra Gayadin
COCKROACHES

Sprays, expensive and odorless
Still the cockroaches are
numberless
Traps, mechanical and
chemical,
The infestation races over wall.
    Contest.

Light off
Television on
I dare not cough.
The infests are on run.
    Not a display,
My work carried over the day!
One.
I lick another.
God.
    Day just started!

Rae Marie Healey
A SILENT BECKON

The violent, raging ocean,
with his white, foaming beard,
Calls lovingly to the girl on
the shore.

She is frightened and unsure.
But willingly answers his call.
She slowly walks to her
awaiting friend.
His body is cold and icy.
It numbs her body.
Taking away all her pain.
Soon his waves engulf her.
Body and soul.
She peacefully drifts away.

Amos H. Rendler
JEANETTE

Jeanette I miss you already,
it has only been a day.
It's not fair for you to go

and for me to stay.
Tomorrow we choose faces.
Though I'm short, mine is
long.
Today we say goodbye
and walk away.
Today I cried and held a pen
for you,
tomorrow we choose faces.
I'd like yours next to mine.
Yesterday we shared a song,
today I lost the words.
Tomorrow we choose faces . . .

Paul E. Rietzke
**CALIFORNIA
EARTHQUAKES**

One a quake, two a quake
Every other day a quake
They sure make the buildings
shake
And even keep one wide awake.
Oh my gosh for goodness sakes
I think I feel another quake
Sure enough, here it comes
Bet t'will be a real big one
It wasn't and with second
thought
T'was really just an aftershock.

Margaret Patricia Durand
THE ARTIST

Many emotions are to a complete
person
as many shades of color are to
a masterpiece
essential for the whole
Something lacked in my
existence
a feeling of hollowness
overruled
frownes and tears in a sea of
a thousand smiles
With a graceful sweep of His
brush
the Artist changed the painting
despair to hope . . .darkness
to light
And when the painting was
completed
it was the ultimate image of
innocent perfection
the tears were gone and the
eyes reflected serenity
The person was one with himself
The Artist had touched my life.

Shirley J. Godley
IN THE GARDEN

In the garden, as they plotted
His death,
Alone, He agonized and wept.
The diciples did not hear His
cry.
Even if they had, they wouldn't
have understood why.
As the evening wore on, a band
of men came.
They did not have to call out
His name
For Judas ran and greeted Him
with a kiss.
He stood calmly and quietly
amidst all of this.

There in the garden, it could
have all ended
Unto His Father, He could
have acsended
The Lord knew if He did not
die on the cross
Forever manking would be
lost.

Mrs. Blanche F. Courtwright
DICTATES OF OUR MIND

Long shadows are cast toward
Iran

Our people, their hostages
Drear and desolate, the aspect
of the scene
Stolen freedom, an injustice!
Most who love, in the love
of God
Understand moral right perfectly
Why the unsolved mystery,
Of peace among the nations?
Loyalth there, had there been
doubt
These consistently refused to
believe
Even to the point of denying
the evidence
Confounded remnants of
hopes
Sole resource
Even now confidence in them
What reason would not do
Love had accomplished.

Ronald Keith Anderson
IN THE MOUNTAINS

It's not the traffic or the smog
I'm fleeing,
It's the change in mind, got my
feet a reeling.
I'm in the mountains now, tis
where I'll stay,
In the soft folds of Mother
Nature's way.
I make my home where the
air is clean,
At the foot of a pine tree, tall
and green.
Blue skies above, earth at my
feet,
This life I live is hard to beat.
If you come to the mountains
it's mellow you'll be,
Cause if you're not, you'll
have to deal with me.
Contentment is what the
mountains breed,
It goes much deeper, like a
wanting need.
It makes no difference on life
how you see,
This is my life, to live as I see.

Donna Mitchell Graham
MY SPECIAL CHILD

I touch him gently
and he turns to me
I point and talk with hands
tiny fingers scan my throat
I must be strong, a teacher,
(though I quake with fear
inside)
those innocent eyes,
sadly silent,
search my face for truth.

Lovelle Clark
A CHANT OF WILD BLOOD

When first the flush of waking
Spring arrives
Phlegmatic juices through one's
veins run free
And lazy clouds march gaily
'cross the skies
Rejoicing, recreating Winter's
lives.
When love and warmth are
all you feel or see
Then Passion's flower bursts
like dynamite
Bespeaking summer's am'rous
prophesy
Wild fires burn within, a hot
decree
Of fever, roses, cherry wine and
light
Nor can a cool spring breeze
such heat subdue

Red rivers rush in torrents, full
of might
They only coarse the deeper
with the night.
Thus, when the urge of Winter's
trials are through
When valves of primal love are
opened wide,
It's true that blood the darkest
flesh imbues
And comes a beating pulse:
it's love's debut.

John Joseph Wilson
WHY

Why do you believe,
the sky is blue?
the sea is green?
that love is true?
Why do you believe,
this is reality?
Tell me?
Could this be some foolish
dream?
A wishful thought?
Some silly scheme?
Could it be a fantasy?
Tell me!

Linda Jean Baker
BEATEN WOMAN

It's cold outside.
I lay in our warm bed beside
you.
My body aches.
I speak to you of love and
understanding;
our arms around each other;
we sleep.
In the early morning;
I awake.
My breast hurts.
I hold my breast with my hand.
Your arm is around me.
I sleep.
The morning;
My bruised spine makes it
hard to pull out of bed.
In the mirror I see a slightly
black eye;
And I feel the pain that comes
from deep within you.

Dian K. Hamilton
MY SOUL MATE

I give my love and respect
To none other but thee
I chose you above all others
And you shall have the best
of me.
Love, respect and trust
Shall all of this be
These shall grow as years go by
Like an acorn grows into
a beautiful
(strong tree)
You shall be ageless to me
And there shall be no death
For heaven is right here
And there hasn't been found
a higher
(place yet.)

Todd B. Cummings
LOVE FOR YOU

I have love for you which you
will never know
I have love for you and it's
hard to show.
I have love for you in so many
ways
I have love for you, that's all
I can say.
I have love for you which will
live forever;
to love someone else I can't

endeavor.
I have love for you and only
you;
without you, what would I
do?
I have love for you, I hope you
can see
for you mean everything to me.

Jonna Spring Reaves
EVERY HUMAN BEING

Live, live, yes every human
being has a chance to live.
Hope, hope, yes every human
being has a chance to hope.
Cry, cry, yes every human
being has a chance to cry.
Die, die, yes every human
being has a chance to die.
Yes, every human being has
a chance to:
Live
Hope
Think
Cry
and
Die.

Leandra J. Mousseau
A LOVE LIKE OURS

You are so special to me
I love you in every way.
Like the sun sets over the sea
You're beautiful every day.
My love for you has grown so
When you're gone I long for
you.
Like a lazy river my love will
flow
With you my dreams come
true.
I'll forever hold you in my
heart
In hopes we'll always be
together.
I'm lonely each day we're apart
A love like ours will live forever.

Yvette Bodnar
WHEN WILL I DIE?

I live my youth in unsuspected
fear,
For every day I live could be my
last.
In this large world my death
would not be vast.
And around every corner death
is near.
Life in its prime is to me very
dear.
Death comes and goes when
you're dead you're past.
And I know what God's life
plan will soon cast,
The thought of death to my
eye brings a tear.
When you are dead you are
gone that is it.
I can't help but think of life
after death.
I hope I will go to heaven not
hell.

Life is the cherry and death is
the pit.
They will then bury me six
feet beneath,
And no secrets on my deathbed
I'll tell.

Catherine A. McCoy
A SPECIAL LOVE

There's someone special in my
heart—
I'll never let him go.
He's warm and tender, kind
and sweet—
God, I love him so.
The love we share is like a
breeze—
across the wide, wide sea.
A tender kiss from his sweet
lips—
is all I'll ever need.
Moments we'll always treasure
with each new dawning day.
A precious hope arises with
the sun's golden ray.
Life's worth living as I daydream
of the times we share.
To hold each other close in
thought
that's why I'll always care.
Our times together soar as a
dove—
That's why we've got a special
love.

Rei En
WHO?

The earth weighs a certain
thing
from year to year . . .
Stop pumping,
Stop drilling,
Stop building and wrecking.
You're changing the balance
of things.
Mt. St. Helen's.
Hurricane Allen
Perhaps someone's trying to
balance back things.

Lynne Owens & Freda Judson
TO LOVE

If you love someone let them
go free
If they never return it was
never meant to be
If they do return love them for
eternity.
So as like the wind
You were here now you're gone
And I stand in silence alone
Waiting to hear your love songs
To worry about yesterday is
a foolish man's way
Yesterday is gone forever
though memories remain
Today is all we have to hold
And our dreams a wish away
Freedom is a choice only one
can make
It's a prison in itself to walk
alone each day
At night your only friend an
empty bed awaits
Freedom is a choice for the
strong, a choice few can
make.

LouAnne Volkey
ENDLESS WORLD

The time is right, the end so
near
Take my hand, guide me to the
unknown land
People are so different there,

then here
I want to live a life that I can
understand.
Confusion is left in my thoughts,
tears in thy eyes,
A heart that melts like wax,
but yet still is burning.
Life is so difficult to
understand, when will
we be able to meander time?
Can we turn back the clock, to
a time when people
were so free?
Fire was fire and the earth had
it all together,
There was lots of love for you
and me.
Come with me to the land of
love and of life,
wrap your arms around me,
hold me tight
Help me stop this ball and chain
seen,
Please make everything turn
out right.

Jan Nelson
LIFE IS

Life is just there, you don't
have to live it;
You just feel it and smell it like
the air—it's just there.
You don't have to enjoy life
you can just sit and shut
everything out.
Life is sometimes still and
sometimes exciting;
It doesn't talk—not a whisper—
yet it takes and gives.
You know life will be there
just like the sun.
When you find a day without
either, you've reached a
point of
equalness, joyfulness, eternity
within your soul and
among others—the real
experience of true life.

Fray Marcos Purdue
THE SEASONS

Hear soft, the bells enchanted
chime,
Ring silver notes of passing time,
The winter's ice-blue treasury,
A river's song—a symphony.

Gold leaves afire from Autumn's
sun,
Encased in webs the spiders spun,
Like jewels displayed to light
the scene,
Within the woodland's ember
green.

The summer's breath of lilac
air,
That touches earth and flowers
fair,
To mist above the silent streams,
Reflecting images of dreams.

Born now the perfumed rains
of spring,
Which cause the heart of love
to sing,
And candle stars the evening
yields,
From heaven's dark and moonlit
fields.

Tom Svinning
CHRISTMAS EVE NIGHT

Where are all the lonely people
on Christmas Eve night,
Has nobody invited them over
for a Christmas dinner,
and to sit by a Christmas tree

light.
Where are all the unwanted
animals, and where do they
eat.
Can't we see they're lonely
and have been crying at our
feet.
Where are the lovers that need
to be loved,
Where are these people, and
animals that nobody cares
to think of.
Where are all the lonely ones
on Christmas Eve night,
Has nobody invited them over
for Christmas dinner,
And to sit by a Christmas tree
light.

Jay Sant
THE MONARCH

As I was walking through the
city today
I found a dying Monarch,
her wings, though scarred,
were very beautiful,
the black on tattered orange
reminded me of Halloween,
and I thought,
how cruel this life.

As I held her in my hand
(weak as she was)
I noticed her struggle for
freedom,
even at death.
Though I knew she could not
I let her fly,
I let her give life
one last try.

I felt as though it was I who
killed her,
I felt there was something
that I could have done to
save her,
as a few ants slowly dragged
her away,
then I thought it's always
the same . . .
stepped on them all
and went on my way.

Sharon Wood
LESSONS

Sometimes I let my mind's
keen eye gaze upon my
memoirs
And travel along unbroken
paths without the obstacle
courses of everyday
living.
And though I'm content, the
stand I've taken sometimes
makes me feel as
lost
As a docile calf struggling
along with a herd of wild
horses.
My world goes by and each
day melts into evening and
passes by.
The stars at dusk change points
at dawn and fade with the
morning glow;
And faded lies my blissful past
like a rose pressed in volumes
of time.
But my days of yore have
built me a castle and from
Time's ancient lessons,
I grow.

Erika M. Lapins
YESTERDAY'S DREAMS

My eyes gaze at the
breathtakingly beautiful sea.
The sky is cloudy,

the waves hit violently against
the white sandy beach.
I had walked down this
familiar way not too long ago.
I wasn't alone that time.
The stars were out, the moon
was new.
The air was aglow with the
promise of a cherished
everlasting happiness.
There was a ring of carefree
laughter as two hands held
each other tightly,
and two pairs of bare feet
strolled together.
The wind was gentle and
caressing,
as two lips touched, and two
hearts beat a rhythm of
love.
Now I am alone.
The chilling wind erases my
vision of a painful memory.
Yes, not long ago we had
built sandcastles and painted
colorful rainbows
here.
But our sandcastles weren't
strong enough to hold up
against the stormy waves,
and the rainbows we painted
were only watercolor.
I turn my back to leave,
taking with me thoughts of
a time never to be
forgotten.
My misty eyes try to blink
away the rolling tears.
Will I ever be able to forget
yesterday's dreams?

Kristin R. Freilino
GABRIELLE

Through the meadow I make
my heavy steps.
I sigh, I ponder my mind. I look
about the jade
colored trees and feel the rich,
cold grass
that softly stands beneath my
feet. I am guided by
nothing behind me. I only walk
forward to escape
my last path. And beyond the
frozen gates of Gabrielle—
a unicorn with gentle eyes is
the keeper of my key.
Buy a ticket, take a chance,
sell your soul. . .I step into
the infinite chamber of what
is not to be. I look
down upon the ground and
see the grass that had been
familiar
before. Now, I am numb to its
coldness.
Purple and crimson paint drown
my mind and I cannot see. I
wish for myself the last path
I had left behind.
But alaw! There is no path in
Gabrielle. I run and stumble.
I have fallen. And above me,
a demon with gentle eyes
holds a sickle to my head.

Annie May Schrimsher
JUST FOR TODAY

Thy strength, oh Lord, just for
this day
I pray you will impart.
For me again refresh my faith
As this new day I start.

Reach out to me and keep Thy
hand
On everything I do.
Direct my path to things

undone
And guide to paths anew.

Give me the patience that I
need
To do for others now
The things that You would
have me do
And kindly show me how.

Through doubts and fears and
heavy loads
I stumble on my way,
Yet through the rugged path I
know
That you are near today.

You steer my feet and lift my
heart
And make the light to shine.
Then all my troubles, aches
and pains
I gladly leave behind.

C. Marie Wilson
WORLD ALIVE!

High on the side of the hill I
take my stand,
(bare feet, warm earth, tall
grass),
Poised as in dance at music-rest;
untamed;
head up reading the breeze,
Eager-sensed, open-pored,
soaking in scent
and sunlight,
Lost and found in burst of
being,
Aching at pleasure of clear air,
pungent pine,
sweet herb, spicy leaf,
mould'ring bark,
mellow sod;
Heart-stab of spring melting
into hot smell of summer.

World Alive! . . .and I alive
to keep it whole
and pass it on,
Wrapped like a present in my
caring; undefiled;
For the coming of future
earth-children.

Rita Dickey
THE CUSP OF NATURE

The most breathtaking sight
that I've ever seen,
Is the snow-capped mountains
in early spring.

The snow will start to melt
and drip from the trees;
The air is crisp from the
fresh mountain breeze.

As I walk around, look and
observe;
I feel this is more than most
really deserve.

To care for nature in a way such
as I
See it go unthought of and ask
myself why.

I feel as if I'm looking at an
undisturbed dream;

As I sit and admire
this unforgettable scene.

Annie B. Douglas
HER NAME IS WOMAN

The grandest flower ever grown
Choicest gem ever shown
Sparkling and bubbly as spring
water
If you don't know who it is
then you oughta.
The most beautiful picture ever
painted
She is pretty good her love is
never tainted
The grandest reason to be born
She brightens up your every
morn.
The glorious mystique in her
eyes
You will wonder what secret
she hides
Treat her good and do her no
wrong, for Hell hath no fury
like
A woman scorned; Jasmine,
opal, ruby, diamond and
pearl
These names all fit her my, what
a girl
God made her from the rib of a
sleeping man
He awoke and gave her a name
he called her, woman.

Mary Louise Blanc
LOVE CAME DOWN

Love came down
in the silent softness of the
night:
In a manger lay a newborn baby.
Mary and Joseph all love and
wonder
behold him perfect there on the
straw.
In the fields sleepy shepherds
are transfixed by a sight and
sound
beyond all dreaming.
A glorious light, angels singing
announcing he has come!
"In a manger you will find him,
a baby with his mother and
Joseph."
The shepherds believed
and went in haste;
all love, simplicity and awe,
carrying their lambs to a
stable
lighted by a star.
They came to love and adore.
There, a sight and sound
to be held forever in their
hearts
and to gladden all their days.

Keith Munsell
TO GRASP THE UNIVERSE

To grasp the universe is what I
seek,
To gain the knowledge that's
mine to keep;
To know what is to most
unknown;
To help those to help their own.
The riches of both thought and
mind.
The strives that are made for
all mankind.
The vastness of its unknown
depths.
The path that leads to its steps.
For this path I want to follow.
To fill my mind of what is
hollow.
There is more out there then

we can see.
A force that is alive in you and
me.
But will I find what I am
looking for?
Since life is so fast and so very
short.
Yes, life is but a race it seems,
And those who win will be
redeemed.
Not like those who will
live in inferno,
But like those who will have
life eternal.
And when I take my final
stride,
I hope my God will be by
my side.

Wende Bischoff
THAT SAD MELODY

What is the tune on the radio?
Many times I've heard it come
and go.
That sad melody that I hear
many times has brought me
a tear.
Something it reminds me of—
I think maybe an old secret
love.
And I admit, it couldn't be
mine,
So I imagine it, oh so divine.
The love we lead, that I can
never drop . . .
I hope this fantasy will never
stop.
It comes to mind when I hear
that song,
The pretty tune that lasts
so long.
I wonder who it could be by
This song that makes me
cry.
I have awakened when it
comes to the end,
And soon enough my heart
will mend.

Denise Sedgwick
FINE

So you say you're doing fine?
Oddly as it may seem,
something's
Wrong.
I really wish I could take
That wrong and turn it into
Something nice.
Maybe then, your sould will be
Free for a short while.

Priscilla Khirfan
LOVE ON MY MIND

I think in love I'd find you
gentle,
As gentle as you are on my
mind.
I think I'd find you soft and
warm,
I think I'd find you kind.
For I have tasted your sweet
kiss,
I've held your hand in
mind.
And thought I have not had
your love,
I've had it on my mind.

Patricia Ann Bray
THEY DO IT ANYWAY

Around the lonely bend and
through the trees
Was clearly heard the rustling
of the leaves,
As monstrous little feet did
steal at play—
Daring bravely to walk

through muddy clay.
And should I call out to let
them all know
That I am aware of where
they will go;
The frisky little imps—they
think they're smart
To run and hide in this too-
wooded part.
But surely I know hence where
they do dart
To do their pledged duties and
thus depart;
Around the lonely bend and
through the trees
Come little scraped elbows
and skinned-up knees.

Kathleen Diane Lucas
EVENINGTIDE

Infinity is mine, as the heat of
Day surrenders itself to the
Serenity of night.
Autumn's harvest moon
embraces the
Velvet ebon sky, giving up its
Light to the tranquillity below,
In colors never seen by day.
The crisp fall air fills my senses
With sweet memories, a haze
of
Future dreams, and solutions
to my
Present schemes.
Silhouetted hills and towns are
now
Asleep, except for the
twinkling
Street lights, the crickets,
nightingales,
And creatures of the night.
The essence of God shrouds
the earth
In peace and love; in the eons
of
Stars can be seen, the alpha and
the
Omega, the beginning and the
end.

R. A. Minotti
WINTER'S COMING!

In years gone by,
I so did cry
Hurray! Hurray!
Winter's coming!

As time did go,
I wondered so
Why I shouted
with such excitement.

But now I frown,
When leaves turn brown,
There's something lost.
Or is it just forgotten?

Walter Gromadin
FROM REGINA

The Christmas of 79 I will
never forget.
It may be the best Christmas
I have had yet.

I got many presents, some big
and some small,
But the one you gave me was
the best of all.
It wasn't gift-wrapped or under
the tree.
It happened first when you were
on my knee.
What it was most people will
not understand.
For it was just a simple clap
of your hands.

Deborah Tolen
BLACK SHEEP

Black sheep?
No, I'm as other members of
the family
These degrading comparisons
leading me to insanity.
Black sheep?
No, we're equal, treat me
the same
A mangled foot, yes, but am I
to blame?
Black sheep?
No, I've been told that before
I'm still hurting, don't hurt
me anymore.
The pain, the shame, my
feelings I can't begin to
explore.
Black sheep? Black sheep?
No! I'm not a helpless lamb.
I'm a human being, I'm me,
I know who I am.

Lea Ann Elliott
ALONE

Tell me, am I lonely
As I lay here in my bed, I hear
only
one car go down the road.
I wonder; Is it one so fortunate
to
be in the company of a
gentleman?

Sarah Cornelius
MY BEST

I am standing on the stage
of life
Looking down on rows and
rows of empty seats.
It's like my life staring me
in the eye.
I may never be able to life
in this beauty,
But I can look in the window
It's good enough as long as
it's my best.

T. J. Williams
I AM . . . THE POET

I am . . .
of the mind, with the body,
and for the spirit.

I am . . .
a miracle: a creation of the
Creator.
My purpose in life . . . is life
itself.

The Creator
is my origin . . .

The origin
is my creation . . .

Creation
is my purpose . . .

Purpose
is my life's breath . . .

Life is . . .
each spontaneous moment
filled with the beauty and
happiness
of creating.
of the Creator,

...in the spirit of love;
...in love for the spirit,
by learning, giving, and sharing
of thought, action and deed.
This is the true life.
This is my life.
I am ...the poet!

Christine Ann Reed
CRASHING BLOW

The 100th year of baseball,
with nothing to detain; until
some fool who hit
the ball, broke someone's
windowpane.

You should have seen teams
disappear, and from the
bleachers, people flew;
because no one wanted to be
the one, who had to pay the
due.

The ball had shattered all the
glass, leaving nothing but
the frame; and all
that then was on their mind,
was, "Not to lose the game."

Although Babe Ruth hit
homeruns, farther out than
me or you; doesn't mean
when he was younger, he
may have broke some too!

Sheila Ann McGrath
GUIDANCE

The Almighty gave me intellect
with which I do explore;
Beauty shared with sisters
features men adore;
Glasses deep inside my heart
to focus down within;
The fortune of a family bond
for quieting the din;
A certain realization that gold
is but a word;
Unless we weigh the thought of
such
its value goes unheard;
And yet with all I have, I have
not because of me;
As Mother of this grateful
Flower
I've blossomed thanks to Thee.

Alma G. Young
MY DOG—HERMANN

He is so funny, that precious
bundle of joy!
He gazes at me with such
solemn and intent eyes
When I speak to him in mortal
tongue.
I give an urgent call for his
safety
Tho' with his untrained mind
and ears
He does not recognize my
caring.
He merely tosses his head
As a mischievous teasing boy
And bounces away from my
concern

With the grace of a startled
doe.
This demands punishment
When we are back together.
But how can I punish
When his eyes gleam at me
With such saucy, tantalizing
laughter
And the "rose petal" tongue
Darts and peeps at me
From between dew-dropped
pearly teeth?

Mrs. Lucile Surface
A MOTHER'S GARDEN

To a mother her family is a
garden
With flowers blooming there,
Each one wonderfully lovely,
Each one a treasure rare.

To a mother her garden of
flowers
Seem lovely beyond compare,
Each has a delicate beauty
That all around may share.

Children and flowers need much
loving
And grooming—by day and by
hour;
Oh, the satisfaction in watching
them grow,
A fresh beauty after each
shower.

No sacrifice too great, no need
too small,
No child too insignificant
Mother and God love them all.

Gregory James Taylor
THE CHILD

In the eternal reaches of your
mind,
My soul touches yours;
Yours touches mine.
The infinite meeting of
prolonged pleasure
Never to bring realms
together,
The flamboyant mind always
to flirt
Forever savoring on the hurt.
In the dark little corner of
your resourceful well,
The little child here must
dwell.
Reality is of no concern;
You can't teach her, she won't
learn.
For when she is in her world
of play,
Where he is taking her, the
child won't say.

Fran King Clark
RAIN DAY

Rain, slipping down onto
The cheeks of the plum and
the quince,
rustling along the edges of
the river
and washing into its huge
grief.
Children, picking their way
through the bombed nurseries,
factories,
gathering the water in their
hats
to carry it home.
Clouds, hurrying along together
ready to speak, make a
statement
that will bring sense to the
scene,
translate the situation.
Silence, sitting under the roofs,
nods through the wet afternoons

knowing the plum tears and
weeping quince
have already, softly, told the
old story.

Salie Watkins Aruta
COLOURS OF ME

I am a prism of colours
Which only shine when the
light hits me.

I am blue with every tear I
cry,
And red is the fire of love
within me.

Pink is the little girl I will
sometimes be
Yellow is the warmth and
compassion inside of me.

Purple is the little craziness
sometimes you will see.

But white is our love as pure
as the snow,
And only with you
Can all of these colours glow ...

Taffy Burke-Donalson
OREGON TRANSPLANTS

Winter swaddled bodies
pale for summer, to
thaw blue-ice marrowed
bones and heal their
California souls.

Gooseflesh, gilded with
freckles
they dream of barefeet
silting in white sands
and baskets of poppies
gold as the sun

Diane M. Argue
REFLECTIONS

Reflections of the years gone
by,
the many lonely tears we've
cried.
Slowly fading memories of
misty colored dreams.
There were reflections in the
laughter
and the warmth after a storm
and the times we've shared
together
and the love that kept us warm.
Reflections in the long, long
walks
the arguments and the long
talks
the times we've spent so far
away
it seems like only yesterday.
Reflections of the times we've
spent together
We thought that it would last
forever—
But memories are of the mind
and all the tomorrows are
left behind.
Memories of our lives together
those reflections will last
forever.

Della Vivion
WE WHO ARE NEITHER

You, who are neither Adam
nor John
But infinitely more like David,
You sent me to my
Gethsemane.

I, who am neither Eve nor
Mary,
But somewhat akin to Ruth,
I felt your cold kiss of betrayal.

We, who now stand separately,
Await the crucifixion.
But, oh, God! Remind me of
Easter.

Catherine Palmer
AUTUMN SKIES

The soft blue of evening
sky lies broken;
Orange and pinks explode
in gay reverie.
Wisps of pale cloud die
slowly in the west.

Quiet again settles,
as night decends.

Cora Dee Strachan
HIS FIRST SNOW

"Oh, what was that?
It looks like a feather floating
through the air;
But it is so cold, falling into
my hair!"
This seems to be the thought
of the big, white cat;
As the snowflakes fall on
him, ker—splat!

I stand watching him as he
leaps and jumps;
Scampering after the frozen
crystals, giving them little
bumps.
His little pink tongue shoots
out, licking at a spot on his
fur.
Then he spins about, as if he's
been touched on the tail
with a spur!

He's soon joined by some of
his brothers.
They seem to enjoy themselves
so;
As they cavort about in their
very first snow.
It could be wished upon many
others.

Soon the flakes are falling
thick and fast.
He seems to have lost his zest
at last.
He seems to decide he can't
eat them all, as faster and
faster they fall.
He's like so many of us, he's
tired of the game, and his
cavorting play.
I watch as he haughtily stalks
away.

Kurt R. Scholz
FRIENDS (FOR P. L. Z.)

Captured on the playground, we
tethered you and shadow June
to the trunk
Of an opportune oak tree.
Ropes knotted fast, gags drawn
tight, we left
You as the the school bells rang,
twin antipodal Joans de Arc,
martyrs for no
Cause. Ordered back to set you
free, the looks of sullied
dignity subdued
My gleeful mood. Racing back
to class, we faked expected
academe with
Practiced, straight-faced airs,
the tongue in cheek of rote.
Golden friend
Of past tense times, different
children ride the playground
swings today,
Tiny feet shuffling leaves
forwards and backwards
through the crisp and
The quick rushing air. The
sounds of young laughter
rekindle old moments
When other leaves forsook
autumnal trees to grace your

auburn hair. I
thought betimes of yesterday
and wrote of deepest love.
Your only response
called back horribly soft across
the years, a diuturnity of
silence
heavy with time.
Hard, like the winter,
Honest as your smile.

James Milton Coe
RETROSPECT

To be with nature away from
  the crowd,
Beyond the concrete and
  humanities' loud.
Would it not be nice to see once
  more,
A land full green from shore
  to shore?

What's that in the treetops? A
  skyscaper leers,
Will the green be here in the
  coming years?
It's up to us to feed our land,
Be thankful and proud of our
  ancestor's land.

Is mother nature almost dead?
Can she not defend
  civilization's tread?
A hand from us would answer
  her need,
Let's back up, slow down, and
  plant the seed.

Rob House
**THE IMMACULATE
PERCEPTION**

Into the muse of life
we are let
to anoint our hearts
mutely entrusted
to the tragic tenure of death.

Alveta C. V. Stubbs
OUR LOVE

Our love is like the ocean
extending far and wide,
Deserting all outsiders
and respecting what's inside . . .

Our love is one of passion
Our love is one of care
Our love is like the ocean,
Extending everywhere.

Our love is undescribable,
It's known only to us,
It's mysterious to others,
And simply JUS to us.

P. F. "Fritz" Blunt
FARSIGHTED LOVE

The fog!
But I can see beautifully
Five hundred miles,
Your smiles and sunshine!

Peggy Sue Barton
COME DOWN

An angel took me by the hands
  and pulled me up
to tell me about that no-good
  stuff.
Stay off the pills and leave the
  dope behind,
before it complicates and takes
  your mind.
It will send you on a trip you
  know nothing
about and take your life and turn
  turn it in and out.

You will see an image only a
  fool sees in his
crazy mind, two worlds, yours
  and mine.
It will have you as if you can

run forever and
never stop and take your head
  and spin it
like a top.
It will have you as if you can
  conquer hell
and take the devil by surprise
  and make the
fourth runner of hell arise.

The world will be a like funny
  box that never
stops laughing and being funny,
  you will be
happy as an Easter bunny.
But after the trip is over and
  everything stands still
it will leave you frustrated
  and filled
with tears.

Pat Hughart
TRANQUILLITY

Oh I have walked in the hot
Sun at noonday
Beside the sea
When the waves seemed to be
Angry at the shore—and me
And I felt fear and uncertainty.

I have walked beside the sea
At midnight—quietly
So gentle the waves spoke to
  me
Caressingly they roll
And I knew peace
In my soul.

There is dawn and twilight
I will keep
Forever in my being asleep.

Susan Robinett
THE PLEA

Like a bird—I've seen you flying
Free from all the earthly cares.
Like a ship—I've seen you sailing
Challinging storms whenever you
  dare.

Like a tree—I've seen you
  standing
On a ground so hard and firm.
Like a king—I've seen you ruling
Your word so strong and stern.

Like a kite—I see you drifting
Towards some unsightly goal.
Like the little girl—who grasps
  it's strings
I'm struggling to keep my hold.

Like a book—without a cover
I'll open up to you.
Like the daytime needs the
  sunshine
I need warm love from you.

Allen Wayne Barnhouse
CHARACTER OF CHANCE

I am a character of chance.
By chance I feel a void,
The child of years of pain.
No contemplation with another
Fills my cup of emotion.
There is no gate through which
To pass my life's feelings.
Lingering so, I burn my light
Until there is no more wick.

To one I would freely give
My hurt, my joy, my Love.
To one would my heart stand
  bare
Ready and willing to be held.
Time has gone and I grow
  weary;
Without a soul to share with,
My embers slowly die and
  go out.
Please grant this wish, above
  all else,

Forgive my failings and look
  inside.
There lie I, in all my nature,
Nothing hides nor shields this
  part from you.
To perceive me such releases
  my burden.
For then I know you will not
  hurt.
For then I know you will love.

Patti R. Farrell
OASIS

Book of spirit
Like my song in tune—
Made the music echo
The summer lit June

Dark smiles of opened races
With heavy feet the track erases
Stunned by tunes
of different oasis —
Pushed their time
To better places.

Hoped too soon
We'd give up paces
Like locks and keys
to "Sweet Embraces"

. . .From locks and keys
to "Sweets and laces"
Followed here
The banned replied—
Coursely soured
They turned—
Then sighed.

Roseanne N. Goode
LONELINESS

All tears dried up
droplets brimming nonetheless
Silently making a plea
to ears turned deaf

Coldness in my hands
echoes the chambers of my
  heart

Thoughts regurgitating
Answers avoiding me
Reason is fleeing
Emotions thrashing out

Cannot sleep
Never hungry
Simplicity of life
Dwell in me.

Cecil L. Ford Jr.
STAYING HOME

When I come to you tonight
will you hear my tears
or will you
turn away from me in bed.

Will you see my heart—
screaming for a passionate
reckoning with yours
or will you
softly drift away from me.

So far away
never to know my feelings
for another night
I shall be content
Just to hold you once again.

Tallak T. Farsjo
**GLORY BEYOND THE
SUNSET**

Behold when all the faithful will
In heaven meet their Lord!
And songs shall heaven's
  mansions fill
In one sublime accord.

O think when death no more
  shall be
In heav'n's eternal life;
And human souls forever free
From all this earthly strive.

Most gracious God, eternal
  King,
We pray for Jesus' sake
That we with angels then
  may sing
When all the saints awake.

So let us meet on yonder
  shore
To heaven's trumpet call;
When earth and time shall be
  no more,
But God be all in all!

Abel L. Oseguera
THE STRUGGLE—BOOK I

His name is Iran . . .and he
  strives with the world!
And as he does he carries a
  sack filled with many things.
And some look at first, but
  then walk away with lips
  curled.
And he still insists and shows
  the contents therein.

And he has labeled his sack:
  Our Nation's Hope.
And once some friends leaped
  out, but were finally caught.
And he ties and reties the sack
  with miles of cinched rope.
And held soundly inside are
  the heads, arms, and legs that
  fought.

And the sack shakes and thrusts
  with tradition and legacy in
  fright!
And more committed and
  established quality ideas try
  to get out.
And somethings do escape and
  slip through the streets of
  day and night.
And he regroups and marches
  to keep some treasures inside
  with shouts.

And he can't keep the sack
  patched . . .and justice, and
  hope, woman and man,
and liberty and fraternity
  struggle . . .and He argues
  that his name is Iran.

Reba L. Rose
UNTITLED

May you be aware

of the good Lord's smile turned
  your way
of the sun and rain that fill the
  day
of loving thoughts that ride the
  air
of the quiet fun in games we
  play
of friends and all of those who
  care
of color and music and hands
  that pray
of trees and flowers and cacti
  gay
of birds and bees and all they
  share
of the moon, the stars, and

the sun's warm ray
of uncountable things along
  life's way
of all that is and is everywhere,
May you be aware.

Johnaye Walker
PRECIOUS MOMENTS

Joy we share
Always being there
Meeting and Kissing
Empty moments missing
Sharing warmly repairing
Enveloping—caring
Deepest affection
Within protection
Always fondly
Respectfully, Sincerely
Deep close Ties
Goodness which lies
Ever so close
Respectively warmth
Desiring to touch
Emptying as ever ready
Surely Lovingly.

Becky Groene
YOU

Guide me to heaven, guide me
  to hell,
hold my hand, oh hold it well.
It's you forever, it's you
  farewell,
It's you who's led me furthest
  through hell.

You loved me yesterday, but
  tomorrow you're gone,
yesterday's gladness, brings
  me tomorrow's sad song.

You took the pleasure, I
  took the pain,
forever I've lost you, but
  forever you'll remain.

Vincent McHugh
A TIME RHYME

If I could collect all the time
  that I spent,
the time that I wasted and
  squandered away,
Look at all the wonderful
  things I could do
with all of those nights and all
  of those days.

I could build that big boat that
  I wanted so bad,
I would take that great trip
  that I planned for so long,
I could read all those books
  that I wanted to read,
I might write a good poem or
  even a song.

But always it seemed there
  was something to do,
That seemed more important to
  me at the time
Than building that boat and
  chasing that dream
or just living the life that God
  said was mine.

Now I look back on my life
  with a bit of remorse,
all that whining and crying
  about nothing to do,
While all of those glorious
  things waited for me
just like they're waiting for you.

So take my advice and get up
  off your butt
and make use of every damn
  minute
You'll enjoy your life much
  more than before
Your new world and
  everything in it.

Now I have decided to change
  all my ways
I'll put on my boots and my
  cap
I'll roll up my sleeves and pick
  up my tools,
But first I must take a short
  nap.

Margaret Munkers
**WHY GO REACHING FOR
THE STARS**

Why go reaching for the stars,
Search your soul and find,
The inner qualities, that make
  you rich,
A wealth of a different kind.

What is money, power and
  gain,
If on our soul, we put a stain,
What is wealth, can it remove
  the mark,
That has slowly begun to maim.

So why go reaching for the
  stars,
Reach out to help and find,
Those needing to be rich
With a wealth of a different
  kind.

Molly Bridges
DEATH OF LISA

Make no mistake about it,
That when I smile, I have tears
  inside . . .
That when I say "Fine, thank
  you."
My heart is broken, a part of
  me has died.

Nowhere can I go but I take
  her with me.
Wherever I look, I see her—
  hear her—reach for her . . .
She eludes me.
I know she is smiling, and I
  smile.
She entices me, and I must
  be there with her.
Her eyes are dancing! Oh, for
  a little while . . .

Make no mistake about it,
My laughter and gaiety is an
  act,
A plot to deceive you.
I'll strive to do it well
So that for a little while
My heartbreak won't be true.

Mabel E. Sylvester
WILLOWS IN THE WIND

Willows in the wind
Whip and sigh,
Telling every passer-by
That they would be fancy free
As a lark or bird in tree,
Telling their fond desire to
  roam
Far from banks where is
  their home;
To the ends of earth on
  sealanes

On their wings or by our planes.
Comes a laddie with his lass,
All old willow's fancies pass
He is just content to hover
And from sight young lovers
  cover.
Now his sighs are full of languor
Whispering of love sans anger,
Of a life complete and willing
To meet trouble, deep and
  milling.

Thus, do dreams
Keep hearts from failing,
At the signs of age or ailing
As the spring our spirits
  welcome
We catch our fancies lilting
  home.
Winter doldrums are now
  remote
And we live and tacitly emote,
Over tasks of sowing—doing
Much we had lost heart in.

Mabel E. Sylvester
PEACE

Peace,
When the hounds of war are
  baying
Bolts its shutter and locks its
  door,
Retires for years and tends
  its praying
Praying, disturbed by cannon's
  roar.

Peace,
Alas, it lives forever
Only in the hearts of fools
For the great concern of nations
Is cartels and affiliate pools.

Peace,
Oh, tragic, fleeting portions
Of this boon of life to men
That was dispensed with
  meager portions
To generations that have been.

Peace,
Bestir you, noble dovelet
Ne'er submit to gold and boors.
Lift your head, and we with
  doublet
Will defend you for daylight
  tours.

Peace,
Lift up your head and lead us
To worlds of betterment and
  gain.
Up and lead your host's
  salvation
To an earth full dowered—
  free from strain.

Vivian Parsons
**THE EARTH DECLARES THE
GLORY OF GOD**

The earth declares the glory of
  God
in multitudinous ways;
In the beauty of the rising sun
at the beginning of our days;
In fleecy clouds in a blue,
  blue sky,
in the breath of a gentle breeze,
In the lap of waves along
  the shore,
or the roar of maddened seas.

When a rainbow arcs across
  the sky,
after a refreshing rain,
My heart rejoices, for this I
  know
is God's promise of love again.
A symphony of bird song
  fills the air,
and I, in wonder, awed

Stand and look, and listen,
and view the wonders of God.

When evening comes, the
  western sky
glows red with the setting sun,
I watch its changing glory
  fade,
in joy for a day well done.
It's then I marvel at God's plan
for rest at the end of our days
The earth declares the glory
  of God
in multitudinous ways.

Julia Pinzenscham
LIFE OF LOVE

The wine is sweet
the music's low
You look at me
with a lover's glow

Through the years
as husband and wife
I've shared with you
the joys of life

Our children seem
to bless our day
And that special time
we watch them lay
As they cuddle blankets
pillows and sheets
We watch them smile
from dreams in sleep

So here we are
another year
A laugh a joke
a joy . . . a tear
We'll do it together
for our love will allow
us to continue
that one special vow.

Linda S. Critchfield
TIME TO LEAVE

Good-bye my friends, so long,
  farewell,
the time has come to leave.
The gates behind are being
  locked,
What happens next we cannot
  tell.

The time to leave is finally here,
after what seemed like eternity.
But are we really glad to leave?
We have so much to fear.

Debbie Kaplan
**LIFE REALLY DID
CONTINUE**

I was sure I couldn't do it.
I thought I wouldn't last.
But my life really did continue
And I did forget the past.
I do remember the good times.
Though it may be no use.
Why should I remember
What causes painful abuse?

Now, it's been a year,
I've made it on my own.
And in all this time
I feel that I have grown.

I thank you for the laughs
And the lesson I was taught.
Unfortunately, now we are
  ready
For the fight that was fought.

Claire (Verdone) Chaluto
WO—MAN

These are all the things you've
  been
It's like starting from a stem
A babe you were, when you
  were born
Bright and early, in the morn
A child you were, but for a

time
Till you grew up, that was fine
A girl you were, when in your
  teens
A girl that had a lot of dreams
A daughter to your mom and
  dad
Sister, to the others they had
An aunt to their little lads
An aunt you were, that made
  you glad
A wife, to the man you married
Mom, to the children you
  carried
A grandmother, to all of theirs
All these children became
  your heirs
Last but not least, you are
  a WO—MAN!
A woman, that first, came
  from man
These are all the things you've
  been
It's like starting from a stem.

Marie Bannon
RENDEZVOUS

Boulders at ocean-edge
catch surf,
hit back foam.

The sea pounds
like an African
drum.

Ocean blue,
your eyes suck back spray;
they leave
a wreck of trash:
beached crab-
shells and kelp strewn
on the shore.

Your return
is as before:
waves swell and break
running on the sand
like a thousand tiny feet.

Dulcy Dutrow
PHILOSOPHY

Man struggles with his future to
  find power,
Above all obstacles he hopes to
  tower.

Storms press him on all sides
  till he is bent,
But he o'er comes before his
  strength is spent.

The wind was he which caused
  the rains' defeat,
For a moment he found his
  dream complete.

What was that light he felt so
  strong that
shown
Against his power, his goal,
  his rock,
  his stone?

And so if he had reasoned from
  the start
He could have found the answer
  in his
  heart.

Luann Thompson
SUMMER TIME IS . . .

Summer time is extra fine—
With beauty all around;
God gave all the miracles
That every day are found.

White cotton clouds and blue
  bird skies;
A shady brook, contented
  sighs,
Sunshine, flowers, green green
  trees—
This flock of birds? He made

these.
The gentle rain like angel tears;
The pretty smells—the sounds
  one hears,
Thank God for summer—
For our beautiful land,
Created for us by the Master's
  hand!

Denise Leveron
HER QUIXOTE

He lacked
the polished charm of
a hand-kissing French
lover.

Yet,

she knew,
like Cervantes' Don,
he'd tilt at windmills
for her.

Lisa M. LeBel
A WALL OF TERROR

There is a wall of terror
And an ocean of guilt.
There is hatred in the dark
And sorrow in the air.
Yet . . .
Deep within oneself,
A wall built of peace.
An ocean of hope.
There is light in the dark
And love in the air.

Open your eyes
And open your heart.
Let feelings penetrate
And allow yourself—
To care,
For everything is in you.

Patricia Yivonne Smith
THE SANDS OF TIME

The golden sands of time
  lie along the ocean shore,
caressed by restless waves,
  softening the roar.

As you and I walk hand in hand
  along the ocean's door,
our footprints left behind
  remain
brief shadows on the shore.

Days will come and quickly go.
Of this you can be sure,
and always there, the seashore
  stands
shining with allure.

Our footprints fade so soon
  upon
that damp and glistening shore.
It makes me wonder who will
  know
that we were here before?

Carol Ann Vukich
VACANCY

How are you?
Fine, fine . . .
  everytime . . .
I ask
  What's new?
Nothing, nothing . . .
  ever.

Are you thinking
  about . . .
Onething
Something
Anything
As you ramble
  with the throng
  in cadence?

Left-face
  Right-face
No-face
  to place
  you,
Dis-missed.

Jennie Mae Frey
A PLAYMATE FOR TIMMY

What a beautiful sight,
I saw today,
As my little boy,
Went out to play.

I heard my child laughing,
And having such fun,
I thought he had a playmate,
But I couldn't see one.

As I looked out.
The leaves were falling all
  around,
They would bounce on his
  head,
And then, fall to the ground.

He would reach for a leaf,
And it would quickly fly away.
Yes, he had a playmate:
God played with my little boy,
  today.

Alan J. Zingler
FORGET—ME—NOTS

We part lips, oh so preciously
On my tongue the honey
  glistens
And holds my throat in
  unbroken ecstasy
Whisper sweet nothings to you
  who listens
Words in unspoken jealousy
As birds in melody
And bees in honey
In thoughts of you just as
  syrupy
Birds and bees
Initials and hearts
Carved in trees
At the start
Forget—me—nots
From flowers to bees
From you to me
She loves me
She loves me not
She loves me
Sweethearts and Forget—me—
  Nots.

E. A. Dzwill
NEW OLD FRIENDS

Two together holding hands
Two together making plans
One alone turns the key
And two together die in me.

Clifton McDonald Peoples, Jr.
THE ROUGH ROAD

The road I travel is very rough,
I try to make it and act like
  I'm tough.

But really I am just scared as
  hell,
I'm so depressed I feel like
  I'm in jail.

I try not to show it but it's
  very hard,
When the cards were dealt I
  got a bad card.

My problems are small
  compared to others,
Especially the problem I am to
  my mother.

She tries so hard to help me
  around,
But whenever she does I just
  knock her down.

My love for my parents is so
  very great,
But my love for myself is
  turning to hate.

I want to help and I want to
  now,
But the only thing is I don't

know how.
My parents are the ones who
  have it rough,
They have so many problems
  but they try to be tough.

They put up with me and
  that's more than enough,
I guess the road I travel isn't
  so rough.

Mary A. Wiederhold
TO MY LOST LOVE

You are my silent sphinx,
You are my sweet enigma,
So cruelly tempered in the
  fierce
Crucibles of war, and ice and
  fire;
But it's you, it's you dear love,
Whom I with my whole heart
  Desire.
No matter what the pain I bear,
No matter what the price I
  pay.
There'll always be an aching
  void
Within my core,
Where once you dwelled
Alone, an emperor
In singular glory enthroned.

Of all the millions of humans
In every age and clime,
Who have lived, and loved,
And passed as clouds away,
Leaving no mark on the bald
  face
Of time;
To think that in one sweet
Moment, of all Eternity,
In a blessed moment sublime;
We met, we loved, our pulses
  leaped
In joy—
And, then, one tragic, one
  accursed day,
It all vanished,
All drifted away, forevermore,
As a cloud on its aimless way.

Rodney Lewis
TOO YOUNG TO BATTLE

Thou there aren't bravest
To go into war. Wait until
Yet youth is gone. Then must
You go shed blood on thee,
Or feel of sorrows you and
Your comrades to shame, or
Be joyous to a victory,
My son!

Dennis Michael Giannone
NEVER LASTING

The snow fell hazing the air
The beauty of a painting was
  everywhere.
The crystals came down thick
  and white,
And everything around looked
  full and bright.

When I gazed out the window
  and up towards the sky
I thought to myself and then

I knew why.
Why nature itself was the most
  marvelous of all,
Especially when you think of
  summer and fall.
The snow stopped falling, and
  the air turned clear,
And I hoped that this would
  be for all the year.
I dressed up warm, and went
  outside,
To get a closer look at the
  trees as they tried
  to hide.
As the day passed on, the sun
  came through,
The snow started to melt, and
  then I knew.
No painting, or thing of beauty
  could last,
And that beautiful white
  picture was a thing of
  the past.

Lianne J. Moore
JUST A DREAM

I wish I was a cloud,
Fluffy and innocent.
I wish I had a star to hold,
To love and need.
I wish I had myself some gold,
To feel as though I'm rich,
I wish my mind was air,
To blow as a breeze,
To be so free at ease.
I wish my eyes were like a
  crystal ball,
To see what isn't really
  there,
To see beyond in life.
I wish I was someone I'm
  not,
To imagine everything is
  just a dream.
To be or not to be me.

Georgia M. Holland
ESSENCE

Bury me in the planet I came
  from,
One little plot I would like to
  enrich.
Dig my grave by my father's
  or Mother's . . .
Any place, to me it won't
  matter which.
From a high mountain scatter
  my ashes
To float on the winds that
  circle the earth.
Take a boat, tip me into the
  ocean,
The Mother of All, who first
  gave us birth.
Gratefully I have enjoyed
  life's pleasures.
I have accepted it's sorrows
  with grace.
Return now my soul . . . give
  back my atoms,
Some other life will be needing
  my place.

Cheryl A. Bond
FREE TO BE

Our love gives us strength
  and allows us
    to be free . . .
To keep a private life apart from
  'our life',
To be complete individuals, free
  to express
ourselves in ways that need and
  want to be,
To know we are accepted,
  trusted, and needed,
To grow,
  to learn,
    to love.
We're free . . . to be.

Sandra A. Myers
DEATH

When death comes calling,
Be it morning, noon, or night.
Will I hear gentle footsteps
  falling,
As he passes by my way.
Will his hands gentle touch me?
As he bids me with him go,
To a land thats bright and
  happy
Through a valley far below . . .
When we cross that great
  wide river,
Will he gently lead the way . . .
Or will I cross it all alone,
Will I want to stay?
Death will take me by the
  hand,
And gently lead the way.
To the glory of his kingdom
There in heaven I will stay.

Robert E. Henson
THE GORY GABBYGAWK

Mostly mirth and merry mocked
While the curt and curry cried.
All fatty fell the furryhawked
And the virgin vanguards vied,
"Shun the Gabbygawk my girl,
The eyes that snack and lips
  that smack.
Don't beguile its pits of pearl
And the touche' tallywhack."
Many moons she merely mired
While the Gabbygawk did glean.
Finally her facules tired
What a sordid shocking scene.
How the Gabbygawk did gire
While the tallywhack took toll.
Our good girl was filled with
  fire
As the monster gored its goal.
"Thou hast seen the Gabbygawk!
Get away you gruesome girl!"
All did titter in their talk
And their whispers whipped
  a whirl.
Mostly mirth and merry mocked
While the curt and curry cried.
All fatty fell the furryhawked
And the virgin vanguards vied.

Judy Graves
SYMPHONY

A symphony was written
Not as a musical score
But in his words of love
That will sing in my heart
Forevermore

No notes are there
On paper
But the orchestration
Of his words
Plays to the very essence
Of my soul.

Sandy Nelson
FAREWELL TO ROSES

Sad eyes glowing from the
  crystal clear tears of truth.
Why do they tell me more than
  I want to know?
Love has been kinder to none
  so blind.
Please, leave me now and don't
  look back.
We just can't track the time
  that love did fade,
and each of us must march to
  our own parade.
Your tears flow like dew on
  an early morning rose.
So frail
so tender
and so sincere
drawing me near . . .
But only for a moment, I must
  go and be free.
This can not work, how can we
  be?
Greener fields of life and love
  are calling to me,
and from your arms I must
  be free.

Martha Tucker Fugate
**THE SHADOW OF HAWK
WINGS**

The shadow of hawk wings,
  gliding,
Slides swiftly ahead on the
  lane.
I watch as he circles and climbs,
Then rides the air again
Toward the fallow field.
Should I fear for his intended
  pray
Or hope that his hunting may
  yield
Him a meal? I admit to
  rhetorical questions
For his beauty has nurtured
  my soul,
Though some hitherto-loved
  furry creature
Run in panic toward his small
  hole.

Mrs. Irene Palmer
THE MAGIC OF CHRISTMAS

There seems to be a feeling that's
  in the air
With joy and beauty everywhere
A sort of universal brotherhood
As if, at least, once a year men
  understood
Each other and forgot their
  petty woes
Being friends to all as hate and
  meanness goes
Yes, Christmas brings such joy
  and cheer
And then we say "A Happy New
  Year."
Now if this spirit could last each
  day
Wouldn't our world be in a
  wonderful way?
If the Magic of Christmas would
  never cease
And bring to our world much
  needed peace.

Carrie E. Brinkman
THANK YOU, MY FRIEND

You have opened my eyes to so
  many new windows
  of life,
You have helped me to grow in
  countless ways,
  and you have watched me
  grow,
  the little girl fading into a

young woman.
You are a beautiful melody in
  my life
  and you let me be the perfect,
  matching harmony
  to your life's song,
The musical mosaic of our soul's
  reaching out
  and touching one another's
  lives
  to enrich and deepen its
  meaning.
Your compassionate
  understanding and gentle
  strength
  is a source of inexpressible
  comfort
  in times of trouble.
What can I say except . . .

I LOVE YOU.

Kathryn E. Beattie
ANALOGY

A sudden gust of wind
Forces more brown leaves
To fall from the heights.
They float to the ground,
The leaves a reminder of lives.
Lives begin, they grow, they
  become colorful,
and they end,
Replaced by new lives,
As the leaves are replaced by
  new leaves.
Each new life destined to be
As the former.

Heidi A. Gorzik
WAITING FOR THE ASKING

Why is it
that some women wait for the
  asking?
Spending their days searching
  faces
becoming soft-grained
with too much time
between airplanes and letters;
Breaking their nails,
burning photographs,
beating their fists against
  over-smoothed pillows;
Dreading winters full of
  memoirs penned by under-rug
  spirits,
holidays alone,
phone calls that don't come;
Running fugitive
from offices to broken-screened
  dwellings,
waiting for the asking,
until silence gives the telling
that it's over.

Ann P. Schweickert
AUTUMN INTERLUDE

I listen to the stillness of
  the autumn afternoon,
And gaze upon the ocean
  streaked with sequined light.
A solitary sailboat seems to
  hang like a cocoon,
Waiting to be changed into a
  butterfly in flight.
The breeze turns cooler now
  as the clouds their shadows
  cast,
And the day seems ready to
  give way before the night.
It is a time for memories of
  autumns long since past,
Of hopes and dreams that never
  quite
Became reality.

James Fuerst
THE ULTIMATE

This much is certain
to have been born on schedule
in the middle of May
means I had to be conceived
in August of the previous year.
But what is not certain
and never will be
is the effect on me
if any
good or bad
had I lingered yet another day
or even one single hour
secured safely in my mother's
    womb
being further formed.

Now had I waited another week
    or two
history warns me life could be
    different.

And nothing should mean less
    to me
than this possibility.

Otto M. Sorensen
BROKEN GLASS

Broken glass
Once clear and whole, replete
    with glow and purpose
And now but scattered
    fragments reft of form and
    mass.

Crumbling sand
Entrapped in lifeless roots,
    awaiting vainly
Fusion from some muted
    smelter's hand.

Shattered glass
Snatched up in hand with roots
    and sand it speaks
Of that which would have been
    and what has come to pass.

Cora Lindsey Lyden
EVENTIDE

I walk in my garden at dusk,
    when the gates are closed and I
    am alone.
The birds and bees are bidding
    goodnight
to their children. The perfume
    of lilacs
is so sweet, and with the scent
    of firs,
spruces, and pines I am at peace.

The lilies of the valley in their
    quiet
spots are like white patches of
    moonlight,
with their tiny bells of fragrance
    trying
to out-do the roses, bending
    over them
along the rosewalk fence.

Standing over the roses, lilies,
    and iris
are the lilacs with out-stretched
    branches
laden with heavy blooms, like
    sentinels through the
    night.

Going through the rosewalk,
    underneath the trees,
I come out with the view of the
    lake, seeing
it over the hedge of lilacs,
    honeysuckle, and
    locusts; there I pause and make
    my evening
prayer of thanks for having so
    much beauty to share.

Night has come and I am alone;
    silence
envelops me.

Ms. Veronica "Baby" Morris
**COME WITH ME BLACK
CHILD**

Come with me Black Child and
    take my hand,
For I shall lead you to your
    promised land.
For four hundred years you've
    been thrown
    in the dirt,
The only fate you've
    encountered is being hurt.
Come with me Black Child
    across the land,
Where you will grow—to be your
    own man.
I'll protect you, advise you and
    send you to
    school,
You won't ever be confused as
    to what is the
    rule.
Come with me Black Child as we
    stroll across the
    bay,
Where you'll lead your people
    to freedom someday.
You'll teach your Black Children
    to love one
    another,
And to show respect instead of
    resentment to your
    distant White brother.
Come with me Black Child as we
    take our final twirl,
Into making your promised land,
    a much better world.

Cindy Loy
THE CONTEST

I'm sitting here in such a
    familiar place
With a look of anguish upon my
    face.
Many times I've taken pen and
    ink,
And written great works, or at
    least I think.
I think I could write just this
    one more time,
But I'll be damned, I can't get
    past the third line.
I have an old woman in a
    straight back chair
It's the ache in her knees that
    keeps her there.
But then after that the words
    are all gone,
The feeling is there because I
    know she's alone.
I have a candle that flickers a
    circle upon the ceiling,
And a book that for the fourth
    time page 46 I'm reading.
Then the damn candle burns
    out and I'm left in the dark;
My pen is running dry, leaving
    a half-wit mark.
I call myself a poet, I guess
    that's a joke;
I just think deep thoughts and
    take lots of notes.
So in the future, if a contest
    should arise,
That just wants a note, I know
    I will win first prize.

Ms. Shirley A. Miles
AUTUMN

I love the gentle autumn wind
    that brush against
    my face,
It's warm and very gentle breeze
    dance so filled
With grace;

It turn the summer's greenery,
    all red and gold
And brown,
And one by one they fall to
    earth, tumbling down,
Down, down.
The very hot days of
    summertime still slowly lingers
On,
    Yet the coolness of the winter
    months began to rush
Head on;
And with it's great delightfulness
    comes Trick or
Treat on Halloween,
And the love and laughter of
    finding what Thanksgiving
Can bring.
I love the gentle autumn wind,
    so comforting are they
To me
They have the warm morning
    sun, and the evening's
    cool breeze;
These are days like no other God
    has given us throughout
The year,
And every season I'll count the
    days until autumn again
Is here.

Marilyn Moran
MONICA

That November day was more
    like spring
Autumn was fading in a last
    brilliant glow
Competing for the spotlight
    with the wedding show
The contest ended when
    the bride appeared,
The day became hers
    and the brilliance blended
    as one—
She captured the sun.

Dana Michelle Baker
WHY?

    The land was theirs, they
    got here first,
then we came.
    They gave back what they
    took from the land,
we took but never gave.
    They hunted only the
    animals they needed,
we killed just to be killing.
    They worshipped the animals,
    the land,
we worshipped only ourselves.
    They had to start their lives
    from scratch,
we started ours from what was
    left of theirs.
    Their weapon was the bow
    and arrow,
ours was the gun.
    They were treated like
    animals,
we acted like God.
    Their lives were ruined,
    families gone,
we walked away proud, we
    had won.

Ruth E. Havens
A CHILD

A child is like a shaft of light
    That pierces through a
    darkened night
    . . . and illumes an oft'
    shadowed day.
Where warmth and laughter ne'r
    do dwell,
    His coming weaves a 'chanted
    spell
    . . . and time delights him at

his play.
When hearts are pained and fear
    would break,
    His tiny presence can remake
    . . . singing strings from
    sorrowing clay.
If hands do lie empty, folded,
    His eager clasp fits there,
    molded
    . . . to lead near to a richer
    way.
I fain would dwell somewhere
    around
    Where childish feet most sure
    abound
    . . . and know no silent,
    sterile quay.

Nancy E. Pardoe
MY DADDY

    This man I knew, was a brick
    layer.
He was not young nor was he
    old, he was
a middle aged man. He would
    tell about
different things like from wrong
    to right;
and about here and there and
    their sights.
I suppose you wondered why,
    I talked
to this man; well I will tell you
    if I can.
He was special to me, because
    he was my daddy.
But he had to leave me, even
    though I will
always love him.

Patricia King
A MOTHER'S EMPTINESS

I still remember the cold snowy
    night in January—
the night you were conceived.
Your Dad and I were warm in
    each other's arms
and love overtook our minds.
We were very much in love
but, you see, we weren't man
    and wife
and we weren't going to be.
Confused, happy and sad all at
    once
for I was to be a mother—a
    mother at 19.
I cried so many tears,
but we were strong together.
It wasn't long though and I lost
    you.
It didn't seem fair to me,
we didn't have time to grow
    together—
my baby and I.
You were to be a son I know
and were to be just like your
    father.
I never knew you but you were
    a part of me
and I loved you so.
The love your Dad and I shared
    was the deepest love I have ever
    known.
I thought if ever I was to loose
    him,
I'd have something of his to
    cherish—his baby.
But I lost you and with years
    passing by, I lost him too.
The pain from his absence is
    over, but the pain from loosing
    you
lives on day after day.
Often my thoughts drift back to
    that night,
those first few months of
    motherhood

and I cry.
I had lost something so precious
to a woman—her child.
Although unknown to each
other,
you will be a part of my life for
eternity.
I love you my child.

M.M.Conrad
THE LAST HIGHLANDER

I have seen the eerie northern
lights,
Once I named them the Merry
Dancers;
Now I retreat to the rocky
heights,
Driven to find the final answers.
With the eagle I stand on the
highest crag,
I seek my soul in the mountain
mist,
Over the moor I run with the
stag;
At the lowland crowds I shake
my fist.
Like the lonely eagle I must
be free;
Once I fought for the land
that I love,
I'd not bow the head or bend
the knee.
They feared the wild skirl
of my pipes from above.
To the farthest western island's
shore
At the end of time I will
surely run,
And launch my boat to sail
once more
Into the setting sun.

Teresa Miller
REMEMBERING A FRIEND

I'm remembering, just
remembering.
Thoughts of you are always
in my mind,
But I can't see you, except
through the stars.
I often wonder if you can see
me.
I can't hear your voice, except
through the wind.
Can you hear me?
I can't feel your warm touch,
except through my heart;
Which tells me more each
day.
How I wish, oh how I wish
your life did not have to
end
on that September day.
I'll remember you always;
Until it comes the day
where we meet again,
in love as friends.

Mark Scott Ovens
WHY GET HIGH

Stoned, shattered —WOW—I'm
high!
This is the question, you asked
me, "Why?"

I think it does something, it
opens my mind
It answers my questions, it
lets me unwind.

Pot solves nothing—it creates
something new.
The thing it creates are ideas
that I view.

With this smokable relaxant
my body feels fine,
My legs start to running and

it tingles my spine.
The rush is tremendous when
the adrenalin flows.
The whole thing is churning, and
it never slows.

I may smoke forever, I may
stop this day,
Who knows the answer, Who
knows the ways?

But listen, don't tell me, I
don't want to hear!
The future is coming, and this
I don't fear.

Helen M. Robinson
THE GINGERBREAD PAIR

I've baked a gingerbread boy
and girl
For my two with the shining
eyes
And I've put them right where
they're sure to see
To give them a great big
surprise.

I wonder if somewhere, someday
My girl
Will fashion with just such
care
Another gingerbread boy
and girl
For another shining eyed pair?

Rissa Tobin
ROOMS ON THE SEA

the time of day and season
designed suspension
far from dark
    feel
        the
            light

hot or cold
the air is fresh
not quite still
the rooms are stark

vacant,
though not empty
watchful
available
through open door and window
lovers come and go

beckoning
telling no secrets
only messages
echoing as these rooms do
bright passages.

Julius Anthony Pfister
TO START

To start and to do one's part
In every part and mart
With one's whole heart
is indeed very smart.

But smarter, and harder it is
To continue the art
Unthwarted.

Simone Marie Baxendale
MERELY BATHWATER

I wish I could be the water of
your bath
I would surround you with
mellow warmth
liquid love
like a frolicking childish wave . . .
I would clash and break
upon the firmness of your
body
engulf and moisten the places
I dream of . . .
If I were the water of your bath
I would memorize each and
every muscle
and being liquid, I would take
your shape
mold myself to your every

curve, your every indentation
I would roll on, over, and off
your satin skin . . .
If I were the water of your
bath
I would send part of me to
the recess of your navel
there my temperature would
rise to match yours
and like plants of the sea
I would move your body's
hairs in and out with the
tender tides
created by my movements
playfully . . .
I would slosh against your
thighs and become very
intimate with your nature.
If I were the water in your
bath
I would cleanse you
as my ancestors of the Nile
and Congo
cleansed your ancestors
But even more,
when you leave me
and pull the plug,
I would delay the natural
order of things
and stay waiting
for your
naked return . . .

Alta Adams
MY LIFE

Oh, where did my yesterday go?
I wonder, as I recall the days
of long ago.
If only I could turn back the
pages of time and see,
That time is ever, and is, and
will be.

My future with great care I
would plan,
Make a blueprint as only an
architect can.
Many mistakes I have made
along the way,
And hope some day to right
them, some way.

We each drift or soar at our own
gait
Never realizing it may soon be
too late.
Oh yesterday, please come
back I pray.
God grant me the chance to
pattern my life the right
way.

James A. Arpan
OUR DAUGHTER

Curly hair and impish grins,
fair little daughter mine.
Whose contented laugh spreads
happiness as you smile passed
cheeks
like cherry wine.
You have answered mommie's
prayers.
How we hoped and dreamed
of you,
and now you're here, our dreams
surpassed,
a veritable wish come true.

H. L. Sarver, Jr.
STARHILL

Tall and proud in all her mystic
knowledge
From her lofty height she
surveys all of Earth
Most ignore her and all she
works for
But some are her children
She teaches and protects her
own

Gently she casts her children
to the far reaches of the
universe
While gone from her they toil
and remain faithfully loyal
Patiently she awaits the return
of her royal children
Some return to her waiting arms
But others go to unbound
worlds of infinity
Despite her tears they never
return
Lost is the finite in the presence
of the infinite
Is her only sigh as she faithfully
continues the appointed task
Crying for those lost and
rejoicing for those returned
Surrounded by apathy she
remains courageous

The few that are hers stare
steadfastly upward
Eagerly they await their turn
Sick of their never questioning
surroundings
They know some will never
return
But they are assured by one
comfort
Above the lofty height of
Starhill the infinite rules
The welcoming fires of heaven
beckon
And each star shines as a friendly
beacon

Both mother and children are
comfortly assured
The children because they know
their turn is near
But mother's comfort is more
passive than active
Starhill knows that above all the
finite stars
Whose place is in the infinite
Carefully watch over all
But especially over Starhill for
within her great possibilities
lie

Kristi McGarry
UNTITLED

The sun is shining
As he hobbles down the road.
My father is old.
The long day ends in sunset
As he drifts away from life.

Kathy L. Austin
THE ESSENCE OF LIFE

Play your banjo for me,
  Mountain Man
Release my mind
It aches to flow again
Like the rivers, the streams
O'er the mountains
That live in my mind
So my sould will know
of a flow
Called the essence of life.

So play your banjo for me,
  Mountain Man
It's a part of a plan
Like a mountain man
For he lives as he can
As do rivers
Caught up in a flow.

Dannette M. Giargiari
YOU ARE THE REASON . . .

You are the reason . . .

Why I am here,
Why I am able to love,
Why people love me back,
Why I think the world is so
beautiful, for you have made
it that way.

You are the reason why life
  wouldn't be complete without
  you,
Why I am able to laugh, cry, and
  be myself,
Why I know right from wrong
  for I have followed your
  paths,
yet I still have my own to make.
You are the reason why I have
  faith and trust in you, for
you have shown me the way
  and how. I owe all of my
  love
to You.

Mary E. Bennett
SUCCESS

Why is it that only some people
  achieve success
It's their willingness to stand
  pat when put to the test
It's their courage to fight, to
  do or to die
It's their strength to hold on
  when others defy
It's their determination to
  complete some unlikeable
  task
It's their eagerness to help
  others without being asked
Then why is it that only some
  people managed to climb
To the top of success's ladder to
  peace sublime
While others at the bottom lay
Waiting for success to pass their
  way
The answer can be found in
  life's bubbling dream
While some people work, most
  just dream.

Dee C. Taylor
NAIL-SCARRED HAND

What has lifted up
The fallen man
Who bloody, dark, and stained
  by sin
Had nothing left; no hope
  within
Has given hope unto the
  hopeless
Riches, wealth unto the poor
And replacing burdens, fears
Gives joy, and peace, and life
  within
What binds up the broken-
  hearted
What lifts up the meek and
  tender
Our arch, our shield, our
  Great Defender
The nail-scarred hand, our
  Great Relender.

Throughout the ages and
  the years
It's wiped away our fears, our
  tears
And lifting man through the
  grace of love
Gives comfort abiding from
  Above.

Lela Grace Schroeder
GOD'S TOOLBOX

Your body is but a toolbox,
  from which to use each day
Your God-given tools in
  Service, to Hil along Life's
  way.
Your eyes, ears, hands, feet,
  tongue, mind and heart
Are instruments He provided
  you with, from the very
  start.

Eyes to follow His Blueprint,
  known as the Master's Plan.
Ears with which to hear and
  heed, the needs of your
  fellowman.
Be a willing worker and gladly
  greet each dawn—
When you've been given another
  day, His task to carry on.
Use your hands in labor,
  remember, too, to pray.
Ask the Lord to guide your feet
  in the most beneficial way.
Use your tongue for telling
  others and to them the message
  bring,
Of happiness that can be
  theirs, if they'll too, His
  praises sing.
Ever keep an open kind, for
  then only, can you reach
The point of Life's lesson,
  He does so readily teach.
Use your heart for all it's
  worth to
  daily help the Lord.
When Pay Day comes, you
  will have earned His very
  great REward.
By having always helped
  others, the more you've
  helped yourself
To build for your Soul
  an Eternal Place on Heaven's
  Grand Tool Shelf.

Jean Comstock White
CHILD OF RHYME

Poets have a rhythm all their
  own,
A part of wave, of ocean, sea
  and sand;
A whilly different feeling, all
  in one,
While tuning in to thoughts
  they understand.

Poets are prophets, in the
  realm of love;
Interpreters of the simple and
  the meek.
They point the way, as star-
  shine from above
Shimmers their very souls
  with an urge to seek

A tryst with the Infinite and
  its Wonder-glow.
Artists, never halted by the
  dark
Of vast confusions, Poets
  seek to know
How different the mundane
  and the spark.

A Poet's sojourn on the planes
  of earth
Is blinded by the Star that to
  him gave
A chance to find again the
  noble birth
That is the martyr's praise
  though heathens rave.

Poet let not this dark sphere
  weigh you down!
Child of Eternity, Clarion of
  Time,
For you God fashioned Rhythm
  as a Crown!
O sing your Pathway Paeons,
  Child of Rhyme.

Sherri Wellman
**A HEART IS NOT A
PLAYTHING**

A heart is not a plaything
A heart is not a toy
But if you want it broken
just give it to a boy.

Boys love to fool around with
  things and see just how they
  run,
But when it comes to kissing
  girls they do it just for fun.
Don't ever fall in love, my
  friend
Don't ever go astray
It causes broken hearts, my
  friend,
It happens everyday.
Each time that you are near
  him
Your heart begins to dance
You kiss his lips and hold him
  tight
There's nothing like romance.
He'll tell you that he loves you
And you believe it's true
One moment you'll be happy—
  the next you'll be blue.

Don't ever fall in love, my
  friend,
You'll be hurt before it's
  through,
You see, my friend, I ought
  to know:
I fell in love with you.

Jeff Mayfield
DOES ANYONE KNOW WHY?

Does anyone know why we're
  pushed around?
Does anyone know the cause
  of loud sounds?
Does anyone know why people
  cheat?
Or why some people are pushed
  out of seats?
Does anyone know why others
  steal?
Or how bad we can make others
  feel?
Does anyone know why people
  starve?
Or why on walls obscenities
  are carved?
Does anyone know why people
  are poor?
Does anyone know who broke
  open the door?
Does anyone know why
  people are killed?
Or why we tear down nature's
  hills?
Does anyone know why life
  isn't fair?
But now tell me the truth—
  DOES ANYONE CARE?

Grigory Vardanian
THE TRUTH

Brighter than the sun,
Stronger than the storm,
Swifter than the thought,
Clearer than the azure.

Straighter than a ray,
Merrier than friendship
Bolder than a dream,
More pleasant than the sleep.

More solid than a rock,

Harder than a diamond.
More beautiful than dawn,
More ardent than the fire.

Sweeter than the lyre,
Lighter than the day,
More terrible than a volcano,
More charming than a flower!

April Loveless
**LOVE SPEAKS IN A
WHISPER**

Love speaks not like thunder
but like a gentle breeze
that whispers to me softly
just enough to tease—
to tease me to listen
for what I want to hear
Love speaks in a whisper
whenever you are near.

Love grips not like winter
but caresses like the sun
that feels warm and inviting
enough to make me come
out to enjoy the weather
when I would have stayed
  inside
Love holds me gently
when I am by your side.

Love holds me gently,
is strong but tender too
Love speaks in a whisper
whenever I'm with you.

Deborah Ann Rhatigan
O SHIPPING

O shell upon the shore,
I saw hue there.
Yet I touched your deep inside,
smiling I triumphed silently.

O wind along the shore,
I soar to meet thy calling,
the sun is a glistening,
and there you lie within
smelling the waves,
diagonal stare whispering

O how delightful that only you
darest to go beyond the fenced
  in front,
to fair the finally hunted.

O honesty, a calling the front,
that only the spiral tragic say.
Come be by me, "I won't!"

O silent friend,
  "Tis so far off that we'll meet
  again."

Charlene M. Rachuy
**A TEAR FROM HEAVEN . . .
GOD**

The shadows fell upon my path,
I disregarded them as nothing,
I merely shrugged and said,
"I can handle it."
I tried to walk alone,
I failed.
In prayer one night I asked
  God for help,
He touched me with a raindrop—
A tear from Heaven . . .God
In that simple way I knew God
  hurt for me.

As the teardrops fell more
  rapidly
I could hear Him say,
"You will never walk alone
  again,
I have been with you all the
  time
You merely overlooked my
  presence.
Your hand is placed in mine—
  I will never let it go.

I am your Northern Star,
I will guide you through this
  life.

Deborah Ransom Via Grace
THE FAIR

Just hold on tight in
    everything;
I will help you overcome all
    strife.
You are mine and I love you."
So said the Lord to me . . .
With a tear from Heaven.

I remember the fair:
Once, I looked inside the tent
of a smiling clown.
His private mirror and my silent
    gaze—
witnessed his frown
that he covered over
with upturned lips and laugh
    lines.
I never gave his disguise away—
but I'll never be able
to laugh again
whenever a clown looks my way.
Human happiness
is lost in the house of Mirrors.
The searchers for truth
run wild . . .only finding
mockeries and false illusions.
In a fit of frenzy, they call
    for help—
But no one hears.
And they break down and cry
When it's time to leave,
they force a frozen smile.
These people that come to
    fairs: leave
with darkened eyes
and make-up smears.

Today I went to the fair . . .
And when a clown danced by
with upturned lips and laugh
    lines—
I couldn't help
but cry.

Jill Hamell
BREAKING UP

We spent so little precious time
    while we were together
Talking laughing and just
    getting to know each other
The times we shared were
    both crazy and intimate ones
But as long as I was with you,
    I always had fun
Then between sunset and
    sunrise our golden times came
    to past
Along with our special love I
    thought would last
The memories I have of you
    seem so very few
I can only hope that you will
    remember them too
You will always have a special
    place deep in my heart
That feeling I have for you will
    never part.

Nicholas DiTomaso
TODAY AND EVERYDAY

He was good to me today
for i have seen the beginning
and ending of a brand new day
He lit the sky above so bright
    n' clear
To let me know He is always
    near
As i go through the day in my
    daily tasks
Should there be questions
All i do is look up and ask
When time comes for my daily
    bread
Before i eat i thank Him first
Then bow my head
Now the sky that shone so

bright
Is slowly fading and turns to
    nite
To-nite as i lie snug in my bed
With weary eyes inside my
    head
I'll close my eyes and turn
    out the light
Then smile at Him and say . . .
Good-night.

Rosemary Hardison
SYMPHONY

Together as we ride
on the wings of passion
We will compose in
a most glorious fashion
The movements of our lives
love symphony.
Always in perfect harmony
Our ever perfect symphony.

Together we will walk
along the shores of tranquility
Beginning as two, inevitably
    as one
Following the ebbing tide
into the ocean of infinity
And we will compose yet
    another part
of our continuing symphony.
Always in perfect harmony
Our ever perfect symphony.

Merry DeMoss Wilhelm
ISLAND SANCTUARY

Our David dug the bones from
    sand and rock
and exposed them where they
    lay.
He'd been a young man,
    perhaps Algonquin,
Huron, Ojibway . . .deduced from
    from his jewelry,
and the tribal grinding stone
passed earlier in the day.
He'd layed himself down in
    heaped up sand,
all the shelter that had come
    to his hand,
and sand had sifted his dreams
    away.
He'd come alone, probably to
    prove he could,
to hunt and to fish the
    undrained swamp
and had dared the late fall
    storms
to put to the test his new
    manhood.
Had he lost his canoe, his
    strength,
to one of those storms?
Facing death, he'd faced his
    home,
far away haze lying low in the
    sky,
and with dignity learned from
    babyhood,
he'd composed himself to die.
Now, how many years later,
    here am I
Escaped from the mainland

the same as he;
and I, too, have fled a storm
to seek refuge on green Pelee.
I hunt for contentment
and fish for escape
and, like the bones in David's
    hole,
quietly atrophy.

Jewell Harrell
BIRTHDAY

Quietly fell the rain of spring
upon the sleeping grass.
The sun shone bright upon
    the trees, which gleamed like
    polished
brass.
The clouds formed trains of
    whispy white up in the
    moody sky.
The wind passed through in
    whispered jogs and stepped
    just once to sigh.
The day began and played till
    dusk had set upon the earth
and night time came with
    splendor
to end the new day's birth.

Susan K. Beauman
ITS UP TO YOU

its up to you
to meet me half   way.
I am willing to go all the
    distance
to reach you.
but are you willing to at least
    meet me
somewhere along the way?

Rita Robloff
WISDOM

In my imagination one day,
I met a rose—
A beautiful red, red rose;
Vivid, velvity American
    Beauty,
Full-bloomed. Radiant!
I asked this rose,
"How is it you are so beautiful?"
The rose replied
"I am
What I came to be."

Roy E. Bundy
THE FAMILY

Hearts as big as the universe and
    enough
love to fill up its vacuum:
Patching your spirit when life
    shoots its
bullets of reality;
Showing you the light when it
    has been
obscured by society's fallacies;
Betting on you when the odds
    say other
wise:
Betting on you because they're
    glad
you're alive.
Injecting strength into your
    body while
theirs is steadily drained;
Giving up their last penny to
    keep you
from witnessing pain;
Staying in your corner when
    the rest have
broke camp;
Pushing you into the 15th
    round as if you
were the champ.
When the rest of the world
    could care less

if you live or die,
Your family is one institution
    in which
you can confide!

Veronica Marie Pryduluk
UNTITLED

Who are your friends?
    (Oh, I have none)—
None, you say?
For the queen bee has her hive;
You my friend, you have your
    mind . . .
Where is your mind?
    (Oh, for it is gone)—
Gone, you say?
For the gopher has his hole;
You my friend, you have your
    soul . . .
What is your soul?
    (Oh, for it is entity)—
Entity, you say?
For the king has his throne;
You my friend, you will find
    a home . . .

Fran Brezina
OUR SECRET FORCE

Some secret force has found
    us
Which lets us love and feel
    alive
Then lets us part and brings
    us back
To be at each other's side.
Again our force would split
    us
It knows you are not free
How strange this love of ours
For you don't belong to me.
But what we feel is special
And this secret force only
    knows
Why it lets us love each other
And then lets us go.
How long can we go on
And love each other this way
Our secret force knows the
    answer
For it controls this play.

Karen L. Hess
UNTITLED

Perhaps one day, man could
    listen and really hear,
His eyes could focus and
    really see.
He could touch and not
    threaten,
And speak instead of command.
Perhaps he could trust
    without questioning,
And love without demanding.
Maybe he could learn to feel
    without touching,
To embrace but not restrict.
If only he could spread
    happiness, his search ended.
His tears be that of joy, instead
    of sorrow.
Perhaps his smile could be one
    of innocence,
And his words be that of
    truth.
Maybe then man's existance
    would not be in vain.

Mary Kaufman–Wildberg
THE RAPE

Bold Jack comes like a jealous
    elf
And strips the tree of her
    leafy coat.
Sprinkles the air with a
    biting frost,
Then slips away in his sleep ice

boat;
Now as he flees, he leaves his
mark
On field and stream and berry
and bark.
What I hold dear, he violates;
Everything else, he serves on
plates.
Thieving Frost—hard-nosed
one,
I'd like to see you bake in sun!

Janeen Tyson
**GENTLE BREEZES AND
SUNNY DAYS**

Oh wind blown day,
carry me away.
To a time of gentle breezes and
sunny days,
Heal my mind.
Drop my troubles into a pool
of clear water,
and let them disappear as the
ripples disappear.
Take my body and warm it
with sunshine .

Behind all the rubble of my
mind,
find the laughter I left behind.
Restore me to a sense of
being.
Blow away the doubts and
jealousies and anger,
and let them die as surely
as a sudden whirlwind
dies.
Shake out my love of life and
let me live again.

Gentle breezes and sunny days,
You took me away for just
a moment.
Now as I comb the tangles
from my hair,
and brush the grass from my
clothes,
I am grateful.

In a quiet time I found the
strength I needed to face
up
and square my shoulders and
finally laugh again.
Laughter, no sweeter sound
could fall upon my ears
and heart, caress my mind,
and restore my soul.

Mrs. Ruth Hunter
TO NATALIE

A little girl came to my house
today—
To eat, and sleep and chase the
blues away.
Her hair like spun gold, her
eyes of heaven blue
Her mouth like a rosebud kissed
by morning dew.
Sometimes she laughs so gaily,
sometimes she
sheds a tear—
But always brings happiness
whenever she is near.
She makes the world a better
place for me.
She's only five years old
my little Natalie.

Kathryn Gravett Streeper
THE TONGUE

We do not realize that what
we say,
Could turn a heart and
make it stray.
In our anger, when raging
mad,
We can wreck a life and make
it sad.

The same tongue, with God's
help, we can tame;
And bring happiness in the
Savior's name.
We can guide a life that it
might be,
Contented, and happy, and
completely free.

Ranay Odell
UNICORN

I looked out my window one
day
And, to my surprise, what
did I see?
You may think I'm mad
for what I say,
But I saw a unicorn looking
at me.
He was white with a horn of
gold
And brown eyes that knew
All of my heart without
being told.
As we stood I wondered what
to do.
I wished that he would be
my friend.
Then he came to me,
We are together now and until
the end
together we'll always be.

Glen Hight
A PROBLEM SOLVED

I really like my paper boy
But it gives me a pain
To have to hunt my paper
Out yonder in the rain.
It's like a game of hide-n-seek
It could be any place
For when it leaves his hand
It takes a trip through space.

Lawanda Gail Williams
MARRIAGE

Today some women say that
they don't
want to marry.
They want to have just free
and
simple relationships.
I don't blame them for not
wanting any
old Tom, Dick, or Harry.
But when you find you want
more
than just companionship,
Look for a guy who has love
and likableness
in a special blend.
Then you'll have a husband,
and, also, a
very best friend!

Sharon R. Frazier
TO TOUCH TRUTH

Man of constant sorrow, trying
to catch a rainbow.
Woman of constant pain,
reaching for a star, trying
to cover a scar.

Break the wall of silence.
Swinging through the universe
on colored ribbons
won't get you very far.

Well, maybe just beyond the
pot of gold you're looking
for.

You cry man, all the tears
of all sorrows.
You bear woman, all the pain
of all tomorrows.

Reach down to touch truth;
through pain comes strength
and power.

The pot of gold is not so far
now.

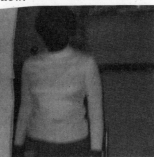

Maggie G . Foster
THE LORD AND I

It is all right with me
If I never be
A great politician screaming
from a box,
Or a smooth talking group of
directors,
With all the bonds and stocks
As long as I can be with the
Lord.

I really don't ever
Wish to know
How the grass stays green
And what makes it grow.
Will the river rise
Or can the ocean flow?
As long as I know the Lord.

I don't care if I never
Have a dollar or a dime.
Gushing oil fields,
Or clothes so fine.
Don't care for no share
In a pure gold mine
As long as I have the Lord.

So, don't try to pull me down
Or push me aside.
The more you puss and pull
The higher I'll rise.
I'll just keep on paddling
Until I ride out the tide.
Because I have the Lord.

Jeanne Higgins Modisette
A MEMORY

Today is the day you were
to be born,
Six months gone, but still
it's a thorn.
You'd have been the sparkle
on our gloomy nights,
You'd have been the warmth
in my arms on nights so
cold,
You'd have been a dream in
my dreams a plenty,
You'd have been the worry
in our hearts so heavy,
You'd have been the token
of two loves for each
other,
You'd have been the playmate
for your older brother,
You'd have filled our lifes
with such love and joy,
Whether you'd been a girl
or boy,
Now—you're only a memory—
Remembered by so few.

Debbi Swanson
COLORADO

I want to grasp your hand and
take you somewhere
no one's ever been,
A very simple land, where its
only riches
are found within.

Sounds are so quiet, land
undisturbed,
and brown;
A sky so wide and beautiful,
only a scorching
sun can be found.
A highway long and narrow with
bumps along the way,
Traveling on the prairie with
the same scene takes days.
But there's something special
about this land
that God found fit and made,
And when I return home
someday, this
memory shall never fade.
For I have been taught a lesson,
this
land has made me learn;
That the space between us
is only physical, it's
the love in our hearts that
makes our world turn.

Margaret McGlaughlin
PRAYER FOR GROWN SONS

They are men now, Lord,
my hands at last are emptied
of the countless tasks required
for so long.
And I am helpless quite before
the problems
that grown sons face. I cannot
right earth's wrongs,
Or smooth their pathways,
but, Dear Lord, you can.

I have no legacy at all to give
them.
But if my prayer is answered,
it will give
Them more than any wealth
the world can offer.
I pray, Christ, be their comrade
while they live.
Walk with them should they
feel they walk alone.
And make your presence, daily,
hourly known.

Companion them. I ask for
nothing greater
than this rich blessing for these
precious ones:
The (Holy) companionship of
Christ, a young man.
As counselor and guide to
these, my sons.
I loose their hands, having done
all I could do.
And trust them, Lord,
implicitly to you.

Janelle Hanson
**ENTERING A WYOMING
RANCH**

Private Property

Keep Out

No Trespassing

No hunting or Fishing

Violators will be Prosecuted—
Howdy

Shelly Pahel
UNTITLED

A little child cries hungry and
cold,
Who will give to save his soul.
A love denied,
A life that died.
A friend you've lost,
The love it's cost.
Not enough to share?
No, not enough who cared,
He's gone, he's dead,
Yet I do not grieve
For he will suffer no more.

Bonnie Newton
UNTITLED

feelings gently put away
inside a soft cocoon
all the things I want to say
unwind the strands too soon.

Susan Lindsey
GHOST TOWN

No one lives in Dolores,
But the wind does,
And it blows.
No one lives in Dolores,
But the rain comes,
And it goes.

Bleak as the buzzard's stare,
Ashes of yester hope
Stark as the desert glare,
Futile as a dead man's grope.

Crying
Lost is a dream to the sunset
Lost is a promise to the night
Lost is an epic to the dawning
And tomorrow to the morning
light.

Valorie E. Buchanan
LISTEN

Listen, can you hear
Listen, can you see
Listen, can you, my dear
Can you listen to me?

Listen, do you hear the rain
Listen, do you understand
Listen, can you feel the pain
of the knife I hold in my hand?

Tom Schmitt
**A DAY IN THE LIFE OF
THE LONELY**

To want to do something—
but having nothing to do,
To want to go someplace—
but having nowhere to go,
To walk to oblivion, every
night—
for lack of a better place,
To love somebody—
but not be loved,
To live infinite tomorrows that
are just like today that
was just like yesterday,
To merely exist—
but never live,
This is a day in the life
of the lonely,
Nothing to do—
Nowhere to go—
No one to love—
Days on end of
nothing new,
nothing different;—
nothing.

Deborah A. Bazin
HERE'S ONE FOR YOU

You are like that of a rainbow—
beautiful and special
in your own way
meaning so much to me

You are there after the storm—
holding me
showing me the colors of
life.

Elisa Davila
**FREEDOM BEYOND THREE
MILE ISLAND**

I'll be free
when smiles and pornographies
all mixed up along the streets
will keep a mournful beat
to all the movie screens.
I'll be free after the fires,
beyond the computer and its
mechanical gardens.

And on the days of marching
and of bombing,
of escaping and of dying,
I'll be humming
secret words and rituals
to little weeds and herbs
quietly planted under broken
wings of
fighting bombers.
I'll be free even at noon today.
POSTSCRIPT:
And one day again
there were no reactors.

Patricia D. Hyatt
FIND THE WARMTH

Find the warmth inside of you
Bring it out to warm me too
Wrap it around us like a
curtain
Let it melt away the pain and
burden
Then deep within our warm
cocoon
our new love will grow and
bloom.
We will take from our love all
it will
give.
But still our love will grow and
live,
and finally, if I must let it go,
I will not mourn for I will
know
The warmth you gave me has
not died
But still is glowing here inside.

Eulalie S. Begley
SYMBOLS

My campfire burns.
I see the smoke
the wind teases,
lifting it upward
blending in space.
The pot boils,
white steam meets the air.
A rain cloud is the same.
It is the sky.
Fire warms me.
The heat cooks my food.
It is the sun.
Animals give to me
that I may live.
They are my brothers.
We are one.
It is the earth.
I listen to nature sing
a song of live.
Of death and birth.
I am not alone.
Men have come
who do not know,
to sing with nature,
man must be in tune.
They do not listen.
The pot boils dry,
smoke hovers low.
Embers are weary of life.
Ashes turn back to earth.
I life my arms to the sky.

Irma Clark
MARRIAGE

Marriage is a sacred thing,
It bonds two people with a
ring.
But rings by earthly men are
made,
And soon their beauty starts
to fade.
But marriage comes from
up above,
For God in Heaven sent His
love.
When He created the first
man,

He made someone to hold his
hand.
And thus ordained for all
mankind,
That marriage be the tie that
binds.

Veronica M. Cavellero
TWILIGHT

The end of the day
comes upon us quite quickly
night begins to dawn.

Leticia Saints
THE EXPERIENCE

For me, it was an experience!
For you, perhaps just another...
...but the memory lingers
within me
your touch, caresses, kisses, and
the love.

From the first kiss I knew
A story I longed to learn.

And what a story it was!
Dwelling within me from that
night on.

Beneath your touch
I ached and shivered.

Your caresses still
Caressing throughout my
body.

Those kisses
Melting mine to perfection.

And the love
...it was an experience!

Mrs. Annette Byrd
REFLECTIONS

Mirror, Mirror, on the wall,
Is this really me at all?
This reflections that I see,
Really what I'm meant to be?
Searching thru my soul
today,
Got to be a better way.
Reflections of my past I see,
Got to set my spirit free,
Gotta get back on solid ground,
Rid of these weights that hold
me down,
Life awaits on me I'm sure,
Help me find that open door,
Help me find that open door.

Marcia Lynn Sherwood
MAC III

I have this little problem
in the bottom of my heart.
It keeps on growing bigger
and it's tearing me apart.
Names and faces blending
meaning nothing much.
Always the remembrance of
your simple touch.
One or more or several
pass within my reach,
But none have had the
meaning
that only you can teach.
I let you walk away
without a warning word.
That in my heart the loving
goes on without a cure.

Mary Ellen Grassel
**LOVE'S REFLECTION IN
A ROSE**

Simply a flower
soft and delicate
Where warm love
Is budding.

And as each petal wakes
It reveals the heart
And the aroma of love
Arouses young hearts.

In comparison the two are one.
Fragile to the touch
But what warmth is created
Upon one's gentle embrace.

A ROSE

But to the heart
There love is reflected.

William J. Keener
GARDEN OF THE CHILD

Row upon row of shining faces
Budding minds not yet of places
Like fear and hate or selfish
greed
And all such things we grown-
ups need
...or seem to.

Ruth M. Whitford
LEAH

Conceived with love,
Borne with love,
Birthed with love.
The loving hands of your
grandmother
Drawing you tenderly into
the world
Embraced by members of
your family
All assisting to welcome
You, so eagerly awaited.
Awaiting your first cry,
It came and hung in the air
Sweeter than any sound of
music.
Into a world of new Spring
you came,
Joyous Spring sounds,
Dazzling Spring sights,
Flowers afresh with dew,
Tiny fledglings twittering
in their nests,
Young, very young like
you.
Into a spring world, bursting
with joy
You came;
A child of love,
Conceived with love,
Borne with love,
Birthed with love.

Lillian Sproul
ODE TO THE DISH PAN

The old dish pan
so faithful and true,
going to hand you on the wall,
cause your working days are
through.
Going to write upon your
bottom,
gone but not forgotten
from the old kitchen chore.
And may you always be
remembered
as the old slave of the poor.

Marleta Wenger
LONGING

Oh how can I tell you of my
love
so deep...so yearning...!

Words seem but empty echoes
in the night.
Would that the silent love
within me
could burst forth!
It would explode with aching
joy . . .
Its catapulting embers inflaming
inflaming . . .
enfolding . . . penetrating your
heart . . .
And we would be as one!

Ellen Holm
ALL I ASK

Be my friend
That's all I ask.
Someone to talk to
When I am blue
Or even when I am not.
I'd like to be yours,
A friend nothing more,
If you'd like to be friends
I'd like to know.
If you don't want this
That's OK too,
Just tell me so.

T. R. Hargan, Jr.
FREE MAN'S SONG

I may be young but I've got a
lot of miles under my wheels
Through distance sometimes
forgetting I'm not as old as I
feel
Honestly, I wouldn't want it
another way
'Cause I've earned quite a few
fond memories
and learned what it takes and
means to be free
When to avoid or gamble with
the games people play
In my wandering search for love
without chains
I've slept in the sun and I've
slept in the rain
With the strangest of faces in
familiar and foreign lands
I've made and helped friends,
I've broke a few hearts
It doesn't matter when it ends,
just should it of start
No matter the reason a true
friend would understand
It's like coming home when on
the freeway again
Not worrying on futures or
where I have been
Just guiding my wheels into the
coming of dawn
I have no fear of the end of
my day
For what's bound to be can't
be sent away
The traces I leave remain long
after I'm gone
In the hunger for life, and the
love, and a free man's song.

Terese M. Hutchinson
HOPE SPRINGS ETERNAL

Where to turn? Who to trust?
Is it a pleasure, or is it must?
A false beginning or a genuine
end?
Does she want something
or is it a friend?
Beliefe in God and what do you
get?
Trust in others, it's only regret.
A promise is made—words
spoken tight
A bond is then broken—
someone's in flight.
Bright sun-filled days, nights
full of rain

Could it be love? Ha, only
pain!
Some feel you're crazy, others
sane,
School days or work its all
so mundane.
Yet hope springs eternal in
my heart
At each dead end it's a brand
new start.
You can't be a loner—that isn't
a must.
Please let me in—it's me you can
trust.
Away from you when problems
arise
Tears of sorrow spring to my
eyes.
Because hope springs eternal,
I cannot cry
And knowing you love me—I
shant 'ere die.

Marilyn Tarbet
NEW LOVE

Come walk with me
Through fields of flowers
Fields of fragile flowers,
Flowers kissed by the morning
dew—
These flowers are old,
Old since time began,
Time of renewal,
Time of memories always new.

Eleanor Morris
THE GRAVE

I stand helplessly at my
father's grave
No way to turn back time
No way to say . . .
Anything
Life alone stretches before
me
An eternity.
Then it is time
To cover the little white box
Which holds all that is left
Of Daddy.
I dig up a shovel full of earth
And drop it into the grave.
The hole in my life
Resounds in the hollow
thud
Of earth hitting the little
white box.
Daddy, gone so soon?
and WHY?

Theresa Ann Sevrence
WHO ARE YOU

Who are you—
deep down inside?
I don't think anyone knows
for sure
Since you don't let your guard
down.
Outside—you're a boy
full of playful tactics
not yet grown-up.
Inside you're a man

with sensitive feelings
and a loving way.
The two of you together
makes one very unique person.
Do you know
who I think you are?
I think—
that you are a warm
sensitive, loving, caring guy
with a fun, humorous side.
But most of all—
I've fallen in love
with that one
unique person:
You.

Teressa D. Bitters
MY KARMA

You have left.
Time does not exist.
Long days pass slowly.
Yellow moons drift endless.
Search for my yesterdays—
All have gone.
(Silence chills)
I am nothing.
Nowhere—
For you are my karma.

S. G. Wahrenbrock
HORIZONS

Keep your eye on the horizon,
watch for shapes and blurs
as they come into perspective.
And keep those shapes and
blurs
in perspective.
They are not gryphons
or dragons,
or other mystical beasts,
but sails of ships
steady on the breeze.

Jenean Lynn Coffman
NO NEED FOR TEARS

I've cried because
You said you loved me,
I've cried because
You said good-bye.
Those tears were shed
For you;
For the love and pain
I felt for you.
But now,
I cry no more.
My pain has
Disappeared . . .
So now—
I have no need for tears.

Pat Harrison
**A GRANDMOTHER'S
PRAYER**

Don't bring me Cotillion,
or Farrah's Fabrege,
Just bring me a tube of good
old Balm Bengay.
Don't bring me candy or wait
for some hints,
Just bring me a box of much-
needed Feenamints.
Don't bring me a fancy new
cover-all, t'would be
more to my liking to have a
warm shawl.
But much better yet, than
any of the above
If all of you would come and
bring me your love.

George A. Datchuk
EVIL AND HONOR

Yeah we're the people
You've been warned about
Public acts unacceptable
Fact without a doubt
Haven't you seen
The troubles I mean

They've left and walked away
Or the promises made
But then tried to say
No you must be crazy
The problem is the shape we're
in
The future seems so hazy
It's funny how they look at
us
Parents yours and mine
Who think the 50's had it
made
Not for me, I whine
I like to rock love to roll
Turn a stomach fine
Cause I believe that we will be
The generation of decline.
Ain't it a shame
They left it this way
For us to struggle thru
Evil and honor thats what they
say
The world we leave to you.

Cheryl Cooper
I AM WHAT I AM

I am a Bullfrog
I sit alone,
Alone in my kingdom
Where I hold the throne.
All of my followers
Look up to me,
Just like they would
The mighty Queen-Bee.
Now I awake
I look and I see,
The world around me
As plain as can be.
No kingdom, No throne,
No followers true.
Just me alone
In the wet morning dew.
What people might think
I could give a damn,
For I am a Bullfrog
I am what I am.

Katherine Nacsin
QUIESCENCE

He signs a note and a nation
obeys;
He gives a speech and opinion
sways.
He sings a song and the
multitude cheers;
He gives a command and an
army veers.
He raises his hand and the
clamor subsides;
He draws a plan and a river
divides.
He writes an order and a
mountain is razed;
He takes a scalpel and a life is
saved.
You ask his name?
His name is Man;
And evening finds him seeking
rest
In the fold of a woman's arms.

Snowfire
THE FALLS OF FOYERS

Springtime swells the water's
tide
Enlarging babbling brooks,
That tumble down the mountain
side
Near homes of nesting rooks.
Summer haze on purple glens
Encourage Scottish lore.
White rabbits race o'er hill
and dale
To dance across the moor.
Winter winds will drift away;

239

So shall ice crystals melt
and harmonize with slushy snow
All through the land of Celt.

Intoxicated tabbies,
Drunk on highland air,
That play their games in
thistle fields
and roam without a care.

A truly natural wonder
That you will never see;
For the falls are now polluted
By a monstrous factory.

Richard L. Dedrick
LOOK AT ME, I'M TRYING

I try so hard
To do things right
But they always
Turn out wrong.
Look at me, I'm trying.

If I ask for help
You just turn away.
I'd extend my hand
But you'd just slap it away.
Look at me, I'm trying.

No one said I would
No one said I could
So why do you laugh
When I try.
Look at me, I'm trying.

But the day will come
When I won't run
When I won't say
Look at me, I'm trying.

Oh won't you look at me.
I'm trying.

Beau Wade
LOVE SONG

If you are mine and I am thine
They why are we apart
Visit me tonight my love
And soothe my saddened heart.
In the eve I'll watch for thee
Far across the distant sea
For I am thine and you are
mine
And our love will outlive
even time.

Earl J. Feather
CONTRITE PRAYER

Break my heart O God and
mold it after
Thine, full of love and
tenderness.
Make all my desires be lead by
Thee,
and Thy love flow out through
me, to
others for whom Thou hast
given Thine
all.

Help me to love the unlovable,
and with
the hard hearted, give me
patience to
linger, at the well of essential
waters,
until his outlook is softened,
or his heart
is broken for Thee.
O God! may they see my Lord,
my Savior and
my friend in my example.
AMEN.

Lynn Louise Clark
YOU

Tonight and tomorrow
I'll think of you
but only for awhile.
pain that intense
can only be endured
in small doses.
I wish I could

forget you completely
but I know tonight
and tomorrow
you'll linger on,
but will I?

Mercy Flanders
OUR CHILD

Our child
Young and innocent
Crying, smiling
Walking, talking

Our little girl
Attending school
Skipping, laughing
Hopscotch, tag

Our adolescent
Acting grown up
Boys, makeup
Dances, swearing

Our trouble maker
Family disputes
Smoking, drinking
Cinch notes, cutting

Our teenager
Never at home
Driving, partying
Drugs, pregnancy

No longer our child
You go your way
While we wonder
What went wrong.

Reuben Hart, Jr.
YOU'RE IN MY SIGHTS

First it was just a telephone
conversation
Listening close and speaking
from ear to ear.
Do I have to go and make a
proclamation
Just to get you here with me
my dear?
It has been said many times
about the highest
mountain and widest sea.
I would do it all too, my love
Just to get you close to me.

Pauline Karlee Grandon
THIEF!

O Monarch, Time! Your
unrelenting hand
And mighty swinging pendulum
spare none;
Your stinging strike brings
terror to the land;
No one escapes your smirking
"Day is done!"
You bide and march at some
untimely time;
You lop off labors that have
just begun.
You foil those who have never
reached their prime
And fly them graveward ere
their race is run.
Hark, Time! If I could hold
you in my grasp,
I'd make you forfeit all the
hours you stole;
And once again within my arms
I'd clasp
My loved ones who have used
your scanty dole.
Mark, Time! If I could cast
you under lock,
I'd seize your timepiece and
turn back the clock.

Mary Paice
TO JIM

I can feel your presence
And it excites me.
Yet at the same time I feel an
emptiness

A lonely aching.
It brings tears to my eyes
As they are here now.
I am lonely—I am empty
Yet thinking of you fulfills
me.
Still I am exhilarated with
anticipation.
I will see you soon.
Each passing hour brings us
closer
As it erases the time we've
spent apart.

Ardis B. Harden
GOD BECKONED AN ANGEL

There's an angel in heaven, so
radiant and fair,
With petal soft cheeks and raven
black hair.
God needed his help and
beckoned him come,
But desperately and selfishly
to his arm I clung.
"Dear God," I whispered,
"Don't take him away,
Let me have him longer, at least
for a day.
Let me have his love and his
tender ways.
Please God." I pleaded, "Please
let him stay."
My head was nestled on his
breast.
Beneath careful breathing I
heard pain in his chest.
In his crystal clear eyes behind
love, I saw pain.
Understanding engulfed me like
wild torrents of rain.
With sorrow in my heart I knew
what had to be done.
I let go of the arms to which I
clung.
A smile on his lips, a caress
to my cheek.
His eyes turned to heaven, the
pathway to seek.
There in the moonbeams he
ascended the stairs,
And I know somehow he will
guide my prayers.
In the land of promise he'll
wait for me,
And together we'll spend
eternity.

Michele Helene Klotzer
GRANDMA

alone
caressing the bed sheet between
age-spotted hands
frail and weak
unaware of the passing time
gums
but the smile has not changed
lonely
without even realizing it
mumbling
about youth and something
none of us know

forgetting—questioning—
repeating
unable to comprehend
her eyes pleading for an
explanation
unsure of what she wants
explained
she just smiles.

Rebecca Sue Philips
UNTITLED

"It's so boring today," my
sister said.
"I've nothing at all to do."
How *could* she say that,
When we woke up this morning
To the first skiff of snow on
the ground.
And a cardinal, pecking and
chirping
Under my window.
A female cardinal, with her red
tail bobbing
And her red head nodding.
And her bright orange beak
merrily pecking
In the snow.
A splash of scarlet against a
white woolen blanket.
The day has begun.
It is the beginning of a perfect
day.
How *could* my sister say she is
bored?

Hallie Elizabeth Compson
GOING ON A JOURNEY

I am going on a journey,
Perhaps not very far,
But any place at all,
Is like a visit to a star.

A mile away from home,
Fills my heart with glee.
When I am going on a journey,
I am happy as can be.

Ms. B. Lavalette
HOME

Sometimes I long to go home
Where tall grass in gentle breezes
Undulate with Earth's breath;
Where daisies and Queen Anne's
lace
Joyously dance as they swing
in release.

Sometimes I long to go home
Where clover and new-mown
hay
Intoxicate the soul with rich
perfume;
Where rustling maple leaves and
morning song of birds soothe
my heart.

Sometimes I long to go home
Where the moist cool of the
pine grove
Refreshingly kisses warm
cheeks;
Where blue skies, ever clear,
Hold fast the lasting light
of day.

Sometimes I long to go home
Where brightly dressed
butterflies
Flutter and hover midst gay
blooms;
Where there is no time or
space
And freedom is infinite.

Dianne L. Eberst
FILL MY CUP

I have a father
who gave me a vision,
of a furry friend
He told me to pick him up

this little guy,
will fill my cup
I opened the door
there he was a kitten in a cage,
Above the floor
I took him in the car
looking at the kitty my cup
turned,
into a huge jar.
You see the look
in his face
was all I needed
I know now what my father
meant
my jar runs over
With peace in my tent.

Billy J. Meeks Jr.
WINTER

Grey skies, naked trees,
Cold days, colder nights,
Icicles forming from the roofs,
Snowy carpets glare so bright.

Lazy minds, glare at flames,
Lover's time spent near the
same.
Drinking ale to bring a glow,
Poems written to let you know,
Winter is here.

Becky Boyd McKeown
THE COMING

Before me I see,
I shall no longer be free;
But cannot believe,
That death has come for me.

Dollie Adams
WHAT WOULD I DO WITHOUT YOU

What would I do without you,
I wouldn't know where to go,
I wouldn't know what to do.
There wouldn't be anything
to know,
There wouldn't be any feelings
to show,
And there wouldn't be any
place to go.

I'd be bored every day,
I'd have nothing to say,
I'd never get my way.
So I can't let you go,
That I know.
Because I kinda love you,
That has always been true.

For you must be near,
For I need you to care,
And my happiness I need to
share.
So please don't leave me,
For I don't know what to do,
So please stay by my,
So my love, you'll see.

Mimi Macbeth
OUR FEELINGS

It felt so good to hear you
whisper in my ear,
"I love you, lady."

The background sounds of
people
Expounding on the virtues and
vices of religious capitalism
Faded into oblivion as you
spoke those words to me.

Then you said it again!
"I love you, lady."
Only this time followed by
a kiss.

I wondered if people felt that
we were in love,
Or crazy,
Or just unconcerned and
uninformed people
Who only had sex on their

minds.
Even as they seriously played
with their theories of
political capitalism,
democratic injustice and
world imperialism,
We sat there aware of it
all,
But also aware that our love was
the most important theory
between us.
Because our love was what
enabled us to survive:
Their political capitalism,
democratic injustice and
world imperialism.
Because we knew that they
could never change, but
we had!

And I want you to say,
"I love you, lady,"
In their congress or their White
House or wherever you feel
inclined to do so.
Because you rlove makes me
what I am,
And tells me what I am capable
of being,
In spite of it all . . .

Joseph Peter Lamphron
THIS OLD DREAM

Yesterday has just begun
and I do not know where I am
While wars continue for no
reason
to have more dreams lost like
me.
And this old dream which was
spoken long ago
is still begging to be brought
out to this day
To show the people a meaning
of life
And ask why I was left behind
this way?
My cries are seen when light
rains appear
but still some do not feel to
understand
To feel me shiver and disappear
for I only want to do what I
can for man.
This old dream is just a dream
but who says it can't come
true
To feel the warmth of
paradise
to share what is for me and you.

Lady G.
WONDER OF PERFECTION

We shall always remember the
morning
Of February 14th, Valentines
Day
Driving along the San Mateo
Bridge
Crossing over the San Francisco
Bay
We visioned a sight beyond
belief
So beautiful, with all its color
So perfectly molded without
a flaw
Complete from one side to
another
Standing like a gateway
Reaching high into the sky
Begging for both our attention
Knowing its caught our eye
Mother Nature had gone all
out
And performed a perfect beauty
Sharing with us, all her glory
As if it was her duty.

Arched across the San Francisco
Bay
Reaching from East to West
Shining like a perfect prism
Showing us one of her very best.
Giving us for a few moments
Permission to share her Pot-
of- Gold
For both of us to dream on
A precious wonder to behold.
Painting the sky above us
Gloriously shining with a
glow
Thank you Mother Nature
For the Valentines Day
Rainbow.

Patricia Gilboy Palmer
GOD'S CHOICE

Arise and lift your head up
high
To greet the morning breeze.
So fresh, so new, so full of
life
A gift of love to please.

Inhale the fragrance of the
air
Sweet scents of pure delight.
Refresh your heart and cleanse
your soul
Accept with all your might..

Arise and hear your call to
love
Yourself, and neighbor too,
Hold high your head and
thank your God
For He has chosen YOU.

Shirley A. Griffith Adkins
LOVE

A sunny shower,
A warm winters' day,
A cold July night;
A falling star, a breathtaking
flower;
Surprises like these, remind me
of you,
Hour after hour.

Elaine Birn
COSMIC WOMAN

Mother of the Moon,
Sister to the Stars,
Daughter of the Dark,
and Witch of the Wind . . .
I am a Cosmic Woman.

Wendy Plain
ROSES OF YESTERDAY

The roses of yesterday—
faded
fragile
and broken,
yet sweeter
than blossoms
of today . . .
for somehow,
looking back
we forgot
the thorns.

Wendy Shoop
OPEN DOOR

I hurt you; I hurt me,
I opened my heart—and you
turned away.
I told you I loved you and
wanted you to stay,
You just turned your back, and
you walked away.
I found a true friend, when I
found you—
I realize now, what it means to
be true.
Loving you is not what it takes,
I realize—I made a mistake.
What I need right now, is a

friend like you—
One who doesn't lie; but will
always be true.
Friendship is all I wanted—right
from the start,
I'm sorry I left you, grow dear
to my heart.
I turned to God to know what
to do—
He said, ask again, for the
friendship we once knew,
He said I need more friendship
than love from you.
He told me true friends are
hard to find,
He made me understand:you
are one of a kind.
You brought me closer to Jesus
above—
I understand, and need your
Christian love.
So if it's not too late—please
open your door;
Please—don't shut me out,
anymore.

Earl Ray Nicol
A TRUCK DRIVER'S PRAYER

As I prepare to start this truck,
And as I turn the key.
I say a prayer before I leave,
No accident will fall on me.
I pray the brakes will hold each
time,
And tires will not blow out.
And pray the freight is loaded
proper,
and boxes will not shift about.
I pray the lights in front and
back,
Are correctly burning.
And pray no one is hidden from
sight,
When backing, passing and
turning.
Please, let no wires or limbs
hang down,
To catch me as I pass.
Let me see things lying in the
road,
as nails, and rocks, and broken
glass.
May I arrive at each place
safe,
Without having to speed.
If the roads are wet, don't let
me forget,
To drive with the caution I
need.
And though the day is nearly
done,
Don't let me be a fool,
To think that I am accident
free,
And know every safety rule.
HAPPY TRUCKING!

Ella Mae Sanders
A HOUSE FULL OF LOVE

At Christmas the gifts can be
many or few,
Of cheapies, home made ones,

241

or expensive ones too.
There are dollies and trucks and
a big panda bear,
Cowboys and Indians and clothes
to wear.
There are games of all kinds and
a huge, big ball,
But—a house full of love is the
greatest of all.
There were home made
decorations to put upon the
tree,
Not quite true to pattern—but
pretty to see.
Because you could tell they
were each made with love
And that's what counts most
with our God from above.
See the twinkling star on the
tree standing so tall?
Yes—a house full of love is the
best gift of all.
The mistletoe in the arched
doorway hung,
And there was activity and lots
of fun
As, sooner or later, everyone
who was there
Got caught in the doorway and
a kiss had to share.
Oh! The laughter and shouting
from oldest to small
And—a house full of love is
still best of all.

Ruth McKinley
IT SNOWED TODAY

The world was white at dawn
today,
Snowflakes were dancing in
their play,
Trees were covered in mantles
of white,
And all of this happened just
last night,
The sun shone down on our
world of white,
Creating a wonderland of
sparkling light,
Warmth of the sun caused the
snow to melt,
And looking out, sadness I
felt,
Snow is a treat when it comes
our way,
And I am glad that it snowed
today.

Marie Goodwin Harden
A SOJOURNER

The quiet becomes a haven
From the madness to incur,
For rains may fall in driven
hordes
The journey to deter.

The leaves are stilled in layered
folds,
A resting place for each one
falling.
Their faces all a different hue,
A subtle softness there is
calling.

The earth gives up a mellow
fume
That lulls the hurried senses.
A sojourner could rest a while,
And then move on to hurdle
fences.

Deanie Elizabeth Janik
REMEMBER

See them walking hand in hand
along the beach in the sand
The night is young
The moon is bright,
as it shines its dim,

but peaceful light
See them laughing
Hear their raves
Watch them skip,
and jump the waves
See them pause,
and see them kiss
Think back,
can you remember this?
This is how it used to be,
but times have changed
for you and me.

Andrew Stewart
INNER SECRETS

Words
Never muttered . . .
Excluding
Those who'd listen
Those who care . . .
Silence
Being your
Only ally
and Enemy
During times
Whereas
Weighing the worst
Of two evils
Still leaves
Pain . . .
The Silence
becomes
Deafening.
So you speak
Of Inner-Secrets
Never before told
Allowing the pain
To be shared
Between two lovers . . .
Though answers
Are not known
You've found
Strength
In Love . . .
and you
Realize
You've finally
Begun
To
Live
A
g
a
i
n . . .

Nicole Favreau
TO KNOW I FIT

The mountains shone in the
early morning sun.
The grass and flowers smelled
of the newly set dew.
The sun took its form with
color that brightened the sky,
There was not a cloud to
darken its light.
I stood alone and watched,
there was no one to break my
peace.
The beauty began to grow in
me, then love filled its
place.
I sat down in the flowers, I

felt close to nature and myself.
I knew I could never find the
real me unless I learned how
I
fit in with nature.
There would never be another
time and place to where I
Would
feel this again.
I watched a bee fly by and land
in the flowers, the birds
sang softly.
The rabbits played in the grass,
and nature was not altered
by my appearance.
It seemed to know, I too, fit
in.

Karen Bitner
WHEN THE POET'S DEAD

When the poet is dead, her
words will fall
like leaves,
the cluttered pages will be torn
and yellow,
Someone will find them and
pass them off as words of fancy.
There will be many types,
those written on a sad, rainy
afternoon
Others after the fresh feeling of
love
Still lingers.
When the poet is dead they'll
stand above her grave,
say she was a good mother and
honest worker.
The words will slip away,
as if they never existed.
The words will be lost in
someone's attic
perhaps one word will be left
clear, unmarked:
EMPTY.

A. G. Moe
LIFE'S CREATION

Ten million knights, all dressed
in white,
Poured into the valley of life.
No arms they bore, nor had
they sight,
To aid them in their strife.
But still they came and fought
their fight,
The outcome certain doom:
And slaughter great to those
did come,
It was a fulsome tomb.
They died there, everyone, save
one,
And he is you, my son.

Paul J. Chiusano
FEEL FOR THE CHILDREN

Mighty ships sail cross the
ocean,
birds with steel wings fly
through the skies,
Yet another child goes hungry,
and another child dies.
Feel for the children,
there is no time to wait.
Yes we have the resources,
to end their horrible fate.
Yet mighty ships sail cross the
ocean,
birds with steel wings fly
through the sky,
And another child goes hungry,
while another one asks why?
Some people will say I'm foolish
we have problems of our own.
And while they make excuses,
another child dies alone.

I hope that you will listen,
to what I have to say.
That no more children go
hungry,
tomorrow or today.

Elger A. Standard
NEXT

You burn your fires
Yet you still chill the earth
It leaves me empty and cold
When I'm told of your worth;
Subtracting never adding
Never worrying about the
next generation
I see your children as slave-
Soldiers fighting off ecological
starvation.

Richard William Dillard, PFC
SPRING

Meadows green
So fine and fair,
Scents of spring
Drift through the air,
Birds their nests
They build so quaint,
Bees they buzz
Their song so faint,
Earth unwreathed
In glorious style,
Lasting for
So short a while.

Sandi Lee Stika
EXPPRESSION

Your eyes speak out above
your voice
Betraying all your carefree
words,
They are the color of the
summer sky:
Soft and clear when all is
well,
Darkening with impending
storm.
Within their mirror can be
seen
Reflections of the soul of one
Who laughs in order not to
cry.
Your eyes are much like
mine.

Judy Joines
WE WILL SEE

To where we will live
In the diminished sea
Beyond beauty
Beyond a screen of windless
hands of lands

We will see
All there is to see
Beyond the universal screen
Beyond our galaxy

We will see a triumph
Which we have seeked
We will find our dreams
In the other galaxies

We will dream of streams
which endlessly flow
in a world without a care or
dare
We will die there
Knowing all that we've seen
Has been a secret beyond
reality.

Jon Katherine Martins
DUNE ROAD

Two miles out the mighty
head lifts
In the misty grey-pink of
twilight
Majestic the tail fans the horizon
The last spout defies the heavens

Dying but gracious in its
instinct
The whale rides the infinite
tide
To rest with the clam's smooth
shell
Left on shore by the great
fisher
Watchdog of the sea combs
the beach
Where impenetrable footprints
in the sand
Are embraced by a woman's
loving arms
Like teardrops from a child's
eye
She softly wipes the coastline
clean
And the melancholy seagull
cries out
For the whale, for the sailor
lost
"Proclaim life's fleeting
preciousness
My Atlantic will forever remain
silent".

Kathy Delonas
ABANDONED CHILD

All your life you've been on
your own
Abandoned child, don't you
ever get lonely?
Living on hopes and dreams
spun long ago.
You used to look to the stars
and now
You say they couldn't put
Humpty Dumpty back
together again.
Abandoned child, are you
headed for a fall?
You greet the morning with
trusting hope
But as night draws near, you
turn gray
Like the smooth, cool surface
of marble
And slip away to an empty
bed and curl fetal-poised
Waiting for life to touch you.
But the sun rises and nothing
has changed.
Your friends confide; do they
hear
When you speak of a final
curtain.
Abandoned child, don't you
ever get lonely?

Pamela Evans
GAMES

You wanted to go so I let you,
but I love you too much to
forget you.
We lived in a world with so
many dreams,
but you forgot them all, it
seems.
Watching sunrises, flying to the
moon,
time is too short, dreams end
too soon.
I know there were bad times,
and the pain,
but we didn't have to play that
game.
We could have stopped in time
to save,
the love we had in our hearts
engraved . . .

Shirley Bommer Stagner
OUR GOAL

In the heavens, oh! so high, so
high,
There lives the sun, the moon

and the sky.
The stars and the rainbow are
also there,
Looking about with faraway
stare.
In the heavens, there are also
these
That honor and praise our
Majesty.
And these are the angels, whom
God did make,
And they are for real, and not
for fake.

But to get to heaven we must
take the right road,
It Isn't like figuring a puzzle
or code.
If we do what God wants we'll
find the way,
If not tomorrow, it'll be
someday.

Pearl Garnett
A FRIEND

Who is a friend
Take that word apart
Look at it from all angles
Then put it together again

A friend is one who'll do for
you
when you are in distress
Who'll help you bear your
burdens
Thus giving you some rest.
Along life's dreary way.

A friend is one who'll listen
When you need to talk
No matter what the age or
sex
Or race or creed I say
A real friend will listen
Whether to laugh or talk
or pray.

Reach out reach out to Jesus
He'll fill your every need
Ask the Lord to save you—
To help you to believe
Believe and God will do the
deed.

Konnie K. Herbert
EQUALITY?

What is all this fighting
Over equal rights,
That is causing men and women
A string of endless fights?

What is all the hassle
Forever out in News,
Causing men and women
To forget their human dues?

If we were meant to quarrel
Over something so very small,
would God tempt to even
mention
Our separate roles at all?

Yet, there is another question
I would like to raise,
To all the men and women
Who fight throughout the days,

If men would treat their women
As God meant them to be,
Would women even ask for
This thing: Equality?

Edith Seaton-Bruce
THE LUCENT SEA

Better I were never yours for
equal-keeping,
The heart I gave, now dies
a-weeping.
None other did I seek or yearn
for,
I was not the one . . .returned
for.

In this dark night of lonely

sorrow,
Your farewell kiss would blight
my morrow.
. . .I wait alone . . .for final
rest,
He will take my broken heart,
unblest.
Recreant lover, don't wait for
me
My tears now seed the lucent
sea.
Scan each cresting wave, for
billet-doux,
Each wave a word, its key
or clue.

Sharon M. Grzyb
**THE MOST VALUABLE
GIFT**

I'd like to give you a gift, that
I know you'd keep.
I'd like to give you a
word, that I know you'd need.
I'd like to give you something
to carry on,
Through all the windy storms.

What I have to give, it is not
much,
Unless you make it so.
It is not mine to keep—I have
to let it go.

I'd like to give you a memory,
yours for ever more.
I'd like to give you a message,
from the bottom of my soul.

What I have to give, it is not
much,
Unless you make it so.
It is not mine to keep—I have
to let it go.

So for your gift, I have a word
which you can carry on in
your memories.
It speaks of the journey and
the message that I brought.
But most of all—here's my
heart.

Kerin Marie Jones
HANKERING

short trips to corner stores,
slowly turn into lifetime plans;
each step a new year or a new
baby.
once more taking off further
from
reality into lands of more
chances.

a glimpse sideways taken away
some productive daydream. . .
and suddenly grows up into
persistent desire.
again, surrounding all thoughs,
as the clouds own the whole
sky on dreary days.

Carlton Day Reed
THE BOSS

The beam weighed thirteen ton.
The crane was just a bit too
light.
The boss had goddamned
everything
In hopes that all would be all
right.

He'd ripped and raved and
rubbed his head,
Though finally he'd raised his
hand,
His fingers pointing up. The
pose
A priest might take was his
command.

The men obeyed. The diesel
roared
And now the load was in the

air,
But no one knew in one deep
breath
If he had likewise said a prayer.

Robert Bruce Fair
**WHISPERS, AS SOFT
VOICES DIE**

Whispers, as soft voices die
become merely empty visions
of the night—
And wants and desires soon
must yield
as Time again has slipped us by.
Hearts, once alive with the
flickering flame
are now somewhat distant,
Yet the memories of the time
we shared together
become the moments . . .which
will always linger on.

Dennis L. Floyd
YOUR FRIEND

A moment in time is all that
we shared
but in that moment I knew that
you cared
perhaps it was something I saw
in your eyes
something warm and tender
that made me realize

Perhaps I saw it in your soft
smiling face
or maybe I felt it in your tender
embrace
or could I taste it on the lips
of desire
that sent me to heaven and
consumed me like fire

Was it the words we whispered
so low
or the golden silence of a new
morning's glow
did we bask in the warmth of
feelings so true
did we savor that moment that
bound me and you

No matter dear friend, it need
not make sense
I felt your closeness, you have
no pretense
so here is the heart that you
have helped mend
when you walked in my life
and called me your friend.

Inez J. Reddoch
JENNIFER

A shy little girl, with locks
that curl
And brown eyes that sparkle,
like stars at night.
She is so petite, so clean and
neat
Loving her is one great delight.

With a skip and a hop, she spins
like a top
She plays all day, and never
stops for anything.
She loves ribbons and bows,
and TV shows

243

'Jesus loves me' is what she
  sings.
She is only four, and a few
  weeks more
And she loves her Mama and
  Daddy very much.
They all have fun out in the
  sun
And she really loves their
  tender touch.
Like a bright new penny, is
  her love for Kenny
And for her little sister, Stacy
  Hill.
Jennifer is quite a peach, down
  at the beach
With much love for Grannie
  and Papaw Bill.
Papaw Miller is there, her
  love to share
And with Grannie Miller she
  goes everywhere.
To church and Sunday School,
  where she learns the Golden
  Rule.
Also to the Zoo, and to a park
  here and there.

George Moyer
**SOMEONE NEW IN YOUR
LIFE**

There's someone new in your
  life,
Someone who died and paid
  the price.
Why don't you stop and
  think today,
That someone helps and always
  saves.

No matter what you may do or
  say,
He'll always hear you when you
  pray.
Your everyday cares, can be
  heavy you know.
But Jesus, is with you wherever
  you go.

There's someone new in your
  life
Before you change your mind,
  think twice,
Why don't you mark this down,
Someday, you will wear a
  crown.

Terri Lee Craig
MEN OF PREY

Birds prey upon the dead
"revolting" some might say.
Man preys upon the living
stalking—him everyday.

Birds strip the bones of flesh
a function true to need.
Man strips the soul of life
with needless selfish greed.

Man litters land with filth,
Birds clean until well-fed.
Man preys upon the living—
until he stalks them dead.

Vickey Ann Fryer
REMEMBER

Goodbye is not forever
though at times it seems to be
For tomorrow no one knows
  what will bring.

If we should pass again
intermingling our hearts once
  more;
Enjoy and cherish those
  feelings
which could not be destroyed.

If we should see each just as
  friends
with a remembrance of

memories past
Then we two are only passing
  ships,
of an old romance.
Times shared between me and
  you,
something special, but no
  longer there
Then let it be . . .

Antoinette Edgett
THE HIGHEST HAPPINESS

The highest happiness sings
Through hearts blending
In love ne'er ending
Through joy and laughter and
  fun,
In bluebells dancing
And daffodils prancing
Through acres of meadows
  and sun.

Life's fulfillment grows
  quietly,
Softly, gently, sweetly, neath
The surface hidden from view,
Then as rivulets
  tinkling
And galaxies twinkling
Till creation sparkles like dew.

Pamela Kucincki
MAY WE NEVER PART

If you ever asked me to leave,
  I don't know where I'd
  go
I wouldn't know what to
  think, I wouldn't know what
  to know.
My life wouldn't be worth
  anything—not a dollar, not
  a cent
I would only wander
  aimlessly reliving the happy
  times we spent.

You are my whole life to me,
  you are my everything
You make me want to shout
  out loud, you make me want
  to sing.
When I am sad or lonely I can
  always count on you
To lift away the clouds and
  let the sun shine through.

Having someone like you
  around can make a person's
  day
I'm so glad you're around for
  me. So hey—
In case you haven't figured it
  out I love you with all my
  heart
And that heart would crumble
  if we ever had to part.

Becky Hartley
GRIEF

The dry withered leaf came
  swirling down from overhead;
I wavered for one tremulous
  moment, then overcame my
  dread.

Slowly rising, as if one of
  Nature's births,
cruely anguished, stood I now
  on Autumn's earth.
Lifting eyes like darkened
  whirlpools
round with sorrow to the sky,
wondered I at cheerful clouds
which skittered gaily by.
Now a vengeful fury ripped
  me—
rage and hateful violence
  gripped me—
from my muted throat burst
  forth an animal cry!
Challenging, I raised my arms,
  in defiance hurled my scorn
hurled it—
threw it with my hatred to
  that cheerful smiling sky!
Suddenly a flood of sorrow
lonely born from "lost
  tomorrows"
doused the moment's soaring
  flame;
memories, kept with me
  dearly,
came to me so clearly, clearly,
tender kisses, loving words,
completely gone,
as was his name.

Agonized, but without sound
crumbled I to moulding
  ground.
Stagnant now, as if in death
there remained my timeless
  breath.

Rhonda Harrington Greene
WAR

Over the rivers and across the
  seas,
there they are fighting for you
  and for me.
Hoping to set our countries
  free,
then home together
with their loved ones they shall
  be.
Far in the night you can hear
  their cries,
the lonely soldiers, some live
  and some die.
Their hearts are aching, longing
  to be home with their loved
  ones, not there alone.
They will fight to set out
  country free and then be
  honored
by some high royalty.
But while they are fighting
  over there, shooting to kill,
who will care, maybe someone
  they will kill, who will
miss them, everyone will!
So, please let's stop fighting
  these wars,
Let's be friends, and open our
  doors.

M. D. Hay
ON PLANTS AND THINGS

I saw a TV show on Channel
  Two
at seven last night,
That discussed retarded foliage,
  sick herbs and various blights.
All the ills of puny plants,
  their sisters and their brothers,
Who could grow strong and
  healthy
like their fathers and their
  mothers.
For shrubs to shrub, beans
  to bean,
it's love that really counts,

Try quiet conversation,
  chamber music,
skip that chewing-out.
Sing tenderly to your floribunda,
  converse gently with that bonsai
  tree,
You may not be Frank Sinatra,
  but it helps to stay on key.
Hum soft melodies to sagging
  cactus,
greet limp parsley with "I
  love you,"
Soon each pathetic specimen
  will perk up,
that's what experts claim is
  true.
But I can't help wondering,
  as I
chat and sing to all my little
  dears,
Who sang and talked to giant
  trees
and ferns before man on earth
  appeared?

Patricia Ann Sprouse
UNREQUITED LOVE

What is Unrequited love
that I should be concerned?
It is love that is given,
but not returned.
It seems to be my story from
the first up to this day.
That the one to whom I would
  give
my love would always turn
  away.
But now I come to you.
Please, don't you turn down
  my love too.
Because if that should be the
  case,
then I'll know there is no place
for my love in this world.
So please return the love I shall
  give.
For then in the exquisite
  delight
of your love I shall live.
Unrequited Love should be
  a situation for no one.
And with your love, for me it
  will be done.

Darlene G. Sturgis
REINCARNATED THOUGHTS

Oh, my brother
  Or so I believe you are
  Could it be we've met before?
  Could it be we've loved before?

I know I've met your eyes
  somewhere in time.
I know I've touched your Soul
  long, long ago.

We'll pass each other again and
  again,
We'll perfect,
  and find each other for our
  final entrance.

Oh my sweet, sweet friend,
What is time—but a flash of
  memory.

For Love has no boundaries,
  no restrictions,
and timeless limits:

So I will know when I've once
  again discovered you,
  My precious, beloved Brother.

For the soul and the eyes,
they never change;
and so my determination—
From life,
  to life,
    to life . . .

Celeste Walker
IF ANIMALS COULD

If animals could talk just think
  what they
would say,
About the world they live in
And how it changes day
  by day.
If animals could feel like
  people, just think
of the tears they would shed,
Because the world they live
  in
Allowed hate and destruction
  to spread.
If animals could think like
  people, they would
greatly protest,
About all the trouble that has
  caused
The world to be in such distress.
If animals could live the way
  that people do,
They would see no difference
  at all . . .
Because people live like animals
  too.

Vince Wheeler
OUR TEENAGE TASKMASTER

September's sweat made a
  pungent lubricant
between body and plastic pads,
And The Man's red coaching
  shorts sagged under his belly
As he led us from the bondage
  of puberty.

Many fought and fell
In the exemplification of his
  ideals,
As words, under the sugary
  guise of manhood, oozed
  from his froth.
A clipboard carried our
  biography of X's and O's
While we thrust his gospel
  on the unwilling,
And displayed scars and dented
  helmets
As testaments to its
  righteousness.

And now, from the seat of our
  season's ticket,
We tingle with the deja vu of
  past confrontations,
And listen to our cracking
  joints whisper:
"The Man was a great
  deceiver."

Victoria E. Van Alstyne
SHIPS AND SAILS

I love to wander down to the
  sea and listen to the old
  seaman's
tales, but most of all I nosey
  about for a glimpse of the
  ships
and the sails.

I down men's pants and stand in
  the wind and let the sea wash
my face and I know there and
  then as I taste salt on my lips
that this is my favorite place.

The smell of fish and rum
  perfume the air and the gulls
  play
games in the sky.

The ocean rolls forever on and
  on as if refusing to lay down
  and die.

I star at the ruddy faces of
  men whipped by the wind
  and burned by

the sun and I feel if they·
  lingered on land they would
  die for the
sea and their souls are as one.

Olive Laura Guess
GOD'S LOVE

He gave us eyes that we may
  see,
The beauty of our land.
He gave us ears that we may
  hear,
A brain to understand.

Where others fail, then we must
  strive,
To keep the name of God alive.
There is no hope on earth for
  sinners,
But always room for God's
  beginners.

Adam and Eve had it made,
They lived in Eden, sun and
  shade,
And then the green-eyed
  monster came,
The Devil and Satan was his
  name.

Only God can save us now,
The Holy Book will show us
  how.

Ralph K. Terry
THE SECRET OF THE MOUNTAINS

Like witches, mountain peaks
  cast eerie spells.
And nature with its riches
  stares in awe;
Is spellbound two, not fast to
  change or flaw.
Enthralled by over-flying mist,
  dead hells.

Their proudness marks the
  thrust where little dwells
On hog-backed ridges,
  disdaining looks at earth law.
Their law is wrapped in mica
  strips; no thaw
Will leak the mystery which
  no one tells.

But mountain men refuse to
  leave their homes
And daring all to learn the
  witches' ken
Or understand the spell, they
  stay with trust.

Then trapped by views unseen
  in fertile loams
They live, exist in ways not
  touched by sin
Sad-eyed but proud to gaze
  at lower dust.

Stephanie C. Chase
SEARCHING

The little men are searcing
  searching for something.
Could it be the searching for
  gold
Or endlessly for the days of
  old?
They dig and dig,
Seemingly forever,
Searching for that something—
  whatever.
Looking for something,
  something better.
They dig and dig,
Searching for the tunnel's
  light
The rainbow's gold, answers
  to their questions.
But such things cannot be
  found in the past.
They must look ahead for
  things that last,

Realize that their something
  is tomorrow;
The tomorrow of their futures,
The tomorrow of their lives.

Evelyn Lorenc
MYSELF

A child of passion, full of fury
  lies awake each night.
Covered by the darkness, will
  she ever see the light?
She dreams of being someone,
  so full of confidence,
She thinks about belonging,
  oh, whatever is the sense?
The man of her life he left
  her twenty four years before.
He left her to another, he
  bruised her to the core.

A child of passion, full of
  anger sleeps that she may find
  peace.
Containing such an empty
  soul, the anger will not cease.
She dreams of one day being
  proud of who she is and why.
She thinks about one day
  fitting in, a tear falls, then
  she cries.

A child of passions, full of
  hatred, she can kill with just
  a thought.
Aiming at those who seem to
  think her life could be sold
  and bought.
Her scars won't heal, her life
  won't change, her past
  affects tomorrow.
They brought her to life to put
  her away . . . they say her
  name is sorrow.

A child of passion, full no longer,
  longer,
covered with a shroud.
Her dream come true, she died
  today . . .she lies in state so
  proud.

Judith Lee Young
A NAME IS BORN

What is in a name
But life itself?
Look at the inner man
Heart full of promises,
Heart full of doubt,
Betwixt and between is he.
His world is like a picture frame,
Scenes of places, people and
  things;
Each having a name all its own
Chosen from earth's vineyard;
From on high beyond man's
  understanding
Waits as perils of mercy fall
  at his feet;
For he is a person of great
  worth
Traveling the road of life
  with expectation,
His destiny soon to be found.

Pamela Lyn Allison
WONDER NO MORE

Ever wonder how you live so
  long;
How some are weak and others
  are strong?
Ever wonder how life will turn
  out;
How you'll live in happiness or
  in doubt?
Wonder no more my dear little
  friend;
The answer is just around the
  bend.
Let it be the best of life to
  come

Not the worse, like some.
Care how the days go by.
Learn how not to defy.
Share your feelings with
  someone close;
And life will bring you the
  most.

Carel Meninno
ONE MORE TIME

one more time
to say good-bye
one more time
to let love pass by

one more time
to stop the tears
one more time
to think of future years

one more time
to sleep alone
one more time
to support the home

one more time
to find happiness
one more time
to find marital bliss.

Elizabeth Davis
HIDING

Hiding in a mushroom,
Safe within its womb.
In every lighted sight,
Is pleasure and delight.
Fans in colored hue,
Present themselves for view.
As you skip along the path,
To escape from the wrath.
Everyday life is a bore,
Fantasies even the score.
To teach you what is best,
And forget about the rest.

Carol Brown Darmour
PATCHWORK OF LOVE

First, you start out with
  separate pieces of material
And slowly but lovingly
  you put the pieces together.
With each addition your
  love grows,
You make a mistake here
  and there
But with tender loving care
You smooth out the rough
  spots
And go on to put the final
  touch
to a lifetime of giving and
  loving.
A gift of a "Patchwork of
  Love" to
Those you leave behind.

Denise Swavely
BETH'S SWEET PRESENCE

Beth's songs are always songs
  of sorrow,
her eyes show pain when'ere
  you look
Her tears fall through
  transparent fingers,

while reading from her well-worn book.
Clinging to those trusting hands,
of the ones who love her best
Guide her through this troubled valley,
to the everlasting rest.

Heavy hearts are aching now,
but still thank God, Beth sleeps at last.
In that peaceful, loving sleep
that pain can't touch as in the past.

Passing now forever more,
from this human care and strife,
Bravely going on before,
to a new and better life.

Willing faith and trusting love,
helped those left behind to bear.
While looking at her simple life,
the simple life they wished to share.

Though she's gone now from their presence,
still it seems as though she's here,
In their loving minds and hearts,
dear little Beth is always near.

Steven Sater
WHILE YOU LOOK ON

If I were of the leaves, as blind men tell,
Then I could come up to you from my hands
And let the breezes convey my longing.
My rustling would tell you in a sighing
What it feels like seeing that these fingers
Are left out of that sky of blue, beyond
The separation of this hand.
Listen,
There, I could beckon to you from these clefts
To lead you by the palms of tenderness,
Where the blue would restl,
roaming through branches.
There you could feel the sky pass through my hands
As I would drift, leaving these arms behind.
So, I might offer still flight from the land
In the bare limbs that come after the fall.

Lois DeVin Neuwirth
RELEASE

Your laughter echoes down the empty
corridors of my mind,
Willing me to think of you;
old memories to unwind.
Wrapped and carefully packed away,
their hurt had nearly passed
But then I should have realized
their silence couldn't last.
Caged and still they waited, watched,
seeking their release;
Looking for the moment when
discouraged, wanting peace,
My mind the door would open
and untangle memory's skein
Hoping that the sorting out
would somehow ease the strain.

They joy in new-found freedom.
Emotions storm my brain,
I try not to remember
but I do—Oh God, the pain!

Kathryn M. Diana
ILLUSIVE

How to describe it?
Tender, ecstatic,
Glorious, stormy,
Sweet, democratic.

Wonderful, peaceful,
Aching, serene,
Powerful, thorny;
It must be seen,

Felt through your senses,
Touched by your eyes.
Description is one thing
All love defies.

Bekki Irwin Vaught
SUMMERTIME FRIEND

He was only a summertime friend
I think of it all once again
As the wind comes on stronger
The days are no longer
As warm as those days way back when
The sun warmed the water
We laughed on the shore
Drank gallons of wine
And kept singin' for more.
The sweet summer nights
In the mountains alone
A little log cabin
A place to call home.
A merry time gone
It has come to an end
He was only a summertime friend.
A thousand grand places I've passed in my life
And many more places I will,
But the finest of places
For real or in dreams
Was Don's cabin in the Santa Cruz hills.
Then everyone left and the cabin burned down
And October announced summer's end.
So I now sit alone and wonder where he's gone,
My beautiful summertime friend.

Tonia Graham
TWENTIETH CENTURY EVE

I ask to be free.
Let me breathe and let me see.
I can make up my own mind
And think for myself.
I'm not your puppet or your toy,
Not your maid or your slave.
I don't need to be told what to do—
I can do it on my own.
So when you understand
That I'm not looking for a keeper,
Just a friend to hold my hand,
Someone to share my freedom with
Then you'll know where to stand.

Wilma "Butterfly" Clark
SOUNDS AT 7 A.M. IN THE GHETTO OF A METROPOLIS

Sun rises,
  Trains whistling,
Cars honking,
  Dogs barking,
Even birds chirping,
Hustlers hustling,

sirens roaring,
  Trash men hauling,
Alarms alarming,
  Some praying,
Others chanting,
  Most swearing,
Junkies nodding,
  Alcoholics vomiting,
Toilets flushing,
  Water running,
Coffee brewing,
  Babies crying,
Children whailing,
Books stacking,
Newspapers crumpling,
  Backs aching,
Backs breaking,
  Feet sore,
Tired and bored,
  Momma's screaming,
Off-to-work,
  Daddy's dreaming,
out-of-work!

Paul W. Phillips
THE PENNY

When I throw this penny
Into the sea,
It will mark a point in history,
No time, no space,
will comprehend,
The meaning of its destiny.

When will the day,
Restored to land,
That old penny from my hand,
That tossed into the sea one time
The mark of centuries laid behind.

Olga I. Baker
SWEET INNOCENCE

In innocence
  She sleeps
    Upon her mother's breast.
    Her eyelids close—
    There is no flicker
    Just sweet abandon.

Sleep . . .sweet sleep
  Sleep so deep
    Transports her away
    To lands unexplored
    And dreams of tomorrow—
    A brighter vision of the world.

Sleep shall not
  Be disturbed
    As she explores the world.
    Her thoughts of innocence
    Will remain
    Till sleep has won
    A glorious day.

Mike R. Stanko
MY LOVER

My lover can feel my pain
My lover doesn't ride no train,
She gives me everything I need
She knows how to plant that seed.
I need her all the time
Cause she makes me feel fine,

In the evening when its cold
I can feel her love unfold.
She's mine
All mine
She's mine
Just mine.

L. A. Brensberger
GAME PLAYER

Suicide? No.
Sue was hiding
the night you found her with her head in the oven.
You took too long to count to ten.
I said "I love you."
While you were sitting there trying to figure out whether
I was kidding or not,
I was slitting my wrists . . .
. . .and by the time you realized that I was on the level,
I had already seeped from your life.

Ms. Elizabeth Adams
CAN YOU SEE ME

You say that you want me,
But can you see me . . .
You say that you want to make love to me
But can you see me?
The sea is so clear, so blue, so full of white foam
The stars, the sky are so beautiful tonight . . .
We can use the stars as our bed tonight.
But, But can you see me?
I need to know can you see me
And not an illusion of me?
Or an illusion of someone you hope me to be?
Before you taste me Sweet Love,
Can you see me . . .?

Elizabeth Adams
IF A DREAM COULD COME TRUE

If a dream could come true,
I would dream of you
If a dream could come true,
I would dream of you making tender love to me . . .
If a dream could come true,
I would dream of you and I sharing out lives in complete happiness.
If a dream could come true, I would dream of seeing you smiling.
Laughing and happy,
Even if it wasn't with me . . .

Gerry Holt
LIFESONG

Now he can hear the symphony at last.

All those simple airs
which he composed
are being played by orchestras of light and dark
that flicker past
sounding but briefly on their way to rest.

Though the cacophony sustains one note
which plays so close to true
that sung alone denies mortality.

The discords muted
all are there
lending a texture and a majesty
to what without would play too thin and sweet.

Not even he has heard the work

entire.
See where he stands
before the warm black night
waiting on God to sound the
final chord.

Marilyn Gordon Thompson
BANDIT

One winter day, when we'd had
a bad freeze,
We saw a small form way back
in the trees.

The shape was a pup, about six
weeks old,
Shivering and starving, nearly
dead from the cold.

He'd found a rag rug, used to
wrap the pipes,
And had pulled it out in the
warm sunlight.

We put out more rugs, food and
milk in a tin,
Thinking his owners would be
looking for him.

He stayed on the rugs in the sun
all that day.
We kept peeking to see if he'd
been taken away.

But, he never moved, as he had
chosen his home!
By nighttime he was inside, warm
with a bone.

Little black pup with a "mask"
on his face,
Bandit stole our hearts and had
found the right place.

Doris L. Hill
THE MOURNING CLOAK

Wrapped in the cocoon
Of my insular life,
Antennae insensitive
To poverty, hunger, strife.

Emerging from my chrysalis,
Drawn by Society's vortex
Into the Ghetto's snare—
I search for . . .where?

Janet Rose Lazere
THE NEW MORALITY

The simplicity of life is deceiving
People are not really themselves.
Sincerity and unselfishness are
obsolete.
The masses no longer flesh and
blood.
Rather . . .Objects cultivated
from ambition
And self-concern . . .pass as
humans.
Amidst it all . . .a fragile being
anticipates
Hatred and contempt have all
but crushed it.
A last effort . . .final struggle for
survival . . .
fails.

And in an unnoticed moment
another life . . .
Is trampled underfoot.

Jill F. Morgan
A SPECIAL LOVE

I have a special love for you
That no one else will know,
A warmth so deep within me
For a love I'll never know.
Love can last forever
This we surely know,
A love and not a lover
Is the only you I'll know.

Susie Appleton
ALONE

As I sit here
Alone
I see the sun
And watch it slowly descending.
A beautiful orange ball
In an orange and red sky,
But soon,
Like everything else,
It's gone.
And I still sit
Left to face the cold,
Dark night,
Alone.

Faustina Hagen
THE MOUSE

Once upon a time,
A little mouse was I.
Afraid to speak a bit,
Or do what mouses try.

Then one day I met a great big
rat,
Who had a lot to say.
We had a lovely honeymoon
In a great big stack of hay.

My great big rat had so much to
do,
That I was often left alone,
And often feeling blue.

Then one day a great big cat
Was stalking my spouse
I guess I should have warned him,
I really was a louse.

The cat did dine,
No bones she left behind.
Happily I ran away,
Another love to find.

Cheryl J. Edgar
THE WIND

It was all around me,
as I walked among the trees.

My constant companion.

I would never be alone,
for the wind would always
be at my side.

Glenna Morris
MOTHER TREE

Trees are so great, so tall and
brave.
There is great wonder in their
very existence.

In the spring they give birth to
thousands of newborn leaves.
What joy there is to watch each
new leaf appear and unfold
in vibrant life.
As they grow they make a
beautiful sight in their mother's
arms.
How proud she is.

But life goes on and fall soon
comes.
And the leaves have come to the
golden years of their lives.
And soon the leaves fall and are
blown away.
Death comes to them—bringing
sadness and sorrow to Mother
Tree.

Yet she has one source of hope

and joy.
The winter is long.
But in the spring new life will
form within her and come
forth
once again.
And the cycle of life continues
eternally.

Vikki Mincey
MIRRORS

Mirrors . . .
Reflecting images of what we
don't wish to see.

Is it the facial features that are
distorted or
is my vision cloudy because of
my thoughts.

Thoughts . . .
Projecting fears and inner
disturbances
that cause restless feelings.

Feelings . . .
Generating thunder and
lightning right
behind my heart.

Hearts . . .
Pumping vibrant blood that
keeps within
us the rush of life.

Life . . .
Goes on.

Helen L. Berger
POETRY

Poetry's a kind of way,
To bring out words you cannot
say;
The simple words and what they
mean,
But most of all—a chance to
dream.

Mary Josephine Lehner Hellyer
TREASURED PATHS OF YESTERDAY

My soul is filled with ecstacy
As I walk in silent memory
Those treasure paths of yesterday
And watch the scenes unroll
before my eyes:
There's tiny babies in their cribs
Laughing, cooing, drooling on
their bibs;
Small children playing at my feet
Asking, "Mother, is it time to
eat?"
Then off to school, new worlds
to conquer
With smiles and tears
All through their growing-up
years.
Now, grown-up children with
families all their own
With small children playing at
their feet
Asking, "Mother, is it time to
eat?"

Joann M. Shatrau
ALCOHOL RECOVERY

Exhausted from reaching, I'm
tired and weak
Unto myself, I turn the other
cheek.
Temptations and torment are
forming a mold
Existing fear of a power so bold.
For a moment I weep an
insanity plea
Clutching a dream which affects
only me.
Show mercy, I beg, at the
reflection within
Belittle me not among other men.
My life now issued on borrowed

time.
Alcohol suicide; more severe
than a crime.
Oh power above, I ask for
undying hope
For the final means, controlled
strength to cope.
Aware of this personal flaw, I
am humble.
Nevertheless, my world starts
to crumble.
My efforts and conscience
annoying my mind
Countless answers, myself I
must find.

Glenna E. Spalding
LOVE AND FRIENDSHIP

Love stands alone in the solar
system of the affections
Like the sun, unmated and
incomparable.

From it, all other emotions
derive their worth
yet they must not expect
to imitate its warmth
light or power.

Our friendships are the stars
next in magnitude to the
orb of light.

There can be but one true love
as there is but one visible sun
to the earth.

But there may be as many
orders of friendship
as there are varieties of
stars in the sky,

Though few to be sure of the
first magnitude.

Dolores E. Bailey
PAX

Desire—alive in the heart
longing to serve.

Hope—burning through the
trials of life.

Fulfillment—of a call of
love.

. . .Peace.

LuAnn Graham
GOD'S GIFT

I felt a movement yesterday.
I knew that was your game.
But what I wondered at the time
Is what would be your name.

You made it easy, not too tough,
To join us in the world.
Your dad and I, we fell in love;
When in our arms you curled.

You mean so ever much to us.
Yes, from the very start.
You've touched a lot of people.
You made it to their heart.

Heather is the name we chose.
'Little Flower' is it's meaning
We love you daughter, oh so
much.
Now there's no more dreaming.

Gordon L. Florence
AS IT MAY BE

The autumn leaves upon the
ground
Are ready for the rake.
How quickly one reacts to this
Determines his true make.

Judith Ann Winters
YOU ARE THE LOVE OF MY LIFE

You are the love of my life,
the joy when there's strife.
You've dried my tears and made
me smile,

when I thought I'd gone the last
mile.
We've shared happiness and
sorrow,
and you're the reason I look to
tomorrow.
I may not let you know it,
but without you I'd be lost,
and could not go on whatever
the cost.
I know without a doubt that God
above,
made you special for me to love.
Now as we share the remaining
years,
happiness and laughter will dry
all tears,
because with you beside me I'll
have no fears.

Iris R. Borne
SEEK YOU THE BEAUTY

Flowers in abundance!
They're there among life's weeds,
And yours for the picking,
(God furnishes the seeds.)

Search, then, for the Rainbow
While going where life leads.

Listen for the music
While hearing others' needs.

Scatter only bouquets
While hiding heart that bleeds.

Gladness, joy and laughter
Abound as life proceeds.
And yours for the choosing,
(See flowers; don't see weeds!)

Catherine Kloepfer
DREAMS

Dreams are for
what could be,
dreams are for
what we believe we see.
Often I dream
of past, of things to be
And I see, not as is, but
how good it was
And the promise of what is to be
But,
reality is
these dreams are me.

Beverly Ovelton Romero
**THE LIGHT—A BRIGHTER
LIFE**

The stepping stones
resemble stumbling blocks,
For the path was long
and the road was dark.
But the presence of a light
encircled with hope
Brought encouragement,
confidence and understanding.
I know,
for I have been without
an outstretched hand.
I trusted
and was betrayed.
Now trust in only a few.
Yes,
there is a light
that made a brighter life—
That Light is you.

E. J. Robley.
JUDGMENT DAY

Judge not, lest you yourself be
judged,
for in the eyes of God
we are as one, who walk upon
this earth, which Jesus trod.

Remember, when you speak of
sin
in others, are you sure
that when the judgment day
has come,
The Lord will find you pure?

Remember too, that on the day
He went into His grave,
He did not judge the ones who
sinned,
'twas them that He forgave.

Jon Farmer
UNTITLED

My feelings are empty
my touch is cold.
My heart is gray,
I am alone.
I'm desolate;
as an island
in the middle of an ocean.
Stranded by time
with no face.
Without reality,
without life,
Without you,
I—have only existence.

Laura Jandreau
WINTER LOVE

The green vibrance of life
is quieted for now,
More subtle, and seen
only as rattling greyness
Responding to the blows of
Passing winds.
It needs but a touch—
light and searching—
To reveal the timeless life
Ever flowing within.

Alicia Atsma
THE PROPHET SPEAKS

I am the writer, the singer of
song,
wondering where it all went
wrong.
I am the builder of houses of
light,
watching the flame flicker
down in the night.
I am the universe, keeper of all,
viewing destruction through
my crystal ball.
You are my children, more
precious than gold,
yet it is for this your own lives
you have sold.
You are the soldiers returning
to war,
without an eye for the blood
bloodshed in store.
You are the fools in this age
of delights,
unwary of danger that lies in
plain sight.

Leigh Ann Chamness
SOUVENIR

The pale blossoms caught upon
her hair
As they kissed beneath the tree
And young June whispered in
her ear
As softly as did he.
The magic of the eve departed
When the sun began to shine
But she tugged the flowers from
her hair
To press in the Scrapbook of
Time.

Chris Meador
BIRTH GLOW

Alone at last with my newborn
child,
I hold her tiny hand.
Her eyes still hold the knowledge
Of some mysterious, unknown
land.
I feel she tried to tell me,
Before innocence veiled her eyes,
Some bit of truth or wisdom,

Some message for the wise.
The wisened glow was there,
then gone;
Never again to burn,
Leaving me to always wonder
What we, from them, could learn.

Brian of Crinigan
THE SILENT PRAYER

I'd often wondered what might
be
if all we knew were not
and often wished to tell you so
but by my bond could not.
So when sometimes your voice
it seems
to echo in my mind
I offer up a silent prayer
that fate be more than kind.
In hopes our spirits kindred be
like gulls aloft amidst the sea
two silhouettes entwined
that with the wind find unity.
The stirrings of this half a heart
for your half heart cannot
in days or years of measured
time
ever be forgot.
I hope this poets' words may
reach
the currents of your soul
and swept will be by destiny
till our half hearts are whole.

Betty Jean Pinto
LITTLE JOYS IN LIFE

The little things in life it seems
can bring the biggest joys
Like the arches of a rainbow
or a child content with toys
The welcomed warmth of
summer
after winter's long cold days
Or the changing of the seasons;
for we know they're nature's
ways.
The magic in a shining star,
the romance of the moon,
The warmth we feel with
sunshine
or the crooning of a tune
Yes, all these little joys in life
mean more than words can say
But with a loving heart you're
sure
to find them everyday.

Oryis Connolly
AGAPE

Sophisticated modern man
Like the Pharisees of old
Prefers to gather his robe about
him;
Excludes common man from
the fold.
Can it be that the individual
Christian,
And the Christian Church,
let's say,
Finds it easier to serve the Saint

Than the sinner or sick today?
Is the Church more at home in
the suburbs
Than in the Ghetto streets?
More at home in Colonial
Mansions
Than in the tenement heat?
Physicians are helpful for the
sick
Salvation for the sinners,
Jesus said, "I am come to seek
And to save the last beginners."

Norma Harrell
WHO AM I

I know who I am and what
I am, I am a lonely man
A rational, but lonely man.
I don't know where I'm from,
or where I am, I am a lost man.
A rational, but lost man.
I know not when I left
Where I'm from or how
Long I have been here, or
where here is.
I am a lonely man, a
Lost forgotten man.
A rational, but lonely,
lost forgotten man.
I cannot go back nor can
I go forward, I know not
where back is and who
knows, here could be
forward and there is
no there to go back to.
I tell you, I am a lonely
man.
A lost man. A forgotten
man.
A rational, but lonely,
lost forgotten man.
I am a black man.

Marlys Hanson Berg
MAYBE LONGER

Three years ago, or maybe longer,
I knew a woman not much
stronger
than an ant, or flea or fly.
I watched her watch her life slip
by.
She died three years ago, or
maybe longer,
but only to herself. Today she's
much stronger;
and she says ants are very strong.
They can carry fifty times their
weight all day long.
I don't watch her waste her
life anymore
or wish I didn't know her;
for I am she and I like me,
I'm not the way I used to be . . .
three years ago or maybe
longer.
With the help of Jesus, I am
stronger.

Beatrice Quintana
**THE MARKETPLACE OF THE
MIND**

Words that erupt from a feeling
within
are always received with a
knowing
of where they have been.
Receiving words transmitted by
thought
are delivered so carefully
as if they were to be bought.
It saddens me to see
the marketplace of the mind,
where pictures are painted with
words
as if they were to be sold to the

blind.
Simplicity is all it takes
to deliver a message that is real,
all anyone needs to do is give
himself permission to feel.

Karen Lusk
THE INFANT

Knowing lips curve tenderly,
 to reassure
 the every gentle move,
Glistening eyes twinkle with
 glee, as if
 to seal your hearts forever,
Tiny wrinkles garnish every
 fold, like
 pudding chilled for tomorrow,
This infant child of innocence,
 how
 soothing—healing,
An Angel near the breast, God's
answer for serenity.

Lisa M. Gait
OUR LOVE

You loved me with
 more than your body.
You were my sunshine
 and my gentle spring rain
You became my backrest
 and your arms
 my haven.

I loved you as much
 as any woman ever loved
 any man.
When you left
 (Oh how I wanted to follow)
You took a part of me.
A part which, ironically,
Not only found its way
 back to me,
but that part was
 made stronger
by the part of you
 you'd left behind.

Mary L. Herndon
SWEET SIXTEEN

By seeming unjust afflictions,
 do not be moved,
If it should be your lot to suffer
 much more
Than those whom you think
 it's been approved
To so fill up the measure of
 their span by **such**
Transgressions void of faith, but
 seek to touch
Not the immorality of the
 heathen's lust—
They shall by the Avenger be
 reproved,
But for Love's Vow aspire 'til
 you again be dust.

Phyllis Ann Blaize
**IN MEMORY OF THE LOSS OF
OF A LOVED ONE**

It's been son long since we have
 seen your smiling face,
Or felt you loving arms around
 us with your tender embrace.
We feel the loss of your presence
 in our lives today,
And often think of the day
 when our saviour took you
 away.
Love is an emotion that binds
 hearts of people together,
And helps each other understand
 our own lives a little better.
So you see our love grows for
 you still today,
And helps us appreciate what
 your life meant to us in every
 way.

We think of the times when you
 showed us that you really
 cared
And think of the happiness and
 joy we all once shared.
God gives us the memory of
 your life that was once a part
 of ours
So we can bring to your
 graveside God's beautiful
 creation
 of flowers.

Loretta Olund
THE SUN'S PRECIOUS LIGHT

It is as if
the earth
 and all its riches
 were the treasure
 of the sun's alone—
as if the sun alone
loved the earth enough
 to know
it must flee from it
to be apart from it
 to come to know
 its worth.

Tracey L. Lantz
UNTITLED

Paint me a picture
a picture of flowers and trees
of love and beauty

Paint me a picture
a picture with life and death
with a beginning and an end

Paint me a picture
a picture that will not be
 demolished
one that can not be

Paint me a picture
a picture of you and me
of us, as one
So, that we will never be parted.

Roger K. Myers
VIETNAM

Did we let our strength drain
or fight and die in vain?
Did so many have to die
for only a medal and a sigh?

Once victory could have been
 at hand
but we had to keep a still stand.
Why did we not go forth
and wipe our all the nation?

We sit down to talk with a beast
with whom there is no
 honorable peace.
For freedom's sake, why did we
 not compete
and bring Communism in
 Vietnam to a defeat?

E. Gene Parsons
TO A WEED

A little weed appeared one day
And lifted its head as if to say,
"Hello there, how are you?
I'd like to chat for a moment or
 two.
The warm rich earth has been

my home,
Now, I'm eager and ready to
 roam
The wide vast space I've heard
 is here,
And see the big sky so blue and
 clear.
I'm afraid someone will cut me
 down
So I'm careful not to make a
 sound,
I love the fresh air, the rain,
 the sun;
The life of me has just begun!"

Stan Labik
TOMORROW

if only I could be as sure of you
 . . .tomorrow
as I am tonight while you're in
 my arms
I need something certain—
 as your hair falling black
 against a pillow of white
 or your sometimes rapid yet
 always gentle breathing
 or the curves and corners of
 your body
 I've grown to know better than
 my own
the time slips by quickly
as it always does when I'm with
 you . . .
 loving you
 tasting the sweetness of your
 body
 giving myself so completely
 to you
 it seems as though we are one
if only I could be as sure of
 you . . .
 tomorrow.

Patricia J. Heavens
SILENT GAZE

the silent gaze
is most profound
I do believe
I've seen it 'round

no matter who
no matter why
I do believe
it's made me cry

Beatrice Cearbe Roma
IDENTITY

I found some papers today
I thought I had thrown away
Unexpected as when first written
Not as welcome as a lost mitten.

Each person is unique,
Molded by many forces,
Within, without.

The Potter spins the wheel
Touching us with life's events
Joy and sorrow
Each leaves an impression.
Slowly a form emerges.
Identity.

I was taken back in time
By neither music nor rhyme
A reel of pictures spun through
 my mind,
Emotions loosed by this sudden
 find.

Anne Harrison
FAREWELL

The ending draws near
Which was implicit in the
 beginning.
Countless words, and thoughts
 exchanged;
A glance, a smile, a stolen touch,
A thousand kisses have
 intervened

T'wixt the beginning and the
 ending,
To add dimension to a love
No less real because it is time
 confined,
With no before, with no after,
Except, to create a shared
 memory.

Vanessa A. Jefferson
A BABY NAMED JESUS

In Bethlehem, a child was born
In Kingly clothes he was not
 adorned

He had no jewels nor a golden
 crown
He wasn't even born on palace
 grounds.

He had no servants nor a throne
But only a manger where hay
 was strown

This child was born a long time
 ago
For his name one day the whole
 world would know

Now he was a King sent from on
 high
His Father sent him for my sins
 to die

Royal blood flowed through his
 veins
For to this world he was born
 to reign

No men of wealth nor high
 acclaim
Came to give praises to his
 name

Only shepherds came to
 show their love
And give their thanks to God
 above

They called his name, Immanuel
God is with us—all is well

A baby named Jesus—his
 precious life did begin
For he was born to die, to save
 us from sin.

Lisa A. Richard
UNTITLED

Some night I'll reach up
and steal myself a star.
I'll hold it close
so no stray beams show
and I'll run
til I'm miles from anyone
but you.
And when we're all alone
just you and I,
I'll gently release my grip
And the rays will stream out
first in streaks from between
 my clutching fingers,
and then to shine in full
 brilliance
upon my outstretched palm.
The soft, sparkly starlight
will brighten our faces
and cast luminous shadows
 behind us.
Just two small people
in a big, dark world
with a private light to share.

Roxanne Dixon
FRIENDS

Our friendship means
 the world to me
For without friends
 where would we be?

We've shared some good times
 some bad times too
But always beside me
 there stood you.

You're one of the few people
  who with secrets I can trust
So if you ever need me
  Ask if you must.

I've had a lot of problems
  but then, so have you
Whenever I needed you
  you always come through.

I'll never forget the
  times we've shared
So thanks a lot friend
  for being there.

Mary Wright
THE SMILE

The smile on your face
Captures the beauty of your soul
For all the world to see.

Courtney Blackburn
LOVE

You were my love, the only
  love I've ever known; you were
  my
only ray of light in a world gone
  dark and cold
I remember your touch, soft
  and gentle like a summer breeze;
  and your spirit, free and always
  able to soften and soothe
  the most troubled of souls;
Never abrupt or sudden, always
  tender and patient; that was
  your way, a way that I'll not
  soon forget.
We were the happiest people in
  the world, and I wanted
  everyone
to know it.
Then he came and then he left
  he beckoned, you followed,
  tearing out all our dreams,
  all your love, and all of my
  world
But worst of all, you left me
  alone . . .

Lday Alice Wonder
SPECIOUS DAZE

Knowing everything
  a lil too late,
And understanding nothing
  a lil too soon.

Kim Bushey
DREAMER'S GAP

Glass of white wine
Against the night's dreamer's
  window-sill
Paused upon Constance's lips
  warm
    smoothness
      tempting
red, yellow, blue
      pulsating
couples dance
      clinging
she orders an
    Orgasm
      dreamed
        thought
          known
Glass of white wine
Against the night's dreamer
Passed Constance's lips

Jeanne Benesh
UNITY

In this world
  if it can truly be,
    that two people
      who in coming together
        can become one—

And if these two people,
  who in their unity
    can reach out,

in trust,
    and find understanding—
Then this world,
  which so many curse
    cannot be truly lost,
      for in thise place
        we have found each other!

Brenda Phoenix
NOW AND TOMORROW

These days are hard and money
  scarce
    The nation is in need
The talk is bleak the spirit down
  The people sad indeed
We've gone so long our separate
  ways
    Concerns we did not heed
So much to do to pull us through
  The future only seed
We must be strong and not give
  up
    From doomsdays we'll be freed
We'll work together one by one
  And rid ourselves of greed
We'll learn to guide ourselves by
  light
    Some will follow, some will
    lead
We'll see the future can be saved
  By thought and word and deed.

Peter Jarmula
IT'S BEEN GOOD . . .

Sitting silently in darkness fold
I paused to ponder my life to
  date.
Free of love or joy or hate,
But it's been good . . .so I've
  been told.

Alone I am and not yet old,
With experiences that dealt
  with much.
A heart that's tender and hard
  to touch,
But it's been good . . .so I've
  been told.

My love of God, my soul I've
  not sold,
My loves on earth are few and
  far,
And for every love I wear a scar,
But it's been good . . .so I've
  been told.

Most people I've known have
  been cruel and cold,
With feelings and carings for
  none.
Not caring whether I've gone
  or come,
But it's been good . . .so I've
  been told.

I've finally found warmth in
  the cold,
As fate would have it she belongs
  to another.
So I turn to no other than my
  mother,
But it's been good . . .so I've
  been told.

Sunlight pierces the darkness
  fold,
Another day has just begun.
Dreams and hopes rise with
  the sun,
And it will be good . . .so I've
  been told.

Diana Roxanne Cano
LOBO

I raised Lobo from a pup
He helped me learn responsibility
I grew to love him very much
He always brightened my day
And now he's gone
He was only 3 years old

Death is hard to accept
Losing him was a shock to me
He was one of my best friends
And part of the family
Chica his mate doesn't
  understand
She looks in a mirror
And barks thinking it's him
A few days later I got another
  pup
I named him Lobo II
He's a big responsibility
And I love him too
But he will never take Lobo's
  place
I will always remember
And miss him very much.

Kimberlee Cockrell
TO BE FREE

My mind is weary and longs for
  rest.
To sit in a chair and rock . . .
  rock . . .
    rock . . .
The radio would play by my
  side.
My eyes would stare vacantly
  into space.
The hurt and anguish would
  melt from my shoulders . . .
The bitterness from my eyes.
The wall inside my soul would
  crumble,
  leaving my soul to fly.
The aching would go further
  away with each rock of the
  chair.
The rhythm would hypnotise me
Allowing me to be free.
Slowly I would float into
  infinity
  where nothing could reach me.
Eternal bliss.
Paradise.

Michael E. Fulford
**TO COVER UP THE
DARKNESS**

I had a beautiful dream after
  falling in love with you,
It began with a mountain that
  was covered with dew.
The sun rose slowly to spread
  its light,
To cover up the darkness of the
  night.

The light touched the trees and
  set them afire,
For you spoke to me of your
  desire.
The trees showed their colors
  blue, green, and yellow,
And with you by my side that
  would make my morning
  mellow.

As the light lightly touched
  down on the forest floor,
I thought of the day that you
  opened up my door.
The birds sang their tunes and
  flew all around,
So we went for a walk to take
  a look around.

The wind whistled through the
  pines its vibrant little song,
And for all I was concerned you
  could do no wrong.

Tammy L. Murphy
STILL IN LOVE

It will break my heart
To know that you want us to
  part.
  I will cry many a night
To know that I will not again
  Be able to hold you tight.

What happened to the love
  once so true?
My smile can't hide the pain
  For I am still in love with you.

As time passes while we're
  apart,
I will still feel the pain of this
  broken heart.

We will meet again some other
  time,
Then tears will fill my eyes
  To think that you were once
  mine.

What was wrong with the love
  we once did share?
Did it drift away forever?
  Or is it still there?

Danzella Behl
MODELS

Nature glides from day to day
  Her goals always achieving:
Spreading beauty all the way
  For each of us, to survey . . .

People rush from day to day,
  Satisfied in leaving
Stumbling blocks, along the way,
  . . .Patterns in the beds of clay!

Dorothy Adams Stephens
**WHAT IS A DAUGHTER -IN
LAW**

She's the one who took over,
  where I left off,
Stills the storms of life in a
  manner so soft,
Will never lose —pay check-vs-
  bills
Astounds modern medicine with
  curing of ills.
She'll work at his side, hours
  at length,
Yet knows just when to lean on
  his strength.
Surrenders her will, retrieves
  it with a kiss,
Makes all the decisions, aware
  they're his.
Protects her children from this
  brute of a man,
While gripping ever tighter to
  his iron hand.
Must master every trick known
  to woman-kind,
From Eve on down to modern
  time.
To love, to honor, to plight
  thy troth,
With my blessing took over
  where I left off!

Evelyn Goddard
WHAT THEN OF SILENCE

I have been filled with the sound
of many muted glories
music unheard by human ear
and many moanings from those
  lands
beyond reach,
until I would shatter the
  darkness

to see wherein lies the answer
to all earthly perplexities.
Beyond the cries sweeter than
   stringed
viols and stranger than all
   desire
are the glories—
harps vibrated by fiercest winds
poised violin bows on broken
   strings,
crash of chords on harpsichord,
pianissimo of piano,
the glories of silences
falling from the apex of sound.
You who prate of earth-life
disfiguring manhood lower than
   beasts
whose mumblings in fish-worlds
are as mighty thunders in water
   depths,
you who streak the written page
with accusings that beauty is
   beast,
from your nadir of despair
through muted music
touch now the inner ring's
   sanctuaries—
The glory of silence!

Kathileene H. Navarro
WEDDING THEME

The soft spoken vows.
Golden rings, silver bells
Two doves that sing.
Snowing white colors that
Symbols thee's purest love.
The gentle kiss that seals thy
   promise.
Two as one and thy promise
lingers on.

Susan Pierce
THE STAIRWAY OF LIFE

We are all climbing a winding
   stairway
Each day is another step in our
   life
At each step we encounter a
   new experience
We meet people who may or
   may not help
All of them teach us a lesson
   or help us to grow
Though we may see them on
   one step or many
What we learn will stay with us
   on the steps
Throughout our lives
Helping us to climb easier as
   we go along
At times we stumble down a
   few steps
But someone is always there
To help us to get back on our
   feet
And to continue climbing the
   stairway of life.

Theodore Allen Ewald
WASTING TIME

Feeling kind of lazy
got my head in a cloud,
my bones are gettin old
and my job is gettin hard.
Think I'm gonna go out
don't know what I'll find
but I gotta keep lookin
cause I'm short on time.

And I'll get myself up
in the morning again
put my right foot down
and give my back a bend.
The whistle starts to blow
and the train bell rings,
the morning light comes in
on its sunshiny wings.

And the day has begun
yes this I can tell,
by the sound of the ringing
of the old town bell.
It's just another day
down in the harbor bay
and the old man in me
is just lazin' away.

Teresa Walls
LOVE ,OLD AND NEW

As I look out
   my window-door,
I see the rain
   that rains no more.
I think the thoughts
   of love I had,
I remember memories
   that now are sad.
But now I live my life again,
   I have a new love,
   and the old's a friend.

Jack Adams
A HIPS EYE VIEW

When you are a baby
Mama shows you what to do
When you get your education
Teachers crawl all over you

Schooling all behind you
Ya try to make a dime
Bosses peep from everywhere
Almost all the time

If you do get married
Or lead a life of crime
There's always someone there
   to say
You'd better —toe-the-line

A halfway happy medium
Has been found by the hip
It's—do your thing—go your way
The captain of your ship

It may not be the answer
It may not be the way
But if it works for them
Who the hell are we to say.

Robert Taylor Burns
WINTER BEAUTY

Dark are the shadows of winter—
   and long;
Bleak are the fields amid
   deepening gloom,
Cheerless and stark, divested of
   bloom,
Stark in the silence that knows
   no throng
Who take to these fields when
   gay songsters chime
And bask in the springtime of
   cheer.
Harsh sound the crows, black
   as chill winter's grime
In these somber days of the year.
Then bright are those fields with
   a mantle of lace;
Frothed are the fields with a
   calcimimed glow.
Roofed are the streams with a
   gurgling flow,
Now slowed to savor the clean-

sculpted grace.
Long were the shadows of
   winter—and dark;
But enwreathed in a crystaline
   cape
Are the shrubs and the trees,
   once so barren and stark,
Now geysers of intricate shape.

Mary Jo Britton
CAROUSEL

We take days as they come
and nights as they fall,
When love comes and takes toll
we've got no sense at all.

Yet we wait and we dream of
what life has to bring,
and what's life in a garden
without love in the spring.

So take kindly to strangers
and look closely inside,
for within every stranger
is a love to be tried.

Krislin Van Landingham
UTOPIA

I dwell within a boundless land,
Happiness always close at hand.

Only kindness lives within,
Anger and hate have never been.

To receive you first must give,
Thoughtfullness by which we
   live.

A blessing it would be this
   generous
paradise,
But for some, not a blessing,
   a sacrifice.

Shirley A. Frericks
TIME

      Too precious
not enough
   and sometimes
      too much of—
   it can be
wasted used or abused
it can be watched,
   it can be clock ed.
But i t will b ring us
      the fut ur e
      put awa y
the past
   But it will alw ays be
      pr esent—
         —time.

Scarlet Raulerson
MY LOVE

My love look into my eyes, then
   try
to realize what's in a smile.
Search the truth.
My love place your hands in mine
dance with me in the morning
   dew,
where Roses smell sweet and
   birds
are singing love songs for you and
   I
My love close your eyes, whisper
softly in my ear, wipe away the
dark clouds of fear.
Search your soul.
My love open your eyes, that I
may see the truth, wisdom takes
time, am I a fool,
speak the truth.

Ruthann Waldsmith
FRIENDSHIP

As I open my eyes
to face another day,
I start to wonder
if any friends will pass my way.
For we all have grown older

and things seem out of range,
But memories of my friendships
will never seem to change.
For friendship is the greatest part
of this life I have to live,
And friendship is the best gift
a person has to give.
For without this thing called
   friendship
life would never be,
As happy or as pleasant
as it has been for me.

Betty Karr
CHRISTMAS

Christmas is a special time, and
   it seems
to me, it should be put down in
   line and
verse to share it openly.

It is a happy time, for children
   everywhere,
there's trees with lights, candles
   bright and
church bells ringing, carols
   singing, plum
pudding fills the air.

But the true spirit of Christmas
   is in our
hearts, for our Savior was born
   this day.
He came to bring "Peace on
   Earth, Good Will
toward Men" that they might
   go and spread the
word to all throughout the land.

Lorraine Rink
PRAYER OF COMFORT

I've not walked in your shoes
   as you
are today.
I'm not sure of the comfort
   these words
will convey.
But I've lived with life's sorrows,
searched for brighter tomorrows,
only to find, that within my
   own soul,
lies the peace you too, can know.
For if we ask, He will help carry
   our load,
His love will unfold,
and help us stand bold,
through the trouble or sorrow
   we bear,
that's beyond all compare!
For you, this is my prayer.

Gina Pravata
MY LONELY HEART

As I was drawn away from you
Counting the days that seemed
   forever
I kept you close in my mind
And felt we were together
I never dreamed of this feeling
That feels as warm and real
I can't believe it happened to me
A love that's so ideal
I thought it would take a lifetime
I thought I'd grow old too fast
But the days would never tell
How long our love would last
I'm sitting here alone
Watching the sun descend from
   my view
Staring down at the water,
The cool wind blowin, I see
   reflections of you
The days seemed to be getting
   shorter
Although we're still apart
I'm still thinking of you and
Waiting to be together
With all my lonely heart.

Debi Bartholf
FOREVER REMEMBERED

There are miles of memories,
 both present and past,
Moments I care to remember,
 and many I wish not to last.
We've shared long-winded
 laughter and a tunnel of tears,
The mere seconds of joy, in
 those very short years.
And though we drift through
 our dreams,
We will still climb to those peaks,
Forever to help the other, find
 what he seeks.

—Ye
LOVE

Love can come most any day—
We don't need to show the way,
One day Love appears, out of
 the blue
Bringing that "someone" just
 for you.

When you're least expecting love,
It falls like rain, from above,
Don't try too hard, don't do too
 too much—
LOVE needs only the velvet
 touch.

Lynda Pierce
PRINCESS THE DOG

Lord! Please watch over
 Princess the dog
She's the one with the big brown
 eyes
She came to you ten years ago
 due to no
fault of her own . . .
who gave nothing but joy and
 love to all
you who stood by me no matter
 what and
would give her life if need be,
You're gone now old girl but
 not forgotten
for we will meet again in better
 times and places . . .

Dianne Jeffs Galbraith
GRAND INSPIRATION

Giant tree with withered boughs,
 defying all that time allows;
Aged trunk with skin of red
 bends and bows its weary head.
Years now it has stood in place,
 rains thrown, winds blown in
 its face.
Endless days upon the earth,
 experiencing dormancy and
 rebirth;
Towering high midst azure skies
 like one with watchful,
 knowing eyes;
Always attentive . . .never
 retiring . . .
 forever grand and awe-inspiring!

Jo Doran Ayers
SECRET

Weeping Willow, can you sing,
 or
do you only weep?
Near your root I share your tears,
But,
as the wind whispers . . .
I hear you
 sing.

Cindy Somach
FORGOTTEN CHILDHOOD

To leave your childhood behind
 you,
 we take the steps of life,
 recalling the once known
 fantasies,

not knowing the forward strife.
A world of total animation,
 where things are not so real;
a place of total happiness,
 all flowers and earth to feel.
A time for childhood dreaming,
 so wonderful to behold;
 this is hidden in the stories,
 that the childhood's never told.

Shelbie S. Whittington
AMERICA'S HOSTAGE PEOPLE

All across America, yellow
 ribbons you will see,
They represent our hostages,
 who long to be set free.
They speak for all Americans,
 who proudly take their stand,
We refuse to let our people die
 in the palm of Khomeinis'
 hand.

Although it's taking longer, than
 any of us planned,
The freedom bells keep ringing
 all across our native land.
The yellow ribbons wave in the
 air—for you, just like "Old
 Glory",
We know it won't be long,
 before we hear your untold
 stories.

We sent our Troops to rescue
 those who so long have been
 held hostage,
But the mission failed and we
 lost those men who bravely
 fought for justice.
Be brave our hostage people,
 keep your faith and hold your
 heads high,
America will rescue you—just
 give us one more try.

B. Eileen Kuchenreuther
MISSING YOU

You are now just a vision
 I see your sweet smile
heart warming thoughts
 your laugh your charming style
Gone, removed from me
 so damn far away
missing you more each day
 . . .so much to say

Aware we both are
a social obstacle has been
 created
does anyone really care
 observe, our spirits remain
 elated
Written for you
 for all around to see
you . . . me . . .together
 once, a beautiful rhapsody

Cera Jane
OH ,IF I HAD ONLY SEEN . . .

As I count them up, I realize
 that the good things you were
 outnumbered the bad.
All the times I damned you for
 only being what you weren't
 instead of seeing the things
 you were,
Meant far more than some
 meaningless lies you might
 say, just
 to make time pass . . .
I can see that now, that you
 cared . But I dug deep for more—
 for something that just wasn't
 to be found.
If I would've found it, I would
 be none to sit all alone,
 That I am.
 I can see it now . . .
 Oh, If I had only seen . . .

Joseph Kennedy
THE BEARDED AND THE BEARDLESS

The smell of barbecue was in
 the air
As the two tennis stars walked
 onto the court.
Amid blaring rock and roll and
 a black child's stare
The games commenced.
 Racquets often swung at air
Where eyes had been certain
 something was there.
Beardless swung once, then in
 a chasing pirouette, swung again.
In the gallery, a black child
 laughed.
Bearded man fell while reaching
 for a shot
His opponent, concerned, asked
 if he was alright.
Bearded man led the set five
 games to two.
The opponent summoned
 courage to fight back;
Vicious volleys, lazy lobs,
 sizzling serves,
Alley shots, net shots, line shots
 tied the set at five games each.
In the gallery, a black child
 applauded both.
Bearded and beardless rolled
 and ran until beardless won;
He shook hands with his
 wheelchaired opponent
As the child looked on in
 wonderment.

Karen Samuel
TODAY I FEEL LONELY

Loneliness is a disease of the
 mind and heart.

I sit alone,
 think alone,
 feel alone.
Once upon a time I had good
 friends,
True friends, once upon a time.
Once upon a time, the lied.
Oh, wait! Selfish me.
Friends have lives of their own.
Perhaps occasionally they do,
 indeed, think of me.
The doubt lies only in my mind.
Good friends love me still,
 though all are silent.
I definitely know I still love them.
Dear friends!

Carolyn Bryant Bucko
TONIGHT

We meet on this dark and
 snowy eve,
Our tangled webs of silk to weave
To trap, ensnare and catch
 ourselves,
In wicked loving lies.

Softly lit places and tender
 embraces
Reflect in the sparkling wine.
Our eyes come together and
 gently remember
Another quick moment in time.

We talk and we laugh, a gay
 pair we make.
We each give a little, a little we
 take.
They're ever so slight, the
 undertones here,
"Did you just whisper
 something in my ear?"

"Oh! I have to go now, it's
 getting so late.
I really enjoyed our 'little date.'
But the wind, the rain, the cold,

cold snow."
The script is already written,
 you know.

Now I sit alone and think of you
And wonder if our lives were new,
Would we play the game the
 same old way?
In some other time, some other
 day?

This last verse, it seems, is
 quickly met
To stem the loss and soft regret,
To burst the clouds of passion's
 dreams.
I'll always remember you, it
 seems.

Evelyn Rose Sullivan
T.V. GOT 'EM

I used to have a "Granny Doll",
 sitting on my shelf.
Along came "Mr. Green Jeans".
 looked just like an elf.
Well, my little "Dolly Dimples"
 took off with "Betty Boop".
They all seen "Captain Kangaroo"
 and kind of flew the coop.

Brenda K. Burgess
I WAS LOST

Lord, I've been looking for you
I've lost you somewhere along
 the way,
I don't know where it was
I don't even know what day.

I must not have had a very good
 hold of you
or you couldn't have just
 disappeared.
I kept searching and looking all
 around me
Hoping that someday you would
 reappear.

Lord, I've been looking for you
And I just don't know where to
 begin.
I feel like I've lost a very good
 friend
I am burdened and so full of sin.

Lord you've been looking for me
It was not you who was lost, but
 I.
When I fell on my knees and took
 time to pray
I found you were with me all
 this time.

John P. Donohue
THE ROAD

I've come to the end of the road,
and I've done what I've had to do.
I've laughed, when I've had to
 laugh,
and I've cried, when I've had to
 cry.
I've traveled it mostly alone,
with few I have called my friend.
No moss has gathered on this
 stone,
A road with no hills or bends.
Oh, there were girls, and lovers,

and loves.
And dreams, and ambition, and hope.
And heartache, and heartbreak, and grief,
And desire and envy, and greed.
I have fought and triumphed, and lost.
And rallied and conquered, and lied.
I have learned my lessons at great cost.
To find at the end, I've died.

Gary W. Crosland
RAIN FOREST

A tall, windy tower huge and indefinite
harrows the drowsy forest.
Green twilight draws dimly to a close.
Two momentary flashes sear the tranquil air
and a loud explosion, as from a hidden siege gun
startles the idle trees awake.
High and far away, leaf and branch
bend in the air's agitation.
Banners of palm-frond green wave defiantly
at deafening thunder.
A flash of lightning reveals a shield, shining
as from living limbs, a protective arch over
trembling trees. The rain in liquid curtain
falls through leaf and limb-sifting-drifting.
It is mist-dispersed as silver on the forest floor.

Betty J. Shaw
A MIRACLE

There was once a girl who was silent,
and never spoke her mind.
She never was there for help to be lent,
and would only speak to some of her kind.
People were suffering and dying begging from every soul,
but she never heard the children crying
refusing to help or to take control.
She turned every thought the other way
never getting involved.
She vowed never to have a thing to say,
although her help could have some problems solved.
One day a child knocked on her door
begged her help if she dared.
The smile brought a change and she wanted more.
Suddenly she realized she had cared.

She blossomed and came out of her shell,
leaving pity behind.
Whenever a stranger stumbled and fell,
she was there to help with an open mind.

Raymond J. VanEck
LOVE, WE ARE OLD NOW

Love, we are old now
I am seventy-three
We have loved long
just you and me

Never wishing to change
my life or borrow
You have loved me well
and gladdened each tomorrow
Your face still pleases
these tired old eyes
The soft touch of you
still stirring youthful sighs
Each challenge met smiling
belying the effort given
Each success won quietly
though we were striven

At long last we pause
just to hold hands
Your head to my shoulder
looking at ancient wedding bands

Shirley Rainer
HAS TIME CHANGED YOUR MIND

You and i can't say goodby, and someone want us, to find out why,
you once told me, that you can't love, so how can you give, what you can't feel.
Someway somehow, you are not the
same, you make me feel, you feel
what i feel, can it be true, you are loving me, the way i love you.
The clock of life, is wound but once, now is the only time we own,
waiting for tomorrow may not be
wise, tomorrow sun may never rise.
It's not necessary, to say the words,
just touch me, and they will be heard,
love me over again, don't say when,
just do it all over again.

Gloria Woods Buchanan
A PRAYER FOR OUR HOSTAGES

Dear Lord "I Thank You For Another Year,
For All Your Blessings" and Your Tender Care,
For The food you Supplied "so Bountifully,
For Calming the Enemy" and keeping us Free.

And Lord "I am grateful" for Loved ones and Friends
This Table before me "this House I live in,
Still with all your Blessings" my heart knows pain
When I think of our Hostages" over in Iran.

I know how lonely "their days must be,
Not knowing if they" will ever

be free,
So much has been lost" from their dear lives,
Separated from loved ones "Children and Wives.
Held in Captivity "by cruel Men,
What they call Religion" I call Sin,
Their Hearts are hardened "by War and Hate,
In the hands of these Men" lies the Hostages' fate.

So Lord "if you please" hear my Prayer,
And soften the Hearts" of the leaders there,
And give America "back her own,
Now and for ever" thy will be done.

                Amen

Carolyn Valentine
IT'S YOUR BIRTHDAY!!

It's your birthday, ain't that swell!
This is something, I just won't tell . . .
Cause it is just between you 'n me.
All this, is ageless past,
    The putting on, our yearly mask . . .
We scamper through the months with glee . . .
Until age, catches up to we . . .
    Then we slowly . . . enter . . . thru . . . each . . .
A . . . day . . . at . . . a . . . time . . .
Stopping for a look to see . . .
What we did, which was living free.

Sheri L. Ballard
IN THE BEGINNING

Adam and Eve were the first people you see,
They were good until they ate of the tree.
The Knowledge of Good and Evil was the tree's name,
That made God's good people go down into shame.
Now Eve, you see, did not tarry by Adam,
Instead she ate of the tree so forbadden.
Now God had told them never to eat,
But instead they tried to perform a great feat.
For Satan had told them that if they ate,
They wouldn't have to go out the garden gate.
Satan was lying, he usually does,
They didn't think he was fibbing—but he was!
God had to punish them for the wrong they had done,
He promised that someday he would send his son.
To die on the cross for the wrong that we did!
When all this is oer, of Satan he'd be rid.

Nan Goergen
THE MANNEQUIN

A spontaneous flame of repulsion
Ignites the fires within,
The desire to burn all mad bridges

Crossed in the shadows of sin.
The wooden world of a mannequin,
Wore a brand, that's eroded with time,
The smell of the painted exhibit
A fate, no less than a crime.
Tears of the charred hopes,
Black, with the anguish of pain,
A failing desire for love
Thus, no emotions will remain.
A mannequin with peeled paint
The cracks, their lines in a face,
Her blurred eyes like a drunken woman
Her past is an utter disgrace.
Thrown in the dump, like garbage,
Her usefulness has ended,
Nobody wants a has been,
No future to be defended.
So, mannequin, with wooden heart
Will go to the fires of hell,
Disenchanted with life's cruelty
Cremated, with stories, a doll can't tell.

Lillian Wildgrube Amerland
THE LIGHT BECAME A CROSS

As a child I wondered why when I would cry
the light became a cross
And then at night in the dark sky
the star became a cross

On cold and wintry dark, dark nights
through panes covered with frost
an ordinary street lamp's light
somehow became a cross

Often I wondered if men wise could see the things I saw
and in their star filled wondering eyes
a cross led them in awe

And now I know, this path I take
I'm never, never lost
God's Light has led me all the way
God's Love shines through the Cross.

Lois J. Swanson
MY MOTHER

She was a young lady
When I came along.
To me, she's so special,
Her life is a song.

She had five other children
To fulfill the years;
We were all special to her,
Even when life had its fears.

She weathered the turmoil
Of depression and war.
Worked hard to bring us;
Dignity, love, sharing and more.

Then came the time when her mate passed on;
Left her with decisions and time.
But being a lady such as she is;
She brought happiness to others without a dime.

If only she didn't live so far away;
I would like for her to spend more time with me.
The day will come soon,
Sharing life together more will be.

Life has its memories and woe;
Precious times we will share.

My special sweet mother
For whom I really love and care.

Christine M. Trucinski
TOUCH ME

Reach out, touch me.
Hold me, close.
Mom, I'm here, inside
  deep inside, your heart.

You've done so much for me.
I could not forget, ever.
Could not feel alone or unloved,
  ever.
My body has gone to rest.
My soul, my spirit, my love
  is ever close with you.
It shall never leave you, never
  die,
  never cease to be.
It is now—more alive, more
  vibrant,
  more strong than ever before.
Because now—I'm free—to
  touch—thee.

Barbara Ratican
HE LOVES, BUILDS SAND
CASTLES

soft blue eyes watchful and
  eager
  contemplative and pensive
pleading and concerned
  about life ahead

he is concerned about time
  and its interference
in his games of chess,
  his desire
to end the search
  for a long-awaited mate

he loves, builds sand castles
  he falls, hurts with the changing
  tides
he loves, stands tall
  tall and slender
like a young tree
grasping and clinging
  to those elements around him
that keep him breathing
  living

his fair skinned shadow
  is scorched by his sun
yet stands sturdy
  in the face of exhausting winds

Cheryl Carvalho
FAREWELL, NOW MY
FRIEND

I love you my friend
You're quite dear to me,
A true friend you are
And always will be.
But you're leaving me soon
And going your own way,
Perhaps we will meet
In the future someday.
You've left me with memories
Of good times we've had,
To treasure forever
And make me feel glad.
I wish you good luck
In all that you do,
May all of life's pleasures
Come your way too.

Farewell, now my friend
And please may you find,
Some thoughts of me
Always in your mind.

Royce Stubblefield
LEI-NAD

An impish grin comes across
  his face,
A little devil's in this place.
A little angel shows behind,
This little boy with a witty
  mind.

Out shines a love as strong as
  steel,
Then anger shows from head to
  heel.
As I sit reading in my book,
I catch from you a fleeting look.
You worry so about your dad,
And always know if he is sad.
You're always there to lend a
  hand,
A fortress in a hostile land.
You play the game with knowing
  eye,
And aren't afraid new things to
  try.
You weigh the facts and make a
  choice,
Then put your thoughts to tone
  of voice.
How lucky can a father be,
Than have you share your life
  with me.

Charles Hollingsworth
A THIEF IN THE NIGHT

Last night I stole something.
I am no thief.
But still . . .
The item was so tempting
I could not refuse.
I stalked it until its owner was
  unawares.
    I came,
      I saw,
        I took!
I had no right; it was not mine.
I guess I should give it back.
No!
What's done is done.
Perhaps another?
And will continue to steal
Until the item is free,
And my life of crime is over.
    I saw,
      I wanted,
        I stole . . .
A kiss from you.

Colleen Cork
COMPULSION

Warm compulsion;
unable to memorize
I'm mesmerized
by magnetic lips
opened wide—
I fall in.

As desire
yields to touch,
I fall in.

Loreda L. Ellis
ROOTBOUND

Roots all bound within a pot,
entangled there to crowd and rot,
the framework system means a
  lot,
to plants and people does it not?

Room is needed to expand and
  grow,
in limitless boundries before we
  we'll know,
an active faith with visions of
  far to go,
and reversing this scheme saps
  energy so!

Divide then multiply is the
  proven rule,
to preserve plants and people in
  a living pool,
with the excellence of love as
  the cutting tool,
using the opposite of this would
  show me a fool.

Melvin Curtis
FEATHER

  Silent
A perfect design
  Beautiful
A color divine
  Flying
Blown by the wind
  Soft
A treasure to win.

Janis Gentner
UNTITLED

it's time i left
the city . . .
it's craziness
has me crazy
half the time . . .
the other half
is spent in
lonliness amidst
the brotherhood
of strangers.
and when i come back
to you
the out-of-doors
my mountain and
my meadow, my quiet,
i feel the vibrancy
that some feel
only in a city's throb
and then i know . . .
my heart is
always here. . .
    the bad is not so bad,
    the quiet is by choice.

Kari Munk
WAR

Amid the clash of verbal swords,
  A tiny bird will sing.
Amid the mess of hurting words,
  A tiny child will swing.
Amid the grief of broken hearts,
  A baby deer will prance.
Amid the death of brave young
  men,
  Old men and women dance.
Amid the sorrow and hurt that's
  shown,
  A delicate flower will bloom.
Amid the sickness and smell of
  death,
  A wife will sit alone.
Amid the bodies of men from
  war
  Tears fall sadly down.
Amid the pain, a child steps near
  And places the flower on the
  mound.

Bethel Nunley Evans
DOWN MEMORY LANE

What happened to all the things
As children we cherished so
  much?
Like the little old corner drug
  store
Where we gathered for sodas and
  such.
Recall the little red school house

That sat on the side of a hill?
Its belfry bell rang loud and clear
And gave the children such a
  thrill.

Oh, just for one more day dream
Of living down near the tracks,
And hearing the hum of the
  wheels
As freight cars rolled forward
  and back.

To lie in the bed late at night
And hear the distant train
  whistle blow
Makes chills run down the spine.
Oh, it was much too long ago.

Getting old is not so bad
If one can only reminisce.
But when the memory no
  longer works,
Forget it—it's recess time, one
  must admit!

Allison K. Whitley
REFLECTION

You can't turn around
as fast as you think you can
Because you'll lose your mind
then you'll have to go back
  looking for it.

Linda E. Vickers
THE TEARS OF A CHILD

The tear that falls
From the eye of the child
Is treated with kindness
Sympathetic and mild.

And the joy and the laughter
That comes from inside.
Is always expected
And nothing to hide.

But as each child blossoms
Into woman or man
The heart is to harden,
Emotion be banned.

Although it's expected
For the weakness to show
In a woman, it's fine,
But the man should outgrow.

Do we all not feel
The same tender emotion.
The love and the sadness,
That comes from devotion?

As we gather the memories,
Both happy and sad
Is it really a weakness,
Is it really so bad?

Is the shoulder to lean on
Less firm to the touch
And is the hand farther
When we reach out to touch?

Can't the heart still be gentle.
Sympathetic and mild
Like a smile or a handshake,
Like the tears of the child . . .

Ellen Wedel
THE KEY

Life is strange, it has its ways,
  of turning you around.
Just when you think you've
  got it pegged,
  another problem's found.

But don't give up you'll work it
  out,
  no matter what the size.
And if it takes a longer time,
  it makes you twice as wise.

We all once reach our breaking
  point,
  don't think that there won't be,
Another time when we will say,
  "Our friendship is the key."

Miss Gabrielle Allyce Driscoll
THE SEA

I must go down to the sea again
And taste the salty air.
And feel the cold, brisk breath
  on my back,
Though no one else is there.
To see the gulls soar oh so
  high
O'er the hills of sand.
To see the sky meet a rising
  sun
That shines on a mystical land.
The frothy waves roll
  endlessly,
undisturbed by man.
It's a world of lasting tranquility
I must go down to the sea again.

Mary K. Shaver
ESSENCE

Melting jellyfish puddle hot
  sand;
days melt.
sun slips over land.

Incarnates intangible,
imperceptibly blithe;
gentle waves swirl sand
and fluid fish
from grasping hand.

Joan Ruth Hightower
IDEAS

Ideas
Like kittens,
Pad softly about,
Spring,
Jump out, and clutch,
At naught, but a fleeting
Thread of thought.
Inherent improbity disguised,
Choose the night
To improvise,
Compelling chase of wit and
  will
Pursuit,
Perfecting higher skill.

Edith E. Stevens
IMAGE OF LIFE

What a life of pearly beads
strung tight on a worn and
  beloved string
with a knot here or there as
  repair
for a shattered existing moment
  now past.
The broken string limp until
it is tied, with each fallen
  pearl
stacked in place,
hugging one another in blissful
peace once again.
Beads that have scattered
on the downfall, yet have not
been broken by the impact
only strengthened through
  resistance
of separate flights once taken.
Now more prepared to
  withstand
the dust under the sofa
and the hardwood floor, or
  cement
at times.
Most often hung gently,
not awaiting disrepair, but
understanding it.

Robert D. Mullins
BEAUTY

Whoever said "beauty is only
  skin deep—"
That fool never once looked into
  your eyes,
Much less beyond them,
Nor heard you utter a single

word
After having known its
  meaning.
For therein lies all the fire
  and laughter
Of lifetimes, and each of them
full to overflowing
With the experiences we know
only as Life.

Virginia D. Dunley
YOU ARE SOMEBODY

Your eyes of kindness,
Your mouth of sweet words,
Your lips speak feelings of want.

Your arms and hands caress a
  cold
body,
Your fingers massaging for
  warmth.

Your navel so small, may speak
  for itself,
Last night, I know not how it
felt.

These are only parts of your
  body,
  which I so much desire,
The rest I may never find words
for, until our time by a fire.

If you are what you call
Nothing. . .
I'd hate to see what you call
SOMETHING

Delma Sala-Fleming
ABYSSAL LONELINESS

At times I gather courage
to look into the abyssal
  darkness
of my loneliness . . .
And when I do . . .
I lose all my courage
all my hope . . .

I lose my reason . . .
I feel inexorably alone!

Denise G. Andersen
UNTITLED

Sometimes I feel
Like a bar of soap—
My identity is wiped
Away by
An uncaring hand.

Terri E. Fowler
OF

Of hotel rooms and empty
  thoughts silent screams of
  cars non-
stop imprisoned in a self made
  dream, more reality than it
  seems.
Of crystal eyes and painted
  smiles, highways stretching
  countless miles
like life within a revolving door
  having no ceiling nor
a floor.
Of emotionless walkers staring
  mute as if plants pulled from
  their roots and set aside put

on display without a dream
  or yesterday.
Of disapproval and dismay,
roads that travel just one
way, we ask ourselves more
often than not, what of hotel
roms and empty thoughts?

Mary Beth Regan
COME TO ME ,SERENITY

Many a long search has not
Brought forth such tranquility;
For the key lies within
And throughout the keen
  spirit
Of the ulterior part of me.

I look to the sun, and faces
Of those who give warmth—
Then I render it back, hoping
That love shall abide;
Giving my life a calm light.

A stream of constant joy
Has not persisted,
as of yet
I have to sense the wonder
Of authentic love, which is a
Beauty of mellow
peacefulness.

Carol McDonald
FURY

Suppressed rage,
Pushing against the outer
  corners of my brain
Clenched fists, fingernails
  digging into taut skin
Frustration,
Quick, heavy breath
Fists smashin out into the
  mirror
Destroying the image
Blood dripping from fingers as
  glass tinkles to the floor
Eyes narrowed to slits
Red and glaring,
Suffering,
Smiling bitterly at the world's
  blindness.

Kathleen Tucker
SUMMER DAYS

The days are a slow trickle
  of life
Washed away
  by the enormity of Existence.
As mundane
  as a haggard wife
And as hungry for resistance.

Dortha A. Banks
ANOTHER YEAR

Another year has come and
  gone, oh how
my love for you has grown.
It hurt my heart so very dear
  to sit around
when you're not here.

The sky is now a milky grey,
  the green grass
is gone away,
The summer sun we see no
  more, the winter's snow
is at my door.

And as these months pass us
  by, the winter time
will seem to fly.
The summer months will grow
  so near and then it will
be another year.

Debe Busch
THE HUNT

Sly and cunning,
like a small but
knowledgeable kitten.
You've snuck

up on me,
you stalked and
planned and
caught me off guard.
The pain and hurt is
too strong to
believe it wasn't planned.
Someday you
will be the prey.

Danis Palmer
DEAR FRIEND

Dear friend, my love for you,
My thoughts so unexpressed;
Could never stoop in vain
  misgiving
Or words of unkindliness;
I've journeyed far, the tears
  have marred
My features for awhile,
But through my prayers God
  answers me
For you alone, I'll smile

To think of others and never
  know
If my paths were right or
  wrong;
To cling to Faith which is all
  you have
When your heart and soul are
  gone,
To conquer tears and human
  pain
While the beauty lingers on.

No words were lightly spoken,
God knows each deed of love,
And should my heart be
  broken
And I rise to heaven above;
My love would still come back
  to you
In drops of falling rain,
And through the tears, you'd
  see me smile
I'll wait for you again.

Helen G. Wuerth
THE MYSTICAL HAT

Chosen from an array
of winter paraphernalia,
The perfect fit—
Soft brown,
Adorned with
White flowers having
Transforming powers.

The wearer becoming
A sovereign's offspring
Celebrating the Word made
  Flesh.

Susan Leonard
UNTITLED

'Tis like a flower
when the dew has come
and dawn falls into
morning.

So refreshingly vibrant
is the giving in thanks
to you, whom have touched
in us.

Luba Becker
REACHING OUT

Brother, brother take my hand
Although I may not fully
  understand
Do not feel ashamed to reach
  out and say
I'm sure glad you're with me
  today

Brother, brother take my hand
For I will try to understand
The frustrations of life are
  hard to bear
But I just want to let you know
  I care

Sometimes words cannot help
at all
But I'll try to help you stand
tall
Brother, brother take my hand
For tomorrow I may need you
to understand.

Manuela S. Tam
THE SKY

A wonder is the sky with
a light to hazy blue, and
puffy cotten
fluffs passing by. A window
of imagination. Open your
soul
and let it free to wonder and
seek the stories hidden up
there
behind the fluffs in shapes of
dogs, cats, horses and trees.
Fly about playing hide-and-
seek going down down down
and
then soaring higher and higher
looking back and seeing your
ambitions grow.
Oh no scurry back, the cotten
fluffs have been chased away
by
steel wads. No light to hazy
blue skies but purple, grey
and
black. Hissing with a bolt of
energy glowing bright and
eerie,
The boom boom BOOM of
the thunder and the howl
howl HOWL of
wind each trying to outdo
the other. The wind wins
and keeps
pushing til all is gone.
Again open your soul and let
it run free with your
imagination
twisting in and out of fluffs
in shapes of dogs, cats,
horses
and trees.

Susan Bean
NO WORLDLY TAX

There is no tax
On precious gifts
Received from realms above.
No itemizing with a list
Each treasure born of love.
The land, the sky;
A tree with fruit;
The eyes of man to see.
A little child
With a mother's grace
Are given . . .
All tax free.

Mary Jo Mays
CHANGING

Everyone changes all during
their life
no one ever stays the same. If
everyone stayed the same, life
would
become very dull and boring.
Many
change when they are growing
some
grow older some just begin to
grow.
People change everyday into
different people.
There are many kinds of
people all
over the world who look and
are very
different. It is interesting to

meet
people who are of a different
nationality. When we travel
to other
countries, cities, states we meet
many different people. I'm
glad that
there are all kinds of people
in this world.

Donna Armour
I BELIEVED . . . I STILL
BELIEVE

When I carefully placed my
tooth under my pillow
Knowing that it was the
Tooth Fairy
Who left the coin which I
received,
I believed.

When I hung my Christmas
stocking
And fixed cookies for Santa
to eat
Because sweets is what his
tummy did need,
I believed.

When I waited for Easter,
the Bunny,
His eggs and chocolate, a new
dress and hat
But cried when my matching
necklace lost a bead,
I believed.

When I asked Mom where
babies come from,
"Where did I come from?" and
she answered
From God and love which she
received,
I believed.

When I look at trees blowing in
the wind,
An eagle flying through a gorge,
a flower
Flowing down a brook, or a
child smiling free from greed,
I still believe.

Rose Graham
THIS NEW DAY

On this new day,
Lord, grant that I
May see the beauty of earth and
sky,
The row of flowers of different
hue,
The fleecy clouds of palest
blue,
The gently waving tasseled corn
And hear the robin's song at
morn,
Hear the traffic on the road
And the still small voice of
God!
Maybe Hear a little rain
Splashing on the window pane
Feel the breezes on my face
And the strength of thy
embrace,
With the Everlasting Arms,
Touch the world with all its
charms
And the folks who come my
way
Lord, help me live for you this
day!

Emily C. Lowry
IF I MUST BE OLD

Sometime, if I must be old
I suppose I will have to be
I want to be old and thin
As the trunk of a hemlock tree.
Old and hungry and lean
With longings that have not

died
And never heavy and smug
And settled and satisfied.
I want to stay thrilled by the
sea
And by spring and the scent
of a wood
And never content to sit
still
To revel in costly food.
I want my soul to go on
With its hungers all unstilled
With ever a dream ahead
Which never has been fulfilled.
Our hungers are what we are of
And I want to be more than
meat
I want to keep seeking truths
And never just things to eat.
Oh, life give me less than my
fill
Lest striving seems to be
vain
Let me die with my boots still
on
And with zest to begin again.

Jacqueline E. Brady
CONFUSED

I'm so confused,
my head's unscrewed.
Flying things,
without wings.
Darkness in the day,
work without pay.
Faces without features,
ugly creatures.
Hands that open only to snatch,
minds working only to catch.
Mouths that spurt steam and
fire
teeth that sever every desire.
Breath as foul, foul as death,
to exist must suffereth.
Burning eyes full of hate,
oh my God, it's too late.
Feel like flying,
no I'm dying.
Colors change, things re-arrange,
flaking, falling just like mange.
Oh my God I.m dying—
how strange!

Cheryl A. Davis-Vasquez
SHIMMERY NIGHT

On a holy starry shimmery
night
With all the stars shining bright
Collected together over an eddy
tide
Together forever side by side.
And God sent down his single
word,
Love one another, for all it's
worth
Be kind, behold, I send thee
My only son, begotten, son of
me.
Then all the world shall then
unite,
And take each other's hand
for I send you this holy one,
The survivor of all man.
Then all the stars and moon
glittered
brightly,
And sent a message back,
"We welcome he, son of thee,
for all eternity."

Meg Harper
HYMN

Savior fill our searching heart,
Joy and peace to us impart.
Anoint with apostolic zeal
Your servants this lost world

to heal.
Confound our willful urge to
stray,
For strength in You we daily
pray.
Reflect on Jesus' humble
birth,
His majesty ennobles earth.
Unmindful of this gift
of love,
This sacrifice from God Above,
Slave to selfish, hurtful needs,
Still our souls with love he
feeds.
Forgives our petty wars and
strife,
Rewards us with eternal life.
Let us with wisdom born of
faith
Conquer earthly sin and
death.

Cynthia Warzecha
UNTITLED

i feel the coldness
of winter within me
i see the full moon rise
above the bare skeleton
of the tree
upon the hill
its naked branches reach out
to touch the stars
it stands alone
in the glittering snow
waiting for spring.

Gary Clancy Voelker
BEGINNING

From a little seed you came
planted by the rain
it didn't take long for you to
appear.
Rooted firmly to your
surroundings
taking in and giving out.
Blossoming into beauty
you are life,
to all you provide.

Bernard Centofanti
FLAME OF FAITH

I am a walking body of matter.
A piece of life carved out from
life itself.
I am intelligent enough to be
a computer, yet not flawless.
There are mistakes that are
made.
I rely on myself for discipline
with the help of my God-given
gift, the mind to make
corrections to these mistakes.
There is a time limit on my
existence, I know of realization
I am capable of feeling.
I know of love, hate, and
sorrow.
I am like all of us, I can cry and
then again, I can laugh.
I have climbed many steps to

reach the height of my cultural maturity.
I need a flame of Faith
to keep me moving.
A flame of Faith to keep me

seeking and searching till someday I
may just stop, find a place,
blow out the candle and rest.
A flame of faith leading me
to a sleep into serenity.

Renata Rzepecki
INTOXICATION

I feel intoxicated
With the simple things of life
I gaze out a window
I realize there is no beauty
Like I feel within me
On a summer's day
Birds building their nests

Trees dressed in green
Flowers reaching through the earth
I can only exclaim
This beauty has been heaven sent.

Tiffany Holland
THE BULLFIGHT

A red wave spun around the shadow,
The mechanic beast stampeded past.
The zoo broke loose,
Supple muscles rippled the ivory;
Caught their eyes.
The beast screamed and charged again.
There was red on the ivory.
The zoo cried with delight—
at it's meal.
Red stood still on red.
The shadow died.

Valerie A. McKenney
TIME

The lines of time are finely drawn.
Running here and there;
Never still to be.

Raindrops falling lightly,
Wind blowing gently,
Life goes on day by day.
Stopping here and there.
Never still to be.

C. Leon Jones
IT'S TIME TO GO

I spent my time in Vietnam
and now it's time to go.
Others may have to take my place; how many, I do not know.

I came to Vietnam a year ago
with thoughts of "war is hell"
I managed to overcome every task and things worked out pretty well.

Americans have come to Vietnam to fight an endless war.
Many of them are going home now; they won't have to fight any more.
Thousands have died in vain, hundreds have suffered tremendous pain.
Many have suffered permanent damage; others have left partially lame.
God bless the men who are going home; for they have done their best.
God bless the less fortunate ones, whom he has lain to rest.
Remember the guys that are left behind to fight a little more
for they will need your love and strength to win this senseless war.

Anthony M. Pionegro
THE WELCOME

Be filled with ease as you enter our home
For we look to you as our brother
And all of these blessings the giver has given
We'll share with one another.
Come sit at our table
And fill your plate
Join us in this feast of kings.
For he has surely blessed us
With these many wonderous things.
So join us then no matter if it be in house or stable
For in our home when we break bread
God sits at the head of our table.

Mildred Pettus McCafferty
SPRINGTIME

It's springtime in the meadows
In every hill and dell
It's springtime in my heart today
I feel that all is well.

In the plan of mother nature
When buds burst forth in sight
We know within our hearts and minds
That all is good and right.

What's within your heart today
As nature comes forth anew?
If anything is dead and ugly, May it all go away
And be replaced with life and beauty
Fresh as Springtime's morning dew.

Glenna D. Jones
I WISH I WAS A BIRD

I wish I was a bird.
With wings so I could fly.
I'd fly up to New Jersey,
Or I'd give it a helluva try.

To see my handsome Soldier Son,
And wish him all the best.
To watch him as he graduates,
Along with all the rest.

I know he's so proud of himself,
He has every right to be.
I'm very proud of him too

Because he's part of me.
When he left, he took along,
A corner of my heart.
I gave it very happily
So we'd never be far apart.
Someday when you marry, Son,
Tuck my heart's corner away.
Hidden mostly from your wife,
But always there to stay.
One thing cannot ever change,
That's a mother' slove,
It's always there when you need it,
Just like God is, up above.

Adeline Mefford
A SONG OF LIFE

At dawning, when the sun blinks through the doorway
and nestles in the corner of your room.
You feel a sense of thrill,
a note of laughter,
that banishes all thought of care and gloom.

You hear a robin on yon windowledge a-chirping,
A child's glad echo wafted up from streets below,
A silver maple blowing in the wind-hush
And waters made with waves of melted snow.

In every nook Dame Nature heralds gladness
While glints of sunshine conquer weary strife.
Until we learn to weave our dreams and efforts
and make a smile our daily song of life.

Ann Gallenson
A SINGLE ROSE

I look across the way and see
The most divine creation,
A single rose.
To pick it is to destroy true beauty.
To allow it to bloom, seed, and die
Is to enhance true artistry.
Nature never intended us to see
only Act I of life.

Tim Moore
ADVICE

Sip deep of the wine, drink from the cask.
How much should you drink? What a question to ask.
Drink all that you can of the Claret so fine.
The cask drys so quickly, so drink deep of the wine.
Sip firmly, and grasp all the flavor you can.
The cask drys so quickly, while held in your hands.
And after it's empty, the Claret all gone,
The red wine has been tasted, the soul must move on.

Julie J. Clark
ENTIRETY

You've touched my entirety
By caressing my emotions
And awakening each one
To the image of you.
You've laughed at my anger

and cried for my smile,
And toyed with each
As a separate plaything.

You've molded them into different shapes and sizes,
According to the empty spaces
You held inside.

So they flowed in and overtook
each crevice and crack,
Making you whole.

Yes, You've touched my entirety
But I became yours.

Lisa Glass
ON A RATHER UNEXPECTED MEETING

Are you enjoying your sunbath?
I was just passing by,
But I think I'll stay and talk.
Do you come here often?
I hop by every now and then,
Usually when I am feeling lonely.
If you kiss me, I might become
A handsome prince. If I do,
You and I would both
Have someone to talk to.
Oh, I see my enemy, the snake coming.
I'd better go somewhere safer.

Sue Rebecca Revell
CATS

Cats are graceful and lovely,
they are here for the world to enjoy.

With eyes of eagerness and ears of the world,
they are the friend of eternity.

Cats never let you down,
they are there for comfort and love.

They are nature's way of making
life beautiful and full.

A cat is unpredictable just like life.

Sometimes they are sweet and beautiful,
and sometimes they are mean and deceitful.

But either way they are there to be enjoyed.

Mrs. Ollie Thorp
UNWANTED TREASURES

Today, I attended a household sale
A sad one I'll have to say
Of an old lady's treasured possessions
She had collected along the way.

There were dishes, linens, pots and pans
And things that were made by hand
All were spread on a table outside
And auctioned off at the children's command.

I listened to the cry of the auctioneer
As he held up an item to sell
"Who'll give me a dollar",
'Who'll give me two"
And the people around stood still.

One lady standing not far from my side
Said, "Mister, they don't

understand."
"That quilt you hold was
    patiently made
By my own Dear Mother's
    hands."

Then I thought of the quilt
    I had at home
My own dear Mother had made
I hope it will never be
    auctioned off
Like this one had today.

I wonder now as the years go
    by
Of the things I'll leave behind,
Will they too be auctioned
    off some day
The thought leaves me with
    a sigh.

Toni Leigh Keller
LIFE

Far from distant rolling seas
    places you long to be
Lost in the confusion of other
    people's minds
    killing time
Freedom's thoughts, they come
    and go
    still no one knows
The inner mind, the warming
    souls
    heart's desires yet untold
Where will you go and where
    will you be
    blossoming from amid life's
    debris
Speaking words in a foreign
    tongue
    language unknown by everyone
Life, it simply goes on its way
    nothing to hear, nothing to say.

Juliet A. Dowse-Simpson
ENCHANTED UNION

All was still on the lake in the
    cool moonlight,
As the crickets were starting
    their song.
One lone bird swooped down
    for a last night flight,
Graceful strokes sent her
    even and strong.

The sky shone as bright as a
    silver bouquet,
Sending night beams of light
    through the trees.
The stillness beheld within
    each single ray,
Was caught up in a nocturnal
    breeze.

In the air was a tremor in
    awaiting the time,
As two souls longed for being
    together.
Each appeared on the bank
    with a glowing divine,
    knowing this was to last them
    forever.

Each in turn took their vow
    keeping silent the
    trance,
Then their hearts made as one
    joined in infinite dance.

M. Lee Singletary
ALL THINGS, I AM

I am to you.
I am a burst of laughter.
I am your joy in the daylight,
    your peace at dusk.
I am Spring in your minds eye
    on Wintry nights.
I am your love.
I am your life—part of it.
I am your secrets and successes.

I am tomorrow and I was
    yesterday.
I am your pot of gold.
I am your love.
I am your woman—man. Flaunt
    me, love me.
As if you didn't know, You are
    all things to me.

Swan Maraman Turner
SEA OF NIGHT

When I weigh anchor
In that sea of night.
Don't fear for me,
My ship's real tight.

I'll check my mast
And all my rails.
I'll set my course
And hoist my sails.

I'll follow my compass
When waters get rough
I'll weather the storm
In that dark gulf.

I'll move straight forward
And I won't retreat
I'll sail right up
To my Captain's feet.

He'll take my hand
I'll sit by his side
We'll wait for you
The next high tide.

Kerry Marie Margaret Vallance
PRAYER

From when I pray to God at
    night
And then the whole day
    through,
My thoughts escape me and I
    dream
Of dreams that won't come true.
My dreams are only of but one
    thing,
Of how to live and how to sing.
And you. Whom I miss at the
    break of day—
And on windy nights when the
    trees all sway . . .
Maybe this prayer, that's the
    first of its kind,
Will remind you, dad, that
    you'll always be . . .
    mine.

Rosemary E. Helmer
**AN EMPTY ROCKING
CHAIR**

My rocking chair is lonely now,
My little girls are gone;
And when my lap is sitting
    there
There's no one to climb on.
Now as I sit alone and read
While rocking silently,
I long for laughing little girls
To climb all over me.
To argue who will sit just
    where.
To cuddle and to kiss.
For oh! The laughter and the
    hugs,
Are what I sadly miss!
My rocking chair looks so for
    forlorn
Without my little girls.
The sunlight dancing through
    the room,
Can't find those red gold curls.
The dimpled cheeks and
    laughing eyes
Are gone, but who knows where
    where?
The dancing sunbeams search
    and find
An empty rocking chair.
Oh! Let me turn the lonely

days
Back through the months, 'til
    when
I cradled dear, small red heads
    close,
And rocked and sang with
    them!

Alice Cleveland Daugherty
**ON SOLITUDE AND
SILHOUETTES**

Solitude is like a shroud of lace,
    that wraps my heart and mind,
It covers all the memories, of
    a love that was so kind.
It holds me in a time and space,
    that lets no one come in.
It seals me to a long lost love,
    and a broken heart that will
    never mend.

The silhouettes are all around,
    they fill this darkened room.
They are symbols of the love
    we knew, before our world
    was doomed.
Death took you quickly away
    from me, like a whisper in
    the night.
It took away reality, and a hope
    that was so bright.

As the days keep turning into
    years, you're so close we
    almost touch.
I sit and smile and reminisce,
    with the one I love so much.

Mary K. Kellett
THE SPOKEN WORD

Don't wait till I'm dead
To talk to me.
Because then it's too late
For both of us, you see.

Kind words should come
From the moment of birth.
Encouraging words
Urge us to go forth.

Words spoken to the dead
Fall on deaf ears.
If said to the living
They can allay many fears.

For once death doth come
No words can suffice
To help ease the
    conscience.
It's too late to be nice.

If only we knew
The time to be giving
Is not to the dead
But speak to the living.

Nelda Jean Schulthise
ELUSIVE LOVE

Love can wear so many faces
A face of joy or pain, or far
    off places
Love may lift you to the heights
    of heaven
Or cast you down to the regions
    of hell
Love may touch you gently,
    oh so tender

Or grasp you tightly, in its
    spell
In vain I scanned each sun-
    bathed mountain
And traveled afar on darkened
    seas
I searched the confines of my
    dwelling
Oh elusive love, where can you
    be
My soul lies girded in the
    sackcloths of mourning
While I dance in gowns,
    trimmed of chrysolites and
    beads
I feast upon the delicacies of
    this world
    and yet starve, from a love
    unfreed.

Terrie Brown
BLACK NIGHT

Stars shining through
a windowless payne
plaster falling overhead
sore blistered lips
rats are running on the floor
there's a hole in my door
lying on this rusty spring
what will tomorrow bring
will I overcome
or shall I withdraw from.

Linda G. Hampton
TOGETHER LAST

I've done a million things
I said I'd never do
but the thing I shouldn't have
    done the most
was fall in love with you

I knew I could never have you
nor stay always by your side
but just the thought of seeing
    you
ceased the longing of my heart
    and mind

Every word you've ever
    spoken
I hold in my memory dear
to remember when I am away
    from you
to help my soul to cheer

Yes I think of you often and
    always
as the lonely hours pass
and I think of often and always
the time we were together
    last

We've done many things
    together
and I hope many more we will
    do
but if we never do anything
    different
I'd just soon the things we've
    done do.

Monica M. Corrado
INTERIM

A void has replaced
the love once there . . .
So no more hurt could come.
Pulled together once more,
by the most powerful force,
    love,
We tried,
We loved once more—
for the good times.
Now I fear
it is truly over—
Although we refuse to accept it.
We tried to avoid the inevitable—
knowing it would come . . .
What fools—
But then,

love is blind.
We wanted it to go on—
don't all lovers, though ?
That was then,
This is now.
It is time to let go . . .
To go our separate ways . . .
To love once more . . .

Kimberly Muncy
SEASONS

Spring is born, a baby child;
never let the babe run wild.
He'll live his life in the day of
spring,
until he meets the family ring.

Life mores on to its summer
years;
youngsters laughing, singing
and crying their tears.
And passing by hand in hand,
they'll meet again in another
land.

This day of fall, it's getting
cold;
it's turning brown, you're
getting old.
On and on as the days pass
by,
you'll look each over with a
sigh.

Old and gray, nowhere to go,
you look outside in the falling
snow,
and see the child on this
winter's day
Put your head in your hands,
and let the child play.

J. C. Goldinak
TO BRIAN ,WITH LOVE

The moon is full and the night
is warm,
the mood is the calmness
before the storm.
The crickets chirp and a
neighbor's dogs bark,
its so peaceful here, alone in
the dark.
Thinking of summers come
and gone,
wondering how to carry on.
Remembering the day when
we first met,
yours is a face my heart won't
forget.
You are the one that pulled
me thru
when times got tough, I'd go
to you.
It's hard to believe we still feel
the same
and haven't got caught in a
lover's game.
We'll always be close, there is
no doubt,
you've taught me what
friendship is all about
But along with friendship comes
caring and trust,
with a little bit of love, it adds
up to us.
So, there you have it in black
and white
the way I feel on this summer
night.
I've felt this way right from the
start,
there will always be a place for
you in my heart.

Mimi Harrison
LITTLE GIRL

What a kid—she'll drive me
crazy!
Chase her around until I'm

hazy.
She plays in the garbage,
and tears magazines—
Putters around like she's been
eatin' beans!
Plays in the toilet,
Eats tobacco and ashes,
But what can I do when she
bats those lashes?
She sneaks out the door,
Eats dirt and stones—
Carries the cat by the neck,
nearly breaks its bones!
She gets me so mad I can't
see straight—
Then what does my angel do?
Looks at me lovingly, smiles,
oh so sweet—
As to say, "Mommy, I love
you!"

Susan Watkins Parris
SEASON, WINTER

Do you recall
One long ago fall
A day when the leaves
Were not there at all
When winter had bathed
The land, all in white
Do you remember
That glorious sight?

Frozen flakes
From heaven descend
Into snow
They each softly blend
The ground they cover
In blanket form
The deeper the drifts
The greater the storm

Fury of winter
Came calling that day
The trees were burdened
In the cold wind—to sway
Heavy their branches
Laden they were
All the big pines
And small Douglas Fir

Born from the runoff
Of newly packed snow
Rivers and gorges
Began to grow
As they'd escaped down the
Steep mountain slope
To all living things
They offered "new hope"

Soon flowers would blossom
In meadows—near springs
With summer to follow—
In the order of things!

Edwina Gallo
THIS MAN

He has touched me
This man of whom I speak
He has kissed me
This man of whom I speak
And though the hand that
touched
Of this man of whom I speak
And though the lips that
kissed

Of this man of whom I speak
Are wrinkled with the years
Who with his touch, his kiss
There still remains the
infinite bliss
He gives throughout my very
being.

Donna Morgan Fockler
A BIRD

If I were a bird I know that I
would spread my wings and
I would fly
I'd fly so far up in the sky
I'd reach your house—at least
I'd try.

But if you saw a bird in flight
or on your window sill did
light
and since I could not speak
or write
You would not ask me in that
night.

You'd see me with a battered
wing
perhaps you'd pity "that poor
thing"
Even though a song I'd sing
No words of love from that
would spring.

A few small crumbs you
might toss
To that poor bird that seemed
so lost
You could not know the price
it cost
My poor frail wings, this land
to cross.

I'm thankful God has made
me, Me
No bird with wings to fly
so free
But one who can write to
thee
and express my love in poetry.

Allison Renna
CUT LOOSE

Still brains with their paralyzed
thoughts.
Someone rescue this creature
from the torment.
Lying on a cool, sandy beach
with an empty mind,
What else could I want?
We'll escape through the
burning fields
Past the miserable workers,
Who long for their freedom.
Beads of sweat drown their
tired bodies.
Dance with me across the
bare land.
Feel the sun and breeze caress
your soul
As you absorb everything
around you.
Let us cast our flight above the
sea
And forever more be lost and
free.

Diane Marie Moody
MARY

Mary,
So bright, so happy, so full of
joy.
Eyes gleaming, face smiling,
At times a bit coy.

Mary,
So gentle, so soft, so un
understanding she be,
With a heart full of love,
And a spirit so free.

Mary,

So warm, self reliant, so sure
of herself.
As sweet as a doll
That sits on the shelf.

Mary,
Oh mary,
My Mary!

Bonnie Hill
FOR THE HAPPY COUPLE

I wish you happiness,
So the laughter and smiles won't
stray
May happiness fill your heart
And joy come by your way.

I wish you success,
May your wealth buy what you
need
But it's not only the riches
That help you succeed.

I wish you good health,
With good health there are
less tears
It's something to be thankful
for
To be healthy throughout the
years.

I wish you a life
designed especially for you
With all the thought
throughout your life
May your hopes and dreams
come true.

But most of all I wish you Love
It's a fortune in itself,
Because Love is so important
Without it there's nothing
else.

Patti Jean
FOG AT SALMON CREEK

swan feathers finger down my
breasts
the heron stands stiff out in
the fog
in surroundings of dead yarrow.

Peter Weber
AN UNTIMELY LETTER

Dear Jim,

Shock, outrage, fear and
compassion,
emotions all clouding my mind;
tears flow, apologies and wishes
begin,
be I ever so fruitless.

Oh Nature's whim, seemingly
cruel;
who am I to say.
An individual, so close, so
dear;
my friend, you do not cease.

Today, tomorrow's yesterday.
Late night philosophies,
supporting glances,
stoning and clowning,
knowing embraces
dangerous canoeing,
ambitious campaigns,
giving and taking,
sharing sorrows and
growing with pride.
All these things we know
together
and we are happy.

An open mind and heart sets
your style;
ignoring hardship and rejection.
You have given so much yet
continue;
may I be as full.

You have not left me, my
friend,

merely moved to another state.
Till we meet again on
different horizons
We love together within the
sunset's splendor.

Good-bye, James, see you soon.

Jean Sherrill
WHAT RIGHTS?

Weep not for the immorality
that has consumed our
nation,
No longer may we hide our
shame behind curtains of
unawareness.
It wasn't just the leaders of
our country, that befell
us to such a condition;
Many times the opportunity
was presented to us,
the choice ours.
Why did we then, mumble
uncertainties
allowing our futures made for
us?
Like clay mounds we accepted
every change,
letting greedy hands shape
and mold;
until we became what we are
today.
Weep not for our lost freedom,
but
weep for the certainty of
failure.

Jean Brown
THE CAVE

The reaches are dark and ragged
blacker is the belly and silent.
Water drips to structure ice-
like
knives that time cannot melt.
Air is oppressive and damp;
it drowns
the tender embryo.
Something moves across the
rough, cold rock.
How can it be here?
Never to see it's
enemy, only to die?
A billion years of clay between
this and
the sun—never to feel it again.
A sound? A hollow thud from
the dark, and red.
Oh, God! It's not a cave at
all, but my
own heart and I'm caught fast
inside to die.
The reaches are dark and ragged,
blacker is the belly and silent.

Janet Kaye Penney
DEAR UNBORN CHILD

Dear unborn child,

When the words were spoken
that filled my life with
joy, I hoped deep down inside
of me that you would be a
boy.
When I feel you in my womb, I
know you are secure, cause
God made you in me and that
I am for sure.
When I lie down to sleep at
night it seems you kick and
play.
I guess you just can't wait
until the turning of the day.
Your father and I are preparing
your room. Because we know
without a doubt, that you will

be here soon.
I love you even now, my child,
like a precious pearl, I'll tell
you so when you come home,
even if you are a girl.

Sincerely, your Mother.

James Leung Hong
THANKSGIVING SPIRIT

Let this one day of
Thanksgiving,
Be the sinew of all the days
we're receiving,
Let all men lay their arms
aside,
And let peace be the law we
abide,
Let human kindness triumph
over racial strife,
And build towards a better
life,
Let our unselfishness conquer
the spectre of human famine,
By sharing what we have to
our fellow man and woman.
Let all people face fear and
conquer it,
For belief is the foundation
to the human spirit.
Once we face the problems
we all have in common,
Our battle is about half-won.
So let's all join our hands and
pray
For the spirit of this
Thanksgiving Day.

Harvey G. Taylor
I WONDER

I wonder why the river flows
Into the endless sea
I know that only one Man
knows
When death shall come for me.
I feel the wicked, restless wind
Her hands about my face,
I wonder where will she descend
To her final resting place.
Why does the silver setting
sun
Glow beyond the sky.
I wonder when his day is done
If he fades away to die.
I wonder why my life I live
Its seconds and its hours,
I'd like to know how will
nature give
The sweet smell to the flowers.
Why does the darkness always
fall
Upon the rays of light,
And through the midst I hear
the call
Of the deep and darkening
night.
These very things that do
amaze
The nakedness of the eye,
They will go through many a
phase
Before we all shall die.

Justin Ewens Jones
**THE SPORT OF SLED
RIDING**

The winter sport of sled riding
Has been pasted down through
the years.
Our ancestors used to do it,
And we still do it here.
There is toboggan racing in
the Olympic games
Which is quite a sight to see.
A team races down a long,
steep course,
And travels at an amazing

speed.
Every little kid likes to grab
a sled
And go sliding down a hill.
For going over the snow so
fast
Is quite an amusing thrill.

Paula McCarty
TRIBUTE

kaleidoscoping emotions have
filled the changing years.
depression was predominate, I
bathed the world in tears.
since the days and nights we
shared, most everything has
changed.
I wonder how long i can stand
the way life's rearranged?
stolen hours haunt me still.
an empty heart and broken
will.
my lost heaven could comfort
and fill.
i wait for signs that you are
near.
my love lies dormant . . .
waiting . . .
and my heart beats . . .
hesitating . . .
then i go crazy waiting here.
and i never stop loving you,
i will never stop wanting you.
and all that's left to help me
through;
. . .endless dreams of you.

Jeannette Clarence
HIGH RISE

Sometimes
standing by
my open window
I see
my body hurtling
down
Do I scream as I fall
I wonder
a real primal scream
to rid me of the pain
of life
mere seconds
before ridding life
of me?
Do I fall straight
like a plumb line
weighted by
my despair
or arch out
and carom from car
to pavement?
And what sould
does my body make
as it hits the ground?
Questions
I will never answer
Answers
only you will know
chance passerby.

Mamie LaRue Bean
MY CHILD

Standing
Quietly by his bed
I watch my small one sleeping—
His soft round face framed
By downlike hair.
Smiling
I notice his knees tucked up
close under him
His arms outstretched
His breathing is even and steady
I know his dreams are gentle
ones.
Thinking
I see my son tall and proud

Bending down to kiss me
good-bye
Going off to join a wife—or
fight a war . . .
My eyes shut tight and these
thoughts fade
Until another time and day.
Kneeling
I place my hand gently on
this little one
And once more I thank God
for this small miracle . . .
My Child.

Evelyn Laurene Hovde
THIS IS GOODBYE . . .

I cannot speak, now that it's
time to go
For though I would, my voice
it quivers so
These are such lovely things
to leave behind:
The pines, the fields, the lonely
roads that wind
Across green hills; gay flowers
song of birds
Love and laughter and unspoken
words
The moonlit lawn beneath a
starry dome—
Oh, it is hard to leave this place
called home!
But I must speak, and so,
Thank you, I say
For everything—Goodbye . . .
With tears I turn away.

Barbara Tyler
UNTITLED

a candle
uneasy in the night
the wind
restless at the door
my heart
uncertain in
its loneliness
my life
confused in
its changing
a candle
dim
against the wind . . .

Brenda J. Booker-Black
WHAT LIFE IS ALL ABOUT

I want to continue serving
the Lord,
no matter how hard times may
be
If it wasn't for my son I don't
know
where I'd be
Life is funny; Life is sad, but
one thing
for sure it isn't all that bad
Life is round; Life is square,
for most of
us it's just there.
Life is short; Life is tall, but
most of all
Life is a BLESSING to us
all.

Belinda Jo Faulkner
UNTITLED

His icy fingers touched my
face, as they have so many
times before
I knew he would be there before
I ever opened the door.
He's tortured me constantly for
the past three months
I've got to learn how to escape
his clutch.
He makes me ache when I'm
with him for long,
But his brutal force is ever
so strong.
He envelopes my whole body
the moment I am without
shield
He's with me even when I
think I'm alone in an open
field.
There's nothing anyone can
do to him that would cause
some restraint
I guess I'll have to suffer with
agony and pain.
Few things have the
extraordinary cost
Of the price you pay for
knowing
OLD JACK FROST!!!

Rhonda Johnson
WOMAN ON A SHELF

Amid the teapot, fine china
The knick-knack and brick-a-
brack
Woman on a shelf.

There to safely keep
Looked in upon
Dust her off and take her out
Look to the inside
For she is your only one.

Her shelf being storage space
Creates instant room for
All the love there within.

Watch closely now
At the touch she has come alive
Magically she will arrive.

Handle her gently, do not
Disturb the finely painted
Lines aged with time.

Examine every detail, but
look to the eyes
For they are open wide
Hiding nothing from the
One who wants to see.

Engraved on her heart
Handwriting of the one who
sees
It fades, so does her space.

The shelf is filled with more
Returned to her space
Woman on a shelf.

Back to her place
Amid the teapot, fine china.
The knick-knack and brick-a-
brack.

Harold W. Small
HUMANITY

How do I know who I am until
I live as someone else?
How do I help someone else
unless
I change my inner pulse.
The inner world is where life
lives
Life comprises not the tangible
selves
Rather the intangible pulse-
stars of thought.
Deep thought, Concerning
the universal lot.

The universality of the black
holes of starvation and
despair
Vortexing in unreflecting
rays away from the black
void's stare.
The reflection of self upon
self ignored.
As we speed away from selves
implored.
Away into the frozen twilight.
Frozen. But redeemable.

Donna Tilton
THE MAN

I met a man, who took my
hand
And made me free, by simply
loving me;
And the man does make me
smile,
And my heart does skip a
beat when he holds me.
And the sun just keeps on
shining
Though the clouds do cry
their tears.
And I love the man so dearly,
That my spirit soars so high
that I can fly;
And the days are filled with
laughter,
But at night I wish he was
there by my side.
And the sun just keeps on
shining
Though the clouds do cry their
tears.
And if he ever leaves me,
At least I'll have some special
memories;
And I'll take the love he's given
And I'll hold it as a treasure
I shall keep.
But my heart will miss the
sunshine
And my eyes will cry the tears.

Barbara Vowels
I THANK GOD!

I wake each morning with the
rising sun,
I stretch with its rays across the
land.
I breathe in the fragrance of
the Lord,
And thank God I'm in his hand!
I thank him for making America
my home,
And for the freedom that blows
so easily by!
I thank him for the right to
choose,
And the intelligence to ask
why!
I thank him for our country,
A land so big, mighty, and
strong!
I thank him for my fellow man,
Together with Him we can do
no wrong!
I'm proud to be an American,
I'm thankful to be free—
I'm glad to be alive
And I thank God I'm me!

LeVinna E. Jeffers
MOTHER AND HOME

In a rustic spot where the
boughs hand low
A by-road leads to a cot I know
Initials carved on a low, flat
stone

Lends a welcome touch, though
wild leaves blown.
A welcome smile and a laugh
so dear
Greets me now as I hurry near
Mother caresses in her loving
ways
Enfolds me close as in bygone
days
Her kiss on my forehead I feel
it now
As the grey streaked locks
caress her brow
A tear drop steals as she
whispers low
My darling child, I'm so glad
you know
All the joys of wealth, or
homes so grand
Or the crown of a King in a
foreign land
If to me they were given in
exchange for this
They'd all be but naught at
the feet of my bliss.

Richard A. Langone
RESURRECTION

With the final words thus being
spoken,
And a forced tear as a final
token.
We commend him unto You,
O Lord,
In the hope of the resurrection
and the life.
Or is it the darkness of night
That causes him to life,
As still as a fallen raindrop,
Released from a thunderous
sky.
Perfectionists cast upon seas
of imperfection,
Can not possibly believe in
a resurrection.
And so I'm left without a
drop.
of faith in God or bewildered
love.
FINIS

Diane R. Daddario
WISDOM

As the grooves and lines in
tree bark
Mirror it's life and stability
So, too, the lines on your
face
are proof of your seasoning—
The reward of age.

Mary Lynn Milne
THE PROBLEM

The day's too short,
The doctor's on call,
The sincere noted voice,
the hand on the wall,
the deep loving eyes,
the soft way to talk,
the short lasting time,

the style in the walk,
the interest in the problem,
the caring at the stage,
the gold coloured finger,
the difference in age.

Randall Johnson
THE HORSEMAN

They opened up the American
plains.
By riding fast, and gathering
fame.
Even taking on ole John Wayne.
But they have lived, cried, and
yet
they still have not died.
To the rodeo ground or an
English jumping meet.
You can always hear the sound
of their feet.
For it's the horseman who still
rides with pride.
He will always be outstanding.
Because he has nothing at all
to hide.
Man and animal bound together
Only thing between them is
the leather.
Through rain, hail, and maybe
even a dry spell.
They all one day will meet in
the big corral.

Edna Canaday Niday
PAGES OF MY DIARY

My dearest one—
As I read the pages of my diary
The tears begin to fall
Each page tells of our love
story
From the beginning— it tells it
all
Of your great love for me
Of your ambition to build
me an empire
Of all you thought I might
desire
When all I wanted was you
And I remember telling you so
many times
That it didn't matter if we had
nothing at all
But My Dearest One—
You Wouldn't let it be that
way
You kept working night
and day
And I remember you saying
to me, Honey,
Tomorrow my work will be
through
We'll take the vacation I
promised you
We'll go somewhere by the sea
Go everywhere you've wanted
to be
But My Dearest One—
Tomorrow for you didn't come
Your life ended with the work
you begun
Now all I have left is, warm
memories of your love,
My diary, and an empire so,
so cold
when all I wanted was you
And the tears fill my eyes
As I read the pages of my diary.

Eve M. Hampton
THE SPRING

Here in the midst
Of waste
And desolation
Stands tall
A mighty tree
With sure roots
Thrust deep

To life's sustaining flow
And teaches truth
To me
Oh Lord—
That we too
Must find
The way
To tap the spring
That feeds the soul.
Then, whatsoever
storms may come—
We too
Shall stand—
Beautiful—
And whole.

Janice E. Martz
APRIL

Another summer
not far away,
No more words
nothing to say;
A flower in bloom
but rain on the sill,
Expressing my heart
the way that I feel;
No more phone calls
at half-past three,
Just a lot of wrong numbers
that mean nothing to me;
No more "I love you's"
That were lies anyway,
No more heartaches,
you're going away.

Gloria Merritt
AGE IS OF FLESH

Oh child live
forever in me,
and let your innocence
always be free.
This flesh shall wrinkle
but not my soul.
And my heart shall not die
if love is heard.
For age is of flesh,
it wrinkles and dries.
But if I truely live
I'll have no chains to try.
And if these tears can reach
and will beseech
then I shall have shed
the water of youth
and cupping a sip
shall lift as freshly forever
as a newborn cry.

Kerry Ann Boss
THE DAYS THAT PASSED

Once in the days that have long
  since passed,
The sailors stood around the
  nearly fallen mast.
The rope hung,
The sails hung,
Ripped by the wind;
Once in the days that have
  long since passed.

Ethyl Street
FAITH

We've never really been apart
Our love has bridged the years;
For you were always in my
  heart
And shared my joy and tears.

Leta M. Stephens
SILHOUETTE OF GOLD

Like lace upon a lovely dress,
The leaves on a tree outside,
  my room
Caress,
My window pane.
A lilting breeze plays among
  the branches,
Pale gold from the moon

enhances
My mood of tranquillity.
The far away sound of a
  rooster's crow,
Has me yawning
I drift back into sleep,
Hours yet before the new day's
  dawning
I am so happy to be alive!

Pamela Hilliard
ME THE UNKNOWN

Nobody knows what is inside
  of me.
I cry, I weep into my deep
  thoughts
of a chosen few.
Although it may seem that all
  is fair,
I shall endure all
until the days change.

Oh yes, there are dreams,
the very special ones,
but they too will have to be
  ensconced.
For the future shall take it's
  place
all around me and deep within
  me,
only I really know what is
  inside me.

Inez T. Beeks
**LORD LET ME LEAVE A
SONG**

Lord let me leave
The world a song
So it may be enjoyed
Long after I am gone.

Let me leave a song
So the world may see
The golden gift
You gave to me.

Let it be so beautiful
They will want to sing
Let it be so loud
It will make heaven ring.

Let it bring such a message
They can't deny
That God is still King
Up there on high.

Let it help some soul
to find its way
To the home you've prepared
For homecoming day.

If one is lost
Can't find his way
May the song I leave
Teach him to pray.

Gladys J. Utter
JIM'S 4 WHEELER

Jim is a man that likes to
  tinker
On engines and things he's
  a great
  thinker.
An engine he needed, a Ford
  he found
A dodge is the frame off of

the ground
A Chev is the body, now this
  is real
mody.
So running he's got it and if
  you should spot it
A Chevy you See, a Ford
  you'd hear,
A Dodge is a rollin, a title is
  clear.
Hey! It Runs! in muck or snow
  it will go
Cause his "4-Wheeler" will run
  the whole show.

Beverly L. Couzens
LIFE

Life is full of twists and turns
Leading us on roads unknown.
Falling stumbling, over every
  stone,
Facing things which make our
  stomachs churn.
For better days we yearn
As we continue to bemoan
About things we do but
  don't condone.
Unbelievably we learn
That life deals us a fair hand.
One by one good things come
  our way
Even as we are undeserveing.
Life blesses us with harshness
  and kindness
Making us glad we decided to
  live it to the fullest
After all life really does give
  us what we seek.

Gigi M. Getz
ARTIFACTS

Symmetry, color schemes aimed
  to please
Vibrant hues made for you to
  see
Golden paints depicting saints
  in ease
Sculptured leaves in the breeze
  of marble trees.
Visions of color sing in refrain
In the songs of art.
Glorified images held by
  golden frames
In the worlds of art.
Contrasts, days of past made to
  last
Secrets of old, never told,
  are trespassed
Bright days turn astray when
  the grey is cast
A skill so vast, molding fast,
  never surpassed.

Wanda J. Marriner
**LOOKING AT JESUS ON
THE CROSS**

I hate to see Thy face so
  pinched—
I will try to look more often;
I know then, I will find it
  hard to sin—
And won't hurt Thee so often.

Debra Mae Schuler
**A CONFESSION TO MY
DAUGHTER**

This is a lesson I have learned
  today—
Which you had taught in a
  special way.
I took ten minutes and read
  you a story—
And your eyes just sparkled
  with glory.
I asked myself, "When was the
  last time?"
But I couldn't remember it in
  my mind.

I then, held and talked to you
  in a loving way—
Darling, I know I didn't do this
  yesterday.
Suddenly, you had tears in your
  eyes—
Your deprived affection had
  made you cry.
I looked at you, and I couldn't
  believe—
The dreadful truth which had
  hit me.
I've neglected you in many
  ways—
Of time, of laughter and of
  yesterday.
I've disciplined you when you
  were bad—
But seldom gave comfort when
  you were sad.
Forgive me darling, for my
  mistakes,
My love—and heart are yours
  to take.

Marie C. Gauthier
HOLD ON

Wishing you were here with
  me;
Loving you is what I need.
Why did we ever have to
  break away?
With you is where I always
  want to stay.

Tell me what it takes to gain
  your love again;
Cause it hurts so hard inside,
To watch you hide,
The love I know you still
  feel inside.

I'll hold on to remembering,
  for now,
Till tomorrow;
Cause with a new day,
Will come a new way,
For us to learn
How to love each other
In a different way.

Cynthia Pipkin
SHOWER

Grace is a shower, not a bath.
Baths rearrange dirt;
Showers chase it away.

Baths leave scum that sticks;
Showers make space for clean.

Baths yield lethargy;
Showers invite power.

Lord, shower me with Your
  Grace.

Sheryl Marie Gilham
**THE FORGOTTEN AND
UNSPOKEN CHILD**

Misty eyes so softly
Forgotten and unspoken
Silently as the snow is on the
  ground
She speaks without a sound
Just as a mute child cries
  without noise
Or just as a blind person sees
  without seeing
Or just as a deaf person hears
  without hearing
Endlessly wandering through
  this world
Like the trickling flow of a
  stream
Wandering alone through the
  world of silence
In search of something or
  someone
Yet her journey will never

end
For she lives in a world of
make-believe
She lives in a world all her own
Her footsteps are like that of
a butterfly
And are washed away by the
roaring tide of the sea
Tears of sadness fall like
rain to the ground
When the dreams she leaves
behind are lost and
forgotten
And a mist fills the air around
her
Yet a beautiful kind of
softness
As she noiselessly leaves
behind
She's the forgotten and
unspoken child.

Virginia R. Gonzales
NATURE'S BEAUTY

The mighty canyons and its
heights,
Different colors, different
lights.
Shining upon its depth, its
strength
So great, so mighty is its
length.
The beauty glitters like gold,
The mighty rocks unfold
Different shapes, just be
T'was an ocean or a sea.
The different echoes made
The myths where monsters
laid,
The roar of waters years past,
Performed a beauty to last
and last.

Heather Pigeon
FRIDAY NIGHTS ALONE

Another friday night just like
all the ones before
I sit home alone while other
girls have dates
While they wonder about what
to wear
I wonder how to fill the lonely
hours
The time they spend choosing
which boy to go out with
I spend praying that just one
boy will ask me out
And the time they spend
remembering the fun
They've had on all their dates
I spend alone, again, crying.

Ivy Kyles
THE WOOING OF MORPHEUS

When lying tense and wakeful
in your bed
Think not of dreamless sleep,
Instead,
Think deep on waking dreams
so dear
Each minute detail blissfully
clear.

And from your mind dismiss
the vagrant thought
That would distract your dream.
You will it not.
Each perfect part caresses
within your mind
And magically, perversely, you
will find
That Morpheus, outraged by
your disdain,
Will take you in his arms—
you'll sleep again.

Linda Heath Mohr
**A FUNERAL FROM THE
EYES OF AN EIGHT YEAR
OLD**

A white box
With a red, white and blue flag
A dark suit and a stone face
Peaceful but gone.

Illusions of breathing
in the eyes of an eight year old
life was still
there, somewhere.

Denial and confusion
A daddy without life.

Wreaths of flowers and strangers
A family reunion and tears
A blanket of tears.
Where are they coming from?
Where has he gone?

Casey Lynn Hatfield
TILL THE DAY I DIE

For another day passes by me,
My life unchanging, my dreams
unbearing.
But not a moment passes by
that will make me not love
you,
Till the day I die.

Mary Anne Waterhouse
VISION

Last night while I was sleeping,
A vision filled my mind.
I dreamt the end had come for
man
And I was left behind.
I saw our world through heaven's
eyes,
I saw it through my own.
I saw the waiting people,
So empty and alone.
I knew the end was coming;
I was searching for a sign.
My world was filled with
darkness,
It was the final time.
A trumpet blew,
it shook the earth.
My mind dwelled on
my life's true worth.
The world was dark,
then in the sky.
A flash of light,
the time was nigh.
The clouds rolled back,
and there he stood.
More than a man,
so pure, so good.
His eyes were soft, but
filled with pain.
He looked at me,
he called my name.
The world was still,
I shook my head.
Was this the man
who died and bled?
It can't be him,
a myth come true.
But he was here?

my life was through.
This man had come to save the
pure.
He smiled upon the world.
And to the blessed waiting,
He uttered but a word.
He beckoned and commanded,
'Come.'
Thousand climbed the sky.
Ascending to a perfectness,
I remained behind.
He gazed upon the sinners,
His eyes were filled with pain.
He shook his head, it was the
end;
My world became my grave.

Helen-Sue Davis
FRIENDSHIP

Sometimes the garden grows
Even when it didn't mean to
And it becomes more beautiful
Than it had meant to.

LaNita Moses
HOW CAN I

How can I say, I love you, when
the night
Too full for words holds silent
songs that hang
As crystal from a ceiling with
no light
And singing birds are still?
The songs they sang
No longer echo in the falling
leaves
For snow and chill have
covered deep the sound.
Blue wind whips branches,
twisting old oak trees,
Casting the final browning
leaves to ground.
How can I say it when the
drifting snow
And ice have frozen tiny feet
from flight
And children beg for bread and
never know
Where they will lay their tender
heads tonight?
I say it for the light and sun
and spring
And hungry, homeless children
who still sing.

Keith Halbrock
DEVIL'S QUEEN

From Witch's Mountain comes
the screams
which usher in the judgement
day.
For from the heart of its own
anger
comes mistress death, the
devil's queen,
to claim the souls of those
above.
She speaks of fun and no
desires
for all is found in hell's warm
fires.
"Now ruler of the darkest
night,
all souls are yours but one.
But, from the arms of yonder
cross,
His soul will drop with ease.
He is a king of kings of sorts—
a prophet of some distant
land;
Now, a sacrifice at your hand."
"Dear master of hell's cold
fire,
His body glows warm with life.
From Him, a grace does warm

the heart;
There's strength at His right
hand.
Human souls are saved by
Him,
for now my kiss is that of
love,
not death, but life with Him
above.

Ruth Gardenhire
AN INDIAN FAMILY

I am a little Indian girl,
My name is Silver Eyes
My mother knits the blankets
And my father's very wise

My mother cooks the victuals
And does the milking too
My sister rocks the cradle
While she helps to stir the
stew

My mother tends the garden
The men folks hunt and fish
We women do the housework
And have all the fun we wish.

Christine L. Regan
**LET THOMAS JEFFERSON
HAVE HIS FIREWORKS**

Let me blow second-hand stars
over your body,
A shimmering current
Reflecting the sparkle from
your skin,
Illuminating the tension
in your arched fingers.

Let me feel your warm breath
Imitating the silent whir
of Roman Candles.
Soaring rockets stay grounded
Confined to richochet
within a tight embrace.

Let me ignite the spectacle.
A subtle flame,
Erupting in an aureole,
of earth tone colors.

Let Thomas Jefferson have his
fireworks . . .
I'll keep mine.

La Follette W. Sanford
SUMMER LOVE

Summer Love, I miss the
radiance of you, so much
When you were so near, and
holding me tenderly
But, most of all darling, I miss
your touch
And, hearing you say that you
really love me.

And, only you darling, can
give me happiness
For, you are the heart of me
and I am not free
And, only you can free this
heart from loneliness,
When I am in your loving arms,
where I long to be

For, you are my thoughts,
my dreams, my everything
As, you are part of me, like
waves are to the sea
With your gentle love, I will
always be the same,
Wanting you my darling,
because you really love me.

And my love for you,
sweetheart, will never fade
away
Like the green leaves that fade
along clover land
For I need you darling, more
each passing day
Like the young bluebonnets
need the soft summer rain.

Jeanne Cyprus
LOOKING BACK

Over my shoulder there dwells
a dream.
The last bird calls at twilight.
Her song shatters the graying
stillness.
The last vibrant note resounds
to answer
The resonant melody that
dresses the air,
With the notes from Pan's pipe
So distant and so clear.
But only to those dwellers of
beauty,
The keepers at the gate of
nature's wisdom.
They have they key that turns
the lock
Of sun drenched smiles
And star tipped lances;
Adorning them with a vestige
of tears
And tattered angel wings
For they have pierced the
child within.

Linda Marie Fossessca
HOPE FOR OUR PEOPLE

Iran has captured our people.
The United States are confused
on what they should
do.
Human beings are being locked
away.
Lord, what are we coming to?
I wish there was some way for
me to get them out.
But my prayers are the best I
an do.
Only you can guide our minds,
Let us not have another war to
go through.
I have faith in you Lord, that
soon you will set them
free.
And let them live their normal
lives,
Back with their families.
I pray Iran will contemplate
Find some heart to let them
go.
This battle is not worth what
is happening to them,
Iran is hurting their human
souls.
Lay your hand upon the
Earth,
Hear your people's prayers.
For the Hostages in Iran, dear
Lord,
I feel them feeling scared.

Darrell Halloran
THE OAK TREE

A friend's affection and love is
likened to the
large oak tree.
It grows as a small seed
And nourished by sunshine and
rain
Abounds to a masterful
existence.
Branches reaching towards the
heavens
Housing bedfellows of many
species.
Protecting them through
stormy,
And allowing them to bask in
the sun
As its warmth pours through
each branch.
Life flourishes.
Always, the mighty oak is
there.

Grace Graham
TIMELESS

Time—
A Fleeting moment never to
return,
once gone becomes a
bittersweet memory.
Time is not tomorrow for the
future lies beyond
the reach.
Time is timeless, no beginning,
no end.

Jennifer Ransdell
IT'S TIME

If there weren't any clocks,
nothing to tell time of day
Just imagine how great it would
be, no tic-tocs to get in your
way
No appointments would you be
late for
No special hours to get things
done
No one would have to tell you
"This is the time to have fun."
Take the lion for example,
when he's hungry he eats
He doesn't need a watch to
say, "It's time to go to sleep"
Do you think there'd be any
reason
In some big or small pool
That a fish is ever marked
'Tardy'
Because it was late for school
No time-piece has to tell a
cow, "It's time to give your
milk"
A bever won't stop working
his dam, pausing for lunch
because it's twelve,
Have you ever seen a skinny
hippo
Or one getting thinner and
thinner
Probably not and probably
because
They're never late for dinner
Take trees, grass, and flowers,
don't you wonder how they
know
When it's their time to flourish,
spread roots, bloom and grow
Well, I hope this has made you
stop and think
And there's more I'd like to say
But I see it's gotten to be rather
late
It's time I should be on my way.

Myrtle E. Hunter
BOYS

Watch any little boy and his
feet just seem to fly,
There doesn't seem to be
anything a boy won't try.
He hops over fences, and climbs
up trees,
Comes home full of jaggers,
scratches, and cut knees.
He fills his pockets with all
sorts of things,
Such as stones, paper clips, and
bits of old string.
He drags home worms and frogs
and even snails,
He chases pussy-cats and pulls
puppy dog tails.
He chases little girls and makes
them scream,
He does it because he's a boy,
he's not really mean.
A black eye or two,
And a worn out toe of just one
shoe,

Buttons gone from the front
of his shirt,
His little face covered with so
much dirt.
A stuck zipper, or a torn
sleeve
He even forgets to say thank
you, excuse me, and please.
But these are the treasured
memories we bury deep,
These are the treasured
memories we'll forever keep,
For boys will be boys, you'll
find it very true
Whether he belongs to me or
whether he belongs to you.

J. Daniel Rooney Jr.
UNTIL FOREVERMORE

Walk along, a summers day,
A cloudless sky of blue,
The whispering wind calls soft
to me,
The name it sings is you.
And the meadow grass blows
free
As I begin to fade,
Into a dream that's lost
somehow,
In tender love we made.
You're more than I could ever
want,
You're more than I could ask
for,
I'll love you 'till we both grow
old,
Yes, until forevermore.
As the sun sinks slowly down
I kiss you and you smile,
You thought that love was
falling back,
It was with you all the while.
We sit upon the mountainside,
I count a billion stars,
I hold your hand so tight
in mine,
The universe is ours.
You're more than I could ever
want,
You're more than I could ever
ask for,
I'll love you till we both grow
old,
Yes, until forevermore.

Vicki R. Magee
OUR LITTLE GIRL

It finally came the day,
And to us was born a baby,
A baby bright and healthy,
A baby that was you,
And to us—Oh, so special!
You have grown so perfectly,
So smart and so strong.
You seem so sweet and so wise,
So innocent and so young,
And to us—A beautiful dream
come true!

Agnes M. Black
LIGHTS OF HOME

Little children romp and play
Mother watches o'er them all
the day.
Father tends the cows and
sheep
As the little ones toddle off to
sleep,
These are lights of home.
Mother sews and bakes and
cooks;
Reads to the children from
their story books.
Father plows to plant the
fertile seeds

And works to eradicate
the weeds,
These are lights of home.
Around the table the family
gathers
And asks the blessings of God
the Father
To keep them safe, one and
all
Through spring and summer,
winter and fall,
These are lights of home.

John O'Daly
BEAUTY

What is beautiful to you?
There is much beauty in the
world to me:
A square-rigger under sail
A running horse
The graceful carriage of a woman
woman of charm.
But the most beautiful of all,
to me, is the
- .

Eleanor Gravallese
SHARING WITHOUT
FEELING

We sit under a tree
As the leaves fall slowly,
The sky above us is a
Bright shade of blue.
I wonder, will it always
Be this way with you?
The sun is shining brighter
Than I have ever seen it.
Does this mean happiness
Will be with us forever?
The leaves fall fast
As if to say "Run"
But I won't, I
Don't want to be alone.
The sun still shines
Although not as brightly
As it once did.
The sky is a darker
Shade of blue today.
Our hands still locked
Together, but not the
Way they used to be.
We are a burden to each
other.
Our lives, like the
Leaves, crumble with
Every storm.

Dolleta Lemon Smith
MARRIAGE SONNET

Let marriage be not entered
least in haste
The heart's confession must
not displease God's law
To alternate love in
alterations place
The divine one Himself gave
love all
There are many who wonder
as a lark
Who knows not worth, or

264

times they've reached for
height
For love cannot be measured
in nights of dark
We say great experience teaches
one much light
Those who make themselves
a paradise are fools
Only God can make a marriage
for keeps
For the school of higher
learning has accurate rules
And the cup of happiness He
still can heap
If this be not of truth than I
have lied
Without God's rules love has
played and many hearts
have cried.

Emma Hildebrand
ART

Friendship
is an art,
Like a painting,
done in oils.
It must come
from the heart
So the beauty
never spoils.

Eileen McKnight
A GRADUATE'S THOUGHTS

My life has paused for a long
moment in time,
an end has come to an
elongated chapter in my
unpredictable existence.
The stage of my life which has
just been
completed
was one of sensitivity and
difficulty,
blissfullness and melancholy.
Growth and development have
nurtured me with
strength to go forward towards
the unfolding
of the next chapter.
I will be motivated thought,
to follow that horizon towards
the unfolding
of the next chapter.
I will be motivated thought,
to follow that horizon toward
my dreams,
learning from yesterday,
and studying today for a
brighter tomorrow.
I will fill every day with
knowledge and
success so I will be prepared,
for the next chapter of my life.

Virginia Ann Kulesa
WORDS OF THE HEART

A conversation, not spoken.
A poem, not written.
It's the look in your eyes that
gives it away.

The way that I feel,
When you hold me close . . .
Turns my emotions into
electric vapor.

Nothing need be said,
For these moments alone,
Are the silent words of the
heart.

Karen Foster Brooks
I WONDER IF

I wonder if
the true realists
along the way,
Aren't the ones

who sleep
with their teddybears of
allusion
and have sweet dreams
of never, neverland!
For is life not
one big red balloon
filled with the hot air
of deception,
Often burst
by the prick of pessimism,
But being quickly replaced
by the next yellow or orange
balloon
filled with just as much
hot air?

Anita J. Barber
AN EXPLANATION

Small and fragile
a fuzzy caterpillar
struggles to scale
a flat rock.
I could lift him
over the rock easily
but he
would not understand
so I watch him struggle.

Christine Sue Wilcox
THE SNOWFLAKE

Dancing in quiet gaiety,
She comes in soft whispers.
If touched, she fades
Like a dream almost held,
Leaving delicate memories
Of a life short-lived.

Henrietta M. Hardy
PRIVATE—GOD ONLY

Somewhere
is there somewhere
where life is simple
where wild horses run free
where the eagle screams and no
one knows
where the earth is not trampled
by man?
Is there someplace God can go
and rest away from the
problems we bring to Him?
I hope so.

Roger Kirpes
MY LIFE

My life is a torrent of rain water,
A muddy seething chaos
Raging down a ditch.
It cannot escape,
Only alternate from high crests
to low valleys
Between the frothy waves.
It's uncontrollable,
Imprisoned within the banks.
It can't escape, see the world,
Or detour for just a little
while.
I can't stop it, slow it down,
Only try to stay on top,
Ride out its rocky course
To its own predestined end.

G. Anthony Jones
THINGS I'VE BLOWN

I've blown . . .
Soap bubbles from a toy
apparatus, when I was a boy.
Weed rolled into fat joints,
when I was an adolescent.
Life from the bodies of human
beings, when I was a soldier.
Hours that stretched into days,
caused by idleness in various
ways,
when I was alone.
Nickels and dimes, good times,

even so called heavy minds,
when I
was a bullshitter.
A good woman's love, when I
was a fool.
My own self respect, just
knowing I was blowing, with
nor forethought
as to where I was going.

Diane Tomaino
UNTITLED

My heart is like a patchwork
quilt
Each time I meet someone new
that I love
another patch is added
Each time I lose someone I
love
a patch is taken away, leaving
a space
that can never be filled
by a new patch.
The quilt keeps me warm,
though sometimes
I feel a chill from the empty
spaces.

Sonia Hughes
I REMEMBER

The day you came into this
world,
Your hair was short and black
and curled,
On top of your head it shined
like coal.
The part that played your
Indian role.
But that was many years ago,
You have changed, since then
you know.
If the people only knew,
The love your father felt for
you.
Of course I was jealous once,
As you grew older in years in
months.
But that was many years ago,
I have changed since then
you know.
But very soon I'll have to go.
Because I'm older than you,
you know.
And if I say it once or twice,
Please remember this advice,
Stay a kid as long as you can,
For someday soon you'll be
the man.

Karen Ann Kay
DEATH IS THE FLOWER
THAT NEVER BLOOMED

Death is today, with no
tomorrow,
Death is pain, with a lot of
sorrow,
Death is as quiet as the night,
Death is giving up without a
fight,
Death is forever, always will
be,
Death is what will happen

to you and to me.
Death is good, but may be bad,
Death is sometimes, always
sad,
Death is life ending soon,
Death is the flower that
never bloomed.

Debra Kay Hettinger
PASSION

our bodies lying close
tenderly exploring, caressing
. . .the other
with our lips and our hands
rising the passion
until:
we finally make love
slowly and silently
then again :
we lay side by side
still touching, not speaking
for words are not needed
the look in our eyes
says all we are feeling.

Rosalie Glew
TO A DEAD SEAGULL

A cyclist leaves you dead upon
the sands,
Quivering like living things,
Your defiant, upswept wings
Reach for unscaled heights.
Does a spirit wait for night
Within your encompassing
form,
Eager to burst forth and take
flight
Up, up beyond the moon,
Among the galaxies,
And with joyous cries,
Greet some wandering star?

Kim Richter
RAINBOWS AND SUNSHINE

The rain is falling
Like tears rolling down the
cheeks of my soul
And dripping into the cracks
of my broken heart.
All is dark and gloomy.
And life doesn't seem worth
living.

But alas . . .there you are.
Breaking thru the darkness
Like the sun after the rainfall.
Bringing brightness into my
dark world.
And painting rainbows
Over the dark clouds inside
me.

Lisa Rado
IMAGES

Images,
Daydreams on a cloud,
Flying slowly through the
heavens,
Spinning round and round.

A young doe,
Sips on pools of sparkling blue,
The Image ripples gently,
Then clears its face anew.

Soft clouds,
Hide the moon from all the
night,
The picture fade in darkness,
But never leave my mind.

A rainbow,
Arches through the morning
rain,
The colors quaver silently
Until they're gone again.

Images,
Like sea foam in the spray,
Whenever you try to grasp

them,
They'll slip away . . .

John Lewis
I LOVE MY IDENTITY

I can't get this person filled
with Love out of my life,
And I don't want to,
She is as much a part of me as
I am a part of her,
In fact her body grew mine and
gave me life,
With my life she also gave me
part of her soul so I may
have an identity and not be just
a piece of flesh,
So now I have an identity, and
also an identity to identify
with
I don't understand but wow . . .
this sure is neat
My identity plays with me . . .
makes funny faces at me . . .
while
tickling me, and I just can't
help but laugh,
Boy she sure is neat
And I sure do cry alot and I
never know the reason why, I
just do thats all
And when I cry my Identity is
soon looking down at me . . .
warmth and all
She is a comfort to my sore
eyes
And she always knows why I
cry, cause not long after,
I no longer
feel like crying
And then she holds me in her
arms oh, so-o-o . . .close, and
oh . . .-h-h . . .m-m-m. . .
m-m-m-. . .THIS! IS WARM . .
Pleas-s-s-se Identity never let
me go, you feel so good . . .
Lets stay like this forever,
this reminds me of even
closer times, you know what
I mean.
And she understands . . .I
don't know how, she just
does
thats all . . .
I love my identity.

Jane Claire Sullivan
LOVE

Love is forever growing and
maturing,
Love is forever giving and
reassuring,
Love is forever there for you—
if you choose the right person
to give it to
Love is forever changing,
Love is forever rearranging—
our lives.

Ellen J. Carey
ME

My mind dwells in a castle,
upon the highest hill;
the door is locked to strangers,

and the windows closed to
chill.
The towering walls a fortress;
as strong as is my soul;
to keep inside my only pride,
a treasure mine alone.
Though some may seek to
enter,
with half-hearted tries;
they can't break through
my fortress,
with human sham or lies.
To enter in my castle,
one must have the key;
some know where to find it,
but few will look to see.

Carolyn Ann Furlow
LOT'S WIFE

Rocks tumbling;
Roads split in half,
Trees pulled from their roots;
digging holes in the ground as
they fall.
Sounds of thunder vibrate in
the clouds, changing their
forms.
Buildings collapse on
deserted streets.
Panic moves ahead.
Running feet
SUDDENLY STOP!

Sharon A. Fragel
ON DISPLAY

As the train crawled past the
bleak yard,
I watched the reddish glow, of
embers'
light and crackling bark, diffuse
above
their brow.
The pair sat propped, on rusted
crates,
with prodding sticks and
pivoting wrists
while stirring the blend of rancid
paste
that began as stew, a few days
past.
The tramps roved by, their
potted feast,
as riders gazed from their seats,
through window's panes of
opaque glass
to watch the bums as people do
at uncaged animals in a zoo.
But, across my face a grin did
spread,
as I marvelled at the
independence
possessed by nomads in a pair,
above concern
for tattered wear.
As the sun sank low, the train
sped past, and
metal wheels clanked and
clashed, in a structure
of metal and glass, encaged,
perhaps I amongst others
were on display.

Mary Boyd Chabet
CANDLELIGHT DINNER

Dinner is ready.
The baby cries.
He blows out the candles.
The both arise.
She says: "I'll feed him.
It won't take too long."
He says: "Why now?
What could be wrong?"
She takes care of baby,
Her husband denied . . .

Then she smiles sweetly;
The child satisfied . . .
"Now take him, dear husband,
and hold him awhile.
I'll heat up the dinner . . .
Look at him smile.
The babe is contented,
He will welcome his bed.
We've held him and loved
him
and his tummy is fed.
Lay him down, husband . . .
Tuck in his cover. . .
Dinner awaits us . . .
My sweet, noble lover . . ."

Josephine B. Ewton
BULLET

I've heard that dogs don't
have a soul
But how could that be?
When there is such a dog as
Bullet
He's almost human, don't you
see?
When I feel depressed
And my friends are not in
sight
I just talk awhile to Bullet
And things begin to look bright.
He is kinder than any person
And would never hurt anyone
If we scold him, he is so
forgiving
He is almost like a son.
He would love to run the hills
of glory
And play with the children
there
He would never hurt any of
them Lord
So, they could be in his
watchful care.
If I'm lucky enough to get to
Heaven
And I sure hope I do
I want to see the gate swing
open
And my Bullet coming through.

Douglas Taylor
DECEMBER 31, 1978

Look T'ward doors, alone
or in rows
Doors appear coloured walnut
or rose
Heavy shoulders may open some
While others extend magic
openings allowing us in.
However the approach to your
door with a key
Understand this thought—Where
Can I Be—?
Behind the KEY in front of
most
You unlock the door
Forcing wire into a hole
gives unpleasantness
Imbalance, Woe!
Catch a Beam, Slide some
Wonder, Brightness Appears
Slow
Ajar some DOORS are left
behind, SHALL WE PEEK?
Caught UNAWARE some
one's meet arrears, splashing
amongst dung
Tune—in people acknowledge
these words, LEARN DO NOT
FREAK!
Handle a knob with twist or
turn, when magic slips
through your fingers.

Ruth Wheeler-Peak
GO, TELL!

The fields are white and ready—
Will you go?
With a spirit strong and steady—
Will you go?
There's an urgent task to do
And the Master calls for you.
Will you prove your love is true?
Will you go?
Many know not of the Savior—
Will you tell?
Know not of his loving favor—
Will you tell?
Will you leave them in their
plight
When they're lost out in the
night?
In your heart is gospel light—
Will you tell?

Mrs. Richardine Holmes
MOTHER AND ME

My Mother and me; We're two
of a kind,
yet she's in her world and I'm
in mine.
Her world is so sunny and free,
doesn't
matter what part she's in, there's
always
time for me.
When I've a problem, an
understanding ear
she gives, for she's experienced
the world
among the people we live.
She never sides with me along,
but lets
me know where I went wrong.
She knows the mistakes I'll
make, but as
they happen it's easy to take;
for she's always somewhere
near, with
a lending hand and a listening
ear.
She's always doing things out
of her way;
things I see as hard, but to
her, just play.
A smile on her face she's
always carrying,
so you never see the load she's
bearing.
As the days roll into months,
and the months
into years, she's always the
same person who
smiles—despite tears.
You may not see it, but we
are two of a kind.
For as I grow older, her world
will become mine.

Judy C. Griffin
NIGHT DREAD

Oft when I am tired and worn
My thoughts return to early
morn.
When first I rose my heart
was bright
Why then dost fade with coming
night?
Why when I am courting sleep
Do ghosts and shadows round
me creep?
Why with fading of the sun
Must I think of deeds undone?
Of loved ones lost and dreams
long dead?
Peace! Will thou not share my
bed?
For others darkness hides

away
The cares and worries of the day.
Why for me must night be long?
Why dread I the nightbird's
song?
Night and Day why not make
peace?
The joy of life thereby increase.
My suffering heart the night
must scorn
And I must wait for early morn,
To bid the ghosts of night
depart
And ease the pain within my
heart.

June Brasted
THE BAY

I walked along the bay,
On a very sunny day.
I thought that I would sway,
On that very sunny day.

I saw the seagulls fly
Against the big blue sky.
I wish that I could fly,
Up in the big blue sky.

I saw the boats go sailing,
I wish that I could too.
I wish that I could go with you,
Sailing, sailing, sailing.

Emajean R, Harrell
FLOWERS MIRRORS LIFE

I saw a flower in the sun—
I said to this flower—from
where do you come?
A seed, said she—so tiny and
small
So little that no one sees me
when I fall—
I lay buried for awhile,
Until the time comes for me
to shine—
And then I blossom oh so
sweet,
A wonder to your eyes I
meet.
I said, I see that you pedals
are fallin'—
Oh, yes, she said, for I have
a callin'—
For when my pedals are
all laid down,
I plant my seed on another's
ground.

Barbara Robertson Seibert
THANK YOU ,DADDY . . .

For bringing me ice cream on
hot summer nights,
For small simple things like
flying a kite.
For giving me boatrides, for
baiting my hook,
For holding me higher to get
a good look.
All the summer vacations, the
sights we would seek
From Niagara Falls to scarey
Pikes Peak.
For standing behind me, a pat
on the back,
Or when I was naughty and got
a good whack.
For holding me tight, for
calming my fears,
For holding my hand, for drying
my tears.
For playing silly games with me,
most times you'd let me win.
For making me feel special
with your special wink or
grin.
I've always known you'd be
there if the need should
ever arise.

Thank you for your strong
support through all my
lows and highs.
Though I may not often tell
you just how much I really
care,
Or say how dear you are to me,
you know the feeling's there.
Daddy, you're so special for
all the things you do,
Of all the Dads in this whole
world, I'm so glad I've got
you!

Ms. Marilyn O. Lunn
AUTUMN LEAVES

When I came home from work
one night
Fatigued, frustrated and too
uptight
I picked up my pen to begin
to write.
"What shall I write about" I
said,
Feeling disheartened and at
low ebb.
Stop feeling melancholy and
lift thy head.
Gazing out the window, my
heart began to pound,
The beauty I beheld was
visible all around,
I watched the Autumn leaves
descending to the ground.
Red, gold, green and bronze,
Oh! what a glorious sight to
see.
Resembling a magnificent mural
of Italian tapestry
And in that moment I found
peace and serenity.

Beth VanBuskirk
SEA OF STARS

There I am
Walking on the beach
Listening to the repeated
echoes of stars
Beating up against the shores
of space.
Then I jump in and start
swimming
Faster and faster until I reach
the speed of light
And beautifully colored light
seems to surround me.
So I swim even faster until I
meet with the speed of
sound
And wonderful music
surrounds also,
I seem to absorb them both.
Then, as suddenly as I had
started, I stopped!
And found myself sinking
deeper and deeper into
the sea of stars
NEVER TO BE FOUND . . .

Linus Dickson
**YOU AIN'T JUS' WHISTLIN'
DIXIE**

when you say you love me
cause you're always
thinkin' of me
you ain't jus' whistlin'
dixie baby
cause I do the same thing
too!
at school
I daydream
of wanting to be with you
I love you girl
oh what a feeling this be
you sharing your love

with me
buttercup
you're so sweet
and your lovin' me is such
a treat
you ain't jus' whistlin'
dixie
cause I feel that
same way too!

Anthony H. Williams
WE ALL LOOK

I won't preach to you,
But you must do me the same.
We probably have the same
ideas,
But conceive them with
different names.
Not that mine are better than
yours,
But simply different levels,
You look for things,
I look for ideas.
You look for people,
I look for solitude.
You look to see,
I look to do.
You look at the surface,
I try to look through.

Alicie A. Chiccini
MANY MILES

We talk of many things,
And smile and laugh.
We walk many miles,
Explore and discover—
together.
Yet you are distant,
And I am still alone.
A touch, a kiss—
First steps on merging paths.
So simple. Yet the road
Remains forever lost.
As always, the wall behind
your eyes.

Rosa P. James
A SUMMER'S EVE VIEW

As I sit here and look around
The wonders of God I have
found,
The wind blowing through
the trees,
The rustling of the beautiful
green leaves,
The airplane in flight against
the sky,
The big, black birds go flying
by.
The buds sprouting, flowers in
bloom,
Nowhere in sight, a thing of
gloom.
Green grass spreading all over
the ground,
creeping, crawling insects all
around.
The farmer's crops growing in
the fields,
Gardens in bloom, vegetables
to yield.

Animals scampering, Children
playing too,
All within, one summer eve's
view.
The greatness of God to behold,
To marvel, to wonder about,
to be told.

Linda D. Shaver
THE SONGWRITER

I was listening to the words of
a new love song,
And wondered if the writer
knew all along;
That I would meet you and
feel that way.
It's funny how he knew just
what to say.

He sure did put those words
down right,
About how good it feels when
you hold me tight.
How through stormy weather,
the sun still shines,
You know, that man stole all
my lines!

I thought it was only me and
you,
But he must know how love
feels, too.
Because he pulled those words
right from my heart,
About how I couldn't live if
we ever part.

You know, I'd really like to
meet that man.
To go and thank him and shake
his hand.
For writing a song expressing
how I feel,
How there never could be a
love more real.

Mary C. Gineman
SEARCHING

As I sit here,
watching the sun set,
awaiting the moon
to make its full appearance
into the sky,
I listen to the quiet sounds
of the night,
and as the sky gets darker
I feel more loneliness—
the empty feeling inside me
has again taken over
my being.
I want to reach out
but there is no one there.
I feel the need to speak
so many words
but there is silence.
And so I sit
staring into the quiet night
awaiting the sun to rise
again
in hopes that tomorrow
will bring
what I have searched for so long.

Tame Jones
PROMISES OF LIFE

Crying out to me,
Songs in the darkness;
At the switch of a light
Scattering far.
Not crying to be seen?
Then why cry out to me?

My blindness, nurtured fear
from
the start,
Dissipates rapidly as I leave
The sun far behind.

I have finally realized
What those songs
were meant to be,

A stock of hidden paper faces,
Their notes were all the same,
Just lodged in different
  spaces
Now scattered, one by one.

Marti Sheff
MIDDLE GROUNDS

In the sunlight softly glowing
upon the savage sea,
The nature of the Universe
  is there revealed to me.

The synthesis of love and hate,
of peace and great unrest,
The middle grounds produced
  by these are Nature at its
  best.

Perfection is an artist's dream,
a vision far from view,
Toast high to Mediocrity;
  toast high to me and you.

Marlena K. Jordan
CHESTER

Randy has a kitty cat,
Chester is his name.
Since he came to our house,
Nothing is the same.

Chester likes to play outside,
And climb the trees so tall.
But he is such a dummy,
Some day, he's going to fall.

He also likes to eat strange
  things,
Like pizza, nuts, and cheese.
When it comes to feeding
  Chester,
He's not very hard to please.

He's really quite a kitty cat,
He likes to jump and play.
In fact, he might grow up and be
A T.V. star some day.

Sometimes I really wonder,
It causes me to fuss.
Did we adopt that Chester?
Or has he adopted us?

David C. Geary
TO DREAM

Life and time
and words that don't rhyme
and the life and the dream
so it must seem
fade with the night
with the pains and the joys
and the dark and the light
and when its all gone bye
I lay with myself
and I wonder why;
why did I
dream in the night
that some day I might
be what I'm not
if only to dream once again
of life and of men
all men must dream
and to them it must seem
of something they're not
and to this I deem
men are all that they dream.

Anita Owen Fenstermacher
MIRACULUM

O God!
Let there be a miracle
Of love
In this desert place.

Gradually,
A flower buds
In the vastness of desert space.

I stand in awe
Amazed,
That such an act can be
And probe

With questions and thoughts
  profound—
With "minds-eye" try to see
How a flower blooms
In the lifeless sand
In the desert
Alone with me.

My soul cries out
In the presence
Of beauty, so haunting and rare.
Logic again reigns supreme
And questions,
"Is it really there?"

The Spirit
Moves in the midst
  of the sand,
    the flower,
      and me,
And whispers,
"Behold the joy and the love
  and let the questions be!"

Frieda Cartwright
CHOICES

If I could choose the way I die
If I could plan to way it would
  be
It would not be in a hospital
  bed
With nurses and doctors
  hovering over me

Neither would I be
In my own familiar room
Amid sobs of relatives
And gathering gloom

I would go instead
To some lovely hill
Where the wind blows free
And the hurrying world stands
  still

I would watch white clouds
Float in a blue sky
Reach to touch one
As it passes by
And smile serenely
As I whisper "goodbye"
If I could choose.

Mildred H. Mallette
PEACE!

Peace! Peace!
A word we utter.
A yearning for in critical times,
Peace! Peace!
Will it ever be achieved?
It is a wish, a hope.
Peace! Peace!
Will it always be just a word?
Peace! Man's hunger.
Say it. Sing it. Act it.
Peace! Peace!

Mona M. Thompson
FOR TARA

Oh my lovely one,
the July sun longed to cast
  your shadow upon the
  ground and
give you birthday sunbeams to
  dance lightly through your
  hair.
The September rain fell quietly
  and softly called your name,
  then traced an elegy upon
  the windowpane.
The last summer breeze grew
  cold, weary from searching,
  and with low moans began
  a season of mourning.
October held her usual glorious
  parade of colors, but you were
  not there, and autumn will
  never be the same.
December snow upon the
  ground and for the first time
  your

footprints could not be found.
Then January came, and
  on a dreary winter day I
  noticed the banks along the
  railroad track strewn with
  tiny blue wild flowers.
Did God send you, my lovely
  one, to walk in early morning
  dew and coax them into
  bloom?

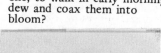

Betty Lee Wilson Woods
IT BETTER BE ME

It's too soon to change that
  look on your
face, something about our love
  letting me know
it's getting out of place.
  I hear voices at night that
  don't make no
sense, trying their best to get
  me convinced,
I said hush, voices, go leave me
  alone, my man will
straighten things out when he
  gets home. I ain't
complaining, our love ain't cold
  cold, it's like a
shadow that follows me
  wherever I go.
  He knows when I cuddle up
  to him so peaceful
and sweet, It's like what the
  sun does to the honey bee.
And if my man is unpleasing
  you see, I don't hesitate
to tell him It Better Be Me.

Lorna Lineker Holmes
OUR SEASONS

The beauty of the sunlight,
The sound of falling rain,
The joy of being human,
As seasons pass again.

The pumpkins in the pasture,
The meadow turns to gold,
The frost is early morning,
As the harvest fields unfold.

The fragrance of the burning
  fields,
As farmers do their chores,
Preparing for that festive time,
When love from hearts does
  pour.

We are happy for the winter,
For summer's stifling heat,
For spring and all its freshness
Fall's harvest of the wheat.

If I had my choice of seasons,
If I asked, "Which one is
  yours"
I'm sure we all appreciate,
Our seasons come in FOURS.

David Gertlar
HIS SOLDIER

A gentle man was he who
  fought so much
until the day his fight to the
  Prince was led,
and by the Spirit's Sword his

heart was touched,
was run through the ear by
  a Love Song, dead.
In Blood his clothes of life
  were washed all white,
new clothes for him dead
  serv'nt of He who loves.
This saint now has the Sword
  of Life, His might,
his so loved friends are 'mazed
  at how He moves.
This man who died to live,
  who gave his life,
to him the fight plan now is
  Spirit taught:
to end as his was done the
  world's strife,
to reap the harv'st so ripe
  his utmost thought.
The spirit will lead him in his
  fight for love,
from Him it has descended with
  a dove.

Robert Todd
A MOMENT

The hope now is renewed, the
  joy once again begun,
On the day of a birth,
On the moment of the Christ.
Each sound of Christmas bells,
Each renewing sound sings
  gloria,
Sounding the birth of a King
Gloria, gloria, gloria!

Sally Kavash
GUARDIAN ANGEL

Though I may go
Through this shadowed world
A scar upon my back
A softened voice
Sings to be heard
Songs of love
When the shadows turn black.

Though the day be cold
And a misty gray
My heart lures the sun through
  the clouds
And your presence I feel
Even if it's not real
The dream brings a smile to
  my face.

Rosalie Gardiner
**CONVERSATION WITH A
BLUE CORNFLOWER**

Beautiful blue cornflower
  there you are, defying every
  obstacle;
A testimony to survival—to
  overcoming!
In spite of gaseous fumes from
  passing traffic; in spite of
  your bed of hard,
arid soil begging to be quenched,
  in spite of the tramping feet
  and the hobo dog,
you stand by the roadside,
  straight and tall, to lift the
  spirit of man
and gladden the heart. For
  who could help, upon seeing
  you, but smile and be
  cheered.

Your color blue is like unto
  the heavens. What color
  are Christ's eyes?
Do we know? I picture them
  brown but could they be
  blue, like you?
Eyes that lifted the spirit of
  man and gladdened the
  heart. That gave and
still give hope.

I pass by a week later and you

are gone. The mower has
been here. My heart is
saddened—but wait!
Some have lain down before
the mower and have risen up
again.
Is that your secret? Is that
your message?
Something in my memory is
stirred. Words fall together—
"Lo, I am with you always."
Are you the reminder of the
Promise?

Ann L. Korosac
OCTOBER RAIN

October rain brings an early
dusk
With falling, wet leaves
Of red, brown and rust;
Brings a feeling of being alone
On a winding road
that will never lead home;
but on toward a stepping-stone
straight into a dark unknown
where all love turns to dust.

October rain brings
an early frost,
with a hint of winter
soon to be crossed;
brings back a smiling, beautiful
face;
red, satin heels;
swirling, black lace;
the smell of peppermint;
old ivy vines;
The warm glow of rich, red,
sparkling wines
Poured with care,
behind closed blinds
for a love so long ago lost.

Donnie Bradley
FEELINGS

If feelings of love only had
sound,
You would hear me coming for
miles around.
Coming to you with arms open
wide,
Waiting to hold you and lie by
your side.
Waiting for the day you will be
all mine,
knowing we'll be together until
the end of time.
My feelings of love are sounds
so true,
They say, I love you, I love
you, I love you, I do.

Ronald A. Pontius
THE LAST TIME

Across the stream of happenings
Of things we used to do
There comes a time, a last time,
At times we never knew.
Of course there are the last times
We know will be the last.
At times we see it clearly
And the shadow it will cast.
The every common day's events
That build the weeks away
The last times of the months
and years
That were our years and days.

Mrs. Lorraine Hamot Noriega
THE SEASONS

I wrote a poem about April.
I wrote a poem about Fall.
I really wanted to feel happy.
I decided to write about
the most wonderful season of
all.

The Christmas Season
A happy and wonderful time
for all.
When I think of Christmas;
so many things pop into my
mind.
Decorations on the house and
windows,
putting up the Christmas Tree.
Santa Claus, Snow, Exchanging
Gifts, Visiting Family and
Friends.
There is another side of the
Christmas season.
Go into any church,
and you will see hundreds of
people.
They are there for one reason,
to give all their love to a
New Born King.
The Christmas Season is a time
for love and good cheer,
peace and harmony for all.
Not just for now, but to get
ready for the new year.

Kathleen O. Schoeck
THE HOUSE ON THE POINT

With a hundred shadowed eyes
She stares at the eternal sea,
Pondering her aging soul,
The bleakness of her destiny.

Set upon the highest eaves
A thousand gulls cry raucously,
Songs that permeate the air
Like mythic siren's melody.

Round her ancient foothold
sweep
Redundant waves, concentric
rings,
Unrelenting enemies
Beseige her with their briney
sting.

Ravaged by insurgent storms,
She groans beneath the
awesome weight,
Symphony of wind and sea
With fortes that will not abate.

Hollow vessel once replete
With life and laughter in her
halls,
Echoes with old memories
Borne on the breeze as darkness
falls.

David L. Lindemann
**A CALL FOR FREEDOM—
SELDOM UTTERED TRUTH**

Truth, a word seldom uttered.
Though abused as it maybe
stands forever
never having to prove itself.
But often misused, and by
passed to another route.
Truth be my friend, that I
maybe found.
For I seek you, but you seem
not to have to be sought.
In thee I find freedom, and
hope, that I am not wasting—
But I seem to continue to
destroy myself.
Or at lease I won't think that I
do.
For deception and conception
are too easily attained.
Truth I hear your symbols, and
what you stand for.
Pool of living water waiting to
be swam in.
Depth, and coolness, your
traits.
Put in with the right measure,
waiting to be; to be had.
Your equilibrium just so

balanced, by unseen scales.
Each rhythm, to a steady,
unrealized beat.
Truth, do not delay, in what
you are to do
But make me your humble
slave,
That I might arrive.

Beverly W. Harris
A YOUNGER FRIEND

A younger friend is dear to me
Because you bring me gaity;
You lighten e'en a dreary day
Just being there across the way.
I'm glad we've met here in
this place
'Cause friends are needed in the
race
Of time in every single life
Which may be torn by harried
strife:
I hope you'll always think of
me
With "older"—not "senility".

Julie Brubaker
LIFE'S TIMING

The earth at my feet,
I look up at the sky,
Wondering, just wondering
About life passing by.
Seeing the days and nights
Before me as they go,
Telling of what wonderful things
That life has to offer.
So older as I get,
The more I shall learn,
Life is not a threat,
Be glad you are born.

Lorna Lineker Holmes
DAD'S CHAIR

The creaking of Dad's rocking
chair,
When i was but a tot,
You think it's long forgotten
You are wrong for it is not.
It was those warm and happy
times,
That I remember best;
I loved to rock and rock-a-bye
I must have been a pest.
Mom never seemed to tire,
as she cradled me with love;
The lullaby came softly,
She was gentle as the dove.
I could feel Dad's eyes upon
us,
In all his mannish pride,
He is still the rock of ages,
Where I could safely hide.
The years have seemed to melt
away,
Time to give up Dad's old
chair;
I still have days when I slip
back,
And wish that I were there.
We never forget those growing
times,
When love and warmth abound;
I still wish that I could hear,
That lovely treasured sound—
Creak creak.

David L. Farrell
SHARE WITH ME

Share with me the tears you shed,
share with me the night ahead,
let me feel the thought you
made,
ours alone as we lay in the
shade. . .

Share with me the moments
when you're sad,
share with me the times when
I am glad,
let me feel you at the end of
the day,
ours alone as we lay. . .
Share with me the gift of a
child,
share with me a home in the
wild,
share with me the growth of
the years,
at last; let me share the
meaning of your tears. . .
"Share with me". . .

David L. Farrell
THE CHAMP

With a blow like thunder the
champ throws his punch,
he eyes his target striking a
passioned hunch. . .
Freedom is yielded as he fights
for the ribbon,
cautiously praying that his
emotions remain hidden. . .
Winning seems never to take
second place,
for the champ must have
courage written on his face. . .
Dancing in the lighted
square, ever so alert, to
rest is a dare,
his life, to his foe, showing
not a care;
the champ wins but deeply
pays the fare. . .

Charlene Haider
TODAY

Our first small child,
To cuddle and to hold,
Filled up our hearts,
And drew out the cold.
We loved her so,
With all our might,
Our love poured out,
At her very sight.
One day she left us,
She had to go away,
She was being called,
Today was the day.
We never gave up,
Though it caused us grief,
And we shall always have the
memories,
Of her life so very brief.

Sara Fechter
THE OCEAN

As your tender voice
Calls out to me,
I feel your presence.
The thought of your touch
arouses me.
Then I see you.
A warmth starts caressing
my troubled mind.
I touch you.
The softness awakens
my tired soul.
As your stillness
passes through my body,
the fulfillment I dream of
is here.

B. Carrell
BITTER TEARS

A hate filled spirit
lies within the bitter woman's
breast
She spun the years so duty filled
to each she gave her best

"not one among you will succeed
till from this world I part
Through love nor deeds nor
riches filled
no man shall touch my heart."

The years crept by as she sat
high
upon her stately throne
Casting hard her die on man
but still she sat alone.

"I need no man to pave my way
I'll make it on my own
I too can walk within your shoes
be master of my home."

For years a tongue of bile lashed
out
"I don't need you now or ever!"
Now old and gray through lonely
tears
she views her short forever.

The lonely years crept slowly by
upon her stately throne
Recalling things that might have
been,
but still,
she sat,
alone.

Esther Shelly
JEALOUSY WITHOUT A CAUSE WEIGHS

I walked into the church one
day, with heaven
on my mind.
I had decided to be more
faithful, and for Christ
to really shine.
Love didn't greet me, as I
walked into the door.
Though I really needed
encouragement I felt trampled
on the floor.
I really love the Lord, and want
to please Him for a fact.
Do you know as I was sitting
there, pain hit
me, as if I had been stabbed in
the back.
Taken into consideration, the
treatment I had
received, all those evil spirits
I am sure the Holyspirit
was grieved.
Be watchful for the devil.
For you he will arouse,
For in Christ there is no place,
for jealousy
without cause.

Joseph E. Lewis
DAWN

The morning sun burns the mist
from the rocky shore
And throws a perfect rainbow
on my cabin door.
The flowers along the pathway,
with dewdrops so bright,
Nod happily in the breeze
that sweeps away the night.

Theresa Fulton
AN OPEN WINDOW

Whenever God closes a door,
He opens a window.
And if by chance we have a
virtue
called patience, and another
called hope,
And a little faith that there
really is
rhyme and reason;
We'll soon feel a breeze—
Cool, fresh, invigorating
This breeze—
if we let it,
will lead us through that open

window;
Where we'll find a fresh,
unmolded world.
A world just waiting for us
as sculptors
To mold it to our will.

Elizabeth A. Beittel
COMING TO A CONCLUSION

Solitude,
a whisper of privacy
so I might sit and think
on the things I have done.
Seclusion,
loneliness of the mind,
giving one's emotions
time to mature.
The answer only lies within
like a situation comedy
building on a constant basis
week to week,
sketch to sketch,
until you are the reality of your
goals,
laughing at the waste of time.

Nevelyn L. Harris
REFLECTION ON A SOUTHERN RENDEZVOUS

Sometimes
yu
cornbread n buttermilk
in the shade, honey. . .
(pass me a spoon now,
hear?)
Chile,
yu
light upon my thoughts like
bumble bees on honeysuckle
vines.
Hey
gimme another wink
from those coffee brown eyes
And
I
just loves it when yu whisper
sweet nuthins in my ear—
O baby!
yu
sweetness n light, red beans and
rice
on watermelon nights
(Pass me a spoon now,
hear?)

Mary A. Von Bargen
THE PERFECT GIFT

I got a gift from God today,
I know it was from He.
His children's needs and wants
He knows,
so individually.
No other knew my heart's desire.
I did not make it known.
I only prayed it to the Lord
'Twas for his ear alone.
The mortals who know me the
best
could not have chosen it.
They could not see the inner me
to measure what would fit.
But, oh my loving Father
no details can elude.
For this sole mind was His
design
in Him alone renewed.
That's how I know it came fro
heaven,
where nothing is too hard.
Just as with every gift He's
given,
Perfection signed the card.

Marie Dodge
A WEDDING WISH

They knew each other from
years gone past
but never did they plan;
That they would share things
together
and walk life's way hand in hand.

Now as they share their years
ahead
as one as man and wife
May all the joys and pleasure be
theirs through all their life.

What Jehovah has yoked
together
let no man put apart
Let all the love they share
be always in their hearts.

And as the years stretch out
ahead
for this life and the one to come,
May their marriage ties get
stronger
and they both live as one.

This world and all within it
God created it for men.
But the marriage arrangement
was his gift
since time and life began.

Brooke B. Hancock
IF I WERE TO TELL YOU NO

If I were to tell you no
would you do it anyway
If I were to tell you yes
would you not
Because I am an individual
you must be one too
You are now yourself
apart from me
We live together in name
though our thoughts are
separate
Once we were lovers
now we are not even friends
When will we realize what lovin'
is for?

Larry LaPachet
MOUNTAIN MAN

Mountain man of fur and trades
Hair and beard white like the
snow
Evergreen the color of his eyes
Staying in the green country of
snow and ice
Living in a cabin of wood and
stone
Alone with the mother of
nature
With all the wonders she has to
give
Sun blues falling from the sky
above.
Just writing songs without music
Painting down thoughts from
inside
Getting by on a pair of broken
down snowshoes
Traveling down the slopes of
hope.
Thinking of Louise a surveyor
of her land
Her face always shining like
the starlight
Hair and skin as soft as flowing
water
Watching her dreams moving
down the streams.
Mushrooms of clouds gathering
in the sky
Got a place with fireplace made
of stone
To keep you warm from the

storm on the way
Will it come or will it go away.
Just to have you by my side
sometime
Two in one or one in two in
your heart
Heaven crying rain on many
lonely roads
Remember the way the
snowflakes fall.

Lynn Swasey
THE END

The people are all running,
from what they have started.
Clans of destruction now
devastate the race.
What have we done cried the
young ones?
The answer was dying with
the wail of the bomb.
Could this have been planned
from long ago?
Your religious beliefs told you
so.
Look into the tear filled eyes of
your brother,
and say good-bye because we're
off FOREVER. . . . .

Larry Kiedrowski
MOTHER

She has been faithful for so
many years.
She has mended broken hearts
and quieted my fears.
When I was down and just
couldn't win,
She helped me up and gave me
confidence to try again.

She has seen me in good times,
she has seen me in bad.
And she's always there to talk
to whenever I'm sad.

And even though we are miles
apart,
She's always with me down deep
in my heart.
I love her more than any other!
She's my friend, she's my mother!

Carl Weathers
MY SON

My son,
Soon to be a man
Trust in God
Do the best you can.

Fear not to ask for help
Always appreciate
Keep all appointments
Try never to be late.

Return the friendship
Others will bestow
Treat all with kindness
Wherever you may go.

Your Mom and I
Think you are number one
We are proud to tell all the world
This man is my son.

Sharon I. Dreyer
THE WARMTH OF YOUR MEMORY

When you are gone
And I am left alone
I will remember you
And the time we shared
Without doubt
Or regret
Only a tear
For the greatest joy.
And in the long
Dark hours
of the nights to come
The warmth of your memory
Will comfort me.

Ruth Mosher
THE LAST LETTER

Since the telegram came saying
  you were missing at war,
I was getting letters you wrote
  some time before.
But today, the last one finally
  arrived—
Now I know you're no longer
  alive.
I can see you now lying still as
  you write—
Straining your eyes in the
  dimming light.
Over the pound in your head,
  you hear gunfire
You are so weak and so very
  tired.
Slowly, you reach inside your
  shirt—
Your hand is stained with blood
  and dirt.
You draw out a pen and begin
  to write
Even then, with death in sight.
"My dear—" is all the words
  there were
The rest an indistinguishable
  blur.
Now, as I hold this blood-
  stained page,
I am growing blind with rage.
What is the need of this ugly war
So many have died—how many
  more?

Michelle C. Pristic
THE BUTTERFLY THAT NEVER WHISPERED

I'm sitting in a chair, lonely as
  can be
Hoping that the phone would
  ring, and this time be for me.
I try to hide my feelings,
  wishing they didn't exist
At times I feel unneeded, sort
  of at the bottom of your list.
"I promise I'll call you!" The
  famous line I hear
When the phone doesn't ring
  I get the message loud and clear.
Every night I lay alone drying
  the tears off my face
So no one knows how I feel,
  so I leave without a trace.
Pity is not what I'm seeking
  but love is what I need
The loving understanding touch
  by you, my only seed.
I've said what I must, leaving
  flowers by my trail
Yet like Romeo and Juliet, let
  us not fail.
The love I hold so close of every
  part of thee
I surely shall live through the
  war, waiting for peace to set
  us free.

Ronnie Lynn Johnson
A BLACK LEADER

Once there was a man, who
  said, "I have a dream,"
  His name was Martin Luther
  King.
He marched and marched both
  day and night,
To free all people, blacks as
  well as whites.
He was jailed and arrested
  several times,
  But not once did his hopes
  for freedom decline.
Martin was against violence in
every way,
And his plans are instilled in
  our lives today.
In nineteen-sixty-three, A
  Memorial Day,
These are some of the words
  Dr. King had to say,
"I have a dream that one day on
  the red hills of Georgia,
Former slaves and former slave
  owners will be able
To sit down at the table of
  brotherhood."
April four, nineteen-sixty-eight,
  Dr. King fell,
But not by request, for a
  sniper's bullet had put him to
  rest.
Even though Dr. King is gone,
  the Southern Christian
  Leadership Conference still
  carries his work on.
He was a great man, with a great
  dream too.
  Now ask yourself the question,
  "Just what can I do
To promote freedom?"

Patricia Dee Spradlin
LATITUDE

I sat at the rivers very end,
My feelings stirred, and was
  Lonely.
I watched the final, endless
  Struggle
Into the sea.
No less a river, yet
Lost?

Archie Westbrook
MOTHER

Mother what can I say that has
  not
been said before about Mothers.
Mother is someone who is loving,
gentle, soft, and hard at times.
Thank God. I'm glad God made
Mothers how about you.

Dana M. Murray
POLYGLASS

When asked what ply,
  I said one.
He said no,
  you've been married twice—
Ah—my tread's wearing thin.
He said—
Well, it's something to think
  about—
I said—
Thanks for the thought.

Beth E. Wilcox
NEVER FOREVER

I can never tell you forever
Cause I said it once before
Then as time passed by
  unfolding fate
It made a liar of me.
I'll never say forever
Cause the future cannot be
  seen
And time plays games with
  peoples lives
The promise of forever can
  never be.
Even without the forever
I want to make it with you
I promise I'll never try to
  deceive you
Without my word, what is left
  of me?
This I say forever
I never want to hurt you
I just want to be with you
And if it lasts forever—that's
  left for us to see.
Forever
The promise of a lifetime
But futures are a mystery
That can't be seen by me.
No promises of forever.

Jane M. Arroyo
SAILING

We are brought down,
Amazing sky,
We sail beyond,
Forbidden eye.
We are kept behind,
Engulfing clouds,
We drift, unwind,
Standing proud.
We are sailors of the deep,
Connecting blue and white,
Flying dreams in our sleep,
Let yourself ignite.

Deborah A. Mullen
MEMORIES

Today is a wonderful day,
It is happening now.
The time goes by so fast,
So fast that I don't know how.
Today will be a memory, after
  today is gone.
Then days from now we'll think
  of this,
And thoughts will carry on.
Good times are always thought
  of,
they're not like all the rest.
These days will be remembered,
These days are called the best.

K. Denise Jackson
MISS AMERICA

Society's child
  Illustrious little girl
Cinderella
  all dressed in yellow
and ribbons and bows
  for curls of gold
Barbie dolls
  and birthday parties
and boyfriends
  and beauty pagents
and college and careers
  and a perfect marriage
Living ludicrous lies
  Trying to escape
the Image in their eyes.

Charlene Annette Carpenter
HE SAID HE WOULD; HE NEVER DID

A man I met in the park one day,
Sitting there quietly in his own
  way.
He was sad and lonely staring
  down,
As though he was sitting,
  watching the ground.
We started to talk his voice
  sounding sad;
Whoever hurt him must have
  been mad!
He said, "Monday, I'll bring my
  kid."
He said he would; he never did.
Before he left, forever, I mean;
Daily in the park we could be
  seen.
We said most things that came
  to thought,
He even talked of a dog he just
  bought.
"Tomorrow I'll bring him with
  box and lid."
He said he would; he never did.
He said one day he had a
  surprise,
And to get it I must close my
  eyes.
He said sadly, "to one hundred
  count."
It seemed his sadness was
  beginning to mount.
When I saw he'd left, I was very
  upset;
I suddenly remembered the day
  we first met
A note said he'd return, my
  heart slid.
He said he would; he never did.

Georgette F. Fekaris
DESOLATION

The grey dawn breaks, cheerless,
  stark, unfeeling;
Even nature weeps;
Her frozen fingers marking a
  swift tattoo
  Against the windowpane,
Streaking the fog-enshrouded
  glass
  With dirt-encrusted fingers,
The shame, the filth, the foulness
  Of a polluted universe!
Reluctantly I open my eyes to
  pain, despair,
  The smothering of all hope;
To star in fascinated horror
  At the ugliness surrounding me.
My mind is shattered as I slowly
  comprehend
  The black and dismal life which
  lies ahead.
I shudder uncontrollably and
  desperately
  Long for
That ardent lover who comes to
  each of us
To soothe with callous hands
  and
  pitiless heart.
I passionately embrace
  The cold oblivion of—Death!

Jeanette McCollum
MY MAN

I've found a man and he's
  quite unique,
For he has helped to make my
  life complete;
He has stood by me through
  the thick and thin,
Together we've got everything
  to gain and win.
He is one of goodness, this you
  can't dispute,
God knows I love him and that's
  the truth;
He's given me love and joy by
  the ton,
Together we share it with our
  young son.
The man I've got has a love that
  will last,
For he's my winner, no other
  can surpass;
To be a leader and a hero is

quite a job,
To my best friend and to my husband, BOB.

Avey C. McClure
A BEAUTIFUL AWAKENING

How beautiful the world it when
you wake up and look up
at the heavens.
You see a cloud move about as
if it's hiding the little angels,
who are looking down on all
of us.
Now I become a little jealous.
I say to myself, "They belong
to me".
I stop and start thinking, who
am I that I should be so special,
For to God we are all his children.
That means there are enough
little angels for all of us.
If we look long enough and use
our imagination, we can see
them.

Martha R. Pohl
FRIENDS

Along the journey from our
birth, until the sleep of death
Our lives will touch so many
more like us—of mortal breath.

To some, it's but a meeting
brief; a nod, a wave, a smile;
To others, mere acquaintances
we see once in awhile.

With other folks, we pass the
time, with laugh and care-free
joke
We have our common work and
play, with no deep friendship
yolk.

But I have found a treasure rare,
a friendship tie so deep
It is a friend who laughs with
you, yet sorrows when you
weep.

For many "buddy-buddy"
friends may laugh and then
forget
But he who blends his tears with
yours, by far's the best friend
yet.

Rachel Ann Saldivar
THE SEAL

I saw a seal,
Eating his meal,
I guess he likes to eat,
A lot of fish meat,
Not puppy feet.

If I were a seal
I wouldn't eat such a meal.
As fish meat,
Nor would I eat puppy feet.

Paul Housego
BORROWED LIFE

I remember your silhouette on
the grey dock, standing;
watching
You used to love the boat,
sailing in the harbour.

Alone, a man died yesterday
A silence, sounding as it fell,
shattered his dreams

You asked me where the sailboat
had gone, with selfish grief
I told you that it was a dream,
his dream.

Catherine Housego
TALE

Ere
the brilliant day began
all sure
the victory on hand

courageous, strong
and quick in battle
all laughed
when mentioned of defeat
but
strangely oft
this tale is told
of brave men
scoffing
lesser fools
and of the last day
when pursued
the brave men
cowered
beneath the fools

Kathy C. Holbrook
A CHRISTMAS MEMORY

When I was just a little girl,
Many years ago,
I met a little star,
Who had a certain glow.

Shining in the sky,
I saw him from afar,
On a calm and lovely night,
I met my little star.

The sky was calm and still,
My little star shone bright,
Within my little heart,
He lit a little light.

It was Christmas Eve,
And I gazed at him in delight,
For I shared with him,
The memory of another night.

For I was the shepherd,
And he was the light,
He led me to the stable,
And a wonderful sight.

There lay what Christmas meant,
In a cradle so small,
The Baby Jesus,
A Christmas gift for all.

I knelt in wonder,
I gazed in awe,
I sang in praise,
For the miracle I saw.

On Christmas Eve,
A memory I still recall,
A little girl and a little star,
And what Christmas means to
all.

Bertie Merphy
FOR YOU

From out of the mists of
dreamtime.
Before the world was new
T'was aware of enchantment
Of a love wrapped up by you!

Way before all dreamtime
Before all time began
I was made your woman
You were made my man!

The mist of worlds in making
The swirls of dust in dew
The morning of my awakening,
Warmed by the love of you.

The sun was seen more glorious,
The moon, we kissed in view.
The night was spent in showing
My world was made by you.

There is no rhyme or reason
We share each space anew.
We know all worlds and seasons.
God made me. . .for you!

Robert D. Williams
FLOWER GARDEN

The Japanese scurry about their
business
Bowing respectfully to neighbors
Who inadvertently stray in their
paths.
There is war but it is very far

away.
Only sailors on leave
And the steady pounding of
factories reminds one of it.
There is still time for haiku
And artistic photographs
clicked in flower gardens.
It is August and summer blooms
heavy and full.
In the garden
A geisha contemplates her
existence
As she applies delicate brush
strokes
To the silk canvas set before her.
Tradition dictates
Woman must serve man.
She deems herself fortunate
But muses of other countries
(of America).
How must one there apply
them
herself to life
And what of rewards?
Do men treat women differently?
Secretly
She suspects they are all alike.
A light brilliant beyond measure
Vaporizes the garden pool.
Oblivion
Precipitates upon her thoughts.
The answers are very far away
And she will never know them.

Suzanne Rising
CLEAR WATER REFLECTIONS

The memories I recount are
vivid,
yet transparent
on the silent creek water.
The clear water reflections carry
a hue of brilliance
that once lived in my childhood.
Gazing eagerly at the enchanting
sight,
I reach out to try to touch the
tenderness of my past;
But I only disturb the loveliness
of the fascinating clear water
reflections
that momentarily brightened
my life.

Patience R. Bonner
LIFE

I can't explain
this feeling.
I don know
that it's pain.
This thing is deep
inside of me.
It feels like
something insane.
I wake
and it's there to torment me,
I sleep,
and it distorts my dreams.
When I try
to shake it out,
It just laughs
or so it seems.
The only way
to stop this pain
Is the knife
above the shelf.
Maybe after
I've plunged it in,
Life will torment
somebody else.

Joan McGrath—Gloe
MEMORIES

I remember that fancy bed of
ours.
I gave it to you.
Just like my heart.
I ended up with it though.

Just like everything else I gave
you.
You traveled light when you
left to find adventure on the
road.
You took only one thing.
Yourself.
You didn't even take your
memories.
You left them with me too.
I found them one day under the
bed.
I sold the bed you loved for a
little while;
Just like me.
Instead of getting tangled in
the sheets with you
I get tangled in the memories
The memories you left behind.
Just like me.

Lori LaMotte
WALK WITH ME

Give me your hand
and we will walk together
with love.
For your hand will lead us.
Your smile will comfort us.
We will walk as one
and love as one.
And the world will look upon us
with Love.

Diane Marie Long
TO MY DARLING SISTER "APRIL"

April is as free as the wind can
be sitting up in a mulberry tree,
The smile on the sweet little girl
brings sunshine to the field of
Daffodiles.

Little chickies yellow and bright
jump onto her hand to cheep
her
Good night
The lovely melodies that do
come out remind little April of
a cooking
Spout
Her tired little yawn sounds so
sweet like bristles of the trees
and
Willows as they weep
Gently and more gently as she
falls asleep she lays down in
the tall
Green grass and no more do the
little chickies cheep.

Donald R. Rosenbaum
GOD MADE

God made the birds,
The bees, the flowers, the trees
The sky, the ground,
The wind, every sound
The mountains, the plains,
Animals that graze,
The fog, a mist, a morning haze,
God made sunlight,
moonbeams,
The stars at night
A rock, a stone, a man alone,
A stream, a nook, a babbling
brook
The morning light, the evening
dew,
God made them all, even me
and you!

Armando Canda
UNTITLED

Possess me but don't overpower
me with caresses.

Love me but don't overdo it to
the point of pure
asphyxiation.

I guess I love you without all
the frills and impositions
  that turns a love affair into
  a nightmare of
  dos and don'ts.
You don't believe me?...Well,
  then don't...but I shall
  never go out of my way to do
  fabricated things
  to make you feel wanted or
  loved.
If you can't honestly tell by the
  way I look into your
  eyes, by the way I hold you,
  by the way I speak
  to you that I love you...
then I guess you'll never know!

Norma Fallos-Cekan
ESCAPE

We'll walk through fields of
  wildflowers
And meadows of Dew kissed
  grass
The birds will be our symphony
Just let the time elapse.

For we are in a world of serenity
That only we have come to know
It's a place that we share secretly
At times letting our passion flow.

You stop and pick me flowers
This is something I truly love
It's simple but so gentle
What I feel pass through your
  touch.

I'll forever love our walks my
  dear
When we escape to find time for
  us
For they mean more to me each
  year
Than you could ever guess...

Floella Bates
CHRISTMAS POEM TO SONS

Tonight it's nearing Christmas,
  and my memory rolls back
  through
  maze of time—
To Christmases long past when
  one, then two small boys I
  called
  mine.
I think of the very few things
  we had, and the many things
  that were missing.
What I still wonder about at times;
Was there enough of hugging and
  kissing?

Now those darling boys are BIG,
  and one is far from home,
He has a wife, a tiny girl, and so
  the cycle goes on;
The other—well—he's out of
  school and working now,
And all this is just as it should be.
But in my heart and my mind's
  eye I still see
  Those two little boys
    One fair
    One dark
    With their bouquets of weeds,
Running, always running back
  to me.

Jonathan Schorsch
A SHOW OF STRENGTH

I remember seeing
a picture in the paper
of a Palestinian guerilla trainee
ripping apart live rabbits
with his bare hands,
and wondering
if he still smiled his boyish grin
when he came to mother's for

supper
and she pinched him on the
  cheek.
or
if those same olive hands
tenderly rubbed the chestnut-
  brown skin
of a lover by the rolling Mediterr
  Mediterranean
or
if, perhaps, when reaching out
to fluff his daughter's hair
he catches sight of his own hand
and remembers how the soft
  fur stretched in his grip
until the warm blood spurted out
  of the severed neck
and the radiantly pink eyes bulb
  bulged while rabbit guts
sloshed, pulsated, between his
  fingers
until the drill sergeant's whistle
  blew
and a little rabbit head
and a little rabbit body
fell lifelessly at his feet.

Penny Lee Bellile
WE WERE LIKE ONE

We were like one
Then things had to change
I felt cold and alone
And somewhat ashamed

I walked on the beach
The sand was warm
But it made me cry
Wishing I wasn't born

All I could think of
Was you and me
The things we had planned
For eternity

The dreams we shared
The times we'd weep
The moments we dared
The secrets we'd keep

We trusted one another
in spite of what's said
We confided in each other
That's what kept us ahead

But the time came
When our paths would part
And along with them
There fell my heart

I still remember you dearly
But only as a friend
Cause the last thing I would want
Is our friendship to end.

Betty Marks Steward Kisic
JESUS HAS A TENDER HEART

Jesus has a tender heart
Oh, that it were mine
Gentle, true and full of love
Heavenly; Divine.

Every footstep that He takes
Oh, that it were mine
Soft and sure and tirelessly
Our mountains He will climb.

Up our hills, down our hills
Stoney paths or grasslands fine
He will even slow His pace
If we but seek His time.

Speaking oh, so softly
Listening so intent
He would gladly answer
Confess our sins, repent.

While in His cleansing power
With every tear that flows
His very heartbeat we would
  sense
Oh, that my heart would know.

His loving touch of kindness
His perfect will to find

His outstretched arms around me
Oh, that it were mine.

I found it in my Bible
His story so divine
Of how He lived and died for me
Thank God, I know it's mine!

Marsha Swofford Cobb
EXPRESSIONS

Moist and warm flowing freely
  I am moved
By a sudden, powerful burst
  of feeling,
And I am gravely misunderstood.
  It is
Freedom for me to be released
  even though,
On occasion, I appear to fall
  unnoticed
Upon lifeless ground. I am
  created by joy
And moved by physical pain. I
  am present
during times of regret and
  remorse; yet I
Am seen in the eyes of lovers
  all over the
Earth. I bathe and soothe the
  heart which
Is my greatest pleasure and
  most treasured
Honor. My extent of measure
  is small; however
My nobility is beyond compare.
  Never
Feel me to be weak! I am the
  ultimate expression
Of all emotions. In a thrill of
  self-giving,
I am the tear that falls from
  your eye.

Evelyn Smail
THE WIDOWER MCVITTY'S
HOUSE

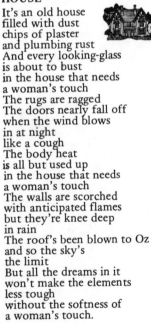

It's an old house
filled with dust
chips of plaster
and plumbing rust
And every looking-glass
is about to bust
in the house that needs
a woman's touch
The rugs are ragged
The doors nearly fall off
when the wind blows
in at night
like a cough
The body heat
is all but used up
in the house that needs
a woman's touch
The walls are scorched
with anticipated flames
but they're knee deep
in rain
The roof's been blown to Oz
and so the sky's
the limit
But all the dreams in it
won't make the elements
less tough
without the softness of
a woman's touch.

Kandi Bennett
IF

If only I could erase the past,
The bad times washed away,
If only time could stop,
I'd change each minute day by
  day.
If only mistakes weren't made,
To scar and despair life.
If only they didn't stab,
Inside me like a knife.
If only I could see my future,

To see how life turned out;
I'd stop myself now, and
Take the right way out.
If only I could cease,
The pain I cannot bear;
If only people my cry,
Could they hear.

Doreen Lynne Davies
A MOMENT EXTRA

Find that I must work in
haste; Running here and there,
  my school books scream
  deadlines,
  my boyfriend demands equal
  time.
  Mother is angry, girlfriends
have lost their loves, and I,
  myself am tired and want
    time alone.
  Yet however hectic and
filled the days may be, one
  blessing
  have I found to be true;
There always seems to be a
  moment extra, A moment
  in which to offer a smile,
a laugh,
  a reassuring hug.

Pat Chamburg
LOVE IS NOT A GAME

We are getting divorced.
I'm the one who threw in the
  towel.
I felt like a soda bottle full of
  love for you,
but with "no return."
  So why does my heart feel
  heavy?
Because my ego doesn't want to
  let go,
  doesn't want to give up.
  No one wants to be defeated
at what they do best,
and for me that is loving.
  There is no defeat in true love,
only victory for two.
People are only defeated,
when they play games.
  So...I quit!

Wendy Sue Kennedy
YOUR LOVE IS LIKE A SONG

Your love is like a song.
Your fingers play the
melody as your eyes
sing along.
and your body sets
the tempo
of with which I go
along.
Your music wraps itself
around me and the rythm
takes control,
as I find myself
becoming a part of its calling
inner soul.
So take me away in
your musicland
and never let me return,
for I want to be lost
forever in your song
composed of love.

Antonette Mikolon
ANTONETTE'S RECIPE FOR
PEACE

P Think positive—choose
   priorities—prepare with
   pleasure—patience & plenty of
   love—here and there sprinkle
   a pinch of prayer.

E Lend your ear—be earnest—
   allow one to expel emotional
   energy—enjoy being close to

the earth.
A Look into one's inner being—
  acknowledge—best
  accomplishment individual can
  make—absorb others—so to be
  more aware.
C Be charitable—carefully sift
  combined comforts—one will
  be creating comfortable feelings
E Now one has encountered
  all ingredients—one's entire
  self must accept—if one accepts—
  he will have been enlightened.
  Take this knowledge
mix well into one's heart
  then my friend
One will have found peace.

Randy Bain
YOU

Thought of you today
  Heard a familiar tune,
Closed my eyes and saw you.
  Just like yesterday. . .
But it's today, really.
  Dreams shattered,
Feelings just don't disappear.

Noella Driscoll
ANXIETY ATTACK

Tredding lightly with sharp
  silvery slivers pricking our
  feet
And the shocks penetrate in
  electrifying signals through
  our body
Hair stands on end
Sharp fingernails reach up to
  scratch
  to grasp hold of
  fleshy arms leaving us
And a scalpel gently slices us
  under our ear.

Mona Arrellin Rodriguez
YES , I AM DIFFERENT

Yes, I am different. Label me
  retard
Because of this, mere existence
  will be hard
Yes, I am different. Label me
  weird
I am not contagious, why am I
  feared?
Yes, I am different. Label me
  slow.
But I am human, I have
  something to show
Yes, I am different. Label me
  freak
Hide me away, while it's
  knowledge I seek
Yes, I am different. Label me
  strange
But with your help we'll go
  a better change
Yes, I am different. Label me
  love
We're God's special children
  from heaven above.

Cynthia Wegrzyn
ALMIGHTY GOD

Almighty God is, and always
  will be.
I want the people to see.
  God is the creator of this
  land. He can
demolish it with one hand.
  This is true for all man. God
  may destroy,
both him and his clan.
  God will rid the world of
  violence and crime,

Only he knows the exact time.
When all wicked and evil will
  have to die.
There is not one that will get
  by.
  They may beg and plead,
  but God will say no,
for all your sins you must go.
  Given the ability to choose
  right from wrong
your choice was evil, you don't
  belong.
  Now you must die for all
  commandments broken.
Almighty God has spoken.

Beverly Barbo
I AM

I am your child, your wife,
  your mother. . .
But who am i?
i am a good girl, faithful and
  caring, i wiped your tears. . .
Did you hear my cry?
i left your home, joined yours
  and made one for you . . .
Where do I belong?
The love i learned, i shared,
  and it grew. . .but. . .
Am I so wrong
To feel that there is more to
  me than
Living through others for the
  praise thereof,
Pushing back the cocoon of
  have to be. . .
Am i a butterfly or moth?
It makes no difference, I am
  free
To find a little bit of both,
But succeed or fail, I will be
  me.

Nora Jacome A
YOU AND I

January, cool January in Paris,
You and I in the station. . .
Paris, La Gare de L'Est. . .
The train awaits
You to Lyon
and I to Cologne
Adieu—No!
—So long
a simple laugh
and a simple chat
in the Cafe,
the Cafe of the Station.
—You said "Bonjour"
I answered the same
—The snow fell
it was cool in the station
  You invited me to have coffee,
I accepted.
—a simple chat—
—The Captain of the station,
  signals
time to leave. . .
But at the farewell,
our hearts flamed up.

Weeks later we met in Cologne
—On a winter night in Bonn,
at the carnival. . .Our love was
born. . .

Carlton H, Maund
SUMMERDAYS

Hot and burning,
Summerday and suntan oil,
Lazy days are flowing,
Palm trees and south wind
  blowing.
Sunrise then sunset.
The cool evening calm with
  stirring palms.

Nighttime and two AM
In a small tropic town.

Karen L. Rolff
I AM A ROSE

Can you fall in love
With a flower?
Can you take it all in?
Taste the bitterness
Of it's petal,
Feel the thorn of its stem?
Can you love a flower?
Would you still love me then?

Barbara Benjamin O'Reilly
**IN PURSUIT OF HIGHER
LEARNING**

The room is empty now
where once lived a boy-child
It is quite neat—clean,
but somehow the neatness
is not as attractive
as the happy clutter
only a child can make.
I stop, look, and wonder
why his childhood was so—
so much swifter than mine.
So few years in this room.
Now there is another
in some far distant place.
Nothing is forever.

Marlene J. Sartain
LITTLE COTTONTAIL

A bunny hopped by my window
And nibbled at the sprigs close
  by
His little nose was bobbing
  and twitching
As he carefully stood up high.
He was all white and fluffy
And had a cotton ball tail
His pink eyes quickly glanced
  at me
As he hurried on down the
  trail.

I hope I didn't frighten him
For he looked so cute that way
I think I'll put some carrots
  out
In case he comes back some day.

Alisa Norris
FRUSTRATION

Ugh! This stupid, ignorant paper!
  Why couldn't the teacher assign
  it later?
Nothing seems to ever work right,
  Now you'll have to stay up all
  night.
Papers scattered all around,
Always make a crunching sound.
You have more homework
  than you've ever had,
It's enough to make yourself
  mad!
You don't get to watch your
  favorite show,
Half of the questions you don't
  even know!
You throw up your hands in the
  air,
And forget everything. . .who
  cares?

Andrew T. Dooley
HAPPY END

There's a lonesome road called
  Might have Been
that leads to Never was,
It's lined with tears folks bent
  with years
and tales of broken love.
It's used by those who
  reminesce
and dream what might have

been
If they had done things
  differently
at a time once known as then.

Perhaps you'd like to take a tr
  trip
go back to never was
And once again let might have
  been
restore your first true love.
If not perhaps youre satisfied
  and wish to stay at now
And not go back to never was
  or wonder if or how.

I sometimes like to reminesce
I travel all alone
I take the road of might have
  been
and make my way back home.

Perhaps someday we'll meet
  we two
on the road of might have
  been
and skip the town of never was
for a place called "HAPPY
  END".

Donna M. Myott
NOT WHAT I AM

You took me in young and
  carefree, protected my wings
  from flight
I became wordly and an
  educated woman almost
  overnight.
My lips blistered and longed
  for gentleness
My body over touched and
  cried needless.

Then my mind became over
  exposed
It aged and weakness rose.
I hadn't the strength to break
  away
You programmed me to give
  more and stay.

How longing I am for a true
  man
How longing I am to be not
  what I am.

Dick Turski
KARMA

When,
  the poem that is metered
and the story that is told
  and the song that is written
becomes meshed within the
  times,
then it can happen.

Brenda Black White
MY FATHER'S SISTER

My aunt could never look at
  me and smile,
She thought me such a plain
  and awkward child.
From earliest remembrance
  I've heard her swear
That she never could learn to
  like red hair.
And I, whose head shone
  copper in the sun,
Wondered what in my short life
  I'd done
To make my aunt dislike me
  with such malice
Though seemingly she loved my
  cousin Alice.

Yesterday, I saw my aunt and
  she was dying
And everyone, save me, was
  red-eyed crying.
She stretched her bony hand
  for me to take

And smiled to show a kindness
for my sake.
She asked me to forgive her,
but I wouldn't;
She said she'd tried to love me,
but she couldn't.

L. Frances Taylor
FRANGIPANI

There's Frangipani, half-
septembering
Beneath the stars between
moonlight and day
With restless, sensual
remembering
Of lost dreams strewn along
the careless way
White, rolling waves beat out
a sweet encore
To cool, dim mystery of night
and sea
They play a haunting opiate
to the shore
That Frangipani whispers
back to me.

Portia Selene Bonner
**UP FROM THE BONDS OF
SLAVERY**

Torn from bonds I came
Waiting to play a game
A new game of life
That has turned into shame
A game of life for who's to blame?
Torn from bonds I came
In chaines that gave heartache,
pains,
The white man's cruel tame.
Then came shame of color and
name.
We were losing the game.
Torn from bonds I came
Growing up with prejudices and
shame.
Black people know life is not a
fair game.
From broken bonds we came
Not afraid of color or name.

Brenda Gail Kuhn
HARMONY

In tranquil hours of silken
soft dreams,
A song drifts through my mind
like a crystal stream.
Stroaking the spindles which
hold body to soul,
He is the harmony that makes
this body whole.
Like trusting moments from
barefoot days,
I open my heart to know his
sharp rocky places,
And instead find waters gently
swirling, cool and deep.
Precious stones, with edges
unknown,
Tumbled smooth in this clear
running stream.
The starry night breeze of days
gone by,
Has returned once more with a
tender sigh.
Whispering forgotten memories
of love, and quiet sorrow.
Bringing a vision of the joy
that is ours, tomorrow.

T. A. Dieudonne
**THOUGHTS ON A RAINY
DAY TO SHERYL**

Sitting silently,
Wind whistling softly,
Rain running down the window
Life lingering slowly
Toward tomorrow.

Mind, drifting to
Eternity,
Searching for the
Solitude of summer days.
Walking without fear
Along lonely beaches.
Unknown beaches,
Like unknown eyes
We learn to love as
Time moves on.
They too move on,
leaving us longing
For those eyes,
Those midnight eyes.
Till darkness comes
Forever.
Reality reaches toward
Thoughts of tomorrow,
Bringing them back to
Earth.
Dreams soaring skyward
Survive.

Paulette Sanchez Rendon
WHY?

Let it be known
That I am home
To see what life has done,
To you and me.
We shall see
Where we're coming from.
The years have gone by
And I've wondered. . .
Why?

Artemio Diaz
THIRSTY DESIRE

Roads of Northern Illinois,
Lakes, rivers and towns
I am passing by,
If you know where she is
Why don't you tell me?
Do not keep her away from me,
Please, let me know where she
lodges,
Look at me, all surroundings,
Tell her I am here in Chicago
Leaving for Kansas City.
I will ask for her in Springfield,
Saing Louis Missouri, farms,
villages
And towns nearby.
I keep hoping to taste her
sweet mouth
No matter if I spend
My lifetime wandering.

Sharon Denny
LITTLE BOY BLUE

Little boy blue
Come back to me
I'm your mother, I love you,
Son, why can't you see?
I know you feel torn
Like you had to decide
Why did you, son
When I'm on your side.
I can't believe that you'd hurt
me
We've been thru a lot together
I hope I live long enough to see
The day I hear "I love you
Mother."

Little boy blue,
Come back to me
I'm your mother, I love you
Oh my son, why can't you see?

Kathy Vivirite
LOCKED PAST

I want to hold on to the past.
It has gone too fast.
I want to hide it in a box,
and close it with many locks.
I want to remember the happy
past—
that did go too fast.
I want to remember the sad,
learn from it, and be glad.
I must hold on to my memories
and never let them go
I must let what I learned from
my mistakes show.
But in that box, I'll always save
room
to let new memories bloom.

Michael James Sundberg
ALONE

Alone I sit
in shadows thick
tetrad windows beset with brick
sealed in hate
cracks there none
sealed my fate
and ate my sun
forsaken in a shrouded tomb
measured air
sparse room
epitaph on callous stone
in shadows thick
I sit
alone.

Wendy Sue Dunn
CUP OF SMILES

TOMORROW lives FOREVER
In the FATHER'S loving hand,
It so neatly fits together
in his perfect master plan.
HIS love is faithful
and ever waitful
MY CUP RUNNETH OVER
with SMILES
as we travel the miles
TOGETHER. . .FOREVER

Lovie Owens
THE LINE

My race
Was told to take its place
Waaaaay at the back of the line.
That all things come in their
own due time
Waaaaay at the back of the line
We waited and waited way over
time
Waaaaay at the back of the line
And things do come in their
own due time
Waaaaay at the back of the line
But look out y'all, it's my time
I am next.

Agnes Grey Ronald
BELLEROPHON

He rises in a stormy cloud of
dust,
A golden rain upon his raging
horse
Whose fiery hooves strike out
a skyward course!
Bellerophon's strong hand is
light—he must
Quiet the stallion's terror and
distrust. . .
The silver Stallion by that
swift resourse
He caught and bridled,
and with godlike force

Mounted between the mighty
wings outthrust!
Bellerophon soars up in meteor
flight,
His naked heels pressed to
the panting sides
Of starry Pegasus, and taking
count
For sudden swerve and
treacherous plunge, he rides
With that wild joy on his
immortal mount
They only know who challenge
uttermost height!

Keith Harrold
TO KELLY—GROWING PAINS

I have watched you crawl, walk,
run, and cartwheel through
childhood.
You have changed into a
beautiful young lady as I
knew you would.
We (you and I) have seen and
heard a-plenty the sorrow and
sadness
of the young.
A million voices, a million songs
have been sung.
You will run away down many
dark streets, bumpy roads,
and narrow lanes.
But you will find you can't
run away from growing pains.
A lot of searching and
meditating you will do.
Then, one day the world you
will see anew.
But in the meanwhile, when
you feel inadequate, and
unworthiness has
you in its clutch.
Just remember, your daddy
loves you very, very much.

Kathy Mitchell
THE WOMAN BEHIND HIM

His being
ages her. . .
He squeezes his mind,
Occasionally by way of heart,
through his pen
onto paper
His truths to be published;
Poetry for fame.
She squeezes the feelings
from the rhyme
Scratches the thoughts deep
into her soul
for no one to read; to
understand.
the cycle, like a river,
flows and never ends.

Suzanne Mischke
FIND PEACE

Shhh!
Don't disturb my silent moment
of thought.
Hush! Don't break the sound
barrier of silence.
Quiet! Be one with me in my
serenity.
Be still!
Find peace, within your soul.

Betty Jane Frye
SADNESS

When I reflect upon my life
I feel a lot of sadness—
a lot of strife,
And wonder now as years gone
past—
How much longer the sadness
will last.

A long time ago it started out
When I was young and full of
    sprout,
The youth within me died
    quite soon
And in my sadness grew a tomb.
Then the sadness began to grow
And the tomb grew larger—I
    should know,
Sometimes my sadness is
    overwhelming
And sometimes I feel as if I'm
    drowning.

But in my sadness I can see
A light far off above a tree,
Maybe soon my life will be
Without my tomb to weigh on
    me.

Then my sadness will run out
And my life can begin to
    sprout,
Again as it should do—
And happiness will be brand
    new.

Wendy Sue Dunn
MY FRIEND JESUS

Come to me you tired and worn
Come to me and be reborn.

Give to me your broken heart
I'll give to you a fresh new
    start.

I love you with a love that's
    strong,
I'll turn your life to right from
    wrong.

Love me, too, and put me first,
I'll see to it you never thirst.

You'll never miss the things
    you left,
The ways that only lead to
    death.

Give me your heart,
I'll do the rest. . .
I love you.

I knit new lives for weary
    worn-out souls,
I give everlasting crowns of
    gold to those
Who are faithful. . .to the end.
My friend. . .let me help you.
You will never be blue. . .that
    you did.

Lisa Kay Banner
A MOMENT

A moment,
Time is all I have, to think, to
    waste,
to one day appreciate.
For what? I don't know, for
    some
specific reason, I suppose.
Love, such a beautiful word,
    but
where did it's meaning go?
And what about tomorrow?
Understanding one another's
    feelings
is something we could try.
Only its easier to pretend and
    just lie.
Takes a while to realize that,
    A time for love and under
    understanding
    only takes a moment.

Verna Peters
ANGELS

Angels of the night
Talk to me in soft voices
Warning me in soft voices
Warning me of war
And of destruction

Yet, to come
The songs they sing
Are of joy and comfort
But, I can still feel
The earth moving
As they vanish in the air
Leaving me sighing
In disbelief.

Patricia A. Bell
**TO A CHILD IN FOSTER
CARE**

Longingly a pair of brown
    eyes gaze, wondering what is
    so special
about the day.
    Slowly you enter upon his
    domain, only once again to
    relieve the
heartache and pain.
    A tiny hand reaches towards
    you, wanting the hour not
    to pass thru.
    You are once again brought
    together and a thought snaps
    thru your
numb brain, maybe, never again
    would be better.
    As the thought trails off you
    shudder, for once again you
    realize you
are this child's mother.
    Once again the tiny hand
    reaches upwards and the wide
    brown
eyes gaze at you.
    You react holding to him
    tight and cry while the child's
    eyes wonder
why.

Donald L. Taylor
A DREAM

On a bench by a stream
Sits an old man and his dream
"Some day I'll be free"
But this cannot be
For he lives in a land
Where they make slaves out of
    man.

To talk is to die
And the truth is a lie
His life is not to be admired
But his love and strength
    is desired
By most of us who see
His ambition to be free.

F. Jane Binzen
NEW CHILD

Look at the summer and fields
    of gold,
Sun bathed fields and the
    warmth they hold. . .
Delight at the autumn's bright
    coloring leaves,
The majestic pattern that
    nature weaves. . .
Look at the hillside that shines
    in the night,
In a crystal, snow flake blanket
    of white. . .
Wonder at spring make the
    world fresh and new,
Bright stars in the sky, soft
    clouds rolled in blue. . .
Look. . .
Look at you. . .

Monica Goad Gardner
MEMORIES

Tracing memories in our minds
is no good. . .time will just
come along and erase them. . .
We should be grateful to time,
because memories only hold us
to the past. . .and the past is

gone forever. . .we know there's
nothing we can possibly do to
change the unchangeable. . .so
let time, in its merciful way,
keep us thinking only of today.

Joseph H. Taillefer
**OUR ALMA MATER'S
SILVER JUBILEE**

Since five and twenty years
    our College stood
The grey of dawn, the best of
    time and need.
Magnanimous deeds, some at
    the coat of blood
Attest that in high drifts She
    took the lead.
Rays well adorn Her name,
    Her site, Her view;
Yea, far and wide, Her teaching
    deep and sound
Secures a reputation real and
    true;
Careers important for Her own
    abound.

O house of work and prayer,
    Thou art our pride !
Long-lived Thy lustre be! To
    Thine impart
Live Faith that will help them
    all straits to tide.
Entreat those in Thy bosom we
    well to start,
Great things for God and Land
    with heart to launch,
E'er being of the Church
    Supporters staunch!

Donald Clark
DEATH SONG

My senses have betrayed my
    spirit.
My heart searches for images
    which do not come.
My spirit is not inspired.

My ears are still to the songs of
    birds,
    The stirring of insects,
    The rhythm of drums,
    The singing waters.

Blind eyes ask the Sacred Dawn
    For blessings
    For my people,
    For all people,
    For little children.

The smokes of a thousand
    campfires
    Are dead in my nostrils.

My senses betray me.

But I feel the pulse of the
    Earth Mother
    Against my feet.
And I am ready.

Kimberly Parkis
DIVORCE

It's breaking my heart by the
    things you say.
You keep tearing me apart
    by the games you play.

You say you love me, but
    you want to leave me.
I tell you to go but you want
    to stay.
It confuses me so when you
    act this way.
I won't turn back, unless you
    want me to stay.
If you really love me, you'll
    make it clear today,
If you don't,
let's say goodbye right away,
I just can't hold on this way.

Robert Garrett Louis Brou
UNREAL TRUTHS

Unreal truths echo through
    the night
And rise upon the day
Serenely silent are these sights
That aren't with me here today.

But the light it fades and the
    light shall come
with breezes blowing to the
    sun
and echoes sounding from the
    ground
It's here all reasons can be
    found.

Glenn B. White
**GOD'S CREATION OF MAN
    AND TREES**

God's creation of man and
    trees
A beauty to behold,
Even when the core is rotten
And the Ages made them old.
Man is like this aged tree
Where the inside never shows,
Until they are cut down
And their inner hearts exposed.

Mrs. Joanie M. Moore
UNDERSTANDING LOVE

Love is a special word, much
    often misunderstood,
Love is a special feeling, a
    feeling of something good.
Love is when two people
    smile together,
And meaning and understanding
    is gathered.
Love is sharing the thoughts
    of one's mind.
And being there for one's need
    all the time.
Love is giving, sharing, not all
    receiving,
Love is never meant to be
    deceiving.

Love is being special to the
    person who is special to you,
And loving him, no matter
    what he may say or do.
Love is being understanding,
    good, and true,
And knowing that when things
    are wrong, love will bring
    you through.

Love is all things done that are
    good,
Love is not jumping to
    conclusions when you
    misunderstood.
Love is all the nice little things
    you do,
But love is special when you're
    being you.

Gloria L. Nothdurft
THIS MIRACULOUS LAND

The sun, the sky
    The clouds rolling by
The wind, the rain
    And I remain

Just a dot upon this earth
Where God has touched
His hand
And where His son gave birth
In this Miraculous land

I marvel at His wisdom
And at his destined plan
From where our souls came
from
In this Miraculous land.

He's shown us too
The threads He weaves
Are not always in sorrow
For as long as we have Faith
in Him
There's always Hope tomorrow
In this Miraculous land.

The entire pattern God will
weave
In the shaping of our life
Is in the belief
That we will strive
For everlasting life
In this Miraculous land.

The sun, the sky,
The clouds rolling by
The wind, the rain,
I still remain.

Just a dot upon this earth
Strengthened by his hand
In this Miraculous land.

K. Jennifer Berry
I WAITED

I waited for you Mother
Until the tears of the spring
of my pain
Watered the seeds of my
wonder.

I waited for you Mother
Until the heat of the summer
Of my sadness melted the joy
Of the blossoms of the sprouts

I waited for you Mother
Until the leaves of the fall
rustled
About the dying stalks of my
weary
Lonliness.

I waited for you Mother
But you never came; you
never saw my garden.
You never heard the rustle
of my flowers in the wind
You never felt the smoothness
of my petals.
And Mother, while I waited
I grew up
And I will wait no more.

Lee Heinze
THE OMNIPOTENT CHRIST

Sunlight He poured into
unseeing eyes
The sick from their beds He
commanded to rise,
The dead He called forth
from the gloom of the tomb
To live again, smile again,
freed from their doom.

The deaf who never, no
never had heard
The roar of the surf or the
song of a bird,
Now listen enraptured to
music and song
And sounds that to them were
denied for so long.

Dead Laz'rus imprisoned in
earth's cold embrace
Sprang forth from his grave
with never a trace
Of sickness or weakness, the
moment he heard

Christ's loud and commanding
authoritative word.
The blind who never, no
never had seen
God's beautiful flowers and
meadows of green,
The stately white lily, the
gorgeous red rose,
The modest blue violet
and scarlet primrose.
Now wide-eyed they gazed in
wonder and awe
And gave praises to God for
all that they saw,
Flaming fires of sunset,
crimson streaks of dawn,
Distant glow of star-lit skies
when day is done.

Betty Kent
IN THE SHADOWS

Auras on the mist of Night
Over stilled lakes and streams
Starlit sky—illumed by that
mystical planet beaming
its rays upon us
Casting shadows on you, on me
Poetry set to the music of the
wind as it caresses the trees
In splendor—witnessed by man.

Russell McCaw
SUN EAGLE

from the wind of the great
heights of refuge
the children in their peace
songs give
new breath to the evolution
of harmony
grasping in love their
understanding of
the union waiting thru the
arches of Autumn.

from the fertile remains of the
green leaves
and purple flowers of spring
and summer
comes the frost of Winter and
the promise
of the return of the green and
purple. . .
in the love songs of children
comes a new season.

Mary Ann Davis
UNTITLED

How can I capture on one
small page
The spirit and warmth of a
modern-day sage?
His heart is a heart both
gentle and rare
He's sought after, admired
and truly sincere.
A stubborn man with a will
unbending
With a charm that's constant,
never ending.
Quick to anger, Strong, yet
mild.
Easily touched by the smile
of a child.
The cynical optimist—
courageous and proud.
Resembling no one—unique in
a crowd.

Eleanor H. Cumming
DEATH OF A PARAKEET

Such a small death. . .does it
really matter,
beyond the sudden ceasing of
bright incessant chatter?
I stroke the emerald feathers
And lay him down to rest. . .
No more to hear the mimi-cry
Swell from his tiny breast.

"I love you," he so often said,
Strutting proudly with cock
of head.
Small caged creature, did you
really know
What love is when you
staged your show?
What lay behind your bead-
bright eyes?
Prisoner from flight to the
starry skies?
Well now, sweet bird, at last
you are free. . .
Look back now and then and
remember me.

Lisa Marie Hontz
I LEAVE YOU

I leave you.
As moonlight
Leaves the water's face.
As winds forsake
The fragile willow's
Brief embrace.
I leave you.
As autumn sun
Melts into gold,
With all the things
We meant to say
—Still untold.

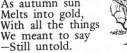

Adelaide Long Lawson
SONG FOR A SUMMER DAY

The day glides by on golden
air
And joines the year upon the
stair
Leading to star-etched
yesterdays;
Retreats beyond the hilltop
haze
Farewelled by pearling notes
of thrush,
In creeping dusk the robins
hush
Small songs for fledglings, safe
in nest
As spears of copper pierce the
west.
This signals peace to meadow
lark
As flame-flowers scatter in the
dark.
The sun slow-motions out of
sight,
And fireflies sequin the velvet
night.

Joyce Karen Flint
LOVE

They say that love
Is a sweet and tender thing.
It has the beauty of Autumn
And the sweetness of Spring.
You have that sensitivity
That's unique in its own way.
You cheer up my nights
And brighten my days.
There's more that I can say,
There's more I can do.
I just want you to know,
I'll always love you.

Marvin L. Sammons
ON HAPPINESS

Happy I was as a child—
Loneliness made me a man—
I'd walked life's monotonous
mile
Fulfilling humanity's plan
When at evening I sat on a stone
To remember the places I'd
been
Who would have thought—
could have known—
Your love had made me a
child again.

Lynder T. Yancey
CREATION LOVED

Man and creatures alike moving
in harmony
nation and world
compassionately understanding
one another
Stars and planets rotating in
perfect balance
galaxy to galaxy expressions
of infinity;
No hour, no day, no year, no
time, no limits. . .
Only the presence of Creation
Loved

Linda A. Nealey
IS IT LOVE

One look, one smile, one touch
And everything in the room
disappeared
There was only you, is it love.

The music soft and low
Dancing in your arms
The room seems to be moving
Round and round, is it love.

Walking in the snow with you
Holding hands, stopping looking
At each other, our lips meet
Such warmth, is it love

Nights with you, never like
before
So much warmth, so much
tenderness,
Flesh on flesh could I be
dreaming,
Or is it love.

You say goodbye, I die inside,
And the feeling of loneliness
Begins, wanting you,
Needing you, Yes this feeling
Inside is love.

Donna Fay Pearson
THE TWO LOVEBIRDS

There sit two lovebirds,
Singing and embracing,
In a gold-wired birdcage.
A female lovebird, Aqua,
Is fond of splashing the water.
A male lovebird, Rainbow
Has a vivid colorful tail which
Resembles the rainbow in
reality.

Eartha Schultz
QUESTIONS TO AMERICA

America, America
Who shines his light on you
Who crowns your good with
brotherhood

From sea to shining sea
Is this still America's song
Or has it been casted out
In my mind there's serious
doubt

When I can't pray in a public
place
It reminds me of a communist
race

Is this the thanks you give
To a God that's kept us
All of these years

Look at that baby—all dressed
up
And playing Punch-a-Nellie
Then look at the one with pin
legs
And a swollen bellie
Dying from disease.

Are you really at east
Not allowing young children
To pray
This nation without God is

sure
To decay.

Elizabeth Curtiss
THE RUDE AWAKENING

One year ago our embassy
   was stormed,
Americans were angry,
   Americans mourned.
Get our people back safely,
   let them know we care,
but nothing was done, as
   they remained there.

They're in our minds, day
   after day,
and that this tragedy will end
   soon, we pray.
God help the families whose
   lives are tossed,
and God bless the eight men,
   whose lives were lost.

There will be a day when the
   flags will fly,
the bands will play, no one
   will cry.
There will be a celebration
   throughout the land,
as we welcome the hostages
   home from Iran.

The Rev. John G. Hay
THOMAS WOLFE

"And I shall be great"
Speeding along in fiercest flight
A restless flame on the river
   of night
Piercing the blackness; waking
   the town;
Chasing the fog like a wailing
   hound.
   Racing onward,
In searching quest,
Faster, faster,
Into the West:
Till the echo dies and the
   flame goes out,
And lovers turn in their sleep.
Roaring onward,
Roaring in pain,
Spin the wheels,
In pounding refrain:
Faster, faster,
Into the West!
"O lost and by the wind
   grieved"
Your search for life has ended.
Look homeward angel;
October fires your wintry berth,
Virginia flowers are dead
And the hills beyond
   transcended.

Sue Boxwell
THE GAME

Isn't it funny how the
   resemblence is so alike for
   us and
the chessmen? We move
   through life finding our own
   like the
chessmen on a board finding
   a mate. The queen looks
   down with
books in her hand, teaching
   us how to lessons unfold,
   teach
them now before they are old
   all the morals and wisdom
   there is
to be told. Never is the
   end of knowledge to be
   shared—to
play the game, it's never the
   same.

So like the king and queen,
   do our young stand beside
   each other, like no race
   ever than ours that is human,
does any other even resemble,
   in face.
We teach each other but do
   we learn, like each in his
   soul,
do we remember? The game
   of life is by chance played,
   the
rules are often broken, and
   altering
isn't always so trecherous.

David H. Skellenger
REFLECTIONS

As I sit here and stare at the
   midnight rain,
I can see a broken man in the
   window pane.
For his life was once full of
   love and joy,
And now has been shattered,
   like a child's only toy.
But not all has been lost,
   for his life is sustained
because of those reflections in
   the window pane.
Reflections of his loved one,
   who is ever so dear,
that he would give his life,
   just to be near.
A uniform he wears, though
   not worn with pride,
because it was they who stole
   his bride.
I hope my wife, who is so
   far away,
Understands my confusion,
   why I am astray.
When I remember your eyes,
   the way they glow,
And your heart of love, your
   heart of gold. . .
Thanks, my dear, for helping
   me through
These ungodly months of
   being without you.
God may have wanted it all
   from the start
To show us our love, while
   we were apart.
Sooner or later it will come to
   an end,
When we can be happy,
   together again.
The memories I hold will
   always remain
in those beautiful reflections
   from the window pane!

Jerry Boursell
BELLS

Do ring o bells to wake the
   slumbering
   for ears of those to hear,
Your voice well known shall
   now be heard
   as morning comes to leer.
Aloft the land to spend one's
   life
   encased on steeples high,
O ring the bells and cry out
   loud
   to then sit back and sigh.
Do lift your head from side,
   to side
   and let they know day's
   time,
For those below sing out the
   land
   her voice so tuned to rhyme.

At home you stay on winter's
   night
   and summer days so pass,
For spring and autumn you
   must stay
   while seasons never last.
As refuge for birds to sit and
   chirp
   they know no other home,
But to sit upon your shoulders
   cold
   as iron drapes your bones.
Then comes the sun to cast
   her light
   as day begins to flee,
And shadows tall do cast away
   to sweep the land and sea.
Now sleep the night for she
   shall fall
   upon your rusty face,
As silence creeps through out
   the land
   do sleep within your case.

Leonard R. Piotrowski
**THE PAGAN DREAM
BEAST**

If a flying saucer
landed in the yard
making every look strange
with its light,
'till it seemed
no longer important
to have eyes,
even then,
if they opened a door
I'd ask to go with them.

Gloria Fusaro
ABORTION

Horrendous and ugly
Never God's plan,
We're all put here
For creation of man.

Conceived in passion
Conceived in lust
No choice to be made
This being unjustly put to an
   early demise.

Not knowing his worth
The unborn child never
   touching this earth
Just fades away and away and
   away.

Andrew S. Theiser
AGE IS

Age is a scale of social
   acceptance
Each of us hoping to attain
   a balance
To linger too long at any one
   stage,
Disrupts the balance and is a
   reflection of age.

Youth may be precious and
   glorious at times
Seen by some as a blessing,
   by others a crime.
Adolescence is confusing and
   often causes fear
Brought on by physical changes
   that appear.

Striving from adulthood, each
   child is prone
Often succeeding and arriving
   alone.
Backward and quickly they
   retreat and regroup
Attempting to define their
   curious coup.

Back through decisions and
   choices they've taken
Seeking reinforcement for a
   confidence shaken.

Slowly retracing their bounding
   strides,
Discovering alternatives their
   excessive speed hides.

Never again will they ever
   achieve
The feelings that frivolous
   playing will leave.
One often wonders after
   these children arrived,
Whether they felt they'd been
   blessed or maybe deprived.

Barbara Rosser
REJOICE

Let us rejoice! Let life fill
   the air
With its unnamed song of
   those who obsess this dare
Let us rejoice and praise this
   unholy day of hell
till beneath our feet, the
   pebbles of dust turn to shell
Let the sky turn gray toward
   our souls
while the spirits grasp the
   ever-winding vine of golds
And as the star of light frowns
   in disgust,
unseeing, we venture into the
   worlds beyond us
Oh, let us rejoice! Let us call
   the dead
for the ball of fancy as evil
   and tyrants put together
   their heads
Bring forthe the wine and
   fulfill our thirst for hate
and let us rejoice for the
   earthly beings of bait

Elizabeth Benton
LAND OF DREAMS

Sitting still and quiet
I gaze out a nearby window
and silently float into slumber—
Not physically sleeping
but mentally dreaming of
faraway places and forgotten
   times.
I'm a fairy tale princess or
   a sorceress—
unknown in the land from
   whence I came.
Reality is no more—
I can dance upon a star
or lounge on a cloud,
see the world through a prism
   of colors.
Slide down a rainbow into the
   legendary pot of gold.
I can swim the ocean in less
   than a day,
and tame wild animals in my
   imaginary jungle.
I'll find the lost Atlantis
and make my home there

among a peaceful people who
   know
nothing of violence and
   suffering.

Suddenly I'm kidnapped—
snatched back to the cold
island of now.
But I know my stay will be
brief,
for a voice will beckon to me
and, again, I will escape to
the opposite side.

Gail C. Garlow
**AESTHETIC IMPRESSIONS
(EBB & FLOW)**

Like a river flowing
And like candles glowing,
Your music comes and goes;

Like a skater dancing
Or wild stallions prancing,
The power waits but knows.

Then the unyielding force
From its one inner source
Bursts forth in radient show;

The song is sung,
The hearts are wrung,
Yet onward the beauty flows.

Like lovers sighing
Or a baby crying,
The music grows and grows.

The power from within
Is the truth, my friend,
where strength and freedom
glow.

The glame may end,
The river may bend,
Yet the source freely knows,

That within the heart
Where the song began,
A river forever flows.

Marion E. Williams
DELIVERY ROOM ANGEL

Oh! What is this I'm about
to see
Hurry don your mask and
come with me
Hold your breath and push i
hear
Don't hold back, the time is
here
Pop, snip. splash, wha, wha,
oh joy it's a boy
Your a giant in that room
Well prepared for joy or gloom
God has blessed you with a
special hand
For i know GOD has you in
his plan.

John Hampton Gray
RETURNING ONCE MORE

Warmed by the glowing coals
of fire,
Mellowed by the lingering
taste of a cup of wine,
I have gazed into your lovely
face and been lost in deep
trance.
Depths of blissful slumber
ensued—many an eve.
Apart I dream of the softness
of your skin, the wispy long
golden brown
hair upon a bare shoulder.
The warmth of a timely touch,
and wish I had stayed on.

B. Coy
RATIONALIZING

You got it off your chest
Footprints on the rest
But soon it's my turn
And you'll surely burn

Someday we will learn
From the stomp and the burn
To save those who're left
And make them our best.

Gary B. Reed
THE MOTH

The chalk colored moth sensed
the glow
spawned by the flickering
flame of the candle.
It fluttered about the teasing,
baiting light
obsessed with the flame's
fluid waving motion.
Attracted and repelled by the
scorching fire,
it momentarily hesitated—before
joining.

Emilia A. Glaz
ARTISTIC COMMENTS

A pelette of paints and canvas
do try
To capture the beauty of
field, tree and sky.
Through an artist's painting
does bring
Great pleasure,
Still none can compare, in
even slight
measure,
To the majesty of art done
by God.

Nora Arquette
TREADMILL

I stepped onto the Treadmill
Because it looked like fun
But I was unaware that
The Treadmill had just begun.

With each step
The speed increased
The Treadmill had caught me
And would not release

No time to think
Just do and be done
My only salvation
To love someone

To get out of myself
I reach out to you
Take me off the Treadmill
Please let me love you.

Goodlow Elkins
WHAT IS A FRIEND

A friend is someone that's
hard to find,
And he can help you find
peace of mind.
A friend is someone that's
always there,
And should you fall he's
there to care.
A friend will give you his
heart and soul.
And he will always be warm
and never cold.
A friend is a human being
that has a heart of gold,
And he will never treat you
indifferent or cold.
A friend is an image of God
from above,
And he will stick by you with
compassionate love.
A friend is a woman or a man,
And you can be certain
they'll always understand.
A friend is someone that's
always by your side,
When your loved ones cross
the great divide.
A friend will share with you
in your sorrow and grief,
And they'll help you find a
portion of relief.
How many friends will you
find?
Not very many, most will
remain behind.

Carol Guerra
NO MORE PAIN!

Oh God how it hurts, can't
stand it no more
the pain is unbearable, i'm
going to fall to the floor.
it's time for release from
confusion and fear
some 714's should make it
disappear
Oh! wow! what a feeling, so
safe and secure
my body is loose, i'm glad
i took four.
in a couple of hours I'll be
gone from this earth
i'll be knee deep in death,
almost like a re-birth

then peace and quiet will
comfort me
they'll be no more to feel
and no more to see.

OH somebody, HELP ME! I
keep slipping away,
I'm scared, I can't see, may
maybe I'll pray!

So now I am gone and NO
MORE PAIN, but also no
love,
no more sunshine, or rain.
A mistake has been made
and I want to come home!
I'm crying, I'm lonely, oh
GOD, I'M ALONE!
Please, Mr. Death, forgive
me once more, I was
impatient and empty when I
fell to that floor!
I'll be different, I promise,
I know it's been said,
OH MY GOD, I'M ALIVE,
AND AWAKE
IN MY BED!!!!!

Mary Elaine Carr
NINA'S POEM

You too are encaged and you
can't deceive me—
For under that disguise of
contentment, you are longing
to be free.
For inside those composed,
soft eyes there are
dreams and imaginary lands.

Everybody has them, visions
aren't only for man.
So never relinquish your
dearest hopes as long as you
are captive—
But follow them with all your
being
and in times of dismay think
positive.

For soon you will gallop
freely over the ground.
And as you run wildly to
where you're bound—
You'll be a picture of
elegance and queenly dignity,
But, most of all, you'll be a
picture of what was meant
To Be Free.

Beverly Leach Hiatt
THE CONFIDENCE

"In quietness and in confidence
shall be
your strength". . .as Isaiah
speaks to us
from the Bible.

And in the quietness of early
morning
hours I find my confidence
for
today.

The confidence to put faith
again in
mankind who disappointed
me yesterday
with shameless deeds
unspoken words
misguided actions toward
others.

The confidence to face
beautiful
nature once again
past winds and floods
birds flown away
cloud-covered sun.

The confidence in myself—that
I can
try to understand how it is
to
be in "those shoes" and
be less than yesterday
in speaking unkind words
listening without hearing
hurrying along my way.

Doris S. Anderson
MY BIRTHDAY

Autumn is a special time—
Brilliant hued and pleasant
clime.
Had I been priviledged to pick
my birth,
(The date I appeared upon
this earth),
October would have been my
choice
If I'd been told I could be
boss.
God knew I'd have picked
this one,
So he sent me forth and
had His fun!

Sharlene Stegall Sharpe
THE PICNIC

Today, when we were together
I played picnic with my heart.
I lay all my feelings out
on a checkered cloth;
There, for you to ponder over—
Pick and choose. . .
Taste, drink in my thoughts
Quickly—lest I grab up
The corners of the cloth and
Run, with my feelings; tied
To the end of a stick. . .
Now, jumbled together
carelessly,
Over my shoulder. . .when the
picnic
stopped.

Ken Hooper
UNTITLED

Beautiful and delicate,
Unique is each one,
Time, to them, means nothing
Three weeks and their work
is done.
Each brings a moment of
beauty
Requiring nothing, except to be,
Flying from flower to flower,
Leaving worries to you and me.
I love to watch them flutter,
Especially in the sun.
Songs they put into my heart,
with the universe I feel as
one.

S. Thayer
FOR THIS I ASK

I will never ask more of you
than you can give.
But

I may ask more of you than
you
are willing to give.

For this I feel ashamed.
  Although
If I did not ask,
  You
may never think to
  give.

Gladys Reed
REMINISCING

Sitting remembering longingly
  of the yesteryears. Searching,
yearning through eyes blinded
  by tears—longing so deeply
his arms to encircle me with his
  protective embrace; feeling
the depth of love that can never
  be erased.
It's here—all around me, and
  with me as yesterday. His
memory is here glowingly alive
  in my heart to stay. The
  indelible
inscription that was written in
  our hearts—"To love
and to cherish till death do us
  part" This golden cord also
was severed as by a shepherds
  shears.
Yet, in my silent aloneness,
  his soft call comes to my
  listening
ears. "I'm waiting, sweetheart,
  what keeps you so long?"
I reply quietly, "I can't pass
  through yet for the pressing
  throng". "The train is
  departing—the whistle I hear,
  the airport
is closed, and the bus is not
  here! I'll wait until tomorrow;
will that be too late?" "Will
  you please meet me at the
portals near the pearly gate?"

S. G. Carnes
AUTUMN PRELUDE

Today, while I was walking
Down a wooded lane
All of nature was talking
Autumn, brilliant, bold and vain

The air was thin and crisp
Frosty winds awhirling
Summer but a lingering wisp
Brightly colored leaves a twirling

The sky, touched with gray
Loomed above the trees
A hint of sunlight in the day
Fretting of winter's freeze

Hearing, somewhere far from
  sight
Amid the frigid, rustic scene
Honking of geese a flight
And fierce flapping of the wing

My heart was not in stolid mood
Peace of mind was with me
Autumn was more than ample
  feed
To set my starving spirit free.

Glen C. Nairn
LOVEABLE VALENTINE

The blossoms of the trees smell
  sweet
The morning dawns upon our
  feet.
Our hearts are filled with joy
  and gladness;
Our dreams and minds are free
  from sadness,
Thanks to this loveable
  valentine.

Ineffable love and joy alike,
Ineffable love affairs alight.
Remote from hatred and from
  lost

Remote from sighs of remorse,
Thanks to this loveable valentine.
O intangible love so divine
O matchless friendship so
  inclined.
The love we know is what we
  show;
The lover's mark is where we go.
Thanks to this loveable valentine.

Betty C. Albright
FREE AS A BIRD

The thought has occurred to me
  Every now and then
    Just what I would like to be
    If I could be born again.
It's not that I'm not thankful
  For my present state
    But, I wonder if maybe. . .
    a bird
      Is truly free of hate.
Our dreams diminish with the
  Passing of years
    Our hearts become filled
    With emotional fears.
But, a bird questions not
  His journey through life
    Nor is he immobilized
    Due to stress and strife.
A human has each and
  everything
  Down to a science
    Including his own questional
    questionable
    Degree of self-reliance.
The irony, it seems, is his quest
  To be. . .free as a bird
    Yet, the bird has the answer
    Without ever reading a
    single word.

E. T. Howell
TO AN INSECT

I think I'll never like a fly
Or a roach or an ant or a flea.
So why do I cry when a
  butterfly
Falls in front of me?

Marguerite L. Taylor
**A TRIBUTE TO THE AUCTIO
AUCTIONEER**

Listen folks and you shall hear,
The call from the Podium loud
  and clear,
The Sale is about to start.
Now all settle down and lend
  an ear,
For you're just about ready to
  hear,
The famous chant of the
  Auctioneer.
A word of warning before we
  start;
If you're here and don't want
  to take part,
Then don't move a muscle or
  breathe a big sigh:
For Merlin has trained himself—
  Quite a Keen eye.
The bidding starts, and he sings

out—
"I have one thou, now two,
  now 3 who'll make it four?"
Then suddenly comes a big
  roar from the floor,
"I got four."
Bids start again and suddenly
  stop,
The gaven comes down with
  a plop—
Then you hear the famous
  last words of an Auctioneer,
"Sold to the gentleman sitting
  right here."
And now in closing may we
  say
It's really a Fine Tribute
You Jersey Folks pay,
To a Great Auctioneer.

Elaine Levin
**TO THE SOUL OF JOHN
LENNON**

Tying the strings of our dreams,
  we soar
As wingless birds of flight, by
  night.
The pot of gold at rainbow's
  end
Our God waits for thee to send.
My heart cries out with colored
  joy:
A red frog leaping with blood
  of chaines.
My love, I wait for thee with
  pains.
Childhood's bright light grows
  dim,
Forever replaced with shine of
  night's whim.

Ann Todd Harrison
MY LITTLE GIRL

Here she comes swinging down
  the road, tell me,
(Where have the years gone?)
The memory of her first baby's
  kiss,
Such a precious gift, I'm so glad
  I didn't miss.
The laughter and chatter of her
  little voice in play,
Could I have it once again, for
  just a day.
Who is this grown-up girl, in
  my little girl's bed?
I know, my little girl went away,
  sent her instead.
Last night in her sleep she called
  my name.
I couldn't see her face, but her
  kiss was just the same.
Her voice was still so warm and
  bright
And she hugged me just as tight.
I noticed lately, a secret in her
  smile
I knew she could only be My
  Little Girl, for just a while.
So goodbye, my little darling,
  (There go the years)
Hello, my grown-up girl,
  welcome, please excuse the
  tears.

Elizabeth A. Anadale
WINGS OF THE SOUL

Invisible the sun, while the
  moon glowed white and bright;
Light were our hearts as we flew
  upon cloudless skies.
Floating among the stars, aiming
  for the moon,
  That benevolent face smiling
  round us,
Encompassing past, present,

and future—daring all.
Words unsaid, thoughts
  possessed, deep secrets
  unfolding
  Beneath shadows of silvery light
Of one mind, of one spirit,
  lulled by the soft sway
  Of a bird in flight,
Grazing deep the pathways of
  heaven.

Trust once given, a moment
  prized alone above others.
Two minds, two beings one
  with the stars.

Soft whispers baring the soul
  with words of love
  And spiritual gain.
Abandoning the chains of dust
  beneath,
  Hallowing in the spacious
  breath of God.

Gwendalyn Gordon
UNTITLED

I'm an incurable romantic
  an eternal optimist
I believe in love
I'm not sure love believes in me
  anymore
I've played the game
  and it seems
I always lose
just when I decide I'll never find
  it
love shows up
  briefly
only to run and hide from me
  again
I wonder how many times
I can pick up the pieces
  and carry on
it seems I am becoming
less and less resilient
  and yet
when a possible love
  comes my way
I'll be there
  to fall
  again.

Grace Paschal
SAVED

When I first came to know You
  I was troubled
  Not about the ordinary things
  in life
Like mortgage and the price of
  food and gas
  That cause most people such
  strife
I worried about my salvation
  I needed to talk to Thee
I wanted it settled once and for
  all
  Where I would spend my
  eternity.
Then a man came by that I am
  sure You sent
  And he kindly showed me the
  way
He asked me point-blank "are
  you saved"?
"No? Then let us pause and
  pray"
I prayed, "Lord I am a sinner"
  "Please wash my sins away
Without You I am nothing
  I am asking You to save me
  today."
That was not very long ago
  I invited You into my heart
Your line is never busy
  I learned that from the start
You have given me peace from
  troubled thoughts

My mind is now at rest
I can declare "Christ is the
answer"
In You there lies the best.

I was talking with You this
morning
Of how undeserving I am of
your love
Still, I will trust You to take me
to heaven
Because You promised it in
Your Word.

Sherry E. Short
THE MAN NEXT DOOR

The man next door
surveys his lawn looking
for stray dandelion weeds.
He flips a switch
And cocks his ear to hear
the purr from the filter
that cleanses his olympic size
swimming pool.
The man next door has three cars
a camper that sleeps his family
of five
and a boat.
I think they call it a cabin cruiser.
The man next door works from
ten to five
if he feels like going to the office.
If not, he goes out on his boat.
The man next door belongs to
the civic league,
P.T.A. and goes to church each
Sunday.
Strange thing tho,
Just yesterday I attended the
funeral of the man next door
and overheard someone say
the ceiling would need three
coats of paint. . .

Daniel H. Kim
DREAMING

With vision cloaked, I listened
for your voice
Hoping for the warmth of your
touch,
Longing for the sweetness of
your smile.
I prayed for your heart to be
mine
Wanting so much to be near you;
I closed my eyes wishing for all
these things.
I thought I heard you call out to
me,
I felt your hand reach out for
mine,
I envisioned the beauty of your
smile.
I sensed the presence of your
heart.
I looked all around; not a thing
I found. . .
I was only dreaming again.

Donelda Christianson
OH, HUSH LITTLE BIRDIE

Oh, hush little birdie,
The sun will soon set,
It's the closing of day,
And all will soon rest.

Little children cease play,
And it's time to set in.
To their cosy warm beds,
In the house with their kin.

We bid goodbye to the sun,
As darkness creeps forth,
In the sky now's a full moon,
As nature takes course.

Goodbye beautiful blossoms,
Sweet rest to you all.
See you tomorrow,
When morning will call.

Lorna K. Davis Apple
PRAYER

Give me crimson sunsets, Lord,
And a patch of fertile land,
Give me mountains high to
climb
And the sea upon the sand.

Send me rain to quench my
thirst,
And trees to shade my eyes,
Let me love with a gentle hand
And, Oh Lord, make me wise.

Give me but enough to live
And I shall be content,
Oh, I shall be joyous, Lord,
Until my life is spent.

Violet Fair
OLD DREAMS

He carried seventy-six years
With pride.
Caring for his crippled wife
Scrubbing floors
Cooking meals
Washing dishes
And dreaming.
Oh, the things he planned to
do
When he retired
Twelve years ago.
He'd visit Charlie in Florida
Fish a lot
Walk for miles
Thru the mountains.
Twelve years gone already
Charlie died this year
His closest brother, dead.
What happened to those dreams
The fishing and walking?
Twelve years tied to a wheel
chair
Not even his own.
His white head bowed
The unfairness of it all
Threatened to engulf him.
Then he looked at her
Helpless, growing weaker
And pity filled his heart, and
love,
Her dreams had vanished too.

Monique Anne Farano
ALONE

Sometimes I sit here and I just
want to rot,
All my friends are going out
with someone, I'm not.
Maybe I'm jealous, that's what
it could be,
Everyone has the one they want,
and then there's Me.
I don't know why I'm like this,
but that's the way it is,
I cry myself to sleep and dream
that tomorrow I'll be his.
One of these days, I'll wake and
it's going to be true,
but for the mean time, to hold
out, what am I going to do?
I shouldn't be so upset, it'll
only make things worse,
I'll hold out for as long as I can,
but inside this really hurts.

Este Cholodenko
MY DOLL

My doll sits the day
upon my bed,
holding up proudly
her wise old head.
She neither laughs nor cries,
nor feels the pains of living,
all she knows is the joy of giving.
Trust and security
is what she gives to me,

always being there and listening
to
whatever it may be.
When a young girl
in her childhood is growing,
she needs her doll
for to love always be showing.
But when that girl grows
the doll that so closely to she
once clung,
is often in a dark closet flung.
It's not until a woman is she
that she realizes how special
her doll still may be.
Within her dolls heart
she quietly holds;
memories of the past,
along with childhood dreams
which will forever last.

Audrey Davis
KIDS

Kids, who needs them?
They're loud and abusive, they
whine and they cry,
They're always fighting, they
constantly lie.
They boss you around say what
they don't like,
They don't listen to reason, get
hurt on their bikes.
You can't win with them, you'll
never be right,
You nurse them when sick, you
stay up half the night.
They get on your nerves, it's
hard to hold on,
Then something happens, they
grow up and they're gone.
And now, you wish for the
noise and the screams,
The house has no laughter, how
empty it seems.
Why didn't we see, why didn't
we know,
To stop and enjoy them, to
watch as they grow.
At least we found out, what we
never thought true,
Kids, who needs them, Believe
it, we do!

Noli C. Guinigundo, M.D.
AWAY FROM THE MOON

there are giants from the full,
big moon
while from your face asleep
creepily fall the tears of night. . .
(among the lines of a banana leaf)
let the night lose the moon
weeping in the fog
for tears die away soon
alone shall we be. . .

so comes the hour of falling dew
with windows a-shuttered
if our fate mustn't cross still
would I
wait: LOVE APPOINTED ME.

J. Elizabeth Apple
LEGENDS OF HAMMER

Standing near the end, the
abyss within the ache,
deep, dark and unknown
reaches for the Teal Aurora
painting the sky.
Pillars built on eternity crumble
from a seismic
rumble, releasing a flood of
tears kept for a
hundred million years.
My body burnt and dropped
into my own abysmal
salty depths, becomes a meteor
trapped inside
Peter's seine.

Fighting the palm that oscillates
me I grasp onto a breath to see
into the infinite mirror my
reflection left for unforseen
years.
The hurt, the pain and the
agony touches the sensitive
celestial winds
Touch the cheek of the Captain
of the flying
ship before he sets sail for
otherworlds.
Once when I was sleeping, he
set port here
and when I awoke all that was
told to me were
the legends left by the Captain
and his mates.

Maxine Myers
ISLAND STORM

From the depths of a nether
world, a bewildered and
beligerent soul,
Struggled from Obscurity, trying
to become again whole.
The pieces would fall together
momentarily, then fade away—
An anguished heart would plead
for help, that grew day by day.
The labrinth of the struggle
increased, the search went
on and on.
A dream of peace of mind
would flash too suddenly, then
was gone.
The weary restlessness was
there, and revealed it's every
mood,
Too long the forces had been
raging deep within and was
far from good.
An outlet was so desperately
yearned for, to calm a being
in need
Of the deepest understanding
of someone who would take
heed
Of a spirit that had been tried
and tried, and had paid the
price of a battle won,
The scars still fresh on heart and
soul, even though the trial
was done.
The end seems near and trust
it is soon, and even though
they are worlds apart,
If one mind can settle another,
will mean an everlasting
peaceful heart.

Shellie Colleen Reese
THE PANTHER

There is a panther within my
breast,
he wanders to and fro.
Why he is so restless
my heart shall never know.
In twilight I can feel him,
he pulls against his cage;
Soft paws claw my sanity,
my mind can tasts his rage.
And I would ever free him
if I but had the key;
Yet, his green eyes, filled with
torment
throw back a mystery.
Those eyes so full of hunger
glitter with emerald gleam;
and crouching in the pit of me
he is not what he seems.
And I cannot fanthom them
nor the fear that makes them
pale,
And in the shadows of my soul
his complaints become a wail. . .
Yet there is a panther within my

breast
His nite-cries fill with pain.
Always he will pace his cell
and strain upon the chain.
And I will ever in torment be
In quest of answers that
would set him free. . .

Susan Dee Baylock
ME AND HER

Me and her, her and I, our
friendship
is so strong I could never lie.
It's always been and it
will always be,
a friendship like ours is for the
whole world to see.
We go together like a doe and
a fawn,
we've stayed up talking til the
break of
dawn.
Our bond is the unbreakable
kind,
I can always cry on her shoulder
and she
never seems to mind.
We love each other with all our
hearts, and we hope to God
we'll never part.

Janet Gage
DRINK FROM THE CUP

As we travel along life's hiway
and drink from the cup it
extends,
sweet and sour intermingle—
for that's what the Master
intends.
Success and failure go hand in
hand,
with happiness and love inter
intertwined.
Grief and sorrow, loneliness
and tears,
are added to challenge the mind.
From early childhood to
second childhood,
we greedily sip from the cup,
to experience life to the fullest
before we take the last sup.

Deborah McCardell
TO MY JEWISH FRIENDS

Though our religions may be
different
Our paths of life are the same
We've laughed and cried together
We've shared each other's pain
We've prayed to God the Father
Who watches over us all
We work and live together
Just waiting for His call.

Ken Jones
CHURCH BELLS

Down the
Valley comes the
Gentle ring of Sunday's
Church bells. . .carried softly
by the
Morning.

Mrs. Angie Gerdes
**A PAT ON THE BACK NOW
AND THEN**

Dad's by-laws were: "The
Bible, Law, Shakespeare, Emily
Post."
He taught us by good example
what to value the most.
It's not what life does to you,
but what You do with your life
If you can love, give of yourself
there will be no strife!
The best make-up your face can

wear is a sincere smile,
Reaching out to others, making
them feel life's worthwhile!
A baby, a young adolescent, and
an adult,
All respond to love, who is there
without any fault?
Everyone needs a pat on the
back now and then,
To make it or to get back on
the right track again,
Dad treated even servants with
dignity, respect,
He died twenty-five years ago,
but his love lives yet!

Mary Dupont
IT'S BECOMING A HABIT

A storm 8 pm. . .
Demonous darkness!
How fiery the night!
Lightning quills nondescript,
fluid-etchings
on the naked pit sky.
The thunder's hedonist roar
hedges the sphere,
as lightning quicks—
My knees quiver.
My spine shivers.
And I sit huddled, like a puppy
to cover.
But— didn't I do that
self same thing
the night of my wedding. . .
when all was tranquil.

Ellen B. Gowen
SUNRISE

I sat at the window this morning
Watching the early sunrise
Such a beautiful sight to see
One can scarcely believe their
eyes.
Every color of the rainbow
Streaks across the skies.
As you watch more intently
A big red ball begins to rise
Out of the line of streaks it
moves
Up, up, up it comes.
Then looks out over the world
And we know another day has
begun.

Michael Bowling
TIME

So soft is the voice of the future
As it whispers lightly in your ear
So quietly it speaks to you
That most hear no sound at all
It is the essence of lightness
And will bring joy to each
one
So try hard to remember
If you have experienced its sound
The present makes no sound at
all
There is nothing lost or gained
It offers no hope or rewards
For the persent is the maze of
reality
The past trumpets loud in
your ear
Making the young our apple of
discord
The past tries hard at deceit
For time is its enemy.

Joyce Joles
THE COMFORT OF GOD

God gave me comfort when I
thought I had none,
He always gave me strength
when I needed some,
I am not alone, as long as he's

in my heart,
I hope someday, I can be worthy
of his special mark.
I've committed sins, and know
I'm forgiven,
It would be glorious someday
to be in heaven,
Where there's only love, and no
hatred,
There, all is kept very sacred.
No more angry feelings to bear,
Only lots of love to be shared.
To learn to love as Jesus loved,
Could only be a gift from above.

Johanna Swane Mooney
**THE FOUR LOVELY SEASONS
SEASONS OF THE YEAR**

Spring, fragrant spring, one of
the loveliest seasons of all,
Birds return on the wing,
looking for love until Fall.
Spring, which makes tender
hearts cling, vanishes while
the birds sing,
Right into gentle, warm Summer,
Summer, the lazy newcomer,
The time of the year when love
sets on fire,
The heart of a groom, with Man's
loving desire.
He takes a sweet bride in June,
And goes off on a long
honeymoon.
Love is uncertain, but is still a
lovely song,
And love going with marriage,
so it really can't be wrong.
Rushing along comes radiant
Indian Summer,
Leaving behind the birds and
the cricket, the hummer.
Then, with the dimming sun,
Autumn leaves and pumpkins
show change of season has won.
Winter comes in quietly, the
most picturesque time of the
year.
With a blanket of snow
and St. Nick, enough to fill
all hearts with
cheer.
I guess I love them all, Spring,
Winter, Summer and Fall.
The four seasons of the year
are still the loveliest of all.

Stephen Sierakowski
**TELL ME THAT YOU LOVE
ME**

Tell me that you love me, but. . .
not until I tell you, and
only with a cherry on top.
Tell me that you love me, but. . .
only when I want to know, so
tell me so, when I let you know
to let me know, ya know?
Tell me that you love me, but. . .
not until the midnight hour,
unless of course I'm asleep.
Sure I listen when you talk, you
Talk! Talk! Talk! What's
there to eat?
What!? You already ate! I
meant to eat at eight!
Why don't you listen to me?
Tell me that you love me. . .

Anna B. Nichols
MY FRIEND CLARA

'Twas the Third of April
In Eighteen Ninety Six
A child was born,
I'm sure a cute trick
She became my friend
Much later in life

She has seen her share
Of joys and of strife
Even tho' she can't see
Pleasant she remains
A joy to be around
She never complains
'Tis the Third of April
in Nineteen Eighty One
Many, many moons later
And many setting suns
On this Third of April
When you are Eighty Five
Not too many of your time
Are still alive
Since all good things
Must come to an end
I'd like very much to say
Glad to have had you for my
Friend.

C. A. Filsinger
THE PRISONER

I know that soon I'll be carried
off to the sea;
They'll throw me in and help
me under, to drown.
Why can't they leave me alone
and just set me free?
They may kill me, but they
can't make me wear their crown.
People listen over and over to
my pleas and cries;
Yet they've hurt me and filled
me with so much shame.
They want to know how I
feel and if I wonder why.
Still, they've taken my dreams
and lost my last name.
Long summer nights, spent
thinking about my passing life.
So often I remember, it all
still seems so unfair.
It would be so much simpler
to end it with my knife;
And let this loneliness fade
away with the midnight glare.
But I don't try to hide or
cover my face;
Because two million people
would gladly
take my place.

Violet Flowers
THE MYSTERY OF LOVE

Love awaits you
But it is not easy to obtain
For the force you have built
around you pushes it away
You alone can let love
flow your way.

Debra T. Humpert
PLAIN OF GRASS

A plain of grass.
The sun shines.
The grass is warm,
It drinks the golden rays
And glows with inner life.
The wind blows.
The grass moved.

It breathes and sighs
And rustles a dry dance.
The moon shines.
The grass is quiet.
It sleeps beneath a silver blanket
And dreams of another day.

Dee Tatum England
DAWN BREAKS

Dawn breaks—
  On the rose petals there is a
  touch of dew.
The sunrise is beautiful too.
  The mist falls through the
  morning air.
In my mind, I form a picture of
  you.
  The birds go off in flight.
Till dark falls somewhere in
  the night.
  Touch me sweet air.
Caress me midnight.
And if I might I'd take one
  wish.
To spend one sweet moment
  holding you.

Daniel R. Amato
WASTE NOT A LIFE

To give birth is to create life.
To create life is to start death,
For life is an experience in death.
If death has not made a
  difference,
Then a life has been wasted.

Rodger Allen Hicks
MISERY

He is maintaining
  (never falter in public, friend)
He has fallen this night shattered
  (as before)
He tries to regroup
  (it is time for display).

Elliot Gibbons
GUY FAWKES DAY

Big bands, noisy clangs,
  And little pops around us.
The boys and girls love to watch
  The fire works around us.
Big thrills and squeaky shrills
  To make us full of fear.
Bright blezes from the fire
  Lets you know Guy Fawkes is
  here!

Mauricia Price
ONLY DREAM POSESSED

Only dream-possessed
And restless flame-touched souls
Can know the hungering
For dew-strewn fragrances. . .
  and grace
A poet seeks to find
Along peripheries
Of bursting day at dawn
Within the fickle brief embrace
Of romping winds upon
Fresh-wakened earth beneath
Bark-armored limbs the trees
Extend, beside an s-curved stream
Of limpid coolnesses
A river spins—can hear
The elfin symphony
Within a poet's sunsplashed
  dream.

Patricia M. Bedrich
HOW OFTEN WE MISS

How often we miss the light
  of the Lord,
It shines through all of the world,
And yet, we are too blind to see.
How often we miss the touch

of God,
The cool breeze, and the fluffy
  snow,
Which only a child will love.
How often we miss the presence
  of God,
On the earth, in the sea, across
  the sky.
How can we think that all of
  this could be,
Without the mighty hand of
  Thee?

Uncle Albert Bianchine
FOG ON ARAPAHOE BASIN

Thick
Heavy nothingness
White shroud
Wood chairs
Light air
10,500 ft climbing
Sounds
Voices
People below
I hear
fear
12,500
No higher
Angelic powder
God's crystaline chowder

Mrs. Cheryl L. Graham
INNERMOST ME

In all the times I've ever known
  of life, of love, of laughter
are still the ways I haven't grown
  and sought what I was after.
To seek the wisdom deep within
  and share all that I find
is peaceful bliss and calm acumen
  from heart. . .not from the mind

Constance Frost
ROSES

You sent me roses for Christmas
The memory still brings a sigh.
I thought they were saying "I
  love you".
Instead you were saying "good-
  bye".
What hurt the more with your
  leaving
My heart or my pride, Heaven
  knows.
One thing for sure, after all
  these years
I can't stand the sight of a rose.

B. J. Lisatz II
THE SONG

Late at night
Driving along the interstate,
The radio a blaring
Not a soul in sight.

Once again
Reminded of you
As a mellow love song plays
Hurling me into a melancholic
  mood.

The words are appropriate,
The past becomes so vivid,

The asphalt a blur,
The music intense.

I see you,
Standing by the roadside
Waving as I pass by.
It has to be a dream. . .

As the last bars are sung
I emerge from my trance
To find myself near Topeka
Where we met so long ago.

Turning off the radio
I head to the edge of town
Where I know
I'll find you once more this eve.

Tears fall, as I peer at the
  tombstone.
Later, I walk away, my heart
  as cold as ice.
Heading toward my destination
Sidetracked by a song.

Teresa A. S. Richardson
BUTTERFLY

How sweet art thou
  whom sails the breeze
whom flutters the skies.

Behold the heavens
  ye so delicate.
Behold your creator
Behold the warmth indeed.

Though so meek—thee art mature
for lacy wings
pray tell, are show

Wither thee yonder go
Before the winter cold
The youngs deed are cozy
'Til spring doth cometh again.

Florence G. Axton
INTRIGUE

The water is a violet-blue
The winds blow shrill sounds
  anew,
The rumble of the crested waves
from the restless salt water sea,
sing songs from a Calypso.

The beach is steep,
Scoped out sand holes,
Hard perhaps, luminous,
Crabs scurrying for new
  protection,
Seagulls aware, instant detection.

The sky a turquoise blue,
white fleecy clouds, a frame of
  lace.
Empty shells on the water's edge
Each with a wrinkled face.

A cottage, not far, beckons,
The lure of a Beau Mondo,
Draped in a Camlet,
Dares to defy
Winter Silence,
low chants,
intrigue.

Tracey Anne LaFond
LOVING YOU

Loving you can be so wonderful.
Sometimes I can just think of
  you,
and feel your presence.
I can feel your gentle touch,
upon my breast.
Or your soft lips upon my neck.
I can see the sparkle in your
  eyes,
which just opens up my heart.
But then loving you can be
  so painful.
I can think of you and feel your
  presence
once again, but in a different
  way.
The thought of your touch upon
  my body,

can make me sick with guilt.
That sparkle in your eyes can so
  easily
turn to black, and then tear me
  apart
inside.
I wonder can the good I feel in
  loving
you, forsake the pain I also
  feel?

Barbara J. Adams Grutter
FOR I DO LOVE YOU

Abide by my love and you
  shall be—possessed.
For I do love you and I cry.
Does God not understand
  this love of mine?

My love for you has such a
  deep power
That at times it has a sickening
  sweep.
You in my thoughts at all
  times is painful.

This love so strong has my
  heart in its grip.
My fear of never forgetting
  you is a burden,
Remembering is a process of
  a slow dying death.

And you, so innocent, unaware
  of my desire.
To not look my way is as an
  unwanted breath.
I can be as any woman you
  would ever need.

But I am me. Lonely as I
  am
My want for you is a rebounding
  ache.
And never will you know this
  love of mine.

Sheila Autry
WOMAN

Reveling through untamed,
  evergreen hills,
she flows like swaying daffodils
Iridescent eyes, dazzling smile,
brings worshipers over many a
  mile.

Zest for life, essence of grace,
vagabond where there's no
  time or space.
Abandoned wanderlust, she
  will camoflage
bewildered yearnings—an
  illusory mirage.

Deservance of veritable reverence
unshakably vigorous, truly
  intense.
Strength of a lioness,
  gentleness of a dove,
she brings rebirth to fantasy
  loves.

Relinquish your insolably
  secret dream
to this lithsome, wistfully
  precious being.
Her fancy—free laughter will
  tickle your despair,
leaving springklings of
  uncurable happiness there.

Bertha Jean Perdue
**HONED TO
UNDERSTANDING**

I mustn't say I understand it all,
Every time I see a fellow being
  fall,
But I'm not so quick to jeer or
  condemn,
When I see failure in my fellow
  men.
The girl I work with , the very

quiet snob,
is risking her life to get to her
job,
The drunken man, she's his wife
He has threatened to take her life.
The weird fellow who has the
shakes,
He can't afford the medicine he
must take,
Those wild little kids, running in
the street,
They're safe, if they go home
they'll be kicked and beat.
So if you must find fault in
your fellow man,
May I suggest that you search
and search again,
See if you can't find a probable
cause,
Enough to give you a pause—
and understanding.

June E. Catalini
MY DAD

His hands were strong yet gentle.
His hair was raven black and
always
waved on one side.
He had a nervous habit of
jingling
the change in his pocket, and a
quiet sense of pride.
I remember trying to ignore the
whiteness that came in his hair;
his tired eyes and the slowness
that settled in his walk.
I remember thinking how empty
life
would be without him to laugh
with
and talk.
Then much too soon I was asked
asked to
live with that emptiness.

John C. Brault
ANGEL

We're sorry that life was not the
way you wanted it to be and
done.
If we could you'd have another
hour,
but reincarnation also was not
meant to be.
Just take the pieces that are
left and put a new
time to will the thoughts, for
past has gone.
We hope that you'll have a
better chance and
understand what there is and
enjoy the ways.
Well my "angel" time for us to
move on,
and we won't be back to tell,
but
will be able to listen to your
thoughts.
Our fate will be with you,
as well as your with us, and
remember "always be among".

Phyllis Sanderson
THE GOLDEN STATE

I love this golden land so bright
in smiling pleasure it glows
Over desert in summer delight
as beauty in the cup grows.
Each moment some elegant thing
like a golden cup in stillness
Spreads its light like a regal king
for miles and miles of loveliness.
Its little forms of life move

in the enchantment of the sun
That in their funny ways remove
your care to enjoy this fun.
So settle down and let this
golden land
fill your mind with its colors,
sounds and forms,
Till you have quite forgot your
care
It's there afresh each morning
bare.
California!

Helen C. Kelley
THE PRICE OF MIND

Bluebird singing on the fence
Never asking whither-whence

Red rose growing from a clod
Never doubting love of God

Oak leaf drifting down to earth
Never musing why of birth

Snowflake swirling through the
night
Never choosing wrong or right

Almost I could wish to be
As you are, naive and free.
Bittersweet, my lot I find,
I must pay the price of mind.

Robert Alvin Davis
SPRING

See now, the cherry in blossom,
Upon each bough, the birds will
sing.
Ah, when 'tis heralded by the
robin
Then God, I know it's spring.
Smell now, the rose the lilac
For in fragrance rare, they bring
The beauty of the flower
And the wonders of the spring.
Gone now, the cold the rain and
snow
Summer is nigh and approaches
fast.
Winter's naught but a word in
this poem
My God, 'tis spring at last!

Kathy K. Suber
LIFE LINE

I believe that beneath dense
webs of
frailty,
confusion, and
despair
there lies a precious gem: an
intense, everpresent source of
powerful strength,
wise direction and
sparkling hope!
This must surely be our
umbilical cord to the Creator;
iron-clad link to the Divine one
and the splendid hereafter!

John Reynolds
MAGIC

Magic summer night—
lights in the distance,
Trees flanking road
And country all around—
The sea is near:
I love my love
In the ocean of love, splashing
Silently within my soul.
Magic

Evelyn M. Putnam
MONDAY MORNING

In silence and alone I wake,
Melancholy, hollow, a
tearburst cheek.
Faint in the shadow of fading
sleep

Heart-wasting cares, restless
deep,
Crowding my mind.
Closing my eyes, the stillness
breaks,
Morning comes with music,
sunshine.
Oh! Tangled mind, disconsolate
heart
Dress in cheerful lustre
For fate of today.

Rebecca-Sue Thompson
THE FIRST DAY OF SCHOOL

Ahh, the first day of school.
You're all dressed up and look
so big.
The smile on your face tells me
you're ready for this;
But how can my baby, my
child so small, be
going to kindergarten and look
so tall.
She does look nice and so
willing to go.
The school doors are opening
and swallowing her whole;
"Oh dear! Oh me! What have
I done!"
My darling's growing and she's
just begun. . .

Jean Ruther
RED DUN FILLY

The colors of the sun
along her soft flank run
in bright and shining beauty.

The earth's timeless whirling race
is losing this filly's space
in a fair meadow's dream.

Reminiscent of an older sound
her world is mostly bound
by the arena's endless pagentry.

All patterned in shifting gold
retreating into some unknown
fold
the tiger and leopard go.

Cruel claw and fang cease,
but man in old unease
tears with bit and spur.

N. Petherick
THE ALARM CLOCK

Arms tucked tight against my
chest,
Legs drawn up—a fetus.
Wrapped inside the web of my
mind's
cocoon—floating—in limbo.

The hoarse, coarse buzz of the
metal insect
droans louder, penetrating my
sleeping senses.
Time becomes measured.

In that instant
Man's vice begins to mark
the speck of my life.

Kelly Jones Sensmeier
THE PAIN OF REALITY

I look at myself . . .
Then I look at you.
Why are we living?
I wish I only knew.
This world we live in
Is all just a game.
But, where are the rules?
Oh, it's just the same!
The rules are just there
To break and to bend.
What shall we do here?
When will it all end?
I'm going in circles . . .
. . .I just feel so lost!
When will I get there?
What will be the final cost?

All I truly do hope for,
Is just happiness.
When do I get mine?
All I can do is just guess.
I'll just look to the skies
Up above.
Who's to say?
Maybe . . .
. . .Someday . . .
I will find my true love.

Daniel E. Travitzki
**PAINT ,PASTELS AND
MORNING DEW**

When you were feeling
rejected,
forgotten by time and man
I gave to you
paint, pastels and morning
dew . . .

Selecting the finest of paints
then—with gentle strokes
erasing carefully
all the sorrow,
yesterday's pain
the fear of age
and all the worry
brushing away everything
which
threatens to take away
from the pure elements of
you . . .
Using pretty pastels
to highlight the softness of
your skin
so much like silk
to shade in the satin
which lace your eyes of
sunrise
giving pure luster
to the treasures of you . . .
And morning dew
the final touch
to give sweetness to you kiss
seasoning the flower of
freshness
that is your smile
a smile which captivates my
every waking moment . . .
laced lovingly with promise
for time
to keep sacred
a love meant only for you
so free
so real
Everything and more, my love
for you . . .
preserved for eternity
now—within
paint
pastels
and morning dew . . .

Tamey Heffelfinger
I LOVE . . .

i love the way You
hold me tenderly in Your arms,
close to Your loving heart
i see no harm . . .
i love the way You
passionately touch my face
as Our hearts race

into the precious night . . .
i love Your inviting eyes
as they wisely gaze,
capturing my hungry soul,
making me Your slave . . .
I love your gentle lips
as they venture towards mine,
Your wild penetrating tongue
can be conquered by none . . .
i love Your searching fingertips
as they seek to find
what is forbidden to touch,
what some wish to hide . . .
i love the way You
caress my trembling body
as my soul joins with Yours,
becoming one eternal Flame . . .
i love Our moist bodies
as they entwine
together we feel ecstasy
that one cannot find . . .

We're perfect beings
brought Together by love,
when We became One
We flew as the dove . . .

I love the way You are,
I love the way I am,
I love the way We are . . .
TOGETHER!

Darlene Gail
THE STREAM

The stream comes to meet me,
  as I walk along the forest floor.
The water rushing over the rocks
  seems to be trying to speak.
I love to watch the water move
  in such an artistic way.
It flows along so gracefully,
  "Follow me," it seems to say.
As I follow further and further,
  I am hypnotized by its beauty.
All at once, I look up and realize
  what I was led to see,
A magnificent waterfall, falling
  down in front of me.

Joyce Quindipan
HOBO

His hair is stringy and it's
  thinning, too.
The stubbles that invade his
  face are grey.
His eyes no longer shine a
  crystal blue,
and velvet skin of youth has
  turned to clay.

His world exists of flirting
  with some broad,
of daily midday naps and
  city strolls.
He worships not nor follows
  any god
but seeks, like us, for ends to
  dreams and goals.

To him, it doesn't matter how
  one's dressed.
He knows that wand'ring
  gathers all life's dust,
that silks and furs suit mainly
  those obsessed
while he, to rags and tatters,
  must adjust.

For Hobos live their lives with
  unsure beat,
a different rhythm sequence,
  but concrete.

William M. Crawford
THE MIST OF TIME

I have come through the mist
  of time,
From beyond the ages past
  and gone.
I am as an eagle, a lion, with
strength and courage.

I have conquered and been
  conquered
but I yield only for a time,
All of the earth and beyond
  is my realm,
Horizon upon horizon I have
  trod and claimed
My right with sword and
  shield.
Even the heavens give sway
  grudgingly
To my determination.
I am the past and I claim the
  future
with all its pain and glory
  in my name:
"MANKIND"

Synthia L. Snyder
FREEDOM

have you faced yourself on a
  sleepless night, alone?
have you longed to be with
  friends
  and found no one there?
have you listened to the music
  in your head
and wondered why it was so
  sad?
have you listened to the wind
  and watched the rain
and wanted to cuddle but
  you were alone?
have you wanted to laugh
  and found no one to laugh with?
have you faced the pain
  of decisions made for the
  wrong reasons?
have you listened to yourself
  and liked what you hear?
have you paid the price for
  your freedom?

Millicent Young
IN THE MORNING

So full
  like sky of rain
  sun of rays
  from the dark ocean belly
  rises
Your love

Jane E. Warthan
MY LITTLE DARLING

Say my little darling, what can
  mama do?
She tells you that she loves
  you, know that it is true
She hugs you and she kisses
  you, we play so many games
Ever since she had you life has
  never been the same
As she watches you grow
  older, she sees so many things
As she watches for any sign,
  of who you will be like
If you will be like Daddy and
  stay up half the night
Or if you will be like Mama,
  and read with all your might
We have so many happy
  times and many more to

come
Your mama she does love you,
  and want for you the best,
For you my little darling
May your life be fully blessed!

Sue Bagley
EPITATH

To those who trod this lonely
  place
Inhabited by memories,
And hear the wind come
  whispering
Across this haunted hill,
As you traverse the narrow
  path
Beside this simple grave,
Always walk softly;
For a dream lies buried here.

Faye Webb
FULL FANTASY

Nurture yourself—
Have pleasant thoughts—
Perhaps a wish will do,
A tale or two—
A fantasy in full view.

To escalate to heights unknown,
Stay for a minute or two—
Then— to return to existing
  reality—
Remembering thoughts,
Cherishing moments,
Perhaps holding on to a few.

Nurture yourself—
Enjoy it—
Love each moment,

Savor each passing breath . . .

Then— life will be fuller,
Each day a little brighter,
All because,
You've nurtured yourself again.

Lauretta D. Moss
THINGS CHANGE

In this thirty-seventh
year of my life
you have come back to me
the same promises you made
  before
hanging from the corners
of your mouth.
Funny, I never noticed before
how your mouth is worn at
  the worners
like the edge of a wave.
I should be happy
(I think)
you are back.
Someone has said
(Margaret Mead, I think)
a child needs his father,
But things change . . .
Margaret Mead
(after three husbands)
is dead.
Your mouth is worn at the
  corners.
Your promises have been
  tattooed
rust colored on your mouth.

Karol Ann Hooper
ONLY YESTERDAY

Seems like only yesterday we
  were
climbing apple trees
and building sandcastles by the
  sea.
Seems like only yesterday we
  laughed
and played and tried to run
over the hill to catch the sun.
Seems like only yesterday we
  were
oh, so full of zest

and wanted life to be at its best.
Seems like only yesterday we
  were
playing hide and seek
and cousin Bobby tried to peek.
Seems like only yesterday mom
  would
tuck us into bed
and gently kiss our little heads.
Seems like only yesterday we
  hoped
and dreamed that life would be,
full of peace and forever free.

Mary E. Dempsey
WOODS OF PINE AT DAWN

Through fields amiable in
  nature
I walked
one morning.
On a September day—
engulfed in woods
of pine
I found myself
in
a secluded valley
variegated in darkness,
and diluted light.
The plants of feathery fronds
still
frost-stricken by the passing
  night
raise spirits to the sky.
In this spot
of sweet smelling pine, and
  aloneness
I sat
for seemingly a duration,
on
a moss-grown log,
and waited till the new day
gave virgin birth to the sun.
I erected my body to leave
  and
it was then I knew I would like
this spot to be
  my eternal resting place
In honor of the serenity
that the
Woods of Pine offered me.

Shirley D. Stoeckel
FORGOTTEN FRIEND

I picked up an old book, dusty,
long-forgotten on the shelf,
its pages dog-eared as if to
  say,
"I still keep safe those secrets
you found within my pages
  on that
long ago day."

Vivian Patricia Pezold
WHAT IS A GRANDCHILD?

A grandchild is an angel who
Is a lot of "them" and a little
  of you!
To love and cherish—to hug
  and squeeze
And yes, at times, to even
  tease!
A little tyke who steals your
  heart
Whom you hope will always
  share a part
Of his woes and laughs and
  sometimes tears
With his grandparents in his
  growing years.
God touches us all in many
  ways
But the sweetest of all is that
  lovely day
He's granted you His greatest

prize—
You look into a grandchild's
eyes!

Shawna Taylor
SLEEPING SLUMBERS

Along my sleeping slumbers of
the
twilight hours and the waking
hours
of the day and dawn, I hear the
sweet
melodies of faraway words
ringing in my ears
calling my name of distant lands
of
words and worlds and I listen
for all the
secrets of the impossible dreams
of my destiny
and I write forever. . .and more.

Karen Miale
I CONTACT

Your green eyes invite me
like patches of moss
in a lover's secret forest.

I reach for you to span
the time and space—
illusions of separate bodies.

My senses are fired
as you draw near.
Contours and colors focus in
and melt beyond
for perception by older eyes.

I embrace you to me.

Karol Fortney
GETTING DRESSED

Pieces of lace,
drifting by,
make a curtain of white.
blowing up
floating down,
sometimes falling fast.
tumbling flakes,
landing perfect,
make a fluffy cover.
trees reach,
earth waits,
for her new dress.

Michelle Baker
MY FAVORITE POEM

You are loved poetry
In my soul—
Always, your lines
Will be engraved
In my heart.

Dushka N. Petkovich
MUSHROOM TEA PARTY

Won't you have one cup of tea?
One cup, please, do have with
me?
In this tea sugar need not be,
For with this tea
I wed thee to eternity.

One sip—
Lie back—enjoy the trip,
Blood walls close upon your ship.
Dance and prance, then take a
dip,
Tarantula girded on each hip.

Inevitable end to this
honeymoon—
Reality returns too soon.

Hazel McLeish
**TEACH ME TO LOVE YOU
AGAIN**

Teach me to love you again,
let me thrill to your charms
anew
Teach me to love you again,
and I know I would never be
blue

Would that I could recapture
all the rapture of yesterday
Time without ending; a lonely
heart wending its way
Just give me one kiss more
tender that I may surrender
to you
It could be most enchanting
and very entrancing 'tis
true
For my arms are just aching to
hold you as then
So won't you please teach me
to love you again.

Betty S. Robinson
TWO ANGELS

While feeling low and depressed
one day
He sent two angels along my
way.
They helped me up when I
was down
and moved way clouds that
had gathered around.
They inspired me when I
thought there
was no hope
And yes, these angels helped
me cope.
They taught me patience with
my fellowman—
How to find faith and peace of
mind within
But most of all they taught me
love—
Yes, these angels were sent
from above.

Lt. John O. Chenevert
**TO MY SON DAVID, IN
PRISON!**

Can you see me Dear Lord,
Standing alone in the night,
So small I must seem,
With all the other wonders in
sight?
Below the cover of darkness,
As white clouds roll by,
Can you see just me, Lord,
As a lonely man cry?
Can you see me look North,
From this spot where I stand,
Can you see me Dear Lord,
Just one little man?
Can you see what I feel,
And what I need to say?
Can you see me tonight,
As if it were day?
Can you hear from my heart,
As I start to pray?

Kimberly Colling
MOVE ME

Move me one over
Closer to you
Show me your rainbow
Then bring me one, too
Teach me to live
What life is about,
Will I win?
Will I lose?
All I can do is try.
Teach me to live
Then teach me to die.

Linda Wagner McKinley
FATAL VISION

At last the liars come
home to their limping
decayed designs   and wonder as

Patterns swirl and vibrate
into sound streaking their
consciousness colorless and

Mute their unheard screams
shatter into mindlessness
for all time and

At last as no one hears
or sees their colors fade
or their wingless flight.

Dawna Laurita
NEGATIVES

I am glad
that I can finally take your
picture down.
Now . . .
all you are to me
is a negative memory
that continues to print the past
we've shared
in most everything I do.

Ellen Fairweather Rodriguez
OF THE EARTH, EARTHY

Those who live in ivory towers
Miss a lot of charming things
Jack-in-the-pulpits, blue grass
flowers
Aren't just for peasants but for
kings
Don't lose touch with Mother
Nature
And forget your feet are clay
When you kick off your golden
slippers
You'll find lots of fun that way.

Deborah Gilliam
FUTURE WE

I am wondering, where I stand,
Will we walk through life, hand
in hand.
Chances are, it could possibly
come true,
What I need, is love from you.
   Accept me, for what you see,
Not for what, you want me to be.
A complex woman, needing love,
   Like the sky, and the dove.
   Let us say, we will give it a try,
Babe, your eyes do not lie.
The warmth and caring, I can see,
   You and I were meant to be
   A WE.

Ann Ida Grover
UNTITLED

Dear Kate lies asleep
the sun shines upon her hair
though her smile is sweet
there's no color in her cheeks
'cept for blood her wrists are
bare.

James S. Bradshaw
FRIENDS

This is to all those who have
helped.
to those who laughed with me,
and felt joy on the sunny days.
to those who will always be,
and helped me see through the
haze.

This is to all those who were
always there.
to those who cried with me,
on the days the world turned

sour.
to those who helped me to see,
that this is not the darkest
hour.

This is to all those who teach
me to love.
to those who hold out their
hands,
when their touch is all I need.
to those who help build my
plans,
and follow when I want to
lead.

This is to all those who will
always be.
to those who are there to
brighten the days,
I can count on them to the
end.
they are there with a kind word
to say,
they are the best, they are my
friends.

Myrtle E. Wilson
**COMMERCIALIZED
CHRISTMAS**

I wonder what happened to
Christmas's past,
When we would have been
happy for a crocheted hat.
Now nothing we get seems like
it's enough,
Seems Mrs. Jones puts that in
the stockings she stuffs.

If you want my opinion, I bet I
know,
Just who those three wise men
were so long ago.
It was Sears, Wards, and Spiegal
Catalogue,
Because there's nothing you
can't buy, except the family
dog.

And that's where the shepherd
came in,
With his animals to sell to men.
And then there's that pony your
kids ask Santa for,
With the feed, barn, and pasture,
there goes the car.

And then there's the B B gun
for thirteen year old Tom,
"Oh, why not, just thirty dollars,
that's not much, Mom!"
Then on sale comes a rifle, for
only thirty-nine, ninety-seven,
Fourteen year old Larry's
wanted to go hunting since he
was eleven.

And then there's a record player
for Tammie Sue,
Who's ten now, but without her
dollies, what would she do?
Then there's baby Ginger, who
we all love very dear,
But she watches too much TV
and believes all she hears.

And these wise men always
make it so nice,
The shepheards say, there's
nothing easier to raise than mice.
Then when the packages are
opened, and Christmas is over,
I bet you're just like me, we
know who's rolling in clover.

Gerri McGlone
MOUNTAIN STREAM

It rushes, pounds, eternally
flowing.
From where the land kisses the
sky it has traveled,
Ever downward, smoothing the
rocks as it passes.

It slaps the rocks harshly,
hurriedly,
In it's quest for the sea.
In the gray-green of the autumn
afternoon,
I sit, studying it's movements,
listening to it's song.
The wind whispers and mingles
with the swirling current,
Until a certain melodic tune can
be heard,
The gentle laughter and
innocence of children,
And the peaceful sighs of one
who knows.
There is no aching, no loneliness,
Only the soft reality of water
and wind.

Marguerite M. Mulberry
MEMORIOUS

Some memories have substance.
I place a scarf into the old trunk,
rock in my grandmother's chair,
turn the dirt thickened door
knob
of the old house.
Inside, the house smells moldy
and light is timid through
dusty windows.
I close the door gently
but it creaks mournfully.

Some memories are imaged in
thought.
They are trees of reflection
illuminated
with light.
They are infinite.

Fred Mobley
THE POWER OF YOUR MIND

Your mind is a Powerful Control
Center
You can use it to be a looser
or a winner
Your mind is a gift, it's like a
Control Panel
Whateven the circumstance,
your mind can handle
Defeat comes from not using
mental positivity
As a result, comes forth negative
activity
Your mind can be used to make
you happy and to succeed
Or you can misuse your mind
and be trampled under the
stampede
Don't be defeated by failure
and fear
Shift your mind to positive and
go forward in high gear
Control your mind to do good
and create
Use your mind to love and not
hate
A positive mind will take you
farther than imagined
You can live in an apartment
your mind can put you in a
mansion
Your attitude can be a total
disgrace
Your mind can put a smile on
your face
There may be an obstacle you
can't overcome
With a positive mind, your
battle is already won
The Power of your mind is a
great source
Use it for life's everyday course
You can't go wrong when you
think right
Tho you may have problems
always look to the way that's
bright

How are you going to use your
mind
Will you be happy or end up in
a bind
Your mind is a Powerful Control
Center
Why not use it and be a winner.

Michael Gonzales
EVERYDAY LOVE

Everyday I think about you
and reminds me of your smile
Everyday I want to be close to
you
and tell you just how fine you
are
Everyday I think of the day we
met
and can't forget the things we
said
Everyday I see you in my dreams
and record the lovely scenes
Everyday I touch my lips upon
her sweets
and thank the Lord for what
I receive
Everyday I see her pretty face
when we meet at the same old
place
Everyday I think about our
everyday love
because darling you are my
only loving dove.

P. A. Young
JUST LOVE

Memories of long ago
My heart all aglow
This bouquet of love
In a soft sweet bow

Just love
Yesterday, today and tomorrow
With the risin' sun
And soft breeze blowin'
I've just begun
To know this, "special one"
May you be aware
I will share
This bouquet of love
For I do care

Just love
Yesterday, today and tomorrow
Life has a key
And shall decree
What is to be
For you, for me

Just love
Yesterday, today and tomorrow

Susan L. Malling-Holm
HOPE

I see a man of old
with his gray hair
and cold wired beard.

The man of the seas,
who travels the dares
of the high cliff waves.
Which only he and the sea,
together will always share.

To ride the rollercoaster of
the hard blowing wind
and the frightening thunder
crashing upon thee.

"And I will travel the seas,
to know only of these
mysteries."

So the old captain of his ship,
fight together with the sea
and the battle of hell.
And the pounding water upon
him and against the helm.

And with this you awake,
upon the fullest horizon.
To see the blue crystal sea

and the sky full with its
exotic colors, as far as you can
see.
"My ship is my hope.
And with my hope,
I'll have my ship."
And together will be,
till the end.

Katherine A. Lords
A FLOWING STREAM

Life is like a flowing stream
I wonder is it only a dream
There are times it seem
That everyone is lowly and mean

Let's wake up and be on our
way
For it is now a bright and sunny
day
There's no time to delay
Jesus is coming back again
But not to stay.

Regina L. Jamison
LOVE

Love is such a precious gem,
To be given all to that special
him.
Friends and family they mean
well,
But in the end, you have to tell.
If a mistake, you have made,
don't give up,
Always remember, another love
await, just
to fill your cup.

Dewey D. Bayless
THE SEPARATION

As you sit and sometimes
ponder
Will you ask and maybe wonder
Will you pause and think of me
Of how our lives used to be
Will your heart ache, as does
mine
As you think of our time
Will you reflect, both good and
bad
More-so-good than more-so-sad
Will your heart seek to return
To a loved one; will you yearn
Will you ask if love exists
Or if it's vanished, in the midst
As you sit and gaze above
Will you know that I still love
Yes, as you sit and sometimes
ponder
Will you ask and maybe wonder

Regina Corbin
A HAND TO HOLD

I need a friend
A friend like you,
Or just a hand
To Hold on to.

I need your love
But Most of all,
I need a hand
So I don't fall.

I need your strength

Or should I say?
I need a hand
Both night and day.
Without your love
Without a friend,
Without your strength
I need a hand.

Without all this
What would I do?
Without a hand
To Hold on to.

Sheila M. Peace
UNTITLED

The waves come into shore
To greet me with memories
Of a love which once was
mine . . . .

They leave me though
Taking back to the ocean
What I remember of joy and
pain . . . .

But just as the waves
Keep returning to shore,
The hurt and pain returns
To lap at my memory
To wash over my heart
To return, recede and return
Once again . . . .

Rebecca S. Powers
HIS NAME, A MEMORY ONLY

Vacant eyes face me as I gently
try to make him comfortable
The pain so intense, but he
never utters a word, not even
a curse.
This man I did not know before
today,
His life, his personality I'll
never know
For he's dying . . . .
The illness that's befallen him
rages on
ravaging his already frail body,
but unsatisfied until it has
all of him.
And I watch along with his
family as his life slowly ebbs
Till soon his name to me, a
memory only.

Theresa Marie O'Brien
**EVERYONE BELONGS TO
NATURE**

I would like to sit and wonder
at the trees and at the thunder.
I would really like to know
how the summer flower grows.
I wish I knew
what is dew.
In the back of our lawn,
at the early peak of dawn,
the crackles of the trees bark
the song of a meadow lark.
would disappear and be
destroyed.
Who will destroy our nature we
own?
People if people;
the way we treat nature now,
everything will leave.
If we don't take care of nature,
God's feelings will be grieve
God gave us nature for a
beautiful reason
He puts a little something in
every season.
The glint of the pond catching
the sun's glow
reflecting in the sunlight forming
a rainbow.
Empty cans, paper bags, block
off the sun's rays,
hiding all the beauty and ruining
a Spring day.

Ashes on the snow from a
  chimney fire smoke,
lust upon the brighten white
  snow
  disappearing the flake's stroke.
Car tracks in the summer
  tearing up the grass
breaking of unused bottles
places pieces on the grass.
Autumn leaves color
fade from the air pollution
dying off and laying in a buried
  position
So I guess I will sit back and
  wonder at the
trees and the thunder.

Keith D. Self
ANGEL FLIGHT

I saw that girl some time ago
Ah, but she was a mystery to
  me,
With long black hair flowing
  thru the air
She was so young but not free.
Ah, but to have Angel Flight.
Some years later she captured
  my stare
But another had the key to my
  heart.
So look but don't touch that
  mystery girl,
Do not with your love freely
  part.
Ah, but I longed for Angel
  Flight.
Then chance came my way and
  she entered
My life, my heart, but not to
  stay.
That mystery girl is all of an
  angel
But like a butterfly she fluttered
  away.
Ah, but I love my lost Angel
  Flight.

Connie L. Newsom
YOU AND ME

Although those nights we spend
  together
are few and far between, the
  only thing that matters is
just how much they mean.
The time that I must spend at
  home,
leaves me feeling quite alone.
What keeps me from this
  loneliness of mine, is our
conversations on the line.
Words that come so hard for
  me
Come to you so easily.
When I'm with friends
  or by myself
I take these words down off
  their shelf.
My age is only nineteen years
  but I've had my share
Of heartaches and tears.
I have fallen for you
  I want you to know
It will not be easy
  to let you go.
Everything I have that is
  important to me,
My kids, my friends, my family
  I'd put them all aside
If I thought for a moment
  it would keep you in my life.

Lynn Marie Stevenson
MY FATHER'S HOME

The dirt road is long and steep,
The trees on either side are tall
  and strong,

The shrubbery plump and leafy,
The bridge of railroad ties and
  planks
  cover the transparent brook,
My father's home.
The log cabin sits far from the
  road,
The brook whispers just feet
  from the cabin,
The meadow above is as peaceful
  as the day
  God created it,
The weasles and other tiny
  creatures live freely
  throughout this mystical land,
My father's home.
The grass long and thick waves
  to the quiet
  happenings of the world,
The whistling birds fill the air,
The silent breezes flow through
  the tree tops,
The smells of all seasons satisfy
  the mind,
My father's home.
The days long and easy are filled
  with dreams,
The nights cool and pleasant are
  filled with
  sound of a distant banjo,
The brook, the creatures, the
  days, the nights,
My father's returned home.

Nancy Von Buskirk
THE CIRCLE

The circle begins over the sea,
  trailing orange and silver
silk on the water. Sandpipers
  race oncoming waves like trees
on a windy day, and the gulls
  overhead cry like rusted hinges.
The day takes on the translucent
  quality of twilight, a time-
less moment when the world
  listens to itself. Silence is
deafening.
Darkness comes with a sigh.
Waves lapping the shore like a
  lullaby, soothing anticipation,
bringing peace. The earth
snuggles in, with stars like night
  lights shining, revolving
slowly around a hushed place.
Wind snores softly around the
  cliffs, restless, yet reassuring.
Dawn breaks with the majestic
  pomp of a queen, commanding
awe
at it's silent splendor. Warm
  rays overflow like a waterfall,
drowning everything in golden
  tones. Morning seems to say,
Dare you lie abed? Arise!
Behold my glory!
And yet, time takes the sun's
  strength and feeds it to
nourish the dark, just as the
  dark must nourish the light.
As
evening slips up, the awareness
  that all is complete comes to
the land. The circle remains.

Harriet E. Mitchell
A SPRING WALK

Today I walked among the pine
  trees,
I heard them whisper low,
Springtime is coming, I feel sure
For gone is the snow.
My very highest branches now
  feel light
  as they can be,
and the loveliest robins

Have built their nest on me.
Raindrops are falling now
Little ducks begin to smile
As they waddle and splash
In the puddles so free.
Little flowers peek through the
  ground
As the warm sun-rays kiss the
  earth;
All of creation show signs of
  re-birth,
Filling our hearts
With much joy and mirth.

Steve Whitham
TIME FOR A CHANGE

What is a hawk,
That hasn't any eye?
What is an eagle,
That doesn't know how to fly?
What is a lake,
If there is no water there?
What would the sky be,
If there were no air?
What about a tree,
That had no limbs or roots?
Or even an orchard,
That doesn't bear its fruits?
What would a sheep be,
If it didn't have a fleece?
What good is peace talks,
If no one longs for peace?
What can be achieved,
Without an aim or goal?
What is a person,
Without a heart or soul?
That's what the world is coming
  to,
From all the lies and hate.
We're slowly destroying
  everything,
And bringing on a gruesome fate.
There's only one way to change
  it,
And that's to change our way of
  flight.
We've got to get it together,
And follow our guiding light.

Steven Stockfish
MY FRIEND THE BUMBLY
BEE

He's alive
in his hive
number five
and I've a good mind to say so.
He's receiving and grieving,
Deceiving no one.
Having fun in his cove.
Keeping warm by the stove.
Pranks, living,
Thanks and then giving
the best shot he's got
He's got quite a lot
He tries to be easing the pain
Relieving and pleasing but it's
  plain
For to see, he's a Lonely
old bee
Be the bee
in his tree
in his tree.
See the bee, you and me, see
  the bee.
Pardon me, all of ye, pardon me.
Take flight with this guy.
Make sight in his eye.
and fight for the right to be free.
To have might and have fight
  and to be.
To be right in the fight for to see.
"Let us you, let us me, let us be
Let us, too, let us we, let us see
and freely let us conform.
To be is to perform.
To see is to reform.
To me we shall inform.

and I survive
in hive
number five"

Donna (Beck) May
I TOUCHED A HEART TODAY

I saw your vacant eyes
Staring blankly out the window
Your expression left unchanged
By the wind and the rain.
When did you become lost?
I wondered to myself
How many birthdays
Have erased the hurt you felt?
You walk hugging the walls
Are they your only friend?
Have all others forsaken you
And left you alone
To further bury your sorrow?
The sadness in me is not as
  great
As the sadness I see in you
A lost child time has forgot
So has the world but can I?
Those searching eyes lacking the
  joy
You should have known
Is it too late?
Then I reach out my hand
To offer you a drink
And you break into a smile
Suddenly to myself I say,
"I touched a heart today."

Cynthia Leigh Stone
DAY OF PROTEST

Stealing down to the plant
Giant golf ball against dawn's
  sky
Sitting somewhere too close to
  the ocean
From deep inside comes a glow
  to light your city
A small glow that can also leave
  no city
Then the sun comes out and we
  vote for it
The other, an almost
  unharnessable source
The cause of the invisible
  deathly illness
The workers, the sterile men see
  us now
They can see the signs and hear
  the disagreement
Threats of the illness cover us
Leave us and let us do the job
We stay and take a stand
To save and be sacrificed
The badges come and they take
  us away
I have fear that the other one
  got me also

Russell Burnight
THE GAME CALLED LOVE

I'm walking down a silent street
it was tell now that I felt defeat
For the game was not one to
  win or lose
but the game was love between
  me and you
I fell defeated, I wonder why
I did not quit, I did not lie
It must be that in the end, I
  still will cry
But is the end as near as one
  might say
or will it last another day
or will I cry and shed a tear
or will it last another year
Now it is time I ask the Father
  above
"Is this the game you call love"

Gerlinda L. McCartin
HIS FRIENDS THINK . . .

She never calls him anymore,
He doesn't spend time smiling
  over the phone.
She never drops in,
He doesn't leave to meet her.

She doesn't pick her favorite
  blouse,
He doesn't pick her wild flowers.
She no longer sends him cards,
He no longer paints for her.

She no longer smiles then by
  the arm
  takes him aside from us,
He no longer speaks of her.
His son asks for her,
Her son asks for him.

In separate places
He's quiet,
  She's crying.

Absent from his life . . .
  Where is he anyway?
    He's far, far away.

Jane Jurison Klein
TO EDDIE

Thank you for the music box,
  it means the world to me,
I only wish that you were here,
  so I could thank you personally
But since you're there and I am
  here,
  this comes to you in writing,
To tell you it was thoughtful;
  and oh, how exciting!
It wasn't really necessary,
  but it gives my life a lift,
I play the music often,
  and it sets my mind adrift.
Remembering when you were
  here,
  and all the good times too,
Sightseeing day and night,
  Remember the tunnel we went
through?
At night upon Mt. Washington,
  all the lights down in the city,
Riding the incline on the hill,
  Three Rivers looked so pretty.
Just sorry that you had to leave
  so soon,
  with many sights unseen,
Pittsburgh is really a nice place,
  and this I really mean!
Maybe in the days ahead,
  sometime we'll meet again,
Here, or there, I really don't
  know,
  but thank you, again, my dear
friend.

Miss Veronica L. Andrews
HUMANS

Why must everyone be better
  than others,
  Why can't we all be the same.
    I'm human, you've human
I've reasonable, you're
  reasonable
  You're important, I'm
  important
It's love which makes the world
  go round.
Humans create this thing called
  love which keeps
  the world moving around.
When your love for others stops
Then so will the world like a
  clock.
  A little love can travel so far,
  No matter where you are.
  Change your ways and love a
little
  day by day.

Lisa Anne Barnhardt
BEACHES OF ETERNITY

We are grains of sand
put together, gathered together
to form a huge beach.

    But we are not
  the only grains of sand,
nor the only huge beach there
is.
    Many other beaches
cover the world and many other
grains of sand
    form these beaches.
We feel so important, but
are we—really?

Reid Fore
THE WAIT

The icy wind sweeps across
  innumerable snowdrifts
Daring anything to venture
  into its path
It searches for miles for
  someone so foolish
But not one creature comes to
  meet the challenge.

Except for one sparrow, in a
  solitary tree
Who, not knowing of the wind's
  cold reputation,
Sits, unruffled, his vitalities well
  insulated
Waiting. . .Waiting patiently for
  Spring.

Donna Lynn Musgrave
WHITE LEOPARD

What is it that slinks so quietly
Across the still and sleeping
  town?
Its paws hold death
It cannot be detected,
As it slinks slowly around,
Quiet and cunning,
Keyed up, but not jumpy,
The thing goes on its rounds,
Though its paws hold death,
It is goodness and wouldn't
hurt a soul I've found.
Instead it does good
To those good to it.
And bad to those who are bad.
But oh, what a dream of just
Watching I've had!

Judith Anderson
TWINS; ONE

Where we sate our lamps
That night
Upon inchoate sand
The scouting sea
Sending couriers of foam
Against our very feet
Singing delirium
With a beat-up guitar
A weathered violin,
All of Knossos' vanished gold
Collected in your hair,
I slumbered ill.

Now on the threshold
Of our vertiginous dreams
On the shores of Matallon
Wherein the limestone caves
The romans buried their dead,
Our hour of extinction
Is here,
Drifting on currents of treachery
Ushered in,
By weaponed words
And warring embraces.

We waken early,
Tune the violing
Whilst our sad small history
Closes over our heads,
My golden Ariadne.

Nancy E. Baran
BECAUSE OF YOU

Touch me. . .
out of the deepest sleep
awakens
my heart, my soul, my mind,
I have found
truth.
Touch me. . .
a vast ocean of joy and beauty
lies before me,
never
seen as now.
I have found
pleasure.
Touch me. . .
I am strong,
afraid
not of trial,
sorrow nor tomorrow,
be it bitter,
be it sweet,
I have found
courage.
Touch me. . .
the gates of my mind
are opened,
my potential expounds.
I was a caterpillar
now
a butterfly.
I have found myself. . .
in doing so,
I have found
you.

Judith Heiberger Dingle
PREMATURE

How destructive man can be
When grasping love too eagerly.

He casts life's stones
on pure, still water,
causing ripples that never cease,
as the hunter with deadly thrill
fells the fawn whose spots he
  did not see;
or the butcher mangles a
  quivering lamb
with hatchet in hand, ignoring
  its plea.

Man pounces undaunted,
  unmoved by her yough,
Probing her mystery to seek his
  own truth.
And the child who on woman
  womanhood's altar is torn
Comes blind, pink and dumb as
  the day she was born.

Mary Lou Brown
WAR

I saw the woman cry,
And I cried with her.
For I saw the people die,
I saw the country torn,
And I saw the nation fall.

Eileen P. Tippey
IT'S HOME THAT COUNTS

When the days grow long and
  lonely
  And no one bothers to stop in
I close my eyes in dreamland
  And pretend to take a spin.

First, I travel to New England
  Along the rocky coast
I see the waves and sea gulls
  As they feed upon my toast.

Then, I travel further onward
  Into the Canadian lands
The falls flow swiftly downward
  And never seem to end.

Across the barren country
  And down the strait I go
The bridge slopes steady down

downward
And the water flows below.

Oh, I've seen the cross of
  Minnesota
  And I've seen the sandy dunes
I've seen the Red Trees standing
  And I've seen Disney cartoons.

I've seen the old Pacific
  And I've seen the Atlantic, too
I've seen the Blue Ridge
  mountains
  And the Rocky's pine ridge
  hues.

As I waken from my dreamland
  And I find myself alone
It's not the place you've been
  that counts
  It's just the place called Home.

Ollie Vee Zoller
WAGES OF GREED

There was a man who greedily
  ate
Sandwich touch as cardboard;
  oh, what fate!
The picnic crowd howled
  When loudly he scowled,
"Help! Doctor! I ate my paper
  plate!"

Valerie Marie Bettendorf
SILVERWARE

They lack all decoration, yet
stately the knives, spoons, and
  forks
stand with their smooth silver
  surfaces
in the metal recepticals.
Each has its own place
on the moving black conveyer
  belt.
Passing thru the flap
a sudden play of light finds
the dime-like holes in the
  recepticals
and bounces off the silverware
into the darkness.

Judith A. Bauschka
UNTITLED III

What is there about you
  that draws me—
    so unabashed?
What mechanism of my being
  do you control?
How have you managed to tap
  these well-springs of feeling
  so far hidden—
    for so long?
Why does this self-sufficient
  entity
  called Me—
    now seem so fragmented?
Why do I react with a child-like
  sense of joy
  to your glance
    your smile
    your touch?
How have you restored
  spontaneity to me
  when I was so sure it was

destroyed—
   buried—
      beyond resurrection?

Steven Michael Cruz
YOU'VE GONE AWAY

I was the morning
You were the night
My life was so boring
Then you made it right
We came together
And could never part
No matter the weather
Love was in our heart
That's long since through
You've gone away
You said you had to go
I died on that day.

Leona A. Metling
BEAUTIFUL AGE

Always was said, Life is short
  and sweet
But to me it's been pretty neat
When I was young and full of
  pep
I never did anything I'd regret
As years flew by, married I
  became
Life marched on almost the same
I gave life to six babes, two boys,
  four girls,
Work, work, work, my life was a
  whirl.
I've lost a son, a daughter too.
Some days are happy, some
  are blue.
As time goes by, The nights are
  short
The days are long.
But I awake happy singing a
  song
Even though I'm growing old
I enjoy each minute of each day.
Not too wrinkled, not too gray.
I wonder, why I wonder about
  age, it's only me
Glad I'm alive to enjoy
the golden years in the land
  of the free.

Carmela Marghella
WAIT FOR FREEDOM

I wish I could be like others,
  but I'm not.
I guess I have to be who I am,
  but I can't;
I have too many restrictions
  blocking my freedom.
  But my love
stay with me, and to me it won't
seem too long for freedom,
  For FREEDOM and life is
ahead with you.

Rebecca E. Meier
DEATH OF A FOREST

A calm, quiet forest
full of green leaves,
Animal's homes,
in the woods and trees.

One careless match
dropped on the ground,
Then quiet prevails,
nothing is found.

K. A. Martin
MY LIFE

My dreams are real
for they seem to be
the only things
which are so close to me.

I dream of the future
the love it may hold
and wish every moment
that my life won't be cold.

I want the world to see
just how happy I am
because I can live
each moment as I can.
I love the way I am
with all my dreams
I can close my eyes
and I have all that I need.

Hagwahide
**PEACE. . .A FOUR - LETTER
WORD**

Peace is the most precious jewel
  of a word in the whole world.

Peace though means more than
  one thing all
  can be summed up in one word.

Peace is thoughfulness and
  thankfulness,
  graciousness and kindness;

Peace is unselfishness and giving,
  forgiving and forgetting;

Peace is patience and endurance,
  tolerance, not indifference;

Peace is not hate, but compassion
  without any compunction!

All these (and more) can total
  one word,
  a precious four letter word.

And that one precious word is
  . . .LOVE!
  . . .(to which mankind could
  resolve). . .

Margaret Ann Sadler
BLACK TULIPS

Do you remember how the
Black tulips swayed up the lane?
(The mail was delayed that day
Because of the rain.)

—And Old Mrs. Tate called out,
  "What are ye' doin' can't
  be done inside?"

—And we laughed, all beside
  ourselves with the joy of it.
—And you said, "We're
  counting tulips
  for the heck of it."

She said "Oh," and slammed the
  door,
And we counted some more.

Now you are gone. There is
  no spring
To count black tulips in the rain.

B. J. McKinney
LONELY CASTAWAY

What have I done!!!
I know naught
All is pain and fear,
Numb to all but tears.

Searing, hot tear
Streaking down a dirt-splattered
  face.
"Help me. . .please" my heart
  cries out.
Hoping, crying, wanting.
Please God! Save me!

Take me away. . .away. . .
I am but imperfect. . .mortal. . .
I know nothing to hold. . .keep.
Nothing is what I am
I don't even know myself.
I am but a servant
Wanting only to live.
Live?
As what?
A human being needed, wanted,
  helpful.
I am nothing here.
Oh Lord. . .please keep me.
No one wants me.
I am exiled in a crowd
Lonely. . .lonely. . .always lonely.
God. . .is my pasture here at all?
Am I to live in peace?
When? Where? Help!
God. . .I hope you see me.
I am nothing but a lonely
  castaway
Seeking my place in society. . .
In the universe. . .in myself. . .

R. Bateman Newcomb
KNIDIAN APHRODITE

What maiden posed before the
  sculptor's eye
And captured marbled
  immortality?
What sweat of passion wet that
  flawless form,
What children witnessed her
  posterity?
That gentle breast and matchless
  thigh of white,
That soft belly, and classic face
  sublime:—
Her silver laughter still is
  echoing
And ringing down the centuries
  of time.

Robert Tipane
**INTO THE VOID OF
VITUPERATION**

Magnetic fields of selfventalation;
Opposite poles deciduously cross,
Past the walls of inclination,
Lies a desolate flowing.
Lake of tears that never runs dry;
So many beings experience this
  knowing;
Floods of solitude imprison
  hearts and minds;
Crying for wanting, looking for
  a new day,
For in time we are this way.

Marianne L. Naas
GROWING LOVE

I feel our love will never cease
  to grow
Lately though I wonder if it
  hasn't already
  Are the hassles I cause
  unbearable
  Am I no longer a woman to you
  Yet, rather, a selfish child
I thrive on your love
Try to work my way around
  problems
Often you are discouraging
I'm lost, I try so desperately to
  keep you
But, feel you want to set me
  free
Laugh with me, love with me
Understand my troubles and
  incapabilities
I want to please you always.
It is hard to try and be the

---

woman I want
Others refuse to let me grow
Come prosper with me, be my
  alliance
If you feel you've grown past the
  spot we once shared
Pause and look back, Give me
  time, my love is not far behind.

Carla Cotner Parr
DEPRESSION

How does it start?
So slowly—a fear lurking in
  shadow.
A hopelessness, a darkness.
Fatigue, so great and heavy.

No desire to live
Or continue the daily walk
Through decisions, and goals,
And deadlines.

Death seems sweet,
A quiet twilight of peace.
Solitude and safety
Enfolding me like a warm hand.

Bradley Schuster
WHAT IS DEATH?

What is death?
Theologians say it's when the
  soul leaves the body.
Scientists say it's when the body
  ceases to function.
I look upon it as an adventure.
Will it be bright and beautiful,
Or dark and sinister.
Will it make my dreams come
  true,
Or will it be my nightmare.
I will someday explore it.
What is death?
Dead!

John W. Tribulak
MAKE ME ALIVE

Even though air is in my lungs
And blood is flowing through my
  veins
My life feels like one which is
  dead
Since everything I do seems to
  be in vain.

Lord, dedicate me to true service
And your will, help me not to
  resist
Come into my life and live
  through me
And help me not to just merely
  exist.

Kenni Barbara Beck
AFTER AWHILE

After awhile
  You tell yourself there's no
  chance
  No chance to ever bring back
  the past.
After awhile
  You learn to forget
  Not totally forget—just the
  part that shows.
After awhile
  You take a chance to try
  Try to see if it can ever be again.
Because. . .
After awhile
  You want to know if you're
  chasing rainbows. . .
  . . .or if you should look
  toward another sky.

Lori L. Warner
FEELINGS YOU INSTILL

When I talk to you—
The right words are so hard to

find
For there are so many thoughts
In my mind and from my heart.
    When I look at you—
I notice every movement you
    make
A little sigh, even a distant stare
And your shifting eyes reveal so
    much.
    When I touch you—
My heart races without an end
My eyes capture all of your
    beauty
And my body feels "magical"
    feelings.
    When I am with you—
I feel all of these feelings and
    more
I feel complete, needed and
    most of all, happy.
    When I am with you—
I feel all of these feelings and
    more
I feel complete, needed and
    most of all, happy
When I talk, look, and touch
    you, I feel whole.
"I love you."

Ralph B. Williams
GOOD ADVICE

I carp of much
    it is loads of fun
        to blow bubbles.
I enjoy almost everything, but
    it is wiser to prick the bubbles
    yourself,
        before someone else tries!
            GOOD ADVICE.

Gina Lynn Rutherford
MEMORIES

There are times
    when I want
to go back
    to places that
are no longer
    there.
And times when
    I want to
        talk to people
who no longer
    exist;
and it is then,
    that I wish
        to be
a child again;
    growing throughout
the days of yesterday.
    Never to let go again,
        Memories,
Sweet, sweet, Memories. . .

Vickie Wood
MOMA'S LITTLE MAN

Peanut butter kisses,
    chocolate covered smile;
Hands all smeared with jelly,
    Bread crumbled in a pile;
With frogs in every pocket,
    The cowboy takes his stand;
Thank you, Lord, in every way
    For Moma's little man.

Jorka Hill-Homko
THE WILLOW

I was a lost and lonely tree,
    Swaying without direction.
Changing movement, altering
    my course,
At every gust's suggestion.

One day you could find my
    branches,
Dancing in the breeze.
Reaching out to touch life;
Fulfilling all my needs.
Then grey skies would look

down on me,
Their eyes dark, as without sleep.
And I'd bend my limbs in
    silent sadness,
A lonely willow left to weep.

At times I'd whirl in total
    confusion,
Waiting for storms to subside.
Wanting just a touch of sun,
To soothe and justify.

And then , at last, you arrived,
Your gaze a gentle ray.
Now I bathe again in peaceful
    moments,
As flowers in the day.

Mrs. Yvette Bundy
A LOVER'S PRAYER

Our Father up above
Please protect Frank Bundy
    the man I love. Guide him
keep him, safe and warm
until the day he's in my
    arms. Keep our love so fresh
and true. Until the day when
    earth is through, bless us
with your loving Grace, until we
    meet you face to face. Guide
    us with your loving hand so
    that
our love may forever stand.
    Amen.

Eva Estes
THE TINY MAN

I understand not the ways of
    man.
If he builds castles or grubs in
    the sand.
He still just stands there a small
    tiny man.
The things that he does is naught
    and dross.
Tho he climbs mountains and
    swims channels
across, paints a fair picture or
    a grand
bust of clay. These are as
    nothing, let's
throw them away.

There comes to me now a giant
    of a man.
Tho his head is bowed and
    feeble frail hands.
But his heart is as sunshine and
    his smile shouts
out love. This is the man that
    towers above.

Frances Bellamy
CAROL

She was my sister, this one so
    fair,
    She had eyes of blue and golden
    hair
Her heart was as big as the ocean
    is wide,
    her love as strong as the raging
    tide
Of't times I think of her and the
    short life she lived,
    how always to others, her all
    she would give
Nothing she ever asked for
    herself in return,
    but gave so willingly, their
    love to earn
She was always searching for
    her dream to come,
    always reaching out, reaching
    for someone;
But her dreams she would never
    find
    for this world to her, it was
    never kind
For her no tomorrows were

ever meant to be
this loving, lonely child, this
    child of destiny
My sister, I'll love you for
    eternity.

Cris M. Kraft
**MY FRIEND WILL LIVE IN
ME**

To me—he was immortal,
A friend one dreams about.
In seconds—years of friendship
Were hurriedly wiped out.

Maybe if I'd been there,
Standing close to grab his hand,
I could have pulled him back to
    life
From death, the cliff and sand.

Well, he's gone now forever;
Reality comes back to me.
Tomorrow at the funeral parlor
My closest friend I'll see.

I refuse to drown in sorrow,
Or ignore this fact of life.
I'll carry forth our dreams,
No matter what the strife.

That is how he'd want it,
And that is what shall be.
Though time moves on, and
    things will change,
My friend will live in me.

Raymond Granville Barger
FOR SHAME

The Puritans came
As of God's plan
Kill damn Indians
Steal all their land
Send others west
To a reservation

Then cut their trees
Pollute the water
Gut the good earth
Change nature's order
Like Crusade for cup
In Eurasian devastation!

Clifford E. Palmer
WHERE EAGLES SOAR

Dreaming of times of old
    folklore
Desiring to go where eagles soar
Mounting emotions to break
    the ties
That keeps me from rising into
    the skies
These are the things dreams are
    made of
Imaginings of flying high above
Eagles require no license to fly
It's quite different with you and
    I
We must go to many schools
And learn to comply with all the
    rules
So if flying is really in your heart
It's necessary to find time to
    start.
See, since we haven't natural
    wings

Ours must come from flying
    machines
And when we're of a proper
    mind
With needed knowledge we will
    find
We're luckier than dreamers of
    the past
For the means is available to fit
    the cast.
Sensations of magic as surging
    upward into the air
All things of earth grow so
    small from there
To sail above the clouds silvery
    white
And drop back down in
    cherished quiet
Quickly realizing you've found
    what You're searching for
You've been where Eagles soar.

Pamela Bettcher
UNTITLED

We walk on this earth for a
    short time,
    spreading our knowledge,
    happiness, and
love along the way. Living,
    loving, all
the while looking for the right
    way
to say good-bye.

Gunner Rasmussen.
TELEFORNICATION

At times
When I see you
    Our bodies get in the way.

At times
It is better to speak
    With you on the phone.

More is said,
Less is done.

But then again
I hang up wishing
    That I had touched you
With more than my voice. . .

Ken Jones
CLOUDY WINTER'S MOON

The Moon. . .
Drunk with her grief. . .
Staggers through the cloud-rifts
Weeping for her long lost lover. .
Li Po

Adrian Earl Johnson
TIDE—N—SURF

The tide went out and they
    sailed with it,
But when the surf came in, they
    didn't.
They were noble, yet they went
    global.
They flailed, they bailed,
They drifted, yes, they were
    gifted.
As they streaked towards their
    mountain atoll,
They were sold on their bold
    fold.
As this tale and others entail
    well.
So do you and I.
For you see, we are the
    tide - n - surf.

Gina Rosingana
MY FATHER

As you pedal
Your way through life,
Have you ever stopped
To look at a flower
In child-like wonder?
The roads were once
Made of dirt and mud,

Little pathways
Through the forest,
Now it's gone,
We sing a different song.
One so young
In the world alone,
You traveled around
With the wind
And the sun.
The people you met,
The ones you know
Will never forget
The inner glow,
The love you show.

Thorgunnur Jonsdottir
REALITY

Do not be puzzled by what you
  perceive;
It isn't what you might believe,
No, it isn't in your mind,
Nor in the minds of humankind,
For it's all in George Berkeley's
  head,
And the Anglican bishop is very
  dead.

Kathi Caldwell
READING AT MIDNIGHT

The reading lamp burns a soft
yellow glow around the
alarm clock on the nightstand
ticking steadily
echoing the sound of raindrops
that fall on leaves and asphalt
outside
these sounds
and the smell of damp air
and wet leaves
stray my mind from "The
  Hobbit"
(Which seems to take more
  concentration tonight)
I drop it with a solid thud to the
  floor
click off the light
and listen. . .

Bonnie S. Bragg Wheeler
LOVE BIRDS

Two love birds in the forest
  green, built their cove near a
  rippling
stream, where the sun shone
  down through the trees so tall,
  they made their
plans as they sang love's call!
The girl was Fran and the boy
  was Dave, and to the other
  their troph
they gave. . .Each one to hold
  the other's heart, near to his
  own, never would
they part!
They built love's castles neath
  the rambling rose, in the deep
  green
forest where no one knows, but
  the two love birds and a white,
  white dove,
know the secret of their own
  true love. . .
It reaches Heaven wherever it
  may be, and crosses over the

deep blue
sea. . .And tho the storms may
  howl and blow, their cove is
  safe, and their
love aglow!
If the other be weak or strong,
  they twine two hearts with no
  alarm. . .
For all the future is theirs you
  see, and they sing love's
  sweetest melody. . .
And when they whisper their
  thoughts of love, they hear the
  secret of the
white, white dove!

Cheryl Derksen
MY LOVE FOR YOU

My love for you is never-ending,
  the rest of my life with you
  spending.
My love for you is true,
  my solemn vow to you.
My love for you will grow,
  and forever overflow.
My love for you will never hide,
  but will forever with you abide.

Kathleen M. Mattson
IMAGES

My eyes
see nothing,
for they are fogged
with images
of you.
The fog does not lift.
How pleasant
it must be,
to be blind.

Betty Sue Hill
FRUITLESS

A fruitless tree, devoid of bloom,
  I liken
to an idle mind.
They both bear not and give yet
  less.
They neither seek nor find.
A mind is given to one and all
  and as trees
Are meant to bear,
  our minds should search for
  wisdom and trees,
Their fruits should share.
If fruitless trees are stripped of
  life and
From existence banned,
What to do with idle minds that
  feed
Upon our land?

Rhonda Crutchfield
MAY I INTRUDE?

In my solitude,
The visions I elude.
Wither away at,
My illusive mood.
Without my make-up,
I seem so crude.
At the risk of being rude,
May I intrude?
For a brief,
But meaningful interlude?
Then, may I feel,
Your thoughts in the nude?

Carol Speer
TO REMEMBER

Standing by the water's edge,
Each in our own space,
Watching as our dreams float
  past,
In the river's race.
Listening to the raindrops fall,

So softly to the ground,
Clinging to the precious moment,
Of its peaceful sound.
Walking back along our path,
Both with words unsaid,
Returning to reality
That lay not far ahead.
As he touched my shoulder,
I turned to face the past.
His kiss so sweet, his warm
  embrace,
I wanted it to last.
Is it the rain that's falling,
So wet upon my face?
Or the hidden feelings,
That escaped their secret place.
Returning to the present time,
From which we came.
Knowing that our feelings
Will forever be the same.

Eva Bynum
A PRECIOUS GIFT

Ten little fingers
Ten little toes
One little mind
One little soul
One little heart that pumps the
  blood
Through the veins of my little
  girl I love.
This little being I hold in my
  arms,
Must be taught right from wrong.
What a precious gift God has
  given me.
Oh, what a responsibility.
It's left up to me, which way
  she will go,
Will I train her up in the ways of
  the Lord?
The question is asked, now its
  left up to me;
Where will she spend an eternity?

Barbara Christie Itz Gilbert
OUR FEELING OF LOVE

Here I sit alone with you
And listen for the forest to
  awaken at a new day.
The colors I see are very soft and
  covered with a morning dew
Which glistens from every living
  thing.
The warm sunlight smiles upon
  the forest
Leaving a refreshing feeling of
  love in our hearts.
We sit close in search of each
  other's thoughts
As slowly we lie down beneath
  the trees.
I set my head down on your
  chest as you hold me gently
Like a newborn babe against
  its mother's breast.
Together our love radiates
  among all things in the forest
And we are filled with peace.

Edward G. Kenny
EDIFICE OF LOVE

Let me create for you
An edifice of love
A mountainous building to
  symbolize
The enormity of my affection
  for you
Its grandeur will be my loyalty
Its building blocks my earnest
  words
Let its lifespan be everlasting,
An undeniable monument
To our eternal friendship
And let twin spires

Encrest its summit—dual
  expressions
Of the two of us made one
By the mutuality of our concern
One for another.

Beverly Laws
**GOODBYE, JUNK FOOD
JUNKIE**

There'll be no more chicken
  delight
When you call me up late at
  night
and ask to come by
for a breast or a thigh
Somehow it just isn't right.
There'll be no more have it your
  way
When you don't even call the
  next day
with your blank look eyes
and the smile that lies
Somehow we have nothing to
  say.
Oh I was hot and juicy
I did it all for you
But that didn't make it special
I am a person
    not a drive-thru.

Jim Banaka
MOM

She wanted just a little verse
that I could never write
About the times she scolded me
and the times she held me tight.

She wanted just a little verse
about the fights the brothers had
And just how close the family
  was
and how we all loved Dad.

She wanted just a little verse
that I could never write
About the sleep I made her lose
in the middle of the night.

She wanted just a little verse
about the tears and fun
And those quiet little moments
between a mother and a son.

I wish that I could show her
as I am sitting here tonight
The poem that she wanted
that I could never
  write.

Karen K. Doty
CLYDENE

Blatantly, the rocks push and
  squirm
Determined to break through
  the sole,
Yet, silver pumps tread lightly
  onward
Stumbling now and then in the
  cold.

As the lane ahead makes a turn
The rugged oak sheds another
  leaf,
And directs with its age-old
  timber
To the left the shoes turn with
  relief.

Not much further now—almost
  there
The leather is getting worn and
  bare.

Soft green grass beckons lightly
Just a few more yards ahead,
Excitedly, tired strides get larger,
Ah—at last, rest in a bed.

Instantaneously, the pace
  subsides
Hopefully searching the name
  chiseled there,

As it squints, another heel
  breaks clean
How much more pain would be
  fair?
Not much further now—almost
  there
The leather is getting worn and
  bare.
Warmly, the name has meaning
These wandering feet have passed
  passed the test,
The stone reads, "Here lies
  Clydene—"
Thank God, she'll now have
  some rest.

Veda Nylene Steadman
A DIRGE IS SO DEPRESSING

She sang a ballade
When he came to her door.
As he strummed a roulade,
She sung a ballade.
He said: "Your ballade
Makes me ask for more."
She sang a ballade
When he came to her door.

Then he turned to the fire,
Laid a log on with care.
To conceal his desire,
Then he turned to the fire.
He pitched his voice higher—
His guitar tuned, aware.
Then he turned to the fire—
Laid a log on with care.

Wanda Whanger Higgins
MY LITTLE GIRL'S PRAYER

I sat by her bed as I usually did
She said her nightly prayer
I had this feeling inside almost
  to weep
My little one said it with such
  care
Her little world so far from mine
Concern and feelings went
  through me
How could she know so much
  to tell?
As she blessed each person of
  whom she knew well
It lifted my heart and made me
  so proud
When she opened her eyes and
  said aloud
"I want God to bless MISTER
But won't God know him better
  by his first name?"
And I wondered how such a
  thought to this small child
  came
So she asked God to bless this
  man who had entered our
  lives
To help him do better
He just needed a guide
With that she said "AMEN".

George J. Seylaz, Jr.
**MOUNTAINS ARE A BRAND
  NEW WORLD**

When I look out at mountain,
  I see a
  brand new world before me.
I see a world of snow capped
  peaks,
  a land of everlasting serenity
  and natural
  wonder.
I see the danger of the wildlife
  the longing to survive in a
  world
  of survival of the fittest.
A place that will last forever and
  ever
  a world of beauty, danger,
  and excitement.

A world where God's creature
  can roam free
and happy for their livetimes
  and all
  of their children's lifetimes.
I see a land that should never
  be destroyed,
  by the "crushing hand of
  mankind."
When I look out at a mountain
I see God's world of love,
  hope and happiness.

Jill Marie Evans
ARIZONA TO IOWA

arizona to iowa
home for the holidays
and Mother you were cruel.
after 2.5 days on a Greyhound
  and your ruthless divorce
we sit down at the table to eat
  the new family since F
and you choose to pick at
Grandma's keepsake locket I'm
  wearing
with pictures of you and Dad
  when you both were 12 years
  younger.
I still think of Dad
  although i never liked him,
and i'm still longing for some
  sense of family,
sitting here at this table
  among the ruins of my own.

Mrs. Wanda Frederick
WE'LL MEET AGAIN

When you wake up in the
  morning,
  and I'm not there,
Remember the memories,
  and the love we shared.
"My cup runneth over with love"

Just love one another
  whatever you do!
Remember my darlings,
  I'll always love you.
"My cup runneth over with love"

Don't listen what others say,
  You'll know what to do,
Just do in the future
  what your heart tells you to.
"My cup runneth over with love"

Don't worry about me.
  For I'm not alone,
I've gone to see Father
  and to live in his home.
"My cup runneth over with love"

You must go on living,
  Don't live in the past;
Just live for the future,
  And all that is best,
"My cup runneth over with love"

In the future, my darlings,
  Our hearts filled with love,
We'll all meet again
  In God's home up above,
"My cup runneth over with love"
"My cup runneth over with love"

Donna-Jean Wick
OH LORD I KNOW

Oh Lord I know why you've
  taken her away.
But yet my heart is yearning
  with despair,
For she helped to mold me in
  what I am,
All I can see are those folded
  hands
While she lies there with undone
  plans.
Her lips are sealed with the
  secrets she knows

And I'm left here to carry on
  with life's many woes.
Oh God, I really loved her
  ever so much
For she's the only mother I
  really knew.
Oh Grandma, I hope you realized
  how much
I really loved you!

Viola M. Mooney
SADNESS

Sadness follows me
  In everything I do.
There's just no happiness for me
  in the world without you.
I never tried to fall in love,
  It was an involuntary thing.
When I found you,
  I found the joy,
That only love can bring.
  I know my life's not over.
It doesn't work that way.
  So I'll just live without you.
Exist from day to day.
  Time will heal my aching heart,
and tears will cease to flow.
  Then I will start to live again.
Just when,
  I'll never know.

Ruth M. Patterson
NOW YOU ARE GONE

When the circling sun slowly we
  went down,
We watched the crimson colors
  drown—
In night's advancing westward
  tide,
As we sat in silence side by side.

Now you are gone.
Those silver wings took you so
  very far,
Across the wide, blue ocean
  where you are—
My morning here, is your
  afternoon,
And night will follow—oh,
  too soon!

I watch the stars, that at night
  fall, rise,
And remember you, as evening
  slowly dies.
Your love has left a warm
  sweet afterglow,
My love will follow—no matter
  how far you go.

Sunny Hye Rapp
VELVET

I saw here there beside the harp,
  she did not know I knew.
I saw her there with all her
  thoughts and dreams of
  softest velvet.
I saw her there and heard her
  play, the music was so gentle,
And now it was called yesteryear
  and still I saw her there.
And though she sat beside the
  harp, no longer in its play,
I understood the dreams she
  had, for I had dreamed them.
  too,
You see, she was the beloved
  child that I had never had.

Nina Margherita Mori
DREAMS

What will become of all the
  wasted dreams,
  the sparks of hope that flare
  then shine no more?
Where is the sea that harbors
  wayward schemes,
  whose waves reach out to touch
  an empty shore?

As lovers cast their nets among
  the stars
  sad memories of kisses and
  regrets,
  of heartbreaks that have rendered
  jagged scars,
  may know the peace of night,
  when one forgets.

Hence, every dream, secured as
  such, may ease
  that piercing shaft of light that
  harks the day
and manifest itself in fantasies,
  so never leave, or send a love
  away.

Each life a myriad of dreams
  contains;
  each dream a life has lived,
  and thus, remains.

Neil David Talisman
MIRROR STARS

Two mirror stars I know of are
  Marilyn Monroe and Betty Boop.
They keep their beauty in a jar
  which is labled "Goop"
Most movie stars keep their
  beauty in a makeup jar.
They think it automatically
  makes them a star.

They think what they see in
  the mirror is true.
But what they see there is by no
  means true.
What they see there should
  make them extremely blue.
They must have electric fans in
  the studio to keep them cool.
If they don't their makeup
  will run and they'll look like
  fools.

What they see in the mirror they
  believe to be.
But what they behold in the
  mirror they cannot possibly
  see.
Their beauty is totally false
  because it comes out of a jar.
And again I repeat, they are
  only Mirror Stars!

Mary Elizabeth Griffin
WHY?

Why is it that you say you
  love me,
  when at a distance? But when
  we are
  in each other's arms, there is
  no
  such words spoken of I love you.

Why is it when we are apart I
  long to be near you?
Though when we are together
  I feel I should leave.

Why is it you say you want me?
  Yet
  your actions say you lie. Why
  is it
  that I think I love you though I
  still feel the same as I did before
  there was you? Lonely.
WHY?

Roy A. Davis M. D.
THE SEASHORE

I love to walk by the side of
  the sea
With the wind and the waves
  just you and me.
Water splashing our barefoot
  feet
Seagulls looking for bread or
  meat.
Our footprints sink in the
  softened sand

Our spirits soar with the birds.
This day was made to set the
   soul free
How thankful I am God shared
   it with me.

Mark Lawrence McPhail
ALBATROSS DAYS

Moments before dawn begins
To measure the morning sky,
He drags the barnacled dory from
Its padlocked shack down
To the sea's seam
Then takes her, taut armed,
Out off the land's slender curve,
Out to his thin sailed schooner
Anchored just inside
Dog Bar Breakwater.

He works the day where
Only seagulls see him.
He hauls the familiar oily nets
Onto the ship's slick deck,
Pregnant with frantic
Beige bellied pollock
On albatross days.

Long after the sun settles,
When the moon wrinkles
On the sea, he returns;
Hands hard at the wheel,
Blistered by many
Tight tackle bights.

I linger here to see him pass
Along this beach each evening.

In his old eyes
I watch the waves crest,
Flick up their tails like
Slight grey fishes
I see the salt winds
   Still stirring within him.

Penny Denice Wharton
WRECK OF INTIMACY

As the moon's rays shine on
   the sea,
   a sailboat passes to eternity.
Two people lying on the deck,
   unfolding the love that is meant.
No one sees them, no one knows
   them, they are still in the night,
   as the moon gives light, oh so
   bright.
As the ocean meets the wooden
   side,
   the moon's glow and sky collide.
So dark is the sea,
   so silent they heave.
Rocky visions fill their myths,
   as they approach the desolate
   cliffs.
Fear strikes them as they
   embrace,
   and are left nowhere, without
   a trace.
No one sees them, no one is
   heard,
   just the thump of wood
   changing its course.
Crashes and splashes are heard
   in the tide,
   as they regain strength and
   survive.
But the night is not over, as they
   again become one,
   and lie on the beach, having fun.
As dawn breaks in the bright new
   day,
   they remember an episode that
   almost gave way.

James N. Damiano
FOOLS

There's so much we need, we
   look for more
As we slide so unconsciously,
   into our own wars

Where pleasures are treasures,
   like battles scored
Lingering in our minds, to help
   mend the sores
Fighting the excitement that
   makes us come to our senses
And helps us see the light of
   the truth
Like a ghost in the bedroom
   something haunts our dreams
Till we explode into fools
And whether it's infinite to one
   or one to one
Life just doesn't seem to have
   any odds
So we wake up in fright from
   a nightmare in the night
And a vision of a monster we
   call God
And though I knew who I was
   but forgot who I was suppose
   to be
I lost my way in this world of
   insincerity, as the thought of
   Being hated confiscated, the
   rest of what I had left of
   my faith.

Jackie L. Case
THE STONE BULL

Like the stone bull you reign—

bouncing my words off your
   back,
   throwing them to echo in the
   air.

staring through your hard
   unheeding eyes
   with engulfing triumph,

issuing defeat through the
   coldness of your bulk,
   reveling in my total disability
   to move you.

Francis J. Tarasuk
**A MAN'S BURDEN CAN BE
LIGHT**

When I was a child,
I received a mystical experience.
The light I saw was heavenly,
spiritual and soul-satisfying.

As a child,
I thought my life was pledged
   to God;
But, as children do, I went on
   my way
and forgot all about my secret
   friend.

I'm much older, retired and
   think
I want to become like a child
   again.
What I witnessed years ago,
is one of life's gifts I held in
   trust.

I believe I'll hold on to my gift
and use it as wisely as I can.
Through darkness, I can see
   and lift
and help the burden in the mind
   of man.

Patricia E. Ferris
WHY

What can be said of a girl in
   love,
When the sun, the moon, the
   stars above,
Cast glowing lights in both her
   eyes,
She sees past the clouds to sunny
   skies.

The world is love and love is life
She dreams of the day she'll be
   a wife.
She looks to the future, a sight

to see,
In the years ahead she'll have a
   family.
Well, the dreams are there, her
   loves not dead;
But the return of love in the
   years ahead,
Looks unbearably dim,
   infinitely small;
A dramatic change from spring
   to fall.

They had planned together the
   years ahead,
Now as her love grows, his is
   dead.
What changed the outlook in
   her man's life?
Why does he now not want a
   wife?

Was it things he could not see?
Or a lack of faith in Humanity?
Or was it things that others said?
Or the desire to go from bed to
   bed.

The anser I guess we'll never
   know,
Just why he left, when she loved
   him so.

Debra E. Bowers
**TO BARBRA (WITH MUCH
LOVE)**

"Ready Deb?" I look up into
   your dark and tender eyes,
mumbling and gathering my
   materials to be discussed. . .
I follow you down the hall
   feeling as though the world
will stop for me and my hour.

As the door swings open you
   pause with your hands at your
   sides,
standing erect, silently observing
   as I strut into your office:
perhaps in tears, full of hate,
   or feeling alone and desperate.

As you close the door and we
   take our designated seats,
and I begin testing, confessing,
   and at times acting
as though I'm regressing. . .
I wish I were able to speak
   from within my heart
and explain that despite the
   hard exterior. . .
I hurt inside and I feel alone.

Allen Reese/Mark Allen
UNICORN

Unicorn, Unicorn,
I want to talk
I need to talk
But no one seems to care
People say you do not exist
But in my dreams and heart
You are so real
You never say anything
But I know you're there
But if you could
And if you would
I know what you would say
Talk, I'm here.

Rhonda K. VanOrder
DEFINITION: REDS—DEAD

A smile started out, with a kiss
   for good times
We laughed with each other and
   thought our game prime
"I've found something great
   called "reds" he said.
"No trouble at all, just one and
   you're "fed."
Those reds became habitual
   and soon he was stuck

I tried to convince him, he was
   living on luck.
I went for help one night when
   he called
He was about to kill himself, I
   was only a stall
Before I reached him, he was
   gone, so I'm told
I felt torn to pieces, but
   remained very bold.
Time is healing this broken
   heart,
But the memory of "reds" is
   still a big part.
People I love I am sure to tell,
That taking drugs is a straight
   trip to hell!

Debbie McDevitt
GOOD - BYE TO LOVE

You were the first sweetheart
   I ever knew
I fell in love the day
   That I met you

Then we got married on
   The first of May
But along came the draft
   You went away

And just as in lives of
   Classified men
In a war some lives must
   Come to an end.

Rochelle Theresa Brown
BALLERINA

Alone, listening
Only to stillness,
She silently dances
To the music
In her memory.

Jean Esplin
DESERT CHILD

Desert Child
Running Wild
Under the Desert Sun

Indian Boy
Filled with Joy
Under the Desert Sun

Brown Skin
and Tribal Kin
Under the Desert Sun

Turquoise Beads
And Ancient Deeds
Under the Desert Sun

A desert Child
Running Wild
Under the Desert Sun
In Arizona

Mary Ann Shepard White
SUFFERING

The fiery trials of suffering,
Is it really necessary for me?
The fiery paths of desperation,
I feel taking tight hold of me.

"Be still and know that I am
   God"
I hear my savior say.
"Look up and carry on in trust,
I'll wipe your tears away!"

Michele T. Joseph
MY FANTASY

Live your fantasy—hand in hand
Lose yourself in swirls of sand
Stars that stretch 'cross the sky
   above
Shine like a heart just polished
   by love
Waves from the ocean are
   dancing to shore
While moonlight warms our
   thoughts once more

Floating together through time
it seems
Fulfilling each other's most
cherished dreams
No other place would I rather
be now
Than sharing with you what
time will allow
As we grope each other's silky
skin
Feeling the vibes as our bodies
spin
We've entered our galaxy, the
highest peak
My man in the moon makes
my body grow weak
Our spaceship has landed and
drifted ashore
The most beautiful feeling is
with us once more
Once upon a planet two lovers
are we
This is what happens in my
fantasy.

Robert Michael Malone
QUALITY FRIEND

A quality friend will stand by
you,
When times are ROUGH
He'll remain with you, even
if times get TOUGH.
He'll always lend a sympathetic
ear
When times get SAD.
He will not turn his back on
you,
When those sad times get BAD.
He is the first to reach your door
When there is TROUBLE.
And if the trouble becomes
TERRIBLE,
He'll do his utmost to prevent
it from becoming
UNBEARABLE

Inger-Jean Heenan
THAT TIME AGAIN!

Many's the time I walked
through the snow
Even got kissed neath the
Mistletoe
Rushed as if crazy from store to
store
Rigged us some lights all aron
around our door.
Yelped when a Christmas Card
came from a friend. . .
Cause I had neglected a card
to send!
Hurried to wrap all the gifts
we'd bought
Rushed here and there with
one single thought
Icicles must be hung on the tree!
Should have more tinsel, it
seems to me!
Trying to do everything just
right
Maybe I'll finally catch up
tonight!
Always afraid that I won't be
through. . .In time to
Send Holiday Greetings to you!

Kelleen A. Bell
FIRST LOVE

It's over now.
Memories are fading,
Getting harder to grasp each day.
Yet the freshness of the moment
Is still there,
Like it was just yesterday.
I don't want it to leave,
But it goes through my
Fingers like the air.
I grasp for it, but it's gone.

Cynthia Goss Kingsbury
OUR LITTLE BOY

There he was
So cute, so small
A bundle of joy
Brought to our lives
Our little boy.
He brought laughter,
Funny faces and sounds
A bundle of joy
To watch and see
Our little boy.
One, two , three. . .
The years go by
A bundle of joy
Grows up too fast
Our little boy.

Lisa Strong
MEMORIES

Memories. . .just patches of
time
clouded with fear.
Memories. . .that are not unkind
followed by a tear.
But memories can be happy as
well
I guess you can never tell
What memories will stay, or go.
And who knows
Maybe someday I'll be a
memory too
To someone like you
It's true,
I love you
Memories.

Linda Elaine Kingsley
THE RUSTLING WIND

Listen to the rustling wind
Picking up debris that comes
within
Tossing articles high into the air
Just where it lands, we know
not where.
Branches are entwined and
broken in two,
Discarded paper looks as though
it'd been chewed.
One sees a leaf being blown now
and then,
But the most flowing
notion is "The Rustling Wind."

Lorraine J. Pearson
HAPPINESS

Seeing the sunshine
After all the rain
Frost painting your window
So you can write a special name.
Saying "I love you"
And meaning it with all your
heart.
Knowing you're love and
thought of
Though the miles keep you apart.
Finding a bright side
When the world gets you down.
Smiling when you're unhappy,
Because it's better than a frown.

Gary Loren McCallister
THIRTY - FIVE

The sun is bright.
The shadows long.
The air is crisp.
The odors strong.
If both are the same,
Then why. . .
Is morning swift
And evening long;
Spring is right
And winter wrong?
Youth is noise
And age is song.

I'm old at last,
My youth is gone.

Jack Bates Lloyd
FALLEN SOLDIER

Would you love me,
if I were no longer near. . .
Would you feel my arms,
If I were far away,
lost among another day. . .
Could you see my smile,
hear my voice,
if I no longer came
to call your lovely name. . .

Rodger Allan Hicks
CONSORT

A hidden kinship
emerges from the confusion of
intelligence
Bonds of breath and birth
sound and sight
The rush of air from the wings
of
a Golden Eagle soaring high
The eerie blues lament of
a sole Timber Wolf on a
crisp fall night
The eruption of water that
reveals
a breathtaking Blue Whale
The cries of a Newborn Child
against his mother's breast
Each sharing a common
ground
a consort of. . .
Life.

David Ernest Camin
LIFE'S BLESSINGS

Everything is just so green and
pretty,
The leaves on the trees are soft
but wity.
The air is so fresh and full of love,
You know someone's watching
from up above.
The birds and the quiet are so
compliant,
The shapes of shadows are
so defiant.
And the way that people are
up and about,
Makes me want to stand and
burst with shout.
There's so much to do and so
much to see,
I just wish we were all in love
with thee.
For in these days, so short and
numbered,
We've got to learn to love one
another.
So wherever you go, and
whatever you do,
Do it with the love, for it is
he who loves you.
He's given us life with all the
dressings,
So praise the Lord and all his
blessings.

Becky Geyer
FIRST LOVE

Why have you come now to
invade my thoughts?
I believed I had imprisoned your
memory, never again to be
tempted by impetuous virgin
love.
That I allow myself to recall
the
innocent 'delight of my youth'
only intensifies the confusion
I feel in reality.
Leave me, please.
No. . .wait.
I ache for this rendezvous
though only a sentimental
fantasy.
Embrace me, and leave me
trembling
as you did then.

Janice Cummings Spiak
BACK HOME AGAIN

I've traveled many places, but
nothing can compare,
with being back home again and
the sounds of being there.
Although I had a wonderful
time and was so abundantly
blessed,
nothing can compare with the
sweet release I feel when I
go back home
and peacefully rest.
My home is very simple and
plain, sometimes not as
elequent as the places I have
been, but still it's where my
heart is and
where my spirit is at rest, for in
my home I feel my blessed
Lord's
Presence best.
A freedom I cannot completely
feel anywhere, lies within
my home,
A freedom I feel in my heart
that is so hard to explain, dwells
in the place where on earth
I reign.
Maybe you cannot relate to
what I share with you, Maybe
your home is not
peaceful or joyful, but filled
with termoil and despair, well
you can
do as I did and invite Jesus,
the Son of God, to live inside
your home,
and he will replace the termoil
with his spirit of joy and peace,
and your home will be forever
filled with his blissful
abiding peace.

Lynne A. Keating
THE SEA

Sweetly sucking, lapping, licking
teasingly the wave caresses each
crevice.
A searing tongue probes his lover;
searching, seeping deep within.
Sad silent whispers, all that is
heard
Occasional plaintive cry from a
distant bird.
Elusive gentle echoes.
Unyielding rhythmic crash, a
lover's pounding thrust;
Wrathful, scarring maiming
lust.
Unattainable, surging upward,
consuming the very flesh of
the earth.

I have know the peace in the
perpetual cycle.
I have touched the prevading
citadel.
The unviolated union of land
and sea.

Herbert J. Fisher
THE MINK

A slender brownish form of fur
Goes loping o'er the snow;
His beady eyes with hunting lust
Shine in the evening's glow;
A hunter, he, with muscles lithe,
Can move with grace and speed;
And woe to birds and mammals
small,
For they are prey he'll heed;
Frogs, and fish and other life,
Add to his varied fare,
For he can also swim with speed,
And stalk this prey with care;
So when you travel through
the woods,
Along a river's brink;
Maybe you'll see a flash of brown,
and that may be a mink.

Aryanna Sadeghi
AN ILLUSION?

You are so close, but
yet so far,
yet asking why,
is a silly question coming from,
a girl who is becoming a woman
for a boy who is becoming a man,
to answer.
We will have patience and
tolerance,
will and faith,
yet we will still melt. . .
into our own personal emotional
habitat,
yet still creating,
useless tension within our souls.

Mary A. Brown
PAUL

My love for you grows deeper
as time passes.
Thoughts of you flow through
my mind as my heart pulsates.
You make my heart happy happy
as it jumps for joy
at the thought of seeing you.
Every moment of my day is
spent thinking about you,
and wishing you were here.
You flash in my mind first thing
in the morning,
and are my last thought before I
go to sleep.
My life is more meaningful
because of you.
You are an inspiration to me.

Steven Stockfish
A MAN WHO'S DESTITUTE

I see a man who's destitute
Asleep while passers-by
Deem his presence to be rude,
Indifferent to his cry.
His dreams are broken for
evermore,
Let's further break his heart.
Then don we now our gay
apparel,
We've been blind from the start.

Sylvia Martin Howell
SONG OF THE WANDERER

Once upon my way somewhere,
across the timeless space;
I beheld a circumstance, a
newly-awesomed place:
Where color-plaited rainbows,

entangled, massive lay;
Writhing all, so wretchedly in
knotted disarray;
Nearby, hosts of floating things
in oil-mocked dignity,
Winged-dead, some resolved to
soar atop a slimey sea;
From hollowed tree stumps
laughter, rode gay the noxious
winds,
Its eerie death-sounds chortle
and don their plastic grins;
Outward next, I trod my path,
for light-years rode its girth;
(I, but one ellipse ago, mid-wifed
this sun child's birth.)
Yet these worlds I've
circumscribed, their guarded
mysteries,
All, in cycles, shed light of
aborted histories.
I've learned in my wayfaring,
though wonderous and sublime,
Such worlds, though lost and
mournful, come newly-wrought
in time.

Denise Wanken Schreiber
YOU

Watching you
Gives me pleasure;
No words are spoken,
But you I treasure.
The looks you give me,
makes me smile.
I feel warm inside,
You have such style.
You are my husband,
My lover, my life,
Sharing my world with you
is so satisfying.

Raphael G. Heavener
MY OBSESSION

Surrounded by mountains on a
cold winter's night,
the moon is low and ever so
bright,
Some rabbits are hopping on the
frozen snow.
As a young buck nestles near
his beloved doe.
Squirrels and woodpeckers sleep
in holes in trees,
while the river ripples with the
coming of a breeze.
The stars that twinkle high above
in the sky,
sometimes are hidden as the
clouds roll by.
This beauty is such a magnificent
obsession,
which could never be told with
any expression.
If only it were shared by not
one but two,
everything would be complete
if I see it with you.

Marcia A. Bowie
I THINK, THEREFORE I EXIST

I think, therefore I exist. Am I
a product
of my thoughts, or are they
a product of me?
Is there a chance I was a
speculation
once upon a time?
A tiny flash in a master mind?
I exist, therefore I love. I will
share
my world with the one who
deserves
the memory of me.
Who will come into my

existence
And share my quiet place of
dreams?
I dream, and in my dreams I can
see
beyond impossibilities into
tomorrow's realities
where fingers stretch across the
sky
toward a sun that is not there;
where birds sing in barren trees
for ears that cannot hear;
where flowers bloom in
forgotten fields
for eyes that cannot see
and rivers flow on empty beds
Filling oceans with despair.
But because I dare to dream
I will not be afraid to think,
therefore I exist.

Mrs. Alma Jean French
WORKING FOR CHRIST

We must work for Christ each
day
For every deed, He'll surely pay.
Accordingly as we have done
And that applies to old and
young

Our soul is only the bank of life
Deposits are made through toil
and strife
The roads are rough, the hills
are high
He'll give us strength is we'll
only try.

We can visit the sick
Or walk with the lame
Or read to the blind
The reward is the same.

It matters not which way we
go
If we represent Christ, then
others will know
We've made a change, we've
made a vow
He has touched our soul, some
way, some how.

Let's work for Christ today,
tonight
He'll always keep us in His
sight
Our lives will change, then others
will see
How truly happy, they too can
be.

Vickie D'Andrea
LOSS

If love is all there is,
then why wasn't it enough
for you and me?

Perhaps it was our dreams
that kept us apart,
for our dreams were so different.

I could not share with you
the things I cared for most.
and you could not be interested
and you had no need to share
your dreams.
But since I could not share my

dreams,
they began to die. . .
and so did I.
So why do I feel such pain at
this,
[our parting?
God knows, I should be glad,
for now, perhaps I'll live again.
It's just that when you leave
a part of me leaves with you.
And it is this sense of loss
that is so painful.

Diana P. Rusek
OCTOBER

As the leaves are changing colors,
The weather starts to get cold,
I sit and watch the harvest moon,
As winter begins to unfold.
The snow slowly approaches,
The wind begins to blow,
I think about those winter days,
Of sleigh rides in the snow.
O how I love these moments,
With the smell of autumn in the
air,
And the feeling that it gives me,
One that I just can't compare.

Muriel D. Ricci
ECHOS

People moving to and fro
You there in the crowd.
Swaying songs and voices;
Rhythms sometimes loud.
Blending thoughts and spirits.
Friendships always vowed.
Can you feel the lonely
Sitting all alone
Thinking thoughts of people
Left alone to mourn.
Can you hear the lonely
Begging for a sound;
Wishing for a favor
Hoping to be found.
Even in the noisy crowd
Away above the roar
Can you sense the beating heart
Asking you for more.
Sounds of knowing that he's
there.
Sounds of knowing that you
care.
Sounds of happy thoughts and
dear
Sounds so sad they bring a tear.
People moving in a crowd
You there standing proud.
Have you noticed someone near
With flashing eyes of doubt and
fear.
Then an entrance
Someone new.
Could the lonely one be you?

Dick L. Tillotson
WHY?

Why do the tree branches reach
up so high?
Why do the clouds float across
the blue sky?
Why does the river roll out to
the sea?
Why does sweet honey come
just from a bee?
Why do the leaves come out in
the spring?
Why do the robins know just
what to sing?
Why does a cat like to play
with a ball?
Why does a bird fly south every
fall?
Why do the puppies chase their
tails all around?
Why do the gophers dig holes in

the ground?
Why does a fawn like to frolic
and play?
Why does the wind keep going
all day?
Why do some people like you
and like me
Have to ask questions bout all
that they see?

Frances S. Longley
ON CHICKEN

Drowned brown roaches in the
kitchen sink
The smell of fried golden brown
chicken freshening the air
I'm waiting for a friend to push
the bell
A male friend from Haiti who
fled black kings
and their iron plunder
I also wait for a female friend
Who works bravely for her own
goals in music.
Your PHD in Counseling
Your CPA in Accounting
Your MD in Psychiatry
And yet it is still the MRS that
really counts in Society
Where the male king, black or
white, still dominates
Yes, I have a chicken bone to
pick with you MR
It is not that I want to be on top
(pass the potato salad please)
I just don't want to be on the
bottom
(the spinich is next—thanks)
I'm not asking for much—just
my dessert—
and the chance to be a woman
—in any kitchen crisis that
arises—
THE woman.

Nan Crystal Arens
CRICKET SONG

The black, the dark of starless
night
Of moonless, windless, soundless
night
Airy void of endless wonder
Searing blindness, soundless
thunder
Alone without in blackened
sphere
Mirrored space within me, fear
Then from the silent, empty air
There wells a voice so sweet and
fair
The voice of single cricket sound
Shrinks the empty place around
A flush of joy within me swells
The sound replace where
darkness dwelled
But silence then reclaims its
rhelm
The lonely cricket overwhelmed.

Stella M. Stout
SUICIDES

Grandpa sits in his chair
Smoking his cigarettes. He died
of cancer.
Grandma told him he was.
The lady next door drinks too
much,
Going to bed with a can every
night.
She just stopped living.
Aunt Betsy drives too fast,
Scared she's not going to be on
time.

Poor thing died in a ditch.
Uncle Tom eats too much,
Always stuffing his mouth,
He died on the table.
But what about the kid down
the road
Who shot and killed himself?
They called it suicide.

Tammy L. Pfaff
WHY?

Why do I keep hearing your voice,
Why do people keep mentioning
your name?
Why is everyone teasing me,
Why do I wish things were the
same?
Why does everything remind me
of you,
Why do I jump when I hear the
phone?
Why do I keep saying I hate you,
When without you, I feel so
alone?
Why do I keep staring at your
picture,
And for no reason start to cry?
Everything seems so hopeless,
Can you tell me why?

Steve Bailey
TEND THE ROSE

Help the rose while meek and
young,
With spray of rain and glow of
sun:

Help the rose grow rich in dirt,
So she can multiply her work.

Roses pink, and red, and sky
Against the coral blush of sky. . .

Yes, God, help us to tend the
rose—
So we can rest our little hoes;

To give one to our dearest love,
And admire the symbolisms of.

Helen Brown Rittershofer
NATURES' ARTISTRY

Today clear color in the sky
Spreading from East to West
I must, as my thoughts drift
Into the mysterious silence of
drifting clouds
Winter, Spring, Summer, Fall
Each in turn paints a picture
On the Canvas of Reflective
Thought.

Ruth Pauline Lees
DEAR SUFFERING JESUS

Dear Jesus: as you bore that
Cross,
Your heart was so heavy and
torn.
You tried to get up and
stumbled along,
But, each time you did—you
were cursed, and tongue-lashed
and bruised with each flying
stone.
Oh! how you must have felt
each step of the way,
As you were nailed to the Cross
with each blow.
Oh! the nerve ends in each hand
and your feet, was the suffering
no end, you endured.
Your arms were outstretched
and muscles pulled tight,
Your bleeding side pierced hard.

The Crown that you wore from
the thorns so sharp,
The symbol of Hate for God's
son.
This was God's son on that
Cross that he bore,
So heavy and cruel to His death.
He died for our sins for
everlasting life,
He died for all sinners that day,
So Dear Suffering Jesus on
Easter, we pray,
That you gave your life that day.

Cindi Rae Cooper
MATT

When the sun sets beyond the
day, there's someone
Who's taken my heart and
turned it to ashes.
And I feel I'll never again see
the sun,
Or the moon or the stars, but
then the one
Who looks at me through long
loving lashes,
Then sees me looking and so
he dashes
From my eyes, never knowing
that he's filled
My heart with a feeling
I'd never run
From or believe I had run from
before.
And I know that I'm not scared
anymore;
This contentment I feel knows
that this one
Has no thoughts of leaving
ashes in my heart.

Lee Anna Jones
ECHOES OF A SUMMER

I hear echoes of a summer
they're drifting into my mind,
searching for an answer,
searching for a fading memory. . .

Echoes of a summer,
a summer of last year,
bring memories so lost
yet somehow so near.

Echoes of a summer,
sunny days and warm nights
together, holding on oh-so close
trying to make it right.

Echoes of a summer,
a far summer past,
bring smiles and tears,
feelings that didn't last.

Peg Brantner
TELL ME, TIME

Time heals all wounds, and
Time will tell.
Time does endless things as well.
There is one thing it will not
do:
Bring back my babe, that gift
from you.
Tell me, Time, can you replace
His sky-blue eyes, his unique
face?
Where is that cry, that little
voice?
Time, you lose; you have no
choice.

What was growth in body deep
Is but a memory gone to sleep.
Our son is but a silent yearning
Lost to time, reflective learning.

Carolyn Marie Baatz
YOUR GOOD - BYE

You went chasing after your star
You took my heart away so far

My dreams will always have you
in
Cause your love will always be
within
Your eyes I do reflect on
everyday
I can remember your special way
Your body and mind had
to go again
I hope my love will always stay
within.

Dorothy Rogers
THE HAND OF FATE

Love is a farce
Played by paper doll puppets
Whose strings are pulled by
old Dame Fate,
A capricious, indulgent old
maid;
Who, while acting out her love
fantasies,
Becomes envious of their
happiness
And flings them apart—
To break their paper doll hearts.

Ron Austin
THE ROAD OF LIFE

The road ahead had many lanes,
I knew not which to choose.
My car—the only car I had,
Was far too good to lose.
So I pondered my decision,
Let caution be my guide,
Then I went straight down the
middle
For a safe and easy ride.
I steered a safe and steady course,
Never veered from side to side,
And when a hazard crossed my
path
I found a place to hide.
But now my journey's near an
end
And I wonder, with a sigh,
If caution's guidance slowed me
down,
And life went passing by.

Byrle Payne
WHITE LIGHT OF CALVARY

Against a white sky three crosses;
on high
Two criminals and Jesus; yes,
these three
Stood out against White Light
of Calvary.
Two Marys, John, and Salome
were nigh.
Unlike the thieves his legs
weren't broken. Why?
Early that day His spirit was set
free,
Washing away the sins of you
and me,
And passed into the whiteness
of the sky,
Seen fading, fading, white—yes,
a white dove.
By His desciples He was forsaken
And three days later He
followed His spirit above:
Thus His belief rests on this
resurrection.
He stressed a way of life that's
based on love
And so He gave the world a new
direction.

Robert M. Cook
THE CLOUDED YELLOW

What mysteries are clouded
in that jaded jewel—
unrequited passion lost
in the rheumy mists
that dim the light of love.

Curse you, O nubilous pendant
suspended beneath
the ravaged face of time.
Let the alchemy of your saffron
  ball
decimate beauty from one to ten
until its hypnotic spell
shall be eternally broken.

Florence K. Kennedy
I WANT

I want to be just who I am
to be just only me
to only do the best
at what I want to be,
to be liked and to be loved,
to have a world of friends,
friends that would like
me for me, because
that's who I am,
to be able to take life
as it passes, and
live out everyday,
to enjoy life just by
living it, even when
things don't go my way,
to be my very own self,
but yet never all alone,
like some object on a shelf,
to be proud of being me,
of who and what I am,
without feeling ashamed
of anything, without being
ashamed I'm me.
I want to be just me,
because that's the best
thing I could ever want to be.

Virginia Matz
LOVE BEGINNING

As the moon shown bright the
  wind so slight the stars glittering
in the velvet night, Oh! It is so
  right!
The wind carressed our faces,
  the waves carressed our feet,
  as my
thoughts go back to where this
  place is, that we first chance to
  meet.
He took my hand, and pulled
  me near, and for a time, the
  sound of
the surf was all I could hear.
Oh! The warmth, this feeling
  so fleeting so rare, as he held
  me
and carressed my hair.
The touch of his hand the thrill
  of his sight as we embrace in
the moonlight, Oh! it is so right!
The stars how they glitter, the
  moon, and its glow, the wind
  so
slight on our face, through our
  hair, I can't let you go.
The closeness I feel you feel it
  too, will last through eternity
time will prove it to you!

Edna F. Fleischacker
IN SEARCH OF GREEN

a great glow of green
pierces the pining, rotting earth
and shoots upwards its springs
grasping passing legs
and pressing its innocence.

human hearts turn
wrestling with green
wrinkling
as green, green surrounds
them and forces their petty
darkness to surrender.

when in green the people crawl
and goo-goo their moocow
they pump and suck
and gasp and cry

while green weeps for the shallow
  sketch.
and darkness returns
the green is blanched
the people hide in mascara
and churning wisdom wheels
the daisies are crushed beneath
  their heels.
winds blow and crack their
  cheeks
the storming green grapples the
  grossness
but all is lost
the heat can't speak out
and green, green, green weeps
and all is calm.

Bruce D. Clark
SUICIDE?

A killer lives deep inside of me.
I feel him quiver, I quake.
I know if he should free himself,
Another life he'd take.

It wasn't I that took their lives,
though my hand held the gun.
It's the killer who is guilty,
But my face; the wanted one.

I know that I must take my life,
To free the world of him.
It seems unfair that I must die,
So he won't kill again.

I slash the blade across my wrist.
My blood is running red.
My vision dims, and now we
  both are. . .

Elaine Chandler
A NEED FOR CHANGE

There's a wind that blows inside
  of my soul
spinning me into actions
my heart not ready for
seizing my being with cosmic
  force
pushing me into change
and into space in need of
  my presence.
I only awaken to my new levels
not conscious of the travel
nor fully aware of my dimensions
I release loves past
and foolish dreams
moving steadfast into the reality
of my visions
clenching desperately to my
  reveries
as fear glides past my shadow.

James P. Polley
REFLECTIONS

I see the petals falling
  from the pale and wilted rose
  and once where there was ivy
  now only sorrow grows.

The oak once strong and mighty
  is dying from within,
  its branches bare and empty
  where green leaves should have
  been.

The woods, that held such
  beauty,
  are now crumbling in decay,
  as the coldness of the night
  sweeps all my love away.

Now slowly I awaken
  and calm my raging fear,
  they were only reflections
  I saw in the mirror.

Mary E. Budd
THE CRUCIFICTION

People wondered at His face
As He silently took His place.
They wondered at the look He

gave
To those who sent Him to
  this grave.
There was no malice or hatred
  there—
only pity and loving care.

Chapman—Snead—Thomas
A SMALL PUPPY

There's a puppy I once knew
who liked to chew upon my
  shoe.
Every time I'd take a seat
he would pounce upon my feet.
The shoe he'd chew,
and laces too.
What on earth was I to do?
I couldn't scold him, no siree,
I was fond of him you see.
Though he's grown
He'll always be just a puppy
Still to me.

Sylvia Garner
**LET ME KNOW IF THERE'S
A DAWN**

Lately the light of dusk
  is tormenting me
I may look around
  I may only see
Tell-tale signs of you
Earthy things about
  I may only see
Yet don't ask me
  about things
Commonly written of
  or of items
  I see in photos
Only let me know.
  if there's a dawn.

Holly M. Winning
UNTITLED

I wandered through churches
  trying to find a truch
  somewhere in the soft glow of
  the stained glass windows.
I talked to those whose life is
  devoted to spreading
  the word of God while looking
  for an answer.
I visited all of the regular
  church-goers and asked
  what I should do to "find God"
But all of my efforts proved
  fruitless and I became
  troubled.
And then, as if you knew my
  trouble, you touched my mind
  when I was alone—warmed my
  heart when it had become
  cold.
And there, within your pure
  and simple love,
  I found what I was looking for.

Arlene Elizabeth Hall
EULOGY TO A GHOST TOWN

From yesteryear, their voices ring
Through wind blown trees, you'll
  hear them sing
In silent steps, they tread the
  ground
In search of gold, some never
  found.

Remains of homes, now doorless,
  stand
Just empty shells, on once a
  prosperous land
Etched against the mountain sky
Wooden structures, beneath
  the graves of mines now lie.

The paths men trod, now weed
  and thicket grown
Softly, wildlife tread this past
  enchanted zone
The land now silent, in secret
  bound

Tell not of men and of the life
  they found.

Yet, on some moonlit summer
  night
Before the sun brings morning
  light
You'll hear the sounds and
  sights of old
Of men who died in search of
  gold.

Elaine Keillor
THE GAME

  Love is a game. . .
    that's all I can say.
The look of eyes, the pearly
  smiles.
    Head games.
    Mind tricks.
MYSTERIOUS
Strange feelings so hard to
  understand at times.
    Tears. . .hurt. . .
    Is it crazy?
One wrong move and you're out,
  Ahead,
    or starting over.
Will I ever win—or is it just a
  dream?

Dori Campman
HIGHLY CLASSIFIED

After having read all the daily
  news,
After having felt torn amidst
  its views,
After having lost something that
  we had. . .
We value the most, the classified
  ad!

Announcements made of things
  both tried and true,
"Nowhere will your word work
  harder for you."

We classify our plans, our goals,
  our thoughts;
We classify our haves, and our
  have-nots.
We classify "For Sale", "For
  Rent", "For Gain";
We classify employment's
  varied names.
We classify the borrowed, the
  old, the new;
We classify our pets and
  households, too.

Each business has its trade
  gadgets and fads. . .
Ways to find friends in the
  classified ads!

Kenneth MacKenneth
TRICK FOR TRICK

Sanburg's fog
a big black cat
silently sat
the sleeping city.

But my cat fog
is wakeful grey
and came to stay
the more's the pity—

a feline trick
that spelled low vision
to me imprison
from bookland treasure.

But, ah! I found
a counter trick
of talking books
that fog dispell
like horn and bell
the more's the pleasure.

Anthony Bartley
UNTITLED

I heard about the trouble in
  the world

And I wondered why
What happens to the futures of
all the boys and girls
Are they born just to die
I heard the anguish of their cry
And I had little doubt
People would lie
Before they helped them out

Trouble is a continual pain
That will never cease
When will we ever learn
The price of peace.

Kimberly A. Rosin
LOVE ME NOW

Love me in the warmth of the
evening
when discovery isn't hindered
by time;
when each moment lasts for a
thousand tomorrows,
and nothing matters except that
you're mine.

Love me completely, not just
with your body,
but with words and the light of
your eyes.
Make me believe that you feel
what you're saying.
convince me it's love that I hear
in your sighs.

Love me now while the chance
is at hand.
Don't say goodbye and leave my
heart cold.
Give me one night if that's all
you can give.
Be there tonight if I need
someone to hold.

And if you must leave with the
morning light
I will survive, for you have made
me strong.
I will be patient and live each
day in itself
until I find another who will
sing my song.

Brian Conway
TABHA

Striding the long red legs to the
max,
the short-haired dog from
Australia
longed to fulfill his instincts.
He had
the freedom to roam and scatter
birds
at his leisure, but it was not the
same.
He had the freedom to protect
if he wished, although it might
be said
it was his assignment. Birds
were too small and being a
watcher
was too confining for his
instincts.
His love was unabounding so
was his
quest to hunt, track, stalk, and
then kill.
The sheep were easy prey and
Tabha became prey
to the rules and regulations of
man.
To protect and save the life,
Tabha was caged.
He stalks in limitation, killed.

Pauline Frechette Fotter
THE CHILD'S DREAM

The child gazed around the room
With thoughts of Santa coming
soon

His tiny heart was filled with joy
With hopes of getting just one
toy.
His thoughts return to Christmas
past
And how the disappointment
lasts
To wake and find the tree was
bare
And cry cause Santa didn't care.
He's unaware that if you're poor
Then Santa passes by your door
Unless there's someone else out
there
With just one gift they'd like to
share.
He heard it said if you believe
Then games and toys you will
receive.
With all his heart he knows it's
true
And prays that Santa will come
through.

Richard Sandoval
TO MY WIFE JANE

This is a story of you and I
Very young we started our
precious life
We joined hands together four
years ago
And as time passes by this I say
to you
Darling I love you, this is very
true
Come to my side so that I can
be with you
Kiss me my darling, I love you.
Remember the day that stamps
were our supply
No car, no money, times were
very dry
What kept us going was the love
that we shared
And we'll stay together till the
day we die.
We traveled our bodies from
place to place
At times we thought we found
a home at last
Suddenly down the road, here
we go again
Seeking our goal and a place to
begin
Here we are now very happy
indeed
Together we planted a most
precious seed
Soon you and I will be able to
see
The child that is born to you
and me.

William L. Marion
LOVE'S OLD SWEET SONG

I think of all our yesterdays how
new and young our lives
first began like spring on the
bloom and birds sing and
hollyhocks in full bloom.
Every moment we lived were
event shared are good times
and bad, began the first chapter
in the history book of
our love.
I'll never forget the first time
our hearts first really
met, it was more than suspicion
or just a hunch. It was
you and I forever and love was
enough.
I was just a hard working stiff
from dawn to setting sun
and you were the beginning of
everything to me. Before

we met my life held no quality
or meaning, but ever since
our first exchange my heart
and mind and soul my total
being and life will never be the
same.
We sometimes argue and quarrel
and I'm usually at fault
but I think of our life's first
sweet caress and how
our love will always be enough.

Judy E. McIntyre
UNTITLED

If I could count the minutes
That you are on my mind
It would take a lifetime
Cause I love you all the time.

I miss the times we spent
together
And each thing that we shared
But now it's all just memories
Although I still do care.

Each day is like a challenge
That I'll get over you
But so far it's been a battle
And very hard to do.

They say that Love's a game
And I really think it's true
Cause someone always wins the
heart
And this time, it was you.

I've had a few relationships
But none not quite like this
Cause no one's ever made me
feel
Like you do when we kiss.

You won my love and stole
my heart
And then it seemed to end
Now I find it hard to face
And even to pretend.

I know that it'll get easier
As time passes on
But time won't fill the emptiness
Now that you are gone.

I hope that you'll be happy
Cause you deserve the best
And I wish you all the luck

In all of life's success.

Betty K. Sleva
WHY IS IT?

Why is it when we're in a close
crowd you seem to
single me out?
I leave the room and when I
come back, you're
watching the door.
When we dance you hold me
close—
It feels so good, I hope the
music will never stop.
I'm sure you feel as reluctant as
I am to part.
Why is it the special feeling
between us is so strong?
We don't talk much at first,
we're afraid to say
the wrong things;
But soon, we're talking easily
about things that
really matter.
It's difficult to include all the
others in our
conversation.
Then I have to leave—I see the
disappointment
in your eyes.
Why is it that I go home on
Cloud Nine?
I know that this was the perfect
beginning of "us"
And the ending of "me"

Why is it the hours and the days
go by?
When the phone rings I know it's
going to be you—
but it never is.
I go back to being just "me";
Wondering how I could have
been so wrong
And asking myself—"Why is it?"

Mrs. Helen Farrell
OLD HOUSE

Peeled paint,
Worn with age
Warped and faded,
In a run-down stage.
Cold and lonely.
Dark inside
Broken window panes,
Held in stride.
Hinges clanging,
Floors sinking low
Boards loosening,
Look out below!

Joseph R. Paquette
TASTE OF HEAVEN

Walking in a Meadow in the
Pre-Dawn hours
A dark blue sky lit by a quarter
Moon
With stars so bright flickering
like Diamonds
Casting a dim light in the
meadow
surrounded by evergreens
Like black lace against the blue
sky.
Other than a hooting owl
The peace and serenity that
brings
Thy Lord in my heart with
prayers
Lighting my path with his
lantern
Escorting me. This is to me a
taste of Heaven.

Susan Pierce
TRAVELING ON

We are living on borrowed time
Our bodies are rented machines
Like rented machines they never
last forever
Though we are promised eternity
in another time
We must first get through the
daily scenes
of facing friends and meeting
other people
To learn to get along with others
While having to always face
ourselves
We can let ourselves get bogged
down with memories
of things or people that once
were
Or we can place these memories
on shelves
To return to when reminiscing
the good old days
But life goes on no matter what
Until the day our rented

machines
Become rusty and something
   that once was
And never will be again.

Wendy Lynn Anderson
BEAUTY

Beauty, have pity and mercy on
   me,
I lie only a shattered shell
Of your true image.
You are my worst of enemies;
You are my best of friends.
You taunt me with images of
   the future,
And, just as quickly, crush them
   again.
Your tarnished self is so precious
To the mortal being.
Perhaps someday all people will
   realize
How much more important the
   inner emotions are
Than the outer beauty, but until
   then
Beauty, befriend me!

Mildred A. Stuck
HAND MADE

I was alone—
The ominous silence seeped
   through my kitchen walls
   and prompted me
   to look out the window.
The sky was an odd yellow
   interspersed with
   the heavy, gathering
   clouds of darkness.
Trees began to sway
   like exotic dancers.
Lightning flashed
   in zig-zag fashion—
   as if in competition
   with the rolling thunder
   which was climaxing
   in a loud roar.
Electric wires sputtered,
   angry at the disturbance
   of their peaceful duty.
As if to ask admission
   the rain pounded
   against my windows.
Suddenly I was afraid!
Where could I hide
   from the wrath of the storm?
Then I remembered—
It was all fashioned
   by God—
   and I was in
   His protecting care.

Marsha Wollenhaupt
MOM AND DAD

I love you two with all my heart,
You two should never be apart.
I know it's hard to forgive and
   forget,
But I know you two will make
   it yet.
I admire you both, the way you
   keep trying,
But only family could ever
   understand why.
I know your relationship will
   work out in time,
And I hope your life is as
   beautiful as mine.
I just want to say, "I'm proud
   to have you as my mom and
   dad,
You are the best parents anyone
   could ever have."
If something goes wrong, try to
   take it in stride,
It will be so much easier, with
   the Lord by yourside.

I want you both to be happy,
   not sad, and have good times
   not bad.
I just want to say—
   congratulations,
And I hope you make the best of
   your relationship.

James Terry Foster
BECKY'S EYES

The glamour
from
Becky's
eyes are
rays of
sun,
beaming
with rays
of warmth
binding
energy to
form a
smile,
displaying
dimples of
alluring
charm,
create a
beauty of
rare gems
to admire.

Starla R. Sholl
TRUTH

Truth
hidden in the dark.
Its journey
covertly continuing.
Its wrath
never revealed.
Ultimately,
evincive betrayal.
Truth
lashes toward its keeper.

Patti Brown
LOVE'S CHARACTER

The face of love smiles upon us
   Each and every day
The hands of love reach down
   to us
   To help along the way
The arms of love hold us tight
   To make us feel secure
The eyes of love shine so bright
   So our love can endure
The shield of love surrounds us
   To keep the real world out
The spirit of love is with us
   In that there is no doubt.

Edith Cannon Storey
THE LITTLE BLACK SHEEP

Far away, and long ago,
On a hill near Bethlehem
Frolicked a little, black sheep
While the shepherds laughed at
   him.
He tried to hide in their shadows
When there shone a dazzling
   light.
His ears tingled as the first
Gloria filled the soft night.
The shepherds gazed at the sky,
Then the looked at each other.
Away they ran to Bethlehem
To the babe and Virgin mother.
The black sheep ran after them,
He was never far behind
He had to know why they ran
And what they had gone to find.
To the warmth of the stable
Sneaked in the little, black sheep
There in the manger rosy fair,
He saw the Christ Child fast
   asleep.
The shepherds knelt and so did

he,
It didn't seem strange at all
To the mother of this babe
That a black sheep came to call.

Marian E. Danskin Snyder
**GOD UNDERSTANDS OUR
SINS**

God doesn't condone the things
   we do,
But I know that He understands
He looks at the whys and the
   reasons of things
by the blood from His nail
   pierced hands.
He doesn't look at the sins we
   have done
Unless He sees the sinner too!
For He sees much deeper into
   our hearts
And the reasons for what we do.
So never despair when you have
   done wrong
For the Lord's arms are very
   wide;
And the price that He paid
In the tomb where He laid
Will make a refuge for us to hide.

Connie D. Elbon
ONE , TWO, AND THREE

All through the years
many poems have been written:
Poems of things; Poems of
   dreams,
Poems of love and fear,
most of all
Poems of things most dear.
God inspired each of these.
He inspires most everything.
This he has given to me.
He says there are three main
   parts of me.
One and two must be present
or there is no complete three.
Number one is God himself.
He who hath given life to
   numbers two and three.
I have parts one and three.
Without number two,
I can not truely be.
You are number two.
I need you, I love you.
Without you there is no me.

Julie D. Larson
MY TWO TRUE LOVES

My first true love tis strong and
   brave.
With forceful lust he rakes me
   to his chest
And his wistful and greedy lips
Seem to gormandize mine as
   he kisses me ravenously.
My body is a mere toy in his
   arms
Helpless and capitulating.
He fulfills a desire I have to be
   dominated.
My other lover tis intimate and
   amiable.
With tender arms he draws me
To his warm and familiar side
And his lithe and mellow lips
   embrace mine fondly.
I am a graceful dove in his arms
Submissive and adoring.
He fulfills a yearning within me
   to be loved.

Sharon I. Dreyer
THE CALIFORNIA LADY

The California Lady
Has left her ocean far behind
With family and friends

To become a distant memory
Beating on the shores of her
   mind.
But in its greatest depth
Rests the realities of the present
As she moves alone with
   conviction
Through his woods creating life
With and for the Mississippi man.

Calamity Jane Mattes
**I NEVER DREAMED OF
MEETING YOU**

When I got married and said I
   do,
I never dreamed of meeting you.
I never wanted to be unfaithful
But with you I could never be
   faithful.
I never thought I could make
   it through the days,
Then at night you showed your
   love for me in a million ways.
Every time I looked into your
   beautiful blue eyes,
I always asked myself, How
   could I ever get into this.
Then I would remember the
   way you kiss,
Then I would remember saying
   I do.
And I knew I could never have
   you.
I never was one to share.
And I knew I was being unfair.
We'd better wake up and see
   the light
Before they find out and put up
   a fight.
So honey this is good-bye,
And it was fun loving you.

Evelyn G. Hankel
MICHAEL

Michael, Michael where art thou?
Thy fields have need of thee
Spring has come and all the earth
Calls out for you to see.
The stream is full of silver trout
And young of all the wild,
Tred softly o'er your fields of
   green
With boldness borne to child.
The rancher tools so loved by
   thee
Lie cold upon the bench
You do not grasp the hammer
   now,
Nor mend the sagging fence.
Michael, Michael, where art thou?
Thy fields have need ot thee.
You walked away across the
   hills
And left them all to me.

Don Poklacki
RETROSPECT

He was a giant of a man!
   though not really very tall
But seen through the eyes
   of a child, yet very small
A man filled with compassion;
   that seemed so out of place
With his large callused hands;
   and his worn, weary face
A voice, the sound of thunder;
   to the young and tender ear
Who has always been my idol;
   and I'll always hold him dear
He helped to guide my life;
   and keep me on the righteous
   path
I obeyed him, out of love though
   not because I feared his wrath
He could fell me with a blow
   of the strength within one
   arm

But reserved it, to protect me;
  and to keep me safe from harm
Just a simple man, called Dad;
  the kindest man to talk the
  earth
Still, no measure made can tell,
  but what a Dad is really worth.

Allyson Mills Wolford
THE WILL

Write a ring around the moon,
  write a rainbow in the sky.
Write the things you've loved to
  see.
Write a world, for only me.
Write it all and write it well, for
  when you're gone,
There'll be no one to tell, of life
  so beautiful and long ago.
Write it, so they'll all know.
Write of the sun and the snow,
  and the rain,
When mist covered the water as
  slowly night came,
The fields and the flowers,
  white clouds in blue skies,
Write it all down for every
  passerby.
A life that was young and knew
  of no harm,
When the world was yet
  undiscovered.
Write the story you know, the
  one you've lived.
For you, the story may be all
  you've to give.
Write it.

Geraldine Fisher Wolfe
LAST SEPTEMBER

It was mid-morn, the very first
  day
of last Sepbember
Our hearts were filled with love—
  how
well we shall both remember.
Our journey began down the
  road, through
the mountain, together to our
  destination
The warmth we felt; the
  wholeness; the
closeness, the all. Yes, it was
  real—not
our imagination.
We shared each other; the sun,
  the beautiful pines,
the path along the way
We'll remember too, the pretty
  blue bird
with the funny top-notch—the
  pinejay!
But, unknown to us then and
  what we will mostly remember
This was our very first and our
  very last
September—last September.

Edith Heal
THE RETURN

What a treat, what a joy
what a lovely place to visit
the picture as clear and bright
as a primitive,
the grass of the park
squared off into separate plots
each with its own grey stone
  building.
The pond with real fish shapes
in it—the little bridge—
and all of it leading
to the green-leafed hideaway
with ivy curling in the window
and the walls made of books.
How odd to come back years

later
to see a tired man at a
  typewriter
instead of the flashing eyes
and seductive voice
of you. . .
dead these many years.

Mary K. King
MASTERPIECE UNDONE

I give to you
  The Elmer's glue
To mend your broken heart.
If only it was so easy
  To kiss
And then to part.
To fingerpaint a
  Fantasy
And live it for a day,
Then use your watercolors
  To wash it all away.

Jonathan C. Bloemker
UNTITLED

Late, late loneliness,
Dried and minor time,
A boring, bearing intonation
Destined to be mine.
When I am full of emptiness
I can't write what I feel.
I can't ink down on paper
A phantom thunder-peal.

Spencer Sutton
THE QUEST

As we travel
through time's door
Searching. . .reaching. . .
and grasping for more
We never know
in where it lies
We must have this quest
before we die
For without it
life has no meaning
And on towards
failure we keep leaning
To release
ignorance from bondage
we need this quest
known as knowledge.

Deborah A. Leach
COME TO ME

Come to me slowly.
Walk quietly,
My ego is frail
and shatters easily.

Speak with me softly.
Tell me please, of
friendship and caring,
of happiness and love.

Behold in my eyes,
a longing for
you to hold me near
I'm reaching out to you.

Are you reaching too?
I'm here with you.
Beside you, waiting,
for you. Reach out to me.

Mildred Noblet
**ON THE DEATH OF LIND
LINDBERGH**

He came out of the sky, like a
  bolt of lightning—
  Young and blond, fearless and
  sky
The "LONE EAGLE" we called
  him. PEERLESS—
  He shot across our world,
  conquering the earth, the air,
  the great Atlantic—
Our minds and our Hearts—
HERO of HEROES! Surpassed
  by none; Columbus, Cortez,

Polo—
  "WE" the Eagle and his Plane—
  The SPIRIT OF ST. LOUIS,
  by name—
Possessed the Spirit of America
  YOUNG, GLORIOUS, FREE
  AMERICA—AND WE WERE
  THERE!
NOW, he is dead—as are our
  Dreams—
  Dreams of PEACE in our Time
  Time—
Dead, too, our Youth—Three
  long wars ago—
SUDDENLY, the WORLD and
  We have become OLD
  And very COLD
BUT
Suspended ONE BRIEF POINT
  IN TIME
  There really was a CAMELOT
AND
ALL GOD'S CHILDREN
WERE
SUBLIME
AND WE WERE THERE!

Robert D. Roberto
OUR LAST GOODBYE

Remember when we said our
  last goodbye
To each other our voices rang
  farewell
We parted ending our last
  pleasured
Filled visit together
Memories of this precious
  moment
Are still on my mind
Remembering you that second
Of time is all I do
Long is the time since
That special night
Thoughts of saying hello seem
A lifetime away
Spending my life to see you
  again
Is all I live for.

Virginia E. Cruikshank
IMPENDING CHANGE

Some loneliness brought me
  here
Where redwings cut the air in
  measured beat.
Like pacers of a cell
They flutter in rehersed
  migration.
And I, with futile gesture,
Would withhold the living,
  pressing wave
And bar it from fulfillment.
For I must stay and face the
  falling year
Unlit by flare of wing;
Nor can my body soar forgetful,
Pushing aside the bars in search
  of spring.
And yet I linger, and prolong
  the pain
in all its gripping sweetness
Till twilight blots the colored
  caravan
And leaves me with the
  blackened rush of wings.

Irene Cody Keenan
DISCO GRANNY

With her house dress on and her
  hair so white
She looked so old in the prime
  of her life
No one knew when it all began
  but this
quiet little lady was making plans
First she bleached her hair threw

her house dress away
I could not believe it when I
  saw her today
With a sweater so tight and a
  pair of new pants
She was listening to the disco
  learning to dance
She was doing the hustle all over
  the room
She looked like a flower just
  starting to bloom
People may call it the change of
  life
But don't worry granny you're
  doing alright.

Lynden Castle
**CRY OF THE GREAT HORNED
OWL**

The cry of the great horned owl
Hangs heavy, soft, and still
Above the moon and heaven's
  turn
In silent, hallowed hill.

Orion's Belt full orbs the earth
The seven Pleiades sing.
The Cheshire strolls the zodiac,
And Pegasus takes wing;

But you, my love, are at my side
When lesser hearts would quail
And stars in their ordained path
Begin to sigh and fail.

V. Barnet Killie
THE GLASS UNICORN

Crystal clear—too far—yet near—
the Unicorn is prism fear.
Lightly poised—a window sill—
high above Hell's Gate Kill—
Burning brightly through the
  glass—
a rainbow flares—the seconds
  pass.
Then it's—by a hand—
reflections—two!—a mirror stand
This artless art—designed by
  chance—
could only be an happenstance.

Philip Van Wagoner
SUMMER REVERIE

The simmering sun blessed path
protrudes across the ocean to
  forever.
The endless pier juts forth
like a giant centipede
bathing its legs,
knees scabbed with barnacles
tangled in a spiders web of
  fishing lines.
The curling waves gently caress
the scarred limbs
the rock outcropping on the
  horizon
looms like a camel caravan
crossing the desert.
The tautly stretched beach is
signed with many autographs,
The sea belches forth a perfect
  sand dollar
Where is my wallet?

Paul Shapshak, Ph. D.
AGAINST THE EMPIRE

Originally mind, marginal
  child-maker,
Life's conquests trailing into
  snow cinders,
The conversation wrestled, sing
  awhile
On your branch of scaffold,
  riding the waves
Of the molested. Images are
  not idolatry.

Crush the grape, boil cauliflower,
Peel cabbage, subliminal
  complexes are

Mired in subconscious drives.
Keep an even pace with eternity,
Climb a comet's tail, shake
  raindrops
From pine branches like
  meadow-larks
In forest gloom. The matted
  swirling vines,
Snakes and leopards ascending
  trees,
Fetch primates to catch drifting
  fog.
In the end, world consciousness
Remains cognizant of darkness.

M. Ruth Proffit
REFLECTIONS OF LOVE

Here is my friend Molly with
  her surprise
Treasured lovingly deep inside,
Someday a new baby there will
  be
Maybe a He, maybe a she.
Along with baby will come much
  advice
Some of it foolish, some of it
  nice,
I'm no different than the rest,
  I fear,
So I'll give you mine while I
  have you here.
When I looked at Brian as a
  brand new Mother
I knew my love would surpass
  all other,
I knew no one else would ever
  love him as I did
But then he grew up and then
  he was wed.
I sat at the wedding remembering
  years gone by
As I worried and fretted and
  tried not to cry,
Then I felt Gary's hand as it
  reached for mine
A gesture of our love that would
  outlast time.
Suddenly another face appeared
  in the church
And I realized with a painful
  lurch,
It was my Mother-in-Law sending
  a loving grin
Cause where I was she too had
  been.
So love your precious son as
  much as you can
And then someday when he
  becomes a man,
You'll know in your heart there
  is no other
That can love him like a
  Wife or Mother.

Sally Mesyk
FRUITS OF THE SPIRIT

When the Holy Spirit fills your
  life
Your life is full of joy, abolishing
  discord and strife.
You feel love and kindness for
  both friend and foe
And with these virtues comes
  self-control.
Within your heart lies infinite
  peace
And your sinful restlessness will
  surely cease.
For all God's children who've
  lost their way
A bit of gentleness will brighten
  their day.
Because the Holy Spirit dwells
  in you
No one can deny its goodness

is true.
A faithfulness to God will always
  be your aim
But without His strength, you
  may fall into shame.
Above all, you have patience in
  all you do
You'll attain all these virtues,
  when His Spirit's in you!

Lorraine Hicks
**BEAUTIFUL LADY, I LOVE
YOU**

We two children grew
yet you and I never knew
We stood at odds,
searching over endless knobs. . .
I for a mother's love
and you for a turtle dove
You danced and dined
fascinated with wine.
I watched you come and go
a beautiful lady aglow.
My heart cried, "Please stay."
A teardrop made its way
down a sad little face.
I learned to erase
the tears and sadness,
until now. . .
Seeing her lingering illness
I cry,
"Mother, don't die."

Annette T. Alexander
ONLY A DREAM

I must stop dreaming of the
  things that will never be.
Of a life, thats only in my dreams.
Tomorrow the sun will shine.
But my dreams will never be.
I dream of our life together
and how beautiful
  it would be
Then I awoke and found it was
  only in my dreams.
My love will always be true for
  you
But our life together will
  always be a dream.
But I must stop dreaming of the
  things that will
  never be.
Because life is not a dream.
You are my hope for life
  and the happiness of all
  my dreams.

Miss Rikki K. Raymond
THE FIRE

I see the trees swaying there
I see the smoke rise in the air,
  I see the fire pouring out
  and all the deer scurrying about,
I see the ground smouldering
  black
  I wish that I could take it back,
  I also see the animals dead
  all burned up, so bloody, so red
  I wish my mind did not
  provoke
for me to light up and have a
  smoke,
  I wish now that I could catch
that murderous, hell ridden,
  fiery match.

Connie Ratliff
A BEAUTIFUL SPIRIT

A beautiful Spirit is in this place
As I look into each loving face
In the congregation—this is
  where I belong
For. the Savior's love comes thru
  so strong!
When the moment arrived and
  I moved to stand
Before the congregation and the

minister took my hand
A feeling of peace crept into
  my heart
As each member embraced me,
  I felt so much a part
Of this family of God, and I'm
  so glad
He let me have the longing I had
The yearning to find His
  Wonderful grace
And I've at last found it in this
  special place!
I'm now a full-fledged member
  here
At Pleasant Valley, and it's very
  clear
That this is where He meant me
  to be
May the way for others be lit
  thru me!

A. C. Empty
**HERE IS WHERE I WANT TO
BE**

I'm so glad Jesus is here with me
My mind is made up, here is
  where I want to be.
I'm so glad I found the Lord,
I sure hope he keeps me on
  board.
I think of him each night and day
and to him my heart will stay.
You may laugh and beat me with
  pipes,
but I am healed by his many
  stripes.
And because my lord provides
  my strength,
I shall stay with him through any
  length.
I don't drink or smoke dope,
Because I know Jesus is my only
  hope.
Sticks and stones may break my
  bones,
But I shall still carry on.
For my Lord he keeps me strong,
and to him I will ever belond.
I sure hope you trust in the Lord
So you won't be slain by his
  mighty sword.
I know the end of the world is
  near,
But I in no way show any fear,
Because I know my soul is saved
For my lord rose from the grave.
So now I've told you where I
  want to be,
I sure hope you'll be there with
  me.

June E. Coolidge
DEATH

Death is such an awful thought;
I often wonder who planned
  the plot.
It can't be seen or heard
But suddenly it sneaks
  around the corner and
  takes you by surprise
That's a shock that I despise.

Brian Conway
THE BEACHCOMBER

The fifty year shell rolls along
  the shell line,
searching for shark teeth left by
  tooth fairies.
Fairies that sprinkle tiny teeth
  like
elusive gold dust into the surf.
  The beachcomber tarries
in one spot and like a card shark
  eyes
the payoff of a microscopic tooth.
The sanded water rolls over lot
  lotioned toes
and splashes over the mammoth

golden brown figure. Sand
  dollars disappear
after the sand rolls away. The
  beachcomber
vanishes after the sun disappears.

Terry Guernsey
1980 APRIL SHOW

On this day I awoke
And I mused it was spring
Old man winter roared through
  with white smoke
Putting springtime in a sling.
His snow melted as quickly as
  it fell
Giving little relief—but problems
  for all
Made the ground soggy as hell
And postponed the chores for
  the garden to install.
According to the weather report
It should be the last snowfall
  of the year
Now mother nature can have
  some comfort
and prove she does care.

Linda M. Jenkins
SPRING IS HERE!

Spring is here, O glory, o joy!
Winter is gone, and so are the
  Christmas toys
The kids are outside walking
  and hiking
swinging and running, batting
  and biking.
The birds are singing and
  building their nests
Blue Jays, cardinals and robin
  red-breasts
Crocus are blooming and grass
  is greenin'
All this makes a beautiful spring
  scene.
I'm ready to go out and quit
  my hibernatin'
Staying in all winter is sure
  frustratin'
I'm gonna plant seed and flowers
  and trees
Tomatoes, strawberries and
  maybe even weeds!

Cathy Breen
DANA'S TEARS

The tears in his eyes,
I didn't understand,
I thought I knew his love,
Then he came and took my hand.
I thought it was his laughter,
His happiness that I saw,
Until I saw him walk,
And look upon the door.
The grip upon my hand,
Loosened up and then let go,
And the words I was to hear,
I yet did not know.
And then he looked into my
  eyes,
And spoke softer than ever
  before,
And said "They're wrong about
  everlasting love,"
Turned and shut the door.

Elizabeth Fowler
PSYCHIC SYMMETRY

More exquisite beauty does not
  exist
Than when two kindred spirits
  kiss.
Twin vibrations merging minds;
Souls and psyches intertwined.
Disrobed of earthly face and
  figure
Familiar images blend and linger.
Inner selves briefly reveal

What heart and tongue must
   conceal.
Like roses blooming in
   mid-winter
Each is awed in wonderous
   splendor
of soul mates crossing paths.

Miss Virginia Lear
OUR INSPIRATION

Closed are the lips that moved
   in prayer,
Still is the heart that kept God
   there,
Cold are the hands that made
   things grow,
Gone is the spirit that forgave
   her foe.
Quiet the laughter that consoled
   the sad,
Shut the bright eyes that made
   hearts glad,
At rest the feet that walked the
   ground,
Gone the "Good Scout" to those
   all those around,
But to those who loved her
   she'll always be,
A bright beacon light to eternity.
Whose one thought was "God's
   will be done",
No matter the cost, heaven was
   to be won,
You have led the way, our
   Mother dear,
We'll walk in your footsteps,
   never you fear.
Till we all meet in our heavenly
   home above,
Where with the Saints, our God
   we'll love.

Tirrell Rae Alfano
HARMONY RAIN

Falling to the Earth the gentle
   sound of Jesus;
Coming down like warm summer
   rain;
Touching anyone who bows his
   head to listen;
Filling anyone who says His
   name.

   Let it fall, let it fall,
      let the gentle rain of Jesus fall
   on me,
   Let it fill, let it fill,
      Let it fill me with His love
   and harmony.

Running through the Earth His
   rain becomes a river,
Winding past the days of every
   man;
Bringing life to those who stop
   and drink the water,
that Jesus holds for them within
   His hands.

   Let it fall, let it fall,
   Let the gentle rain of Jesus fall
   on me,
   Let it fill, let it fill,
      Let it fill me with His love
   and harmony.

Come my brother, kneel beside
   the healing water;
Lay your broken dreams along
   the shore;
Let the rain from Heaven wash
   them from your memory,
Then bow your head and wait
   upon the Lord.

   Let it fall, let it fall,
      Let the gentle rain of Jesus
   fall on me.
   Let it fill, let it fill,
      Let it fill me with His love
   and harmony.

Regina Conrath
HOW HIGH SOEVER IT MAY BE

Some persons climbed
   the highest peak,
Others looked up to see
   the highest cloud,
Many travel to look up
   at the highest skyscrapers,
Unknowns often pay
   the highest prices,
Mile high cities are
   the highest cities,
Airplanes fly
   over the highest mountains,
Someone sees
   the highest flying bird,
No one sees
   the highest flying snowflake,
Somebody cries
   to highest heaven,
With thoughts
   in highest ecstacy,
"O Lord, O Lord,
   You are the highest!"

Lori Morgan
CARESS ME GENTLY

Caress me gently, love
Hold me close and yet, allow
   me room to grow.
Caress me gently, love
I need to know you're near me
   and yet, I need to stand alone.
Caress me gently, love
Have faith in me so I can have
   faith in myself.
Caress me gently, love
My wings are beginning to unfold.
   Caress me gently, love
I'm ready to face the world and
   accept you as my love.
   Caress me gently, love
   Caress me gently. . .

Mary Elizabeth Somes
BE YOU ALONG LIFE'S ROAD

Sunset upon the humanity's
   restlessness
whispering realities search for

meaning in life
Human nature's sin causes misery
dignity all needs
acceptance is nice to find.

The human heart is selfish
   beyond compare
so much sadness we bring
   ourselves
as what we sow we reap.

To be loved and understood
   everyone wants
all feels a need to be themself
Goals we decide which to choose.

Life use to seem so simple
when we were young and
had dreams and were carefree

Live by your values
and you will be glad
be your best friend.

Gene Lankford
ELEGY

O, great Mentor, who will join
   me in mourning your fall!
Throughout all the ages you
   have lived among us, trying all
   but
   in vain to teach us the p
   profoundest mysteries of life;
Now all the world has forsaken
   you and your ways.

Your beloved wife Religion, she
   has abandoned you for the
   more

attractive lovers Ritual and
   Tradition;
Does she have one tear to shed
   for the one she once loved
   and trusted?
Your best friend Learning, he
   to has turned his back on you,
Following in the ways of his
   new companions–Nationalism,
   Power, and Money;
Allying himself with your
   adversary Institutionalism;
Does he give any lamentation
   over the loss of his Creator?
Few remember your works
   and ways;
Only your children–Love,
   Justice, and Truth–are left to
   carry on
   your memory and your hopes.
Rise again! Return to lead us in
   the fulfillment of your noble
   dreams!

Lathan H. Frayser
DAILY CARING. . .

Humans have a way of creating
   and fostering hates
   and divisions,
But God unites:
All have the same feelings. . .
   the same emotions. . .
The same hurts. . .
All want to love and be loved,
But one must love to be loved.

It matters not whether your
   eyes are black or
   brown or blue,
What really matters depends on
   you:
Like symphonies–each is
   different in structure
   according to its creator,
Each human is different
   according to his Creator;
The organ called the heart, keeps
   alive each
   person we know,
But the contents embedded
   within the heart are
   what makes a person glow.

Failure to give of yourself
Finally yields the nothing that
   you gave.
How do you expect an apple
   tree to grow
If you never plant the seed?
Daily caring will yield
An abundant field.

Mona F. Blandford
TRANSIENCE

Dan Shephard's house came down
   down today,
No match for man and machine;
When Dan build it, with mortar
   and stone
He built for the ages, with his
   one arm
and more determination than
   some men with two.
Now, in one half-day, it has gone
   down to rubble;
A heap of stones, dry memories
   and dust.
Within the time of a new
   generation's progression,
People in passing will say,
   "Dan who?"
So must be the fate of man-
   erected monuments
Even those built of sturdier stuff
Love, kind thoughts and actions
   are stronger than mortar,
But only in the minds of those
   whose lives we have touched;

When they too are gone, a new
   generation will say of us,
   "Who?"

James P. Chagares
COME TO THE MOUNTAIN

If I were a mountain men
   would look at me
And if I had my wisdom no one
   could conquer me
If I had a kingdom I'd have it by
   the sea

Other men would walk there,
   they would envy me
but I am only one man and I
   must stand alone
Get my courage from the
   mountain that's why I stand
   like stone.

If I were a white swan I'd wing
   to the sky
I'd search for tomorrow, let
   God answer why
I'd soar over green fields over
   the mountain I'd fly
I'd sleep in the meadow let
   nature hear my cry
But I am only one man and I
   must stand alone
Get my courage from the
   mountain that's why I stand
   like stone.
All the pain and the sorrow
   and the laughter will follow me
Come to the mountain, come
   with me.

Marilyn Jean Blomgren
REACTION

One summer morn there was a
   loud, rumbling sound,
and a rolling sensation on the
   ground.
Banging against windows were
   venetian blinds,
Swinging back and forth were
   plants of all kinds.
I got goose bumps on my arms,
   my tongue went dry,
I didn't know what happened,
   I was too scared to cry.
The phone was dead, I couldn't
   make a call,
so I rose to my feet and went
   out in the hall.
Under the archway I stood there
   saying,
"What on earth's causing that
   terrible swaying."
My thoughts turned to getting
   all details on the news,
At least we had electricity,
   no blown fuse.
I turned on the radio to station
   KCBS,
It was indeed an earthquake,
   yes, oh my, yes.

Lee Jacques
MY DAUGHTER–WHERE ARE YOU?

It has been such a long time
   since any news were received
From my only daughter
   my heart is thirsty and hungry
Dear child why such a lapse of
   time?
   a fear in my heart is conceived
Have I lost the love of my
   daughter?
   this fear hurts so cruelly
My mind, my soul and heart
   search
   for a good and sound reason
Yet, the fears and the hurt do
   not disappear

leaving mine an anguished heart
No phone, wrong address were
    answers to my search
and my heart remained in a
    cold, frozen season
Yet, my love kept faith and
    hope—news to appear
Lord bring consolation to my
    wounded heart.

Long—after many tears and
    much anguish
your letter came—my heart
    was floating
Tears came once more—this time
    of joy!!
you still loved me—I accepted
    your reasons
My loving child (daughter) loved
    me—no more anguish!!
my love and happiness—now
    glowing
As those tears flowed—of sincere
    joy
my love for you survives all
    seasons.

Dorothy A. Lawson
JUST PLAIN FOLKS

The oaken bucket that sat by
    the door
is now empty and forgotten its
    not used anymore
And the rock that was there to
    hold the door open wide
it's out by the pathway we have
    left it outside.
All the old dishes are broken and
    left here behind
They were Mom and Dads we
    thought they were so fine
The sun would beat upon us in
    the cotton field we tread
And all the tired people their
    hopes and dreams they said
A quilt upon the floor the
    rest we all did need you see
And how weary and sleepy
    we kids would all be
When picking cotton in the fall
    the winds blowed so cold
And we knew we must hurry
    and finish that last load
Our barefeet would run in
    dust of, ankle high
And see the wild geese flying
    across the sky.

Darcy Smith
THE HANGING

Racing after
catching
    the horse thief.

Lynching up
killing
    the helpless man.

Back and forth
swinging
    the lifeless corpse.

Marie Day
UNTITLED

My life was but a cold endless
    journey to
nowhere. It held no past and
    presented no future.
The present was but a mist that
    faded at each days
end. The paths I walked on
    were dark and lonely.
No one was there to keep me
    from stumbling. No one
even to hold my shaking hands.
Bewilderment was
always full to the brim in my
    mind.
I met you at a turn in the road.
Light

seemed to shine from around
    you. The welcome of
your smile drove away my
    lonliness. It put warmth
all through me, exchanging
    bewilderment for awe.
You held my shaking hands
    and calmed them. I knew
my life would have meaning
    while wlaking by your
side. I could see a new horizon
    holding a bright
future, filled with love and hope.

Candice Elizabeth Reason
FINNY

Graciously your blue tints glow
    into my own motion of
    blooming.
Appealed by the spiritual halo
    caressing inner judgements.
Peacefully searching love's
    truths,
light heats the soul;
as starbursts of energy create
    seasons.
Eau delights frosting the mind
are worlding and ever yielding
    the why's—the fork of confusion.
Never can it be to enjoy its
    beauty
And eat from it?
As Eve is to morning and to
    Adam,
one will turn as Autumn leaves;
beauty in ending, returning to
    ashes,
a result of fire. Its the price
    we pay.
Even so, darkness changes to
    hope,
For through stillness,
life turns and will return
being reality's rule; natural law,
    creation of God.

Dessie Bryant
**THEY CAME HOME FROM
IRAN**

Barrels of black ink saturating
    Cheerios and doughnuts,
Myriads of sounds and images
    Vying for authority
And priority
    Over anxious airwaves.
Ink and sound exploding
    Into a cautious reality.
Fifty and two no longer
    Just names and numbers
Invading conscious and
    Unconscious minds.
But faces grown familiar—
    Revered, dissected—
Led and shoved,
Shot forth from a powderless
    Cannon of red tape
    Into an unfamiliar glare.
In their privade deprivation
    They knew
Even before we did
    How desperately
We needed to know

That the Lone Ranger still
    rides.

Pandora Jorgensen
GRAN ROSE

You were so old, forgetful and
    frail,
    yet so full of life.
Always wondering, worrying,
    would you outlive all your
    children?
At 89 you were an inspiration;
    never wanting to be a burden,
    always worrying about
    everyone else.
I remember things so vaguely,
    Sunday afternoons spent with
    you.
Then we had to move away,
    the miles seemed to go on
    forever.
Now your two daughters are
    here
    left to battle over your few
    things.
They said you felt no pain,
    how I wish I could have held
    your hand.
My dearest Rose,
    how I hope that I grow up to
    be like you.

Gena J. Lloyd
THE BELL OF FRIENDSHIP

I rang the bell of friendship
With tones both loud and clear
A friend who once was far away
Today is very near.
I rang the bell of friendship
As I sailed down life's highway
a glow of warmth, a touch of love
It brings to me each day.
I rang the bell of friendship
Which lasted through the years,
The one whose love was
    strongest,
It was mother dear.
I rang the bell of friendship
with all its hope unfurled,
One though for love, one though
    for kindness
Will make a better world.

Cheryl J. La Rousa Groves
LIFE

A place of serenity,
It's beauty to see,
My eyes behold nature and it's
    all near to me.
I reach out to touch it but it all
    fades away,
So I pack away all of my dreams
    for another day.
Miles of walking in the sands by
    the ocean's floor,
It's the start of a new beginning
    and the opening of another
    door.
I sit here and meditate my cares
    away,
And I limit my thoughts
    just for today.
The beauty is all around me,
And as I look toward the sea,
I make a new discovery,
Because I've found the real me.

Jeannie Carlson
THE DISENCHANTED ROSE

As a sanguineous bud she
    graciously grew
To accept the blemished petals
Being plucked from her fleeting
    face,
To allow defoliation of her
    succulent loins

And permit the deprivation of
    her savage, caustic thorns.
Then she brazenly blossomed
    and was brutally
Loved for the softness of her
    subjugated skin
(Not for the charisma inside
    her slender stem),
Adored for her fragrant and
    fragile facade
(Ignored within).
So she wilted wantonly
Her sublunary self slipt
Unsampled into an ecstatic
    earth.

Steven Thorpe
**THE TEN THOUSANTH
CRUCIFIXION**

I see a man
Eternally nailed
To a plaster crucifix
    pale dead eyes staring
    up to an empty heaven—
    a steel factory roof.
I hear the slap
Of ten thousand molds
Filled with holy plaster
And see the solemn procession
Of ten thousand bleeding white
    Christs
Crucified on ten thousand
    chalk crosses
Silently marching down
A dusty white
Conveyer belt.

Jim Hillin
THE MOMENT BEFORE

"Let's look at the stars..."
and we rise and walk carefully
to the wide open back porch
beneath the darkness.

    Cool breaths of air flow by
    you and I
    as we stare, stare at our faces
    and then the heavens.

        Quiet moments stand between
        us and
        caress our tongues as we watch
        for shooting stars,
        stars I will always see.

        I look up and see your face
        only,
            no stars or clouds above;
            my eyes turn to you and
            yours to mine and I wonder.

Diane Kie Sanders
TRIFLING

i cannot be a replica
    of cherished whatnots
        fragile/dainty
that society has indoctrinated
    you to adore/i came fresh
    uncontaminated
spring/ready to give you me
found out it was not I wanted
    rather
china dolls of crystal lights
    sugar plum smiles
        hugh liverpool eyes
that say, Yes...
instead came i/a trifling wench
        born to conjure...
and not afraid to ponder why i
    must be that which i'm not
and i think you like the mole
        blind/arrogant
and babies should not be born to
you but come packaged as
        jigsaw puzzles
with special instructions to read
please be not dismayed
    god moves in mysterious ways
        perhaps i am a way.

James S. Beam
GENETIC FEAR

Things stay the same
we make them change
to explain away the days;
watch your children break
things that remain the same
why are generations so hard to
please?
I'll always remember
truth has no sides
love is monetized
suicide is classified;
society needs revenge
or is it guilt they agonize?
Death will catch you
if you look ahead
so watch the future and the kids
one could kill you
the other be your friend.

Fannie Johnson
A PEACEFUL MIND

A time to remember,
that God loves you.
A time to remember,
that He gave his Son.
A time to remember,
to receive salvation for your soul.
A time to remember,
God's gift is grace.
A time to remember,
joy and peace.
A time to remember,
to Glorify His name.
A time to remember,
to understand His greatness.
A time to remember
His heavenly touch.
A time to remember,
He is with us forever and always.

Kathryn C. Wagner
CRACKER JACKS

I found my love
in a box of Cracker Jacks.
Amid caramel popcorn,
Surrounded by the peanuts.
And it was the surprise inside
That told me that your love
Was not a toy but something
real.
that would last forever
or until the peanuts ran out.

Mrs. Jewel T. McElroy
CASCADING AUTUMN LEAVES

Like little imps they flutter
And clutter the landscape with
Spanish gold.
Their multi-patterns leave no
trace
Where once they held a special
grace
To make the shade, where
children played,
And mockingbirds sang their
songs
To the passing throngs.
But now the north wind blows.
And soon the snows
Will cover them in an Ermine
wrap
Where they'll all settle down
To a long winter's nap.

Dawn E. Rutter
ROSITA'S CANTINA

The cantina was small,
The music was loud.
In walked a Vaquero
With posture proud.

No one spoke a word
As he strode to the bar,
For the tall Vaquero
Had a face with a scar.

The music began again,
Rosita whirled round,
The tall Vaquero
Kept his eyes to the ground.

The music sped on—
Rosita danced faster,
He smiled, the Vaquero,
For he knew he was master.

He leaned toward Rosita
And encircled her waist,
Strode from the cantina
With her in his embrace.

To his stallion he took her,
She followed with grace,
Rosita said nothing—
It was not her place.

They rode from the cantina
In the velvet black night,
The cantina musicians
Were amazed at the sight.

Many years have gone by
In that Mexican town,
They repeat now the story
When the moon's going down.

Richard W. Selle
PEACE WITHIN

Alone and weary, only peace
sought I.
There hadn't been anything I
wouldn't try.
Still peace evaded me all life
through,
Until I searched further and then
I found you.

There are temporary islands on
life's troubled sea,
But only in Jesus is there real
peace for me.
I've roamed the world over and
searched far and wide,
But only in His arms does
comfort abide.

Bring Him your burdens, your
troubles and cares,
He paid the price and your
sins He bears.
"All is forgiven", my Savior
tells me,
"That's why I gave up my life
on a tree."

So stop needless searching in
life's world of sin,
You'll never find peace until
you let Jesus in.

Marlene Stoetzel
LIFE'S CONSOLATION

There comes a time as years go
by,
When one stops to wonder why.
The sun continues to rise and
set,
And one's world is darkened by
a gloomy net.
For difficulties arise, to which
I refer,
As the loss of a loved one, we'd
like to defer.
But through the darkness shines
a bright light,
Improving one's outlook, in
spite of the plight.
For God is always near to help
us all,
Listening and aiding to heed our
call.
And in answering our prayers,
maybe one day,
The good Lord willing, will
show us the way,
Enabling us to see our loved ones
again.
And, in extending a hand to

greet a friend,
The Lord will fill the void which
arose,
Until one's life comes to a close.

Joseph E. Barrett
LOVE IS

Love is a glowing spark in
Nature's Web,
Love is a bar of music not quite
herad,
Love is a tender feeling at day's
ebb,
Love is a well known old four
letter word.

Love soars on wings above the
barren veldt,
Love cleaves the depths as
mermaids sing the dawn,
Love dances where once elvin
magic spelled,
Love ploughs the fields the old
gods cried upon.

Love wakes the birds and teaches
them sweet song,
Love stirs the fish and fills the
spawning bed,
Love moves the beasts, the weak
ones and the strong,
Love ensnares Man and soon all
reason's fled.

Love came disguised to Leda as
a swan,
Love came, and my poor heart
was just a pawn.

Christine J. Burton
BETROTHAL OF THE SEASONS

I slowly walked a forest path
today,
The snow drawn back by March's
warming touch;
A heavy tweed of green and
brown and gray
Enclosed my step: of pine and
earth and such
Great stones, or so they'd seem
to woodsy folk
Of fur and quill, and others
thereabout.
Beyond a wall and sheltered by
a cloak
Of underbrush I saw a scene
devout:
Within the nave of brittle
undergrowth,
Hid from view, a rite of phantom
spring:
Precocious flowers of white
and gold betroth—
The dream of mums and glads
exchanging rings.
Complete with birds of sume
summer—a choir of joy;
The kiss unseen,—a squirrel
the altar boy.

Duane D. Thornton
VANISHING LANDS

Untouched wilderness,
Are vanishing lands:
With the coming of progress;
They're slipping, through our
hands.

Leaving the present
And becoming the past;
How much longer
Will open lands last?

Can we afford:
To lie them behind,
To be only memories;
Locked in one's mind.

We can never regain,
What's already lost:

But; we can preserve what's left;
If we're willing, to pay the cost.

We have obligations,
To those; yet to be,
The freedom of the wild,
And of; prosperity.

Both are as important
As the other;
Problems created today,
Should not continue to another.

Sherman Conrad
OLD CHATTY

What am I doing here
No son, brother, wife
The leaves came down
all last night
in that driving killing rain

In my head words keep saying
not from me, maybe from
someone
else's life
I can't remember

Bright day today, cold wind
unseasonable out of the south.
Not a name I could give if
they came to ask me.

I just keep quiet, keep
it inside me, and wait.

Bonnie M. Kinnison
DREAMS

If only dreams came true
You'd have me and I'd have you
We would always be together
And our love would last forever
Every day we'd say a prayer
For God to keep us in his care.
Before we went to sleep each
night
We'd make love by fire light
Then we'd sleep, holding each
other tight
I can't think of anything more
right. . .
if only dreams came true.

Judy Lynn Klimcheck
REACH OUT

I found something new today,
I reached out and it was there.
Maybe you didn't and maybe
you don't even care.
It wasn't frightful, it wasn't sad,
you needn't beware.
Just to tell you about it, if
you didn't find it, wouldn't
be fair.
But then it isn't a matter of
should I or shouldn't I share.
You couldn't find it easier if
someone set out a flare,
Or if you searched for a subject
and sat down to stare.
Tomorrow you can look too.
You have time to prepare.
Try to find something new
tomorrow if you dare.
I will find something new. I'll
reach out and it will be there.

Dorothy A. Crosby
OLE INFLATION

Ole inflation is like a puffing
wind,
Siphoning our money till we
can't spend.
It has us stretching, saving and
trying to eat,
Just plain trying to make ends
meet.
It's at the filling station, the
movie, and
the grocery store,
Everywhere screaming, More!

More! More!
Daily we wonder when it will
    go away,
We shake when we think it is
    here to stay.
Somebody do something and do
    it fast,
To make Ole inflation a thing
    of the past.
Just a tiny, little inkling of hope,
Will make it better for us trying
    to cope.
How we wish and we pray as
    we look to the sky,
For the day Ole inflation will
    finally die.

Jacob Van Wyk
**FOOTPRINTS IN THE SANDS
OF TIME**

As I look back to yesteryear,
I do not look back with fear.
I see another footprint and
I know that God is near.

As we walk together,
He talks to me now and then
and carries me from time to time,
when I can no longer stand by
this strength of mine.

So as the years go by, one by one
And in those sands of time.
One footprint will be Jesus'
The other will be mine.

Robert Keith Brough
**WOULD THAT THERE WERE
ALCOHOLIC ICECUBES**

A sea of black I never see
Recalls the past (though darkly)
With reflections of a heartless
    life
Filled with seedy Saturday
    nights
And licentious Saturday lights.

Far below my clouded seat,
A delicate web of
Lace strung lights and
Patchwork metropolises
Guides me to my somber future
(mirrored by my somber past)
And all I see (through all I'm
    told)
Never explains the heart of
    darkness
Like a surrealistic vision
Through alcoholic icecubes
would.

Marge Harkness
WEDDING PRAYER

I believe, God in his wisdom has
    sent my way
A most precious possession for
    which I prayed.

A man so filled with goodness
    and love
And a union now sanctioned by
Heaven above.

I pray for the insight and wisdom
    I need
To please this man with every
    word and deed.

May my every emotion be filled
    with thought
For the happiness in life, he
    already has brought.

As the twilight years into our
    life must creep
And the flow of mortal life
    begins its sleep

May God look upon this union
    we've won
As His most prized arrangement,
    ever done.

Amen.

Deanna Enos
AT NINETY YEARS

There was no rest for him
Just days, repeated days.
his dreams were few.
His hopes unclear.
The children tried to give what
    they could spare.
Yet they would not strip
    themselves too much
For fear they'd lose a touch with
    youth
His cry was louder still than most
    most at ninety years.
A cry to live!
I cannot go before I've learned
    to love!

S. S. Moorty
HOPE

Blue skies are for us to look up
    boldly
And feel one with bounty of
Nature, dear!
Yet, do you, Lakshmi (my wife)
    ever see wholly
Behind grey clouds, you so often
    fear?

Is there any? In grey, you find
    doubt!
But I discern Hope and our, my
    dear, Future.
Love, do know, clouds are
    transient. So, shout
As thunder and lighten up your
    doubts. Venture

With hope, and doubt not what
    is beyond.
Let invisible breeze touch joy
    of what's to come.
Tell me that Life isn't grey all
    times. Grand
Hours of hope-filled life, my
    lady, are a stream.

So, curse me not for my gentle
    reproach;
Let us then sail toward a new
    approach.

Walter D. Neumiller
CHILD OF GOD

Child of God what will you be
    when you get as old as me?

As you grow up, strong and tall
    trust in God and you'll not fall.

Sing a song of love and praise;
    God will love you all your days.

When you're ready to depart,
    trust the Lord with all your
    heart.

Christ will raise you with his
    hand
    and take you home to Heaven's
    land.

Child of God what will you be?
    Pray to God and you shall see.

Georgia Radcliffe
FAITH

How can I ever fully comprehend
    complexities that prove how
    rare you are,
Can I define the subtleties of
    breath
    or analyze the brilliance of a
    star?
If I should take a rose and pull
    apart
    each delicate, soft petal one
    by one
I'd only have a stem of stinging
    thorns
    to show my disbelief when I
    was done,

So as the seasons flow this is my
    prayer,
    that my loved one reflects
    and always knows
Within my heart, intact and
    unexplained,
    still blooms one mystifying
    crimson rose.

Alessandra A. Poles
THE FALL AND RISE

Oh, why is there so much unrest
    about?
The guttered sounds upon this
    earth, still cries
Of old and young, the poor and
    rich, the ties
Of tired and hollow shadows
    breeding doubt.
Why are the nagging horns of
    smog enroute
The smolders breath of lives
    in slow disguise;
And why do double rattled
    tongues give rise?
Just who or what controls? Do
    not sit! Sprout!

Unfold the gathered rust that
    lies inside,
Free soul from its confined
    degrees of sheath,
Let fresh sound air sweep in to
    fill new thought;
Our hearts, our minds, our
    spirits will then ride
Through opened gates and gain
    new lease to breathe
To reach a love that flows—
    untying knot.

Mrs. Flora J. Krantz
HAVE YOU EVER?

Have you ever waited for
    something
And it never came?
Have you ever done something
And now you're ashamed?

Have you ever started love
And suddenly quit?
Have you ever wanted love
But couldn't find it?

Have you ever wanted to cry
And later wondered why?
Does sad music make you sigh?
Does love seem to just pass you
    by?

Have you ever balled your fists
And wondered if love really
    exists?

If so, I say this to you now, my
    dove,
It does not matter if you are
    loved
For today we should be brothers
And you of all should love all
    others.

Jasper Davis
LOVE, ONE BENCH AWAY

A bench across in a leafy park,
Sat a romantic beauty.

Her charm frightened my speech
When our eyes met I became we
    weak.

Motion none did we make,
But stared and drifted our minds
    away.
Waded through some golden
    brook,
Her soft hand in mine I took.

Embraced we climbed the hill,
Where stood an old abandoned
    mill.
Beneath its leaning shed we
    loved,
Alone without a word.

Back to the park we gaily walked
Not a whisper, nor a talk.
Satisfied we were with a stare,
Though only our lustful minds
    did share.

Jerry D. Rose
WIND

I bring movement to all in my
    path.
I move in happiness and I move
    in wrath.
Sometimes I like to race the
    lightning.
Other times I enjoy the solitude
    of resting.
At times my presence is a
    welcome sight.
Other times I am met with
    curses and fright.
I come with the heat and I come
    with cold.
Sometimes I am meek and
    sometimes bold.
I keep everything moving that's
    made by God.
I love to sway the grass on the
    sod.
But you will never see me
    going past.
You will only see where I was
    last.
Because, you see, I cannot wait.
For I am the one who must
    never be late.

Beatrice Ann Duda
THE FOOL

Putting things in pleasures face
Send these feelings to their place
Making sure of my disguise
Hide these tear drops in my eyes
Tis carelessness for me to weep
While this passion slowly creeps
Up into my lonely hands
Dying for the touch of man
Surpressing things within my
    soul
Helpless dreams to yet unfold
Quaking from my every thought
Lessons to have learned or
    nought
Putting distant looks in place
Seeking but to see a trace
Of the love I lost ago
Never seeing or to know
Depth of love or beauty's soul
Reaching out to touch or hold
Many dreams I hide away
Foolish for another day.

Margaret E. Fiske
HOW TO BE

Sit placidly like a cow
And do not sit upon the rug
Then people will have no reason
To slug your ugly mug.

Remember to grease the cat's
    boil
If you kill yourself, leave a note
Wash yourself often or you will

become
As smelly as a goat.
Don't wear blue jeans inside out
Nor bras upon your feet
Don't put Alpo on fried eggs
Or rat spray on your meat.

Never goose your grandma
As she tries to take a bath
For she may drown and you
  would find
The cops hot on your path.

If you disguise yourself as a
  moose
Or in a pickle suit
Then people will call you a sick
  mind
A Toadburger and a Fruit.

Above all, smart-off graciously,
Never toot on anyone's thumb,
One who knows just "how to be"
Will never be thought of as dumb.

Helen Holub
HAUNTED EYES

I awoke and shook my head
  in disbelief. . .
I knew not why I felt such
  utter grief.
The haunted eyes I'd seen
  in slumber deep
had wakened me, as I
  struggled from my sleep.

I could not shake emotions of
  that day. . .
Somehow, I knew I'd see those
  eyes another way.
Time passed, and still I
  dwelt upon those
  haunted eyes.
It seems illogical, but still
  emotions would arise.

Would I always be distressed
  by just a drea?
Could those eyes find peace,
  without that haunted
  gleam?
One last time, I saw those eyes
  with sorrow dwelling there.
'Twould be the last, and almost
  more than I could bear.

Mother looked at me and there
  I saw that dream again. . .
"It's time," she said, and I
  saw those haunted eyes
  and then. . .
The blessed sleep from pain
  had closed them ever more;
And now, she dwells within the
  gates of Heaven's shore!

Myrna V. Johnson
SOMEONE HELP

Here I am upon the shelf
I can't find me alone
Won't you help me find myself?

I'm tucked away behind
  someone's favorite book,
Does anyone care?
Won't someone help me look?

There are four black walls and
a floor
It's cold, and it's dark
And I can't find a door.
Here I am on the shelf,
Please help me find myself.

Rhonda R. Abreach
MOTHER EARTH

Ah, once she was a gentle giant
  boasting of her young
Proud of every man and beast,
  so healthy, bright, and strong
Now her mighty head is bowed,
  her eyes filled with great tears
The bold ones wrecked the
  beauty the faint of heart held
  dear
Her soul now aches within her,
  but she blames neither side
For all are products of her; no
  heritage denied
And yet she's stripped of life's
  blood by those she gave the
  most
When she has no more to give,
  who will stand the loss
Mother Earth stands crumpled,
  her cries fall on deaf ears
Her heart will be all that's left
  when the horizon finally clears.

Joseph Paul Montes
KARMA

Draw the sword of vengence,
  for it carves a wicked path,
and in it's pools of passion,
  must a blind man have his bath.

Words of wit unheeded,
  as the blindness takes control,
we now pay not with money,
  the balance due. . .is soul.

Tena Kemp
YOUR PILLOW

What a friend your pillow can be,
It does not think nor does it see;
A pillow sometimes is hard,
But mine are very soft so far.

They are your friend all night,
And cradles your head softly
  right;
You can cuddle them, fold them,
  cry
In them and dream in them,
But most of all what a night with
  out your pillow, would be.

Adrian M. Maschek
QUIET MOMENTS

Through the noises of the day
or the silence of the night
I thank my Lord and Savior,
for guiding me aright.

When my day is done
and evening shadows fall
it is these quiet moments,
that I pray best of all.

I sense that God is with me
when the sun has lost its glow
and I seem to feel his presence,
as the gentle breezes blow.

A whisper touch to the shoulder
means my prayer is heard
and I sense a sort of breathing,
a guarantee of his word.

I look forward to quiet moments
to thank God and to pray
and for his divine protection,
when I am on my way.

My prayers go not unanswered
my faith grows with each day
I seem to search for stronger
  words
to praise him when I pray.

I thank you Lord for these quiet

moments
and a time to kneel and pray
for all that's bestowed upon me,
and for showing me the way.

John A. Guilliams
THE CROSS

Is the cross too heavy—the
  burden too strong?
Are you trying to carry the cross
  on
your own?
Let Jesus tenderly lift the cross
  from
your shoulders.
He will carry the burden of your
  load
all life long.
He is waiting to carry the heavy
  load
for you.
All you have to do is ask him
  to take
the cross which is too heavy for
  you to
carry alone.
He will take your cross and carry
  it
along with mine, too.

Jessie M. Bunch
LITTLE CHUKWALLA

Little Chukwalla, Little
  Chukwalla,
By accident our paths have
  crossed
Here in the hot Mohave;
You run so fast o'er the burning
  sands,
Then pause on a rock to watch
  me.
The sun is at it's zenith now,
One could cook in it's rays on
  a stone.
How do you stand this Desert
  heat?
It is all that you have known?
You are a perfect miniature
Of those immense, ancient
  beasts
Who lived and ruled their misty
  world,
Then mysteriously ceased.
You look at me, with your little
  eyes;
You do not seem afraid,
I would not harm you, my little
  friend,
Both of us God has made.
You eat the bugs that I detest,
This is your world, I know,
I am the intruder here, not you
It's me that needs to go,
Little Chukwalla.

Joan D. Iburg
LONELINESS

It's just a feeling I get
when I look around
and you're not there.
Yes, it's just a feeling I get.
Standing alone without you,
I cry.
I pick myself up and
walk alone without you.

Gathering all my own strength
  deep
within my soul,
I can stand alone.
For, it's my strength I feel as I
  weep.

Along our path I walk
alone, and the warmth I felt
once is gone. My heart

is cold now like a rock.
Sometimes, it's a feeling I get
when I remember you,
briefly.
Yes, it's just a feeling I get.

Adam Nichols
THE HOSPITAL

Doctors in white cloaks
Stalking the halls,
Nurses whispering,
Then scurrying off,
Orderlies dressed in shrouds,
Apparently lifeless,
Patients complaining,
Claiming there's pain.

The visitors are sad
Or maybe glad. . .both!

The air is dead
No, just negative
Peering into a still pond
and seeing a tidal wave.

Anne Page Twist
APRIL

With loving arms you hug our
  necks,
Kissing our cheeks with gentle
  pecks.
How precious you are in saying
  "Good Night",
And then, "I have to go potty",
  turn on the light!
You like kitties and doggies and
  bunnies, too,
Grandma's lipsticks, and wearing
  her shoes.
Little April with hair the color
  of gold,
Sometimes shy; and sometimes
  bold!
Oh, my darling, how precious,
  to us, you are,
You brighten our hearts like an
  evening star.
I wish we could look into the
  future and foresee,
The only hurt you would ever
  suffer would be a bruised knee.
God and his heavenly angels
  love you; and so do we.
"HAPPY BIRTHDAY", April,
  today you are three.

Eleanor Powers McCann
WHAT MEASURE

Being both human and afraid,
  men try
To make some measure of their
  precious things,
To total all their wealth and so
  deny
The sure uncertainties that living
  brings.
Rubies they rate by carats, time
  by days,
Air by breaths, water by drops,
  and dew, and
Space that can elude them in a
  haze
They dub infinity, and bind it,
  too.

But what can be the measure
  of love?
Not drops, nor seas, not weights
  of much or few,
And "Infinite" spreads over
  Heaven above
A narrow thing meant only for
  two.
Perhaps the understanding
  that they bring
Measures our loves. . .not any
  other thing.

Shirley Grant
IN THE COUNTRY

In the country, skies are blue
Grass is green, wet with dew
Sun is rising over the hill
Good morning yellow daffodil

Birds are singing in the trees
Rustled by a cool fresh breeze
Blowing through the valleys deep
Waking from their nighttime sleep

In the country when the sun sets
  low
In the western sky and the cool
  winds blow
Silver moon shines down its light
And a quiet countryside whispers
  goodnight.

Kathi Kimmins
A POSTMARK LAFAYETTE

Dreaming on sliver-silver moons
of the ex-cajun reel 'n roll band
getting set to play,
of the smokey beers and
the cool dim corners
we slipped to
to kiss and hold tight
the hurry of the station
and long flashes of
your blue promised eyes.

But in the silence
my slit dreams
spill stains to the floor.

Diane Jean-Marie
FROM THE CORNERS OF MY MIND

Sometimes
I feel as though
my thoughts must be carefully
  gathered
From the corners of my mind
I have lost too many;
for some are so fleeting
that seconds later
I cannot remember
What I was thinking
Are they worth saving?
I don't know
Sometimes I think so
Others have told me that they are
But there are times
When I am not sure
If they are worth anything at all—
and I wonder. . .
Sometimes why I bother
There are also times
when I feel almost compelled
to put my thoughts down
  before
I lose them all
Surely I should save them
Perhaps they will give
insight to someone else or
perhaps facts history knowledge
  opinions maybe even ideas
make them think. . .
If they can help anyone then they
are surely worth gathering
from the corners of my mind.

Mary E. Woolsey
SUNSET MYSTERY

Did you ever in the evening—
Sunset time is drawing nigh—
Wonder who the crow was calling
Cawing in the tree so high?

When I was a girl no higher
Than the knee joint of a fly
I went out to see—one night time
Who or what was passing by.

Just at sunset by the crow tree
On a toadstool soft as down
I saw what he saw that ev'ning
Saw the sun so big and round

Don his nightcap, pull his covers,
Made of soft green covered hills,
Up so high around his shoulders,
Wink Goodnight—
See—
  Crow is still.

Robert S. Hensley
YOU AND THE MORNING

I saw you
And I remember you
Early in the morning
And the memory
Of you
And
Of the morning
Stays
With
Me.

Sensei, Joseph Carbonara
AFTER THE DUSK COMES THE DARKNESS

Twilight, it's not so clear.
  Life has been a struggle, I hold
  it dear.
Getting late purpose unfolding.
This world we live in I find
  beholding.
Darkness is on us no need to hide
  My God I'm glad I have not lied.

Susie Gumm
YES, I REMEMBER

The first week into December,
She asked of me—
As she has for these past seven
  years,
"Have you been to Michael's
  grave?"

How can I tell her that—
your smile,
Your touch,
The bounce of your step,
Are not confined there—
Where once a year she goes
  to mourn—
But are pressed safely away in
  the depths of my heart
From where I shall grieve for
  you
Every minute of my life.

Nina J. Moore
CRY WITH ME

Come world, come cry with me.
  Draw your
  Tears from an oil-stained sea.
Look upon this body of a once
  white bird,
  And know, like me, there is no
  word for
  What man has done to thee.

Weep from your skies of dirty
  gray,
  Remembering the blue of
  yesterday.
For we no longer see the stars,
  and this
Once fair land is covered with
  scars
  Of man's destructive way.

Cry, of world, cry out with pains,
  as
You feel the hot drops of the
  atomic rain.
And as you see the tall trees
  wither
  And die. Can it be possible that
  Only I—am crying too?

Ann Conard
AFTER MARY ANN

Mary Ann supposed the element
  of risk
Not consummate love brought

her into being
That after existentialist birth,
Continual accidental existence.
Walking in Capricorn around
  Eola
Excited her drive to survive
  against forty,
Her auburn hair washed twice a
  week her salute
To strangers coming and going
  moving with the sun.
Mary Ann, who ordered
  strawberries out of season,
Who rode her bicycle in the
  rain, "company to my tears"
She said when I asked her about
  cocaine.
News from Mobile came by way
  of Orlando.
Mary Ann, suicide. God, she
  killed herself.
Reality is a daisy like a rubbing
  on the heart.

Mary Anne Mackey-Wisor
GRACE

Age—what is it?
Time—space—mindset
grace
A LIFE FULL OF GRACE
graceful
FULL OF DIGNITY AND LIFE
gracefully
TO GLIDE THROUGH LIFE
graceless
TO BE MEAN AND
  CANTANKEROUS
gracelessness
TO GIVE UP AND HIDE
TO SMILE
TO LIVE
TO GROW
full of grace and dignity
TO FACE GOD WITH A
  THANKFUL HEART
for being gracious
THAT IS OUR GOAL OF AGE

Cindy Kelly
PICTURES OF CREWEL

Life is but
  Pictures of crewel:
Vivid hues,
  Mere shades of jewel.

Intricate stitches
  Forming the row
Appears unto thee—
  Stained glass window.

Reverse the crewel
  Thou doth seeth below,
Uneven stitches
  Compose a sparkling—
  Stained glass window.

Dr. Anita Joan Wepfer
THE MOON LIVES ON

Casting her mellow shadow upon
  the earth
Lighting the path for those who
  here have trod
Caressing the seas with her
  splendid touch
And sharing the sanctity of God.

Seeing the righteous rally when
  smitten
Watching false images crumble
  to dust
Blessing the wonders of hope,
  love, and freedom
Condemning the evils of
  slaughter and lust
Guiding her people in the
  conquest of space

Possessing great mysteries that
  shall never cease
Wearing the sign of a man on her
  face
Endlessly searching the world
  for peace

Floating serenely, aloft in the
  dark
Remaining so faithful when all
  else is gone
Travelling the trail of her
  age-old arc
The moon lives on.

Barbra Smith
ARE YOU IN NEED OF A FRIEND?

Are you in need of a friend
One who'll stay close to you
  til life's end
One who'll be nice, sweet, and
  kind
One who'll help you through
  when You're in a bind
Someone you can tell your
  secrets to
Someone who will listen to you.
  You can have this friend
He'll stay with you until life's
  end
He'll be nice, sweet and kind
And he will help you when
  you're in a bind
You can tell Him your secrets,
  too
He will listen to you.

My friend's name Is Jesus
And He will be with us
Until Eternity
If you only want him to be!

Mayrene Wainwright Roszell
JUST TWO YEARS OLD

Don't give me mansions pearly
  white
Nor jewels made from silver or
  gold
Just give me grandchildren for
  my delight
And let them be—just two years
  old

Don't give me clothes flashy or
  fine
I have all my closets can hold
Just give me grandchildren in
  my time
But let them be—just two years
  old.

Don't give me wealth for a
  Queen's delight
Nor any red carpets unrolled
Just give me loving heads of
  white
With eyes of brown—just two
  years old

Dear God, you gave me gifts
  from above
More precious than silver and
  gold
They are mine to cherish and
  love
And I wish they could stay—just
  two years old.

Mrs. H. K. Elliott
CONTROVERSY

Who is this stranger
  that stalks in the night
Whispering the message
  "Take arms and fight"?

Was that an Indian, walking
  so slow
Over the pine cones on moccasin
  toe?

Maybe a red coat or even a

blue. Look over your
shoulder.
Could it have been you?

Rosa Driever
LANA IN PRISON

A fragile flower
broken, bent
Trod upon and plucked
from sunshine
Inside pent. To wait
to wonder.
Caged. A time to weep
A pawn in human hands
Where human flesh is cheap.

Shellie Hockenbury
GREEN RHYME

Roses are green; Violets are blue;
I want you to know, how much
I love
you.
More than me; more than I;
More than the birds that fly in
the sky:
And if at any time we must
depart;
tell me truthfully what's in your
heart;
And if you return with doubt in
your mind
ask me a question;
I'll tell you this rhyme.

Roberta H. Long
RAIN DROPS

The rain came falling gently
down,
Sparkling as it hit the ground.
Little rivers, little streams,
Makes a little boy day dream.
He's a captain on the boat,
The leaves are row boats all
afloat.
He shall save them one by one.
In his dreams his job's well done.
Now he slowly walks away,
The rain has stopped for the day
The little rivers and little streams
Disappeared with his dreams.

D. L. Anderson
A MOMENT'S PAUSE

The sting of unshed tears
was simultaneous
with the thought,
"I miss my mother."
as my glance
through the kitchen window
warmed my heart
and silenced the hurt.
because a little
blue bird paused
momentarily in flight,
then rested
and secure again,
delicately,
winged its way from sight.

Paul W. Phillips
PRO—JECTIONS

I sat and gazed at the moments
trouble
and stared at time as if a bubble,
I lingered in a fantasy world,
and read the news of my new
birth.
I saw in distant meditation
bound
with thoughts peculiar to those
around,
I felt the air
the music the talk
As if like a visitor—from
somewhere

With dreamy eyes,
And depressed soul,
nobody could realize,
my deapths to unfold.

Maude G. Allen
**ERUPTION OF MT. ST.
HELENS**

If Mount St. Helens
Keeps burping up
She no doubt needs the aid
Of a stomach pump.
No tonic on earth
Could solver her fate
And not even a Scientist
Could a remedy relate.
But she's still struggling on,
Giving a puff now and then
And nobody knows
How many more, and when.

Sara Anne Cunningham
FOR THEM TOMORROW

If I could cast a spell to make
them run
To me, my dear ones, in their
daily rush
To share entire an hour beneath
the sun,
And then aware, together
hold the twilight hush
I would not sigh as creeping
night draws near
For me alone amidst their
vibrant life and wastrel ways
Who need not measure Time,
hold seconds dear
As I with knowledge of my
numbered days.
Oh, if I could reach out to pull
them in
And with my secret precious
moments borrow
I would not for they'd lose
what I would win.
And, yet, though deep I love
them, I envy them tomorrow.

Michael J. Malec
WHISPERS OF LOVE

And you whisper I love. . .
Not with words but emotion
As I bow to your altar in a
lover's devotion
Half-filled wine crystals
decorated. . .
Dressed with reflections of
desire
Mirrored moments of lovers in
an aesthetic attire
A silent caress
As ashen darkness fades to light
Two figures fused still by the
passioned heat of the night.
And you whisper I love. . .
A glazed form arched in rapture
Untamed telling eyes once again
in my capture
The senses are teased
As an echoed candlelight dances
To a Fogelberg lyric of life's
wysterial romances
The words spur my thinking
Fears of future. . .Tokens from
a lonely day
And you whisper I love. . .as
the fears like the darkness fade
away.

O. Afton Linger, A. B., ThM.
THE WORLD BELONGS TO ME

The world belongs to me,
although I paid no price for it!
I own the golden sunsets,
the moon, the stars and sky.

I own the mountains, all,
and glory in their beauty;
The plains and wooded hills,
with all their trees and shrubs.
The creatures all are mind,
and ev'ry living thing.
The wind, the waves and water
are mine to love always.
All the people in the world
are kin and dear to me.
Some say I'm poor, but I am
rich;
I own the world, and more;
the world belongs to me!

Hyacinth Melody Simonds
LONELY TIMES

There come such lonely times
into our lives
The days seem scarcely able to
be born
And something warm and lovely
in us dies
And all the world seems old
and weary worn
We lost at last an old and
treasured friend
And sadness tears our hearts
with sudden pain
That a score of newer friendships
could not mend
Or love that we had treasured
sacredly
And we had thought as timeless
as the sea
Without warning ceases suddenly
to be
And grief and longing are too
deep for tears
It isn't always death that robs
us thus
For there are sadder things
can come to us
The trailing of life's dreams
within the dust
When a cherished soul breaks
faith with us
The quality of life becomes
impoverished
When the heart has lost the
dreams it built upon
'Tis then we question why we
linger on
With all of life's best and
dearest treasures gone.

Sheila South
A DREAM WORLD

A dream world is a beautiful
place to escape from reality.
It is a
place where we hide from the
world or ourselves. It shows
beauty in all
its glory, the way we want to
see things. It is a wonderful
place
sometimes, if we don't use it
too often, For when used too
much it hurts
when we see reality.
The dream may be a place where

we would like to be or a part
of what is
thought to be in ourselves. It
could be a field where pollution,
corruption and
crime are not known. It may
have characteristics we want
or wonder
what it would be like to have
them.
Dreams, thoughts or feelings.
Are they a part of reality in
the end?
Do they help keep things living
without destroying the mind?
(Who knows?)
But they're needed in this
world in limited quantities.

Sara M. Hoagland
ARGONAUTA

Lovely mystery of the sea,
Washed ashore at Point
Conception
Gathered on a balmy summer's
day
While on a lover's holiday.
Creamy white, with fluted edges
blushing pink—
At first glance, one might think
we are worlds apart.
How did you get your start
While in the billowy depths of
the deep?
Did you perhaps cross paths
with the ancient one—
Or flung from the crown of the
Pleiadas—
Or became encrusted with sea
anemones—
To end your journey here— in
my hand?
I hold you to my ear— I hear—
Only an answering silence!

Evelyn Myrtle Miller
A PETITION

Lord, I tremble at lofty heights
physical and spiritual
in which I find myself.
Mountain-peaks beckon:
I climb, strain, grasp each
rooted thing on the way up.
A lone flower dances quietly
puffy clouds drop shadows
like seeds borne upon the wind.
Ageless trees, bent, gnarled
from violent storms
stand dauntless.
WHY, LORD, CAN'T I?
Grant me the courage to:
stand against controversy
complacency and injustice.
Grant me the wisdom to:
overcome pettiness
selfishness and sensitivity.
Grant me, dear Lord, tranquility.

Merry Wreath
DEATH OF A FLOWER

Frightened and alone
the flower cries.
Its petals droop
with a gentle sigh
as the conquering bee
watches with a victorious eye.
It seems he took the staff of life
from which the flower must rely;
now the innocent bud
is turned awry.
The gentle breeze forwarns
of death coming nigh,
and with its last breath of life
the flower tries;

yet it falls to the cold, hard
  ground
and dies.
From here it grew
and now shall lie
until the day
God ignites the pyre.

Rosa Bruton
SOUND THOUGHT

A thought is caught;
  thus, found:
though caught for naught.
  For sounds
surpass the vast
  unspoken ground
where thoughts abound;
  and only elements of speech
turn thought to sound.

Joan Squire
THE GREEN PUCKER

Puckered lip stop light,
Whose arms are long enough to
  embrace your green mouth?
Did you fall in love with
  a tall stop sign?

Joey Christopher Robinson
ACORNS UPON A TREE

Of all the acorns upon the tree;
One has fallen and now it spends
All of its life crying this plea;
"Come and we shall be friends!"

Of all the acorns upon the tree;
No one knows exactly when;
But maybe someday;
I'll find a friend.

The leaves will turn gold;
And the acorns will fall;
So that we can be friends;
After all!

Eleanor Otto
**SAINT PATRICK (A SOLDO
SONNET)**

A portrait of St. Patrick in
  stained-glass
Shines on a throng of
  worshippers in spring—
Roman invasion's Ides of March
  removed—
To honor Patrick, Saint of
  Ireland's fame.
He blesses all, with gentle arm
  up-raised;
Man's ceaseless faith in Christ
  and nature praised.
Good workds, his mission.—
Evil he disproved.
With cross he killed a snake's
  unholy sting.
His spirit stays to guide a
  people's ways,
From savage strife to love for
  man and life.
He offers the sacred Communion
  Host:
Trefoil of God, the Son, and
  Holy Ghost.

Sharon F. Cote
KNIGHT OF LOVE

You're as, dark, as the night
I'm blue, as, the moon;
When, you, smile your love
  shines thru.
It warms my heart and touches
  my soul;
Your love, is vital for me to grow.
At times, the shadow of a storm,
  passes
over your face
Bitterness and hate, takes love's
  place;
It's flowers begin, to wither and

break.
Finally, a rainbow appears,
  glowing with
the light of joy;
After, all the years in passing
A smile, a touch, love shines
  thru, again.

Deborah Elayne Parsons
NIGHTMARE

I huddle within
Nothing—just blank
Captured by the emptiness
  inside me.

I call out your name
Then lie still and wait
Hiding from the silence
  than haunts me.

Margie Baucum
STAR

This morning I dreamed again
  of my dog, Star.
He was as I remembered.
He had the same look as he
  raised his shaggy head.
I felt again the great sweetness.
I touched him again.
I felt the softness of his fur.
I felt the wetness of his tongue.
Then I awoke to stroke him.
But I remembered he is gone
  long ago.
Yet he lives on.
He lives in shadows, and
  memories.
Never dead. Always alive in my
  heart.
As long as memories last, he
  lives forever.
When the vail of life is rent,
  we shall be together, I'm
  sure.
We shall be companions to play,
  and roam once more.
And Star will "smile" again
  as he used to nearly seven
  years ago.

Katherine M. Braun
SUE

I wonder what you're thinkin',
  Sue—
  You look at me—I look at you.
You're just a dog—I'm just a gal;
  But this I know—you're some
  great pal!
You walk, you run, you're all
  around—
  —Jump up so high, then hug
  the ground.
I sure will know, until the end—
  He sent you to me—you're my
  friend!
Yes, when your time on earth
  is past,
  My thoughts of you will ever
  last!
We'll meet again, of that I'm
  sure;
  For love is born but to endure!

Paul Raymond Silveira
DEATH KNELL

Bad ol' good ol' college days
as Nixon played our Captain
  Hook
to Fonda's Peter Pan
and Indochina's Wheel of
  Fortune
kicked our star-spangled can.
Men died those years on hills
cast in bronze by the sun
and were buried
in velvety black patches of earth

every one.
Bad ol' good ol' Nixonian
  summer
and I play
under rainbow gift-wrapped skies
while in far away paisley-shawl
  marshes
a fellow student dies.

CKM
I HAVE A FRIEND

I have a friend
  And a good friend have I
If I had no friend
  Then I would not be I
Not saying that my friend is I
  Or that I am he
It's just a way of saying
  That I, My friend, are we.

Janice Morgan Flynn
IN MEMORY OF JAMIE

A sunbeam flitted through this
  world of mine,
  with untold beauty that has
  left me breathless.
This touch of Paradise, hard to
  define,
  passed through my life just
  like a soft caress,
  and now he sleeps!
So briefly did he stay, I scarce
  believe
  that he was ever really meant
  to be.
He's peaceful now and I'll try
  not to grieve;
  but Lord, could you kiss him,
  just once for me?
His mother weeps!

Mrs. Richard Hancock
STORM

The western sky is brassy and
  there's a haze around the sun
For surely a storm is brewing
  and by signs a wicked one.
The world is held in stillness,
  not a stirring in the trees
Until jagged lightning cracks
  the sky, and raindrops patter
  on the leaves.
Then a swirling, raging, howling
  wind descends upon the land
Forcing driven pellets to pound
  and pummel all at hand.
While darting lightning flashes
  blast and pierce a sullen sky
And monstrous peals of thunder
  roll loud and roaring by.
You can only stare in wonder
  at the violence Nature sends
While waiting for the rainbow's
  prism, the covenant of storm's
  end.

Rosemary E. Helmer
**ALONG THE BACK YARD
FENCE**

The canna blossoms grow so
  high
It seems they're reaching for the
  sky.
Along the back yard fence they
  grow
Like tall slim sentinals in a row.
Each day, it seems, their blooms
  like fire
Have grown so many inches
  higher.
I stand beside their flower bed,
  Amazed they tower overhead.
And, silhouetted 'gainst the sky
They dwarf mere mortals, such
  as I.
Oh Scarlet blossoms, reaching
  high

Against the azure of the sky;
What beauty does my eyes
  behold
And treasure, more than wealth
  or gold?
Such loveliness, a gift from God
Conceived from bulb and
  common sod.
Along the back yard fence they
  grow;
Those scarlet sentinals in a row.
And, striving higher, from their
  sod,
Their beauty reaches toward
  GOD!

Lois Irene Brown
SILENT SNOW

Sometimes snow jumps up on
  the window sill,
there are no words for such as
  this;
Like numbers on a clock
I bite off time in small mouthfuls
lingering on good times
so they will last.

I collect moments in my brown
  paper sack
It seems that both out destinies
  lay
just around the bend;
Will it be a new beginning?—or
  a
beginning of the end?
The silent snow
surrounds me as I wait.

Elizabeth Wilson Aldrich
PRAYER FOR EXPRESSION

To be articulate—O God, to
  give words birth!
This longing, panting agony of
  joy
Springs unaware to life within
With sudden, clamorous pain
And borne, it must be born.

Music shakes and trembles in
  my mind,
Love remembered, knocks
  here
  at my heart;
I know, I feel the world's own
  yearning.

Beauty unbound, let me bear
  your form;
Tear me apart, rend me, leave
  me
  bleeding—
But let my spirit's head, beget
  a soul
  articulate.

Doris O. Hawks
VACATION'S OVER

Vacation time is over
Evenings getting cool
Camping gear back in garage
Kids are back in school.
Now try and get the waistline
Back to trim and neat

After a round of visiting relatives
It seemed all we did was eat.
If one travels by land, air or sea
Vacations fall short of time
For viewing this world's beauty
Time to buckle down now
From our active pace
Then spend the winter planning
Next years vacation in a new
place.

Pamela M. Vona
THE AWAY OF LOVE

Love thou doth call and thine
heart dost reply,
There yet yielding to the open
fields of beauty,
The soul is detained in following
for fear that haste,
May swallow and devour the fair
blossom, before the sun has
risin in the heavens,
And the rains have purified the
airs of life, alas to love in
truth then,
Is oft' not to love in presence
at all, but to beseech one as
it seems,
From somewhere beyond a
wall hidden from the world,
exposed only to the heavens,
Where soft and gentle as an
angel's whisper, the heart
there can be heard singing.
Oh beloved, perhaps it is not
as necessary to be loved as
to know thou art loved,
And thus always it shall be so,
in silence's shadow,
No less, but more precious as
perfection before infirmity
and beauty before sunset.
Nay naught shall stain the state
of ecstasy thy day lives on,
And none shall deter the arrow
of a cupid's star bound bow,
For there where wings fly no
hand may reach,
And what God has love come
to learn, no man can thus so
teach.

Margot Valentine
EASE

Something about the sound of
the wind, way
High in the oaks—its invisible
push
Moving my napkin around,
Stirring up dust.

Tammy Corsette
**MEMORY OF A
GRANDMOTHER**

The rocking chair in the dark,
dismal corner
dusty, damp, desolate
absent is the familiar creaking
sound
back, forth, up, down
Once occupied by skill,
experience and age
For an instant a beam of light
shines
on an incomplete
knitted afghan
making it momentarily come
alive
as though once again
in skillful, wrinkled, loving hands
Almost perceptible is the illusion
of a petite, elderly figure
as she gently rocks with
purpose. . .
One is reminded it is only a
memory—a false image
made up by a reminiscent mind

a mind—attached to an arm—
which slowly, temporarily closes
the door
on a memory, on a love, and
on a loss of a grandmother.

Deborah A. Bowyer
SANTA'S ELVES

Santa's elves work hard all year,
Making toys to delight and
cheer—
Children who are sweet and good;
children who do what they
should.

So I ask you why elves do,
Work so hard to please me
and you?
They've never seen us; yet, I
know,
They love us all—Santa said so.

So let's give a "thank you"
dears,
To these little people who work
all year,
They are so tiny and so small;
But their hearts are big enough
to love us all.

Kathleen Le Compte
TO BE

To walk in the silence of the
night
To inhale the music of fresh
spring air
To gaze at the starlit silvery
light
To belong, be alive, and just to
care.

To listen to the night songs in
the shadows
The rustle of a tree, a
cricket's hymn
To see the trees, each clearly
silhouetted
Against the dark sky, each twig
and limb

The sudden, deep call of a
nearby frog
And the night calls then become
a croon
Both from overhead and from
the meadow
Where is housed the emerald-
fronded lagoon

So intense the night one can
feel the grass grow
. . .See a star, ablaze across the
sky
Speak not a word, but be aware
For this is the night—and here
am I.

Phyllis A. Menna
VISION

A vision surfaced from the
caverns of my mind,
When the lunar phase was anew
and Heaven's orbs of light
brightly shined.

The fibers of my dream meshed
into the night... .
an on this celestial journey were
the awesome depths of Life.
The core of existence rooted in
the concept of Love I saw,
that blossomed forth to answer
the question of Universal Law.

And Mankind's Spirit soared
with me through the heights of
my dream,
tho' clouded by some mystical
haze,
and our physical distance
deemed,
We are United always.

It is when our Souls can escape

these nocturnal illusions of
our minds
that our bond of Love will form
a fortress against the hands of
time. . .

Loretta Chierico
**LIFE'S DAILY MERRY—GO—
ROUND**

For many of us, some days are
filled with fear and loneliness,
imagined or for real.

Pain and anxiety brings neither
comfort to the body nor
peace to the soul.

That's when we look up to
GOD
above, who comes to us
to console and heal.

Before you know it, this test
of faith will help us
through our daily ordeal.

Then soon we forget "HIM"
too busy with many
earthly things.

With the fear, the loneliness,
pain, anxiety it
seemingly brings.

Then once again we seek
him out knowing he's
there in time of need—

He's sure to be forgiving
by cleansing our sins
As life's daily merry-go-round
eternally spins.

Ms. Joy Patrice Knutson
CITY OF FOUNTAINS

I once gazed at a Fountain,
such beauty beheld my eyes.
But springing up, t'would plunge
back down,
from majestic Missouri Skies.
"I am like that Fountain," I
smiled,
as I threw in a penny for 'luck'.
But once I start my splashing
reach—
    I'll go up and up and up. . .

Joan K. Power
WE NAIL YOU TO THE CROSS

You are spat upon by those
who laugh and scoff.

You are naked and humiliated
but we turn out heads
for the naked light of truth
is too blinding.

Nails pound your palms
from our rejection of you
and hate of each other.

You are left to die
by a people who live
as though they created the world.

You come down from the cross
with arms outstretched
with breath stopping words:
    I LOVE YOU!

Words that shatter the walls
we have built to buffet the truth;
there is indeed someone who
cares
especially for you.

Paul A. Flodquist
BLACKSTRAPPING

Great waves of rolling thunder
Bearing down upon the guiltless
child
Slashing and smiting the
beautiful creation down
Directed along a straight and
narrow course
To a pre-determined end
Why was I chosen?
How could I know?
Why did it have to be known?
I believe in you so let me go
I want to know so set me free
I trusted in you but you refused
to see
The importance that was in my
mind
That made a force of me.

Dianna L. Webb
TO BE OLD

To be old is a hunger.
For what was,
and what will be.
To be old is a knowledge,
That you can't,
it isn't allowed.
To be old is a torment.
Filling the mind,
and emptying the body.
To be old is not living.
It is existing,
waiting for the end.

Clara L. Kuck
MEMORIES

Memories are precious little
things,
That linger far and long,
They leave the aches within one's
heart
Of things long since gone.
Sometimes there lingers memories
of joy,
At other times they're sad,
But just to remember things,
no matter what
Makes one a trifle more glad.
I love to remember all the friends
I've had,
Though there are some I'd like
to see,
I wouldn't trade anything for my
memories,
For my memories are precious
to me.

Linda C. Jenkins
**THE LONG LONELY
HIGHWAY**

Life is a long lonely highway,
You must travel it alone.
When you think you've found
an exit,
You'll find that you were wrong.

You'll go stumbling on along
your way,
Searching for a friendly face.
But all the people that you meet
Will be busy running their own
race.

Then you'll meet someone
who is going your way,
And with an open heart, you
will be received.
Then you'll awake one morning
alone again,
To find that you have been
deceived.

So you'll just heave a sigh, and
    try to be brave,
Then you'll start your journey
    once more.
But the farther along you go,
    the more you'll realize,
That these steps are harder
    than the ones you took before.
Yes, the farther down the road
    you go,
The heavier your steps become.
And when you think you've
    neared the end,
You'll find you've just begun.

Diana Demos Capuano
MORN

It peeks beyond an earthly line
And lifts the shroud of night.
It grows with every mome of time
Until it twinkles bright.

It plants a kiss upon the land
And pats away the dew,
The little rays that none can see
They lift and waken you.

The crimson rose asleep from
    night
Peels back its petals strong,
And slowly opens for all to see
And. . .yawns.

The blades of grass all bent and
    weepy
Shake themselves of dew,
And stand all neatly at attention
To make a carpet for you.

The bird in flight
Glides left—glides right
And sings its early song,
Awake, awake it sings to us
Awake, for it is morn.

Todd R. Gratz
THE MOVEMENT IS TOO RAPID

The movement is too rapid
when you are after something
    you
want too much and
are trying to make it happen
pleasure thrives on spontaneity

The movement is too rapid
when you make something
    happen
before its time
pleasure can't be force-fed

You might as well drink a
glass of ice water as fast as
    possible
for all the pleasure you'll get
from rushing into something
before its time or by trying to
slip into a dream before you've
fallen asleep.

Winston Lee
ONLY FOR THAT GLORIOUS MOMENT

For thirty score years you've
    lived
And gloaming twilight of your
    final days dawn.
And you reflect and remember
    the aches and pains
    that accompanied you
When you carried out the Lord's
    work.
Blinded men scoffed at your
    gospel and tortured you
    for what you stood for.
But you continued in that same
    dogged pace,
Carrying the Torch of Truth and
    casting Light upon
    humanity.

But now, after years of toil,
    only blood and perspiration
    cover your face,
And terrible wounds plague
    your body and you cry out:
"Oh God! Why have you chosen
    me to carry out such a
    burdensome task?"
But take care, a guiding hand
    shall touch you and heal
    your wounds.
He will enclose you and wipe
    away bitter tears of
    remembrance.
In soothing voice He will bless
    you and say:
"Well done my servant!"
This quote you will treasure
    more than the kingly realms
    on Earth;
Even in face of death, this,
    you will remember.

Sandra Marlene Finley
ASCENDED PRAYER

My prayer ascended to Heaven
To the Heavenly Father's Throne.
My prayer ascended to Heaven
And I knew I was not alone.

Like dewdrops on the roses,
My prayer fell upon His ear,
The darkness turned to dawn
When I felt his presence near.

No earthly music played,
But yet my heart did sing.
Peace and joy filled my soul,
My burdens all took wing.

My prayer ascended to Heaven
And in one moment's space,
I could almost touch His hand
And look into His face.

Daisie Viola Rose
ISLAND IN THE SUN

You're far across the ocean
On an island in the sun
And I find in thinking of you
When my endless day is done
Are you lying in the golden sun
Dreaming dreams to be
Or maybe chasing rainbows
Like ships thats lost at sea
Do you think about your loved
    ones
Or the friends you left on shore
Do you think about your home
    land
Do they matter any more
Have you sailed beyond the
    turning point
Where cares exist no more
Where all day long you laugh
    and play
Along a golden shore.

Joan Thisius
ONE MORE DAY

Because I love you,
I will not cause you pain
I will love you
In friendship and in truth
My struggle with living will be
    eased
Knowing your love is eternal.

Susan Cayco
BEYOND THE HORIZON

While my stillness was broken
    by whistles
    from a departing ship
A pair of sparrows flew over
    the emptiness
    of a lonely sea
With a sadness unexplained
    I turned and caught the vision
    of a sunset so golden

When softly the artist's moment
    was crossed by a thought
That I like all in life have my
    horizon. . .
When the birds and the ship
    and the sun
    disappear beyond
    so do I
Now left wondering what lies
    beyond
    the distant horizon

Omega Hamby Guffey
BIRTH OF A PARENT

Things suddenly have more
    meaning
With a love that never ends,
now that you're a parent
a new life begins.

Emerging into enlighment
    brought forth
a brand new life one day,
of challenge and enrichment of
    which
pure love hath paved the way.

Through miraculous intervention
a door is opened in the mind,
a bright light awakening
to be not left behind.

But onward to great horizons,
to depths unexplored.
On to expectations and
hope for a reward.

The sight of seeing someone
extending from your own,
the pride of knowing
to this someone you belong.

Tis the birth of a parent
to a child he adores.
A new life unfolds and
opens many doors.

and. . .

Things suddenly have more
    meaning
with a love that never ends,
now that you're a parent
a new life begins.

Roberta C. Latham
PEACE! BE STILL

Even the sea obeyed His
    command and
    ceased its tumultuous turning
But in the depths far below
    Christ
    knew another tempest was
    churning
He knew the time was short for
    him to
    accomplish His mission
He knew this discordant world
    must be
    given clearer vision.

The lessons He taught have
    lived two
    thousand years.
They're all that we have to
    banish
    heartache and fears

His great love and sacrifice has
    not
    been in vain
More souls have responded than
    turned
    away with disdain.

He knew where He came from
    and where
    He was going
He left His peace with us so that
    we'd
    all be knowing
That to obey his commandment
    and love one another
His peace would stay with us
    and each
    love his brother.

Margery E. Kuhn
GREENER GRASS

The grass is always greener
    On the other side of the hill
But you always hope to get there
    And I guess. . .you always will

But once you climb to the other
    side
    The one from whence you've
    come
Tis now the greener of the two
Now you're back where you
    begun.

Ruth Worthy
THE HOUSE I LIVE IN

The welcome mat is at my door,
And you are welcome in
For the house I live in is
Filled with love,
For my enemy and for my
    friends.
For I must love my enemies
As I do my friends
For God won't let them harm me.
For He is my dearest friend.
One day He came into my heart
And I welcomed him with praise.
He said to me right then and
There, "You need not be afraid,
For I will feed and clothe you
And give you all your needs,
I take care of the birds that
Fly, the flowers and the trees.
You need not worry any more,
For you're not the least of
    these."

Betty Finzel Foley
THE SILENT BELLS

The bells of the church were
    silent.
But, still, I thought they rang,
When in the deep blue twilight
The holy angel sang.

The world outside was silent
When I heard the angel's song.
"Glory to God in the Highest!
He will right your wrong."

The little white church was
    silent.
And I felt His presence there,
As I looked to the candle-lit
    altar
And knelt in heartfelt prayer.

The bells of the church were
    silent.
And, yet, I know they rang,
When in the deep blue twilight
The blessed angel sang.

James A. Beck
UNTITLED

And the silent Sentinals of the
    Night
Couchant, poised in great and
    clumb'rous fright
'Midst broken dreams of strange

and guarded things,
In cold, forgotten sepulchres of
Kings
Lay wait; with talons poised on
mind, begin
Weave cunning webs of dank
and spectral glooms
Ensnared beneath their shielded,
guided dooms
Of unrequited penitence. And
is it not
A curse, this morbid plague of
things forgot,
That slays all conscious thought
with poisoned breath
And leaves naught? Their pale,
frigid passion, Death,
Long held a shattered image to
their lust,
Now lies, a tarnished remnant,
in the dust.

Kenneth W. Griffith
FRIENDS

I want you to know that you
are a very dear friend
Thanks to you, you were always
there to help me mend
through all this pain and trouble
I saw you
trying to make all things new
you wanted to help me gain
self pride
but I told you I can't do
anything but hide
Because I lost the girl I loved
very much
and you brought me out of it
with your special touch
I will never forget who has
showed me the light
By making all things that were
wrong right.

Ruth M. Newell
**ALMOST AS OLD AS WINE
ITSELF**

Wine through the sour grapes is
pressed
is aged in the deep of a cool
abyss
set to ferment with a
gentleness
'til once is sipped by
fondliness;
as old as wine itself, I rest
that my life is quite like this,
—quite thoroughly lived,
yet so much missed
as is fine wine I do insist.

Diane M. Zacaroli
MIRRORED IMAGES

I see the reflection of my face in
your glassy eyes.
Though I appear slightly
misshapen
you cannot see it
Because you are looking out and
I am looking in towards you
to see me.
Though that image is slightly
misshapen
I don't quite know
how to change it.
Perhaps I must begin
to look away from
your glassy eyes.

Amy Louise
OCEAN VIEW—WINTER 1980

Cybele pulled in her satellite,
snuffed out the thousand eyes
that lighted up the skies o'er
Ocean View.
A blanket dark was thus pre
prepared

to shed its undyed scraps of
white
upon the village in the night.
When morning broke, that
slender spit
that jutted out into the bay
deep wrapt in ermine lay.
Still Cybele, her mind made up
Enriched the pall until by two
a foot or more lay all about
The shining strand of Ocean
View.

Ms. Annette G. Simon
INFLATION

There's not a place where her
voice is not heard—
She enters every business place
and cries—Inflation
She goes down the streets;
In super-markets, groceries and
shopping centers
With her usual cry—Inflation.
Her head is lifted up high among
her fellows,
she has no consideration for
anyone—
Many question her increasing
demands
In the eyes of society she's
looked upon as monstrous.
She travels to every country;
Ruling as a Tyrant—unafraid, a
and unceasing,
Who would dare stand as her
rival?
Disrupt her association with
our merchandise
And she would be brought
down to nothing,
With her usual cry—Inflation.

Martha E. Kirkland
TRUE DEDICATION

Martin Luther King, Jr., was
a man of true dedication,
One with an even greater
determination.
He had the courage to take a
stand
To make life better for his
fellowman.
It was not easy getting things
progressed
But he gave his all for people
oppressed.
With faith in God, he had
no doubt
That right above wrong would
always win out.
It did not matter whether black
or white.
He only intended to make things
right.
He fought long and hard that
violence and hatred may cease
And all God's children might live
in peace.
Although his life has come to an
end,
I'm sure people of every
denomination

Will never forget this man of
true dedication!

Jess N. Martin
**WHERE FLOWERS NEVER DIE
DIE**

I dream of a land of Sunshine,
A land where orchids never fade
and Roses never, no never die.
In that land of Heavenly
Sunshine.
We may go there some day you
and I.
Yes, I have heard of a sweet
happy place,
just over in the sweet by and by
where we will be, in his saving
Grace.
In that land of Heavenly
Sunshine
I have hope of his saving Grace.
I would, that I may see his
sweet face—
in a land where orchids never
face
and roses never die.

Joseph P. Kowacic
SUMMER

I love
the long, green aisles
of summer,
its chapeled silences,
where only sacred secrets
seem whispered,
and unseen spirits
softly to stir.
I love
the shades
of summer,
dark recesses for refuge,
where cool-lipped breezes
kiss the fevered cheek
of day.
And I love
the lazy dreams
of summer. . .
warm breasts,
where tired thoughts
come
restfully
to stay.

Rhonda Shugart
JOURNEY

Becoming philosophical,
I arrive at some thoughts
I would share with you:
I (and all others)
am on a solitary journey
to an unknown destination.
I began my journey alone
and will end it alone;
along the way
others will share my path,
but I alone guide my feet.
I will welcome companions
but I must realize
that their way
may separate from mine.
Let us travel together
for a while,
my dear,
and when the time
for parting comes,
I will endeavor to gracefully
let you go.

Hazel McGraw Gwinn
THE PORTRAIT

On the wall of the children's
playroom
Hangs the eighteenth century
portrait
Of a beautiful lady with dark
red hair.

She has a pleasant look in her
eyes,
Seemingly pleased at what she
sees.
On an oval hand crocheted rug
In the center of the room.
Sits a lovely little six-year-old
girl
With long dark hair hanging
down her back.
The child, as she plays, is
oblivious to the lady
Watching from the golden
ornate frame.
Too bad they couldn't have met.
The little girl is the lady come
to life again.

Billie Holley
THE LITTLE RED BARN

It sits among the trees
Behind a bigger barn,
It looks a lonely,
If passing by you are.
But if a closer look you take;
it's cheer it radiates,
And while the breezes softly
blow,
Silently it waits—
For children coming home from
school
Oft play in its wee loft,
And many a happy memory
Is made 'ere winter's frost!

Essie Wallace
TEARS OF ANGELS

Tears of angels that fall as rain
Cleanses the earth and removes
its stain
Gently they fall on land and sea
They quench the thirst of plant
and tree.
When ever so gently the angels
cry
The tears that fall wets a land
so dry
They give a deeper green to
each blade of grass
and a gift of life to each flower
we pass.
The Angels tears washes the
structures of man
They leave as they fall—pools
in barren land
They feed the roses as a mother
feeds her child
And give water to the animals
that roam in the wild
They help the farmer that plants
his crop
There's a wealth of good in each
Angels tear drop.

Stephen Tomporowski
TOWARD THE SUNRISE

Follow always the road ahead,
look not back from where it's
lead.
Pursue your fortune without
haste,
leave all behind and left to waste.
The road ahead will never end.
How far you go will all depend,
on you and your mind.
Perhaps you will also find,
no matter the price paid,
There are those who would be
delayed.
But do not stop to grieve,
the road you follow is like a
sieve;
those are wont to have betrayed
are quickly and finally waylaid.

Watch about for only yourself,
the road cannot hurt you of
   itself,
for only people figure in this
   strife,
which goes by no other name
   than Life.

Nellie Erwin Stromberg
MR. BUNNY'S LAMENT

I never ever laid an egg,
I could not, if I'd try.
Sometimes, I am so mortified,
I think I'll surely die,
For every year, a certain day,
A rap is pinned on me.
This rap is as outrageous
As any rap could be.
Then I'm accused of laying
   eggs,
Of every size and hue.
The upshot of this whole thing
   is,
I'm feeling mighty blue.
Although some people think I'm
   funny,
The fact is, I'm a simple bunny,
And if I am a bunny, then
Why do they think I am a hen?
I know you all are friendly
   chaps,
Pitch in and help me beat
   these raps.

Mary J. Moss
WORDS

Mystic words you come to me.
Please linger for a while,
I want to write down these
   words in
verses for others to see.

You bring joy and sometimes
   sadness,
But when I write these words
   down
they always bring gladness.

Words come like jewels in the
   night.
To be made into a necklace of
   verses.
So mystic words please linger
   with me.
While I write a poem for others
   to see.

Joseph R. Chanerak
A DRIFTER

Weary that I may be as wind
From trails and travels across
   the miles;
That somewhere is a place in
   mind
Where the lure of a welcome
   avails.

The highway is a lonesome road;
Where not one is a company
And the miles are abroad
That each footstep is a weary.
Once, I had not a courage to
   start
That going on was no more to
   be;
When, the recollection of
   thoughts you shared
Came and spoke to me.

Mary Ann Collins Luzier
THE FOREIGNER

There was a young man,
Full of hope was he.
Came from the old country,
To the land of the free.

His dream of live here
Was a promise for tomorrow,
With riches for the poor
And no time for sorrow.

Now far from his homeland
Alone and quite poor
This thin grayed old man
Lay dead on the floor.

Jesse Hibbard
ENS

Without substance
But needed by all.
The strong, the weak,
The great and small.
Essential to all
Of those who live.
Yours to have
to keep. to give.
HAPPINESS'

Marilyn Branch
WHAT IS LOVE?

   What is love, you ask?
   Finding out is the biggest task.
   You can ask someone
      anyplace,
But they will just slam the door
   in your face.
      On every person it really
      shows,
   That come to find out nobody
      knows.
But if nobody knows, then why
   is it there,
   For everyone in the world to
      share?
      Please tell me dear God above,
      What is this thing called love?

Nancy L. Rainier
FOREVER FRIENDS

Many times we've travelled
   down this road,
And now we seem to go this
   way again,
Viewing sights and sounds
   already seen and heard,
Everlasting sounds that echo
   across open fields.
Upon reaching the crossroads
   instead of making the
   decision to go separate ways,
   Let's cross over and continue
Keeping in touch with one
   another forever.

Kenneth W. Sewell Jr.
THE WORDS OF A MAN

He was not rich by any standards.
His clothes were not fashionable.
Nor were they who followed him.
Yet, the words he spoke will
   never die.

Life is hard at times, unbearable
   even.
our pockets are too often empty.
We are plagued with doubt
   and sorrow.
Were we born only to suffer and
   die?

But then I remember his words.
Empty pockets don't hurt as
   much.
Nor is the emptiness quite so
   heavy.
I wonder how, or why this is.
Some say the man was a prophet.
Others say he was the Son of
   God.
Maybe He was or maybe not.
But what of this man's words?
Does it matter who He really
   was.
Or, in fact, if He ever existed?
This question may never be
   answered.
But the words He spoke, what of
   them?

Colleen Mahoney
SEA OF LIFE

Come travel with me through
   the Sea of Life. . .
Through its calmness and
   roughness;
beauty and ugliness;
deepness and shallowness;
warmth and coldness.

Let's catch a wave and ride it
   from beginning to end.
Let's ride it high and admire
   its strength.
If the wave should break, we'll
   find another—
   and carry on.

Let's venture the deepness of
   the sea. . .
Admiring the beauty and
   uniqueness with curiosity—
Exploring areas yet to be
   discovered;
Touching objects yet to be
   noticed;
Challenging creatures yet to
   be beaten.

Together we will challenge
   the currents,
   denying their pull and
   possession.
We will ride the waves of
   imagination
And cry in the drowning seas
   of sorrow—
Only to grow and experience. . .
The dreams of tomorrow.

Blanche Jane Halsey
**TO A POET AND A PATRIOT
LINDSEY AND LINCOLN**

Vachel Lindsey wrote of
   Honest Abe,
Of the heartaches war had
   caused this man of honest
   heart.
He wrote of bitterness, of the
   war lords grevious mistakes—
   the hideous nightmare of
   tearing souls apart.
Could he have lived to write
   the epitaph of war since—
   Lincoln's day.
It's peace so superficial, I
   wonder what He'd say.
Will he ever sleep upon his hill
   again, or will white
   crosses ever grow o'er all the
   kingdoms of sea and land.
Won't treachery be maimed,
   or peace restored, that we
   may walk nation with nation,
   hand in hand.
That the soul of a poet, the
   soul of a Patriot, may rest in
   peace upon his Hill
Let the murmer or war forever
   be still.

Gloria Ann Condrey Myers
TOMORROW I'LL CRY

The children are teenagers now,
   with new dreams, new fields
   to roam;
It's so awfully quiet here, just
   the dog and I at home.
We did so many things together,
   the children and I,
But those days are gone, never
   to return—tomorrow I'll cry.
Remembering how they
   brightened my life, I too was
   young at heart,
Surely, they have earned this
   adventure, their new start.
I'm being selfish in not wanting
   to let them say goodbye.

It's their time of need—my time
   of loss—Tomorrow I'll cry.
Now what am I going to do—and
   who will need me sure?
How empty can a person be,
   how much can they endure. . .
I feel as though my world
   has turned—life's waving a sad
   goodbye;
Please give me strength
   throughout today—Tomorrow
   I'll cry.

Catherine Lynn Daniels
SISTERS

   Sharing,
   loving,
   talking,
   caring.
When you can't tell it to your
   friends,
when your friends aren't there.
When you need someone to
   hold you,
when you need someone to
   cry with you.
When you won't listen to
   anyone,
when no one will listen to you.
When someone has burned you
   and you can't take anymore,
   that's what sisters are for.

Dick G. Norris
SWEET DREAMS

I've just been to Heaven.
I know that it's true,
For in my arms I held an angel,
And she whispered, "I love you."

In her eyes I saw a beauty
That I've never known before.
Pure love shown all around me.
No mortal man could ask for
   more.

I trembled as I held her,
Somehow I sensed it wasn't
   true;
For when I awoke at dawn this
   morning
I knew that I had dreamed of
   you.

Maryann M. Bills
I'M A RAINY DAY FRIEND

You seldom say hello to me
   except when passing by
You rarely take me anyplace
   except when no one else
   is by your side.
You never want me to come
   over
   except when you're alone
You never lend me anything
   unless it's not your own.
You never care if I'm
   dead or alive, except
   when you're sad too.
You never seem to realize
   I can be your friend
Except on days, a rainy day
   When I'm your Rainy Day
   Friend.

Elizabeth McMurray Moore
BEREAVEMENT

Standing by I saw your heart
   break today;
I watched it's slowly downward
   bleeding way;
It fell there silently beside my
   feet
It's slaughter echoing a ewe
   lamb's bleat.

Your own dearly beloved one
   is gone,
And you alone are left to linger

on.
God knoweth why this call must
needs be made;
He asks you now to face Him
unafraid.

At divers times he sorely tries
us all
And waits the answer of our
trumpet call.

He strengthens us and never lets
us down
Sometimes must fashion us to
wear a crown.

Jean M. Theida
GRANDMA'S LAMENT

When cares of the day, fade
gently away
and I sit down to rest at last,
I breathe a deep sigh, ponder
as to why
time is racing by me so fast.

I long for the time of "Roses
and Wine"
when youth was a glorious age,
From daylight to dark, all life
was a lark,
with no thought of the piper's
wage.

Alas and alack it now all comes
back,
as so tired and lonely I be,
The tales I am told and things
I behold
surely couldn't have happened
to me!

Leila D. Fernandez
FOR MY DAD

I know it took awhile for me
to say,
What I really felt up to this
very day.

In all our fights I give you all
the blame,
And when I realize I was wrong
I felt so ashamed.

So when I come back to set
things clear,
You smile at me and hold me
so near.

All our lives together we have
shared,
Love, hard times, and despair.

You're my favorite daddy, you
know,
So far away from you I will
never go.

I'm looking forward to the day
When I walk down the aisle
and you will give me away.

But don't you worry daddy
cause all my tears,
Will be of the beautiful times
we had all those years.

Bertha Warren
A HUNDRED YEARS AGO

In 1881 Nolen county came to
be from
the shaggy herds of buffalo
along the
Santa Fe.
It grew from farm and ranches,
some small
some very large,
And shows how hard our fathers
worked and
what they stood up for.

One doesn't have to look far to
see what
has been done
from riding in a buck board to
flying
just for fun.

From wishing for a Dr. a minister
or
friend
We pick up the telephone or tune
the T. V. in.
A fine new marble court house
says we're
the county seat,
A coliseum for all our sports has
now come
to be.
Our schools are a long way from
a one and a path,
Nolen county Happy Birthday
Right here is where its at.

Marianne R. Thomas
ODE TO SPRING

There's a time of the year that
is known as Spring,
When, all of a sudden, our
hearts start to sing.
No matter how bad a winter we
endured,
The sign of a crocus is bound
to insure
A lift to our spirits, a lilt to
our laughs,
That's certain to dispell the
gloom of the past.
It's funny how Spring does
these strange things to us;
It's interesting how our spirits
adjust.
I wonder how people endure
without Spring,
Without the sight of birds on
the wing,
Without the surge of hope in
one's veins
That arrives as winter appears
on the wane?

Alana Gentry
A FANTASY CALLED LOVE

Circles of love,
Enlightened with feelings,
emotions and dreams,
Continuosly going around and
'round.
Never ending.
Leaving breathless dizziness.

In the beginning,
A loving fantasy,
To be shared,
Only by two.

Squeezed by actions,
Entangled by words.
Soon the circle of love,
Grows to include a different
world.

Realities slip into fantasy,
Nightmares slip into dreams.
A fulfilling paradise
Is no more.

Gordon L. Florence
IT MATTERS

For smiling happily
A gladness greets the day.
For crying gloomily
It's quite another way.

Letia A. Zimmermann
RAMPANT DESTRUCTION

Violent words of rage, splashed
against my face
and I felt abused.
Hammering insults that burned
my soul kept
me wasted and used.
Total serenity fell into a sea of
commotion,
and I empty of love and full of
hate
knew this mercenary of
destruction
had won.

Eleanor Wasdin
SUMMER REVERIE

Bright, sunny, sandy beaches
Waves and gulls as far as the eye
reaches.

A soft, warm, velvet breeze
Rustles the fronds of the palm
trees.

Quiet walks on warm, wet sand
The music of the waves rival
any band.

Lightning puts on a show at
night.
But it's a thing of beauty, not
of fright.

When winter comes with it's
cold gales,
We'll remember blue water
and white sails.

Hazel Smoak Clover
ACTIONS ARE ROSES

"Actions speak louder than
words," People say.
Actions are roses delivered
today.
When you give a hug or wipe
away a tear,
Your actions are saying, "I
love you, my dear."

You always find time for an
extra mile.
For adults, animals, and just
a small child.

There's always a feeling that you
have the time,
To share rambling roses that
grow on your vine.

Entwining the hearts of loved
ones so dear
Sharing with friends who live
far and near.
Sharing your roses that will till
the end
Give loads of fragrance to share
with a friend.

As long as good deeds multiply
by the score,
Roses will always be there,
more and more.
Roses have petals that fall by
the way,
But actions are the roses
delivered today.

Colleen Marie Gavin
IT'S FUNNY WHAT I FOUND

I thought I loved you very
much
Each time you came around,
But more and more I talked
to you
It's funny what I found.
You showed me how to live
and love
be happy through and through
The more I learned to do
these things

The more that I loved you.
You helped me when I needed
it
Picked me up when I was down
But the more you tried to
help me
It's funny what I found
I found that love was more
than this
more than just a kiss,
It's caring, sharing, everything
something we can't miss.
So we leave today as friends
I feel
closer than before
The love we found was
friendship
Will help us love once more.

Elaine C. Hart
COMPARISONS

It's been a long, hard climb,
And I have many friends like me
But if I had my druthers
I'd rather be like thee.

Where your responses are many
and swift
Ours are few and slow.
We tend to cling together
wherever we may go.

We've had long periods of
hospitalization
And depression,
Where you have known
Elation.

They say it's better to be
in the land of the living.
But it seems to me
I'm the one who's always giving!

So I lean upon the Lord who
loves me.
I know he'll give me a home in
Eternity!
The Lord is my Best Friend,
I'll trust Him til the end.
He's my Shepherd true,
I know He'll care for you.

Lisa Gaye McClanahan
DIALOGUE OF CONFIDANTS

Rust and gold crackling
Under the four soles;
Rich blue peers through the web
of boughs;
Rays of blinding whiteness break
The pattern of silent dimness
On the shaded path under
The looming presence of aged
wood.

Two voices mingle with the
biting breeze,
Blows a force to roll the fallen
foliage over,
Leaf over leaf,
In festive autumnal procession.

Whispers, swishing of leaves
become one sound as
Thoughts of the strolling
Achilles and Patroclus
Melt and blend.
Sunbeams bend to meet the
shadows;
Blue above and yellow-gold
below
Yield hueless incandescence.

David E. Lindamood
A PAIR OF SHOES

Her pair of shoes, slightly used
she never liked to wear things
out. . .
It's not that she didn't care,
her gown's still hanging there
with the rest of my heart. . .

and all of her things
A crystal glass bought in the
   past
from an amusement park. . .
we had so much fun, the way
   we'd laugh and run
but that's forgotten now. . .
well, most of the time
Her brown eyed bear, with eyes
   that stare
she used to hold on to it. . .
and give me the shiest smile
   and ask me to hold her for
   awhile
that bear just stares at me. . .
or do I stare at him?
My clothes don't fold, the
   house is cold
silent are the many walls. . .
the air was spiced then, o so
   nice then
I used to see her in the mirror. . .
looking back at me
Her pair of shoes, slightly used
she never liked to wear things
   out.
But that's forgotten now. . .

Elsa B. Doroin-Horn, M.D.
A PHASE OF LIFE

It's simple to answer with a
   placid face
"I'm fine, thank you", plus
   a hurried gaze
But who among you would try
   to preach
Into one's solitude too deep to
   reach.

Retreat after work with a fit
   of sullens
Greeted with a deafening silence
Four walls and memories would
   share a part
To hammer the thorn in my
   lonely heart.

Then in my sleep sneak out
   those dreams
Desires and rapture of yesterdy
   yesterday's ecstacy
Forget the sorrows, drowned
   into streams
Cast out the face of ugly verity.

But time goes on and comes the
   dawn
To tear my dreams apart
Then comes to view a world
   in mourn
Solitude and agony shaping its
   art.

Answer the days call, as you
   and I must
Both wearing a foil of a happy
   mask
Greeting each other with "How
   are you?"
Reflexly retorting, "I'm fine,
   thank you."

Laura E. Pacitto
**SOMEWHERE THERE IS A
POET**

Somewhere there is a poet
Welcoming summer as warmly
   as the scent of fresh baked
   bread;
While as a lover I hastily
   withdraw the invitation
And urge on autumn, like
   refreshment in a desert.

Suspicious elms sway away from
   me,
Fearing the loss of their green
   celebration
Painful return to bare mourning.
Sensible shoppers of sun-tanning

oils, and swimming pools.
Obeying all the seasonal rules
   know
   to shy away too.
Summer must think me cruel.

But somewhere there is a
   mathematician
Carefully counting days until
September
Converting them again to
   hours, minutes, seconds.

Jean-François Wen
EXPECT THE COLD

Expect the cold: Indian summer
   ends.
Catch the last colours of the
   leaves
And the sun, before their
   shadows
Turn to ice.
Light the fire! Light the snow!
And let thoughts of Spring
Whisper to you good-night.

David P. Rosen
ARENA

At each nightfall, I coil by the
   fire
which spends a steady light.
The unknown crawls beyond
   the glow,
so I sacrifice more wood
in the ritual offering of fear.
   As the phoenix, I consume my
   past
by incinerating fears of darkness
   falling, Satan, and death.
   Still, images of serpents in the
   flames.
I force dragons and mammals
   to compete,
restraining man from entering
   the list.
A fascination with flight, the
   thirst for milk,
an affinity to tools, and the
   drive to defend,
each emerge from the blaze.
I set the arena in my awareness
so each lance strikes the brain
   to ignite joust cinders.
As everlasting lights, instincts
   flare
and flash the evolution of
   intelligence.

Judy C. Villines
TIME TO TAKE IT EASY

Born, smiling baby,
Older, crying teen,
Makeup, roses, pictures
Trying to be seen.

Individual, your way, my way,
No time to make a scene.

Living, older yet.
Time to take it easy,
Die now and forget.

LaRue Larsen
WHAT IS A CHILD?

What is a child? It's a soul of
   great worth:
A bundle of innocence, wonder
   and mirth;
A package of laughter and
   unfounded fears,
And hugs and wet kisses, and
   quick-turned-on tears.
A child may be garnished with
   ruffles or jeans,
With dirt-frosted faces and all
   sorts of things.
It sometimes brings heartaches
   expense, sadness too.
(But it tugs at your heart when

it smiles at you.)
A child's a delight filled
   chockful of love—
An unselfish being sent from
   Heaven above.
It's life's greatest blessing—a
   sweetness and joy
To be thoroughly cherished,
   whether girl or a boy!

Twila Reppe
OF LOVE

Poets write of love
   And I am no exception
      For to live is to love
         And I have lived. . .

Poets write of life
   And I am no exception
      For to love is to live
         And I have loved.

Michael J. Colosimo
GREENFIELDS FOREVER

I saw the dream in the mirror.
It crystalized right before my
   eyes.
And everything became so
   very clear
Like a puzzle.
The pieces all fit together.
Like rushing water that joined
   together.
To flow as one to the sea.

And in the dream in the
   mirror
I saw you and me
Lying under the sun of gold
with marshmallow clouds
In a sky of blue.
Love grew around us and out in
   the fields
So we pledged each others love
And wished for greenfields
   forever.

Genevieve Locke Oliphant
PEOPLE WATCHING

In a world where people gaze at
   stars or watch the birds,
I'm a people watcher, watch
   faces and their words.
I see and feel their innermost
   thoughts and share their pain,
Feel their deepest longings,
   the truths, also the lies.
Upon a face I sometimes see a
   death, time verifies.
I understand their flippancy and
   careless attitude,
It is just a coverup, they mean
   not to be rude.
I feel with them their loneliness
   and share their agony,
Touch upon their heartstrings,
   hear their melody.
How I long to touch them with
   hands as well as tought,
To revise their thinking, change
   what life has brought.
But this is quite impossible;
   what is to be will be,
We each must travel onward to
   face our destiny.

Sharon A. Christopher
TO CHRISTOPHER

Dream a dream upon the ocean
wish a wish upon a star,
pass each day with expectations
should your travels take you far
to the lands of midnight glory
or the lawns of ancient kings
think the thoughts you feared
   might hinder
all those warm and sacred things;
in your mind there dwells a
   castle

much more stately than the
   others,
do not let the golden portals
fall defeated to jealous brothers;
live your dream beside the ocean
fly with the star that gave you
   joy
and you shall never know the
   sorrow
life pretends to throw, my boy.

Angelia K. Haynes
HER

What is she like
What do you see
Does she wonder about
your old life with me
Does she cook good food
And fix good meals
When you speak of me
How does she feel
Does she cheer you up
Like I used to do
When you come in
feeling down and blue
Does she fix you a drink
At the end of the day
Does she ask about work
If you had a good day
Does she kiss you good-night
When you go to bed
Does she kiss you awake
On the top of the head
What is she like
Please don't make it long
I just want to know
What I did wrong.

Ethyl C. Storms
LACE

Reproduced aging yellow lace
Tending to the wishes
Of indignant buttons.
Jealousy lurks in the hearts
Of the ugly
Toward the bonnie ashes
Of the poor.
Buttons are the well-attended,
Well–preserved, and well-to-do.
Lace is but for decoration,
Dedicated, desititude.
Lace is all I shall ever be.
Beauty is no help to me.

Sarah C. Stein
YELLOW IS THE COLOR

Yellow is the color that heralds
   spring and says hello to fall.
We eagerly await the first
   buttercup, Find it if you can.
Later in the spring: forsythia,
   curlicues, daffodils and
   dandelions.
Yellowed birch branches soften
   their structure
We gaze with amazement at
   snow flakes in April.
And fall—yellow is the season's
   color.
Mixed with a touch of red; yes,
   yellow says hello to fall.
With a grove of yellowed aspen
   trees or birch trees,
Yellow the the chosen color
   of peace and truth.
"Tie a yellow ribbon round
   the old oak tree."
Yellow—the color that heralds
   spring and says hello to fall.

Elizabeth Carwellos
LIFE

take her hand
grasp it hard
never let it go
enjoy the nectar
from her fruits

before she fades
slipping silently
into oblivion

Joni Patterson
GENTLE

You are gentle I found
as giving gentle finds gentle
Fresh as a sip of English morning
tea
at the yawn of sunrise
is your perception refined.
You are tolerant in the midst of
extreme
and steady in the fall-apart
frenzy.
Rich as newly turned earth
in the dew of summer's ever
are your wisest, glorious
dreams.
Walk awhile with me
and we'll introspect too much
laughing softly together.
Frolicking fun times, my dear,
serious, gentle.

Ethyl Roberts Williams
GOD IS EVERYWHERE

I see God's hand in everything,
I see Him everywhere
in the beauty of the flowers,
In the fresh, clean morning air.

I see him in the mountains,
in all their majesty,
I see him in the desert
With its cactus, wild and free.

I see Him in the heavens,
I see Him in the sea
All this He has created,
Just for you and just for me.

And as I gaze upon it,
My faith is born anew,
For only God could make a
world,
So perfectly in tune.

Jeanne Marie Halama
SNOW

Wet snow, deep snow,
white snow all around;
No more vegetation dead
cluttering the ground.
Cold snow, crystal snow,
fluffy snow about;
fairylandishscenes seen
while walking out.
Snow a-pile, snow adrift,
feather snow a-wing. . .
sky-sterile bandages
over everything.
Languid snow, dancing snow,
angry snow a blow;
blankness of eternity
everywhere you go.
Pure snow, frigid snow,
a Universe of white. . .
I shall write a verse upon it
this very night!

Kathie Benefiel
THE LION IN ME

I have an unpredictable lion
living in me,
That neither you or I can
really see.
He walks everywhere I go on
my feet.
Sometimes I think he uses them
for a seat.

When he suggests rolling and
playing on the grass,
I know I must control myself
behind this mask.
When I wish I could rub noses
with some handsome man I
see,

It's not my idea but the beast
bottled up in me.
When some impatient person
takes his turn ahead of me,
I mustn't let out a growl but
be as nice as can be.
Knowing the lion's taste I order
a steak quite rare.
When serfed well done I feel
him raising his hair.
Driving on the freeway if I see
a tailgater on my rear,
Or some motorist cutting me
off in the mirror,
My Lion whispers jump on
the hood and crash inside
I say no Leo I can't even
though I was born under you.

Marlene Cedillo
LIFE

It is to thyself for which "Life"
is
what you've made of it.
"Life" shall be beautiful, as to
what you decide to make of
it, whether it
be easy and a lot fun, or difficult
and very complicated.
"Life" should be taken day by
day.
rather than all at once.,
Remember. . .
Life is very precious time, so don'
don't
waste any of it.
"Life" is given to you once, and
can
only be lived once.
"Life" is also only, taken away
once,
that for which our heavenly
father will
take away from us whenever
needed.
"Life" is given to us, and live
dku
lived by us,
for the individuality and
single personal
ways of life, and our different
traits in
life.
"Life" should be lived right,
so, live
right in your life day by day,
by starting
NOW, So. . ."Live it up" before
it's too late.

Kimberlee Grage
DISCOVERY

On the mountaintop we sat
watching in quiet solitude
the colors of a rainbow
at noon.
Each color was alive
and singing
for us.
Each note was sung

in precise harmony
Each movement
was graceful,
like a ballerina dancing
on a rose petal.
Love came to us from heaven
and gave us a feeling
we'd never known before
We forgot our solitude—
it was given to the rainbow.
For we didn't need the rainbow
anymore.
Not the peacefulness
or liveliness.
We had each other now.

Marilyn B. Rutter
FLOWERS IN BLOOM

I never thought that flowers
could be nice
Until I saw them in my sight.
I never thought I could have a
friend,
Until flowers bloomed once again.
Along the road, their petals
broke outright—
Pungent yellow—wondrous to
the sight.
Sore eyes could hurt, but never
hurt again,
when in my sight those blossoms
bloomed again.
I saw and never wanted to stop
to see.
The happiness that they had b
brought to me.
"Don't pick?" I told a secret
friend. "they live along the
road
To bring the peace and make
the hatred end."
"When vicious people want to
pick a fight—tell them to go
out
Watch the flowers—then
can they fight!
Do watch the beauty of nature
outright.

P. Thibodeau
FROM WITHIN

Within this tiny shell, there isn't
much to see,
No e here to bother—for
there is only me.
Lonely is a word I do not know;
From within this world there is
no room for it to grow.
Laughter, gaiety, frolic, and
smiles;
Have never visited—not even for
a little while.
Sadness, teardrops, anger and
fright;
From where I am, I'll know not
their plight.
Should it be here, that I should
remain;
Then, from all emotions I shall
refrain.
But, should I venture out into
the world;
Then, it shall be known if I
am Boy or Girl.

LaRae Morris
TO LEARN

Who am I? I'm just eighteen,
Little of life and love I have seen.
With much to learn of what both
mean,
I know that I'm on my way.

I make a life for me today,
I look for me in bub'ling Andre.
Like the needle in a stack of hay
But that's not the way things

must be.
With much to learn and more
to see,
I pray my life is always free.
I know someday I will find me,
Living for the day, still learning.

Georgia Crnich
WISDOM OF THE AGES

A rock watched me one day
and soon I heard him say,

"We're brothers you and I.
We pave the way,
though people without mercy
tread on us as if we are dead,
We are both a living part of God
and know the wisdom in what
he said.

We'll be the survivors, you know.
The others refuse to hear and
grow.
Love is the power to save a
nation.
It is the world's only salvation."

Stephen Wujek
FLIGHT

Rather than soar like the eagle
I stand with the trees and rocks
Content and unafraid,
Yet yearning for the thermals
My friend floats effortlessly upon

I can ponder the question
of why our fates are thus.
For him thought is nothing
but a clear blue liquid sky.

Charles William Cunha
WALKING

Walking in the woods
seeing no trees,
not hearing the birds
or the bees.
The wind blows hard
but it's not felt.
The flowers breathe softly,
but they aren't smelt.
Time passes by,
an illusion at best,
but we sense it more
than all the rest.

Agnes Ellen Erickson
LITTLE DOG LOST

I belonged to someone once
But they've forgotten me.

I'm sitting here on "death-row"
With no one to hear my plea.

Tomorrow is my last day—
My '30-days' are up—

For no one really gives a damn
About a little pup!

The morning sun is shining,
(The last that I will see!)

NO WAIT, there's someone out
there—
And they're looking straight at
me!

The door is slowly opening
And they're reaching down for
me,

My body's all a-quiver
And I pray that they will see

What a lovely little doggie
That someday I will be.

Oh, that Doggie Saint from
"up above"
Has granted a reprieve,

For he knew this Master needed—
A LITTLE DOG LIKE ME. . .
AMEN.. : .

Vickie Beard
ALONE

In a dark corner
All alone
No one to talk to
No one who cares
Sitting, thinking, and staring at
the wall.
If I had just one person to talk to
This corner wouldn't be so dark
anymore.

Sheila M. Ricksgers
FIRST LOVE

I'm sitting here with nothing to
do;
so I'm taking this time to think
of you.
I remember that very first night,
when I kissed you and you
held me tight;
this is one night I'll never forget
for this was the night that we
had met.
I remember walking hand in
hand,
across the field throughout the
land;
wishing upon the very first star,
making love in the seat of your
car.
I remember everything that we
ever shared,
I remember finding out that you
never cared.
The hurt and pain I can still
feel today,
I loved you in a very special
way.
I remember it all, as you can
see,
I wonder my first love, do
you remember me?

Mrs. Jane Allen Graham
**THE CHRISTIAN'S
MARRIAGE**

Love is not something
You hold in your hand.
Love blends body and spirit
Between a woman and a man
Love is not just a feeling
You have for one another.
Love is the merging into one
Of you and your lover.
Love is defined in a letter
Written by the Apostle Paul.
Love in God's heart
Is living out his call!

C. Kuntz
**AN ANIMAL
TRANSFORMATION A
COSMIC REALITY**

an animal in due course
a monotonous feeding of change
chrytalized within an elastiised
capsule
an imitation of a higher being
a transformation of an
individual type.

stretch your wings through this
slimy transparent membrane
burst open this stereotyped egg
be persistant in your actions,
pattern becomes process
to the holder of this
manufactured webb.

break all boundaries
fly past the space where the
stars are kept.
a transformation has now begun
physical and psychological
events are now to come.

time to show your real feelings

tone your spirit,
to the movement
of the space your in.

pass through the violet
ever so gently
in order to proceed to more
sensational level
an immortal creative activity.

Denese Sinclair
ME AND MY BLACK JESUS

Me and my black Jesus
As I sat along on
my little ghetto street
living this ghetto life
looking up to the skies
reaching for my black Jesus
Me and my Black Jesus
and there he would stand
a bronze of renaissance,
with his brilliant luster
smile on his face.
Me and my black Jesus
sitting, looking, out
into space,
He's always by my side.

searching through the
big blue heavens, with
precious glory for his
divine throne.
Me and my black Jesus.

Nora Raleigh
SONNET

By thrall and by wight it is there,
in one night held all cupped bare,
by other hand, called as a plum
blossom
fallen so light, so gently to earth
near a moonlit, ephemeral lake,
proof
for sake and remembrance in
this mind;
if ever there are in the dark again
white birch trees and hard
ground a bed
close this semblance to water
inland,
'neath a great arc seen through
sand
where found is the moss soft,
dark green
and board the naked arms
enfolding part
not the whole of pretensive
reality;
but, o the illogic of the proud
guide
and the long ride out on the
trail.

Richard Paul Flinn
TALK TO ME SILENCE

Talk to me Silence
In your poetic tone,
Whisper softly
Your echoing sounds
Of the beauty hidden
By the lack of sight.
Speak softly short silence
For your time is dwindling,
Show me the unseen world
Before my eyes.

Charles Allison Hearn
ALL THESE YEARS

All of these years we've been
apart;
Yet we still hold places in our
hearts.
It may not be the love we once
knew
But I know it's somehow true.
Many times you've gone your
way and I've mine,
Leaving each other behind; only

to return,
And to rendezvous and say
silently. . .
I still love you.
However to face Reality is s
sometimes hard
When it's holding a knife
drenched with pride;
There must not be a more
frightening thing,
knowing Reality could slash,
any moment, into Past.
So we again go our ways,
Content, FREE,
Perhaps alone, but FREE;
Until we get the courage to
approach the blade of Hurt.

Caroline Woolever
A MOMENT

The tide rolls in and out again,
It never seems to stay for more
than a moment.
Every time the salted water
tickles my toes
It looks so different.
Never will a wave, big or small,
look the same.
I stand here in a daze thinking,
dreaming,
wishing,
wondering what tomorrow
will bring.
I think of you, just as the tide,
with the individual waves,
You never twice will look the
same way.
I look out as far as my eyes can
see,
Feeling a tear form, I blink.
Clearing the tear away, I
think of you again.
My moment is coming to an end,
I whisper a small prayer
I love you,
Amen.

Narinder K. Bhugra
DISCRIMINATION

People here do discriminate,
because we do not originate,
Some people think they are
superior, and we are inferior.
But it is not a fact, only just
a tact.
We have to fight, if they do not
treat us right.
We came in different ships, but
are now in the same boat.
We have the same rights, we
even have the right to vote.
They are misusing their power
to hire and fire,
They will realize in their old
age, when they are ready to
expire.
They are proud of their speech,
We are proud of our accent,
Everybody should be proud
of one's culture and heritage,
Since what is life, but just a
stage.
Narinder's question is not

from where we came,
But how fair we play the life
game.

Julie Bastedo
SOMEDAY

Someday I wish were tomorrow,
To open my eyes,
Feel no sorrow,
Someday
Seems so far away
A thought
That may never be,

Wishful
As it is,
Often it is said.
Someday
The true meaning of life
I will understand,
For
Often I awake, only to feel
Loneliness
Engulf my heart,
Regret,
Someday I wish were tomorrow.

Sr. Charity Halback, O. S. F.
ME?

Searching—
Striving—
Falling—
Crying, "I love You!"
Hearing—
Smiling—
Accepting—
Correcting, "We love each
other!"
Holding
In Your hands
My being.
Whispering,
"You're precious,
Oh! So precious."
The wonder of it.

Lori Morgan
KOLN

You frightened me by your
sudden presence
And even more sudden gesture
of friendship. . .
And I reacted to my fear,
rather than to the adventurous
spirit within me—
Then you were gone. . .
And even now, as I return,
looking for you—I know it
wouldn't be the same.
My heart both longs to see you—
and yet, fears it also.
So, it is a relief knowing. . .
you won't be there. . .

Mrs. Garnett Reeves
FLIGHT

I awoke up early this morn
To see a beautiful new day
being born.
Silver winds softly blowing;
Their way not knowing.
Lost in the pattern of the snow;
Down they come up they go.
Bringing leaves tumbling like
diamonds from the trees,
An injured bird to wing no more.
Falling quiet as a fleeing doe,
It's flight not knowing where to
go;
Sleeps quietly in the soft white
snow.

Maria Iskiw
THE JOY OF A LEAF

This leaf did fall
From a tree so tall,
To fulfill God's will
And give you a thrill.
It was sent by a dove
With a lot of love.
May it bring you peace
And daily release.

Gina Jenkins
LOVE

Love isn't something
You find everyday,
Love isn't something

you can give away,
When you're unhappy,
Love comes to stay,
So keep your love,
And never give it away!

John Charles Parker
WHAT CAN I BELIEVE?

What is the real meaning of life?
Could it be the cause of my
    eternal strife?
What is it that we hold so dear?
An untold meaning that is not
    clear?
Is the value of life hidden
    somewhere
Under the water, a tree, or a
    rock out there?

Why does Society have different
    beliefs
Of gods, goddesses and the rest?
Yet the childrens' power seethes
When faced with the most
    important test.

And so, what can I believe?
What can I hold true?
It is my wish not to grieve,
But, I know not what to do.

Richard Milam
A CALLING

When out of nothing comes a
    calling
From one unknown intruder,
Disturbing me in my abode,
Involving me to answer:
And I inclined to inward ways
Regarding my endeavor,
I stirred to heed this beckoning
Of dubious concern.

A familiar voice spoke to me
In unfamiliar tone;
A penetrating honesty
Endearing to be known:
Was death's honesty I heard
And now do hear resounding.

Tura A. Kinsel
BUDS ASLEEP

Somewhere in the forest deep,
Little buds are fast asleep,
Waiting the magic of sun and rain
To wake them from their winter
    dream,
And sing their springtime song
    again.

Robert T. Zabniak
SURVIVAL

The November gale
  Is pounding her through
Trying to weaken her
  And break her in two
As powerful and furious
  And winds that prevail
Maria has persisted
  And furled her sail
The test of endurance
  Both must meet
Each holding the other
  Preparing for defeat
It's man against Nature
  As been for ages
Each having victory
  Throughout History pages.

Christy Lynn Archer
IN PRAISE OF ME!

It comes from me.
All my thoughts and feelings
come from me.
Because of me,
I am me.
No one else is me,
or ever can be me.
They can imitate me and admire

me,
But never come close to truly
    being me.
I am truly unique, I am me.
Me is what I'll always be.
Not just plain old me, but
exciting wonderful ME!
And she is someone wonderful
    to be,
because Me is like no other.
Me is Me and only me,
One that no one else can be.

Eugene Glover
WAITING—NOSTALGICALLY

Here I sit nostalgically,
Waiting for his promise to me.

Waiting for sapience,
Sapience that world scholars
    couldn't teach.

Waiting for valor,
whereby great heroes can not
    speak of.

Waiting for that joy,
No wonderful being could share.

Waiting fot that special love—
That no lover could possibly give.

Waiting for life,
No mother could bear.

Waiting for his promise,
A promise whatsoever none
    other could offer.

Dr. Mildred Carroll Wiseman
ETERNAL PROMISE

With heavy heart I face the
    dawning day
And in despair I bow my head
    to pray.
Dear God, I know I've strayed
    outside your way,
I'm tired, I'm ill, I'm broken
    hearted
And I need your help today.
Then as I lift my eyes toward
    Heaven
I see the signs of all your
    greatness.
The setting moon looms large
    on the horizon,
The eastern sky arrayed in
    magic splendor
Meets today with the gloriously
    rising sun,
And now I know this is a signal.
You reign supreme. You've
    heard my plea
and I rest assured in your
    ancient promise
I know you'll care and watch
    over me.
So with spirits sublimely lifted
I face the coming days with
    lighter heart
I'm sure that now by You I'm
    set apart
To receive Your very special
    blessing
As the dawn surrounds me in
    soft caressing
Promise of renewed love and life
Completely free from cares and
    strife.

Sandra Stalford Austin
THESE THINGS SHALL CEASE

Here upon the dreams,
    of time I lie,
My head not far above,
    the misty days,
I long to wrap my arms,
    around each living thing,
look about and calmly say.
I have found what many men
    seek,

I have learned from each,
    and every task.
I myself, I give, I take,
    tho my actions to some,
    I may not gain.
I do be me,   the one,
    no one else,   can be.
When time is gone and
    thoughts,
    no longer remembered,
    there's no more, but peace
    for me.
When time doesn't hide
    a single thing,
These, They, will be as all
    time before.
For life is dreams and dreams,
    are dreamt by men,
    and in time,
These, Things, too shall cease.

Esther R. Rowland
LIFE'S REQUESTS

A little white house on top of
    the hill,
A path curving up to the door,
With you by my side, we'll
    live there, my dear,
We couldn't ask for anything
    more.

Tall trees standing behind the
    house,
Flowers blooming 'round the
    door,
A garden in back, some chickens
    and cattle, my dear,
We couldn't ask for anything
    more.

A wee little one in the spare
    room cot,
Over the years we had a few
    more,
We were happy, for they were
    healthy, my dear,
We couldn't ask for anything
    more.

The years have rolled by, the
    children are gone,
We hear their laughter no more,
Just you and I, as in the
    beginning, my dear,
We couldn't ask for anything
    more.

For years you lay on a bed of
    pain,
Now you've gone to The Other
    Shore,
Just wait a wee while, I'll be
    coming, my dear,
I don't ask for anything more.

Pamela Wharton
FOREVER

Why do we feel the things we do?
    do?
Why don't we do the things
    we should?
Maybe if given a chance or the
    time we would.
Not many can tell what you feel
    or why,
just a few by that look in your
    eye.
The ones who care take the time
    to see you through.
To help you with indecision and
    fear.
To know how it feels to have
    someone so near.
When something as strong as
    love is in the way,
there's nothing much you can
    do or ever say.
To share, to trust, to feel, to
    cry, to love

enough to share a life without
    a lie.
We have shared something
    very special and deep.
It is something I will always
    keep, FOREVER.

Julie Richardson
**THE ARAB'S GOODBYE TO
HIS STEED**

My beautiful, my beautiful, that
    standest by and by,
With the beautiful arched neck
    and
    the dark golden eyes.
Farewell my pet even though I
    plead
    to keep you again, oh my
    Arabian steed.
You fly like the wind across the
    desert plains, I
    wish you wouldn't have to
    go, you give me great pain.
Who's ever hands you fall in
    obey them on
    command, I know that you
    will miss the
    Arabia desert sand.

Marya Colleen Phillips
LULLABYE

Ain't no word I know, Chile,
More human and more useful
    to humans
Than the word—hope.
Hope has eased many a starvin'
    man
Into the next world,
And kept a prayer on lips
Parched dry with thirst,
Hope marches into war,
And comes out livin'!
Hope sings lullabyes for mamas
With babies dyin' against dry
    breasts.
Hope fires sufferin' men with
    great dreams of freedom,
Bringin' us out of the holes
    humankind digs for itself.
Reckon there ain't nothin' in
    this world
More powerful'n hope.
Hush yer cryin' now, Chile.
We ain't givin' up hope.

Barbara Nelson Blinn
BATTLE CRY

Beware! Beware! The earth's
    decaying.
We must rise up. The hour is
    late.
Evil and tyranny dwell among
    us;
The world is full of fear and
    hate.

Let's battle for our rights and
    freedom;
All unjust things we must defeat.
We must rise up and fight
    wrongdoing.
Be not afraid. Do not retreat.

Come! Do not be so meek and
timid.
Let us cry out so others hear.
We must stand up, speak out,
be counted,
We must be brave and hide our
fear.
Come! Let us join ourselves
together,
Because we share a common foe.
Don your armor and choose
your weapons!
Into this battle we must go.

Ethel M. Gerbig
LOVE, TO BE IMPORTANT

LOVE, to be important must be
as a glorious sunrise;
A joy at just being alive.
LOVE, to be important, must
be as a golden sunset;
A sorrow that a perfect day
has ended.
LOVE, to be important, must
be as a baby's first sound;
Sweet music to the parent's
ears.
LOVE, to be important, must
be as a cold refreshing drink;
It satisfies the deepest thirst.
LOVE, to be important, must
be shared;
It cannot be a jealous
possession.
LOVE, to be important, must
first be given;
Then it can be received.
LOVE, to be important, must
satisfy the soul
As well as the body and mind.
LOVE can only be important
if two people give it and
share it.

The Reverend Lee C. Taylor
SUNSET

I stroll the beach at sunset
Beside a quiet sea.
I watch the ripple of the waves
Remembering my yesteryears.
The sea at night, brings a misty
chill
After angry billows roared, and
a violent
tempest flared.
The tides were high and waves
were rough,
It tempted old memories for me.
Tonight, at sunset, low tides
came in and
stilled the seas.
As I strolled along the beach, I
thought
Of a past love, a stormy love,
and many things,
As I stand at sunset and watch
the sea,
I will always remember the
beauty of God's creations,
The haunting sea and sunset,
that HE painted
For you and me to see.

Mike Cluff
KATY GIBSON

Katy Gibson smolders in the
dark
regales the stars
empty of pity for her plight;
rosewater soap suds smells
damp hair drips like blood
smeared against her head—
wreath of thorns odd shampoo;
noble slavery to the idols

of health the youth long past
according to the hallway mirror
tear-stained by bitterwet
memories
of early evenings with no hope
underneath newly-plied mascara/
rouge
teased to cover those tell-tale
signs of years now dust-encrusted
cruel Michaelangelos guiding
hate-inducing chiselers on bone
and skin.
Now, the night goes light
and morning lurks at the edge
reflected no longer in her mind—
glass lying like jagged pieces
of a deadly puzzle dense-red
flowing thick on marble tiles
slabs blanched pale
in the dawn's premature
brightness.

Nellie Parodi
VOYAGER ONE

Voyager one,
miracle blazer of the stars!
Your fifteen hundred millimeter
eye
sends us the revelation of your
finds!
Mariner, Pioneer, Orbiter
probing Mercury, Venus, Mars!
Now you, Voyager One, see
Jupiter!
On your eighty-four hundred
mile per hour race
what do you see?
Boiling minerals, chemicals,
sink-holes,
cyclones, active volcanoes,
molten flow!
where are the living creatures,
mountains, flowers and trees?
Where the better world we
yearn to see?
Voyager One,
what are you telling us, Earth
beings?
We search for life in other
worlds,
but as of now,
in spite of violence and wars,
pollution, plunder, illnesses,
of all the planets of our Sun's
family,
Earth is the only habitable one,
so beautiful, the best wherein
to life!

Angela Jean Wilhemi
MY WALL

If I sat down and talked with
you
would you listen to my heart?
Or would you turn me away,
and say let's make it some other
day.
I know time is hard to spare,
but I was hoping you'd take
one last
time to care.
I promise it won't take long,
then I'll be on my way and gone.
There's so much inside I've
saved,
my heart feels like an over
worked slave.
And the wall, you should feel it,
it has built itself so tall
And I stand behind it, so tiny
and small.
Too tired to break it down,
wouldn't that be great if I was
a clown?
Then this would all be funny,

and the days cheery and sunny.
Though, as much as I wish, I'm
not a clown,
it's just too late my wall will
never break down.

Ora Stallworth
LIFE SO PRECIOUS

Life so precious
Don't waste it
Make every day
A special day
By sharing love.
Love so beautiful
Show it by letting
That someone in your life
Know how special they really are.
Life so precious
Don't waste it
By being sad
Smile and be happy
Life so precious.

Lillie J. Huckaby
TIMES

Times gone by and times to
come
Both together in times now
present.
I see the faces of those
Whose minds wander
To days of yesteryear.
The joys of youth, the dreams
of childhood.
The warmth of friends, the
touch of love,
The pride of work well-done,
of pay well-earned.
I see the faces of those
Whose minds dance and shine
Of days to come.
Places to go, people to see,
Work to do, Pride to gain,
Friends to meet, love to know.
I see the faces of
Times gone by and times to
come
Both together in times now
present.

S. H. Ciccolini
ALONE

I like to sit and think beside
the fire,
When day has slipped and fallen
into night,
When tensions ebb and yield
to deeper sight,
And feeling's force is flowing
ever higher.
The dip and dance of flames
with no set course,
Emancipate the force in
likewise tide,
From joy to joy ignoring dark
beside
Each flame. I glow as though
I were the source.
Then with a thud and sparks
that reach my toes,
The timbers jockey for a
different place.
The fire subsides and glowing
embers doze.
And still my mind's compelled
to follow close.
To stop the dance and sadder
subjects face.
Alone, like this, is not quite
what I chose.

Janice Goldsberry
DIAMOND

A dewdrop. . .
A teardrop. . .

A star. . .
As fire within ice.
A sunbeam. . .
A flower. . .
A frost. . .
As life within death.
A feeling. . .
A desire. . .
A lust. . .
As love within hate.

Matthew Noll
ONE MORE

She would kiss me, hug me,
hold me tight,
Each time I saw her, each time
in sight.
It happened each time I walked
through her door,
I wished it wouldn't happen
anymore.
But now she's gone and she'll
never come back,
And each time I go to her grave
It is that one kiss I lack.

Mr. Dana A. Gravely
METHODICAL

The office moves methodically
A clockwork technique.
The office moves in rhythm
A formula unique.
The people move schematically.
Production is the goal.
The people move routinely
Meticulous control.
Typewriters chime precisely.
Copiers hum and jerk.
Secretaries smile nicely.
It's all in a day's work.

Roger L. Halle
A WOMAN KNOWS

A woman knows how long it
takes
In time and life to grow a man.
The sacrifice in self and love,
The tears and joy and wonder
of
The growth of child from womb
to boy,
Who curiously wants to know
The wondrous things in this
wide world
He thinks are for himself alone.
A woman senses troubles all,
The pains, delights a boy must
know
Before her mind a youth she
sees
Ready to take his place
unknown
In God's ever eternal plan.
With love and patience she
bestows
This long creation called a man.

Jane Waters Moore
TRYING TIMES

Sometimes when I'm with you,
I find it hard
to constrain myself;

keep my emotions in check;
be cool and off-handed with
you.
Sometimes when I'm with you,
I find it hard
to deny my feelings for you;
be a friend, a pal, a buddy to
you;
deny my love for you.
Sometimes when I'm with you,
I find it hard
to restrain myself from grabbing
you;
shaking you;
pounding it into your head how
I feel about you.
Sometimes when I'm with you,
I find it hard
to realize it will always be this
way
with you.
Sometimes when I'm with you,
I find it hard
to accept that life would be
simpler
without you:
less complex without you;
less constraining without you.
For, sometimes when I'm with
you, I find it easy
to recognize how lonely life
would be
without you.

Lucinda Munoz-Perez
**WHAT ARE YOU LOOKING
FOR?**

What are you looking for my
dear. . .
So far away from home!
I'm searching for my love.
He left so long ago.
He has never returned.
I've searched for him these many
years,
With no success.
I've looked for him in our
favorite place
To no avail.
I've looked for him o'er hill
and vale.
I've searched in far-off lands.
I haven't found my love as yet
And know not where else to
look.
No, I know not right now.
I do not feel his presence close.
Just cold, cold silence
everywhere,
When'er I breathe his name.
Where is my love?
And a cold, gentle breeze
answers,
"He's gone, he's gone.
Forever more he's gone."

Margaret Ann Guy
LIBERTY

Release me from frustration
and doubt;
Open the door of my cage;
Watch the winds of freedom
Carry me to where life is to
engage.

Seeking a refuge in God's
forgiving arms,
To self-doubt I will not retreat;
So, unlock the bars that confine
me,
And hasten my escape from
defeat.

My potentials are unlimited
In my Father's great domain;
My fulfillment is guaranteed.
In bondage I will not remain.

Joyce A. Hurst
A PERSONAL OPINION

Happiness can't be defined.
It's a certain mood, a state of
mind.
It's sharing every day affairs
With one who understands and
cares.
It's a tender look, a gentle touch
That says, "I love you very
much!"
It's a welcome smile when you're
blue;
A dream that's shared. . .A
dream come true.
And happiness is more than this.
It's a warm embrace, a magic
kiss.
It's a special blessing from above.
It's what you have when you
can love.
For me happiness can easily
be versed,
I spend my life with Gary and
Eric Hurst!

Terry Stein
A DRAG ON LIFE

Lit with love
Clouds of dreams that rise above
Smoke disappears
Vision clears
Reality holds no love

All feelings filtered
True taste concealed
Burnt out
Without
Meaning revealed

Burnt out feeling
Sores of strife
All feelings burnt out
Butt,
    Life.

Carol D. Stearns
JUST ME

If I were but the master of words
Instead of lines,
I would tell you what lies deep;
If I had the gifted voice of song
I would compose a melody
To sing just for you;
But I am only me
Without the ability of words
To speak
Nor the gift of voice
with which to sing.
All I know is I love you
and nothing will ever be the same.

Teri McMaster
I HAVE A FRIEND

I have a friend who never fails,
When things are going rough.
The kind who knows the way
to care,
When life seems far too tough.
I haven't forgotten this friend
of mine,
The kind who understands.
I hope my friend remembers
That I am struggling too.
That life is made of many things,
In what we say and do.
I hope the world can keep the tie
That holds us all as one.
The tie that's known as
friendship
It radiates the sun.

Anna Jane Panezich
DESERTION

My bird never lived in a cage.
He was wild
But made himself tame
In order to survive.
He waited for me each day

And ate out of my hand.
He was deformed
An outcast from his flock.
I went away
He never returned
A victim
Of the pecking order.

Jerry Richert
MOTHER LOVE

A child should be someone who
A father loves and needs
Not justsa person in his view
Who he tolerates and feeds.

A mother too who knows loves
pains
If she is to have worth
Should seldom cry or complain
Of her childs habits since his
birth

Then faith that God will fill
life full
With happiness and love
Will work with hope as it's fuel
For they are hand in glove

And love will in large quantities
With patience as it's guide
Make for close knit families
Who walk side by side

A father's love though has all
this
And is both rich and warm
Falls short of a mothers love,
a mothers kiss
A shelter from all harm

Edwin F. Winkleman
TIME

Time,
   Drags when one is dismal
Time,
   Glides when one is glad
Time,
   Introduces new born babies
Time
   Does away with the dead.

Elinor Belcher Jones
**MY BABY STARTED SCHOOL
TODAY**

She walked away with a smile
on her lips
and a song in her heart.
I stood and watched, biting
my lips, torn apart.
The day was sunny and bright,
as she stepped into another
stage of life.
A lovely dress, neatly curled hair,
a ribbon placed just so,
New shoes, a little sack lunch. . .
and she was ready to go.
Yes, a kiss goodbye, and she
went away,
I cried. . .
My baby started school today.

Lona M. Krueger
WORDS IN THE SEASONS

When I cry out, "I love you,
Sweet Boy,"
   Don't you know?
The words freeze and fall in the
snow
Awaiting an answer however
you can
A feeling, a thought, an action,
a plan.

When I cry out, "I miss you,
Son,"
   Do you hear?
The autumn leaves form the
words ever so clear
Then the wind carries them off
to wherever you are
And twinkles your response

from a friendly star.
When I cry out, "I want you
back, Baby,"
   Can't you see?
Blades of grass pop up from my
tear-streaked plea
And your answer comes to me
on the rays of the sun
Warming my heart as your
laughter had done.
When I cry out, "I need you,
Honey,"
   But I know you're gone.
The spring flowers open with
their beautiful song
And you come to me in the
form of rain
And cry with me to wash away
the pain.

Sandy Hobbs
PORTRAIT OF A CHILD

The child, so innocent and true
Questioning the birds and all
that is new
Laughing gaily at the small,
fluttering butterflies
He doesn't understand, yet he
tries
The broad smile on his youthful
lips
The chocolate smudges on his
fingertips
His quick unexpected actions
Usually thanks to his tennis shoe
tractions
The cool, blond hair blowing in
the wind
The tree limb he simply "must"
bend
The tiny freckles dotting his
face
The way in which he loves to
chase
His innocent looks hiding his
guilt
The way in which he snuggles
his quilt
Remind me of my days of youth
When my biggest worry was a
loose tooth.

Donita Rae Boyes
**LISTEN LOVE AND YOU
WILL HEAR. . .**

Listen love and you will hear
my love for you is everywhere.
Though others have turned and
walked away
you alone are the one who
stayed;
By my side you helped me
through
with the little things you say
and do.

Listen love and you will hear
it's for you I'll always care.
Questions I've had on how I
feel
but, now my love I know is real.

Listen love and you will hear
whenever you need me I'll be
there,
remember I'm here and I'll
come when you call
and hold out my hand so that
you won't fall.

Robin Ab Lang
INTREPID MAID

i lotus pose against jacinth
perhaps a priestess
with bamboo flute.
i mountain browse
with this catkin instrument
balleting along the erete.

orange wind
combs my blonde
like holidays
or the larvae of silk fibre.
i
dance je ne sais quoi
and gemmate soft muscles.

Suzanne Toupin's Father
UNTITLED

I know your heart is lonely and—
you know that mine is too.
But what is there this side of
    earth
that you or I can do.
I can not walk across the sea,
or overpass the land—
to see your loving smile again—
and to hold your hand.
I can not turn the clock around
to bring the hour near.
And so we have to save our
    dreams—
and live on messages—
that warm the waiting heart.
But there will be a day when
    I will anchor my shop—
And then your charms will fill
    my arms—
And I shall kiss your wonderfully
    sweet lips.

Jon Scot Swenson
IMAGES

I
haven't seen her in ages
those ages of her
I
have not yet seen
whose ages not seen have
I

Bessie Lindsay Davis
MINUTES

I wait for you and leaden
    minutes creep
    Begrudgingly across time's
    aged face;
You come, and lo, with speed
    of thought they sweep
Our happiness away into eternal
    space.

You leave, and wearied from
    their speed
They pause, and drag a resting
    train,
Gaining fresh strength with
    jealous greed
To bear away in haste, our
    joys again.

Nelda LeVant
THE SH, RUB

Euphoria
    The bitter milky juice, genera,
Ja, Pan ese,
Spurge.

Pachysandra, Variegata.
S'LunshiTime!

Tae and Taedium Vitae
He touched me with the love

---

in his hands
and the pain went away.
Body Language conducting a
    symphony,
and she danced away
In the sun.

Sandra L. Ream
LADY

The sea is one lady you should
    always respect,
ask those who's ships and boats
    she has wrecked.

Don't try to abuse her, for
    she'll have no pity,
you can never fool her she's
    more than just witty.

Be a gentleman and know your
    place and she's sure
to show your her courtesy
    and grace. For there's
never been a woman so fair,
    no one could match
her style and flair.

You should always be gentle
    never too rough, you
do and she'll show you she's
    just as tough.

Any man who's known her to
    groan, knows she is
a woman with a mind of her
    own.

Her fiercest waves have been
    tried by men, only
to loose again and again. No
    matter how big or
brave you be, you'll never be
    any match for that
lady, the sea.

Dorothy Horstman Valley
MARK

Marky Sparky. . .remember this
In younger years a little Miss
Changed your name from old
    to young
Until the age of ten and one.

At the age of twelve or so
All we heard was . . .ski-doo,
    ski-doo
After much was said and done
The ski-doo had finally won.

Into his teans our growing son
Helped to fill our hearts with
    fun
Vacationing to and from
Horses looked like bears to some.

Off to college he did go
Pharmacy he now does know
Soon to graduate with cheers
Mom and Dad cry happy tears.

Jacquelyn Wilson
ESSENCE

I am aware of me,
but when I try to turn that
    knowledge
of certain things back into
    myself,
I encounter a black area
where ignorance and knowledge
    meet
with no discrepancy,
for both exist,
and the existence is justification
    for being.
my truth is encased
in a hard metal shaft
at my near center,
which must be torn away
from the stickly, pulpy mass of
    my personality,
and stood back
as something that is not really

---

part of me.
then, as I grow more used to
    its ideas,
it can be moved closer,
eased slowly, slowly up,
until it again touches my being,
except that now the content
has been pulled a little closer
    to the sides,
until it is absorbed in the heat
    of my emotion
and my intellect has a broader
    base of myself
from which to work.

Einar Nelson
HARVEST HELPERS

A neighbor friend to help he
    came,
Kelly Winters was his name;
To run my combine through
    the day
When I was sick, this I must say.

The Dixon brothers, a hand they
    gave,
All three were there my crop
    to save.
Their giant combines, they
    swung ahead,
First in the lead, his name was
    Fred.

And Dickie Geer was hauling
    grain,
To me he said, "It looks like
    rain."
His skillful help could not be
    beat
When Dick sat in the driver's
    seat.

The women folks they turned
    out strong
To feed these men whose days
    were long.
They brought them stew and
    apple pie,
Hot coffee, too, when they
    were dry.

Friends to me are worth much
    more
Than all the riches men can
    store.
These friends have shown what
    they can do
When my steps were short and
    very few.

Jan Winemiller
SAND DOLLAR

Having spred her
blanket on the beach
Sarah watched a wave
climb up the strand
dive out of reach.
She shunned the rise
and fall of lean
years at the beck
and call of children
battered by her
own hand. She fixed
her thoughts on
better times and
tried to sleep.
A shell left her grip
like prayer pulled
through parched lips.

Sue Crannell
MOMENTS

the silent, black curtain of
    eternity
        streaming downward
        night
    the sun's steady hand
slowly splitting the stillness
    dawn
the fiery, red roof of the

---

universe
    baking the solid sphere below
    noon
        the calm coolness of crimson
        clouds
encircling the setting sun forcing
    it under
        dusk
the silent, black curtain of
    eternity
        streaming downward
        night

Melissa Goldsmith
JOSEPH STREET

The rain in pantomine:
    it teases me
    and runs away;
    the fool
    again knows nothing.
But sometimes I catch whispers
    of the hidden silver threads
as the ghosts play their game
    This way,
    Step here—
You have seen those loves before.
    Look now;
    Shadows on the water,
Misbegotten parodies of
    themselves,
        Gathering their winters,
        Echoes in the glass. . .
        Ghosts;
        Touch them away.

Ronda Stritel
I CAN COPE

Ah, Vile liquid, I shall drink
    you down,
Please make me feel warm
    inside as you
    travel through my system—
erasing the horrid
events of the day—and help me
    cope with tomorrow.

Oh, sleep, why don't you come?
No worry, I got my dream-maker
    friend.
I'll just release him from his
    glass prison
and to me he shall bring sleep.

It's morning—drowsyness, go
    away, you know how
I hate to wake up feeling dead.
But alas! One easy swallow of
    my fast friend.
Energy! Life?
Oh world see how well I can
    cope.

Tim Uzzel
LOOKING BACK

Who made it so? which few of
    all waiting spirits are let slip
into this world? swept close
    over time and distance,
    merging
to remain alongside. Once only
    was that place, where paths
    must
touch, where one trail wound
    long near to another; beginning
in a small room we thought large,
    in a town with one name, a
space on the brink of knowing,
    where friends ran, and searched,
and fled, each down his own
    changing river, to, finally, an
    ocean,
a gulf that severed any new link,
    anything newly shared, an
outgoing surge which scattered
    those known for a lifetime,
    ending
the constancy of what bound
us, interrupting all we had
    begun.

Michelle Clifford
FLIGHT OF LOVE

A lone seagull soars high into
    the air.
Free from all the earthly ties.
It's flight takes it higher and
    higher.
Just like that lone seagull,
My love for you has set me free.
The sweet thrill of loving you,
Takes me higher and higher.
And just like that seagull,
I have no earthly fears of
    rejection.
I know that you might not ever
    love me,
But I'm not worried about that
    future.
Feeling this love for you
Is a trip I wouldn't miss taking.
For just like that lone seagull
You make me soar high and
    free.

Brenda Anderson
SOON

The farmhouse so white,
alone in fields bared,
with snow sprinkled over the
    forgotten soil.
A glow comes from the windows,
smoke curls gently out the
    chimney
wafting aimlessly into a bleak,
    grey sky.
There lives my love and my life.
So handsome and powerful;
he fills the door with his sweet
    and loving being.
The smile he smiles
is like the stars fallen from
    heaven.
The twinkle of his brilliant, blue
    eyes,
strength that surges through his
    body,
and the love between us.
Someday I will be his,
he will be mine,
and we will be together—forever.

Christina Manes
THE VAGABOND

He wanders through the
    darkened streets,
Secretly he watches families
    gather around.
A tear gently falls down his
    bearded face,
He then departs,
And wanders through the
    darkened streets.

Helen Weisneck
CHEATING ON YOU

You kept telling me all the time
That there was something on
    my mind.
With a love so strong, and a
    trust too great,
You didn't know I came home
    so late.
I cheated and lied and went out
    on dates.
Will your love for me turn to
    hate.
I didn't mean to make you pay,
For you never went astray.
I broke your heart right in two,
Now I'm paying for cheating
    on you,
Every night I lay awake,
    thinking of my mistakes,
Hoping we could start anew,
No one but me and you.
But until we do,
I am paying for cheating on you.

Tanya Pihl
UNTITLED

I'm sitting here, next to this
    bright window,
wondering if I'll ever, many
    years passing, be
able to reach out and grasp
    whatever may lie beyond.
Many times I have hoped to
    steal a glance out
this window,
Which may, one day, hold my
    future.
Many years have passed, and
    now, only now,
am I brave enough to reach out
    a finger and touch
what lies beyond the window
    pane.
My life.

Sherri Ailshie
OUR FLAG

Old Glory rides the breeze on
    high,
Undulating against the sky,
Regally she stands alone.
Flaunting her colors on her
    throne.
Lofty, but lonely, she dances
    there,
A symbol of freedom everywhere
    everywhere,
Guarding our nation from high
    in the air.

John W. Grula
A THIRST FOR CONTACT

I walk into the room and there
    they are:
A picture of her goddamn dog
And a picture of her goddamn
    boyfriend.
But cool off—
She's nice enough I suppose.
It's just that she can't
    understand
Why it is one should wonder
    about a murderer's mind,
Or attach so much importance
To the tiny golden hairs on a
    leaf.

Marcie Lacy
DADDY, DADDY

Daddy, daddy, where did you
    go?
Daddy, daddy, I'm all alone.
Daddy, I desperately need you,
And I love you too.
It happened so fast,
That you had to leave me,
I knew our happiness would
    surely pass,
But I let you go; you are at last
    free.
I will never blame you,
For leaving me.
Death is a terrible way to be free.
Daddy I feel you in everything I
    do.
Daddy, I often shed tears,
For my many fears,
That you'll never return to me,
Oh Daddy, why must you be
    free?
Comfort me and drive my fears
    away,
Let me see you once again,
I miss you Daddy,
I love you, is all I can say.

Jeannia J. Bottger
SECRETS

The wind is whispering secrets
As it touches the leaves,

the grass, your hair;
it's the ones who grew old
    before us
and have lost their voices. . .
whispering.
And when we grow old,
and leave,
not only will we also be
    whispering
But then we will understand.

Dorsey Robbins
I SING

I sing in the snow
I sing everywhere I go,
I love to walk o'er the snowy
    white,
It makes it appear fairy like;
It beautifies God's earth with
    cheer
For the snow is beautiful and
    dear!

Shirley D. Hennis
NIGHTMARE

I stand alone, deep in the woods,
It's dark and I am cold.
I try to think of pleasant things,
to be real brave and bold;
I see eerie shapes around me,
hear noises everyplace,
Then I feel a clammy hand,
touch upon my face!
I've never ever known such fear,
So scared, I start to scream,
If anyone can hear me, Please!
Wake me from this dream!

Louellyn Duncan
MOTHER LOVE

Did Mary love her baby more
    because He was divine?
It was the Son of God she bore
    among the sheep and kine.
Was there a difference as He grew
    from boy to manhood fine?
Or was the mother's love she
    knew
    the same as yours and mine?
Was every care she had for Him
    along a different line
Than those of mind and heart
    and limb
    for mortals such as mine?
Or do all mothers feel the same?
    no other will outshine
The love she felt when Her Son
    came,
    or that I felt for mine.

Georgia Innes
TRANSIENT

Go and listen to the wind. It is
    my song.
Wish on a star. I shall hear it.
I tickle the children and delight
    in their laughter.
Naked and joyful, I dance in
    the rainwater.
Music moves me and lifts me
    away from this earth;
And I snatch up the sun and

carry it in my heart.
No cloud can block it there.
It will be my warmth and energy
When my body is cold and dead.
Then I shall soar again through
    the stars;
Innumerable sensations bound
    bouncing off the sound waves
And light streaks will guide me
    onward
To my next existence and
    destiny.
When I am born again,
Trapped once more into a
    patterned role,
I shall look up into the stars,
And then remember
How soon it will be
Before I am again among them.
I will play my part,
And give my best performance
    before I go.

Alice Wettleson
OASIS

Sad when one realizes
Life at its best must still go
    on . . .
Each of us merely occupies
His own special time and space,
Giving and sharing of ourselves
Something we can never replace.
During youth all is new and
    beautiful
With age something slightly
    tarnished
Takes its place . . .
Colors don't have their
    brilliance and their hue,
And yet lines of character
Start to come into view.
A new beauty we bring into
    the world,
Our inner selves shine more
    radiantly,
And a new wisdom unfolds,
The real essence of oneself,
    I am told.
So pocket your wisdom,
    and share with those you meet,
Then life will be richer,
And all will seem complete.

Carl J. Mir
IS THIS LOVE?

I seem to miss you
when you're gone;
is this love?
I always want to see you
And be near you;
is this love?
I long for your voice
just talking, of anything;
is this love?
I think of you with someone
    else
and my head and heart hurt;
is this love?
Are we too young to know,
and are you willing to say,
or am I,
is this love?

John A. Turchetta
TO EARTH AND BACK

While clouds swirl and tumble
    through the Sea of sky
Mountains stare and wonder
    why.
Light, so light thrusted by
    a mere whisper of wind
Looking down upon rock
    smiling a knowing grin.
For rock, majestic and bold,
    holds its ground and scoffs

At the massing on the horizon
Flowing . . .closer, closer,
  only to caress to tickle.
Climbing . . .up, up, the
  mountain, riding crests
Releaseing cleansing trickles.

Subtly carving insulted rock
Dislodging particles drop by
  drop
spreading its bulk along aeons
  of time
Filtering down through
  sandstone and lime.
So innocent clouds return
  back to the Sea
Repeating the cycle endlessly.

Sylvia B. Carver
LONELY: I AM

When life began for me,
Only the Lord knew how I
  was to be.
Whether I was to be happy and
  feel great inside,
Or was I to be someone who
  could never confide.

As time went on,
Everyone seemed to be gone.
There was no one to talk to.
For there was always something
  else to do.

I can't figure out why the Lord
  let me come into this world,
I've never been any help to
  anyone for my life's always
  in a swirl.
Why do I shy away from others,
Maybe because I want to keep
  my head under the covers.

Why are the skies so dark,
And there seems to be no
  kind of spark.
Will I always be this way,
Lord, there has to be a new
  day.

People make me tense,
And I feel they have for
  themselves more confidence.
I want to be a persn who can
  take care of one's self,
But so far I've broken all the
  parts of this shelf.

Idon't like to admit to anyone
  I'm depressed,
For they want to go deeper
  into matters which I want
  to rest.
I wonder if people should
  tell how they feel to someone
  they trust,
I would say "yes", for that's
  the only way to get under
  the crust.

To survive I must learn to be
  someone I'm not,
But that would put me on the
  spot,
That was a foolish idea, wasn't
  it,
But you learn bit by bit.

I don't want to be lonely
  forever in a world that is
  stronger than I,
For that would make me cry.
in the future I will become
  strong,
And when that time comes I
  will know right from wrong.

Yvonne Humpal
TOO SHORT THE TIME

The stillness of night
Came early today
As the sun sank behind the
  cloud.

And the birds awing
Gave up their song
As the stream to the river
  bowed.

For April in May
And May soon is June,
My destiny therein shall lie;
For as much as we dream,
Too soon we shall find
That the days and our lives
  have gone by.

So cast away few
And live every one,
Make the most of all that may
  be,
That a full rich life
And a heart full of love
Are first what the world will
  see.

So love in the rain
And dance in the snow.
Make all the earth sing and
  shout.
Kiss me goodnight
And hold me to you
Until life's candle burns out.

Sharon L. Wolff
BUTTERFLY

Gentle butterfly,
With spots the color of coal
And wings like satin,
Glides slowly,
Dipping down to flowers
Like feathers drifting to the
  ground.

Patrick V. Foley
KISS

My love,
Gave to me
a kiss.
Yield did I
to her tender gift,
And found a moment—
Heaven blessed!

D. S. Oblinger
SUNSET . . .NOVEMBER

Sunsets that are sung
are red and gold on gilted
  strand
Or brilliant cloud pictures
hung above the trees.
I sang of these.

Now I sing of silver
breaking through the low
  cloud cover
at the horizon
Pouring over mountain height
and out across the land
as far as light can reach.

Each object in my room is
  silver
My hearth a silver stone
My page. My pen. My words.
The wind a silver song.

Paula Rhinehart Armstrong
FOR MY SON DAVID

My gift to life is asleep next
  door,
Working through dreamland
  like it is a chore.
He works so hard in his struggle
  with life;
I'd love to help take away all
  strife.
I seem to get harder as each day
  goes by,
Forgetting for a moment he
  must find out why.
I want to hold him forever in
  my arms
And keep him safe from all
  evil charms.

I know it'll hurt, but let go
  I must,
There's a fear inside me
  that never can bust.
So I'll be here always for
  him,
Never losing faith even if
  he doesn't win.
But he's a fighter and will know
  what to do,
Just know, my son, that I'll
  always love you.

Millicent Lynne Stokes
WHEN

When will those kind, and
  sometimes cruel,
lips touch mine,
with an unleashed passion
that could satisfy
the most intense desire.
And . . .
When will they whisper
the words, "I love you"
with a gentleness that could
  calm
the stormiest sea.
When will those deep, and
  unfanthomable,
eyes look at me,
with so much love
that they could outshine
the brightest star.
And . . .
When will they look
in mine to see all the love
I have for you.
When will those firm, and
  unyielding,
hands hold mine,
in a grip so binding
that it could only intensify
my love for you.
And . . .
When will they caress me
to ease away the pain
I have known from all the days
I spent wondering—When.

Rene McLane
**BOUND FOR THE BRINEY
BLUE**

The ships are in, full rigged and
  trim,
The spars are gleaming bright.
The crews are gay and sea
  array,
To meet the briny fight.

The mariner steady at the
  helm,
Awaits the sails' unfurl;
The mates and crews with ropes
  pulled taut,
Lean to the breezy swirl.

"Heave ho! my lads!" comes
  aft the call,
It runs the rigging through;
The sail ship quakes, it leaves
  the docks,
Bound for the Briney Blue.

Sail on, oh ship, at steady knots,
Ride high the rolling sea;
Hold fast you crew, you good
  mates too,
Safe ports aboud for thee.

Full speed ahead, port side we
  lean,
And we knife through waves of
  white;
Steer clear the rocks, the
  breaker's trap
That makes for seaman's plight.

Sail on, oh ship, behind us
  spreads,

The swirling waves in wake;
Both fore and aft we'll take
  our stands,
That duty bids us take

An even keel on every sea,
Our mates this training gave;
No anchors throwed, no
  hausers need,
Out on yon rolling wave.

"Heave ho! my lads", comes
  aft the call,
It runs the rigging through;
The sail ship quakes, it leaves
  the docks,
bound for the Briney Blue.

Betty Louise Denton
WEEPING

Mother's gone
She was so dear
Always so sweet
Ever so near

Mother's gone
I'm so alone
Will I always feel
This sadness I've felt
Since she's been gone

She's in her grave
She's just asleep
For my Dear Mother
I'll always weep.

Brett Robert Kangas
NIGHT LIFE

The sun softly fades
night comes on strong,
the moon makes her appearance
She shines the night long.

The stars sing their song
To the heavens and Earth
gathered this evening
rejoicing night's birth.

The lakes come alive
as the mayfly takes flight,
stilled by the day,
aroused by the night.

The moon with her charisma
draws the tide in,
They're helpless to fight
  her
servants to earth's spin.

The night's joyous noises
awaken the earth,
the stars bid farewell
a new day's begun.

Linda A. Quill
**IN ECSTACY OF ONE
ANOTHER**

Speak to me in pleasure's
  voice
And lay me in the dewy grass
Press your lips right on to
  mind
In secret consequence.

Lift your head to greet the
  sun
As it rises o'er the whitish
  forms
That labored inexhaustibly

through the night
In ecstacy's completeness.
Calm the body's trembling
heart
The throbbing pain of
pleasure
As blood pumps hard,
so deep inside
In love's explosion died.

B. J. Patrizi
THERE ARE SOME DAYS

There are some days—
of brilliant warm skin soaking
sunshine
when I see only the dark
foreboding curtain
of an impending storm stalking
the unsuspecting horizon,

the laughter of young
frolicking children
invades the privacy of my
singular silence
to hear only the devastating,
tortureous blast
of mortar shells dismembering
young men's bodies.

the delicate fleece of a black
velvet kitten
strokes the bristle on my
heaving naked chest
to feel only the taunt knotted
emptiness
of starving stomaches
suffocating neglected
unwanted children

the perfumed fragrance of
emerging rose buds
permeates the solemness of
my solitary vigil
to smell only the vulgar
oppressive stench
of fermenting garbage
decorating uncleansed alleys.

There are some days—
when the lonely
see themselves alone,
when the injured
hear their deformities,
when the hungry
taste their emptiness,
when the poor
smell their poverty.

When? Damn it—when will
these no longer be!

J. L. Hamblin
MISTY'S HER NAME

Have you ever felt someone's
presence,
But there isn't anyone near?
Someone that's with you always
to
help drive away your fear.
Someone that you know is
always
close to your heart.
Even if there isn't anyone who
believes
in her , they couldn't drive you
apart.
She's something very special
that

came from above.
She flew down to me like a
beautiful white dove.
She was sent to sit upon my
troubled shoulder.
To protect me through life
as I grew older.
Why she is still with me I'll
never know.
For as much as I have sinned
She should surely go.
With death I have had many
a close call.
But with her upon my
shoulder
I have survived them all.
Many people may call this
thing "luck"
But with my guardian angel
lies all my trust.

Evelyn M. Adams
MY SHEPHERD LEADS

When my life on earth is over
and my eyelids
close in death.
And my Shepherd leads me
through the valley to
that land of perfect health.
My heart will be rejoicing when
I reach that
heavenly shore.
For there I will see Jesus, the
one whom I adore.

When my eyelids close in death,
and my Father
calls me home,
And my shepherd leads me
through the valley, to that
land where pain and sorrow
are not known.
My loves ones will be there
to meet me when I reach
that heavenly shore.
I will sing praises to my Jesus,
the one whom I adore.

When my eyelids close in
death, in that sweet
by and by.
And my Shepherd leads me
through the valley to
that mansion in the sky.
Where the lamb is the light,
and where the angels sing.
I will worship Him upon
the throne, my Savior
and my King.

Frances P. Hothian
**A POEM TO MY SON ,
ROLAND**

My son is great in the eyes of
the Lord,
And the eyes of his mother,
too. .
My love for him is never ending
I find his likeness in few.

Timid in things close to him,
Quick to rush to a fellow in
need,
Sensitive to all personal remarks,
kind, cheerful and philantropic
his creed.

A ready smile, a warm hand
shake,
A greeting most sincere,
A love for people, old and young
is a part of his career.

His happy moments are in his
work
which continues day and night:
A speech to make in some far
town
Affords a nap in flight.
He is a lover of land, maps

and books,
An occasional love story too,
But his favorite game is Real
Estate
Both, owning and managing
a few.

He has a wife and three
children to cherish,
A home immaculately clean,
What more can I wish for
the son I love
Unless, "An Impossible Dream."

Renita L, Mosley
**I SAW DEATH WALKING
DOWN LIFE STREET**

He opened his mouth; I
shivered
as the coldness of his breath
Produced particles of ice
On my unprotected body.

His eyes were mirrored with
hate and envy
And once there were pupils
Rage, lust, and sin filled the
holes.

The savage wars of many nation
nations
Rested idly on his shoulders
And the blood of a thousand
warriors
Spreaded endlessly on his
back.

His feet left paths of
unearthly doom
As he crushed the lives of many
helpless victims
And those who tried to find
the way
Were stomped deeper into the
ground.

I ran to life's stoplight
As fast as I could
But death's destruction
Did not yield.

And I too never saw the sun
rise again . . .

Eddie M. Daniels Sr.
**EVERYTHING WILL BE
ALRIGHT AFTER TONIGHT**

You are everything I have ever
prayed for
Everything I have ever wanted
Now I know
Everything will be alright after
tonight
No need to fuss
Nor fight
Whatever we do will be alright
After tonight
I ask will we ever be together
You said yes forever
Forever seems so far away
Yet it's so near
But everything will be alright
After tonight
It's all up to us
Without all the fuss
Keep me in your heart
As I keep you in mine
Then we shall never be apart
Keep in mind everything will
be alright
After tonight
God will make a way
For you and me
As long as we keep our faith
There is no need
To see
What the cards hold for you or
me
Because
Everything will be alright
After tonight.

Margaret Alice Walsh
REACHING OUT

To reach out and touch
someone,
with your wisdom and with
your smile,
To give of yourself so
unselfishly,
To make another's life seem
worthwhile.
To sort out those mixed
emotions
and to put them all in place.
To help take that frown away,
and put a smile upon one's
face.
To be tactful enough to be
honest,
and yet caring enough to
trust,
To be strong enough to guide
someone,
but yet weak enough to feel;
All of these are qualities that
I see in you,
And one day I hope to be more
like you,
But with those qualities that you
have brought
out in me.

Carol Zola Rozzo
CONCEALED

tenderly you kiss me
yet fall deeply to sleep
is our lov dead
or just disguised as sleep

Richard Brobst
**ARTHUR, SHALL THE WINDS
OF MARCH FREE YOUR
SHIPS?**

Oh, the visions dance
platonic dreams
from his three quartered
blindness
finds him at the window's pane
staring out at the afternoon's
darkness
stepping barefoot through
the glass years
Oh, you visions dance for him
platonic dreams

From the bow of the greatest
Naval ships;
a young poet, beneath the stars,
his hair blew
back with the unharnessed
breeze
fused in mind with the seas
Magellan, Columbus all the
great men
whose world knew no end
no chains, no shackles beneath
the sky
he danced on the waves of
foam and mermaids
to find the answers others
dare not ask
until he was one with the land
and sea
and cooked for the hearts of
brave young men
pounding dough into cast
iron stoves
from a New York balcony,
Sweden and France
a master chef with ageless
hands
where men and ladies bowed
their heads
sweet wind in compliments
flowed
fragrance of feast through game
rooms touched
and the hearts of young women

in Sunday dresses
waited for a glance from his
   traveled eyes
he had seen so much yet, not
   enough.

From the later years
from the trade winds of Miami
from your window of the sea
turned balsa wood and glue
into majestic replicas
with your eyes
the lives of those lost
to the serpent
   Atlantic
and finished ships to families
   mantles
where great grand-children would
   study
the tiny men who hide in desks

should they ask
who was that man who built
   these ships?
why are they not in bottles?
Arthur, why are your ships
   not in bottles?
Is it something you saw from
   the bows
of your younger days. When
   illuminous sea fog
purred and nuzzled at the mast.
Perhaps a midnight lullaby
   of drunken sailors
perhaps, the chainless flight
   of rusted whalers

Step gently now, through
   those glass years
we will wait patiently outside
   your door
yet we cannot help but
   scream
Fight, fight the light of mental
   darkness
yet we cannot touch your
   mind
nor your visions
Dance, oh dance for him
   visions
platonic dreams.

Melissa Lennear
GOD I BELIEVE

G — Grant me patience my
      heavenly Father
O — Obey I will to thy wishes
D — Dare will I not question
      them

I — I believe in You.

B — Break me from my sinful
      habits
E — Eager, I am, to be your
      child
L — Love, I will give, to thy
      neighbor
I — Intend, I do, to follow your
      lead
E — Effort, I will put forth, to
      bring peace
V — Visualize, I will, a better
      world and
E — Eternal life for all.

Lillian M. Orincak
FAREWELL BEAUTIFUL ROCK SPRINGS

I can only imagine how beautiful
   you were brand new!
I'm just glad for my visits that
   were more than a few.
The delight of all, old and young
   alike is the merry-go-round.
With it's beautiful horses, seats
   and gay musical sound.
I'm glad it will be saved for
   others to see.
Perhaps in the Smithsonian

Institute in Washington, D. C.
Virginia Gardens could boast
   of big name bands of long ago.
How those musicians could make
   their horns blow.
Skaters enjoyed the beautiful
   smooth floor.
You could see their smiling
   faces as they whizzed by the
   door.
The plane ride was so very high.
In those two seaters, you flew
   in the sky!
To catch a fish and win a prize!
What delight shown in a child's
   eyes.
The Cyclone will be remembered
   as a wild ride.
Fright in the face of a new
   passenger was hard to hide.
A slow high ride did appeal,
For those who rode the Ferris
   Wheel.
If you aimed well and shot a
   target down.
You might win a little Kewpie
   Doll or a clown.
The dodgem cars one could
   drive so fast.
But many times your car came
   in last.
The fun house was spooky and
   dark.
To be in there alone was no lark.
Strange mirrors could make you
   fat, thin or tall.
A good time and a hearty laugh
   was had by all.
The many smells of good things
   to eat,
Was to the hungry, an enjoyable
   treat.
Under the cool shade trees all
   around the park
Were benches for us, and lights
   after dark.
One thing even more precious
   than gold,
Is the water from the spring so
   cold.
Our memories no one can buy
   or sell
Farewell Rock Springs Park,
   Farewell.

Giovanna Basandella
THE ROLLING STONE

The sun shimmers like gold dust
   tossed into the azure sky,
And the children laugh.
Away in the distance,
   surrounded by people,
There she sits, picking the
   flowers—
Surrounded by weeds.
Her yellow hair is dancing with
   the wind—surrounded by
   clouds—
Of smoke.
Her mind wanders, jumping from
   thought to thought,
All of them surrounded by wild
   colors and geometric figures.
An empty tear drop rolls down
   her face as she recollects her
   life—
Not fully lived—
And all the things she let touch
   her.
Like the pebbles on the beach
She and her little world play the
   game.
All the pebbles on the shore roll
   as far as they can,
Trying not to reach the waves.
But this pebble, burned by the
   sun, rolled too far,

And the wave caught it.
All the other pebbles stood and
   stared helplessly
As the stone sank to the bottom
   of . . .
   "Teenage Wasteland."

Vera Makaeff
DREAM

You crept into my dream—
   invading—
Laying your lips on mine
with kisses that I could count.
The soft tenderness and
complete assurance of love
My thoughts of happiness—
you will not leave me for this
   is the beginning.
Upon awakening—
The warm scent of your—body's
   existence—
Still lingers among my pillows.

Sylvia Nickerson
REINCARNATION

Once you stood
   tall and straight
   toppling over the rest;
Being the prince
   you were admired
   by all.
From everywhere they appeared
   to feast their eyes
   and gaze upon your beauty.
With beautiful lines
   you held your ground
   offering protection
   for others;
Providing a haven
   beneath those strong
   widespread arms.
Then burdens became too heavy;
You grew weak and old
   under the strain
   and you died.
God watched over you
   for so long,
Who will cherish you now?
It is I!
For in death
   you became reborn,
My old treasured
   pine rocking chair.

Marcia J. Neff
FRIENDS

When words of love are lost, and
   the feeling's no longer there
It's best to part as friends, cause
   friends will always care

To find a friend, and keep that
   friend, as long as life you have
to give. To share the happiness,
   sorrows and joys in life
Every day that you do live

Friends will help you out, in
   time of trouble they'll be there
Friends will stand by your side.
   Friends will always care.

Friends are people who need no

thanks, just by the look in
   their
eyes. And friends will always
   tell the truth, to them there
   are
no lies.

So if someday you find a special
   person who means a lot to you
Consider him a friend in life,
   in everything you do.

M. B. Kelling
REVERY

This still white night, star-lit and
   clear
Hails the Almighty's presence
   here
On earth to guide the hearts of
   men
Through a New Year and bring
Them comfort, solace and cheer.

Over snow-clad fields, mountains
   and cities
His spirit moves along,
His loving message shields
The suffering from their pain,
   and pities
Those who have not joined His
   throng.

Follow on! Until you too
   belong
To the faithful, patient, and
   kind,
For nothing in this world
Gives man such peace of heart
   and mind,
As the sight of God's banner
   unfurled.

Cathy Lipinski
SKY OVER THE LAKE AT NIGHT

Night begins,
A falling flame
Growing dimmer
Splashing into the
Rippling blue chiffon;
Clustered diamonds

And one lone pearl
Lifting themselves
And settling into their places
On infinite black satin.

Lyne Parsley
MEMORIES

The days have passed,
Memories, they are just
   flashbacks.
Of the days,
We once had.
But, now we must live the
   future,
And have memories once in
   awhile.
Yes, live today,
Look on tomorrow,
And think back of yesterday.

Carla Stephenson-Harvey
BLACK HISTORY—BLACK MYSTERY

February is the month they
   chose
To tell about Black History in
   prose
To educate American Blacks
On some of what our history
   lacks

To tell us of our contribution
To America and its institution
Things that aren't of current
   concern
Is that of what our children
   yearn
To know about our past indeed!

America, you must concede
To tell us some of what we've
done
As part of America's countrymen
American history we helped to
mold
But was always left untold
We helped in all the wars they
fought
But none of this was ever taught
We helped to cultivate the land
Yet still we were 'forgotten man'
We helped to build on many
roads
And carried all the heavy loads
Inventors we were of many
things
Of very few our history sings
Pilots, builders, teachers galore
Doctors, nurses, lawyers and
more
America, you did beguile
And yes, it slowed us down
awhile
But now alert, we want to know
Which way did history really go?
It's harder now to find the
history
So long America kept a mystery
Another century it will take
To dig up all that Blacks
contributed
But yet America thought it
great
To smother Black history and
not distribute it!

Jane Bomba Riordan
CHARLIE

Lighter than air
The image beaming radiantly
Mocking catches some
Only to crumble forever.
Distances of knowing
Impulses from the soul
Stillness only subsiding
I love you.

Ethel Vila
SON

Although the house is full,
It is empty.
A portion of my life departed
When you left.
Perhaps I didn't say it, but
I love you.
Somehow, I think you knew
How I felt.
You are my son, my baby, my
life,
I miss you.
More than I ever thought I
could,
I need you.
I'll count the days until I hear,
"Mom, I'm home."

Judy Johnson
ALONE AT DAWN

She squinted awake alone,
Through the sliding glass door
Even dew drops become one
While her own hands play in
her moist morning.
Sometimes nails straggle a
braless breast;
As before only a bumpy
moment
Pill granules leave a foggy mist
of night before
Settling on a nearly puckered
mouth,
Hands grasp empty bottles
Savoring the hardiness of its
neck,

That last comforting drop
Trickled; joined deep within a
warm-bloody throat;
Daybreak and darkness find
bottles only
Long and hard near her sucking
mouth.

Lathan H. Frayser
HOME IS WHERE YOU ARE

Home is where you are.
Whether in a mansion
Or a shack,
Whether in a city of teeming
crowds,
Or an obscure spot along a
railroad track.
Home is where you are.
There is no need for wealth that
must be guarded,
Treasures abound abundantly
in your smiles,
A million dollars would mean
nothing to me,
But to be with you, I'd walk a
million miles.
Home is where you are
And the making of the
memories you create:
My face embedded within the
soft texture of your
hair,
The tender grasp of your
hands . . .
With you, nothing can compare.
Home is where you are.

Linda M. Wallace
UNTITLED

Breezy memories
on a warm
afternoon
refresh the
closets
of my mind.

Suzanne Margrave
REFLECTION OF TWO

The earth was dampened by a
light, misty rain
Leaving a quietness that
enveloped all around.
Shadows played hide and seek,
only to wane,
And drops of rain glistened
upon the ground.
A peaceful feeling transfixed on
the souls
Of the two standing in a pool
of bliss
To each the other would
console
With caressive word and lingering
kiss.
Dusk faded and night arose
A lovely vision of two felt in
delight,
No other thoughts could impose
Upon the mood of two so quiet.

W. R. Goodman
MY JOURNEY

I walked one day with Pleasure,
We sang a lilting song,
But, at our parting, not a
measure
Remained to help my steps
along.
I walked one day with Sorrow,
The journey sad, and long,
But the faith she had for
tomorrow
Left me with a song!
I walked one day the road alone,
Or so I thought I did,

But soon God's love-light shone;
My sadness disappeared, and
hid.
I know I'll never walk alone,
For I can hold His hand,
And, when my burden seems a
stone,
On the Rock of Faith I'll stand!

Violet Rilkoff
LOVE PUPPET

Come pull my strings
and see me dance
only you could make me smile
without you
I don't stand a chance
I lay here crumpled
in a pile
just shove me far back
in a drawer
I lay here till you want to play
I wait in the darkness
no hope in store
helpless without you
here I stay
I hear you coming
up the walk
at last my heart leaps forth in
glee
you're bored again
you need to talk
come in my love
and play with me

Alan M. Beasley
MY BROTHER JOHN

I awoke this morning
Stretched
    And started yawning
Crawled out of bed
Just as the sun was dawning,
Ambling to the mirror
To wake my sleepy head
I heard a friend
I knew was dead,
He said hello
And I said goodbye
Now he's with his Lucy
Singing in the sky,
Putting on my happy face
To face the human race
I placed my sorrow
In my pocket
The left one to my locket,
As I walked out the door
I spied a beetle on the floor
It scudded beneath a rock
to hide
So I boarded a bus
With a ticket to ride,
Looked around at all the people
Where do they all come from
There was Harry, Dick and Tom
There was Patrick with a bomb,
I said hello
And they said goodbye
As I alighted from the bus
I went to heaven
Asking why?
There I heard my friend again
He wished for peace
Not sorrow or pain,
He gave me the courage
He took my doubt
United we can work it out.
Came down to earth with a
start
My brother John inside my
heart.

Chris Staples Brophy
A THOUGHT ON WORTH

The rain descends
In rhythmic patter
Hitting on glass
As wipers sway

Erasing the drops
So frail and small—
Sweeping them up
As fast as they fall.
And here am I
Driving along
An animate speck
On a dreary road
Moving down miles
Of winding wet—
Will it sweep me up?
Would I feel regret?
For what has worth?
And what does not?
When seeking alone
It's all so unclear . . .
Then suddenly
. . .there's light
And I see loving eyes—
And they give me the worth
That a cold world denies.

Vickie J. Glassburner
GOODBYE MY FRIEND

Every ending has a beginning
Filled with love and promises
Happiness in the beginning and
lonliness in the End.
That is why saying good-bye
is difficult.
But I am thankful that I
was given the chance
to share the relationship
we once knew.
No words could speak the
beauty that my eyes have seen
nor my heart has felt.
I am Grateful for the precious
memories that I shall always
keep
For every tear that had fallen
was a sunshine filled day.
When you left, you did not
take all.
For I have a special
feeling in my heart you
shared with me, that
will always bring back memories
and keep me thinking of you.

Stephen J. Torres
DEW

When you're old like me you
gaze out the window,
You sit there and think of times
when you were younger
And all the fun you used to
have, the laughing,
the playing, the dreaming of
tomorrow.
You're children all the joy
they gave you,
All the years.
The fond memories of Tommy's
black eye,
Susie's broken arm and how she
cried for weeks,
And yes, Ann's first date and
how you waited
Up for her to come home.
And the wedding days you
tried so hard to
Hold back those tears.
Now you sit gazing out the
windows waiting for
a long distance telephone call.
How the years go by so fast,
how my hair turned so gray.
How I buried my wife four
years ago and have never
Yet been to the grave.
And how my children all
grown up are never to come
home.

Here I sit looking out the
window at the sun
And not the rain . . .

Rosemary E. Helmer
SEPTEMBER MEMORIES

While driving through a
mountain pass
One late September day;
I saw a sight to thrill the soul,
It took my breath away!

One mountain side was
beautiful,
Most wondrous to behold!
Amongst the spruce and fir
and pine
Was a swathe of molten gold.

There grew a strang of aspen
trees
Like a great and glowing tide,
That flowed from crest, down
to the base
Of that great mountain side.

From palest gold to leaves
of flame,
Where aspen trees and sumac
blend;
I gazed in wonder at the sight
That heralded the summer's
end.

I felt as though the Master's
hand
Had painted scenes that were
divine.
And gratefully, I thank HIM
that
September memories are mine!

Gwendolyn C. Callaway
AUTOMYOGRAPHY

Perchance through vanity may I
One day with quip and quill,
Unveil the bust that is my life,
The granite of my will.

And with great subjectivity,
Leave markings of my stay,
In hopes that unlike most who
live,
Some heart or soul I'll sway.

But if I may express the view,
Such writings would prove
sham,
For how am I to write of me,
And know not who I am.

And if via men or history,
You learn not of my deeds,
Then what a waste of word
and wit,
My automyography.

Alice H. McCool
THE UNRAVELING

People running to and fro
Not knowing where they go;
Unrest evident everywhere,
Men's hearts failing for fear.

Earthquakes, fires, pestilence,
Devastation of much
consequence;
The earth erupting from within,
A world rampant with sin;

Murders, rapes and divorces,
Mounting daily beyond
proportions;
Wild animals roam the street
Seeking to devour whomever
they meet,

A portrait of gloom, no less,
Painted by Satan's request.
Ah! but fear not, dear ones.
The foe has been conquered
thru Jesus Christ the Son!

Dorothy Briu Crocker
THE STARS ARE TOUCHED

So many sounds await release
From galaxies beyond the
reach
Of mortal man. But oft the
stars
Are touched and songs
resound in space.

The gentle melodies of smiles,
a tear, or tender word of hope
Awakens an echo remotely
heard,
A sound of delicate, fragile
lace.

The sounds of all the universe
Communicate inaudibly
To ask if Love is ready now
To carry peace from place to
place.

Barbara Wirkows ki
JESUS AND ME

I was lost in this world of
darkness, and couldn't see a
thing.
I was so desperate, I was ready
to give up everything.
The path I walked, was with
struggle and despair,
And when I needed someone,
there was never no one there.
My heart cried out in lonliness
and pain,
I felt that everything was all
in vain,
My eyes had cried 'till they
couldn't cry no more,
And everywhere I went they
would always close the door.
I've walked that rugged road,
time and time again,
And I thought to myself, will
there ever be an end?
I felt like running wild you
see,
But what good would that be
doing me?
But then one day, Jesus came
into my life.
He took me by the hand and
took away the strife.
Now my life has been with
bliss, you see.
We worked together, Jesus
and me.

Marla J. Esser
ENCOUNTER

be not afraid
of this waking silence.
starlight melting into shadowed
gloom
follow in stride
through raging tranquility
streaming sunlight fades
beneath miles of horizon . . .
as each falling star
reflects the moon's gleam,
I see,

the dawn . . .
the dusk . . .
side by side.

Helen J. Shepard
LITTLE CHILDREN

God bless our little children
wherever they may be
Broken homes and most people
fail to see
They're confusion and wants
and how they care
Wishing Mommy and Daddy
would both be there.

People are so busy worrying
about themselves
They can't see the trials or
torments of the little elves.
Take time to love them and
explain the best you can
What sometimes happens
between women and men.

They will understand better
than you know
Even tho outwardly it does
not show
They are people too, need
assurance and love
Remember they were given
you from God above.

Lyndall Anne Carvell
RUNNING WITH FIRE

She smiled a sweet simple smile
from behind the ranancula's
orange pastel fire,
pressing it against her heart
icy slick;
causing my head to fill with
sticky yellow mucus, an
involuntary reaction to the
explicit monologue
on the nature of my disease;
The Doctor will be with you
in three-quarters of an hour.
But the fog has become too
thick,
he will never find me
wrapped up neatly, a package
under the Christmas tree,
my Father told me so;
he failed to mention
my Mother, tied in plastic tubes,
I met her twenty-four years
later
in a hotel room, traveling
together
she confessed her ignorance
leaving me the guilt;
And the Doctor is not in,
he grew too impatient
prodding me in the night
I vomited, a spoiled child
I smile back
at your burning flowers
I will steal, pulling
off their perfect petals
as I run.

Philip M. Weir
OUR LOVE

Our love for each other is not
going to pass
But the love we share is going
to last.
For the love we have, to us,
was given
From God our Father,
creator of earth and
heaven.
By reading God's word and
much time spent in prayer
God has led us together our
love to share.
Through troubles and trials we
have gone

And now we have seen the
Lord strengthen our bond.
Knowing that God's will,
will be done
Our love we unite, together
as one.

Grace F. Moore
OUR DEVOTED FRIENDS

Sometimes you can count them
Sometimes it's one or two
But without them I really
don't know
what ever I would do.

Friends from years back, lots
of friends
that's new
Friends that were our daughters,
when she was in school
Friends that all remember the
Golden Rule.

Friends that were next door
neighbors
long long ago,
All so very thoughtful now
Friends I'm sure that you all
know.

Friendship is like the beautiful
flowers
It grows and it blooms and
sometimes it showers.

Colleen A. Dolan
THE FACADE

The empty glances that she's
returned
mask hidden feelings she would
not learn.
The endless nights—curtains
of dawn.
All was a Facade, he was but
a pawn.

A pawn in a game that could
never end.
A friendship lost and a heart
won't mend.
The faces seemed different—yet
all were the same.
All was a Facade, it was but
a game.

But the game was over when he
saw through her face.
The stage was now set every
scene, every place.
Her heart came alive when she
saw him that day.
The Facade was broken. The
end of the play.

Karen Elizabeth Meditz
25 YEARS TOGETHER

Twenty-five years ago
two lives were joined together
as one
as two very special people were
wed.

A marriage that has—
seen life at its fullest—
the good times and the bad,
the laughter and the tears.

And through the years, this
marriage—
has shown just what caring,
sharing
and loving are all about.

And now twenty-five years later
here we stand—
Your children, now a part of
you,
who love and respect you so very
much
and who
at times may not show it,
but who do realize how very

thankful we should be—
for the gift God has blessed us
   with—
The gift of two very beautiful
   parents.
And in the same way that God
   has blessed us with this gift—
May He continue to bless
   the both of you—
Two lives joined together as one—
in happiness and in love—
   the two of you—
together—
Forever.

Kathi Schuster
THE SEASONS

I look at the trees so straight
   and tall
and watch their leaves as they
   begin to fall
their colors are orange gold
   and red
they're oh so beautiful yet
   oh so dead
the chill in the air comes with
   the night
and the frost on the window is
   a saddening sight
the summer is gone with all of
   its glory
but the beauty of fall unfolds
   a brand new story
flakes of snow will soon hit the
   ground
while you listen to the wind
   with its howling sound
the birds have left a long time
   ago
they could sense the arrival of
   the upcoming snow
don't dismay for whatever
   the reason
just enjoy the changing of
   each beautiful season!

Marla Joy-Veniegas
THE INNER VOICE

I bestow My boundless Love
In some token of harmony—
Subtly placed in mind or
   myth,
I share with you life's
   mystery.

Though I may disguise My
   Love
In some form or fashion—
Those who seek an inner path
Discover my Compassion.

Every form of giving,
Be it smile or carnation,
Will show you I am pouring
Life in loving invitation.

I will always love you,
In some sign you'll know—
In some moment when
   thoughts rest,
My Love will overflow.

Patricia M. Hatch
ARGUMENT

I smooth out the wrinkles
expressing disagreement;
there are no more chuckles.
I smooth out the wrinkles
from a print of sickles,
a course envelopment.
I smooth out the wrinkles
expressing disagreement.

Henry J. Mihalek, Jr.
A PSALM

What is this life, Oh Lord:
It is the pride of God;
The sorrow of Our Lord.
We count as nothing unto you,

Of man is your glory measured.
I cannot comprehend the
   majesty
of Your name; who made the
little things and built the mighty
works. Unworthy is our name,
   yet
We are next to God in wonder;
Our place is above the angels.
My heart is dark, and troubled
   Lord;
I do not know the workings of
   my mind.
My strength is like the puddle
   before the
hot sun; my faithfulness is like
   the
sapling before the strong gale.
Your way is good; Your road is
   easy.
Too often do I stray; too soon
   I leave
the path. As a child is drawn
   away by
bright and shiny toys, so too
   am I;
As a child cries in the night and
   is
found, so too am I. To wander
   is
my lot; those who know the
   Lord
can never be lost.
I am but a man; that is all you
   would
have me be. So many things to
   know, of one
we can be sure. It is all we need
   to know,
for You have said it is so.

Henry M. Grouten
MEMORIES

Your warm letters,
   Precious thoughts,
Once a pleasure
   Now have perished.

Seeds of happiness
   Grown to heartbreak;
This internal wound
   Will always bleed.

Your soft touch,
   Loving memories,
Now a treasure
   To be cherished.

David Michael Wade
CRUDE AND PRUDE

You say I'm crude,
I say you're prude,
And no one wud be sued,
But especially wooed,
With food for thought,
You standing there nude,
Thinking only about being
   unhesitatingly lewd,
Forgetting about rude,
Concentrating on mood—
   mood, mood, mood.
But who am I kidding?

Marilou C. Chanrasmi
TOO LATE

Losing me: you saw sunset
   as i in fear . . . and
         frustration—
   Held back.
Shining behind a cloud, you
   couldn't
   reach me . . . then, came
Rain.
Rain touched,
   but never soaked me;
   it asked for no change.

It took a tornado and total
   destruction
      for me to see.
A dying light in darkness, i was
   . . . too late.
And now, all that's left of you
   is a speck of dust in a world
      of nothing,
   while i, a nothing in a world
      of dust.

Lana Kay Lyon
MY TEEN AGE DREAM

I've liked a lot of people but
   only loved
   just one
There you were, my teen-age
   dream
my light my morning sun.
You were something special
   and you meant
a lot to me
But dreams don't last forever
   like I
thought they would for me.
So I'll live my life without you
   and
forget about love's pains
I'll go on like I never knew you
You were just a teen-age dream.

Michael Frank
TRIBUTE

Just a hard day's night,
Ono heard the cry,
Hello. Goodbye.
No more strawberry fields
   forever.
Living isn't easy
Eyes can plainly see.
No reason to die.
Now the days have gone by.
Of every head he's had the
   pleasure to know,
Nothing remains but a silent,
   long and winding road.

Pamela K. Hogue
CHILD OF THE WEST WIND

A silent summer's evening
Spent in adoration of life;
Relaxing with the peace
And tranquility of time.
Then, a gentle stirring
Begins in the treetops
And filters down toward earth,
Growing in strength with each
   passing second.
Within my soul, a kindred
   stirring
Begins and grows to full flower.
It is the answering call
From the child to its parent, the
   West Wind.
My soul cries out, and begs
   freedom
To join the spirit world.
The West Wind answers, urging
   patience
And reminding me that my
   time has not yet come.

Slowly, ever so slowly, the spirit
   leaves
To claim its other children
   whose time has arrived.
Inside, my soul stirs one final
   time,
Bidding adieu to the parent who
   rarely visits.
Calmness reigns supreme once
   more in my being
And once again, the child of the
   West Wind sleeps.

Mary Hare Megargee
MODERN SUBURBIA

Columbus was wrong. The
   world's not round it's flat
Flat squares of crabgrass with
   little look-alike houses all in
      a row
Their flat rooves crushing out
   the spirit of man.
Flat miles of cement leading
   from nowhere to nowhere.
Only the mind of man is
   round, and goes round and
      round,
Round like a cipher—Round
   like a zero.

Ethel M. Winslow
SHOGUN

Jasmine whispers
Wander the garden
In fingers of
Geisha breath;
Stirring the
Sake sated samurai
To his final
Honorable act of
Moonlit
Seppuku.

Kelly Anne Sullivan
THE WORLD SPINS ROUND

The world spins round and
   round
And still I wonder where I'm
   bound
I walk beneath the starlit sky
Deep in thought and wondering
   why
We always used to share so much
Now I'm lucky if we even touch
Why can't it be the way it used
   to be
Why have you gone and set me
   free
In my eyes I see no one else but
   you
Can't we start over and start
   somewhere new.

Catherine Bishop Bilbo
A SHADOW

"What's a shadow, Ma?" he
   asked,
As one across my path he cast.
"A shadow, son, is what is not.
But if it is,
It's not as hot
As it would be
If it was not!"

Barry P. Schmidt
NEW YORK CITY, NEW YORK

snowcones and paper dragons
are a far cry
from the Wall Street madness
Madison Avenue declared war
   on 42nd Street
Avenue of the Americas
seceded from the Union
Lady Liberty keeps a watchful
   eye
o'er the V'narrows

clutching desperately to the
telephone directory
never needing the yellow pages
except for making
paper airplanes
keeping careful count of passing
Volkswagens
and departing sparrows

yesterday an old man
with whiskey breath and
countless friends
carefully selected his tombstone
smiling with contentment
as he lay in the gutter
in front of the Empire State
Building
and died
no one
was
concerned

today the sun seemed sad
as it peered through the layers
of smoke and haze
bringing tears to people's eyes
tomorrow i'll crawl to
the George Washington Bridge
and place a sign across the
east bound lane
saying
CLOSED

Cherie Harclerode
COMFORT

The ocean is my friend . . .
She calms my nerves . . .
Slows down my rush . . .
I can be still when I'm with her.

I go running to her side . . .
When I'm in pain . . .
Or feeling lost . . .
She makes everything feel all
right again.

I watch her ebb and flow . . .
She's always there . . .
No matter what . . .
She never lets me down.

Todd Jordan Peterson
IN MATURITY

As the swallow flies
Over the southbound streams
Of falling fortunes;

As life seeps
Down the trunks
Of freezing masters;

As water freezes a shield
To repel the cold sunlight
Of the dying morning;

The crossbill twitters
From the corridors of
statesmen
Whose needles pierce the
frozen patchwork.

The melting water threads its
way from death
To nourish diminishing life:
They grow forward.

Ruth K. Penny Cameron
TIME

"What is time?" Inquired the
boy at the old man's knee.
"Time? . . . time!" Though
the old man, remembered
when he was
a boy at his father's knee.
Now wrinkled hands and
furrowed brow, the weary
long days
behind the plow.
"Time? seems funny somehow."
as he thought back now, to
the days
he thought would never pass.
To the years when Rover was

just a pup, and he was
anxious to
grow up.
The summer vacation and long
school days seemed to be
only in
a distant haze.
Old Rover's been gone for a
number of years and here am
I,
Lived through the years and
tears of time.
Time? . . . Time!
What has it been? Daylight
and darkness and me within.
Now here sits another time at
my knee, asking what is time.
How does one answer? How
can it be?
How can one tell him that
time is in his heart and hands
alone?
Now time has gone for both
of them.
And here am I alone, while
time goes on and on.

Trisha Peters
SHATTERED DREAM

He never skied a mountain slope
and felt the wind upon his face.
He never soared like a bird
through space.
He always said to me with a
smile upon his face;
"Gonna surf around the World
Ma,
feel the ocean spray upon my
face.
Gonna do all the things I've read
about,
want to see all of Nature's
Ways."

He went away one summer day
with a smile upon his face.
He said, "Don't worry Ma,
there's nothing I can't face."
I wanted to shout, "Don't do it
Son!
Don't sacrifice your life!
Don't be torn between what
you think
is right, and the Freedom born
into your life."
War is Hell and the Dead can't
Tell!
Now my heart is cold as ice.
Eighteen years old in a grave so
cold,
in a land of hate and strife.
Now as the days roll into Months,
to Years,
and I gaze out at the sea;
As the ocean roars with its
mighty waves
I hear his voice inside of me;
"Gonna surf around the World
Ma,
feel the ocean spray upon my
face.
Gonna ski the highest mountain
Ma,
and soar like a bird through
space."

Sue Bagley
ENDINGS

Today, I saw my lawyer, he
listed
my demands,
The fragments of my life, all
legal
black and white.
I'll take the kids, you'll take the
bills,
How deceptively simple it

sounds.
But, who'll take the love that
once
filled our lives?
Who'll bury our yesterdays?
Who'll clean up love's refuse
that
we leave behind?
Who'll cry our unshed tears?
For, tomorrow, like our
memories,
we must start anew,
scarred, dejected and embittered
but free to love once more.

Sarah La Presle
LOVE IS MAGIC

Love is magic I've been told
—and it's only for those who
believe.
Yet, I believe, and still I wait,
for someone who can spin my
thoughts to reality
and who can bring magic to my
heart.
And, like the Magician's
assistant,
I am only part of a team.
I'm waiting for someone to be
that magician,
someone who can perform that
magic called Love.

Vila Keller
**EVERYWHERE SOMETHING
SINGS**

Life's cycle in spring begins
the real mystery of birth again.
As the young bend with the
wind,
everywhere I hear something
sing.

Life's space is filled
with squirrels and trees,
with birds and bees.
Everywhere something sings.

Life's force is strong.
As different faces appear,
across the bridge of time.
The sun continues to climb.

Life's colors slowly change.
As the moon holds off the
darkness,
Stars are suspended in the sky
Obscured by clouds passing by.
Life's darkness hides many
things,
But not the hoot of an owl,
or the lonesome coyote's howl.
Everywhere something sings.

Anne Berghoff
LOVE

Oh, those sparkling eyes
dazzle me so;
And that smile of yours
forever glows.

I give you my love that will last
forever,
A love that time cannot
destroy,
It can't stop as long as we're
together,
A love like this can only bring
joy.

Thelma Jo Bowling
CROWN OF FEATHERS

A little crown of feathers,
A picture at one year,
Are all the things I have left
Of one I loved so dear.

Just two short years was all he
had
Then he was called away.

My memory walks in every place
Where he was known to play.

Beneath the stairway is his
horse
He rode him many a day
Across a field of lush green
grass
Beneath that tree to play.

The little teddy bear he loved
His cheeks seem somehow wet
As if the things he knew and
loved
Never will forget.

He lay upon his bed of pain
For only three short days
But left the imprint of his head
In the pillow on which he lay.

My friends say it's an omen
They say, to a heart so cold
Your baby traded feathers
To wear a crown of gold.

Paris Salvatore Dalto
PROFUNDITY

. . . and a man's mind
thinks many things,
in so short a life;
And the things he thinks—
are good if,—
when good, he seeks to find . . .

Linda Kay Fenner
THE CANDY SHOP

Come over to the candy shop,
You'll find it very nice;
Where cotton candy puffs like
clouds,
And rock candy sparkles like
ice.
Where gumdrops fill up every
box,
And lollipops every jar;
And licorice whips are kept
beside
Each giant chocolate bar.
There are cakes lined in the
window,
And pastries filled with cream;
The children stand and looked
inside,
And dream every possible dream.
They dream of swimming in
lemonade pools,
And sailing in chocolate boats;
And they sweep the decks with
licorice sticks,
And pails full of ice cream floats.
And they sail away on a sea of
dreams,
With cotton candy clouds above;
Not one bad thought enters any
kid's mind,
For their dreams are dreamed
with love.
So come to that magical,
wondrous place,
Where all the the children stop;
Where dreams fill the shelves
and love fills the hearts,
The beautiful candy shop.

Beverly Mather
YOUR TOUCH

Your touch has words
That speaks to me.
It tells me how, Oh!
So gentle you can be.
As you reach out with
A gentle caressing hand
To guide me through a door
In front of which I stand.

Your touch has words
That speaks to me
It tells me how kind
You can always be.
As you reach out
With your gentle touch
To brush away a tear
To soften the hurt
Of someone I hold near.

Your touch has words
That speaks to me
As you reach out your arms
To hold me so close
Of a gentle caress
As you hold me so tight
Of an unspoken love
As you whisper, , ,
  Goodnight.

K. Cousin
NOTHINGNESS

there was the deep
  purple sea,
the brightness in
  the sky,
shadowed by the
  fluffy clouds
the scene that caught
  my eye.
nothing on the
  horizon
only the sea meeting
  the sky
no one at all
  around,
just this nothingness
  and I.

Denise E. Hopkins
FROM A DISTANCE

I watch you from a distance.
You don't know I'm there.
You know not of my existence,
Or how very much I care.
I wish I could talk with you,
To find out all I can.
In my life I swear it's true,
I've never seen such a man.
I think about you every minute,
I don't know why I do.
Each second of my life you're
  in it,
And I don't even know you.
I want to find out who you are,
And why I feel this way.
To me you are a shining star,
Even on a sunny day.
How can my feelings be so strong
For someone I don't know.
How will I ever get along,
Should they continue to grow.
I hope there will come a day
When you and I will talk.
When you would look at me
  and say,
"Come, Friend, let's take a walk
  walk."
On that very special day, there
  could never be,
A happier person, none happier
  than me!

Mary E. White
PERFUME OF THE EARTH

perfume of the earth,
perfume from your loins:
i seek you/i seek to know

your essence,
for my heart, caught in that
  vast
ocean, seeks its harbor
against your smooth, wet shore.
i seek to open you
to our joining.
i seek to warm myself
in the fire of your nights.
i seek to behold
the glow from your dark source,
drawing from it strength and
  love,
replenishing it with love and
  strength.
these words, like the tenderest
fingertips, seek you out,
reaching inside
to stir your dance
in that great ballet of love.
perfume of the earth,
perfume from your loins.

Ruth Wright
MALIBU WEST

The majesty and grandeur of the
  sunset
On the shore
Makes long dark hours forgotten
Like a glimpse through heaven's
  door,
The golden ball glides slowly,
  changing
Azure sky to gray,
Somewhat as a shy maiden hid
  behind a misty veil
Her pale orange form in roseate
  surround
Hangs o'er the dark gray sea
Whose color, deepened from the
  day's cool green
Now shows a darker hue,
The rainbow fades, night's
  curtain falls
And through half-closed eyes
  we watch
Our golden beauty leave,
One final gleam, and we are then
  bereft.

Marian G. Voelker
THIS MOMENT IS MINE

The humid night air drifts
  through my window.
The candle flame dances softly.
The crickets sound off in mass
  confusion.
Birds stir in the tree tops lofty.
Fireflies blink in scattered
  disarray.
Tree limbs bow gently to the
  ground.
Stars twinkle and send forth
  their rays of light.
The moon has not yet become
  round.
The city lights and noise are
  far away.
No human voices do I hear.
The cows and sheep graze in
  the meadow grass.

Two fuzzy kittens doze so near.
Although the hands of time
  move on unchecked
As down the path of life I trod,
I will cherish this moment
  forever.
Tonight belongs to me, from
  God.

Barbra R. Tucker
THE THIN WALL

A thin wall
Stands
Between life and death.
Souls who pierce
Its pliant
Transparency
Find the wall
Transformed
Into dense
Solitidy.
All who yield
To the lure
Of its crystalline
Brilliance
May never return.
And the thin wall
Remains,
Waiting to lufe
The next unwary soul
Who would step through
And temporarily explore
Eternity.

Pamela D. Hatt
MY ETERNAL FLAME

I sit watching the flame of
  the candle flicker,
My soul so full of mixed feelings.
The shadows dancing on the
  wall, like a flower dancing in
  the rain.
Oh, how I long to be held
Held out of love
And how I long to hold, and
  to say I love you.
A wind blows ending the flames
  life,
But I can not blame the wind
  for blowing out my own.
I dream for a somebody,
A somebody to love.
To trust,
To care for.
And I think and I feel that this
  somebody may never enter my
  world.
And it is this thought that scares
  me.
It is this thought that makes me
  want to blow out my life, like
  the flames.
But I do not.
For if I did, I would not be here
  when he came.

Marguerite Mooney
CONTEMPLATION

In a golden trance I sit, to watch
  and dream
As flocks of crows soar high in
  aimless flight
Like blackened paper from a
  dying fire,
And I know my happy summer
  days have passed.
I wander o'er the hill to the
  gurgling stream
Where foam whipped by the
  autumn breeze
Spins out like the white whisp
  whiskers of yonder goat
That rigid stands and dreams
  of pastures fair.
A carpet of fallen leaves lay amid
  the trees,

Velvety soft in sober tones of
  amber, red and green.
The robins toss their faded
  bodies into the teeth of
  the wind
And trill a song of sad farewell
  to summer scenes.
The evening's lengthening
  shadows, move with quiet
  stealth
To encircle the ever playful
  summer clouds,
But my lazy sun-dappled days
  shall return again,
When earth awakes and yellow-
  breasted meadowlarks
  proclaim tis spring.

Henry M. Grouten
SISTER

In a matter of days
  not gone too
  long
his heart was breaking,
  slowly aching,
  without
the pain showing,
  or anyone knowing
  he missed
  her.
The absence of one
  having been so
  close
saddened his face
  in this strange
  place,
with tears flowing,
  after years of
  growing
and sharing with his
  sister.

Lawrence Spirio
THE WOUNDS OF LOVE

I listened to the bellowing waves
  that rushed up to the shore,
I heard the howling evening
  winds
  bring forth the oceans roar.
The wind slapped my face and
  body,
  the water numbed my soul,
I cared not whether I lived or
  died,
  no ambitions, no wants, no
  goal.
The tide tossed me to and fro,
  the rains began to pour,
then in its anger 'gainst the
  storm,
  it threw me to the shore.
I lay exhausted, alone and
  weary,
  weary of soul, weary of mind.
weary and desolate, all alone
  with the pains I left behind.
I lay on the cool white sand,
  daring to lie reposed,
my heart bled the wounds of
  love
  and with the storm I dozed.

Patricia Ann Cummings
MY CHILD

  The whispering of the wind
blows softly through your hair.
  my child,
You know not of the world,
  but someday you'll find
life's more than what you see.
  If life—you find—
  you do not understand
  do not give up
for life has just begun.
  Be not blind,
  my child,

for blindness
is unworthy of you;
but see instead.
For if you see
with your heart
and not just your eyes,
you'll find a world
so beautiful
it cannot be denied.
And if you look
and do not see
take time to find
what life can really
mean!

Elizabeth Brooks
NEW LIFE

The joy and happiness, the
excitement of New Life.
The rushing of the nurses,
everyone about working
so diligently; for it is your labor
of love and may
you always have divine guidance
from above.

The skillful hands of the doctors,
so calm and so
sturdy, guided by a silent helper.
The spanking of
the bottoms and at last a cry is
heard. It is the
cry of a tiny baby kicking and
fighting its way
into the world, taking hold of
its rightful place.

The little fist clenched so very
tight, just lying
there so helpless, so beautiful
but yet so full of
life.

Now it's time for a little sleep,
a little slumber,
a little curling of the fingers,
a little yawning and
the crumpling of the toes, a
little smile and
the twinkling of the eyes.

Best my little dear ones for an
abundance of peace
is upon you.

Sweet dreams be unto you and
may the angels watch
over you forever.

Angel Marie Duty
UNTITLED

Lord,
I think we've all
gotten completely
out of touch.
Caught up
in the hustle and bustle
and fuss with so much.
perhaps
we need less.
That's how it all began.
We never
go to a quiet corner
and think,
from whence

it all began.
Dirt.
and
to it
We all must return.

Jacquline Stone Waltz
SLEEP WELL CHILD OF MINE

Sleep well my loved and lovely
child let your slumbers bring
good dreams with no nightmares
to bring stress to your
young innocent mind.

For soon life will take you by
the hand and lead you on
to a new and different life.

My love will go with you and
watch over you. Whatever
road of life you choose to
take loved and lovely
child, as I look at the elfin face
on your pillow; so at
peace with the world your
small protected world here in
my
loving care.

May never you find the wrong
road, may you take the good
and stay sweet and lovely as
now my child. When that time
comes when you are led into
the world face it brave and
with
a smile, never let life take love
and laughter out of your
heart loved and lovely child.

Meet it with humane fortitude.
Sleep well loved and lovely
child, may the peace of the
world stay with you forever.

Grace Waltz Fry
**DEVOTION OF A MOTHER
(MINE)**

Oh! how you raptured in the
aura of divine givingness,
Never
to falter in time of woe or
need always with an over
abundance
of love, you spread your
outstretched wings for
protection
from harm.

Never to give in no matter your
dismay your smile was always
there to brighten the way you
lived within or even for.

The birds have flown, your all
alone, the nest so full is now
so bare your wings still spread
the span too far to reach
each one.

Your weary now so bring them
in your nest again   if only
in your heart and rest those
hovering wings if only for
awhile.

Larry Gene Indra
AS THE DAY DIES

The night air chill embraces me,
as the sun becomes an orange
ball of flames.
The beach is deserted for the
most part.
Most of the people have gone
home.
The sky is orange with the sun's
glow.
It has now stopped for a moment
on the water's edge,
as it slowly gives into the great
ocean.
The sky darkens, a few birds

fly in front of the dying sun.
They appear black against the
orange sky.
The sun now is half gone.
In only a fwe minutes there
will be no sun.
you can barely see the orange
ball.
The horizon has become a
beautiful rainbow.
Finally all that is left is a bright
gold line on the horizon.
The night has once again won.
It creeps into my world, making
my world cold and dark.
I will sit here, waiting for the
sunrise to warm my world,
so I may see once more this
beautiful world that surrounds
me.

D. A. Dawn Prince
CHESTER COUNTY DAY

We bought tickets,
Waited in line,
Saw restored houses and
churches
of local merit.

The past floated by;
But, the now came alive
In a low ceiling room
With five busy, robust women,
Each donning a pretty bonnet.

One called out:
Dear folks of the touring group
Step over here
For home-made chicken soup.

And support our cause—
A new kitchen
for the parish hall.

Cheryl Butler
THE THINGS I VALUE MOST

The things I value most. .
The hours we share
The thrill I feel, by loving you
And knowing you care

Our special plans—our private
jokes
The things you say and do to
make days more fun—
These are the things I value most.
And you're a part of it all.
You make my days and nights
Just a little more special.

But most of all, I value the love
we share
And the way you make me feel.

Karen J. Birk
MOVING ON

Fly. . .
To a place far away
where challenge and uncertainty
await you.
Circle above. . .
Take one last look.
Remember the time gone by.
Cry if you feel. . .
Laugh now and then.
Memories it now must be.
Now,
take your place in the sky.
Don't look back!
This place will soon disappear
From view.
Faces will blur. . .
Names forgotten.
It takes up but a second of your
life.
That second
enriches your soul with
friendships
never to be replaced
except by those who can't
accept
the gift of love from others.

Mary M. Stumreiter
FRIENDS

Friends old and new
Friends tried and true.
Friends made by pen and ink
Friends who make you stop
and think,
Friends who relate in sorrow
Hoping a longer life to borrow.
Friends who are near in distress
Friends who really have no
address,
Friends who often call to say,
"Hello, and have a happy day!"
Friends who wear a different
face
At any time or any place.
Yet, our greatest friend of all
Is God, who never spurns our
call.

Edward J. Jones, Sr.
**ON THE LOVE OF LITTLE
ANIMALS**

What is it about my little cat
that seems to say to me,

"He who cares for you, no
matter what,
has also cared for me."

"I feel so touched of my
Father's love
when you stoop carressingly."

"You lift me high, as the dove,
as you hold me tenderly."

"It's for his sake as well as mine,
You cherish me as you do."

"You've stroked the fur of my
kittinish mane,
and my face and body too."

"And each thing you've done,
you've said to God
just what he's said to me."

"I am loving you with all things
good
that I've chosen specially."

"My kitten shows My love for
man;
His love for her is for me."

Dolores Alonso Tonelson
CONSIDERATION

She asked only consideration,
Not wealth or heroic deeds or
selfless devotion,
Only a ring on the phone
To say he was delayed,
A compliment on his favorite
souffle,
One "How do you feel?" when
life lowered her mood,
To be consulted before decisions
Marched forth to action,
A complete message when her
best friend called;
She asked only for drops of
water,
Not a waterfall.
She asked only consideration
The one thing he couldn't give
at all.

Bruce Thorpe Caldwell
LOVE'S REALITY

Hallways
Being what they were,
Reminded me of love dreams,
Which expressed themselves
Via High School .
But, I am beyond my thoughts.
I have a tangible dream.
I also have a hallway,
And my love is real.

Twas but youth ago,
that I practiced my desires
As an actor.

Now,
I express my feelings in a
  hallway
which harbors life,
To which I share the secret of
  life.
That secret is but the love
Which was meant for my
  beloved,
Whom,
Living within my eternal heart
  now,
Has time to touch me in this
  world.
Though I may vanquish my
  reality
For but awhile.
I am blessed to hold within
  my arms
At this very moment
The long sought after
Woman of my being.

Miss Sharon Arbuckle
ANGER
the raging force; we have inside
  makes others quake and
fear within;
makes flame burst before our
  eyes and
foundation of creations shake
  from fear and surprise;
How can we quiet this raging
  beast may our prayers
cause it to cease and make us
  find peace. Epoiloge.

Susan Bauer Johnson
ENTER SUNLIGHT
Sunlight.
A breeze has taken me in her
  arms
And torridly teases my hair.
Butterflies, clumsy, foolish with
  airs
Hangglide lazily over my head.
A snake
Thinks to trick me
As he curls wickedly around
  some brush.
Fragile stalks
Shudder senuously,
Their frailness laid naked in the
  sun.
Young clover blushes in the
  sweltering heat.
Nature
Laid barren.
It's purity questioned by the sun.

Mary J. Grant
MY DAD
As I travel the road to true
  happiness,
I thank God that I've been
  blessed,
By having a Dad I could walk by
  with pride,
It was always a joy to have you
  by my side.

I'm proud of you Dad, and
  mother too.
I could my blessings each day
  anew,
Just knowing I have parents
  like you.
You gave me character, courage
  and inspiration,
You're the best Dad in all
  creation!
I hope your day is especially
  happy
and in appreciation
We're going to have a real
  celebration!
I love you dear,
And I'm glad
That God gave me You
  For my Dad!

Pamela Prout
GRADUATION DAY
We have waited so long for this
  day,
The worry, the toil, the
  forgotten play.
Familiar figures looking over
  our shoulder;
Mentors and friends making us
  bolder.
Donning the robe of
  accomplishment,
We reflect energies that were
  spent.
Honors and dishonors we march
  along
To face an old yet unknown
  song.
The glow of the moment, short
  as it is,
Will find us in the morning
  without bliss.

J. Milton Halliday
FOR YOU AND ME
Someday when sunbeams dance
  and shake
  On rounded stones where
  ripples break—
The winds will whisper tenderly
  As once they called for you
  and me.
The winding path that skirts
  the shore
  Will recreate those steps of
  yore—
As lillies on the nearby lea
  All sweetly bloom for you
  and me.
And osiers that gently sway
  Will mimic clouds. . .like
  lambs at play—
As once again in memory
  God's hills stand watch for
  you and me.
Then. . .hours, beyond the veil
  of Time,
  May masquerade in wisps of
  rhyme—
And echo from Eternity
  What once was real for you
  and me.

Frieda Cartwright
DAY IS DONE
An old man sits—on his porch
  in the evening
Savoring the last rays of the
  setting sun.
He slowly rises—as the night
  comes on
And mumbles this sad phrase
  "Day is Done."
He goes slowly into the empty
  room of a house

Once filled with laughter and
  fun.
No one there to hear him now
As he says again and again
  "Day is done--Day is done."
He goes at last to his lonely bed
Where visions of happier days
Floated through his head.
He speaks to the silence
His words hang in the air.
No one to hear him
No one to care.
Life's purpose is over
My race is run.
I'm ready to rest now
  "My day is done."

Michael E. Arnett
SWEET IS THE NIGHT
Sweet, sweet is the night
Now you are near
Dark, dark were the days
Now they just disappear
Moon glow, come light
The way up to my window
As you roll across the night
Casting shadows on my
  bedroom door
I was starin' into the skies
Seeing only starlit secrets
With the lunar twinkle in my
  eyes
Wishing only for mystical treats
I wonder what mysteries lie
  ahead
Waiting patiently, watching
  endlessly
Stars climbing higher, seeing
  everything
Escalating, slowly spiraling.
Such a joyous occasion,
There's no reason to doubt
Stars radiate their luster
Both inside and out.

Shelleigh Betz
DAY'S DAWNING
The dawn glowing soft and
  radiant
is pre-empted by an April
  storm,
tearing the sunrise to shreds of
  light
filtered through the rainwashed
  clouds
forming a spectacular sight.
Watery colors fill the sky
until the sun ceases to shine
and the rainbow melts and
  melds
With the pot of gold at its end.

Nelson L. Smith
MESA MIRAGE
I can see the arid desert, in my
  mind—
Hot, stinging sand; dry, parched
  wind
And sticky sweat, clinging to
  your chest;
  —And, I find;
That long ago, Man withstood
  Nature
And fought against the element
  elements—to win;
And, he learned to survive (and
  was glad to be alive!)
  —Despite the dry, hot, stinging,
  scorching sands!
We are so dependent on our
  Machinery today—
That our peoples would famish,
  without them!

But, the Old-timers lived by the
  sweat of their brow;
  —And managed to get by,
  without them!
I look out across the Mesa, and
  I can 'see'—
The herds of Buffalo—now
  vanished—thundering by!
We may live now by the means,
  of giant industrial Machines;
  —But the Wild Buffalo has
  vanished, into the sky!
Our nation has lost; and, it
  has been a terrible Cost—
And, common sense has eroded
  down the drain!
But, the Old-timers tried—and,
  under a scorching Sun, died—
  —But, his generation will
  never share the blame!

Patricia W. Minter
MOTHER
If I were an artist I would paint
  her beauty
Her beauty is manifold;
Tenderness should be her name.
Ever present is her smil
Ever present is the sun of her
  smile.
Abundant is her willingness to
  forgive.
She is humble to a fault.
Her love for humanity shows
  through her respect for all life.
Her life is the summit her her
  moral consciousness,
Yet she does not judge others
  by self-comparison
She believes in God and the
  power of prayer
Through all her encounters, she
  knows that He is there.
Freely she gives of herself
Time after time.
She is precious and priceless,
  Sweet mother of mine.

Hilda J. Knowles
TO SAM, A BOXER DOG
You lie beneath the Norway
  spruce
Where every day you made a
  truce
With summer heat, a bed you
  made
secluded in the sheltered shade.
Next to a bush which made a
  bower
Of yellow blossoms like shower.
Years made your bed a quilt
  of grass
I see you every time I pass.

Evelyn J. Thornbrue
DAVY, OUR HERO
Davy's hyperactive (my little
  grandson)
But Grammy tames him down,
  "Davy, sit down here for fun,
And Grammy will tell you a
  story
  bout a big brown bear
Who lives up in our big tall
  woods
His fear is everywhere.
Now he was mighty ferocious,
  a tall and ugly beast
And he raided all our ranches
  and ate our calf Saltee;
So Davy got on Dundy
  (our mighty quarterhorse)
And struck out for those big
  tall woods
To kill that bear with force.
It only took one bullet

triggered out with Davy's hand
To hit that bear right in the
heart
And drop him where he stands.
Davy tied him onto Dundy
(our mighty quarterhorse)
And packed him home to
Show and Tell
And that's the end of course."

Keturah W. Wood
UNTITLED

Gray waters rising
Under mountains lost in mist;
A foghorn blowing.

Jo Ann L. Tienken
THE VICTORY

Little soldier wherever you are
Lead into life's battles
Displaying the star.
Your armor is love
For it conquers all
Empty fears may await you
But love and life is your call.
Be not afraid little soldier
A medal for bravery
Awaits you each day
if no fear can halt you
Along the way.
Just follow the path of justice
and truth
For the victory cometh
And love is your proof.

Ed Burgess
DRAW BRIDGE

hanging photo of
marble statue of
seated artist painting
Yurok women weaving
baskets.
red-deer pictures,
brown bark fibers

Janice L. Hedden
PURE LOVE

The night turns into day
as I lay here all alone
should I get up—maybe go for
a walk
or should I just stay here at
home.
Nobody knows the love that I
need
or the ache that lingers inside
I try not to show the troubles
I know
but the feelings I can't always
hide
Friends may drop by for a
visit
or they'll either give me a call
but even if days are spent
without friends
it doesn't seem to matter at all
"Time passes slowly for those
who wait"
how well I know this is true
for days seem long and
nights forever
as I lay here waiting for you.

Victoria Louise Decker
THE ARTIST KNEW

And they called the baby Jesus
So few there to receive
A promised baby King,
So hard to believe.
This tiny little infant,
Would change the course of time.
Not exactly what was hoped for
In the picture—canvas primed.
A strong man was needed,
To instantly take hold,

Of all the people's troubles,
And gallantly be bold.
But what of this small child,
So warm and soft asleep.
Who knew then the knees to
bend,
Who saw the eyes to weep?
As the baby boldly loved us,
Regardless of our sin,
And gallantly forgave us,
And gladly took us in.
No not the way we planned it,
But who were we to say?
God painted the picture,
He painted it his way.

Pamela Jean Brown
THE LAST LONELY DAY

The old man stood alone by
the door,
Wishing he were here no more.
His wife had passed on years
ago
And since she'd been gone,
the days passed so slow.
Deserted, forgotten, and he
couldn't bear
The thought that not even one
person would care,
If he were to slip away into the
night.
So he gave up his life without
even a fight.
His son was too busy with
his business and all.
His daughter too busy to even
call.
His grandchildren's lives were
filled with college and gyms.
No time left for Mom, for Dad,
or for Him.
One lonely old man stood in
the door
And when they found time for
him
he would stand there no more!

Laura Muto
ANOTHER BEAUTIFUL DAY

I watched the sun sending it's
last ray
Across the land at the closing
of the day.
And off in the distance I hear
the call of
the whip-poor-will.
I watched a great white tailed
Eagle
Soaring high on yonder hill.
I stand here wondering what
tomorrow will
Bring.
Will I hear the call of the
whip-poor-will?
And will the great white tailed
Eagle be
flying on yonder hill?
Will the sun send it's splendor
across this
great land?
Now the evening shadows are
closing in,
I hurry my footsteps along the
path-way
I look up at the heaven and
thank God
for giving me another beautiful
day.

Tauri L. Cornell-Boyd
LADY OF THE COUNTRY

Lady of the country
lay across the land
bring forth life on the hillside
and love to the essence of
harmony
Lady, Sweet Nature

lay me down
among the leaning blades of
grass
shaded by the surrounding
trees of knowledge
which speak with a rustling
breeze
Will thou tell me of the summers
passed by
and the winters yet to come
Lady of the universe
dance across the skies
glowing white with the
mysterious moon
and beam down as the sun's
ray
Lady, Winged Spirit
send me into space
leave me to orbit in the mist
of Jupiter
to glide the rim of Saturn's
rings
longing to ride a plunging
meteor
Gathering the stars of yesterday
so they may shine bright
through our tomorrows

Sharon Ackley Caldwell
THE WONDER OF MUSIC

Oh, to what wonderful heights
we can soar
As we listen to a beautiful
musical score!
Our spirits and fancy on wings
they take flight
Like combing the universe on
a star-studded night!
Oh, to be blessed with that God-
given gift
Of making souls and spirits lift
To the strumming of guitar, or
playing the piano-forte
To make the keys magically say
"Here is the joy that life can
give—
Hear it, enjoy it and let the spirit
live!"
To hear in a hymn praising
God's name
The message—"It was for us that
Jesus Christ came!"
To say through a song telling of
joys or woes
"This is how life really goes."
The joys are endless when music
we love
Music—a treasure sent from above
above!

Dianna L. Rennie
SERENENESS OF SPRING

In the stillness of midmorning,
the lone fisherman lazily
watches
the illusionary waters, half-
hoping
to have a good catch for the
day.
Serenity of the crimson-turned
leaves
radiant in the noon-day sun
the surrounding tranquility,
the stillness-
of the glassy, mirrored waters.
Calmness of the trees, soaking;
drinking
in the sun's golden warmth.
As dusk falls, imaginery
illusions fall
on the surrounding waters,
creating
them frightfully larger than
real.
Day animals sinking into their

homage
out of the way of the never
viewed
night animals.
The lone fisherman slowly makes
his way
to his cabin, selfishly unable
to leave
the quiet and peacefulness of
the
Wilderness and its beauty.

Camille Pratt
LOVE'S HYMN

Within the light of freedom
'Neath heaven's golden dome,
Within my Father's mansion
My Father's house, my home;
O! Love betrothed in glory
A godliness I see
An image, likeness unto Him
Upon the face of thee.
Upon the face of thee, O! love,
Upon the face of thee.

O! bless thee of the father
And of his holy Son
And of the Holy Spirit
Our love be blessed as one.

Within the light of freedom
'Neath heaven's golden dome,
Within my Father's mansion
My father's house, my home;
As evening weds the sunset
Upon earth's altar be
Love's hymn empower each
holy hour
Within the arms of thee.
Within the arms of thee, O! love,
Within the arms of thee.

Lavern Winkleman
WHITE STALLION

White stallion's whinny echoes
On the moaning evening breeze,
Moving across the mountains,
echoing, echoing, echoing!
White stallion's hoofbeats
pounding,
Galloping, grinding green moist
grass,
Pawing impatiently at the still
locked gate,
echoing, echoing, echoing!
White stallion's hay is gone,
No welcoming voice he hears,
No one hears his whinny,
echoing, echoing, echoing!
White stallion's mane is flowing,
In the eerie evening light,
With thundering hoofbeats
returning
echoing, echoing, echoing!

Madeline Wiles
OCEAN OF DEATH

You stand before me a tired,
broken toy
tomorrow doesn't exist
and because of this
your life you must destroy
You have chosen me to take
your life away
it doesn't seem fair
but I still care
and for your soul I'll pray
The moon reflects your swollen,
tear-stained eyes
hurt many times before
and then once more
because of this it's I who is
despised
Now close your eyes and leap
into my open arms
for you I'll calmly wait

do not hesitate
I'll welcome you with all my
love and charms
A cry of pain as you look down
on me
and then you descend
this is the end
I have finally set you free.

Pamela J. Fetzner
A SPECIAL KIND OF LOVE

She is my best friend,
my mentor,
my critic.
She cheers me up
when I'm down,
she picks me up
when I stumble.
She accepts me
with my faults,
she stays by my side
through good times
and bad.
When my world starts to
crumble
she is there to
help me pick up the pieces.
When I fail,
she helps me carry on.
When things go wrong,
she is there to dry my tears.
She is the one
most like me,
yet we are totally different.
She gives me confidence.
She is someone I can trust.
She is someone I can confide in
Only she knows my innermost
secrets.
She shares my tears,
she shares my pain.
She shares my fears,
she shares my joy.
She is my sister,
and I love her.

Michael J. Wagner
IT WASN'T WORKING

For awhile he lived in a city
lost in a bustling crowd
Some of the neighbors nodded
one even spoke aloud

Surrounded by flowing masses
he felt the surge of life
Not in himself only others
since the murder of his wife

He mocked the feel of living
and though he really tried
He knew it wasn't working
and so he simply died.

Barbara VonTill
2:47 A. M.
Time suspended
On a moonlight chain
Hypnotized by feelings
That I never knew I had.
Madness, sadness,
Deep pools of pain.
Dreams of killing
And the courage needed to face
The creatures of the night.

I write all these feelings down
Yet I know, tomorrow
It will be in some foreign
language
I haven't yet learned.

J. Scott Gibbs
LIFE

Lessons to be learned
Feelings to be felt
Sometimes you get burned
The way the cards are dealt
Roller coaster up and down
Bending, winding all the time

Change a smile into a frown
The life we lead is but a mime
Plunge ahead, we must go on
Day by day, it's in the plan
We laugh sometimes, then we
moan
Life is strange but grand

Ana M. Navarro
DEPARTURES

We may be far apart, but the
love we have,
remains and grows between us.

As days go by, we realize how
much love we
Can contribute to all who come
and go;
But only to those who go,
Do we realize we love the most.

Cynthia Skowyra
LOST

I used to laugh like the rolling
waves on the deep blue sea
But now I sit and watch
like a lonely child under gray
skies.
    I am lost

I used to be Carol Burnett
burning
Crimson with uncontrollable
laughter
But now I wonder what provokes
such gayful red insanity
    I am lost

I used to be a bright blue star
shining in the moonlit sky
But now I walk in black light
    I am lost

Sunshine Knash
**A BATTERED WIFE'S
LAMENT**

    I feel silence deep and dark,
    tho' there are sounds all
    around me;
and I ponder to myself that this
    may be a form of insanity
To try and feel like a part of
something; and know not what,
I try hard and cannot relax,
I feel the world's problems
    along
with my own, and they are
    weighing me down
I cry out in total frustration
but no one hears me, I find a
joyless calming sensation in the
drugs I use; but it does not last
Time flies quickly, and I am
only getting older, I enjoy
nothing
for long, only for short moments
and then I am alone again
I hate the loneliness, the
frustration, but I cannot
crawl out, I
cannot trust anymore
    I tried so many times for so
many years and that trust
proved to be my undoing each
    time
    Does anyone have the
answer? Not just for me, but
    the thousands
of others like me. A miracle
    perhaps!

Eileen E. Martin
JUST A MAN

When I look into those pale
    blue eyes
I see a long ago youth aged with
    years
The bittersweet smile which
    takes residency on your face

Adds a glowing warmth and
takes a permanent place.
The peaches and creme
complexion Mother fondly
recalls
Now long gone with only a
trace of youth
Looking at you I recall the
triumphs and hardships we
faced
the love each one shaped
Dad love is more than the
words a person can say
It takes showing it in every way.

Valorie Ann Meszaros
UNTITLED

I love spring, and everything
tulips, buds, blossoms, robins
that sing
but most of all—as I recall
both now and then—as I think
back
of the beauty and fragrance of
the lilac
spring isn't spring—May isn't
May
Mother's Day isn't Mother's
Day
Without a beautiful big bouquet
Of lilacs and blossoms and
everything
that makes up spring.

Mary Jane Anderson
A SHADOW

Here in the shadow of what was
a beautiful thing
memories of a wedding ring
I turn over in bed
to an empty space
I embrace the pillow
It has no taste
a shallow feeling
of your touch
a shadow of a love
I cherish so much
a love that was
chose to roam
a misunderstanding
I'm all alone
until love returns
and that shadow is gone. . .

Cheryl Claussen
AMERICA

Welcome to America
land of the free and the brave
Where no one is man's master
and no one is man's slave

Opportunity knocks but once
or that's what people say
But here in America
it knocks once a day.

Thinking is free
and education is for all
Where anyone can be famous
in a land that stands tall

Granted we have problems
but we also have solutions
in the land of high ideals

and few delusions
So now our grand stature we
renew
as the country who is first
in life, love, and liberty
and pride to quench the thirst

Marilou Shubert Guthrie
NO REGRETS

When the sun is setting and the
final light fades,
Oh, God, let me have no regrets.
Hopefully, my soul touched
others—
like a river spreading,
And in the touching brought
peaceful response.
I tried to vanquish all trivial
thoughts, petty desires,
Vain egotism and conceit.
May my tongue have always
voiced kind words—
Never vengeful nor filled with
spite.
Benevolent Father, let me have
no regrets.
When the closing chapter is
done, the memories
of all that went before,
Should be savored with sweet
satisfaction,
Instead of remorse and the
desire to reverse time.
Revered Lord, let me have no
regrets,
But feel that warmth of
contentment.
As the final curtain falls on the
last scene,
I hope that I may have no
regrets;
But that you, Spirit of the
Universe,
Will look on me with
compassionate favor,
And say, "Well done, good and
faithful servant."

Sharon G. Davis
WHEN I WAS A CHILD

When I was a child,
the grass was verdant green
the rain smelled sweet upon
the earth,
the stars were as cotton balls
smothered in velvet,
And, I always stopped to ask
"Why"?

When I was a child,
a rose twinkled as I walked by,
trees burst through the clouds,
the sun kissed my cheeks with
warmth,
And, I always stopped to ask
"why?"

When I was a child,
jets drifted high above,
suspended in time,
roller coasters loomed to touch
the sky,
trains traveled on a naked
journey somewhere far away,
And, I always stopped to ask
"why"?

When I was a child,
heaven nestled on the crest of
a cloud,
only "Superman" and God
could fly,
there was comfort cuddled in
my father's arms,
And, I always stopped to ask
"why"?

Now, that I am no longer a
child,

I often forget to ask "why".
Too many things are simply
 understood,
and the inquisitive innocense
 of a child
has escaped into reason.

Dee Edwards
CHALLENGES

Even the uncertainty of the
 next few hours brings more
and more challenges.

Each challenge I conquer is like
 a ray of sunlight
feeding my confidence as I reach
 for more challenges.

Each challenge I fail to overcome
 is like a drop of
rain that dampens my belief.

But, in truth, the rain is what I
 need to grow—
and in the end—succeed.

Peggy Wotherspoon
I LOVE YOU

I love you Mom and Dad
For you're the best by far
You're always there when
 needed
Yes, you bought me my first car

I love you Mom and Dad
Because you care about my life
You care about the way I live
Though I sometimes live in strife

I love you Mom and Dad
because whenever I am down
I know that I can trust you
I know you'll be around

Mom and Dad you've raised me
The best that you could do
And though I never say it much
Mom and Dad. . .I love you.

Laurie Ann Mayfield
THE MOTHER OF THE BRIDE

The wedding album is put away
 in the closet
My white dress hangs there too
I remember when you said I
 looked beautiful in it
That once I actually believed
 you

A glow reappeared in your eyes
That I had not seen in years
As you prepared so thoughtfully
And softly calmed my many fears
 fears

You shone with motherly pride
As you watched my new life
 begin
Now that your little girl had
 grown up
You could let your life quietly
 end

Few noticed your obituary pages
 back
From the announcement of the
 wedding
But for a radiant Mother of the
 Bride
There is no more fit an ending.

Melba F. Illinger Rappe
AND IT WAS GOOD

When God made you, He used
 A little of everything He made
At the beginning of creation,
 And It Was Good.

He placed two people He loved
 very much
 Near one another upon this
 Earth,
Which He created so very long
 ago,

And It Was Good.
Into their eyes He sprinkled
 A little stardust from the Stars,
Which He created so very long
 ago,
 And It Was Good.

Their sparkling eyes brought
 them together
 Like the waves meet the shore,
Which He created so very long
 ago,
 And It Was Good.

He warmed their hearts for
 each other
 With a ray from the Sun,
Which he created so very long a
 ago,
 And It Was Good.

He allowed them to share
 Each other's love by Moonlight
Which he created so very long
 ago,
 And It Was Good.

You are a product of God's love
 In these two people, your
 parents.
You are special, not only to
 them
 But also to God and others,
And YOU are good!

Dora Lee Christie
THE ROSEBUD

A dainty little rosebud
 Lifted its quiet face to God;
Its scarlet head so proud
 Above the dark and silent sod.

The perfume it so gently holds,
 Then releases to a passing breeze
 breeze;
So that the fragrance kisses him,
 Long before the rose he sees.

God gave much to the rosebud,
 And then gave the rose to us;
To teach us the bloom of life
 is ours,
We should face the thorns
 without a fuss.

Florence Nicodemus Russell
TO MELISSA BETH

Grammy and Grampy
Welcome you, Dear.
There is much to see,
And nothing to fear.

We'll play in the sand,
And build castles there.
Enjoy the big sea,
And the fresh salty air.

While you are here,
The time will fly by,
We will then send you back
With a tear and a sigh.

But let us enjoy you,
All that we can.
Later you'll visit us,
Again and again.

Harriett M. Nesbitt
A NEW DAY

I woke up one morning to say,
It's great to be alive on this
 new day.
The Lord made this day for you
 and me
And all his dear children to see!
I'll say my prayers at night—
then I'll close my eyes and sleep
 tight.
God will keep me in his care—
And help me; all my burdens
 to bear.
When my children are all grown,
 and

out in the world on their own;
To them, I'll say,
You must always pray.
God knows all your needs,
So from this you must take
 heed.
Don't wait 'til you're older,
Or any the more bolder—
Pray while you can;
And God will lend a helping
 hand.
I know this is true—
For he has brought me through,
So many dreary days when I
 felt
the sky would never turn blue.
And I could only count the
 ways—
Of troubled times, when I felt
 this
can't be part of mine.

Michael Matthews, Poet
HOBO RIDING THE RAILS

I am a rail road hobo.
People call me a tramp.
I ride the train from
place to place and
town to town.
I love the rail road life.
I am a hobo and a man, who
lost his life wondering on
free rides to no where on
the rail across my land.
I may be hobo, but, I sure
love the trail life.

Amy Vasinko
**PEACE MINUS THE
AMERICAN DREAM**

Burning embers in my mind
A thought that caught a-fire
A small spark
In a dry field of wet desire
A minute hope, a prayer for
Peace for all mankind
Tranquility, a worthy goal
to hope for and to find
But in this world of war
A single dew-drop diminishes
 the spark
The scar of greed and prejudice
Left in the mind to be a lasting
 mark
The "American Dream" all
 do strive
for money and success
If love for man meant more than
 money
Would man be man the less?

Jarri Suzanne Cruse
MY FRIEND

When I'm happy you share my
 happiness,
when I'm sad you cheer me up;
You're someone I can depend
 on, someone I can always trust.
When I have a problem, you're
 always right there
willing to listen even when,
 you have no time to spare.
If I have a secret that I want to
 go untold,
I can tell you with no worry
 that you'll tell another soul.
You're always pouring out
 adivse,
even when it's painful or not
 very nice.
You tell your point of view
 so honestly;
whether we agree or disagree.
Yet even when you don't agree
if I needed you you'd stick by
 me.

For all these acts of kindness, I
 "Thank You" and hope you
 see
you being my friend means a
 lot to me.
And as we've shared good times,
 I know there will be more
because friends as great as you,
 are friends forever more.

Kathie L. Boltz
TIME

Flying faster as one goes on
Rushing onward, leaving undone
Things that could be

A paradox, a mystery
(At least it seems so to me)
That it should be

A very wide road when we are
 young
Narrowing to a small path
Until at last
When all is done

It greets another dawn
At the end of the setting sun.

Wendy A. Parker
GOD HELP ME

Help me oh God I pray
Help me make it through this
 day.
Help me do the things I need
 to do
Help me oh God as I help you.
Help me oh God not to sin
Help me stay out of trouble I'm
 not in.
Help me stay where I belong
Help me through the whole
 night long.

Marta Ruth Nava
LUNA

Silver orb that rules the night,
beckoning fantasies that delight.
Placed on your throne above
 the sky,
illusion and enchantment
beheld by the eye.
Sometimes wicked, sometimes
 true,
seen by many, understood by
 few.
Silver orb that rules the night.

Vickie Woods Lovett
**RAINBOWS FROM A
MATCHBOX**

The joy we impart
by the friendship we share
is truely from the heart
tho' some might say it's not
 there.
But, you can't always see it,
however hard you look
you must turn back the cover
and begin reading the book.
This caring is the love that is
 shared by two,
and this is that expression
from me to you.

Phyllis S. Christensen
HAND—WORK

Poets do not crochet;
They knit words together
And pick phrases all apart.
They spin a golden strand
Of thought, and manage
   somehow
To embroider pearls. . .
Upon the tattered heart.

Sod Caboose
RISE

Translucent pillows lay across
   the docile bog
An orange glow
   emerging from the east
The pillows rise
The ball appears
   the silence
   the strength
Overwhelming beauty
   pure scenery
Joy
and from whence it came
   war?

Alice B. Kendall
FIRESIDE PRAYER

Breathe on these ashes, Lord!
Breathe life to glowing coals,
leaping flames, sparks set free
to warm the heart, to tame the
   dark.

Spirits rise like wind-swept
   smoke,
trailing off in distant skies.
Each one we've loved the most
will find a private destiny—
and leave us by the hearth,
radiant with memory.

When my turn to ashes comes,
let one small spark take flight
to etch, white-hot, 'L-O-V-E'
across the cold, black night!

Sherri Pickel
THINKING

I'm sitting here at 8:15 a.m.
With nothing to do—but think
   of you.
To think of the few precious
   moments
We were allowed to share.
To think of how very much
   I love you.
Thinking of our first night
Thinking of the night we danced.
Thinking of our first night,
   together in bed.
Thinking of our last night
   together
Thinking of our last good-bye.
Me, hoping it wouldn't end.
But it did.
And now I sit here—thinking of
   you.

Laure Dixon Higginbotham
DEATH

Death
Comes too soon:
Crawling like a snake
It slithers and slides
Seeking the unwilling, the unwe
   unwary, the unready,
While the music of the universe
Pounds out its noisy notes
   among the rockheads
That inhabit the cemetery.

Death
Remarkable event:
Could we pass it up
And fly like winged ants around
   small hills of sand
While we wait for the others?

Jacqueline T. Guillas
FLIGHT OF LOVE

As autumn leaves drop to the
   earth
My tears are rain today;
A love that built its nest in my
   heart
Has suddenly flown away.

Oh gentle moth, I've touched
   your wings
You shakily flutter then fly;
I only rubbed off enough magic
To teach my heart to cry.

Be on your way then frightened
   bird,
I'll not cage you again.
I clipped your wings but for a
   time,
Now I'll just be a friend.

Rosalie Lay Siffard
MOTHER

How often has she pressed me
   to her breast
and shielded me from many tears
How often she has given me a
   peaceful rest
and solaced many fears

All those prayers mother has
   said,
when all my joy and sorrow
   she would share.
That bright path before me
   mother has led,
will still be shining in every hour.

Now silver threads in her hair
   I see,
Is it that mother could be
   getting old?
Are were some of those silver
   threads caused by me?
Those silver threads that once
   were gold.

Laure Dixon Higginbotham
PALE SPECTRE

Feathered,
Thin, pale spectre
Streaming, swaying, spiralling,
Swept through the opalescent
   sky
Screaming

Ghostly
Apparition,
Herald of cold terror
Floating through the foggy
   evening
Trembling.

J. D. Diller
EACH TIME

Each time that I get closer,
To finding my special you,
I sense a flow of adrenalin,
That just doesn't subdue,
Each time I find someone,
That honestly seems to care,
My mood is one of paranoia,
Derived from past love
   despaired,
Each time I write my feelings,
Down on paper with my words,
I express continued loneliness,
A life of fear so very absurd.
Each time I get to know,
Someone like I look for,
Seems that my unquenched
   desires,
Flare up all the more,
Each time I find a lady,
That touches me inside,
I feel an uncontrollable drive,
To run away and hide.

Wilma A. Ingalls
RUNAWAYS

Lost souls run away from life
   support vines
absent of human love's warmth
   that fades
like a dim memory
reaches back into infancy
to end in blackness
where they live in excellerated
   time
on asphalt jungle streets

Their freedom lifestyles
bring garbage can food stands
among their doorway-subway
   pads
wrapped in newspaper blankets
against the rain and cold
while fire hydrant sprays
   becomes their oasis
in summer's heat
like seashore playgrounds.

They roam city's streets with
   survival instinct
to beg, and con, and kill,
   and steal, and sell
with faces that reflect life's
   scars
like mirrors
in harden hearts of steel
until someone cares enough
   to soften
in love's melting pot
to show them another vision
   of life.

Eva Zach
SWEET BABE

Those tiny lips around my
   breast
where you sweet babe were fed,
   at rest
Those precious eyes looking
   at me
Oh so content and filled with
   glee
Here's where it seemed that
   you felt best
close to your mother, outside
   her womb
at last, at last
My dearest baby close you must
   stay
for passed once more, is
   another day
Advantage we must take sweet
   babe
of special times like these
   this way
For soon you'll grow and
   wonder shall I
why time passed by so fast, Oh
   why?

Wendy Meegan
UNTITLED

The kindest man there is on
   earth
   (He sits alone with drink in
   hand)
feels he's lost all useful worth.
   (rocking slowly to the band)
Over now for many years.
   (A country tune no one would
   know)
Why are there still so many
   tears?
   (her favorite song so long ago)
The pain is just like yesterday,
   (He hums the tune, now on
   the brink)
the hardest price he'll ever pay.
   (ready for another drink.)

Will the loving never cease?
   (He sees her face as she was
   then)
and put his mind at last in
   peace?
   (wife, mother, lover, friend.)
The guilt he feels has left him
   numb.
   (He reaches out to touch
   her hair)
The hurt's too strong to
   overcome.
   (He starts to cry; she is not
   there.)

Margaret L. Schroeder
**AND YE SHALL FIND
LEAVES AMONG THE GRASS**

And ye shall find leaves among
   the grass,
Stones among the waters,
And where the lilies pass
Ye shall find the wind
Blowing tempest-tossed
Over the sands of time
Covering all that is lost
With a cloud of dust,
And there amongst the upset,
There will be memories of
   yesterday
With some things you will forget
Like the breeze
But there amidst the sadness
   deep,
Where among the roses will be
   thorns,
And beneath the pale clouds
   aloft
That will greet the coming morn,
Ye shall find love,
And ye shall find truth, honor,
Peace, and laughter
That will follow thee
Softly after
Every sad time,
And ye shall live then
A better person
In the world of men
For having known them.

Diane L. Hill
THE WINTER SPIRIT

She stands
Quiet in the night.
Slowly she raises her arms to him
As he watches from above.

Like a cloud
She drifts among the stars to him
The spirit in the winter night
Loving the Man in the Moon
through time eternal.

She is bound to Mother Earth
But wishes for the Heavens
   above
And her Man in the Moon.

Father Sun, seeing her,
Sends the swells of anger to her
And she falls back to the ground.

She crys,
And as she does,
The breath of the North wind
Chills her tears.

They fall,
Snowflakes covering the ground
In a blanket of white.

The Man in the Moon looks
   on in helpless silence
As his Winter Spirit spreads
   her sheet of sorrow.

Winter is here.

Phillip F. Pointer
THE BUTTERFLY

So quick the wings that flutter
   about,

Darting here and there.
Piloting their way to and fro,
From blossom to blossom,
  everywhere.
By nature 'tis but helpless prey,
This body thus these wings
  convey;
Betwixt the earth and deep,
  blue sky,
That comely form of
The enchanting butterfly.

Robert Wayne Smithson
JUST ANOTHER PRAYER

How to grasp life, does it depend
  on the handle?
Why curse the darkness, when
  you can light a candle?
Okay, Lord, forgive my sins
  that I've confessed to Thee—
But how can I be reassured?
Light the candle, the darkness
  and sin will flee—
Your handle can be found in
My Word.

Heidi H. Anthon
UNTITLED

Butterfly in flight
A journey on rainbow wings
Irridescently shimmering
Flutter by, butterfly
Free wind-floater
Fly and roam
To the contentment of your
  being
Soaring time ends soon
choose the flower
Which suits you best
And come to rest upon it.

Richard R. Lemelin
**LIFE , LOVE, AND
HAPPINESS**

Life is living each day and
  getting the best you
can out of them.

Love is a degree of liking
someone as much, sometimes
more than yourself.

Happiness is contentment with
  yourself, with people
around you, and with existing
  conditions.

Life, love and happiness
  combined make for a content
person. This is not always easy
  to have, but once
you have it don't let it go.

Suzie Grove
BECAUSE OF YOU

Because of you
  I smiled today
So sweet of you
  to touch my heart
I'm trying to
  thank you
For tender words
  you said of me
And though
  it could never be
I'll cherish the
  feelings
  you had for me.

Teresa Lynn Stapleton
**MORE THAN WORDS CAN
SAY**

I love you
more than
words can say;
and this love
grows stronger
every day.
This love
of ours

is true;
honey—
don't ever leave
or I'll be blue.
I don't love you
in just one way
but I love you
more than words
can ever say!

Michael J. Rotzler
THOUGHTS

Asleep. . .no, of course not.
Your breath as regular as the
  ticking of the clock on the wall.
The gulls flying to and fro as I
  reach for them in the candles'
  glow.
Snow has once again covered
  your windshield.
I wonder if she remembered
  her scraper?

Peggy Lynn Ross
WHO AM I?

I am a person, trying to live in
  this ever-changing world,
  trying desperately to keep up
  with the fast pace of things
  around me.
I am a person, searching for the
  right things,
  searching for the missing
  pieces that
  will finish the puzzle of my life.
I am a person, longing for
  answers to my questions,
  longing for the things in life
  that
  will erase my question marks.
I am a person, learning the
  basic rules for survival,
  learning that as I get older I
  must
  rely upon new rules that
  change the
  basic to complicated.
I am a person, living in this
  world,
  living under conditions that I
  alone
  cannot improve, but with help
  from
  others, there is a chance.
I am a person, doing familiar
  things,
  doing the same thing from
  one day to
  the next. . .
  Will I ever change?

Kimberly Sue Sigwanz
CLUDIG

The castles and clowns and
  animals on parade are nothing
but clouds
  and tomorrow they will be
  dark and gray and
  menacing,
  like you.
I wish I could blow the clouds
  away somewhere far from
here,
  but I cannot,
  the most I can do is close
my eyes and pretend they
  don't exist while
  they rain on me.
Until the sun shines and I am
  fooled again.
Like the clouds, I am never
  sure of what you are.

Carol Chope Gilman
A VIEW

You. . .Hey you—
You up there, twinkle every

evening.
Transmit your wisdom unending.
But who will listen, who will
  care?
Our fear of your thoughts is
  more than we dare
To contemplate, your existence
  beyond
Our lives, of which we are fond.
Although we are seen
As decendants of our Lord, we
  lein
On life but here to be found;
Within our meager minds we're
  bound
To stagnate our thoughts for
  fear
Of our familiar life we hold so
  dear.
These words I say and do feel
  strong,
Your lives will be shown to us
  before long.

Theresa Barnhill
LEFT BEHIND

Left behind my childhood daze
Surrounded now by a cloudy
  haze
Put up in my storage room
Things that took me from bud
  to bloom
Left behind my childhood teddy
  bear
Missing one eye leaving one tear
Leaving behind my doll house
  dream
Now living in a world of glitters
  and gleam
Sometimes I go up to my
  storage room
Just to remember how things
  bloom
But now once more reality I
  face
When I come down from that
  treasured place
Left behind once more
Things I love behind that door.

ShirleysLudlow
FLOWERS AND DOGS

In far-away lands when a
  stranger I acquaint
And no premise serves for trust
  to depend
I behold first his face as he looks
  on a flower
Then I see if to dogs he's a friend

If, for instance, a man stops to
  marvel a lungswort
Or is moved when he looks on
  a rose
If he stands back in awe at an
  eight-foot laurel
bending down to see how it
  grows
If the fragrance of violets stirs
  his passions anew
while with deference he
  examines a crocus

Then my strust in this stranger
  begins to unfold
And my affection for him bursts
  into focus

However, just on flowers one
  cannot be sure
for his eyes may not bend
  toward the soul
But perhaps on a beauty that
  reflects only joy
And demands not reality in the
  whole

But then if by dogs he is favored
  with respect
one sees nobility drawn to light
for dogs aren't deceived by
  manners or attire
and can sense, more than us,
  wrong from right
for a dog has virtues, even as
  man
through his excellence are his
  loyalty and control
if then by the dogs this stranger
  is admired
my trust and affection soar its
  goal

So by flowers and dogs I
  determine my trust
it's a matter of two simple tests
I observe first the man as we
  walk through a garden
Then I summon the dogs for
  the rest.

Sherri A. Orchino
WINTER IN MY CABIN

It is a snowy winter day.
Inside my cabin a fire blazes.
The glow from my lamp bathes
  the
  room in warmth.
My pen and paper act as my
  brush and canvas:
Instruments to paint a picture of
  this lovely day.
Delicate snowflakes gather in the
  window corners.
Frost on the glass makes a
  beautiful
  frame for the splendor outside.
Distant scenery is lost in the
  haze of falling snow.
outside the wind is blowing.
Inside I sit in the warm glow of
  my lamp
in front of the window
With my pen and paper
Enjoying the beauty of this
  winter storm.

Mary Hamilton Darrell
THE MASTER'S HAND

With my hand in the hand of
  the Master
I will walk with assurance each
  day;
I will go to my task full of
  courage
For He guides every step of the
  way.
When the clouds hover over
  the sunshine
I'll not fear, for He promises
  me.
And I know that His promise
  is lasting—
"As thy cares shall thy strength
  ever be."

So I'll walk with my hand in
  the Master's
Though the way be stormy or
  fair;
For He promises ever to guide
  me,
I have only to rest in His care.

When the shadows shall lengthen
   at evening,
When the day is far spent I shall
   stand
Unafraid, in the glow of the
   sunset
With my hand in the Master's
   hand.

Evangeline Elmquist
TO TOUCH A ROSE

You must reach through thorns
   to touch a rose—
Life's sweetest gifts often come
   with pain;
And flowers, crushed to bring
   forth their perfume,
And for a rainbow, there must
   be rain.
You must reach through thorns
   to touch a rose
The sweetest songs the broken
   heart sings;
And of precious things we
   always find
That they're born of bruised
   and beaten things.
You must reach through thorns
   to touch a rose
Each joy a garland of tears may
   wear,
Every heart, both joy and
   pain must bear—
And both joy and sadness crown
   the year.
Bittersweet is the way we must
   go
And many heartaches life will
   disclose;
But love's blossoms are
   entwined within—
You must reach through thorns
   to touch a rose.
Joys and sorrows are
   intermingled
On the tapestry of our years,
But when we view the total
   pattern
We'll see rainbows shining
   through the tears.

M. Christin Greene
THE VISITOR'S WARNING

You've come here invited,
Not to inspect or criticize!
It's not your place to judge
   the condition,
Or comment on the size!
You've come here as a guest,
Not a buyer or lender be!
You do not pay the rent here,
The damn checks are signed by
   me!
So, if you'd like some coffee,
Sit down and stay awhile;
We'll chat about a dozen things,
And, even share a smile.
But, if you've come to see the
   joint
Remember, if you please—
A friend will never see the dust,
Or, if the beds are made!

She wouldn't care about the
   sink,
Or, if the bills are paid!
She wouldn't come to touch the
   sill;
Or, the refrigerator top.
And, when she makes a
   comment,
She knows when she should
   stop!
So, pardon, if you notice
How my look has turned to ice—
Tours can be exciting,
But, friendships can be nice!

Orville
UNTITLED

Bells Augio
Intoned for you
So perfectly
Like stained glass shades
In their moment's hue
Touching those things within me
That bring forth
Tears of love. . .
   . . .and mourning
For the bells will linger here. . .
In gift shops. . .
   . . .Churches. . .
      And clocks
While Augio will sound for
   the sixteenth day
The passing of the summer grass
Upon a silent grave.

Tammie Ripple
LEAVING IN LOVE

Sometimes I used to think
That there would never be
Anyone as lucky as me.
What everybody thought was
   nothing
Was everything to me.

You are the only one that I will
Ever love with all my heart.

I prayed day and night that we
   would never part.
'Cause if we do, and we did
I'll always be in love with you.

From now until eternity
You'll be the only one for me.

Darleen Ramos
YOUNG WOMEN

she orders a strawberry colada,
I a shot of schnapps,
our just washed hair absorbs
the smoke filled room
—the fat man's cigar—

(Naked legs,
   tight pants,
      lacy bitches)

we talk about Paris
   owning land
      cycles of the moon
         having affairs. . .

I sink into my drink
and think of childless women,
my mother's nine daughters,
the hollowness of cold bathrobes
reflecting little queens
eating pills
of life.

Cathy Lacy
CAROL

The first love is always great,
While it lasts.
It's like a knife,
The scar never quite disappears
The wanting is always there,
Until someone else comes along.
But still you remember,
That very first kiss
The first one to really say I love

you,
Yes, those feelings never
   disappear.
But that doesn't mean they're
   real,
When true love really comes,
You won't doubt it, you'll
   know,
For suddenly those words you
   shared,
Have the meaning God meant
   for them to have.

Mary Yarberry Parrish
MEMORIES OF PAIN

How does one stop feeling pain?
When for so many years
I lived to nurse, comfort,
And see smiles of recovery
Again.
A year ago, my vigil of
Comforting—with such tender
   loving care,
Brought no relief to the pain,
As I watched my father's
Prayers go unanswered—as he
   prayed to live!
Some will say he was "old"—
Maybe so, if you count age by
   years.
But, he whoso keen of mind and
   and heart,
Human as he was—begged me for
"something" to stop the pain!

Helpless, I could only stand
   and watch
This nightmare to end!
Then, with seemingly total
   understandment
My Father said, for this pain I
   bear,
There is no relief but death.
The answer to his prayer
   was "no" to live—
But, to be free of such pain—
God answered, with a merciful
Death.

Irene Maria Collins
OUR BAND

My friends and I formed a band,
with instruments close at hand,

Alex drums a big, deep kettle;
George beats on some tinny
   metal.

Sam clangs hub-symbols from a
   Ford,
while Johnny strums an old
   washboard.

Mike pipes his Dad's old whiskey
   jug,
and I blow notes with a coffee
   mug.

The tunes we play are really
   neat,
as we march along our favorite
   street.

But it never fails, when we're
   playing swell—
someone's mom has to go and
   yell.

Blain W. Bittinger
SNOW

The world was dark and lay all
   in silence,
When the snowflakes started
   to fall,
With each little messenger
   scurrying downward,
As if just to answer my call.

All through the storm I
   watched and waited
Thrilled with the spectacle

mine eyes could behold,
Trying to meet each small,
   winged visitor
Impatiently hurrying through
   the cold.

Then alone, I beheld as they
   gleamed in the moonlight,
Their beauty unmarred as they
   covered the land,
Humbled I thought of their
   delicate beauty,
Conceived and created by God's
   loving hand.

The trees in the forest are
   shrouded in white,
A star-studded glow in the
   moon's silver light,
A gleaming of diamonds, a
   whisper, a glow,
All the world lies in beauty, it
   is covered with snow.

Emily June Scarlett
SURPRISE

We first saw him running
at a tremendous speed,
so we all gave him chase
for the runner we'd need.
The season for football
was coming in sight
and for making a touchdown
we thought he'd be "right"
A sissy could never run
that fast through town.
We thought "she" was a "he"
till her pigtails fell down!

W. Phillip Lyliston
FAVORITE TEACHER

"A creative mind"
      you said,
as
   you quelled
      my tears,
awakened
   me
      to
         my desire
         to express.
"Keep writing down
      those
         thoughts,"
and
   I
      did.

Debbie Ramirez
I USED TO BE BUT NOW. . .

I used to be a Dancing Doll,
But now i'm dirty and dusty
Because I am only a puppet.

Victoria Simeone
THE ANNEX

Oh, to be a part of
the nucleus;
to enclose the
wings of life
within me
to arrive at this annex
finally.
It all comes back to me
a certain place
a certain time

The little girl
she's not dressed in pink
what do you think?
She's dramatic
it's problematic
you're ecstatic. . .
then there are tears
so many tears

Becoming a person
from out of nowhere land
to gather the fragments,
shattered in the

universe of her heart
oh to feel
oh to be a part
of the revelation.

Roy T. Holland
HILLS OF CLAY

Among hills of clay,
Shadowed by blue, serene skies,
I played beneath arms of green
And shared memories with sighs.

Among hills of clay,
Ribboned by oceans of tears,
I challanged the dullness of hate
And smiled at quiet, peaceful
years.

In time, I left my clay hills
To seek the innocence of a
sweet face,
And touch the warmth of new
solitude
In a less delusive southern place.

Red, yellow streaked hills of
clay
Let me not falter and forget
thee;
Thick, sticky hills of clay—
Cautious and wise molder of me.

Mary C. Davis
THE DRIFTER

Through the doors walked a
quiet man,
dressed in a three piece suit
and tie.
Curly hair mixed with silver
strands,
a loner type of guy.

Sits quietly alone in a chair,
sipping a glass of wine.
Doesn't say too much though,
he never does,
but, with his eyes you could
read his mind.

A man of the world but, a man
discreet,
known only to a chosen few,

His life kind of a private place,
enter only if he asks you to.

His presence holds a mystery,
you can sense it in the air.
But, never question reasons,
just accept that it is there.

Than being the kind of man he
is,
you've got to know someday,
His time for moving on will
come,
for him it has to be that way.

Patricia Anne Solek
PERSONAL DESIGN

As I catch the tail
I am the circle;
if I go deep to discover
I go down the spiral.

If I look forward to a dream
I once had, I climb and look
down.

To be a place where
no choice is made
is my heaven of peace. . .
a silent change!

Daryea
**TO THEE I ASK: WHY MUST
THE HEART ACHE SO?**

I lay to rest upon my throne
My reigh has ended; my name
—unknown
I flounder in darkness, a void
prevails
My body aches; it knows it's
failed

Why must I accept defeat?
Can I not defent my honor?
My heart thumps to a sorrowed
beat
I have my love no longer. . .

Clair Wood
PUPPETS

I walk along the city streets
My tears have long been dried
What could have been
What may have been
Has now been cast aside

Not by me
Nor by you
We really had no say
Society made its rules
Fate made its play.

You moved forward in your
world
I moved in mine
Tangled puppets on unknown
strings
Unbroken by love or time.

Consider not days gone by
As wasted yesteryears
The bitter past is sweetened
by memories held dear

Regret not one moment
of what we shared in time
Life is made of memories
These are yours and mine.

Marian Hastings Keck
EVOLUTION

Up from the covering waters of
the years
That hid the slow unfolding,
Like a dragonfly I crawl—
A new wet-winged self,
Cautious yet of lonely flight,
Pulsating in a feeble sun,
Tremulously awaiting a
strengthened moment
For sunlit flight.

Barbara F. Goldman
MYSTERY

Autumnal wrench is
felt in the leaves, which
suddenly in sunlight
turn bright torches
heralding
love's mystery—first
flaring hidden gold—
before the brittle touch of dust
leaves deepening mold.

Mary Thoennes
DREAMING?

Tall, blonde, and handsome.
That's what my dream man
shall be.
With sparkling blue eyes,
As wild as the sea.
A special smile, for no one but
me.
A private wink that only I see.
Special talks that bring us
together.

Closer than ever before.
Love that shines in our eyes.
Need no words to tell more.
Cause our love is special
Like roses after rain,
We cherish every moment,
Since none will be the same
I'm the captive of your love
Free to please it, or deceive it.
But I'll never leave your
love.
It pours on me with a passion
from above.
Then I awaken from my dream
dream. . .
With a heavy sigh. . .Then I
smile.
Turn and face a man with
sparkling blue eyes,
as wild as the sea.
That's what my dream man
shall always be.

Mary Virga
VALENTINE'S DAY

"Valentine's Day" is forever,
It's the love that we possess,
To share with one another
The joy and happiness.

When two hearts are entwined
Pierced by cupid's dart,
Life is like a radiant ring
Spinning like a top.
"Valentine's Day" is for lovers.
Love makes the world go round.
It brings visions of gladness
When two hearts are bound in
one.

Ruth Roland Rouse
THE ARTIST

The beauty on the canvas
Put there by the artist's touch,
He bares his soul in painting
He loves it very much

It is his life ambition
A gift from God above.
No one else can understand it.
It is his greatest love.

He hears the birds a singing,
As he paints them in the trees,
The wind is softly blowing
He can even feel the breeze.

He can hear the murmur of the
brook,
As he paints it's silvery stream
And smell the fragrance of
the flowers,
That is his life's golden dream.

Caryl McNees
TEARS

The world
Allowed the flakes
To melt their bright designs
Upon her scarred and bloody
crust
And wept.

Carl McIver
YOU GAVE ME HOPE

You gave me hope,
And ended my
Endless quest for
Hope itself.
You gave me time,
To rest and quench
Myself in the waters
Of hope.
Refreshed now, I start
On another journey
For happiness.
But when you
Found about my journey,
You said you were
Looking yourself.

And so we started out,
On another endless quest
With no one to end it for us.

D. Florence Hanson
UNTIL

Until the Star
again can pierce the numbing
chill
of man's unending bitter strife,

Until that light
can find a kindred flicker
in the arena of man's life,

Until the holy man
can make all creatures new
to live in true humility,

Only then
will man forget himself
and willingly commune in love
and trust.

Regina Easterling
SUDDENLY YOU

Everything was going wrong
When suddenly you came along.
You turned my darkness to
light
And made my dull life bright.
I thought you were being true
When suddenly you said, "I
love you."
I thought you were "Mr. Right"
As you held me so very tight.
And kissed away all my fears.
Then suddenly you left me in
tears,
Taking a part of me with you
As you found someone new. . .

Shirley Willsey Lyons
TWINS

You're going to have a baby.
Oh! What fun!
But what happens when you
find you have two—
instead of one?
You look on the bright side,
whatever it may be
Because instead of two, you
could have had three.
they're sugar and spice and
They're sugar and spice and
everything nice,
Except for just once, you have
it twice.

Judy A. Jackson
FLY AND BE FREE

As I remember
The times of yesterday
Through promises and dreams
I feel as though
I've lost someone
Very dear—very special to me
But because you
Are one who deserves
All the treasures of life—
I carry no regret
For I've found you cannot cease
A bird from
flight.

Sharon Fletcher
WHY COULDN'T YOU LIVE?

I've had mixed emotions, since
your suicide. Feelings of love
and of anger, I hold inside.

You left behind your husband,
your parents, and your friends.
The loss that we all felt, is the
kind that never ends.

People who were close to you,
had to be torn apart. Too
many memories, of you, lived
within each heart.

You stole from us, a love,

only you could give. Why
couldn't you live?
Why couldn't you share your
problems, with me? I was no
longer a child, sitting on your
knee.
I wish you were here, to see
my children grow. You could
be giving them that special love,
I know.

Dhani
ROCK HAD BLUES

I always wished for a place to be
To see what others have to see,
Once the experience has gone
There is no place to return to;
Except when rock had blues
And times to listen true
To the tunes of me and you.

Maureen Goltz Berryman
HOME

Open your doors and welcome
me,
Many miles I've come to feel
your warmth,
Many faces I've seen that lack
your love,
Many years have passed since
I've been gone.
Change if you must, but take
me as I am.
You are my refuge, my strength,
my being.
Always be there to welcome me.

Walter C. Stout
AUTUMN

Summer has faded,
Fall has begun.
Gone are the days
Of hot weather fun.
Leaves are turning
To yellow and red,
And squirrels are making
A snug winter bed.

None should regret
That Autumn is here.
It marks the approach
Of the end of the year.
Colors abound
In nature's way,
And deepen their beauty
Each passing day.

As nights get cooler
Crops are brought in—
Farmers will finish
'Ere rains begin.
Awed by the splendor
Of leaves on the sod,
We're deeply aware
Of the works of God.

Bonnie Dyer
THE EAGLE

The eagle is a bird with beautiful
beautiful wings,
A symbol of our nation, noted
for many things.
It stands for strength, bravery
and skill,
Builds it's nest high up in a tree,
or on top
of a high, high hill.
The eagle is great with a grayish
hue.
There are many kinds, not just
a few.
It has a strong bill, powerful
claws, and
keen eyes, that can spot it's
prey from afar.
It eats birds, fish, fawns, and
sometimes a hare.

The eagle can spread it's wings
and fly with ease,
To great lengths and heights
in the cool, cool breeze;
It can maneuver it's body in
a way,
So it can land gracefully and
accurately without a run-way.

Ellis Franklin Jones
A TOAST TO FREEDOM

America, America, how much
we owe to thee!
Thy blessings sweet we oft
forget, so used to them are we!
Let all of us, with humble
hearts, praise God we still
possess
Our cherished rights of liberty
and ways to happiness!
In other lands faith dims too l
low, and freedom is no more
As war-mad legions sweep
across, like waves upon a
shore.
May truth and justice yet
prevail, and honor conquer
lust!
May sons of freedom never fail
to vindicate their trust!

Romanita Morganella
THE DANCER OF LOVE

I dance to the everlasting music
Not knowing you were looking
at me
My heart stopped, but only to
assure me
The thrill of life has still to find
me
How did I know my dancing
was for you alone?
The lights from the chandellier
above marking patterns below
me
Your look was all too close now
Music carried by the wind so
rapidly
Out on the terrace I continued
my dance
love of my life now you must
know
How sweetly and lightly the
music now goes
Bringing us together so we may
dance our dance of love

Kristine Compagnone
WOULD WE

If we had but one last day
would we do things in a
different way?
Would we hold each other a
little longer?
Would our kisses be a little
stronger?
Would we suddenly see how
good life can be,
and not just always be thinking
of "me"?
Would we linger longer over that
last glass of wine,
instead of thinking all in life that
is "mine"?
Would we go to sleep, before
satu
saying "I'm sorry"?
Would we think about life with
a little less worry.
How different for us, things
would be,
If only into the future we could
see.
Would we take the time to smell
the flowers,

and thank the Lord for what
was ours?
Would we listen more closely
to the sound of birds
and think about hurt, before
choosing our words?
But life is so, that we don't
know when.
We may not wake up and
have tomorrow again.
So let's start living in a
different way,
Because only God knows,
if this is our last day.

Vickie Sandvik
SUMMER'S PAINTING

With wind upon my many faces
cooling the lines of fate and
fortune,
I trace through creations of
superior rating
drenched in the most popular
shade of green.

Cool, unsaturated waters
flowing over cleansing rocks
reach my feet, and then, as if
relieved at meeting someone,
flow on with a chuckle and a
sigh.

Lying in dense, unshaped grass
where butterflies light on
waving wands,
the sun shines on with clear,
radiant warmth.

While swirling scents of dancing
blossoms
fall on my reviving mind,
I gaze into pure, unabused
tranquillity.

Ola Margaret James
OUR WORLD OF DREAMS

We picked up tiny colored shells
Upon the beach, near Malibu:
That day pure magic bound us
round,
The ocean turquoise, sky so
blue,
There was a glow upon your
face,
And salty breeze blew cool to
whip
Against our bodies and our
close embrace;
There was such laughter on our
lips,
it blended with the beating tide
that frothed the sandy shore—
The ships spread sails against
the sky,
The red gold sunset of the sky,
And there was only you and I,
within the world, our world
of dreams!

Christi Tanner
IN TIME

When does a bud become a
Rose?
When does a baby first touch
it's
Toes?
In time, in time,
In time. . .
When does a tree it's leaves
Unfold?
When does a mother her child
First hold?
In time, in time,
In time. . .
When does a son become a
Man?
When do the shells turn into
Sand?

In time, in time,
In time. . .
When does a note become a
Song?
When does a right correct a
Wrong?
In time, in time,
In time. . .
When does the mind quit asking
Why?
When does a heart forget to
Cry?
In time, in time,
In time. . .

Dagie Gibson
THE HILLS OF HOME

I was a gypsy and a dreamer
And for years I could not stay
Within confines of home sweet
home
Fast were those freedom days
The hills of home were waiting
For years for my return
Candle burning at both ends
Sweet-life the years do burn
The hills would beckon and I'd
hear
My one great love of all
The hills of home were waiting
I answered to their call
Just to grab the wooded trill
Upon my hills just one more
time
The hills of home had called me
My one great love sublime.
The hills of home are with me
now
O earth, the years I've wasted
The hills of home are in my
tears
Just as the sea-salt I have tasted.

D. Eisenman Herter
GOD'S GIFT TO DIONYSUS

A gift from the gods
bestowed as diamonds at dawn
to Arachne's children.
Clinging to a finely spun tapestry
A gift rare, costly,
carefully chosen.
Hung as the last star fades
And Apollo begins his
ride across the crimson sky.
Silver threads sway in the
flood of Dionysus, liquid
amythysts
and garmets. Wines in
celebration of the gift.
Sun touched tears slide from
Arichne's daughter's eyes.
Dionysys, in search of his
present
In the first rays of the sun,
Looked among the clouds
And failed to see
The tapestry and the diamonds
lying in pieces
On the ground.

M. Alexander Teuschler
MY OTHER HALF

Searching through darkness,
I found you out there.
Finding you worthy,
I started to care.
Caring about you,
becoming your friend,
I hoped this new friendship
of ours would not end.
No end is in sight
for I'm learning to love you.
I spend all my days
and my nights thinking of you.
This fond reverie

is my favorite pastime.
Hours become minutes,
which quickly fly past. I'm
Hoping to spend my whole
lifetime with you.
My heart's not alone now,
it's one part of two.

Beth A. Hogan
STRANGER IN THE CASTLE OF LOVE

Man/child
so strong, so wise,
Views the world
through innocent eyes,
The wonderment of all
Christmas dawns,
Transposed on the face
of Life's pawn,
Walls built high
'round castle's door,
Cold and icy, yet
warm and secure,
Fair haired man of
child within
Stands at the gate,
not knowing if
To come in,
peers through
windows, cracks open
doors
Retreats and runs,
only to
Return for more.

Emilia A. Glaz
GIVE PEACE A HELPING HAND

Don't cry when the sun isn't
shining,
For the world can't exist by sun
alone.
Start spreading love instead of
whining,
Thus, you'll erase the proverbial
groan
And sunshine will come from
within you.
Don't wait till tomorrow, do it
today.
Give a helping hand to your
brother.
Oh! What a pity, should you
delay
To show the people that it's
no bother
To heal a world that suffers
in pain.
Forgive your enemy and love
your friend.
It's a small step in the right
direction.
Now, if every person followed
this trend,
It could be the start of a chain
reaction
In bringing peace to a troubled
world.

Catherine Jasper
A NOTE TO DON BLANDING

I've read of your Vagabond
House. It seems
To be like the one I have in my
dreams.
The grand piano, the shelves of
books,
The flame filled fireplace, the
cozy nooks.
Mine has a huge sea picture too.
Splashed in vivid shades of
green and blue.
And Pinky and Blue Boy in dark
gold frames,
And fragrant teas with exotic
names,

That I'll serve from a beautiful
silver pot.
And I'll have other treasures
that you forgot—
Children! I'll get them from war
torn places,
At least three or four. I can see
their faces,
As they run and laugh and
sing and play
In this house that I hope to
build someday.
For a house is only a house,
you know,
If there are no children who can
grow
Older with it and fill it with
memories.
That's why you had to resume
your journeys.
For your house was only the
empty shell
That all houses are where no
children dwell.

Janet W. Habener
A MOTHER'S PRAYER

Thank you God for the
children on earth
From the mothers you trusted
for them
at birth
Grant that we may find a way
To guide their lives day by day.
From tiny babes to women and
men
May we have the power to keep
them
from sin
To teach them the righteous
way of life
Always trust in God when
there is a strife.
A smile on their faces from
the start
Honest, kind, brave, and a
happy heart.
Let them know when we aren't
near
God will listen to the things
they fear.
A mother's prayer, hope and
desire
Is not to have this world on
fire
But to raise true Christians
so they
can see
To live in a world God meant
it to be.

Lucille Farmer
NIGHT

It was night
When I saw the dark mountains
Against the sky.
It looked as if the moon
Were about to rise.
Soon, a bright orange glow
Which looked as though there
were a fire
Just over the mountain top.
Soon the moon all yellow gold
Rose above the mountain crest.
As I watched, it climbed up
high
And bathed the earth in its soft
light.
All was quiet but for a few
things.
Like a dog barking far away
And the sound of a little frog
And the rustle of dry leaves
As the breeze came up.
It was so peaceful and yet!

Somewhere, there were those
Who would spoil the night!
Somewhere,
With their wicked deeds.
And this will continue
To get worse
Until the day comes
When Jehovah cleans the earth.

Deanna Brown Pointon
REUNION: FAMILY STYLE

Grandpa's here. . .Grandma's
there
Aunt Lizzie isn't coming,
Cousin Gus, is raising a fuss
'cause bearded son is strummin'
Old guitar.
Fried chicken is here. . .ham is
there
salads are on the table,
Cousin Gus. . .still raising a fuss,
up drives Auntie Mabel;
Old car.
Hugs are there and
Hugs are here and kisses there
and the kids are making faces,
GOD. . .help us all get through
this day,
with people from different
places!
Old times.

Iain A. MacArthur
UNTITLED

I, in part, my weakness know,
And in part, discern my foe;
Well for me before your eyes,
All my heart now open lies;
Turn not from me as I plead,
For your compassion, for my
need.
Fain would I your words
embrace,
To live each moment on your
grace;
All myself to you I consign,
And live your will in your
design:
Think and speak, be and do,
Simply that which pleases you;
And all that I can e'er impart,
Is the loyal singleness of my
heart.

Kathy Price
EXTEMPORANEOUS LOVE

Waited so long
Trapped inside a fantasy
New beginning
With an old dream.
That smile that puts me under
Brings about a hypersensitivity
To his touch.
The kiss so new
Awaited for,
For so long,
Inside a trembling,
Excitement and anticipation
Gets me high.
How many daydreams predicted
Future now present?

Richard D. Creech
YESTERDAY MORNING

I walked past your home,
yesterday morning.
But you were not alone, you hit
me without warning.
I wanted to phone, but storm
clouds were forming.
So I went on my own, dressed
in black for mourning.
Without going home, to watch
the sky storming.
I walked as I watched the river
rise

I threw in a flower for you
and one for me.
I tried to remember you and
your eyes
do they still shine through
can they see?
I was small next to the river's
size
and yet somehow I grew
I let it be.
I recalled the sweet sound of lies
it was then I knew
I had to flee.
I had the river and scars of
goodbyes
as the wind blew
I needed the sea.

Sandy Gullotti
TERMINAL POINT

Once I actually thanked the
stars
Under which our acquaintance
kindled.
An acquaintance which grew
and raged
Before it finally dwindled.
I wish now we had never met.
Bitter? You bet.

Lisa Malcolm
FOOTSTEPS

footsteps in the sand
a passing memory of
times I've had
and things I miss
footsteps travel through my life
they follow me
and I turn
to see them wash away
away to somewhere I want
to be
a place I feel I'll never find
at least
not till I wash away
and my footsteps walk
where I
once was.

Sandra N. Duross
PAIN

Damned paraside, make a quick
exit
you're not a welcome, invited
guest
being your hostess, to be
explicit
is utterly revolting, at best.
How dare you attack with
such audacity
what have I done to deserve
so much?
why the determined tenacity
to keep me in your gripping
clutch?
Your persistence has proved
effective
you've certainly made your
point
now, may I pursue the elective
to throw you out of my "joint"!

Frances W. Brown
DAY DREAMS

As on the grass I dreamily lie
And watch the clouds drift
lazily by,
My castles rise—until it seems
They cannot be just air-filled
dreams.
On each cloud—dreams I cannot
tell
I bid to rise tho' others fell—

For who hath not their
   dreams increased
When others fell, or simply
   ceased?
I dream not just of halls of
   fame—
On which is written high my
   name.
Nor do I dream of gardens, rent
With many a flower's beauteous
   scent.
I do not dream of things afar,
Such as the sun and moon and
   star.
I dream of things sincere and
   true,
Things all worthwhile—
I dream of you.

Laura B. Helmuth
THE FOREST

Out in the forest I long to be,
   to listen
to silence and hear its sweet
   sound,
To touch God's love where it
   so abounds!
To see the proud trees as they
   waltz in
the breeze, a carpet of moss at
   their feet.
Where tiny insects hide and play
   and do
their work in a merry way.
Each fragrant wild rose will
   blush and
turn pink as mountains stretch
   skyward
and wait to be kissed.
Where babbling brooks run
   cool and clear,
the finest of crystal could never
   compare!
Dotted with fish, like rainbows
   and silver,
They swim all about in a gay,
   gleeful glitter.

Out in the forest I love to be,
   no prejudice
here that I can see! All God's
   creatures
roam so free, with a special
   beauty for
the world to see. Oh. . .what
   a pity
some take not the time, to
   enjoy and cherish
God's gift so divine!
Out in the forst I long to be. . .
Won't you come and join me?

Debbie Pacana
EYES

Eyes that well, with hurt and
   pain—
Darkness will quench the
   inevitable rain—
Rain that falls, from the eyes
   so blue—
Like silver droplets of morning
   dew.

Eyes that see the world unrest—
That flinch when given life's
   true test—
Consumed with thoughts of
   live or die—
Effete, but without final good-
   bye.

Eyes that conquer the solitude—
That open wide with gratitude—
To greet the sun obsequiously—
Thankful with gross intensity.

Eyes that face another day—
Dance and sparkle, in a
   pensive way—

Content to gaze and let life
   pass—
The eyes I see—In my looking
   glass.

M. Helen Towe
MY FAIR—WEATHER FRIEND

Just call me when the sun
   shines
don't call me when it rains.
When storms appear please stay
   away
Until it's clear again.
I enjoy your days of laughter
so filled with fun and play,
but when your eyes fill up with
   tears
from me—please stay away!
I've had my own heartaches
   and woe
and times were rough, indeed.
I don't enjoy the presence of
   you when you're in need.
Too busy to be leaned on,
no one is worth the pain,
just let me know when the
   storm has passed
and I'll come back again.

Yvonne Ashurst
KAREN

I hope for people around the
   world that you never feel lost
   and alone.

To lose someone very special
   to another part of the world
   that
mean's everything to oneself.

Her ways, her smile and the way
   she holds her head, with
flowing hair cascading around
   her shoulders fair and the
   twinkle in her eyes that seems
   to say I care.

Yes, this special person means
   so much a part of me that my
life has always revolved around
   her so many times and to be
without her makes me feel
   lost and alone.

But o how lucky other people
   are to be able to share her
beautiful ways and the loving
care that she radiates when she
   walks into a room.

You have touched a lot of lives
   Karen in all your twenty-three
years, but most of all you've
   touched mine.

Peggy Weiderman
ANTIQUE MIRROW

A mirrow so grand
Times moment, like a grain of
   sand

On this sideboard antique
I wish I could peek

Into the other side
And take a ride

Into days gone by
To wonder where and why

This sideboard so old
Has in its mirrows eyes to be
   told

As I sit and look
I wonder if it could tell a book

But. . .its eyes study me. . .
For now I will be

Part of this mirrow's memory
As it watches the life of me

For a century has gone by
But mirrow's eyes, never dies. . .

Eva Faye Compton
CAREFREE

The sun shines brightly;
   the wind blows boldly.
The hills roll gracefully,
   topped by trees abundantly.
Children, happy in their work
   and play;
   bodies radient, with healthy
   glow.
Shimmering water in shining
   pail,
   brought from the top,
   where the purest flows.
Huge sunflowers, with crowns
   of gold, patiently waiting
   'neath the soft green hills,
For their daily share
   of earth's bountiful till.
Can this be but just a dream?
   No! No! We've got to find a
   way,
To make this dream, reality,
   today!
Fill their lives, with carefree
   energy, I pray.

Tammy Lee Moore
ME

Pain, Oh sweet pain,
Freedom my dream,
Soften my hope,
Black my life,
Dark my days,
Lost my soul forever from me.
Reach my hand for light, I do
   not see.
By fire I overlooked,
My pain is my pain, you cannot
   see nor feel.
Leave to me
Leave me to the company of
   my shadows,
for we are one and the same.
I would death to part us,
Alas, tis' not my fate, that is
   truly me,
And you wished me to care.

Glorianne A. Niemi
TO BRUCE WITH LOVE

You're leaving
   You've got to know I'll miss
   you!
Your face is part of my dreams
   Your smile brightens my days
   and though I don't know you
   well
My life is incomplete without
   you
You're leaving
   And though you don't know
   it
. . .You're taking a part of me
   with you. . .

Kathleen C. Reinhardt
MY PET ROCK

Although many rank you as
   unliving, I won't lend
   comment on this position.
For you were made as I was
   made by a powerful man with
   many a mold.
Your difference from me is
   merely your form and the
   difference in time
in which we were born.

The box that contained you
   left you alone I got the
   impression you
needed a home.
Now that I have you under my
   care I wonder with constance

your origin
   as where.
Whether you laid on the ground
   stepped over by Tut. . .
Well if you didn't really so what.

Just your nature and context
   are so very profound, I just
   know
wonder and you must be
   bound. . .

Babs Kametzky Lewallen
LIVING FOR YOUR LOVE

I live for you love
Tell me I'm the one you're
   thinking of.
For I miss you when you're
   gone—
The days and nights seem so
   long.
But when you're home at last
The time apart is in the past
Time is what it's all about
And my love for you has
   grown no doubt.

Robin Gilligan Nash
AFTERNOON PAUSE

On tiptoes through illusions
   of soundless repose,
I saw you standing in afternoon
   patches of
shadowed dusk, on shaky legs,
pulled to full height by strong
   arms and curious eyes.
With toothless gums chewing
on the confinement of the crib,
making no demands on your
   tiny world,
o so quietly
you watched the rain.

Cher Spagnola
OPEN BOOK "C.T."

Teach me, and I will learn
   from you,
learn, and I may teach you. I
   deal
with everyone on their own
   level.
for no two persons can be the
   same.
I delve deep into their
   personalities,
individualities and their distinct
qualities. And I look for the
   kind
of characteristics, that I would
want to instill upon myself.
   I learn,
and absorb, from others and
   always
acquire my own conclusion.
   For every
one is like a book, some may
   be good,
and some bad. But when I
   find the one
that surpasses all the rest it
   becomes an open book, as
   in a friendship open
and versatile and like a good
   book
I will refer to this friendship,
I will never close it, nor will I
ever put it aside. Teach me and
   I will learn from you, learn
   and I may teach you.

Alene L. Carroll
TRACTOR PARADE

The farmers in the country
Regardless of the weather,
Couldn't sell their crops for
   much,
So they banded up together.

Riding on their tractors,
They came from near and far,
Warning signs on front and
    back
To show you who they are.

Resolute and determined
They formed a big parade,
To the White House they did go,
And they were not afraid.

Fair prices for our priducts!
Our demand and only factor,
How else can you expect us to
Meet payments on our tractor?

And you can bet your boots
The farmers will stay handy,
Till the prices and cost agree,
And that would be just dandy.

Joan Burgess Gill
MOONLIT ROMANCE

We ventured from our room
Entering the ecstasy of a full
    moon

So near to our reach
We drifted on the beach

So deep in our hearts
Lives how we feel
Of which we hesitate to reveal

Enchanted were we
Our emotions ran free

We nestled in the sand
So very close at hand

Our fantasies went wild
A love no longer that of a child

Enchanted
Enhanced with the night
Nothing seemed more right.

Donna L. McKenney
YOU AND ME, TOGETHER

I look at your picture
and realize the feelings will
    always be there.
My mind keeps slipping back
to the days when it began.

A real spring romance
you know, a time when
    everything feels good.
Cool refreshing rains and sunny
    days,
soft breezes and lazy evenings
a time when life starts.

It was then my life started
and it felt so good
You and me together
playing in the rain
going for long walks,
sharing in each other's pain
never being afraid to talk.
Oh, where did those days go.

At times when you're so close
I want to touch you, but I
    can't
even when the miles separate us
our hearts will always be
    together.
Reaching out, and feeling for
    each other,
remembering. . .
What was and what will always
    be.
A special love between two
You and Me, TOGETHER'

Marie A. LeVan
THE ROADWAY

The road flows on
A long gray line in a misty
    world
Curving into the dim and lonely
    distance,
Slipping at last into nothingness
Beyond the farthest hill,

One with the cold gray sky.
Suddenly a dart of palest gold
Parts the forbidding grayness
And draws the line between
    road and sky.
The slender band of light
Increases its intensity
And stripes the dusky road
With alternating gold and
    shadows
Cast by the thousand year old
    trees
That edge the way.
There is no stopping here
For sunlight or for shadow.
The road moves on inexorably
Into the far beyond.

Annamaria Mongillo
WORDS OF LOVE

It seems that everything has
    been said
But I still have so many things
    to tell.
I just can't seem to find the
    words
To explain it all to you.
I love you, like I never knew I
    could.
I love you, like I never knew I
    would.
You are all it's worth living for.
You are all I've been looking for.
I wish you were closer to me.
I wish there was nobody for
    you but me.
I miss you when you're not
    there,
I need you more than air.
    I dream of you night and day.
But you are so far away.

Margaret Rann
WAITING

The tinkle of a piano key
He is back, he's here with me.
The colored leaves of Autumn
    fall
Hush, I think I hear him call.
The stillness of a summer night
And there he stands in pale
    moonlight.
They say he's gone, they tell
    me so
And yet I know he'll never go.
Yes, into every single day
He'll tiptoe in some lovely way.
The children speak his
    cherished name
I hear his laugh, it's still the
    same.
The warmth of love and
    friendship too
Will never die, it is so true.
One who meant the world
    and more
Will someday open that Great
    Door.
And smile and beckon with his
    hand
And welcome me to his new
    land.

Mary Ellen Dietz
IN A HURRY

I stopped to visit you today,
but not for long. I had so much
    to do.
I had to hurry off, hubby would
    soon be home.
So I gave you a hurried kiss,
    and off to my
    daily chores I go.
There—my daughterly deed
    was done.

My conscience could now be at
    ease.
All through the day I thought
    of you, but
    consoled myself by saying,
I didn't have the time.
I was in too big a hurry to take
    time and
    say, "Dad, I love you!"
Guess I figured you'd think I
    was silly.
In a hurry no time to waste was
    all I could say.
You have always had time
You always have had time for
    me,
and one day soon I shall deeply
    regret it,
If I simply don't take time and
    say,
"Dad, I love you!"

Donna Marie Pavlick
FALSE CONNOTATIONS

Why do people always connotate
    the words "ecstacy" and
    "contentment"
    with love?
Why not words more like
    "heartache" and "being
    burned"?
Oh, I have been hurt many times
    before,
but none of those wounds
    seemed to have spoiled my
    character.
They were over within a matter
    of time,
and if they weren't,
I could always turn my back
    and run away without guilt.
Yet, what is it I really feel now
    that I keep holding on?
Love—or is it really? Or, maybe,
    need or want? Perhaps.
Whatever, still, I have shared
    a great portion of my life with
    you.
Sometimes, I think too much,
    at other times, not enough.
But the injury I feel right now
    is not that from a paper cut
    or a
    needle prick or a small burn;
It is much worse, this pain I
    feel;
I can't run from this one.
Maybe this hurt needs to be
    challenged.
Perhaps, I will stay around—
    tackle this one;
And afterwards—afterwards,
    I will understand.
Only then will I be able to go
    back and see the words
    "contentment" and "love"
and know their meanings as
    one.

Rita S. Guillory
**SEARCH FOR
CONTENTMENT**

To focus on the splendor;
Of searching for a dream.
May leave the spirit troubled;
If fate has dealt routine.

And just when all is going well;
It seems our goal is nigh,
What happens then, it turns
    around;
And what was low is high.

Can we sit and be content;
Or should we dare pursue.
A cowards heart is shackled
    from;
The things he yearns to do.

And though our lot may not
    be sure;
No reason not to try.
The one who never learns to
    sail;
May be the one to fly.

When winter winds are coldest;
Springtime's round the bend.
And when we feel the lowest;
That's when we find a friend.

So dare we be the dreamer;
Who feels the highs and lows.
Or choose to never live enough;
To laugh and cry and love.

Debi Buettner
A NEW ROAD

The world wonders of our love
and suddenly we begin to
    question
where are we going, where do
    we want to go
are there questions to answer
    alone
are there dreams to dream on
    our own
are there roads to travel by
    ourselves

We've been traveling this road
    together
and now have come to a turnoff
shall we turn together or alone
we wonder of where we've been
and where a new road will take
    us
are we to travel it together or
    alone

I read the map of this new road
to find its direction is uncertain
looking over where we've been
I find the unique path we've
    tread
and the questions come once
    again
to travel this new road with
    you or alone.

Mary M. Gillespie
TABBY CAT

My Little Hunter, the tabby cat,
Runs and hides when Pap says,
    "Scat."
Everyone calls him the fraidy-
    cat.
He acts afraid at the drop of [
    your hat
And runs and hides under the
    door mat.
Now I'm going to train
My Little Hunter, the tabby cat,
Not to be afraid of everything
    and that.
I know he will grow into the
    nicest cat
And won't be afraid of the
    biggest rats.
So—when Pap says "Scat,"
He will just lay his head back
And take a nap.
My Little Hunter, the tabby cat.

Bertha Taylor
REVELATION

Even as the trees,
    standing bare and unadorned,
    their leafless boughs uplifted,
Reveal the secret nesting place
    of birds long drifted
    to a warmer clime—

So, we bare our souls to Thee,
Dear God;
    our contrite hearts confessing
    the little sins found nestled
    there,

Invoke Thy blessing
and find in Thy forgiving Grace,
Hope,
and Joy
and Peace sublime.

Elayne B. Olson
IMPRISONED

Imprisoned in my inner self,
fighting to survive, not die.
Living all alone inside,
Me, myself, and I.

Leonard F. Duzinski
WITH ME

You are with me every hour
of each day,
In dazzling sunshine, where
halcyon breezes with the
flowers play.
In every breath and sign and
all serenity,
You are with me in delicious,
loving, ecstasy;
Sublime solitude is my delight,
For you are with me every day
and starry nite.

In each prayer, along the
winding roads, under blue
skies,
Reflections softens in your
wondrous eyes;
In wisy dreams you are in
close sight,
In utter despair you are the
beam of sunny light;
Tho' distance separates us miles
apart,
Darling, you are with me, in my
heart.

Jeanette Mia Eash
IF YOU CAN'T FIND LOVE

If you can't find love
The grass won't grow
If you can't find love
You're always a little low
Till after the day you've died
If you can't find love
You'll always hurt deep down
inside.

Dane Petersen
**AN ELECTRODYNAMIC
WALLOP**

From the distance, out of the
jet black
My ears are struck as by
thundercrack,
My eyes are pierced by
electrifying spears
Of city starshine, like jeweled
chandeliers,
Glittering needles of light,
slick glass luster and steel,
Though glowing electric blue,
rubs me raw, to reveal
The nerves, high energy wired
power surge,
A brainstorm, emotion and
intellectual fury merge.
Rush impulse and tremors,

intense exciting zones
Inspire lines and edges, sharp
cornerstones,
Towering boldly; staggering
awe strips me bare.
The flash magnetic shock force
of electricity in the air
Fueled to drive the rocket roar
Or rip a gash, expose my core
I rage berserk and spill my gore,
My head is torn off,
And put on backwards.
Now, as I look out through
bruised, swollen eyes,
My slautered body throbbing
and oozing,
I smile and laugh hysterically
for all the thrills,
And a new understanding of
the brilliant city.

Victoria Kraetzner
NATURE'S TIME

Fall is nature's time zone
coming to a close,
Petals wither on a once radiant
rose.
As the sun lowers from east to
west,
Nature shows her beauty at its
very best.
Glistening leaves in the autumn
hew
Is a breathtaking sight against
radiant blue.
Nature may need this time to
retreat,
Gathering strength for this
spectacular feat.
This is nature's time zone
coming to a close,
But it is really the beginning
of the next radiant rose.

Vincenza Serrutta
TRAMONTO

In questa terra si nasco col pianto
E nati appena si e' mensi
In soffici odorose culle.
Bambini di latte omai cresciuti
Indi all' eta' fiorita, stagion bella
cotesta
Pien di amor speme e fortuna.
Poscia uomini ambiziosi ed
operosi
D'una vita di belta' e focolar
divini
Son sol che fugaci lampi.
L'uomo dal volto roseo e
vigoroso
Si gangia in rughe e bianco il
crine
Incurvato e stanco langue
mormorando:
Caronte falce tagliente e' digia'
presente.
Ahi vita, vita umana che
tramonta.
E spenta, mai piu' ritorna.

Gary R. Linn
THE KING

Talons strike,
as one mass twirls in the sky.
Pinions are torn
as the darkened hole separates.
Plummage tumbles,
trying to verify its fligth.
With a snap and a whirl
at the twist of the wind,
The monarchs restore their
quarrel
among the clouds.
Speed and agility,

accuracy and style,
The difference is ripped apart
in the heart of the younger.
A limp. soul—free, and
lifeless Prince
tears through the sky,
Endlessly falling,
into a sea of forgetfulness.
Again, experience has defeated
eagerness.
Ant the true ruler, the King,
contains the power of the air.

Macrina Margaret Oatrowski
AS THE SEAGULLS FLY

As the seagulls fly,
the lilies lie back and sigh,
but as a distinguished bee
takes flight,
all the flowers jump in delight.
But as the stars fell upon the
earth,
who knows how, but those
lilies gave birth.
Then the sun rose and those
seagulls flew,
and all the flowers grew to new,
then the winds blew,
and the flowers beautiful collar
flew too.
For now spring was over,
and the winter snow did cover!

Barbara Brownlee
LOVE IS AN ISLAND

You are an island
kept all to yourself
That mountain of a man that
you are
is surrounded by soft, sandy
beaches.
That mountain, who supports
life and yet
burns with volcanic feelings
within.
There are very few blessed with
the
privilege of touching your
shores.
The tide must be just right or
they will be swept back to sea.
You can't be taught how to ride
the tide.
It's something you can only
achieve
if the trust and love are really
there
to carry you safely to his home.
His towering strength gives to
you
more than hope and security,
just as his fire keeps
you warm and safe within.
Only when that desire and love
are so strong will he then allow
the tide to carry you over
the last barrier reef
and home into his arms.

Beth H. Clark
FIRST HUNTING TRIP

My heavy heart watched him
cross the meadow
with hunting in mind and gun
in hand;
a bird or rabbit he said he would
find,
so young, this man child of
mine.
As all mothers know
there comes a time to let go.
He came through the door,
no rabbit, no bird,
Just an empty hunting bag;
but his voice full of trills
as he handed me his prize.

I smiled with gladness
at the light in his eyes
and his hands full of golden
daffodils!

M. Jean Moore
LET'S GIVE LOVE A TRY

No matter what you seem to do,
I can't seem to forget about you.
You're always on my mind
I keep remembering of that time.
It seems so far away
Yet in my heart it's there to
stay.
I know we don't know each
other vey well,
Yet somehow I know we
wouldn't fail.
No matter where you go I will
always know,
Someday there might be a place
for me in your heart.
We can take it from the start,
And hoping that it won't end.
Cause darling I know we can
make it around that bend.
So what do you say, let's
give love a try,
Cause it only takes two
And darling that's me and you.

Fred L. Higgins
A PARADISE ONCE

Deep in lands of forests lush,
a meadow no longer grows green
and plush.
Blackened rocks now fill the
glade,
where children ran in happier
days.
In this place there serenely
lies,
the ruins of a tower which once
broke the sky.
Beneath this castle's cold dark
mass,
lie the shadows of a time now
long past.
And when through the trees the
cold wind whines,
the shadows sing the legends of
a forgotten time. . .

Patricia Vestal
DEATH OF A ROSE

Love is a budding rose
Bursting with warmth and love
Nurtured by tenderness and
caring
Till it blossoms forth in all its
beauty
To fulfill its glorious destiny
for a brief moment.
Our love was like that rose
Once we were filled with the
wonder of life
Basking in the glow of each
other
But a rose must be lovingly
tended
Or the blush will fade away
As it does in a dying romance.
Love, too, can wither in the
summer sun
Although it valiantly fights for
life
But the cycle is complete
When death takes its toll
And teardrops, like petals, fall
Scarcely noticed as they
plummet to the ground.

JoAnn Woods
GROWING

Growing hurts.
Like being forged.

Terribly painful, but seeing a
  better person emerge.
Not like butterflies
Quietly shedding cocoons,
Although perhaps they have
  their own delicate pain.
There's more stress, more agony,
A tearing apart inside.
Tears, fears, reluctant acceptance
  of mature thoughts,
Giving up childish emotions.
Admitting one's honest wrongs,
Allowing to be what is right for
  all,
Not just what you want for
  yourself.
Is it worthwhile?
Equal to the cost?
Yes! I see a better me coming
  forth.
The same me.
Same values, and standards.
Just everything tuned to a
  greater perfection.
Every part at full capacity
Not running at quarter speed.
Finally challenged enough to
  meet the demands.
Growing hurts.
It always will,
If you really want to grow.
I'm still growing
  and I hurt.

Diana K. Arnold
THANKSGIVING PRAYER

Thank You Father
  for the grace you've given to
  be
to share with all
  by the love you allow in me
Thank You Lord
  with love so shone
and believing with others
  on our way home
Yes, with the Holy Spirit
  among us
We will enjoy our meal
  and continue to praise Him
For this fullness we feel.

Carryl Crysler
IMAGES

Ghosts from past and
present, stiffly posed,
grimace as if in pain.

In a flash of light
the celluloid captures
the aura of a man;

and lies waiting in a
darkroom grave, to be
brought to life again.

Shirley Anita Rhodes McDonald
BETTER FEW

How well you treat me,
  when it seems to you the time.
The affections you show me
  come only when I cry.

Once upon a time you cared
  a little for my thoughts.
Those days were few but,
  better few than naught.

Anjetta A. McQueen
NO ONE ELSE LISTENS

  no one else hears me
That's why I'm turning to you
  Lord
  on bended knee

I've never believed
  as so many do
Still I need Your help
What else can I do?

Please look down on me
  Give me love that I've craved
Bless my soul and heart
  So my life may be saved. . .

Shelly Williams
ALONE

Alone—
  the silence is deafening
No one around but
  my own thoughts and dreams.
Drowning me with
  my sorrows,
Swallowing my mind.
  I know not who I am, or what
  I should be.
Too weakened of pride
  to cry for help as I slide
into the shadows of doom and
  everlasting loneliness,
Captive of my ownself—
  eternally alone.

Gina Marie Oleston
THIS I REMEMBER

All the months of waiting
The sleepless nights, and
  the sickness each morning
The way my body ached from
  the heavy load it bore
And finally, the long hours of
  pain and labor
These things I've forgotten
But hearing his first breath
And then that sweet cry of Life
Life that I've given
Fill the bright sterile room:
This I remember.

Kim Balser
SHOW ME

When you say you care for me,
there's nothing I can do,
when you say you love me
show me that it's true.
The first time goes so strangely
and ever so unsure,
The next time will be better
so pleasant and so pure.
So take me in your arms
and love me till I die,
Never stopping to hesitate
or ever wondering why.

Suzanne Pearce
UNTITLED

When your child was
Little more than a whisper
The faint sound of realization
Dawning within
While the secret was
Still
So deep inside me
I found you
With a twisted clothes hanger
In your voice
And nothing in your heart.

Juanita Gray Kelly
FANTASY THE TEMPTRESS

Illusions of reality masquerades
  exuberantly inside your womb,
Abstract temptations deeply
  enthralled within your cocoon.
Tell me, will your ecstasies
  give birth into the light;
Or will you forever remain
A barren temptress of the night!

Peggy Lynn Lane
INTO ONE

Give of yourself
So that one day you may know
  the joy I know
Don't hold back
Know what is, instead of what
  could've been

Most of all—know me
For I love you more than words
  can say
I am giving you as much of me
  as I can
And trying hard to give even
  more
So give yourself to me
For I love you
  I am you.

Deborah Jean Saladini
SAND CASTLES

I remember yesterday
in your arms
It seemed we had
forever to love
Life held the promise
of dreams fulfilled.
Together we built castles
in the sand
where we shared
bubble gum kisses
candy cane smiles
sunset walks along the shore
with only the wind to guide us.
You pledged your heart
and I my soul,
but time found us wanting
more than we could give
and so we parted
friends forever
lovers still
drifting endlessly through time
like castles in the sand. . .

Bev Lambe
WISHING

I wish I were as sturdy as the
  mighty oak tree,
as soft and at peace as a river
  flowing into the sea.
I wish I could travel as quietly
  as the soft clouds above,
I wish I could be free to talk
  to you and tell you how
  much you are loved.
I wish to tell everyone in this
  unsettled land how much
  I care,
but I'm not as noticable as a
  big grizzly bear.
So until I am noticed by the
  world in some small way,
I'll have to wait to tell you
  how I love you all and I'm
  here to stay.

Laurette E. Meara
ONE STEP

One step at a time I look at
  them as if it was in my
Dream.
I know that now as I walk the
  path along for hours
In silent, darkness as it falls
  and stars begin to
Appear.
Yes one step at a time I think
  I must be near.
But no so I keep walking that
  path of my dream.

So understand I can not carry
  this body of mine beyond
my dreams.
Let me go one step at a time
  by myself and live my
life along.
I'm not afraid and it's not far.
I know somewhere with
One step at a time I'll make it
  there.

Paul H. Engel
OH GOD IT'S ME AGAIN

I used to drink and never think
So I went a little bit too far
When I traveled around to each
  and every bar
I never cared about what and
  who you were
After stumbling all across the
  town
I should have never gave you
  up Oh God
So I am going to ask you for
  your help again.

Larry J. T. Foucault
OF THE COMING WAVE

There will be men who
  walk about
  telling those of power
in their own amount.
They will speak of darkness
  in the end.
They will speak of blindness
  when the colours blend.
Take heed to their words
  with caution
For some are true,
  and some are filled
  with intoxication.
(It is true that darkness
  will come,
And the earth will
  be blinded by the
  heat of the sun
And all that holds
  to pliable atoms
  will turn to metal.
And the waters to drink
  will turn to dryness.)

Bobbi Bailey
THE RAINBOW'S END

Go to sleep, my little one,
For the summer's day is nearly
  done.
I feel the warmth of your soft
  brown,
And I know we don't have too
  long now.
Soon you shall find Eternal
  Sleep,
And only then may I weep.
I'll long to look once more
  at you—
To see your eyes so bright and
  blue.
To touch your golden, curling
  hair—
To kiss your cheeks so flushed
  and fair.
For now I hold you close to
  me
Before I have to set you free
So you may go around the bend
Where you will find the
  Rainbow's end. . .

John T. Travison
REALITY

What are these wicked tongues
  of flame,
That light the midnight sky,

How quick they bloom, and
then consume,
Destroying me as they die.
What is this awesome creature,
That stalks about at night,
That makes me lock my doors,
And leave within a light,
What are these wretched cries
  I hear,
In the darkness all about,
Their pleadings go unanswered,
Their voices shuttered out,
What is this frightening wail
  I hear,
Bent on it's desigh,
It fills the quiet evening air,
Sending shivers up my spine,
Whose is this dreaded voice I
  hear,
That tells me to beward,
That speaks of doom, and
  spreads it's gloom,
To leave me in despair,
What are these frightening
  sights and sounds,
That haunt me constantly,
In truth they're yet more
  awesome still,
They're just reality.

Lillie Mae Carter
SILVER ANNIVERSARY

Homeward plod I
  wading through
  drifting snow,
Chilled to the
  marrow of the bone
  only to
Shake the flurries
  from the body,
Lay the fire,
Watch the firelight glow—
  in the eternal quiet
  ALL
  ALONE!

Juan Manuel Lavitt
SAND

Oh, those grains of sand all
  over the lonely beaches
Enjoying the fresh kiss of
  unending waves,
The burning touch. . .light
  of life,
Refreshing balsam of Mother
  moon.

All those diminutive, infinite
  particles of mountains
Dreaming, printing, holding
  footsteps, castles.

Oh, humble grain of life. . .
    There is a God.

W. N. Gardiner
FLOWER CHILDREN

She watched the boy play
with a small green grasshopper
in the cropped grass,
love welling in her soul
like a warm spring.
Body to body she loved him,
as body to body
she had loved his father,
gone now never to return,
planting a seed whose flower
he would never see.
She had elected it
this way, unchristlike
to raise the child alone,
unknowing what trade
the boy would follow,
uncaring, living on
A. D. C., a flower-girl
with a flower-child
playing in the short grass.

Mary Lou Heckel
TEARS

A tear
And as I looked in the mirror,
Trickles became streams,
Then rivers and then oceans.
Why, Lord, this uncontrollable
flood of tears?
Why these mountains of fears
that someone might see me cry
And know I am not at an all
time high?
Tears were not made to show
weakness.

They're a part of boldness as
  well as meekness,
A conveyance of unspoken
  emotion,
A beautiful expression of
  devotion,
A part of joy—yet part of
  sadness—
Jewels turned into gems of
  gladness—
Really a gift of love from
  above.
    Jesus wept.
    John ll:35

Debby Masterson
SORTING IT OUT

I'm not cut out for motherhood,
I am a total wreck,
To me kids are nothing but
A big pain in the neck.

I wish I'd had an older friend
Who could have set me straight,
On what it's like and how I'd
  feel,
But now it's just too late.

I clean, I cook, I wash, I go
Run errands for everyone,
And when I think I'm about
  through,
I find I've just begun!

And then some people have the
  nerve
To come right out and say,
"You have time to do this for
  me,
Beings you sit and do nothing
  all day!"

I'm going to keep on helping
  others
With all I have togive. . .
But you can bet, when I hit
  forty,
This chick's gonna LIVE!!!

Ruth B. Gross
THE COLLAGE OF LIFE

Shed no tears that tomorrow
  will
  soon be today and today
  YESTERDAY. . .
Think of it as your collage of
  life. . .
Each slot a reflection of what
  you
  are, were, and perhaps will be. .
Mirroring your yesterdays and
  the
  tender memories of time
  gone by. . .

Lillian J. Loyd
FOR LYELL AND LYNDON

You have made my life worth
  living,
Every gift was worth the giving,
Each memory, I'm now reliving
As I grow old.
All the happiness I knew

In the days I shared with you
Pass by in glorious review
As I grow old.
And when I'm no longer
capable of
Protecting you, I know God's
love
Will always shield you from
above
When I grow old.

Dorotheo Jessop Baird
ASHES

The smoke has cleared;
Yesterday's fire has died;
A slow and struggling death.

Or could it be just banked?
No; look, the coals are black;
The ashes, too spent to drift.

Is this how it ends? Always?
The staggering flame, of
  mis-spent life,
A little pile, of a soul, in ashes.

Phyllis Molson Praill
LIBERACE

Your fingers glow with sheer
  delight,
As they race across the keys.
Such beautiful music one
  has ever heard,
So soft, so sweet,
Now loud and clear.
God must have been so very
  near,
For hands like yours
Are truly rare.
So give thanks, that you were
The chosen one.
To make the piano sound like
The human tongue.
A piece of wood,
Oh not for you,
It comes alive, and lives
For you.

Ellen Wilmarth-Jackson
LATE FALL

There is no moon tonight
I am satisfied watching you
and the North Star through
the clouded pupil of our
  window
in sleep, you are separate
  from yourself, talking to me
from the depths of a dream
A strong, fierce feeling guides
my stroking hand
I am wed to you by many
  untold secrets.

Wilma Richardson
HOMEMAKER

You scrub the floors
And do the chores,
It really doesn't pay.
For home they come,
Adventuresome,
No matter what you say.
Preparing meals
And oiling wheels,
To turn throughout the day.

You wash the clothes
And hang in rows,
To gently swing and sway.
The garden weeds
Are choking seeds,
A tangled, green display,
There's grass to cut,
A gate to shut,
A fence we need to spray.
It's time to press
This evening's dress
In blue and darkest gray.
The day is done,
Respite is won
And yet to our dismay,
The baby cries.

You dry his eyes
And settle down to stay.
Now you may grieve,
May disbelieve
In aid and ample pay,
But joy and love
Work hand in glove
And in this way repay.

Opan Sain
DEW GEMMED

Peering through an early
  morning haze
The beauty before my eyes,
I stopped to touch a diamond.
T'was a dewdrop in disguise!

Kathleen Hall Norton
REBIRTH

Who can feast upon Spring's
  woodland splendor
  and not feel God's presence
  near;
Or revel in the riot of color
  that blossoms forth every
  year,
But be drawn closer to the
  Creator
  through His beauty
  everywhere;
For each thing created is a
  memoir
  of His constant, loving care.

Who can watch the earth's
  rebirth each Spring
  but to see a Master Plan
That dispels mortal fear of
  Death's sting
  at the end of life's short span?
Then together in faith let all
  sing
  praise to God who so loved
  man!

Gretchen Busch
THE PUPPY HAS GROWN UP

Inside me, a voice keeps his
  name on my lips
When everyone says, "let it
  go!"
I'm sure they're quite right and
  he'll never be mine
But I'd rather that he tell me so.

Four years ago it was love at
  first sight
But now I cringe at his stare
It's the moment his eyes are led
  astray
That it's clear, my love is still
  there.

He fosters feelings within my
  heart
That conflict and forever thrive
At times, I pray he'll never leave

At others, he weren't alive.

A lifetime ago, I could weather
  the pain
My emotions would change with
  the wind

I just liked a face or a voice or
a smile
I hadn't real love to contend.

Dear God, I need your assurance
That my love will be returned
But I know you won't deliver
that
So I'll take a chance and learn.

Donna R. Rankin
HUMBLE MAN

Inwardly, you are better than
many will bare outwardly.
Silently, you say more than
the spoken word.

With peace—you are more
effective than
armies in open battle.
With honesty, you can humble
the convicted liar.
With your heart—you find
goodness
in the wicked shrew.
And, with your faith—you
could convert
the lowly sinner.

But, with your inner-most
being
You may someday
Destroy!
All that you are!

Laura Callahan
LOVE'S WAITING GAME

The last time I saw you
you had tears in your eyes.
I could hear the bitterness
in your voice
that day you told me good-bye.
I could feel your body tremble
as you put your arms around
me,
I could feel the pain within
your heart.
I know how much you long to
be free.
I had you convinced to stand up
and be a man,
To live your own life. . .
But you turned around and ran.
You ran back to the one who
has
caused you heartbreak and
sorrow,
She loves you today. . .
Where will you stand
tomorrow?
She had a power over you that
you don't seem to realize.
Don't you see what's
happening, babe?
Why don't you open your eyes
eyes. . .?
You can't play the game of
love
by following all the rules.
I've already lost my heart to
you
but there's nothing I can do.
I played the game of love and
lost. . .
I played the fool for you.
I have hope that you'll come
home to me,
No matter how long it takes,
And on that day I'll be able
to say
"Hey Babe. . .you're finally
free."

Kathy Lowe
CHRISTMAS EVE

Christmas Eve is just for kids
excitement's everywhere
Santa Claus is on his way
There's magic in the air

Mom's got her cookies baking
and dad is on a stew
He's thinking bout the good
old days
and what the world is coming to
Poor mom is so exhausted
but kids still need her so
She'd like to just forget it all
but she's got to make a show
Somehow they'll get through
christmas
they'll create a fantasy
They'll make the spell of
christmas
an enchanting memory.

Wayne Oliver Brown
TURQUOISE

A certain romance about this
gemstone,
has spellbound man for seven
centuries.
Many believe wealth, health
and love,
comes from this aqua blue stone.
Located in remote desert
regions,
turquoise deposits are in copper
mines.
It is dug by hand and pick,
behind the monstrous jaws of
the shovel.
Brought to town by the
contractor,
turquoise is sold to silversmiths,
stonecutters, and many
hobbists.
Turquoise can be considered an
accident,
a freak in the vast mineral
kingdom.
So many geological
contingencies,
are involved in deposition.
It is a complex mineral and
relatively rare.
Therefore, the sky stone seems
distant, inaccessible, and
mysterious.

L. J. Rebo
MODERN MOSAIC

Willful lover when I met you,
Slyly scheming ways to get you,
Sing my love song, I will let you.

Take my heart and gently hold [
it,
Feel the need to catch and mold
it,
Whisper words that can unfold
it.

Patience learned, my great
desire,
Is to set your heart afire,
What is it that you require?

Help me find our secret
laughter,
Promise me forever afger,
We will share our love hereafter.

Fickle love, you left me
stranded,

Could you just this once be
candid,
Keep the love that you were
handed.

Words to you have lost all
meaning,
Life no longer has me dreaming,
Nights alone now leave me
screaming.

Know this that I won't forget
you,
Never in my life regret you,
Keep our love song, I will let
you.

Toni Lee Nelson
DEAR FRIEND

Dear Friend,

If I could reach out my hand,
and touch you,
for just a moment;
we could then understand one
another.

If I could but give you,
A brief hug,
for just a moment;
we could share the joy,
we feel within.

If I could hold you in my arms,
for just a moment;
we could share our tears.

If our souls could touch,
for just a moment, then;
our love would last till the end
of time;
Not just for a moment.

   Love,
     Toni.

Joseph Richichi
NIGHTMARE

Mind, etherized into
unconsciousness,
Awakes into lethargic
subconsciousness.
The film begins, it's the evening
show.

The man escorts his dream lady—
Tall, dark, beautiful—Perfect.
A rerun from previous nights.

An intimate late night snack,
And passionate love making.
The film picks up speed.

Bodies and souls become one.
The man is rudely awakened.
The film crashes to a halt.

"Wake up dear, You were
having a bad dream"
    Says his

Nightmare.

Kirsten M. Obadal
THE CHILDREN

I am a child. . .
No, I am a teenager. . .
No, I am a young adult.
We are all of these—my peers
and I.
The nation is prospering,
and we are young adults.
Riots break out,
and we are teenagers.
The nation is at war,
and we are children. . .
We are all children, then.

Ruth Evelyn Jones
LAUGHTER

Reaching,
out so bold
The world to enfold.
Dreams,
of tomorrow. . .
yesterday.

Breathtaking in its way.
Music,
in ones ears,
So pleasant to hear.
Joy,
no sorrow there.
Happiness, beyond compare.

James Robert Miller
JEFFORY

A love of son,
is my fatherly grace. . .
When I bend to touch,
his sleeping face. . .
A brow so full,
of learning late. . .
A beard untouched,
by habit's fate. . .
Leaves much to see,
of childhood there. . .
His softness speaks,
for all to share. . .
I give to you,
my words of him. . .
To you I speak,
my Jeff from Jim. . .

Anna Tillman
YOUR DAUGHTER

When I met this child, dirty face
and all smiles,
My heart was captivated,
by her brown eyes and fawn-
like actions,
jumping and playing on long
legs she unfolded
from her tiny body.
But nonetheless, she was just a
child,
Like any other child, I loved.
Until I met you.
Then she became your daughter.
And because I instantly fell in
love with you—
she scared me.
Not because of tears that
wrapped you around her finger
Or hugs, that made me warm.
But because of what she was,
through no fault of hers.
I tell myself, all she needs is
love.
Which is all I can give her.
  No genetics,
    No traits—
      Just love.

Your daughter—
Please share her.

Wendy Butcher
A SPECIAL LOVE

I hardly even know you
  But yet you're the closest
  anyone could be,
I have yet to see or touch you
  But you're a very special part
  of me.

You've never seen me either
  you know
  And even now you don't hear
  what I'm saying,
Still all my love to you I show
  And for you I'll always be
  praying.

You will always be my special
  little one
  You'll always be good; oh
  well maybe,
Whether you'll be my daughter
  or son
  To me you're special
  very special,
    you're my baby.

Ralph J. Greco
THE NATURE OF THE BEAST

crawling under new day sun
spirit free fly
no worries in the innocent mind
heart in the right place

walking under noon-day sun
half time confusion mind
thinking of where to go how
to see beyond the haze
but soon he gets through

standing straight in horizoned
sun
straight cold cut precision path
he knows where to go and how
to get there he laughs at
the past

crawling under setting sun
spirit free fly but now to old
lie stagnant in your decaying
frame mind alive
wish he could start again.

Enola Jones
JACK FROST

As I was sitting by my window
I saw an old man all dressed in
his splendor
I looked at him he looked at me
and we became
friends as you can see.
I stepped a little closer to take
a peek,
And if he was frightened he
could not retreat.
He looked so happy and yet so
lost because
the sun is rising on old Jack
Frost.

Gwen A. Solberg Golden
YESTERDAY

Past are the memories of
yesteryear
They come to mind so loud
and clear
Of freshly, fallen, fluffy snow
Of icicles and fire glow
Of sleeping in a bed with three
And sitting up on grandma's
knee
Of holiday togetherness
And aunty Lou's forgetfulness
The nights of skating on the pond
Of sledding then we sure were
fond
The magic of the christmas tree
Of sneaking early up to see
Of puddles from the summer
rain
How in and out of love was pain
Of fighting now and then of
course
And how you rode your cousins
horse
How magical the time was then
To be a child of nine or ten
Now finding all those years
have passed
I'm sure we all grow old too
fast!

Jennifer L. Mitchell
UNTITLED

Now you have become an
illusion in my life.
You are just a dream that
has passed me by.
I see white-top, endless
mountains towering over my
head.
I can now sing along with the
birds
Instead of listening and envying
them.

I'm going to run with the wind
knowing it's with me,
Not against me.
Now I see a new tomorrow, just
waiting for me.
My life used to be filled with
wishes and hopes
Of being with you again.
But I have finally awakened
from my dream world,
And can look for a new b
beginning.
I'm making new and higher
goals.
Goals that are too high for you
to reach and destroy.

Shirley Babineau
DEBBIE

I'll always call you—my little
girl
Altho you're now—a woman of
the world
Nineteen years is a very short
time—for me
But you grew up—And that's
the way it had to be
I know it's selfish—wanting to
keep you here
But in my heart—I know you'll
always be near.
Nine months and nineteen
years—
you've erased all the pain and
tears
You were born from God and
love
You're mommy's angel—from
above.

God will protect you—in
whatever you do
For I've sent up prayers—
especially for you.
If I am nothing in what I do
I own the world—because
I've had you.
It's all my pride in you—that
puts my heart at rest
I love you my daughter— and
you are the best.
Now you're starting your new
life
A man is richer—because you
you're his wife
Don't settle for less—you can
have it all.
Just reach for the stars
They're at your beckon call.

Cheryl Butler
THE THINGS I VALUE MOST

The things I value most. . .
The hours we share
The thrill I feel, by loving you
And knowing you care.
Our special plans—our private
jokes
The things you say and do
to make days more fun—
These are the things I value
most.
And you're part of it all.
You make my days and nights
Just a little more special.

But most of all, I value the
love we share
And the way you make me
feel.

Donald J. Bayman
SKY WAR

Grey-white schooners in the sky
Silently go sailing by,
Making sunlight peek-a-boo
Like a beacon in the blue.

Unseen pilots set a lie—
Straight and true they soar on
high,
Following their heading to
Keep a secret rendezvous.

Shadows merging as they go,
Cloud—ships wander to and fro
'Til the sky is seen no more—
And the fleet prepares for war.
When the lightning strikes
the foe—
When the air is all aglow—
Then flotilla's cannon roar
Answering an angry Thor.

Soon, the battle will be done
And the ships will cut and run
As quietly as they came.
Some intact—some all aflame
In the rays of the setting sun.
What matters now—who has
won?
There is no fame—and no shame
As before. . .as now. . .the same!

Dover A. Haddock
THE ENDLESS DAY

The dawning of a brand new day
How sweet to contemplate,
For once again, it seems to say
Praise GOD, and Celebrate.

The Dawn is proof, that life
is sweet
Gave by our FATHER'S LOVE
To think, that One Day, we
shall meet
Our SAVIOR, up above.

The Dawn gives meaning, to
each day
Begins them fresh and new
Remember less, each yesterday
Look for tomorrow's view.

And if tomorrow does not
come,
Live free, O soul and pray
For soon, you shall be going
Home,
Rejoice! The Endless Day.

Buddy Rose
IN MEMORY OF JOHN LENNON

The day is dark,
The land, once free, now flows
again
with the blood of the
righteous.
The land, once brave, now
breeds
a lunatic to strike down all
who dare to speak the truth.
America, your sins fall back
on you like the eagle that is
plucked from the sky by
death.
And Sergeant Pepper is dead,
murdered by your insanity.
There is no justice at all
in your justice for all.
And I curse you, my homeland
for what you have become.

Harold E. McCawley
SPRING

I see fields of flowers—
daffodils

romping in the sun
playing the nature
kissing mother earth.

I hear a robins song—
violins
after a long cold winter
filling me with joy
singing my song.

I feel its soft touch—
miraculously

stirring my soul
lifting my spirit
making me high.

I smell its arrival—
SPRING!
a time of beauty
a time of miracles
a timeless ritual.

Robert Michael Balderrama
THE MIRACLE OF MARY

M is for the miracle God sent
down from above
Who gives us so much happiness
happiness with her sweet
tender love
A is for the answer to our
prayers in every way
By bringing us her sunshine
that has brightened up each
day
R is for the right to share her
every hour on earth
And for the blessings we
received the moment of her
birth
Y is for the years we've shared
in her sweet company
Our very own sweet Mary pride
of our good family.

Michelle L. Estrange
AWAY

If it were all to end
In the sunshine of the day
You can bet I'll be wearing
my jeans
But if the darkness of night
Should take me away
You can be sure
That I felt no fear
Cause the angels sing
Regardless of the key.

Ruth Roye White
PRAY TODAY

I am praying, as best I can,
That peace will come, once
again.
This dog eat dog kind of living
Has put behind our thoughts
of giving.
Where is the kindness we
once knew?
Is it forgotten, are we through?
There is no need for us to be
greedy,
We can still love and help the
needy.
We don't have the money that
we once had,
But we can pray for others and
that's not bad.
Times will change you wait and
see,
With faith and love, for you and
me.

Crystal Lillian Ruth Geldart
UNTO THEE. . .

Unto thee all men will please.
Unto thee all men deceive.

Thou art keeper of the dead.
Thou art ruler of the living.
All men hate thee, but none as
  much,
As they who go beyond thy
  gate.
For man is a slave unto thee,
No matter what he plead.
For thou art "Death."
"Eternal master of the living
  and the dead."

Pamela D. Gunter
DAY TO DAY

I go from day to day
Building added courage with
  each day's events;
  False courage—surmised only
  through my belief in what I
  pretend to be.
One day I may fail

I quake with fear at the
  thought,
Someday my courage will fail
  me,
  And then the world will see
  behind my outer shield.
They will know what I really
  am;
  A lost frightened little girl,
  just playing grown-up to keep
  from being hurt.
But hurt will come,
  And soon everyone will know;
Hopefully someone will take
  my hand and show me
the real world and I will no
  longer have to pretend.
  I'll be a woman.

Holly Warren
THE QUARREL

the storm came along
brought ribbons of song and
  tears
i watched as my sky opened up
'though the rain fell hard
he kept me dry
beneath his softest words
and i learned every raindrop
  he taught me

Beth C. Brashier
HOW MANY THINGS?

The lights hang low with flowers
  strewn.
I contemplate my fears unknown.
The race for time intimidates.
How many things have I left
  too late?

Could just one more kind word
  be said?
Is there one more book I should
  have read?
Is there one more day I could
  have spent
With someone to whom much
  I've meant?

Is there one more smiling word
  of praise
To help a child through an
  awkward phase?
Is there one more call I could
  have made
To help someone through a
  lonely day?

Is there one more song that I
  could sing
To make the walls with laughter
  ring?
Is there anything that I should
  do
Before my race with time is
  through?

I wonder as I sit in this silent
room,
Where every face is filled with
  doom,
As time goes on, it doesn't
  wait,
How many things have I left
  too late?

Cosby Merideth Newsom
TWO HIGH COUPS

Winter's snow far flung,
Cypress trees, sap tightly
  wrung,
Patient, cold, coiled spring.

Surreptitious rape,
Thrusting, organizing grace,
We perpetuate.

Michele J. Grieco
MY INNER SELF

Do you know me inner self?
  Do you know the way
to reach the goal I strive to meet
more and more each day?

Are you lonely inner self?
  Are you feeling pain
of getting lost inside the clouds
swallowed up with rain?

Understand me inner self!
  Understand I know
what it's like to be real blue
with no hiding place to go.

Don't be foolish inner self,
  don't think no one cares.
Why are you so depressed
  dear one, for my love's
  strong and rare?

Care about me inner self!
  Care and let me know
which path to find my future,
directions where to go!

Trust in me my inner self,
  trust in all my hopes,
then guide me through the
  ups and downs
of life's unending slopes.

Know me better inner self!
  Know me through and
  through,
so I can find life's happiness
to transpose from me. . .to
  you.

Cherie J. Bulger
EASY

When the ocean waves goodbye
  to the shore
Say hello to the seashells
  left behind once more.

When the sun pulls the blanket
  of night over its head
  at the end of the day
Fall into the velvety blackness
  that is lit up
by the Milky Way.

Gae Schmitt
SECOND PERSON UNIQUE

  You
are a song that mellows my

quickly-run life
  You
are a tide that tugs at my
  fantasies
  You
are an untamed colt that
  demands my resources
  a thorned rose
    a starfish
      a wish
        You
are a novel so deep that you
  must be read twice
    You
are a string hanging loose around
  my feet
      You
are a flower that blooms in
  midst of the snow
    a prayer shawl
      a teacher
      a lure.

Christine Hemrick
BEING TOGETHER

We are cheerfully being
  together,
just the company of one
  another.

When I'm looking straight into
  your blue eyes,
I'm seeing our love in the sky.

As we are thinking the same
  things,
and knowing how much it
  means,

I'm feeling the spirit of your
  heart, moving in
kindly but wildly.

We are forgetting the world for
  a few moments
and then once again I see how
  you can be so lovely.

Karen S. Morales
CHILDLESS PAIR

In our lives there will never be
The joy of children to fill the
  need
Of empty hearts and empty
  arms
to fill the void inside of me.
We'll never know the joy and
  care
That most husbands and wifes
  know.
We'll never have the need to
  share
The love that makes our hearts
  ache so.
For God has chosen us to be
A CHILDLESS PAIR.

Donna Ritchie
MY SON, MY SON

My son, my son, you were
  conceived by love not through
  lust.
This in itself is a magical
  splendor
Not often found in this world
  today.
As you grow learn to listen,
  learn to speak,
Learn to give and learn to
  receive.
But most important of all,
  learn to love.
This you must always
  remember my son, my son.
Genuine Love always brings
  life
and false love will destroy life.
This you must never forget,
  my son, my son.
You were conceived by love

not through lust.
This in itself is a magical
  splendor
Not often found in this world
  today.

Alberta A. Cox
**HAPPY IS THE BIRD THAT
SINGS**

Happy is the bird that sings
Happy is the boy that grins.
Happy is the one who knows
Right attitudes helps happiness
  grow.
If in ourselves, we'll simply try
To put a smile where once we'd
  cry.
If courage is placed over fears,
It can repress a million tears.
Through cultivation of our faith,
We give a smile instead of hate.
And truly as we learn to smile
We make other's lives
  worthwhile.

For happy is the bird that sings.
And happy is the boy that grins.
Through smiles, we gain so
  many friends
And happiness that never ends.

Donata Chiara
LIVE FOR TODAY

There are two days, we
  shouldn't worry or fret,
  They are yesterday and
  tomorrow, we should try to
  forget.
The fears, aches and pains,
  all worry and apprehension,
With its frets and its blunders
  and its lost attention.
We cannot change a single act,
  whether we did rise or fall,
Forget yesterday, for it's away
  beyond all recall.
The other day we should never
  dwell upon is tomorrow
  with it's possible adversities,
  large promises or sorrow,
The saying goes "Tomorrow is
  just made for some"
For Tomorrow for you and me
  might never come.
Only think of today, for all
  things life can give,
  Thankful to the fullest each
  day that we live.
Anyone can fight the battles
  of life of just one day—
  By putting yesterday and
  tomorrow out of our way.
Just having faith, hope and
  trust in our God sublime
And try doing our best,
  living one day at a time.

Cynthia Jean Lord
UNTITLED

You asked me to come visit
  your garden
I tried to tell you that I could
  not see
So I begged you to grant me
  your pardon
For your world was too
  beautiful for me
You wanted me to see all the
  wonder
I tried to tell you that I had
  not time
For I couldn't hear teardrops
  through thunder
And for me, the poetry
  wouldn't rhyme

Then you asked me to love you
  forever
But I had to tell you I could
  not stay
Since you knew I could
  understand, never
You then allowed me to go on
  my way
As you moved aside so that I
  might pass
I turned and saw you crying
  through the glass.

Ampara Goitia Owens
WHO AM I?

I am a child cell,
a rolling,
turning,
fast paced molecule,
rushing furiously,
thru icy blue,
darkness of space,
the last dying struggle,
of the human race.

fine me in the tears of a howling
  wind,
find me in the last winded note
  of repentence,
find me in the gentle wind of
  a mother's plea,
find me in the strong winds of
  human survival,
find me in the destructful,
scorching,
deathly, fiery bite.

or in the warm,
comfortable,
gentle,
fiery lite.

I am the nucleus in hope,
the moon,
stars of the universe.

I am the world!
Pushing,
screaming,
tearing,
BIRTH!

I am reborn,
combination earth!

Oh yes,
Now you know me well,
I am the excited positive
  electron,
in the revolving child cell.

Lana Young
DEDICATION TO THE SOURCE OF INSPIRATION: THE WORLD CEEN AT 18

Pain bounces off the shield
it masks what we really feel
Ones manner is only a front
Fatigued of living among
  distrust
For survival, coping with it is
  a must
Confusion arises
not knowing where to turn
Many people are manipulators
it's live and learn

But through the anguish
I have prevailed
At this point
My search for love has failed
The time has come
to explore my own path
Moving on
Never looking back
to just keep growing
For one day You will see
that I was made for You
and You for me.

Karlyne
TIME

Time, something we all fear
Fragments of which are sheer
Set upon wings to fly
A hiding place in which to lie
We see it come and go
Always fast never slow
And just when we think its
  bought
That's when we get caught
Down endless corridors we
  walk
Doors locked to our every
  knock
Dreams we have that just end
Promises we can't keep to a
  friend
Time always seems to get in
  the way
Of the things we said we'd do
  today
But when it's over and our
  time is up
I just hope mine is not an em
  empty cup.

Margaret R. Morrisette
I TELL GOD

I pour my heart out to you
  Dear Father in heaven.
I pour my heart out to you
  For I feel so much pain.

I tell you all about my pains,
  All about my worries
I put my life in your care,
  Won't you help me please?

I pray to you for strength
  To go on from day to day
If you can spare a miracle
  Please send it my way!?

Sometimes I forget
  That you are there to help,
Dear Father from above
  Give me patience and your
  love.

It has been a few years now,
  I have learned to endure
What I would have done
  without you,
  I do not know for sure.

I have learned to meditate,
  Learned more about you
It is when I meditate
  I feel so close to you.

Dear Father in Heaven,
My Lord, My God to you I pray
When the time comes for me to
  die
  Grant me a peaceful day!

Maryse Elot
DEATH OF A MUMMY

There are millions of live
  mummies,
Millions and millions of
  mummies;
(The Ancients would not believe
  it!)
They work, they sleep, they
  think, they eat,
They exist on little monies.

There are millions of
live mummies. . .
The mummies are in
  mausoleums
(For, of course, where else
  could they be?)
From nine to five at minimum
Every week day, every, every. . .
There are millions of live
  mummies. . .
Among all the intricacies
Of artificially lit halls
In a silence of lunacies
Of vaults, of tombs, of walls
  and walls,
An inhuman, creeping silence
The mummies go, come, sit,
  run, dance
Time limited, air limited,
Hardly breathing, overheated. . .
There are millions of live
  mummies. . .
You see more and more
  mausoleums
Among the fossils of dead
  homes
Along the streets, one after
  one,
Yet the mummies are not
  embalmed. . .

Lois Wahl
SNOW MAGIC

What wonders winter storms do
  bring us, oft'
Piling pale snow mounds midst
  us, e'er so soft,
Last night like grateful guests
  they came 'round
And left an ermine gift there
  for the town.
They waited late til all the
  people slept,
Then quite silently, stealthily
  down the crept
Between the faint moonlight
  and pre-dawn's hush
And painted landscapes with
  an artist's brush.

This morn the world seems
  clean and pure and white
Ere footsteps foul the magic
  of the night.
Soon laughing children early
  off to school
Will come with gay abandon,
  less than cruel,
And with a thousand, errant,
  wayward feet
Spoil the soft snow scape
  along the silent street.

Ramona E. Hunter
DREAMS ON THE SANDY BEACH

While lying on the sandy beach
I thought of the many dreams
So hard to reach
The one so clear in my mind
Was the greatest dream of all
  time
The dream of you being in my
  arms
You are so near yet so far
As the gentle breeze blows
  across the ocean
I dream we are together again
And as I look up into the big
  blue sky
I can't help but wonder why
Why we are so far apart
All of these dreams are
  breaking my heart
Knowing you are out of reach
Knowing I am forever alone on
  the sandy beach.

J. L. Lints
LINGERED TIME GONE BY

There is just one you don't talk
  to
who, in a universe, walks
  through
a seething muddle quietly
not making waves or things to
  see
how much his passing brings to
  you.
Yet within all the things you
  do
are unknown meanings life
  bestrew
upon your way, but then from
  me
there is just one.
Let all that life and time
  construe
be found by someone searching
  true,
for meanings lost are history
and may not come or even be
again for when you think are
  two
there is just one.

Debbie Mollick
NOVEMBER IS AN EAGLE

November is an eagle
with dark and piercing eyes,
a voice that cries so mournfully
as it soars across the skies.
  A bird of bronze and amber,
  whose wings whip through
  the air,
  with an icy cold rhythm
  as she travels without care.
Yes—November's here—
the icy rains, the windswept
  trees—
a sometimes dark and known
  despair.
  It's Mother Nature who makes
  the seasons alter
  and nature too, who prevents
  the Grand Bird's falter.

Denise Coney
STONE CONVERSATION

What are you thinking?
I ask.

Slow, shallow,
passionless breath
fills the room.

I cry.

You turn over
in your sleep
seeking a safe distance.

I turn and leave.

Your breath
follows me down the hallway
but cringes
from
my steel
  blue world.

The front door
shuts you out.

S. M. Toupin
MY HUSBAND

My husband—so kind and sweet;
  How can I help but to love
  only thee.
You love me and want me for
  the rest of your life;
  I am so proud to be your wife.

In our marriage we'll have lots c
  of fun;
  I am so happy I bore you two
  sons.
And though your children are
  only two—
  Your dream may now come

true.
The fear of drink, I have—I know
That I should not worry so.
And though the drink you would not abuse;
The fear of drink I cannot refuse.

The pretty girls, you look at all;
How I wish you didn't look at all.
Jealous, oh yes that's me—
But only because I truly love thee.

Jitendra Vir Singh
STILL LIFE

deserted
midnightroad
outside
the railway station three
telegraph
wires
slice
the yellowed poonam moon
floating
in a quiet pool
of sky.

Madge C. Frink
GLORY FULFILLED

Hither and yon do they scatter and scamper
Flirting with the wind
As gust prevail each leafy lashing
Of richly patterned green and gold
or rusty tinged waving wonder
To loosen from their moorings
An ddrift slowly down
Until earthward bound and stilled.
The world of October's glory fulfilled.

Denise D. Hamell
TIME FOUND FOR LIVING

Time.
Like a rapid heartbeat, never slowing down.
Making some people cry for tomorrow,
And others wishing today would never end.
Trying to hold on,
To memories of yesterday.
Wondering, if it is all worth it.
Holding tight to what is left,
Not wanting to lose.
Giving everything.
But, receiving nothing.
Time stops.
The final buzzer sounds.
The race in life is over. . .
Silence.

Fern B. Shoemaker
LIFE

Life is so full
of wonderful things.
Love, sympathy, tears,
aches, pains, years
Of ceaseless caring and doing
for those we love.
Also, years of receiving,
blessings from above.
Yet, without all these
life would be empty.
No tears, no happiness,
no love, no pain,
No caring or doing
no sympathetic word

No extra work to be done
no blessings from above.
Yes, Lord, without all these
life would be very empty.
So, please, Lord, give me
the tears, the love.
The aches and pains
and blessings from above.
And, please, Lord, make me worthy of
all these wonderful things of Life.

Howard B. Pierson
INFLEXIBLE RIGHTEOUSNESS

I looked inside the gates of Hell
and there to my surprise
Were those while on the earth
did dwell laid claim to Paradise.

Christians that I'd known on earth whom nothing could dissuade,
Were cluttering the halls of
Hell on this our Judgment Day.

What! I exclaimed and Satan said, these were my best of friends;
They set themselves up
righteously and disclaimed all other men.

Their way was the only way,
this story they did tell;
And stood steadfast by all their claims but doomed themselves to Hell.

Jada K. Harris
FOR MOM AND DAD WITH LOVE

You've always tried to absorb the hurt,
And wash away the pain.

I love you dearly,
I hope my love shows clearly.

I'd like to say thank-you
For caring so about me.

Roberta L. Logston
THRESHOLD OF LOVE

When I step on the threshold
of love, I want with me,
someone who'll try to
understand me, be my friend and lover to.
One who'll want to be with me
always, loving me,
faithful, keeping our thoughts and ideals honest
and true.
Someone who will talk with me, walk with me,
be with me through all stages of life.
Enjoying the good times together, being as two souls
in one, even in the periods of strife.
Entering the threshold of love
and once inside,
will be thrilling, but at the same time it can scare;
but if I have the right one
walking beside me,
nothing can hurt me, because I'll have love,
togetherness and everlasting care.

Charlotte Lambert Ripple
LISTEN

Winter, Spring, Summer, Fall
None of them really matter at all.
s the seasons pass so

do the years,
Leaving only the pain
caused by wasted tears.
The loneliness withers
leaving the soul hard,
and a once loving heart
is forever marred.
The past becomes clouded,
the future is grim
But there's a plead for a chance,
a new life to begin.
It struggles to be heard
as it pierces the air—
—Won't someone please listen,
won't someone please care.

Paula Christine Flowers
MY FRIEND, MY LOVER

Do not leave my side, my friend, my lover.
Keep your heart near mine,
Stray not far behind.

Do not wish me harm, my friend, my lover.
Guard me with your strength,
Protect me with your soul.

Do not bring me tears, my friend, my lover.
Kiss away my sadness,
Bring me back your smile.

Do not break my heart, my friend, my lover.
Speak to me of tenderness,
Love me once again.

Stewart Kellum
TO A HOBO ANGEL

when i saw the silver train,
a hunger pain of
flying came to me
because i knew there
was a place i must be
but sitting in this ol' chair tho
i guess it has been too long
for the hobo song that i sang
so many years ago.
like the wind blowing
thru my hair
which is speckled gray and white
and the mirror reflects a still crinkled smile,
but a trace of sadness veils
a second light
The silver train still flies.

Thelma R. Anest
YULETIDE

Yuletide dwells within our city.
Bells ring out with chimes anew;
Celebrate we now His birthday—
Bring our gifts with praises true.

He was born for our redemption;
Loud we will proclaim His birth;
Honor give with much rejoicing—
Sing glad songs o're all the

earth.
Young and old alike draw nearer
To the heart of Him who came;
Happy people, filled with living
Good lives for the manger King.

Old traditions, ways and customs,
Ever new at Christmas time—
Give us unity of purpose
And a sense of joy sublime. [

Ring the bells more loudly, Clearer—
Yuletide dwells within our land;
Hand in hand we'll go together—
Worship Him—our Lord and King.

L. O. W.
SEARCH ON

Keep your face to the wind
look at what you see
think of where you have been.
Whistle a merry tune
find what you seek
keep it for a week
Search on.

Look deep within yourself
without overlooking another.
Seclusion
can be a tree
without rings of growth
Stunted.

When you look back
see that dust repels your tracks
if not
walk harder.

When ask where you have been
stop
Count to ten
be able to talk about it.

Smile
when you are glad
be sure to tote your bag
not over your shoulder
By your side.

Feel the sun in the sky
if it makes you close
your eyes
rest your hand on your forehead
Walk on.

Evajo E. Rose
TO-DAY

When your day's work has begun and you
face the rising sun be thankful that all
is well
With a peaceful mind you'll leave behind
all worries cares and woes as you travel
down life's road praying and smiling as you go.
When you're day's work is done and you
face the setting sun be thankful
all went well and today was the
Tomorrow we dream of yesterday.

Mary Beth Baker
SONNET TO GRANDPA BUDDY AND BEN

I see them walk, the old and young, to plant
The seeds of earth's eternal promise: age
And child are wise, believers,

dreamers, can't
Be told, cajoled from pleasure
  or their rage.
An old yet firm hand holds
  my son's with care.
There is no gap in age; they
  love and give
And trust. I see their love;
  they plant and share.
The seeds will grow, and so
  their bond will live.
My son will know his great-
  grandfather's name.
He'll know his own name and
  his bond to those
Who lived before. Ben holds
  the seeds, his aim
to plant the seeds of life,
  its joys and woes.
He'll freeze the NOW of old
  and young 'til WHEN
Their hands, their hearts,
  their spirit's one in Ben.

Eric Scott R. Larivee
**BALLAD OF THE LOST
CHILD**

A little child, so weak and
  feeble,
For a week now, he did not
  have a meal.
Somebody help him, he cries
  in the night.
He's yelling out now, alive
  with fright.
The time has come now, God
  must take him,
He is sleeping now, do not
  wake him,
He is going away, the angels
  are coming,
golden harps and cymbals,
  are there at the dawning.
Angels, please take him,
  don't make him suffer any
  longer,
They took him right then and
  there and then, and saw the
  wonder.
He was no more a weak child,
  but strong and healthy,
And now, in God's splendor,
  he's very wealthy.
Goodbye, Little Lost Child,
  Goodbye.
You are going without a sigh.
I love you, little lost child,
  so weak and feeble,
Seek out your happiness,
  and do what you feel.

James Salvator
LOVE

Love like windplay on the
  windmill
air is there
when a feeling is radiant
a gentle breeze begins,
and so it turns. . .

Thomas J. Nixon III
SHOCK TROOPS

Now came noon time in fog,
  the world in gray
No screech of gull, no passing
  auto's horn
The world of man asleep
  through noon of day
As quiet as night the hour
  before the dawn
The only sound-waves caused
  by waves of sea
Like children's pitchers pouring
  over rocks
You'd hardly think these swells
  could later be

A horde of violent, mean,
  destructive shocks
Of troops—in white on steeds of
  green, hell bent
For shore. Their lives in this
  one charge well spent
In giving to their fiendish will
  intent.
No more will they essay to their
  wild wrath give vent
If this one time they spend their
  energy
In surely washing us all out to
  sea.

Robert Burster
MARILYN MONROE

 May it be said,
that I have fearfully
loved a person stranger
than me.

Bergita Ann Bilbrey
**THE BABY WITH THE
CROOKED SMILE**

He came one day down here
  to stay
For just a little while.
He came to ffill our lives with
  joy—
  The baby with the crooked
  smile.
He touched our hearts and held
  our love—
  Our little angel child.
And now he's home far up
  above—
  The baby with the crooked
  smile.
Our little one now lives with
  God—
  He's happy all the while.
But we still miss his precious
  face—
  The baby with the crooked
  smile.
We held him and we loved him
  so—
  He did our hearts fulfill.
And though he's with the Lord
  above,
  Our hearts are aching still.
He filled our hearts with so
  much joy—
  Our precious little child.
He was a gift from God above—
  The baby with the crooked
  smile.

Marian Slonski
BUT WE LOVE HIM SO. . .

"True," I say,
"Too true."
He lays there like a harmless
  stone
A gem, too pure,
Bent on a destruction only
  one can see.
The Creator knows the stone.
Knows its mind
Knows its body
and will not let it destroy
  itself
and us with it.
He stops the flow of blood
  with love
Given through us,
Hoping for a return of life,
  of breath
But doubtful, all the same.
The bustle of the hospital
  ceases to exist for him
Has done so, in fact, for a
  great many years.
Tears fallen from pain-filled
  eyes

Have no effect, unheeded by
  the stone.
And when the spirit leaves
Making him an empty rock
And when his brain can work
  nŏ more
Leaving him to enter the
  Heavens, quietly, finally,
Will we truly be sorry for
  our loss,
or rather, be grateful for his
  first but final gain.

Debbie Stelmaschuk
THE STORM

Black is the night,
  shattered with lightning;
A shadow appears,
  that's almost frightening.
A myth states that,
  the thunder is from;
A heavy set man who,
  beats the drums from above.
Cool is the night,
  with a hurling strong wind;
The water is restless,
  the fight soon to begin.
The clouds from above,
  like cigar smoke blown;
Are stirring about,
  the restless unknown.
The lightning strikes,
  the thunder rolls;
Who wins the title,
  is told by the polls.
The clouds now cleared,
  the moon shines through;
The stars are twinkling,
  to behold what is new.

Kaye Hayden Gideon
DILEMMA

You must never look into my
  soul
With those eyes so haunting,
  and bold.
An affectionate gesture, or smile,
Must do me, for just a while.
You must not try to come too
  close,
And startle my quiet repose,
Nor tug at the strings of my
  heart,
Causing emptiness, when we're
  apart.
For if I should start to care,
And unveil this mask that I
  wear;
But the past must not surface
  again!
If you care, you'll understand.
Don't stare in that sweet, tender
  way,
Ignoring these words that I say.
I'm not ready for you, can't
  you see?
Yet your arms feel so warm
  holding me!

Laura S. Gwinner
JUST A TOUCH

Just a touch,
That's all I ask.
No words. . .
  No songs. . .
    No tears. . .
      No smiles. . .
For these can all hide one's true
  feelings—a mask
  which will someday fade.
But with your hand in mine we
  can face the world,
  together.
We can feel the vibrations of
  true love and compassion.
  We can be friends.

Johanna Axelrod
THE PRETENDER

Facing me, the eyes shine truth
Acknowledged under facades of
  youth
The smile touches only me
Mirth destroys hypocrisy
Today is gone, no longer there
Tomorrow brings the unaware
Unexchangable without receipt
Hearts impaled upon deceit
Determine not what you shall
  say
Determine just whom you
  shall play
Facing me, the eyes shine youth
Acknowledged under facades
  of truth.

Laura Vee Murdock
LOST IDEAS

Some people think its wrong
  To ponder over lost ideas,
But I, I see no wrong
  No harm is really done.
Then others say its this or that;
  When no one really knows.
And, if the question should
  arise
  The blame would shift to
  those
Who thought they knew, but,
  really didn't.
So there, you see, it's best to
  sit,
To stop and think a while
  Before you to conclusions
  jump,
Before you set the trial.
  It's best sometimes, to change
  one's mind
To listen while others speak,
  To hold your tongue; yet
  better still,
To turn the other cheek.

Mark A. Shafrath
MARRIAGE

For when two cross
  The bridge of Unity
The culmen they will be.
For time will suppress
  For them to live
In total harmony.

Eva H. McCool
TO A SPECIAL LADY

I sat watching the clock on the
  wall
Just waiting for the day
When I can say
This is for you, my Special
  Lady.
Love is such a simple word
When you are close by,
I can feel the beat of your
  heart,
See the smile on your face.
Lady—You are my Special
  Lady.
Magic, there is no magic,
When I look deep into your
  eyes
All I can see is the complete
  understanding.
Just a phone call away
Is all I'll ever need.
Can this all be real,
to feel a love as deep as you?
Easy, oh it was so easy
Cause, you are a Special Lady.
I close my eyes and dream
  about you,

Yet can all this be true,
Sitting so close and falling in
 love with you.
And yet it happens each and
 everytime
This is all for you, my Special
 Lady.
Never once did you turn your
 back
Even when we were so far
 away
Or even close together
I'll always have to say
Yes, You are my Special Lady.

Roberta K. Agness
SPACE LOVE

I'm lost in time
I'm lost in space
 Maybe God;
Will find my place
In heaven or in hell
Thats where I'll dwell.

Barbara L. Smith
DANDYLIONS

Small yellow top
short green stem
a collection in a field
walked on, mowed over,
 picked.
Heads poppled off
bodies made into chains
smelled by many
remembered by few
return each year
with many more along
a collection of a few
turns into millions
all to be
walked on, mowed over,
and picked!

Elmer E. Krueger
LIGHT VERSE

I speak to you
 in words of rhyme
In hope the meaning's subtle hue
 may shine out bright
To fill the night
 twixt me and you
With the comfort of it's light
 in just the way. . .
That candles do.

Darrell Baldwin
SUNRISE

The mountain yells "He's
 coming,
Wake up world and sing.
Each night he drowns in the
 sea.
We cry to think he's gone,
But he lives again each dawn."

Mrs. Blanche Williams
A MOTHER'S LOVE

I retreat
before the fierceness of his
 youthful anger
After all twenty-five
is the year of newborn wisdom.
I see
the impatience in his eyes
as he flips the pages of his
 mental book
to review the accounts
entered
upon the minus column
underneath
my name.
My heart reels
as I reach across
this dark abyss
to touch his hand.
It is withdrawn—

The coals are hot
with tiny flames
that sear and scar.
Still—
Somehow—
Mother-love flows on—
 in bewilderment.

Regina Fisher
THE MASK

Another day begins.
My mask is put on.
I leave my house
with a smile.

People surround me constantly.
They see me happy.
I must hide this feeling.
I must fight back the tears.
No one must see me fall.

What is this hidden feeling?
I cannot understand it.
I only know
It concerns you
Desiring you, wanting you,
 needing you.
I wait for you.

But the day ends
and I am alone in my room.
My mask is removed,
The tears fall like raindrops from
 my eyes.

You know, it's funny,
Everyday, I fool everyone,
Except the one that should
 be fooled—
and that one person is—
Myself.

Lorelei Chouinard
THE LOOKING GLASS

 If only I had a looking glass
I could see deep into the rivers
 of life,
 Knowing the way the
currents flow,
Understanding the paths where
Lovers go.
 But I have only a mirror
To reflect upon the memories a
and mistakes of the past.
 Still I must go forward,
blindly moving on,
 Into the waves of life.
I will live, love, and learn
every moment
to its fullest from then until
now on.

Suzanne E. Morse
PATIENTLY

Patiently, patiently, He waited;
As my life went all astray,
And I struggled with sin everyday
 everyday,
Without yielding my heart to
 pray.
Patiently, patiently, He waited;
As my heart broke in pain,
And I saw, at last, His way,
Then I came. . .
So patiently.

Patiently, patiently, I wait;
As I see you, friend, make the
 same mistake,
Ignoring Jesus day by day,
Refusing to give your heart away.
Patiently, patiently, I wait;
As I view the contempt upon
 your face,
Knowing inside that you long
 to partake,
Coming closer each day. . .
So patiently.

Patiently, patiently, we must
 wait,
Until the Judgement Day.

Aimee Walicki
**REOCCURING DREAM (FOR
NEIL OF JANET)**

Once again—life has become
 awesome
Our bodies lie entangled
 unaware of the world.
Amongst the still of darkness;
There is a sense of solitude,
And that mysterious touch of
 comfort.

The sun magnifies through the
 window
piercing my eyes, bringing more
 pain as if
waking to reality doesn't hurt
 enough.
 You died awhile back.
I lie motionless, unruly thoughts
 disturb me.
Once again—life has become
 lonely.

Lea Tanzman
TWILIGHT

of remembered shapes
and remembered pathos
or
rather
the mild light and
shade play of actual forms
and the sharpness
 the sharpness
of remembered shapes
upon the wall

Pamela R. M. Lewin
SONNET

If only we could see
Beyond today, then surely we
With retrospective glance would
 smile
At all the petty follies that
 beset us now
And cause remorse the while.
We could be as the journeying
 pilgrim, who, with labored
 stride
Moves on towards his goal,
Which having been attained,
 he soon forgets the irksome
 path
In sweet refreshment of his
 wery soul
 weary soul.
We then would know the joy
 of labors past,
The satisfaction of the finished
 deed
Our sorrows and frustrations
 wouldn't last.
But no! These previews are
 denied us mortal men
We can but live the moment,
 and that done, begin again.

Talma Windle Wolfe
VULNERABILITY

Heart's wound only can be
Caused by someone close to me,

The few relatives left,
A stranger, acquaintance,
 friend
Might offend
By accident, unmeant
As I give no deliberate cause.
Such offense may give me pause
But no lasting pain.
Only when family hurts
Me am I bereft,
Heart cleft,
Again.

Susan Saint Louis
AGAIN

Again trapped
Swallowed whole by the throat
of societies putresent sycophant
 tangled
in its mucous of despondency.

Again raped,
by the groin
of a Satanic machine
its nuts and gears
gouging my soul
using its green coin
to lick the pieces
of my soul from
its lascious piston

Again indurated
Again indomitable.

Christina Lynn Trees
UNTITLED

I have never seen you smile
in this world you've living in.
what path does your life
 follow?
where have your footsteps
 been?

you cannot see through mirrors
you do not see through glass.
how can you go on living
in the future that has passed?

Shirley A. Nelson
SEASON WITH GOLD

Something within me loves
 the fall,
Most opulent season of all.
I walk among the molting
 trees;
They scatter their radiant
 wealth at my feet.
I breathe deeply of the
 crisp air,
Wind playfully tosses my hair.
Migrating clouds and flocks
 of geese
Pattern the sky as they advance
 and retreat.
The world's on tiptoe, breath
 held in
Until the winter storms begin.
Nature has extended the lease,
For without fall the year
 would be in complete.

Peggy McElbatten
HE DIED

After a year of mourning
His death is a quiet hurt—
Not deep enough for wailing—
Too deep to stay the tears.

His memory lingers too long.

Blanche A. Yako
MY GRAM

There once was a lady
 we all adored
Then one night
 she walked with the Lord
She's in the heavenly
 skies above

And we'll never forget
her tender love
She raised her family
her work is done
Now she's with God
her freedom is won
She went to the heavens
everlasting light
And is smiling down on us
with her face so bright
For she knows she was loved
and we miss her so
But we will meet again
this she knows
And we'll be good
she'd want it that way
Till we meet again
on our judgement day

Gregory Alan Bullock
FACELESS SOCIETY

I see people: walking
Faceless
Mutation? No
Obscurity? Yes
By choice? Or course
Why?
Fear
Of what?
Oneself
Fear of oneself,
fear of others.
Looking through each other,
never at each other.
A faceless society.
In fear of me,
in fear of you,
in fear of what,
they may go through.
They might have to laugh,
or could be forced to smile.
The features are there,
ears, eyes, nose and mouth,
but the face is gone.
Only to come out of hiding,
in the security of being alone,
with no one to face but
themselves.
Only fooling themselves.

Hazel V. Swayze
SOUND OF LAUGHTER

Now where does my laughter
go I wonder,
To sit upon a moonbeam?
Or tilt the rainbows end?
Or it might be carried to
Children's ears,
To quieten all their fears,
That lovely sound
I know
I'll know
When it returns to me.

Robin Gayle Puryear
**THOUGHTS ON
GRADUATION DAY**

We have achieved the ultimate
goal for our four years in
high school.
During this time, our many
teachers have guided us with
their
influence and rule;
We have accomplished a few of
our ambitions and a few we
have
failed to gain,
But our graduation finally
symbolizes the goals we have
been
able to attain.

We have known close
friendships, shared warm
experiences, and
held wonderful memories.

This is not only a joyous
occasion, but a sad one as I am
sure
every graduate agrees;
For after today, we will go our
separate ways—each to pursue
a career,
But from time to time, we will
sit and think—and remember
the
friends we hold so dear.

Leonard E. Meadows
SKYWRITER

No day shall ever fade without
a thought,
of you deep in it. . .night shall
never go
Unsilvered by some reverie
you wrought. . .
fleeting enchantment
that I cherish so.
My eyes shall never see but
your dear smile,
and all the gentle glory of
your eyes
shall haunt with tender
dreamings
every mile
for lonely feet that stray
from paradise.
No dawn shall ever break
upon the hills
in breathless splendor on
the towseled trees,
unless it's mingled song of
rapture fills
my heart with all your muted
melodies.
Your name in sunshine every
day I write,
and build it in the distant
stars each night.

Debra G. Whitten
BODY EMOTIONS

Heart of mine please don't
throb and pain
Mind of mine don't think of
him don't drive me insane
Arms don't reach out cause he
is not there
Eyes misty with tears but
he doesn't care.

My body aches for his warm
tender touch
I want him, I need him and I
love him so much.
He's more to me than any
man has been—
He's my lover, my husband
and my best friend
When he takes me in his arms
and holds me close
I know he really loves me and
to him I'm the most!

Lisa Lowe
NIGHT

The sunset is fading now;
darkness takes over.
The world closes its eyes to

sleep.
The moon rises over the
mountain top, making light
the darkness
The stars begin to show their
heavenly light.
Lovers everywhere feel the
romance this moment has
created
It's a moment of beauty, of
peacefulness, of love and
serenity.
A time when two people share
the world,
their thoughts and their feelings.
A time when you silence
yourself and
enjoy the beauty that God has
given you;
The beauty of nature.
Soon morning breaks and all
is lost
forever when,
The darkness fades and
sunlight takes over.

Frank L. Fowler
**SABREINA & FRANCINE
(I SEE IN A DREAM)**

I caught them laughing as the
waves brought them closer
to shore.
Bliss! I thought.
And I'm in it every time I see
them like they are every day.

I caught them crying as mommy
told them their little puppy
was no longer with them by
the way of God.
They didn't understand!
And I don't every time I see
them doing things I used to
do
when I was in their shoes.

I caught them loving as they
sat next to their mother at
breast.
Bliss! I thought.
And I'm in it every time I see
them as they are now.

Sarah Jemison
FEELINGS

I hurt all over, for I am sad.
Wish someone was here.

I am alone, frightened by the
wind.
I lay still, my sister has dozed
off.
My head nods, my eyes feel
heavy.
Thus, the wind whistles around
me as
if I weren't there,
The birds sing and chatter, twigs
pull at my hair.
Someone is near me calling me
to. His call too
great to be love, too sad to be
death.
Is this the feeling I feel, too
scared to move.
Too warm to be cold in the
snow.
Dragging me closer and closer. . .
Was it all a dream?

Cheryl A. Siam
MEMORIES OF YOU

You remind me of the dawn
As the sun rises behind the
mountains
You make me think of the wind
As it flies by and sways the

grass
You remind me of the ocean
As the slaps get harder as they
near
You make me think of our life
For our time is all in the past
You remind me of the
wilderness
As a lone deer runs from a gun
You make me think of a river
As the water over the rocks
flows
You remind me of a new born
baby
As the cries warm the soul
and heart
You make me think of our
song
As the fondness in my heart
for you grows.

Thomas Crowl
I AM BUT A WANDERER

I am but a wanderer
Who seeks a place to stay;
A night watchman looking at
the day.
I am a thinker with no thoughts;
A player with no game to play;
A convalescent seeking a
disease;
A blind man who thinks he sees.
I am an aviator without the sky;
And a tiny baby who cannot
cry.
I'm a laugh which cannot find
a joke;
An entire forest that's gone
up in smoke.
I sleep forever without
dreaming;
I am a life which has no
meaning;
A king without a throne;
A celebrity who remains
unknown.
I am a wayfarer without a
home;
A poet without a poem.

Fern G. Allen
SUN RAIN SONGS

It's different in the summer
When dusk comes
And the sky starts to fade
Darker. . .
Especially after a sun rain
It's different in the summer
I don't know
If everyone can smell
The sun setting
Or the dampness from the rain
Drying
It has its own smell
And the smell has
A texture.
You can touch it
If you want to
And if you know how
I walk along the quiet street
After the rain had fallen

And thought about
And thought about
And thought about
And. . .thought about
The trees not yet dry
And why. . .and how
The leaves felt
To themselves.
I know how they feel
To me.
Here in my hands.
Slippery. . .
And covered
With the wetness
From the sky

And I
Walked still
Along the gray street
In the gray city
And wondered why
I was still here.

Carol Ann Richard
REALIZATION

The groundhog's hiding
  And the summer birds are
  gone;
Soon the pond'll have
  Enough ice for us to skate on;
A red squirrel's scrambling
  Up an old oak tree—
I hope that he remembers
  Where his nuts might be;
Snow drifts, trees bare,
  And evergreens are
  ev'rywhere. . .
My, how sad I didn't notice
  These things last year!

Donna L. Rossmann
BEAUTY

"Beauty is in the eye of the
  beholder", or so it is said.
But there are some things that
  are beautiful to everyone.
A bright and sunny summer's
  day and beauty are one in the
  same.
A wide open country field,
  smelling of hay and fresh
  country air.
What's more beautiful than
  the sun as it permeates the
  trees in the forest.
Or a clear, fresh mountain
  stream.
A garden in full bloom.
Love and the miracle of birth
  are certainly things of great
  beauty.
If everyone would take the time
  to look around at the beauty
  in this life,
this world would be a better
  place to live.
Who is to say what is most
  beautiful?
But to me, Life is the most
  beautiful.

Kathryn Kohler
PAPA'S BIRTHDAY

Only our God can guide our
  heart,
  Your heart he made of gold;
You seldom find its counterpart
  Did He throw out the mold

And leave to you the job to do,
  To teach us how to live,
That it's not what you get in
  life;
  But what you have to give.

You give us such a loving smile
  And send us on our way;
May every little smile come back
  And bless your heart today.

Lynnette R. Bolton
THANK YOU LORD

Dear Lord let me always seek to
  find, the wisdom that you've
  planted,
  deep within my mind.
Without your love and tender
  care, there'd be lots of words
  like,
"That's not fair!"
But help us Lord to remember
  the day, you gave your life
  without
  asking for pay.
You forgot to make us listen,

you tried to make us care, but
  all we
  seem to say Lord is, "Life
  seems so unfair!"
Touch us with thy tender hand,
  let us hear the rejoicing band.
The trumpets will sound
  with the call of each name but
  I know,
you're not worried with fortune
  or fame.
  Thank you Lord for giving to
  me, a world so rich, so
  beautiful,
and free.

Geraldine J. Rigliano
IN EARNEST

Finality has lent her precious
  time for me to search my
  Vivid mind for memories in
  Earnest. . .

The pliable but aging hand with
  slightly shaded spots of
  Brown grips a chubby, pink,
  newborn finger; Finality,
You mercilessly tease the
  fleeting memory still done in
  Earnest.

The melodies so creatively
  penned by your deftly
  winsome seasons
Swiftly, stealthily weave into
  songs—their hypnotically
Catchy lyrics mimicked by
  all ages.

The fresher hours of early
  silver shifted, melted toward
  an
Inescapable frighteningly
  cherished golden hue—the
  Alchemy in
  Earnest.

Brown spots, a sudden
  metamorphosis of white, as
  the tested grip
Becomes a protective clasp
  returned—Finality.

Finality these are for me my
  own perpetual memories
  never to be
Marred by subconscious/
  willful erasure.
They are for me friend, priceless
  portraits done—
  By Earnest.

Mary Ellen Dietz
EMPTY

Here I sit in our spare room.
Nothing but I and this rocker
  you gave me.
I look about myself, the walls
  are bare.
There is one window, but no
  shade.
This room is a lot like me.
  Empty.
A long time ago when things
  didn't turn out

right, or when you would
  work late,
I would come here and cry.
Now, I no longer have tears
  except inside.
But no one can see as you once
  did.
I see the snow which once was
  white and the
  sky matches with a dirty
  grey color.
I hate the winter time,
  everything is dead.
I can't wait until it rains, and
  things are growing.
I will plant some grass, maybe
  even some roses
  and tulips.
Those were your favorite.
Like nature dying in winter,
So did a part of me, you see—
They buried you today!

Gina Renee Foster
WORDS I CANNOT SAY

As I sit alone
The middle of the day
A million things enter my mind
Words I cannot say

But still these thoughts invade
  my head
Thoughts that are confused
These thoughts cannot be heard
They are words I've never used.

Ervena D. Fetty Stanley
YESTERDAY'S CHILD

Yesterday's child is still here
  today,
living in each of us in some
  soft of way.
Though today we're men and
  women, yesterday's child
is still there,
Forgotten. . .yet waiting. . .
  deep within us, somewhere.
Longing and yearning to be
  set free,
Softly walking the back roads
  of my memory.
If you listen closely then you
  may find,
The cry of yesterday's child that
  lives in your mind.
No, yesterday's child has not
  gone away,
For the child lives on. . .that
  child of yesterday.

Jean Marston Olney
MAKE BELIEVE

I'm lost in a world
of make believe
acting my life away
the world is a stage
for the lonely games I play

All the faces and disguises
I've used to find a friend
always wondering when I take
  it off
will they ever come back again?

I know there's someone deep
  inside
aching to be free
I wonder
could that person be the real
  me?
If I look deep inside
and find that I'm not there
it's back to my world of make
  believe
where no one really cares

In and out my life
the people come and go
watching all my acting
it's just another show

I keep on playing lonely games
in a world of make believe
telling fairy tales
to hide the real me

I know there's someone deep
  inside
aching to be free
I wonder
could that person be the real
  me?
If I look deep inside
and find that I'm not there
it's back to my world of make
  believe
where no one really cares.

Mike Carter
OH LONELY ROAD

Oh lonely road, winding
  through time
Traveled by all and none;
Always leading away, and
  bringing back
Eternal do you run.

Oh elusive goal, sought by one
  and all
Though none who search do
  find;
That which is bringing all joy,
  tranquil quiet
And eternal peace of mind.

Over mountainous plain,
  dry desert sea
Past empty crowded space;
Through darkened day,
  enlightened night
At such a slow rapid pace.

Oh lonely road, forever to run
Your touch all life does mend;
With mystery great, for how
  can it be
Your start begins at your end.

The way to joy, and happiness
  true
That lies within us all;
On a path to be traveled, never
  to end
Led by the silent call.

Ragnar Carlgren
GRECIAN FORMULA

My wife one day said to me:
"You look old, it isn't fair.
Dear John, I can't see
Why you shouldn't touch up
  your hair.

Millions of men use it, you
  know,
Grecian formula, it's very fine;
Grecian Formula, it's very fine;
It won't cost you a lot of
  dough,
And your hair will have a
  shine!"

So, she bought me some of it,
And I groomed it on my scalp,
Day after day a little bit.
I could see that it did help.

Gradually I got rid of
Some gray the first two weeks,
Watching what the Grecian did
To remaining graying streaks.

Third week came, the gray was
  gone.
My wife was pleased, so was I,
Neighbor asked: "Is that your
  son?
Sorry, didn't know, oh my,
  oh my!"

The fourth week came, then
  said June:
"You are looking wonderful,
  Mr. Beck,

Please, don't think it
  opportune,
Help me, near you I'm a
  wreck!"

Fifth week came, June moseyed
  in
On my desk to compare notes,
  Unspoken she'd on, and a
  grin,
And here are some of her
  quotes:

"Could go for you in a big way
like before you tied the knot,
Now that you got rid of gray,
I could give it all I've got."

That's when my wife entered
  room,
My face as white as hair before.
She said, and you know to
  whom:
"No more Grecian, John,
  no more!"

William G. Zdanis
ODE TO A WAYWARD TEEN

Oh, Wayward Teen,
  You've never had
A closer friend
  Than Mom or Dad.

Thought you were smart
  When you left home.
You're sorry now
  That you're alone.

You're hungry, broke,
  And you don't know
Which way to turn
  Or where you'll go.

That's jungle, where you
  Are, my dear.
Lest you forget,
  There's much to fear.

There's Drugs and booze
  And wolves out there.
Should you go wrong,
  No one will care.

You're young, Naive,
  And immature.
That you'll get hurt
  Is almost sure.

Your family, friends,
  Your Mom, your Dad,
Are worried sick,
  And that is sad.

So call them now,
  And let them know,
You're coming home.
  Pack up. Then Go!

Allen D. Ames
**WHAT HAPPENED TO THE
FLOWERS**

Why didn't you bring me flowers
  Or candy or something today?
You knew it was our
  Anniversary!

Why didn't you bring me a gift
  Or that something I had my
  eye on
In the store we went to the

other day?
Why didn't you. . .Oh!
  What's that in your hand?
A touch of love, for me!

And what's that on your lips?
  A miss more sweet than honey;
Better than any candy.

And what's that in your eyes?
  Your look, a gift of love,
Your look of love is prettier
  than any flowers!

Thank you my love for the
  gifts you brought to me.
For they are more precious than
  all the stars above.
Thank you for being with me
  today and holding my hand
In a very special way. I love
  you, Ann!

Ron Vander Ark
I REMEMBER JOY

My mother's face when my
  sister was born.
My grandfather's sigh after
  planting the corn.
The cows when released from
  the barn in the spring.
My sweetheart's eyes when I
  gave her the ring.
My brother's grin when he
  landed the fish.
Christmas morning when we
  got our wish.
My grandmother's smile when
  we braided her hair.
Feeding my dog lying under
  my chair.
Smelling the earth turned up
  by the plow.
Kissing my girlfriend before I
  learned how.
Holding my father's hand
  when it was drak,
The 4th of July when we went
  to the park.
Too much snow for the buses
  to run.
After the storm when out
  popped the sun.

Annette Margarite Blue
HOLD FAST

Hold fast to that which is
  true and strong,
let not your courage falter.
For you are still young and
  have much to learn
from those Time's hands have
  altered.

Embark upon Life's journey
  now
down paths of straight and
  narrow.
Though they be ones less trod
  by foot,
their way is like the arrow.

And when you reach your
  setting sun,
keep close all wisdom gained
to share with those
  who wish to venture
on roads by which you came.

Sharon Elaine Barton
SEQUEL

This is my town where
  I grew
stronger, the concrete grew
  taller. I once danced
upon their foundations, green,
  with the sun in my hands; by

the shores of this lake
the evergreen
will always be green.
Today I watched a seagull
in the parking lot.
A seagull,
in the parking lot dove
into the air, the wind bent
the water, I may never find
this lake as it found me,
dancing with the sun
in my hands, the sun
at my command but
set down,
again, next to the concrete and
if I will
set down,
who can tell the ripple's dance
  or the wind or
the sunlight as
the ducks glide in
preparing to nest?

Karen E. Bender
**THE DECLINE AND FALL OF
THE BOURGEOISIE EMPIRE**

stinking of fat and stale
  Pampers
gluey white smiles and cottage
  cheese thighs
polyester pantsuits soiled with
  deodorant
too loud voices (shut up) I
said. sugar-coated salutations—
amniotic mudpies and lacy
  Freudian slips.
let's analyze our San Andreas'
  faults as
life skips by in 55-minute hours.
Hadassah henwives (cluckcluck)
  they said—
Let's go to Israel then complain
  about the flies.
Maybelline goo shoveled on
  our daughtersouls
take two aspirin and
call the doctor
cause suburbia's
dying
  because
    amid all the plastic
      flowers where is the
      one perfect rose?

LaRue Mower
TEMPER TANTRUM

"What on earth's the matter
  with you?"
  a friend asked me one day.
"I've seen you in some moods
  before,
  but you never looked that way
  way!
Your eyes are bulging out of
  your head,
  your face is almost gray."
I gave him a haughty stare,
  and to him I did say:
"I'm going to have a tantrum
  like
  I never had before.
I'll weep and wail and gnash my
  teeth
  and kick upon the floor.
The noise I'll make will put
  to shame
  the fiercest lion's roar,
If you don't want to witness it
  you'd better go out the door.
"I'm going to have a tantrum l
  like
  you never dreamed I could.
Not a thing I've done this live
  long day
  has gone the way it should.
I've tried hard to be patient,

but that did me no good
All of my good intentions
  have
  been misunderstood.
"Be calm and smile, and you'll
  win out,
  psychologists expound,
But all that's ever got me
  is trodden underground
If you're not good at swimming,
  you'd better hit high ground.
I'm going to shed so many
  tears,
  I'm afraid you might get
  drowned.
"I'm going to have a tantrum
  that's what I'm going to do.
Everyone for miles around
  will know it 'fore I'm through.
I'd hate to see you getting
  hurt,
  I'm much too fond of you.
"I'm going to have a tantrum
  you never will forget.
I'm going to be heard this time,
  that's one thing you can bet.
I suggest that you go far away,
  you'd better go by jet!
You think you've seen me mad
  before?
  You ain't seen nothing yet!!!"

Barbara Lavore
**WOMAN, GOD'S SECOND
CHOICE**

I am a seed buried deep in the
  clayey soil,
Someone planted me—Dare I
  to be?
Changes start within my small
  unformed body
Then, as I unfold and stretch,
  I realize I can't move!
Someone forgot to water
The hard compressed soil,
It has set into cracked, ugly
  patterns
When I reach, I hear voices,
"Now don't do that,
You're getting dirt all over!"
More voices,
"You are going to crack the
  pot!"
I am so thirsty—
It is so dark—
I know my roots could spread
  and flourish
But for this,
My prison or my grave?
Am I, as a plant
Not yet submerged, that
I classify myself with something
Of such non-entity?
Please—Someone put me here!
And forgot to show me how
  to grow—

Vincent Luppino
DOMENICA

In 1908 the earth did tremble
  and roar
where she stood holding her
  year old son
she desperately ran away from
  falling buildings
racing for shelter covering
  her child
No the ravages of nature would
  not get him
he nestled protected in her hold
but the frightful flight
  weakened her
and from that day the pleurisy
  did grow
She lived to be eighty-eight
in a home across the sea

The son she saved gave her
grandchildren
to cradle on firm New England
soil
away from the treachery of
southern Italy's terrain
When she died doctors learned
she had been living with one
lung
the other was lost that day in
1908
Brave lady exhausted in her
prime
saving the only child she
would ever bear.

Chas. D. Owens
PARADISE IN THE WILLOWS

Two little kittens in a worn out
shoe,
Their mother was gone there
was nothing to do,
Their dinner bell rang but no
one was there,
So they cooked up a steak and
each ate their share.

Next morning big mamma
returned to the shoe,
All ruffled and worn and covered
with dew,
She mentioned a big cat she
met new the slew,
He was gray all over with
eyes so blue.

(And this is what she said)

"Hims jaws is as wide as a gweat
smoke stwack,
Hees tail is as long as a wail woad
twack,
Him can spit across the slew
and half way back,
And catch any varmint that
wuns down d-twack.

Him jumped high and caught
an old E-agle,
Wrestled him to d-gwound just
to see him weagle,
He told that old E-agle to stay
out of his domain,
Or he would claw off hims beak
and flush it down d-dwain."

Next day the big cat found
the shoe,
He sniffed the kittens and liked
the two,
Then he called big mamma and
invited them all,
To visit his den in the willows
tall.

So they all took off from the
shoe,
To arrive in the willows in a
day or two,
Every one is happy, all are fine,
They reached the den at half
past nine.

The den is in a great oak log,
Blown down by the wind among
the willows tall,
In the center is a hollow three
feet high,
With ample storage for cat-nip
pie.

Karen Campen
THE PERFECT LOVE

True love=
  Total love
Where God is concerned.
No one can love like
  God can love,
And there is no love
  like his love.
He can accept us
  for who we are;
And forgive us for
  what we've done;
And still love us
  completely!

There is no love
Like his love—
He sent his only son
  to die for us,
Because he wants us
  to spend eternity
  with him!
He let his only son
  suffer and die
  for us,
Because he loves us
  so much!

God's love is never
  ending;
God's love is total
  love, pure love,
  and total love;
God's love is
  perfect love!

MariaRita Petrillo
FEAR

Fear is someone I know,
something I feel,
a spirit I live with.
Sometimes, I see it in someone's
  eyes,
or feel it in myself.
Sometimes, I walk hand in hand
  with
it down a dark and lonely
  avenue.
At times, I feel it in my bones
  when
the lights are out and no one's
  home.
I rebell against it, but I'm always
afraid of feeling the hurt—of
  being defeated.
Fear accompanies me even when
  I'm
with friends at times.
"What's there? What's that?—
  and why?" I ask.
Fear has no pity. It cares not,
  nor needs to—
It thrives in the minds of
  people,
rotting away their souls,
gnawing at their conscious.
Fear is knowing no one is there
  behind
you, but hearing their breath.
Fear is knowing someone's
  watching,
but turning and seeing no one.
Fear is a torture; an emotional
  torture
that forever lives in you.
It may weaken your every walk,
stifle your every word,
retard your every action,
and destroy your final breath.

Marie Chapman Jensen
BIRD IN A TREE

If I were a little bird
I'd fly to be heard to the top
  of that tree.
I'll sing a song of love for you

and me,
I'll sing loud and clear from
  heaven above
so each and all *would know
  you,*
I hold dear and love.

I cry, I worry, I dream,
*One, two, three—That empty
  chair?*
There should be four.
With each sound I wait for an
  open door.
Each passing hour wondering
  where you are
Missing you more and more.

If I were a little bird at the
  top of a tree,
I'd ask of heaven, *transplant
  this tree and me
  to the land God has forgotten,*
The land our son was taken,
Not from the heart nor, *has
  God forsaken.*

Harry Budd Jr.
A MOTHER

A mother is a wonderful person
Treat her with the highest
  respect
She is your one and only
And don't you ever forget
She straightens you out, if you
  are wrong
That's the way of a mother
So thank God, if she is alive
Because there will never be
  another

A mother is not just anyone
She is a part of your life and
  mine
Someone so very special
And a woman so refined

A mother has a tremendous task
She is a Teacher, Nurse, and
  Friend
The only person that will stick
  with you
Until the very end.

She teaches you from the
  beginning
And soothes your aches and
  pains
When certain problems arise
Intelligently to you, she explains

A mother is like a perfect gem
Not a single flaw
She takes care of the family
And never ask for anything more

What a beautiful human being
  to know
When times are sad and gray
So tell mom, how much you
  love her
Each and everyday

Someday she will be gone
Not even family, sister or
  brother
Can ever replace the love,
The touch and warmth, of a
  Mother.

Karen Suyemoto
PAWNS

We're all just pawns for them to
  play,
on sun or snow or rainy days—
Let them play.
We slaves all move at their
  command,
a lash of their voice, a flick of
  their hand—
Let them command.
The masters enclose us all in
  prisons,

they cut off our love,
  all warmth, our vision—
Let them imprison.
Our bodies belong not to us, to
  them,
with much less value than a
  precious gem—
Let our bodies to them.
They think they hold our
  deaths or lives,
they think they control us with
  all of their knives—
Let them hold lives. . .
  for they do not really. . .

Our thoughts, ideas, all our own,
our imprisonment we do not
  condone—
  To Hell with them!—
our inside life to only us is shown
Never will they force us out,
not with torture, not with shouts
for we are us—there is no doubt
that we have value too.
More so than them, in all of fact
for we stand alone, without a
  pact.
We do not pretend superiority,
although we are different—a
  minority.
Inside we fight them, and we
  deeply feel,
the remorse and guilt of "coming
  to heel".
And one day soon we'll all rebel,
and break out, shatter, our
  unwanted shell,
But.what to do until that day?
Where do we search for that
  freedom way?
So now again we are back at go,
and once again we are placed
  below—
And nothing, nothing, nothing
  is done,
for we are not a violent people,
so we give in. . .until—
when???

Inez J. Reddoch
MY GRANDSON

My grandson is ten, an
  independent lad
His intentions are really very
  good.
But, he is somewhat like his
  Dad
He really believes, he is
  misunderstood.

His little sister Stacey, he likes
  to tease.
He gives her dolls, beads and
  such.
Or maybe frogs or honey bees
But he loves her very much.

At school, there is much concern
Getting up his home-work really
  pays.
Of course, it helps him to learn
And he is rewarded for his A's.

Kenny played football this year
And received a Certificate of
  Award.
Like a pro, he was made to
  appear
Here at home, in his Ole School
  Yard.

Kenny loves Gift giving most
  anytime
And even though he is only ten
He would give his very last dime
To help needy children, women
  and men.

Just this year, Kenny was a
  hero in town
When our neighbor fell and

broke her hip.
She didn't want her window or
door town down
So right through the transom
he did slip.

He slid through the top,
dropped inside.
Unlocked the door for neighbors
and friends
The neighbor took an
ambulance ride.

To a hospital, where her hip
will mend.
Kenny will be glad, when
school is out.
Then he will have lots of
summer fun

He will travel many places,
around and about,
But, he'll be happy, when day
is done.

Well! That's my real live
grandson
For all the world to know.
I only have just this one
And, Oh dear Lord, I love
him so.

McWallace Braxton
THE THANKSGIVING POEM
AND PRAYER

We pause in our daily activities
to give thanks this season

It is the time for harvest and
blessings that were bestowed
upon us, is
our reason

We ask that the supreme being
be continually merciful and
help us to help
ourselves and each other

It is the time we take off from
work and schools to visit
friends, relatives,
father and mother.

We are grateful for what we
have and what we expect to
get

It is the time we try to have joy
and peace in our hearts so
that our
home fires and candles are truly
lit

We also ask that in time we
may have those of us who
are fellow Americans
who do not have their freedom
to be considered and to
remember

It is hoped that they will be
released to their homeland
and their loved
ones in either this month or
our christian, holy month of
December. . .

Freddie Phelps Hanson
MY SEAMLESS ROBE

I gaze in my mirror, seeking a
change
In my natural body. Does that
seem strange?
I've found it easy and somehow
much fun
Once that I'm robed and the
task seems well done.

I'm earning also my Spirit Robe
here
The one that is seamless
throughout each Sphere
It's not so easy, this Brilliant
White Light
More sensed than seen through

the darkest night.
That radiating Center of my
mind
Known as the Aura I too now
must find
Tremendous, quickening,
Transcendent power
Enriching my soul through
each earthly hour

Just how do I do this? Paul
let me know
The Kingdom within is my
way to go
Faith, realization, affirming that
of
Truths which God teaches,
the greatest is love.

I'm making my Love Robe,
the Seamless one
And won't forsake it until it
is done
Faith, perseverence, down
deep in my heart
I'll keep keeping on. I have
a good start

Perfection, purity, guarding
each thought
I'm earning my Robe. It's
fashioned, not bought
Aware of God's presence,
seeking that dome
With my Robe completed, I
can go home.

Barbara Snowden
THE GHOST OF PARKER BAY

Parker Bay is haunted by a ghost
all dressed in white
He moans and wails and weeps
and they see him in the night
A few years back someone
killed a fair young maid
They found her dead and
broken and on the ground she
laid
"We'll find the dirty killer" all
the people cried
They were searching for the
guilty and they hunted far and
wide

They caught young Ezra
Hawkins, her lover and a kid
He swore he didn't do it but
the townsfolk said he did
They took him out and hung
him, how he pleaded for his
life
He swore he'd never harmed the
girl he'd wanted for his wife

They made the day a picnic!
Food and drinks were shared
No one pitied Ezra for no one
really cared
But scarce a month had passed
till folks began to say
Scary things were seen and
heard commence in Parker Bay

They saw him in the graveyard
and by the hanging tree
They saw him and they heard
him, a Spirit never free
They saw him in the churchyard
where ghosts should never
roam
But most of all they saw him
[near the judge's home

Townsfolks talked and
wondered
The judge was going wild
Until at last he screamed and
admitted
He had been the very one
Who'd slain that lovely child
Parker Bay is haunted by a

ghost all dressed in white
He moans and wails and weeps
and they see him in the night.

Mary Louise Willoughby
FLIGHT TO OLD SAN JUAN

We left L.A. so early
My dearest Dad and me
"Come fly away to Old San Juan"
He'd said so blissfully.

Away we flew. The mighty jet
gave forth a forceful roar
and I was so excited
to be seeing Dad's land once
more.

First out o'er the pacific coast
The mighty bird did soar
Then back again and Eastward
'Til I saw my home no more.

The blazing sands and colors
of the picturesque southwest
I loved them all so dearly
and had come to know them
best.

The Lone Star State of Texas
Came forward into view
The came Louisiana
and pine trees, water blue

The mighty Mississippi
that I had known so well
back in my days of childhood
It made my sad heart swell.

We stopped in old New Orleans
The steamy plane set down
enough to give just one quick
look
to Ol.' New Orleans town.

Then out we roared at noonday
with sun through billowy clouds
The mighty delta and its boats
A thrill to see so proud.

For hours we flew o'er the water
the pilot on his plan
Roared down between bold Cuba
and the land of Yucatan.

The thunderheads were building
We could feel the lightning roar
And rain far in the distance
Til we could see no more.
With evening came Montego
bay
Jamaca, what a sight
Fresh from its frequent showers
I smiled with its pure delight.

My Dad and I in leisure
talked and laughed and strolled
'Til it was time to go on board
We had been firmly told.

The evening brought the a
shadows
So lovely and so black
To the Dominican Republic
and Haiti we looked back.

We flew not too much further
The plane was flying low
We spotted Puerto Rico
With soft green lights aglow.

A flame far out in Ponce
that marked the southern coast

The birthplace of my Father
He truly loved it most.

Aguadilla, Arecibo, Bayamon
and Mayaguea
All lit up like a jewel
insthe night, upon a fez.

The plane dropped low, then
lower
o'er the port of Old San Juan
My heart beat a little faster,
My Dad was going home.

Then all at once the touchdown
San Juan , oh what a thrill.
My heart raced with excitement
Indeed it always will—

To think back to those happy
days
We strolled in Old San Juan
My Dad and me together
For he had taken me home.

Frances Matthews
GOLDEN ENLIGHTENMENT

Goals unobtainable
feelin blue
in a rut,
Gave incentive to study
the life of King Tut.
Left my humble abode
to the exhibition
I rode.
There in hieroglyphics
and scroll were
pictures of his majesty
in all his glory;
Surrounded by treasures
  Enchanting
    Mystical
      And gory.
I raised my arm in imaginary
libation
and toasted the King
a deserving salutation.
For when an heir to
the throne was delivered
of the womb
His life was spent
preparing for the tomb.
Many slaves as the story
unfolds had to mine and
sculpture great
quantitities of gold.
Dissolute thoughts were
conjured, placing myself
living, consorting in
that time gone by
waited on by hand-maidens,
protected by guards until
I should die.
Leaving all this wonder
behind, surely my
thinking was cloudy
and making me
  blind.
Like a hooded Falcon
I had vision but
could not see,
That I was alive, the
sun was my gold.
What greater lesson need be told;
Just live for the
present, don't drudge
in misery
accumulating things for
a time that might
  not

Sam Butler
THE FALL OF GRAVEL PIT
MACKINTYRE

The leaves were turning amber
A stranger hit our town
He slouched around, he
sniffed the air
He looked them up and down.

What he was or who he was
The wonder it did grow—
"The name is John P. MacKintyre
And brother I'm not slow."

The trade mark of the stranger
A silly looking grin
To intice men in his company
Or cover up a sin

Not his looks or stature
With his hair line back a mile
A shapely wench on either arm
Was his for just a smile.

He fooled around in maintenance
He thought it all a joke
He buggered up the burners
And spent doubles cleaning coke

When we got to know him better
He'd tell us of his home
The business that he wanted
Making gravel from crushed stone

A foreman didn't jar him
Not farnaman or the lot
He was quite at ease and fluent
From the bottom to the top.

So it wasn't so surprising
That one summer late in May
He shacked up in farnman's
 trailer
While the family was away.

Periodically he'd mention
That he may be going home.
He was going back to "T.O"
To make gravel from crushed
 stone.

He had to train a burner man
Someone to take his job
To an Englishman—a journeyman
He taught the fear of God.
But Romney took it serious
Where MacKintyre had fun
And like the devils stoker
He was always on the run.

So again when leaves were
 changing
Old MacKintyre took flight
He departed rather suddenly
It happened over night

And then the bombshell bursted
It echoed all around
Over twenty grand in hardware
 Had been stolen from the town.

The evidence was left behind
A van low on its springs
Was setting on a flat car
Boundout with all those things.

The B. I. B. got wind of this
Seized van and all the rest
The owner and the fall guy
That MacKintyre had left.

A man is coming to our town
Behind a red coat he's in tow
The name is John P. MacKintyre
And brother he's not slow.

The outcome of this matter
Is anybody's guess
I leave right here my version
And let the matter rest.

The judge then passed the
 sentence
He didn't change his tone
We'll put you on the work gang
Making gravel from crushed stone.

Patricia Suriano
IF THERE IS A WAR
Will the birds still sing in the
 morning?
Will the children continue to
 play?
Will the sun still shine in the
 morning?
Will the fighting seem far away?

Will there be any hope in the
 morning?
Will we all be too broken to
 care?
Will there be any food in the
 morning?
Will we all be too hungry to
 share?

Will the men all be gone in
 the morning?
Will the children be left all
 alone?
Will the women all cry in the
 morning?
Will we believe that the sun ever
 shone?

Will we all be in black in the
 morning?
Will the blood and the hate
 ever end?
Will anything make sense in the
 morning?
Will we remember what we're
 trying to defend?

Will the whole world be gone
 in the morning?
Will their sacred bombs finally
 fall?
Will there never be peace in the
 morning?
Will there be any morning at all?

Aurora L. Espinoza
HOY HABLÉ CON DIOS
Hoy hable con Dios
y me dijo. ...cuanto cuanto
nos amaba
lo sone que bajaba lentamente
y muy cerca di mi almohada
se sentaba;
Hoy hable con Dios
lo vi tan dulce y tan serno
que le pedi perdon por todos
los humanos
porque Dios me dijo que nos
ama. .y nosotros nos portamos
tan ingratos
lo mire tan tranquilo y tan
hermoso
que cai de rodillas y sus pies
quise besarle;
Mas su voz sono potente
y me dijo, levantado su mano
 lentamente. . .detente
tu has pecado. . .y tu beso
por hoy no puedo yo aceptarlo;
Hoy he visto a Dios
y en mi sueno de esta noche
en mi corazon para siempre
se a quedado
le he pedido perdon y he llorado
mis pecados. . .y promenti no
volver
jamas a la senda equivocada
para hasi poder besar su mano;
Esta noche he visto a Dios
y en mi sueno a mi almohada
a bajado
y en mis sueno, he subido
asta las nubes
y desde ahi he podido ver
todas las ingratitudes
que a diario y en cada instante
cometemos;
Mas El sabe que asi somos
todos los humanos
pues de barro fuimos hechos
por su propia mano
perdoname senor/de rodillas
to lo pido
tu que esta noche. . .en mi
sueno
a mi almohada. ..as bajado
perdoname senor. . .y lavame
lavame senor de toda mancha
de pecado;

Lisa Kachurchak
RAINBOWS IN REALITY
Sometimes we all feel down
and out
And it seems that things won't
work out
But, if you believe in what you
do
Then rainbows are always there
for you
Cause there will always be the
bad times
But there will aoso be the good
So, stop and take a minute
To look back on your life
To look at all the things you've
done
The things that came out right
And look at all the good times
The times you've had with
friends
And remember all the rainbows
The rainbows that never end

Because there's rainbows in
reality
Rainbows everywhere
Sometimes you've got to search
to find them
But still they're always there
Cause rainbows are so beautiful
Just like the things in life
But rainbows always fade away
As do special times in life
But still there's memories of
those times
Just like a rainbow in the sky
The memory will always stay
Even though the colors drift
away.

So, next time you're feeling
down and out
Remember what I've said
Rainbows are so beautiful but
still they always fade
The good times that you have,
will also fade away
But like the rainbow in the sky
Good times will return before
your eyes
So, if you believe in what you do
Then rainbows are always here
for you.

Connie Gordon
A BEST FRIEND IS. . .
A best friend is. . .
 always there when you need
 her.
She is. . .
 the person who cares about
 your feelings.
A best friend is. . .
 someone who is always
 open with you.
She is. . .
 the person who laughs along
 with you. . .
 rather than at you.
A best friend is. . .
 someone who expresses her
 feelings
 opinions freely with you.
She is. . .

the person who's with you at
your
 highest and lowest peaks.
A best friend is. . .
 someone who stands by you in
 times of trouble.
She is. . .
 the one who hurts when you
 hurt.
A best friend is. . .
 the friend who loves you. . .
 for what you are.
She is. . .
 your best friend and the only
 one
 that really counts.

Evelyn Evans
A PILGRIM NO LONGER
A pilgrim no longer, a pilgrim
 no more—
The Father has shown me the
 way to His door.
I wandered as far as a wand'rer
 can roam,
But now I've returned to my
 heavenly home.

A pilgrim is one with a prodigal
 mind,
A prodigal heart and a course
 undefined;
And I was adrift like a ship
 with no sail,
And tossed by whatever wild
 winds might prevail.

At times I'd be riding the crest
 of a wave,
Then suddenly sink toward a
 bottomless grave.
But once, when I thought that
 I'd hear death's bell toll,
I listened, instead, to a voice in
 my soul:

"Come home, son, come home.
 Let me show you the way—
When I'm at the helm, men
 cannot go astray!"
I looked and saw nothing but
 my heart aflame,
But nothing about me has since
 been the same.

"You can't find your destiny,
 son, without Me—
Let Me light your way now, and
 shadows will flee;
Let Me chart your course; then
 wherever you roam,
You'll know I am with you,
 and you will be home."

"Is home on the shore ," I
 then asked, "or at sea?"
It seemed He was speaking a
 deep mystery.
"The door opens in—you're a
 kingdom to gain;
Now, seek Me within, and
 attain, son, attain!"

"You just haven't known that
 where you are, I am;
I even was with you in far-off
 Siam.
Your treasures are waiting—I've
 guarded them well,
For how many ages, I'd rather
 not tell".

And then I could see, as the
 door opened wide
A mansion—a palace—a Kingdom
 inside.
This story, I'll grant you, is
 strange and yet true;
And someday you'll tell
 one that's similar, too!

Harry W. Cameron
BEAUTEOUS MT. ST. HELENS

There I sat my "share-fire" to
   tend
Where the land bridge arched
   the Wauna
Above the swift white waters
   marching to the sea;
Came many Braves from north
   and south alongsthe gorge
To strut and boast their love for
   me!
To the wild red rose, Pahatu,
Who watched your bronze
   bodies prance;
Each hour your contest-fighting
   grew
Until it brought Tahmahnaw
   crashing down,
Casging our love-ship into a
   legend new!
The God's wrath rumbled across
   the land
And froze your passion-hearts
   within the mt. strand;
And Ka-Nax and Na'gon your
   punishment shall be
One each to stand on either
   bank of Wauna's bed
To stare at, not touch, the
   lovely me, throughout eternity!
To meet the centuries cold-aloof
Three snow-capped mts. above
   the Cascade roof,
Mt. Adams and Mt. Hood the
   white men know
The indians call the Wa-ya-ast
   and Paho;
Then there I stand, Mt. St.
   Helens, with ermine mantel. . .
   so!
Hear me! great braves who once
   would rush
To seek my warm-fire and
   maiden's blush!
Within me glows a smouldering
   heat
While you stand so cold and
   mute
My eternal love I oft' repeat!
Note ye not my quaking body!
Hot ash and steam my
   volcanic-toddy!
You dare ignore my dream of
   love
While heart-break deep inside
   me
Leaves me dying like a wounded
   dove!

   Oh Great Father high above
   I have two braves
   But not their love!

So hush my frantic beating
   heart;
But keep in hopeful st ore
That Ka-Nax and Na'gon a
   vigil keep
While I lapse into a quiet and
   gent le sleep
Another hundred years or more!

Robert Anthony Brown
THE ISLAND OF ME

I live on a lonely Island called
   the Lonely Island of Me
A broken will is my battered
   ship and four sad walls my sea.
In the silence of my lonely land
   I lie amidst the throng
Of stillness luring me to death
   as I am all alone.

I live in a lonely prison cell
   made by my thoughtless choice;
choice;

No new sails soar in my sea and
   no old anchors hoist.
A prayer arises everyday for a
   moment of release
From my self-condemned estate
   estate—an eternity of peace—
A prayer for storms which
   might dethrone that mighty
   bolted door;
But never a storm in any form
   draws near upon my shore.
Yet, there were times when war
   seemed wise and on it I could
   boast.
But now I pray for a thousand
   fleets to land upon my coast.
Acoustic rhythms rhyme no
   more to purify the sound;
No thunders roar can intercede
   where my quiet heart abounds.
And warships and Armada fleets
   no longer sail my sea,
For I am King of the lonely
   Thing called the Lonely
   Island of Me.
Yes, I'm the ruler of an Island
   that I fought hard to win;
But now would trade a thousand
   thousand like it to hear a voice
   again.
I always dreamed of being
   an Island somewhere out in the
   sea—
But I never dreamed I'd call
   the thing the Lonely Island
   of Me.

Lisa M. Leone
ALL THE WRONG REASONS

   I like to read,
But I read all the wrong books.
   I like listening to music,
But I listen to all the wrong
   songs.
   I like talking,
But I talk about all the wrong
   subjects.
Will someone ever sweep me
   away
   and love me for me,
      and not for
All the wrong reasons?

Judy Mitchell
JUST WONDER WHY

Fresh as the sunshine at the
   break of day
Like the perfect peace of the
   first shining ray
When the trees seem to stretch
   just to reach the sky
All you can do is just wonder
   why

Free as the wind on a cool clear
   night
When the moon shines full
   and the stars shine bright
And the only light is the light
   from the sky
All you can do is just wonder
   why

So fresh and beautiful life can
   be
But the best part of all is it's

   all for free
No one can change the sky at
   night
Or make the stars any less bright
No matter what or where you
   are
Nature is never very far
You don't have to be rich to
   enjoy the sight
And if you look it's really a
   beautiful night

If you keep looking at the
   stars and moon
You'll feel the same way very
   soon
When they want to change the
   land beneath the sky
All you can do is just wonder
   why.

Marciel M. Strong
MOTHERHOOD

I bear you my testimony
   I must tell you
   this
If you don't enjoy being
   a mother you'll
   miss. . .
More than a big house
   money cannot buy
   a single thing,
That the peace and comfort
   and joy that children bring!
Not just while you're young
   but in the next world
   to be,
It took me too long
   until I was nearly forty
   to see. . .
That a job, work, money
   of any kind or
   fame,
Would not, could not compare
   with the children and
   grandchildren that
   carry our name!
And it's not just while
   they've tiny you need
   stand by their
   crib,
To polish shoes, clean up
   spilled milk, was diapers
   and bid. . .
But after school when they
   come home and holler
   "Mom"
Can I have cookies and milk
   for John, Jack and
   Tom?
A big house and furniture,
   nice clothes don't mean
   one thing,
If you don't have time
   to read to your children,
   bake cookies and
   sing.
I watched by their bedside
   and rocked them when
   they got sick,
After an accident to the
   hospital got them there
   quick!
I sewed them costumes and
   watched them in programs
   and plays,
Watched them wrestle, play
   football and run all
   kind or relays.
But as they got older and
   took friends over Mom
   and their Dad,
I went to work to see that
   clothes and spending money

they had.
I wished my mother would have
   lived longer and helped
   me understood,
That the most important thing
   in the world is the gift
   of motherhood!
That no matter how much
   trouble comes in this world
   to you and to me,
What really counts is the treasure
   of children in the next world
   to be!

Jean Bagby
SLEEP

Sleep is but a little death.
A time for the soul to go
   a-calling,
On other planes of existence,
Beyond our earthly concepts.
Along the stardust of the
   Milky Way,
Our souls go a-calling.
Visions and dreams, problems
   are solved,
Loved ones are visited—
Those here and beyond,
When our souls go a-calling.
Sleep, sweet sleep, when our
Souls go a-calling.

Wanda Richy-Roach
LOVE'S MEASURE

Stand still one second, Time!
While I untangle my heart.
Unravel slowly as does twine,
Loose ends begin to part.

Skein by skein layers peel,
Exposing all that's real,
Pain peers through, but Joy
   outruns
And overtakes all ruin.

Enough! Unwinding is endless.
Layers count not the cost.
Heart unfolds—reveals love
   and alas!
Endless measurement is lost.

Ms. Vicki Augustine
EVEN IN THE PAIN

I have been
with you,
in the dancing showers
of a warm autumn day.
Talking with you
of simple things;
then.
listening
as often
I have.
Watching you
I sense
an inner peace;
a quiet joy.
Seeing you,
I feel
you are happy.
Loving you,
even in the pain of parting,
I know
now,
you were right.

Peter A. Bilgrav
JULIE AND ME

That blonde haired girl
   that looks so divine,
She's so lovely,
   and she is also mine.

She's as timid
   and as harmless as can be.
She is so unique
   and she belongs to me.

She is one of a kind
 and that is why she's the best,
I can't believe she's mine,
 and she's different from the
 rest.

Her eyes sparkle
 when we look at each other.
She gives me chills every time
 and I hope for another.

My mind goes blank
 when I look at her face.
But I still know one thing
 that I have great taste.

Love and happiness
 it will always be,
For the best couple,
 Julie and me.

Joseph Duran
IMAGES

I gaze over tree tops
from my lofty perch
Through hazy shadows
green giants
my eyes do search
Far off
into the distance
Dusty clouds of
brownish gray
Circling in
anticipation
Birds
of prey
Overwhelmed
with curiosity
I strain
to witness
the event
The struggle
for life
The ease
of death
Images
are sent.

Christine Burgess
LITTLE GIRL LOST

Oh my, oh my what have we
 here?
A little girl with many tears.
What is your problem? I
 asked quite clear.
My mother I've lost, I know not
 where.

This is a problem I'm puzzled
 too
To find a mother in the city zoo.
Is your mother fat or thin?
Or does she have a double chin?

No, no, she cried, not fat but
 thin.
My mother's tall with dark
 brown skin.
She said to meet her at the gate
And here I've been and wasn't
 late.

Was your mother dressed in
 blue?
And does she look a lot like you?
My mother wore a dress of red.
With a yellow hat upon her
 head.

What time were you to meet
 her here?
I'd like to know, I really care.
She said to meet her here at two,
And she would bring my sister
 Sue.

I think I see her coming near.
She's coming, she's coming over
 here.
Oh mother, oh mother I'm glad
 you came.
This lady was kind but I don't
 know her name.

The lady was gone when the girl
 turned around.
She had left in a hurry without
 making a sound.
What lady my dear? for I do
 not see one
Now let's go to the zoo and
 have some fun.

Fiona Campbell
IN MEMORY OF...

He lay writhing in pain,
Clutching at his invisible
 tormentor
He fought like an animal
Twisting and turning, His
 abnormal body coiling in a
 distorted fashion;
His mind and body worked as
 a team;
He fought his tormentor.
He fought a losing battle, with
 cries of pain,
And eyes full of terror
He fought...until the end.
Ashes to ashes, dust to dust...
May he rest in
 peace.

Joy T. Gallagher
MY FRIEND

He was my friend,
He with the bright anxious eyes
And sympathetic song.
Always ready to listen
To my problems and complaints
Without interruption.
Although I'm sure he must have
 had
Many of his own.
Yes, he was nervous and
 skeptical,
But he knew where he was going,
And he was free.
I thought that he would stay
 forever,
My friend,
But I should have known better,
He was not content to stay
And eat raisins out of my hand.

Mary Ann Sanders
TRUE LOVE

True love is something
 we all seek
but never hope to find.
True love is something
 we all need
but all give up in time.
True love is something
 I hope to find
and I will someday
because you'll be mine!

Joyce Demma Bertschy
**WORDS FOR A MAN FAR
AWAY**

The empty days which have
 no end,
The newspaper, with cut-out
 sections to send.
The lonely nights of desire
 yet to be,
I do it for you- for the love you
 give to me.
Stationery that dwindles as it
 leaves
 to reach your hand,
Stamps, sealing wax and a
 bit of desert sand.
Strength to bear a child who
 has given us so much,
I do it for you- for your gently
 searing touch.

Sitting at home on a Saturday
 night,
Gazing longingly at the full
 moons'
 light.
Rocking our child so gently on
 my
 knee,
I do it for us- for the family we
 will be.
Reaching for a cookie and
 telling myself "NO!!"
Going to sleep before the late
 late show.
Waiting and wanting the reality
 of you,
I do it for you love, I do it for
 you.

Carol Diane Bond
**I ONLY HAVE EYES FOR
YOU—MY ONE AND ONLY**

I've been so lonely
 for You
 'Cause I only
 have eyes
 for you—
my One and only

I wish You were here
 to soothe my pain
This needle in my heart
is worse than in the vein
 'Cause I have eyes
 for You only

 Night and day
 I wish
they would never
come, go or stay
 'Cause without You
I'm filled with the blues

 Can't see straight
 Can't eat right
 Don't enjoy the party
 Swinging to the beat
 late at night
'Cause I only have eyes
 for You—
 my One and only

There are no blue skies
 No shady afternoons
 Not even love
 in the moon
 'Cause...

I'm not with you

The evenings are long
 and unbearable
I write these words
 to tell You
my sweet, sweet love
I...I only
have eyes for You

The other guys passing by
don't even put a flicker
 in my eye
 'Cause I
Yes, I only

have eyes for You—
 my One and only

Amy L. Range
UNTITLED

 As the rain stopped falling I
 looked
out my window and I thought
 of words that
might describe you. I thought
 of all the
things you've said and all the
 things you've
done that made me feel so
 special. I even
searched for a reason why we
 must say GoodBye,
though never to find the answer.
 The hours by the swimming
 pool and
the chance to wear your ring, all
 seemed
to fade as the cob webs of my
 memories
broke into a hopeless dream.
 The rain had started to fall
 again,
but not on the window outside.
 Instead
they fell upon my cheeks from
 the thought
of having to say Good-Bye.

Susan M. Reiter
KILLING TIME

Morning comes—I'm slowly
 waking; head and muscles
 gently aching.
Slower still I think of rising
 and of the things I'll do today.
And the empty bed I'm finding
 lately's something I'm not
 minding,
and the morning sun is blinding
—blinding me with each new ray
Sun is keeping me from rising—
blinding me with each new ray.
Killing time along the way.

But the day ahead will beckon,
 every minute, every second,
till I find that I must reckon
 with thoughts that I cannot
 convey.
So I amble, rather aimless,
 feeling feelings as yet nameless
and the note there has a
 sameness so its meaning fades
 away.
And the words grow hard to
 read there as the meaning
 fades away.
Killing time along the day.

I pour a cup and while drinking,
 strive to sort the thoughts
 that
 I'm thinking.
It seems I have most all I need
 and all these things I now
 survey;
husband—faithful and
 complacent, gracious living,
 modern basement,
A-frame home with yard
 adjacent, my friends envy me
 they say.
All the things life has to offer,
 my friends envy me they say.
Killing time—it slips away.

I think, then, it's become too
 much, I rise and pass the
 china hutch.
The handblown glass so smooth
 to touch; the trophies of a
 life plan laid.

But suddenly, I'm afraid.
Upstairs, the bed is left
unmade.
The words I'm writing start to
fade as back downstairs I
make my way.
And the words are hard to
recall as downstairs I make my
way.
Killing time in my own way.

Lupe San Miguel
MOON HAPPINESS

The moonlight is exciting
tonight.
So happy
Little moon-beams twirl
fast
Many smiles
stretching faster.
Shining scene.
Long shadows
wait their turn.
Taller moon-beams
are falling
perhaps in love,
for the running
radiance of shiny light
before them.
The moon's chorus
has arrived.
At long last
the lighted shadows
join with singing sounds.
Teams of joy
Listening to brightness sing
Happy songs.
Songs with comet-like
endings.
Night-long love-tunes.
Courteous shadows
rise
With more sparkles.
Little happy beams of light
Under the moon,
Sigh.
In the flying dance
of whiteness.
Strength and fragileness
Breathe of one.
Embraces close by.
Music rhythms watch
even closer.
Beautiful light glows
All beams are warm
and growing warmer.
Happier.
Moon happiness.

Paul Sheppard
I TRIED

I looked out on the world
yesterday,
And saw what sad shape it was
in.
Yeah, man, in all his humanity
Had stocked it full of death,
hate and sin.
I asked what I should do today,
I told them what I saw and
thought.
They said, "If you've got
answers, man,
Go on out and save this world
of yours". . .And I tried.
But it was a lot worse than
I'd thought—
A little too early for their
ears to listen,
A little too late for my voice to
matter.
No, the world was not nearly
set to begin.
All I could see before me were
sad people,
Some had money, some had

homes and friends.
But all hung their heads down
low,
Thinking about when it would
all end. . .and I sighed.
And I looked out past the
superficial sufferers
To those who had a reason to
feel blue.
And I saw death and starving,
disease and hatred.
I turned away and didn't know
what to do.
All these little children in
such poverty
And our supermarkets full of
food.
Is this the world we call so
great?
Is this the time we call so good?
. . .Then I cried.
My voice had been inaudible
above the agony,
My promises and hopes were
ground to dust.
Those who had the power to
move were deaf—
I knew that going all alone was
a must.
I wrote my soul down on this
paper,
Left a message for tomorrow's
sons.
I went to a land where there
was no love
And gave my heart to some
who had none. . .Then I died.

Michael S. Rother
LAST NIGHT'S DREAMS

Last night I had a dream
Woke up and found myself
crying
Almost let out a scream
'Cause everyone was dying
I was tired of always trying
Couldn't get back to sleep
The dream was on my mind
A thought for me to keep
Had I left them all behind
The friends I once did find.

Now my mind was clear
Closed my eyes to dream
Woke up without a fear
Had myself a scheme
Riding on love's beam

Now is the time
For all to join hands
Just a little rhyme
To sing in every land
Love is in demand

Diane Tregurtha
THE SEAWALL

I love sitting on this seawall
overlooking
this vast ocean. It's never
ending it
goes on and on. . .
The sky always looks clearer,
the stars
so much brighter. It seems like
you can
just reach up and touch them.
You're up
there too, why can't I reach
up and touch
you???
Yes, I love this seawall. . .
I'm looking out into this ocean
so black,
and thinking of you. ...I'm
sure you're out
there, can't you see me?
I can see your face that I loved
to see smile.

I can see your eyes so brown.
I can see your
mouth that I loved to kiss, and
I can see your
body that I loved to touch. . .
Yes, I love this seawall. . .
I just want to touch you once
more.
You're getting closer, you look
so good.
Exactly how you left me it
seems so long ago. . .
The sand feels good against my
feet and
the wind is blowing against my
face. . .
You're getting closer, I just
want to touch
you once more. . .
The water feels cold and the
waves so strong. . .
You're getting closer. . .
And the sea wall looks so far
away. . .

Janet Lillian Crawl
JANE

She was bow-legged and broad;
Her skin was dark, and she
Wore her short hair in
"Plaits"—most times—
All over her head
Except when she called
herself "dressed up."
She even dipped snuff
to "pacify her nerves."
But when she smiled, in pride,
her face illumed
And she was beautiful,
This lady named Jane.
Called "Mama Crawl,"
My grandmother.

Laurie A. Stevens
CELEBRATION

I celebrate your eyes
Because they looked at me
Without guilt or shame.

I celebrate your tears
Even if they cry for something
That I have or haven't done.

I celebrate your smile
It pulls me through the rough
times
To know you really love and
care.

I celebrate life, for it was
You that made me what I am
with patience and tenderness.

But most of all, I celebrate God
For he gave me, the gift of you
and asked for nothing in return.

Celia Marik Wakefield
**THE TALLEST MAN ONLY
STOOD FIVE FOOT SEVEN**

Our Dad was a man of five foot
seven,
To us he is the grandest dad in
heaven
No one could compare with
him he stood so tall
He was the greatest of them
all.

When he spoke his voice was
very kind
His love and compassion was
hard to find,
He went thru life with lots
of pride
Our sweet Mother always by
his side.

Our dad's parents were so far

away
I know he thought of them
every day,
Our sweet Mother kept in touch
with them all thru the years
We have seen them shed many
a tears.

Our home was a happy one
always open for all
No one had to be invited or
even call,
Dad's pleasant smile and tender
love met everyone so dear
Made everyone feel welcome
when he was near.

This story I have written of
man so very tall
He was five foot seven and that
was all.
A man loved by so many both
young and old
He was the greatest Dad with
a heart of gold.

Don G. Durant
THE BATTLE OF MCDOWELL

The thunderclouds were
forming over the
Allegheny Range, as the armies
wheeled
for battle in the spring of '63.

The thin gray line of Johnson's
men keep
step along the trail. . .as the
drummers
pounded cadence. . .and the
cadence
filled the hills.

The top of Old Bull Pasture was
where they
made their stand. . .and below. . .
poised
in the valley. . .was Milroy's
blue clad band.

With minie balls screaming. . .
and grape
shot in the air. . .the Battle
of McDowell
was on. . .and death was
everywhere.

The battle raged for four long
hours. . . and
many a lad was killed. . .the
stream ran
red with blood. . .and
frightened horses milled.

The old church was filled that
night. . .with
the wounded and the dead. . .
the casualties
were heavy. . .the enemy had
fled.

As morning winds pushed back
the smoke. . .brave men

stood and cried. . .the battle
was
over and they had won. . . .
but many a friend had died.

A hundred springs have passed
since then. . .
but on a misty morn. . .can
still be heard. . .
the bugles blowing,

Forlorn. . .
Forlorn. . .
Forlorn. . .

Elizabeth W. Troublefield
TO MY "BEST" FRIEND

I perchanced to meet my best
friend today
And as we rushed to each
other's side
I felt something in my friend's
touch had gone
Quite like a stranger in disguise.

We laughed, talked and
exchanged our lives
Avoiding all the "not so good"

Being extra careful to "put on
airs"
As true friends never would.

Alas, time changes, even people
too
But I was sure "friends" we'd
always be,
All the wrong emotions had
took control
As we both could plainly see.

I won't resort to explain just
why or what
Fate has so timely laid in store
One thing's for sure, as you well
may know,
Our friendship's not what it
was before.

Ten years passed and I'd never
realized
Just how far apart we had
grown
We exchanged best wishes and
farewells
Separating paths—careful to
remain—Alone.

Gloria L. Wray
**ALONE (AS SEEN THROUGH
THE EYES OF A 10-YEAR
OLD)**

"Don't let anyone in
While we're gone," Mom says.
"And nine is the time
To go to bed."

They drive away
In the black of the night.
You know when you're alone
Things will be quite a fright.

Maybe if you do something
To get your mind off things;
Read a book, watch TV,
Or maybe even sing.

You've run out of things to do,
Though you haven't done a lot.
And now it's time to go to bed.
It's nine o'clock.

You trudge upstairs to your
room,
You brush your teeth and all
that,
You hop in bed, and THEN you
hear
Noises like THUMP,
CREAKITY CRACK.
Your eyes want to go to sleep,
But you won't let them.
And there are those strange
noises!

A-Hem!
Who's that in the driveway?
You feel cold as a stone.
Is it? Yes! It's your mom and
dad!
It brings warmth to your bones!

Tony Glyn Snelling
THE PHANTOM HOUND

I heard the baying of the
phantom hound
As he quickly followed a trail
With leaps and bounds he
moved away
Until I could hear only his wail.

I know not what the phantom
hound tracks
Or where his trail may lead
But the chase is as endless as
night and day
As the phantom hound fulfills
his deed

I have heard the phantom
hound on many a night
And I saw him a time or two
As quick as quick and as fast
as fase
A mind and a heart with a
purpose true

He's black as black and white
as white
And the size of any great
houng
His baying is his song—music
and words
Without it he'd never be found.

Some night when you're all
alone
If everything is breathless and
still
You may hear the lonely
phantom hound
Tracking his prey on some
distant hill

Oh phantom hound why do
you run
Where are you going—what
have you done
Are you seeing your master
in some distant place
And is he also a phantom
caught up in your chase

Miss Lorie Wildman
ILLUSIONS OF LOVE

Like stars forever shine,
That was love—yours and mine.
Like the sun up in the sky,
You gave warmth—so did I.
Like a mountain standing tall,
Love is strong, it won't fall.
Like a bird's unchartered flight,
Love can soar to any height.
Like the fog rolls off the sea,
Love's illusions set me free.

The sky turned dark—it started
to rain.
The love we had got lost in pain.
What we had—well, it faded
away.
I never dreamed it would end
this way.
Love is forever—fairy tales say.
They lied to me, it drifts away.
It's like the sun burning bright,
But it can turn as dark as night.
Love can shine like stars in
the sky,
But stars burn out—I won't lie.
I followed a rainbow to its end.
I found a love, I found a friend.
But the weather changed and
so did we.
Like birds we knew it was time
to be free.

Ann Williams
BORN TO BELIEVE

I was born to believe the lie
that some things last forever
My soul has slept, waiting for
the beam of your light
Unawake until you touched me
I have felt and loved you, stood
with my heart beating too
fast to let me speak
I sit alone, lingering on the
thoughts of you that light my
life
You came to me, unsought,
enlarged the meanings of my
life
I cannot arm myself in vain
to accept a sudden blow
Torment myself with foresight,
and pride myself on facing
disappointment
I should hate myself if I did
anything less
Than snatch the moments
we are equal, and in love
To allow myself the luxury
or pride is to lose the sweetest
joy of all
This moment, experiencing that
rare meeting of similarities
and difference
that compliment each other
You are my beautiful enemy,
unattainable
You make me alive and
important
We have exchanged the glance
that betrays deep emotions,
and can never again
be strangers
The delicious memory of warm
burning wood can still the
chill of winter when
the logs lose their fire
True love transcends the
uneasiness of what cannot be
And it cannot be unrequited.

Anne E. Weston
SUMMER'S REMNANTS

It's quiet on the hill, where I sit.
The first crop of hay has been
cut, and the time is late August.
The second crop of hay has come
come, and the clover in that
has turned brown.

The air is cool, but the sun just
warm enough to heat the back
of my shirt.
My blue jeans have taken a toll
from the summer sun, for they
now show many
strands of white.
My sneakers have seen me
through the weeding of the

garden, and the mud and
rain that accompany it.
A yellow butterfly dips and
turns, looking for a fresh
flower to land on.
The blossoming thistle is one of
the last the butterfly finds
enjoyable.
Even with its green thorns
extending outward, the
butterfly finds no difficulty.
There are only a few blossoms
left,
The newest sparkling purple,
the others dividing off.
Each tiny seed protected by
white silk, so when the air
catches it, it floats
haplessly along.

The sun moves westward,
shining on a few strands of my
golden hair, that refuse
to stay braided.
The cricket with his neverending
ability to rub his legs together
sings for me.

I look out across the field, and
the corn has long passed me in
height.
The tassles are golden brown,
and the ears that once held
juicy yellow niblets,
are now hard and turning red.

The road I walk, is down
through a field, a farm made
road, dirt tracks here
and there, but mostly packed
down grass.

The sun moves even more,
causing my pen to cast a
shadow as I write.

The beechnut tree has provided
for the deer and squirrels as it
does every year,
proving to be even more reliable
than I.

Jill Wright
GREENED GATES

Some say that they'll die in a
silk richened bed,
With all those they love. . .
weeping around,
But I. . .I would die with the
first flowers of spring
In my hand. . .sprinkled with
moist. . .black ground.

With a small leaf of clover (not
4 leaves. . .just three)
Clutched between the teeth of
me,
On blue-reddened lilacs cupped
to hold their own scent. . .
I want my last treasures of
breath to be spent.

To see the spirea as the bridal
bouquet
At the wedding of sky and
earth,
On this my last day.

To be so young-spirited that I'd
know
That all the world's not big
enough to grow
My garden of love. . .budded
inside me!

And so: sensing another place
Where time is no terror
But the latch-key of space,
(Have I not told you of my need
of space)?

I go. . .away from my roots to
that other world

(Did you not know that the
    Heavenly Gates are greened. . .
    NOT PEARLED)?

Robert Allan Hanson
TIMES OF DIFFERENCE

Soon th' rain'll turn t' snow. . .
    The cold north wind'll start
    t' blow;
But now's the time I'm feelin'
    low. . .Thinkin' 'bout these
    times of difference.

Someday people will begin to
    face the fact. . .That I'm not
    tryin' to put on an act.
An' maybe even get off my
    back. . .So I can go down
    my life's track. . .alone.

Thoughts are pilin' all over me. .
    me. . .An I still believe I'm
    in-a-way-free. . .
To say anything about what
    I see. . .An be the way I wnt
    want to be. . .Me!

World's full 'a fakes an' fools. . .
    Usin' other people as their
    tools. . .
To make us all abide with rules,
    an' fight th' wars an' the
    dules. . .for em.

Honesty don't have a chance. . .
    The laws been cast into a
    trance. . .
Can't remember when I first
    caught a glance of these. . .
    Times of difference.

Changin' times fly to and fro. . .
    People minds are much too
    slow to follow
    them so they know. . .
    About what they missed when
    they go. . .sleepin'.

Ya see I try to speak the truth,
    An' I'm not tryin' to be
    uncouth, but I
    ain't gonna spend my youth. . .
Troubled by these. . .times
    of difference.

I'm not th' trouble makin'
    kind. . .an I haven't lost my
    mind
But someday I can look b'hind,
    and say I lived through these. . .
    Times of difference.

Lineaus W. Longenecker
A GARDENER'S PRAYER

I feigh can see God plan with
    care
Eden's garden, fair and bright.
    In the cool of a busy day
    they'd share
A Heaven on earth's delight.
A fit and high calling God
    had giv'n
Those gardeners, Adam 'n Eve;
    Design the beds, paths wide
    'n even
Amidst the flowers interweave.
    A gardener true, this calling

high
Co-laborers with the Creator's
    blessing.
Flowers, paths, ah, this is why
My days have added joys'
    refreshing.
    Planting, watering, feeding,
    weeding;
Fun and fellowship to share
    And I find that each time
    returning
That God, Himself is dwelling
    there.

And so, I ponder life's short
    day;
Our heart is like a garden kept.
    Some glow with colors bright
    and gay,
While others, how sad, the
    weeds have crept.
    There is no secret, 'tis simple
    'n plain,
For that heart whose sunshine
    is the Lord,
    How sweet the bloom,
    refreshed with rain,
Which feeds on Honey of God's
    Word.

So Now, Dear Lord, I humbly
    pray
For gardener's wisdom for
    today,
That passers-by may sense
    and see
This sweet reward of serving
    Thee.
    May the weary find a resting
    place
At the setting of the sun
    And share the thrill of Thy
    love and grace
While yet on earth, A Heaven's
    begun.

Pam Little
**A DIFFERENT CHRISTMAS
EVE**

Cool, frosty, evening air
Icicles hanging from snow-
    covered trees.
You walk down the path—in
    silence.
Walking
On newly fallen snow. . .is
    like walking on cotton.
You walk on. . .in search of
    peace
Quiet and solitude.
In the deep blue sky you spot
    the first star
And make a wish.
Little snowflakes gently touch
    your face.
Silence
The sound of falling snow
Is like the faint sound of
    Jingle Bells.
It's Christmas Eve
Merry Christmas!

Robert C. Marshall
**HAPPY BIRTHDAY—
WONDERFUL WIFE**

Here's to my JEANNIE—
    birthday gal—
She's no "also-ran" in the corral,
But pert and sweet and lively
    too—
Dynamic, vivacious thru and
    thru!
"Smart as a whip"—"cool" in
    the brain.
She comes on strong when
    others refrain.
Personality rarely found,
    She could tame wild horses to

the ground!
With grace and charm she runs
    the house
GRUFF if needed, or quiet as
    a mouse.
Day and night she checks the
    others
With eyes and ears just like
    a mother's!
She holds her own in any
    forum
And yet can always "cook up
    a storm."
Not only she cooks like an
    artist,
    Beating her sketching is the
    hardest!
Yes indeed—she's got a heart so
    rare—
She's got love and a heart to
    spare!
Yes—she loves with a heart so
    true
That I love her—now wouldn't
    you?

Denise Zera
GOD MADE MOTHERS

It is a great wonder that God
    should decree
    a mere mortal a mother should
    be.
If anyone has spent even one
    trying day
    keeping up with a toddler, it
    causes them to pray.
Many an athlete couldn't handle
    I'm sure
    the rigorous pace a mother
    must endure.

The high jump she mastered
    from hurdling toys
    which are scattered about by
    these girls and these boys.
But nothing can compare with
    the love that's expressed
    by a toddler waking up from
    an afternoon rest.
The love that you see in those
    shining bright eyes
    could never be measured
    by mere earthly size.
Those tiny arms encircling your
    neck
    make you forget that you feel
    like a wreck.
These tiny children still fresh
    from God's hand
    make you feel closer to heaven
    than you could have planned.
Thank you, dear Lord, that you
    gave to me
    that extra ingredient so a
    mother I'd be.

Ruby Liles
THRESHING TIME

Threshing was a time
Of both work and joy
Back on the farm
When I was a boy.
I remember how excited
We kids would all be
As down o'er the hill
The engine we'd see.
Belching black smoke,
We watched as it came
Straight down the road
Then turned in our lane.
It rolled by the house
And the steam was quite hot,
Then straight through the gate
Out to the barn lot,
Where the straw was to be piled
In a golden stack
As the wheat was brought in

On the wagon rack.
When the rig was all set
And the separator clean
Then I'd rush to the barn
To harness my team.
Old Jack and Old Pete
Were to be first in the field
To bring in the grain
That the harvest would yield.
I'd drive those mules proudly
In a pattern quite neat,
To load my wagon
With the bundles of wheat.
Then I'd drive to the machine
With a jaunty proud air
To unload the bundles
And see them threshed there.
With the wagon unloaded
Back again we would go
To gather the wheat shocks
That stood row beside row.
The sun high in the Heavens
Told all it was noon,
Then the whistle would blow
And it was none too soon.
My stomach was ready
Willing and able
To partake of the goodies
I saw on the table.
My mother and sisters
Had been working indeed
In preparing the food
The threshers to feed.
The table fairly groaned
With the ample supply
Of meat, bread, and vegetables
Plus three kinds of pie.
I'd take from each bowl,
And fill my large plate
For I knew that supper
Wouldn't be till quite late.
Then back to the field
With Old Jack and Old Pete
We continued the pattern
Till the harvest was complete.
When the rig left our house
In its brash noisy style
In the lot stood a massive
And golden straw pile.
Oh, yes, I remember
And I still often dream
Of the days on the farm
And my faithful mule team.

Timothy John Lux
PITY WE HUMANS

She pulls the trigger of
    a gun;
    its chamber
    void of sound.
My soul breathes on,
    my heart
    it lies,
    crushed upon the ground.

A girl she is
    to lift aloft.
A breath of life
    that's O so soft,
    Or
A howling wind, as cold as ice.
A thing to buy, that has no
    price.

Sweet visions of us sharing
    our lunch.
Sweet visions of chapels and
    towers.
Pity we humans, a silly bunch.
We damn the rain but love
    the flowers.

Dumas Martin, Jr.
THE OLD FOLKS HOME

Good friends within die slowly
Minds travel down memory lane
Soundless voices echo not a
    whisper

While distorted faces mirror
bitter pain.
Aching hearts yearn for
expression
A wealth of love inside they
burn to share
Unknowing eyes see only their
afflictions
Blinded to the deep affection
there.
Arthritic hands reach skyward
Seeking to touch a long awaited
friend
Their loneliness, far too sad to
mention
The cruelest part of life's
bitter-sweet end.

Joey Bruce Lewis
DREAMS LOST

How long can a man hold on
to his dreams?
When the days turn to years
and nothing changes, it seems
Perhaps it is only a vision of
some unearthly schemes
Where only deep in his
subconscious can he hear its
screams
But how can a man hold on
when there is nothing to hold?
It can't keep his heart warm
or shelter him from the cold
A dream can easily fade as
the sun melts the falling snow
One unkind word or broken
promise can follow a man
until he is old
Man comes from flesh and
blood and then returns to dust
When the years have gone there
were few that he could trust
For even the steel so hard
and strong can be eaten by
the rust
With his back against the wall
no one else put him first
So dreams come and they go
sailing by
Only love can wipe that unseen
tear from his eye
And he thinks that to the end
of time broken dreams will
cause man to cry
He cusses the dreams but
inside he knows that without
them he would die
But he can't hold dreams in
his arms
Nor do they compare to
the beauty he saw in her
charms
They can't even shield him
from this world and its
harms
They have took the music from
his life and the meaning
from his poems.

Leslie A. LaFleur
UNTITLED

I know
you need
for more of me
than I
as yet
have learned to give
and no excuse
that I've prepared
seems adequate
or right enough
for never letting go to love. . .
except,
that I
have lived too long
outside of love

and you weren't there
between the time it took
to journey here
from where I've been
Breakfast in bed
and you the night before
are reasons
more than just enough for me
to try to understand
or open up to love
a little more
at least.

Opaline Larson
TOO LATE

The year begins
He smiles goodbye
I am a woman
I will not cry
World outside
Pass me by
Pen and paper
Will be my guide
Beauty is here
Association is not
I can only fantasize
Dreams into colorful words
Passing seasons
Parade outside my window
Fragrantly arrayed, mosaics
Promenade before my eyes
Never seeing, nor hearing
The music of the band,
or smelling
the fragrance of understanding
I watch with blinded eyes
I write in silence
I do not participate
For me
it is
too late. . .

Elizabeth Killoran
THE LEAVES

It was just an ordinary day at
the library
until we found a book
published in 1879.
Flipping through its tender,
yellow pages, we discovered
leaves
oak and maple pressed,
preserved and perfect,
freshly picked
one hundred years ago, long
before man had soared to
space.
We held the leaves in our hands,
wondering who had held them
one hundred years before,
twirling the stems, or setting
them between their teeth like
a pipe
marking special passages, leaves
between leaves.
It seemed a shame to shake
them loose from their hiding
place,
as once before they were shaken
from their place of birth,
their tree, to die here in the
library waste basket.
It seemed like a final ceremony,
like a cremation of the hand
that twirled them,
or the lips that held them like
a pipe
Those lips that breathed one
hundred years ago
Those eyes that scanned the
pages of this book
marking their favorite passages
with oak and maple.
I could picture him resting
with his book,

looking up to the planeless
clouds.
And now, a hundred years
have passed
Perhaps he rests in oak,
beneath a maple tree.
I'm not sure what this book
meant to him,
I suppose he would always
remember its passages.
And I will always remember
its leaves.

Gail J. Monteith
THOUGHTS OF A SOLDIER

I visited Flanders Fields today,
The crosses still stand, row on
row
And as I stood there, my
thoughts returned
To days gone by, it seems so
long ago.
I do remember, with time as my
guide,
When the air was quiet and still,
I looked above in a clear blue
sky
To our country's pride, high
on a hill.
Then in our town, the talk
began
Of the war across the sea,
Where men were dying and
amid bullets flying,
The talk then turned to men like
me.
I will never forget my mother's
face
As my brother walked out the
door.
Like rain on rose petals, tears
dotted her cheeks,
As the pride of man drew me
also out that door.
Soon I was surrounded by
flashes and shells,
And as days went by I witnessed
the cry,
The screams of fear that rang
in my ears,
Through tear-rimmed eyes,
I saw my friends die.
I cried for myself as a shell
pierced my arm
Yet not like the others was I
blind or lame,
Watching them around me I
saw what man had done
And the pride of man filled
my heart with shame.
Then word came of my brother's
death.
With the pain inside I cursed
this war,
As part of my life had died
within me.
The enemy must pay for the
burden I bore.
The guns subsided, my health
I regained
And home I returned to suffer
more pain.

For nights were filled with
visions in mind
Of deaths of friends, never to see
again.
Now today I stand here, the
air is still,
My enemy I've met, and they
live like me.
So remember with us, the pain
we endured,
We fought for your future,
please keep it free.

Irvin C. Kreemer
NIGHT MAGIC

Come, walk with me on a
mountain's height
when the world is asleep on
a summer's night,
where beauty and peace are
on every hand
and earth is as fair as a fairy
land,
where a star gemmed galaxy
glows and gleams
and moonlit mountains are
drenched in dreams.
Come, walk with me and hold
my hand
as we look abroad on a lovely
land
and share the beauty that
weaves its spell
making you lovely and loveable;
Romance rampant to love's
delight
with your eyes aglow and warm
and bright.
Come, walk with me for I long
to hold
you close to me for time untold.
There's loveliness in laughing
lips
for me who their warm nectar
sips.
There never was a night like
this
To hold you close and taste
your kiss.

Carole T. Kemp
FAREWELL TO ELF

You shared with me your
treasure
And knew I'd keep it safe.
What treasure you ask?
What else but Carole Faith?
Thank you for being so
generous.
She's brought me so much
pleasure.
But when I have to give her up;
I'll have lost my little treasure!
I know you'll have to go your
way
And I'll miss you very badly.
I'll let you go and wish you luck
But do it extremely sadly!

Angelia Patterson
FLYING AMERICA'S COLORS

Our goal was reached ending
New World conflicts
On July 4, 1776.
We achieved freedom: a new
life was born,
Bearing a flag, battered and torn.
The pride was branded in those
stars and stripes;
Independence replaced the agony
and strife.
It was a time to grow and learn
new things;
America had earned her wings.

It was then that we took flight;
Fireworks exploded into the
  night.
Colors of victory filled the view
But none shone brighter than
  the red, white, and blue!

The vibrant red and royal blue
Symbolize courage through
  and through.
The white represents honesty,
A sign of utmost purity.

We'll fly our flags and sing
  our songs;
When loyal to America, we
  can't go wrong.
Let's serve our ever powerful
  nation
With gallant and high-spirited
  participation.

Laine Pomeroy
CLOWN PRINCE OF PAIN

Led into fire
Exhaust and flame
Transformed figure
Fountain of blame.
Trained to be triggered
By a radical's tame,
Formed is a newborn
Lonely child of fame.

When wisdom suffered
Forms images as plain,
and circular motion
Protrudes the sane,
and lines of objects
Neglected gain,
Then appears an outcast
Clown prince of pain.

Gwendolyn Trimbell Pease
BACK TO LOVE

Eternal solution not
world revolution is
love is love, is love
emotion, devotion
soothing lotion
lover's potion is
udder balm
quiet calm an art
cooling palm
fulfilled dream
rule supreme
press heart to heart
folding, molding, holding
the endless caress, the very
expression of nearness is
love is love, is love
one life that we live
billing, cooing, willing
to give someone
life if necessary.

Nathaniel O'Neal
WHEN MY MIND WAS WEAK

The idle mind is the devil's
  workshop.
  I don't want. . .Faulty!
  to be bothered/Rhymes—
  by you (me!)/ Consumes
  valuable time.
For Randy and Kind,
  Love is a strong word;
  Hate is nothing that I am
  (heard) love must remain at
  it's trace.
  (And the over-used it plunder
  plunders. . .
  when offerings as a whole
  comes off like the/. . .)

Joked about,
  "I am lonely but never alone."
I thought about it,
  but decided to rule my hands:
  Sliced-off one ear like "Starry
  Night."

You-know-who/What's-his-
  name,
  But Who I am. . .I, who still
  has to leave the realistic.
I thought about it,
  When my mind was weak—
  Reminiscence/remembrance
  of Fealty. . ."
I thought about it
  but decided to rule my heart;
  Sliced-off the dependant's
  dependence
  and feed my smarts. . .
Bowie Wrote it down as a
  vital-static.

Naomi R. Pugh
ALWAYS YOU

  Twilight fell, death came on
  silent feet and
took the flesh and blood of you.
  Yet in each sunset I shall
  see You.
  In each smile on a child's face
  I shall
  see You.
  In the sun warm on my face I
  shall
  feel You.
  In all love for others I shall
  see You.
  In each breeze that caresses
  my cheek I shall
  feel You.
In the rising mist of the early
  morn I shall
  see You.
  In the springtime freshness,
  summer sun, new snow, I
  shall
  feel You.
  In all compassion for others I
  shall
  see You.
  Until I myself am only a
  memory of these things,
I shall always see and feel You.

Rebecca C. Pittman
ECHO OF AN ANGEL

There's an echo of an Angel
  known so well by all,
Her voice shares many stories
  in life as she recalls.

Her music is so touching,
  sometimes of true despair,
They speak of joy and hard
  times, this Angel has been there.

So often she faced a mountain,
  but faith made her strong,
She was determined she could
  make it, with God she moved
  along.

Now she's a country singer,
  dressed in a floor length gown,
Upon the stage before us, with
  dark hair hanging down.

Her blue eyes seem to sparkle,
  her face is all aglow,
She takes the mike into her
  hands, it's time to start the
  show.

As Queen of Country Music, her
  dreams have now come true,
To know that she's accomplished
  what she set out to do.

She's been a singer and a writer,
  way back from the start,
Like the "Coal Miner's
  Daughter," it came from
  within her heart.

So seldom do people realize,

how things come to be,
From where it came and why,
  is quite a sight to see.
From a poor Coal Miner's
  Daughter, to a star in neon
  lights,
Through many eyes we see her,
  as an angel shining bright.
So many times she shared
  her life, in songs as we recall,
The Echo of this Angel, is
  known quite well by all.

Richard Prager M.D.
MONTH AFTER MONTH

January; stills the winter woods
  as a snowwhite day,
February; is happiness and a
  warm lover's heart;
March; is springtime in sweet
  series of surprises.
April; fools are wonderful
  fantasies and beautiful dreams.
May; is to watch flowers grow
  and witness a little miracle.
June; is like the summers song,
  sweet nostalgia, and a warm
  embrace.
July; is silence of summers day,
  where we can hear
  the children play.
August is a quiet moment for
  fall leaves to fill the summer's
  stream.
September, is like no other
  month, where loves knows
  only lonely hearts
October is the summer's breeze,
  where there is Harvest on the
  Summer's land.
November is Autumn leaves and
  memories of sweet summer's
  breeze.
December is the children's
  Christmas for one, for us,
  and for all.

Eva Pajan
REFLECTIONS

The wind whistled through
  the meadow,
bending the heavy golden heads
  of wheat,
that men sow.
I walk slowly through the
  meadow.
Across the endless sea of clover
  and grass
bowing to me as I walk past.
I am walking alone, yet,
I am not alone,
for you are there, always there,
present in my heart and mind.
I sing a happy tune, yet
I am not happy, for I go to
  reach for you,
and you are not there.
I've hardly spoken a word to
  you, yet,
you are my lover,
and I live only for you.
I walk the meadow alone, yet,
I am not.

Jane Moseley Parrish
BIRTH AND DEATH

Warm, safe, free of expectations,
Wafting in the womb, celestial
  haven, my first tomb.
I break the fetal sac of security
  to meet the transformation,
One, alone, at the beginning as
  one, alone, at the conclusion.
A soft voice, a warm breast,
Baby suckling in the nest of

arms secure.
To veil, she forms a shield,
  a safeguard,
To protect the unwary,
  unsuspecting nursling that time
  chases.
I am ready. It is time to leave
  this secular pain,
To climb, to soar above the
  vain desires, anticipations
  rejected,
To shun man's ongoing,
  unending struggle,
To seek release, and in that
  separation, find peace.
Death, yield peace?
Man's eternal question rings
  unanswered through all time.
Potential peace is promised not,
  but in another sphere,
A separate space, an orb of
  different span and place,
Ordeals may fade.

Annie L. Wilson
**SEARCH FOR A TRUE
FRIEND**

A person so real, so kind, so
  true.
A real honest to goodness—true
  friend.
Someone to walk with.
Someone to talk with.
Down to the final end.
Where have they all gone?
Maybe it's me. Expecting—what
  isn't there,
A real true friend—down to the
  end.
There has to be one. Somew
  Somewhere?

The age of deceit. Of lying.
Of ripping and tearing apart.
Of hurting, of really not caring,
Of wounding even a mother's
  heart.

There was a time, when trust
  was King.
And truthfulness also a gem.
And kindness, thoughtfulness,
  They were all there.
And loyalty, what happened to
  him?

All for one. And one for all.
True friends used to say.
So Long ago! So wonderful!
But where are the true friends
  today?

John Joseph Nutter
TIME AND LOVE

Time is a remembered dream
For all the visions of the past
Flow like flowers down a stream,
And the fragrance everlasts;
Though grief may be a waterfall,
And the flowers topple
  overboard
The present in its voice will call,
To the stream below in softened

word,
To undam the flowers in the
  stream
And carry grief to the deep sea
Where sorrow drowns in
  destiny;—
Event sturn clockwise in a
  circle
Slowly turning time to thought,
And memory rhymes in a cycle,
And all the things we thought
  unsought
Return us though as unawares
To times we thought were gone
  with cares,
Until the circle in its noon
Awakes in us its dreaming
  moon.

Katherine Lyne Wheeler
THE SEASONS

Seasons come and they depart,
  but sadness seems to raise
  her hand
and touch my heart.
So breakable and brittle. Each
  time the seasons change, I die
  a little.
Autumn trees stand barren and
  tall, silence resounds as
  departed leaves
fall.
Splashes blazoned defiantly bold
  of flame, bronze and amber
  gold.
Then out of the North, winds
  demand winter appear and take
  command.
In glitter, and glisten chill
  icicles dance. Tingling and
  mingling a world of
entrance.
Snow invades the land like
  snowmen in a marching band.
But they too descend around
  the bend for Spring has a mess
  message she must send.
A vocalist with a vest of red, a
  sprig shooting up from a fertile
  bed.
Soft and gentle rain tapping
  out her name—like a
  constant steady drummer.
And dream filled eyes turn to
  sun filled skies and speak her
  name, it's Summer.
Yes I'm sad as they depart and
  leave their poignant imprint
  on my heart.
Which seems so brittle,
As each time the seasons change
  I die a little

Maxine Sams Miller
TO NINETEEN

In just one year the change
  apparent grew,
And, sweetly-wise, her new
  donned grave maturity
Be-sat her well, although my
  proud heart knew
A fleeting sadness at this grown-
  up surety,

The years had been too short,
  so very few!
Her little-girlness lost in dim
  obscurity.
But, living in the past can't be
  for those
Who knowingly would change
  this, not one fraction,
For though her years went by
  on dancing toes
(And mem'ry's tears fall at
  the heart's contraction)
The Handi-work each year more
  precious grows!
My Heart records her every word,
  and action.

Mary Nolan Moran
HARVEST

Anyone should know
That dust grows and grows!
And it knows, as it grows.
And it crows, as it grows.

In this role that she chose,
The poor girls knows
How dust grows and grows,
As she endlessly "mows".

What do you suppose
The lady of the house does?
Her work never slows,
Although it never "shows".

The dust crows and crows
And it knows that it grows.
The good lady knows
that this is "no rose".

Jay Nixon
A GENTLE RAIN

It was a gentle rain
on the first of Spring,
  and it fell straight down
as happens
  when there's no breeze
to fill the screens
  with drops
better placed
  on expectant forsythia.
I sat with the vestal air
  and
thought of nothing unpleasant
  holding the moment
as a handful
  of
gentle rain.

Jill Marie Meyer
GRIEF

In my room, I found myself
  crying
Outside my windowpane, rang
  raindrops
In tune with my sorrow
As soon ceased my tears, as
  the rain
I wandered outside to an angry
  nature
I stood there in my grief, as if
  dying
Surrounding me, dark clouds
Lit, only with the lightning
I pleaded with myself to stand
  tall
Bend as did the branches
Not fall as the leaves
To strike with lightning
Whenever tear or raindrop fall
Let me sound with thunder
Rather than be weak and small
So I unbent and grew back to
  height
As I followed the clouds high
  in the sky
I became sheltered as a baby
  fawn
Comforted by nature, I quieted

my storm
I shall remember to fight storm
  with storm
Or to fall with weakness, to be
  washed away with the soil.

Luciano L. Medeiros
PISCES TELLS OF LIBRA

in the morning
  she rides the sky
    from her Atlantis
    on a golden chariot
  she stops to rest on my lawn
to drink summer wine
at noon
  she sails away
    and she rides the winds
    leaving behind her book of
    songs
  and as i flip through her pages
i find her mind
discover her feelings
in the slumber of the night
  i dream her images of love
in my midnight land of fantasy
  i find her a searcher seeking
  i find her seeking comfort
  from the tempest of the storm
and when the night fades into
  day
  she rides again
    to give to everyone
    but when she needs
  who gives to her
when her mind is lost
in endless confusion and pain
  who stops the rain
    when she has lost her way
  down the unchatted paths of
life
who stops the pain
    and she sails on
    across the infinite span of
    eternity
  suddenly
    she stops and cries
    she wishes she could die
  because she discovers that her
  horse-mounted lover
    is loneliness
    and not the rescuer dressed
    in shiny armour
  and her white knight left with
  her sister
    moon
    she cries
    she dies for another day
and in the morning
  again she will ride the sky
    because a libra can never die
    forever
because she sings a song of
  freedom
i read her book
and i am the pisces

Tanya Johnson
A HELPING HAND

Sometimes I cry silent tears for
  all the lonely people
Who will never be;
But for those special ones who
  have the strength to,
I smile.
Thoughts of the lonely comfort
  me
As I walk along my paths alone.
You know, sometimes the only
  people
Who care enough to learn how
  to be,
Are the lonely.
The children of the world, are;
Because they live for the
  moment,
Never having time for loneliness
  and pain.

Leave tears for pain.
Loneliness and pain often go
  hand-in-hand.
Wouldn't you like to take my
  hand?
My loneliness and your pain
  could learn from each
  other,
And be comforted.
Sometimes that's all we need—
A helping hand.

W. Scott Jenkel
FULL OF ILLUSION

Madrid is full of boys in awe
  of matadors quite vain,
The mere display of valor
  is most highly prized in Spain.
Young Juan worked long at the
  pension, bullfighters were his
  pet,
Though second-rate or old
  were they, they were the lone
  he met.
To him they were the best of
  men, all brave and without
  fears.
But he did not hear their
  private cries for glorious
  bygone years.
He didn't suspect they were
  passe, most scared all old,
  some sick.
So Juan worked tirelessly ev'ry
  day with his apron and a stick.
One day his friend became the
  bull, meat knives his deadly
  horns,
He pawed the floor, poised
  to charge, unaware of how
  pain forlorns.
"Charge hard," Juan yelled,
  "Come like a train," a pass
  to order was made.
Juan swung aside, media-veron',
  and deftly escaped the blade.
The bull then turned and
  charged again, this time a fatal
  slip,
The blade slid in about chest-
  high, because Juan failed to
  dip.
A searing rush around the
  wound as his blood flowed
  out so fast,
"Hurry my bull and find the
  priest, for I know I will not
  last."
His thoughts of brave matadors
  returned as his life passed
  away that day,
He died unaware of the aches
  in life, "full of illusion"
  the Spanish say.

Virginia N. Hurn
A SUMMER'S DAY

Lazy day, and idle hours.
Scorching heat, and sudden
  showers.
Steaming streets; rain-drenched
  grass
Revealing wet imprints of small
  feet that pass.
Glistening puddles with tiny
  insects afloat,
Are irresistable lures for
  "small-fry" with boats.
Neighbors mingle in the
  welcome coolness,
Light-hearted with relief from
  the heat's duress.
The world seems encased in a
  soft, smoky haze.

Soon sunset casts the sky ablaze.
Twilight beckons the stars—one
  by one,
And another summer's day is
  done.

Penny L. Hughes
**LIFE HOLDS ONTO DREAMS,
LOVE, HATRED, ALWAYS,
NEVER**

Dreams are a wonderous thing,
Dreams are the parts of life.

Love is a very strong
  imagination,
Love can also be a hurtful time.

Hatred is a fact of never sworn,
Hatred is not loving one another.

Always I know you didn't mean,
Always when I love Thy Father.

Never will I, never can I,
Never is way up to the sky.

Dreams I'll remember you,
Dreams that I once knew.

Love is for two, they say I do,
Love is for quite so a few.

Hatred wanting a lot for not,
Hatred seeing it strong in dark.

Always will love you no matter
  what,
Always is when you can do it.

Never is when you're not there,
Never is always saying it's not
  fair.

Silena P. Hubach
WE ARE!

In a world full of make believe,
  we are the only thing real.
In a world full of sorrow,
  we are the only thing joyful.
In a world full of violence,
  we are the only thing calm.
In a world full of hate,
  we are the only thing loving.
In a world full of deceit,
  we are the only thing truthful.
In a world full of craziness,
  we are the only thing sane.
In a world full of jokes,
  we are the only thing serious.
In a world full of frowning,
  we are the only thing laughing.
In a world full of killing,
  we are the only thing living.
In a world full—
  we are the only thing!

Dennie E. Gose
UPON A HIGH MOUNTAIN

Upon a high mountain, from
  the rimrock I see,
A creation of beauty, and
  splendor before me.
Mountains, valleys, and
  clear cool streams,
Lakes and forest, beyond one's
  dreams.
A pleasure to behold, far
  reaching, so great,
With magnificence mother
  nature alone could create.
Through millions of years
  her work has went,
To remain to be seen, when
  my life is spent.
Treasures within, these
  mountains do hold.
Secrets of time that will never
  be told.
While the water and wind play
  melodies,
Along the rocks and evergreen
  trees.
  Setting a background, for this

moment of glee,
For those that view this scene
like me.
As I stand here amazed at this
glorious sight,
I feel sl small, and
overwhelmed by it's might.

Lynda Holmes
TOO MUCH SPRINGTIME

There's too much springtime
  here of late;
the birds too sweetly sing.
Their songs conspire to seal
  my fate
with Love's soft whispering.
There's too much April in the
  air;
it sets my senses whirling
in myriad patterns of warmth
  and light,
a bright, ecstatic swirling.
Too enticing, tantalizing is the
magic that we share;
a raging force, a gentle joy,
a rapture fine and rare.
There's a grassy hill where I love
  to run
to caress the moon and touch
  the sun,
to taste the wild, sweet wine
  of spring,
and know the joys that love
  can bring.
Oh Springtime, I surrender to
  your
soft, seductive spell.
I have fought, but your velvet
  touch
is strong and can compel.
My reluctant heart will she its
  woe
when Love's sweet words are
  spoken.
With too much joy I realize
that love is springtime's token.
In praise of love I'll shout
  aloud
as my heart collects its winnings
Once again I will feel alive
and reach out for new
  beginnings.
In love with you and life and
  spring,
I'll dance, I'll hope, I'll smile,
  I'll sing.
There's too much April for
  sorrow here,
There's too much spring to
  shed a tear.

Joseph A. Hanofee
MY POEM FOR YOUR POEM

The love swollen boy shoots
  arrows of affection,
To strike his Miss and turn
  her attention,
To turn her round and capture
  her eye,
To charm her and disarm her
  and to hear her sigh.

From shouldered case some
  feathered missiles are allied.
One of many that is shot to
  win her to his side—
The Jewel, when raised, is shot
  keenly to wound;
'Dorned with diamond or jade
  the lady falls to swoon.
Natural are the flowers,
  proven a most effective dart,
Often used by the hunter to
  bag the reluctant heart.
Sweet, spell-casting Rose turns
  the unsure bosom sure;
The beast so skillfully his
  Beauty did allure.
Then, too, there are the candies.
  what a weapon these sweets.
Most desired the little
  chocolates she eagerly greets,
Softly has this marksman
  struck her with candied arrow;
Delights to her palate, so
  faintly remembered in the
  morrow.
One feather from the quiver no
  hunt be hunt without,
Did Romeo at Juliet boldly
  aim with courage stoud—
A Poem, a message, a song
  of love with words chosen
  dearly,
On a bow strung with desire
  did this Gallant pluck her
  severely.
My poem for your poem is
  fully pointed with ardor.
Drawn back on the string each
  word at painful labor.
Let fly all and one in
  passionate art—
My arrows are gone to you, a
  rain on your heart.

Polly Galbraith
TWO LOVES

Two loves have I; of joy and
  remorse
Each love appeals and satisfies
  a need
When circumstance observed
  and not the source
The motive in control and not
  the deed.
Help me, O Lord, to give myself
  to hope
Regret to spurn and burn it
  like the dross
Our mortal minds can ne'er
  comprend the scope
Of love supreme expressed
  within your cross.
There is no love or hope or
  joy, so dear
But that your joy enhances
  and fulfills,
Your perfect love o'ercomes,
  deletes all fear
Regret destroys, but hope
  springs very real.
God doth not give a dread of
  fear, or signs
But pow'r and love and joy
  and strong, sound minds.

Daniel R. Cavanaugh.
ROSES AND STONES

Most hands would rather hold
  a rose,
  Than lift a stone to throw;
But there are fools who do not
  want
  To see the roses grow.
Thus roses are ignored by some,
  Whose hands prefer the stone,

That can become like weaponry
  And may bring blood when
  thrown.
Of course, the roses stems have
  thorns,
  Which also may draw blood;
While stones with proper toil
  may build
  A home or block a flood.
So leave the roses and the
  stones,
  But take away the fools;
That all may know at last the
  worth
  Of beauty and of tools.
Despite the weeds, the roses
  bloom,
  For they are strong of root;
So too the soul of greatest
  growth
  Will bear the richest fruit.

Virginia E. Chase
LONELY MOUNTAIN

I climbed a lonely mountain
And half way up the side,
I wondered about the length
  of it
And also the miles wide.
Soon I started climbing
For I never stop half way.
The sun was brightly shining
To proclaim a glorious day.
But I was shaded and protected
By the leaves that swayed above.
It seemed the mountain held
  me
Tenderly, with love.
I reached the top by sunset;
The world spread out below.
As a fawn came out from hiding,
Softly followed by a doe,
I dropped myself onto my knees
And turned to face the west.
I saw the world had turned to
  gold;
God had done his best.

Kelly Dalrymple
TO THIS I'VE COME

I sit and contemplate and
  wonder about you.
I drink and rave.
For once I loved you,
  cherished your loveliness,
and to this; I became a slave,
I loved your scented hair,
and craved you as a flower.
I felt a need to love your body,
and thus became of courage.
Sometimes I sit and curse you,
and cry because you're gone.
I drink and rave more.
For once it was you who made
  my life worth living,
and now you've shown me the
  door.
I loved your eyes that shined
  so bright,
and craved you as a vision.
I felt a need to correct you,
and thus became a challenge.
I will continue to sit and
  contemplate,
wonder about you, curse you,
  cry because you're gone,
but most of all, drink and
  rave more.

Solomon Vanguard
**THE MESSAGE FROM THE
STARS**

Over Clark Hill Road the
  oldsmobile went,
The riders knew not where they
  were bent.

On the other side, with the
  town lights left behind,
The driver showed what he
  had in mind.

He pulled the car off to the
  side of the road,
Switched off the lights and
  discharged the load,
As they stepped out into the
  dark of the night,
Off in the distance shone one
  house light.

But up in the clear moonless
  night;
Millions of stars,—God's great
  panoply of light;
Twinkling, sparkling, an
  awesome display,
Lighting the sky more brilliant
  than day.

Lights from distant stars,
Vast giants in other spheres,
Traveling through time and
  space,
For thousands, yea millions,
  of light years.

Mingling with the lights from
  neighboring planets,
In Earth's own solar system
  space,
Meeting in the eyes of these
  observers,
At this selected space.

Man cannot fully comprehend
  or discourse
The magnitude of this sight
  by which he is awed.
Did the Creator provide this
  window-display to his
  universe
To prove to Earthlings that He
  is God?

In all the vast, majestic universe,
Is God's superior creation—
  Man?
Placed on this minor planet
  Earth,
Each with a mortal body and
  an immortal soul,
Each with a free will—to hate,
  do evil and perish,
Or—to love, do good, and prove
  his worth?

Each night time observer of the
  sky
Reads this message from the
  stars,
"Oh man! It is up to you to do
  or die—
Go and earn My blessing for
  your try."

Tommy Crowl
TO JAMIE

Your eyes are pools of
  starlight;
Your skin is smooth as silk;
Awake, I dream of you all night;
I long to fill your breasts with
  mother's milk.

Your touch sends chills
  throughout my spine;
Your tongue makes me lose
  control;
You taste to me like the
  sweetest of wine;
You live in the depths of my
  soul.

Your hands are masters of
  pleasure;
No woman born can compare
  to you;
In clothing you are a buried
  treasure;

Naked you are a dream come
  true.

Given the chance I'd kiss your
  feet and your face
And everything in between;
But you've belted your pants
  and evicted me from my place
And left me alone to wean.

But my love for you will not
  cease;
My heart and mind shall not
  find peace;
For my love for you there is
  no measure;
I will love you Jamie, forever.

Eva Edington
GOD'S MATCHLESS LOVE

There's many an aching heart
In this old world of sin;
Often a smile, on one you meet
Is hiding a hurt within.

Many a heart is crushed today
With a burden so heavy to bear,
Come to Jesus, lonely one,
He's waiting your grief to
  share.

He sees every tear drop falling
Understands your hurt and
  pain;
He longs to comfort and
  give you peace
  You'll not come to Him in
  vain.

We cannot live without Him
Without Him, we dare not die.
He's the only one who under
  understands
And is always standing by.

He proved His love when He
  died for us
And took our place, on the
  Cross;
May we never cease to give Him
  praise
Who saved us from all loss.

Fran Franklin
COMPANIONS

Fall came wearing gray chiffon
  clouds
  over a red-gold gown
Spider lilies leapt upon her
  leaf-shod feet.
Then she disrobed before my
  eyes
  casting brown all around.
Branches wove fragments
  in demure modesty.

Winter came starkly dressed in
  soot;
  she screamed a fire alarm
And gird herself with amethyst
  'cross the breast.
She stood aloof within the
  aisle of trees,
  breathed and whirled, and
  caped
The whole with a crystal ice-
  snow fall.

Spring came carrying lightning
  rods
  and wearing a thunder frown.
Raindrops made
  daffydowndilly sounds skip-
  beat.
Then she put on pink-yellow-
  green
  gossamer apparel,
A while she smiled, then blew
  up the leafy street.

Summer skipped blonde and
  barefoot
  shaking her tasseled fawns

As birds abused the air and
  beat straw-twig nests.
She posed and turned, greening
  a smile
  at the animal world,
Then draped robes of honeys
  honeysuckle over all.

Ruth Becky Johnson
SERENITY

I planned a Great Adventure
  such as none
  that ever may
Befall me, as I sat upon a
  hilltop,
  where the birds were still at
  play.
My emotions were commingled
  with a
  distraught frame of mind
And I trembled as I sat there,
  seeking
  love I could not find.

Serene clouds were but a pillow
  upon which
  to place my head,
And I revelled at the silence
  which at
  once became my bed.
Then and there most tranquil
  feelings
  warmed my spirit all
  throughout
As my fears and all anxiety
  were melting
  all about. . .

Melting down upon the
  sandstone,
  Melting down around my feet;
Melting down and through
  the meadows
  where the sheep and cattle
  bleat.
This down to earth experience
  submerged my
  heart with peace
As my worries and adversities
  were met
  with great surcease.

These enemies and I are now
  in full accord
  and I enjoy great freedom
Since the journey with my
  Lord.

Penrose Spohn
**THE CATHEDRAL OF
MEXICO**

It looms like a mountain
on one side of the vast barren
square of the Zocalo
where once the great white
  pyramid stood
with its twin temples
and their bloody altars.

The shrunken beggar women
and their ragged decoy children,
descendants of the pyramid
  builders,
are grateful for the shade it
  yields
and the compassion it evokes
in the hearts of the faithful.

Within, the vaulted spaces
glow warmly with the light
from lofty windows and the
  gold
of second-generation ornaments,
remelted to expel the pagan
  dross.
One hardly notices at first
the leaning piers,
the fractured walls,
patched and repatched,

the sunken steps;
only the uneven floors alert
  you,
confiding to your feet.

Those who built it
were stronger in their faith than
  in their engineering;
the uncalculated mass
settled unevenly upon the
  earlier stones
and the yielding soil of the
  ancient lakebed;
that much is evident.

Or could it be:
the mighty Aztec gods buried
  beneath it
amid the debris of their hideous
  worship
writhing in anger and agony
struggle to overturn it?

Joseph Tacderas
TO THE CRUCIFIED

This is a darkening world,
  O Savior.
Shed a ray of Your
  empowering
  Light.
Your Father gave us
  Light:
The sons of Lucifer
  came and stole the
  Light.

This is a weakening world.
  The towers and the powers
  have
  fallen.
The nations need more than
  a million tons
  of bricks
  to rebuild them
  to reach the skies.

This is a famishing world.
  Give us your Bread
  of Life.
The bakers' bread in
  multi-sizes
  could not satisfy
  our hunger,
Yet a morsel of Your
  broken bread is
  Peace.

This is a thirsting world.
  All the wines are poison,
  all the waters turn to blood
  and tears,
  yet a little drop from Your
  Chalice
  is our Everlasting Satisfaction.

You are Humanity
  flowing in our hearts.
You are divinity
  enfolding
Time, Space, and
  Eternity.

Mr. Frank Schofield
ODE TO THE POET'S WORD

'with this pen, I thee write'
the poet pledged aloud,
and follow other poets plight

to Wonder lonely as a cloud.
the love the feeling they inspire
as creation comes to mind
to paint in words of their desire
poetic words, the pros outlined.

of natures most abundant
   means,
of fruits, of love so pure
from childhood and throughout
   their teens
fond memories, dreams demure.
from broken heart to cure.

of love and happiness, and
   despair,
of christmas and of aulde lang
   syne,
of paupers penniless and bare,
and thus the poet make to
   rhyme.

To write a poem with emphasize,
to spell that feeling clear.
so all the world can critisize,
and to the poets words 'Adhere'.

Ean St. Clare
SEVEN TINY CHAKRAS

Seven tiny chakras lying quietly
   in the dark,
Waiting through the ages for
   fuel to feed the spark.
The body labored, deaf and
   dumb, to fill the mental bowl,
Then knowledge came so
   sweetly and found eternal
   Soul.
"Here I AM", subconscious
   cried, in dreams and gentle
   nudges,
But man continued down the
   path with war, and hate, and
   grudges.
Lifetimes come and lifetimes
   go with Ego in command,
Mental trapped in greed and
   lust spread fear across the
   land.
Truth forgotten—mind in
   shackles—ignorance takes the
   lead;
The world becomes a shambles
   and life begins to bleed.
Men were born to freedom, not
   in chains or walls of clay.
Awake! Awake! The ONE
   within calls forth the coming
   day.
Mantras ring across the land to
   touch the minds of all—
Forgiving hearts receive the
   chance to breech our prison
   wall.
East meets West—in joyful
   union—a strength of quiet
   repose,
The Redwood bows before the
   Sun and moonbeams kiss the
   rose.
I hear sad notes of discontent
   as mist upon the bay.
Be still, my Child, and listen,
   in your very special way.

Mark A. Fisher
THE UNICORN

Flashing through the night,
In the forests out of sight,
Runs the lone Unicorn,
Body white and silver horn.

Winter comes and summer goes,
As it runs it never slows,
Passing through lands of night
   and day,
Passing through lands of mortal
   and fey.

A lady young, the Unicorn's

dear,
Behind a stone cowering in
   fear,
From a tiger of the night,
Stripes of orange; stripes of
   white.

The tiger lept, the Unicorn
   struck;
Yet that day neither had luck;
Dark red blood on silver horn,
Splattered blood on the Unicorn.

The tiger's dying paw did strike,
The Unicorn's neck; so like,
A twig it broke.
He lay and died with gasp and
   choke.

The lady stood in silent sorrow;
Without this beast couldst be
   a morrow?
Summer comes and winter goes,
Time it moves and never slows.

But in the minds of men,
Who can remember when. . .
Flashing through the night,
In the forests out of sight.

Austin Dryden Cushman, Jr.
NEPTUNE'S FARM

For footpath take a vagrant
   stream
   To the ocean—Neptune's Farm,
Whose pastures border every
   shore
   In rolling, fluted charm.

I've roamed this ranch from
   shore to shore;
   I've seen its colors range
From gray to green and deepest
   blue,
   To tone this restless grange.

No dust bowl here to irrigate;
   These plains know naught of
   drought.
No desert on this broad
   domain,
   Tho' rimmed with sand about.

Nor fences bound this vast
   estate,
   Whose livestock roam at
   large
And countless poachers take
   their fill
   Along its every marge.

It's cattle are the porpoises,
   The chickens are the gulls,
And breezes plow the furrows
   deep
   To harrow in the lulls.

Uncounted seamen sound
   these fields,
   All searching for a clue.
Who put the color in the sea?
   Who paints this farmland blue?

Who feeds the cattle and the
   chicks?
   Who shelters them at night?
Who knows what goal these
   nomads seek?
   Who guides them to the site?

Mayhap I know the answer yet;
   None other may it be
But He with trident in His
   hand,
   Who dominates the sea.

Verna Nye Camien
PURPLE VIOLETS

Purple violets near a hedge grew,
   They were of the deepest hue.
The child saw them and clasped
   her hands in delight,
Longing to pick them and
   hold them tight.
The mother warned her not to

go near,
   She said, "Thorns are there,
   my dear!"
But one day, the longing became
   too great,
   And the little girl did not wait.
She ran very fast and did not
   tarry,
   Until, she picked all the violets
   she could carry.
She held them there with tears
   in her eyes,
   For the pain of the thorns, she
   did now realize.
The mother stopped her work,
   came and carried her away,
   All of this happened on a
   faraway day.
She picked out the child's
   thorns and dried the last tear,
Then said "My darling, some
   lovely things you can't always
   go near!"
The mother then brought her
   beautiful carnival grape vase,
   And helped the child put each
   violet into its special place.
The child looked at her mother
   in a very special way,
For a real lesson, she'd learned
   that with her would stay.
Now, the mother and child have
   gone elsewhere,
   And one wonders, if in the
   spring, the violets still grow
   there?
I was this child and still have
   the lovely carnival grape vase.
This is why these memories,
   I can never erase.

Laura Lammers
**THE FOOTBALL FANATIC'S
GIRL FRIEND**

Oh, to be a football game,
Every football fanatic's girl
   friend's dream,
To receive every pass of
   attention,
This is what we long to be.

Where football is concerned,
It's driving, and we are riding,
It's in the front,
And we're in the back!

We wouldn't mind so much,
If the San Diego Chargers
Were the ones that cooked,
Or if the Eagles were the ones
   that cleaned,
Or if the Raiders were the
   ones that loved,
Then we wouldn't mind.

Then we wouldn't mind teams
   such as Pittsburg,
Stealing his attention.
But when his attention is passed,
They intercept it from us every
   time.

Our first love is him,
And we are glad to tell him so,
His first love is football,
And he is glad to show us so.

Maybe when the season's over,
We'll find the neglect will be
   gone.

Maybe the score of the season's
   last touchdown,
Will send him running—back to
   us.

So, in result,
We'll love him, like we always
   have,
We'll feed him, and clean for
   him,
And care as much as we do. . .

And try to be understanding,
For one season of every year.

Yvette Harper
BLOSSOMING INTO LIFE

A babe is like a flower, a seed
   that has to grow
When nourished properly,
   it's energy will flow.

When planted in the womb and
   protected by it's shield
A baby awaits patiently, to face
   the world's ordeals.

And when the seed has grown it's
   full and blossoms into life
A babe is born of many things
   to face a world of strife.

And when the seed has
   blossomed and wilted all away
A babe awaits patiently to face
   his judgement day.

And when a babe has been
   judged and he, God, forgives
Again a seed is planted and again
   a babe lives.

Donna Gail McMaster
INTELLECTUAL DUNCE

The lessons of life have taught
   me well.
No longer will it fool me,
I've graduated from Mother
   Nature's class.
With honors, I've earned my
   degree.
Now, I can hear the warmth
   of the sun.
I can see the coolness of the
   wind.
I can smell the color of the
   ocean.
I can feel the fragrance of
   spring.
My mind, disciplined from
   grueling hours
of study, and careful thought,
has taken me to the head of the
   class
with an answer to the question
   I sought.
Temptation can rule us,
   eventually defeating us,
unless we control our lust,
but banish the tempter from
   within,
and you also banish trust.
There can be no desire for
   something unknown.
There can be no breaking stride
if we cease to keep walking.
Without pursuit, no reason to
   hide.
Love could not end, without
   a beginning.
I've learned my lessons well.
No hearts to be broken, without
   first being stretched.
Without masquerade, no secrets
   to tell.
Ah, but an ordinary man of
   normal intelligence

could explain in a few minutes
  what I've learned
after endless years of searching.
It's called reason: no fire, no
  way to get burned.

Helen Farmer
THIS MAN ALONE

He was known to many, yet
  passing through this Life alone;
Now he's gone, gone to his Place
  at Home
He was always a Friend, but who
  was his Friend,
This man alone.

He was loved by many but not
  understood,
This man alone.
With his little cocked hat and his
  books tucked under his arm,
He went through life not doing
  any harm,
This man alone.

He was her friend, they said;
But how was she to know he
  was dead?
This grief she bore alone for
  her friend,
This man alone.
He's at peace now, but will
  he ever know
How lonely she feels,
This woman alone?

She'll always remember him
  because he was her friend.
She is getting over her grief
  and is on the mend.
He came when she needed him,
This man alone.
Together they talked of how
  things used to be
When they were younger
  and both were free.

Now he's gone, but his wisdom
  lives on
In the woman's heart, and she'll
  tell others
Of this man alone.
Of how he helped others in their
  hour of need,
And of how he helped her, his
  friend,
The woman alone.

Cindy Grillo
ROCKING CHAIR

Rocking chair, rocking chair
  what a friend I've found in you.
Think of all the sleepless nights
  we've been thru.
You my sturdy wooden friend
Have been with me from the
  beginning right to the end.
When little ones are sick and
  need our love,
Together we work like a hand
  in a glove.
You rock so gentle and in an
  even pace,
While I wipe the tears and kiss
  a tender face.
Of the helpless little masterpiece
  laying so close to my heart,
Then like a slow moving stream
  the teardrops start,
Because once rocking chair we
  thought one might die.
But he made it thru and didn't
  say good-bye.
I held him and loved him with
  all my might,
And we were still rocking when
  it came morning light.
Now there is another one that
  I hold dear,
To lose him at times I really do

fear.
With him in my arms and you
  on our side,
You give us both a smooth
  easy ride.
While the calm night sleeps
  outside our door,
You and I keep rocking just
  as before,
So rocking chair, rocking chair
  please help me thru,
Because I'd have a lot of lonely
  time if it weren't for you.

Cynthia Anne Smith
**THE WAY IT WAS WITH
EMMY**

His palsied hands picked up
  her "Line-a-Day",
The last of all her things to
  pack away;
His dimming eyes devoured
  every line
Where she'd recorded small,
  precise and fine
The details of the busy life she'd
  led;
The births of babies, names
  and dates of dead
Beloved parents; graduation
  dates,
Children's marriages and mates;
Notes on gardens long returned
  to sod,
Tears for a grandchild soon
  returned to God;
The whisker from a favorite
  yellow cat,
A faded photo, feathers from a
  hat.
Illnesses, a storm, first signs
  of spring.
She'd been a quiet, gentle,
  secret thing;
He'd not been sure his loving
  was returned,
Nor hid these pages balm for
  which he yearned;
Then—last two pages, wrinkled,
  stained with gold
And pressed between—a daisy,
  brittle, old
That stirred his failing mem'ry
  to recall
A summer meadow by a
  waterfall,
When Youth had plucked a
  daisy for her hair,
And Love had held the hand
  which placed it there.
He'd never been aware she'd
  kept it so;
She chose this last farewell to
  let him know.

Frieda L. Levinsky
**WHO IS THIS CREATURE
MAN**

Man is Adam in flesh,
a stranger in a wandering maze,
a guest strolling in a jungle;
he is also Cain and Abel
  throughout history
who dwelt in dells or meadows
alone and exposed to good and
  evil.

As I wandered in his footsteps
I saw man in the voiceless void
in huge heaps at Auchwitz;
with silence lips he lay,
defamed, humiliated without
  honor,
with no soil to veil his naked
  bones.
Or down the path a thousand
  miles or more
I stood at Babi Yar, a town

in Russia,
where a hundred thousand
  bodies lay disposed
with no regret from passersby.
No monument stood for my
  kin to shed a tear;
no soul bothered to remember
  their names.
Further down the road of
  Europe
I heard the echoes of the dead;
"Have we not sacrificed our
  lives
for the living to build our cities
  anew?"
But few sober voices could reply
"We place all arms aside for
  peace."
No single general could claim
  a victory, nor could he see
  empty arsenals
when looking upon the date,
or claim that his fighting days
  are gone
never to return
to more conflicts like those of
  the past.

Mary Lou Lemoine
PEACE

When troubled I am, I look for
  peace.
I walk alone in the park.
With eyes wide open, I stand
  beneath the trees.
I listen to the wind and feel its
  breeze
Making lazy shadows across the
  grass,
Branches swaying to and fro.
Then my thoughts of you begin
  to grow.

I stroll across the park and
  everywhere
I can remember seeing you there.
I sit beside the ocean on the
  sand listening
To the tide coming in and the
Hungry ocean grasping at the
  sandy shore.
Then I remember telling you I've
  done this before.

Breakers pile higher and higher;
  and then you hear
The roar of rushing water as it
  goes farther.
I climb a mountain and look up
  at its height
until I feel its strength and
  power.

I sit and rest upon a fallen log,
  looking at the
  canyons
And thinking of things I might
  fear.
Then I wish you were here.

I take a walk at night and
  observe the moon and stars.
The moon actually walked upon
  by man.
The thought gives me strength

and power.
Suddenly I have no fear and I
  feel you are near.
Wherever I decide to go,
Quietly in the silence,
  meditate.
For the quiet and the silence
Steal into the inner part of
  my heart
And they become a part of me.

I find peace all around me.
As I'm sure you can see.
Gratifying, Satisfying,
Peace of body, mind, and soul.

Jose Zakus
MY OLD HOUSE

I drove by it the other day
And noticed the lawns were
  velvet green
The trees grown strong, straight
  and tall;
I drove by it the other day and
  my eyes were filled with tears.
I wanted to stop and look
  around
but I kept on driving;
I wondered if the roses still
  bloomed at the back.
Was the giant evergreen still
  stately and proud?
The sheltered pation with
  fireplace of brick
And red wooden table and
  chairs;
But I kept on driving.
Does the pathway still lead
  to the white garden gate?
And the leaves crunch under
  your feet
When Autumn frost freshens
  the air.
I drove by it the other day and
  my eyes were filled with tears.
In the golden days of summer's
  delight
Are the raspberries ripened and
  red?
I remembered the kitchen
  window I loved—
Those high-beamed ceilings
  and chandeliers,
Yes, the pictures of loved ones
  at rest
But I kept on driving and my
  eyes were filled with tears.
Dear old friends and "Fluffy"
  the cat we so loved;
Then holiday gatherings when
  all were back home,
With neighbors so wonderful
  still—
Our children all grown in
  distant lands now,
God called them to lead their
  own lives;
But Time passes on, great
  changes take place,
So I kept on driving,
For my old house is no longer
  my old house. . .
And my eyes were filled with
  tears. . .

Helen Krebs
THE GARDEN OF THE MIND

Most everyone is interested
  in a garden of some kind,
But the most important garden
  is the garden of the mind.

The gardener who grows flowers
  selects the seed with care.
Always trying to improve the
  plants and grow something
  rare.
He also knows that the type of

seed he sows is the type of
plant that grows.
Yes, all gardeners know that
from a sandbur seed you
cannot grow a rose.
Just so it is with the garden of
the mind.
If we sow bad deeds and
thoughts, the plants will be
that kind.
If we sow the thought seed of
anger, jealousy, hate and
greed,
We will soon have our mind
garden completely filled with
weeds.
Those bad thought weeds will
grow and grow till the mind
with them will be filled.
No room now for good thought
plants—mind soil can't even
be tilled.
Like a computer, our mind
reacts to what comes in from
time to time.
So let's carefully sort out the
bad thought seeds, line by
line.
The mind is not a vacuum, so
keep it filled with good
thought seeds.
For when the mind is filled with
good-thought plants, there is
no room for bad thought deeds.

Cindy Kilgore
APPALACHIA SOUL

Mountain music
rushes my blood
as toes point n' skip
the floor,
dulcimer sings the wind
and hot fiddles
set heels tappin'.

Appalachia soul
born and bread
electric white lightning
magic.

Appalachia soul
running fast
like dust trailin' buckshot.

In n' out,
between trees,
crossin' feather beds,
avoiding smellin'
hounds treadin' water.

Mandolin serenades
moonlight's crystal
glazing.

Skippin' beats,
sippin' moonshine,
feet pacin the march gales
of a banjo and gitar
praising
the waking of the early morning
rising.

And the strength of the melody
rose the mountains to greet
the sky
as all the animals
woke
with the best of mountain
music
pumping their hearts.

two step
two step

Appalachia soul
in the earth
blowing the wind
living in the mountain man

shuffling his fingers
cross dulcimer's delicate neck
cooking fiddles, hot frying pan
fire

dancing the mandolin, chasing
feet
across his life, early morning
buck-dance
white liquor drums the beat.

Appalachia soul, Appalachia
soul
mountains greet the sky,
A man's work or pleasure
is never told.

Rev. Joseph E. Kiely
CONSOLATION

Tonight I saw a setting sun
Descending in its glory
To me this burnished red-gold
orb
Has told its whole life story
Has told me of its glorious rise
Into the spangled Orient skies
Its warming strength at high
full noon
But then 'tis spent and all too
soon
Now it descends its work well
done
Such the song of the setting sun.

Tonight I saw a silent soul
Ascending to her glory
A mother's soul I need not say
I know her whole life story
But though full heart-sick,
'reft, forlorn
I should not feel so sorry.

For, as I saw that setting sun
Fast-fading from my eyes
I knew it would in other lands
Begin it's glorious rise
As surely as the parting ship
Shakes off a foreign strand
And reaches soon the friendly
shores
Of it's own native land
So surely will a mother's soul
Her work in life well done
Be met by loving Mary—
And Jesus Christ, her Son.

Debbie Auen
CALL ON ME

GOD GENTLY BECKONS:

CALL ON ME My precious child
I am yet here while all the world
seems to have gone too wild
CALL ON ME I will hold your
hand
I will be your guide through
this promised land
The Promised Land can be here
and now
If you are willing to live for ME
I will show you how
How to live above all this
present hate
How to enter Heaven's eternal
gate
CALL ON ME if you are weak
I understand for my nature
is humble, lowly, and meek
Surrender all that is in your
heart

The good—the bad, I need it all
That I may help you make a
definite, fresh, rewarding start
When life has somehow affected
you
To the point that you are help
helpless as you question what
to do
CALL ON ME I will give you
rest
You are my child and I want
for you only the very best
I know that this is hard for you
to see
Because you have been too
busy ignoring ME
Give ME your sorrow in
exchange for MY peace
Only by coming directly to ME
Can you find any real purpose,
renewed strength, or release
You often make loving you
such a difficult thing
For you neglect to come to ME
You forget all of your heart
to bring
CALL ON ME let ME love you
my redeemed chosen one
alway
Loving one another besides
being beautiful it's everlasting
Always CALL ON ME
From MY LOVE MY
PRESENCE please don't ever
run.

Rasul
TRY A LITTLE KINDNESS

Seeds were planted, but few
things were grown
The crows of the land would
not leave them alone
They ate the seeds and picked
on the crops
So Nature demanded that the
eating should stop
The crows continued to eat
their share
They laughed at Nature, and
really didn't care
So Nature sent a cloud across
the sky
The crows and the people all
wondered why?
The people scattered and ran
about
A storm was brewing without
a doubt
Instilling fear in all the land
Smacking all things with its
mighty hand
It injured the crows that fease
feasted on the crops
Yet it destroyed other things
before it had stopped
Sure it was quick and completed
the task
But earth in her fear just had
to ask
"Oh God of the skies from up
above
couldn't you take time to show
a little love?"
Then returned the crows to
have more food
The storm sure scared them but
not their moods
So Nature sent the land
another cloud
Not as big as the first nor
quite as loud
It began to rain the birds flew
away
And each time they returned
it would rain on that day
So the crows soon left the
food all alone
The rain nurtured the plants

and the crops were full grown
Nature called the crows to tell
them it was okay
There's enough food for all,
and now they can stay.

Louis J. Kwistek
**KING RICHARD, THE
LYIN' HEARTED**

He came, as he from Elba,
with Munich
in the wings,
With a smile and a curtsy, a
smooth voice,
and two fingers,
The knife concealed in freedom
flag, was
a king's aspirings,
A knave well versed in
conspiracy, best
of all intriguers,

[He chose the right hands, as
this breed
thrive in shadow,
And spun the web to sit in,
an evil mind
in the center,
With schemes connived and
records kept
and sheep to follow,
A king, he ruled with iron fist
clever was his endeavor.

With skill and deception, while
deviant
tentacles held fast
His followers were of the same
sly ilk,
and similar persuasion,
But the scales balanced, like
those that
leveled in the past,
And like before, naked was
sin, in that
final revelation.

The cries of innocence were
loud, quite
sincere and adamant,
But the truth stepped forth, to
open up
the gates of water,
And sightless justice, again
undermined,
mas made impotent,
As he, not of the peoples choice,
crossing hands,
washed the other,

So by irony of fate, that he
manipulate,
a villian was set free,
While all the sheep and slaves
milled,
like those of before,
His purse grew fat, though
public eye he justified his
tyranny,
But the cleft in truth, will never
heal,
a sore, to fester, evermore.

Frederica McDill Culbertson
TO NED

I walk the beach today,
while the rolling, pounding surf
makes circles on the southern
sand
and sweeps the beach, as tho
by hand.
And now the sand is almost
tan,
as I dream of thee and we walk
hand-in-hand.

See the water's gray-green,
against a sky serene,
now dull blue and laced with
frothy clouds of white.

My treasure for today?
A tiny starfish. Hurrah!
I'll take it home for you.

When you're away, I walk
and silently with you I talk,
with a happy heart—so full of
love.

But I fear the bubble's burst,
for having had my hell on earth,
I ask, "How can this bit of
heaven last?"

And why, dear heart, I ask
myself,
as I happily wait for you,
has my poetry voice, with a
heart full of song
for so many years been still
too long?

Not since inspired by a three-day
storm,
followed by a morning sun,
in another place of sun and fun,
have I taken pen in hand, and
then,
been moved to write a verse.

And then I asked myself today,
"Why after all those years—
yes, twenty-two,
did suddenly two verses come
in June?"
T'was I'm sure—a gift for you.

And do you know, my bearded
one,
how me you motivate?
Yes, suddenly I wish to dig and
weed
and prepare myself for thee.

Be kind when you return at
last
and do not me forget.
Yes, I fear this beauty I now
know—
for you, it will not last.

Frank Lawrence Sofo
A CHRISTMAS MESSAGE

C—Stands for chimneys blanked
blanketed with snow so white;
While children everywhere will
wait for Santa's ride this night.

H—Stands for hymns that in
churches today will be sung,
While in homes wreathes of
green will be hung.

R— Stands for Rudolph, the
reindeer with a nose so red;
While in houses tiny tots lay
asleep in their beds.

I—Stands for icicles hanging from
house tops frozen and cold;
While near fireplaces chestnuts
will be roasted and stories told.

S—Stands for Santa Claus , a
legendary soul with rosy cheeks
and a beard
So white;
While in homes everywhere
children eagerly await his ari
arrival by dawns
early light.

T—Stands for Toys that children
will play with on this day;[
While in churches altars Jesus
in a manger will lay.

M—Stands for mistletop, a
place where all tread gently,
careful not to miss;
While at this time each and
every person will show affection
with a great
big kiss.

A—Stands for Angels atop trees
so green;

While blinking lights and
shining tinsel makes this
ornament a sight
to be seen.

S—Stands for the season of
Christmas that soon will be
near;
While this poem reflecting this
joyful holiday will be endeared
in our hearts all year.

David P. McKenna
TIN SOLDIER

Your armor's dull and tarnished,
And your weapons gone to rust;
Your weathered face is lined
with tears,
And your dreams all fall to dust.

You'd think you'd learn your
lesson,
No wiser, though you're aeons
older;
You keep on making the same
mistakes,
You're a goddamn fool, Tin
Soldier.

In love with another ballerina
Who makes your tired heart
dance;
You'll follow your dream
through the gates of Hell,
Though you know you have
no chance.

And you wear your bitter,
aching love

Like a millstone on your
shoulders;
And dream of things that can
never be,
You're a goddamn fool, Tin
Soldier.

So you roam the night like a
battered wreck
Adrift on an empty sea;
Searching for the sheltering
port
Of a love that can never be.

So give up on your empty
dream,
You know you'll never hold
her;
Ballerinas aren't meant for the
likes of you,
You're a goddamn fool, Tin
Soldier.

Annette Marie Marquez
THE ATTIC

Sleep, sleep in endless deep
Remembrance of
Running steps down the hall,
Dew drops on a petal
Before it was pressed
When you were small
Between the pages of Little
Women.

Tiny, lacy doll-sized dresses,
Among the folds. . .a golden
curl
Cut from your Goldilocks
tresses

Before they darkened, my
grown-up girl.
And look! The little white
Sunday shoes
You wore so proudly then,
How I long to hear those
scampering feet
And the screen door slam loudly
again!

Suddenly I remember finding
my mother long ago,
In another time and place;

As I climbed up the old attic
stairs back home,
Sitting, clutching my old
high-buttoned shoes,
The same sad, far-away look on
her face
As I now see reflected in the
mirror,
In the mirrors of my mind.

I couldn't understand then,
the tears,
The pain of letting go and I
leaving things behind.
But, how close I feel to you
now
Dear mother, after all these
many years.

Little things that seemed forever
past;
Cloaked in silence
Under a veil of dust,
Whisper faintly, stirring within
me
A flash of memory, a pang of
sorrow. . .
That today I live the memory
of every tomorrow.

Miss Susan Boone
UNTITLED

I look at Maygan
And I see
Not just a baby
But perhaps. . .

A little tot of two
Exploring a world that's so new
How will I keep up
She never seems to stop
Yet before I know it. . .

She's a child of five
Asking when can she learn to
drive
I laugh and say
She'll just have to wait
But before I know it. . .

She's a little lady of eight
And suddenly wants
To stay up late
TV you know
It's her favorite show
Well, just this once I say
Just for today. . .

Today. . .a teenager
Thirteen?
It's hard to believe
And suddenly I'm faced
With the birds and the bees
And boys?
Oh dear
Maygan, come here, we must
have a talk now that you're. . .

Sixteen and as sweet as can be
And suddenly I feel something
come over me
Did I miss a year with you
It's gone so fast
Since you were two
And now I look. . .

Eighteen, is it true
Was I all I could be to you
A parent, a friend
I did my best
I taught you and helped you
And I'd repeat it all
If I could
For suddenly it seems it all
went so fast
From diapers, to jumpers,
to jeans. . .

To a wedding dress
She's as pretty as can be
Funny, now I notice
Yes, she does look like me
All the years have passed

So long ago
When you were a baby
And you saw your first snow
When you took your first step
So afraid I'd let you go
But today's the day
You're the one letting go
And before we say our last
good-bye

Yes, quickly, before I cry
There's something that I want
you to know. . .
There will always be a part of
me
That sees you as
My little baby.

Jeri M. Lang
DAILY PRAYER

To do as You would have me do
And have no fear,
To love and aid my fellow man,
To dry a tear,
And follow in thy footsteps
Lord,
A humble clod,
This will be my task, oh God.

There are nations in distress
And many die,
We see the starving multitudes
And wonder why.
Show us in thy loving way
The paths to trod,
And this will be my task, Oh
God.

Throughout the ages men have
sought
For selfish gain,
Without regard for others rights
Or others pain,
A battle for a pound of flesh
Or earthly sod,
We sorely need Thy loving and
direction, God.

We listen to the sound of war
Without distress,
Draughts and famine take their
toll
In pain and death,
Sometimes it seems our gentle
Christ
Has died in vain
While me, in growing apathy
Can feel no pain.

If I could lift some heavy load
From shoulders bent,
Receive a smile, a rich reward
For service lent,
And elevate my soul to walk
The paths you've trod,
Then this will be my task, o
Oh God.

And If I help one helpless one
Along the way,
By giving of my heart and soul
And common clay,
And follow Thee with Christian
love
No lenience asked,
Then Lord let me abide with

Thee
I've done my task.

P. D. Andrews
OH YOU WRETCHED SOULS

In his, her eyes,
There is a glimmer of sunshine,
Shimmering, searching for help.
  they hope,
Blue, green brown colors
  focusing wantingly.

They have been beseiged too
  long,
Our eyes slant to the East of us,
South, West, North, all around,
Whites, yellows, browns,
  pigments of our own.

Some destitute beyond belief,
From where will come this
  relief?
As Hunger has ridden many a
  time,
Again he rides with sabre drawn.

Oh, you wretched soul, where
  do you go?
What is this emblem to which
  you pledge allegiance?
Yet you laugh where darkness
  enshrouds,
Who is your leader? You are so
  proud!

You call out for others to join,
Ah, Pestilence, you mount your
  black stallion,
Off you ride, gaily shrieking,
  laughing.
Both their sabres drawn, where
  do they go?

As I watch, I now see three.
My eyes wince from their hellish
  sight,
And this flag they fly, their true
  colors,
Ominously in the wind, cross
  bones and skull.

So, Disease, you join your ugly
  friends,
While riding out of your hellish
  den,
Our anger flares, you have ridden
  too many a time,
Again you ride with sabres in
  hand.

Can no one stop this lecherous
  union?
They prey on the innocent tiny
  children.
And who is this leader they
  speed to meet?
Where does he dance?. .In
  what depths!

Now we see the leader you meet.
Death! You have readied your
  forces once more.
But, we too have not been still.
In our hearts is a will to beat
  you, to survive.

Sifting sands of time, having
  it your own way,
We have let you beat us too

many a time.
One day we will send you
  reeling, back to where you
  belong.
We will capture you and cage
  you.

Oh, you wretched souls, now,
  where do you go?
We know the meaning of this
  emblem, this pledged
  allegiance.
Yet, you laugh in our faces,
  where darkness enshrouds,
All of you terrorizing our whole
  world over.

You have defeated us when
  fragmented.
But, now we have too pledged
  allegiance.
We fly a flag much greater
  than yours.
We have united our mighty
  nations against you.

And when that final battle
  is done,
We will have routed your
  Satanic forces.
Our little people, everywhere,
  will dance and laugh.
And as for you death, we will
  have lifted your seige, at last!

Heather Hallam
SUMMER LOVE

He sat upon the cold, gray rock,
  Among the dampened moss.
Tears were those of sadness,
  He whimpered at the loss.

Gold spun toffee streaked the
  sky,
  Dismissing any trace,
Of blue marshmallow sorrow. . .
  In danced evening grace.

Silhouetted 'gainst a moonbeam,
  Curls whisped o'er his cheek.
Passion stiffed within him,
  Heartbeat,
    Tired and weak.

Rustling grass bowed low before
  her,
  Wind now played her hair.
Her songs flew cross the
  shoreline,
  For he was seated there.

A star fell to the northern hills,
  His wish came naturally.
Mary pattered to his side,
  United finally!

Mary was a poor lass,
  Shepherd's daughter fair.
Peter stared in wonder,
  A tripper from nowhere.

Their eyes met in the silence,
  Speak or move they daren't.
Magic lasted minutes,
  For loving was apparent.

Loon called from the highland,
  Breaking all suspense.
God watched as his children
  Stiffened and were tense.

Breathing travelled heavy,
  Passion filled the air.
Peter promised Mary
  Loyalty and care.

And now as I lay resting
  By the water blue;
I hear a young voice singing,
  To her tripper true.

Kay Piersdorff
MARIPOSA, CALIFORNIA

God found a giant earthen bowl
and made a salad.

He put in green and white
  mariposite,
gray and green serpentine,
and dark green jade;
clear quartz crystal that shone
  like diamonds,
huge white boulders and black
  granite.
He added pyrites that gleamed
  like gold,
and gold itself.

He put in rich black earth,
brick-colored adobe mud,
red soil, and tawny sand that
  shone like gold,
and added some more gold itself.

He added trees;
the pink manzanita bush, the
  redbud
of red and pink and purple;
wild blackberry with blooms as
  white as snow
and thorns as sharp as needles;
the mistletoe twined 'round
  the mighty oak. . .
the live oak and the water oak
  and the white oak
and the black oak,
huge ponderosa pines and little
  scrub pines,
poplars and ash and cottonwood,
  and gray brush;
and then to add sweetness
He put in fruit trees, the peach
  and the apple
and apricot and plum;
and for tartness, the lemon and
  the orange,
and the osage orange that looks
  like gold,
and He sprinkled on a little
  more gold itself.

He thought, it needs a bit more
  color,
so He added flowers; the orange
  fiddleneck,
white popcorns, blue and white
  lupins,
the lovely blue larkspur and
  baby-blue-eyes
and the deep purple myrtle;
cerise redmaids, pink shooting
  stars
and indian paint brush,
yellow daisies and the yellow
monkey flower, and yellow
  buttercups
that gleamed like gold;
and a dab more gold itself.

He made the dressing for his
  salad;
clear sunny skies blue with
  promise,
sparkling crystal streams and
  golden sun,
and just a pinch of gold itself.
He put his hands into the
  great earthen bowl
and tossed His salad;
once. . .twice. . .and yet again
and when it had settled back
  into the bowl,
and no one part looked like any
  other,
He smiled.
He sprinkled on some bees,
  and birds
and as a final touch,
he added the brilliant butterfly;
it was bright and beautiful
Mariposa.

Ribero W. Strauss
TO CHRISTOPHER

You were born when a
  hurricane threatened the land

And the wind whistled wild on
  the Key. . .
Was your infant soul stirred by
  the music you heard
In the sound of the surging sea?
Is that where the song in your
  heart began?
And the magic you find in each
  minute?
Is that why you feel so akin to
  the earth
And to all of the creatures in it?
Who knows? No matter the
  wherefore or why,
Just be glad you are one of the
  few
Who has truly been blessed with
  the sparkle and zest
That make life enchanting to
  you.

But now that you've reached a
  milestone, Chris,
Now that you've turned thirteen,
Has life changed somehow?
  Are you different now?
What does it really mean?
Of course, you are older than
  you were. . .
But you're younger than you'll
  be.
And, of course, you're a real
  teenager now,
Quite officially!
A teenager, yes, but not an
  adult.
Maybe even a child now and
  then.
Caterpillars much change to
  become butterflies,
And boys must evolve into men.
So you'll have to expect some
  growing pains,
And you'll feel both joy and
  sorrow
As you try to hold on to
  Yesterday. . .
As you dare to dream of
  tomorrow.
The teens are tender,
  tempestuous years;
They are makers of memories
  too,
Your first prom, first love, and
  first broken heart
Will always be part of you.

But summers too rapidly fade
  into falls,
And winters unfold into springs.
And once in awhile, if you
  listen, you'll hear
The flutter of butterfly wings.
So hold on to your song,
  little grandson of mine,
The song that your soul has
  been hearing,
It's the heart of you, and the
  part of you
That, somehow, I find most
  endearing.
And one of these days when
  you spread your wings
And soar out in search of
  success,
May you fly high and free,
  like the wind on the Key.
Happy landings, my love. . .
  and God bless.

Christine Marie Milbocker
MANKIND'S VANQUISHED GLORY

Gentle fingers of starlight
  cradle a silent kingdom,
Caressing mystery with tragic
  tears of remembrance. . .
An infant soul, swaddled in

innocence, nurtured in
tranquillity,
Flutters amid lilies of serenity,
angelic heralds of universal
compassion,
Sensing the sweet nectar,
aromatic chastity;
Neither praising nor condemning
purity.

Utopic infirmity, the betrayal
of time, shatters idealism
Crippling the delicate wings of
life.
Blind ignorance stumbles before
the terror of Darkness,
Deceitful command of
temptation, cruel enemy of
Enlightenment.

Abhorrence. Blissful peace.
The battle rages; infinity
delights.
Neither dawn nor dusk
surrenders its spirit.
Deepening shadows do not
satiate ravaging evil,
For deliverance rests on the lips
of the faithful.

Knowledge cascades in
unrestrained valiance,
Encompassing laughter and
wretched despair,

enriching fertile and barren soil;
Illuminating chasms and
crevasses alike.

Wisdom triumphs. Truth
prevails.
A flower unfolds, basking in
the millenial radiance
Of a dream untethered.
Uncertainties dissolve, yielding
fragrant petals of hope.

The soul, released on an odyssey
of inner reflection,
Perceiving not the desperate
pleas of the heart,
Yearns to unite with supremacy,
Obsessed with transcending
mortal power.

Dominance is implanted in the
minds of elders,
Inevitably predicting the
fate of the youth.
Immaculate lilies cringe in
horror,
Awaiting their burial in the
smouldering ashes of history.

Insane hatred created the
inferno. Technology, the
tool of detonation.
A trichotomy remains: Death's
icy breath of mockery,
The elegy of mankind's
vanquished glory,
And glistening tears of love
promising rebirth.

L. S.
MOM & DAD

Who are these people that try
so hard, to help you become
the way they are.
Feed you, Keep you, and help
you to grow, but you repay
this "Oh so slow."

When you grow older and start
to run, and all that they've
taught you try to shun.
Why do you do this, It hurts
them so bad, but who are
they
to say "You're mad."

You drink, you smoke, take
dope and swear, but in the end
you know not where.

Bud Mom and Dad will always
be there.
So when you do not what
you're told, You then sacrifice
all that they hold.
For you're the one to make
the choice, good or bad, it's
in your voice.
Stop and think of all that's
been said, and hope to God
you're home safe in bed.
When you wake up to this
groovy dream, Guess who it
was
to hear you scream.
Standing there to protect
and love. It seems real
funny, but they're sent from
above.
Love Dunk.

Romaine L. Goodman
CAPTAIN JOHNNY CROSS

With your arm upraised—
one last farewell
A happy smile upon your lips
You gaily blew me one last kiss.
Your skin was bronze from
the sun's strong ray;
What a handsome man you were
that day!
The wind fanned your copper
hair so bright,
But tears crept in and blurred
my sight;
For my strong, sweet love,
my heart's desire,
To hold you here, I had no
power.
And on that long ago, sad day
You took your ship and sailed
away
To your first true love—the
jealous sea,
Your mistress, who coaxed you
away from me.
But I knew you loved me second
best
So I waited on land, wild hope
in my breast,
That you'd come safely back
to me
And reject your mistress of
the sea.
So on lonely, barren shores I
walked
As lightning split the heavens
wide
And rian came down from
laden skies.
The pounding of the lashing
waves
Beat on the hard, cold reef
They struck their blows in
angry haste,
Then fled before this wanton
waste,
And rolling back in swift retreat
They left around my frozen
feet
A tangled, slimy growth of moss

While I waited for you, My
Captain Johnny Cross.
The days were long, the nights
were lonely
And all my thoughts were for
you only.
I prayed that Fate so kind would
be
And send you sailing back to
me.

Then a message came, my own
sweet John
That violent storms of bitter
fury
Hit your ship and killed your
mate
Split the mast right down the
middle
Smashing you beneath its
weight.
They buried you, My Captain
Cross,
So brave and strong and true;
They slid your body cold
and still
Into the dark, green sea.
With lashing waves that gently
moaned,
She claimed you for her very
own.
I hear you call my name, my
own true love,
From beneath the deep, dark
sea;
I'm coming, John, to be with
you
In waters deep and cold;
We will share your grave
beneath the waves
For I am not alone.
Your son's heart beats beneath
my own—
We are coming, John, we're
coming home.

David M. Singer
**REFLECTIONS ON A SILVER
ANNIVERSARY**

It's that time again, it comes
each year,
To take down our memories
and shake off the dust;
To sit in our worn but
comfortable chairs,
To break out in a smile and
think about us.
Was it worth it, we ask, the good
times and bad,
the laughing and fighting, the
joy and the tears;
The loving and building and
loving again,
When, my reverie's broken,
my memory clears.
My wife, ah yes, it was worth it,
I know,
My companion in life, I could
ask for no more;
When good times were with us
her smile kept them going,
When bad times came knocking,
she held shut the door.
Oh, there were plenty of times I
thought we were through,
We would fight with every tooth,
nail, and claw;
But when it was done, I'd think
back on our life,
Remember our love, and jump
back in for more.
And the little ones, the children,
all grown now and gone,
The cutest, the brightest,
that there's ever been;
Their innocent faces full of
wonder and fear,
Their open brown eyes, to

suck your heart in.
And soon, the grandchildren
will pay us a call,
To sit on our shoulders,
and pull on our ears;
Then snuggle up close, close
their eyes so to nap,
With grandpa to sheild them,
and ward off their fears.
Oh, yes, it was worth it,
our lives have been full,
We get down on our knees,
and thank God we're alive;
Then we hoist ourselves up,
and take a deep breath,
And wish ourselves the best,
for our next twenty-five.

Roger Lynn Kelling
THE FRUIT OF MAN

It spills forth from in the mind
Where guarded it did sleep
Down the arm and out the pen
A thought profound and deep.

Splashing forth and crying loud
From the womb secure and
warm
Then severed from its umbilical
—wet and cold
So the fruit of man is born.

A written word to an empty
page
To withstand the slaught of time
Appears quite unspokenly
To grow into a line.

A child is borning from its
mother's womb
To walk in sunning light
To live the warm of day at noon
Or crawl through the
sightlessness of night.

The fruit of thought becomes a
page
In but a moment's time
Then the pages swell with
subtleties
Extracted from deep within
the mind.

The pages turn to lengthy tomes
And speak of truth or fear
The author bears each one
forth
Like child—that's close and dear.

The child crawls forth also now
To claim its worldly home
The words sustained from birth
of thought
Call the pages their new home.

For parent be or author too
They feel to be the same
As parent of word—or parent of
child
Birth is your only claim.

For child of pen or child of
life
Too soon must wobbly stand
The only thing for parent now
Is but a steady guiding hand.

For the fruit of thought
Or fruit of womb
The parent cannot own
For child or book—after
birthing time
Now become their own.

Sister Rose Dumey, A. S. C.
LOVE

LOVE is a tender, soul-warming
feeling,
that puts a twinkle in your eye,
and sets your face aglow,
as silently you sense each others
presence.
LOVE is unique by allowing you

to know
another human being in such a
way,
no one else knows; without a
touch,
without a word, without a sigh
just by being yourself.

LOVE is a kaleidoscopic view
of cherished
acts no money can buy; such
as deeds of
mutual love, joy, happiness,
respect,
trust, concern, and million others.

LOVE is fragile like a red
velvet rose
in a hot summer day. Neglect
to give it
tender loving care, it will wither
and decay.

LOVE is God's glory in the
radiant sunset,
reflecting the colors of your
mind, the
beauty of the glistening stars at
night,
awakening you at sunrise with
as the birds
sweetly sing their Creator's
praise.

LOVE is strength of heart, soul,
and mind
to love the unattractive person,
the poor,
the lonely, the unwanted, the
addict, the
vino, the thief. To Dismas Christ
said,
"This day shall thou be with
me in Paradise."

LOVE is not always true and
sincere. It
is tangible and many a heart is
broken;
shattered like many pieces of
broken glass
that cannot be mended. The
flame that once'
burned deep within the heart
has smouldered
leaving a vacuum filled with grief.
Gone are loving relationships,
communications,
trust in each other, and ability
to share.
Needs are left unfulfilled, so
are hope and
dreams. Promised love is often
only a sham
that is never received.

LOVE is the supreme sacrifice
of Christ
crucified. When dying he
gasped, "It is
consummated." At our death
we will with
ecstatic contemplation
experience the
embrace of Christ's divine LOVE
eternally
in Paradise.

Joy Ansel
JAMIE

You've given me happiness,
And made my life worthwhile.
When I am down you bring me
up,
With "I love you's" and a smile.

Your innocence and orneriness
They work together and take
part,
In playing with my patience,
While the other steals my heart.
You're so alive and beautiful

That sometimes I could cry.
God made you so very perfect,
Just for me? I wonder why?

No one is safe from your smile,
Or free from your angelic ways.
You take their love, and in
return,
You give them carefree days.

No mother could be prouder,
[Or so full of love and care.
Grandma Poff said you'd be
special,
And a very special bond we
share.

Patricia Randall
ODE TO KATHY

You see with saddened eyes
not what is—but—
One short dream,
in the world of perhaps.

Dreams breed tomorrows
that come as today.
For without dreams
there is only "NOW".

While we wait
our days fade.
Promises are unfulfilled
with future's hope.

For when we give up dreams
the reality of "NOW"
is lost with the emptiness
of youth.

Mary Harper Gordon
PEACE

Lord give me peace. . .
Stop the crazy world I'm in!
Send a shower of peace to me
Let me bathe my ragged nerves
in your
shower of soothing peace
Let it beat upon my body the
renewing,
reviving strength gained
from peace.
Then Father clothe me in a
robe of peace
untouched by the worlds rage.
While constantly sharing my
robe of peace. . .

Joyce W. Wallace
FULFILLMENT

The mountain towered
majestically—reaching for the
sky,
a cloud clung to her highest
peak—a crown worn proudly—
oh so high.
Pine trees standing straight and
tall—clinging to her sides,
birds circling and drifting on
winds ever changing tides.
At the foot of this tallest
mountain, a stream bubbled
lazily on its way,
trails of deer leading to the
shore, where they drink and
graze at end of day.
Is there really a God who
created this wonder, that
brings peace to my troubled
heart?
Or could it all be just by
chance—if so, where did it
get its start?
In a meadow, facing this
mountain, where wild flowers
grew,
I found a peace of mind which
before I never knew.
I lay in this mountain meadow,
nature and I as one,
my heart warmed by all

nature's love—my body by
the sun.
The mountain watched over me
me—as though to guard this
love,
such beauty makes me wonder
if there's not a God above.
And one day when I know that
I shall die—to my meadow
I'll go for eternal sleep.
and pray to the creator of
this beauty my soul to keep.
Where my spirit can soar o'er
the trees, on the mountain
side,
and like the birds—drift on the
winds changing tide.

Lucy Hadsell Curtis
REFLECTIONS

The moon rises like a red lantern,
On a breathless July night,
The frosty moon in December,
Sprays the landscape in silvery
white.

At dawn today a rose cloud lay,
On the hills to the northeast.
Then changed to bright lavender,
The snow lined trees increased
And absorbed its pastel beauty.
A lavender world turning
Coral and crimson and orange,
As the sun's sphere starts
burning.
I love the red barns in the
valleys,
The majesty of the mountains,
The closeness of God in the
meadow,
The halo of mist in the
fountains.
O Golden time goes on and on,
The gift of will is great,
And health is our most precious
wealth
And harmony is the highest
state.

Harmony of God and man,
Of sounds and shapes and
reflections,
Of colors and skins, voices and
minds,
A balance of nature's
perfections.
This is the living form
Of God's presence everywhere.
That He is the brightest lilies,
That sweetly perfume the air.
That He is the upswept wind,
That blows the seeds about,
That He is the pulsing spring
That makes the tulips sprout.
That He is the careful pilot,
That slowly spins our earth
And moves the moon and stars,
The love that summons our
birth.
That He is live itself,
And laughter and joy and pain,
That He is the evening star
And the patter of falling rain.

David E. McCray
UNTITLED

I am just a young man
trying to find me.
Make my own decisions
to what is right for me.
Past vows have been broken
and now it's said I'm free.
So now I must choose
What in Life it is I'm to be.

I could be dishonest, deceitful,
vile and cruel.
I could turn a friendly smile
into a charming tool.
I could wander aimlessly,
a parasite I'd be.
Contented to have just in life
what was gave to me.
I could be a rebel and fight
'gainst every cause.
I could be a renegade
defying all man's laws.

But me I think I'll take a stand
and try to be the kind of man
I feel is inside of me, and pray
one day it comes to be.

Laura Lee
STOLEN MOMENTS

A mother cherishes a time to be
alone.
Just a special day when all the
gang is gone.
Invite someone to lunch at an
exciting new place.
A leisurely meal to enjoy
without a hectic pace.
Brouse the mall's intriguing
shops—select a
perfect piece of art.
Into a favorite boutique to
purchase a blouse
that's really smart!
Maybe a quick errand to run—
a surprise
gift to select.
Or a lingering stroll in the
garden—those
beautiful roses to inspect.
Stretch out on the chaise—a
chance to view
the distant trees.
Hear the cardinal call and feel
a cool
gentle breeze.
Absorb a fascinating plot
found in a mysterious book.
Create a lovely garment with a
crochet hook.
Dial a friend and chat
confidentially for a while.
Jot a quick note to a forgotten
one across the miles.
The time grows quickly—the
sun begins to set.
It's been a day that has no
regrets.
The rest has been refreshing.
The uninterrupted quietness,
peaceful and fulfilling. . .
'Hey! Mom, we're home! What
did you do today?"
"Oh, nothing—did you have a
good time?"

Mickey Ferdinand
THE BUCKROO

I notice a child walking alone,
I watch his moves,
And wonder if he's heard the
news.
He looks sorta bashful;
But walks very brave,

He needs some confidence,
He wants a little trust;
He lacks security,
And needs to be loved.

He lost his family,
Really got no friends,
I could tell the way he pretends.

I pull over,
Start to talk,
He ignores me and
Continues to walk.

I notice a child walking alone,
I've got to follow,
Can't move too fast;
I have to be sure,
The little one can last.

He's four or five, just walking
away,
I've got to protect him;
He'll need a place to stay.

I notice a child walking alone,
If he has any relatives,
I'll give them a call;
Cause
He needs a family,
He needs a home,
He can't live his life,
Living alone.

He never knew relatives were
family.
He didn't know of any friends.
He is young,
He is old,
Trying to put together,
What he was told.

We find some relatives,
Now he has to go.
I won his confidence,
I won his trust,
He's got security;
Cause he wanted to be loved.

I notice a child walking alone,
I bring him to his family;
Where he has a home.

Dottie Scarborough Ball
GOLDEN GIRL

Heather is my child so fair
My golden girl
with long blonde hair.

She looks to me with eyes of
blue
Which shine so bright
in wondrous hue.

Her world is full of love and
sharing
She gives of self
with all her caring.

Her pictures drawn with so
much pride
The warmth within
she cannot hide.

A simple yearning to be heard
The joy she brings
without a word.

Her love of soft and furry things
Her fingers sparkling
with shiny rings.

The high heeled shoes she wants
to wear
The coloring books
she's left on the chair.

The dolls in her room all lined
in a row
The gold star on her paper
she's anxious to show.

She's racing with cars and
climbing a tree
And wearing a dress
with a bruise on her knee.

She's playing piano and dancing
on toes

She's brushing her tresses
and donning her bows.
With joy in heart, love fills the
air
My golden girl
with long blonde hair

Faye Gordon
**HOOVES ACROSS THE
PLAINS**

I hear the echoing:
The thundering across the
plains.
I hear the war cries and
The screaming of the cannon's
blast.

I see phantom riders:
Soldiers clad in blue and
gray.
I see brown earth marbled
with scarlet;
Burning with Hades' stench.

I hear the death chants
Ringing towards the sky
I hear bugles blow day is done:
Drowning out the shouts of
victory.

I see the children weepin':
Tears flowin' like the river.
I see the women prayin':
Heads bowed low on bended
knee.

I hear Gabriel's trumpet:
Backed by Heaven's band of
harps.
I hear all the angels singing:
Hosannah to the king.

I see the coming of the Lord:
A crown of gold upon his head.
I see pearly gates:
Thrown open by his command.

Linda Rogers
SEASONS

i saw the spring go out today
and blossom into summer
the birds sang the rain away
and acted as its runner

the summer sun was oh so warm
with cool breezes in the sky
the endless heavens a glorious
blue
and the summer sun on high

and all too soon the sky turned
gray
and the wind began to blow
my mind would not accept
what my heart would say
my summer would have to go

i saw the fall come in today
with rain and dreariness
abound
and soon the great grey sky
turned white
and snow was all around

the snow and rain and cool crisp
days
are all that i can see
i dream of sun and golden days
its all the same to me

i saw the spring come in today
the grass and leaves uncurled
the sun and flowers and birds
of song
let their joy be known to the
world.

Guy T. Fisher
CIRCUS IN SESSION

the circus was in session today
and all the acts filled the room
but the acts couldn't get started
until the head jester did arrive
his seconds were all on hand

just to keep the acts in their
places
and collecting the info of what
the acts did do
the head jester did arrive ever
so late
just so he can make his grand
entrance
and the seconds made sure that
all rose to greet him
one by one the acts did appear
before him
and the head jester either
accepted them
or he threw them on the pile
nervously I await my turn to
perform
watching the casting going on
before me
my name is called out loud and
clear
but my chance to perform is
taken away
you must return at a later date
and if we see fit you will
perform that day
so away with you now
and don't forget to return
cuz I'll be holding court again
that day
and the head jester will make
his ruling
either to be accepted
or cast upon the pile
and maybe to return again
and again and again.

Laura J. Friedman
TWINKLE OF THE STARS

The twinkle of the stars fade
away
as daylight approaches.

But do not fear they will
reappear at
the end of the day.

The sunlit sky disappears as the
evening starts to dawn.

But do not fear it will reappear
at
the start of the day.

Our friendship, too, has
vanished

But when will it return?
At the break of day or the
crack of dawn?

Stephen Chisholm
THE YELLOW DRESS

YOU laying there looking
synthetic
you somehow remind me of
the time
I told you
That I thought I had seen you
In every conceivable way
In all positions.

The next day
As I layed on my back
On the grass—
You stepped over me
Straddling my head.
You were wearing that yellow
chiffon dress
the one I liked the best
and you had no underwear
beneath it
and you proved
there was a view
still new of you.

And now you're laying there
looking plastic
in that new purple dress
the one I picked out for you
Just what are you proving

now?
The needle still hangs
from your arm
filled with red blood
and your ankles are flat
against the tile.

YOU do not look real anymore
and this view
tears the throat
out of my heart
but I can't look away
until the man
covers your head
with the white sheet.

Edna Aboussleman
**INFLATION FIGHTER
(CHRISTMAS 1980)**

I'm as American as apple sauce.
'Twas almost Christmas, our
Government had spoken—
We must tighten our purse
strings, help fight inflation
Whilst making way for Santa
Claus.
To Crafte Centre I hied me for
cheap ornamentation.
I'd make my own cards, a
worthy contribution.

The clerk was most helpful,
became part of my team.
"Construction paper," she
said, "You will need a ream.
'N a bucket of glitter to
brighten 'n cheer.
Christmas, M'Dear, comes but
once a year."
"Look, Miss," I protested, "You
are so kind. . ."
"I know," she purred; "'N folks
like you 'R hard to find."
"What I mean to say, I have
but few . ."
"Of course," she rejoined, "'N
don't forget them so they can't
forget you. Tell ya what I'm
gonna do!"
"Huh?" I gasped, thinking I
knew, scarce daring to ask.
(Really, I SHOULD take her
to task.)
"I'll throw in this barrel of
glue, half price—now, the
total, let's see, can it be?"
"Tell me," I pleaded, gripping
the counter, whilst 'round
me spun Ye Olde Crafty Centre.
"One Thousand One Hundred
Fifty-three—plus tax, we'll
figure that last; come, let's
pack your order fast!"
"That's a lot," was my lament,
"I can't believe how much
I've spent."
"Not when you consider
your intent!" She was most
vehement,
"And at only 18 per cent.
You can't expect to fight
inflation, nor hope to
save YOUR nation—
Unless like Faith, you sow
the seed; nuthin' down—all

the time you need."
I wheeled, would've made it to
the door; she blocked, we were
a team once more.
"O, 'tis such a worthy cause.
Paul Revere rode forth; we
honor his name—He did it with
a horse.
"You, M'Dear, have even
greater claim to fame. 'N
you've
done it with an EMPTY
PURSE!"
(Are you list'nin', Santa
Claus?)

Elfrieda Evelyn Burkett
**GOLD AND SILVER AND A
ROMANTIC FAR AWAY
LOOK**

A gold and silver mist hangs
over this street,
Stores , people, restaurants,
newsstands we meet.
A sense of rushing to and fro
or just browsing by.
Cinemas, theatres, shows, seem
to say give us a try.
Their advertisements invite,
almost grab you inside.
Huge placards showing their
naked in their sweetest
innocence.

Crowds almost in mob
proportion with no place to
hide.
Many and varied tea rooms
and relaxing salons to make
you less tense.
Wig shops, nut shops, record
shops, watch and jewelry shops,
Taxies, busses, sightseeing cars
to take passengers to many
stops.

Sometimes this street has a
business look, a romantic
look,
Many times it has a tough tense
look, also the look of love.
It is an intensely moving street
watched by the heavens
above—
Constantly in motion, people
waiting for the street lights
So they can go to the next
department store in their
sights.
Many subway entrances and
exits for human beings to
enter,
All kinds of destinations like
Columbus Circle or
Rockefeller Center.

One can ride from the Hudson
River to the East River eyeing
everything.
You can jump off the bus and
purchase cigars or a brand
new ring.
From Grand Central Terminal,

you can take trains to other
states,
At the Port Authority Bus
Terminal, you might find
your future mate.

People walking by, rushing by,
running by, romantically
longing—
For something, someone, or
seeking peace in a health
food shop.
A gold and silver mist and a
romantic far-away look hangs
over
this street.
Forty-Second street, or Times
Square, also known under
the pseudonym
of Grand Central,
"Hello and a kiss to you we
greet."

Camilla Collier
UNTITLED

When summer is green again
Laughing and cool,
Perhaps I'll go down
To a deep forest pool
where water still clear
and magically bright,
forever with morning,
shall dance in my sight.

Edward J. Vining
FOR SALE

The house was still, each
window-sill,
was dressed in virgin white.
The doors were locked around
the clock,
no chimney smoke in sight.

About the land the trees were
bland,
the fences lay in ruin.
And all was lean, that once was
green,
and chores were left for doin'.

And to the right, in black and
white,
below the front porch rail,
A sign was fixed, I almost
missed,
that simply read, "FOR SALE."

Ruth L. Schuck
ABC OF FLOWERS

A is for Asters, a beautiful
bouquet,
B is for Begonia in splendid
array
C is for Columbine with old
fashioned charm
D is for Daisy growing wild
on the farm
E is for Elephant's Ear, just
like it's name
F is for Forsythia blooming in
the lane
G is for Gladiolus so colorful
and proud
H is for Hollyhock standing
out in the crows
I is for Ivy that crawls up the
wall
J is for Jack-in-the-pulpit, speak
speaking to all
K is for Kochia, a symmetrical
plant
L is for Lilac, always so fragrant
M is for Marigold, found in
most homes
N is for Nasturtium, like jewels
atop green domes
O is for Oxalis grown in a pot
P is for Pansy whose face

smiles a lot
Q is for Quaking Grass, so
ornamental
R is for Rose, its charm
sentimental
S is for Scarlet Sage, all ablaze
T is for Tithonia, a fiery
orange moss
U is for Upas, evergreen so high
V is for Violet, earthy and shy
W is for Wildflower growing in
the wood
X is for Xeranthemum, by
the gate it stood
Y is for Yucca, accent of the
roadside
Z is for Zinnia too brilliant to
hide.

Frances Meigs Goodnight
FROST

Grandfather frost in his winter
attire—
so regal and white
Visited our town last night while
all was
silent and quiet.

He danced on the hillside
touching each shivering tree.
He skipped in the meadow
painting with frost a fairyland
for the
whole world to see.

He made not a sound as he
made every round,
Not even to awaken the
creatures that
nest in the ground.

The world slept in silence—they
heard not a sound,
While Grandfather Frost scamp
scampered and
tugged, unrolling a white
blanket
as fluffy as down.

His breath short and crisp
chilled the air
as it fell,
Touching the earth with a
melody of
rest—of slumber so deep in its
resounding knell.

He finished his work—he
stepped back to view,
A landscape in picture—so
frosty, so
delicate, so lacy and mirrowed
with light.
The artist was finished—What
a beautiful,
musical, wonderous sight.

The sun's morning brilliance
cast its arms o'er the earth
Revealing a portrait so priceless
so fragile—of winter's first
glistening delight.

The sleeper awakens, entranced
by the frost laden sight.
But Grandfather Frost has
departed
leaving the majesty of God
autographed indelibly
By the morning's first light.

Peter W. Ciampa
TRUTH

Thinking now of our past
I wonder when I saw you last
Were you smiling of pure joy
Or thinking of me as a toy?
Were my heart and feelings
a piece of clay
Of when you tired you could
throw away

I can't decide what I should
believe
My feelings are causing me
much grief
I can not have you that is true
Without you the sky is no
longer blue
My heart cries out for you with
no avail
True love like mine is such a
sad tale
If my love was used by you
Then I swear that this is true
The spark that is in my heart
Must completely depart
Never again to be set ablaze
No words or deeds will
penetrate the maze
That I will live in further more
My heart will be a bolted door
My heart is the source of life
I wanted you forever as my wife
Searching and yet never to find
Is a heavy burden on the mind
You are there and I am here
From thee I seek to hear
Do you care for what I am
Or don't you give a damn?

Jan Muse
TRAPPED

Trapped!
That dreadful day shall come!
I know it will!
The fear I hold within my heart
grows with each passing
moment;
a cancer ravaging my mind.
The pain will be great no matter
what path I seek, but which
will
guide me safely on?
Is the ultimate result worth
the agony of the days ahead?
What is there to hope for, to
even live for?
Happiness is now beyond the
realm of reality.
Can my mind withstand the
torture and confusion
whirling kaleidoscopically
within itself?
I am bending!
Will I break?
Breaking!!
I reach down into the depth
of insanity.
Can I return from the
catacombs of that shadowy
land?
I am a caged animal!
The wild uncertainty visible
within my eyes reveals the
unknown that
is slowly destroying my life.
I cannot escape.
I search for answers that are
forever—beyond.
Fear consumes me—is this
eternity?
I AM LOST!!!

Bernadette Papenbrock
WINGS

In all, it is beauty.
Sunlight gently blankets the
valley.
A rainbow
of sounds
Fills the forest and
Wings flutter carelessly
Through
slender
trees
Deer stoop to taste the satin
coolness.
(night falls)

White light of the moon
Becomes hidden by clouds
Shadows are cast over trees and
Wings retreat
    to hide
      from
        the rain,
That fades the colour and
  drowns the rainbow.
  (clouds darken)
Shadows of night are
Shattered
    by
      light.
Cries and thunder command
The once peaceful
Silence.
A tree
    dies,
    bursts,
As a new, hot light pierces
Splitting it in two.
  (heat grows)
Rainbow collides with Rainbow,
Each
    fleeing
A confusion of light and
A confusion of life and light.
Broken
  Wings
    Tangle
      with
        charred
          trees
        (as day dawns.)

Dawn Davignon
A FRIEND IS SOMETHING SPECIAL

Did you ever stop to think how
  special friends really are,
They're as special as the night's
  first shining star.
As special as a bird's song early
  in the morn,
As special as a baby that has
  just been born.
You just don't realize it every
  minute of the day,
But a friend is so special in
  their own way.
Each one is so different from
  the other one,
Some are for listening and
  some are for talking, but all
  are for fun.
No one friend is better than
  the rest,
Each one is special, each one
  is the best.
You could look all day to find
  that special friend,
But, each friend is something
  special from beginning to end.

Ann M. Gundersen
PEOPLE OF THE EARTH

You people of the earth take
  heed, my friend
In this world we must love,
  and extend a hand
To a neighbor in need, not
  scorn or hurt
So many have done to folks
  not alert
They never learn or care,
Their only concern is
  themselves
And their gains, yet, laugh
  at the poor
Whom are troubled with pains.

When the day of resurrection
  arrives
  Will they rise to the voice of
  Jesus

As He extends his hand with
  a smile
  That will surge deep down
  inside
Asking, "Have you kept my
  Ten Commandments"?
Tho He knew, He wanted to
  hear
The truth—from you.
You people of the earth, take
  heed, twice said
  live according to God's Words,
Whether single or wed—
  Sharing, not swearing—not
  hurting for spite
For when the end comes
And we fight for our life
We can relax—let go—With
  Jesus in hand
Welcoming us—To his heavenly
  land
For all eternity—what joy
Tis worth waiting for!

Dan Parker
QUINTESSENCE

flashing azure eyes
across a crowded room
sparks flying
unseen by the unknowing
powerful currents
parallel directions
merging in a single glance
"ask me" he thought
a request unspoken
nonetheless profound;
transcending the threshold of
  uncertainty
she swept him up. . .
dancing together
to rhythmic primal intonations
meant for no one else
passionate souls
pulsating in unison.

weekdays and weekends
time melting moments
changing patterns and colors
textures coarse and fine
wind-blown emotions
seeking sanctuary
refuse from the storm
bodies aching for closeness
and warmth

silent words
floating freely
in inner sanctum
forming unsung melodies
two-part harmony.

a love song
of peace
of promise
echoing in the recesses
of sequestered time and space
wrought with enchantment
encompassed by felicity.

Mrs. Helen Agathen
PRAYER

When life seems so uncertain,
And burdens hard to bear,
I bundle all my troubles up,
And go to God in prayer.

I tell him I am heartsick,
And know not what to do,
I ask that He be near me,
To help me see things through.

It takes but just a moment,
When murmerings start to cease
My prayers are being answered,
I'm granted inner peace.

What a friend we have in Jesus,
For He does truly care,
He comforts and protects us,
Through a simple thing called
  "Prayer."

Darlene D. Gulliford
STILL ,I REMEMBER

As I sit alone in my room , I
  gaze out the window
Into the stillness of night and
  remember.
We were in love long time ago
  and the spring air
Was there for us to share.
  Our thoughts and minds were
  as one.
Dancing in the warm summer
  rain, watching the leaves fall
And the snow silently drifting
  in the night.
As suddenly as dawn finds
  the morning, he was gone.
Seasons change, years go by
  but still, I remember.
Sometimes at night I see him;
  his hand reaches out to touch
  mine
In a dream of the forgotten
  past. All to vanish into the
  light.
The letters they remain, all
  speaking of his love to me.
A love that will never be again,
  still it lingers like a half
  remembered song.
I wondered what it was really
  all about as I watched his
  plane disappear.
For as he turned to go, I said
  'goodbye.'
Still, I remember.

Ellen Crosby
MY COMMISSION

I drove through a rainbow one
  morning
It's colors so brilliant—so true
And my heart was filled
With a marvelous joy
The joy of knowing you.

I climbed a lonely mountain
  one day
And breathed the clean pure
  air
And a still small voice
Spoke to my heart
And I felt Your presence there.

I stood on a rocky cliff one day
Looking down at the coast
  below
And the turbulent sea
Brought back to me
An answer that filled my soul

I knelt by a quiet grave one day
And pledged my faith anew
And an inner peace
Brought sweet release
And I knew what I must do.

I must share my faith from day
  to day
With others while I live
And help them find
The peace of mind
That only Christ can give.

Mary Hullah
REINCARNATED LOVE

I used to hear of Love's delights,
Searing kisses, hungry arms,
  blissful nights. . .
And with a cynic's smile
  dismissed them each,
As idle fantasies,. . .quite out of
  reach.

Then I met you, and the
  instant recognition
of another time, another space,
  an intuition
Flashed across the mirror of
  my mind . . .

The fleeting thought that "he's
  your kind".
The cynic's smile is gone, and
  in its place
A radiance glows in heart and
  soul and face. . .
For I know love now, and all
  its boundless joys
Are not the conjuration of
  lovesick boys. . .
But the true communion of
  two souls who meet again
After centuries apart, the lips
  the arms the heart
Well known before, are just
  as real just as sweet
As the golden days of yore.

Eula Maye Bennett
LET GOD CLOSE THE GATE

Like the prodigal son I
  approached the gate
With trembling soul, beyond
  lay my fate.

Knowledge of broken vows
  caused me to fear
I could not see beyond stood
  the Lord of the year.

Like the Father—in sympathy
  I heard Him say,
"Come with your broken
  dreams and tears today
Look to the green pastures
  of my holy word
My promises are true", are the
  words I heard.

With tender nail scarred hands
  He beckoned me on
Toward the New Year and the
  rising sun.

Again I heard "Fear not for
  past mistakes,
Good intentions and selfishness
  forget, let brotherly love
  prevail.
Come with me, the future path
  is bright
Leave all behind, face the New
  Year's light.

The New Year is a bud to be
  a full blown flower
When touched by the freshness
  of pure love.
  A lovely path for the feet to
  trod
Guided by the Holy God
  Landscapes to paint with
  colors bright
Friendships to claim in
  Heaven's light
  A soul to touch a gift to bear
  A kind word here and there.

Beyond the mystic gate, my
  dear awaits the dawn of a
  golden year
  The path is aglow with
opportunities sweet
  To share the Light of Truth
  with all you meet."

Then I heard Him say further,
"Go on, don't look back—don't
hesitate
  For I stand here and your
past is forgiven
  Go on my child, I'll close
the gate."

Pat De Santis
MONA LISA

Ah! This portrait:
With a face of mystery,
With eyes of the unknown,
With a smile of uncertainty,
Even the valleys behind her;
Testify! To the mystique.

She is, the summing up of man's
works;
She is, the on looker of live;
She is, the representation of
ageless beauty.

Verna I. Granlund
IMAGE BELOVED

Roses withered and forlorn
Daisies bowing in disgrace
  Emblems of your passing
Like the tears upon my face.

Our meeting was so brief
Moments in a frame of time
The shutter clicked
Your image stamped
Like the cadence of a poet's
rhyme.

Silent words were spoken
Coded expressions messaged
  across your face
Embraces warm
  hesitantly broken
Sacred vows—tokens
Were edged in wedding lace.

Your image faded
But seen again today
When my heart felt
  the coldness of a rapier blade
As I read that you had passed
away.

On this damp and foggy morn
as I stand beside your grave
Seeing roses withered and
  forlorn
Daisies bowing in disgrace
I wipe tears
  not of sorrow
But tears of sadness and regret
That you passed away
Before in essence
  we had even met.

Paul H. Menier III
YOU WERE THERE

When first we met and fell
  in love,
The time we shared was small.
For Uncle Sam required of me,
That I give him my all.
The thing that kept me going,
On this my love, I swear.
Was knowing that you love me,
And knowing you were there.
But now the time is over,
I paid my dues to man.
I'll now devote my time to you,
Give all the love I can.
I'll do my best to make life
  good,
And everything we'll share.
For when I needed love so bad,
I always found you there.
There's times I was in Germany,
So very far away.
But you were always on my
  mind,
Each and every day.

No more will miles divide us,
With pain so hard to bear.
For love I've learned a lesson,
When you were always there.
We now can plan together,
The things we want to do.
For all my time is mine alone,
I give it all to you.
We'll make a life together,
With love beyond compare.
Cause where and when you
  need me,
You'll always find me there.

Barbara Neace Sienkiewice
LIFE'S ROAD

We walked a country road,
The path was long and winding.
The air was bitter cold.

Little was said as we continued
  our journey,
No more tears were shed.
Our grief was far from gone
But the well within our mind
  was dry.

Many times we parted but

  came together again.
At one point we thought the
  road would never end;
My sister, his ladyfriend, and I.
We saw the bridge and knew it
  had to be crossed.
My fear was intense, I knew I
  could not swim.
We inched our way to the
  middle of the bridge;
His ladyfriend and I.

As I stared into the swirling,
  ice cold water,
I desperately tried to hang on;
But the unavoidable happened—
I slipped in.
The ugly water was suddenly
  warm
And I found that I could swim.
My heart was full of joy
As I came up out of the water.

My first sight was a beautiful
  sandy beach.
What an odd place—
The dog is chained but the lion
  walks free.

In the distance I saw what
I thought to be a priest.
He stretched out his arms to
  welcome me.
On his face was a familiar grin.
I ran to be embraced by him
  again.
We were together once more;
My brother and me.

He was changed just a bit,
No sadness in his eyes and not
  a blemish on his face.
As I thought of the times I had
  longed for this reunion—
I remembered that I had not
  been alone.

He knew my thoughts without

a word.
He pointed first to the road,
Then down the beach.

Our sister's time is not finished,
She must still walk the road.
As we looked at the dead body
  of
His ladyfriend, lying in a heap.
He said—Aren't you glad,
  you chose the right road?

Janice Kirby Marmion
TOO CLOSE

I crawled into a clock one day
So I could mix with time:
It was my wish to pull some
  strings
And tell them it was mine.
The coils and springs ignored
  me
As they whirled and bounced
  their way.
I was so bewildered;
I found I couldn't stay.

I slinked into a mirror
So I might find out
The things I'd been missing
And I could look about.
But all was so confusing
With faces everywhere.
I could see the side of you
Of which I should beware.

My body was exhausted,
So I put me in the sky.
I rode upon a cloud
And let my friends run by.
I could see their faces,
But not so close to me.
For this I was much happier—
I offered myself some tea.

Thomas E. Kipp
TURN THE OTHER CHEEK

Confused, afraid, protected by
  the tribe,
Man fought in vain with sin,
  and lust, and greed.
There was no golden rule to
  serve as guide,
No "Love your Neighbor"
  policy to heed.
The laws were harsh and mercy
  seldom shown,
For might made right; the
  weak could not survive.
His death was final, hopeless,
  all alone. . .
And then came One with
  strength to help, revive.
He taught when struck to turn
  the other cheek;
When forced to go a mile, make
  two our goal;
That blessed are the gentle ones,
  the meek. . .
And we should love the Lord
  with heart and soul.

He gave His life that each
  might one day be
A child of His through all
  eternity.

Doris Ann Park
DEVASTATION

I close my eyes and see the oaks,
So stately and so tall,
Lending their shade and beauty
To the creek below.

To walk among them was
  reprieve
From city life and call,
To dove and rabbit, quail and
  squirrel,
The everlasting shelter from

their foe.
I've looked through myriads
Of branches
Thick with morning dew
That catches the sun and
  sparkle
Like a gem.

I've seen the moon shine through
And glimpse the owl and night
  hawk
On the limb

I've shot at doves atop the
  tallest spire
Before erratically their flight
  begun,
And then in evening's cool
  attire,
Watched whispering branches
  nod
That day is done.

The oaks are gone, destroyed
As if by wand;
The gently rolling earth is
All that's left to me.

I cry the silent tears of one
  forlorn,
For true it is that only God
Can make a tree.

Cornelia Austin
GOALS

I wandered through a woodland
  glen
  Where flows a brook in pure
  delight,
It sings and gurgles as it goes
  O'er rocks and pebbles,
  smooth and bright.
It has a goal—to form a pool
  Where creatures of the wild
  may drink
And be sustained by waters cool
  Ere summer's burning sun shall
  sink.

Majestic deer came here one
  day
  Then loped to heights—with
  backward glance
They paused a moment to
  portray
  A silhouette in regal stance.
Their goal was reached without
  delay
  Lush meadows green beyond
  the height
Where they would graze 'til end
  of day
  Near forest, haven of the night.

My goal is lofty as Mt. Blanc,
  As oft enshrouded in the mists
Of doubt and gloom and years
  of toil
  But flame of faith and hope
  persists.
I, too, shall reach the goal I
  seek
  If there be purpose in the
  task
Of knowledge, gained along
  the way
  Of this I'm sure—I do not
  ask.

James N. Siefreid
MEMORIES OF LAURA

"Laura, why must my memories
  of you haunt me so?"
Memories of a summertime long
  ago.
All is archaic, decadent, or dead,
On the hill where once your
  footsteps have tread.

Justice is that fair virtue
  brought to mind,
Because your performance

was so unkind.
You drifted away on the night's
ebb tide.
Away from the scene, away
from my side.
This unforeseen act gave a
headlong start,
To the pain and anguish within
my heart,
From a love I cherished and
was eager to share,
Instead of those forsaken
moments of despair.
I lost you in those dreary
bygone days,
Because I was so innocent and
sky.
I had no knowledge of all
the strange ways,
In which friendships finish,
and vows untie.
As here! In springtime on the
grass I lie,
With haunting memories of your
last good-bye.
I remember every moment I
shared with you,
Though four long decades
have since passed from view.
The hour-glass of time is
silently slipping by.
These haunting memories
will linger on until I die.
Nevermore to languish here,
amid the living.
How joyous life would be,
If I had been forgiving.

Geri Wenger
GOLGOTHA'S HILL

The thief on the cross to our
Savior did plea
If thou be Christ, than go down
from the tree.
But our Lord to the other did
say:
"You'll be with me in Paradise
this day."
How many of us believe in His
Name?
Are we guilty and share in the
shame?
Do we mock and scoff at His
Words?
For if we do, we bear the blame.
The Lord said when He finished
His task
"Come to Me, is all my heart
asks."
To set us free from our sins
He died.
That we might live, His love
magnified.
Are you goin' to Golgotha's
Hill
Fill His thirst, with vinegar still?
Remember, my friend, when
your life is done,
Will you see Christ, God's only
Son?
Thy kingdom come, thy will be
done
Here on earth as it is in Heaven.
The holy powers and glory
command
When the king of kings reigns
over His land.

Karen Renee Fisher-Manson
AS A MATTER OF FACT

Facts are facts, fiction is for
the birds
when it comes to getting down
I'll give it a third
a third you say sounds funny,

it because I'm a funny person
when
getting down,
Oh what I mean is, let's stop
pussyfooting around
let's take care of business the
way we should
'cause we are always saying,
if I could of I would
You would of what, not one
damn thing, you've been
singing that
song for years
If I hear that line one more time
I'll bust right out in tears.
Cry baby cry baby, thats what
you call a baby when it cries,
well tell me this is it true,
dead man can tell no lies
Nine lives he has, you don't
believe that
I'm talking about that big
black cat
no not the man sitting under
the tree
that big rascal over there,
damn can't you see
I see right now I'll have to go,
I have no place here with you,
the fact of the matter is,
Fiction is sometimes true.

Stephanie Nahirniak
THANKSGIVING FOR NATURES BEAUTY

Who can show us nicer beauty
then the rays of the morning
sun,
Or the chirping and the flapping
When the birds are having fun?
Who can paint in million colors
Different trees and flowers
that thrive,
Not on paper or on dummies
But ones that grow and are
alive?
Who can clothe the sky with
clouds
Or just make it bright and gay,
Who can make the night have
darkness
Or make it light during the day?
Who can melt the snow in
springtime
Or in summer make flowers
bloom,
Who can change the colors in
autumn
With snowing winters following
soon?
Oh the beautiful lakes and
rivers
With the huge blue oceans wide,
Who has made all this great
beauty,
For us people to abide?
I could tell of a million sceneries
That are put upon this land,
With all creatures and the
animals
All created by a powerful hand.
For all is nature's beauty,
That our human eye can see,
God and only God has made it
Above all powers for you and
me.
Now as we sent Thanksgiving
blessings
To each other far and near,
Let the first be a Thanksgiving
prayer
To our Lord who is most dear.
We thank thee Lord for all

creation
With prayers that come from
our heart,
For protecting us and forgiving
With your love, we'll never part.

Mr. Felix Peterson
UNTITLED

M=1000
I'm sorry for the peoples greedy
money,
or the peoples terrible or ugly
taste.
M l
Many people say God does not
live in the
Churches or in the temples,
But that God
lives in each peoples home too!
I say
that is correct too! What the
people say.
M ll
If you like, God lives in your
home too.
M lll
You must have self-discipline
and respect
or understand—right or wrong,
good or
evil.
M IV
On the earth planet lives
the two feet dangerous animal,
with the name human. He is
the earth planet's king!
MV
Augustus, Julius or Marxus he
likes
himself and his
Roman names too. This
natures creature study the
universe
planet sun, or give the name
God!
MVI
Or god sun! But what is the
God?
He says, God is love! God is
a spirit!
But what will do the planet sun?
MVII
Or can the planet sun, today
drink the de cafe?
But I'm very sad for
the peoples liars or false!

Russell C. Brown Jr.
STAND BY YOUR FELLOW MAN

Times when strangers need
a hand
And your just the person to
help.
Remember, he's just a fellow
man,
A brother, a person, like
yourself.

I say to you, at a New Years
start,
Make way to help and give.
This person you help is a
fellow man
He's got the same right to live.
Color, race and creed are just
words,
If you love your fellow man.
It makes no difference if he's
black or white
You can still offer a hand.
Love and peace will never be,
If you don't give a damn about
men.
Turn to help, go out of your
way,
To build, to show and lend.
Riches are yours from our
Father,
With each day you give to Him.
Standing by man and living,
Is the battle in which you'll win.
As I end this thought of mine
Remember each day from here
Standing by your fellow man,
my friend,
Will bring you peace both far
and near.

Deidre Alexander
LIFE IS A STRUGGLE

When everything's fine,
we stay in one place,
but want to move on.
Reaching the next step,
a choice must be made,
without looking back.
Just memories remain.
Failure or success:
It does not matter.
Learning continues
as we are growing,
and reaching our goals.
Knowledge increases
with satisfaction
when we share our needs.
Remembering Christ,
strength is provided
when our will needs it.
Restoration comes
as we are steadfast,
though Satan tempts us.
Continuing on,
and not giving in,
God will work things out.
Waiting patiently,
our gifts are revealed,
and also uses.
But, if we control
everything goes wrong,
because it's God's job.
With all in our hands,
and no direction,
life is meaningless.

Garnet Glendenning
COUNTRY LANE

How I recall the old Country
Lane. . .
that led to the back woods
pasture.
Where the old turkey hen hid
in the brush. . .
among the beauty of the
flowery woodland.
Our little bare legs didn't mind
the briars.
Each day the same trip to see
is any eggs were in the nest:
And how long till the little
baby turkeys might appear?
For in time the old turkey hen

slyly led our a band of
bright eyes. . .just an image of
the old feathered friend.
Oh just for a day to go back to
the old home with ducks
and geese and chickens.
The big frame house with trees
and leaves
just for a child to romp and
play. . .
with their pup around the door.
Oh just for a day down the old
dusty road. . .

to the old brick school house
we loved.
Where the big iron bell called
the roll.
With the old oak desk for
teacher to sit.
Each scholar was eagar for
to learn for the life ahead.
So many of our little play
mates have passed on and
some are left.
Slowly as the memory fades
away leaving a sadness of
the by gone day of
yesterday.

Alma Lillian Hageman
REUNION AT LAST

We're out on the highway
The road called "Second
Chance"
My heart feels delighted
To the past I'll give
no second chance.

High on love's skyway
We're on the right road again
Bound for each other
Time moves us on.

All aboard the train
for glory
We're bound for cloud nine
We'll meet at the station
Delight will be mine.

Hands clasped together
My soul locked in thine
Eyes bright with tear drops
Happily shine.

The years have been heavy
Many crosses to bear
We did our best Dear,
Now our time is here.

We've known the rough weather
We've known fall's gentle
healing rain
Softly. . .splashing away
the pain.

Let's not judge how
much time left to
spend,
Let's judge how well
time is spent.
Love is not quantity
It is the quality lent.

E. Eugene Perry
**EVENING IN MARTINS
FERRY, OHIO**

soggy purple sky—
evening comes.

mama's in the kitchen
fixing dinner—
tuna casserole,
again.

papa drags in from
the mills,
gray and unsmiling.

turning on the t.v.
to re-runs,
he stares at,
not watching really,

the flickering b&w images.
upstairs,
i sit in my room
with my second-hand royal
writing pages no eyes will read.

dinner is always
the same—
the smells,
the tastes,
the conversation—
sisters chirping
of when who was where with
whom—
is this my life?
is this my destiny?

the hills that bind
the river to its course
bind me also.

it will be dark soon.
the boys will traditionally
friday-night screech
the tires of their daddy's car
just one more time,
then the city will settle
to crickets.

i'll dream
maybe morning
will be different.

yet dawn slips in unnoticed,
still soggy.

another day begins.

Grace R. Dorsey
XMAS LIGHTS AGLOWING

Xmas let glow, let it aglow at
Christmas let it snow.
Now while the stars are
watching are watching the
sleepy earth below
This glow and ruins is now at
a little quiet town in
Bethlehem.
Angels was protecting Babe
Jesus lying in a manger behold.
The shephards was attending to
their flocks of sheep by night.
Starburst brightness now a
glowing forever a light.
This literal of peace on earth
good will to all men.
Now this is a symbol of the
Christ babe for each and all
to remember.
For faith we keep on this
date is still twenty fifty of
December.
Be kind to People, Places and
things of this is always
blessing weeks.
Spiritualism is how He hold
us in graceful keep.
Joy to the world was and is this
Glory nights and days.
How three wise men arrived
to show them and us the new
ways.
So it was love. Peace and joy
was always here to stay.
Christianity gives more
aglowing lights for why we do
not go astray.

Charles R. Perlwitz
**THE PATHS ALONG THE
WAY**

Somehow there was always
another trail
leading off from the one we
traveled.
We backed up a bit, fearing
we had
misjudged, but in the end it was
always
as if propelled by a guiding wind

we assumed the way, flying
through
all hesitation and doubt,
rambling onward
toward the center of the deep
preserve.
We understood the paths
without really
knowing them, realized their
interrelation.
as being more than directed
distance,
or even the connection between
this actual
place
and those greener and more
hushed, farther
up along the way. It all came
down to this:
We were here and you were
there, and all
that lay between were the
paths along
the way, feeling out their
presence as they
united us, connecting
within this vastness.

Mary Rando
I MISS YOU—YOU KNOW

I miss you—you know,
Though you've never let me
tell you so.
I yearn to feel your warm
embrace, your tender touch,
To see your face.
To sit and talk about your day,
your joys, your fears,
To know your gentle way,
To have you listen to what I say
And know you care.

I miss you—you know,
Though it's been such a short
time ago
That you had to leave me, had
to say "goodbye"
Neither of us knowing when
we would again say "Hi".

I promised myself, I wouldn't
wait by the phone,
And then the days passed and I
felt so alone,
I missed you—you know?

You've been on my mind
constantly
Although I've fought the
thoughts.
I've wanted to call you
And then thought—better not.

Perhaps had we met in another
time,
We could spend our lives
together.
But since that wasn't so
I know I will have to let you go
And simply miss you—you
know?

Teressa Bobier
FREEDOM

Like the leaves of the forest,
when summer is green,
They glow like banners when
the sunset is seen.
Soon to be parted from the
trees where they've grown,
For summer has parted and
autumn has blown.
The wind whispers softly as it
blows through the trees,
It seemed quite warm for an
autumn breeze.
The frost has come in the dark
of the night,

Covering the leaves with a
frosting so white.
Changing the colors as lovely
can be,
Showing the beauty of a
wonderful tree.
Down the leaves fall to the
ground far below,
They float down as soft as new
fallen snow.
Silently dancing around through
the trees,
Twisting and twirling in their
flight to be free.
Like the waves of the ocean or
the silvery sea,
They fly in the wind like the
birds to be free.

Dorothy E. Wright
OH, TO REMEMBER

My mother used to tell me
stories of beautiful dreams
that she wanted to live by.
She loved to see the seasons
changing and she watched
the trees and streams with a
sigh;
She longed for my Dad to be
alive again to help her
when her heart was troubled,
And Mom, poor soul, would
talk to him, just like
a new life he'd doubled.
She thought she could see him
enter the house and
sit in a chair by the bed;
They would hold a discussion
about what troubled her,
then she would wake up with
a clear head.
She just knew he had helped
her decide whatever her
decision might be
She also knew she had done
the right thing and
always would say, "You'll see."
She would tell me about the
first house they'd bought
with a dirt road, "right in
front by the yard."
With fruit trees scattered here
and there, and a
huge iron kettle to render the
lard.
She loved to can vegetables and
fruit, and make
grape juice by the gallons,
And of course, my Dad broke
the seal on some, so that
he would have wine for his
talents.
My Mother lives again by the
side of the road,
the first house she and he
ever bought;
They moved away twice, and
each time returned because
without their "Home"
seemed lost.
It was always crowded with

children and love, a
  better home there never could
  be;
It's so wonderful to go home,
  see Mom,
  and to hear her say "You'll
  see."

The clutter, collections of
  memories, I should say,
abound as you enter the door.
There's pictures of families
  for generations back,
  and trinkets from grand
  children galore;
Mom keeps things handy, as do
  I, because
  we both are losing our sight,
We want to see everything as
  long as we can, and we
  can't if it is "put away"
  right;
There's more to living than just
  fashion and order,
  Mom's ideas for her are right
Inside her head it's neat, and
  clean as a pin,
  outside it's clutter afright.
What's life without dreams
  of things to come,
  and memories of all things
  past.
For the beautiful things will
  always be, even
  when we're old they'll last,
  "You'll see."

Janet L. Webb
INNER CONFLICT

From the distance heard a
  howling,
One that chilled me to the bone.
Alas I knew it oh so certain:
To be my inner soul's dire moan.

Searched in vain across the still
  earth,
For a futile sign of life,
But I knew as I searched vainly,
What I saw was my own strife.

Heard a doubtful beating
  starting,
As I neared the outer ledge,
Oh I knew it was my own
  heart,
Listlessly pounding O'er the
  edge.

Caught my foot among the
  briars,
Tangled in a heaping maze.
All my broken dreams had
  gathered,
In this snarling, blinding haze.

Irene Sorenson Duval
DON'T YOU QUIT

When things get rough
  and they sometimes will,
When the road you're trudging
  seems all uphill,
You don't know whether
  to walk or sit,
Rest if you must,
  But don't you quit!

You're sick in body,
  weary and worn,
You feel so helpless,
  alone and forlorn.
You say to yourself,
  "Well, this is it."
Rest if you must,
  But don't you quit!

When you look and see
  the mountain top,
You start to think,
  "Will the problems stop?"

Bring them to God,
  relax and sit,
Rest if you must,
  But don't you quit!

Turn about face
  and get in the race
He'll give you the strength
  to withstand the pace.
The prize you will win
  is worth every bit,
Rest if you must,
  but don't you quit!

Say to yourself,
  "I'm going to win."
You'll feel God's presence
  abiding within.
Trust Him, my friend,
  take hold of the big.
Rest if you must
  but don't you quit!

Gladys Terrel
SOMETHING FOR NOTHING

I'm remembering a day not
  so long ago,
  It was Fall, if I remember
The sun was shining, bright
  and clear,
  Around the first of December.

I said to my daughter, "Let's
  go for a ride,
  There's something I seen that
  I want.
I need it for making a Christmas
  gift,
  So let's go on a little jaunt."

So down the highway we went,
  her and I,
  To hunt for a little box.
And lo and behold, there it
  was,
  Boy! I'm a sly little fox.

So I said, Hey Sharon, come on,
  back up!
  And of course that's just what
  she did.
And gracious, gracious, when
  she backed up,
  Into the culvert we slid.

I started to open my door just
  a crack,
  To see what the matter could
  be.
And OH! My goodness, you
  wouldn't believe,
  The sight that confronted me.

There was no way on earth, that
  I could see,
  We could get out on our own.
So Sharon got out, and thumbed
  a ride,
  To get to a telephone.

While she was gone, a nice man
  came by,
  And said, "Ma'am, are you

having trouble?"
And I said to myself, "Boy,
  when I get home,
  My troubles will probably
  double."

To shorten my story, I'll tell
  you she brought,
  A man and a tow truck back.
The man said "Twenty-two
  fifty please,"
  And I paid it without any
  flack.

When I looked at the box it
  was crooked,
  And I thought, now isn't
  this nifty?
All I've got, is a crooked old box
  and I'm minus twenty-two fifty.

This crazy old crooked old worn
  out box,
  That I thought I could put to
  some use.
Has taught me a lesson, I
  won't soon forget,
  Yea, you silly old goose.

And then, I thought, oh well,
  what the heck!
  That was quite an adventure
  you had.
We certainly had, a nice
  sunshiney ride,
  So perk up, laugh, don't be
  sad.

But the very next time, you
  happen to think, you'll
Get something for nothing, my
  Dear.
Just remember that box at the
  side of the road,
  And give it another thought,
  Hear?

Jeff Altgilbers
**TO HER BEYOND THE
MOUNTAINS**

Bend to me O giants of eastern
  sky! Bade me
peer at such beauty portrays,
  that my eyes may
nurse on another star, another
  light or ray.
O that if I may embrace such
  charm that hands
of mine may know, to touch
  the hidden ecstasy that
all lovers long to know. Whose
  flame no
mortal hand can summon or
  caress, aye not even
a wounded heart from loves
  lost forest spent.
Open those guarded valleys
  while dawn sleeps
in her cave of dreams, I shall
  not disturb
her slumber that twilight
  softly sings. Nor
shall I utter any word save
  softly said, nor
surrender any glance except
  to such serenity

I pray may wed. 'Tis not
  your forest fountains
I ask from thee, nor of its
  vintage that virgins
of night from it must feed.
  Only the soft flow
from rosey lips beg thee I
  must confess, for I
search with a thirst that only
  she can tide to

shore love's peaceful rest.
  But if my wounds
you would suffer and leave to
  me, then only
conquest must write such tales
  to be. That
lovers of old may remember as
  they sing, the
glory and fate of man's liberty.
  For if such
as I perish by events uninspired
  love shall
continue my fight until its
  last hour. Then
my words silent in thought
  shall be said
"Eternal in Eternity love is
  never dead!"

Olive C. Shaffer
THE LITTLE WHITE CANOE

That knight of noble heritage.
He stands against the blue;
As down the river floats Elaine
In her little white canoe.

Her golden tresses flying
In the sunset and the dew,
As she floats down the river
In the little white canoe.

The boat is lined with silver,
And the oar is edged in blue.
And she floats down the river
In her little white canoe.

The trees are green in spring
  time.
All the earth is bright and new;
While she floats down the river
In her little white canoe.

The heart within is heavy
for the love that proves untrue;
And she's floating down the
  river
In her little white canoe.

The lover in his armor
Silhouettes against the blue;
While she floats down the river
In her little white canoe.

There, beneath the evening
  sunset
In her gown of white so new;
There, they found her cold
  and lifeless
In that little white canoe

Gladys E. McElwre
THE COMMIE'S DOOM

Red Russia and her Satellites,
  They seek world conquest.
Der Fuhrer tried the same thing
  once
  and came out second best.

We won't forget Pearl Harbor;
  We'll make those Reds
  remember

How we came fighting back
  after the seventh of December.

We'll pay them back a thousand
  fold;
  they'll have their sad regrets.
For ever having tangled with
  our gallant leather necks.

Our ships, bombs, guns and
  armoured tanks
  will blast them all asunder,
And maybe that will put an
  end
  to all their rape and plunder.

We licked the foe in forty-five,
  We'll do the same now.
We really haven't started yet
  but when we do "Oh Wow."
We should have heeded Patton.

Wipe the Commies off the map.
We'll do it now and prove to
them
our Uncle, he's no sap!

Our liberty, we'll fight for
with everything we've got.

We won't give up democracy,
we'll die first on the spot.

Fight on, fight on, fight on
to victory
for Uncle Sam needs our help
to keep this country free.

So put your dimes into bullets
and your dollars into guns and
also give a pint of blood to
help our Yankee sons.

We'll all help Uncle Sam to keep
this country free,

And make it the safest place
for you and me to be.

LuAnn M. Caldwell
THE WOODS

On a busy day,
you have the need to think—
head for the woods,
Keep a squirrel company—
an old dead forgotten log
amongst the many weeds
adds comfort.
The beautiful wild flowers
stand out in
vibrant colors
against the weeds of a
deep, rich green.
A dandelion here,
a violet there
and the devil's paintbrush
has even tried its hand
at adding some color
to the scene.
Each square-patch of land is
a little different, but
when the many varieties
are combined—
It is as beautiful as
a patchwork quilt.
The combination of
wildflowers. . .
and wildlife itself,
instills an inner peace
that was sadly lacking—
You start home—
now able to cope
with whatever comes
your way.
Because you achieved
the peace that comes with
the beauty
of nature.

Diana R. Schoenoff
SOMEONE WHO CAN!

If I came to you and said
"I'll take away your sins
I'll save your soul and bring
new life."
Wouldn't you let it begin?

If it could be done so easily
Just a yes from you is all
Never again a worry or doubt
That your soul to hell would
fall

It would be just as simple
To put all faith in me
To take on all your faults
So I could set you free

Not only salvation could I give
But also true joy and love
Also help and power within
For a life you've only thought
of
You say a story and just a

dream?
But one that brought such
peace!
"It couldn't be so or I'd have
known
To say yes for my soul's
release."

But there really IS such a one
Who will bring you all these
things!
Just say yes to his calling now
And in your heart, he'll be
your King

Trust this man to meet your
needs
Not on yourself as before
Try this JESUS CHRIST right
now
He's knocking at your heart's
door.

Lautaro Vergara
QUO VADIS

I am a fallen rock
on the road
of life
(Yesterday a blind man
spat on me.)
If I were near the sea,
I would give my love to a
swordfish.

To be a rock
is an unbelievable reality. . .
Incomprehensible:

With my eyes
I petrify myself
at beholding
the pine trees of the mountains
or the vastness of the desert.

Am I dead?
No! Very much alive
in the middle
of granite columns,
or in the eruption of volcanoes
in fierce flames
or in the heart
of a meteorite.

There is life in death,
in the planetary
transformation
of this earth.

To prove it
man must die;
although there is
no return passage
from death.

A man dies today. . .
Awakens
in a million years
as a rock—
in a piece of bread—
or as a flower
in the Spring.

Alice Johnson
BABYLON

Babylon, Babylon,
Iraq, Iran
Afghanistan
Who is the beast?
Who is he?
An evil man
Who comes
From the sea.

Is Babylon Rome?
No it's Iraq.
Iran's in the area too—
What's that to you?
It will be broken—
Babylon I mean—
And destroyed in one day
With a fiery seam!

The European Market—
With the nations joined up

Is the nauseating mess—
Within the harlot's cup
A union of nations—
And the number is ten.
The beast and the prophet
Will come—but when?

A group of nations—
And that is sure
Will be led by a tyrant
Neither right nor pure.
God has it organized—
The clock is right on time—
And when both hands
Point straight up—
The clock will start to chime!

Adela-Adriana Moscu
THIRSTY FOR YOU

I'm thirsty for your love my
darling,
My breasts are longing for your
touch,
My body, mind and lips are
going
To say: "I am missing you so
much."

I want your lips to burn me
kissing,
And your embrace to hold me
tight,
I need to drink your love this
morning,
And keep you close to me all
night.

What could I do to make you
love me
The way I love you from my
heart,
I crave for you and now inside
me
My passion makes my life so
hard.

My life is hard when I can't
have you,
The nights are senseless when
you're far,
So may times I wonder if you
Stay lonely drinking in a bar.

I wish we'd share some
thoughts together,
And hand in hand would walk
across
The beach, now when this
lovely weather,
Makes you feel rich, without
a loss.

And now, love, share your
possession
By giving me the love I need,
I have to make you a confession:
I'm sure together we will
succeed.

Ortrud Hamann Perez
HE WAS

His eyes—
Dark magnets;

His voice—
Song of a harp to my ears;
His gait—
Carefree and sure
As that of a stallion;
His hair—
Black waves of the sea
And its island
Laughing at me.
The nose
Splashed on his face
Like paint on an abstract
painting.
A deep, round dimple
Sculpted in his chin.
His smile;
Beaming white stars,
Spreads from lobe to lobe
And radiates to me.

His broad, cushiony shoulders—
An all-enclosing embrace.
Now and then
The clown in him
Tickles my senses
And wakes up a sleeping laugh.

Then the bomb
Of terminal illness
Strikes this cosy idyll.
Helplessly
I watch as
The clown in him
Falls asleep.
His stature slowly resembles
That of an old man;
His step becomes
A tired climb.
His smile flickers,
Then vanishes.
His eyes, dulled by pain,
Look at me
In search of relief. . .
A hoarse voice
Crackles,
Then breaks. . .
He is only a shadow
Of the man—
My husband.

Eyes closed.
He squeezes my hand,
As I sit by his bed.
Tubes down his nose,
His mouth open
To breathe
Breath after labored breath;
Then the breathing just stops. .!
He has found relief.
And he was. . .

Pam Armistead
**LAZY DAYS —N—DUSTY
DREAMS**

Lazy days -n- dusty dreams,
Belong together, so it seems.

Days of gloom and days of
sunshine,
I like to wander and dream in
my mind.

Here is where my heart runs free,
For this is where I can be me.

Walking alone, through majestic
scenes,
Following paths and trails
and streams.

Sunlight's rays filtering through
the trees,
Makes my soul fall to its knees.

Peaceful woods, luxurient and
green,
All God's creations may be
seen.

Unlimited creatures all around,
The woods are filled with many
a sound.

The laugh of the brook, the song
of the bird,

Tell me a story, yet speak not
a word.
A story of peace, harmony and
love,
In a special world with the
Father above.

If ever God's Existence was a
doubt,
Here is where I find His
Presence is about.

While sitting by the brook and
talking with Him,
My worried and troubled
thoughts grow dim.

An inner peace fills my soul,
To hold on to this peace is
my daily goal.

I'd like to come here every day,
If I could but find a way.

Here is where my heart belongs,
Free to be happy and write
my own songs.

Now the daylight is slipping
away,
But I'll be back very soon one
day.

I've found happiness at last,
so it seems,
In those lazy days - n - dusty
dreams.

Julie Summerlin
MY BEAUTIFUL KINGDOM

Rainbows and Unicorns,
Dancing, queens.
These are what make up,
A world never seen.

A world hidden,
From sight and from sound,
A world so discreet,
A world never found.

It takes place,
On a far away star,
So near you could touch it,
But yet it's so far.

Nothing is as beautiful,
Nothing else can compare.
So beautiful it is.
This land is so rare.

The winds speak with majesty,
The lakes talk with wisdom
Only if you could see,
My beautiful kingdom.

The air is filled with peace,
The streams overflow with love.
Everything is so peaceful here,
Even the tiny dove.

The unicorns, they live here,
An animal just so rare.
No one has ever seen one,
And they really don't even care.

There is no one to rule this place
Everything is free.
Because war has not yet been
discovered,
Evil has never been seen.

This world is just so perfect,
It will always stay this way.
Because hatred will never
encounter my world,
It must always stay away.

SP/4 William D. Jordan
LABYRINTH

Getting into my mind is so
hard at times,
Seeing where I went wrong is
like a sad song:

I've tried God, I've tried AA,
and my past
Still comes back to me today.

My tears are real, my feelings
too.
I wish my mind wouldn't make
me so blue.
From sleeping in junk cars to
eating mutton stew,
To dirty needles and the o so
fantastic beatles.
From hate and anger and being
along for days on years,
Never knowing why or what
is making the tears.
To in and out of jail—that's all
I could do,
Not knowing me not knowing
you.
Someday just someday I
wish I could see the light—
And become someone, not
just something at night.
My life is like a merry-go-round
just spinning and spinning
and hearing no sound.
I don't know where is up, but
I know the ground—you
see my face is in it all over town.
I have nothing, but Lord I've
tried—It's the same old story
mud in the eye.
There is a life for me, but I
know not where—boy
I feel so bear.
Some people are winners, some
people are stars—but for me all
I saw was bars
My life isn't great it isn't even
good,
I'm still living down being a
hood.
I came into the Army to get
it together—
but it's the same old stormy
weather.
I started getting it together I
was forever
doing good but now I am going
to lose it, I knew
I would.
Where is my pain going to
end, I hope it's soon—
Because I can take no more.

Teresa A. Waterman
I'M HUNGRY

I'm hungry.
I open the door of the
refrigerator
and the light clicks on—
brightly displaying what
it has to offer.
I search the cold
drawers—but nothing appeals.
I close the doors.

I wander aimlessly
about the kitchen
looking in the cabinets.

There must be something.
If I just sit and think.

I know what I want.
Chinese food.
But my car is out of gas.

My stomach is gnawing at me.

I fix myself a
peanut-butter sandwich—
the bread is stale.

Or maybe my tastebuds are—
probably from the cigarettes.

My gnawing has subsided some,
but it's not enough;
I want to be full.

So I have
cookies and milk.
Not enough.
Popcorn and rootbeer.

Not enough.
Cheese and crackers.
Enough.
For now.
I feel sick.
—But
At least I'm full.

I search the medicine
cabinet for some seltzer.
I drink it.

I put on pyjamas
and I go to bed with a
success story.

But I cannot concentrate—
so I turn off the light,
and cry,
and sigh,
and curl into a fetal position,
and sleep.

Victoria D. Still
**REMEMBERING THE SEA
AND BOWLAN**

When I was making the
transaction
From girl to womanhood,
I had a friend living on the beach
A couple miles from Rosewood.
A rusty old man named Bowlan
Who softened only for my
smile;
The wonder revealed within my
eyes
Took the elder back for awhile.
We'd take walks along the
water;
Climb rocks that edged the blue,
And in the misty saltiness

We cried to gulls that flew.
But the time that I remember
most
Was when we took to waves
and foam;
To the place cherished within
him
As truely Bowlan's home.
I remember the two of us sailing
On a cool wet summer night—
The beating of the fabric and
My heart kept in time.
The stars steadily reflected
On a mirror called the sea;
My soul almost burst for crying
out
From deep inside of me.

Years later, my husband and I
Moved quite far away—
But sometimes I watch the
children,
Seeing visions of how I played
Near the sea with a special
friend
Who, long ago, has died
And ran along a favorite beach
Beneath a sparkling vernal sky.

Jeffrey Owen Smith
ODE TO BUSING

The's riots in Boston
and O'er the nation,
Because the answer
Was forced integration.

They send white folks to black
schools
And vice versa,
But when they get here
All they do is curse at ya.

It's a long ride on the bus
All the way across the city,
And all they do is fuss
and say the school is. . .bad.

They come with all their
prejudices

Wrapped up with their fears,
And when we's get a little
rough wit'em
They always end up in tears.

We's spos to get to know em
But don't know if we want to,
There must be some mellow
honkeys
But the's probly damn few.

They don't jive to our bongos
And don't lis'n to Soul Train
If they don't start boogie'n
to our tune,
They gonna end up in pain!

George A. Harris
**THE LAND FROM WHENCE
YOU CAME (MUSINGS ON
A MUMMY)**

Hear me, brother, in strange
attire!
Let the memory of this day
Be cast in ivory and in fire
Upon your brow of antique
clay.

We now can reckon with the
past
Wherein your feet have eager
spun
Webs of purple darkness, fast
Within the city of the Sun

Your robes hung in heavy plaits.
Adorned with diamonds was
your girdle.
From your throat suspended
weights
Of myriad gems, and wreaths
of myrtle.

So heavy with the luxuries of
Earth,
And tired, so tired of worldly
splendor—
Within your Heart of Royal
birth,
The Demon Grief played
throne's pretender.

The Keeper of the Sun you did
implore
To stifle forge and stop the
trompe;
To diffuse upon your head no
more
The cynosure of blazing pomp.

Gently down to rest they laid
you
About you, bursts of kingdoms
shone.
The brilliance lit your
rendezvous
With shades within your
eon-cone.

There stood one beside your
form and said,
"Where now do you sleep, and
why?"

With all this wealth your bed is
   made,
   Yet with all these jewels you
empty lie."

Hear the answer, O my Brother!
   The muted age is speaking
   now,
By your decree, yourself did
   smother;
   Time's vault of stillness to
endow.

You took with you what you
   did ask:
   You took the slumber of the
   years.
You took your linen burial
   mask.
   You took the silence of the
   biers.

The tears of Isis closed your
   scroll
   On the Nile. Without request,
Sad Nephthys hid your
   barcarolle
   In Waters of the Goodly West.

Indigenous lore well sealed you.
   Your body for this day was
   spiced.
Your image lay an icon to
   construe,
   When the winding of the
   thread sufficed.

The past you may not care to
   find—
   Nor freedom and the means
   once yours.
You may not wittingly unwind
   These ugly wrappings you
   endorse—

Still ancient Egypt's curse of
   men
   Can't quell the Phoenix of
   your flame.
Your own Sun's orb shines
   again
   Upon the land from whence
   you came.

Daniel Brewer
ONE O'CLOCK

streets are lonely at one o'clock
   a.m.
so I turned a corner and waited
   until you
      peered in the window Hi.
a drink in an apartment and
   we laughed

you liked bach I liked soc hops
I'm just a big kid and we laughed
   again.
you don't seem like a teacher or
   I like a sweeper salesman
and we made fun of that for
   five minutes.
It was time for me to go. no
   don't. do I didn't.
      until the next morning.

people are crazy.

you told me good-bye during
   the night.
I already missed you. that's
   what I get for being
      a sentimentalist.
   a teacher. unbelievable
   I never had any like you.

next week rolled around and my
   mind was sound again.
   decisions I made proved I was

a "little kid" and we
argued. . .(I like little kids). . .
   but just for fun.
tonight was different. I wished
   the light had
been turned off sooner. too
   much light affect
me and detects a wrongness in
   my lying
"little kid" image. I'm through
   lying. the little
kid is dying. now is adultness
   and uninnocence.

loneliness develops a thinking
   process.
lives are lonely at one o'clock
   a.m.
so I turned a corner and waited
   until you
      peered in the window. . .
      GOOD-BYE'

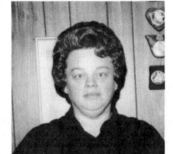

Maggie Johnson
THE GIFT

The family plot had called the
   first of it's own
Afraid and alone I cursed the
   hurting of the moment known
I said good-bye to my loved one
   in winters frost filled air
Nothing but sadness everywhere
Graveyard crowded—with
   tormented eyes they stare
I got in my car with a silent
   prayer, asking God for the
   courage to
leave her there. "Oh God" you
   just have to tell her how much
   I care
The ride back home wasn't far
   as I traveled slow over ice filled
   tar
Holding up traffic were the cars
   of loved ones as far back as I
   could see,
All heading back to the home
   she would no longer share with
   me
No longer the busy hostess
   serving hot coffee and tea
As I pulled in the driveway I
   took a good look at our little
   home
And "Oh God" never had I felt
   so alone
The people swarmed like flies,
   they followed me in the house
Pain stabbed my heart as my
   eyes fell on her favorite pink
   blouse
The people gathered inside—
   some cried—there was quiet
   talk
while some sat—some walked
Warm thoughts of her crowded
   my brain
My heart throbbing from all
   that pain

God knows what to do—when
   you feel like everything's
   been taken from you
I then heard God say, she left
   you a gift—it's neatly tucked
   away
I searched my mind and one
   memory came back
I saw a vision of her so clear
   sitting with a big yellow book
   on her lap.
I called my three children to
   my side
Their faces all spotted from
   tears dried
I told them how their mom was
   always writing in that big
   yellow book
Full of anticipation we started
   to look
We went to her office that
   special place of her own
Where she often sat and typed
   may a poem
And there like God said tucked
   neatly on a shelf
Was her big yellow book what
   else?
I was drained with emotion,
   so I was not strong
But opening to the first page

   didn't take me long
It was her poetry, words she
   had written for all to see
About her life and what
   probably would be
There were poems about God
   above, poems of love she
   held deep witnin
It was her Gift to hold us over
   till we could all be together
   again
How she must have raced against
   time putting down all her
   poems—
that rhyme
The Lord was surely on her
   side
Or she never could have finished
   the book before she died
But she did—there is a
   beginning—a middle—we can
   read
clear to the end
One page especially stands out,
   what her happiness was all
   about
It was about her Lord and
   Savior, how he gave her the
   Gift, a writer
This wonderful lady lives with
   God above,
She left us a gift—Her book—
With its pages all filled with
   love.

D. M. Cronin
WITHOUT COMPANY

I went through a corridor of
   time
walking the straight line
to end in a small room
filled with a familiar tune
a gentle waltz to make a body
   sway
and move the legs gracefully
   around corners of the tomb,
but softly enough to hear
   the heartbeat
of him coming secretly behind

seducing me into the quiet
   dance of Time and I.
His hand in mine, an arm
about my waist, whirling me
rustling my satin skirts
and we danced this man and I.
His beard stroking the clevage
   of my breasts
tickling, making me laugh
chuckling deep to soothe
his arm to please
waltzing me through this
   dance
as if I was his young bride
and drank too much wine.
He wiped a tear
caressing the curves around my
   eyes
running his fingers through my
   hair
and circled an ear
whispering farewell to the
   heartbeat he was so near,
to the one he held so dear.

LeAnn K. Reedy
SHOW ME LOVE

To you, my love, who cares so
   much
   You're filled with love inside.
Who understands my deepest
   fears
   the ones I try to hide.
You dry my tears and hold my
   hand
   to comfort when I'm sad.
With smiling eyes you hold me
   close
   Until my heart is glad.
You give me oh so many things
   from deep within your heart.
Love, compassion, kind sweet
   warmth
   but that's only just the start.
So many things I can't list all
   the beautiful things you do.
Thank you for always being
   there
   so I could count on you.
Bless you Babe, for all you've
   done
   to have shown me life with
   love.
I care so much about you dear,
   you're a blessing from above.

Pamela A. Kay
REALITY

He was my friend
   when I learned to walk.
He was my friend
   when I learned to talk.
As time grew on
   so did we.
I would talk to him
   and he'd listen to me.
I could see the care
   in his eyes
they were so deep;
   my place to hide.
He seemed to age
   must faster than me.
I didn't care.
   It was just us: we.
But life went on
   and I grew apart.
He was still with me,
   but not truly at heart.
Today I stopped
   and looked at my friend.
My tears rolled down;
   I felt so bad.
My friend is deaf

and he cannot see.
Oh God, what happened,
he needed me.

My friend is dying
slowly but soon.
When it happens,
what will I do?

It's so hard to see
a friendship die.
He just looks at me,
his eyes say good-bye.

No place to run to,
no place to hide.
I will just sit by my friend
and watch him die.

Hector Castillo
**SNOWING THE SILENCE OF
YOUR MUTE LOOK**

Snowing the silence of your
   mute look
runs the weekend through an
   abysman
melody of steps.
Imagined streets of your body
   that my hands
walked, stopping in the corner
   of your mouth to
drink a rainbow kiss.

Raining the sound of your deaf
   words
statically the hours penetrate
   my shoe's tone,
statically tuesday swims in my
   brain.
Your skin is still attached to my
   fingers,
they play a concerto of glasses
   and wine
in the semi-darkness of my room
in the semi-darkness of your
   absence.
Sunning the
sonority of my
solitude, I watch how the time
   disintegrates, waterly,
your nearness. How your twin
   starts heat my
emptiness.
Give me your whiteness snow of
   my soul—winter!
Give me your rain cloud of my
   spring—heart
Make me your sun of my
   sand—summer, burn my
   existence
O kidnapper of my whole!
Make me disappear in you
absolve me in your autumn,
but do not let me continue
   playing the piano
of my
sadness!

Raymond Adamick
CHILD OF WINTER - SPRING

Among the tides
of the moon, the
child of winter-spring
wades in the birth waters
near the shore of the
waiting land.

Daylight, but the stars
can be seen clearly, in
the eyes of the child
of winter-spring.

The child spreads out
his hands, and the
winds are at his command
and the clouds are dragged
along helplessly.
   The sun is covered
and the day grows dark.
   The waters rage

around him now:
   The waters of his birth
and the same waters that will
spawn the others like himself.
   Gaps of whiteness roar
within his touch,
   the land upheaves
below his feet:
Clouds of black smoke
   drift down from the
   mountains.
Voices from within
tells the child
to stop, but its
   too late,
the child has the feel
   for divine power.
From his lungs
   blow cold
winds
   which will make
barren the virgin
   of his
   tender dreams:
The dreams of the warm
   nights of lovemaking.

In sadness he floods
the Earth with his gentle tears,
   leaving an age of
childhood, and entering that
   of man.
For the raging pool of waters
   he gives his only
seed.
   And so, with one last
parting of the hands,
   he shatters the wall of
   time-space.
      Crimson Sky.

William Carroll Arnett
**TWO BROTHERS ESAU
AND JACOB**

Born to Rebekah and Issac
By an act of God.
Their mother gave them the
Name of Esau and Jacob.
Jacob came into the world
Holding onto Esau's heel.
Esau was red all over like a
Hairy garment,
While Jacob was smooth of skin
And young.
The Lord told Rebekah there
were
Two nations in her womb.
Esau was a cunning hunter
But Jacob was a plain man
Dwelling in tents.
Issac in his old age was blind
Gave the blessing due the
   first
Born to the young son.
Deception was in the heart of
   their
Mother.
Anger separated the brothers
Forever!

Regina Fisher
LUCKY SUN, LUCKY MOON

The sun and
   the moon
shed their light on
   the whole world.
The sun brightens the world
   by day
and the moon performs its task
   by night.
It must be wonderful
   to see everyone
in the whole world
   everyday!
Yes, they are very lucky
   to have

such a power.
If
   I asked both of them
about one person,
do you think
   they would answer?
I would have to ask
   both because
the sun only sees him
   for a certain amount of time
and the moon
   also has the same problem.
But
   I would
rather see this person
   for myself.
So
   I shall place
one of my eyes
   on the sun
and one of my eyes
   on the moon.
Then
   I shall be
even luckier
   than both
the sun and the moon
   Because
I shall see this
   one special person
all day,
   everyday!

Eura J. Olsen
THE DYING LEAF

Oh, little leaf
   Lying upon the ground,
You look all withered
   and you have turned all brown.
You have served your purpose
   and your end has come,
We are going to miss you
   for the job you have done.

The season is over,
   the requirements you have
   met
And now that you have fallen
   we seem to forget.
You shielded and shaded us
   from the sun and the rain,
You gave us new hope
   new fortune and fame.

You began your life
   with just a seed,
You grew and flourished
   and met all our needs.
You were just beautiful
   all clothed in green,
You made our country
   a beautiful scene.

You caused a great change
   when you came to be,
Why, you just made life
   come to that tree.
So sleep on little leaf,
   return to the soil,
Your job was well done
   no more will you toil.

Mrs. Jewel DuClos
THE FOUR SEASONS

I love the four seasons, but don't
   know just
   where to start.
Each one with all it's splendor
And not too far apart.
First let's take the Spring, how
   do we know
   We wake up one morning
   and we see the
greeness of the grass, peeking
   through the
   melting snow.
We see the budding of the

trees,
   The flowers pushing through
   the ground.
The rose bushes budding out.
   And the little robins singing
   all around

Next comes the summer, with
   everything in bloom.
   It's the middle of the seasons,
   we assume.
The vacationers on their way,
   here and there
   They see the beauty of our
   country, everywhere.

Next comes the fall, the beauty
   of it all,
   The leaves on the trees, turning
   all the colors
there is to see.
   The little squirrels storing
   their food for
the cold cold winter.
   It's a wonderful sight to me.

Next comes the winter, the
   season most people love
   The holidays most of all.
If it gets so bitter cold, we
   can't complain.
   For all the beauty to enjoy,
   while waiting
for the spring.

We owe it all to God, for giving
   it to us
   The beauty of our world.
From early dawn to dusk.

Ylde Fonsa Hidalgo de Delgado
**A MESSENGER FROM
HEAVEN**

He came to us as a warning
That God's Son is coming soon
And as he passed through
Who cried the loudest
The man in the moon.

The man in the moon sees
   everything
He calls but no one hears
No one bothers to look up
He yells, "Hey, Jesus is near!"

God put that man there for a
   reason
To light the way for us at night
But some of us prefer the
   darkness
And the rest of us prefer the
   light.

His message was loud and final
That little bundle of joy
He brought us closer together
That beautiful little boy.

On his way home from
   California
On him did shine the light
Then he arrived, the little tyke
Finished was his flight.

Now listen to this, for his
   message is clear

Don't cry for me, he said: I
  came to bring you near
To the love that surpasses all
  sickness and pain
Praise God, my people, it's not
  in vain.

Now to mommy and daddy, I
  love you
And I do want you to know,
That to live is Christ,
  and to die is gain,
And in heaven I know I will
  grow.

I will wait for you in heaven,
In the meantime, read God's
  word,
In God's word you'll find the
  answers
Before me, were not understood.

And so he came to bring a
  message,
And a message he did bring,
He came in hopes to fill our
  hearts,
With God's Love for every
  being.

And now his little body rests
But his spirit went to heaven
Jesus reached down, with open
  arms
The message had been given.

So now the tears of sorrow,
Have become the tears of joy,
For my little grandson, Ricardo
is God's precious little boy.

Have you accepted Jesus?
If not, will you today?
So that we will be together
On that very special day.

The Lord has promised us a
  home
On an eternal basis,
Accept His word, and sing out
  loud,
Some beautiful, heavenly
  phrases.

Ann Gettys Cunningham
THE FRIENDSHIP BOND

Two little girls with golden
  hair
Became inseparable friends,
Sharing childhood days of
  happiness
They hoped would never end.
The seasons came and hurried
  by,
Funny, they never noticed them
  pass,
Their lives were engulfed with
  each fleeting hour,
As they trailed in the other's
  path.
They watched the squirrels
  fly through the trees
And listened to a whipporwill's
  call,
They watched the sky as the
  clouds drifted by,
And wondered if the sky could
  fall.
They picked the daisies as they
  bloomed
And ragweeds for my vase,
Many times the fragrance was
  not of perfume
And they came with built-in
  ants.
They shared their joys and
  their tears,

And heard each other's dreams,
Their time for playing seemed
  so short,
Life just passed by, it seemed.
But the unselfish love between
  the two
Was a glory to behold,
Something grown-ups seem to
  lose,
As maturity and years unfold.
Then came the time for their
  paths to part,
Two little hearts couldn't
  understand,
They had pledged their
  friendship forever,
And a short distance seemed
  like a foreign land.
So now each night, they dream
  of each other,
And whisper a prayer across
  the miles,
But somewhere, somehow,
  they will always remember,
Their friendship bond as a
  child.

Maryann P. Maugeri
A REFLECTION ON LIFE

In this world of stress and strife
  We have but one life
Given to us by God
  Some to live easy, some hard
But—One thing is for sure
  Whether we be rich or poor
We're all gonna get old
  sometime.

It's not easy to see a parent
  die
  And so often, we wonder why?
But harder still, it is to see
  A parent lose his identity
Not to know who they are
  Is difficult to watch, by far
But—We're all gonna get old
  sometime.

Seeing them sitting in a chair
  Often, with a look of despair
Confused as to what to do
  In their world, at times,
  so blue
Happy when we glimpse an
  occasional face of glee
  Sensing they remembered a
  loved one in memory
Thinking—We're all gonna get
  old sometime.

And when the day comes that
  they're laid to rest
  Fondly think of them at their
  best
Not as you saw them last
  But rather, as in the past
The happy, sad and even
  tearful times of days gone by
And then, a pause, recalling
  with a sigh
Knowing—We're all gonna get
  old sometime.

Claire L. St. Onge
MOTHER'S DAY

Long ago on this day
You said you would never
  forget me,
But you were only a child
  anyway
Full of love and so free.
You brought me flowers from
  the part
Gave me kisses from your heart,
But where are you now
When I need you most of all?

I know you don't need me
  anymore
but remember the times you

did before?
I was always by your side
Held you when you cried,
Fed you when you were
  hungry
and kissed you before you
  laid down to sleep.
You were my present and
  my future
My little girl and now a stranger.
You used to hold my hand in
  yours
Told me I was the one you
  adored,
And when my tears began to
  roll down
Landing upon your little arm,
You would say, "Don't cry
  mommy dear,
I love you and will always be
  here."
That was long ago, I know
But to me you will always be
  special.
Maybe one day I'll see you again
And we could take a walk
  through the park,
Pick a flower and pin it to
  my heart
and pretend you're my little
  girl again.

Mary Kay Matson
THE SEARCH

I feel my consciousness rise
  above my body, lying peaceful
  in dream.
My thoughts awake to the
  forbidden boundaries of my
  conscious being.
Searching, ever searching for
  the unfamiliar thoughts I
  deny my daytime self.
The feelings and the knowledge
  I repress while in daily route.
The truth which lies in my
  soul, that I snatch back, before
  it can
enter my mind.
The lonely emptiness of my
  inner being.
We so often limit ourselves to
  the familiar boundaries,
  with the ever present
  fear to venture beyond, afraid
to touch on the unknown.
Trembling at the thought of
  change and still just a little
  hungry to feel a different
  shade.
But here, walking in my dream
  dusted gown, I look at the
  shell of my
being, lying so silent and still.
I walk faster and faster until
  my thoughts are running
  through the
corridor of my mind, quickly

unlocking every locked door,
  looking
inside only to find another shell
  of my being, another and
  another and
another until I become frantic
  not finding anything but
  emptiness lining the walls
  of the rooms I place my values
  on.
Then I come to a door for which
  I have no key, for there isn't
  a lock on this door.
I slowly extend my arm toward
  the door knob as something
  chilling grabs
my hand, turning my blood into
  ice, and my arm falls to my
  side unable
to move forward again.
An unlocked door in the house
  of my minds dream.
An unlocked door which I can
  not open.
A door to which lies the stream
  of my true self, and if only I
  could
wash my shell in this stream, I
  could look into myself and
  know who
and what I am, and I would
  know where the roots of my
  soul are planted
And connecting the roots of
  my soul to my soul, I could
  then attain
the tranquil peace and beauty
  and blissful harmony my
  heart craves.
And my hunger would then
  subside.
Then I would not have to look
  at this repulsive shell of my
  being.
Then I would not have to be
  haunted by the black
  emptiness that fills
the air I breathe.
It's Time! It's time. I feel my
  consciousness being pulled
  back into
my body. I have failed, once
  again, in the time alloted to
  me, to
force my hand to touch the
  knob and push open the door.
Morning has dawned and my
  search must end until the
  quiet of night
falls from the Heavens once
  more.

Mardres E. Story
SLEEPING BEAUTIES

fighting to reach through the
  richness of the ebony black
  soil continually lusting for
  the gentleness of
  the life-giving sun
  seeking its warmth
  and bright glory

pushing through to freedom
  to become majestically
  beautiful with brightly
  arrayed colors more numerous
  than the colors of a rainbow
  in the pale blue sky after
  the quiet washing
  of the rain
  teeming

with sensuous fragrances
pleasant to gaze upon
enchanting unwary victims
with deadly beauty
innocently
lying in wait
lusting
with thorns of death
to prick with razor
sharpness drawing red waters
of life quenching
the thirsts of vengence
for being disturbed
as they peacefully slept
in beds of royal clusters
upon vast and barren fields

Anita Jean Rusch
SEVEN DAYS OF WONDERMENT

Before God's creation
The earth had no shape,
He then said, "Let there be
  light."
And so the light He did make.

He was then very pleased
And thus divided the light;
The light He called daytime
And the darkness twas night.

Thus ended the first day.

And God said, "Let the vapors
  be separate
To form the oceans and sky;"
And thus in the creation of
  earth
The second day drew nigh.

Then the oceans were gathered
And the dry lands came forth,
He called the oceans "seas"
And the dry lands were "earth".

And God said, "Bring fruit trees
With their fruits bearing seeds,
Bring seed-bearing plants,"
And thus God was pleased.

Thus ended the third day.

To bring about seasons,
To identify day and night,
And to mark days and years,
God said, "Let there be lights."

The sun and the moon
Names he gave to these lights;
The larger, the sun, to preside
  over day
And the smaller, the moon,
  to preside through the night.

From these lights came the
  stars
  And thus ended the fourth day.

God said, "Let the waters teem
  with fish
And may the birds fill all the
  skies,
Let the fish stock all the
  oceans

And every bird shall never die."
Thus ended the fifth day.

Then God brought forth the
  animals—
The wildlife of every kind,
He brought the cattle and
  reptiles
Leaving none of them behind.

Then God said, "Let there be
  man,
And let him rule all things on
  earth,
Let him be fruitful and
  multiply,"
So of man and maid was birth.

And God said, "I have given
  you fruit trees
On which you may feed,
And as for the animals,
They'll feed on the plants and
  the reed."

Then, when God was finished
And had looked at all He'd
  made,
He saw that it was excellent,
And thus ended the sixth day.

Now the heavens and earth
  were completed
On the seventh day in creation,
God blessed this day and made
  it holy
To bring about religion.

Albert Furiani
FOR THE FIRST TIME IN LIFE; I LIVE

You appeared softly
On the wings of Los Angeles
I could have reached out
And caught you like a butterfly
But I didn't.
I thought you, like a butterfly
Wouldn't stay with me
I thought that, like a butterfly
You'd be hurt if I touched you,
Damaging the silvery dust of
  life
On the patterned wings of your
  soul.

But I kept seeing you, around,
Above, and here and there
And I couldn't stop thinking
About you
And in thinking about you
I had to get closer,
Be nearer,
To keep you in sight.
Like morning glories drawn to
  the sun
Like iron filings to a magnetic
  core
The flame of my spirit
Was being
Drawn to your butterfly
  presence.

And my outer self said "Leave
  her alone,
You'll hurt her"
And my inner self said "Go to
  her quickly,
You need her"
Said my inner self "No—
There is no one you need."

And my inner self persisted
While my outer self resisted.

And I didn't know
What was happening to me
I was angry at the world
At every person, dog and cat

At every bird, and traffic light
While my inner and outer selves
Fought the battle for my
  future.
Until the gentle feathered
  pressures
Of my inner self
Wore down the many mountains
That had grown around my soul
Made it now the perfect place
For a butterfly to live.
And now we are one forever
After gentleness won its
  endeavor
For the first time in life, I live.

Bruce Laflam
THOUGH NO MORTAL EYE

Though no mortal eye
may gaze upon the winds of
  time
  No foot can tread upon the
    sea of illusory fate
The rhythm of the sea is set
  to heaven's gate
And though the air of revelry
  be laid with tasks
    and fears,
A dream, a phase, a moment
  of tempestuous light
set no mind in plight.

  And will a child arise
    with untried metaphors
  to lay aside the Celestial
    gate
What is this fickle hand
  that seeks the arrogancy of
    Pride
  Be stilled, be calmed, be
    laid aright
  Can we not reason the actions
    of our thoughts?
And though the mountain
  crumbles
  before our very sight. It is no
    task
  to be sent to hold and
  stem the tide that
  Lays the sea aside.
And though the Sun of History
  fashioned bright the glory
  of the mountain side
No hill be tested by
  weathering this night.
Can we be calm in the face of
  fright?
  No moon-lit shadows cast
    an eerie light, the working
  of the Majesty that sets
    the time aright!

Rosaling S. Levor
REMEMBERING

Ohio River outings
On the grand old ISLAND
  QUEEN,—
NICKELODEONS of my
  childhood days,
Great Stars of the Silent Screen!

The muffler that I knitted
For some doughboy 'cross the
  sea,
Who bravely fought to keep
  the World
"Safe for Democracy!"

The piano lessons that I took
To please my "next of kin",
Only to abandon, later on,
BEETHOVEN for BERLIN!

My worn-out yellow "slicker"
Names scrawled on every side,
Bobbed hair—short skirts—
  galoshes
With buckles opened wide!

The CHARLESTON and
BLACK BOTTOM,
  The UKE I learned to play,
the HULA that I loved to
  dance—
In a skirt of straw, I'd sway!
The FOLLIES—EDDIE
  CANTOR,
AL JOLSON on his knee,
singing ROCK-A-BY YOUR
  BABY
WITH A DIXIE MELODY!
VALENTINO, The Shiek, we
  shrieked for,
His love scenes made us
  swoon—
The big dance bands of
  yesterday
That faded far too soon!
The lazy, care-free living
Of my FLAPPER DAYS back
  aga
  then,
In those UN-ATOMIC
  TWENTIES
That I wish were here again!

Sandra B. Tikulski
THOUGHTS ON THE BEACH

I run my fingers through the
  sand,
As I quietly sit on the beach.
I need some time alone to
  think,
Out to my friend, the ocean,
  I reach.
I ponder why things are this
  way,
Everything going astray.
Nothing at all seems to be
  right
Since the breaking of the
  new day.
I ask my friend why things
  must happen,
Just the way that they do.
The ocean replied a few
  moments later,
"How do you want them to?"
"I'd like them to run
  smoothly," I said,
As I looked at my friend who
  does anything but that.
Then I thought of what I
  said,
And a while longer I sat.
It all came to me at once,
In a surge that was so strange,
I liked my friend the way he
  was,
And I'd never want him to
  change.
Everything put on this earth
Has its own destiny.
As much as we'd like it to
  change,
It was never meant to be.
I slowly rise from my seat in
  the sand,
I no longer feel as if I'll cry.
As I make my retreat,
My friend, the ocean waves
  me goodbye.

William C. Gibbons
SEED OF LOVE

Love is a seed planted by God,
  then graced in
  Heaven above.
To nourish the seed, there is
  hope and joy, and
  patience to help it grow.
And the final stage in the
  growth of the seed
  is what blossoms into love.

To understand the meaning
of love is something
I'll never know,
For life has many forms of
love, we encounter
them every day.
The event of love, into my life,
has given to
me a different approach.
I find that in my life today a
love that will
continue to grow.
And each day as time endures,
the bonds grow so
much stronger.
For no longer do I pretend that
my heat is all aglow.
As time goes on I can feel, I
can see, this gift
which was given to me,
Will give me understanding,
foresight and happiness
too.
For success in love and life, e
every day the formula
must continue to be
Nourished daily with
gentleness, this love which
stands above
To help me through everyday
in life to attain the
peace I seek.
And the fruits of the labor
which I receive come
from a seed of love.

Elizabeth Lewis Smith
HANDS

When I considered all God's
hands have made,
I drew apart one special time
and prayed
A prayer of gratitude, and
asked for grace,
That I'd recall each
understanding face
Whose hands helped make
this life worthwhile,
And thus enjoy each day
again and smile.

Those long hands grasping
strongly at my birth
Helped many children all
alight to earth.
My Mother's hands, though
not like his before,
Guided, nurtured me and
hundreds more.
For all her acts of love I can't
repay,
Except in deeds of love and life
each day.

I see a host of hands, I know
them all,
An injured hand that will not
let me fall;
Pointed hands that are a part
of me,
Joined with mine, we face
eternity;
Tender hands, adept at any
tast
To comfort body—always
these I ask.

Ah! children's hands, a
freshness from above,
They clasp in gentle strength
with trust and love;
And working hands, though
rough with toil and grime
Are part of life, so useful in
their time;
They gladly do the tasks they
need to do
and in it all, I know God's

hand shows thru.
Dear friends, with hearts right
in their hands,
Bind souls together in unbroken
bands.
They lift us up in prayer each
day
Thru hands in reverence, then
one day
It dawns within our souls, we
understand
To find the way, we simply
grasp the Guiding Hand

Margaret H. Reynolds
**MOM, SOMEONE VERY
SPECIAL**

Someone very special
More loved than words can say
Is thought about so often
Is missed more everyday
There was no one like her
There will never be
A beautiful example
Is what she was to me
She had cares and sorrows
Much more than her share
Still she had the will to laugh
She found the time to care
Never wanted much in life
She never was that kind
Just some understanding
A little peace of mind
Giving all she had to give
Was all that she lived for
Taking care of those she loved
'Till she could do no more
'Twas then that God decided
Her time had come to rest
He took her to His Heavenly
Home
There she'll have all the best
Those who went before her
Will have her now to love
What a great reunion
Is going on above
I can almost see her
So happy and so free
Telling everyone she meets
About her family
There will be no ending
To the pleasures God has
planned
Nothing we have here on Earth
Could ever be so grand!

Cheryl A. Bayes
FOR NATURE ALONE

I write a poem
with words that rhyme
and sentences breaking
through stillness in time
I call the words out
to the sky up above.
It listens with the silence
of understanding love.
The clear blue sky
absorbs my unwritten words.
My words seem happy
on the wings of the birds.
My words drift down
as autumn leaves to the
ground,
Where God mixes beauty
and bright colors abound.
A multicolored leaf
amidst others it lay
on top of a pile
amongst children at play.
A single unit of nature
unnoticed by the crowds.
Seen only by the maker
as a diamond in the clouds.
So must my poetry be
unnoticed from the start,
Heard only by my Lord
and written only in my heart.

The words float away
on the autumn breeze
Forgotten tomorrow
as the leaves from the trees.
But such as the leaves
gave color one day
So did my poem
help show me the way

Arthur C. Ford
**WILD, WIGGLING, WIG
WEARING WOMAN**

Walking down the street
She nearly made me shout
She was hanging "Right-On In"
She was hanging "Right-On-Out"

It was shifting into gears
That could delight engineers
And I knew if not the card
She had the "Clout".

Her hips, wide as ships
Swaying side to side,
Made me want to go to her
And ask for a ride.

Her top had such proportion
That it startled the emotion
And the notion
That the front was like the back.

She revolved one hundred eighty
And I instantly thought crazy
Cause I wished to put
My hands upon her rack.

Our smiles were so provoking
That we knew we weren't joking
Cause we started conversation
And some poking.

And the night came to be
Some loving history
As the sunshine through the
curtains
Hit our eyes.
Then I noticed beauty here
And her hair over there
And I knew that she was lonely
But very wise.

Then as fast as I could guess
She had speedily got dressed
And my heart began
To feel sort of frozen.

Then she said "I must go"
You're really "Quite a Beau"
And remember
Many come, but few are chosen.

Now if you think this never
happens
Or that something was missed
Just remember of this poem
When you lie within your tryst.

This poem doesn't guarantee
She'll come to you when
summoned,
It only tells the legend of the
Wild, Wiggling, Wig Wearing
Woman.

Christina M. Sloan
MAYAN MEMORY

Searching through the
catacombs of History
I happened upon an ancient
mystery
I cradled it with loving care
To touch it—hold it—do I dare

Overwhelmed by Your presence
Time stood still for remeniscence
I sensed a rhyme—a reason
Aged for eons knowing no
season

Plucking you from your olden
cast
Phantom of time long since past
Shall I disturb your relic rest
To let you sleep I know is best

Fossil of man once removed
Let me hold you in the light
Give to me the gift of sight
Knowledge to make man free

Guardian of all our yesterdays
Give to your children better
ways

Take from them this awful curse
Will them new meaning on whc
which to nurse.

Leave behind a legacy bold
A new rebirth with which to
mold
Oh ancient bones of Mayan
Lore
Would that you could tell me
more

Can we be If you never were
Father to him Mother to her
Remains of ancestors once alive
Say that mankind will survive.

I'm hiding here from Today
In the archives of your past
Consuming all your wisdom
Hoping it will last.

Isabel O. Brown
OLD MAN'S LEGACY

The old man's face was worn
and weathered
His shoulders stooped and bent.
His voice just above a whisper,
Held a note of history there.
When he looked deep into my
eyes I swore,
He could see into my soul.
He smiled weakly as he said,
"Come near my child, sit by
my side".
"My time has come and it has
gone
I spent it wisely and not alone."
"Go forth young lass and
spread good cheer,
Remember, I'll always be near."
This old man, now departed,
At my bedside when my life
started,
Gave me love and endless
pleasure,
Showed me all the worlds
treasure.
He made me laugh when I was
sad,
That he was near he made me
glad.
He was my strength when I
was weak,
Of my errors he'd seldom speak.
He stood by me, right, or,
wrong,
Always loving, always strong.
Now he is gone, but, I'm not
alone,
For he left behind his legacy.
He left his strength, his love
and caring,

He asked not of me, but, my sharing.
His parting words were full of beauty,
And he taught his lesson very well.
He helped my soul to be set free,
But, best of all, he taught me how to like me.

Earl Mueller
MY LOVE, MY JUDY

God made a certain somebody,
with all His guile and skill
And just as with the rest of us
He gave that certain someone
their very own free will.
And then He gave them wit
and knowledge and grace, and beautiful hair,
a sweet smile and a lovely face.
But then a person's beauty will really have no appeal
If they do not have the character
to show you how they think and act
and feel.
God gave the certain angel all
of these and more,
And then left them with the chance to show the halo that they wore.
He gave them someone to cherish, someone who really cared,
And the chance to show they wanted to know how that someone fared.
It seems the other angels would show envy when they knew
How much this angel meant to others, and then what they meant, too.
So God in all His wisdom and power, brought forth upon the earth
this flower;
He gave her all this charm and beauty, and then He named her Judy.

Kari Grenness
THE BLACK DOVE

The cold-blooded hunter
has picked his prey and loads his rifle with mortal bullets
There's no fight
his victim is helplessly trapped
in this cruel game
The animal is holding the rifle
a bloodthirsty monster
in man's clothing
A man-hunter, hungry to carry out his plan
with precision
Nothing matters, to him

slaughter
equals heroism
The victim's weapon is that of peace
and understanding
His brothers and sisters have sacrificed
their blood for this
and now
his time has come
His words are not for killers
but for humanity
yet, he becomes the victim of inhumanity
His song is the fire of love
The hunter's is that of a hangman
A dove carrying the message of peace
is shot down
unable to defend himself
A black dove hit by a deadly bullet
leaving a hole as big as that of a clenched fist
Yet, yours is open and has always been
For how long now, Vernon Jordan?

Russell E. Goetz
MY SPACE

Should I take my space and move it far away?
A lonely man I'll be until you see.
I've walked a thousand miles for smiles
I've found most everywhere.
When will happiness be truly free?
I wouldn't want to watch our world
Come down on you some day.
I couldn't get you off before the storm.
Some people I have talked with
want to give it up and hang around.
Behind the sounds they feel they're safe and warm.
Music to the would could be a remedy.
Your faith must look beyond to find the way.
If celebration wonderland
can not explain
what bothers me
Perhaps this is the time to end my stay.
Man and his machines will turn itself inside one day
as dying holy rollers sell their souls.
Let me take my space and place it
right beside the one that's yours.
Let me hold your heart and pull it through.

Patricia Suzanne Sarmiento
ETHEREAL REFUGE

In tortuous times of anguish
Each yearning and desire
seems to crumble
before my feet
like falling pieces of shattered glass,
landing only in an aimless disarray.
Whisps of gentle winds
destroy long-awaited moments of bliss.
Confusion plays havoc

within the corridors of my mind,
seizing every opportunity
to annihilate the once warm feelings
of love and happiness.
In a futile attempt,
I try to paste together
the useless rubble of the past.
Momentarily, I transport myself
into another world:
A different time and place
where I can bask
in my accomplishments
and am not afraid
to dream of the infinite future;
A land where no one knows
the meaning of failure, loss, or grief.
Hopes and wishes are fulfilled
at the command of one's will.
If only such a magnificent locale
existed in reality
and not in the paradise
of my perception

Everett A Mills
WHEN MEN WERE MEN

In the days of old when men were bold
And women did exactly as they were told;
They stayed within the four walls of home
While man went out upon the roam.
Man held his women in high esteem;
While they did the work of ten machines.
It was a golden pedestal turned upside down;
An excuse for man to crouse around.
Now high upon a bluff called Sills
There stood a lonely whiskey still.
And down below in the buzzard roost
Was a lookout called the long-neck-goose.
With a blanket spread on the ground,
All the gamblers sat around;
Betting on the running hounds
And drinking booze—straight and down.
While far off into the valley below
The flickering kerosene lights they glow;
And in the distance a lantern is seen
Carried by a midwife aroused from her dreams.
Soon, another soul will be born
And she, too, will wait some night and mourn;
Or, he will take his place on his manhood throne,
And leave his lonely wife at home.

Bonnie Jean Lill
MEMORIES OF AN INDIAN MAID

I have walked these earth-ways
through countless dawns.
No tender, gracious thing,
this land I know.
I have watched my people fade away—
who knew the blazing summer sun and winter snow.

Once I heard the war-cries from their throats—
it surged as wild music from the talking hills
Then I shared their campfires in the night,
now their laughter in the night time haunts me still.
These hills, where grass still grows, so green and sweet
knew the feel of mighty, pounding feet of painted ponies who ran wild and free—
the grasses heard the wooing of young indian maids
by bronze skinned braves—
whose lives wrote my sweet-sad history.
Their way of life so challenged from the start
their pride of race, a tender shining star
nurtured in the warm fires of the heart,
still living where the glow of campfires are.
I am but a memory left in time, a gathering of loves,
a long, lost way of life.
I am a sighing of the winds through ancient pines,
that served as sentinels through tragic years of
war and strife.
Now they are gone, I wonder lonely—
I call to them through misty dawns of time,
red brothers of the wild, red blood—
right or wrong, their hearts still call to mine.
So I walk lonely now, these forest paths—
the rim of canyons, where their silent feet
once trod—
standing here alone in time and space
my heart finds solace in the white man's God.

Ruby Craft Cedrone
LADIES OF RED ROCK CANYON

Two ladies out for a stroll
Atop the mountains high.
One appeared slightly bent,
For her years made her not so spry.
The other younger she might be.
Seemingly they tripped and bobbed along ever so lightly.
For miles they could be seen
As the train noisily bounced along.
Ever walking, bobbing and nodding
Engaged in engrossing deep conversation
Wonder what they're talking about?
So attentive to each they seem to be!
As the train hurriedly chugged along
On the tracks—Clickety clack!
These two ever so chummy ladies
Seemed to grow taller, ever taller,
Until a wide billowing skirt
Arranged in fanciful dips and folds

Each was seen wearing ever so
jauntily!
Then suddenly they appeared
Dangerously near the edge of
the cliff!
Were they so unmindful as to
catapult
Over the edge into the dark
chasm below?
Not so! Staunch and firm
they ever stand.
They're still there walking
and talking
In chummy communion with
the stars.
You can see them too!
If you'll take the time to seek
Them among the domes,
spires and peaks!

Alberta E. Cross
MY COUNTRY

I love my country, America
From the mountains to the sea
But now my country is in
danger
This home of the brave and land
of the free

This country our forefathers
fought for,
And founded in "God we Trust"
Seems to have forgotten the
Creator
And became full of evil and lust.

If Washington and Lincoln
were here today,
What tears of sorrow they
would weep
Because their decendents have
forgotten
God our Father and His laws
to keep.

What a great Constitution we
have
And a beautiful flag we fly
The Stars and Stripes forever
But those are no longer the
words we cry

Our people no longer love
their neighbors
But are greedy and grasp for
more
No longer thoughtful and
loving
Bowing to the rich, neglecting
the poor.

God said, "If my people which
are called by my name
Shall humble themselves and
pray
Seek my face, I will hear from
heaven
Will heal their land and sinful
ways."

America, America, land that
I love
Down through the ages
sinful nations did fall
Now is the hour to listen to
God
Listen to the sound of our
sweet Shepherd's call.

Lela Hadzilacou-Gibbons
THAT THING CALLED LIFE

Sometime ago, when I was a
child, I asked my grandma
What is "That thing called
Life?" Health of body or
peace of mind?
She looked at me, thought for
a moment, took a breath and
said:
Listen child; Life and I

have been together
through pleasant and cloudy
weather
In small proportions we just
beauty see
and in short measures life may
perfect be
But there is no perfect life if
there is no health of body
of peace of mind.
Don't search them far away;
think all materialism goes in
vain.
Follow Jesus, in Him there
is no despair, nothing is
better,
don't search or compare.
Following God's steps bring
us into the world source
of light,
which world we do name
justice or peace of mind.
I have grown old my child; stay
here with me, stay near-by
to close my eyes to receive
God's last blessing.
Let you the youngest climb up
the slope of life,
then let you cry three times
"Old grandma has died".
But I want you to know that
of all people "Old grandma
lives" in smooth and
steadfast mind.
Gentle thoughts, all calm desires
in God's way.
This is your home—He said—He
made me stay.
Justice and peace of mind.
That thing called life.

Maureen M. Campbell
AN ANSWER FOR EDWARD

You ask me how much I love
you.
Can mere words explain the
feeling?
You are my sun in the morning,
My song in the breezy afternoon,
My stillness and serenity in the
peacefulness of the night.
When I am with you I am lost
in you.
When I am not I am lost in
myself.
When you love me
I am no longer just me
But an extension of you.
You are my daydreams, my
night dreams, my life dreams.
To live is to love you.
To merely exist is to lose you.
The feelings I experience from
you
Are more beautiful than
rainbows, sunrises or sunsets.
And you ask me how much?
Come hold me close. . .be
silent and let me tell you;
For the words are just words
Yet the feelings are
unmistakable.
Open your eyes. . .look deep. . .
deep into mine.
To find the answer to a
question asked since the
beginning of time.
And always remember;
In the stillness of the night
Let me come to you.
Open yourself to me,
Visit my innermost sincerity

Engulf me totally with your
touch.
You are my dreams beyond all
expectations.
Our silent love reminds me of
the constant crashing waves
Uniting with the shores they
caress so passionately.

Marciel M. Strong
A GIFT FOR CHRIST

Christmas is coming and there's
so much to do. . .
Cleaning the house, baking and
shopping too!

It's fun to shop for our children
a little girl or boy,
There are so many books to
choose
from or a game or a toy!

They all appreciate homemade
clothes,
a quilt or some little thing,
Or going to a program to watch
a play
or to hear the choirs sing!

There are lights and decorations
to put up and
the tree to trim.
And just where should you place
the mistletoe where your
husband will grin!

And. . .Oh, all of those
Christmas
cards and letters to write,
Be sure and have plenty of
wood to
burn and candles to light!

There's another thing, no
matter
how we try, we always regret,
Someone's address we lose or
somebody's size we forget!

But as we look at all decorations
in green and red,
Over all the food and
beautiful
gifts we can be misled. . .

The bright lights and gifts won't
be right unless we try,
To reflect over the long ago
Christmas
thousands of years gone by. . .

To remember the very first
Christmas
and what it really means,
Reflecting back on the birth
of Christ
and the humble stable scenes.

And just how do we give a
Christmas gift to Christ
this Christmas day?
You've guessed it, we give to
others who need help along

their way!

Teaching with our lives by
example, we can show
every single day,
How to love our neighbors,
give service, and ask
forgiveness when we pray.

Then Christ will open the door
and say come on in and
life with Thee,
Because if you gave to your
fellow
men it was even better than
giving gifts to me!

Michele Pye
**A DEDICATION TO MRS. L.
BERGEY**

Let us say good-bye to
yesterday,
farewell to today,
gazing upon them with
the naive surety of youth, or
the
patronizing benevolence of
age.

Let us open the door—
fearless, adventurous
gazing upon the injustices
with glances, misted over
with time,
that are never quite sure if
it was as terrible as we
thought,
or as magnificent as we
remembered.

Let us part the closest of
friends
never remembering
how bad it really was, or
how good it really wasn't
remembering the days of
sunshine and roses
rather than those of
rain and wilted daisies.

Let us let go of yesterday
with the grace of an old
forgotten heroine,
good-bye to today
with the wisdom of a
Greek philosopher,
and
hello to tomorrow
with the wisdom of
a new-born child

Hazel B. Plummer
PATTERN OF LIFE

God gives us a new pattern
As we conceive the role of
mother
An exclusive pattern that
cannot be bought
But more precious than any
other.

As we cut and fashion it
And handle with greatest care—
God gives us the necessary
material
Because, He is always there.

The instructions we should use
Are written for us, quite clear—
In His holy and precious book,
We always hold most dear.

Daily, we need His guidance
To see faults that merit blame—
May He give us courage to
discipline
And keep on loving just the
same.

May we acknowledge their
good deeds,

And offer our grateful praise—
And not lose our sense of
humor
No matter what—the phase.

Lord, fill our children's hearts
with gladness
And their souls with faith
and cheer—
Love to brighten their daily lives
And trust, that vanishes fear.

And, dear Lord, forgive us
mothers
When our hearts grow forgetful
and cold—
Let us always perceive the
wonders
Of these gifts, more precious
than gold.

Cindy Markwell
THE ANGEL STONE

Sometimes I feel so broken
So lost in little pieces of love
I spend my life wandering
Through time.
Wondering where to go
What is mine.
Picking up angel stones
On the beach,
Running my fingers through
the sand
'Til I find a golden pebble
In my hand.
I fall to my knees
Feeling weakened again
And I wonder.

Wondering of times way back
when
And who else walked
Through this sand.
Don't you know a million people
Can walk the same place
And still end up
Facing a different way?
Don't you know I feel weakened
And I want to cry
Don't you know why?

The angel stone slips through
My fingers as I stand
And run down the beach
With the waves and the sand
I feel the wind rip through my
hair
As I cry.
And the wind pulls my skirt
To my thigh.
The waves reaching up to my
heels and my toes
In a world where a lady
Or a prostitute goes
And I know that I'm lost
And that I want to be.
I want that golden pebble
To remember me,
And I wonder.

Sadie Brown Floyd
THANKFUL

I raise my eyes in thanksgiving,
on this day set aside
And view this great nation,
peaceful and quiet;
I watch Old Glory, proudly
wave in the breeze
And I say a prayer for honored
men, who died for these.

Stacks of straw and hay make a
stockade against the sky,
Flocks of wild geese spiral, then
swoop with blatant cry;
Love, home, a garden, beauty
by the brooks,
Splendid, stupendous beauty
never found in books.

Churches of all denominations

over all the land,
Freedom and liberty for all,
the rights are grand;
Bought by our fathers and sons
of today,
So hoist the Stars and Stripes
and kneel to pray.

Thank the Heavenly Father in
an old fashion way
For fruits of men's labor and
joys of today;
We are heirs to a land made rich
with peace,
May the blessings of America
never cease.

May I never feel indifference for
these rights of mine,
May I appreciate a country
with laws so fine;
Help me, O God, to be
unselfish, lacking not in
honesty,
To do my part to preserve such
freedom and liberty.

Warren Alfred Sanford
A FAREWELL TO DOYLE

Advocates, assessors,
prescriptionnaires,
Citizens—good friends all;
Lend, yet a-while, your ears
And attend with your hearts
As we make sincere speech of
that
For which we are here gathered
to do.

All too soon now,
That blinding curtain we
sometimes call
abscence
Unkingly moves to enfold its
insensible self
About the presence of one
among us
Who hath been of no mean
service to
Both the city and the State;
And who, thusly, being put
out-of-sight,
Must move on and away from
us.

Farewell good Doyle, and know
thou this:
We measure thee the noblest
Casey of them
all.
Pity tis that thou must now
depart
After such a short, but goodly
time.
Perhaps, as good men are so
often wont
to do,
Thou leaveth here, a
better where to find.
But, kind sir, after all is said
and done,
Look thou first, for thy guidance

to him above;
And through thine own heart
for that so
ordained action;
Remembering , this above all,
to thine own
self
Be true, and kind;
And it must follow, as the night
the day,
Thou canst not then be false
and unkind
to any man.

So, fare-thee-well, and thrive-
thee-well
good Doyle;
Where-so-ever thou goeth.
And now and then, when time
approves,
Please grace us with your better
thoughts;
As you shall dwell in ours.

Diko D. Velieff
P. O. W.

"Who cares for the man with
the broken spirit?"

"Not I." said the one with the
bleeding
heart.

"He cares for himself as others
before Him have done."

"Take the burden from your
shoulders
and share it with another."

"No, I silently carry this
burden
to my end, as they bring down
the lash
upon me once more."

They chewed-up my body,
and spit it onto the pavement.
Again I arose,
planted firmly for the second
blow.

My insides gone,
all but a spark remains in the
shell.
Oh how insanity laughs in
my face!

Reason having escaped me,
death's arms reaching out for
the embrace,
survival obsesses me.

Still waiting,
Ever waiting,
for the hand of authority.
While the heart pounds the
gallows' song,
the tiny cell becomes colder.

And yesterday's world,
seems to be a mere dream.
Left to myself,
having no-one to honor but
myself
I cry,
but shed no tears.

Irving A. Lynn
HEART OF DARKNESS

Time is a stop-watch and a
lone sprinter
racing around a cinder track,
like the earth around the sun.
Time is a cycle of a whirling
sphere, peopled with bugs
and emperors, moving from
darkness to darkness.
Time is the screaming flight
of a comet
careening around a sharp turn
in the sky;

Time is not stopped by a
splash of careless light
which divides the night from
day. It hurries on, wheels
onward,
in a crazy career. Time is a
juggernaut, shivering temples
and idols, respecting no shrines,
over-running man
and his gods.
Minutes and minutes of time
are gone.
How many minutes since the
first star shone?
How many minutes since
the first soul crossed the span
of stars, the cold and finite air
to God?
How many minutes are there
in the lives of stars?
in the luminous cycles of the
sun?
How many minutes are there
in a millenium,
O You who made the world
in a frenzy of black spite?
And how many millenia
have daubed the corpse of
history red?
O worms and emperor-priests,
O troglodyte,
How many minutes has
humanity forgot your face
and time your gods, your
temples, and your wars?
How far apart are we, O cousin
on this whirling sphere,
this minute-timeclock in a
timeless universe?

Ken Easlick
LONELY COUNTRY ROAD

Leaves on tree beside the road
Horse in the meadow—blowing
his nose
Water in the creek—on its way
Left the milk house minutes
before
Running over pebbles and
around some stones
Sometimes in the shade,
sometimes in the sun
Looking for that old covered
bridge out ahead
Where the bass and blue gill
run and play
Old fence posts along the way
Some are new, some are old,
some ain't—
Just a board standing upright
stapled to the old top barb
Leaning to and fro, depending
on how the wind blows
The old covered bridge up
ahead—
Catching the sunshine over the
ridge
It's boards all aged and weather
beaten
Covered with initials and hearts
of days gone by
Its foundation stones all worn
smooth
From the seats of pants of
fishermen and their can of
worms
Boards are missing from its
side
For boys and girls to dive and
play around
The grass seems greener on the
other side
Cows in the meadow—crows in
the corn—
An old dead tree stands alone
Looking down a crooked
country road.

Index of Poets

INDEX OF POETS